Renault Clio
Service and Repair Manual

A K Legg LAE MIMI & Peter T Gill

Models covered *(4168 - 8AL1 - 352)*

Renault Clio Hatchback (plus most features of Van), including special/limited editions

Petrol engines: 1.2 litre (1149cc), 1.4 litre (1390cc) & 1.6 litre (1598cc)
Turbo-Diesel engines: 1.5 litre (1461cc)

Does NOT cover 1.9 litre turbo-diesel engine or Renaultsport 172, 182 or V6 models

ABCDE
FGHIJ
KLMNO
PQ

A book in the **Haynes Service and Repair Manual Series**

ISBN **978 1 84425 744 7**

British Library Cataloguing in Publication Data
A catalogue record for this book is available from the British Library.

Printed in the USA

Haynes Publishing
Sparkford, Yeovil, Somerset BA22 7JJ, England

Haynes North America, Inc
861 Lawrence Drive, Newbury Park, California 91320, USA

Haynes Publishing Nordiska AB
Box 1504, 751 45 UPPSALA, Sverige

Contents

Contents

REPAIRS AND OVERHAUL

Many people see the words 'advanced driving' and believe that it won't interest them or that it is a style of driving beyond their own abilities. Nothing could be further from the truth. Advanced driving is straightforward safe, sensible driving - the sort of driving we should all do every time we get behind the wheel.

An average of 10 people are killed every day on UK roads and 870 more are injured, some seriously. Lives are ruined daily, usually because somebody did something stupid. Something like 95% of all accidents are due to human error, mostly driver failure. Sometimes we make genuine mistakes - everyone does. Sometimes we have lapses of concentration. Sometimes we deliberately take risks.

For many people, the process of 'learning to drive' doesn't go much further than learning how to pass the driving test because of a common belief that good drivers are made by 'experience'.

Learning to drive by 'experience' teaches three driving skills:

- ☐ Quick reactions. (Whoops, that was close!)
- ☐ Good handling skills. (Horn, swerve, brake, horn).
- ☐ Reliance on vehicle technology. (Great stuff this ABS, stop in no distance even in the wet...)

Drivers whose skills are 'experience based' generally have a lot of near misses and the odd accident. The results can be seen every day in our courts and our hospital casualty departments.

Advanced drivers have learnt to control the risks by controlling the position and speed of their vehicle. They avoid accidents and near misses, even if the drivers around them make mistakes.

The key skills of advanced driving are **concentration,** effective all-round **observation, anticipation** and **planning.** When **good vehicle handling** is added to these skills, all driving situations can be approached and negotiated in a safe, methodical way, leaving nothing to chance.

Concentration means applying your mind to safe driving, completely excluding anything that's not relevant. Driving is usually the most dangerous activity that most of us undertake in our daily routines. It deserves our full attention.

Observation means not just looking, but seeing and seeking out the information found in the driving environment.

Anticipation means asking yourself what is happening, what you can reasonably expect to happen and what could happen unexpectedly. (One of the commonest words used in compiling accident reports is 'suddenly'.)

Planning is the link between seeing something and taking the appropriate action. For many drivers, planning is the missing link.

If you want to become a safer and more skilful driver and you want to enjoy your driving more, contact the Institute of Advanced Motorists at www.iam.org.uk, phone 0208 996 9600, or write to IAM House, 510 Chiswick High Road, London W4 5RG for an information pack.

Working on your car can be dangerous. This page shows just some of the potential risks and hazards, with the aim of creating a safety-conscious attitude.

General hazards

Scalding

• Don't remove the radiator or expansion tank cap while the engine is hot.
• Engine oil, automatic transmission fluid or power steering fluid may also be dangerously hot if the engine has recently been running.

Burning

• Beware of burns from the exhaust system and from any part of the engine. Brake discs and drums can also be extremely hot immediately after use.

Crushing

• When working under or near a raised vehicle, always supplement the jack with axle stands, or use drive-on ramps. ***Never venture under a car which is only supported by a jack.***

• Take care if loosening or tightening high-torque nuts when the vehicle is on stands. Initial loosening and final tightening should be done with the wheels on the ground.

Fire

• Fuel is highly flammable; fuel vapour is explosive.
• Don't let fuel spill onto a hot engine.
• Do not smoke or allow naked lights (including pilot lights) anywhere near a vehicle being worked on. Also beware of creating sparks (electrically or by use of tools).
• Fuel vapour is heavier than air, so don't work on the fuel system with the vehicle over an inspection pit.
• Another cause of fire is an electrical overload or short-circuit. Take care when repairing or modifying the vehicle wiring.
• Keep a fire extinguisher handy, of a type suitable for use on fuel and electrical fires.

Electric shock

• Ignition HT voltage can be dangerous, especially to people with heart problems or a pacemaker. Don't work on or near the ignition system with the engine running or the ignition switched on.

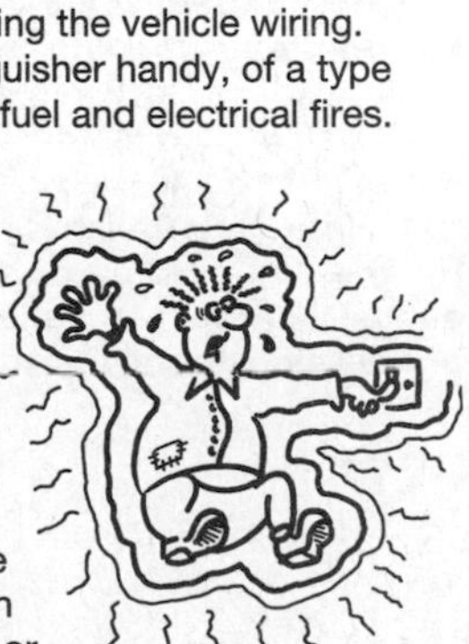

• Mains voltage is also dangerous. Make sure that any mains-operated equipment is correctly earthed. Mains power points should be protected by a residual current device (RCD) circuit breaker.

Fume or gas intoxication

• Exhaust fumes are poisonous; they often contain carbon monoxide, which is rapidly fatal if inhaled. Never run the engine in a confined space such as a garage with the doors shut.

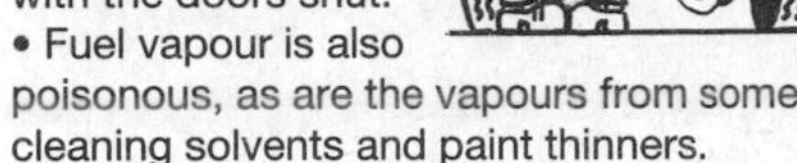

• Fuel vapour is also poisonous, as are the vapours from some cleaning solvents and paint thinners.

Poisonous or irritant substances

• Avoid skin contact with battery acid and with any fuel, fluid or lubricant, especially antifreeze, brake hydraulic fluid and Diesel fuel. Don't syphon them by mouth. If such a substance is swallowed or gets into the eyes, seek medical advice.
• Prolonged contact with used engine oil can cause skin cancer. Wear gloves or use a barrier cream if necessary. Change out of oil-soaked clothes and do not keep oily rags in your pocket.
• Air conditioning refrigerant forms a poisonous gas if exposed to a naked flame (including a cigarette). It can also cause skin burns on contact.

Asbestos

• Asbestos dust can cause cancer if inhaled or swallowed. Asbestos may be found in gaskets and in brake and clutch linings. When dealing with such components it is safest to assume that they contain asbestos.

Special hazards

Hydrofluoric acid

• This extremely corrosive acid is formed when certain types of synthetic rubber, found in some O-rings, oil seals, fuel hoses etc, are exposed to temperatures above 400ºC. The rubber changes into a charred or sticky substance containing the acid. *Once formed, the acid remains dangerous for years. If it gets onto the skin, it may be necessary to amputate the limb concerned.*
• When dealing with a vehicle which has suffered a fire, or with components salvaged from such a vehicle, wear protective gloves and discard them after use.

The battery

• Batteries contain sulphuric acid, which attacks clothing, eyes and skin. Take care when topping-up or carrying the battery.
• The hydrogen gas given off by the battery is highly explosive. Never cause a spark or allow a naked light nearby. Be careful when connecting and disconnecting battery chargers or jump leads.

Air bags

• Air bags can cause injury if they go off accidentally. Take care when removing the steering wheel and/or facia. Special storage instructions may apply.

Diesel injection equipment

• Diesel injection pumps supply fuel at very high pressure. Take care when working on the fuel injectors and fuel pipes.

Warning: Never expose the hands, face or any other part of the body to injector spray; the fuel can penetrate the skin with potentially fatal results.

Remember...

DO

• Do use eye protection when using power tools, and when working under the vehicle.

• Do wear gloves or use barrier cream to protect your hands when necessary.

• Do get someone to check periodically that all is well when working alone on the vehicle.

• Do keep loose clothing and long hair well out of the way of moving mechanical parts.

• Do remove rings, wristwatch etc, before working on the vehicle – especially the electrical system.

• Do ensure that any lifting or jacking equipment has a safe working load rating adequate for the job.

DON'T

• Don't attempt to lift a heavy component which may be beyond your capability – get assistance.

• Don't rush to finish a job, or take unverified short cuts.

• Don't use ill-fitting tools which may slip and cause injury.

• Don't leave tools or parts lying around where someone can trip over them. Mop up oil and fuel spills at once.

• Don't allow children or pets to play in or near a vehicle being worked on.

Three petrol engines and one diesel engine are available in the Clio range. The petrol engines are in 1.2, 1.4, and 1.6 litre sizes, and the diesel engine is 1.5 litre. All petrol engines use a fuel-injection system, and diesel engines use a direct injection system. All the engines are of excellent design and, provided regular maintenance is carried out, are unlikely to give trouble.

The Clio is available in 3- and 5-door Hatchback body styles, with a wide range of fittings and interior trim depending on the model specification.

Fully-independent front suspension is fitted, with the components attached to a subframe assembly, and the rear suspension is semi-independent, with torsion beam and trailing arms.

A five-speed manual or sequential gearbox, and electronically-controlled four-speed automatic transmission are available.

A wide range of standard and optional equipment is available within the Clio range to suit most tastes, including an anti-lock braking system.

The Clio is conventional in design, and the DIY mechanic should find most servicing work straightforward.

Your Renault Clio Manual

The aim of this manual is to help you get the best value from your vehicle. It can do so in several ways. It can help you decide what work must be done (even should you choose to get it done by a garage), provide information on routine maintenance and servicing, and give a logical course of action and diagnosis when random faults occur. However, it is hoped that you will use the manual by tackling the work yourself. On simpler jobs, it may even be quicker than booking the car into a garage and going there twice, to leave and collect it. Perhaps most important, a lot of money can be saved by avoiding the costs a garage must charge to cover its labour and overheads.

The manual has drawings and descriptions to show the function of the various components, so that their layout can be understood. Then the tasks are described and photographed in a clear step-by-step sequence.

References to the 'left' or 'right' are in the sense of a person in the driver's seat, facing forward.

Project vehicles

The main project vehicle used in the preparation of this manual, and appearing in many of the photographic sequences, was a 2002 Renault Clio dCi Expression fitted with the 1.5 litre K9K diesel engine.

Acknowledgements

Certain illustrations are the copyright of Renault (UK) Limited, and are used with their permission. Thanks are also due to Draper Tools Limited, who provided some of the workshop tools, and to all those people at Sparkford who helped in the production of this manual.

We take great pride in the accuracy of information given in this manual, but vehicle manufacturers make alterations and design changes during the production run of a particular vehicle of which they do not inform us. No liability can be accepted by the authors or publishers for loss, damage or injury caused by any errors in, or omissions from, the information given.

The following pages are intended to help in dealing with common roadside emergencies and breakdowns. You will find more detailed fault finding information at the back of the manual, and repair information in the main chapters.

If your car won't start and the starter motor doesn't turn

- ☐ If it's a model with automatic transmission, make sure the selector is in the P or N position.
- ☐ Open the bonnet and make sure that the battery terminals are clean and tight.
- ☐ Switch on the headlights and try to start the engine. If the headlights go very dim when you're trying to start, the battery is probably flat. Get out of trouble by jump starting (see next page) using another car.

If your car won't start even though the starter motor turns as normal

- ☐ Is there fuel in the tank?
- ☐ Is there moisture on electrical components under the bonnet? Switch off the ignition, then wipe off any obvious dampness with a dry cloth. Spray a water-repellent aerosol product (WD-40 or equivalent) on ignition and fuel system electrical connectors like those shown in the photos. Pay special attention to the ignition coil wiring connector and HT leads.

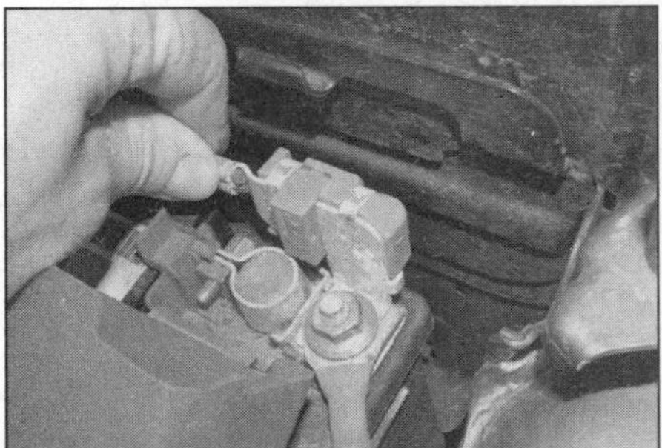

A Check the condition and security of the battery connections.

B Check that the spark plug HT leads or ignition coil wires are securely connected.

C Check that the fuel injector wiring harness is secure.

Check that electrical connections are secure (with the ignition switched off) and spray them with a water dispersant spray like WD-40 if you suspect a problem due to damp

D Check all multi-plugs and wiring connectors for security - make sure the ignition is switched off

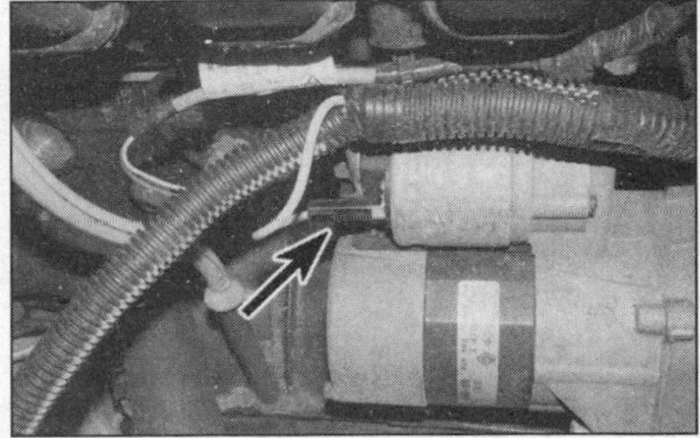

E Check the connections on the starter motor are secure.

Jump starting

When jump-starting a car using a booster battery, observe the following precautions:

- ✔ Before connecting the booster battery, make sure that the ignition is switched off.
- ✔ Ensure that all electrical equipment (lights, heater, wipers, etc) is switched off.
- ✔ Take note of any special precautions printed on the battery case.
- ✔ Make sure that the booster battery is the same voltage as the discharged one in the vehicle.
- ✔ If the battery is being jump-started from the battery in another vehicle, the two vehicles MUST NOT TOUCH each other.
- ✔ Make sure that the transmission is in neutral (or PARK, in the case of automatic transmission).

Jump starting will get you out of trouble, but you must correct whatever made the battery go flat in the first place. There are three possibilities:

1 The battery has been drained by repeated attempts to start, or by leaving the lights on.

2 The charging system is not working properly (alternator drivebelt slack or broken, alternator wiring fault or alternator itself faulty).

3 The battery itself is at fault (electrolyte low, or battery worn out).

1 Connect one end of the red jump lead to the positive (+) terminal of the flat battery

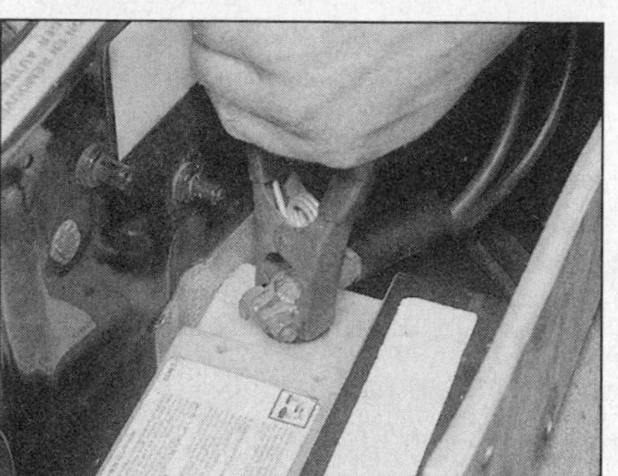

2 Connect the other end of the red lead to the positive (+) terminal of the booster battery.

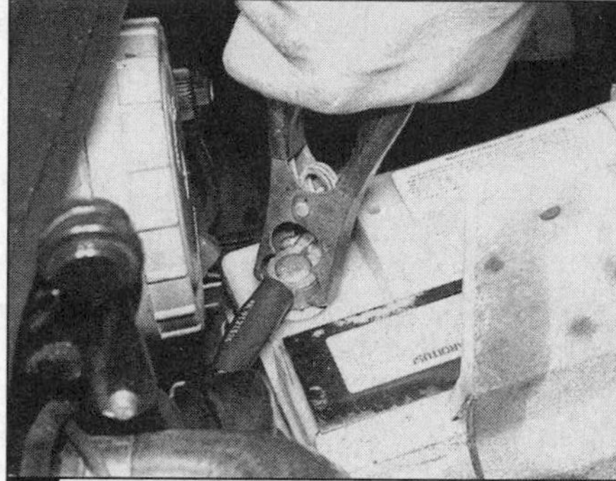

3 Connect one end of the black jump lead to the negative (-) terminal of the booster battery

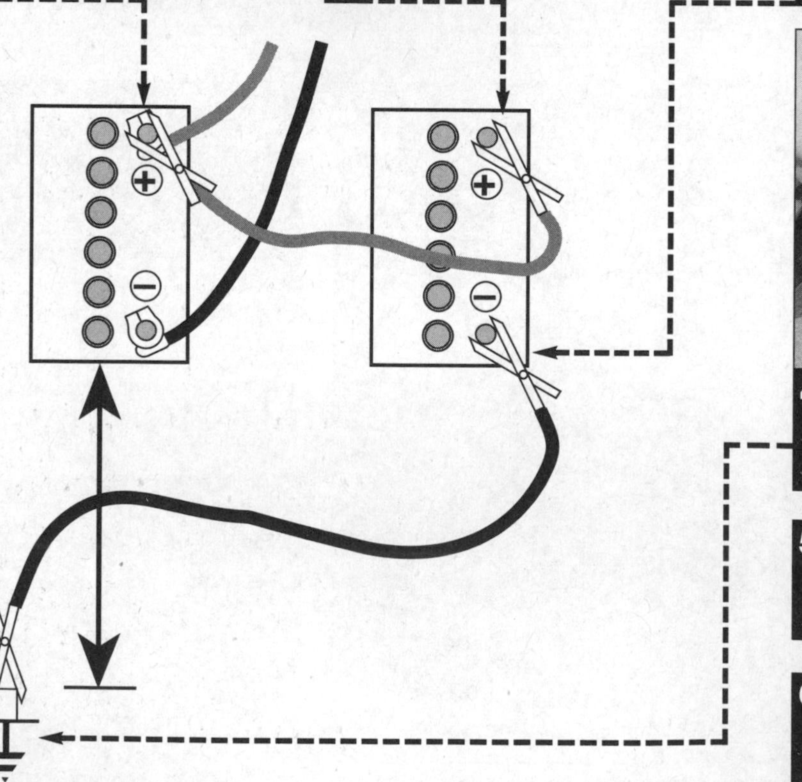

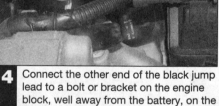

4 Connect the other end of the black jump lead to a bolt or bracket on the engine block, well away from the battery, on the vehicle to be started.

5 Make sure that the jump leads will not come into contact with the fan, drive-belts or other moving parts of the engine.

6 Start the engine using the booster battery and run it at idle speed. Switch on the lights, rear window demister and heater blower motor, then disconnect the jump leads in the reverse order of connection. Turn off the lights etc.

Wheel changing

Warning: Do not change a wheel in a situation where you risk being hit by another vehicle. On busy roads, try to stop in a lay-by or a gateway. Be wary of passing traffic while changing the wheel - it is easy to become distracted by the job in hand.

Preparation

- ☐ When a puncture occurs, stop as soon as it is safe to do so.
- ☐ Park on firm level ground, if possible, and well out of the way of other traffic.
- ☐ Use hazard warning lights if necessary.
- ☐ If you have one, use a warning triangle to alert other drivers of your presence.
- ☐ Apply the handbrake and engage first or reverse gear (or Park on models with automatic transmission).
- ☐ Chock the wheel diagonally opposite the one being removed – a couple of large stones will do for this.
- ☐ If the ground is soft, use a flat piece of wood to spread the load under the jack.

Changing the wheel

1 The spare wheel and tools are stored in the luggage compartment under the carpet. Unscrew the retainer securing the tool holder and spare wheel.

2 Lift out the tool holder.

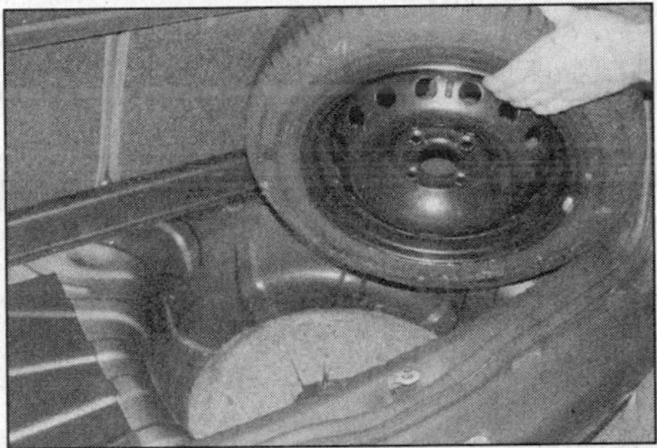

3 Lift out the spare wheel.

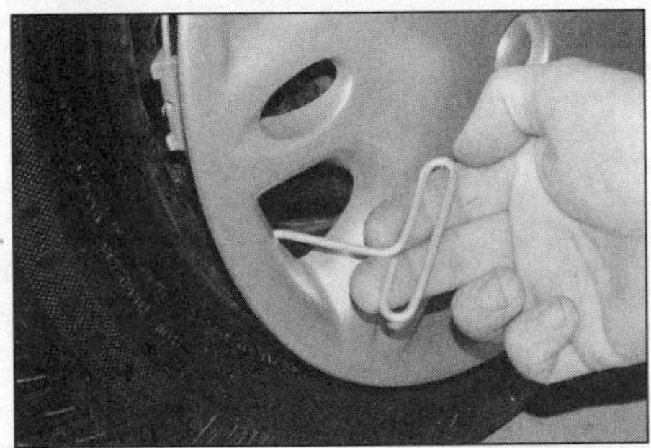

4 Use the hook provided to remove the wheel trim (where fitted).

5 Slacken each wheel bolt by half a turn.

6 Locate the jack below the reinforced point on the sill (don't jack the vehicle at any other point of the sill) and on firm ground, then turn the jack handle clockwise until the wheel is raised clear of the ground.

7 Unscrew the wheel bolts using the brace provided, and remove the wheel. Fit the spare wheel, and screw in the bolts. Lightly tighten the bolts with the wheelbrace then lower the vehicle to the ground.

8 Securely tighten the wheel bolts in the sequence shown then refit the wheel trim. Stow the punctured wheel back in the spare wheel well. Note that the wheel bolts must be tightened to the specified torque at the earliest possible opportunity.

Finally...

- ☐ Remove the wheel chocks.
- ☐ Stow the jack and tools in the correct locations in the car.
- ☐ Check the tyre pressure on the wheel just fitted. If it is low, or if you don't have a pressure gauge with you, drive slowly to the next garage and inflate the tyre to the correct pressure.
- ☐ Have the damaged tyre or wheel repaired as soon as possible, or another puncture will leave you stranded.

Identifying leaks

Puddles on the garage floor or drive, or obvious wetness under the bonnet or underneath the car, suggest a leak that needs investigating. It can sometimes be difficult to decide where the leak is coming from, especially if the engine bay is very dirty already. Leaking oil or fluid can also be blown rearwards by the passage of air under the car, giving a false impression of where the problem lies.

Warning: Most automotive oils and fluids are poisonous. Wash them off skin, and change out of contaminated clothing, without delay.

The smell of a fluid leaking from the car may provide a clue to what's leaking. Some fluids are distinctively coloured. It may help to clean the car carefully and to park it over some clean paper overnight as an aid to locating the source of the leak. Remember that some leaks may only occur while the engine is running.

Sump oil

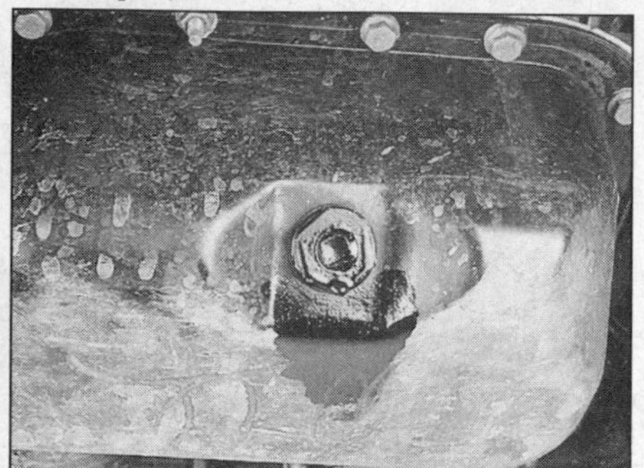

Engine oil may leak from the drain plug...

Oil from filter

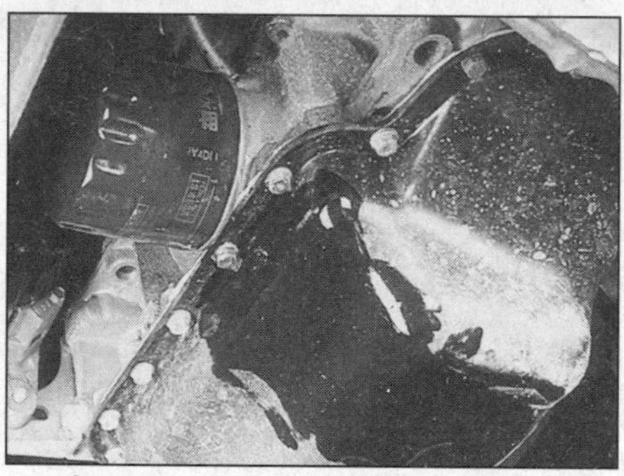

...or from the base of the oil filter.

Gearbox oil

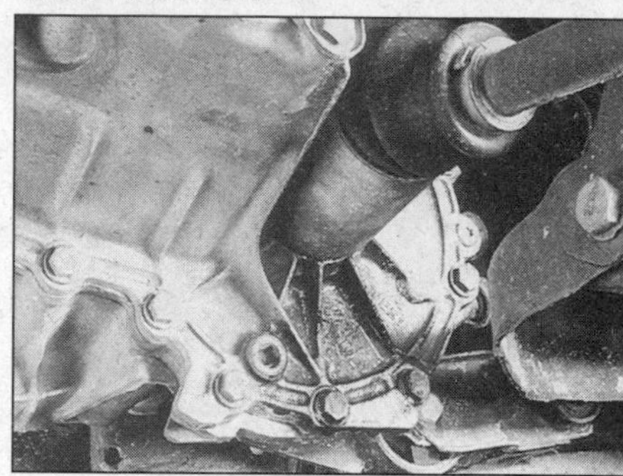

Gearbox oil can leak from the seals at the inboard ends of the driveshafts.

Antifreeze

Leaking antifreeze often leaves a crystalline deposit like this.

Brake fluid

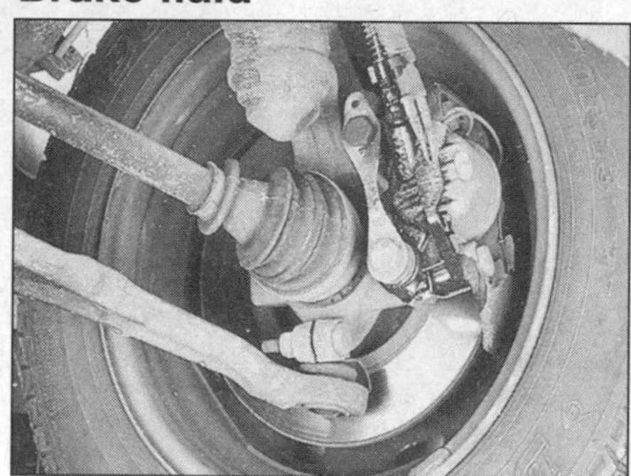

A leak occurring at a wheel is almost certainly brake fluid.

Towing

When all else fails, you may find yourself having to get a tow home – or of course you may be helping somebody else. Long-distance recovery should only be done by a garage or breakdown service. For shorter distances, DIY towing using another car is easy enough, but observe the following points:

- ☐ Use a proper tow-rope – they are not expensive. The vehicle being towed must display an ON TOW sign in its rear window.
- ☐ Always turn the ignition key to the 'on' position when the vehicle is being towed, so that the steering lock is released, and that the direction indicator and brake lights will work.
- ☐ Before being towed, release the handbrake and select neutral on the transmission.
- ☐ Note that greater-than-usual pedal pressure will be required to operate the brakes, since the vacuum servo unit is only operational with the engine running.
- ☐ The driver of the car being towed must keep the tow-rope taut to avoid snatching.
- ☐ Make sure that both drivers know the route before setting off.
- ☐ Drive smoothly and allow plenty of time for slowing down at junctions.
- ☐ On models with automatic transmission, do not exceed 25 mph and do not tow for more than 30 miles.
- ☐ A towing eye is provided in the tool kit in the luggage compartment. To fit the towing eye at the front, screw it into the threaded hole located below the left-hand headlight unit. Tighten the eye using the wheelbrace.

Introduction

There are some very simple checks which need only take a few minutes to carry out, but which could save you a lot of inconvenience and expense.

These *Weekly checks* require no great skill or special tools, and the small amount of time they take to perform could prove to be very well spent, for example:

☐ Keeping an eye on tyre condition and pressures, will not only help to stop them wearing out prematurely, but could also save your life.

☐ Many breakdowns are caused by electrical problems. Battery-related faults are particularly common, and a quick check on a regular basis will often prevent the majority of these.

☐ If your car develops a brake fluid leak, the first time you might know about it is when your brakes don't work properly. Checking the level regularly will give advance warning of this kind of problem.

☐ If the oil or coolant levels run low, the cost of repairing any engine damage will be far greater than fixing the leak, for example.

Underbonnet check points

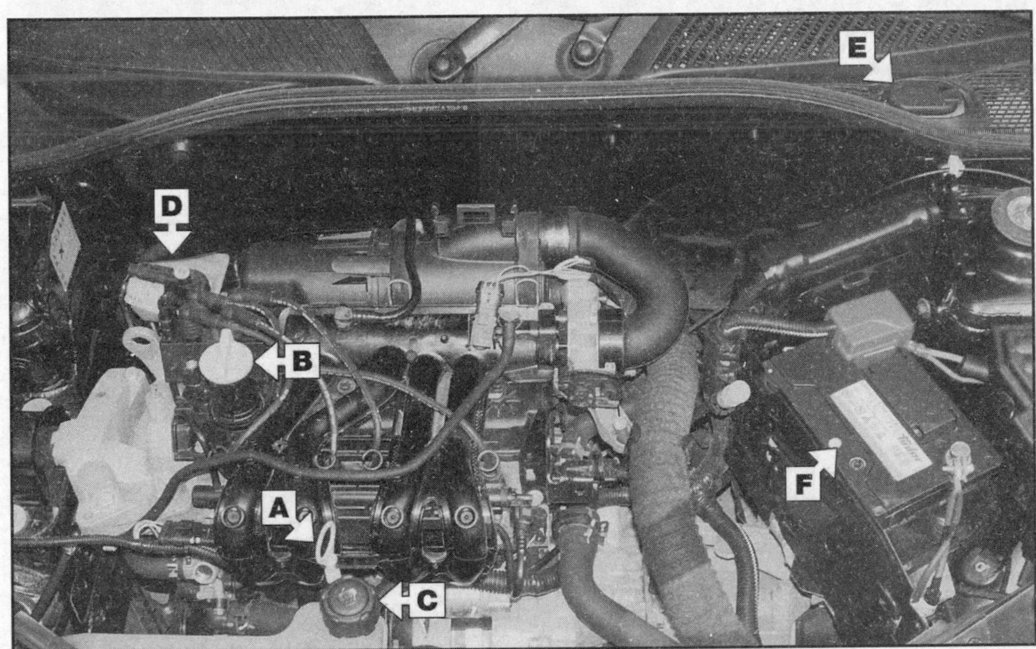

◀ **1.2 litre 8-valve (D7F) petrol engine**

A *Engine oil level dipstick*
B *Engine oil filler cap*
C *Coolant expansion tank*
D *Brake fluid reservoir*
E *Washer fluid reservoir*
F *Battery*

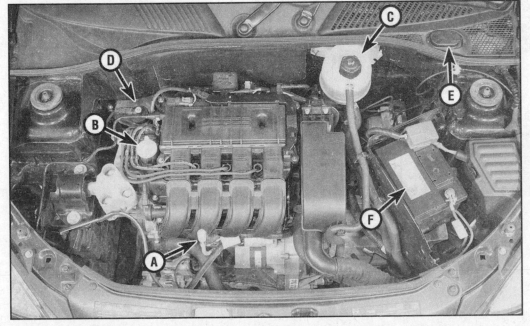

◀ **1.2 litre 16-valve (D4F) petrol engine**

A *Engine oil level dipstick*
B *Engine oil filler cap*
C *Coolant expansion tank*
D *Brake fluid reservoir*
E *Washer fluid reservoir*
F *Battery*

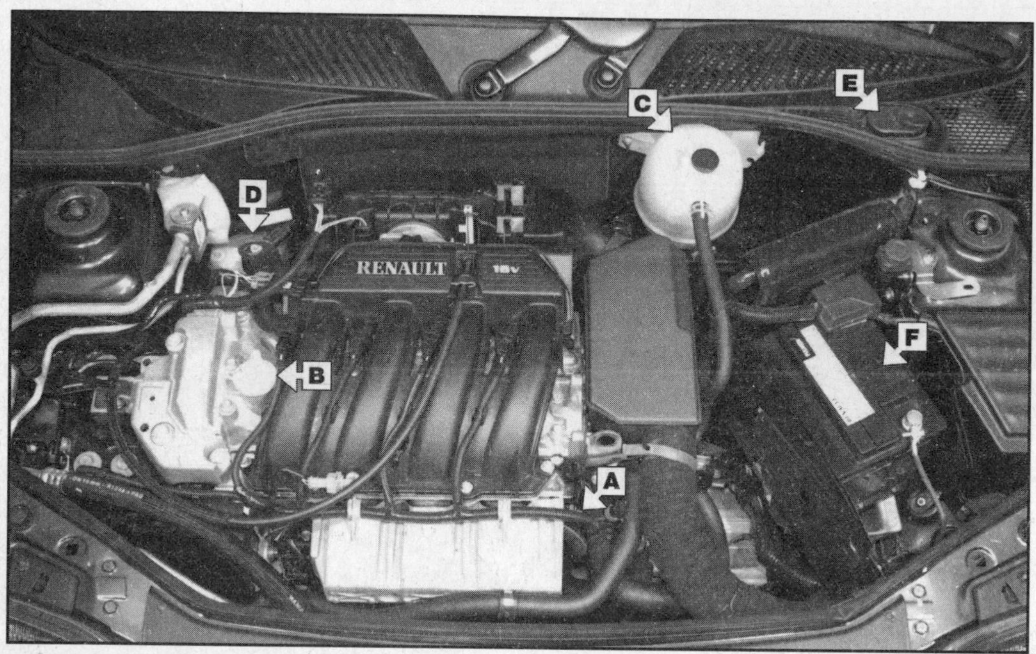

◀ **1.4 litre 16-valve (K4J) petrol engine**

A *Engine oil level dipstick*
B *Engine oil filler cap*
C *Coolant expansion tank*
D *Brake fluid reservoir*
E *Washer fluid reservoir*
F *Battery*

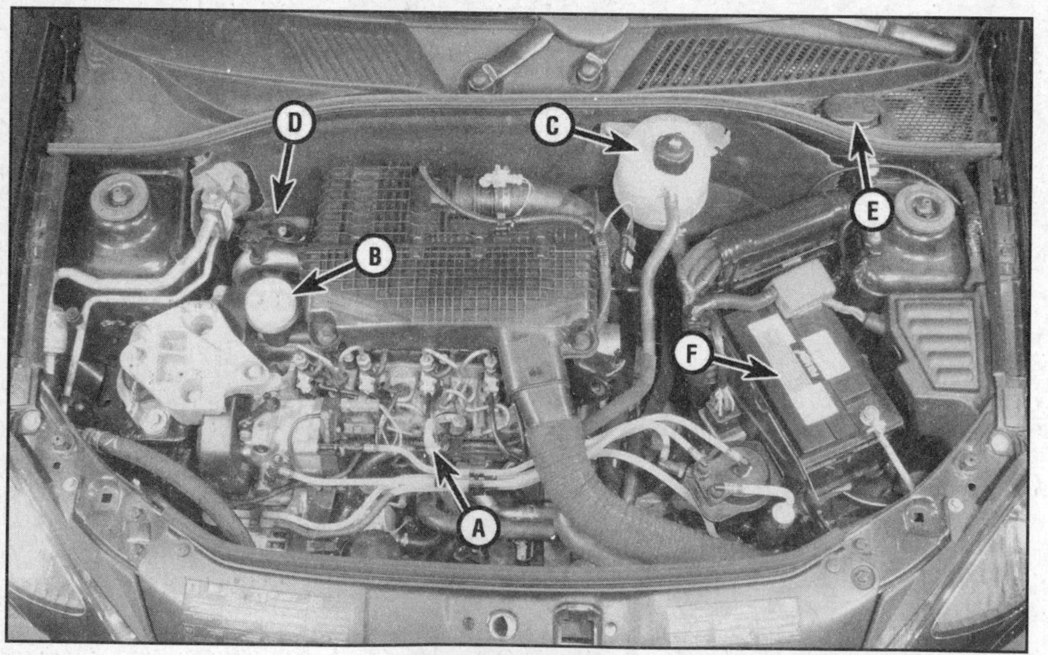

◀ **1.5 litre (K9K) diesel engine**

A *Engine oil level dipstick*
B *Engine oil filler cap*
C *Coolant expansion tank*
D *Brake fluid reservoir*
E *Washer fluid reservoir*
F *Battery*

Engine oil level

Before you start

✔ Make sure that your car is on level ground.

✔ Check the oil level before the car is driven, or at least 5 minutes after the engine has been switched off.

If the oil is checked immediately after driving the vehicle, some of the oil will remain in the upper engine components, resulting in an inaccurate reading on the dipstick.

The correct oil

Modern engines place great demands on their oil. It is very important that the correct oil for your car is used (See *Lubricants and fluids*).

Car Care

● If you have to add oil frequently, you should check whether you have any oil leaks. Place some clean paper under the car overnight, and check for stains in the morning. If there are no leaks, the engine may be burning oil.

● Always maintain the level between the upper and lower dipstick marks (see photo 3). If the level is too low severe engine damage may occur. Oil seal failure may result if the engine is overfilled by adding too much oil.

1 The dipstick is brightly coloured yellow and is located on the front of the engine (see *Underbonnet Check Points* for exact location). Withdraw the dipstick.

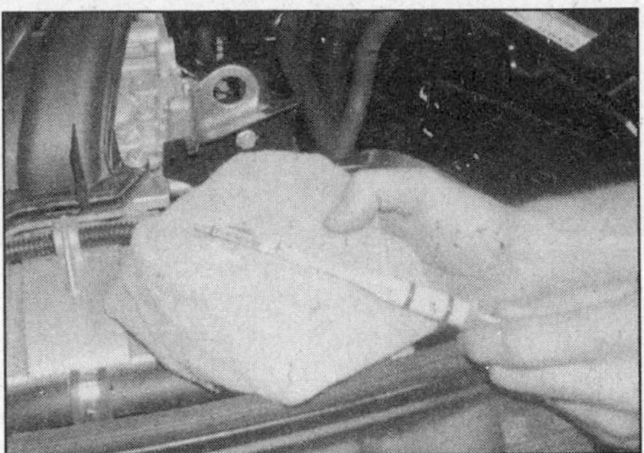

2 Using a clean rag or paper towel remove all oil from the dipstick. Insert the clean dipstick into the tube as far as it will go, then withdraw it again.

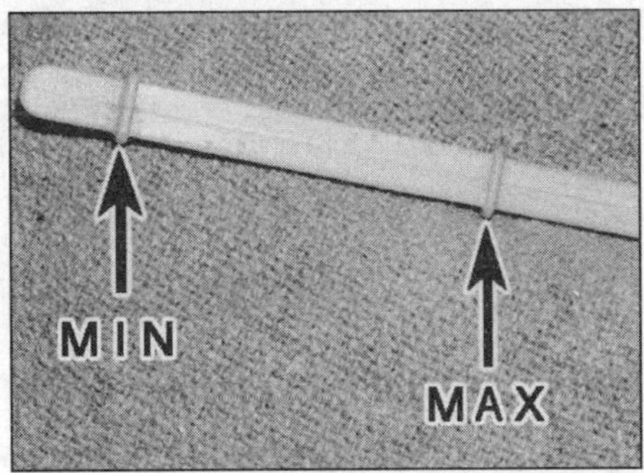

3 Note the oil level on the end of the dipstick, which should be between the upper (MAX) mark and lower (MIN) mark. On some engines the MAX and MIN marks are indicated by notches. Approximately 1.5 litres (depending on engine) of oil will raise the level from the lower mark to the upper mark.

4 Oil is added through the filler cap. Twist the cap anti-clockwise and withdraw it. Top-up the level. A funnel may help to reduce spillage. Add the oil slowly, checking the level on the dipstick often. Do not overfill.

Coolant level

Warning: DO NOT attempt to remove the expansion tank pressure cap when the engine is hot, as there is a very great risk of scalding. Do not leave open containers of coolant about, as it is poisonous.

Car Care

● With a sealed-type cooling system, adding coolant should not be necessary on a regular basis. If frequent topping-up is required, it is likely there is a leak. Check the radiator, all hoses and joint faces for signs of staining or wetness, and rectify as necessary.

● It is important that antifreeze is used in the cooling system all year round, not just during the winter months. Don't top-up with water alone, as the antifreeze will become too diluted.

1 The coolant expansion tank is located either at the front of the engine compartment, or at the rear. The coolant level should be checked with the engine cold, and it should be between the MINI and MAXI marks on the tank.

2 If topping-up is necessary, wait until the engine is cold. Slowly unscrew the expansion tank cap, to release the pressure present in the cooling system, and remove it.

3 Add coolant (a mixture of water and antifreeze) to the expansion tank, until the coolant is up to the MAXI level mark. Refit the cap, and tighten it securely.

Brake fluid level

Warning:
- ***Brake fluid can harm your eyes and damage painted surfaces, so use extreme caution when handling and pouring it.***
- ***Do not use fluid that has been standing open for some time, as it absorbs moisture from the air, which can cause a dangerous loss of braking effectiveness.***

- ***Make sure that your car is on level ground.***
- ***The fluid level in the reservoir will drop slightly as the brake pads wear down, but the fluid level must never be allowed to drop below the MIN mark.***

Safety First!
- If the reservoir requires repeated topping-up this is an indication of a fluid leak somewhere in the system, which should be investigated immediately.
- If a leak is suspected, the car should not be driven until the braking system has been checked. Never take any risks where brakes are concerned.

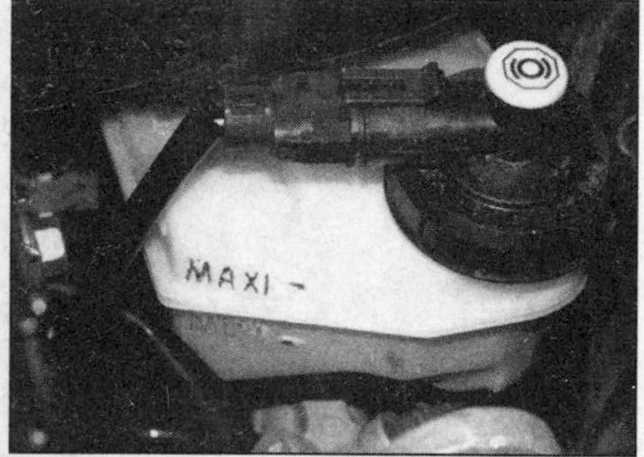

1 The MAXI and MINI marks are indicated on the front of the reservoir. The fluid level must be kept between the marks at all times.

2 If topping-up is necessary, first wipe clean the area around the filler cap to prevent dirt entering the hydraulic system. Unscrew and remove the cap.

3 Carefully add fluid, taking care not to spill it onto the surrounding components. Use only the specified fluid; mixing different types can cause damage to the system. After topping-up to the correct level, securely refit the cap and wipe off any spilt fluid.

Screen washer fluid level

- Screenwash additives not only keep the windscreen clean during bad weather, they also prevent the washer system freezing in cold weather – which is when you are likely to need it most. Don't top up using plain water, as the screenwash will become diluted and will freeze in cold weather. ***On no account use coolant antifreeze in the washer system - this could discolour or damage paintwork.***

- Check the operation of the windscreen and rear window washers. Adjust the nozzles using a pin if necessary, aiming the spray to a point slightly above the centre of the swept area.

1 The reservoir for the washers is located on the rear left-hand side of the bulkhead. If topping-up is necessary, open the cap.

2 When topping-up the reservoir a screenwash additive should be added in the quantities recommended on the bottle.

Tyre condition and pressure

It is very important that tyres are in good condition, and at the correct pressure - having a tyre failure at any speed is highly dangerous. Tyre wear is influenced by driving style - harsh braking and acceleration, or fast cornering, will all produce more rapid tyre wear. As a general rule, the front tyres wear out faster than the rears. Interchanging the tyres from front to rear ("rotating" the tyres) may result in more even wear. However, if this is completely effective, you may have the expense of replacing all four tyres at once!

Remove any nails or stones embedded in the tread before they penetrate the tyre to cause deflation. If removal of a nail does reveal that the tyre has been punctured, refit the nail so that its point of penetration is marked. Then immediately change the wheel, and have the tyre repaired by a tyre dealer.

Regularly check the tyres for damage in the form of cuts or bulges, especially in the sidewalls. Periodically remove the wheels, and clean any dirt or mud from the inside and outside surfaces. Examine the wheel rims for signs of rusting, corrosion or other damage. Light alloy wheels are easily damaged by "kerbing" whilst parking; steel wheels may also become dented or buckled. A new wheel is very often the only way to overcome severe damage.

New tyres should be balanced when they are fitted, but it may become necessary to re-balance them as they wear, or if the balance weights fitted to the wheel rim should fall off. Unbalanced tyres will wear more quickly, as will the steering and suspension components. Wheel imbalance is normally signified by vibration, particularly at a certain speed (typically around 50 mph). If this vibration is felt only through the steering, then it is likely that just the front wheels need balancing. If, however, the vibration is felt through the whole car, the rear wheels could be out of balance. Wheel balancing should be carried out by a tyre dealer or garage.

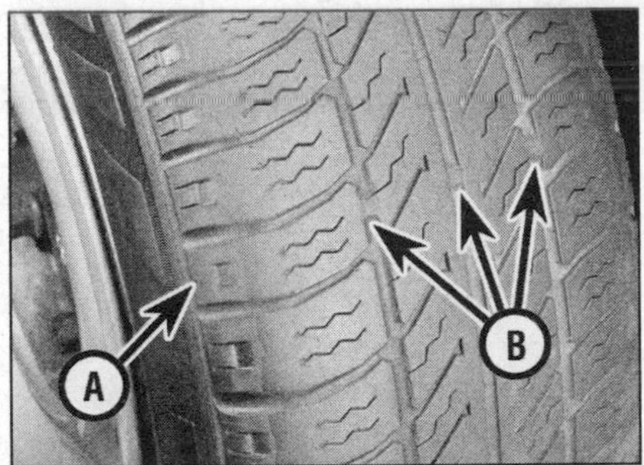

1 ***Tread Depth - visual check***
The original tyres have tread wear safety bands (B), which will appear when the tread depth reaches approximately 1.6 mm. The band positions are indicated by a triangular mark on the tyre sidewall (A).

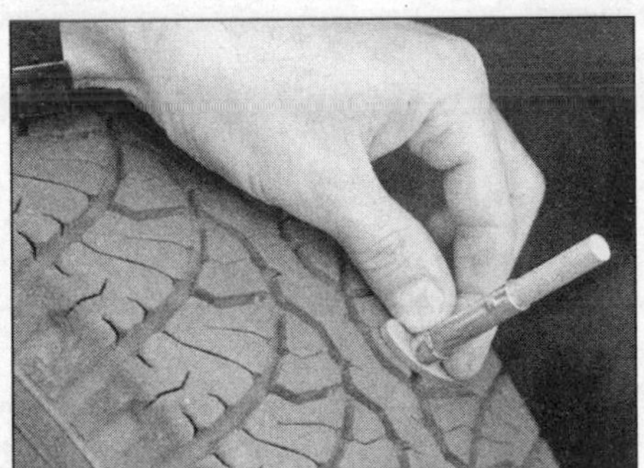

2 ***Tread Depth - manual check***
Alternatively, tread wear can be monitored with a simple, inexpensive device known as a tread depth indicator gauge.

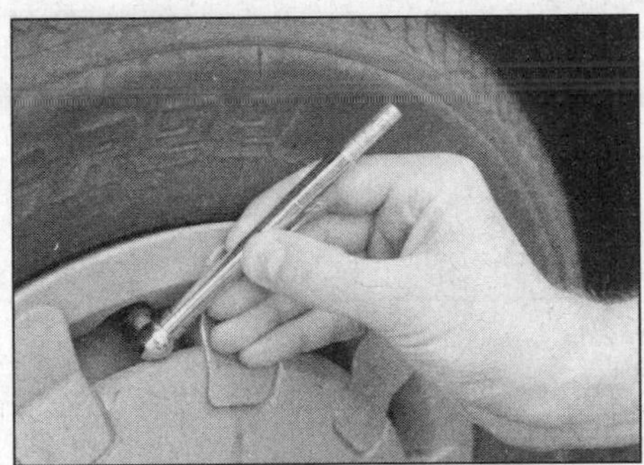

3 ***Tyre Pressure Check***
Check the tyre pressures regularly with the tyres cold. Do not adjust the tyre pressures immediately after the vehicle has been used, or an inaccurate setting will result.

Tyre tread wear patterns

Shoulder Wear

Underinflation (wear on both sides)
Under-inflation will cause overheating of the tyre, because the tyre will flex too much, and the tread will not sit correctly on the road surface. This will cause a loss of grip and excessive wear, not to mention the danger of sudden tyre failure due to heat build-up.
Check and adjust pressures
Incorrect wheel camber (wear on one side)
Repair or renew suspension parts
Hard cornering
Reduce speed!

Centre Wear

Overinflation
Over-inflation will cause rapid wear of the centre part of the tyre tread, coupled with reduced grip, harsher ride, and the danger of shock damage occurring in the tyre casing.
Check and adjust pressures

If you sometimes have to inflate your car's tyres to the higher pressures specified for maximum load or sustained high speed, don't forget to reduce the pressures to normal afterwards.

Uneven Wear

Front tyres may wear unevenly as a result of wheel misalignment. Most tyre dealers and garages can check and adjust the wheel alignment (or "tracking") for a modest charge.
Incorrect camber or castor
Repair or renew suspension parts
Malfunctioning suspension
Repair or renew suspension parts
Unbalanced wheel
Balance tyres
Incorrect toe setting
Adjust front wheel alignment
Note: *The feathered edge of the tread which typifies toe wear is best checked by feel.*

Wiper blades

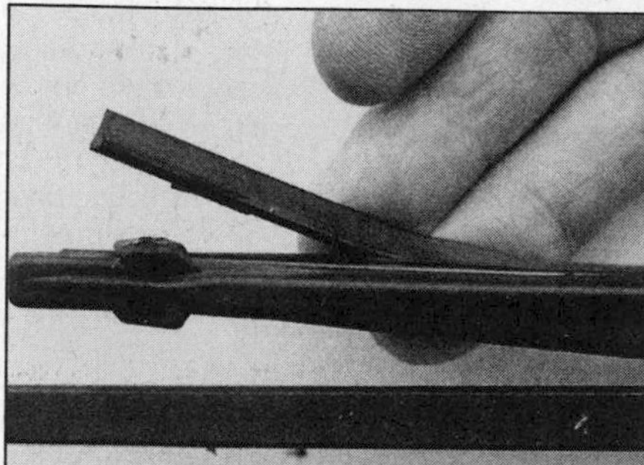

1 Check the condition of the wiper blades; if they are cracked or show any signs of deterioration, or if the glass swept area is smeared, renew them. For maximum clarity of vision, wiper blades should be renewed annually.

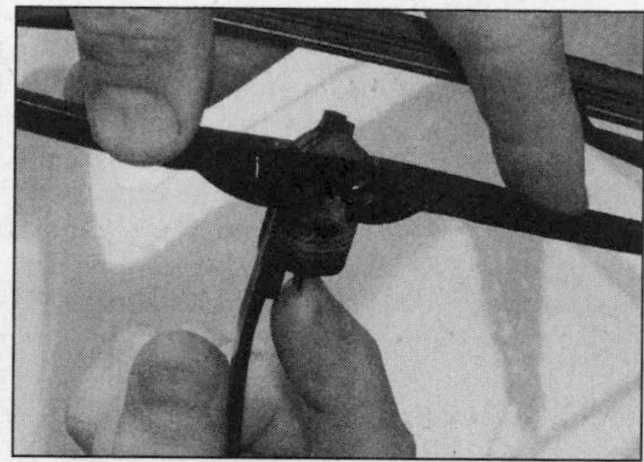

2 To remove a wiper blade, pull the arm fully away from the glass until it locks. Swivel the blade through 90°, then squeeze the locking clip, and detach the blade from the arm. When fitting the new blade, make sure that the blade locks securely into the arm, and that the blade is orientated correctly.

Battery

Caution: Before carrying out any work on the vehicle battery, read the precautions given in 'Safety first!' at the start of this manual.

✔ Make sure that the battery tray is in good condition, and that the clamp is tight. Corrosion on the tray, retaining clamp and the battery itself can be removed with a solution of water and baking soda. Thoroughly rinse all cleaned areas with water. Any metal parts damaged by corrosion should be covered with a zinc-based primer, then painted.

✔ Periodically (approximately every three months), check the charge condition of the battery, as described in Chapter 5A.

✔ If the battery is flat, and you need to jump start your vehicle, see *Jump starting*.

1 The battery is located on the left-hand side of the engine compartment. Where necessary, prise open the plastic cover for access to the positive terminal. The exterior of the battery should be inspected periodically for damage such as a cracked case or cover.

2 Check the tightness of battery clamps to ensure good electrical connections. You should not be able to move them. Also check each cable for cracks and frayed conductors.

HAYNES HiNT

Battery corrosion can be kept to a minimum by applying a layer of petroleum jelly to the clamps and terminals after they are reconnected.

3 If corrosion (white, fluffy deposits) is evident, remove the cables from the battery terminals, clean them with a small wire brush, then refit them. Automotive stores sell a tool for cleaning the battery post . . .

4 . . . as well as the battery cable clamps.

Electrical systems

✔ Check all external lights and the horn. Refer to the appropriate Sections of Chapter 12 for details if any of the circuits are found to be inoperative, and replace the fuse if necessary.

✔ Visually check all accessible wiring connectors, harnesses and retaining clips for security, and for signs of chafing or damage.

If you need to check your brake lights and indicators unaided, back up to a wall or garage door and operate the lights. The reflected light should show if they are working properly.

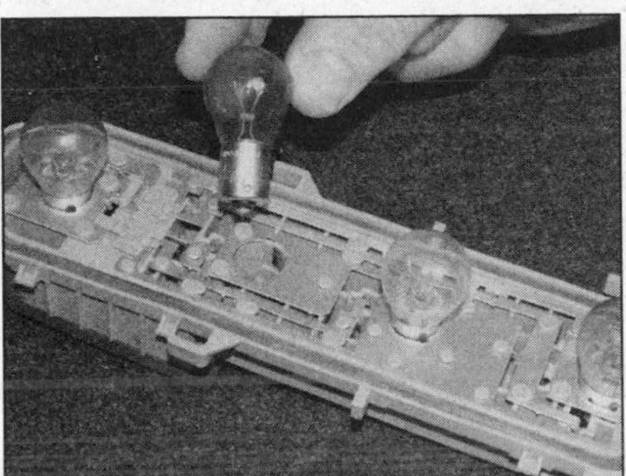

1 If a single indicator light, stop-light or headlight has failed, it is likely that a bulb has blown and will need to be renewed. Refer to *Electrical fault finding* in Chapter 12 for details. If both stop-lights have failed, it is possible that the switch has failed (see Chapter 9).

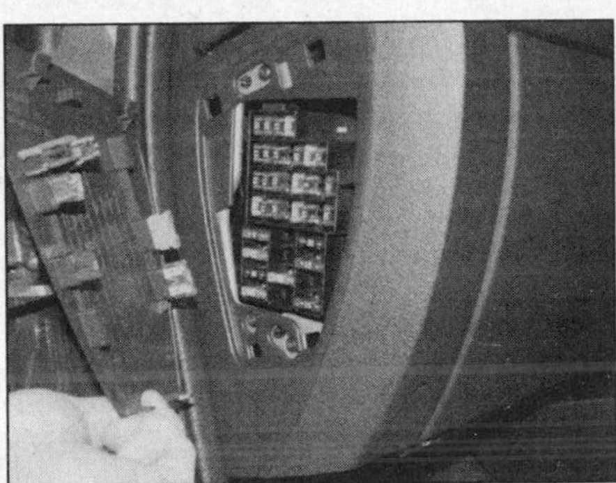

2 If more than one indicator light or headlight has failed, it is likely that either a fuse has blown or that there is a fault in the circuit (see Chapter 12). The main fuses are located on the left-hand end of the instrument panel. Open the left-hand door then prise off the fusebox cover. The fuse locations are indicated by symbols on the rear of the cover. Additional fuses and relays are located in the left-hand side of the engine compartment.

3 To renew a blown fuse, remove it using the plastic tool provided. Fit a new fuse of the same rating, available from car accessory shops. It is important that you find the reason that the fuse failed (see *Electrical fault finding* in Chapter 12).

Lubricants and fluids

Petrol engine	Multigrade engine oil, viscosity range SAE 10W/30 to 10W/50, to ACEA A1, A3 and A5
Diesel engine	Multigrade engine oil, viscosity range SAE 10W/40 to 10W/50, to ACEA B3 and B4
Cooling system	Ethylene glycol-based antifreeze – RX Glacéol type D coolant
Manual gearbox	Elf Tranself TRJ 75W-80 gear oil
Automatic transmission	Elf Renaultmatic D3 SYN, Dexron III ATF
Sequential gearbox	
Gearbox	Elf Tranself TRJ 75W-80 gear oil
Hydraulic control fluid	Elf Renaultmatic D3 SYN, Dexron III ATF
Brake fluid reservoir	Hydraulic fluid to SAE J1703F or DOT 4

Choosing your engine oil

Engines need oil, not only to lubricate moving parts and minimise wear, but also to maximise power output and to improve fuel economy.

HOW ENGINE OIL WORKS

• Beating friction

Without oil, the moving surfaces inside your engine will rub together, heat up and melt, quickly causing the engine to seize. Engine oil creates a film which separates these moving parts, preventing wear and heat build-up.

• Cooling hot-spots

Temperatures inside the engine can exceed 1000° C. The engine oil circulates and acts as a coolant, transferring heat from the hot-spots to the sump.

• Cleaning the engine internally

Good quality engine oils clean the inside of your engine, collecting and dispersing combustion deposits and controlling them until they are trapped by the oil filter or flushed out at oil change.

OIL CARE - FOLLOW THE CODE

To handle and dispose of used engine oil safely, always:

• Avoid skin contact with used engine oil. Repeated or prolonged contact can be harmful.

• Dispose of used oil and empty packs in a responsible manner in an authorised disposal site. Call 0800 663366 to find the one nearest to you. Never tip oil down drains or onto the ground.

Tyre pressures (cold)

Note: *Pressures apply to original-equipment tyres, and may vary if any other make or type of tyre is fitted; check with the tyre manufacturer or supplier for correct pressures if necessary. The pressures are also given in the vehicle handbook.*

	Front	Rear
1.2 litre models		
Normal use	28 psi (1.9 bar)	26 psi (1.8 bar)
Full load	29 psi (2.0 bar)	28 psi (1.9 bar)
1.4 and 1.6 litre models		
Normal use	32 psi (2.2 bar)	29 psi (2.0 bar)
Full load	33 psi (2.3 bar)	30 psi (2.1 bar)
1.5 litre diesel models		
Normal use	32 psi (2.2 bar)	29 psi (2.0 bar)
Full load	33 psi (2.3 bar)	30 psi (2.1 bar)
Emergency spare wheel		
1.2 litre models	33 psi (2.3 bar)	
1.4 and 1.6 litre models	35 psi (2.4 bar)	
1.5 litre models	29 psi (2.0 bar)	

Chapter 1 Part A:
Routine maintenance and servicing – petrol models

Contents

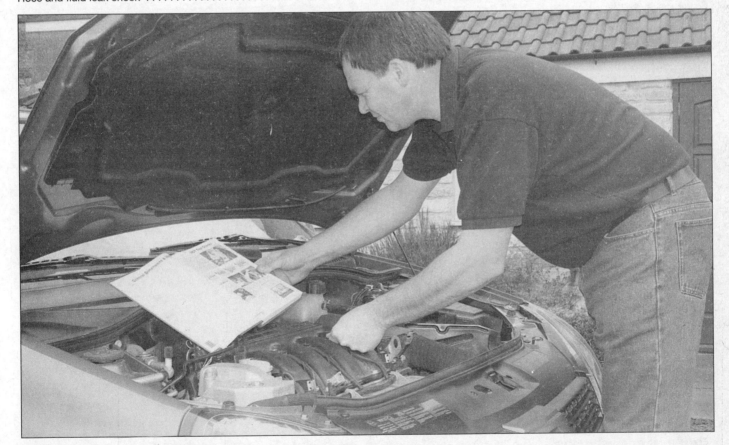

Degrees of difficulty

Easy, suitable for novice with little experience 	**Fairly easy,** suitable for beginner with some experience 	**Fairly difficult,** suitable for competent DIY mechanic 	**Difficult,** suitable for experienced DIY mechanic 	**Very difficult,** suitable for expert DIY or professional

Lubricants and fluids

Refer to *Weekly checks* on page 0•18

Capacities

Engine oil	**Excluding oil filter**	**Including oil filter**
1.2 litre:		
D7F engine	3.5 litres	4.0 litres
D4F engine	3.5 litres	4.0 litres
1.4 litre K4J engine	4.25 litres	4.9 litres
1.6 litre K4M engine	4.25 litres	4.9 litres
Difference between MAX and MIN dipstick marks	1.5 to 2.0 litres depending on engine	
Cooling system		
1.2 litre:		
D7F engine	4.5 litres	
D4F engine	5.0 litres	
1.4 litre K4J engine	5.7 litres	
1.6 litre K4M engine	5.7 litres	
Manual and sequential transmission	3.4 litres	
Automatic transmission	6.0 litres	
Fuel tank	50 litres	

Cooling system

Antifreeze mixture:	**Antifreeze**	**Water**
Protection to –23°C	35%	65%
Protection to –40°C	50%	50%

Fuel system

Specified idle speed (non-adjustable)	750 ± 50 rpm
Idle mixture CO content (non-adjustable)	0.5% maximum (0.3% at 2500 rpm)

Ignition system

Firing order	1-3-4-2	
Location of No 1 cylinder	Flywheel end	
Ignition timing	Controlled by ECU – see Chapter 5B	
Spark plugs:	**Type**	**Electrode gap**
1.2 litre D4F engine	Bosch VR 8 SE	0.9 mm
	Champion REA 8 MCL	0.9 mm
All other engines	Bosch FR 7 DE	0.9 mm
	Eyquem RFC 50 LZ 2E	0.9 mm

Brakes

Front disc brakes:	
Pad thickness (including backing):	
New	18.0 mm
Minimum thickness	6.0 mm
Rear disc brakes:	
Pad thickness (including backing):	
New	15.0 mm
Minimum thickness	6.0 mm
Rear drum brakes:	
Shoe thickness (friction material only):	
New:	
Leading	4.6 mm
Trailing	3.3 mm
Minimum thickness	2.0 mm

Torque wrench settings

	Nm	**lbf ft**
Roadwheel bolts	90	66
Spark plugs	25 to 30	18 to 22

The maintenance intervals in this manual are provided with the assumption that you, not the dealer, will be carrying out the work. These are the minimum maintenance intervals recommended by us for vehicles driven daily. If you wish to keep your vehicle in peak condition at all times, you may wish to perform some of these procedures more often. We encourage frequent maintenance, because it enhances the efficiency, performance and resale value of your vehicle.

If the vehicle is driven in dusty areas, used to tow a trailer, or driven frequently at slow speeds (idling in traffic) or on short journeys, more frequent maintenance intervals are recommended.

When the vehicle is new, it should be serviced by a factory-authorised dealer service department, in order to preserve the factory warranty.

Every 250 miles (400 km) or weekly

- ☐ Refer to *Weekly Checks*

Every 9000 miles (15 000 km)

- ☐ Renew the engine oil and filter (Section 3)

Note: *Frequent oil and filter changes are good for the engine. We recommend changing the oil at the mileage specified here, or at least twice a year.*

Every 18 000 miles (30 000 km) or 2 years, whichever comes first

In addition to all the items listed previously, carry out the following:

- ☐ Renew the pollen filter (Section 4)
- ☐ Check the handbrake (Section 5)
- ☐ Check the brake pads and discs (Section 6)
- ☐ Check the operation of the clutch (Section 7)
- ☐ Check the condition of the auxiliary drivebelts (Section 8)
- ☐ Check the condition of the seat belts (Section 9)
- ☐ Check the operation of all electrical systems (Section 10)
- ☐ Check the condition of the exhaust system and mountings (Section 11)
- ☐ Check the suspension and steering components (Section 12)
- ☐ Check all underbonnet components and hoses for fluid leaks (Section 13)
- ☐ Check the tightness of the roadwheel bolts (Section 14)
- ☐ Check the bodywork and underbody for damage and corrosion (Section 15)
- ☐ Check the front and rear shock absorbers (Section 16)

Every 36 000 miles (60 000 km) or 4 years, whichever comes first

In addition to all the items listed previously, carry out the following:

- ☐ Renew the spark plugs and check the ignition system (Section 17)
- ☐ Renew the air filter element (Section 18)
- ☐ Check the rear brake shoes and drums (Section 19)
- ☐ Check the manual or sequential transmission oil level (Section 20)
- ☐ Check the front wheel alignment (Section 21)
- ☐ Check the operation of the air conditioning system (Section 22)
- ☐ Carry out a road test (Section 23)
- ☐ Renew the timing belt (Section 24)*
- ☐ Renew the brake fluid (Section 25)
- ☐ Renew the coolant (Section 26)

* **Note:** *Although the normal interval for timing belt renewal is 75 000 miles (120 000 km), it is strongly recommended that the interval is reduced to 36 000 miles (60 000 km) on vehicles which are subjected to intensive use, ie, mainly short journeys or a lot of stop-start driving. The actual belt renewal interval is therefore very much up to the individual owner, but bear in mind that severe engine damage may result if the belt breaks.*

Component location – petrol models

Underbonnet view of a 1.2 litre 8-valve petrol model (D7F engine)

1. *Engine oil filler cap*
2. *Engine oil level dipstick*
3. *Front suspension strut upper mountings*
4. *Ignition HT coils*
5. *Brake master cylinder fluid reservoir*
6. *Air cleaner*
7. *MAP sensor*
8. *Inlet manifold*
9. *Coolant expansion tank*
10. *Windscreen/headlight washer fluid reservoir*
11. *Engine management ECU*
12. *Battery*
13. *Engine related fusebox*
14. *Air inlet duct*

Front underbody view of a 1.2 litre 8-valve petrol model (D7F engine)

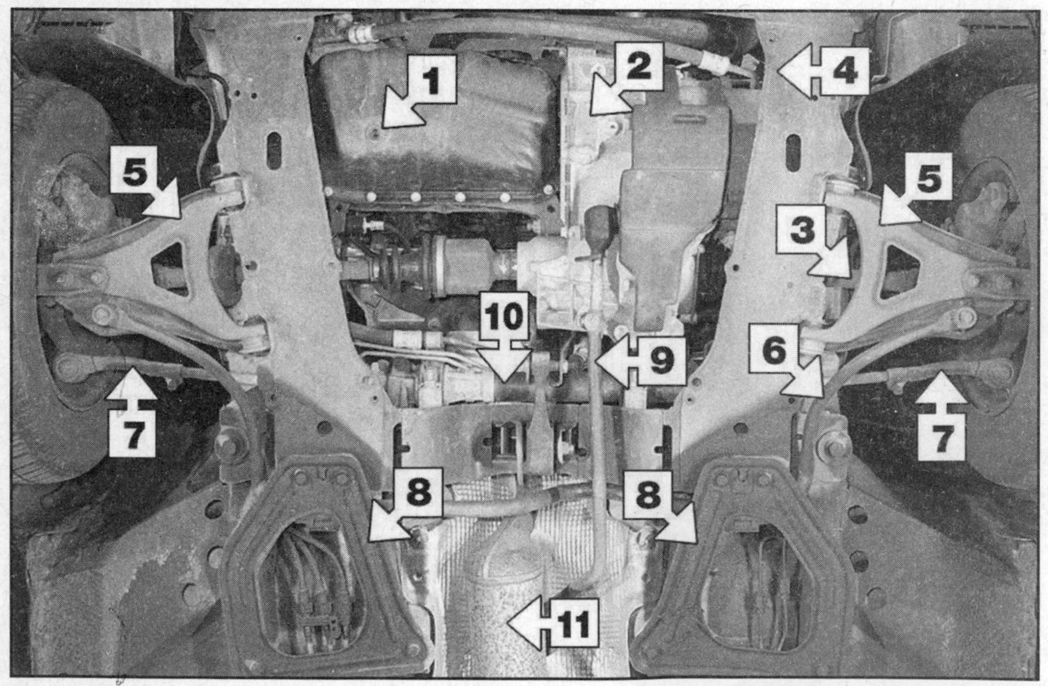

1. *Engine oil sump drain plug*
2. *Manual transmission*
3. *Driveshafts*
4. *Front suspension subframe*
5. *Front suspension lower arms*
6. *Front anti-roll bar*
7. *Track rod ends*
8. *Front subframe rear links*
9. *Gearchange rod*
10. *Power steering gear*
11. *Exhaust catalytic converter*

Rear underbody view of a 1.2 litre petrol model

1 *Fuel tank*
2 *Handbrake cables*
3 *Fuel tank strap*
4 *Fuel feed and return lines*
5 *Rear brake compensator*
6 *Rear axle assembly*
7 *Rear coil springs*
8 *Exhaust rear silencer and tailpipe*
9 *Shock absorbers*

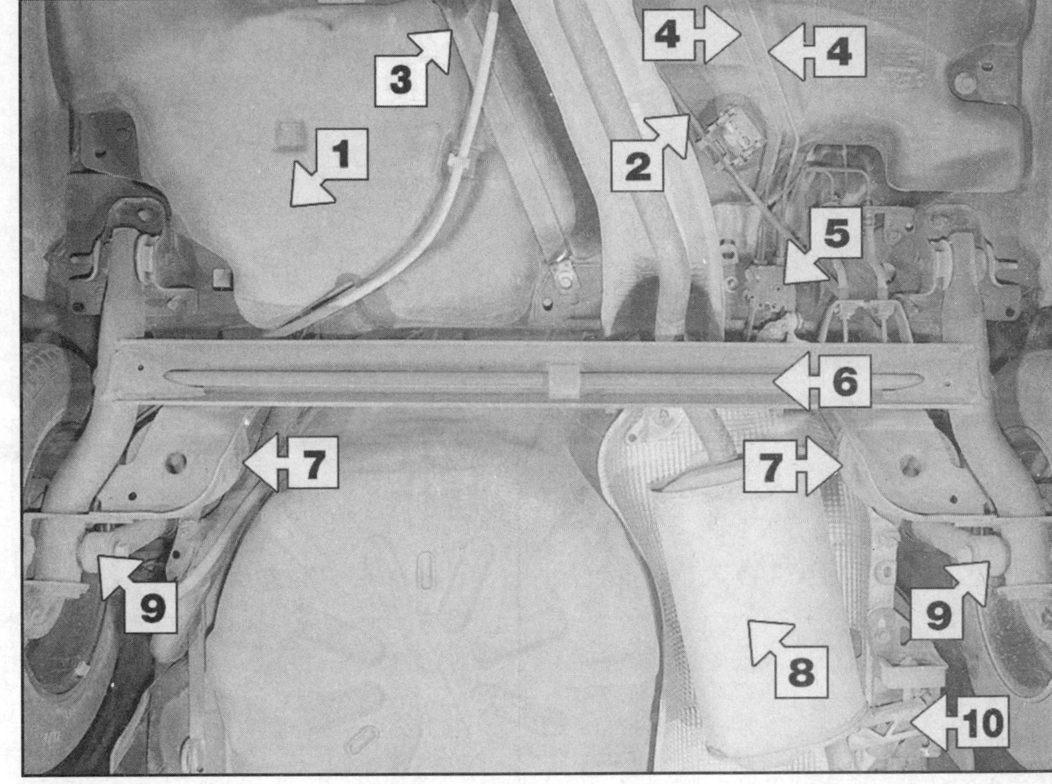

Underbonnet view of a 1.2 litre 16-valve petrol model (D4F engine)

1 *Engine oil filler cap*
2 *Engine oil level dipstick*
3 *Ignition HT coils and leads*
4 *Alternator*
5 *Front suspension strut upper mountings*
6 *Brake master cylinder fluid reservoir*
7 *Air cleaner*
8 *Coolant expansion tank*
9 *Engine management ECU*
10 *Battery*
11 *Engine related fusebox*
12 *Air inlet duct*

Front underbody view of a 1.2 litre 16-valve petrol model (D4F engine)

1. *Engine oil sump drain plug*
2. *Manual transmission*
3. *Exhaust catalytic converter*
4. *Gearchange rod*
5. *Front suspension subframe*
6. *Front suspension lower arms*
7. *Driveshafts*
8. *Steering gear*
9. *Front anti-roll bar*
10. *Track rod ends*
11. *Front subframe rear links*

Underbonnet view of a 1.4 litre 16-valve petrol model (K4J engine)

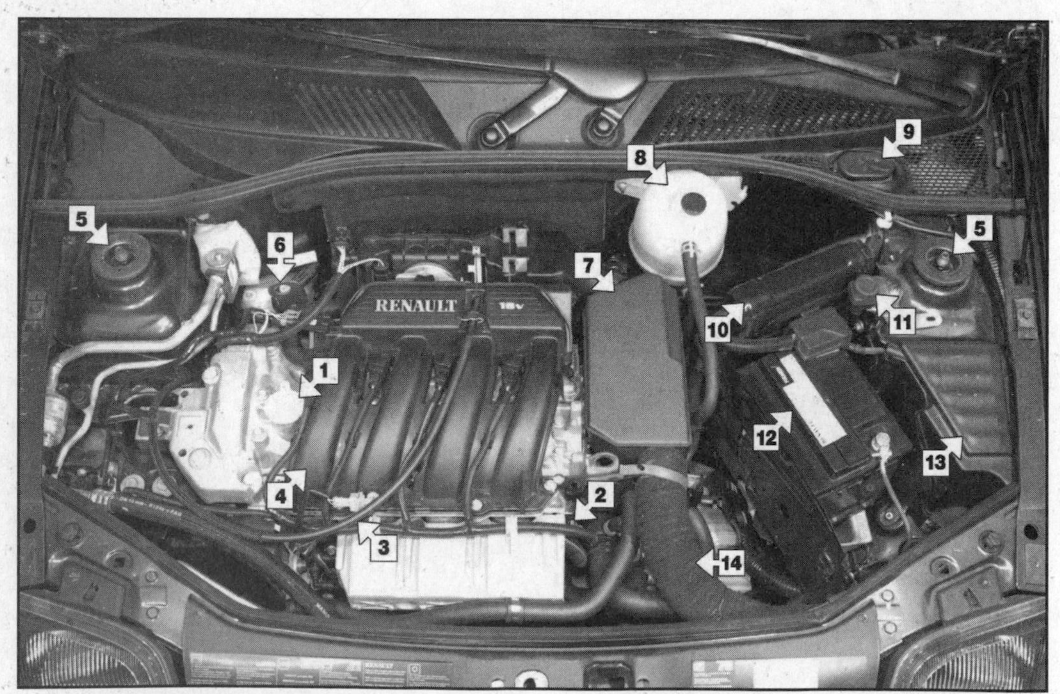

1. *Engine oil filler cap*
2. *Engine oil level dipstick*
3. *Accelerator cable*
4. *Inlet manifold*
5. *Front suspension strut upper mountings*
6. *Brake master cylinder fluid reservoir*
7. *Air cleaner*
8. *Coolant expansion tank*
9. *Windscreen/headlight washer fluid reservoir*
10. *Engine management ECU*
11. *Fuel cut-off inertia switch*
12. *Battery*
13. *Engine related fusebox*
14. *Air inlet duct*

Front underbody view of a 1.4 litre 16-valve petrol model (K4J engine)

1 *Engine oil sump drain plug*
2 *Manual transmission*
3 *Driveshafts*
4 *Front suspension subframe*
5 *Front suspension lower arms*
6 *Front anti-roll bar*
7 *Track rod ends*
8 *Front subframe rear links*
9 *Gearchange rod*
10 *Steering gear*
11 *Exhaust catalytic converter*

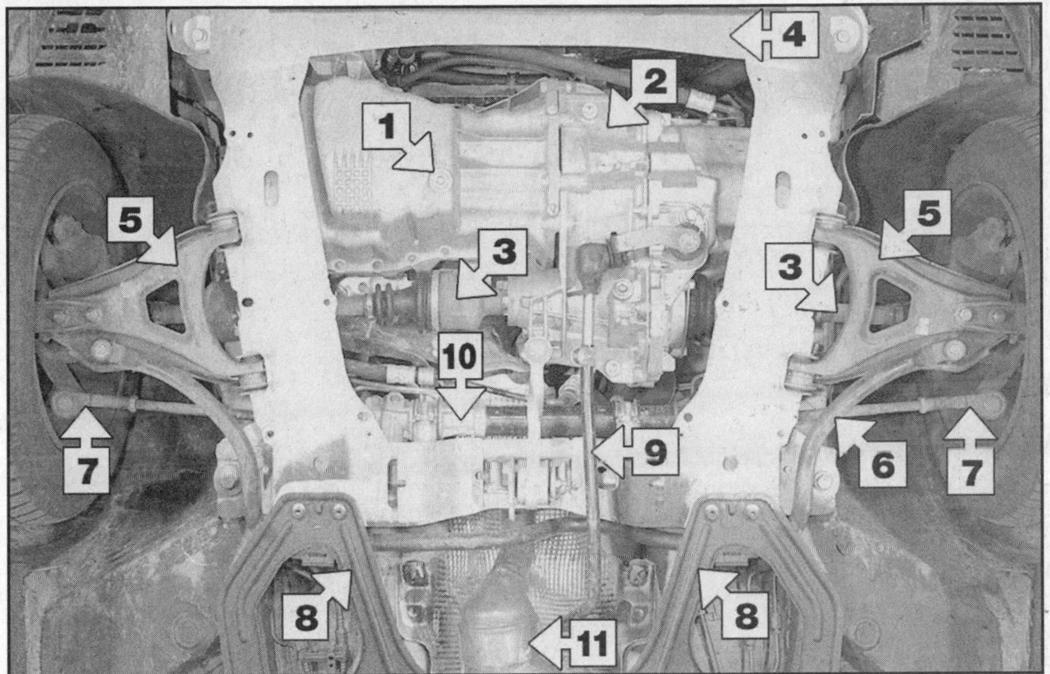

Maintenance procedures

1 Introduction

This Chapter is designed to help the home mechanic maintain his/her vehicle for safety, economy, long life and peak performance.

The Chapter contains a master maintenance schedule, followed by Sections dealing specifically with each task in the schedule. Visual checks, adjustments, component renewal and other helpful items are included. Refer to the accompanying illustrations of the engine compartment and the underside of the vehicle for the locations of the various components.

Servicing your vehicle in accordance with the mileage/time maintenance schedule and the following Sections will provide a planned maintenance programme, which should result in a long and reliable service life. This is a comprehensive plan, so maintaining some items but not others at the specified service intervals, will not produce the same results.

As you service your vehicle, you will discover that many of the procedures can – and should – be grouped together, because of the particular procedure being performed, or because of the proximity of two otherwise-unrelated components to one another. For example, if the vehicle is raised for any reason, the exhaust can be inspected at the same time as the suspension and steering components.

The first step in this maintenance programme is to prepare yourself before the actual work begins. Read through all the Sections relevant to the work to be carried out, then make a list and gather all the parts and tools required. If a problem is encountered, seek advice from a parts specialist, or a dealer service department.

2 Regular maintenance

If, from the time the vehicle is new, the routine maintenance schedule is followed closely, and frequent checks are made of fluid levels and high-wear items, as suggested throughout this manual, the engine will be kept in relatively good running condition, and the need for additional work will be minimised.

It is possible that there will be times when the engine is running poorly due to the lack of regular maintenance. This is even more likely if a used vehicle, which has not received regular and frequent maintenance checks, is purchased. In such cases, additional work may need to be carried out, outside of the regular maintenance intervals.

If engine wear is suspected, a compression test (refer to Chapter 2A or 2B as applicable) will provide valuable information regarding the overall performance of the main internal components. Such a test can be used as a basis to decide on the extent of the work to be carried out. If, for example, a compression test indicates serious internal engine wear, conventional maintenance as described in this Chapter will not greatly improve the performance of the engine, and may prove a waste of time and money, unless extensive overhaul work is carried out first.

The following series of operations are those most often required to improve the performance of a generally poor-running engine:

Primary operations

a) *Clean, inspect and test the battery (refer to 'Weekly checks').*
b) *Check all the engine-related fluids (refer to 'Weekly checks').*
c) *Check the condition of the auxiliary drivebelt(s) (Section 8).*
d) *Check the condition of all hoses, and check for fluid leaks (Section 13).*
e) *Renew the spark plugs (Section 17).*
f) *Check the condition of the air filter, and renew if necessary (Section 18).*

If the above operations do not prove fully effective, carry out the following secondary operations:

Secondary operations

All items listed under *Primary operations*, plus the following:

a) *Check the charging system (Chapter 5A).*
b) *Check the ignition system (Chapter 5B).*
c) *Check the fuel system (refer to Chapter 4A).*

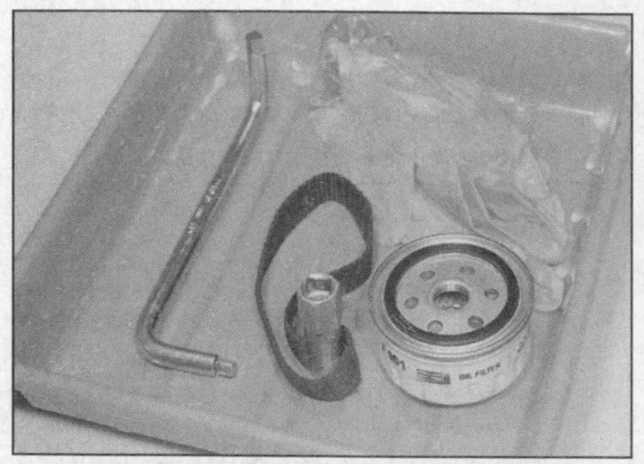
3.1 Tools and materials necessary for the engine oil change and filter renewal

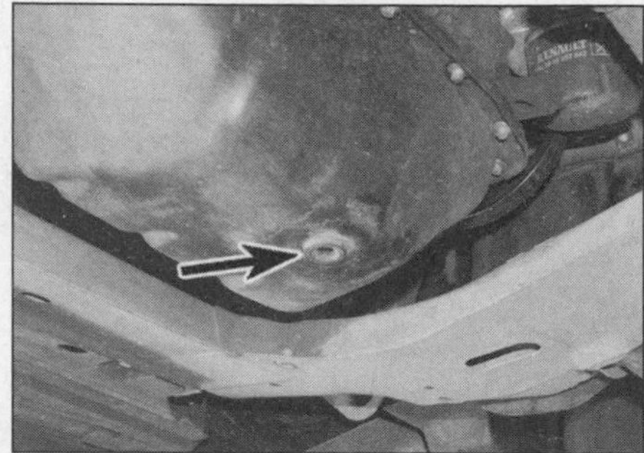
3.2 Engine oil drain plug

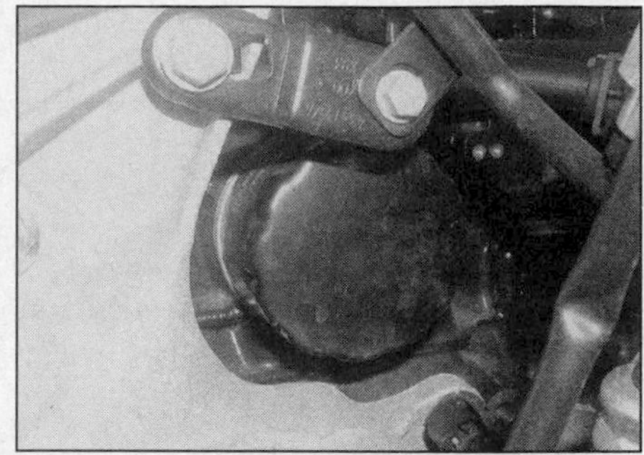
3.5a Oil filter location – K4J and K4M engines

Every 9000 miles (15 000 km)

3 Engine oil and filter renewal

1 Before starting this procedure, gather together all the necessary tools and materials **(see illustration)**. Also make sure that you have plenty of clean rags and newspapers handy to mop-up any spills. Ideally, the engine oil should be warm, as it will drain better and more built-up sludge will be removed with it. Take care, however, not to touch the exhaust or any other hot parts of the engine when working under the vehicle. To avoid any possibility of scalding, and to protect yourself from possible skin irritants and other harmful contaminants in used engine oils, it is advisable to wear rubber gloves when carrying out this work. Apply the handbrake, then jack up the front of the vehicle and support it on axle stands (see *Jacking and vehicle support*). Alternatively, raise the vehicle on a lift or drive it onto ramps. Whichever method is chosen, make sure that the car remains as level as possible, to enable the oil to drain fully. Remove the engine undertray where applicable.

2 Remove the oil filler cap from the valve cover, then position a container beneath the sump. Clean the drain plug and the area around it, then slacken it half a turn using a special drain plug key **(see illustration)**.

If possible, try to keep the plug pressed into the sump while unscrewing it by hand the last couple of turns. As the plug releases from the threads, move it away sharply so the stream of oil from the sump runs into the container, not up your sleeve.

3 Allow some time for the old oil to drain, noting that it may be necessary to reposition the container as the oil flow slows to a trickle.

4 After all the oil has drained, wipe off the drain plug with a clean rag and renew its sealing washer. Clean the area around the drain plug opening, then refit and tighten the plug securely.

5 Move the container into position under the oil filter. The oil filter is located on the front of the cylinder block on K4J and K4M engines, and on the rear of the cylinder block at the timing belt end on D4F and D7F engines **(see illustrations)**.

6 On the K4J and K4M 16-valve engines, there is only limited room between the subframe and the sump, and it is very difficult to reach up to the oil filter. However, it is possible to gain access through this space, and it is not necessary to remove any body or engine components **(see illus-tration)**.

Canister-type filter

7 Using an oil filter removal tool, slacken the filter initially. Loosely wrap some rags around the oil filter, then unscrew it and immediately position it with its open end uppermost to prevent further spillage of oil. Remove the oil filter from the engine compartment and empty the oil into the container.

8 Use a clean rag to remove all oil, dirt and sludge from the filter sealing area on the engine. Check the old filter to make sure that the rubber sealing ring hasn't stuck to the engine. If it has, carefully remove it.

9 Apply a light coating of clean oil to the sealing ring on the new filter, then screw it into position on the engine. Tighten the filter firmly by hand only – do not use any tools. Wipe clean the exterior of the oil filter.

Paper filter element

10 Unscrew the plastic filter cover – this should be possible by hand, but a strap wrench may be used if necessary. Note that using a chain-type filter wrench may damage the cover. Anticipate that the cover will be full of oil – have a container ready to pour it into. Recover the large O-ring seal from the cover groove – a new one should be supplied with the new element **(see illustration)**.

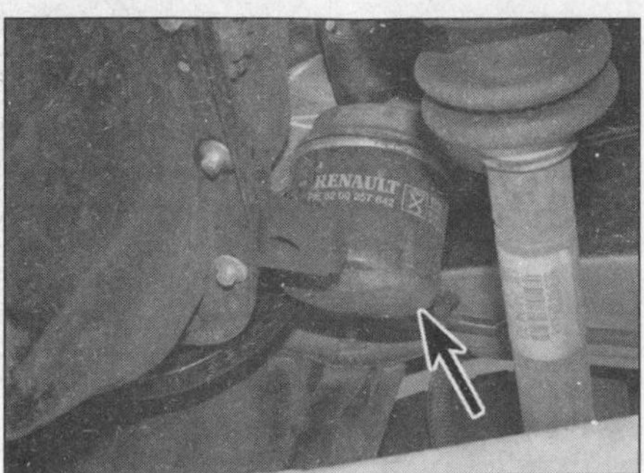
3.5b Oil filter location – D4F and D7F engines

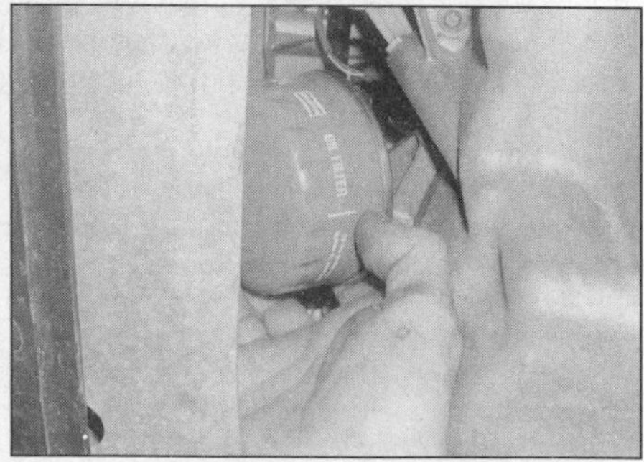
3.6 Removing the oil filter – K4J engine

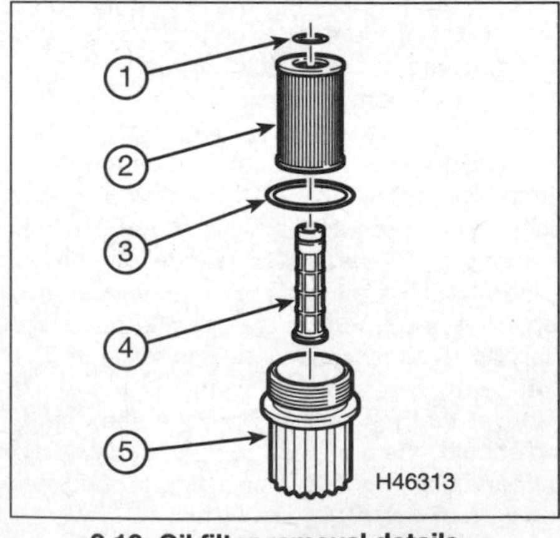

3.10 Oil filter removal details – paper filter element

1 O-ring
2 Filter element
3 O-ring
4 Spindle
5 Filter cover

11 Pull the filter's centre spindle downwards to release the filter element, and remove it. Recover the small O-ring from the base of the spindle – again, a new O-ring should be supplied.
12 Withdraw the filter element from the spindle. Wipe the spindle clean, and fit a new element to it. Fit the new O-ring to the groove at the base of the spindle.
13 Refit the spindle and element into the oil filter housing, and push it home firmly to locate the O-ring.
14 Fit the new O-ring to the filter cover, then screw this on firmly by hand only – do not use any tools.

Both filter types

15 Remove the old oil and all tools from under the car, then, where necessary, refit the undertray and lower the car to the ground.
16 Fill the engine with the specified quantity and grade of oil, as described in *Weekly checks*. Pour the oil in slowly, otherwise it may overflow from the top of the valve cover. Check that the oil level is up to the maximum mark on the dipstick, then refit and tighten the oil filler cap.
17 Start the engine and run it for a few minutes, checking that there are no leaks around the oil filter seal and the sump drain plug. Note that when the engine is first started, there will be a delay of a few seconds before the oil pressure warning light goes out while the new filter fills with oil. Do not race the engine while the warning light is on.
18 Switch off the engine and wait a few minutes for the oil to settle in the sump once more. With the new oil circulated and the filter now completely full, recheck the level on the dipstick and add more oil if necessary.
19 Dispose of the used engine oil safely with reference to *General repair procedures* in the Reference section of this manual.

Every 18 000 miles (30 000 km) or 2 years

4 Pollen filter renewal

Note: *The pollen filter may not be fitted to all models.*
1 With the bonnet open, remove the windscreen half-scuttle grille from the right-hand end of the bulkhead.
2 Undo the retaining screw and slide the cover forwards to unclip from the pollen filter housing **(see illustrations)**.
3 Note the direction arrows on the filter and housing, then carefully extract the filter element by squeezing its central folds together **(see illustration)**.
4 Fit the new element using a reversal of the removal procedure, but make sure that the direction arrows are aligned with each other.

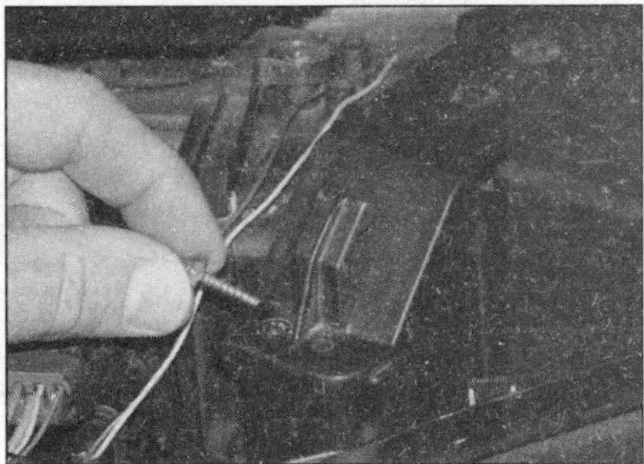

4.2a Undo the retaining screws . . .

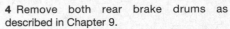

4.2b . . . and unclip the cover from the pollen filter housing

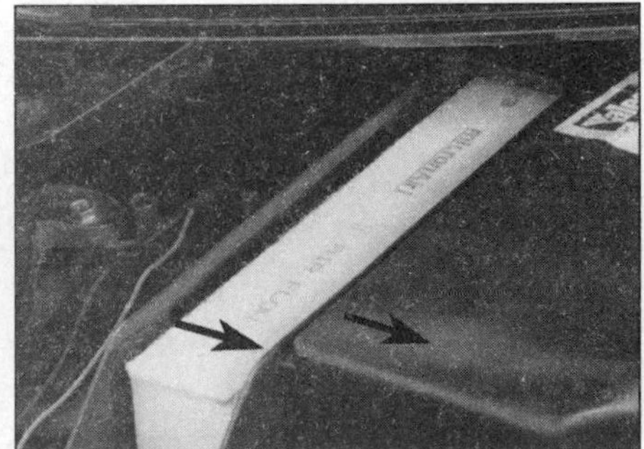

4.3 Removing the pollen filter element. Note the direction arrows on the element and housing

5 Handbrake check

1 The handbrake should be capable of holding the parked vehicle stationary, even on steep slopes, when applied with moderate force. The mechanism should be firm and positive in feel, with no trace of stiffness or sponginess from the cables, and should release immediately the handbrake lever is released. If the mechanism is faulty in any of these respects, it must be checked immediately as follows. **Note:** *On models with rear drum brakes, if the handbrake is not functioning correctly or is incorrectly adjusted, the rear brake self-adjust mechanism will not function. This will lead to the brake pedal travel becoming excessive as the shoe linings wear.*
2 Handbrake adjustment is made beneath the vehicle on the cable adjuster nut **(see illustration)**.
3 Jack up the rear of the vehicle and support it on axle stands (see *Jacking and vehicle support*). Undo the heat shield retaining nut(s) and lower the rear of the heat shield to gain access to the handbrake cable adjuster nut. Slacken the locknut, then fully slacken the cable adjuster nut.

Models with rear drum brakes

4 Remove both rear brake drums as described in Chapter 9.
5 Check that the knurled adjuster wheel on the adjuster strut is free to rotate in both directions. If it is seized, the brake shoes and strut must be removed and overhauled as described in Section 12 of Chapter 9.
6 If all is well, back off the adjuster wheel by five or six teeth so that the diameter of the brake shoes is slightly reduced.
7 Check that the handbrake cables slide freely by pulling on their front ends. Also check that the operating levers on the rear brake trailing shoes return to their correct positions, with their stop-pegs in contact with the edge of the trailing shoe web.
8 With the aid of an assistant, tighten the adjuster nut on the handbrake lever operating rod so that the lever on each rear brake assembly starts to move as the handbrake is

5.2 Handbrake cable adjusting nut located beneath the vehicle

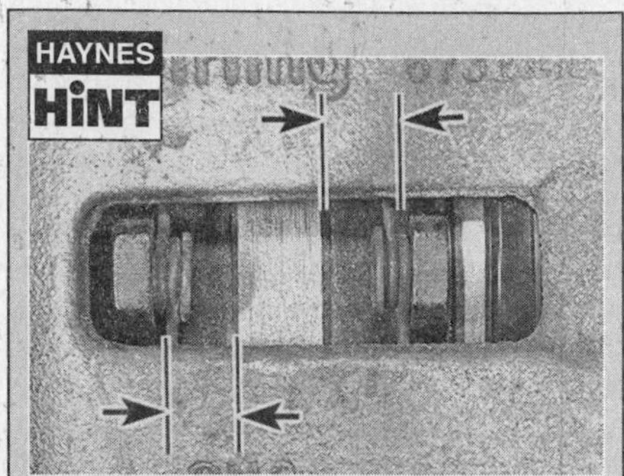

For a quick check, the thickness of friction material remaining on each brake pad can be measured through the aperture in the caliper body.

moved between the first and second notch (click) of its ratchet mechanism. This is the case when the stop-pegs are still in contact with the shoes when the handbrake is on the first notch of the ratchet, but no longer contact the shoes when the handbrake is on the second notch. Once the adjustment is correct, hold the adjuster nut and securely tighten the locknut. Refit the catalytic converter heat shield retaining nuts.

9 Refit the brake drums as described in Chapter 9, then lower the vehicle to the ground.

10 With the vehicle standing on its wheels, repeatedly depress the footbrake to adjust the shoe-to-drum clearance. Whilst depressing the pedal, have an assistant listen to the rear drums to check that the adjuster strut mechanism is functioning; if this is so, a clicking sound will be heard from the adjuster strut as the pedal is depressed.

Models with rear disc brakes

11 Check that the handbrake cables slide freely by pulling on their front ends, and check that the operating levers on the rear brake calipers move smoothly.

12 Move both of the caliper operating levers as far rearwards as possible, then tighten the adjuster nut on the handbrake lever operating rod until all free play is removed from both cables. With the aid of an assistant, adjust the nut so that the operating lever on each rear brake caliper starts to move as the handbrake lever is moved between the first and second notch (click) of its ratchet mechanism. Once the handbrake adjustment is correct, hold the adjuster nut and securely tighten the locknut.

13 Refit the heat shield retaining nuts (where necessary), then lower the vehicle to the ground.

6 Brake pad and disc check

Note: *Drum brake checks are in Section 19.*

1 Firmly apply the handbrake, then jack up the front or rear of the vehicle (as applicable) and support it securely on axle stands (see *Jacking and vehicle support*). Remove the roadwheels.

2 For a quick check, the thickness of friction material remaining on each brake pad can be measured through the aperture in the caliper body **(see Haynes Hint)**. If any pad's friction material is worn to the specified thickness or less, all four pads must be renewed as a set. Pad wear warning contacts are fitted to the inboard pads, but this should not be used as an excuse for omitting a visual check.

3 For a comprehensive check, the brake pads should be removed and cleaned. This will allow the operation of the caliper to be checked, and the brake disc itself to be fully examined for condition on both sides. Refer to Chapter 9 for further information.

7 Clutch check

1 Check that the clutch pedal moves smoothly and easily through its full travel, and that the clutch itself functions correctly, with no trace of slip or drag. If the movement is uneven or stiff in places, check that the cable is routed correctly, with no sharp turns.

2 Inspect the ends of the clutch inner cable, both at the gearbox end and inside the car, for signs of wear and fraying.

8 Auxiliary drivebelt check and renewal

Note: *Where applicable, the tension of the belt is checked midway between the pulleys at the longest point. The tension can only be checked and set using the correct electronic measuring tool (Hertz or Seem units). If access to this equipment is not available, have the belt tension checked by a specialist with this equipment or your Renault dealer (The procedures in this Section assume that the Renault special tool is being used).*

Checking

1 The auxiliary drivebelt is located at the right-hand side of the engine.

2 Numerous different drivebelt configurations may be encountered, depending on engine type and whether the vehicle is equipped with air conditioning **(see illustrations)**.

3 Due to their function and material makeup, drivebelts are prone to failure after a period of time and should therefore be inspected and, where applicable, periodically adjusted.

4 Since the drivebelt is located very close to the right-hand side of the engine compartment, it is possible to gain better access by raising the front of the vehicle and removing the right-hand wheel, then removing the engine undercover (where applicable) and wheel arch liner from inside the wheel arch.

5 With the engine stopped, inspect the full length of the drivebelt for cracks and separation of the belt plies. It will be necessary to turn the engine (using a spanner or socket and bar on the crankshaft pulley bolt) in order to move the belt from the pulleys so that the belt can be inspected thoroughly. Twist the belt between the pulleys so that both sides can be viewed. Also check for fraying, and glazing which gives the belt a shiny appearance. Check the pulleys for nicks, cracks, distortion and corrosion.

Renewal – D4F and D7F engines

Alternator

6 Slacken the alternator upper and lower mounting bolts **(see illustration)**, then move the alternator until the belt can be slipped from the pulleys.

7 Fit the belt around the pulleys, ensuring that the belt is of the correct type if it is being renewed. Take up the slack in the belt by swinging the alternator away from the engine

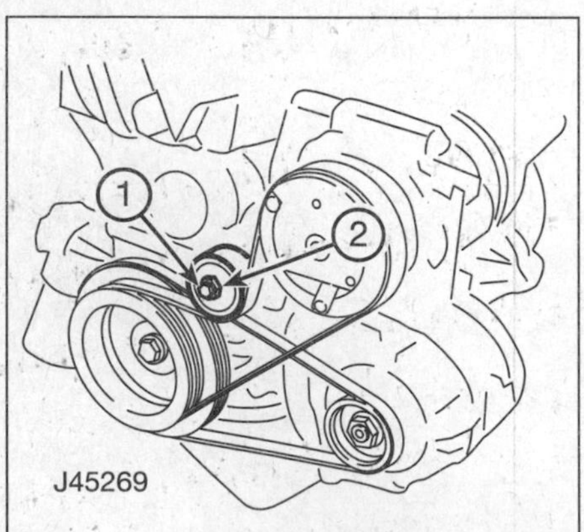

8.2a Auxiliary drivebelts – D4F and D7F engines

Slacken bolt (1) and turn nut (2) clockwise

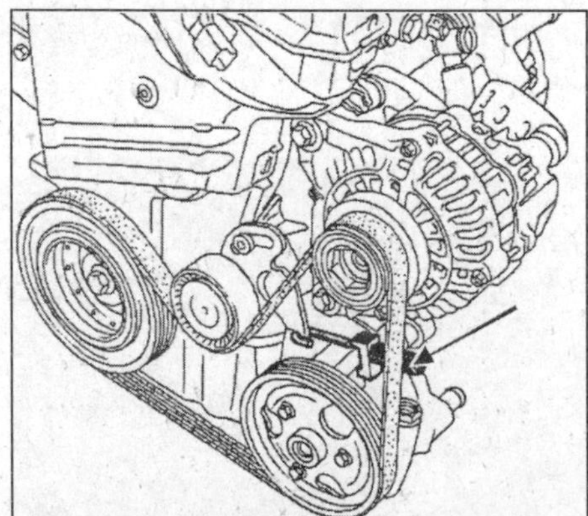

8.2b Using the Renault tool to pull the tensioner and adjust the belt – K4J and K4M engines

8.6 Alternator drivebelt tensioner adjustment bolt (arrowed) – D4F engine

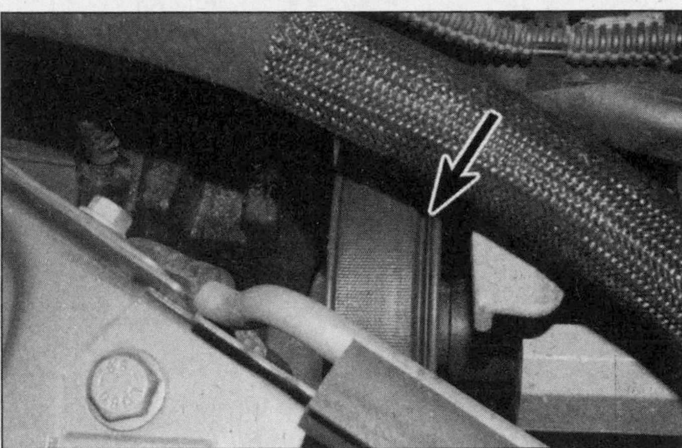
8.16 Note the inner groove (arrowed) on the pulley is left clear – K4M engine

and lightly tightening the mounting nuts and bolts.

8 Position the alternator to achieve the correct tension of 260 ± 5 Hertz (see note at the start of this Section), then tighten the mounting bolts fully.

9 On completion, where applicable, refit the power steering pump drivebelt.

Air conditioning compressor

10 Working in the engine compartment, slacken the belt tensioner pulley centre bolt, then using a spanner turn the outer nut clockwise to release the tension on the belt **(see illustration 8.2a)**.

11 Noting the fitted position of the belt, slip the drivebelt from the pulleys.

12 Fit the belt around the pulleys, then take up the slack in the belt by turning the tensioner pulley with a spanner. Position the pulley to achieve the correct tension of 210 ± 5 Hertz (see note at the start of this Section), then tighten the centre bolt.

Renewal – K4J and K4M engines

Note: *Before removal of the belt, note the fitted position. On models without air conditioning, the alternator pulley has six grooves, the belt has five. In this case the outer groove is left unused, so that the run of the belt is straight. On models with air conditioning, the compressor pulley has six grooves, the belt has five. In this case the inner groove is left unused **(see illustration 8.16)**, so that the run of the belt is straight.*

13 Apply the handbrake, then jack up the front of the car and support securely on axle stands (see *Jacking and vehicle support*). For improved access, remove the right-hand roadwheel, then remove the wheel arch liner, noting that it may be necessary to drill out the securing rivets on certain models.

14 Loosen the bolt(s) securing the tensioner bracket to the engine.

15 Loosen the locknut and back off the tensioner adjustment bolt until the drivebelt can be removed from the pulleys.

16 Fit the drivebelt around the pulleys making sure that it is correctly located in the grooves **(see illustration)**.

17 Position the tensioner to achieve the correct tension of 108 ± 6 Seem units (see note at the start of this Section) for the alternator drivebelt.

18 Fully tighten the tensioner bracket bolt and the locknut for the adjustment bolt(s).

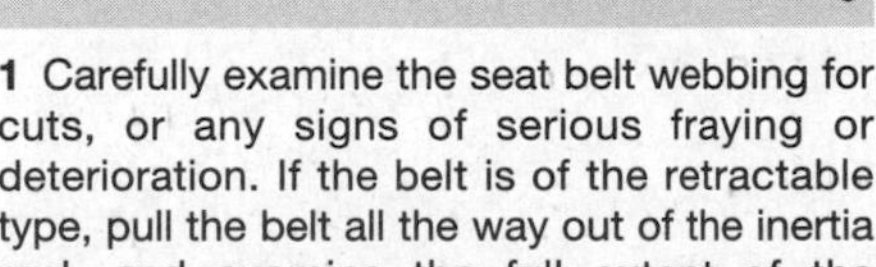

9 Seat belt check

1 Carefully examine the seat belt webbing for cuts, or any signs of serious fraying or deterioration. If the belt is of the retractable type, pull the belt all the way out of the inertia reel, and examine the full extent of the webbing.

2 Fasten and unfasten the belt, ensuring that the locking mechanism holds securely, and releases properly when intended. If the belt is of the retractable type, check also that the retracting mechanism operates correctly when the belt is released.

3 Check the security of all seat belt mountings and attachments which are accessible without removing any trim or other components **(see illustration)**.

9.3 Checking the security of the seat belt mountings

10 Electrical systems check

1 Check the operation of all electrical equipment, ie, lights, direction indicators, horn, etc. Refer to the appropriate Sections of Chapter 12 for details if any of the circuits are found to be inoperative.

2 Note that stop-light switch adjustment is described in Chapter 9.

3 Visually check all accessible wiring connectors, harnesses and retaining clips for security, and for signs of chafing or damage. Rectify any faults found.

11 Exhaust system check

1 With the engine cold (at least an hour after the vehicle has been driven), check the complete exhaust system from the engine to the end of the tailpipe. Ideally, the inspection should be carried out with the vehicle on a hoist to permit unrestricted access, but if a hoist is not available, raise and support the vehicle safely on axle stands (see *Jacking and vehicle support*).

2 Check the exhaust pipes and connections for evidence of leaks, severe corrosion and damage. Make sure that all brackets and mountings are in good condition and tight. Leakage at any of the joints or in other parts of the system will usually show up as a black sooty stain in the vicinity of the leak.

3 Rattles and other noises can often be traced to the exhaust system, especially the brackets and mountings. Try to move the pipes and silencers. If the components can come into contact with the body or suspension parts, secure the system with new mountings or if possible, separate the joints and twist the pipes as necessary to provide additional clearance.

12.3 Check for wear in the hub bearings by grasping the wheel and trying to rock it

4 Run the engine at idling speed. Have an assistant place a cloth or rag over the rear end of the exhaust pipe, and listen for any escape of exhaust gases that would indicate a leak.
5 On completion, lower the car to the ground.

12 Suspension and steering check

Front suspension and steering

1 Raise the front of the vehicle, and securely support it on axle stands (see *Jacking and vehicle support*).
2 Visually inspect the balljoint dust covers and the steering rack-and-pinion gaiters for splits, chafing or deterioration. Any wear of these components will cause loss of lubricant, together with dirt and water entry, resulting in rapid deterioration of the balljoints or steering gear.
3 Grasp the roadwheel at the 12 o'clock and 6 o'clock positions, and try to rock it **(see illustration)**. Very slight free play may be felt, but if the movement is appreciable, further investigation is necessary to determine the source. Continue rocking the wheel while an assistant depresses the footbrake. If the movement is now eliminated or significantly reduced, it is likely that the hub bearings are at fault. If the free play is still evident with the footbrake depressed, then there is wear in the suspension joints or mountings.
4 Now grasp the wheel at the 9 o'clock and 3 o'clock positions, and try to rock it as before. Any movement felt now may again be caused by wear in the hub bearings or the steering track rod balljoints. If the outer balljoint is worn, the visual movement will be obvious. If the inner joint is suspect, it can be felt by placing a hand over the rack-and-pinion rubber gaiter and gripping the track rod. If the wheel is now rocked, movement will be felt at the inner joint if wear has taken place.
5 Using a large screwdriver or flat bar, check for wear in the suspension mounting bushes by levering between the relevant suspension component and its attachment point. Some movement is to be expected, as the mountings are made of rubber, but excessive wear should be obvious. Also check the condition of any visible rubber bushes, looking for splits, cracks or contamination of the rubber.
6 With the car standing on its wheels, have an assistant turn the steering wheel back-and-forth, about an eighth of a turn each way. There should be very little, if any, lost movement between the steering wheel and roadwheels. If this is not the case, closely observe the joints and mountings previously described. In addition, check the steering column universal joints for wear, and also check the rack-and-pinion steering gear itself.

Rear suspension

7 Chock the front wheels, then jack up the rear of the vehicle and support securely on axle stands (see *Jacking and vehicle support*).
8 Working as described previously for the front suspension, check the rear hub bearings, the suspension bushes and the shock absorber mountings for wear. **Note:** *The handbrake will need to be in the released position before checking the rear wheel bearings.*

A leak in the cooling system will usually show up as white- or rust-coloured deposits on the area adjoining the leak.

13 Hose and fluid leak check

1 Visually inspect the engine joint faces, gaskets and seals for any signs of water or oil leaks. Pay particular attention to the areas around the valve cover, cylinder head, oil filter and sump joint faces. Bear in mind that, over a period of time, some very slight seepage from these areas is to be expected – what you are really looking for is any indication of a serious leak. Should a leak be found, renew the offending gasket or oil seal by referring to the appropriate Chapters in this manual.
2 Also check the security and condition of all the engine-related pipes and hoses, and all hydraulic and braking system pipes and hoses. Ensure that all cable ties or securing clips are in place, and in good condition. Clips which are broken or missing can lead to chafing of the hoses, pipes or wiring, which could cause more serious problems in the future.
3 Carefully check the radiator hoses and heater hoses along their entire length. Renew any hose which is cracked, swollen or deteriorated. Cracks will show up better if the hose is squeezed. Pay close attention to the hose clips that secure the hoses to the cooling system components. Hose clips can pinch and puncture hoses, resulting in cooling system leaks. If the crimped-type hose clips are used, it may be a good idea to use standard worm-drive clips.
4 Inspect all the cooling system components (hoses, joint faces, etc) for leaks **(see Haynes Hint)**. Where any problems are found on system components, renew the component or gasket with reference to Chapter 3.
5 With the vehicle raised, inspect the fuel tank and filler neck for punctures, cracks and other damage. The connection between the filler neck and tank is especially critical. Sometimes a rubber filler neck or connecting hose will leak due to loose retaining clamps or deteriorated rubber.
6 Carefully check all rubber hoses and metal fuel lines leading away from the fuel tank. Check for loose connections, deteriorated hoses, crimped lines, and other damage. Pay particular attention to the vent pipes and hoses, which often loop up around the filler neck and can become blocked or crimped. Follow the lines to the front of the vehicle, carefully inspecting them all the way. Renew damaged sections as necessary. Similarly, whilst the vehicle is raised, take the opportunity to inspect all underbody brake fluid pipes and hoses.
7 From within the engine compartment, check the security of all fuel, vacuum and brake hose attachments and pipe unions, and inspect all hoses for kinks, chafing and deterioration.
8 Check the condition of the automatic transmission fluid cooler pipes and hoses, where applicable.

14 Roadwheel bolt check

1 Remove the wheel trims, where applicable, then slacken the roadwheel bolts slightly.
2 Tighten the bolts to the specified torque, using a torque wrench.

15 Bodywork and underbody condition check

1 Once the car has been washed and all tar spots and other surface blemishes have been cleaned off, carefully check all paintwork, looking closely for chips or scratches. Pay particular attention to vulnerable areas such as the front panels (bonnet and spoiler), and around the wheel arches. Any damage to the paintwork must be rectified as soon as

possible to comply with the terms of the manufacturer's anti-corrosion warranties; check with a Renault dealer for details.

2 If a chip or light scratch is found which is recent and still free from rust, it can be touched-up using the appropriate touch-up stick which can be obtained from Renault dealers. Any more serious damage, or rusted stone chips, can be repaired as described in Chapter 11, but if damage or corrosion is so severe that a panel must be renewed, seek professional advice as soon as possible.

3 Always check that the door and ventilation opening drain holes and pipes are completely clear, so that water can drain out.

4 The wax-based underbody protective coating should be inspected annually, preferably just prior to Winter, when the underbody should be washed down as thoroughly as possible without disturbing the protective coating (see Chapter 11, Section 2, regarding the use of steam cleaners). Any damage to the coating should be repaired using a wax-based sealer. If any of the body panels are disturbed for repair or renewal, do not forget to replace the coating and to inject wax into door panels, sills and box sections, to maintain the level of protection provided by the vehicle manufacturer.

16 Shock absorber check

1 Viewing over the roadwheels into the wheel arches, check for any signs of fluid leakage around the front and rear shock absorber bodies, or from the rubber gaiters around the piston rods. Should any fluid be noticed, the shock absorber is defective internally, and should be renewed. **Note:** *Shock absorbers should always be renewed in pairs on the same axle.*

2 The efficiency of the shock absorber may be checked by bouncing the vehicle at each corner. Generally speaking, the body will return to its normal position and stop after being depressed. If it rises and returns on a rebound, the shock absorber is probably suspect. Also examine the shock absorber upper and lower mountings for any signs of wear.

Every 36 000 miles (60 000 km) or 4 years

17 Spark plug renewal and ignition system check

Warning: High voltages are produced by the electronic ignition system. Extreme care must be taken when working on the system with the ignition switched on. Persons with surgically-implanted cardiac pacemaker devices should keep well clear of the ignition circuits, components and test equipment.

1 The correct functioning of the spark plugs is vital for the correct running and efficiency of the engine. It is essential that the plugs fitted are appropriate for the engine, the type being specified at the start of this Chapter. If the correct type of plug is used and the engine is in good condition, the spark plugs should not need attention between scheduled servicing intervals. Spark plug cleaning is rarely necessary, and should not be attempted unless specialised equipment is available, as damage can easily be caused to the firing ends.

2 To remove the plugs, first open the bonnet and unclip the engine upper cover **(see illustration)**.

3 On models with the D7F engine, where applicable, unclip the plastic spark plug lead tool from the HT lead cover on the top of the engine, then use the tool to disconnect the HT leads from the spark plugs. On D4F engines, pull the plastic tubes upwards to disengage the HT leads from the spark plugs **(see illustrations)**.

4 On K4J and K4M engines, remove the ignition HT coils from the top of the spark plugs as described in Chapter 5B **(see illustration)**.

5 It is advisable to remove any dirt from the spark plug recesses using a clean brush, a vacuum cleaner or compressed air before removing the plugs, to prevent the dirt dropping into the cylinders.

6 Unscrew the plugs using a spark plug

17.2 Unclip the cover from the top of the engine – D4F engine

17.3a Unclip the plastic spark plug lead removal tool . . .

17.3b . . . and use it to disconnect the HT leads – D7F engine

17.3c Disconnecting the HT leads from the spark plugs – D4F engine

17.4 Removing the ignition HT coils – K4J and K4M engines

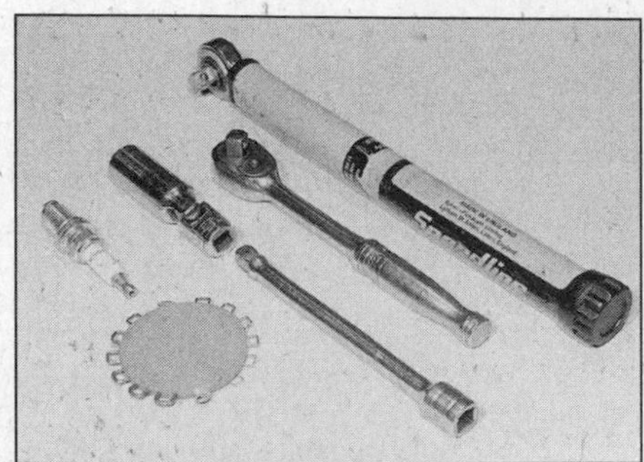
17.6a Tools required for spark plug removal, gap adjustment and refitting

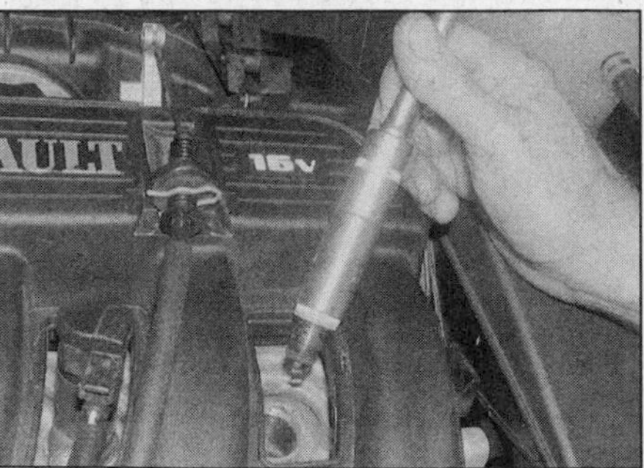
17.6b Using the spark plug deep socket to remove the spark plugs – K4J engine

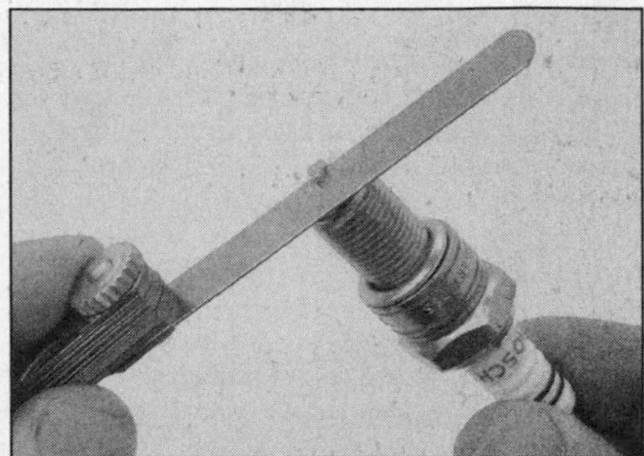
17.12 Measuring the spark plug gap with a feeler blade

spanner, box spanner or a deep socket and extension bar. Keep the socket in alignment with the spark plug, otherwise if it is forcibly moved to either side, the ceramic top of the spark plug may be broken off **(see illustrations)**. As each plug is removed, examine it as follows.

7 Examination of the spark plugs will give a good indication of the condition of the engine. If the insulator nose of the spark plug is clean

17.13 Measuring the spark plug gap with a wire gauge

HAYNES HiNT

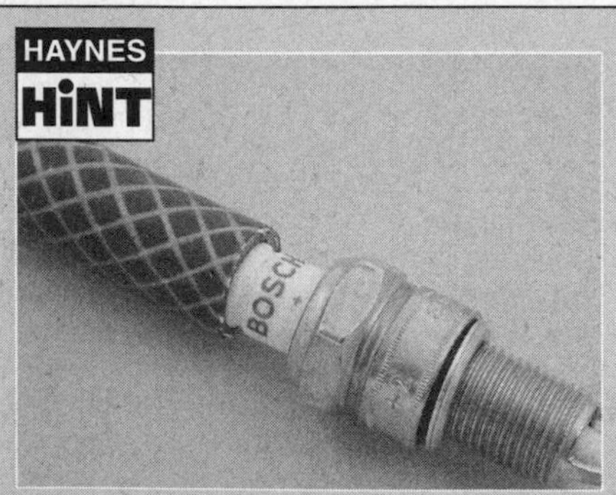

It is very often difficult to insert spark plugs into their holes without cross-threading them. To avoid this possibility, fit a short length of rubber hose over the end of the spark plug. The flexible hose acts as a universal joint to help align the plug with the plug hole. Should the plug begin to cross-thread, the hose will slip on the spark plug, preventing thread damage to the aluminium cylinder head.

and white, with no deposits, this is indicative of a weak mixture or too hot a plug (a hot plug transfers heat away from the electrode slowly, a cold plug transfers heat away quickly).

8 If the tip and insulator nose are covered with hard black-looking deposits, then this is indicative that the mixture is too rich. Should the plug be black and oily, then it is likely that the engine is fairly worn, as well as the mixture being too rich.

9 If the insulator nose is covered with light tan to greyish-brown deposits, then the mixture is correct and it is likely that the engine is in good condition.

10 If the spark plug has not completed its service interval, it may be refitted, however, check that the condition of the plug and the gap is correct before refitting. If, due to engine condition, the spark plug is not serviceable, it should be renewed.

11 The spark plug gap is of considerable importance as, if it is too large or too small, the size of the spark and its efficiency will be seriously impaired. For best results, the spark plug gap should be set in accordance with the Specifications at the start of this Chapter.

12 To set it, measure the gap with a feeler blade, and then bend open, or closed, the outer plug electrode until the correct gap is achieved **(see illustration)**. The centre electrode should never be bent, as this may crack the insulation and cause plug failure, if nothing worse.

13 Special spark plug electrode gap measuring and adjusting tools are available from most motor accessory shops **(see illustration)**.

14 Before fitting the spark plugs, check that the threaded connector sleeves are tight, and that the plug exterior surfaces and threads are clean. Apply a little anti-seize compound to the threads.

15 Insert each spark plug into the cylinder head and screw them in by hand, taking extra care to enter the plug threads correctly **(see Haynes Hint)**.

16 Tighten the plugs to the specified torque using the spark plug socket and a torque wrench.

17 The spark plug (HT) leads, where applicable, should be checked whenever new spark plugs are fitted. On the D4F and D7F engines, unclip or open the lead holder and release the leads. Ensure that the leads are numbered before removing them, to avoid confusion when refitting. Check inside the end fitting for signs of corrosion, which will look like a white crusty powder. Push the end fitting back onto the spark plug, ensuring that it is a tight fit on the plug. Using a clean rag, wipe the entire length of the lead to remove any built-up dirt and grease. Once the lead is clean, check for burns, cracks and other damage. Do not bend the lead excessively, nor pull the lead lengthwise – the conductor inside might break. Disconnect the other end of the lead, and check for corrosion and a tight fit. If an ohmmeter is available, check the resistance of the lead. Check the remaining leads one at a time.

18 On models with the D4F and D7F engines, check that the HT leads are correctly located in there retaining clips or holder. On the D7F engine refit the plastic spark plug lead tool. Reconnect the HT leads to their respective spark plugs.

19 On K4J and K4M engines, refit the ignition HT coils with reference to Chapter 5B.

18 Air filter element renewal

Removal

D7F engine

1 Push down the air cleaner cover retaining clip on top of the air cleaner casing, and simultaneously twist the cover towards the rear of the engine compartment (anti-clockwise looking from the right-hand side of the car). Remove the cover from the air cleaner element housing **(see illustration)**.

2 Withdraw the cylindrical-shaped element from the housing **(see illustration)**.

D4F engine

3 Unclip the coolant hose from the air cleaner housing, then undo the two retaining bolts **(see illustrations)**.

4 Unclip the air cleaner cover and withdraw the filter from the housing, noting its fitted position **(see illustration)**.

18.1 Removing the air cleaner cover – D7F engine

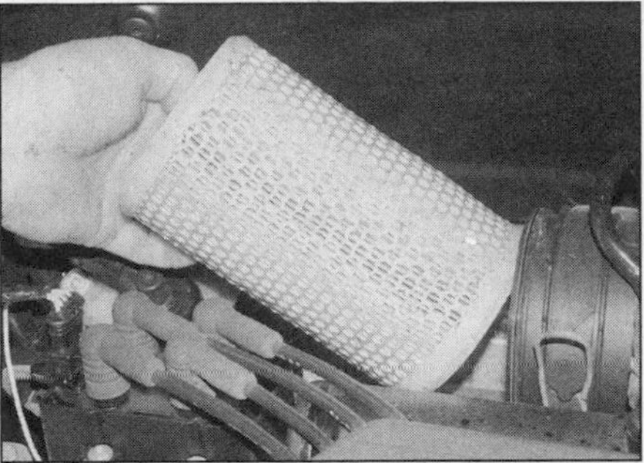
18.2 Removing the air cleaner element – D7F engine

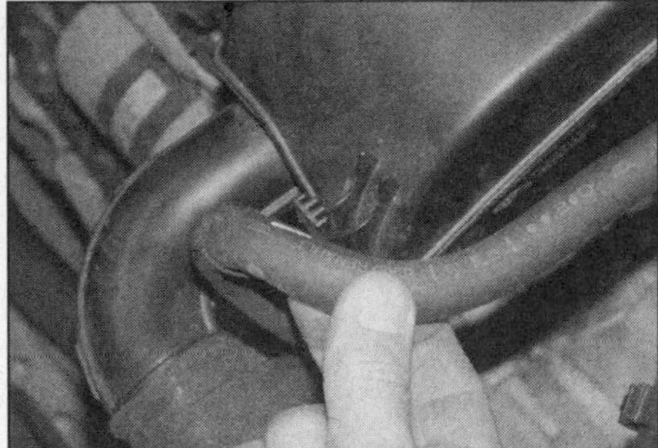
18.3a Unclip the hose from the housing . . .

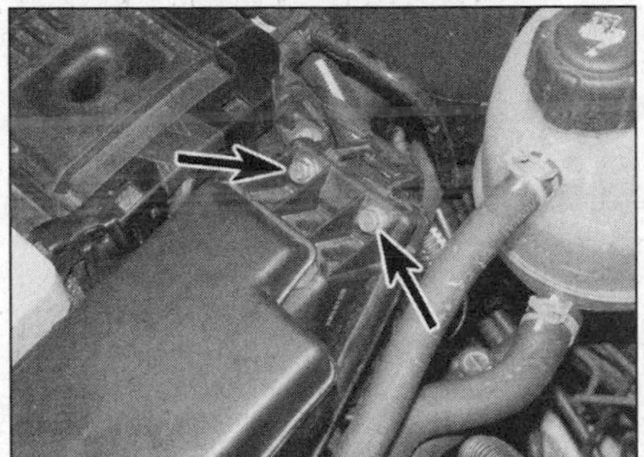
18.3b . . . undo the two retaining bolts (arrowed) . . .

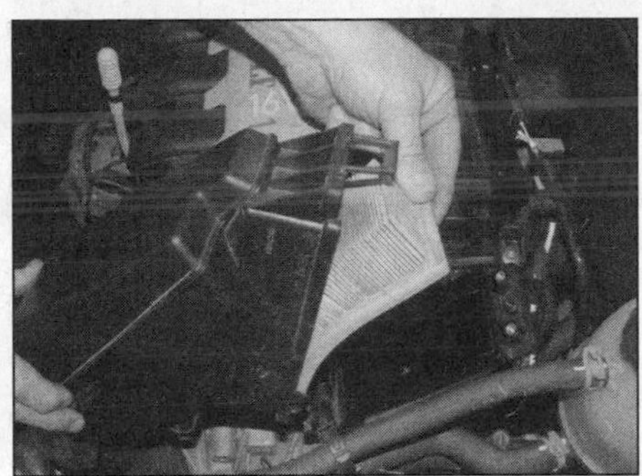
18.4 . . . and withdraw the air filter – D4F engine

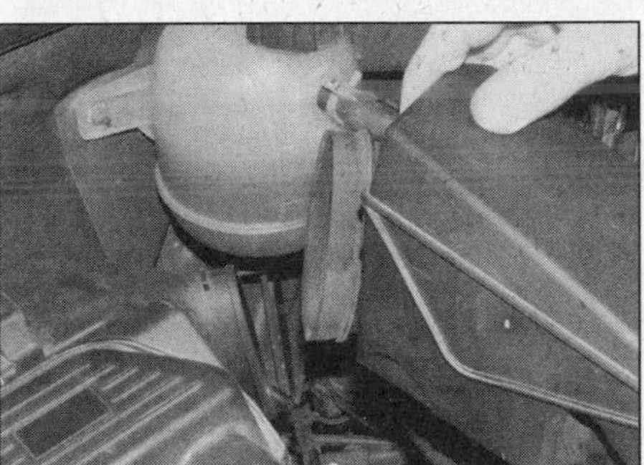
18.5 Unclip the air inlet duct . . .

K4J and K4M engines

5 The air filter element is located at the left-hand rear of the engine. First unclip the air inlet duct from the air cleaner housing **(see illustration)**.

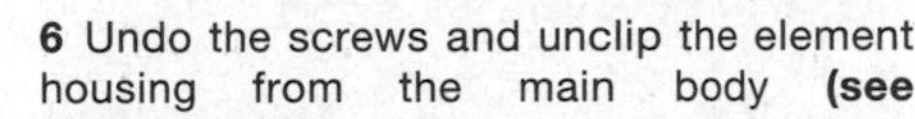

6 Undo the screws and unclip the element housing from the main body **(see illustrations)**.

7 Note how the element is fitted, then withdraw it from the housing **(see illustration)**.

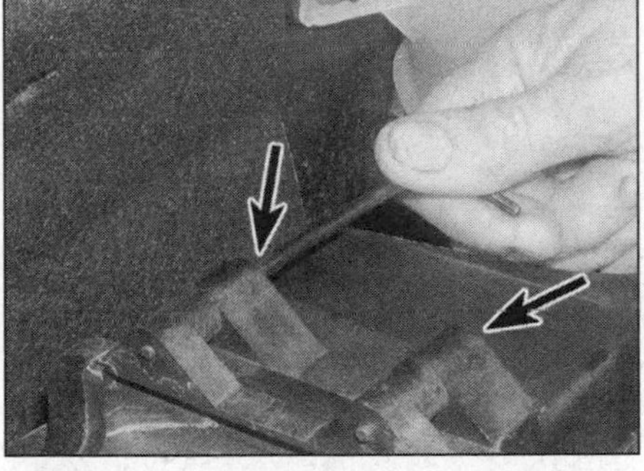
18.6a . . . undo the screws (arrowed) . . .

18.6b . . . unclip the housing . . .

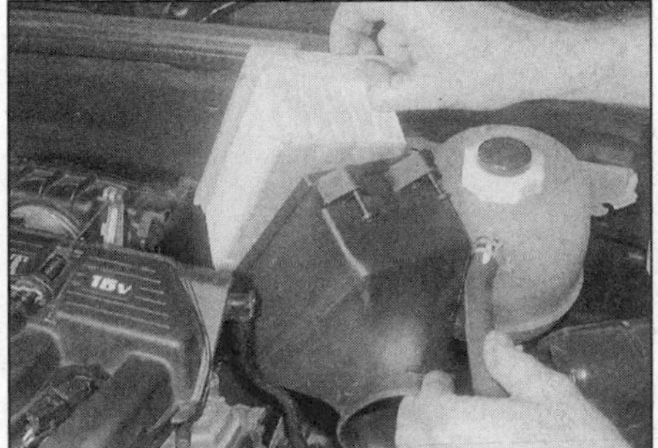
18.7 . . . then withdraw the element from the housing – K4J and K4M engines

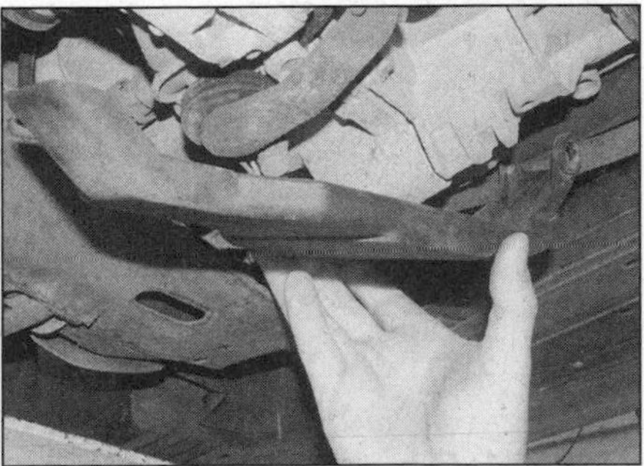
20.2 Unclipping the bottom cover from the transmission

Refitting

8 Clean the inside of the air cleaner body and cover, being careful not to get dirt into the inlet duct.

9 Fit the new element using a reversal of the removal procedure.

19 Rear brake shoe and drum check

1 Remove the rear brake drums, and check the brake shoes for signs of wear or contamination. At the same time, also inspect the wheel cylinders for signs of leakage, and the brake drum for signs of wear. Refer to the relevant Sections of Chapter 9 for further information.

20 Manual and sequential transmission oil level check

1 Either position the vehicle over an inspection pit, or jack up the front and rear of the vehicle and support it on axle stands (see *Jacking and vehicle support*). The vehicle must be level for the check to be accurate.

2 Remove the engine undertray or unclip the cover, as applicable, from the bottom of the transmission **(see illustration)**.

3 Clean the area around the filler/level plug

20.3 Transmission oil filler/level plug (arrowed)

located on the front facing side of the transmission, then unscrew and remove the plug **(see illustration)**.

4 The oil level should be up to the lower edge of the filler/level plug aperture **(see illustration)**.

5 If necessary, top-up using the specified type of lubricant until the transmission oil level is correct. Fill the transmission until oil starts to flow out and allow excess oil to drain out.

6 Once the transmission oil level is correct, refit the filler/level plug and tighten it securely.

7 Refit the engine undertray cover or transmission bottom cover as applicable, then lower the vehicle to the ground. Note that frequent need for topping-up indicates a leak, possibly through an oil seal. The cause should be investigated and rectified.

21 Front wheel alignment check

Refer to the information given in Chapter 10.

22 Air conditioning system check

The air conditioning system must be checked by a Renault dealer using dedicated test equipment.

23 Road test

Instruments and electrical equipment

1 Check the operation of all instruments and electrical equipment.

2 Make sure that all instruments read correctly, and switch on all electrical equipment in turn, to check that it functions properly.

Steering and suspension

3 Check for any abnormalities in the steering, suspension, handling or road 'feel'.

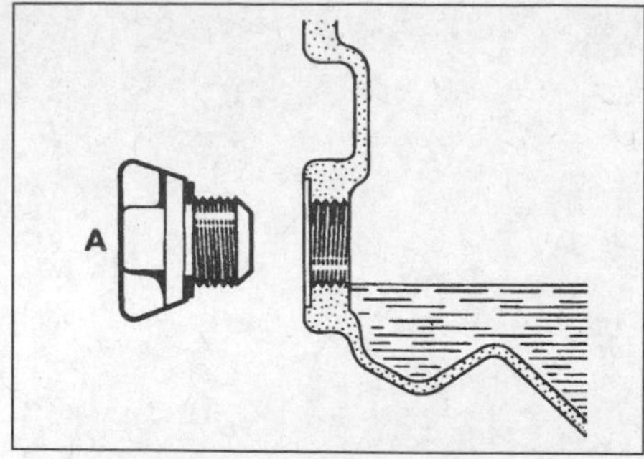

20.4 Manual and sequential transmission filler/level plug (A) – correct oil level shown

4 Drive the vehicle, and check that there are no unusual vibrations or noises.

5 Check that the steering feels positive, with no excessive 'sloppiness', or roughness, and check for any suspension noises when cornering and driving over bumps.

Drivetrain

6 Check the performance of the engine, clutch, transmission and driveshafts.

7 Listen for any unusual noises from the engine, clutch and transmission.

8 Make sure that the engine runs smoothly when idling, and that there is no hesitation when accelerating.

9 Check that, where applicable, the clutch action is smooth and progressive, that the drive is taken up smoothly, and that the pedal travel is not excessive. Also listen for any noises when the clutch pedal is depressed.

10 Check that all gears can be engaged smoothly without noise, and that the gear lever action is smooth and not abnormally vague or 'notchy'.

11 On automatic and sequential transmission models, make sure that all gearchanges occur smoothly, without snatching, and without an increase in engine speed between changes. Check that all of the gear positions can be selected with the vehicle at rest. If any problems are found, they should be referred to a Renault dealer.

12 Listen for a metallic clicking sound from the front of the vehicle, as the vehicle is driven slowly in a circle with the steering on full-lock. Carry out this check in both directions. If a clicking noise is heard, this indicates wear in a driveshaft joint (see Chapter 8).

Braking system

13 Make sure that the vehicle does not pull to one side when braking, and that the wheels do not lock when braking hard.

14 Check that there is no vibration through the steering when braking.

15 Check that the handbrake operates correctly, without excessive movement of the lever, and that it holds the vehicle stationary on a slope.

16 Test the operation of the brake servo unit as follows. Depress the footbrake four or five times to exhaust the vacuum, then start the engine. As the engine starts, there should be a noticeable 'give' in the brake pedal as vacuum builds-up. Allow the engine to run for at least two minutes, and then switch it off. If the brake pedal is now depressed again, it should be possible to detect a hiss from the servo as the pedal is depressed. After about four or five applications, no further hissing should be heard, and the pedal should feel considerably harder.

24 Timing belt renewal

Refer to Chapter 2A or 2B.

25 Brake fluid renewal

Warning: Brake hydraulic fluid can harm your eyes and damage painted surfaces, so use extreme caution when handling and pouring it. Do not use fluid that has been standing open for some time, as it absorbs moisture from the air. Excess moisture can cause a dangerous loss of braking effectiveness.

1 The procedure is similar to that for the bleeding of the hydraulic system as described in Chapter 9, except that the brake fluid reservoir should be emptied by syphoning, using a clean poultry baster or similar before starting, and allowance should be made for the old fluid to be expelled when bleeding a section of the circuit.

2 Working as described in Chapter 9, open the first bleed screw in the sequence, and pump the brake pedal gently until nearly all the old fluid has been emptied from the master cylinder reservoir. Top-up to the MAXI level with new fluid, and continue pumping until only the new fluid remains in the reservoir, and new fluid can be seen emerging from the bleed screw. Tighten the screw, and top the reservoir level up to the MAXI level line.

Old hydraulic fluid is invariably much darker in colour than the new, making it easy to distinguish the two.

3 Work through all the remaining bleed screws in the sequence until new fluid can be seen at all of them. Be careful to keep the master cylinder reservoir topped-up to above the MINI level at all times, or air may enter the system and greatly increase the length of the task.

4 When the operation is complete, check that all bleed screws are securely tightened, and that their dust caps are refitted. Wash off all traces of spilt fluid, and recheck the master cylinder reservoir fluid level.

5 Check the operation of the brakes before taking the car on the road.

26 Coolant renewal

Cooling system draining

Warning: Wait until the engine is cold before starting this procedure. Do not allow antifreeze to come in contact with your skin, or with the painted surfaces of the vehicle. Rinse off spills immediately with plenty of water. Never leave antifreeze lying around in an open container, or in a puddle in the driveway or on the garage floor. Children and pets are attracted by its sweet smell, but antifreeze can be fatal if ingested.

1 With the engine completely cold, remove the expansion tank filler cap. Turn the cap anti-clockwise, wait until any pressure remaining in the system is released, then unscrew it and lift it off.
2 Where applicable, remove the undershield, then position a container beneath the radiator bottom hose connection.
3 Loosen the hose clip, pull off the hose and allow the coolant to drain into the container.
4 To assist draining, open the cooling system bleed screw(s). See the cooling system layouts in Chapter 3, Section 1.
5 When the flow of coolant stops, reposition the container below the cylinder block drain plug where fitted. It is located either on the front left-hand side or rear right-hand side of the cylinder block. Remove the drain plug, and allow the coolant to drain into the container.
6 If the coolant has been drained for a reason other than renewal, then provided it is clean and less than two years old, it can be re-used.
7 Refit the radiator bottom hose and cylinder block drain plug on completion of draining.

Cooling system flushing

8 If coolant renewal has been neglected, or if the antifreeze mixture has become diluted, then in time, the cooling system may gradually lose efficiency, as the coolant passages become restricted due to rust, scale deposits, and other sediment. The cooling system efficiency can be restored by flushing the system clean.
9 The radiator should be flushed independently of the engine, to avoid unnecessary contamination.

Radiator flushing

10 Disconnect the top and bottom hoses and any other relevant hoses from the radiator, with reference to Chapter 3.
11 Insert a garden hose into the radiator top inlet. Direct a flow of clean water through the radiator, and continue flushing until clean water emerges from the radiator bottom outlet.
12 If, after a reasonable period, the water still does not run clear, the radiator can be flushed with a good proprietary cleaning agent. It is important that the manufacturer's instructions are followed carefully. If the contamination is particularly bad, insert the hose in the radiator bottom outlet, and reverse-flush the radiator.

Engine flushing

13 To flush the engine, first refit the cylinder block drain plug.
14 Remove the thermostat as described in Chapter 3, then temporarily refit the top hose at its engine connection.
15 With the top and bottom hoses disconnected from the radiator, insert a garden hose into the radiator top hose. Direct a clean flow of water through the engine, and continue flushing until clean water emerges from the radiator bottom hose.
16 On completion of flushing, refit the thermostat and reconnect the hoses with reference to Chapter 3.

Cooling system filling

17 Before attempting to fill the cooling system, make sure that all hoses and clips are in good condition, and that the clips are tight. Note that an antifreeze mixture must be used all year round, to prevent corrosion of the engine components. Also check that the cylinder block drain plug is in place and tight.
18 Remove the expansion tank filler cap.
19 Open the cooling system bleed screw(s).
20 Slowly fill the system until the coolant level reaches the MAXI mark on the expansion tank.
21 Close the bleed screw(s) when coolant free from air bubbles emerges.
22 Start the engine, and run it at a fast idle speed (do not exceed 1500 rpm) for approximately 4 minutes. Keep the level topped-up to the top of the expansion tank filler neck.
23 Refit and tighten the expansion tank filler cap.
24 Allow the engine to run at 2500 rpm for approximately 15 minutes, until the cooling fan cuts in and out.
25 Stop the engine and allow the engine to cool for at least 30 minutes.
26 Recheck the coolant level with reference to *Weekly checks*. Top-up the level if necessary and refit the expansion tank filler cap. Where applicable, refit the engine undershield.

Antifreeze mixture

27 The antifreeze should always be renewed at the specified intervals. This is necessary not only to maintain the antifreeze properties, but also to prevent corrosion which would otherwise occur as the corrosion inhibitors become progressively less effective.
28 Always use an ethylene-glycol based antifreeze which is suitable for use in mixed-metal cooling systems. The quantity of antifreeze and levels of protection are given in the Specifications.
29 Before adding antifreeze, the cooling system should be completely drained, preferably flushed, and all hoses checked for condition and security.
30 After filling with antifreeze, a label should be attached to the expansion tank, stating the type and concentration of antifreeze used, and the date installed. Any subsequent topping-up should be made with the same type and concentration of antifreeze.
31 Do not use engine antifreeze in the windscreen/tailgate washer system, as it will cause damage to the vehicle's paintwork. A screenwash additive should be added to the washer system in the quantities stated on the bottle.

27 'Service' light – general

The Clio has a warning light on the instrument panel which may light up with the word SERV or SERVICE. Despite appearances, this is **not** a service indicator light, as featured on some other cars – it is actually an engine management light, and if illuminated, it indicates that a fault has been logged in the engine ECU. The only way to put this light out is by using the Renault XR25 diagnostic tester – see Chapter 4A, Section 12.

Notes

Chapter 1 Part B: Routine maintenance and servicing – diesel models

Contents

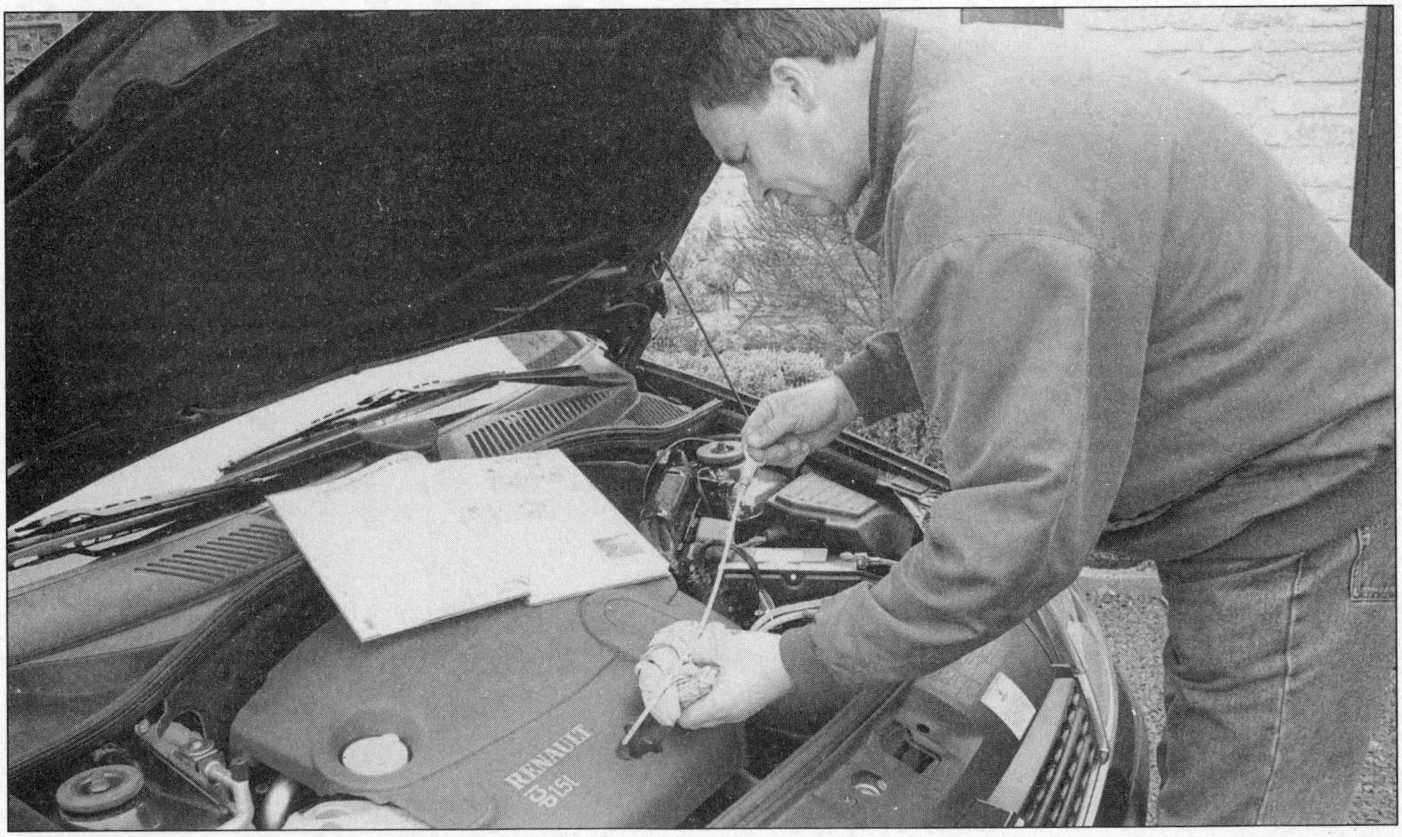

Degrees of difficulty

Easy, suitable for novice with little experience 	**Fairly easy,** suitable for beginner with some experience 	**Fairly difficult,** suitable for competent DIY mechanic 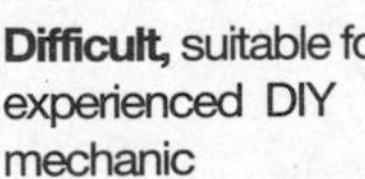	**Difficult,** suitable for experienced DIY mechanic 	**Very difficult,** suitable for expert DIY or professional

Lubricants and fluids

Refer to *Weekly checks* on page 0•18

Capacities

Engine oil	
Excluding oil filter	4.5 litres
Including oil filter	5.0 litres
Difference between MAX and MIN dipstick marks	approximately 1.5 litres
Cooling system	5.5 litres
Manual gearbox	3.4 litres
Fuel tank	50 litres

Cooling system

Antifreeze mixture:	**Antifreeze**	**Water**
Protection to –23°C	35%	65%
Protection to –40°C	50%	50%

Brakes

Front disc brakes:	
Pad thickness (including backing):	
New	18.2 mm
Minimum thickness	6.0 mm
Rear disc brakes:	
Pad thickness (including backing):	
New	15.0 mm
Minimum thickness	6.0 mm
Rear drum brakes:	
Shoe thickness (friction material only):	
New:	
Leading	4.6 mm
Trailing	3.3 mm
Minimum thickness	2.0 mm

Torque wrench setting

	Nm	**lbf ft**
Roadwheel bolts	90	66

The maintenance intervals in this manual are provided with the assumption that you, not the dealer, will be carrying out the work. These are the minimum maintenance intervals recommended by us for vehicles driven daily. If you wish to keep your vehicle in peak condition at all times, you may wish to perform some of these procedures more often. We encourage frequent maintenance, because it enhances the efficiency, performance and resale value of your vehicle.

If the vehicle is driven in dusty areas, used to tow a trailer, or driven frequently at slow speeds (idling in traffic) or on short journeys, more frequent maintenance intervals are recommended.

When the vehicle is new, it should be serviced by a factory-authorised dealer service department, in order to preserve the factory warranty.

Every 250 miles (400 km) or weekly

- ☐ Refer to *Weekly Checks*

Every 9000 miles (15 000 km)

- ☐ Renew the engine oil and filter (Section 3)

Note: *Frequent oil and filter changes are good for the engine. We recommend changing the oil at the mileage specified here, or at least twice a year.*

Every 18 000 miles (30 000 km) or 2 years, whichever comes first

In addition to all the items listed previously, carry out the following:

- ☐ Renew the pollen filter (Section 4)
- ☐ Check the handbrake (Section 5)
- ☐ Check the brake pads and discs (Section 6)
- ☐ Check the operation of the clutch (Section 7)
- ☐ Check the condition of the auxiliary drivebelts (Section 8)
- ☐ Check the condition of the seat belts (Section 9)
- ☐ Check the operation of all electrical systems (Section 10)
- ☐ Check the condition of the exhaust system and mountings (Section 11)
- ☐ Check the suspension and steering components (Section 12)
- ☐ Check all underbonnet components and hoses for fluid leaks (Section 13)
- ☐ Check the tightness of the roadwheel bolts (Section 14)
- ☐ Check the bodywork and underbody for damage and corrosion (Section 15)
- ☐ Check the front and rear shock absorbers (Section 16)

Every 36 000 miles (60 000 km) or 4 years, whichever comes first

In addition to all the items listed previously, carry out the following:

- ☐ Renew the air filter element (Section 17)
- ☐ Renew the fuel filter element (Section 18)
- ☐ Check the rear brake shoes and drums (Section 19)
- ☐ Check the manual transmission oil level (Section 20)
- ☐ Check the front wheel alignment (Section 21)
- ☐ Check the operation of the air conditioning system (Section 22)
- ☐ Carry out a road test (Section 23)
- ☐ Renew the timing belt (Section 24)*
- ☐ Renew the brake fluid (Section 25)
- ☐ Renew the coolant (Section 26)

* **Note:** *Although the normal interval for timing belt renewal is 75 000 miles (120 000 km), it is strongly recommended that the interval is reduced to 36 000 miles (60 000 km) on vehicles which are subjected to intensive use, ie, mainly short journeys or a lot of stop-start driving. The actual belt renewal interval is therefore very much up to the individual owner, but bear in mind that severe engine damage may result if the belt breaks.*

Underbonnet view of a 1.5 litre diesel model

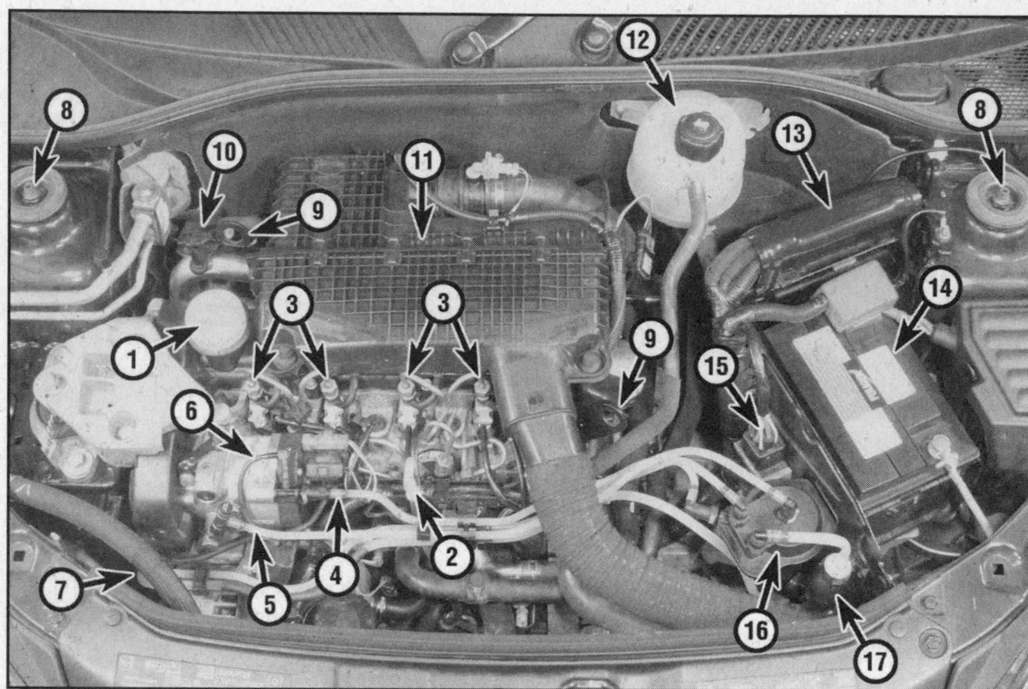

1 *Engine oil filler cap*
2 *Engine oil level dipstick*
3 *Fuel injectors*
4 *Fuel return pipe*
5 *Fuel supply pipe*
6 *Fuel injection pump*
7 *Auxiliary drive belt*
8 *Front suspension strut upper mountings*
9 *Engine lifting eye*
10 *Brake fluid reservoir*
11 *Air cleaner element*
12 *Coolant expansion tank*
13 *Fuel injection electronic control unit (ECU)*
14 *Battery*
15 *Pre/post-heating control unit*
16 *Fuel filter*
17 *Fuel system priming bulb*

Front underbody view of a 1.5 litre diesel model

1 *Steering gear*
2 *Hydraulic brake pipes*
3 *Gearchange link rod*
4 *Exhaust downpipe*
5 *Rear engine mounting link*
6 *Fuel pipes*
7 *Subframe mounting bolt*
8 *Anti-roll bar*
9 *Front suspension lower arm*
10 *Right-hand driveshaft*
11 *Engine oil drain plug*
12 *Transmission*
13 *Front lower arm balljoint*
14 *Steering track rod end*
15 *Front subframe*

Typical rear underbody view

1 Fuel tank
2 Handbrake cables
3 Fuel filter (not fitted to diesel models)
4 Fuel feed and return lines
5 Rear brake compensator
6 Rear axle assembly
7 Rear coil springs
8 Exhaust rear silencer and tailpipe
9 Shock absorbers

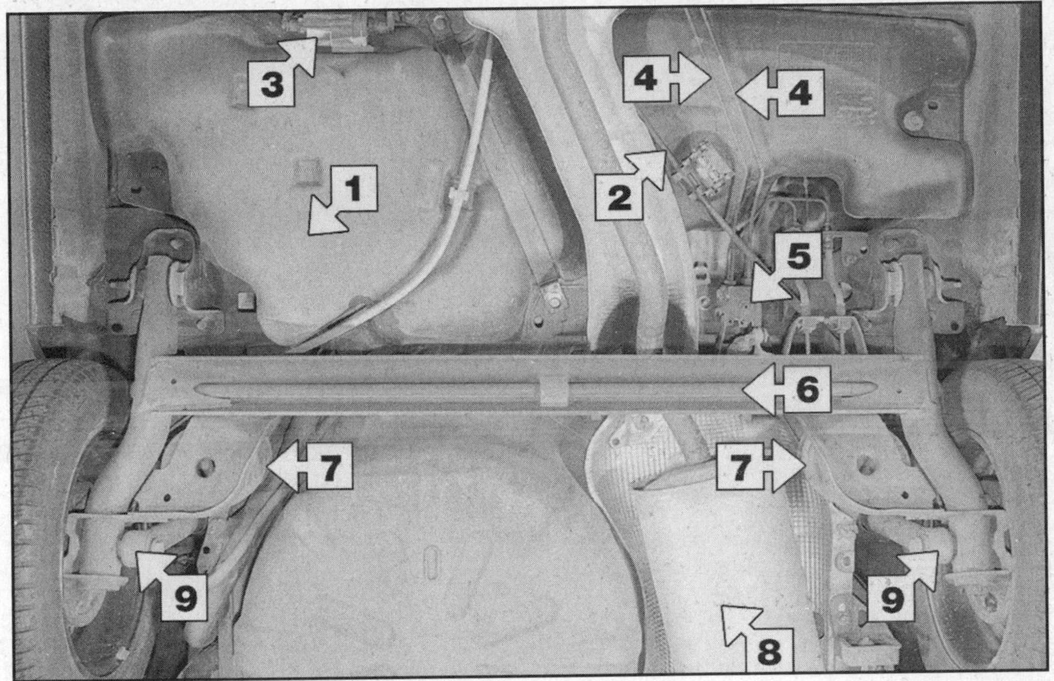

Maintenance procedures

1 Introduction

This Chapter is designed to help the home mechanic maintain his/her vehicle for safety, economy, long life and peak performance.

The Chapter contains a master maintenance schedule, followed by Sections dealing specifically with each task in the schedule. Visual checks, adjustments, component renewal and other helpful items are included. Refer to the accompanying illustrations of the engine compartment and the underside of the vehicle for the locations of the various components.

Servicing your vehicle in accordance with the mileage/time maintenance schedule and the following Sections will provide a planned maintenance programme, which should result in a long and reliable service life. This is a comprehensive plan, so maintaining some items but not others at the specified service intervals, will not produce the same results.

As you service your vehicle, you will discover that many of the procedures can – and should – be grouped together, because of the particular procedure being performed, or because of the proximity of two otherwise-unrelated components to one another. For example, if the vehicle is raised for any reason, the exhaust can be inspected at the same time as the suspension and steering components.

The first step in this maintenance programme is to prepare yourself before the actual work begins. Read through all the Sections relevant to the work to be carried out, then make a list and gather all the parts and tools required. If a problem is encountered, seek advice from a parts specialist, or a dealer service department.

2 Regular maintenance

If, from the time the vehicle is new, the routine maintenance schedule is followed closely, and frequent checks are made of fluid levels and high-wear items, as suggested throughout this manual, the engine will be kept in relatively good running condition, and the need for additional work will be minimised.

It is possible that there will be times when the engine is running poorly due to the lack of regular maintenance. This is even more likely if a used vehicle, which has not received regular and frequent maintenance checks, is purchased. In such cases, additional work may need to be carried out, outside of the regular maintenance intervals.

If engine wear is suspected, a compression test (refer to Chapter 2C) will provide valuable information regarding the overall performance of the main internal components. Such a test can be used as a basis to decide on the extent of the work to be carried out. If, for example, a compression test indicates serious internal engine wear, conventional maintenance as described in this Chapter will not greatly improve the performance of the engine, and may prove a waste of time and money, unless extensive overhaul work is carried out first.

The following series of operations are those most often required to improve the performance of a generally poor-running engine:

Primary operations

a) Clean, inspect and test the battery (refer to 'Weekly checks').
b) Check all the engine-related fluids (refer to 'Weekly checks').
c) Check the condition of the auxiliary drivebelt(s) (Section 8).
d) Check the condition of all hoses, and check for fluid leaks (Section 13).
e) Check the condition of the air filter, and renew if necessary (Section 17).
f) Check the fuel filter, and renew if necessary (Section 18).

If the above operations do not prove fully effective, carry out the following secondary operations:

Secondary operations

All items listed under *Primary operations*, plus the following:

a) Check the charging system (refer to Chapter 5A).
b) Check the preheating system (refer to Chapter 5C).
c) Check the fuel system (refer to Chapter 4B).

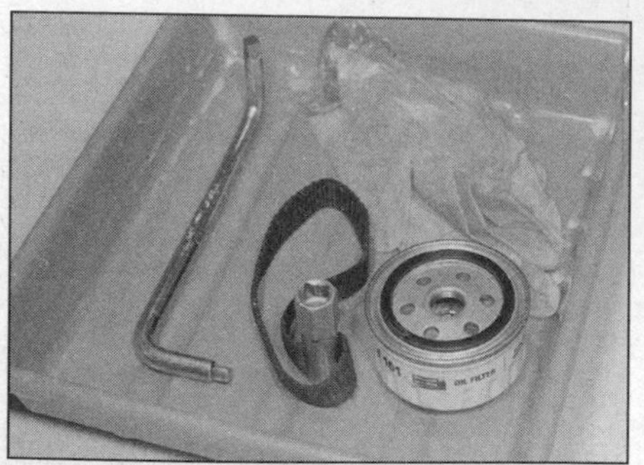

3.1 Tools and materials necessary for the engine oil change and filter renewal

3.2 Engine oil drain plug (arrowed)

3.5 Oil filter location on the front of the engine

Every 9000 miles (15 000 km)

3 Engine oil and filter renewal

1 Before starting this procedure, gather together all the necessary tools and materials **(see illustration)**. Also make sure that you have plenty of clean rags and newspapers handy to mop-up any spills. Ideally, the engine oil should be warm, as it will drain better and more built-up sludge will be removed with it. Take care, however, not to touch the exhaust or any other hot parts of the engine when working under the vehicle. To avoid any possibility of scalding, and to protect yourself from possible skin irritants and other harmful contaminants in used engine oils, it is advisable to wear rubber gloves when carrying out this work. Apply the handbrake, then jack up the front of the vehicle and support it on axle stands (see *Jacking and vehicle support*). Alternatively, raise the vehicle on a lift or drive it onto ramps. Whichever method is chosen, make sure that the car remains as level as possible, to enable the oil to drain fully. Remove the engine undertray where applicable.

2 Remove the oil filler cap from the valve cover, then position a suitable container beneath the sump. Clean the drain plug and the area around it, then slacken it half a turn using the special drain plug key **(see illustration)**.

HAYNES HiNT ***If possible, try to keep the plug pressed into the sump while unscrewing it by hand the last couple of turns. As the plug releases from the threads, move it away sharply so the stream of oil issuing from the sump runs into the container, not up your sleeve.***

3 Allow some time for the old oil to drain, noting that it may be necessary to reposition the container as the oil flow slows to a trickle.

4 After all the oil has drained, wipe off the drain plug with a clean rag and renew its sealing washer. Clean the area around the drain plug opening, then refit and tighten the plug securely.

5 Move the container into position under the oil filter, located on the front of the cylinder block **(see illustration)**.

6 Using an oil filter removal tool, slacken the filter initially **(see illustration)**. Loosely wrap some rags around the oil filter, then unscrew it and immediately position it with its open end uppermost to prevent further spillage of oil. Remove the oil filter from the engine compartment and empty the oil into the container.

7 Use a clean rag to remove all oil, dirt and sludge from the filter sealing area on the engine. Check the old filter to make sure that the rubber sealing ring hasn't stuck to the engine. If it has, carefully remove it.

8 Apply a light coating of clean oil to the sealing ring on the new filter, then screw it into position on the engine **(see illustration)**. Tighten the filter firmly by hand only – do not use any tools. Wipe clean the exterior of the oil filter.

9 Remove the old oil and all tools from under the car, then, where necessary, refit the undertray and lower the car to the ground.

10 Fill the engine with the specified quantity and grade of oil, as described in *Weekly checks*. Pour the oil in slowly, otherwise it may overflow from the top of the valve cover. Check that the oil level is up to the maximum mark on the dipstick, then refit and tighten the oil filler cap.

3.6 Slackening the oil filter with a removal tool

3.8 Applying clean oil to the seal

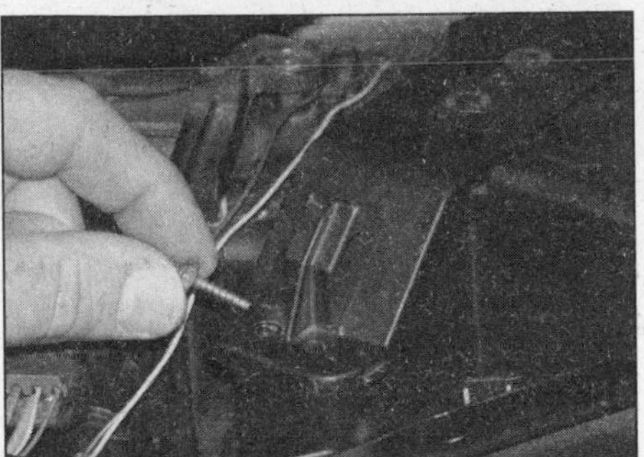

4.2a Undo the retaining screws . . .

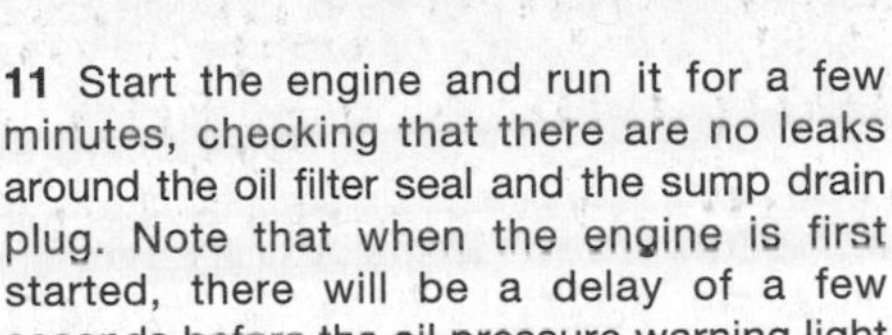

4.2b . . . and unclip the cover from the pollen filter housing

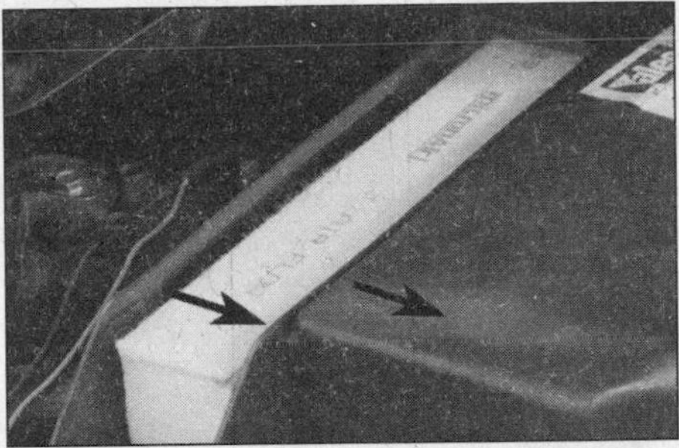

4.3 Removing the pollen filter element. Note the direction arrows on the element and housing

11 Start the engine and run it for a few minutes, checking that there are no leaks around the oil filter seal and the sump drain plug. Note that when the engine is first started, there will be a delay of a few seconds before the oil pressure warning light goes out while the new filter fills with oil. Do not race the engine while the warning light is on.

12 Switch off the engine and wait a few minutes for the oil to settle in the sump once more. With the new oil circulated and the filter now completely full, recheck the level on the dipstick and add more oil if necessary.

13 Dispose of the used engine oil safely with reference to *General repair procedures* in the Reference section of this manual.

Every 18 000 miles (30 000 km) or 2 years

4 Pollen filter renewal

Note: *The pollen filter is not fitted to all models.*

1 With the bonnet open, remove the windscreen half-scuttle grille from the right-hand end of the bulkhead.

2 Undo the retaining screw and slide the cover forwards to unclip from the pollen filter housing **(see illustrations)**.

3 Note the direction arrows on the filter and housing, then carefully extract the filter element by squeezing its central folds together **(see illustration)**.

4 Fit the new element using a reversal of the removal procedure, but make sure that the direction arrows are aligned with each other.

5 Handbrake check

1 The handbrake should be capable of holding the parked vehicle stationary, even on steep slopes, when applied with moderate force. The mechanism should be firm and positive in feel, with no trace of stiffness or sponginess from the cables, and should release immediately the handbrake lever is released. If the mechanism is faulty in any of these respects, it must be checked immediately as follows. **Note:** *On models with rear drum brakes, if the handbrake is not functioning correctly or is incorrectly adjusted, the rear brake self-adjust mechanism will not function. This will lead to the brake pedal travel becoming excessive as the shoe linings wear.*

2 Handbrake adjustment is made beneath the vehicle on the cable adjuster nut **(see illustration)**.

3 Jack up the rear of the vehicle and support it on axle stands (see *Jacking and vehicle support*). Undo the heat shield retaining nut(s) and lower the rear of the heat shield to gain access to the handbrake cable adjuster nut. Slacken the locknut, then fully slacken the cable adjuster nut.

Models with rear drum brakes

4 Remove both rear brake drums as described in Chapter 9.

5 Check that the knurled adjuster wheel on the adjuster strut is free to rotate in both directions. If it is seized, the brake shoes and strut must be removed and overhauled as described in Section 12 of Chapter 9.

6 If all is well, back off the adjuster wheel by five or six teeth so that the diameter of the brake shoes is slightly reduced.

7 Check that the handbrake cables slide freely by pulling on their front ends. Also check that the operating levers on the rear brake trailing shoes return to their correct positions, with their stop-pegs in contact with the edge of the trailing shoe web.

8 With the aid of an assistant, tighten the adjuster nut on the handbrake lever operating rod so that the lever on each rear brake assembly starts to move as the handbrake is moved between the first and second notch (click) of its ratchet mechanism. This is the case when the stop-pegs are still in contact with the shoes when the handbrake is on the first notch of the ratchet, but no longer contact the shoes when the handbrake is on the second notch. Once the adjustment is correct, hold the adjuster nut and securely tighten the locknut. Refit the catalytic converter heat shield retaining nuts.

9 Refit the brake drums as described in Chapter 9, then lower the vehicle to the ground.

10 With the vehicle standing on its wheels, repeatedly depress the footbrake to adjust the shoe-to-drum clearance. Whilst depressing the pedal, have an assistant listen to the rear drums to check that the adjuster strut mechanism is functioning; if this is so, a clicking sound will be heard from the adjuster strut as the pedal is depressed.

Models with rear disc brakes

11 Check that the handbrake cables slide freely by pulling on their front ends, and check that the operating levers on the rear brake calipers move smoothly.

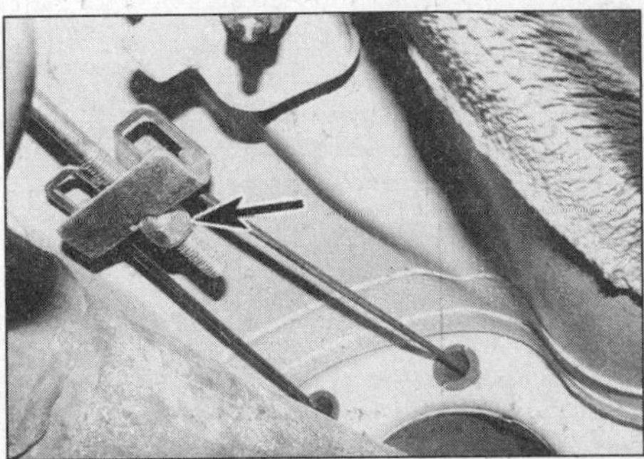

5.2 Handbrake cable adjusting nut (arrowed) located beneath the vehicle

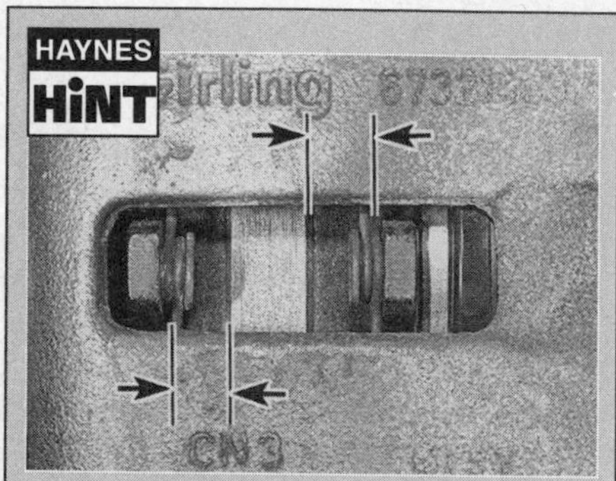

For a quick check, the thickness of friction material remaining on each brake pad can be measured through the aperture in the caliper body.

12 Move both of the caliper operating levers as far rearwards as possible, then tighten the adjuster nut on the handbrake lever operating rod until all free play is removed from both cables. With the aid of an assistant, adjust the nut so that the operating lever on each rear brake caliper starts to move as the handbrake lever is moved between the first and second notch (click) of its ratchet mechanism. Once the handbrake adjustment is correct, hold the adjuster nut and securely tighten the locknut.

13 Refit the heat shield retaining nuts (where necessary), then lower the vehicle to the ground.

6 Brake pad and disc check

Note: *Drum brake checks are in Section 19.*

1 Firmly apply the handbrake, then jack up the front or rear of the vehicle (as applicable) and support it securely on axle stands (see *Jacking and vehicle support*). Remove the roadwheels.

2 For a quick check, the thickness of friction material remaining on each brake pad can be measured through the aperture in the caliper body **(see Haynes Hint)**. If any pad's friction material is worn to the specified thickness or less, all four pads must be renewed as a set. Pad wear warning contacts are fitted to the inboard pads, but this should not be used as an excuse for omitting a visual check.

3 For a comprehensive check, the brake pads should be removed and cleaned. This will allow the operation of the caliper to be checked, and the brake disc itself to be fully examined for condition on both sides. Refer to Chapter 9 for further information.

7 Clutch check

1 Check that the clutch pedal moves smoothly and easily through its full travel, and that the clutch itself functions correctly, with no trace of slip or drag. If the movement is uneven or stiff in places, check that the cable is routed correctly, with no sharp turns.

2 Inspect the ends of the clutch inner cable, both at the gearbox end and inside the car, for signs of wear and fraying.

8 Auxiliary drivebelt check and renewal

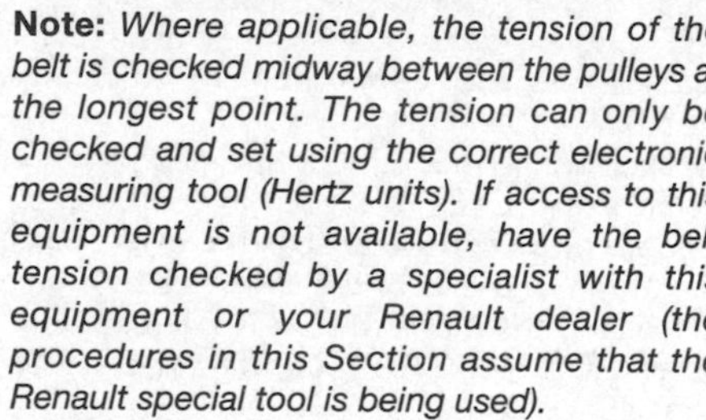

Note: *Where applicable, the tension of the belt is checked midway between the pulleys at the longest point. The tension can only be checked and set using the correct electronic measuring tool (Hertz units). If access to this equipment is not available, have the belt tension checked by a specialist with this equipment or your Renault dealer (the procedures in this Section assume that the Renault special tool is being used).*

Checking

1 The auxiliary drivebelt is located on the right-hand side of the engine.

2 Due to their function and material makeup, drivebelts are prone to failure after a period of time and should therefore be inspected, and if necessary adjusted periodically.

3 Since the drivebelt is located very close to the right-hand side of the engine compartment, it is possible to gain better access by raising the front of the vehicle and removing the right-hand wheel, then removing the engine undercover (where applicable) and wheel arch liner from inside the wheel arch.

4 With the engine stopped, inspect the full length of the drivebelt for cracks and separation of the belt plies **(see illustration)**. It will be necessary to turn the engine (using a spanner or socket and bar on the crankshaft pulley bolt) in order to move the belt from the pulleys so that the belt can be inspected thoroughly. Twist the belt between the pulleys so that both sides can be viewed. Also check for fraying, and glazing which gives the belt a shiny appearance. Check the pulleys for nicks, cracks, distortion and corrosion.

5 Renault technicians use a special tool to check the tension of the auxiliary belt, see note at the start of this Section.

Renewal

Note: *Before removal of the belt, note the fitted position. On some models, the compressor pulley has six grooves, the belt has five. In this case the inner groove is left unused, so that the run of the belt is straight.*

6 Using a spanner on the outer nut on the tensioner, turn the tensioner clockwise to release the tension on the belt **(see illustrations)**, then lift the drivebelt from the pulleys, noting its fitted position.

7 Using the spanner on the outer nut on the tensioner, hold the tensioner clockwise, to allow the new belt to be fitted around the pulleys, making sure that it is correctly located in the grooves.

8 Using the specialist tools (see note at the start of this Section), check that the belt has the correct tension of 233 ± 5 Hertz. If the reading is not within the tolerances given, then a new belt or tensioner will be required.

9 Run the engine for about 5 minutes, then recheck the tension.

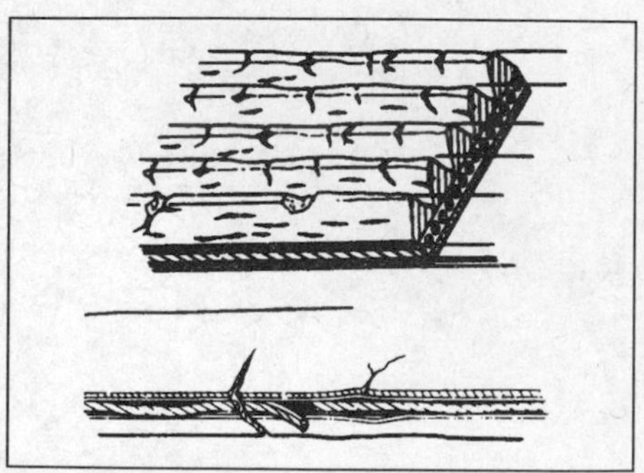

8.4 Checking for drivebelt wear – multi-ribbed type shown

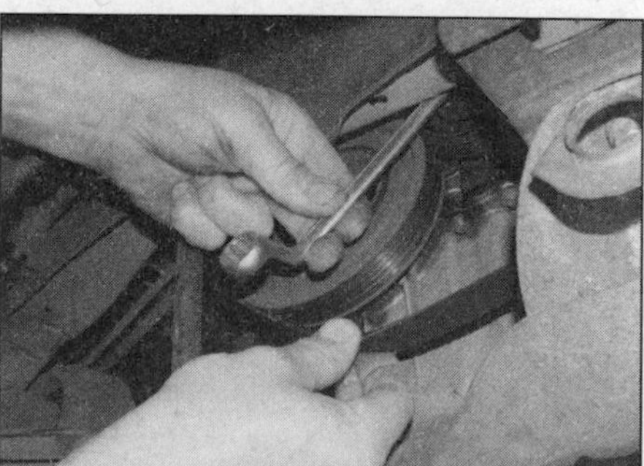

8.6a Turning the spanner clockwise from under the vehicle . . .

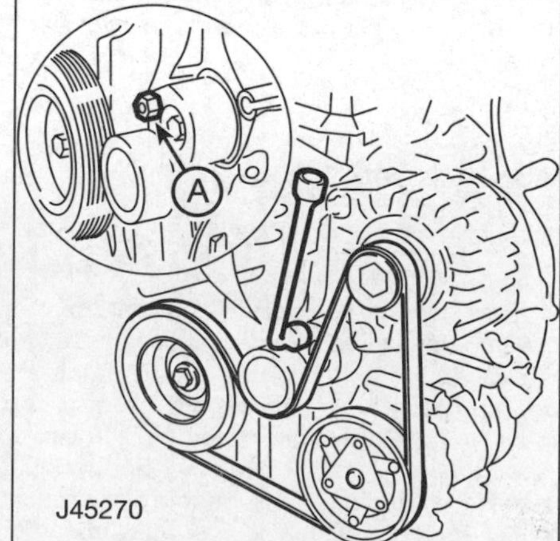

8.6b . . . or from above, using hexagon (A) on the tensioner pulley

9 Seat belt check

1 Carefully examine the seat belt webbing for cuts, or any signs of serious fraying or deterioration. If the belt is of the retractable type, pull the belt all the way out of the inertia reel, and examine the full extent of the webbing.

2 Fasten and unfasten the belt, ensuring that the locking mechanism holds securely, and releases properly when intended. If the belt is of the retractable type, check also that the retracting mechanism operates correctly when the belt is released.

3 Check the security of all seat belt mountings and attachments which are accessible without removing any trim or other components **(see illustration)**.

10 Electrical systems check

1 Check the operation of all electrical equipment, ie, lights, direction indicators, horn, etc. Refer to the appropriate Sections of Chapter 12 for details if any of the circuits are found to be inoperative.

2 Note that stop-light switch adjustment is described in Chapter 9.

3 Visually check all accessible wiring connectors, harnesses and retaining clips for security, and for signs of chafing or damage. Rectify any faults found.

11 Exhaust system check

1 With the engine cold (at least an hour after the vehicle has been driven), check the complete exhaust system from the engine to the end of the tailpipe. Ideally, the inspection should be carried out with the vehicle on a hoist to permit unrestricted access, but if a hoist is not available, raise and support the vehicle safely on axle stands (see *Jacking and vehicle support*).

2 Check the exhaust pipes and connections for evidence of leaks, severe corrosion and damage. Make sure that all brackets and mountings are in good condition and tight. Leakage at any of the joints or in other parts of the system will usually show up as a black sooty stain in the vicinity of the leak.

3 Rattles and other noises can often be traced to the exhaust system, especially the brackets and mountings. Try to move the pipes and silencers. If the components can come into contact with the body or suspension parts, secure the system with new mountings or if possible, separate the joints and twist the pipes as necessary to provide additional clearance.

4 Run the engine at idling speed. Have an assistant place a cloth or rag over the rear end of the exhaust pipe, and listen for any escape of exhaust gases that would indicate a leak.

5 On completion, lower the car to the ground.

12 Suspension and steering check

Front suspension and steering

1 Raise the front of the vehicle, and securely support it on axle stands (see *Jacking and vehicle support*).

2 Visually inspect the balljoint dust covers and the steering rack-and-pinion gaiters for splits, chafing or deterioration. Any wear of these components will cause loss of lubricant, together with dirt and water entry, resulting in rapid deterioration of the balljoints or steering gear.

3 Grasp the roadwheel at the 12 o'clock and 6 o'clock positions, and try to rock it **(see illustration)**. Very slight free play may be felt, but if the movement is appreciable, further investigation is necessary to determine the source. Continue rocking the wheel while an assistant depresses the footbrake. If the movement is now eliminated or significantly reduced, it is likely that the hub bearings are at fault. If the free play is still evident with the footbrake depressed, then there is wear in the suspension joints or mountings.

4 Now grasp the wheel at the 9 o'clock and 3 o'clock positions, and try to rock it as before. Any movement felt now may again be caused by wear in the hub bearings or the steering track rod balljoints. If the outer balljoint is worn, the visual movement will be obvious. If the inner joint is suspect, it can be felt by placing a hand over the rack-and-pinion rubber gaiter and gripping the track rod. If the wheel is now rocked, movement will be felt at the inner joint if wear has taken place.

5 Using a large screwdriver or flat bar, check for wear in the suspension mounting bushes by levering between the relevant suspension component and its attachment point. Some movement is to be expected, as the mountings are made of rubber, but excessive wear should be obvious. Also check the condition of any visible rubber bushes, looking for splits, cracks or contamination of the rubber.

6 With the car standing on its wheels, have an assistant turn the steering wheel back-and-forth, about an eighth of a turn each way. There should be very little, if any, lost movement between the steering wheel and roadwheels. If this is not the case, closely observe the joints and mountings previously described. In addition, check the steering column universal joints for wear, and also check the rack-and-pinion steering gear itself.

9.3 Checking the security of the seat belt mountings

12.3 Check for wear in the hub bearings by grasping the wheel and trying to rock it

Rear suspension

7 Chock the front wheels, then jack up the rear of the vehicle and support securely on axle stands (see *Jacking and vehicle support*).

8 Working as described previously for the front suspension, check the rear hub bearings, the suspension bushes and the shock absorber mountings for wear. **Note:** *The handbrake will need to be in the released position before checking the rear wheel bearings.*

13 Hose and fluid leak check

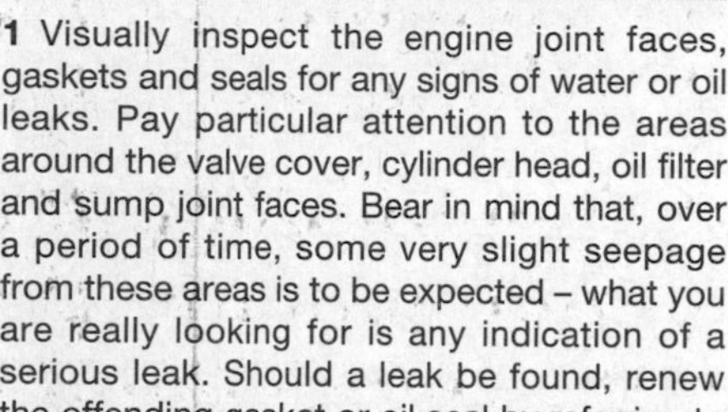

1 Visually inspect the engine joint faces, gaskets and seals for any signs of water or oil leaks. Pay particular attention to the areas around the valve cover, cylinder head, oil filter and sump joint faces. Bear in mind that, over a period of time, some very slight seepage from these areas is to be expected – what you are really looking for is any indication of a serious leak. Should a leak be found, renew the offending gasket or oil seal by referring to the appropriate Chapters in this manual.

2 Also check the security and condition of all the engine-related pipes and hoses, and all hydraulic and braking system pipes and hoses. Ensure that all cable ties or securing clips are in place, and in good condition. Clips which are broken or missing can lead to chafing of the hoses, pipes or wiring, which could cause more serious problems in the future.

3 Carefully check the radiator hoses and heater hoses along their entire length. Renew any hose which is cracked, swollen or deteriorated. Cracks will show up better if the hose is squeezed. Pay close attention to the hose clips that secure the hoses to the cooling system components. Hose clips can pinch and puncture hoses, resulting in cooling system leaks. If the crimped-type hose clips are used, it may be a good idea to replace them with standard worm-drive clips.

4 Inspect all the cooling system components (hoses, joint faces, etc) for leaks **(see Haynes Hint)**. Where any problems are found on system components, renew the component or gasket with reference to Chapter 3.

5 With the vehicle raised, inspect the fuel tank and filler neck for punctures, cracks and other damage. The connection between the filler neck and tank is especially critical. Sometimes a rubber filler neck or connecting hose will leak due to loose retaining clamps or deteriorated rubber.

HAYNES HiNT

A leak in the cooling system will usually show up as white- or rust-coloured deposits on the area adjoining the leak.

6 Carefully check all rubber hoses and metal fuel lines leading away from the fuel tank. Check for loose connections, deteriorated hoses, crimped lines, and other damage. Pay particular attention to the vent pipes and hoses, which often loop up around the filler neck and can become blocked or crimped. Follow the lines to the front of the vehicle, carefully inspecting them all the way. Renew damaged sections as necessary. Similarly, whilst the vehicle is raised, take the opportunity to inspect all underbody brake fluid pipes and hoses.

7 From within the engine compartment, check the security of all fuel, vacuum and brake hose attachments and pipe unions, and inspect all hoses for kinks, chafing and deterioration.

14 Roadwheel bolt check

1 Remove the wheel trims, where applicable, then slacken the roadwheel bolts slightly.

2 Tighten the bolts to the specified torque, using a torque wrench.

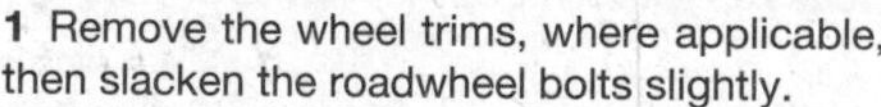

15 Bodywork and underbody condition check

1 Once the car has been washed and all tar spots and other surface blemishes have been cleaned off, carefully check all paintwork, looking closely for chips or scratches. Pay particular attention to vulnerable areas such as the front panels (bonnet and spoiler), and around the wheel arches. Any damage to the paintwork must be rectified as soon as possible to comply with the terms of the manufacturer's anti-corrosion warranties; check with a Renault dealer for details.

2 If a chip or light scratch is found which is recent and still free from rust, it can be touched-up using the appropriate touch-up stick which can be obtained from Renault dealers. Any more serious damage, or rusted stone chips, can be repaired as described in Chapter 11, but if damage or corrosion is so severe that a panel must be renewed, seek professional advice as soon as possible.

3 Always check that the door and ventilation opening drain holes and pipes are completely clear, so that water can drain out.

4 The wax-based underbody protective coating should be inspected annually, preferably just prior to Winter, when the underbody should be washed down as thoroughly as possible without disturbing the protective coating (see Chapter 11, Section 2, regarding the use of steam cleaners). Any damage to the coating should be repaired using a suitable wax-based sealer. If any of the body panels are disturbed for repair or renewal, do not forget to replace the coating and to inject wax into door panels, sills and box sections, to maintain the level of protection provided by the vehicle manufacturer.

16 Shock absorber check

1 Viewing over the roadwheels into the wheel arches, check for any signs of fluid leakage around the front and rear shock absorber bodies, or from the rubber gaiters around the piston rods. Should any fluid be noticed, the shock absorber is defective internally, and should be renewed. **Note:** *Shock absorbers should always be renewed in pairs on the same axle.*

2 The efficiency of the shock absorber may be checked by bouncing the vehicle at each corner. Generally speaking, the body will return to its normal position and stop after being depressed. If it rises and returns on a rebound, the shock absorber is probably suspect. Also examine the shock absorber upper and lower mountings for any signs of wear.

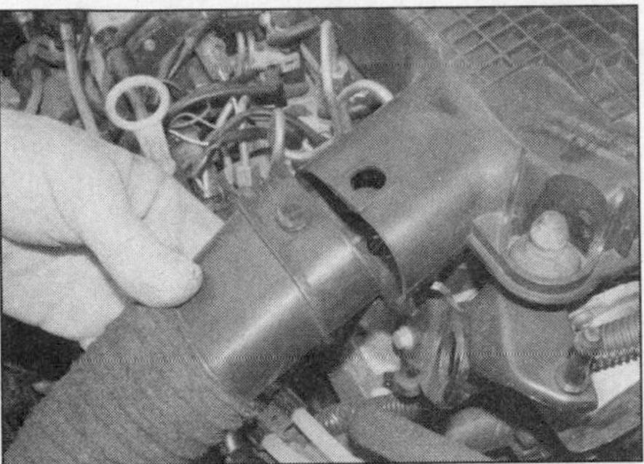
17.1 Disconnecting the air intake pipe

17.2a Undo the retaining screws . . .

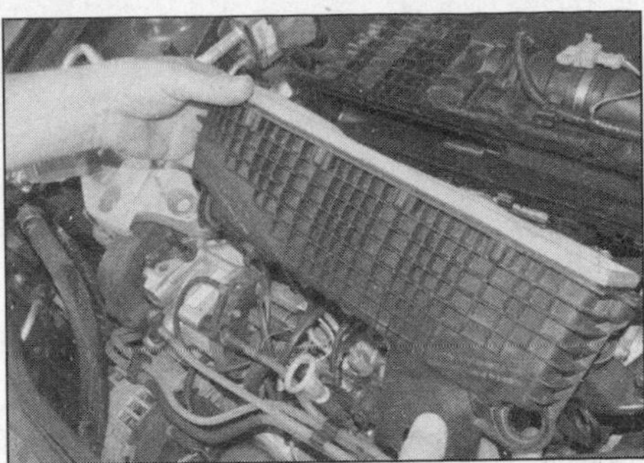
17.2b . . . release the air filter housing . . .

Every 36 000 miles (60 000 km) or 4 years

17 Air filter element renewal

1 Unclip the cover from the top of the engine and disconnect the air intake hose from the front of the air filter housing **(see illustration)**.
2 Undo the four retaining screws from the top of the housing and withdraw it from the top of the engine **(see illustration).**
3 Lift the element from the air filter housing, noting its fitted position **(see illustration)**.
4 Clean the inside of the main body and cover, then insert the new filter element.
5 Make sure the housing is located correctly – the bottom supports must locate securely, and the top must engage correctly to make a good seal.
6 Tighten the retaining screws across the top of the housing and refit the air intake hose and engine cover.

18 Fuel filter renewal

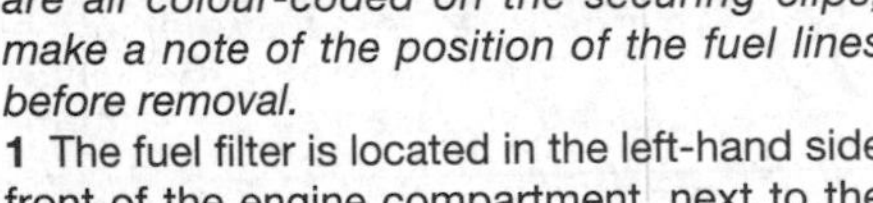

Note: *The fuel lines on the top of the fuel filter are all colour-coded on the securing clips, make a note of the position of the fuel lines before removal.*
1 The fuel filter is located in the left-hand side front of the engine compartment, next to the battery. A water drain screw is provided on the base of the filter unit **(see illustration)**.
2 Place a suitable container beneath the drain screw. To make draining easier, a suitable length of tubing can be attached to the outlet on the screw to direct the fuel flow.
3 Release the securing clip and disconnect one of the fuel lines **(see illustration)**, then open the drain screw by turning it anti-clockwise.
4 Allow the entire contents of the filter to drain into the container, then tighten the drain screw.
5 Holding the new filter next to the old filter, disconnect each fuel line in turn off the old filter and connect them onto the new filter.
6 Unclip the old filter from its mounting bracket on the battery tray and clip the new filter in its place **(see illustration)**. Dispose of the old filter using the correct method.
7 Open the drain plug on the new filter and squeeze the hand pump **(see illustration)** until the fuel flows through the filter, then securely tighten the drain plug. For further information, see Chapter 4B to prime and bleed the fuel system.

19 Rear brake shoe and drum check

1 Remove the rear brake drums, and check the brake shoes for signs of wear or contamination. At the same time, also inspect the wheel cylinders for signs of leakage, and

17.3 . . . and lift out the air filter element

18.1 Fuel filter drain screw (arrowed)

18.3 Disconnecting one of the fuel lines

18.6 Dispose of the old filter and fit new filter into mounting bracket

18.7 Squeeze the hand pump to fill filter with fuel

20.2 Unclipping the cover from below the engine/transmission

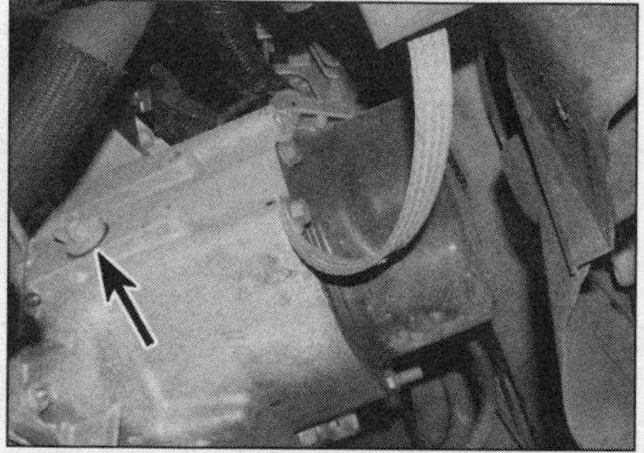

20.3 Transmission oil filler/level plug

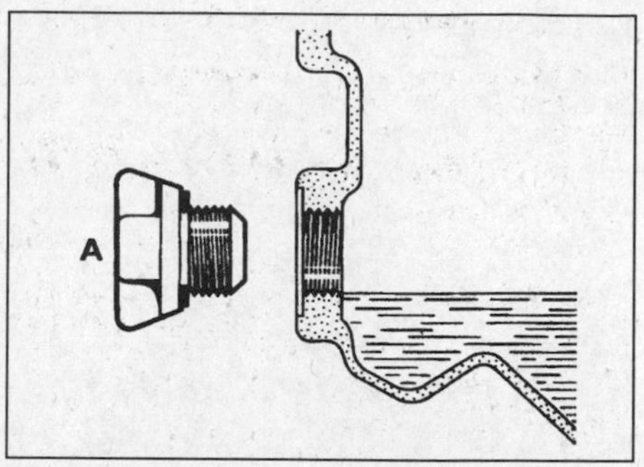

20.4 Manual transmission filler/level plug (A) – correct oil level shown

the brake drum for signs of wear. Refer to the relevant Sections of Chapter 9 for further information.

20 Manual transmission oil level check

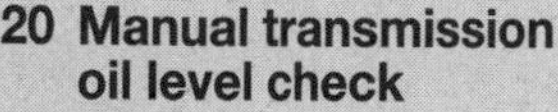

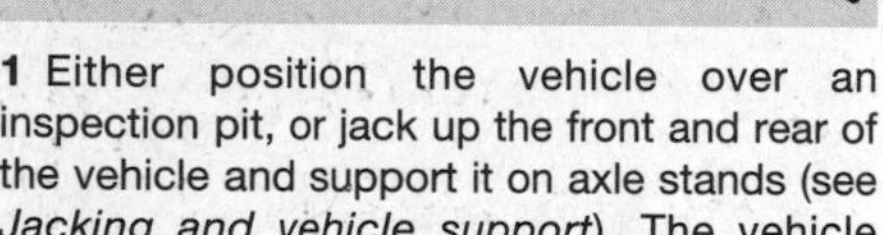

1 Either position the vehicle over an inspection pit, or jack up the front and rear of the vehicle and support it on axle stands (see *Jacking and vehicle support*). The vehicle must be level for the check to be accurate.
2 Remove the engine undertray or unclip the cover, as applicable, from the bottom of the transmission **(see illustration)**.
3 Clean the area around the filler/level plug located on the front facing side of the transmission, then unscrew and remove the plug **(see illustration)**.
4 The oil level should be up to the lower edge of the filler/level plug aperture **(see illustration)**.
5 If necessary, top-up using the specified type of lubricant until the transmission oil level is correct. Fill the transmission until oil starts to flow out and allow excess oil to drain out.
6 Once the transmission oil level is correct, refit the filler/level plug and tighten it securely.
7 Refit the engine undertray cover or transmission bottom cover as applicable, then lower the vehicle to the ground. Note that frequent need for topping-up indicates a leak, possibly through an oil seal. The cause should be investigated and rectified.

21 Front wheel alignment check

Refer to the information given in Chapter 10.

22 Air conditioning system check

The air conditioning system must be checked by a Renault dealer using dedicated test equipment.

23 Road test

Instruments and electrical equipment

1 Check the operation of all instruments and electrical equipment.
2 Make sure that all instruments read correctly, and switch on all electrical equipment in turn, to check that it functions properly.

Steering and suspension

3 Check for any abnormalities in the steering, suspension, handling or road 'feel'.
4 Drive the vehicle, and check that there are no unusual vibrations or noises.
5 Check that the steering feels positive, with no excessive 'sloppiness', or roughness, and check for any suspension noises when cornering and driving over bumps.

Drivetrain

6 Check the performance of the engine, clutch, transmission and driveshafts.
7 Listen for any unusual noises from the engine, clutch and transmission.
8 Make sure that the engine runs smoothly when idling, and that there is no hesitation when accelerating.
9 Check that the clutch action is smooth and progressive, that the drive is taken up smoothly, and that the pedal travel is not excessive. Also listen for any noises when the clutch pedal is depressed.
10 Check that all gears can be engaged smoothly without noise, and that the gear lever action is smooth and not abnormally vague or 'notchy'.
11 Listen for a metallic clicking sound from the front of the vehicle, as the vehicle is driven slowly in a circle with the steering on full-lock. Carry out this check in both directions. If a clicking noise is heard, this indicates wear in a driveshaft joint (see Chapter 8).

Braking system

12 Make sure that the vehicle does not pull to one side when braking, and that the wheels do not lock when braking hard.
13 Check that there is no vibration through the steering when braking.
14 Check that the handbrake operates correctly, without excessive movement of the lever, and that it holds the vehicle stationary on a slope.
15 Test the operation of the brake servo unit as follows. Depress the footbrake four or five times to exhaust the vacuum, then start the engine. As the engine starts, there should be a noticeable 'give' in the brake pedal as vacuum builds up. Allow the engine to run for at least two minutes, and then switch it off. If the brake pedal is now depressed again, it should be possible to detect a hiss from the servo as the pedal is depressed. After about four or five applications, no further hissing should be heard, and the pedal should feel considerably harder.

24 Timing belt renewal

Refer to Chapter 2C.

25 Brake fluid renewal

Warning: Brake hydraulic fluid can harm your eyes and damage painted surfaces, so use extreme caution when handling and pouring it. Do not use fluid that has been standing open for some time, as it absorbs moisture from the air. Excess moisture can cause a dangerous loss of braking effectiveness.

1 The procedure is similar to that for the bleeding of the hydraulic system as described in Chapter 9, except that the brake fluid reservoir should be emptied by syphoning, using a clean poultry baster or similar before starting, and allowance should be made for the old fluid to be expelled when bleeding a section of the circuit.
2 Working as described in Chapter 9, open the first bleed screw in the sequence, and pump the brake pedal gently until nearly all the old fluid has been emptied from the master

cylinder reservoir. Top-up to the MAXI level with new fluid, and continue pumping until only the new fluid remains in the reservoir, and new fluid can be seen emerging from the bleed screw. Tighten the screw, and top the reservoir level up to the MAXI level line.

Old hydraulic fluid is invariably much darker in colour than the new, making it easy to distinguish the two.

3 Work through all the remaining bleed screws in the sequence until new fluid can be seen at all of them. Be careful to keep the master cylinder reservoir topped-up to above the MINI level at all times, or air may enter the system and greatly increase the length of the task.

4 When the operation is complete, check that all bleed screws are securely tightened, and that their dust caps are refitted. Wash off all traces of spilt fluid, and recheck the master cylinder reservoir fluid level.

5 Check the operation of the brakes before taking the car on the road.

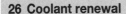

26 Coolant renewal

Cooling system draining

Warning: Wait until the engine is cold before starting this procedure. Do not allow antifreeze to come in contact with your skin, or with the painted surfaces of the vehicle. Rinse off spills immediately with plenty of water. Never leave antifreeze lying around in an open container, or in a puddle in the driveway or on the garage floor. Children and pets are attracted by its sweet smell, but antifreeze can be fatal if ingested.

1 With the engine completely cold, remove the expansion tank filler cap. Turn the cap anti-clockwise, wait until any pressure remaining in the system is released, then unscrew it and lift it off.

2 Where applicable, remove the undershield, then position a suitable container beneath the radiator bottom hose connection.

3 Loosen the hose clip, pull off the hose and allow the coolant to drain into the container.

4 To assist draining, open the cooling system bleed screw located on the thermostat housing.

5 When the flow of coolant stops, reposition the container below the cylinder block drain plug located at the rear right-hand side of the cylinder block. Unscrew the plug and drain the coolant into the container.

6 Flush the system if necessary as described in the following paragraphs, then refit the drain plug and secure the bottom hose. Use a new hose clip if necessary. Refill the system as described later in this Section.

Cooling system flushing

7 If coolant renewal has been neglected, or if the antifreeze mixture has become diluted, then in time, the cooling system may gradually lose efficiency, as the coolant passages become restricted due to rust, scale deposits, and other sediment. The cooling system efficiency can be restored by flushing the system clean.

8 The radiator should be flushed independently of the engine, to avoid unnecessary contamination.

Radiator flushing

9 Disconnect the top and bottom hoses and any other relevant hoses from the radiator, with reference to Chapter 3.

10 Insert a garden hose into the radiator top inlet. Direct a flow of clean water through the radiator, and continue flushing until clean water emerges from the radiator bottom outlet.

11 If after a reasonable period, the water still does not run clear, the radiator can be flushed with a good proprietary cleaning agent. It is important that the manufacturer's instructions are followed carefully. If the contamination is particularly bad, insert the hose in the radiator bottom outlet, and reverse-flush the radiator.

Engine flushing

12 To flush the engine, remove the thermostat as described in Chapter 3, and disconnect the bottom hose.

13 Insert a garden hose into the thermostat housing and direct a clean flow of water through the engine. Continue flushing until clean water emerges from the radiator bottom hose.

14 On completion, refit the thermostat and reconnect the bottom hose.

Cooling system filling

15 Before attempting to fill the cooling system, make sure that all hoses and clips are in good condition, and that the clips are tight. Note that an antifreeze mixture must be used all year round, to prevent corrosion of the engine components. Also check that the cylinder block drain plug is in place and tight.

16 Remove the expansion tank filler cap.

17 Open the cooling system bleed screw on the thermostat housing.

18 Slowly fill the system until the coolant level reaches the MAXI mark on the expansion tank. Close the bleed screw when coolant free from air bubbles emerges.

19 Start the engine, and run it at a fast idle speed (approx 2500 rpm) for approximately 4 minutes. Keep the level topped-up to the top of the expansion tank filler neck.

20 Refit and tighten the expansion tank filler cap.

21 Allow the engine to run at 2500 rpm for approximately 15 minutes until the cooling fan cuts in and out.

22 Stop the engine and allow the engine to cool for at least 30 minutes.

23 Recheck the coolant level with reference to *Weekly checks*. Top-up the level if necessary and refit the expansion tank filler cap.

Antifreeze mixture

24 The antifreeze should always be renewed at the specified intervals. This is necessary not only to maintain the antifreeze properties, but also to prevent corrosion which would otherwise occur as the corrosion inhibitors become progressively less effective.

25 Always use an ethylene-glycol based antifreeze which is suitable for use in mixed-metal cooling systems. The quantity of antifreeze and levels of protection are given in the Specifications.

26 Before adding antifreeze, the cooling system should be completely drained, preferably flushed, and all hoses checked for condition and security.

27 After filling with antifreeze, a label should be attached to the expansion tank, stating the type and concentration of antifreeze used, and the date installed. Any subsequent topping-up should be made with the same type and concentration of antifreeze.

28 Do not use engine antifreeze in the windscreen/tailgate washer system, as it will cause damage to the vehicle's paintwork. A screenwash additive should be added to the washer system in the quantities stated on the bottle.

27 'Service' light – general

The Clio has a warning light on the instrument panel which may light up with the word SERV or SERVICE. Despite appearances, this is **not** a service indicator light, as featured on some other cars – it is actually an engine management light, and if illuminated, it indicates that a fault has been logged in the engine ECU. The only way to put this light out is by using the Renault XR25 diagnostic tester – see Chapter 4B, Section 1.

Notes

Chapter 2 Part A:
1.2 litre petrol engine in-car repair procedures

Contents

Degrees of difficulty

Easy, suitable for novice with little experience 

Fairly easy, suitable for beginner with some experience 

Fairly difficult, suitable for competent DIY mechanic 

Difficult, suitable for experienced DIY mechanic

Very difficult, suitable for expert DIY or professional 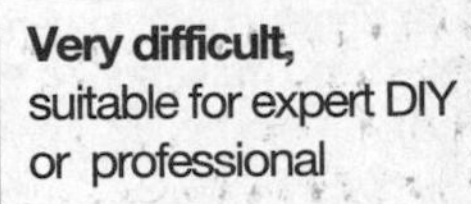

Specifications

General

Type	Four-cylinder, in-line, single overhead camshaft (SOHC) operating 8 valves (D7F) or 16 valves (D4F)
Designation:	
8-valve	D7F
16-valve	D4F
Bore	69.0 mm
Stroke	76.8 mm
Capacity	1149 cc
Firing order	1-3-4-2 (No 1 cylinder at flywheel end)
Direction of crankshaft rotation	Clockwise viewed from pulley end
Compression ratio:	
D7F	9.65 : 1
D4F	9.8 : 1
Camshaft endfloat:	
D7F	0.07 to 0.148 mm
D4F	0.08 to 0.178 mm

Valve clearances (cold)

D7F:	
Inlet	0.10 mm
Exhaust	0.20 mm
D4F:	
Inlet	0.05 to 0.12 mm
Exhaust	0.15 to 0.22 mm

Lubrication system

System pressure:	
At idle	0.8 bar
At 4000 rpm	3.5 bars
Oil pump type	Two-gear

Torque wrench settings

	Nm	lbf ft
D7F 8-valve engine		
Camshaft sprocket bolt	45	33
Connecting rod (big-end) cap:		
Stage 1	14	10
Stage 2	Angle-tighten a further 39°	
Crankshaft oil seal housing	9	7
Crankshaft pulley/sprocket bolt:		
Stage 1	20	15
Stage 2	Angle-tighten a further 90°	
Cylinder head bolts:		
Stage 1 – all bolts	20	15
Stage 2 – all bolts	Angle-tighten a further 90°	
Stage 3 – all bolts	Wait for at least 3 minutes	
Stage 4 – bolts 1 and 2	Slacken fully	
Stage 5 – bolts 1 and 2	20	15
Stage 6 – bolts 1 and 2	Angle-tighten a further 200°	
Stage 7 – bolts 3, 4, 5 and 6	Slacken fully	
Stage 8 – bolts 3, 4, 5 and 6	20	15
Stage 9 – bolts 3, 4, 5 and 6	Angle-tighten a further 200°	
Stage 10 – bolts 7, 8, 9 and 10	Slacken fully	
Stage 11 – bolts 7, 8, 9 and 10	20	15
Stage 12 – bolts 7, 8, 9 and 10	Angle-tighten a further 200°	
Engine/transmission mountings (see Section 17):		
Left-hand mounting central nut	62	46
Left-hand mounting to body	21	15
Left-hand mounting to transmission	62	46
Rear mounting	62	46
Right-hand mounting central nut	105	77
Right-hand mounting to engine/body	62	46
Exhaust manifold	25	18
Flywheel bolts:		
Stage 1	18	13
Stage 2	Angle-tighten a further 110°	
Inlet manifold	15	11
Main bearing cap:		
Stage 1	20	15
Stage 2	Angle-tighten a further 80°	
Oil pump	9	7
Roadwheel bolts	90	66
Rocker shaft bolts	23	17
Sump	10	7
Timing belt tensioner bolt	50	37
Valve cover	11	8
D4F 16-valve engine		
Air conditioning compressor	50	37
Alternator:		
Upper bolt	25	18
Lower bolt	50	37
Alternator mounting bracket	50	37
Camshaft:		
Stage 1 – sprocket end bearing cap bolts 1 and 2	9	7
Stage 2 – rocker arm rail bolts	5	4
Stage 3 – bolt 3: fully loosen, then tighten to	7	5
Stage 4 – bolt 3	Angle-tighten by a further 50° ± 6°	
Stage 5 – bolts 4 to 12	Repeat Stages 3 and 4 in turn in the correct order	
Camshaft sprocket bolt:		
Stage 1	30	22
Stage 2	Angle-tighten a further 45° ± 6°	
Clutch	20	15
Connecting rod (big-end) cap:		
Stage 1	14	10
Stage 2	Angle-tighten a further 39° ± 6°	
Coolant outlet	9	7
Coolant temperature sensor	15	11
Crankshaft oil seal housing	9	7

Torque wrench settings (continued)

	Nm	lbf ft
D4F 16-valve engine (continued)		
Crankshaft pulley/sprocket bolt:		
Stage 1	40	30
Stage 2	Angle-tighten a further 70° ± 6°	
Cylinder head bolts:		
Stage 1	20	15
Stage 2	Angle-tighten a further 230° ± 6°	
Engine/transmission mountings (see Section 17):		
Left-hand mounting central nut	62	46
Left-hand mounting to body	21	15
Left-hand mounting to transmission	62	46
Rear mounting	62	46
Right-hand mounting central nut	105	77
Right-hand mounting to engine/body	62	46
Exhaust heat shield	15	11
Exhaust manifold	25	18
Flywheel bolts:		
Stage 1	18	13
Stage 2	Angle-tighten a further 110° ± 6°	
Inlet manifold:		
Stage 1 – all side bolts	Hand-tighten	
Stage 2 – side bolts 4 and 5	6	4
Stage 3 – side bolts 4 and 5	Slacken fully	
Stage 4 – all side bolts	10	7
Stage 5 – upper bolts	10	7
Knock sensor	20	15
Main bearing cap:		
Stage 1	20	15
Stage 2	Angle-tighten a further 76°	
Oil filter	20	15
Oil level sensor	38	28
Oil pump	9	7
Oil pump strainer	9	7
Roadwheel bolts	90	66
Rocker arm rail bolts:		
Stage 1	Tighten camshaft end bearing caps	
Stage 2	5	4
Stage 3	Slacken fully	
Stage 4	7	5
Stage 5	Angle-tighten a further 50° ± 6°	
Spark plugs	24	18
Sump:		
To crankcase	10	7
To clutch housing	40	30
Timing belt lower and intermediate cover	10	7
Timing belt tensioner nut	24	18
Timing belt upper cover	33	24
Valve cover	12	9
Water pump	9	7

1 General information

This Part of Chapter 2 Is devoted to in-car repair procedures for the 1.2 litre petrol engine. Similar information covering the other engine types can be found in Parts B and C. All procedures concerning engine removal and refitting, and engine block/cylinder head overhaul can be found in Part D of this Chapter.

Refer to *Vehicle identification numbers* in the Reference Section at the end of this manual for details of engine code locations.

Most of the operations included in this Part are based on the assumption that the engine is still installed in the car. Therefore, if this information is being used during a complete engine overhaul, with the engine already removed, many of the steps included here will not apply.

Engine description

The engine is of four-cylinder, in-line, single overhead camshaft type, mounted transversely in the front of the car.

The cylinder bores are machined directly into the cast-iron cylinder block. The crankshaft is supported within the cylinder block on five shell-type main bearings. Thrustwashers are fitted at the centre main bearing to control crankshaft endfloat.

The connecting rods are attached to the crankshaft by horizontally-split shell-type big-end bearings, and to the pistons by interference-fit gudgeon pins. The aluminium alloy pistons are of the slipper type, and are fitted with three piston rings, comprising two compression rings and a scraper-type oil control ring.

The overhead camshaft is driven by the crankshaft via a toothed rubber timing belt which also drives the water pump. The camshaft operates the valves via rocker arms located on a rocker shaft bolted to the top of the cylinder head. On the 16-valve engine, each rocker arm operates two valves.

A semi-enclosed crankcase ventilation system is employed.

Lubrication is by pressure feed from a gear-type oil pump, which is driven directly from the timing end of the crankshaft.

Operations with engine in place

The following operations can be carried out without having to remove the engine from the car.

a) Removal and refitting of the cylinder head.
b) Removal and refitting of the timing belt and sprockets.
c) Renewal of the camshaft oil seal.
d) Removal and refitting of the camshaft.
e) Removal and refitting of the sump.
f) Removal and refitting of the connecting rods and pistons.*
g) Removal and refitting of the oil pump.
h) Renewal of the crankshaft oil seals.
i) Renewal of the engine mountings.
j) Removal and refitting of the flywheel.

** Although the operation marked with an asterisk can be carried out with the engine in the car after removal of the sump, it is better for the engine to be removed in the interests of cleanliness and improved access. For this reason, the procedure is described in Part D of this Chapter.*

2 Compression test – description and interpretation

Note: *A compression gauge will be required for this test.*

1 A compression check will tell you what mechanical condition the top end (pistons, rings, valves, head gasket) of the engine is in. Specifically, it can tell you if the compression is down due to leakage caused by worn piston rings, defective valves and seats or a blown head gasket. **Note:** *The engine must be at normal operating temperature, and the battery must be fully-charged, for this check.*

2 Begin by cleaning the area around the spark plugs before you remove them (compressed air should be used, if available, otherwise a small brush or even a bicycle tyre pump will work). The idea is to prevent dirt from getting into the cylinders as the compression check is being done.

3 Remove all of the spark plugs from the engine (see Chapter 1A).

4 Disable the engine management system by removing the main engine protection fuse from the engine compartment fusebox.

5 Fit the compression gauge into the No 1 spark plug hole – the type of tester which screws into the plug thread is to be preferred **(see illustration)**.

6 Have an assistant hold the accelerator pedal fully depressed, while at the same time cranking the engine over several times on the starter motor. Observe the compression gauge – the compression should build-up quickly in a healthy engine. Low compression on the first stroke, followed by gradually-increasing pressure on successive strokes, indicates worn piston rings. A low compression reading on the first stroke, which does not build-up during successive strokes, indicates leaking valves or a blown head gasket (a cracked head could also be the cause). Deposits on the undersides of the valve heads can also cause low compression. Record the highest gauge reading obtained, then repeat the procedure for the remaining cylinders.

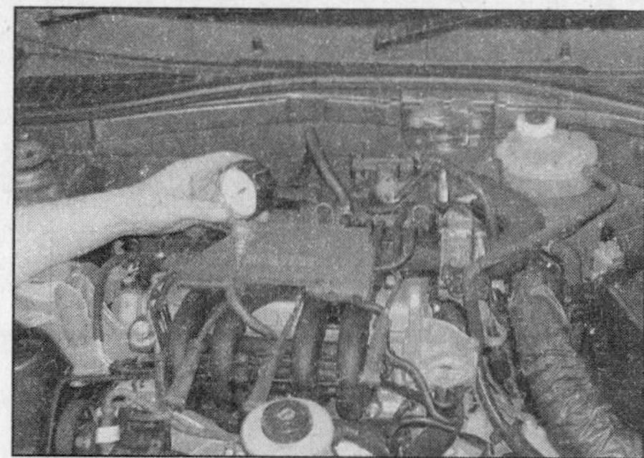

2.5 Carrying out a compression check

7 Add some engine oil (about three squirts from a plunger-type oil can) to each cylinder, through the spark plug hole, and repeat the test.

8 If the compression increases after the oil is added, the piston rings are worn. If the compression does not increase significantly, the leakage is occurring at the valves or head gasket. Leakage past the valves may be caused by burned valve seats and/or faces, or warped, cracked or bent valves.

9 If two adjacent cylinders have equally low compression, there is a strong possibility that the head gasket between them is blown. The appearance of coolant in the combustion chambers or the crankcase would verify this condition.

10 Actual compression pressures for the engines covered by this manual are not specified by the manufacturer. However, bearing in mind the information given in the preceding paragraphs, the results obtained should give a good indication of engine condition and what course of action, if any, to take.

3.6a Remove the plug from the aperture in the lower engine mounting bracket/upper timing belt cover – D7F engine

3 Top Dead Centre (TDC) for No 1 piston – locating

1 Top dead centre (TDC) is the highest point in the cylinder that each piston reaches as the crankshaft turns. Each piston reaches TDC at the end of the compression stroke, and again at the end of the exhaust stroke; however, for the purpose of timing the engine, TDC refers to the position of No 1 piston at the end of its compression stroke. No 1 piston is at the flywheel end of the engine.

2 Apply the handbrake, then jack up the front right-hand side of the car and support it on axle stands. Remove the right-hand roadwheel.

3 Remove the plastic liners from within the right-hand wheel arch to give access to the crankshaft pulley bolt.

4 Remove the spark plugs as described in Chapter 1A.

5 Place a finger (D7F) or inverted screwdriver handle (D4F) over the No 1 spark plug hole in the cylinder head (nearest the flywheel). On the D4F engine, the spark plugs are deeply recessed at the bottom of metal tubes. Turn the engine in a clockwise direction, using a socket or spanner on the crankshaft pulley bolt, until pressure is felt in the No 1 cylinder. This indicates that No 1 piston is rising on its compression stroke.

6 On the D7F engine, remove the plug from the aperture in the top of the lower engine mounting bracket/upper timing belt cover. On the D4F engine, remove the plastic upper timing cover. Look through the aperture, and continue to turn the crankshaft until the TDC timing mark on the camshaft sprocket is aligned with the reference mark on the top of the bracket/timing belt cover. If the lower engine mounting bracket/upper timing belt cover has been removed, the reference mark on the camshaft sprocket should be aligned with the reference mark at the top of the valve cover **(see illustrations). Note:** *The camshaft sprocket has five reference marks. Only the rectangular reference mark on one of the teeth represents TDC. The other semi-circular marks are used to adjust the valve clearances. Due to parallax, it is tricky to see whether the reference marks are aligned when the lower engine mounting bracket/upper timing belt cover is fitted. Provided that the crankshaft sprocket timing mark is aligned with the mark on the oil pump flange (see paragraph 7), and the camshaft sprocket reference mark is visible through the hole in the engine mounting bracket/timing belt cover, No 1 piston is at TDC.*

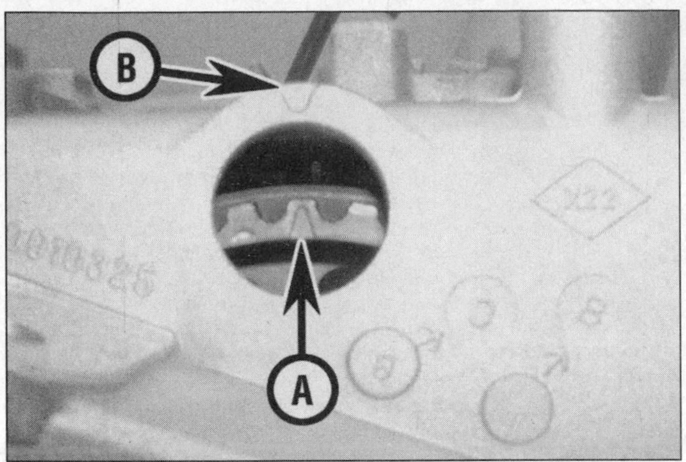

3.6b The TDC timing mark (A) on the camshaft sprocket should align with the reference mark (B) on the top of the lower engine mounting bracket/upper timing belt cover . . .

3.6c . . . or the reference mark (C) at the top of the valve cover

7 If the crankshaft pulley is now removed (see Section 5), the timing mark on the crankshaft sprocket should be aligned with the TDC mark at the bottom of the oil pump flange **(see illustration)**. If necessary, the flywheel may be locked to the cylinder block by inserting a suitable bolt through the special hole in the left-hand front of the block and locating it in the hole in the flywheel. Renault technicians use a special tool for this, and it is worth displaying a warning on the steering wheel as a precaution against someone attempting to start the engine with the tool in position.

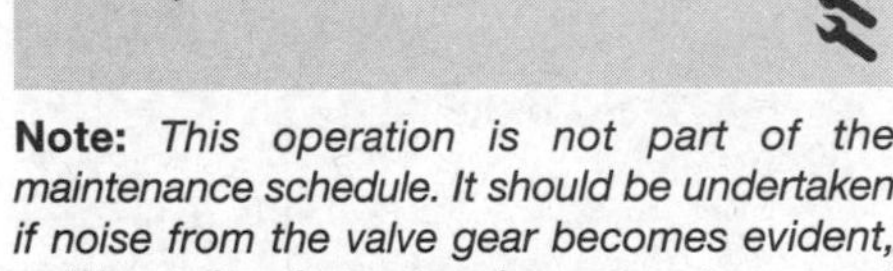

4 Valve clearances – adjustment

Note: *This operation is not part of the maintenance schedule. It should be undertaken if noise from the valve gear becomes evident, or if loss of performance gives cause to suspect that the clearances may be incorrect. A new valve cover gasket will be required.*

1 Remove the inlet manifold, as described in Chapter 4A.

2 Unscrew the bolts, and remove the valve cover and gasket. Discard the gasket, a new one must be used on refitting.

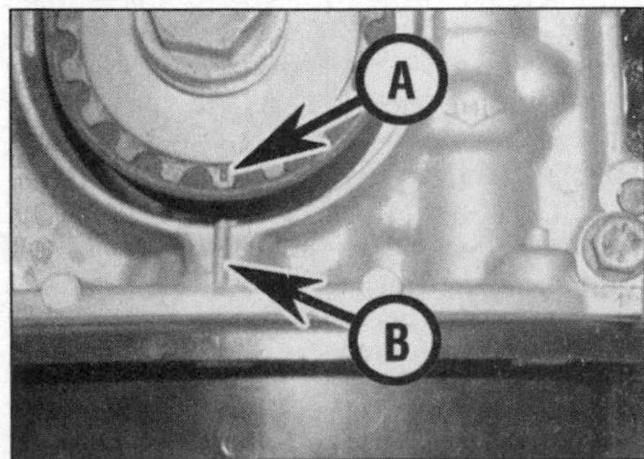

3.7 The timing mark (A) on the crankshaft sprocket should be aligned with the timing mark (B) on the oil pump flange

3 Remove the spark plugs, with reference to Chapter 1A, in order to make turning the engine easier. This however is not essential.

4 Draw the valve positions on a piece of paper, numbering them according to their cylinders, from the flywheel end of the engine (ie, 1E, 1I, 2E, 2I and so on). The inlet valves are on the inlet manifold side of the cylinder head, and the exhaust valves are on the exhaust manifold side. As the valve clearances are adjusted, cross them off.

5 There are two methods of adjusting the valve clearances; the 'camshaft mark' method and the 'exhaust valve open' method. The 'camshaft mark' method can only be used on the D7F engine, however, the 'exhaust valve open' method can be used on both engines.

Camshaft mark method

D7F engine

6 Turn the crankshaft to bring No 1 piston to TDC on compression, as described in Section 3. Do not lock the crankshaft in position. Continue to turn the crankshaft until the first of the valve clearance adjustment marks (semi-circular marks) on the camshaft sprocket is aligned with the reference mark on the engine mounting bracket/upper timing belt cover, or the valve cover, as applicable (if necessary, temporarily refit the valve cover to check this) **(see illustration)**.

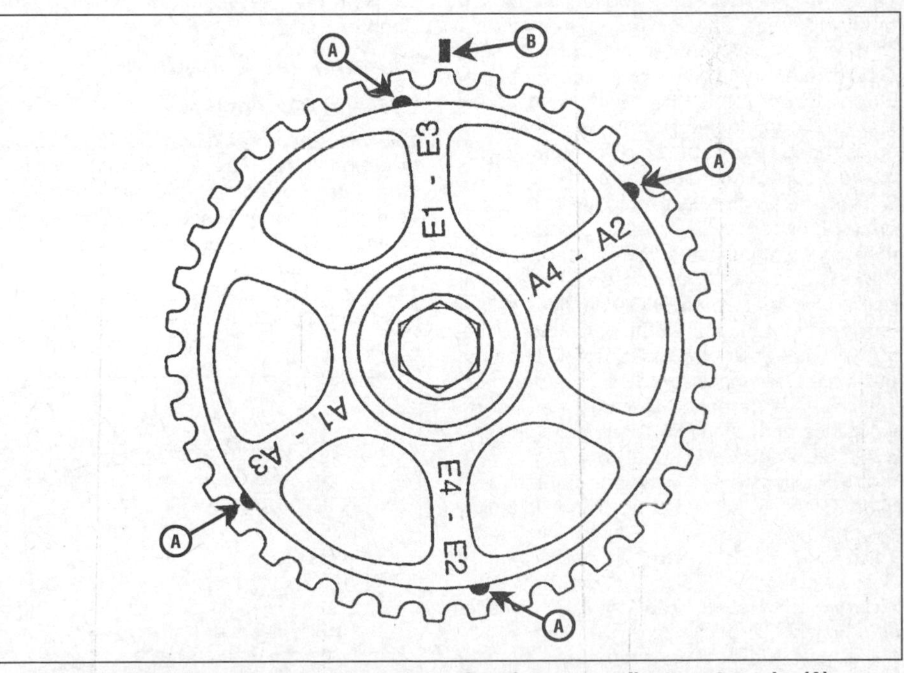

4.6 On the D7F engine, the first of the valve clearance adjustment marks (A), marked E1-E3 on the camshaft sprocket spoke, should be aligned with the reference mark (B) on the valve cover

4.7a Check the valve clearance using a feeler blade . . .

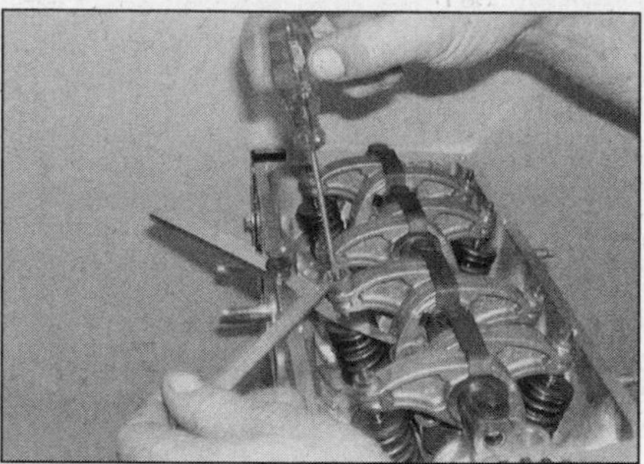
4.7b . . . and adjust if necessary using a ring spanner and screwdriver - D7F engine

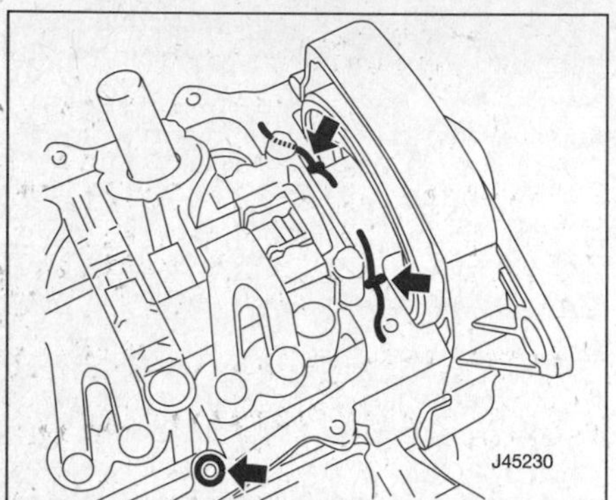

4.18a On the D4F engine, apply beads of sealant to the camshaft right-hand end bearing cap . . .

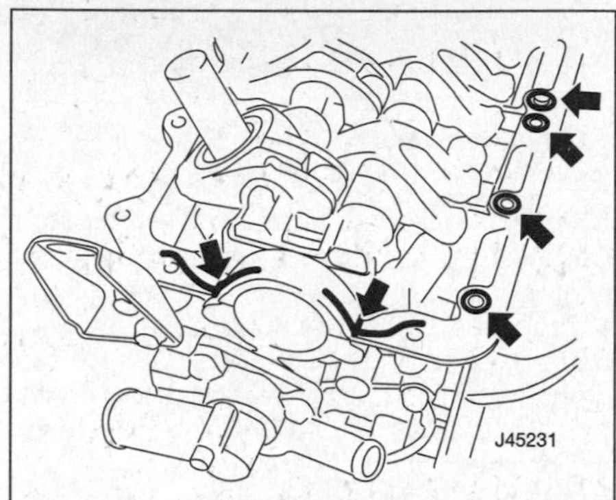

4.18b . . . to the left-hand end bearing cap, and around the valve cover mounting bolt holes

7 Insert a feeler blade of the correct thickness (see Specifications) between the No 1 cylinder exhaust valve stem and the end of the rocker arm. It should be a firm sliding fit. If adjustment is necessary, loosen the locknut on the rocker arm using a ring spanner, and turn the adjustment screw with a small screwdriver until the fit is correct **(see illustrations)**. Hold the adjustment screw, tighten the locknut and recheck the adjustment. Repeat the adjustment procedure on No 3 cylinder exhaust valve.

8 Turn the engine in a clockwise direction until the second valve clearance adjustment mark on the camshaft sprocket is aligned with the reference mark on the top of the timing belt cover or valve cover (as applicable) **(see illustration 4.6)**. Adjust the valve clearances on No 1 inlet and No 3 inlet valves. Note that the valve clearances for the inlet and exhaust valves are different. Continue to adjust the valve clearances in the following sequence.

Valve clearance mark in alignment*	Valves to adjust
First	No 1 ex. and No 3 ex.
Second	No 1 in. and No 3 in.
Third	No 2 ex. and No 4 ex.
Fourth	No 2 in. and No 4 in.

** Turning crankshaft clockwise from camshaft sprocket TDC mark*

9 Remove the socket or spanner from the crankshaft pulley bolt.

10 Refit the spark plugs, with reference to Chapter 1A.

11 Refit the valve cover using a new gasket, and tighten the securing bolts to the specified torque in a spiral sequence working from the centre outwards.

12 Refit the inlet manifold as described in Chapter 4A.

Exhaust valve method

D7F and D4F engines

13 Turn the crankshaft in a clockwise direction until No 1 exhaust valve is completely open (ie, the valve spring is completely compressed). Note on the D4F engine, each rocker arm operates two valves at the same time.

14 Insert a feeler blade of the correct thickness (see Specifications) between the No 3 cylinder inlet valve stem(s) and the end of the rocker arm(s). It should be a firm sliding fit. If adjustment is necessary, loosen the locknut on the rocker arm using a ring spanner, and turn the adjustment screw with a screwdriver until the fit is correct. Tighten the locknut and recheck the adjustment, then repeat the adjustment procedure on No 4 cylinder exhaust valve(s). Note that the clearances for the inlet and exhaust valves are different.

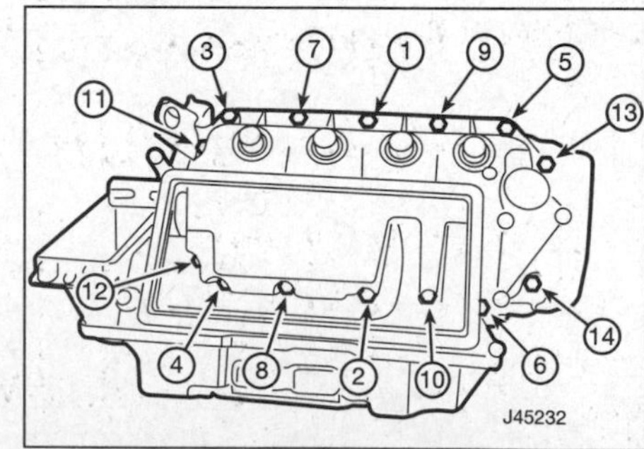

4.19 On the D4F engine, tighten the valve cover bolts in order

15 Turn the engine in a clockwise direction until No 3 exhaust valve is completely open, then adjust the valve clearances on No 4 inlet and No 2 exhaust valves. Continue to adjust the valve clearances in the following sequence.

Exhaust valve fully open	Inlet valve to adjust	Exhaust valve to adjust
1E	3I	4E
3E	4I	2E
4E	2I	1E
2E	1I	3E

16 Remove the socket or spanner from the crankshaft pulley bolt.

17 Refit the spark plugs, with reference to Chapter 1A.

18 On the D4F engine, apply beads of sealant to the camshaft end bearing caps and around the valve cover mounting bolt holes **(see illustrations)**.

19 Refit the valve cover using a new gasket, and tighten the securing bolts to the specified torque. On the D7F engine, tighten them in a spiral sequence working from the centre outwards. On the D4F engine, tighten them in sequence **(see illustration)**.

20 Refit the inlet manifold as described in Chapter 4A.

5 Crankshaft pulley - removal and refitting

Removal

1 Apply the handbrake, then jack up the front of the car and support it securely on axle stands. Remove the right-hand front road-wheel.

2 Remove the plastic liner from inside the wheel arch for access to the crankshaft pulley.

3 Remove the auxiliary drivebelts with reference to Chapter 1A.

4 The crankshaft must now be held stationary in order to loosen the crankshaft pulley bolt. To do this, have an assistant select first gear, and apply the footbrake firmly.

5 With the crankshaft held securely in place, unscrew the pulley bolt and recover the washer, then remove the pulley from the crankshaft **(see illustration)**.

Refitting

6 Refitting is a reversal of removal, bearing in mind the following points.

a) *Ensure that the locating pin on the crankshaft sprocket engages with the corresponding hole in the pulley.*

5.5 Removing the crankshaft pulley, complete with bolt and washer

b) Tighten the pulley bolt to the specified torque, in the two stages given in the Specifications.

c) Refit and tension the auxiliary drivebelts as described in Chapter 1A.

6 Timing belt covers – removal and refitting

Upper timing belt cover

1 On the D7F engine, the upper timing belt cover is incorporated in the right-hand engine mounting lower bracket (refer to Section 17). A plastic cover is fitted on the D4F engine.

Centre plastic cover

Removal

2 Remove the right-hand lower engine mounting bracket/upper timing belt cover, as described in Section 17.

3 Unscrew the two securing bolts and withdraw the centre plastic cover **(see illustration)**.

Refitting

4 Refitting is a reversal of removal, but refit the lower engine mounting bracket/upper timing belt cover as described in Section 17.

Lower plastic cover

Removal

5 Remove the crankshaft pulley as described in Section 5.

6 Unscrew the securing bolt, and remove the lower plastic cover **(see illustration)**.

7.8 Slacken the timing belt tensioner nut and turn the tensioner pulley clockwise

6.3 Removing the centre plastic timing belt cover

Refitting

7 Refitting is a reversal of removal, but refit the crankshaft pulley as described in Section 5.

7 Timing belt – removal, inspection, refitting and adjustment

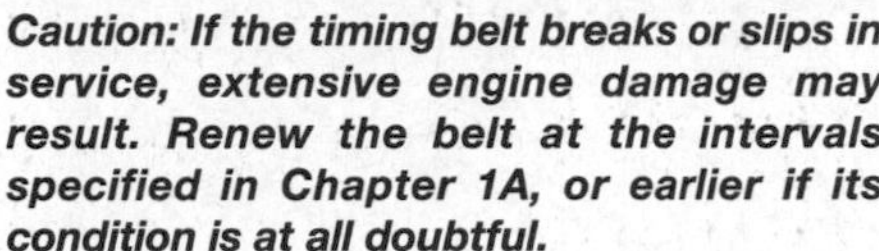

Caution: If the timing belt breaks or slips in service, extensive engine damage may result. Renew the belt at the intervals specified in Chapter 1A, or earlier if its condition is at all doubtful.

Removal

1 Disconnect the battery negative lead.

2 To improve access, remove the bonnet as described in Chapter 11.

3 Remove the crankshaft pulley as described in Section 5.

4 Temporarily refit the crankshaft pulley bolt, and turn the crankshaft to bring No 1 piston to TDC, as described in Section 3. Lock the engine in this position with the special tool or a suitable bolt, as described in Section 3.

5 Carefully, position a trolley jack and a large block of wood under the sump to support the engine. Raise the jack to just take the weight of the engine.

6 Remove the right-hand upper engine mounting bracket, and the lower mounting bracket/timing belt cover, with reference to Section 17.

7 Remove the two plastic outer timing belt covers with reference to Section 6.

8 Slacken the timing belt tensioner nut, and turn the tensioner pulley clockwise to relieve the belt tension **(see illustration)**. Slip the timing belt from the sprockets and pulleys. With the timing belt removed, do not turn the crankshaft or the camshaft until the belt has been refitted.

Inspection

9 Check the timing belt carefully for any signs of uneven wear, splitting or oil contamination and renew it if there is the slightest doubt about its condition. If the engine is undergoing an overhaul and has covered more than 36 000 miles (60 000 km) since the original belt was fitted, it is advisable to renew the belt as a matter of course, regardless of its apparent condition.

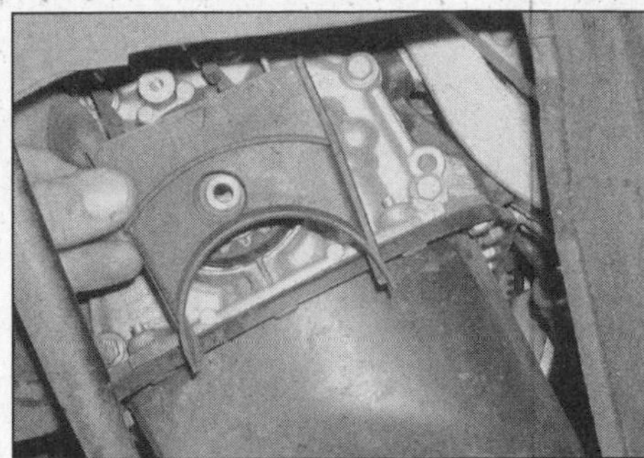

6.6 Removing the lower plastic timing belt cover

10 If signs of oil contamination are found, trace the source of the oil leak and rectify it, then wash down the engine timing belt area and all related components to remove all traces of oil.

Refitting and adjustment

11 Ensure that the timing marks on the camshaft sprocket and crankshaft sprocket are still aligned with the relevant mark on the valve cover and the oil pump flange (see Section 3).

12 Fit the timing belt over the crankshaft and camshaft sprockets and around the water pump pulley, ensuring that the belt front run is taut, ie, all slack is on the tensioner pulley side of the belt, then fit the belt around the tensioner pulley and turn the pulley anti-clockwise. Where applicable, line up the two timing reference marks on the belt with the timing marks on the crankshaft and camshaft sprockets. Do not twist the belt sharply during refitting, and do make sure that the belt teeth are correctly seated centrally in the sprockets and that the timing marks remain in alignment (see Section 3) **(see illustrations)**.

D7F engine

13 Renault recommend that a special timing belt tensioning tool (Tool Mot. 1273) is used to tension the belt. Alternatively, the following method can be used to tension the belt approximately, but in this case it is strongly recommended that the tension is checked using the Renault special tool at the earliest opportunity.

7.12a Where applicable, align the timing reference marks on the belt with the timing marks on the crankshaft sprocket . . .

7.12b . . . and camshaft sprocket

7.15 Hold the belt tensioner in position and tighten the tensioner bolt to the specified torque – D7F engine

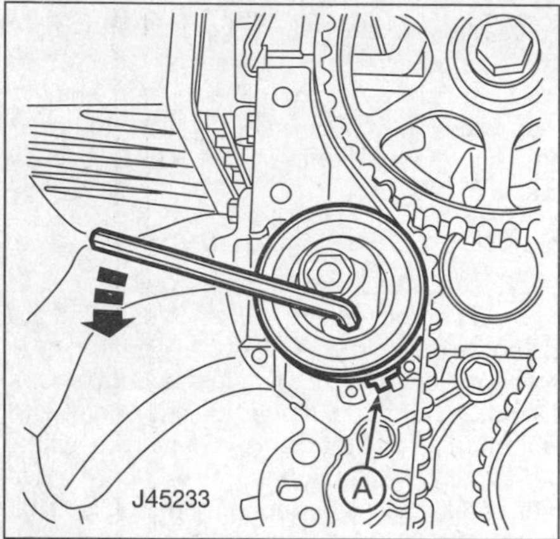

7.17 On the D4F engine, initially adjust the tensioner so that the index pointer is at the front of the timing window (A)

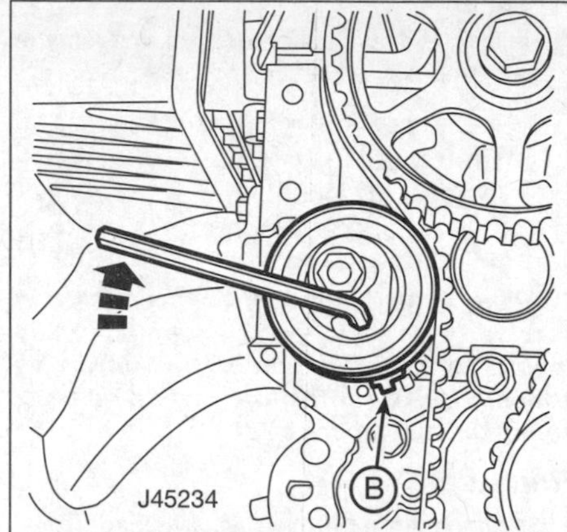

7.19 On the D4F engine, align the pointer in the middle of the timing window (B) after turning the engine six complete turns

14 Engage a pair of angled long-nosed pliers with the two holes in the tensioner pulley, and use the pliers to turn the tensioner anti-clockwise as necessary until the belt run between the tensioner and the crankshaft sprocket can just be twisted through 45° under moderate pressure with the thumb and forefinger. Alternatively, the check can be made on the belt run between the water pump pulley and crankshaft sprocket.

15 Hold the tensioner in position using the pliers, and tighten the tensioner bolt to the specified torque **(see illustration)**.

16 Remove the locking tool and temporarily refit the crankshaft pulley bolt, then turn the crankshaft clockwise through two complete revolutions, and align the timing marks again (see Section 3). After checking that the locking tool enters the flywheel correctly, remove it.

D4F engine

17 Locate a 6.0 mm Allen key in the tensioner eccentric hub and turn it anti-clockwise to bring the index pointer to the front of the timing window **(see illustration)**. Tighten the tensioner nut to the specified torque.

18 Remove the locking tool and temporarily refit the crankshaft pulley bolt, then turn the crankshaft clockwise through six complete revolutions, and align the timing marks again (see Section 3). After checking that the locking tool enters the flywheel correctly, remove it.

19 Fit the Allen key, then loosen the tensioner nut and turn the eccentric hub until the index pointer is in the middle of the timing window **(see illustration)**. Tighten the tensioner nut to the specified torque.

All engines

20 Refit the two plastic outer timing belt covers.

21 Refit the lower engine mounting bracket/ timing belt cover, and the upper engine mounting bracket, with reference to Section 17.

22 Carefully lower the trolley jack and wooden block from under the sump.

23 Refit the crankshaft pulley as described in Section 5.

24 Refit the bonnet as described in Chapter 11.

25 Reconnect the battery negative lead.

8 Timing belt tensioner and sprockets – removal, inspection and refitting

Camshaft sprocket

Removal

1 Remove the timing belt as described in Section 7. Note that there is no need to remove the timing belt completely, provided that it is slipped from the camshaft sprocket. **Do not** rotate the crankshaft or the camshaft until the timing belt has been refitted.

2 Slacken the camshaft sprocket retaining bolt and remove it, along with its washer. To prevent the camshaft from rotating, a tool can be fabricated from two lengths of steel strip (one long, the other short) and three nuts and bolts. One nut and bolt should form the pivot of a forked tool with the remaining two nuts and bolts at the tips of the forks to engage with the sprocket spokes **(see illustration 8.6)**. Alternatively, if the valve cover and rocker shaft are removed, the camshaft can be held stationary using a suitable spanner on the flats provided on the timing belt end of the camshaft. **Do not** allow the camshaft to rotate as the sprocket bolt is being loosened.

3 Withdraw the sprocket from the camshaft.

Inspection

4 Clean the sprocket thoroughly, and renew it if it shows signs of wear, damage or cracks.

Refitting

5 Refit the sprocket, ensuring that the lug on the sprocket engages with the cut-out in the end of the camshaft **(see illustration)**.

6 Prevent the sprocket from rotating by using the method employed on removal, then tighten the sprocket securing bolt to the specified torque setting **(see illustration)**. **Do not** allow the camshaft to turn as the bolt is tightened.

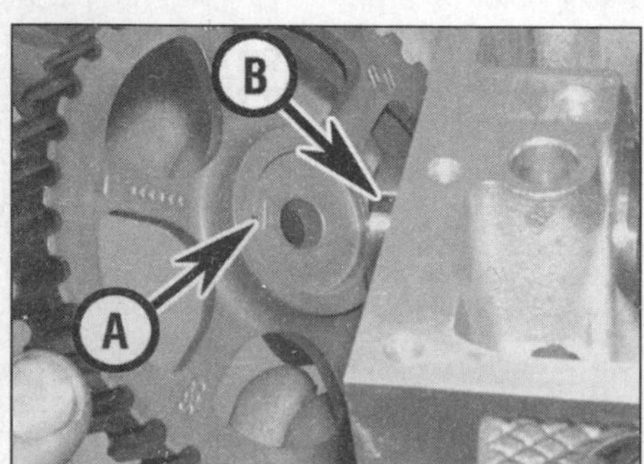

8.5 Ensure that the lug (A) on the sprocket engages with the cut-out (B) in the end of the camshaft

8.6 Preventing the camshaft sprocket from turning using an improvised tool whilst tightening the sprocket bolt

7 Refit and tension the timing belt as described in Section 7.

Crankshaft sprocket

Removal

8 Remove the timing belt as described in Section 7. Note that there is no need to remove the timing belt completely, provided that it is slipped from the crankshaft sprocket. **Do not** rotate the crankshaft or the camshaft until the timing belt has been refitted.

9 Remove the sprocket from the end of the crankshaft.

Inspection

10 Clean the sprocket thoroughly, and renew it if it shows signs of wear, damage or cracks.

Refitting

11 Refit the sprocket to the crankshaft, ensuring that the lug on the sprocket engages with the cut-out in the end of the crankshaft. Note that the sprocket flange should be innermost, and the TDC mark on the sprocket should be aligned with the corresponding mark at the bottom of the oil pump flange **(see illustration).**

12 Refit and tension the timing belt as described in Section 7.

Tensioner pulley

Removal

13 Remove the timing belt as described in Section 7. Note that there is no need to remove the timing belt completely. **Do not** rotate the crankshaft or the camshaft until the timing belt has been refitted.

14 Unscrew the securing nut and recover the washer, then withdraw the tensioner pulley from the stud on the water pump body (D7F engine) or cylinder head (D4F engine).

Inspection

15 Clean the tensioner pulley, but do not use any strong solvent which may enter the pulley bearing. Check that the pulley rotates freely, with no sign of stiffness or free play. Renew the assembly if there is any doubt about its condition or if there are any obvious signs of wear or damage.

Refitting

16 Fit the pulley to the stud on the water pump body (D7F engine) or cylinder head (D4F engine), ensuring that the direction of rotation arrow is visible on the outer face of the pulley, then fit the washer and the nut, but do not tighten the nut at this stage. On the D4F engine, make sure that the notch on the tensioner engages with the rib on the cylinder head.

17 Refit and tension the timing belt as described in Section 7.

Water pump pulley

18 The water pump pulley is integral with the water pump, and cannot be removed separately.

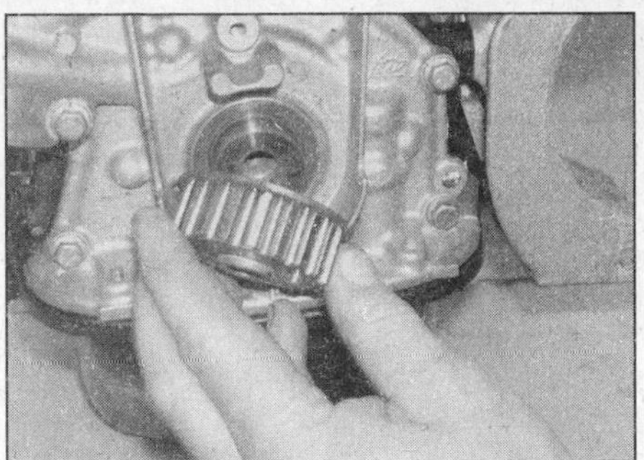

8.11 Refitting the crankshaft sprocket

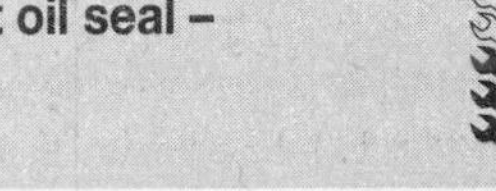

9 Camshaft oil seal – renewal

1 Remove the camshaft sprocket as described in Section 8.

2 Note the fitted depth of the seal, then prise out the old oil seal using a small screwdriver, taking care not to damage the surface of the camshaft. Alternatively, the oil seal can be removed by drilling two small holes diagonally opposite each other and inserting self-tapping screws in them. A pair of grips can then be used to pull out the oil seal, by pulling on each side in turn.

3 Inspect the seal rubbing surface on the camshaft. If it is grooved or rough in the area where the old seal was fitted, the new seal should be fitted slightly less deeply, so that it rubs on an unworn part of the surface.

D7F engine

4 Wipe clean the oil seal seating, then dip the new seal in fresh engine oil, and locate it over the camshaft with its closed side facing outwards **(see illustration)**. Make sure that the oil seal lip is not damaged as it is located on the camshaft.

5 Using a metal tube (such as a large socket), drive the oil seal squarely into the bore to the depth noted before removal of the old seal (or less deeply if there is evidence of a wear groove on the camshaft) **(see illustration)**. A block of wood cut to pass over the end of the camshaft may be used instead.

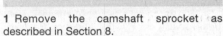

D4F engine

Note: *On the D4F engine, the oil seal is extremely fragile, and is supplied with a fitting protector/guide. The seal itself must not be touched.*

6 Renault technicians use a special tool (Mot. 1587) to fit the oil seal. The tool consists of a threaded rod, metal tube and nut. The rod is screwed into the end of the camshaft, and the protector/guide located on it. The metal tube is then fitted against the oil seal and the nut tightened to press the seal into the cylinder head/bearing cap. If the Renault tool cannot be obtained, a similar tool can be made out of threaded rod, metal tube, a washer and nut.

7 Press the oil seal squarely into position. Note that the Renault tool is designed to locate the seal at the original depth, however, if the camshaft sealing surface is excessively worn, position it less deeply so that it locates on the unworn surface.

8 After fitting the oil seal, remove the protector/guide and remove the tool.

All engines

9 Wipe away any excess oil, then refit the camshaft sprocket as described in Section 8.

10 Camshaft – removal, inspection and refitting

Note: *A new camshaft oil seal will be required on refitting.*

Removal

1 Remove the cylinder head as described Section 11, and place it on the workbench.

D7F (8-valve) engine

2 Progressively unscrew the bolts holding the rocker shaft and retaining plate to the cylinder head, and withdraw the rocker shaft assembly **(see illustration)**.

3 Slacken the camshaft sprocket retaining bolt and remove it, along with its washer. To prevent the camshaft from rotating, a tool can be fabricated from two lengths of steel strip (one long, the other short) and three nuts and bolts. One nut and bolt should form the pivot of a forked tool with the remaining two nuts

9.4 Locate the oil seal over the camshaft . . .

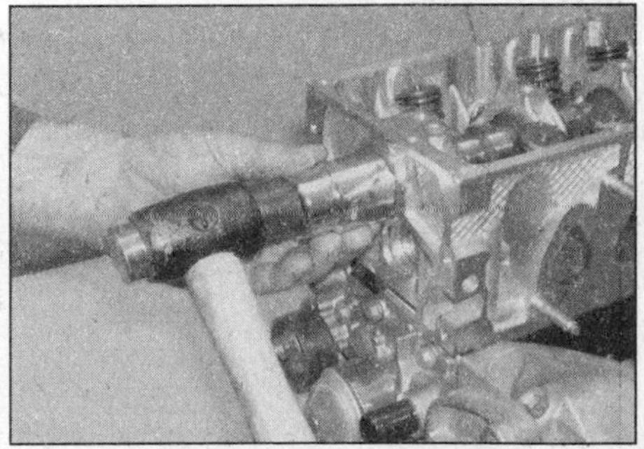

9.5 . . . then drive the seal into position using a large socket or tube

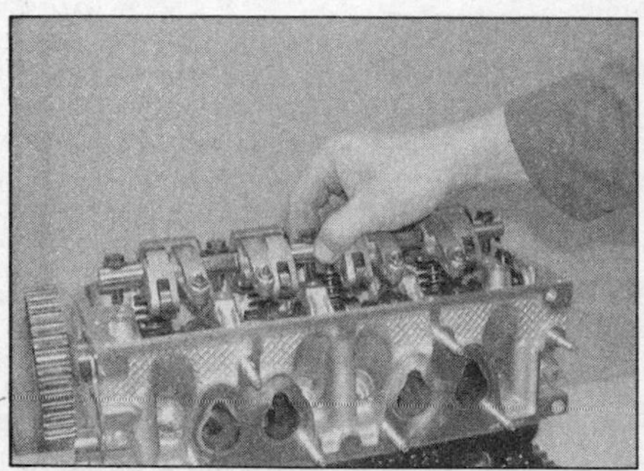

10.2 Withdrawing the rocker shaft assembly

10.3 Removing the camshaft sprocket bolt

and bolts at the tips of the forks to engage with the sprocket spokes. Alternatively, the camshaft can be held stationary using a suitable spanner on the flats provided on the timing belt end of the camshaft. Remove the camshaft sprocket **(see illustration)**.

4 Using a dial gauge, measure the endfloat of the camshaft, and compare with that given in the Specifications **(see illustration)**. This will give an indication of the amount of wear in the thrustplate.

5 Remove the camshaft oil seal, with reference to Section 9.

6 Unscrew the two bolts and lift the thrustplate out from the slot in the cylinder head **(see illustrations)**. Note which way round the thrustplate is fitted so that it can be refitted in the same position.

7 Carefully withdraw the camshaft from the sprocket end of the cylinder head, taking care not to damage the bearing surfaces **(see illustration)**.

D4F (16-valve) engine

8 Slacken the camshaft sprocket retaining bolt and remove it, along with its washer. Refer to paragraph 3 for details of a suitable tool to hold the sprocket. Remove the camshaft sprocket.

9 Using a suitable tool, lever out the camshaft plastic end cover from the left-hand end of the cylinder head. A new one will be required for refitting.

10 Using a marker pen, identify the camshaft bearing caps, the rocker arms and the two rocker shafts for position on the cylinder head. The inlet rocker shaft is the one at the front of the head.

11 Progressively unscrew the 10 bolts retaining the rocker shafts and camshaft bearing caps on the cylinder head.

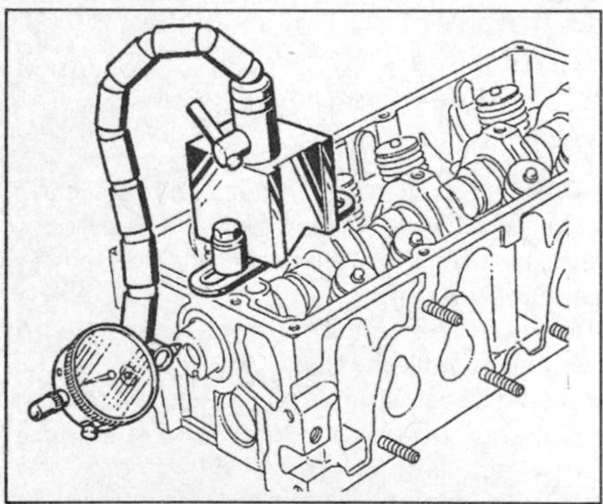

10.4 Measuring camshaft endfloat using a dial gauge

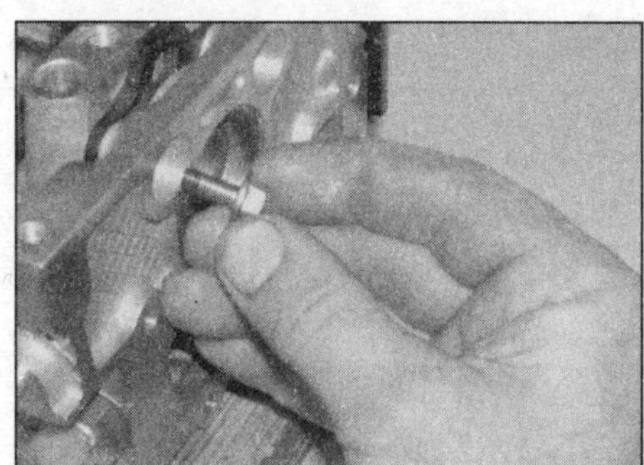

10.6a Unscrew the two bolts . . .

10.6b . . . and lift the thrustplate from the slot in the cylinder head – D7F engine

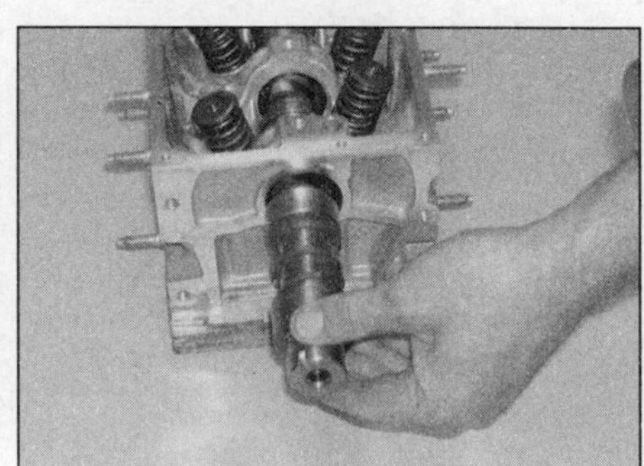

10.7 Removing the camshaft

12 Lift off the rocker shafts and arms, keeping all the components identified for position.

13 In order to measure the camshaft endfloat, the rocker arms must be removed from their shafts, then the shafts and camshaft bearing caps temporarily refitted. Tighten the bolts in their correct order to the specified torque and angle.

14 Using a dial gauge, measure the endfloat of the camshaft, and compare with that given in the Specifications.

15 Remove the rocker shafts and bearing caps again, then refit the arms to their correct shafts and retain them by temporarily inserting the end bolts.

16 Carefully withdraw the camshaft from the cylinder head, taking care not to damage the bearing surfaces.

Inspection

17 Examine the camshaft bearing surfaces, and cam lobes for wear ridges and scoring. Renew the camshaft if any of these conditions are apparent.

18 Examine the condition of the bearing surfaces on the camshaft (and bearing caps on the D4F engine), and in the cylinder head. If the surfaces are worn excessively, the cylinder head will need to be renewed.

Refitting

D7F (8-valve) engine

19 Lubricate the bearing surfaces in the cylinder head and the camshaft journals, then insert the camshaft into the head.

20 Refit the thrustplate (if the original thrustplate is being refitted, ensure that it is fitted the correct way round, as noted before removal), then apply locking fluid to the threads of the retaining bolts, insert them, and tighten securely.

21 Measure the endfloat as described in paragraph 4, and make sure that it is within the limits given in the Specifications. Excessive endfloat can only be due to wear of the thrustplate or the camshaft.

22 Fit a new camshaft oil seal with reference to Section 9.

23 Refit the camshaft sprocket, making sure that the tab engages with the cut-out in the end of the camshaft. Hold the camshaft stationary using the method employed on removal, then insert the bolt and tighten it to the specified torque.

24 Refit the rocker shaft assembly and retaining plates, then insert the bolts and tighten them to the specified torque.

D4F (16-valve) engine

25 Lubricate the bearing surfaces in the cylinder head and bearing caps, then lower the camshaft onto the head.

26 Apply 2.0 mm wide beads of sealant on the cylinder head **(see illustrations)** in the No 1 and No 5 bearing cap positions.

27 Refit the bearing caps in their correct positions, then insert the two bearing retaining

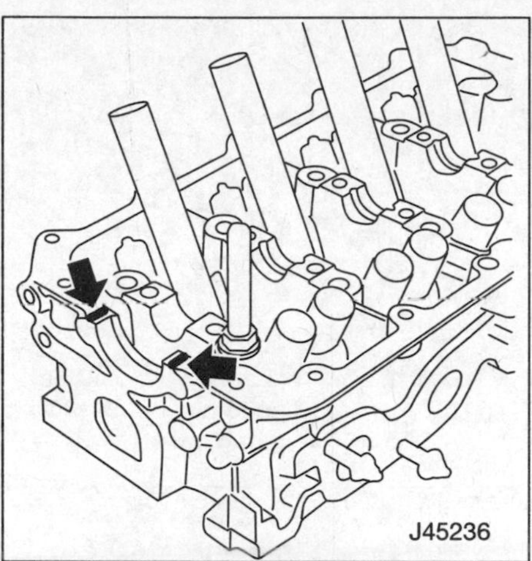

10.26a Apply beads of sealant on the cylinder head in the area of the No 1 bearing cap . . .

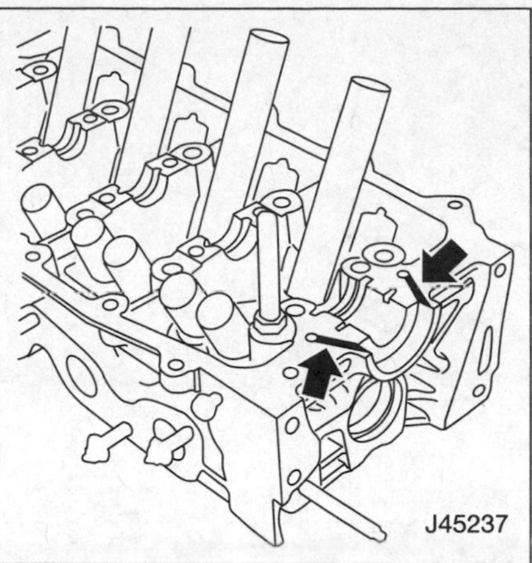

10.26b . . . and No 5 bearing cap (caps numbered from the flywheel end of the engine)

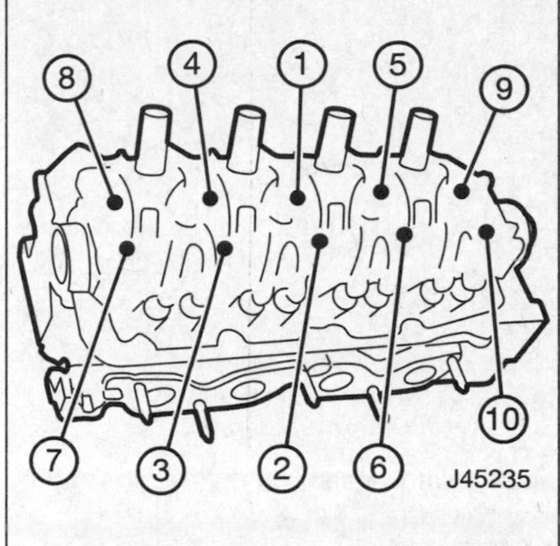

10.28 Cylinder head/rocker shaft bolt tightening sequence – D4F engine

bolts at the sprocket end, and tighten them to the specified Stage 1 torque.

28 Refit the rocker arms and shafts, insert the bolts, and tighten them in the correct order **(see illustration)** to the specified Stage 2 torque.

29 Loosen bolt 3 fully, then tighten it to the Stage 3 torque and Stage 4 angle.

30 Working on one bolt at a time and in the correct order, repeat the procedure given in paragraph 29 on the remaining bearing cap/rocker shaft bolts.

31 Fit a new camshaft oil seal with reference to Section 9.

32 Refit the camshaft sprocket, making sure that the tab engages with the cut-out in the end of the camshaft. Hold the camshaft stationary using the method employed on removal, then insert the bolt and tighten it to the specified torque and angle.

33 Carefully drive a new camshaft end cover into the left-hand end of the cylinder head. Renault technicians use tool Mot. 1605 to do this, however, a suitable metal tube may be used.

All engines

34 Adjust the valve clearances as described in Section 4.

35 Refit the cylinder head as described in Section 11.

11 Cylinder head – removal and refitting

Note: *A new cylinder head gasket and a new valve cover gasket will be required on refitting.*

Removal

1 Apply the handbrake, then jack up the front of the vehicle and support securely on axle stands (see *Jacking and vehicle support*). Remove the front right-hand roadwheel and, where fitted, the engine compartment undertray.

2 Disconnect the battery negative lead.

3 To improve access, remove the bonnet as described in Chapter 11.

4 Drain the cooling system as described in Chapter 1A.

5 Remove the timing belt as described in Section 7. Make sure that the engine is adequately supported on the trolley jack.

6 Pull out the oil level dipstick then disconnect the brake servo vacuum pipe from the inlet manifold.

7 Remove the air cleaner assembly and disconnect the accelerator cable as described in Chapter 4A.

8 Disconnect the fuel supply and return hoses located on the right-hand end of the cylinder head.

9 On models with air conditioning, loosen the bolts securing the compressor to the engine.

10 Disconnect the HT leads from the spark plugs. To do this, unclip the special tool located in the HT lead holder, engage its end with each lead and carefully pull to disconnect.

11 Disconnect the charcoal canister pipe and the fuel vapour hoses from the solenoid purge valve.

12 Disconnect the wiring from the ignition module, fuel injectors, idle speed stepper motor, throttle position potentiometer, and air temperature sensor (thermostat housing).

13 Release the hose clips, and disconnect the heater hoses from the water pump, and from the support at the transmission end of the valve cover **(see illustrations)**.

14 Release the wiring harness from the clips at the rear of the valve cover extension **(see illustration)**.

15 Remove the inlet manifold, throttle body and fuel rail as described in Chapter 4A.

11.13a Disconnect the coolant hoses from the water pump . . .

11.13b . . . and from the connector at the transmission end of the valve cover

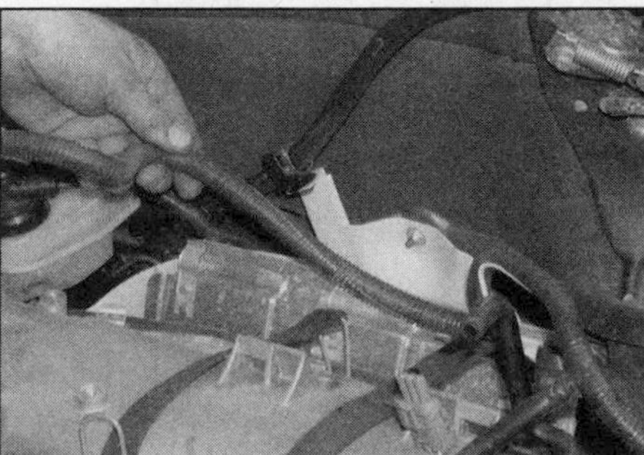
11.14 Release the wiring harness from the clips at the rear of the valve cover extension

11.16 Disconnect the coolant hoses from the thermostat housing

11.17a Remove the rubber plug . . .

11.17b . . . for access to one of the valve cover securing bolts

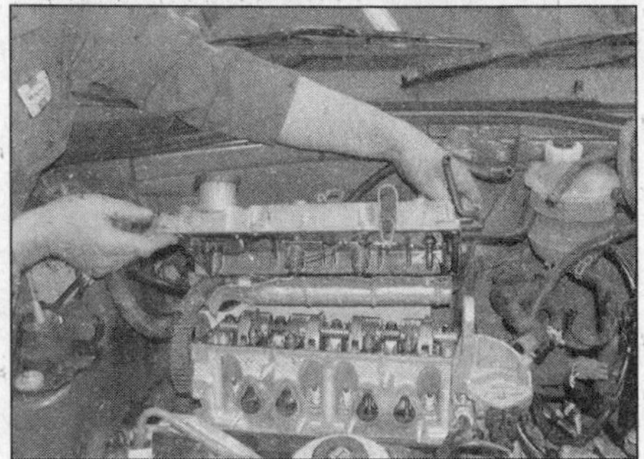
11.17c Removing the valve cover

11.19a Progressively unscrew . . .

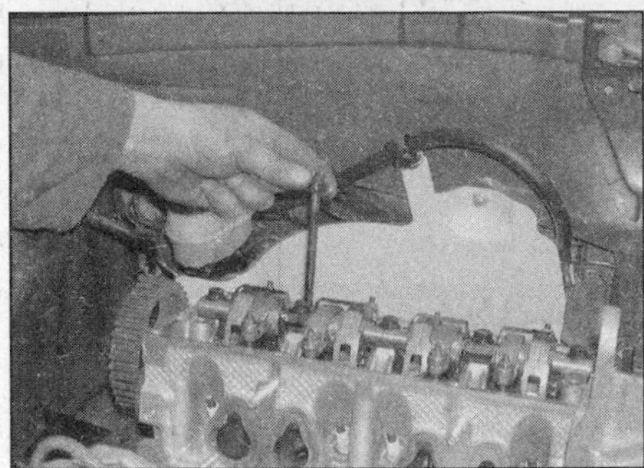
11.19b . . . and then remove the cylinder head bolts

16 Loosen the clips and disconnect the hoses from the thermostat housing **(see illustration)**.

17 Unscrew the securing bolts, and withdraw the valve cover and gasket. Note that on the D7F engine, one of the valve cover securing bolts is hidden under a rubber plug at the camshaft sprocket end of the cover **(see illustrations)**.

18 Disconnect the exhaust downpipe from the manifold and, if necessary, remove the exhaust manifold completely as described in Chapter 4A.

19 Working in the reverse order of the tightening sequence **(see illustration 11.33)**, progressively unscrew (ie, slacken each bolt by one turn at a time) the cylinder head bolts. Withdraw the bolts **(see illustrations)**.

20 Release the cylinder head from the cylinder block and locating dowels by rocking it. Do not prise between the mating faces of the cylinder head and block, as this may damage the gasket faces.

21 Carefully lift the cylinder head from the block **(see illustration)**. Recover the cylinder head gasket, and discard it.

22 If desired, the camshaft can be removed as described in Section 10, and the cylinder head can be dismantled as described in Part D of this Chapter. If necessary, unbolt the thermostat housing and lifting eye from the left-hand end of the head. Remove and discard the housing gasket.

Refitting

23 The mating faces of the cylinder head and cylinder block/crankcase must be perfectly clean before refitting the head. Use a hard plastic or wood scraper to remove all traces of gasket and carbon. Also clean the piston crowns. Take particular care, as the soft aluminium alloy is damaged easily. Also, make sure that the carbon is not allowed to enter the oil and water passages – this is particularly important for the lubrication system, as carbon could block the oil supply to any of the engine components. Using adhesive tape and paper, seal the water, oil and bolt holes in the cylinder block/crankcase. To prevent carbon entering the gap between the pistons and bores, smear a little grease in the gap. After cleaning each piston, use a small brush to remove all traces of grease and carbon from the gap, then wipe away the remainder with a clean cloth. Clean all the pistons in the same way. Clean the head bolt hole threads in the cylinder block and remove all oil, if necessary using a syringe.

24 Check the mating surfaces of the cylinder block/crankcase and the cylinder head for nicks, deep scratches and other damage. If slight, they may be removed carefully with a file, but if excessive, machining may be the only alternative to renewal.

25 If warpage of the cylinder head gasket surface is suspected, use a straight-edge to check it for distortion. Refer to Part D of this Chapter if necessary.

26 Wipe clean the mating surfaces of the cylinder head and cylinder block/crankcase. Check that the two locating dowels are in position at each end of the cylinder block/crankcase surface.

27 Check that No 1 piston is still positioned at TDC with the camshaft and crankshaft sprocket marks correctly aligned (see Section 3). **Do not** rotate the camshaft and crankshaft until the timing belt has been refitted.

28 Fit the new cylinder head gasket to the

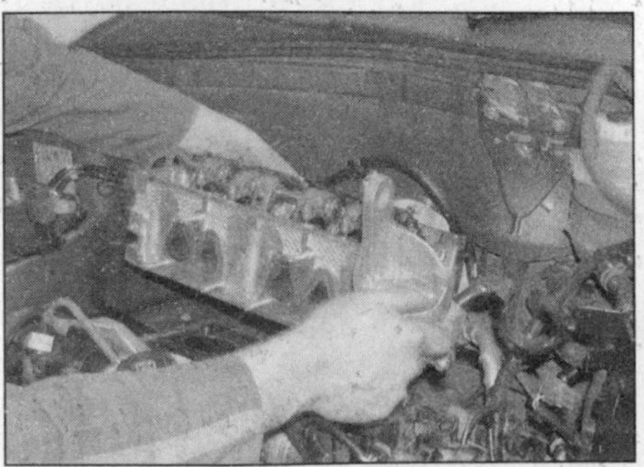
11.21 Lift the cylinder head from the cylinder block

11.28 The cylinder head gasket TOP marking should be on the inlet manifold side of the engine cylinder block, ensuring that it locates correctly over the dowels, with the TOP marking visible on the inlet manifold side of the engine **(see illustration)**.

29 As necessary, reassemble the cylinder head with reference to Part D of this Chapter, and refit the camshaft as described in Section 10. Where removed, refit the thermostat housing together with a new gasket. Also refit the lifting eye where removed.

30 Lower the cylinder head into position, locating it on the dowels.

31 Apply a light film of clean engine oil to the threads of the **new** cylinder head bolts, and to the undersides of the bolt heads.

32 Carefully fit the new cylinder head bolts, and screw them in, by hand only, until finger-tight.

33 Tighten the cylinder head bolts to the specified torque in sequence, and in the stages given in the Specifications at the beginning of this Chapter **(see illustration)**. The first three stages precompress the gasket, and the remaining stages form the main tightening procedure.

34 Reconnect the exhaust downpipe to the manifold with reference to Chapter 4A.

35 On the D4F engine, apply beads of sealant to the camshaft end bearing caps and around the valve cover mounting bolt holes as shown in Section 4.

36 Refit the valve cover using a new gasket, and tighten the securing bolts to the specified torque. On the D7F engine, tighten them in a spiral sequence working from the centre outwards. On the D4F engine, tighten them in the sequence given in Section 4.

36 Reconnect the hoses to the thermostat housing and tighten the clips.

37 Refit the inlet manifold, throttle body and fuel rail as described in Chapter 4A.

38 Refit the wiring harness to the clips at the rear of the valve cover extension.

39 Reconnect the heater hoses to the water pump and to the support at the transmission end of the valve cover, and tighten the clips.

40 Reconnect the wiring to the ignition module, fuel injectors, idle speed stepper motor, throttle position potentiometer, and air temperature sensor (thermostat housing).

41 Reconnect the charcoal canister pipe and the fuel vapour hoses to the solenoid purge valve.

42 Reconnect the HT leads to the spark plugs.

43 On models with air conditioning, tighten the compressor mounting bolts.

44 Reconnect the fuel supply and return hoses located on the right-hand end of the cylinder head.

45 Reconnect and adjust the accelerator cable, then refit the air cleaner assembly with reference to Chapter 4A.

46 Reconnect the brake servo vacuum pipe to the inlet manifold, and insert the oil level dipstick in its tube.

47 Refit the timing belt as described in Section 7.

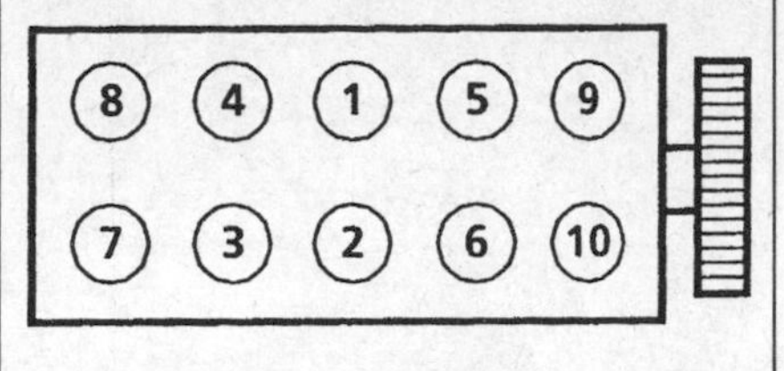

11.33 Cylinder head bolt tightening sequence

48 Refill the cooling system as described in Chapter 1A.

49 Refit the bonnet with reference to Chapter 11.

50 Where applicable, refit the engine compartment undertray.

51 Refit the roadwheel and lower the vehicle to the ground, then reconnect the battery negative lead.

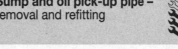

12 Sump and oil pick-up pipe – removal and refitting

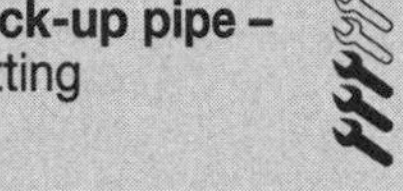

Note: *A new sump gasket and a new oil pick-up pipe O-ring will be required on refitting. On later D4F engines, an aluminium sump is fitted instead of the previous steel type.*

Removal

1 Disconnect the battery negative lead.

2 Apply the handbrake, then jack up the front of the vehicle and support it on axle stands (see *Jacking and vehicle support*). Remove the engine compartment undertray.

3 Drain the engine oil, with reference to Chapter 1A if necessary. Also pull out the oil level dipstick from its tube.

4 Disconnect the wiring from the oil level sensor **(see illustration)**, then unscrew and remove the sensor from the sump. If necessary use a half-moon wrench.

5 Where fitted, unbolt the cover plate from the gearbox bellhousing **(see illustration)**. On the later D4F engine, unscrew the bolts securing the sump to the clutch housing.

6 Progressively unscrew and remove the sump securing bolts.

7 Release the sump from the crankcase, then rotate it to the rear in order to release the oil pump strainer from the sump partition.

8 Lower the sump and withdraw it from under the vehicle. Where applicable, recover the gasket (note that the sump is sealed in production using sealant).

9 Unscrew the two bolts securing the oil pick-up pipe to the bottom of the oil pump. Remove the bolts, then withdraw the oil pick-up pipe and recover the O-ring **(see illustration)**.

Refitting

10 Clean all traces of sealant or gasket from the crankcase and sump mating faces, and wipe the mating faces dry.

11 Locate a new gasket on the sump, noting that the flat surface of the gasket should face the crankcase.

12 Refit the oil pick-up pipe to the bottom of the oil pump together with a new O-ring **(see illustration)**. Tighten the bolts securely.

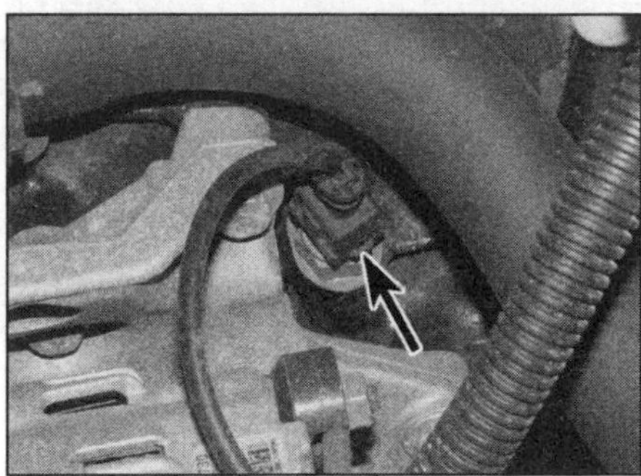

12.4 Oil level sensor wiring plug – D4F engine

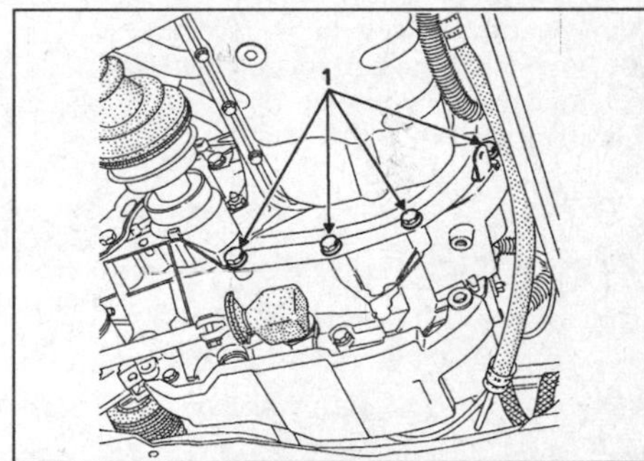

12.5 Gearbox bellhousing cover plate securing bolts (1)

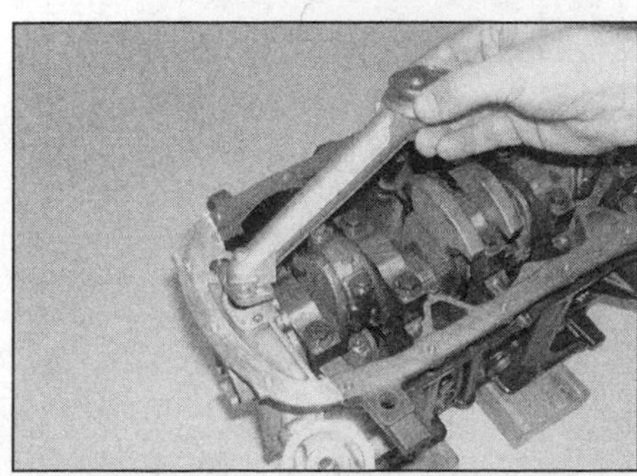

12.9 Removing the oil pick-up pipe (viewed with engine removed and inverted)

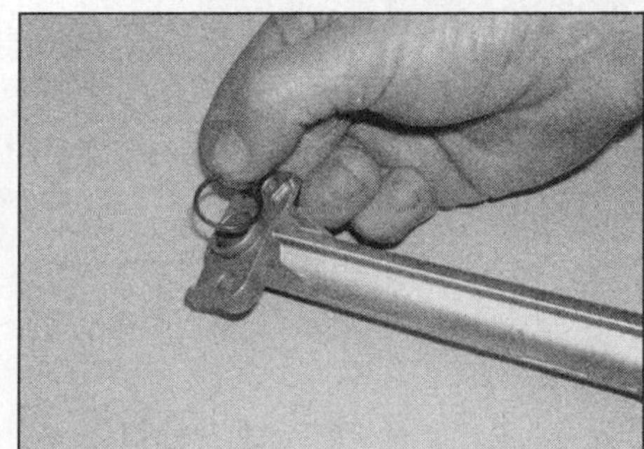

12.12 Fit a new O-ring to the oil pick-up pipe

13.6 Withdrawing the oil pump – viewed with engine removed and inverted

13 Offer the sump onto the crankcase, rotating it as necessary over the oil pick-up pipe, and at the same time ensuring that the gasket remains in place. Insert the bolts and hand-tighten at this stage. On later D4F engines, also hand-tighten the bolts securing the sump to the clutch housing, and make sure that the sump side face is in contact with the housing.

14 Tighten the sump-to-crankcase bolts progressively and in diagonal sequence to the specified torque.

15 On later D4F engines, tighten the sump-to-clutch housing bolts to the specified torque.

16 Refit the gearbox bellhousing cover plate where applicable, and tighten the securing bolts.

17 Refit the oil level sensor to the sump and tighten securely, then reconnect the wiring.

18 Refit the oil level dipstick to its tube.

19 Refit the engine compartment undertray, then lower the vehicle to the ground.

20 Reconnect the battery negative lead.

21 Refill the engine with oil as described in Chapter 1A.

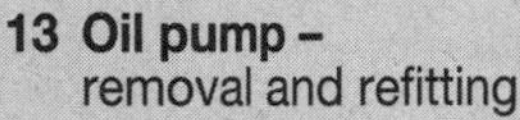
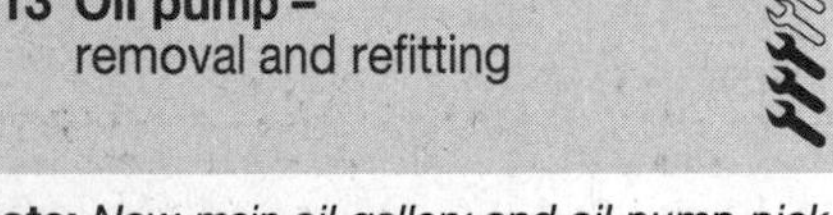

13 Oil pump – removal and refitting

Note: *New main oil gallery and oil pump pick-up tube O-rings will be required on refitting, and Rhodorseal 5661 sealant or a suitable alternative will be required.*

13.11 Apply a bead of sealant to the cylinder block mating face of the oil pump

13.7 Recover the O-ring from the main oil gallery in the cylinder block

Removal

1 Remove the timing belt as described in Section 7.

2 Temporarily refit the right-hand lower engine mounting bracket/timing cover to the cylinder head, and tighten the securing bolts.

3 Connect a hoist and lifting tackle to the lifting eye on the right-hand lower engine mounting bracket/timing cover, and raise the hoist to just take the weight of the engine.

4 Working under the vehicle, withdraw the trolley jack and block of wood from under the sump, then remove the sump and pick-up pipe with reference to Section 12.

5 Withdraw the crankshaft sprocket from the crankshaft.

6 Unscrew the securing bolts, and withdraw the oil pump from the cylinder block **(see illustration)**.

7 Recover the O-ring from the main oil gallery in the cylinder block **(see illustration)**.

8 Prise the crankshaft oil seal from the oil pump.

Refitting

9 Commence refitting by cleaning the mating faces of the oil pump and cylinder block.

10 Fit a new O-ring to the main oil gallery in the cylinder block.

11 Apply a 1.3mm wide bead of Rhodorseal 5661 (available from a Renault dealer), or a suitable equivalent, to the cylinder block mating face of the oil pump **(see illustration)**. The bead must be on the inner side of the mounting bolt holes, and completely around the oil supply hole.

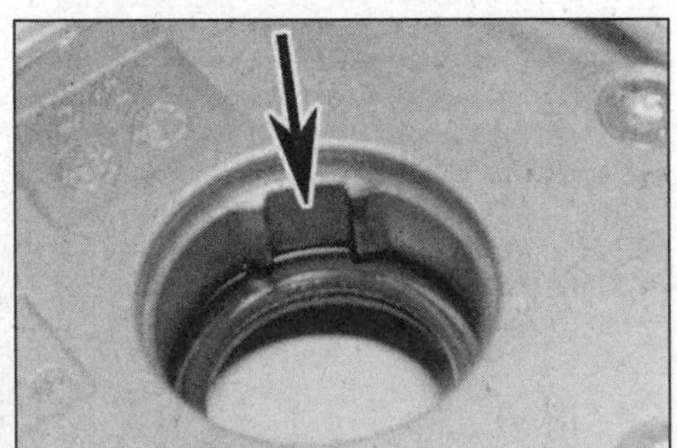
13.12 Ensure that the flats on the crankshaft engage with the cut-outs (arrowed) in the oil pump rotor

12 Slide the oil pump over the crankshaft, ensuring that the flats on the crankshaft engage with the cut-outs in the oil pump rotor, and that the positioning dowel engages with the hole in the oil pump **(see illustration)**. Wipe away any excess sealant.

13 Refit the oil pump securing bolts, and tighten progressively to the specified torque.

14 Fit a new crankshaft oil seal with reference to Section 15.

15 Refit the crankshaft sprocket, ensuring that the lug on the sprocket engages with the corresponding cut-out in the end of the crankshaft.

16 Refit the sump as described in Section 12.

17 Place the trolley jack and block of wood under the sump to support the engine, then disconnect the lifting tackle and hoist.

18 Unbolt the right-hand lower engine mounting bracket/timing cover, then refit and tension the timing belt as described in Section 7.

14 Oil pump – dismantling, inspection and reassembly

No spare parts are available for the oil pump, and no wear limit specifications are provided for the internal components. If wear or damage is suspected, a new pump assembly should be fitted.

15 Crankshaft oil seals – renewal

Timing belt end oil seal

1 Remove the crankshaft sprocket, as described in Section 8.

2 Note the fitted depth of the seal, then prise out the old oil seal using a small screwdriver, taking care not to damage the surface on the crankshaft. Alternatively, the oil seal can be removed by drilling two small holes diagonally opposite each other and inserting self-tapping screws in them. A pair of grips can then be used to pull out the oil seal, by pulling on each side in turn.

3 Inspect the seal rubbing surface on the crankshaft. If it is grooved or rough in the area where the old seal was fitted, the new seal should be fitted slightly less deeply, so that it rubs on an unworn part of the surface.

4 Wipe clean the oil seal seating, then dip the new seal in fresh engine oil, and locate it over the crankshaft with its closed side facing outwards. Make sure that the oil seal lip is not damaged as it is located on the crankshaft.

5 Using a metal tube, drive the oil seal squarely into the bore to the depth noted before removal of the old seal (or less deeply if there is evidence of a wear groove on the crankshaft). A block of wood cut to pass over the end of the crankshaft may be used instead.

16.5a Unscrew the mounting bolts . . .

16.5b . . . and lift the flywheel from the crankshaft

16.8 Using a suitable tool to prevent the flywheel from turning when tightening the securing bolts

6 Refit the crankshaft sprocket as described in Section 8.

Flywheel end oil seal

7 Remove the flywheel as described in Section 16.
8 Proceed as described in paragraphs 2 to 5.
9 Refit the flywheel with reference to Section 16.

16 Flywheel - removal, inspection and refitting

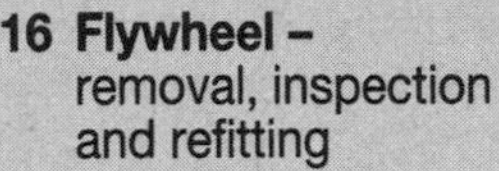
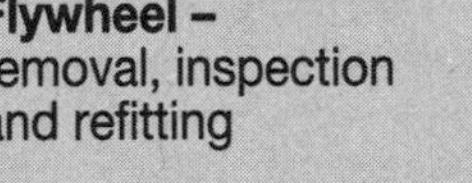

Note: *It is recommended that new flywheel bolts are used on refitting. Suitable thread-locking fluid will be required to coat the threads of the flywheel bolts.*

Removal

1 Remove the gearbox as described in Chapter 7A or 7C.
2 Remove the clutch as described in Chapter 6.
3 Mark the flywheel in relation to the crankshaft.
4 The flywheel must now be held stationary whilst the bolts are loosened. To do this, locate a long bolt in one of the transmission mounting bolt holes, and either insert a wide-bladed screwdriver in the starter ring gear, or use a piece of bent metal bar engaged with the ring gear. Alternatively, a suitable tool can be made up and bolted to the cylinder block **(see illustration 16.8)**. Do not insert a bar or tool into the engine speed (flywheel) sensor teeth on the flywheel.
5 Unscrew the mounting bolts and withdraw the flywheel from the crankshaft **(see illustrations)**. Be careful not to drop it – it is heavy.

Inspection

6 Examine the flywheel for scoring of the clutch face, and for wear or chipping of the ring gear teeth. If the clutch face is scored, it may be possible to have the flywheel machined, but renewal is preferable. If the ring gear is worn or damaged, it may be possible to renew it separately, but this job is best left to a Renault dealer or engineering works. The temperature to which the new ring gear must be heated for installation is critical and, if not done accurately, the hardness of the teeth will be destroyed.

Refitting

7 Thoroughly clean the flywheel and crankshaft faces, then locate the flywheel on the crankshaft, making sure that any previously-made marks are aligned. Note that the flywheel bolts holes are offset, so the flywheel can only be fitted in one position.
8 Apply a few drops of locking fluid to the threads of the new flywheel bolts. Fit the bolts, and tighten them in a diagonal sequence to the specified torque in the two stages given in the Specifications. Prevent the flywheel from turning using the method used during removal **(see illustration)**.
9 Refit the clutch with reference to Chapter 6.
10 Refit the gearbox as described in Chapter 7A or 7C.

17 Engine/transmission mountings - inspection, removal and refitting

Inspection

1 Apply the handbrake, then jack up the front of the car and support it on axle stands (see *Jacking and vehicle support*). Where fitted, remove the engine compartment undershield.
2 Visually inspect the rubber pads on the two front and one rear engine/transmission mountings for signs of cracking and deterioration **(see illustration)**. Careful use of a lever will help to determine the condition of the rubber pads. If there is excessive movement in the mounting, or if the rubber has deteriorated, the mounting should be renewed.
3 Lower the vehicle to the ground.

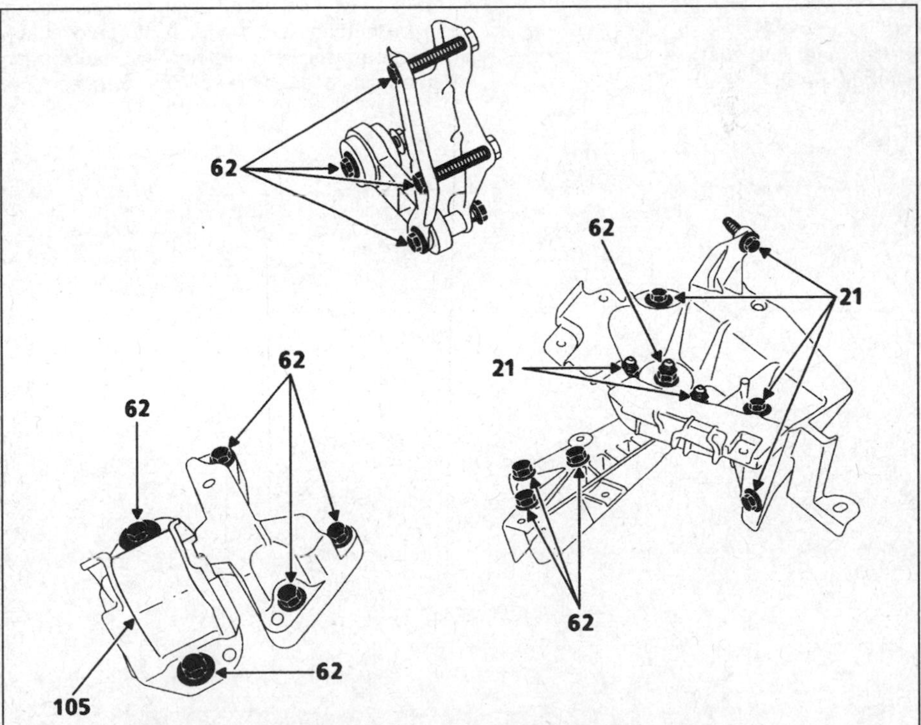

17.2 Torque wrench settings (in Nm) of the engine mountings

17.5a Right-hand engine mounting – D7F engine

17.5b Right-hand engine mounting – D4F engine

Renewal

Right-hand mounting

4 Support the right-hand end of the engine with a trolley jack and block of wood beneath the sump.

5 Unbolt the mounting brackets from the engine and inner wing panel **(see illustrations)**.

6 Fit the new mounting using a reversal of the removal procedure, but tighten the nuts/bolts to the specified torque wrench settings.

Left-hand mounting

7 Connect a suitable hoist and lifting tackle to the left-hand engine lifting bracket, and raise the hoist to just take the weight of the engine and gearbox.

8 Remove the battery as described in Chapter 5A.

9 Remove the fuel injection ECU as described in Chapter 4A, Section 13.

10 Release any wiring harnesses, cables, hoses, etc, from the mounting bracket/battery mounting.

11 Unbolt the battery mounting side plate from the bracket and remove it.

12 Carefully mark the position of the mounting bracket/battery mounting on the body to enable the bracket/mounting to be refitted in its original position.

13 Unscrew the two nuts securing the mounting bracket/battery mounting to the gearbox mounting, then unscrew the four bolts securing the bracket/battery mounting to the body, and withdraw the mounting.

14 Refitting is a reversal of removal, but tighten the mounting bracket/battery mounting bolts to the specified torque.

Rear mounting

15 Apply the handbrake, then jack up the front of the vehicle, and support securely on axle stands (see *Jacking and vehicle support*). Remove the engine compartment undertray.

16 Working beneath the car, unscrew the bolts (counterhold the nuts with a second spanner or socket) securing the rear mounting link to the brackets on the subframe and cylinder block, noting the locations of any washers and spacers on the bolts. Withdraw the link from under the car.

17 If desired, unbolt and remove the brackets from the subframe and cylinder block.

18 Refitting is a reversal of the removal procedure, but tighten the securing nuts and bolts to the specified torque.

Chapter 2 Part B:
1.4 and 1.6 litre petrol engine in-car repair procedures

Contents

Degrees of difficulty

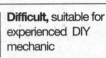

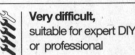

Easy, suitable for novice with little experience 
Fairly easy, suitable for beginner with some experience 
Fairly difficult, suitable for competent DIY mechanic
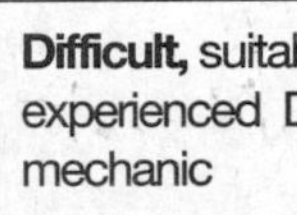
Difficult, suitable for experienced DIY mechanic
Very difficult, suitable for expert DIY or professional 

Specifications

General

Type	Four-cylinder, in-line, double overhead camshaft (DOHC) engines
Designation:	
1.4 litre models	K4J 712, K4J 713
1.6 litre models	K4M 748
Bore	79.5 mm
Stroke:	
K4J engine	70.0 mm
K4M engine	80.5 mm
Capacity:	
K4J engine	1390 cc
K4M engine	1598 cc
Firing order	1-3-4-2 (No 1 cylinder at flywheel/driveplate end)
Direction of crankshaft rotation	Clockwise viewed from pulley end
Compression ratio	10 : 1

Timing belt tension value

Fitting/checking value	30 ± 10% SEEM units
Minimum operating tension value	26 SEEM units

Camshaft

Endfloat	0.08 to 0.178 mm
Camshaft bearing journal diameters:	
No 1 to No 5 bearings	24.979 to 25.000 mm
No 6 bearing	27.979 to 28.000 mm

Lubrication system

System pressure:		
At idle	1.0 bar	
At 3000 rpm	3.0 bar	
Oil pump clearances:	**Minimum**	**Maximum**
Gear-to-body	0.110 mm	0.249 mm
Gear endfloat	0.020 mm	0.086 mm

Torque wrench settings

	Nm	lbf ft
Camshaft phase-shifter cover	15	11
Camshaft phase-shifter sprocket (inlet camshaft)	75	55
Camshaft sprocket (not inlet phase-shifter):		
Stage 1	30	22
Stage 2	Angle-tighten a further 84°	
Connecting rod (big-end) cap – oiled	43	32
Crankshaft pulley bolt:		
Stage 1	40	30
Stage 2	Angle-tighten a further 115° ± 15°	
Cylinder head bolts:		
Stage 1	20	15
Stage 2	Angle-tighten a further 240° ± 6°	
Engine/transmission mountings (see Section 12):		
Right-hand mounting to engine/body	62	46
Right-hand mounting central nut	44	32
Left-hand mounting to transmission	62	46
Left-hand mounting to body	21	15
Left-hand mounting central nut	62	46
Rear mounting	62	46
Flywheel/driveplate bolts	53	39
Front suspension strut-to-swivel hub bolts	See Chapter 10	
Main bearing cap:		
Stage 1	25	18
Stage 2	Angle-tighten a further 47° ± 5°	
Oil pump:		
Mounting bolts	25	18
Sprocket bolts	10	7
Oil separator to cylinder head upper section	13	10
Roadwheel bolts	90	66
Rocker arm adjustment screw locknut	15	11
Rocker shaft bolts – oiled	23	17
Strengthening bracket/flywheel cover:		
On engine	50	37
On transmission	25	18
Subframe-to-underbody bolts:		
Front	62	46
Rear	105	77
Sump:		
Stage 1	8	6
Stage 2	14	10
Timing belt idler pulley	45	33
Timing belt tensioner pulley:		
Pretighten	7	5
Final	27	20
Timing cover (upper)	41	30
Valve cover bolts:		
Stage 1 – bolts 22, 23, 20, 13	8	6
Stage 2 – bolts 1 to 12, 14 to 19, 21 to 24	12	9
Stage 3 – bolts 22, 23, 20, 13	Slacken fully	
Stage 4 – bolts 22, 23, 20, 13	12	9

1 General information

How to use this Chapter

This Part of Chapter 2 is devoted to in-car repair procedures for the 1.4 and 1.6 litre petrol engines. Similar information covering the other engine types can be found in Parts B and C. All procedures concerning engine removal and refitting, and engine block/cylinder head overhaul can be found in Part D of this Chapter.

Refer to *Vehicle identification numbers* in the Reference Section at the end of this manual for details of engine code locations.

Most of the operations included in this Part are based on the assumption that the engine is still installed in the car. Therefore, if this information is being used during a complete engine overhaul, with the engine already removed, many of the steps included here will not apply.

Engine description

The engine is of four-cylinder, in-line, overhead camshaft type, mounted transversely in the front of the car. Double overhead camshafts are fitted.

The overhead camshafts are each mounted in the cylinder head by six plain bearings with matching caps, and are driven by the crankshaft by a toothed rubber timing belt, which also drives the water pump. On the K4J and early K4M engines, the camshaft sprockets are both conventional, however, on the later K4M engine the inlet camshaft sprocket incorporates a phase-shifter which provides variable valve timing by advancing the inlet valve timing during certain operating conditions. The phase-shifter is activated by the engine management ECU via an electrically-controlled solenoid valve located on the top, right-hand side of the cylinder head. The camshafts operate the valves by hydraulic tappets and roller cam followers located below the camshafts in the cylinder head.

The cylinder block is of cast iron. The K-series engine has conventional dry liners bored directly into the cylinder block. The crankshaft is supported within the cylinder block on five shell-type main bearings. Thrustwashers are fitted at the upper centre main bearing to control crankshaft endfloat.

The connecting rods are attached to the crankshaft by horizontally-split shell-type big-end bearings and to the pistons by gudgeon pins which are an interference-fit in the connecting rods. The aluminium alloy pistons are fitted with three piston rings, comprising two compression rings and a scraper-type oil control ring.

A fully-enclosed crankcase ventilation system is employed; crankcase fumes are drawn from an oil separator on the cylinder head, and passed via a hose to the inlet manifold.

Lubrication is by pressure feed from a gear-type oil pump, which is chain-driven direct from the crankshaft.

Operations with engine in place

The following operations can be carried out without having to remove the engine from the car:

a) Removal and refitting of the cylinder head.
b) Removal and refitting of the timing belt and sprockets.
c) Renewal of the camshaft oil seal.
d) Removal and refitting of the camshaft.
e) Removal and refitting of the pressed-steel sump.
f) Removal and refitting of the connecting rods and pistons.*
g) Removal and refitting of the oil pump.
h) Renewal of the crankshaft timing belt end oil seal.
i) Renewal of the engine mountings.

* **Note:** *Although the operation marked with an asterisk can be carried out with the engine in the car after removal of the sump, it is better for the engine to be removed, in the interests of cleanliness and improved access. For this reason, these procedures are described in Part D of this Chapter.*

2 Compression test – description and interpretation

Note: *A compression gauge will be required for this test.*

1 A compression check will tell you what mechanical condition the top end (pistons, rings, valves, head gasket) of the engine is in. Specifically, it can tell you if the compression is down due to leakage caused by worn piston rings, defective valves and seats or a blown head gasket. **Note:** *The engine must be at normal operating temperature and the battery must be fully-charged, for this check.*

2 Begin by cleaning the area around the spark plugs before you remove them (compressed air should be used, if available, otherwise a small brush or even a bicycle tyre pump will work). The idea is to prevent dirt from getting into the cylinders as the compression check is being done.

3 Remove all the spark plugs from the engine (see Chapter 1A).

4 Disable the engine management system by removing the engine protection fuse from the engine compartment fusebox.

5 Fit the compression gauge into the No 1 spark plug hole – the type of tester which screws into the plug thread is to be preferred.

6 Have an assistant hold the accelerator pedal fully depressed, while at the same time cranking the engine over several times on the starter motor. Observe the compression gauge – the compression should build-up quickly in a healthy engine. Low compression on the first stroke, followed by gradually-increasing pressure on successive strokes, indicates worn piston rings. A low compression reading on the first stroke, which does not build-up during successive strokes, indicates leaking valves or a blown head gasket (a cracked head could also be the cause). Deposits on the undersides of the valve heads can also cause low compression. Record the highest gauge reading obtained, then repeat the procedure for the remaining cylinders.

7 Add some engine oil (about three squirts from a plunger-type oil can) to each cylinder, through the spark plug hole and repeat the test.

8 If the compression increases after the oil is added, the piston rings are worn. If the compression does not increase significantly, the leakage is occurring at the valves or head gasket. Leakage past the valves may be caused by burned valve seats and/or faces, or warped, cracked or bent valves.

9 If two adjacent cylinders have equally low compression, there is a strong possibility that the head gasket between them is blown. The appearance of coolant in the combustion chambers or the crankcase would verify this condition.

10 Actual compression pressures for the engines covered by this manual are not specified by the manufacturer. However, bearing in mind the information given in the preceding paragraphs, the results obtained should give a good indication of engine condition and what course of action, if any, to take.

3.7 Using a screwdriver, prise the camshaft sealing plugs from the left-hand end of the cylinder head

3 Top Dead Centre (TDC) for No 1 piston – locating

Note: *A TDC pin from a Renault dealer (Mot. 1489) or automotive tool shop is required for this operation.*

1 Top Dead Centre (TDC) is the highest point in the cylinder that each piston reaches as the crankshaft turns. Each piston reaches TDC at the end of the compression stroke and again at the end of the exhaust stroke; however, for the purpose of timing the engine, TDC refers to the position of No 1 piston at the end of its compression stroke. No 1 piston is at the flywheel end of the engine.

2 Apply the handbrake, then jack up the front right-hand side of the car and support it on axle stands. Remove the right-hand roadwheel.

3 Remove the plastic liners from within the right-hand wheel arch to give access to the crankshaft pulley bolt.

4 Remove the spark plugs as described in Chapter 1A.

5 The engine must now be turned in order to check for pressure in No 1 cylinder (nearest the flywheel) as the piston rises on the compression stroke. As the spark plug holes are deeply recessed, it is not possible to place a finger over them, however, the inverted handle of a screwdriver may be used instead, or alternatively simply listen for air being forced out of the No 1 spark plug hole. Turn the engine in a clockwise direction, using a socket or spanner on the crankshaft pulley bolt, until air is forced from No 1 cylinder; this indicates that No 1 piston is rising on its compression stroke.

6 Remove the air cleaner and resonator from the left-hand side of the engine with reference to Chapter 4A.

7 Using a screwdriver, pierce the centres of the two plastic plugs at the left-hand end of the cylinder head, and pull out the plugs **(see illustration)**. With No 1 piston approaching TDC, the grooves in the ends of the camshafts should be positioned approximately at 30° angle from the horizontal, with the offset below the centreline.

8 Unscrew the TDC plug from the left-hand front of the cylinder block, then fully screw in the TDC pin **(see illustrations)**.

9 Carefully turn the crankshaft clockwise until the crankshaft web is in contact with the TDC pin. At this point, the No 1 piston is at TDC on its compression stroke, and the grooves in the ends of the camshafts will now be positioned horizontally. Renault technicians use a special

3.8a Unscrew the TDC plug . . .

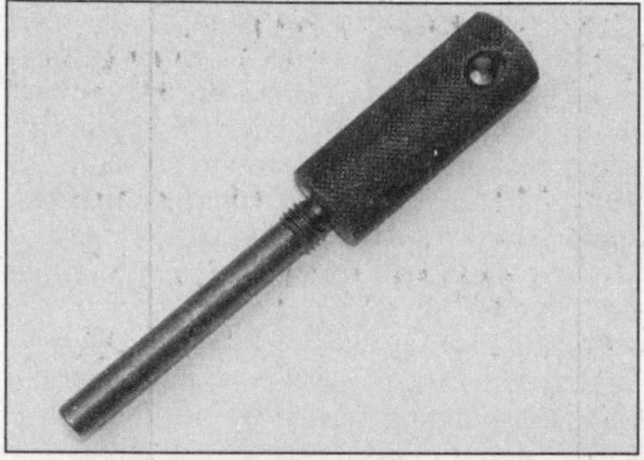
3.8b . . . obtain the TDC pin . . .

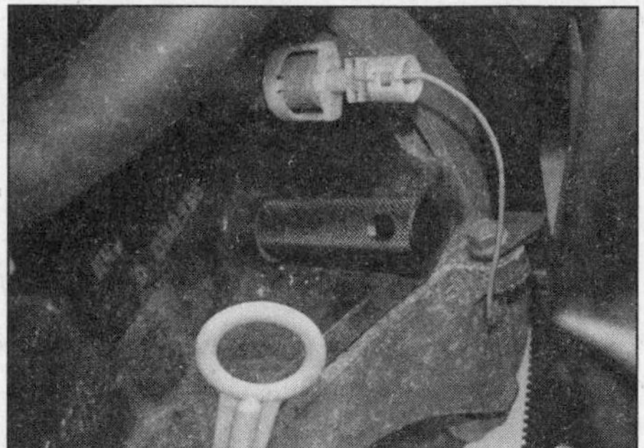
3.8c . . . and screw it into the cylinder block

tool to lock the camshafts in their TDC position. The tool is attached to the left-hand end of the cylinder head to hold the camshafts with their grooves horizontal, and a similar tool may be fabricated from metal plate if necessary **(see illustrations)**.

10 Note that the crankshaft sprocket is not keyed to the crankshaft, therefore if the crankshaft pulley/sprocket is removed it is important to have an accurate method of determining the TDC position of No 1 piston.

3.9a The special Renault tool used to lock the camshafts in their TDC position

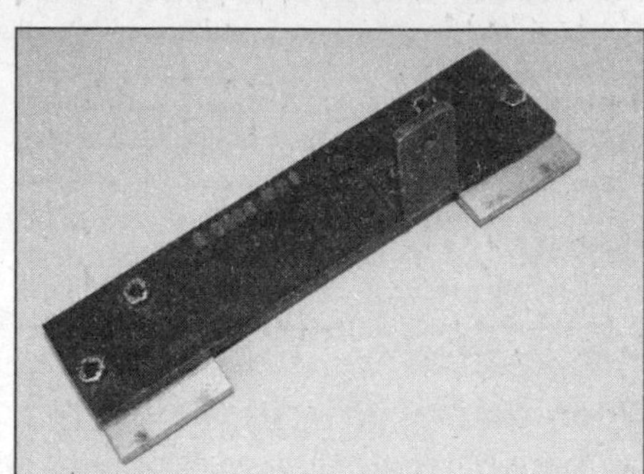
3.9b Home-made tool for locking the camshafts

4 Timing belt – removal, inspection and refitting

Note: *A Renault TDC pin (Mot. 1489) or approved alternative is required for this operation, and may be obtained from most car accessory shops. Also, a Renault camshaft locking bar (Mot. 1496) or alternative will be required (see text).*

Note: *Renault state that the timing belt must be renewed whenever it is removed, and also that the tensioner and idler pulley must be renewed whenever the timing belt is renewed.*

Caution: If the timing belt breaks in service, extensive engine damage may result. Renew the belt at the intervals specified in Chapter 1A, or earlier if its condition is at all doubtful.

Removal

1 Disconnect the battery negative lead (refer to *Disconnecting the battery* in the Reference Section).

2 Apply the handbrake, then jack up the front right-hand side of the vehicle and support on axle stands (see *Jacking and vehicle support*). Remove the right-hand roadwheel. Where fitted, remove the engine compartment undertray.

3 Remove the right-hand wheel arch liner(s), after pulling out the plastic retainers and removing the screws **(see illustration)**. This is necessary for access to the crankshaft pulley and bolt.

4 For improved access to the right-hand side of the engine, we found it beneficial to remove the front bumper (see Chapter 11) and engine compartment front crossmember (5 bolts). The engine is very close to the right-hand inner body panel.

5 Remove the auxiliary drivebelt as described in Chapter 1A.

6 Set the engine at TDC for No 1 piston as described in Section 3.

7 Carefully, position a trolley jack and a large block of wood under the sump to support the right-hand side of the engine. Raise the jack to just take the weight of the engine **(see illustration)**.

8 Remove the right-hand upper engine mounting bracket from the engine and body with reference to Section 12. At this stage, we

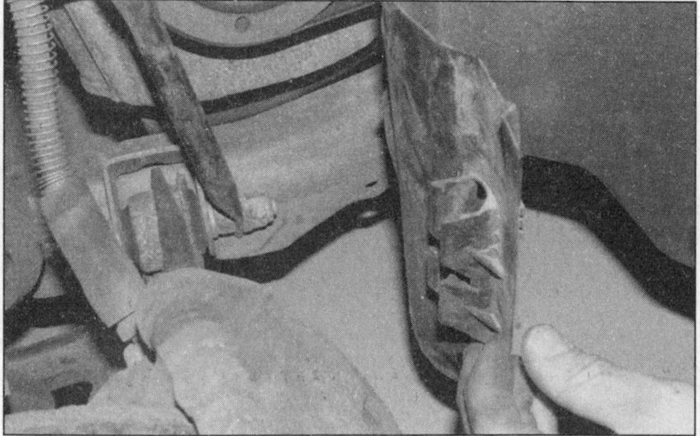
4.3 Removing the wheel arch liner

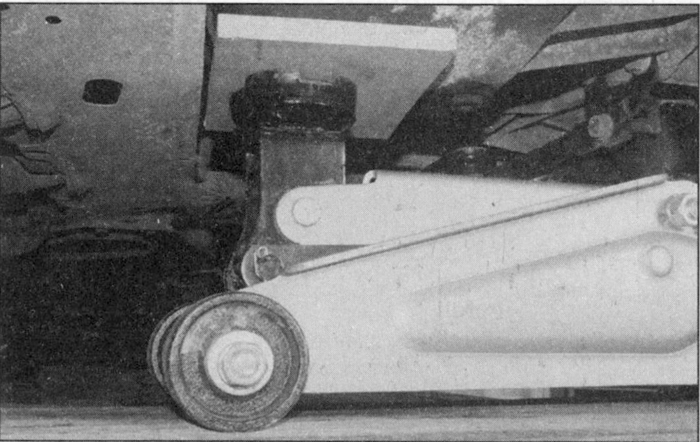
4.7 Support the right-hand end of the engine with a trolley jack

4.8 Removing the alternator

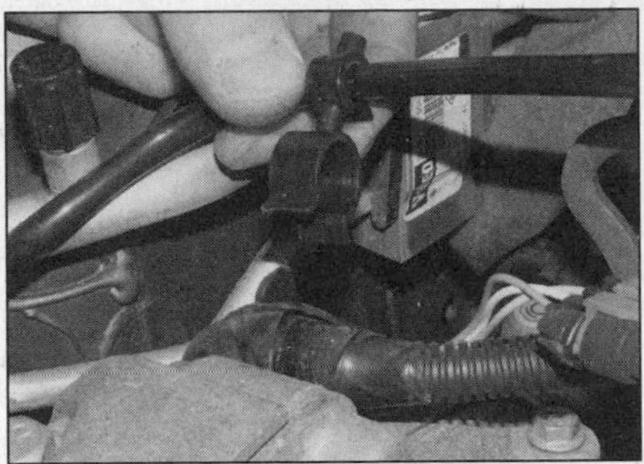
4.9a Unclip the vacuum pipe . . .

4.9b . . . then disconnect the wiring loom and position to one side

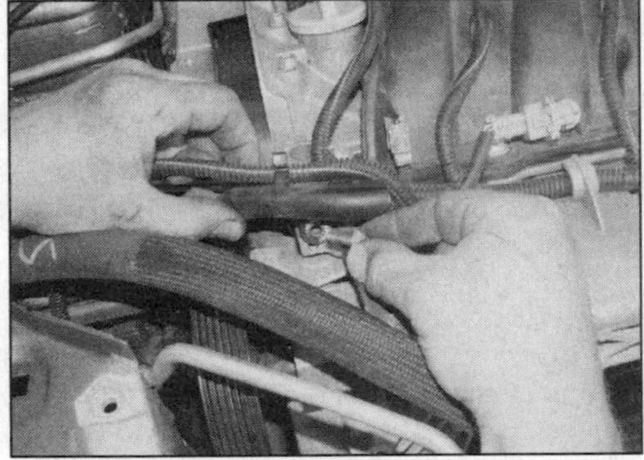
4.9c Unbolting the wiring support bracket from the right-hand front of the engine

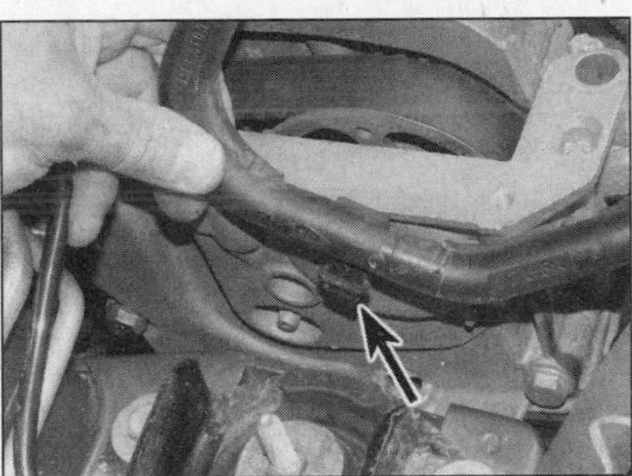
4.9d Note how the wiring loom conduit locates in the upper timing cover

4.11a Use a screwdriver to prise out the plastic plugs from the left-hand end of the cylinder head

also removed the alternator for improved access **(see illustration).**

9 Remove the wiring loom from the right-hand end of the engine by disconnecting it from the inlet manifold and unbolting the support bracket at the right-hand front of the cylinder head. Also unclip and disconnect the vacuum pipe from the inlet manifold. Release the loom from the upper timing cover and position it to one side **(see illustrations).**

10 Unclip the fuel pipe(s) from the lower timing cover, then remove the air cleaner and resonator as described in Chapter 4A.

11 Using a screwdriver, pierce the centres of the two plastic plugs at the left-hand end of the camshafts, and pull the plugs from the cylinder head. With No 1 piston approaching TDC, the grooves in the ends of the camshafts should be as shown **(see illustrations).**

12 Unscrew the TDC plug from the left-hand front of the cylinder block, then fully screw in the TDC pin **(see illustration).**

13 Carefully turn the crankshaft clockwise

4.11b Turn the crankshaft until the slots in the camshafts are initially positioned at approximately a 30° angle from the horizontal, with the offsets below the centreline

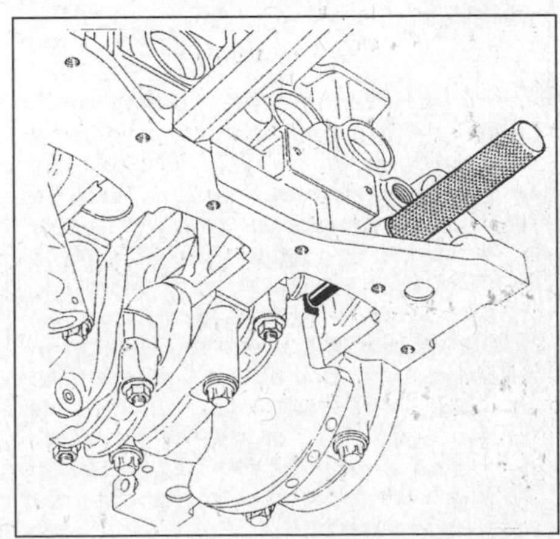
4.12 TDC pin on the left-hand front of the cylinder block

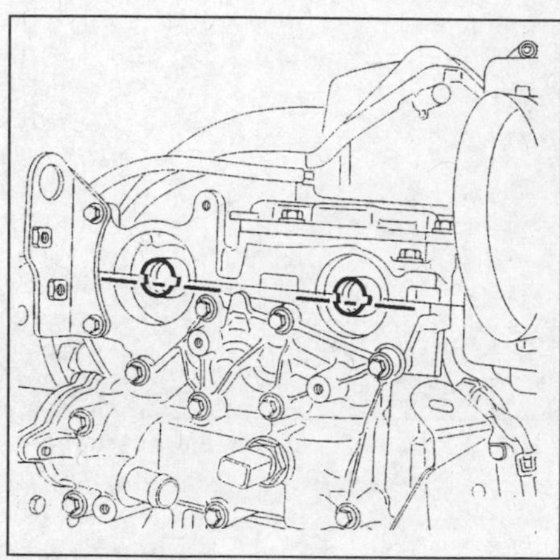

4.13a With the crankshaft at TDC the grooves in the end of the camshafts will be positioned horizontally

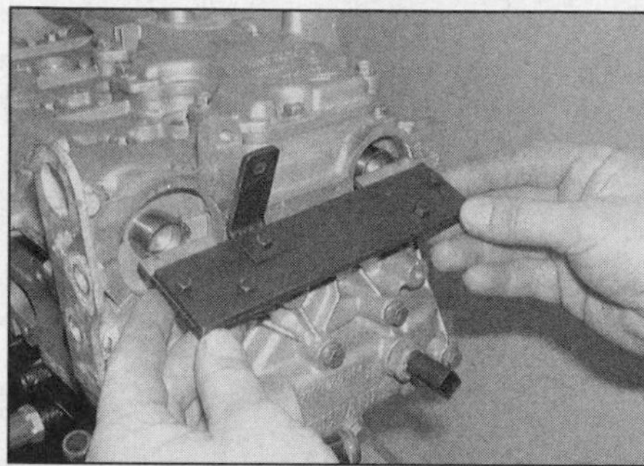

4.13b Engage the camshaft holding tool with the camshaft slots . . .

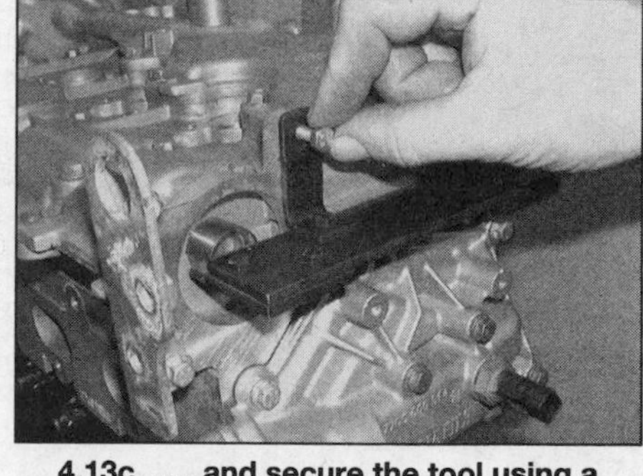

4.13c . . . and secure the tool using a suitable bolt screwed into the cylinder head

until the crankshaft web is in contact with the TDC pin. At this point, the No 1 piston is at TDC on its compression stroke, and the grooves in the ends of the camshafts will now be positioned horizontally. Renault technicians use a special tool to lock the camshafts in their TDC position, however, a length of metal bar may be fabricated **(see illustrations and Tool Tip)**.

14 Before loosening the crankshaft pulley bolt, note that the crankshaft sprocket is **not** keyed to the crankshaft, therefore if the crankshaft pulley is removed it is important to have an accurate method of determining the TDC position of No 1 piston (refer to paragraph 12). Although the sprocket is not keyed to the crankshaft, there is still a groove in the crankshaft nose which is at the 12 o'clock position when piston No 1 is at TDC. To prevent the crankshaft from rotating while the pulley bolt is unscrewed, first remove the metal bar from the camshafts then, on manual transmission models have an assistant engage top gear and depress firmly the brake pedal. Alternatively, and on automatic transmission models, the crankshaft may be held stationary by unbolting the crankshaft speed/position sensor from the top of the transmission and wedging a screwdriver in the starter ring gear teeth through the sensor's opening in the bellhousing. Unscrew the crankshaft pulley bolt, then remove the pulley **(see illustrations)**. **Note:** *The bolt is very tight*. The bolt may be re-used if its length from under the head to its end does not exceed 49.1 mm. If the length is greater than this, renew the bolt.

15 Unbolt the lower timing cover followed by the upper timing cover **(see illustrations)**.

16 Loosen the timing belt tensioner, then turn the tensioner hub anti-clockwise to release the tension.

17 Check if the belt is marked with arrows to indicate its running direction, and if it is to be re-used, mark it to ensure correct refitting. Release the belt from the camshaft sprockets, water pump pulley, crankshaft sprocket, tensioner pulley and idler pulley and remove it from the engine.

18 Clean the sprockets, tensioner and idler and wipe them dry. Also clean the cylinder head and block behind the timing belt running area.

TOOL TIP

To make a camshaft holding tool, obtain a length of steel strip and cut it to length so that it will fit across the rear of the cylinder head. Obtain a second length of steel strip of suitable thickness to fit snugly in the slots in the camshafts. Cut the second strip into two lengths and drill accordingly so that they can be bolted to the first strip in the correct position to engage with the camshaft slots. Secure a suitably drilled small piece of steel angle to the first strip so that the tool can be bolted to the threaded hole in the cylinder head upper section.

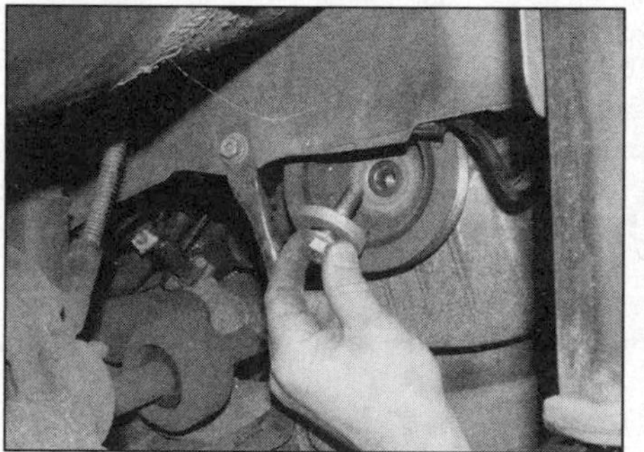

4.14a Unscrew the crankshaft pulley bolt . . .

4.14b . . . and remove the pulley

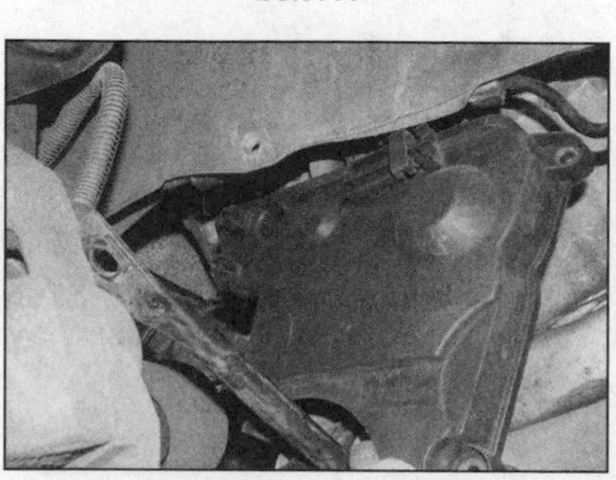

4.15a Removing the lower timing cover . . .

4.15b . . . and upper timing cover

Inspection

19 Examine the timing belt carefully for any signs of cracking, fraying or general wear, particularly at the roots of the teeth.

20 Renew the belt if there is any sign of deterioration of this nature, or if there is any oil or grease contamination. Renew any leaking oil seals. The belt **must** be renewed if it has completed the maximum mileage given in Chapter 1A.

21 Thoroughly clean the nose of the crankshaft and the bore of the crankshaft sprocket, and also the contact surfaces of the sprocket and pulley. This is necessary to prevent the possibility of the sprocket slipping in use.

Refitting

22 Check that the lug on the rear of the tensioner is correctly located in the groove.

23 Check that the camshafts and No 1 piston are still at TDC. Fit the timing belt on the crankshaft sprocket, then locate it around the water pump and idler, over the camshafts and around the tensioner. Make sure that the belt is taut between the camshaft sprockets, and the correct way round if refitting the original.

24 Check that the idler retaining bolt is tightened to the specified torque.

25 On the K4J (1.4 litre) engine two types of tensioner have been fitted; Version 1 is identified by having a fixed and adjustable pointer, whereas Version 2 has a fixed notched plate and adjustable pointer. On K4M (1.6 litre) engines, only the Version 2 tensioner is fitted. The adjustment procedure varies for each version.

Version 1 tensioner

26 With the belt fully engaged with the pulleys, slacken the tensioner and tension the belt. To do this, use a 6.0 mm Allen key to turn the index finger on the tensioner 7.0 to 8.0 mm to the right of the static index, then retighten the tensioner to the specified torque **(see illustration)**. Check that the camshafts and crankshaft are still at TDC.

27 Refit the crankshaft pulley and tighten the bolt to the specified torque. This can be done with the timing pin still tight in the cylinder block, and the crankshaft web resting against it. If the original bolt is being re-used, lightly lubricate the threads with engine oil. If a new bolt is being used it should be fitted dry.

28 Remove the locking tool from the camshafts and the TDC pin from the cylinder block. Turn the crankshaft clockwise two complete turns, then reset the piston to TDC as described earlier.

29 Remove the locking tool and TDC pin, then unscrew the tensioner fastener by one turn only. Using the Allen key, align the index finger with the static index pointer by turning it anti-clockwise. Tighten the tensioner fastener to the specified torque.

30 Turn the crankshaft two complete turns and recheck the TDC position and tensioner index setting.

Version 2 tensioner

31 Using a 6.0 mm Allen key, turn the index pointer until it is opposite the shallow notch at the front of the fixed notched plate **(see illustration)**, then pretighten the nut to the specified torque. Check that the camshafts and crankshaft are still at TDC.

32 Refit the crankshaft pulley and tighten the bolt to the specified torque. This can be done with the timing pin still tight in the cylinder block, and the crankshaft web resting against it. If the original bolt is being re-used, lightly lubricate the threads with engine oil. If a new bolt is being used it should be fitted dry.

33 Remove the locking tool from the camshafts and the TDC pin from the cylinder block. Turn the crankshaft clockwise two complete turns, then recheck the TDC position and tensioner index setting. If necessary, loosen the nut and use the Allen key to reposition the index pointer in line with the shallow notch. Finally, fully tighten the tensioner to the specified torque.

All engines

34 Refit the upper timing cover and lower timing cover, and tighten the bolts securely.

35 Refit the TDC plug to the cylinder block and tighten securely.

36 Fit two new plastic plugs in the cylinder head on the left-hand end of the camshafts. Renault technicians use special tools to drive the plugs into position, although suitable sockets or blocks of wood may be used instead **(see illustration)**.

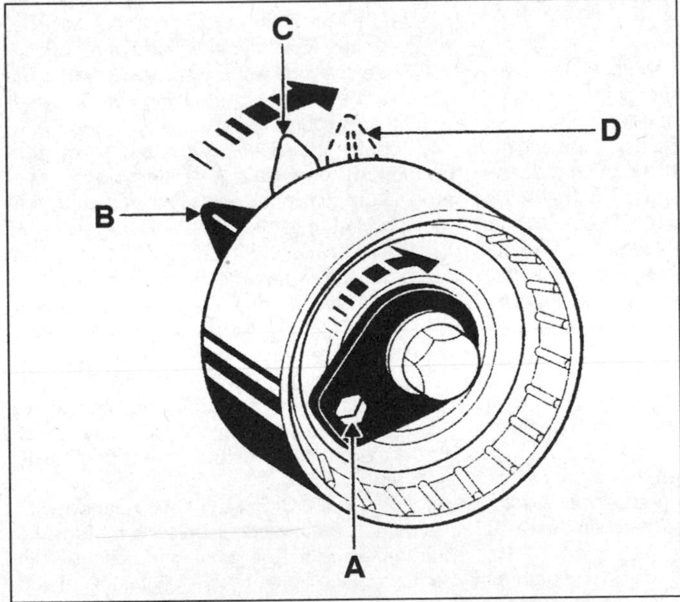

4.26 Version 1 timing belt tensioner pulley details

A Slot for Allen key in tensioner arm
B Position of moving index pointer in the at-rest position
C Fixed index pointer
D Moving index pointer positioned 7.0 to 8.0 mm to the right of the fixed index pointer

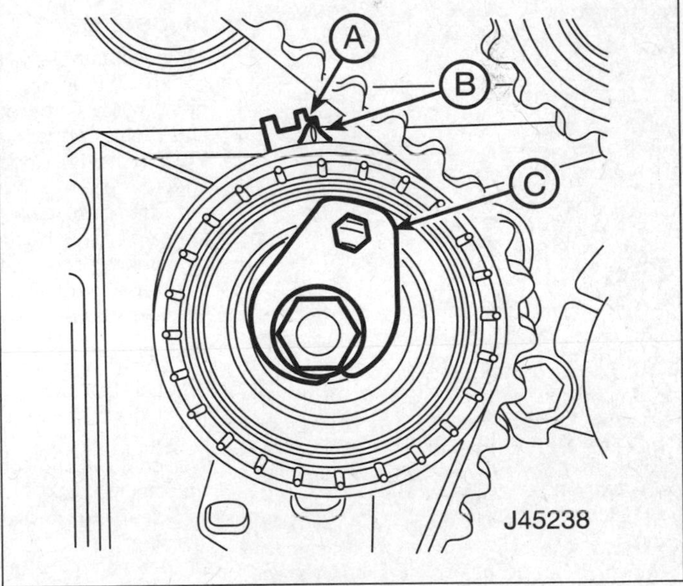

4.31 Version 2 timing belt tensioner pulley details

A Shallow notch
B Adjustable index
C Eccentric adjustment

4.36 Fitting new plastic plugs to the cylinder head using a large socket

37 Refit the air cleaner and resonator with reference to Chapter 4A.
38 Clip the fuel pipes to the lower timing cover.
39 Reconnect the vacuum pipe to the inlet manifold and attach the wiring loom to the upper timing cover. Refit the support bracket and tighten the bolts, reconnect the wiring and attach it to the support.
40 Refit the right-hand upper engine mounting bracket to the engine and body with reference to Section 12. Lower the jack and block of wood from the sump. Where removed, refit the alternator at this stage.
41 Refit the auxiliary drivebelt with reference to Chapter 1A. Where there is an extra unused groove, check that the belt is located on the correct grooves as noted on removal.
42 Where removed, refit the crossmember and front bumper.
43 Refit the right-hand wheel arch liners, and engine compartment undertray, then refit the roadwheel and lower the vehicle to the ground.
44 Reconnect the battery negative lead.

TOOL TiP

Tool Tip 1 To make a camshaft holding tool, obtain a length of steel strip and cut it to length so that it will fit across the rear of the cylinder head. Obtain a second length of steel strip of suitable thickness to fit snugly in the slots in the camshafts. Cut the second strip into two lengths and drill accordingly so that they can be bolted to the first strip in the correct position to engage with the camshaft slots. Secure a suitably drilled small piece of steel angle to the first strip so that the tool can be bolted to the threaded hole in the cylinder head upper section.

5 Timing belt sprockets and tensioner – removal, inspection and refitting

Caution: The timing belt sprockets are not keyed to the camshafts, neither is the crankshaft sprocket keyed to the crankshaft. Before starting work, make sure that you have the necessary tooling to accurately set the camshafts and crankshaft to TDC.

Removal

1 Remove the timing belt as described in Section 4.
2 Slide the crankshaft sprocket from the nose of the crankshaft, noting which way round it is fitted.
3 Use a suitable tool to hold each camshaft sprocket stationary while the fasteners are loosened, then unscrew and remove the fasteners and withdraw the sprockets from the camshafts. Note that on later K4M engines, the inlet camshaft sprocket incorporates a phase-shifter, and it is necessary to unscrew a cover for access to the retaining nut.
4 To remove the tensioner, unscrew the centre fastener and withdraw the unit from the stud on the water pump. Note the groove in the water pump cover for the tensioner lug.
5 To remove the idler, unscrew the centre bolt and withdraw it from the cylinder head.

Inspection

6 Inspect the teeth of the sprockets for signs of nicks and damage. Also examine the water pump pulley. The teeth are not prone to wear and should normally last the life of the engine.
7 Spin the tensioner pulley by hand and check it for any roughness or tightness. Do not attempt to clean it with solvent, as this may enter the bearing. If wear is evident, renew the tensioner. **Note:** *Renault state that the tensioner and idler pulley must be renewed whenever the timing belt is renewed.*

Refitting

8 Locate the idler on the cylinder head, then insert the bolt and tighten to the specified torque.
9 Locate the tensioner on the stud on the water pump cover, making sure that the lug engages the groove. Fit the fastener loosely at this stage.
10 Set the engine at TDC for No 1 piston as described in Section 3. Slip the crankshaft sprocket off the end of the crankshaft and check that the keyway in the crankshaft is uppermost. Note that although there is a keyway in both the crankshaft and crankshaft sprocket, a Woodruff key is not used.
11 Using a suitable solvent, thoroughly clean the end of the crankshaft, crankshaft sprocket bore, and the crankshaft and sprocket mating faces. Similarly clean the camshaft ends, camshaft sprocket bores and mating faces. It is essential that all traces of oil and grease are removed from these areas to allow the sprockets to be securely clamped when the pulley and retaining bolt/nuts are refitted. If the sprockets slip in service, serious engine damage will result.
12 Check that the camshafts are still correctly positioned with their slots parallel to the join between the upper and lower cylinder head sections, and the offsets below the centreline. If necessary, temporarily refit the old camshaft sprocket fastener and turn the camshafts slightly using a spanner to correctly align the slots.
13 The camshafts must now be retained in this position either by using Renault special tool Mot. 1496, or by fabricating a home-made alternative **(see Tool Tip 1)**. Engage the Renault special tool or the home-made alternative with the slots in the camshafts and secure the tool to the cylinder head using a suitable bolt. With the crankshaft against the TDC pin and the camshafts secured with the holding tool, refit the crankshaft sprocket to the end of the crankshaft.
14 Locate the camshaft sprockets on the camshafts so that the Renault logo engraved spokes, or phase-shifter marking, are at the 12 o'clock position. Fit the sprocket fasteners loosely at this stage. A clearance of between 0.5 and 1.0 mm should exist between the fasteners and the sprockets. Where applicable on later K4M engines, mark the rocker cover in line with the mark on the inlet camshaft phase-shifter and check that the phase-shifter is neither advanced or retarded.
15 Slide the crankshaft sprocket onto the nose of the crankshaft, making sure it is the correct way round.
16 Locate the new timing belt over the crankshaft and camshaft sprockets, and around the tensioner pulley, making sure that the sprocket marks remain vertical.
17 Refit the crankshaft pulley and the retaining bolt and washer. If the original bolt is being re-used, lightly lubricate the threads with engine oil. If a new bolt is being used it should be fitted dry. Tighten the bolt so that there is approximately 2.0 to 3.0 mm clearance between the bolt and the pulley. The crankshaft and camshaft sprockets must all be free to turn for the timing belt to be tensioned correctly.
18 Using a 6.0 mm Allen key engaged with the hole in the tensioner pulley arm, turn the pointer to the setting positions described in Section 4 (according to tensioner version) and tighten the retaining fastener.
19 Turn the exhaust camshaft sprocket clockwise through three complete revolutions to initially settle and pretension the timing belt; use the mark on the sprocket and rocker cover to count the number of turns. Note that three revolutions of the camshaft sprockets will turn

***Tool Tip 2** To make a camshaft sprocket holding tool, obtain two lengths of steel strip 6 mm thick by 30 mm wide or similar, one 600 mm long, the other 200 mm long (all dimensions approximate). Bolt the two strips together to form a forked end, leaving the bolt slack so that the shorter strip can pivot freely. At the end of each 'prong' of the fork, drill a suitable hole and fit a nut and bolt to engage with the holes in the sprocket.*

the crankshaft sprocket through six complete turns. The exhaust camshaft sprocket can be turned using a suitable forked tool engaged with the holes in the sprocket **(see Tool Tip 2)**. During this operation, ensure that the camshaft and crankshaft sprocket retaining nuts/bolts remain slack to allow the sprockets to turn freely.

20 On models fitted with the Version 1 tensioner (see Section 4), unscrew the tensioner fastener by one turn only, then use an Allen key to align the index finger with the static index pointer by turning it anti-clockwise. Tighten the tensioner to the specified torque.

21 On models fitted with the Version 2 tensioner (see Section 4), check that the tensioner pointer is still aligned with the shallow notch on the fixed plate, and if necessary, loosen the fastener and use the Allen key to reposition the pointer. Finally, fully tighten the fastener to the specified torque on completion.

22 Moderately tighten the crankshaft pulley bolt, then remove the TDC timing rod and fully tighten the bolt to its specified torque while an assistant holds the crankshaft stationary with a screwdriver engaged with the flywheel ring gear. Do not tighten the bolt with the timing rod in position.

23 Refit the timing rod and set the crankshaft to TDC, then check that the camshaft locking tool is in position. The camshaft sprockets must now be held stationary while the fasteners are tightened in the specified stages. Renault technicians use a metal plate bolted to the cylinder head which clamps the two sprockets stationary, however, the tool used to hold the pulleys on removal can be used provided care is taken not to move the camshafts or crankshaft during the tightening procedure.

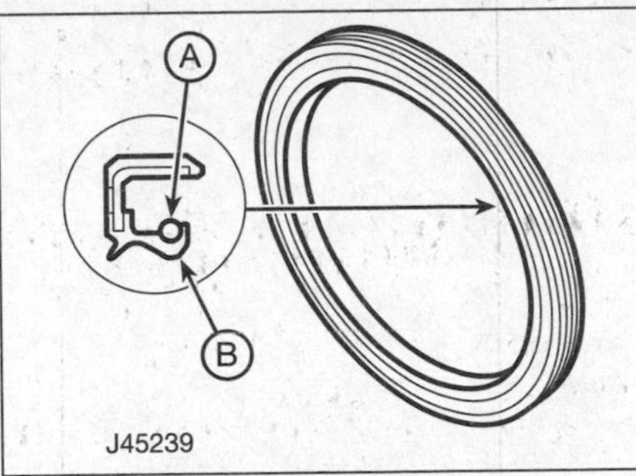

6.0a Camshaft oil seal Version 1

A Internal spring
B V-shaped sealing lip

24 Remove the timing rod and locking tool, then turn the crankshaft clockwise through two complete revolutions and recheck the timing for a final time. Remove the timing tools.

25 Where applicable, refit and tighten the cover on the phase-shifter sprocket.

26 Fit two new camshaft sealing caps to the left-hand end of the cylinder head, carefully tapping them into place with a large socket or similar tool.

27 Refit the upper timing cover and lower timing cover, and tighten the bolts securely.

28 Apply a little sealant to its threads, then refit the TDC plug to the cylinder block and tighten securely.

29 Refit the air cleaner and resonator with reference to Chapter 4A.

30 Clip the fuel pipes to the lower timing cover.

31 Reconnect the vacuum pipe to the inlet manifold and attach the wiring loom to the upper timing cover. Refit the support bracket and tighten the bolts, reconnect the wiring and attach it to the support.

32 Refit the right-hand upper engine mounting bracket to the engine and body with reference to Section 12. Lower the jack and block of wood from the sump.

33 Refit the auxiliary drivebelt with reference to Chapter 1A. Where there is an extra unused groove, check that the belt is located on the correct grooves as noted on removal.

34 Refit the right-hand wheel arch liners, and engine compartment undertray, then refit the roadwheel and lower the vehicle to the ground.

35 Reconnect the battery negative lead.

6.4 Smear a little grease on the oil seal . . .

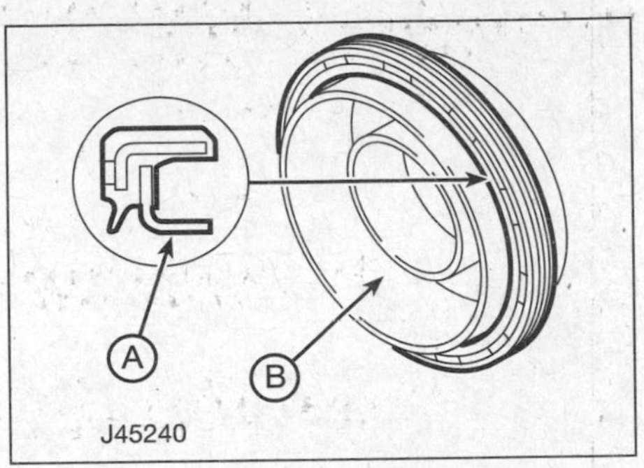

6.0b Camshaft oil seal Version 2

A Flat sealing lip
B Fitting protector

6 Camshaft oil seal – renewal

Note: *There are two versions of camshaft oil seal fitted* ***(see illustrations)****; version 1 has an internal spring and V-shaped sealing lip, version 2 has a flat sealing lip without an internal spring. Version 2 is extremely fragile and must only be handled by the protector. The oil seals are not interchangeable and the fitting procedure for each is different, as described in the following paragraphs.*

1 Remove the camshaft sprocket as described in Section 5.

2 Note the fitted depth of the old oil seal. Using a small screwdriver, prise out the oil seal from the cylinder head taking care not to damage the sealing surface on the camshaft. Alternatively, the oil seal can be removed by drilling two small holes diagonally opposite each other and inserting self-tapping screws in them. A pair of grips can then be used to pull out the oil seals, by pulling on each side in turn.

3 Inspect the seal rubbing surface on the camshaft. If it is grooved or rough in the area where the old seal was fitted, the new seal should be fitted slightly less deeply, so that it rubs on an unworn part of the surface.

Version 1 oil seal

4 Wipe clean the oil seal seating, then smear a little oil on the outer perimeter and sealing lip of the new oil seal **(see illustration)**.

5 Locate the seal squarely in the cylinder head, then drive it into position using a metal tube or socket which has an external diameter slightly less than that of the bore in the cylinder head **(see illustration)**. Alternatively, the oil seal can be pressed into position using a metal tube, washer and nut.

Version 2 oil seal

6 Renault technicians use a special tool (Mot. 1632) to fit the oil seal. The tool consists

6.5 . . . before driving it into the cylinder head with a suitable socket

of a threaded rod, metal tube and nut, and a machined shoulder to locate the protector/guide on **(see illustration)**. The rod is screwed into the end of the camshaft, and the protector/guide located on the shoulder. The metal tube is then fitted against the oil seal and the nut tightened to press the seal into the cylinder head/bearing cap. If the Renault tool cannot be obtained, a similar tool can be made out of a threaded rod, metal tube, washer and nut.

7 Wipe clean the oil seal seating, then press the oil seal squarely into position. Note that the Renault tool is designed to locate the seal at the original depth, however, if the camshaft sealing surface is excessively worn, position it less deeply so that it locates on the unworn surface.

8 After fitting the oil seal, remove the protector/guide and tool.

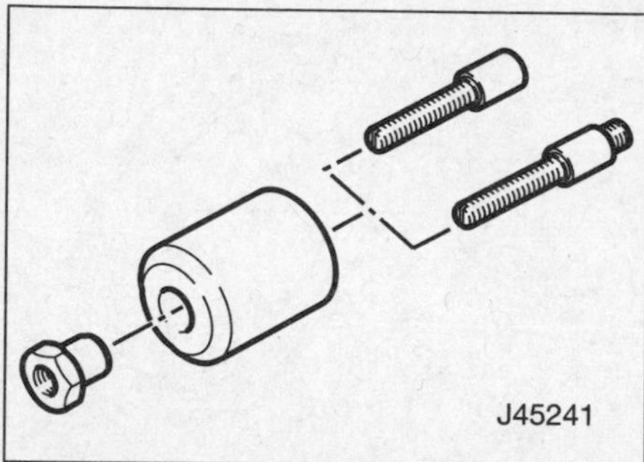

6.6 Renault tool for fitting the camshaft oil seal

All types

9 Wipe away any excess oil, then refit the camshaft sprocket as described in Section 5.

7 Camshafts – removal, inspection and refitting

Removal

1 Disconnect the battery negative (earth) lead and position it away from the terminal.

2 Remove the timing belt as described in Section 4.

3 Remove the camshaft sprockets as described in Section 5.

4 Where applicable, disconnect the accelerator cable from the throttle housing with reference to Chapter 4A.

5 Disconnect the fuel supply and return hoses from the fuel rail with reference to Chapter 4A.

6 Remove the injector gallery protector, then disconnect the wiring from the injectors and coils and position it to one side.

7 Unbolt the inlet air duct unit, then remove the cooling system expansion bottle and position it to one side.

8 Unbolt the catalytic converter mountings and remove it from the exhaust manifold.

9 Remove the throttle body as described in Chapter 4A.

10 Disconnect the wiring from the oxygen sensor.

11 Unbolt and remove the exhaust manifold support strut and the engine lifting eye.

12 Disconnect the brake vacuum pipe from the inlet manifold.

13 Unbolt and remove the inlet manifold.

14 Remove the ignition coils as described in Chapter 5B.

15 Unbolt and remove the oil separator unit **(see illustration)**

16 Progressively unscrew the valve cover/bearing cap retaining bolts, then release the cover by using a copper mallet to tap the lugs at each rear corner and using a screwdriver to lever up the lugs on the front of the cover. Once the cover is free, lift it squarely from the cylinder head **(see illustration)**. The camshafts will rise up slightly under the pressure of the valve springs – be careful they don't tilt and jam. Remove the cover/bearing cap.

17 Identify each camshaft for location and TDC position, then carefully lift them from the cylinder head. The inlet camshaft should have the marking AM on it and the exhaust should have the marking EM. If these are not visible, identify the camshafts with dabs of paint. Remove the oil seals from the camshafts, noting their fitted positions.

18 Obtain a box with 16 compartments and mark the valve positions clearly on it. Remove each hydraulic cam follower and place it in its compartment for safe-keeping **(see illustration)**.

19 Obtain a metal box with 16 compartments identified with the valve positions, and fill it with fresh engine oil. Remove the hydraulic tappets from the cylinder head and place them in their correct compartments, making sure that they are completely immersed in the oil **(see illustration)**.

Inspection

20 Inspect the cam lobes and the camshaft bearing journals for scoring or other visible evidence of wear.

21 If the camshafts appear satisfactory, measure the bearing journal diameters and compare the figures obtained with those given in the Specifications. If the diameters are not as specified, consult a Renault dealer or engine overhaul specialist. Wear of the camshaft bearings will almost certainly be accompanied by similar wear of the bearings in the cylinder head, which will entail renewal of the cylinder head upper and lower sections together with the camshafts.

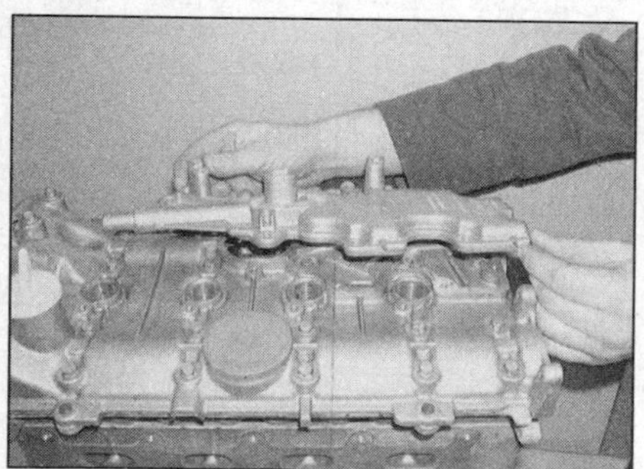

7.15 Undo the eight bolts and remove the oil separator housing

7.16 Removing the valve cover/bearing cap from the cylinder head

7.18 Lift out the cam followers and place them in a marked box or containers

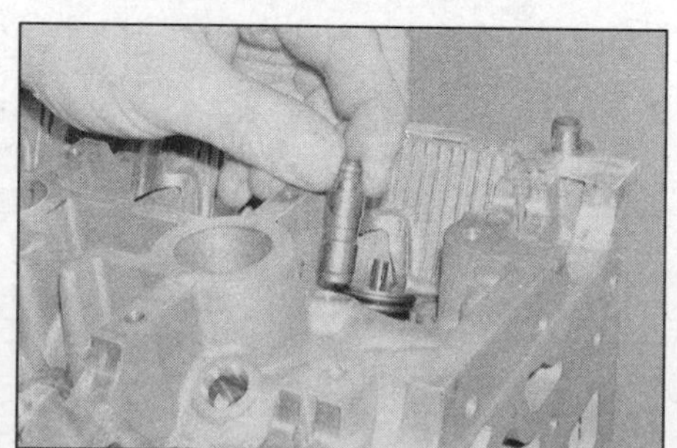

7.19 Lift out the tappets and place them upright in a marked box or containers filled with oil

7.29a Refit the camshafts in the cylinder head . . .

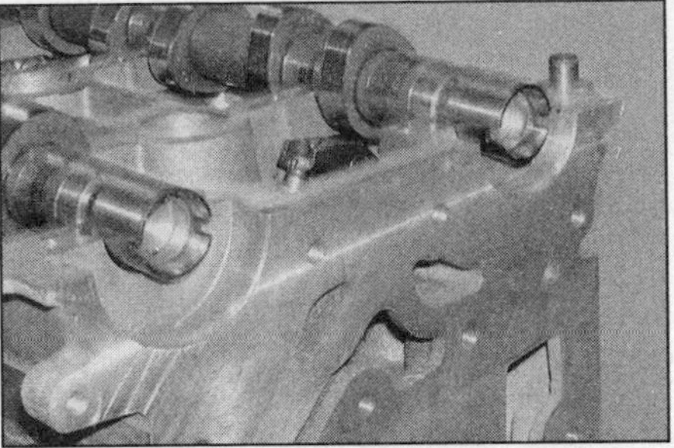
7.29b Position the camshafts in their TDC position so that the grooves are horizontal and the offset is below the centreline

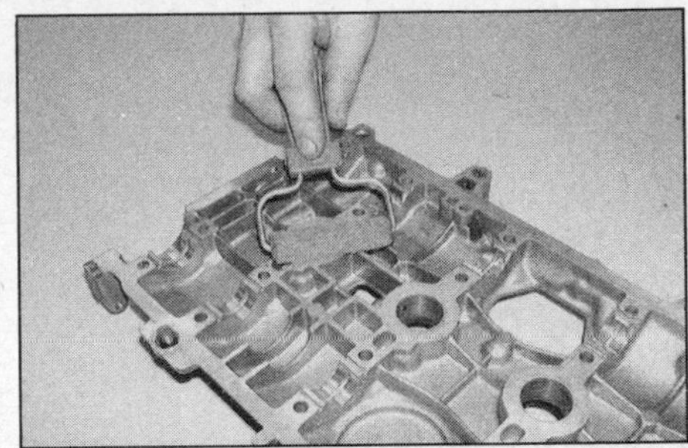
7.30 Apply an even coating of Loctite 518 gasket solution to the mating face of the valve cover/bearing cap

22 Inspect the cam followers and hydraulic tappets for scuffing, cracking or other damage and renew any components as necessary. Also check the condition of the tappet bores in the cylinder head. As with the camshafts, any wear in this area will necessitate cylinder head renewal.

Refitting

23 Clean the sealant from the mating surfaces of the valve cover/bearing cap and cylinder head.

24 To prevent any possibility of the valves contacting the pistons when the camshafts are refitted, remove the TDC pin or dowel rod used to lock the crankshaft, and turn the crankshaft clockwise a quarter turn.

25 Lubricate the tappet bores in the cylinder head with clean engine oil.

26 If the hydraulic tappets have not been kept immersed in oil, the oil will drain from them and they will need to be reprimed before refitting. To check whether they require repriming, depress the top of the tappet with a thumb – if the piston goes down, the tappet requires repriming. Renault recommend that the tappets are immersed in diesel fuel and operated until they are primed.

27 Remove the hydraulic tappets from their compartments and insert them in their correct positions in the head.

28 One at a time, remove the cam followers from their compartments and locate them on the hydraulic tappets and valve stems.

29 Lubricate the bearings and journals of the inlet and exhaust camshafts with fresh engine oil, then carefully locate them on the cylinder head in their correct positions and at TDC as previously noted. The grooves at the left-hand end of the camshafts must be horizontal **(see illustrations)**.

30 Check that the valve cover/bearing cap mating surfaces are clean and dry, then apply Loctite 518 (or a suitable alternative) to the cover surface using a roller **(see illustration)**. Make several applications until the colour is **reddish.**

31 Locate the valve cover/bearing cap on the cylinder head, insert the bolts, and progressively tighten them to the specified torque in the sequence and stages given in the Specifications **(see illustration)**. Make sure that the camshafts are located correctly on the cam followers and in the cover.

32 Check that the oil separator mating surfaces are clean and dry, then apply Loctite 518 (or a suitable alternative) to the separator surface using a roller **(see illustration)**. Make several applications until the colour is **reddish.**

33 Locate the oil separator on the valve cover, insert the bolts, and tighten them to the specified torque in sequence **(see illustration)**.

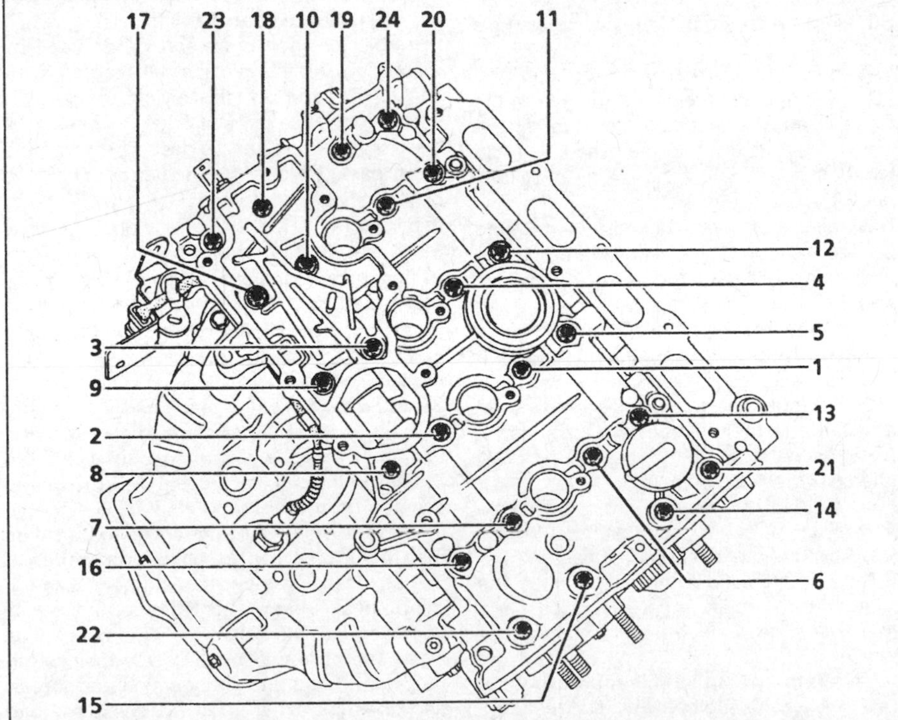

7.31 Valve cover/bearing cap retaining bolt identification

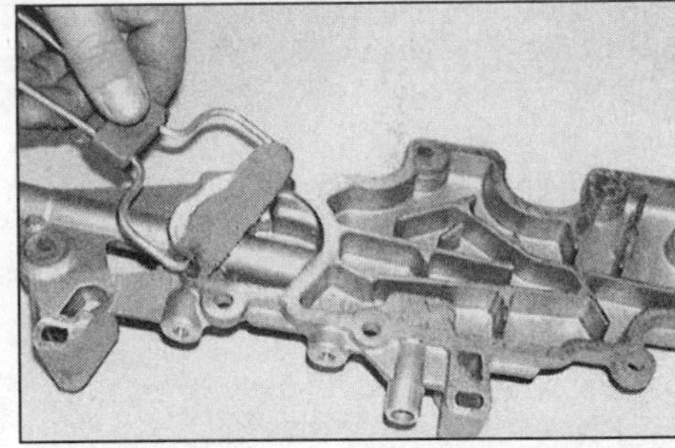
7.32 Apply an even coating of Loctite 518 gasket solution to the mating face of the oil separator housing

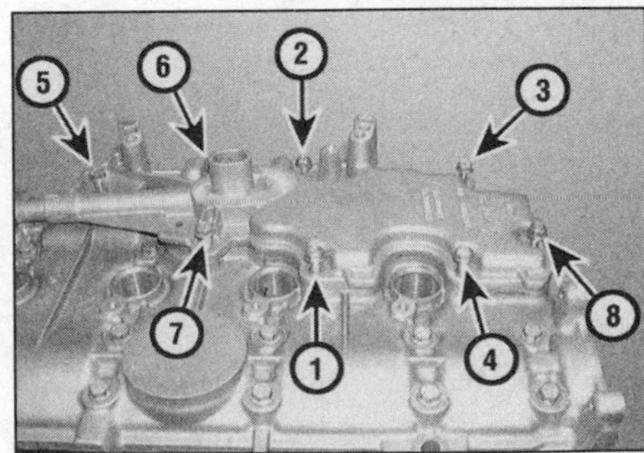

7.33 Oil separator housing retaining bolt tightening sequence

34 Refit the ignition coils with reference to Chapter 5B.

35 Refit the engine lifting eye to the cylinder head and tighten the bolts securely.

36 Refit the support bracket to the right-hand side of the exhaust manifold, and tighten the bolts securely.

37 Reconnect the wiring to the oxygen sensor on the rear left-hand side of the engine.

38 Refit the throttle body with reference to Chapter 4A.

39 Refit the catalytic converter to the exhaust manifold with reference to Chapter 4A.

40 Refit the inlet manifold together with new seals with reference to Chapter 4A.

41 Reconnect the brake servo vacuum hose to the inlet manifold.

42 Refit the expansion bottle to the bulkhead.

43 Reconnect the wiring to the ignition coil and fuel injectors, and attach the wiring loom to the front of the engine.

44 Reconnect the fuel supply and return hoses to each end of the fuel rail, and tighten the clips.

45 Refit the injector gallery protector.

46 Where applicable, reconnect the accelerator cable to the throttle body with reference to Chapter 4A.

47 Refit the camshaft sprockets as described in Section 5.

48 Refit the timing belt with reference to Section 4 of this Chapter.

49 Remove the trolley jack and block of wood from under the sump.

50 Reconnect the battery negative lead.

51 Refill the engine with fresh oil, with reference to Chapter 1A.

52 Refit the engine undertray and lower the vehicle to the ground.

8 Cylinder head – removal, inspection and refitting

Note: *In addition to any other parts required, have a new timing belt, cylinder head and cylinder head cover gaskets and (possibly) a set of new cylinder head bolts ready for reassembly. Renault state that the tensioner and idler pulley must be renewed whenever the timing belt is renewed.*

1 Disconnect the battery negative lead (refer to *Disconnecting the battery* in the Reference Section).

2 Remove the bonnet as described in Chapter 11.

3 Carefully, position a trolley jack and a large block of wood under the sump to support the engine. Raise the jack to just take the weight of the engine.

4 Remove the timing belt and camshaft sprockets with reference to Sections 4 and 5 of this Chapter.

5 Remove the engine undertray, then drain the cooling system with reference to Chapter 1A.

6 Drain the engine oil with reference to Chapter 1A.

7 Where applicable, disconnect the accelerator cable from the throttle body with reference to Chapter 4A.

8 Unbolt and remove the injector gallery protector and remove the inlet manifold.

9 Disconnect the fuel supply and return hoses from each end of the fuel rail.

10 Disconnect the engine wiring loom at the front of the engine, and also disconnect the wiring from the ignition coil and fuel injectors.

11 Refer to Chapter 3 and remove the expansion bottle from the bulkhead positioning it to one side, then unbolt and remove the inlet manifold with reference to Chapter 4A.

12 Refer to Chapter 4A and remove the catalytic converter from the exhaust manifold. Remove the throttle body as described in Chapter 4A. Disconnect the wiring for the oxygen sensor on the rear left-hand side of the engine.

13 Unscrew the bolts and remove the support bracket from the right-hand side of the exhaust manifold.

14 Unbolt the engine lifting eye from the cylinder head.

15 Disconnect the brake servo vacuum hose from the inlet manifold.

16 Remove the ignition coils with reference to Chapter 5B.

17 Unbolt the oil separator from the top of the valve cover.

18 Progressively unscrew the valve cover retaining bolts, then release the cover by using a copper mallet to tap the lugs at each rear corner and using a screwdriver to lever up the lugs on the front of the cover. Remove the cover.

19 Identify each camshaft for location and TDC position, then carefully lift them from the cylinder head. The inlet camshaft should have the marking AM on it and the exhaust should have the marking EM. If these are not visible, identify the camshafts with dabs of paint.

20 Obtain a box with 16 compartments and mark the valve positions clearly on it. Remove each cam follower and place it in its compartment for safe-keeping.

21 Obtain a metal box with 16 compartments identified with the valve positions, and fill it with fresh engine oil. Carefully remove the hydraulic tappets from the cylinder head and place them in their correct compartments, making sure that they are completely immersed in the oil.

22 Disconnect the wiring from the temperature sensor on the thermostat housing at the left-hand end of the cylinder head.

23 Release the clips and disconnect the radiator top hose, heater hoses and expansion tank hose from the thermostat housing.

24 Unbolt the wiring loom support bracket from the left-hand end of the cylinder head.

25 Unbolt the engine lifting eye from the left-hand end of the cylinder head.

26 Remove the spark plugs as described in Chapter 1A.

27 Progressively unscrew and remove the cylinder head bolts in the **reverse** order to that shown in illustration 8.39b.

28 Lift the head from the cylinder block, followed by the gasket.

Inspection

29 The mating faces of the cylinder head and block must be perfectly clean before refitting the head. Use a scraper to remove all traces of gasket and carbon and also clean the tops of the pistons. Take particular care with the aluminium cylinder head, as the soft metal is easily damaged. Also, make sure that debris is not allowed to enter the oil and water channels – this is particularly important for the oil circuit, as carbon could block the oil supply to the camshaft and cam followers or crankshaft bearings. Using adhesive tape and paper, seal the water, oil and bolt holes in the cylinder block. Clean the piston crowns in the same way.

To prevent carbon entering the gap between the pistons and bores, smear a little grease in the gap. After cleaning the piston, rotate the crankshaft so that the piston moves down the bore, then wipe out the grease and carbon with a cloth rag.

30 Check the block and head for nicks, deep scratches and other damage. If slight, they may be removed carefully with a file. It may be possible to repair more serious damage by machining, but this is a specialist job.

31 If warpage of the cylinder head is suspected, use a straight-edge to check it for distortion, as this can be associated with the head gasket blowing. No regrinding of the cylinder head is allowed. Refer to Part D of this Chapter for further information.

32 Clean out all the bolt holes in the block using a pipe cleaner, or a rag and screwdriver. Make sure that all oil is removed, otherwise there is a possibility of the block being cracked by hydraulic pressure when the bolts are tightened.

33 Examine the bolt threads and the threads in the cylinder block for damage. If necessary, use the correct-size tap to chase out the threads in the block and use a die to clean the threads on the bolts. In view of the severe stresses to which they are subjected, owners may wish to renew the bolts as a matter of course whenever they are disturbed. If any of the bolts shows the slightest sign of wear or of damage, all the bolts should be renewed as a set. The bolts may be re-used if their length between the bolt head underside and thread end does not exceed 117.7 mm – if any one bolt is longer than this dimension, renew all the bolts as a set.

8.35 Locate a new cylinder head gasket on the cylinder block . . .

8.37 . . . and carefully lower the cylinder head into position

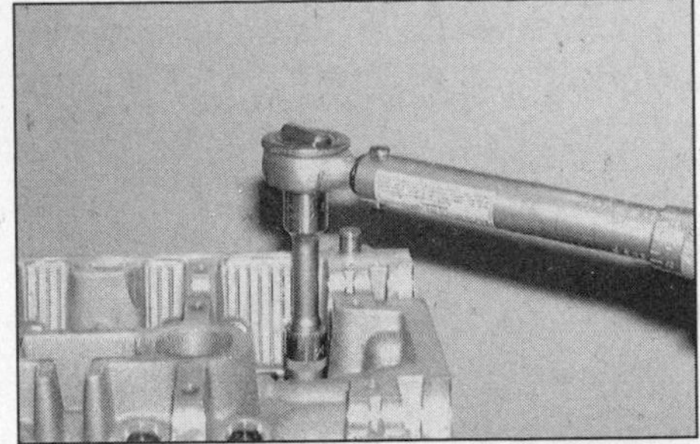
8.39a Tighten the cylinder head retaining bolts to the Stage 1 torque setting using a torque wrench

Refitting

34 It is recommended that No 1 piston is positioned half-way up its cylinder before refitting the cylinder head as a safeguard against the valves touching the tops of the pistons. Turn the crankshaft clockwise until No 1 piston rises to the mid-cylinder position.

35 Position a new gasket on the block making sure it is the correct way up **(see illustration)**.

36 If the lower inlet manifold was removed, it can be refitted at this stage, with reference to Chapter 4A, making sure that the timing end is flush with the end of the cylinder head before tightening the bolts.

37 Carefully lower the cylinder head onto the block making sure that the gasket is not displaced **(see illustration)**.

38 If new bolts are being fitted, **do not** lubricate their threads, however if the old bolts are being refitted, lubricate their threads with fresh engine oil. Insert the bolts and initially screw them in finger-tight.

39 Tighten the cylinder head bolts to the specified torques in sequence and in the stages given in the Specifications **(see illustrations)**. The first stage precompresses the gasket and the second stage is the main tightening procedure. When angle-tightening the bolts, put paint marks on the bolt heads and cylinder head as a guide for the correct angle, or obtain a special angle-tightening tool. Note that, provided the bolts are tightened exactly as specified, there will be no need to retighten them once the engine has been started and run after reassembly.

40 Refit the spark plugs with reference to Chapter 1A.

41 Refit the engine lifting eye to the left-hand end of the cylinder head.

42 Refit the wiring loom support bracket to the cylinder head and tighten the bolts.

43 Reconnect the radiator top hose, heater hoses and expansion tank to the thermostat housing and tighten the clips.

44 Reconnect the wiring to the temperature sensor on the thermostat housing.

45 If the hydraulic tappets have not been kept immersed in oil, the oil will drain from them and they will need to be reprimed before refitting. To check whether they require repriming, depress the top of the tappet with a thumb – if the piston goes down, the tappet requires repriming. Renault recommend that the tappets are immersed in diesel fuel and operated until they are primed.

46 Remove the hydraulic tappets from their compartments and insert them in their correct positions in the head.

47 One at a time, remove the cam followers from their compartments and locate them on the hydraulic tappets and valve stems.

48 Lubricate the bearings and journals of the inlet and exhaust camshafts with fresh engine oil, then carefully locate them on the cylinder head in their correct positions and at TDC as previously noted. The grooves at the left-hand end of the camshafts must be horizontal.

49 Turn the crankshaft clockwise to position No 1 piston at TDC. Refer to Section 3 if necessary.

50 Check that the valve cover/bearing cap mating surfaces are clean and dry, then apply Loctite 518 (or a suitable alternative) to the cover surface using a roller. Make several applications until the colour is **reddish.**

51 Locate the valve cover on the cylinder head, insert the bolts, and tighten them to the specified torque in the sequence and stages given in the Specifications **(see illustration 7.31)**.

52 Check that the oil separator mating surfaces are clean and dry, then apply Loctite 518 (or a suitable alternative) to the separator surface using a roller. Make several applications until the colour is **reddish.**

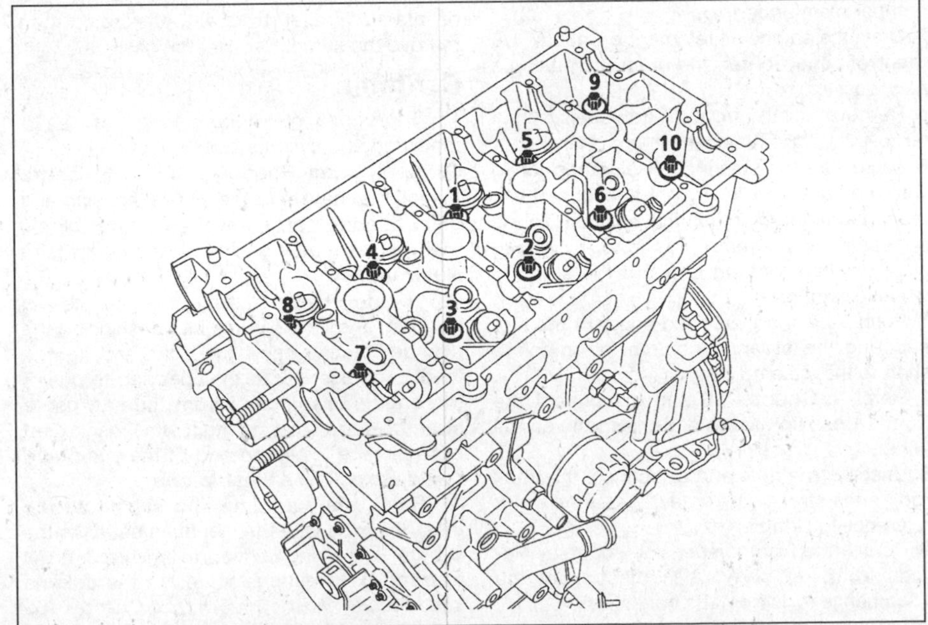

8.39b Cylinder head retaining bolt tightening sequence

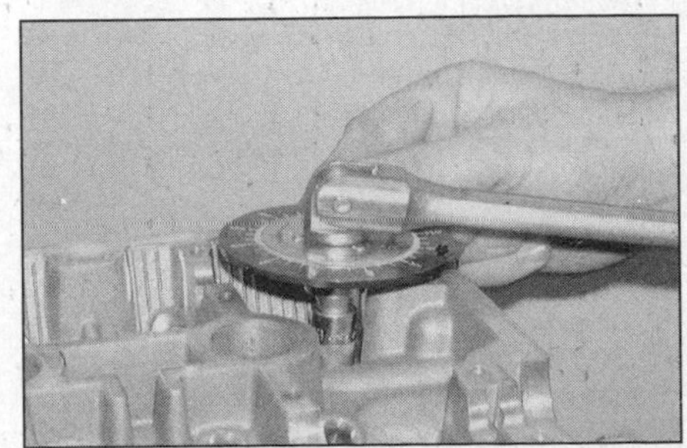
8.39c Using an angle tightening gauge to tighten the cylinder head retaining bolts through the Stage 2 angle

9.18a Apply sealant to the joint areas of the oil seal housing . . .

9.18b . . . and main bearing cap . . .

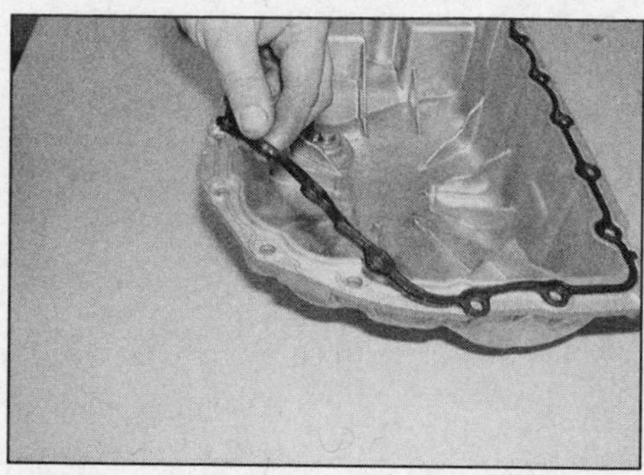

9.18c . . . then locate a new gasket on the sump

53 Locate the oil separator on the valve cover, insert the bolts, and tighten them to the specified torque in sequence **(see illustration 7.33)**.

54 Refit the ignition coils with reference to Chapter 5B.

55 Refit the engine lifting eye to the cylinder head and tighten the bolts securely.

56 Refit the support bracket to the right-hand side of the exhaust manifold, and tighten the bolts securely.

57 Reconnect the wiring to the oxygen sensor on the rear left-hand side of the engine.

58 Refit the throttle body with reference to Chapter 4A.

59 Refit the catalytic converter to the exhaust manifold with reference to Chapter 4A.

60 Refit the inlet manifold together with new seals with reference to Chapter 4A.

61 Reconnect the brake servo vacuum hose to the inlet manifold.

62 Refit the expansion bottle to the bulkhead.

63 Reconnect the wiring to the ignition coil and fuel injectors, and attach the wiring loom to the front of the engine.

64 Reconnect the fuel supply and return hoses to each end of the fuel rail, and tighten the clips.

65 Refit the injector gallery protector.

66 Where applicable, reconnect the accelerator cable to the throttle body with reference to Chapter 4A.

67 Refit the timing belt and camshaft sprockets with reference to Sections 4 and 5 of this Chapter.

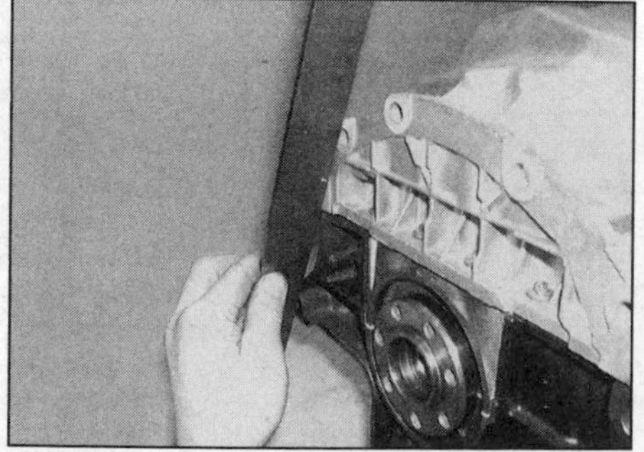

9.19 If the engine is removed, use a straight-edge to maintain the alignment between the left-hand end of the sump and cylinder block

68 Remove the trolley jack and block of wood from under the sump.

69 Refit the bonnet with reference to Chapter 11.

70 Reconnect the battery negative lead.

71 Refill the engine with fresh oil, with reference to Chapter 1A.

72 Refill and bleed the cooling system with reference to Chapter 1A.

73 Refit the engine undertray and lower the vehicle to the ground.

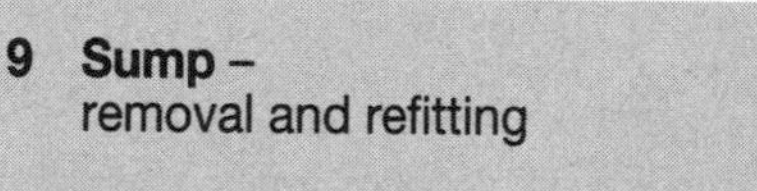

9 Sump – removal and refitting

Note: *An engine lifting hoist is required during this procedure.*

Removal

1 Disconnect the battery negative lead.

2 Jack up the front of the vehicle and support on axle stands. Remove the engine compartment undertray.

3 Drain the engine oil referring to Chapter 1A, then refit and tighten the drain plug using a new washer.

4 Remove both front roadwheels, then remove the right-hand wheel arch liner.

5 Make sure the steering wheel is positioned with the front wheels straight-ahead, and use tape or string to hold it in this position. This is necessary to prevent damage to the airbag rotary switch located beneath the steering wheel central pad.

6 Push back the gaiter and unscrew the bolt securing the steering column intermediate shaft to the steering gear pinion.

7 Refer to Chapter 10 and disconnect the front suspension lower arms from the swivel hubs.

8 Unscrew the nuts and disconnect the track rod ends from the steering arms with reference to Chapter 10.

9 Detach the front suspension subframe tie-rods from the body. Also disconnect the gearchange rods from the transmission.

10 Loosen only the bolts securing the rear engine mounting link to the body.

11 Unscrew and remove the front bumper lower mounting fasteners.

12 Where necessary, unbolt and remove the exhaust manifold heat shield and remove the catalytic converter with reference to Chapter 4A.

13 Where necessary, unbolt the power-assisted steering pipe supports from the cylinder block. Also unbolt the multi-function support bracket (for PAS pump/air conditioning compressor/alternator).

14 Unbolt the front suspension lower arms from the subframe with reference to Chapter 10.

15 Unscrew each subframe mounting bolt in turn and substitute them with lengths of threaded rods and nuts. These are required to lower the subframe approximately 13.0 cm in order to remove the sump. With the rods in position, lower the subframe until the gap between the subframe and body is 9.0 cm at the rear mounting and 13.0 cm at the front mounting. As the subframe is being lowered, disconnect the steering gear pinion from the column intermediate shaft.

16 Unscrew the bolts securing the sump to the cylinder block. Tap the sump with a hide or plastic mallet to break the seal, then remove the sump. Recover the gaskets.

Refitting

17 Thoroughly clean the mating surfaces of the sump and cylinder block.

18 Apply some Rhodorseal 5661 sealant to the joint areas where the oil seal housing and main bearing cap meet the cylinder block, then locate a new gasket on the sump **(see illustrations)**.

19 Locate new half-moon gaskets in position, and lift the sump into position on the cylinder block. Insert the bolts and tighten them progressively to the specified torque. If the engine is removed from the car, use a straight-edge to maintain the alignment between the left-hand end of the sump and cylinder block **(see illustration)**.

20 Raise the subframe and substitute the threaded rods with the mounting bolts. As the subframe is being raised, make sure that the steering gear pinion locates in the column intermediate shaft correctly (see Chapter 10). Tighten the bolts to the specified torque (see Chapter 10).

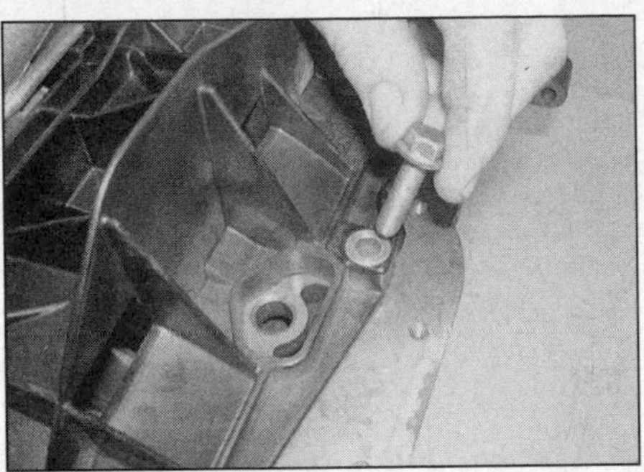

10.2 Unscrew the anti-emulsion plate retaining bolt(s)

10.3a Remove the anti-emulsion plate . . .

10.3b . . . then tilt the pump to disengage its sprocket from the drive chain

10.6 Slide the drive sprocket together with the chain from the crankshaft

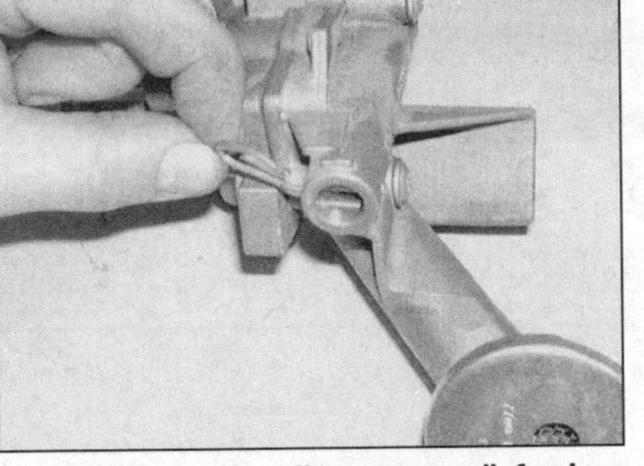

10.7a Extract the oil pressure relief valve retaining clip . . .

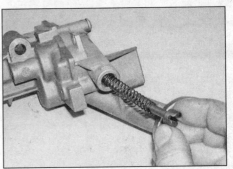

10.7b . . . remove the oil pressure relief valve spring retainer and spring . . .

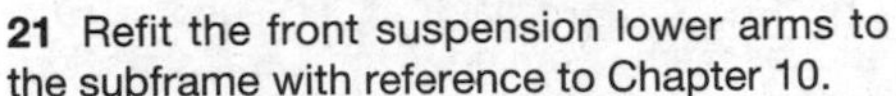

21 Refit the front suspension lower arms to the subframe with reference to Chapter 10.

22 Where applicable, refit the multi-function and power steering pipe supports.

23 Refit the catalytic converter and exhaust manifold heat shield with reference to Chapter 4A.

24 Refit and tighten the front bumper lower mounting fasteners.

25 Tighten the rear engine mounting link bolts to the specified torque.

26 Reconnect the gearchange rods to the transmission, and refit the front suspension subframe tie-rods to the body.

27 Refit the track rod ends to the steering arms with reference to Chapter 10.

28 Reconnect the front suspension lower arms to the swivel hubs with reference to Chapter 10.

29 With the front roadwheels straight-ahead, refit and tighten the bolt securing the intermediate shaft to the steering gear pinion. Locate the gaiter over the shaft, then remove the tape or string from the steering wheel.

30 Refit the wheel arch liner and right-hand front roadwheel. Also refit the engine compartment undertray, then lower the vehicle to the ground.

31 Reconnect the battery negative lead.

32 Fill the engine with fresh oil with reference to Chapter 1A.

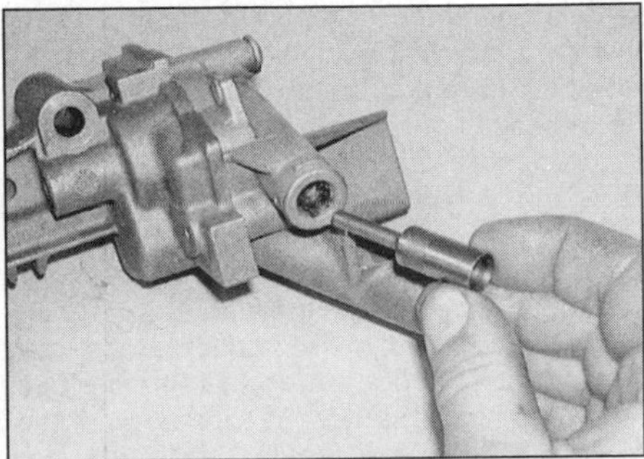

10.7c . . . followed by the plunger

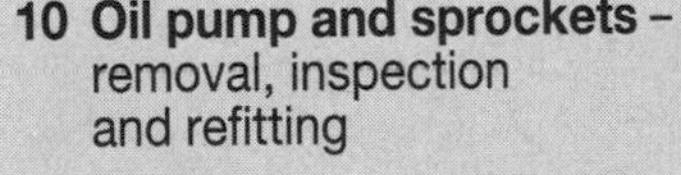

10 Oil pump and sprockets – removal, inspection and refitting

Removal

1 To remove the oil pump alone, first remove the sump as described in Section 9.

2 Unscrew the oil pump mounting bolts and the additional bolt(s) securing the anti-emulsion plate to the crankcase **(see illustration)**.

3 Withdraw the oil pump slightly and remove the anti-emulsion plate. Tilt the pump to disengage its sprocket from the drive chain and lift away the pump **(see illustrations)**. If the locating dowels are displaced, refit them in their locations.

4 To remove the pump complete with its drive chain and sprockets, first remove the sump as described in Section 9, then remove the crankshaft timing belt end oil seal housing as described in Section 11.

5 Remove the oil pump as described in paragraphs 1 and 2 above.

6 Slide the drive sprocket together with the chain from the crankshaft **(see illustration)**. Note that the drive sprocket is not keyed to the crankshaft, but relies on the pulley bolt being tightened correctly to clamp the sprocket.

Inspection

7 Extract the retaining clip, and remove the oil pressure relief valve spring retainer, spring and plunger **(see illustrations)**.

8 Unscrew the retaining bolts, and lift off the pump cover **(see illustration)**.

9 Carefully examine the gears, pump body and relief valve plunger for any signs of scoring or wear. Renew the pump complete if excessive wear is evident.

10 If the components appear serviceable, measure the clearance between the pump body and the gears using feeler blades. Also measure the gear endfloat, and check the

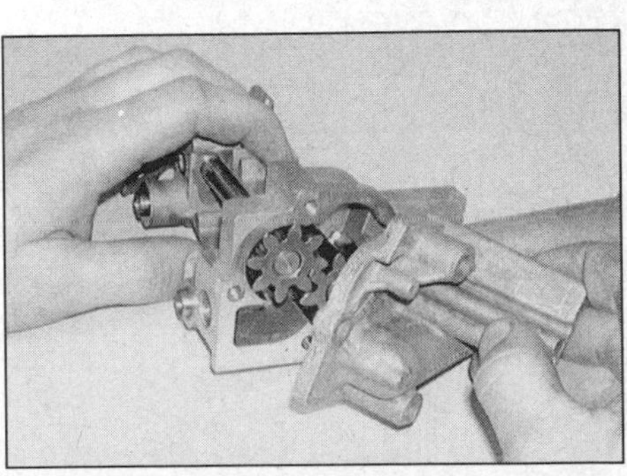

10.8 Unscrew the retaining bolts, and lift off the oil pump cover

10.10a Using feeler blades, measure the clearance between the pump body and the gears . . .

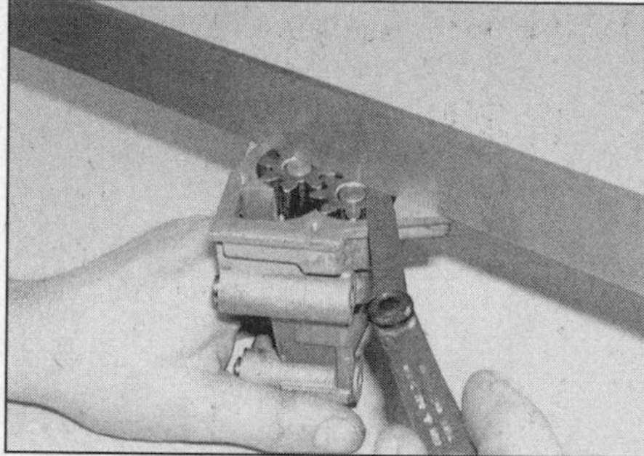
10.10b . . . and measure the gear endfloat

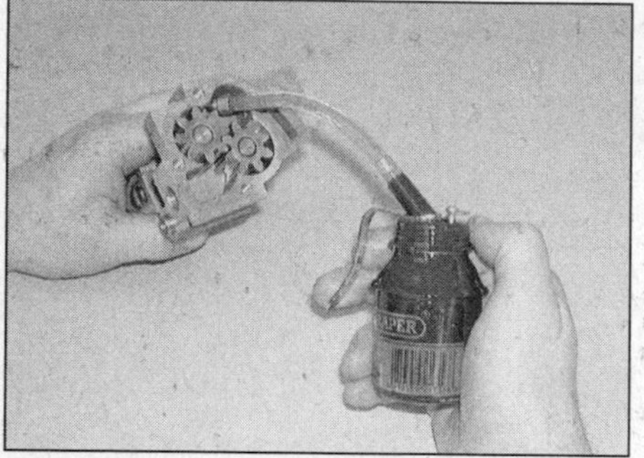
10.11 Fill the pump with oil, then refit the cover

10.13 Ensure that the oil pump drive sprocket is fitted with the projecting boss facing away from the crankshaft

flatness of the end cover **(see illustrations)**. If the clearances exceed the specified tolerances, the pump must be renewed.

11 If the pump is satisfactory, reassemble the components in the reverse order of removal. Fill the pump with oil, then refit the cover and tighten the bolts securely **(see illustration)**.

Refitting

12 Wipe clean the oil pump and cylinder block mating surfaces.

13 Locate the drive sprocket onto the end of the crankshaft, ensuring that it is fitted with the projecting boss facing away from the crankshaft **(see illustration)**. Engage the pump with the dowels, fit the two retaining bolts and tighten them to the specified torque.

14 Refit the anti-emulsion plate and secure with the retaining bolt(s).

15 Refit the oil seal housing as described in Section 11.

16 Refit the sump as described in Section 9.

11 Crankshaft oil seals – renewal

Timing belt end oil seal

1 Remove the timing belt and the crankshaft sprocket with reference to Sections 4 and 5. An alternative, though longer, method is to remove the sump and oil seal housing, and fit the new oil seal on the bench.

2 Note the fitted position of the old seal, then prise it out of the oil seal housing using a screwdriver or suitable hooked instrument. An alternative method of removing the oil seal is to drill carefully two small holes opposite each other in the oil seal and insert self-tapping screws, then pull on the screws with grips. Take care not to damage the surface of the spacer or the seal housing.

3 With the oil seal removed, where applicable slide the spacer from the crankshaft, noting which way round it is fitted.

4 Examine the spacer for excessive oil seal wear and polish off any burrs or raised edges which may have caused the seal to fail in the first place. If necessary, the spacer can be refitted so that the new oil seal contacts an unworn area. Clean the oil seal seating in the housing.

5 Smear the lips and outer perimeter of the new seal with fresh engine oil and locate it over the crankshaft with its closed side facing outwards. Using hand pressure, press the oil seal squarely into the housing a little way, then use a socket or metal tube to drive the oil seal to the previously noted position – take great care not to damage the seal lips during fitting **(see illustration)**. Do not drive it in too far or it will have to be removed and possibly renewed.

6 Slide the spacer onto the crankshaft and carefully press it into the oil seal, while twisting it to prevent damage.

7 Wipe away any excess oil, then refit the crankshaft sprocket and fit the new timing belt with reference to Sections 5 and 4.

Flywheel/driveplate end oil seal

8 Renewal of the crankshaft left-hand oil seal requires the engine and transmission assembly to be removed as described in Chapter 2D so that the engine and transmission can be separated on the bench (see Chapter 7A or 7B), the clutch (where fitted – see Chapter 6) and the flywheel/driveplate (see Section 13 of this Chapter) can be removed.

9 Prise out the old oil seal using a small screwdriver, taking care not to damage the surface on the crankshaft. Alternatively, the oil seal can be removed by drilling two small holes diagonally opposite each other and inserting self-tapping screws in them. A pair of grips can then be used to pull out the oil seal, by pulling on each side in turn.

10 Inspect the seal rubbing surface on the crankshaft. If it is grooved or rough in the area where the old seal was fitted, the new seal should be fitted slightly less deeply, so that it rubs on an unworn part of the surface.

11 Wipe clean the oil seal seating, then dip the new seal in fresh engine oil, and locate it over the crankshaft with its closed side facing outwards **(see illustration)**. Make sure that the oil seal lip is not damaged as it is located on the crankshaft.

12 Using a metal tube, drive the oil seal squarely into the bore until flush. A block of wood cut to pass over the end of the crankshaft may be used instead.

13 Refit the flywheel/driveplate with reference to Section 13. Refit the clutch as described in Chapter 6, reconnect the transmission to the engine and refit the engine/transmission unit as described in the relevant Chapters of this Manual.

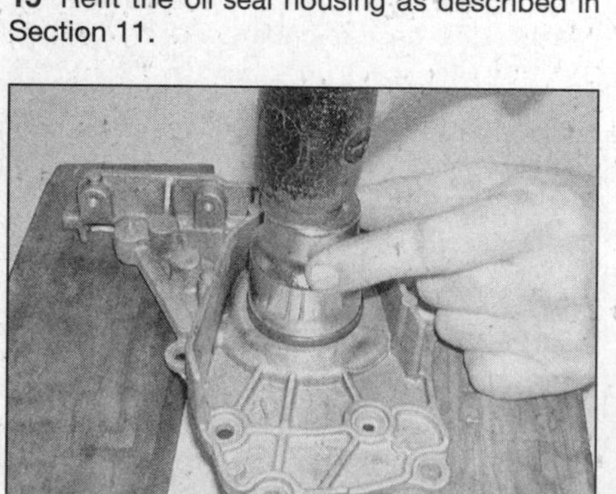
11.5 Using a socket to drive the new crankshaft oil seal into the housing

11.11 Fitting a new crankshaft flywheel end oil seal

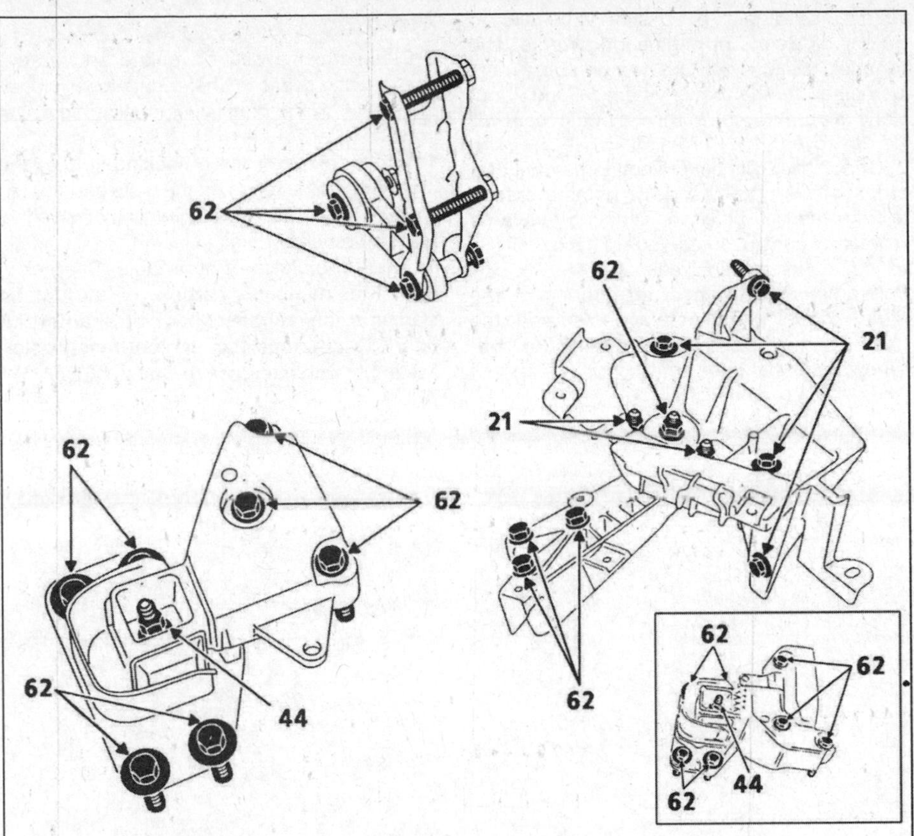

12.2 Torque wrench settings (in Nm) of the engine mountings

12 Engine/transmission mountings – inspection and renewal

Inspection

1 Apply the handbrake, then jack up the front of the car and support it on axle stands (see *Jacking and vehicle support*). Where fitted, remove the engine compartment undershield.

2 Visually inspect the rubber pads on the two front and one rear engine/transmission mountings for signs of cracking and deterioration **(see illustration)**. Careful use of a lever will help to determine the condition of the rubber pads. If there is excessive movement in the mounting, or if the rubber has deteriorated, the mounting should be renewed.

3 Lower the vehicle to the ground.

Renewal

Right-hand front mounting

4 Support the right-hand end of the engine with a trolley jack and block of wood beneath the sump.

5 Unbolt the mounting brackets from the engine and inner wing panel and remove the guard plate **(see illustrations)**.

6 Fit the new mounting using a reversal of the removal procedure, but tighten the nuts/bolts to the specified torque wrench settings.

Left-hand front mounting

7 Remove the air inlet ducts from the left-hand side of the engine as applicable, for access to the engine/transmission left-hand mounting. Remove the battery as described in Chapter 5A.

8 Support the left-hand end of the transmission with a trolley jack and block of wood beneath the sump.

9 Unbolt the mounting brackets from the transmission and inner wing panel.

10 Fit the new mounting using a reversal of the removal procedure, but tighten the nuts/bolts to the specified torque wrench setting.

Rear mounting

11 Apply the handbrake, then jack up the front of the vehicle and support it on axle stands (see *Jacking and vehicle support*).

12 Unbolt the link bar from the transmission or bracket, and from the subframe **(see illustration)**.

13 Where applicable, unbolt the bracket from the transmission.

14 Fit the new mounting using a reversal of the removal procedure, but tighten the nuts/bolts to the specified torque setting.

13 Flywheel/driveplate – removal, inspection and refitting

Note: *Removal of the flywheel or driveplate requires the engine and transmission assembly to be removed as described in Chapter 2D so that the engine and transmission can separated on the bench.*

Removal

1 Remove the manual gearbox or automatic transmission as described in Chapter 7A or 7B.

2 On manual gearbox models, remove the clutch as described in Chapter 6.

3 Mark the flywheel/driveplate in relation to the crankshaft to aid refitting. Note that the flywheel/driveplate can only be refitted in one position, as the bolts are unequally spaced.

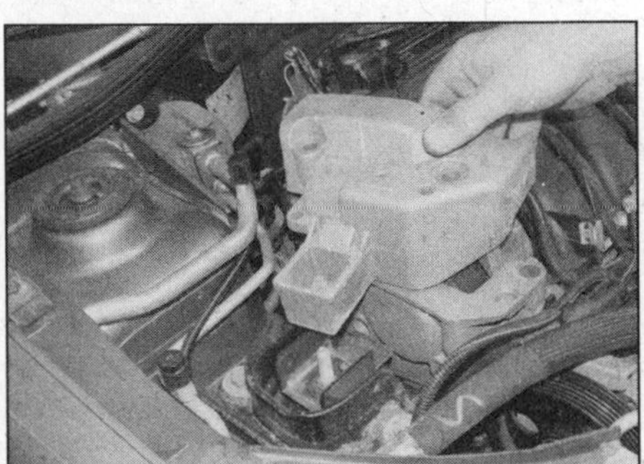

12.5a Removing the right-hand front engine mounting . . .

12.5b . . . and guard plate

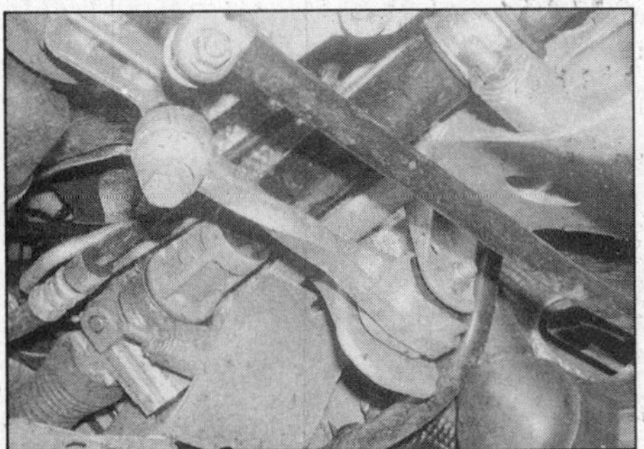

12.12 Engine rear mounting link

4 The flywheel/driveplate must now be held stationary while the bolts are loosened. To do this, locate a long bolt in one of the transmission-to-engine mounting bolt holes, and either insert a wide-bladed screwdriver in the starter ring gear, or use a piece of bent metal bar engaged with the ring gear.

5 Unscrew the mounting bolts, and withdraw the flywheel/driveplate; be careful – it is heavy.

Inspection

6 Examine the flywheel/driveplate for wear or chipping of the ring gear teeth. If the ring gear is worn or damaged, it may be possible to renew it separately, but this job is best left to a Renault dealer or engineering works. The temperature to which the new ring gear must be heated for installation is critical and, if not done accurately, the hardness of the teeth will be destroyed.

7 Check the flywheel/driveplate carefully for signs of distortion, and for hairline cracks around the bolt holes, or radiating outwards from the centre. If damage of this sort is found, it must be renewed.

8 Examine the flywheel for scoring of the clutch face. If the clutch face is scored, the flywheel may be machined until flat, but renewal is preferable.

Refitting

9 Clean the flywheel/driveplate and crankshaft mating surfaces, then locate the flywheel/driveplate on the crankshaft, making sure that any previously-made marks are aligned.

10 Apply a few drops of locking fluid to the mounting bolt threads, fit the bolts and tighten them in a diagonal sequence to the specified torque wrench setting.

11 Refit the clutch, if applicable (Chapter 6) and the manual gearbox or automatic transmission as described in Chapter 7A or 7B, then refit the engine/transmission assembly with reference to Chapter 2D.

Chapter 2 Part C:
Diesel engine in-car repair procedures

Contents

Degrees of difficulty

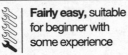

Easy, suitable for novice with little experience 	**Fairly easy,** suitable for beginner with some experience 	**Fairly difficult,** suitable for competent DIY mechanic 	**Difficult,** suitable for experienced DIY mechanic	**Very difficult,** suitable for expert DIY or professional 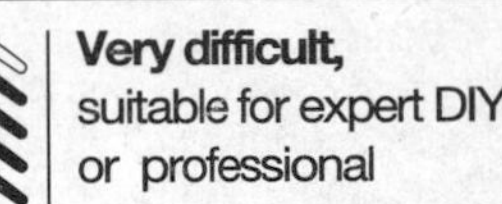

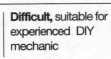

Specifications

General

Type	Four-cylinder, in-line, single overhead camshaft
Designation	K9K 700 (65), 702 (80), 704 (65), 710 (65) or 712 (100)
Capacity	1461 cc
Bore	76.0 mm
Stroke	80.5 mm
Firing order	1-3-4-2 (No 1 cylinder at flywheel end)
Direction of crankshaft rotation	Clockwise viewed from timing belt end
Compression ratio	18.25:1

Compression pressures

Engine warm – approximately 80°C:	
Minimum pressure	20 bars
Maximum difference between cylinders	4 bars

Camshaft

Drive	Toothed belt
Number of bearings	6
Camshaft endfloat	0.08 to 0.178 mm

Valve clearances

Inlet	0.20 + 0.05 – 0.075 mm
Exhaust	0.40 + 0.05 – 0.075 mm

Lubrication system

System pressure (at 80°C):		
At 1000 rpm	2.0 bars minimum	
At 3000 rpm	3.5 bars minimum	
Oil pump type	Gear-type, chain-driven off the crankshaft right-hand end	
Oil pump clearances:	**Minimum**	**Maximum**
Gear-to-body	0.110 mm	0.249 mm
Gear endfloat	0.020 mm	0.086 mm
Oil level sensor resistance	6.0 to 20 ohms	

Torque wrench settings

	Nm	lbf ft
Air conditioning compressor	21	15
Alternator	21	15
Big-end bearing caps:		
Stage 1	20	15
Stage 2	Angle-tighten a further 45° ± 6°	
Brake vacuum pump	21	15
Camshaft bearing caps	10	7
Camshaft sprocket:		
Stage 1	30	22
Stage 2	Angle-tighten a further 84°	
Clutch	8	6
Crankshaft main bearing caps:		
Stage 1	27	20
Stage 2	Angle-tighten a further 47°	
Crankshaft pulley bolt:		
Stage 1	20	15
Stage 2	Angle-tighten a further 130° ± 15°	
Cylinder block TDC blanking plug	20	15
Cylinder head bolts*:		
Stage 1	25	18
Stage 2	Angle-tighten a further 255° ± 10°	
Cylinder head coolant outlet	10	7
Engine right-hand cover:		
Stage 1 – bolts 1 and 6	8	6
Stage 2 – bolts 2 to 5 followed by 1 and 6	12	9
Engine/transmission mountings:		
Right-hand mounting to engine/body	62	46
Right-hand mounting central nut	37	27
Left-hand mounting to transmission	62	46
Left-hand mounting to body	21	15
Left-hand mounting central nut	62	46
Rear mounting link to subframe	62	46
Rear mounting link to transmission	105	77
Exhaust gas recirculation valve	21	15
Exhaust manifold	26	19
Flywheel*	52	38
Front suspension subframe:		
Front	62	46
Rear	105	77
Glow plugs	15	11
Heat exchanger connector	45	33
High-pressure fuel pump	21	15
High-pressure fuel pump sprocket:		
Stage 1	15	11
Stage 2	Angle-tighten a further 60° ± 10°	
High-pressure pipe	38	28
High-pressure rail	28	21
Injector flanges	28	21
Knock sensor	20	15
Multifunction support	40	30
Oil filter body	45	33
Oil level sensor	22	16
Oil pressure sensor	22	16
Oil pump	25	18
Roadwheel bolts	90	66
Sump (refer to text):		
Stage 1 – bolts 1 to 8	8	6
Stage 2 – bolts 1 to 8	15	11
Stage 3 – bolts 9 to 20 followed by 1 and 2	8	6
Stage 4 – bolts 9 to 20 followed by 1 and 2	15	11
Timing belt tensioner	25	18
Turbocharger oil delivery pipe	23	17
Turbocharger oil return pipe	9	7
Turbocharger-to-exhaust manifold	26	19
Valve cover	10	7
Water pump inlet pipe	20	15
Water pump	11	8

* **Note:** *Use new bolts.*

1 General information

How to use this Chapter

1 This Part of Chapter 2 is devoted to in-car repair procedures for the 1.5 litre diesel engine. Similar information covering the other engine types can be found in Parts A and B. All procedures concerning engine removal and refitting, and engine block/cylinder head overhaul can be found in Part D of this Chapter.

2 Refer to *Vehicle identification numbers* in the Reference Section at the end of this manual for details of engine code locations.

3 Most of the operations included in this Part are based on the assumption that the engine is still installed in the car. Therefore, if this information is being used during a complete engine overhaul, with the engine already removed, many of the steps included here will not apply.

Engine description

4 The engine is of four-cylinder, in-line, single overhead camshaft type, mounted transversely at the front of the vehicle.

5 The cylinder block is of cast iron with conventional dry liners bored directly into the cylinder block. The crankshaft is supported in five shell-type main bearings. Thrust washers are fitted to No 3 main bearing to control crankshaft endfloat.

6 The connecting rods are attached to the crankshaft by 'cracked' horizontally split shell-type big-end bearings and to the pistons by gudgeon pins. The gudgeon pins are fully-floating and are retained by circlips. The aluminium alloy pistons are fitted with three piston rings, comprising two compression rings and a scraper-type oil control ring.

7 The single overhead camshaft is mounted directly in the cylinder head, and is driven by the crankshaft via a toothed timing belt.

8 The camshaft operates the valves via inverted bucket-type tappets, which operate in bores machined directly in the cylinder head. The valve clearances are adjusted by changing the tappet buckets which are available in 25 different thicknesses. The inlet and exhaust valves are mounted vertically in the cylinder head and are each closed by a single valve spring.

9 The high-pressure fuel injection pump is driven by the timing belt and is described in further detail in Chapter 4B.

10 A semi-closed crankcase ventilation system is employed, and crankcase fumes are drawn from the cylinder block and passed via a hose to the inlet tract (see Chapter 4C for further details).

11 Engine lubrication is by pressure feed from a gear-type oil pump located beneath the crankshaft. Engine oil is fed through an externally-mounted oil filter to the main oil gallery feeding the crankshaft, auxiliary shaft (where fitted) and camshaft. Oil spray jets are fitted to the cylinder block to supply oil to the underside of the pistons. An oil cooler is mounted between the oil filter and the cylinder block.

Operations with engine in place

12 The following operations can be carried out without having to remove the engine from the vehicle:

a) Removal and refitting of the cylinder head.
b) Removal and refitting of the timing belt and sprockets.
c) Renewal of the camshaft oil seals.
d) Removal and refitting of the camshaft.
e) Removal and refitting of the sump.
f) Removal and refitting of the connecting rods and pistons.*
g) Removal and refitting of the oil pump.
h) Renewal of the crankshaft oil seals.
i) Renewal of the engine mountings.
j) Removal and refitting of the flywheel.

** Although the operation marked with an asterisk can be carried out with the engine in the car after removal of the sump, it is better for the engine to be removed in the interests of cleanliness and improved access. For this reason, the procedure is described in Chapter 2D.*

2 Compression and leakdown tests – description and interpretation

Compression test

Note: *A compression tester specifically designed for diesel engines must be used for this test.*

1 When engine performance is down, or if misfiring occurs which cannot be attributed to a fault in the fuel system, a compression test can provide diagnostic clues as to the engine's condition. If the test is performed regularly it can give warning of trouble before any other symptoms become apparent.

2 A compression tester is connected to an adaptor which screws into the glow plug hole. It is unlikely to be worthwhile buying such a tester for occasional use, but it may be possible to borrow or hire one – if not, have the test performed by a garage.

3 Unless specific instructions to the contrary are supplied with the tester, observe the following points:

a) The battery must be in a good state of charge, the air filter must be clean and the engine should be at normal operating temperature.
b) All the glow plugs must be removed before starting the test and the wiring disconnected from the injectors.

4 There is no need to hold the accelerator pedal down during the test because the diesel engine air inlet is not throttled.

5 The actual compression pressures measured are not so important as the balance between cylinders. Values are given in the Specifications.

6 The cause of poor compression is less easy to establish on a diesel engine than on a petrol one. The effect of introducing oil into the cylinders ('wet' testing) is not conclusive, because there is a risk that the oil will sit in the swirl chamber or in the recess on the piston crown instead of passing to the rings. However, the following can be used as a rough guide to diagnosis.

7 All cylinders should produce very similar pressures; any difference greater than that specified indicates the existence of a fault. Note that the compression should build-up quickly in a healthy engine; low compression on the first stroke, followed by gradually increasing pressure on successive strokes, indicates worn piston rings. A low compression reading on the first stroke, which does not build-up during successive strokes, indicates leaking valves or a blown head gasket (a cracked head could also be the cause).

8 A low reading from two adjacent cylinders is almost certainly due to the head gasket having blown between them.

Leakdown test

9 A leakdown test measures the rate at which compressed air fed into the cylinder is lost. It is an alternative to a compression test and in many ways it is better, since the escaping air provides easy identification of where pressure loss is occurring (piston rings, valves or head gasket).

10 The equipment needed for leakdown testing is unlikely to be available to the home mechanic. If poor compression is suspected, have the test performed by a suitably-equipped garage.

3 Engine assembly/valve timing holes – general information and usage

Note: *Special Renault timing tools are required for this work, or tools obtained from an automotive accessory shop.*

Caution: Do not attempt to rotate the engine whilst the crankshaft and camshaft timing pins are in position. If the engine is to be left in this state for a long period of time, it is a good idea to place suitable warning notices inside the vehicle, and in the engine compartment. This will reduce the possibility of the engine being accidentally cranked on the starter motor, which would cause considerable damage.

1 Top Dead Centre (TDC) is the highest point in the cylinder that each piston reaches as the crankshaft turns. Each piston reaches TDC at the end of the compression stroke and again at the end of the exhaust stroke; however, for the purpose of timing the engine, TDC refers to the position of No 1 piston at the end of its compression stroke. No 1 piston is at the flywheel end of the engine.

3.13 Fitting the crankshaft TDC pin

3.14 Fitting the camshaft TDC pin

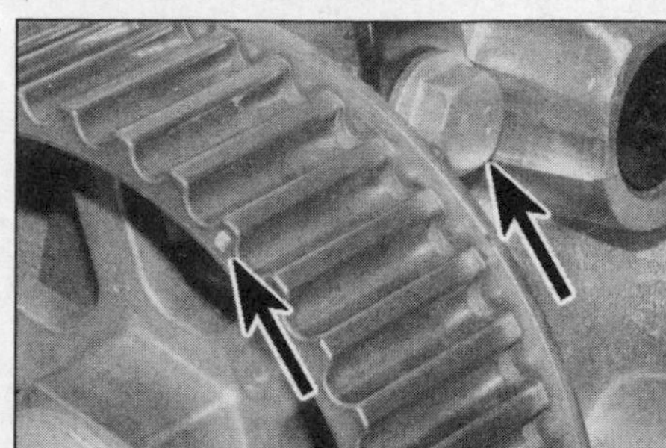
3.15 The mark on the high-pressure pump sprocket must be aligned with the bolt head on the cylinder head

2 When No 1 piston is at TDC, the timing hole in the camshaft sprocket will be aligned with the hole in the cylinder head so that the timing pin can be inserted. Additionally, if the crankshaft timing pin is fully screwed into the cylinder block, it will just contact the timing flat on the crankshaft web.

3 Setting the TDC timing is necessary to ensure that the valve timing is maintained during operations that require removal and refitting of the timing belt. Note that the engine does not have a conventional diesel injection pump, however, it is still necessary to align a mark on the pump sprocket with a bolt head on the cylinder head.

4 To set the engine at TDC, the right-hand engine mounting support and cover must be removed for access to the camshaft sprocket. First jack up the right-hand front of the car and support on axle stands. Remove the front right wheel, engine undertray and wheel arch liner.

5 Remove the auxiliary drivebelt with reference to Chapter 1B.

6 Support the right-hand end of the engine with a support bar across the engine compartment, with a hoist, or alternatively with a jack and block of wood beneath the sump. Unbolt the right-hand engine mounting from the engine and body, and unclip the upper timing cover.

7 Unbolt the high-pressure pump position sensor from the lower timing cover.

8 Release the fuel pipes from the support clips, then remove the lower timing cover by releasing the clips and pulling out the plastic bolt. If necessary, slightly raise the engine to facilitate removal of the timing cover.

9 Unbolt and remove the engine mounting support bracket.

10 Unscrew and remove the plug from the TDC hole on the left-hand front of the cylinder block.

11 The crankshaft must now be turned using a spanner on the crankshaft pulley bolt. To enable the engine to be turned more easily, remove the glow plugs (Chapter 5C) or the fuel injectors (Chapter 4B). Before removing the injectors, consider that Renault stipulate the high-pressure fuel lines must be renewed after removing them. New high-pressure fuel lines are expensive.

12 Turn the crankshaft clockwise until the timing hole in the camshaft sprocket is approaching the hole in the cylinder head.

13 Insert and tighten the special TDC pin into the cylinder block timing hole **(see illustration)**. **Note:** *If the pin is not available, an alternative method of determining the TDC position is to use a dial gauge on the top of piston No 1 after removing the fuel injector or glow plug.*

14 Slowly turn the crankshaft clockwise until its web contacts the timing pin. Now insert the remaining timing pin through the hole in the camshaft sprocket and into the cylinder head **(see illustration)**. The engine is now positioned with No 1 piston at TDC on its compression stroke.

15 Check that the mark on the high-pressure injection pump sprocket is aligned with the bolt head on the cylinder head **(see illustration)**.

16 On completion, remove the timing pins and refit all removed components.

4.2 Disconnecting the crankcase ventilation hose from the valve cover

4.4 Valve cover retaining bolts

4 Valve clearances – checking and adjustment

Note: *This operation is not part of the maintenance schedule. It should be undertaken if noise from the valve gear becomes evident, or if loss of performance gives cause to suspect that the clearances may be incorrect. Adjustment involves removing the camshaft and changing the tappet buckets which are available in 25 different thicknesses.*

Checking

1 Loosen the clip and disconnect the air hose from the rear of the air filter. Unscrew the mounting bolt and remove the air filter assembly.

2 Disconnect the crankcase ventilation hose from the valve cover **(see illustration)**.

3 Release the fuel return pipes from the clips on the valve cover.

4 Unscrew the bolts and remove the valve cover from the top of the cylinder head **(see illustration)**.

5 During the following procedure, the crankshaft must be turned using a spanner on the crankshaft pulley bolt. Improved access to the pulley bolt can be obtained by jacking up the front right-hand corner of the vehicle and removing the roadwheel and the lower wheel arch cover (secured by plastic clips).

6 If desired, to enable the crankshaft to be turned more easily, remove the glow plugs (Chapter 5C) or the fuel injectors (Chapter 4B). Before removing the injectors, consider that Renault stipulate the high-pressure fuel lines must be renewed after removing them. New high-pressure fuel lines are expensive.

7 Draw the valve positions on a piece of paper, numbering them 1 to 8 from the flywheel end of the engine. Identify them as inlet or exhaust (ie, 1E, 2I, 3E, 4I, 5E, 6I, 7E, 8I).

8 Turn the crankshaft until the valves of No 1 cylinder (flywheel end) are 'rocking'. The exhaust valve will be closing and the inlet valve will be opening. The piston of No 4 cylinder will be at the top of its compression stroke, with both valves fully closed. The clearances for both valves of No 4 cylinder may be checked at the same time.

4.9 Using a feeler blade to check the valve clearances

9 Insert a feeler blade of the correct thickness (see Specifications) between the cam lobe and the top of the tappet bucket, and check that it is a firm sliding fit **(see illustration)**. If it is not, use the feeler blades to ascertain the exact clearance, and record this for use when calculating the thickness of the new tappet bucket required. Note that the inlet and exhaust valve clearances are different (see Specifications).

10 With No 4 cylinder valve clearances checked, turn the engine through half a turn so that No 3 valves are 'rocking', then check the valve clearances of No 2 cylinder in the same way. Similarly check the remaining valve clearances in the sequence shown **(see illustration)**.

Adjustment

Note: *A micrometer or dial gauge and probe will be required for this operation.*

11 Where a valve clearance differs from the specified value, the tappet bucket for that valve must be changed with a thinner or thicker one accordingly. On new tappets, the thickness is stamped on the bottom face of the tappet, however, the original tappets do have any thickness stamped on them. It is therefore prudent to use a micrometer or dial gauge to measure the true thickness of any tappet removed, as it may have been reduced by wear **(see illustration)**.

12 To access the tappet buckets, first remove the camshaft as described in Section 8. Remove and refit each bucket separately, to avoid confusion **(see illustration)**.

13 The size of tappet required is calculated as follows. If the measured clearance is less

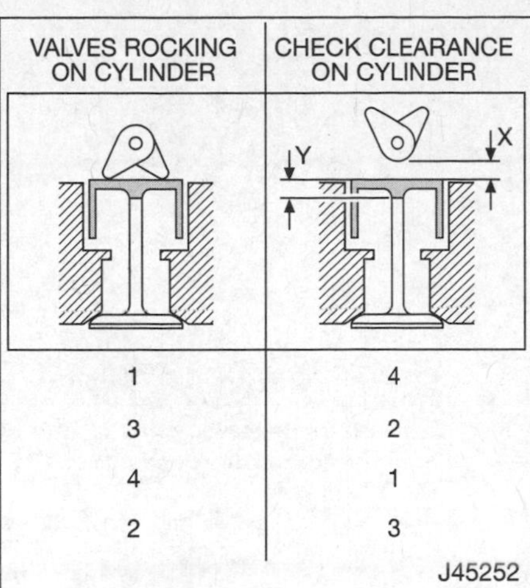

4.10 Valve clearance measurement

X Clearance
Y Tappet thickness

than specified, subtract the measured clearance from the specified clearance, and deduct the result from the thickness of the existing tappet. For example:

Sample calculation – clearance too small
Clearance measured (A) = 0.15 mm
Desired clearance (B) = 0.20 mm
Difference (B – A) = 0.05 mm
Tappet bucket thickness fitted = 3.70 mm
Tappet bucket thickness required =
3.70 – 0.05 = 3.65 mm

14 If the measured clearance is greater than specified, subtract the specified clearance from the measured clearance, and add the result to the thickness of the existing tappet. For example:

Sample calculation – clearance too big
Clearance measured (A) = 0.50 mm
Desired clearance (B) = 0.40 mm
Difference (A – B) = 0.10 mm
Tappet bucket thickness fitted = 3.45 mm
Tappet bucket thickness required =
3.45 + 0.10 = 3.55 mm

15 Working on each separately, lift out the bucket to be renewed, then oil the new one and carefully locate it in the cylinder head **(see illustration)**.

16 Refit the camshaft with reference to Section 8.

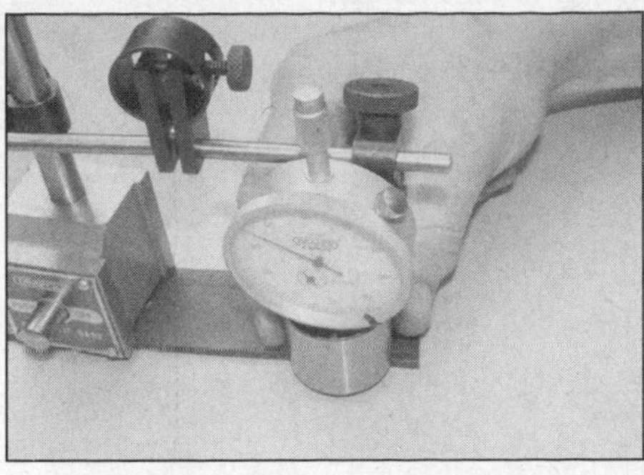

4.11 Using a dial gauge to measure the thickness of the removed tappet

17 Where removed, refit the glow plugs (Chapter 5C) or the fuel injectors (Chapter 4B).

18 Remove the spanner from the crankshaft pulley bolt.

19 Wipe clean the contact surfaces on the valve cover and cylinder head, then apply four beads of sealant, 2.0 mm wide, to the camshaft end bearing caps (Nos 1 and 6) **(see illustration 8.25)**.

20 Refit the valve cover and tighten the bolts to the specified torque in the order given **(see illustration 8.26)**.

21 Secure the fuel return pipes in the clips on the valve cover.

22 Reconnect the crankcase ventilation hose.

23 Refit the air filter assembly and tighten the mounting bolt, then reconnect the air hose.

5 Timing belt – removal, inspection and refitting

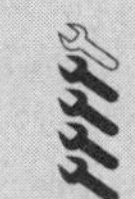

Caution: If the timing belt breaks in service, extensive engine damage will result. Renew the belt at the intervals specified in Chapter 1B, or earlier if its condition is at all doubtful.

Removal

1 Disconnect the battery negative lead (refer to *Disconnecting the battery* in Reference).

2 Jack up the right-hand front of the car and support on axle stands. Remove the front right wheel, engine/radiator undertray and wheel arch liner. Also remove the engine top cover **(see illustrations)**.

4.12 Removing a tappet bucket

4.15 Lubricate the tappet bucket before refitting it

5.2a Removing the engine/radiator undertray . . .

5.2b . . . and engine top cover

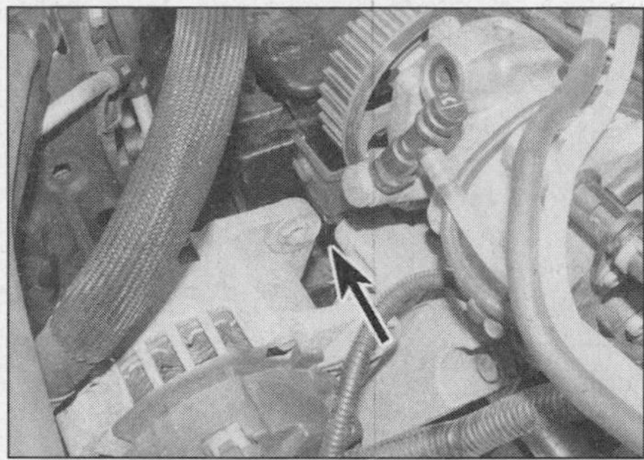

5.3a Swivel the alternator away from the cylinder head for improved access

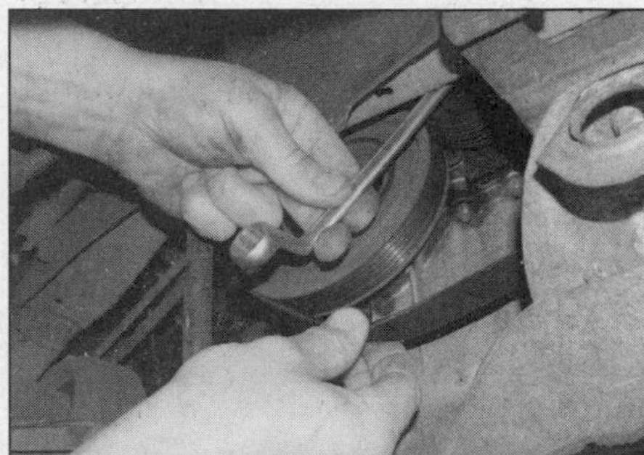

5.3b Removing the auxiliary drivebelt

5.5a Unscrew these bolts . . .

5.5b . . . and remove the right-hand engine mounting . . .

3 Remove the auxiliary drivebelt with reference to Chapter 1B, then unbolt and remove the drivebelt tensioner. For improved access, unscrew and remove the alternator upper mounting bolt and loosen the lower bolt, then swivel the alternator away from the cylinder head **(see illustrations)**.

4 Support the right-hand end of the engine with a support bar across the engine compartment with a hoist, or alternatively with a jack and block of wood beneath the sump. If a hoist is being used, remove the bonnet with reference to Chapter 11.

5 Unbolt the right-hand engine mounting from the engine and body, then release and unclip the plastic upper timing cover **(see illustrations)**. There is no need to unscrew the centre mounting nut.

6 Unbolt the high-pressure pump position sensor from the lower timing cover and disconnect the wiring **(see illustrations)**.

7 Release the fuel pipes from the support clips, then remove the lower timing covers by releasing the clips and unscrewing the plastic bolt **(see illustrations)**. Note that the bolt is refitted by simply pressing it into position. If necessary, slightly raise the engine to facilitate removal of the timing cover.

8 Unbolt and remove the engine mounting support bracket **(see illustration)**.

5.5c . . . then release the clips . . .

5.5d . . . and remove the plastic upper timing cover

5.6a Removing the high-pressure pump position sensor . . .

5.6b . . . and disconnecting the wiring

5.7a Release the fuel pipes from the support clips . . .

5.7b . . . then remove the lower timing covers

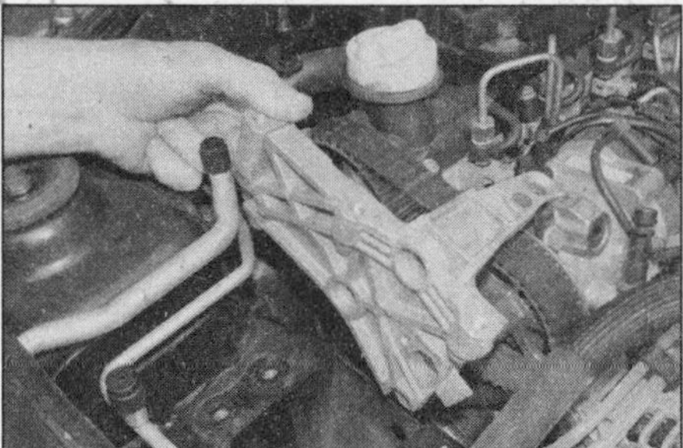
5.8 Removing the right-hand engine mounting support bracket (note the bracket extension is fitted *beneath* the timing belt)

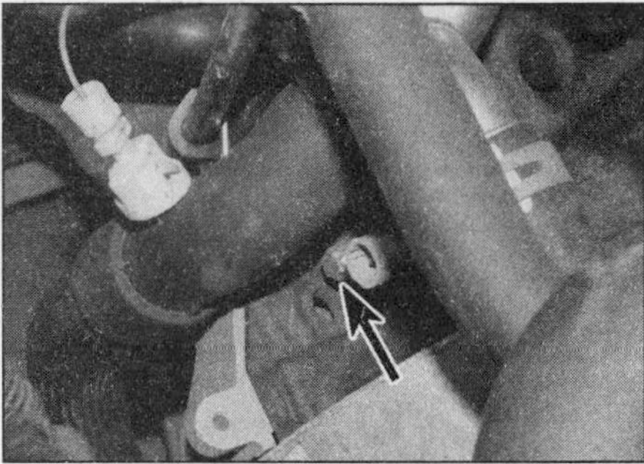
5.9 TDC hole blanking plug

5.13 Using a bolt as a TDC pin through the camshaft sprocket

9 Unscrew and remove the blanking plug from the TDC hole on the left-hand front of the cylinder block **(see illustration).**

10 The crankshaft must now be turned to the TDC position using a spanner on the crankshaft pulley bolt. To enable the engine to be turned more easily, remove the glow plugs (Chapter 5C) or the fuel injectors (Chapter 4B). Before removing the injectors, consider that Renault stipulate the high-pressure fuel lines must be renewed after removing them. New high-pressure fuel lines are expensive.

11 Turn the crankshaft clockwise until the timing hole in the camshaft sprocket is approaching the hole in the cylinder head.

12 Insert and tighten the special TDC pin into the cylinder block timing hole.

13 Slowly turn the crankshaft clockwise until its web contacts the timing pin. Now insert the remaining timing pin (or a suitable bolt) through the hole in the camshaft sprocket and into the cylinder head **(see illustration).** The engine is now positioned with No 1 piston at TDC on its compression stroke.

14 Check that the mark on the high-pressure injection pump sprocket is aligned with the bolt head on the cylinder head.

15 Temporarily remove the timing pins while the crankshaft pulley bolt is being loosened.

16 Before loosening the crankshaft pulley bolt, note that the crankshaft sprocket is **not** keyed to the crankshaft as is the normal arrangement, therefore if the crankshaft pulley is removed it is important to have an accurate method of determining the TDC position of No 1 piston. Although the sprocket is not keyed to the crankshaft, there is still a groove in the crankshaft nose which is at the 12 o'clock position when piston No 1 is at TDC. Unscrew the crankshaft pulley bolt while holding the crankshaft stationary. Have an assistant engage 4th gear and depress firmly the brake pedal. Alternatively, remove the starter motor or where applicable remove the cover plate from the transmission bellhousing, and have an assistant insert a screwdriver or similar tool in the starter ring gear teeth. With the bolt removed, ease the pulley from the crankshaft **(see illustrations).**

17 Reposition the crankshaft at TDC and insert both timing pins again.

18 Loosen the tensioner locknut, then turn the tensioner clockwise to release the tension. If necessary, use a 6.0 mm Allen key in the eccentric hub plate to move the tensioner **(see illustration).**

19 If the original belt is to be re-used (contrary to Renault's recommendation), check if the belt is marked with arrows to indicate its running direction, and if necessary mark it. Similarly, make accurate alignment marks on the belt, corresponding to the timing marks on the camshaft, high-pressure fuel injection pump and crankshaft sprockets. Check that there are 18 inclusive teeth between the timing marks on the camshaft and injection pump sprockets, then release the timing belt from the camshaft sprocket, high-pressure injection pump, water pump pulley, crankshaft sprocket and tensioner **(see illustration).**

20 Do not turn the camshaft or the crankshaft whilst the timing belt is removed, as there is a risk of piston-to-valve contact. If it is necessary to turn the camshaft for any reason, before doing so, turn the crankshaft anti-clockwise (viewed from the timing belt end of the engine) by a quarter turn to position all four pistons half-way down their bores. Leave the TDC pin tightened into the cylinder block.

21 Clean the sprockets, water pump pulley and tensioner and wipe them dry, although do not apply excessive amounts of solvent to the water pump and tensioner pulleys otherwise the bearing lubricant may be contaminated. Also clean the rear timing belt cover, and the cylinder head and block.

Inspection

22 Examine the timing belt carefully for any signs of cracking, fraying or general wear, particularly at the roots of the teeth. Renew the belt if there is any sign of deterioration of

5.16a Unscrew and remove the crankshaft pulley bolt . . .

5.16b . . . and remove the pulley

5.18 Loosen the tensioner locknut . . .

5.19 . . . then release the timing belt

5.26 Align the timing marks on the belt with those on the camshaft and fuel injection pump sprockets

this nature, or if there is any oil or grease contamination. The belt must, of course, be renewed if it has completed the maximum mileage given in Chapter 1B.

23 Thoroughly clean the nose of the crankshaft and the bore of the crankshaft sprocket, and also the contact surfaces of the sprocket and pulley. This is necessary to prevent the possibility of the sprocket slipping in use.

Refitting

24 Check that the crankshaft, camshaft and high-pressure fuel injection pump sprockets are still positioned at TDC, and that the groove in the crankshaft nose is pointing upwards. If the pistons have been positioned half-way down their bores, turn the crankshaft clockwise until the web contacts the TDC tool.

25 Check that the tensioner peg is correctly located in the groove in the cylinder head.

26 Align the timing marks on the belt with those on the camshaft and fuel injection pump sprockets **(see illustration)**, ensuring that the running direction arrows on the belt are pointing clockwise (viewed from the timing belt end of the engine). Note that the belt should be marked with lines across its width to act as timing marks. Fit the timing belt over the crankshaft sprocket first, followed by the water pump pulley, fuel injection pump sprocket, camshaft sprocket, and tensioner. There are 18 inclusive teeth between the timing marks on the camshaft and injection pump sprockets.

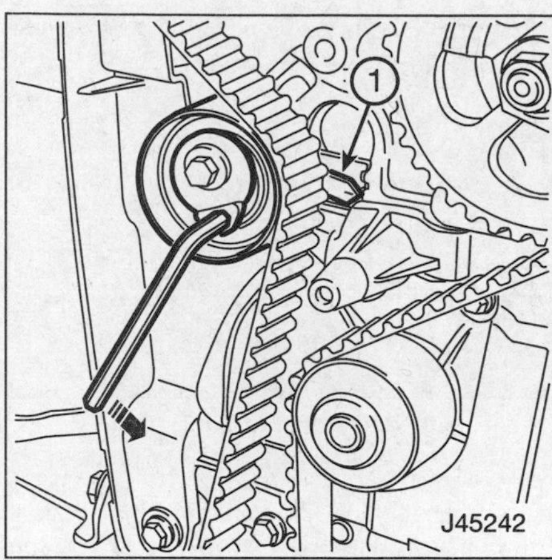

5.27a Pretension the timing belt by positioning the tensioner pointer (1) as shown

27 With the timing marks still aligned, use the 6.0 mm Allen key to pretension the belt by turning the tensioner anti-clockwise until the index pointer is positioned below the timing window **(see illustrations)**. Hold the tensioner stationary and tighten the locknut to the specified torque. This torque is critical, since if the nut were to come loose, considerable engine damage would result.

28 Refit the crankshaft pulley, then insert the bolt and tighten to the specified torque and angle. This can be done with the timing pin still tight in the cylinder block, and the crankshaft web resting against it. After tightening the bolt, remove the timing pins from the cylinder block and camshaft sprocket.

29 Turn the crankshaft two complete turns in the normal direction of rotation, but just before the camshaft sprockets are aligned, refit and tighten the crankshaft timing pin. Slowly turn the crankshaft clockwise until its web is contacting the timing pin, then check that it is possible to insert the remaining timing pin through the hole in the camshaft sprocket and into the cylinder head. If so, remove the timing pins.

30 Hold the tensioner with the Allen key, then loosen the locknut a maximum of one turn, and turn the tensioner clockwise until the index pointer is positioned in the middle of the timing window **(see illustration)**. Tighten the locknut to the specified torque.

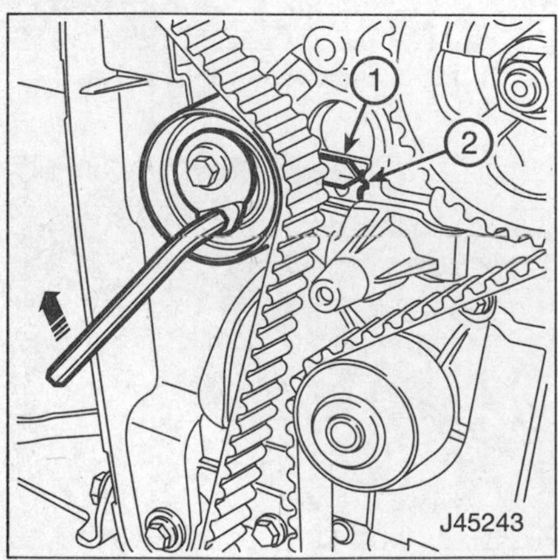

5.30 Position the pointer (1) to its final setting in the middle of the timing window (2)

31 Apply sealant to the threads, then refit the blanking plug to the cylinder block and tighten it to the specified torque.

32 Refit the engine mounting support bracket and tighten the bolts to the specified torque.

33 Refit the lower timing cover and locate the fuel pipes in their clips.

34 Refit the high-pressure pump position sensor on the lower timing cover and tighten the bolts.

5.27b Pretensioning the timing belt

35 Clip the upper timing cover onto the lower cover, then refit the right-hand engine mounting to the engine and body and tighten the bolts to the specified torque.

36 Refit the auxiliary drivebelt with reference to Chapter 1B.

37 Refit the engine undertray and wheel arch liner.

38 Refit the front right wheel and lower the car to the ground. Tighten the wheel bolts to the specified torque.

39 Reconnect the battery negative lead (refer to *Disconnecting the battery* in the Reference Section).

40 If removed, refit the bonnet with reference to Chapter 11.

6 Timing belt sprockets, idler pulley and tensioner – removal and refitting

Crankshaft sprocket

Removal

1 Remove the timing belt as described in Section 5.

2 Slide the sprocket from the crankshaft, noting which way around it is fitted **(see illustration)**.

Refitting

3 Thoroughly clean the nose of the crankshaft and the bore of the crankshaft sprocket, and also the contact surfaces of the sprocket and pulley. This is necessary to prevent the possibility of the sprocket slipping in use.

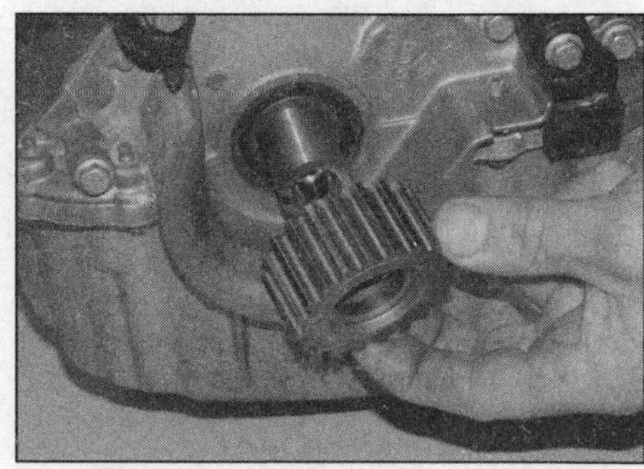

6.2 Removing the crankshaft sprocket

4 Slide the sprocket onto the crankshaft the correct way around.
5 Refit the timing belt as described in Section 5.

Fuel injection pump sprocket

Caution: Do not remove the sprocket described in paragraph 6.
Note: *A suitable puller will be required for this operation.*

Removal

6 Note it is strictly forbidden to remove the high-pressure pump sprocket where it is marked with the number 070 575 **(see illustration)**. All other sprockets may be removed as follows, however, note that if it is being removed for pump renewal, a special Renault tool is available to enable the pump to be removed without removing the timing belt; refer to Chapter 4B for details of the procedure which entails using a sprocket support tool.
7 Remove the timing belt as described in Section 5.
8 Hold the sprocket stationary using a suitable gear-holding tool. Alternatively, an old timing belt can be wrapped around the sprocket and held firmly with a pair of grips. Unscrew and remove the central securing nut.
9 Use a puller to release the sprocket from the taper on the pump shaft. Recover the Woodruff key from the groove in the pump shaft.

Refitting

10 Refitting is a reversal of removal, bearing in mind the following points.
- a) *Ensure that the Woodruff key is correctly engaged with the pump shaft and sprocket.*
- b) *Tighten the sprocket securing nut to the specified torque.*
- c) *Refit and tension the timing belt as described in Section 5. Make sure that the mark on the sprocket is aligned with the bolt on the cylinder head.*

Camshaft sprocket

Removal

11 Remove the timing belt as described in Section 5.
12 Hold the sprocket stationary using a suitable gear-holding tool. Alternatively, an

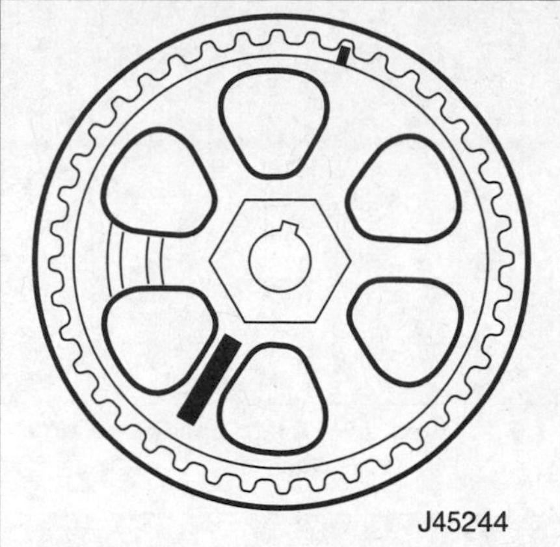

6.6 Do not remove this high-pressure injection pump sprocket marked 070 575

old timing belt can be wrapped around the sprocket and held firmly with a pair of grips. Unscrew and remove the central securing nut.
13 Release the sprocket from the camshaft, noting the integral spline on the sprocket and the corresponding cut-out in the end of the camshaft **(see illustration)**.
14 Recover the Woodruff key from the end of the camshaft.

Refitting

15 Refit the camshaft sprocket, making sure that the integral spline locates in the camshaft cut-out. Insert the bolt and tighten it to the specified torque and angle, holding the sprocket stationary as during removal **(see illustration)**.
16 Refit and tension the timing belt as described in Section 5.

Tensioner

Removal

17 Remove the timing belt as described in Section 5.
18 Unscrew the securing nut and remove the washer and pivot bolt, then withdraw the tensioner assembly from the engine **(see illustration)**.

Refitting

19 Refitting is a reversal of removal. Refit and tension the timing belt as described in Section 5.

7 Camshaft oil seals – renewal

Timing belt end oil seal

Note: *There are two versions of camshaft oil seal fitted* ***(see Chapter 2B, Section 6)****; Version 1 has an internal spring and V-shaped sealing lip, Version 2 has a flat sealing lip without an internal spring. Version 2 is extremely fragile and must only be handled by the protector. The oil seals are not interchangeable and the fitting procedure for each is different, as described in the following paragraphs.*
1 Remove the camshaft sprocket as described in Section 6.
2 Note the fitted depth of the old oil seal. Using a small screwdriver, prise out the oil seal from the cylinder head taking care not to damage the sealing surface on the camshaft. Alternatively, the oil seal can be removed by drilling two small holes diagonally opposite each other and inserting self-tapping screws in them. A pair of grips can then be used to pull out the oil seals, by pulling on each side in turn.
3 Inspect the seal rubbing surface on the camshaft. If it is grooved or rough in the area where the old seal was fitted, the new seal should be fitted slightly less deeply, so that it rubs on an unworn part of the surface.

Version 1 oil seal

4 Wipe clean the oil seal seating, then dip the new seal in fresh engine oil, and locate it over the camshaft with its closed side facing outwards. Make sure that the oil seal lip is not damaged as it is located on the camshaft, and if necessary, temporarily wrap some tape around the end of the camshaft to protect it **(see illustration)**.
5 Locate the seal squarely in the cylinder head, then drive it into position using a metal tube or socket which has an external diameter slightly less than that of the bore in the cylinder head **(see illustration)**. Alternatively, the oil seal can be pressed into position using a metal tube, washer and nut.

6.13 Removing the sprocket from the end of the camshaft – note the integral spline

6.15 Removing the timing belt tensioner

6.18 Angle-tightening the camshaft sprocket retaining bolt

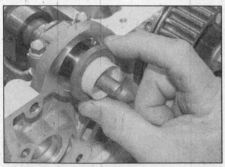

7.4 Locate the new oil seal on the end of the camshaft . . .

7.5 . . . then drive it into position using a socket

7.6a Screw the rod into the end of the camshaft . . .

7.6b . . . locate the new oil seal and protector onto the camshaft . . .

7.6c . . . then tighten the tool to press the seal into position

Version 2 oil seal

6 Renault technicians use a tool (Mot. 1632) to fit the oil seal. The tool consists of a threaded rod, metal tube and nut, and a machined shoulder to locate the protector/ guide on. The rod is screwed into the end of the camshaft, and the protector/guide located on the shoulder. The metal tube is then fitted against the oil seal and the nut tightened to press the seal into the cylinder head/bearing cap **(see illustrations)**. If the Renault tool cannot be obtained, a similar tool can be made out of a threaded rod, metal tube, washer and nut.

7 Wipe clean the oil seal seating, then press the oil seal squarely into position. Note that the Renault tool is designed to locate the seal at the original depth, however, if the camshaft sealing surface is excessively worn, position it less deeply so that it locates on the unworn surface.

8 After fitting the oil seal, remove the protector/guide and tool.

All types

9 Wipe away any excess oil, then refit the camshaft sprocket as described in Section 6.

Flywheel end sealing

10 No oil seal is fitted to the flywheel end of the camshaft. The sealing is provided by a gasket between the cylinder head and the brake vacuum pump housing, and on certain models by an O-ring fitted between the vacuum pump and the housing. The gasket and the O-ring, where applicable, can be renewed after unbolting the vacuum pump from the cylinder head (see Chapter 9).

8.7a Removing the brake vacuum pump and gasket

8.7b Offset drive in the pump which engages the slot in the end of the camshaft

8 Camshaft and tappets – removal, inspection and refitting

Note: *A new camshaft oil seal will be required, and suitable sealant will be required for the camshaft bearing caps and valve cover.*

Removal

1 Removal of the camshaft will normally only be required for access to the tappet buckets (eg, for valve clearance adjustment) or during cylinder head overhaul. For cylinder head overhaul, remove the head as described in Section 9.

2 Remove the camshaft sprocket as described in Section 6.

3 Loosen the clip and disconnect the air hose from the rear of the air filter. Unscrew the mounting bolt and remove the air filter assembly.

4 Disconnect the crankcase ventilation hose from the valve cover.

5 Release the fuel return pipes from the clips on the valve cover.

6 Unscrew the bolts and remove the valve cover from the top of the cylinder head.

7 Remove the brake vacuum pump with reference to Chapter 9. Note the position of the offset drive inside the pump which engages the slot in the end of the camshaft **(see illustrations)**.

8 Using a dial gauge, measure the camshaft endfloat, and compare with the value given in the Specifications **(see illustration)**. This will give an indication of the amount of wear present on the thrust surfaces.

9 If the original camshaft is to be refitted, it is advisable to measure the valve clearances at this stage as described in Section 4, so that any different thickness tappets required can be obtained before the camshaft is refitted.

10 Check the camshaft bearing caps for identification marks, and if none are present, make identifying marks so that they can be refitted in their original positions and the same way round. Number the caps from the flywheel end of the engine **(see illustration)**.

11 Progressively slacken the bearing cap bolts until the valve spring pressure is

8.10 The camshaft bearing caps are numbered from the flywheel end of the engine

8.12 Removing the camshaft from the cylinder head

8.13 Removing the tappets

8.20a Apply 1.0 mm wide beads of sealant to the camshaft end bearing cap-to-cylinder head contact areas as shown

8.20b Apply the beads of sealant . . .

relieved. Remove the bolts and the bearing caps themselves.

12 Lift out the camshaft together with the oil seal **(see illustration)**.

13 Remove the tappets, keeping each identified for position **(see illustration)**. Place them in a compartmented box, or on a sheet of card marked into eight sections, so that they may be refitted to their original locations. If any of the valve clearances measured in paragraph 9 is incorrect, use a micrometer to measure the thickness of the old tappet from its upper surface to the inner surface which contacts the valve stem. Refer to Section 4 and obtain new tappets of the correct thickness.

Inspection

14 Examine the camshaft bearing surfaces and cam lobes for wear ridges, pitting or scoring. Renew the camshaft if evident.

15 Renew the oil seal at the end of the camshaft as a matter of course. Lubricate the lips of the new seal before fitting, and store the camshaft so that its weight is not resting on the seal. Alternatively, the seal may be fitted after refitting the camshaft.

16 Examine the camshaft bearing surfaces in the cylinder head and bearing caps. Deep scoring or other damage means that the cylinder head must be renewed.

17 Inspect the tappet buckets for scoring, pitting and wear ridges. Renew as necessary.

Refitting

18 Oil the tappets (inside and out) and fit them to the bores from which they were removed; where applicable, fit the new tappets to their correct bores.

19 Oil the camshaft bearings. Place the camshaft without the oil seal onto the cylinder head.

20 Wipe clean the upper sealing edge of the cylinder head, then apply four beads of sealant, 1.0 mm wide, to the camshaft end bearing cap (Nos 1 and 6) contact areas as shown **(see illustrations)**.

21 Refit the camshaft bearing caps to their original locations, then insert the bearing cap bolts and progressively tighten them to the specified torque **(see illustration)**.

22 If a new camshaft has been fitted, measure the endfloat using a dial gauge, and check that it is within the specified limits.

23 Fit the new oil seal with reference to Section 7.

24 Refit the brake vacuum pump with reference to Chapter 9.

25 Wipe clean the contact surfaces on the valve cover and cylinder head, then apply four beads of sealant, 2.0 mm wide, to the camshaft end bearing caps (Nos 1 and 6) as shown **(see illustration)**.

26 Refit the valve cover and tighten the bolts to the specified torque in the order given **(see illustration)**.

27 Secure the fuel return pipes in the clips on the valve cover.

28 Reconnect the crankcase ventilation hose.

29 Refit the air filter assembly and tighten the mounting bolt, then reconnect the air hose.

30 Refit the camshaft sprocket as described in Section 6.

8.21 . . . then refit the camshaft bearing caps

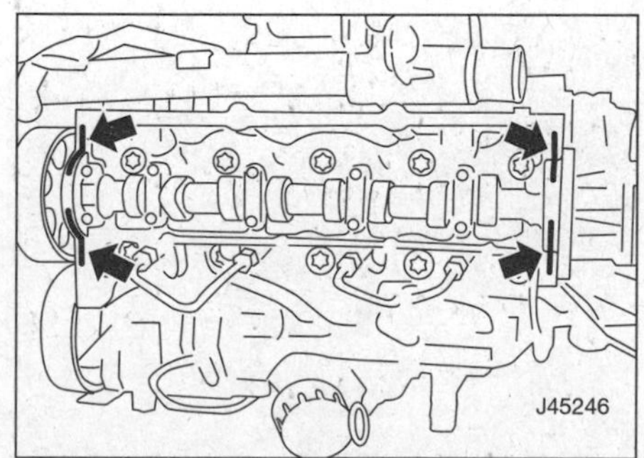

8.25 Apply 2.0 mm wide beads of sealant to the camshaft end bearing caps as shown

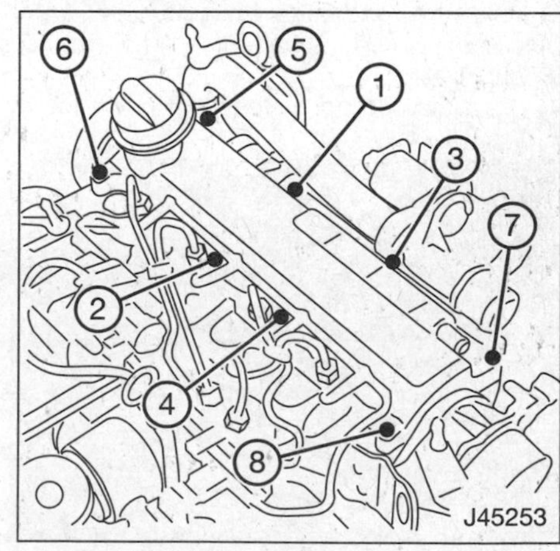

8.26 Valve cover tightening sequence

9.5 Disconnecting the wiring from the coolant temperature sensor

9.8 Releasing the wiring

9.9 Coolant hoses on the left-hand end of the cylinder head

9.12 Removing the timing belt tensioner roller

9.14 Removing the inner timing cover

9 Cylinder head – removal, inspection and refitting

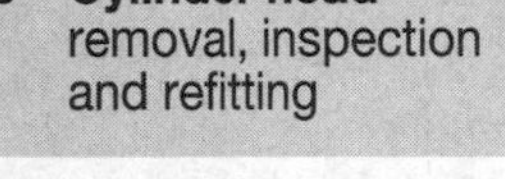

Note: *A new cylinder head gasket must be fitted and all cylinder head bolts must be renewed. Sealant for the valve cover will also be required.*

Removal

1 Before starting work, allow the engine to cool for as long as possible, to ensure the fuel pressure in the high-pressure lines, and the fuel temperature, are at a minimum (refer to Chapter 4B).

2 Disconnect the battery negative lead (refer to *Disconnecting the battery* in the Reference Section).

3 Drain the cooling system with reference to Chapter 1B. Refit and tighten the plug after draining.

4 Remove the timing belt (Section 5) and, if necessary, the camshaft sprocket (Section 6).

5 Disconnect the wiring from the following sensors:

a) Air intake temperature (before turbocharger).
b) Air intake temperature (after turbocharger).
c) Air pressure (after turbocharger).
d) EGR valve control.
e) Air filter.
*f) Coolant temperature sensor **(see illustration).***

6 At the rear of the high-pressure injection pump, disconnect the wiring from the fuel temperature sensor and low pressure flow adjuster.

7 Disconnect the wiring from the four fuel injectors and glow plugs. If necessary, remove the glow plugs from the cylinder head. Before removing the injectors, consider that Renault stipulate the high-pressure fuel lines must be renewed after removing them. If the removal of the cylinder head is just to renew the gasket, leave the injectors in position together with the fuel lines and high-pressure pump. New high-pressure fuel lines are expensive.

8 Release the clip securing the fuel return pipe and wiring, and release the wiring from the lifting eye **(see illustration)**.

9 Remove the hoses and coolant temperature sensor from the left-hand end of the cylinder head **(see illustration)**.

10 Disconnect the exhaust downpipe and detach the catalytic converter from the turbocharger as described in Chapter 4B. Note, however, that the converter cannot be completely removed from the engine compartment, as the right-hand driveshaft is still in position; place or tie it to one side. To remove the turbocharger, unbolt the two support struts.

11 Unscrew the union nuts and remove the turbocharger oil return pipe from the cylinder block and turbocharger.

12 Unbolt and remove the timing belt tensioner roller from the cylinder head **(see illustration)**.

13 Unbolt and remove the auxiliary drivebelt tensioner from the cylinder block.

14 Unbolt and remove the inner timing cover from the cylinder block and head **(see illustration)**.

15 Loosen the clip and disconnect the air hose from the rear of the air filter. Unscrew the mounting bolt and remove the air filter assembly. Also, unbolt the air cleaner support brackets **(see illustration)**.

16 Disconnect the crankcase ventilation hose from the valve cover **(see illustration)**.

17 Release the injector fuel return pipes from the clips on the valve cover **(see illustration)**.

18 Unscrew the bolts and remove the valve cover from the top of the cylinder head **(see illustration)**.

19 Refer to Chapter 4B and observe the precautions necessary when disconnecting the high-pressure fuel injection pipes. In particular, all disconnected pipes and components in the following paragraphs must be plugged to prevent entry of dust and dirt into the fuel system, and all removed high-

9.15 Removing the air cleaner support brackets

9.16 Disconnecting the crankcase ventilation hose from the valve cover

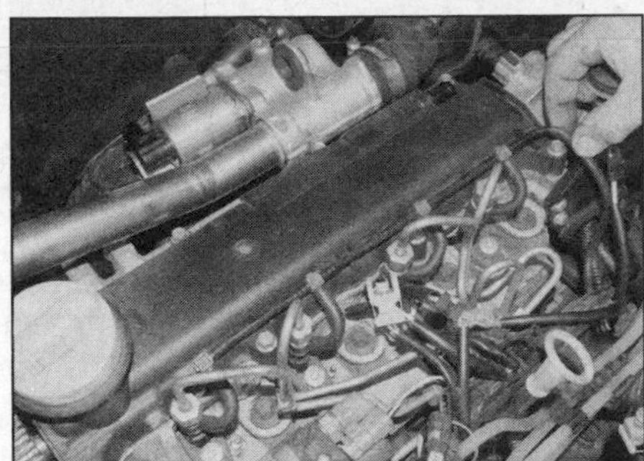
9.17 Removing the injector fuel return pipes

pressure pipes must be renewed after removing (refer to paragraph 7).

20 Loosen the union nuts and disconnect the four high-pressure pipes between the fuel rail and injectors.

21 Loosen the union nut and disconnect the fuel supply pipe from the fuel rail.

22 Disconnect the wiring from the fuel pressure sensor on the fuel rail **(see illustration)**.

23 Disconnect the quick-release vacuum pipe from the brake vacuum pump on the left-hand end of the cylinder head **(see illustration)**.

24 Unbolt the air filter support bracket. Also, unbolt the engine oil level dipstick tube from the cylinder head and remove it from the sump **(see illustration)**.

25 The cylinder head assembly complete with high-pressure pump and ancillaries is very heavy. If they are to be left attached, it is advisable to use a hoist and suitable lifting tackle connected to the lifting eyes to lift the cylinder head. Alternatively, before loosening the cylinder head bolts, remove the turbocharger, manifolds, and high-pressure pump from the cylinder head with reference to the relevant Sections of Chapter 4B.

26 Before removing the cylinder head, turn the crankshaft anti-clockwise (viewed from the timing belt end of the engine) by a quarter turn to position all four pistons half-way down their bores. The TDC pin can remain in the cylinder block if necessary, however, remember that it is in position and do not turn the crankshaft further anti-clockwise.

27 Progressively slacken the cylinder head bolts in the **reverse** sequence to that shown **(see illustration 9.37)**. With all the bolts loose, remove them **(see illustration)**.

28 Lift the cylinder head upwards off the cylinder block **(see illustration)**. If it is stuck, tap it with a hammer and block of wood to release it. **Do not** try to turn the cylinder head (it is located by two dowels), nor attempt to prise it free using a screwdriver inserted between the block and head faces.

29 If necessary, remove the camshaft and tappets (Section 8).

Inspection

30 The mating faces of the cylinder head and block must be perfectly clean before refitting the head. Use a scraper to remove all traces

9.18 Removing the valve cover

of gasket and carbon, and also clean the tops of the pistons. Take particular care with the aluminium cylinder head, as the soft metal is damaged easily. Also, make sure that debris is not allowed to enter the oil and water channels – this is particularly important for the oil circuit, as carbon could block the oil supply to the camshaft or crankshaft bearings. Using adhesive tape and paper, seal the water, oil and bolt holes in the cylinder block. Clean the piston crowns in the same way.

To prevent carbon entering the gap between the pistons and bores, smear a little grease in the gap. After cleaning the piston, rotate the crankshaft so that the piston moves down the bore, then wipe out the grease and carbon with a cloth rag.

9.23 Disconnecting the quick-release vacuum pipe from the brake vacuum pump

9.27 Removing the cylinder head bolts

9.22 Disconnecting the wiring from the fuel pressure sensor on the fuel rail

31 Check the block and head for nicks, deep scratches and other damage. If slight, they may be removed carefully with a file. Machining of the cylinder head or cylinder block is not recommended by the manufacturers.

32 If warpage of the cylinder head is suspected, use a straight-edge to check it for distortion. Refer to Chapter 2D if necessary; if the warpage is more than the maximum, the cylinder head must be renewed, as regrinding is not allowed.

33 Clean out the cylinder head bolt holes in the block using a pipe cleaner, or a rag and screwdriver. Make sure that all oil is removed, otherwise there is a possibility of the block being cracked by hydraulic pressure when the bolts are tightened. Examine the bolt threads in the cylinder block for damage, and if necessary, use the correct-size tap to chase out the threads. The cylinder head bolts must

9.24 Removing the engine oil level dipstick tube

9.28 Using a hoist to lift the cylinder head from the block

9.35 Locate the new gasket on the cylinder block

be renewed each time they are removed, and must not be oiled before being fitted.

Refitting

34 Where removed, refit the tappets, camshaft and camshaft sprocket with reference to Section 8 and 6. Turn the camshaft so that the sprocket is at its TDC position.

35 Ensure that the cylinder head locating dowels are fitted to the cylinder block, then fit the new gasket the right way round on the cylinder block **(see illustration)**.

36 Carefully lower the cylinder head onto the dowels and gasket, then insert the new bolts and hand-tighten. **Do not** oil the threads or heads of the new bolts.

37 Tighten the bolts in sequence, and in the stages given in the Specifications **(see illustration)**.

38 Turn the crankshaft clockwise by a quarter turn until the internal web contacts the TDC timing pin.

39 Refit the turbocharger, manifolds and injection pump to the cylinder head with reference to the relevant Sections of Chapter 4B.

40 Refit the air filter support bracket and tighten securely.

41 Reconnect the vacuum pipe to the brake vacuum pump.

42 Reconnect the wiring to the fuel pressure sensor on the fuel rail.

43 Reconnect the fuel supply pipe to the fuel rail and tighten the union nut.

44 Refit the four high-pressure pipes to the fuel rail and injectors and tighten the union nuts to the specified torque.

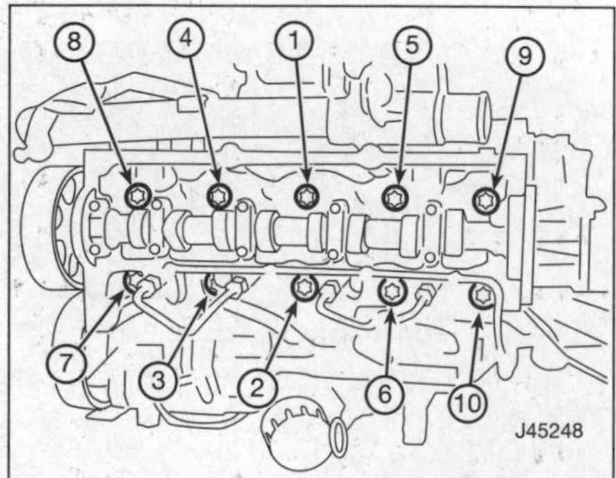

9.37 Cylinder head bolt tightening sequence

45 Wipe clean the contact surfaces on the valve cover and cylinder head, then apply four beads of sealant, 2.0 mm wide, to the camshaft end bearing caps (Nos 1 and 6) and refit the cover with reference to Section 8. Secure the fuel return pipes in the clips on the valve cover and reconnect the crankcase ventilation hose.

46 Refit the air filter assembly and tighten the mounting bolt, then reconnect the air hose.

47 Refit the inner timing cover and tighten the mounting bolts.

48 Refit the auxiliary drivebelt tensioner and tighten the mounting bolt.

49 Locate the timing belt tensioner roller on the cylinder head and hand-tighten the securing nut at this stage.

50 Refit the turbocharger oil return pipe and tighten the union nuts.

51 Refit the turbocharger and reconnect the exhaust downpipe and catalytic converter with reference to Chapter 4.

52 Refit the coolant temperature sensor and coolant hoses.

53 Secure the fuel return pipe and wiring with the clip.

54 Where removed, refit the injectors and glow plugs then reconnect the wiring.

55 Reconnect the wiring to the fuel temperature sensor and low pressure flow adjuster on the rear of the high-pressure injection pump.

56 Reconnect the wiring to the air intake temperature sensors, air pressure sensor, EGR valve and air filter.

57 Refit the timing belt as described in Section 5.

58 Reconnect the battery negative lead (refer to *Disconnecting the battery* in the Reference Section).

59 Prime and bleed the fuel system as described in Chapter 4B.

60 Refill and bleed the cooling system as described in Chapter 1B.

10 Sump – removal and refitting

Removal

1 Disconnect the battery negative lead (refer to *Disconnecting the battery* in the Reference Section).

2 Jack up the front of the vehicle and support on axle stands. Remove the engine compartment undertray and both front wheels.

3 Drain the engine oil referring to Chapter 1B, then refit and tighten the drain plug using a new washer.

4 Remove the right-hand front wheel arch liner (Chapter 11).

5 Undo the front bumper mountings on the front suspension subframe.

6 Set the front wheels straight-ahead, then secure the steering wheel in this position using tape or string. This is necessary to prevent damage to the driver's airbag clock spring and connections located beneath the steering wheel central pad.

7 Push back the gaiter and unscrew the clamp nut and bolt securing the steering column intermediate shaft to the splined steering gear pinion shaft.

8 Refer to Chapter 10 and disconnect the front suspension lower arm balljoints from the swivel hubs. Also, disconnect the steering track rod ends from the steering arms on the swivel hubs.

9 Working under the car, unbolt the link brackets securing the subframe to the underbody on each side.

10 Refer to Chapter 7A and disconnect the gearchange at the transmission end only.

11 Under the rear of the engine, unbolt the rear engine torque link from the transmission and loosen only the bolts securing the link to the subframe.

12 Mark the position of the subframe on the underbody to ensure correct refitting. One way to do this is to spray paint around the subframe mountings using an aerosol; the outline of the mountings will be marked clear on the underbody.

13 Unscrew each subframe mounting bolt in turn and substitute them with lengths of threaded rods and nuts. These are required to lower the subframe approximately 11.0 cm in order to remove the sump. With the rods in position, lower the subframe until the gap between the subframe and body is 11.0 cm. As the subframe is being lowered, disconnect the steering gear pinion from the column intermediate shaft. This is the recommended method, however alternatively the subframe can be lowered onto axle stands or blocks of wood using a trolley jack.

14 Unscrew the oil level sensor from the cylinder block **(see illustration)**. Also, remove the oil level dipstick.

15 Unscrew the bolts securing the sump to the cylinder block. Tap the sump with a hide or plastic mallet to break the joint, then remove the sump. Recover the gasket and discard it as a new one must be used on refitting. If necessary, remove the baffle plate from inside the sump.

Refitting

16 Thoroughly clean the mating surfaces of

10.14 Removing the oil level sensor

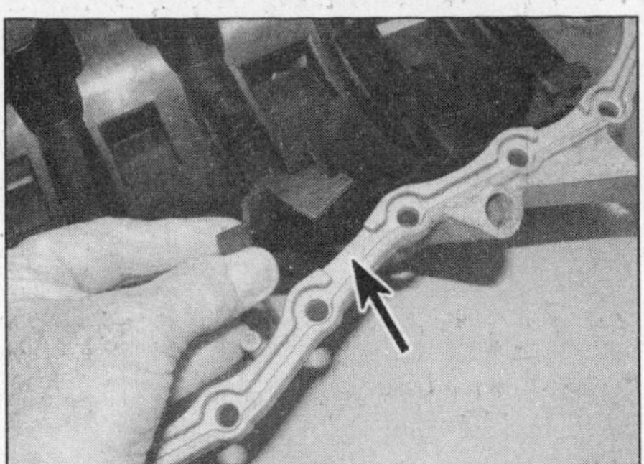

10.16 Make sure the tabs are located in the cut-outs when refitting the baffle plate

10.17a Apply sealant where the right-hand cover meets the cylinder block . . .

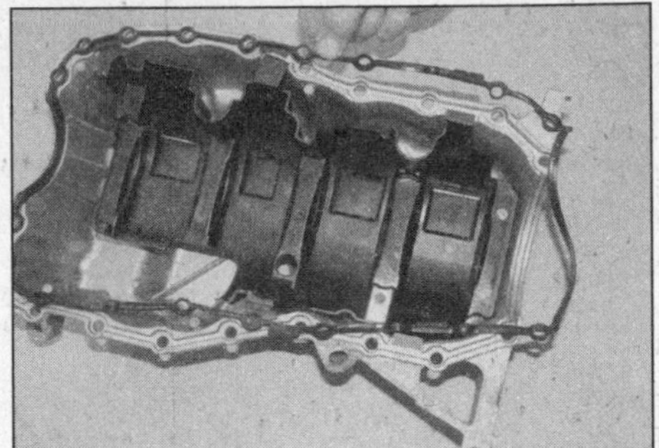

10.17b . . . then locate a new gasket on the sump

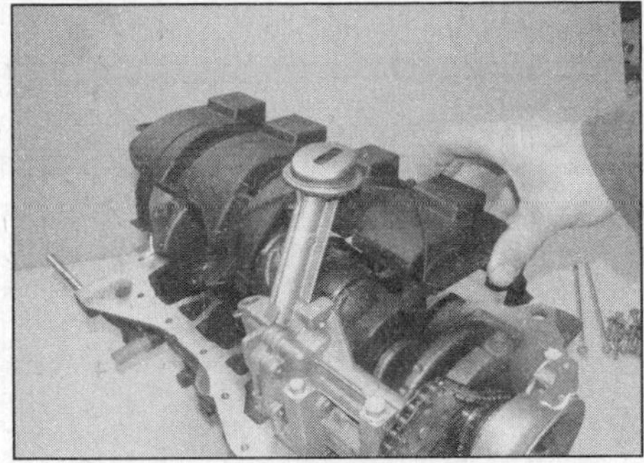

10.18a With the engine inverted, refit the baffle plate . . .

10.18b . . . before refitting the sump

the sump and cylinder block. Where removed, refit the baffle plate making sure that the tabs are correctly located in the cut-outs near the sump joint face **(see illustration)**.

17 Apply some Rhodorseal 5661 (or similar) sealant to the two points where the engine right-hand cover meets the cylinder block, and to the angled areas on the right-hand cover and oil seal housing, then locate a new gasket on the sump. The gasket must be located over the baffle plate tabs **(see illustrations)**.

18 Lift the sump into position on the cylinder block and use a straight-edge to align the flywheel end of the sump with the corresponding end face of the cylinder block. Insert the bolts the use a Torx key to tighten them in sequence to the specified torque, and in the stages given in the Specifications. If the engine is inverted on the bench, it will be easier to locate the baffle plate under the oil pump suction tube before refitting the sump with the new gasket **(see illustrations)**.

19 Refit the oil level dipstick and oil level sensor.

20 Raise the subframe and substitute the threaded rods with the mounting bolts. As the subframe is being raised, make sure that the steering gear pinion locates in the column intermediate shaft correctly (see Chapter 10). With the subframe positioned as previously-noted, tighten the bolts securely.

21 Refit the engine rear torque link and tighten the bolts to the specified torque.

22 Reconnect the gearchange with reference to Chapter 7A.

23 Refit the subframe link brackets and tighten the bolts.

24 Refit the front suspension lower arm balljoints and steering track rod ends with reference to Chapter 10.

25 With the front roadwheels straight-ahead, refit and tighten the bolt securing the intermediate shaft to the steering gear pinion. Locate the gaiter over the shaft, then remove the tape or string from the steering wheel.

26 Refit and tighten the front bumper mountings on the subframe.

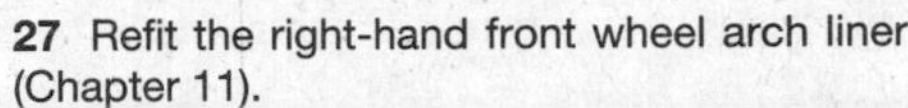

27 Refit the right-hand front wheel arch liner (Chapter 11).

28 Refit the engine compartment undertray and both front wheels, then lower the car to the ground.

29 Reconnect the battery negative lead.

30 Fill the engine with fresh oil with reference to Chapter 1B.

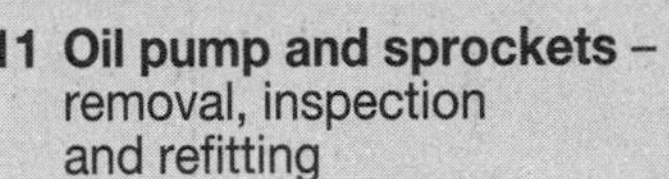

11 Oil pump and sprockets – removal, inspection and refitting

Removal

1 Remove the sump as described in Section 10.

2 Unscrew the two mounting bolts and withdraw the oil pump, tilting it to disengage its sprocket from the drive chain. If the two locating dowels are displaced, refit them in their locations.

3 To remove the drive chain, first remove the crankshaft sprocket as described in Section 6, then unbolt the engine right-hand cover from the cylinder block. Prise out the oil seal with a

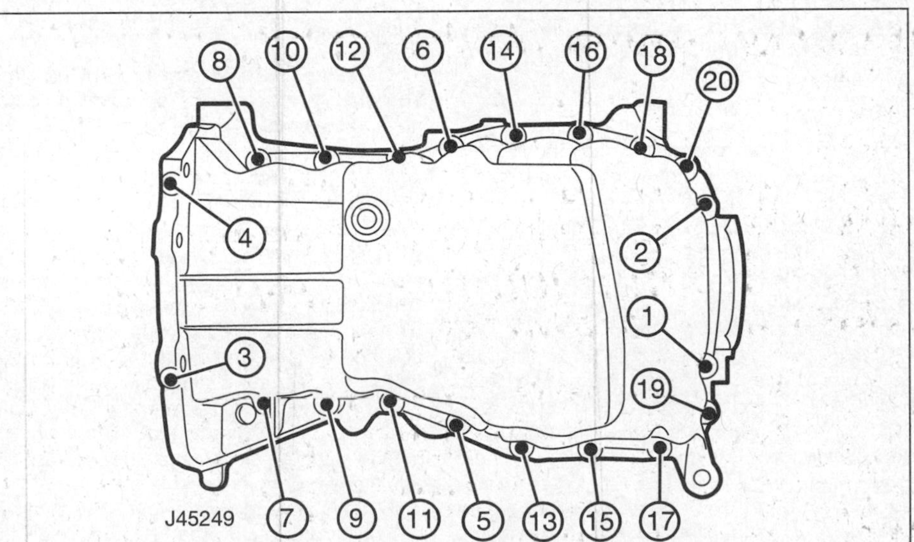

10.18c Sump bolt tightening sequence

11.3 Fitting a new oil seal to the right-hand cover

11.4a Oil pump and mounting bolts

11.4b Removing the oil pump and drive chain

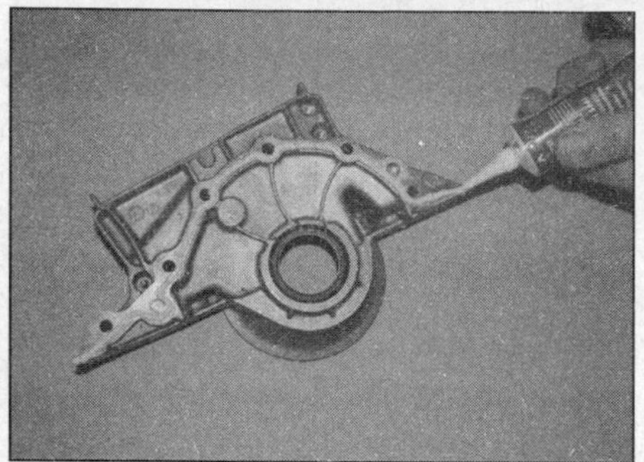

11.13a Apply sealant to the mating faces . . .

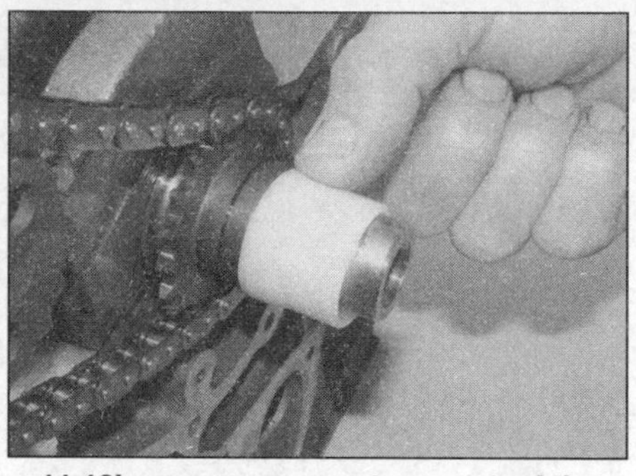

11.13b . . . wrap some tape around the nose of the crankshaft . . .

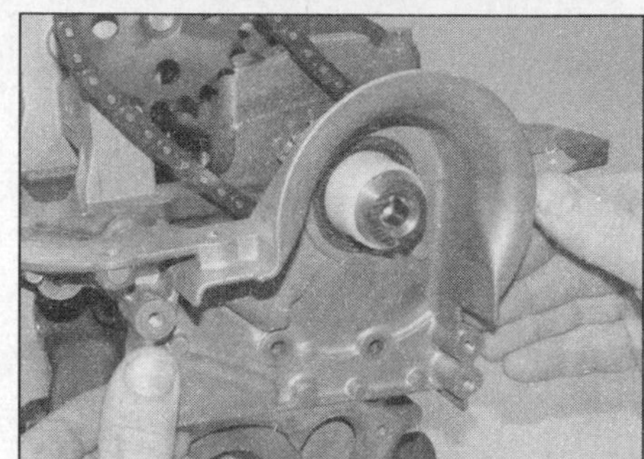

11.13c . . . and fit the right-hand cover

screwdriver, and discard it as a new one must be fitted on reassembly. If necessary, the new oil seal may be fitted with the right-hand cover on the bench **(see illustration)**.

4 Slide the oil pump drive sprocket and drive chain from the nose of the crankshaft **(see illustrations)**. Note that the drive sprocket is not keyed to the crankshaft, but relies on the pulley bolt being tightened correctly to clamp the sprocket. It is most important that the pulley bolt is correctly tightened otherwise there is the possibility of the oil pump not functioning properly.

5 Unhook the drive chain from the drive sprocket.

Inspection

6 Unscrew the retaining bolts and lift the pump cover over the driveshaft. Withdraw the idler gear and the drivegear/shaft. Mark the gears before removal, so that they can be refitted in their original position.

7 Extract the retaining clip and remove the oil pressure relief valve spring retainer, spring, spring seat and plunger.

8 Clean the components and carefully examine the gears, pump body and relief valve plunger for any signs of scoring or wear. Renew the complete pump assembly if excessive wear is evident (no spare parts are available).

9 If the components appear serviceable, measure the clearance between the pump body and the gears using feeler gauges. Also measure the gear endfloat and check the flatness of the end cover. If the clearances exceed the specified tolerances, the pump must be renewed. There should be no discernible wear or distortion of the cover.

10 If the pump is satisfactory, reassemble the components in the reverse order of removal. Fill the pump with oil, then refit the cover and tighten the bolts securely.

Refitting

11 Wipe clean the oil pump and cylinder block mating surfaces and check that the two locating dowels are fitted in the cylinder block.

12 Engage the drive chain with the drive sprocket, then slide the sprocket onto the nose of the crankshaft.

13 Apply a 1.5 to 2.0 mm wide bead of silicone sealant (preferably Renault Threebond) to the right-hand cover sealing face, making sure that the bead runs below the bolt holes. Refit the engine right-hand cover, insert the bolts and tighten them to the specified torque in the stages given. If a new oil seal has already been fitted, wrap tape around the nose of the crankshaft to protect the oil seal, and remove it on completion **(see illustrations)**. First pretighten the bolts furthest from the crankshaft (Nos 1 and 6), then fully tighten the intermediate bolts (2 to 5), and finally fully bolts 1 and 6.

14 Tilt the oil pump and engage the sprocket with the drive chain, then position it on the dowels and insert the two mounting bolts. Tighten the bolts to the specified torque.

15 Refit the sump with reference to Section 10.

12 Crankshaft oil seals – renewal

Timing end cover oil seal

Note: *The new oil seal is extremely fragile and must only be handled by the protector.* ***Do not*** *touch the surface of the oil seal.*

1 Remove the crankshaft sprocket, as described in Section 6.

2 Note the fitted position of the old seal, then prise it out of the right-hand cover/housing using a screwdriver or suitable hooked instrument, taking care not to damage the surface of the crankshaft. Alternatively, the oil seal can be removed by drilling two small holes diagonally opposite each other and inserting self-tapping screws in them. A pair of grips can then be used to pull out the oil seal, by pulling on each side in turn **(see Haynes Hint opposite)**.

3 Inspect the seal rubbing surface on the crankshaft. If it is grooved or rough in the area where the old seal was fitted, the new seal should be fitted slightly less deeply, so that it rubs on an unworn part of the crankshaft surface.

4 Renault technicians use a tool (Mot. 1586) to fit the oil seal. The tool consists of a threaded rod, metal tube and nut, and a machined shoulder to locate the protector/guide on. The rod is screwed into the end of the crankshaft, and the protector/guide located on the shoulder. The metal tube is

HAYNES HiNT

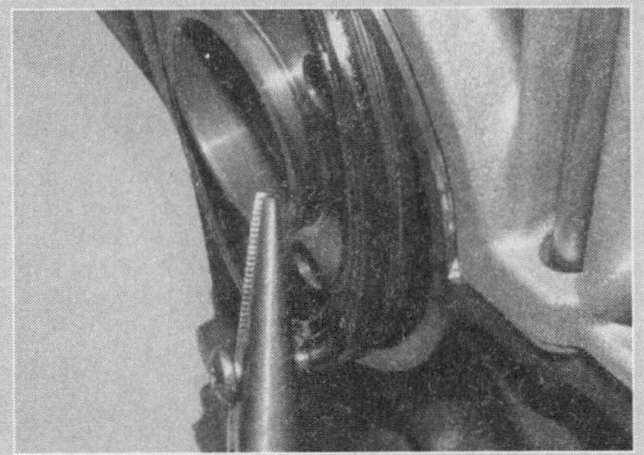

Oil seals can be removed by drilling a small hole and inserting a self-tapping screw. A pair of grips can then be used to pull out the oil seal by pulling on the screw. If difficulty is experienced, insert two screws diagonally opposite each other.

then fitted against the oil seal and the nut tightened to press the seal into the right-hand cover. If the Renault tool cannot be obtained, a similar tool can be made out of a threaded rod, metal tube, washer and nut.

5 Wipe clean the oil seal seating, then press the oil seal squarely into position. Note that the Renault tool is designed to locate the seal at the original depth, however, if the crankshaft sealing surface is excessively worn, position it less deeply so that it locates on the unworn surface.

6 After fitting the oil seal, remove the protector/guide and tool.

7 Refit the crankshaft sprocket as described in Section 6.

Flywheel end oil seal

8 Remove the flywheel as described in Section 13.

9 Renew the oil seal as described in paragraphs 2 to 6 inclusive **(see illustration)**.

10 Refit the flywheel with reference to Section 13.

13 Flywheel – removal, inspection and refitting

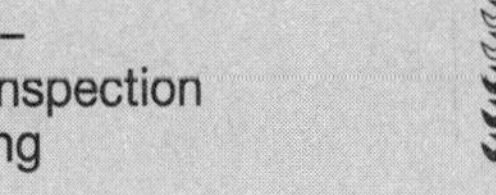

Note: *New flywheel bolts must be used on refitting.*

Removal

1 Remove the manual transmission as described in Chapter 7A.

2 Remove the clutch as described in Chapter 6.

3 The flywheel must now be held stationary while the securing bolts are loosened. To do this, locate a long bolt in one of the engine-to-gearbox mounting bolt holes and insert a wide-bladed screwdriver or length of bent metal bar in the starter ring gear or use a suitable locking tool **(see illustration)**.

4 Unscrew the securing bolts and withdraw the flywheel from the crankshaft. Note that the flywheel bolt holes are offset so that the flywheel can only be fitted in one position. Discard the old bolts as new ones must be used on refitting.

Inspection

5 Examine the flywheel for scoring of the clutch face and for wear or chipping of the ring gear teeth. If the clutch face is scored, the flywheel may be machined until flat, but renewal is preferable.

6 If the ring gear teeth are worn or damaged, the flywheel must be renewed.

Refitting

7 Clean the flywheel and crankshaft faces, then coat the locating face on the crankshaft with Loctite Autoform, or an equivalent compound.

8 Locate the flywheel on the crankshaft and insert the new securing bolts, then tighten them in a diagonal sequence to the specified torque. Hold the flywheel stationary as during removal **(see illustration)**. **Do not** oil the new bolt threads as they are supplied with locking compound.

9 Refit the clutch as described in Chapter 6.

10 Refit the manual transmission with reference to Chapter 7A.

14 Engine mountings – renewal

Inspection

1 Apply the handbrake, then jack up the front of the car and support it on axle stands (see *Jacking and vehicle support*). Where fitted, remove the engine compartment undertray.

13.3 Hold the flywheel stationary using a screwdriver in the starter ring gear

12.9 Fitting a new oil seal to the flywheel end of the crankshaft

2 Visually inspect the rubber pads on the right- and left-hand engine mountings and the rear torque link, for signs of cracking and deterioration. Careful use of a lever will help to determine the condition of the rubber pads. Check that all the mounting bolts are securely tightened; use a torque wrench to check if possible. If there is excessive movement, or if the rubber has deteriorated, the mounting should be renewed.

Renewal

Right-hand mounting

3 Connect a hoist and suitable lifting tackle to the engine lifting brackets to support the engine/transmission assembly while the mounting is removed. Alternatively, the

13.8 Fit new flywheel bolts

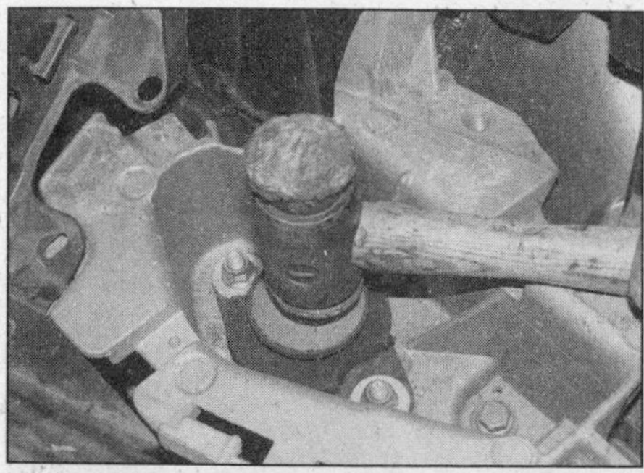

14.14 Use a soft-faced mallet to release the stud from the left-hand mounting bracket

14.22 Removing the engine rear torque link

assembly can be supported using a jack and a suitable block of wood to spread the load under the sump.

4 Unscrew the centre nut securing the engine bracket to the body-mounted bracket.

5 Unscrew the bolts and remove the bracket from the engine, and at the same time unclip the upper timing cover.

6 Unscrew the bolts and remove the mounting/bracket from the body.

7 Locate the new mounting/bracket on the body, insert the bolts and tighten to the specified torque.

8 Refit the bracket to the engine, insert the bolts and tighten to the specified torque.

9 Lower the engine making sure that the bracket locates on the body mounting correctly. Remove the hoist or trolley jack.

10 Refit the centre nut and tighten to the specified torque.

Left-hand mounting

11 For improved access to the mounting, remove the battery as described in Chapter 5A. The battery tray can also be unbolted.

12 With the front of the car supported on axle stands, remove the left-hand roadwheel.

13 Using a jack and block of wood, support the weight of the transmission/engine.

14 Unscrew the centre nut securing the lower mounting to the upper/body bracket, then slightly lower the transmission/engine. If necessary, release the stud from the upper bracket using a soft-faced mallet **(see illustration)**.

15 Unscrew the bolts and remove the upper bracket from the body.

16 Unscrew the bolts and remove the lower mounting/bracket from the transmission.

17 Locate the new mounting/bracket on the transmission, insert the bolts and tighten to the specified torque.

18 Refit the upper bracket to the body, insert the bolts and tighten to the specified torque.

19 Raise the transmission/engine making sure that the mounting stud enters the upper bracket correctly. Refit the centre nut and tighten to the specified torque. Remove the hoist or trolley jack.

20 Refit the battery with reference to Chapter 5A.

21 Refit the roadwheel and lower the car to the ground.

Rear torque link

22 With the car supported on axle stands, unscrew the bolts securing the rear mounting link to the brackets on the subframe, engine and transmission **(see illustration)**. Withdraw the link from under the car.

23 If necessary, unbolt and remove the brackets.

24 Refitting is a reversal of the removal procedure, but before fully tightening the bolts attempt to rock the engine/transmission assembly in order to settle the mountings. Tighten the mounting bolts to the specified torque.

Chapter 2 Part D:
Engine removal and overhaul procedures

Contents

Degrees of difficulty

Easy, suitable for novice with little experience 

Fairly easy, suitable for beginner with some experience 

Fairly difficult, suitable for competent DIY mechanic

Difficult, suitable for experienced DIY mechanic 

Very difficult, suitable for expert DIY or professional

Specifications

General

Engine codes:	
1.2 litre SOHC:	
8-valve petrol engine	D7F
16-valve petrol engine	D4F
1.4 litre DOHC petrol engine	K4J
1.6 litre DOHC petrol engine	K4M
1.5 litre SOHC diesel engine	K9K

Valves

Valve spring free length:	
D7F engine	43.00 mm
D4F engine	40.20 mm
K4J and K4M engine	41.3 mm
K9K engine	43.31 mm

Cylinder head

Height:	
D7F engine	113.5 mm
D4F engine	99.0 mm
K4J and K4M engines	137.0 mm
K9K engine	127.0 mm
Maximum acceptable gasket face distortion	0.05 mm
Refinishing limit	No refinishing permitted
Valve protrusion in relation to head surface	0.00 ± 0.07 mm

Cylinder block

Bore diameter:	
D7F engine:	
Class A	69.000 to 69.015 mm
Class B	69.015 to 69.030 mm
D4F engine:	
Class A	69.000 ± 0.015 mm
Class B	69.015 ± 0.015 mm
K4J and K4M engines:	
Class A	79.500 to 79.510 mm
Class B	79.510 to 79.520 mm
Class C	79.520 to 79.530 mm
K9K engine	N/A

Pistons and piston rings

Piston diameter:	
D7F engine (measured 40.0 mm from crown):	
Class A	68.965 ± 0.005 mm
Class B	68.975 ± 0.005 mm
D4F engine (measured 9.0 mm from bottom of skirt):	
Class A	68.976 ± 0.006 mm
Class B	68.984 ± 0.006 mm
K4J engine (measured 45.7 mm from crown):	
Class A	79.475 ± 0.005 mm
Class B	79.485 ± 0.005 mm
Class C	79.495 ± 0.005 mm
K4M engine (measured 42.0 mm from crown):	
Class A	79.475 ± 0.005 mm
Class B	79.485 ± 0.005 mm
Class C	79.495 ± 0.005 mm
K9K engine (measured 56.0 mm from crown)	75.94 ± 0.007 mm
Piston ring end gaps (installed):	
D7F engine	N/A
D4F engine:	
Top compression	0.20 to 0.35 mm
Second compression	0.35 to 0.50 mm
Oil control	0.20 to 0.90 mm
K4J and K4M engine:	
Top compression	0.15 to 0.35 mm
Second compression	0.40 to 0.60 mm
Oil control (2 rails and expander)	0.20 to 0.90 mm
K9K engine:	
Top compression	0.2 to 0.35 mm
Second compression	0.7 to 0.9 mm
Oil control (2 rails and expander)	0.25 to 0.5 mm
Ring gap spacing (all engines)	120°
Piston protrusion (K9K engine)	0.192 ± 0.093 mm

Crankshaft

Main bearing journal diameter:	
D7F and D4F engines:	
Standard	44.000 mm ± 0.01 mm
1st undersize	43.750 mm ± 0.01 mm
K4J, K4M and K9K engines:	
Standard	47.990 to 47.997 mm
1st undersize	47.997 to 48.003 mm
2nd undersize	48.003 to 48.010 mm
Crankpin (big-end) journal diameter:	
D7F and D4F engines:	
Standard	40.000 +0 – 0.016 mm
1st undersize	39.750 mm +0 – 0.016 mm
K4J, K4M and K9K engines:	
Standard	43.97 ± 0.01 mm
Crankshaft endfloat:	
D7F engine	0.060 to 0.235 mm
D4F engine	0.045 to 0.235 mm
K4J, K4M and K9K engines:	
New	0.045 to 0.252 mm
Maximum	0.852 mm

Torque wrench settings

Refer to Parts A, B, and C of this Chapter.

1 General information

How to use this Chapter

This Part of Chapter 2 is devoted to engine/transmission removal and refitting, to those repair procedures requiring the removal of the engine/transmission from the vehicle, and to the overhaul of engine components. It includes only the Specifications relevant to those procedures. Refer to Parts A, B or C for additional Specifications, and for all torque wrench settings.

General information

The information ranges from advice concerning preparation for an overhaul and the purchase of new parts, to detailed step-by-step procedures covering removal and installation of internal engine components and the inspection of parts.

The following Sections have been written based on the assumption that the engine has been removed from the vehicle. For information concerning in-vehicle engine repair, as well as removal and installation of the external components necessary for the overhaul, see Parts A, B or C of this Chapter.

When overhauling the engine, it is essential to establish first exactly what replacement parts are available. At the time of writing, very few under- or oversized components are available for engine reconditioning (the exception being for the diesel engine). In many cases, it would appear that the easiest and most economically-sensible course of action is to replace a worn or damaged engine with an exchange unit.

2 Engine overhaul – general information

It is not always easy to determine when, or if, an engine should be completely overhauled, as a number of factors must be considered.

High mileage is not necessarily an indication that an overhaul is needed, while low mileage does not preclude the need for an overhaul. Frequency of servicing is probably the most important consideration. An engine which has had regular and frequent oil and filter changes, as well as other required maintenance, will most likely give many thousands of miles of reliable service. Conversely, a neglected engine may require an overhaul very early in its life.

Excessive oil consumption is an indication that piston rings, valve stem oil seals and/or valves and valve guides are in need of attention. Make sure that oil leaks are not responsible before deciding that the rings and/or guides are bad. Perform a cylinder compression check to determine the extent of the work required.

Check the oil pressure with a gauge fitted in place of the oil pressure warning light switch and compare it with the value given in the Specifications. If it is extremely low, the main and big-end bearings and/or the oil pump are probably worn out.

Loss of power, rough running, knocking or metallic engine noises, excessive valve gear noise and high fuel consumption may also point to the need for an overhaul, especially if they are all present at the same time. If a complete tune-up does not remedy the situation, major mechanical work is the only solution.

An engine overhaul involves restoring all internal parts to the specification of a new engine. **Note:** *Always check first what replacement parts are available before planning any overhaul operation – refer to Section 1. Manufacturer main dealers, or a good engine reconditioning specialist/ automotive parts supplier, may be able to suggest alternatives which will enable you to overcome the lack of parts.*

During an overhaul, it is usual to renew the piston rings, and to rebore and/or hone the cylinder bores; where the rebore is done by an automotive machine shop, new oversize pistons and rings will also be installed – all these operations, of course, assume the availability of suitable parts. The main and big-end bearings are generally renewed and, if necessary, the crankshaft may be reground to restore the journals.

Generally, the valves are serviced as well during an overhaul, since they're usually in less-than-perfect condition at this point. While the engine is being overhauled, other components, such as the starter and alternator, can be renewed as well, or rebuilt, if the necessary parts can be found. The end result should be an as-new engine that will give many trouble-free miles. **Note:** *Critical cooling system components such as the hoses, drivebelt, thermostat and coolant pump MUST be renewed when an engine is overhauled. The radiator should be checked carefully, to ensure that it isn't clogged or leaking (see Chapter 3). Also, as a general rule, the oil pump should be renewed when an engine is rebuilt.*

Before beginning the engine overhaul, read through the entire procedure to familiarise yourself with the scope and requirements of the job. Overhauling an engine isn't difficult, but it is time-consuming. Plan on the vehicle being off the road for a minimum of two weeks, especially if parts must be taken to an automotive machine shop for repair or reconditioning. Check on availability of parts, and make sure that any necessary special tools and equipment are obtained in advance. Most work can be done with typical hand tools, although a number of precision measuring tools are required for inspecting parts to determine if they must be renewed. Often, an automotive machine shop will handle the inspection of parts, and will offer advice concerning reconditioning and renewal. **Note:** *Always wait until the engine has been completely dismantled, and all components, especially the cylinder block/crankcase, have been inspected, before deciding what service and repair operations must be performed by an automotive machine shop. Since the block's condition will be the major factor to consider when determining whether to overhaul the original engine or buy a rebuilt one, never purchase parts or have machine work done on other components until the cylinder block/crankcase has been thoroughly inspected.* As a general rule, time is the primary cost of an overhaul, so it doesn't pay to install worn or sub-standard parts.

As a final note, to ensure maximum life and minimum trouble from a rebuilt engine, everything must be assembled with care, in a spotlessly-clean environment.

3 Engine removal – methods and precautions

If you have decided that an engine must be removed for overhaul or major repair work, several preliminary steps should be taken.

Locating a suitable place to work is extremely important. Adequate work space, with storage space for the vehicle, will be needed. If a garage is not available, at the very least a flat, level, clean work surface is required.

Cleaning the engine compartment and engine before beginning the removal procedure will help keep tools clean and organised.

The engine can be removed complete with the transmission and subframe by lowering it from the engine compartment. Alternatively, the transmission can be removed first, then the engine lifted from the engine compartment. An engine hoist will be necessary; make sure the equipment is rated in excess of the combined weight of the engine and transmission. Safety is of primary importance, considering the potential hazards involved in removing the engine/transmission from the vehicle.

If this is the first time you have removed an engine, a helper should ideally be available. Advice and aid from someone more experienced would also be useful. There are many instances when one person cannot simultaneously perform all of the operations required when removing the engine/transmission from the vehicle.

Plan the operation ahead of time. Arrange for, or obtain, all of the tools and equipment you'll need prior to beginning the job. Some of the equipment necessary to perform engine/transmission removal and installation safely and with relative ease, and which may have to be hired or borrowed, includes (in addition to the engine hoist) a heavy-duty trolley jack, a strong pair of axle stands, some wooden blocks, and an engine dolly (a low, wheeled platform capable of taking the weight of the engine/transmission, so that it can be moved easily when on the ground). A complete set of spanners and sockets (as described in the Reference section of this manual) will obviously be needed, together with plenty of rags and cleaning solvent for mopping-up spilled oil, coolant and fuel. If the hoist is to be hired, make sure that you arrange for it in advance, and perform all of the operations possible without it beforehand. This will save you money and time.

Plan for the vehicle to be out of use for quite a while. A machine shop will be required to perform some of the work which the do-it-yourselfer can't accomplish without special equipment. These establishments often have a busy schedule, so it would be a good idea to consult them before removing the engine, to accurately estimate the amount of time required to rebuild or repair components that may need work.

4.2 Removing the wiring loom from the battery guard plate

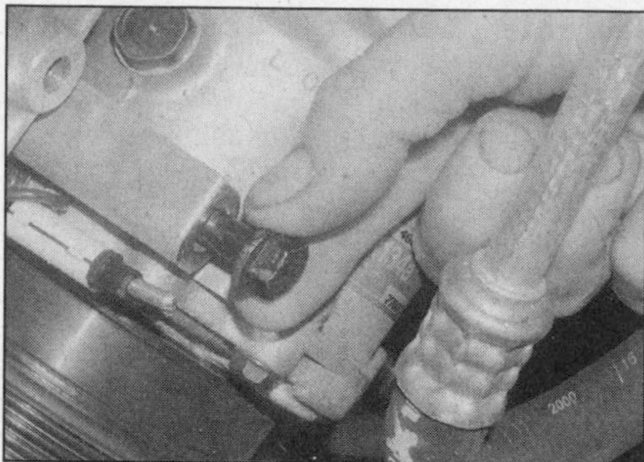

4.3a Unbolting the air conditioning compressor from the engine

4.3b Unbolt the air conditioning condenser from the radiator

4.3c Suspend the air conditioning condenser from the bonnet without disconnecting the refrigerant lines

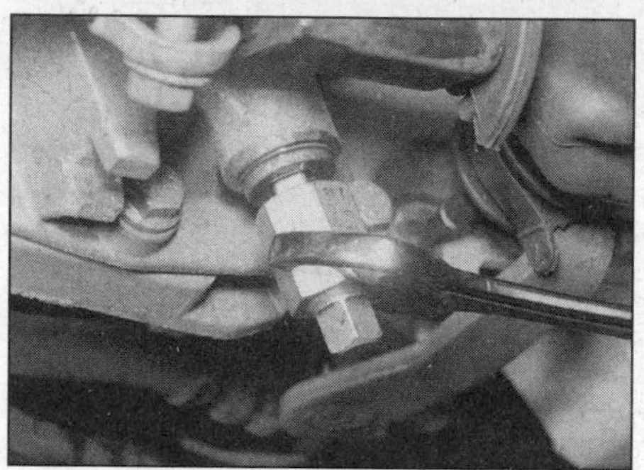

4.4 Unscrewing the drain plug from the manual transmission

4.5 Disconnecting the radiator bottom hose from the water pump pipe

Always be extremely careful when removing and installing the engine/transmission. Serious injury can result from careless actions. By planning ahead and taking your time, the job (although a major task) can be accomplished successfully.

4 Engine – removal and refitting

Note: *Read through the entire Section, as well as reading the advice in the preceding Section, before beginning this procedure. In this procedure, the engine and transmission are removed as a unit together with the subframe, lowered to the ground and removed from underneath, then separated outside the vehicle. However, if preferred, the transmission can be removed from the engine first (as described in Chapter 7A, 7B or 7C) – this leaves the engine free to be either lifted out from above or lowered to the ground.*

Removal

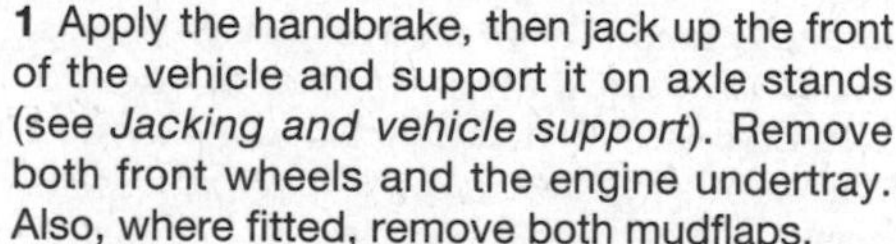

1 Apply the handbrake, then jack up the front of the vehicle and support it on axle stands (see *Jacking and vehicle support*). Remove both front wheels and the engine undertray. Also, where fitted, remove both mudflaps.

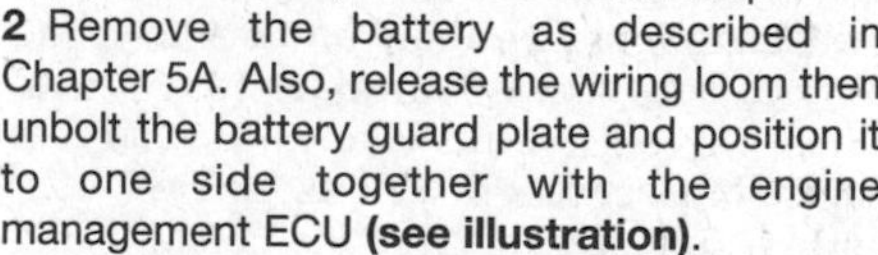

2 Remove the battery as described in Chapter 5A. Also, release the wiring loom then unbolt the battery guard plate and position it to one side together with the engine management ECU **(see illustration)**.

3 On models fitted with air conditioning, the refrigerant circuit must be evacuated by a refrigeration specialist, or alternatively, the compressor can be unbolted from the engine (Chapter 3) and tied to one side while the engine/transmission is being removed. If the radiator is to remain on the subframe when the engine assembly is lowered, also unbolt the condenser from the radiator and tie it to the bonnet **(see illustrations)**.

4 If necessary, at this stage the engine and transmission can be drained of oil/fluid **(see illustration)**.

5 Drain the cooling system as described in Chapter 1A or 1B. To do this, the bottom hose must be disconnected from the radiator or water pump pipe **(see illustration)**.

6 At this stage, either the driveshafts and swivel hubs can remain attached to the subframe and transmission, or alternatively, the front suspension lower arms may be disconnected from the swivel hubs and the driveshafts pulled out of the transmission (refer to Chapter 8).

7 To leave the driveshafts and swivel hubs attached to the subframe and transmission, remove the left- and right-hand brake calipers and tie them to the front suspension coil springs, then remove the ABS sensors (Chapter 9) – do not disconnect the brake hydraulic system. Unbolt the front suspension swivel hubs from the bottom of the struts with reference to Chapter 10; the driveshafts will remain attached to the swivel hubs **(see illustrations)**. **Note:** *The ABS sensors are very often difficult to remove from the swivel hubs, and rather than destructing them, they may be left in the carriers and their wires disconnected at the connectors located just inside the engine compartment.*

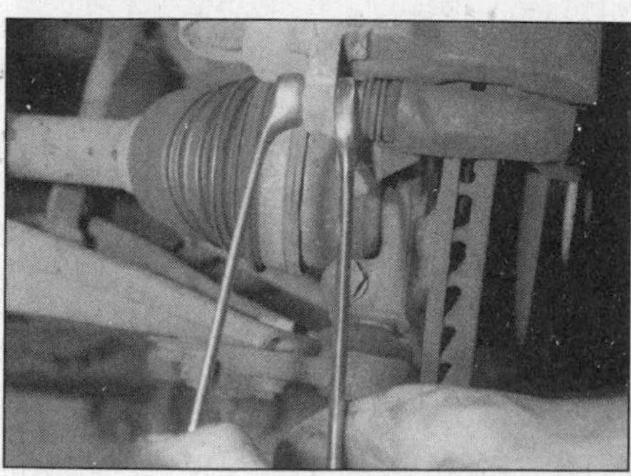

4.7a Unscrew the mounting bolts . . .

4.7b . . . remove the left-hand brake caliper . . .

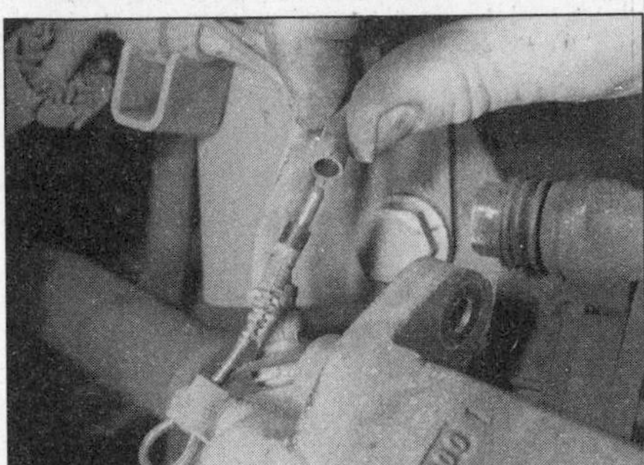
4.7c . . . and disconnect the pad wear warning wiring

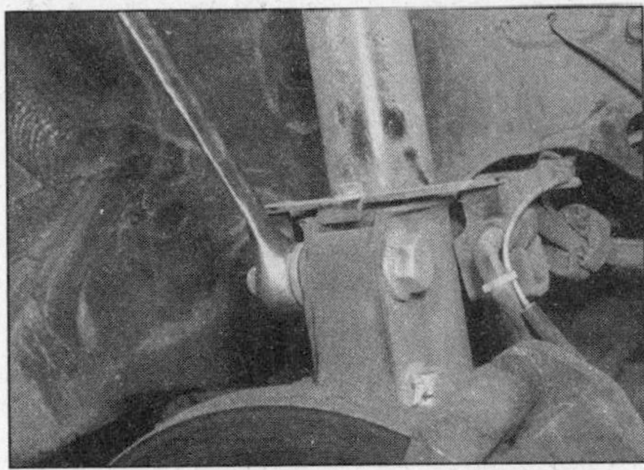
4.7d Unscrew the nuts . . .

4.7e . . . and tap out the bolts securing the swivel hub to the bottom of the suspension strut

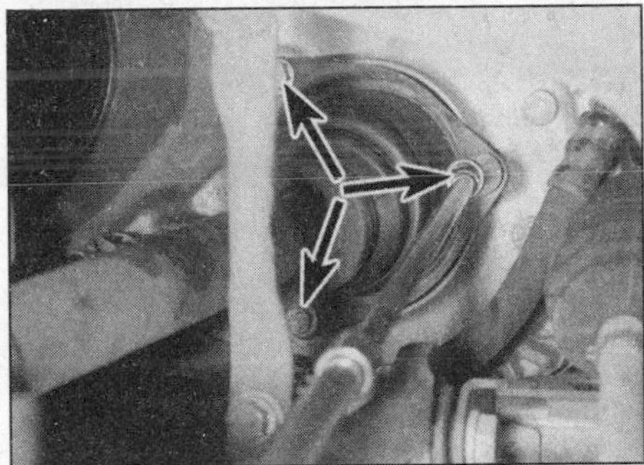
4.8a Removing the three bolts securing the left-hand driveshaft inner rubber boot and metal ring to the transmission

4.8b The right-hand driveshaft is splined to the transmission output shaft; no roll pins are fitted on later models

4.11 Removing the electric fan assembly from the rear of the radiator

8 To disconnect the driveshafts from the transmission, detach the front suspension lower arms from the bottom of each hub carrier (Chapter 10), then remove the driveshafts from the transmission with reference to Chapter 8 **(see illustrations)**. Tie the driveshafts to one side of the engine compartment.

9 Remove the front bumper (Chapter 11) after disconnecting the front foglight wiring and removing the radiator grille.

10 Remove the engine top cover and air intake hoses.

11 Remove the radiator (Chapter 3). Alternatively, release the radiator upper mountings from the crossmember and secure the radiator to the engine; the radiator can then remain mounted on the subframe while the assembly is removed. If necessary, remove the electric fan assembly from the rear of the radiator **(see illustration)**.

12 On petrol engine models, disconnect the wiring from the purge valve located on the carbon canister beneath the right-hand wing. Also, disconnect the fuel supply hose and the carbon canister hose on the inlet manifold.

13 Where applicable on early models, disconnect the accelerator cable.

14 Unbolt the engine management ECU from its support behind the battery.

15 On manual transmission models, disconnect the clutch cable at the transmission (Chapter 6).

16 On diesel models, release the fuel filter from its support then disconnect the fuel supply and return hoses and unclip them from the valve timing cover **(see illustrations)**. Also remove the connector from the accelerator pedal position potentiometer, where fitted.

17 On diesel models, remove the vacuum pipe from the brake vacuum pump. Certain models with the D4F petrol engine may also have a vacuum pump fitted.

18 Where applicable, remove the rear-mounted coolant expansion tank and place it to one side. Disconnect the relevant wiring at the fusebox in front of the left-hand strut mounting **(see illustration)**. Alternatively, the wiring may be disconnected from the engine after noting the location of each wiring plug.

19 On the bulkhead at the rear of the engine, disconnect the hoses from the heater matrix stubs **(see illustration)**.

20 Unbolt the earth cable from the

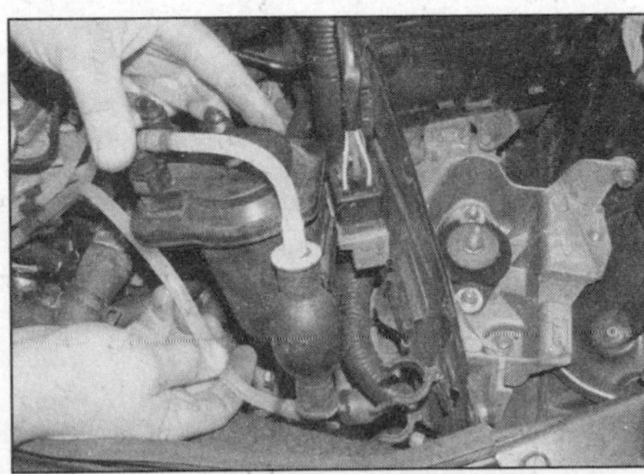
4.16a Removing the fuel filter – diesel engine

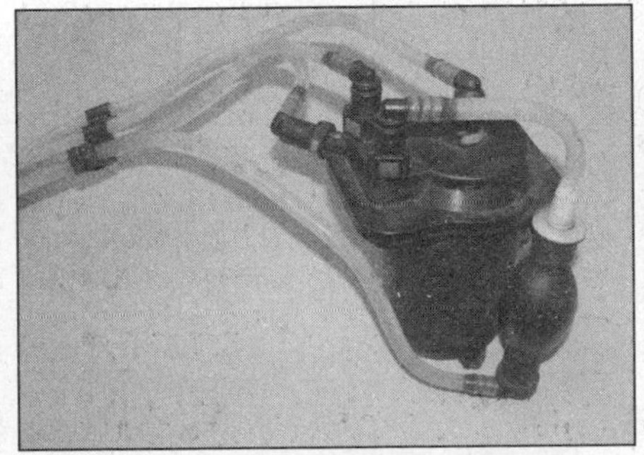
4.16b Fuel filter, showing fuel lines – diesel engine

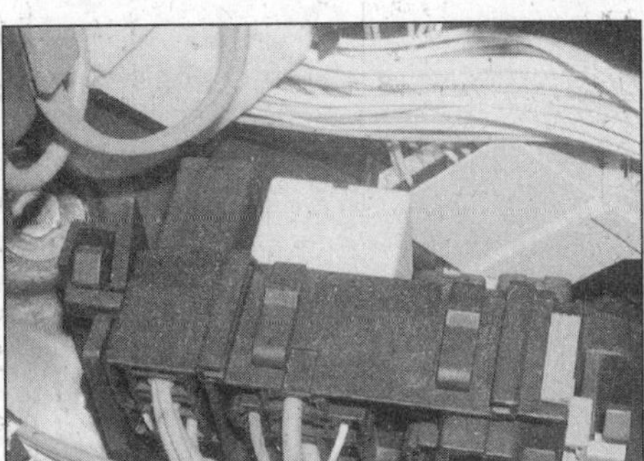
4.18 Engine wiring harness at the left-hand side of the engine compartment

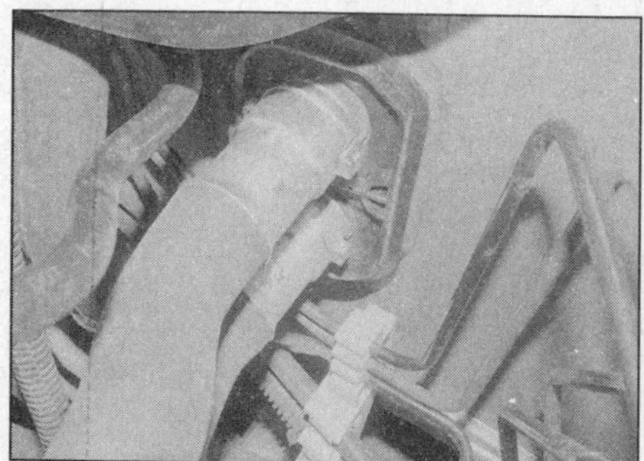

4.19 Heater hoses on the bulkhead

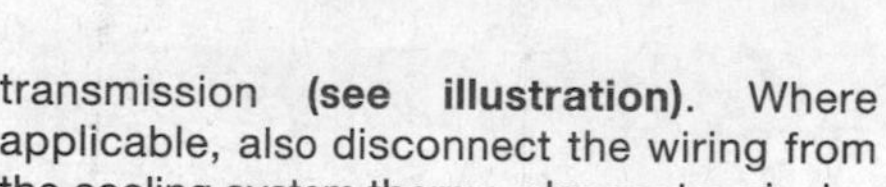

transmission **(see illustration)**. Where applicable, also disconnect the wiring from the cooling system thermo-plunger terminals.

21 Check that the front wheels are pointing straight-ahead, then secure the steering wheel in its central position with tape or string. This is important, as subsequent damage to the airbag clock-spring may occur if the steering wheel is turned beyond its normal range.

22 Working in the driver's footwell, push back the cover then unscrew the nut and remove the clamp bolt securing the steering column intermediate shaft to the steering gear pinion **(see illustration)**.

23 On petrol models, disconnect the wiring from the oxygen sensor located upstream of the catalytic converter at the rear of the engine compartment, and the second oxygen sensor located downstream of the converter beneath the car.

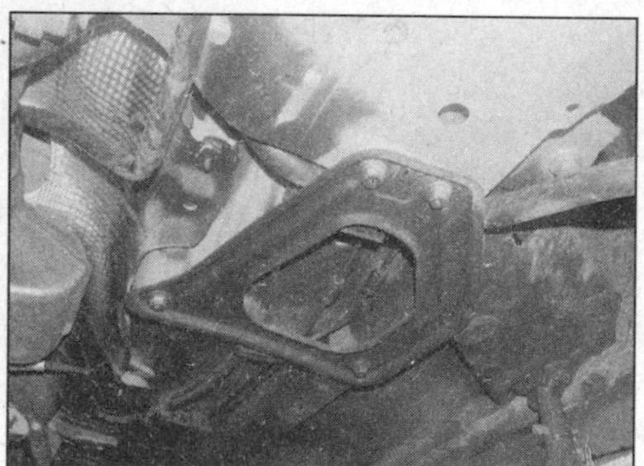

4.26 Subframe rear support plates

4.34 Lower the engine and transmission from the engine compartment

4.20 Gearbox earth strap securing bolt (arrowed)

24 Working beneath the car, unbolt the clamp and release the exhaust intermediate section from the catalytic converter (petrol models) or front pipe (diesel models).

25 Disconnect the gearchange from the transmission with reference to Chapter 7A, 7B or 7C. On petrol models, it will be necessary to remove a plastic cover from the gearbox, and remove two heat shields from the underbody.

26 Unbolt and remove the rear support plates from the underbody and subframe **(see illustration)**.

27 Wedge a block of wood between the transmission and subframe to support it while the assembly is being removed.

28 Unscrew the central nut from the left-hand engine/transmission mounting, and release the stud by gently tapping it with a mallet.

4.29 Right-hand engine lifting eye

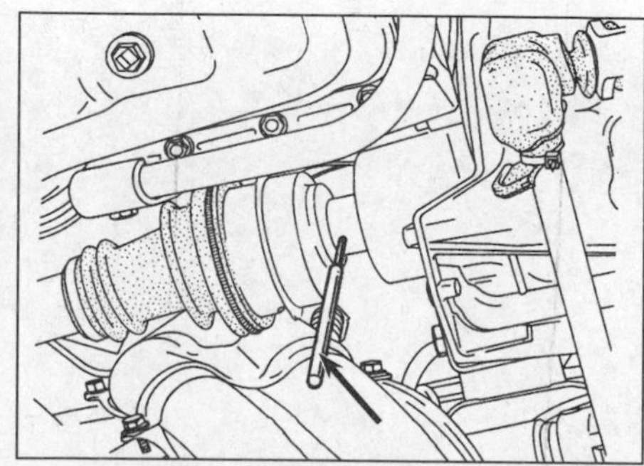

4.35a Using a pin punch (arrowed) to drive out the driveshaft roll pin – early models only

4.22 Pull back the rubber grommet, then remove the bolt securing the bottom of the steering inner column to the steering gear

29 Connect a hoist or engine lifting bar to the engine lifting eye, and support the weight of the engine **(see illustration)**.

30 Remove the right-hand engine mounting (Chapters 2A, 2B or 2C) from the engine and body. If preferred, the mounting central nut can remain tightened and both mounting bracket sections removed as one unit.

31 At this stage, Renault technicians fit a special tool between the right-hand end of the cylinder block and the subframe to support the engine, however, blocks of wood may be used instead provided that they will remain in place during the removal operation. Make sure that the engine and transmission is adequately supported so that it will not tilt or become unstable when removing the subframe assembly. Disconnect the hoist or lifting bar.

32 Mark the position of the subframe on the underbody to ensure correct refitting. One way to do this is to spray paint around the subframe mountings using an aerosol; the outline of the mountings will be marked clear on the underbody.

33 With the help of an assistant, support the subframe with two trolley jacks and lengths of wood. Position the jacks beneath the subframe adjacent to the lower suspension arms.

34 As an aid to removing and refitting the subframe, unscrew the front mounting bolts and substitute them with lengths of threaded rod; the rods will act as guides for the subframe, and if necessary, washers and nuts can be fitted to temporarily hold the assembly in place. Carefully lower the assembly to the ground **(see illustration)**, and at the same time disconnect the column intermediate shaft from the steering gear pinion. Make sure that the assembly clears the engine compartment components.

35 The engine and transmission must now be removed from the subframe and separated from each other on the workbench. If still fitted, remove the driveshafts together with the swivel hubs, and the steering gear, with reference to Chapters 8 and 10 **(see illustrations)**.

36 Support the engine/transmission with a hoist, then disconnect the subframe.

4.35b Power steering pump location on early models – D7F petrol engine

4.35c Power steering pump location on early models

4.38 Separating the transmission from the engine

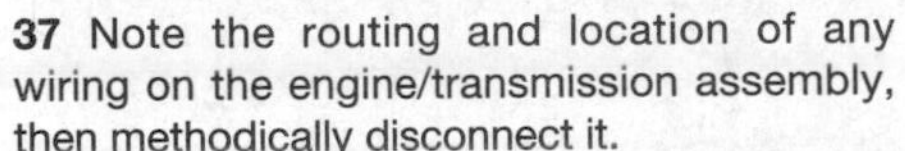

37 Note the routing and location of any wiring on the engine/transmission assembly, then methodically disconnect it.

38 Remove the manual, sequential or automatic transmission from the engine with reference to Chapter 7A, 7B or 7C **(see illustration)**.

Refitting

39 To reconnect the transmission and engine, reverse the operations used to separate them. Above all, do not use excessive force during these operations – if the two will not marry together easily, forcing them will only lead to damage. *Do not tighten the bellhousing bolts to force the engine and transmission together.* Ensure that the bellhousing and cylinder block mating faces will butt together evenly without obstruction, before tightening the bolts fully. Reconnect any wiring on the engine/transmission assembly, routing it as noted on removal.

40 With the engine/transmission supported on a hoist, refit the subframe beneath.

41 If applicable, refit the driveshafts and swivel hubs to the transmission and subframe with reference to Chapters 8 and 10.

42 Manoeuvre the engine/transmission/subframe assembly under the car on the trolley jacks, then raise it into the engine compartment, making sure that the subframe locates on the threaded guide rods. At the same time reconnect the column intermediate shaft to the steering gear pinion.

43 Align the subframe with the previously-made markings, then insert the bolts and tighten securely.

44 The remainder of the refitting procedure is the direct reverse of the removal procedure, noting the following points:

a) *Tighten all fasteners to the specified torque wrench settings, where applicable.*
b) *Ensure that all sections of the wiring harness follow their original routing; use new cable ties to secure the harness in position, keeping it away from sources of heat and abrasion.*
c) *Ensure that all hoses are correctly routed and are secured with the correct hose clips, where applicable. If the hose clips cannot be used again; proprietary worm-drive clips should be fitted in their place.*
d) *On vehicles with manual transmission, adjust the gearchange with reference to Chapter 7A.*
e) *Refill the cooling system as described in Chapter 1A or 1B.*
f) *Refill the engine with appropriate grade and quantity of oil, where necessary (Chapter 1A or 1B).*
g) *Refill the transmission oil or fluid (see Chapter 1A or 1B).*
h) *Where applicable, the refrigerant circuit must be recharged by a refrigeration specialist.*
i) *When the engine is started for the first time, check for coolant, lubricant and fuel leaks etc. If the engine has been overhauled, read the notes in Section 18 before attempting to start it.*

5 Engine overhaul – dismantling sequence

1 It is much easier to dismantle and work on the engine if it is mounted on a portable engine stand. These stands can often be hired from a tool hire shop. Before the engine is mounted on a stand, the flywheel/driveplate should be removed (Part A, B or C of this Chapter) so that the stand bolts can be tightened into the end of the cylinder block/crankcase.

2 If a stand is not available, it is possible to dismantle the engine with it mounted on blocks, on a sturdy workbench or on the floor. Be extra careful not to tip or drop the engine when working without a stand.

3 If you are going to obtain a reconditioned engine, all external components must be removed first, to be transferred to the new engine (just as they will if you are doing a complete engine overhaul yourself). **Note:** *When removing the external components from the engine, pay close attention to details that may be helpful or important during refitting. Note the fitted position of gaskets, seals, spacers, pins, washers, bolts and other small items. These external components include the following* **(see illustrations)***:*

a) *Alternator, air conditioning compressor and mounting bracket (Chapter 5A).*
b) *Coolant pipe.*
c) *Air conditioning compressor mounting brackets.*

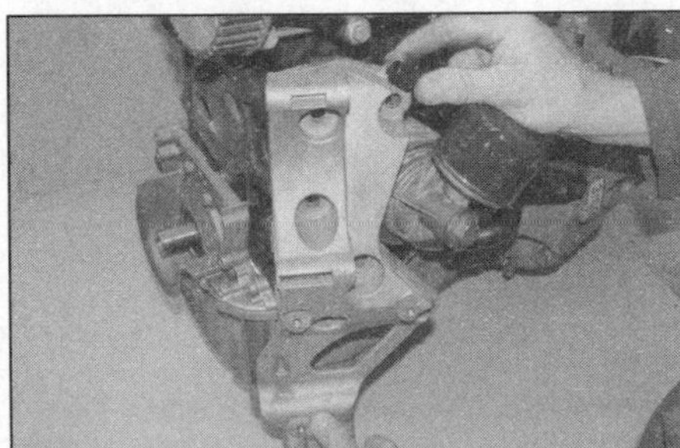

5.3a Removing the alternator and air conditioning compressor mounting bracket – diesel engine

5.3b On diesel engines, unbolt the coolant pipe from the cylinder block . . .

5.3c . . . and pull it from the water pump inlet

5.3d On petrol engines, unscrew the bolt . . .

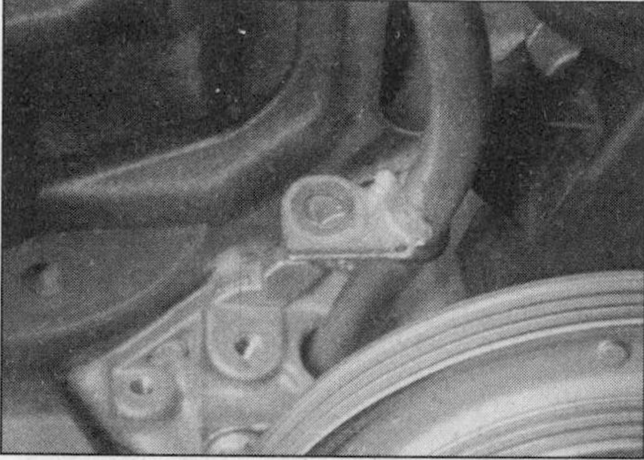
5.3e . . . lift the oil filler tube and dipstick from the front cover . . .

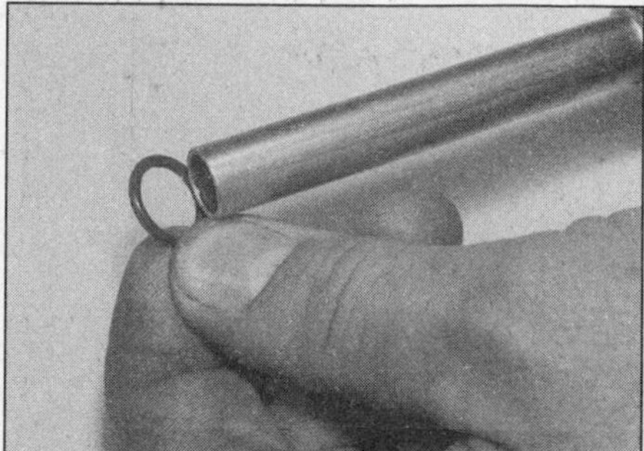
5.3f . . . and remove the sealing O-ring

5.3g On the diesel engine, unbolt the cover (noting the location finger) . . .

5.3h . . . then disconnect the hoses . . .

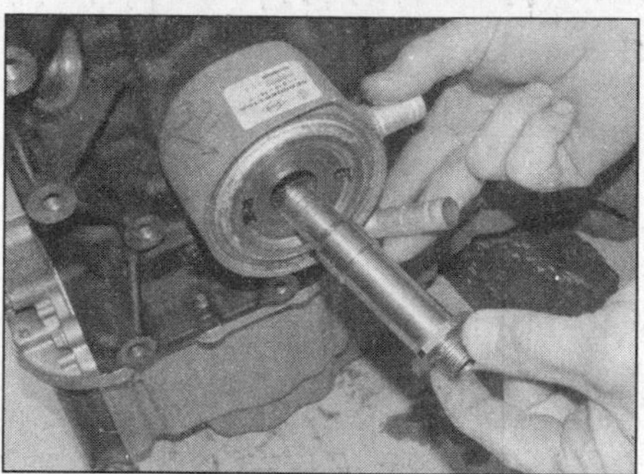
5.3i . . . unscrew the special bolt . . .

d) HT leads and spark plugs – petrol models (Chapters 1A and 5B).
e) Fuel injection system components (Chapter 4A or 4B).
f) Brake vacuum pump – diesel models (Chapter 9).
g) Thermostat and housing, coolant pipe and hoses (Chapter 3).
h) Oil filler tube and dipstick.
i) All electrical switches and sensors.
j) Intake and exhaust manifolds (Chapter 4A or 4B).
k) Oil filter (Chapter 1A or 1B) and oil cooler.
l) Engine/transmission mounting brackets (Chapter 2A, 2B or 2C).
m) Flywheel/driveplate (Chapter 2A, 2B or 2C).

4 If you are obtaining a 'short' engine (which consists of the engine cylinder block/crankcase, crankshaft, pistons and connecting rods all assembled), then the cylinder head, sump, lower crankcase (where applicable), oil pump and timing belt will have to be removed also.

5 If you are planning a complete overhaul, the engine can be dismantled and the internal components removed in the following order.

a) Alternator and mounting bracket (Chapter 5A).
b) Intake and exhaust manifolds (Chapter 4A or 4B).
c) Timing belt and pulleys (Chapter 2A, 2B or 2C).
d) Water pump (Chapter 3) ***(see illustration).***
e) Cylinder head (Chapter 2A, 2B or 2C) ***(see illustration).***
f) Air conditioning compressor mounting brackets.
g) Flywheel/driveplate (Chapter 2A, 2B or 2C).
h) Sump (Chapter 2A, 2B or 2C).
i) Oil pump (Chapter 2A, 2B or 2C).
j) Piston/connecting rod assemblies (Section 10).
k) Crankshaft (Section 11).

6 Before beginning the dismantling and

5.3j . . . and remove the oil cooler

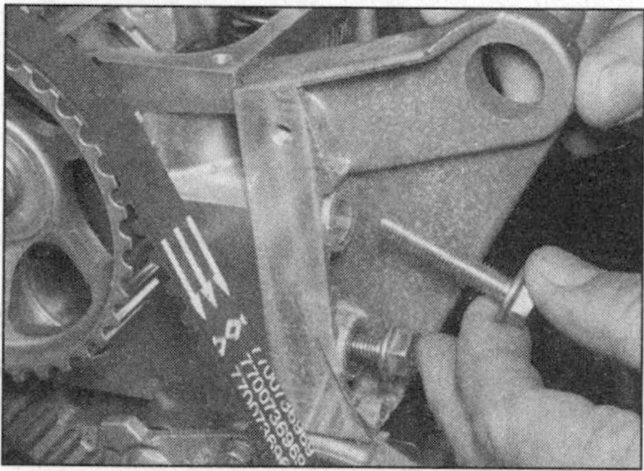
5.3k Removing the front engine lifting bracket – petrol engine

5.5a Unbolting the water pump from the cylinder block – petrol engine

5.5b Removing the cylinder head – SOHC petrol engine

6.2 Thermostat housing on the left-hand end of the cylinder head – diesel engine

6.3 Engine rear lifting eye bolts

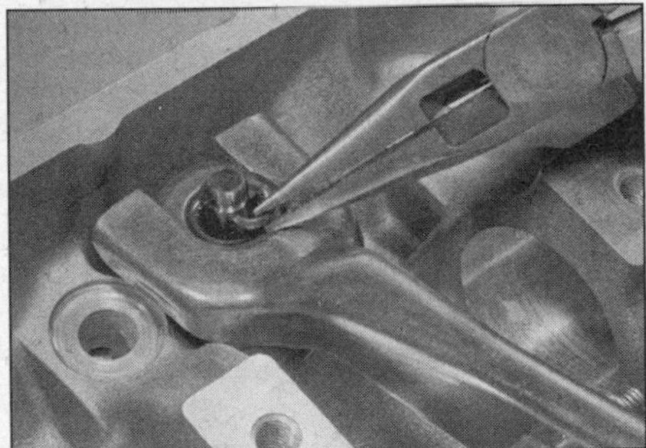

6.4a Remove the split collets . . .

6.4b . . . then lift off the cap . . .

6.4c . . . and valve spring

6.4d . . . followed by the spring seat

overhaul procedures, make sure that you have all of the correct tools necessary. Refer to the Reference section at the end of this manual for further information.

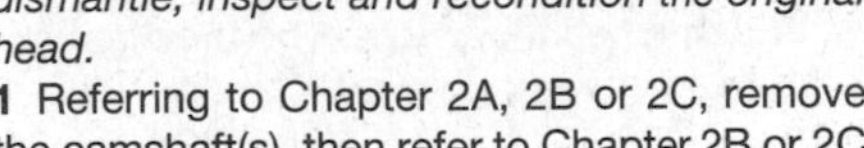

6 Cylinder head – dismantling

Note: *New and reconditioned cylinder heads are available from the manufacturers and from engine overhaul specialists. Due to the fact that some specialist tools are required for the dismantling and inspection procedures, and new components may not be readily available (refer to Section 1), it may be more practical and economical for the home mechanic to purchase a reconditioned head rather than to dismantle, inspect and recondition the original head.*

1 Referring to Chapter 2A, 2B or 2C, remove the camshaft(s), then refer to Chapter 2B or 2C and remove the tappets.

2 On diesel engines, remove the brake vacuum pump (see Chapter 9), thermostat housing **(see illustration)**, the fuel injectors, injection pump (if removed with the cylinder head) and glow plugs (Chapter 4B or 5C).

3 On all engines if necessary, remove the inlet and exhaust manifolds, the engine lifting eyes **(see illustration)**, and coolant outlet elbow.

4 Using a valve spring compressor, compress each valve spring in turn until the split collets can be removed. Release the compressor and lift off the cap and spring. If, when the valve spring compressor is screwed down, the valve spring cap refuses to free and expose the split collets, gently tap the top of the tool, directly over the cap, with a light hammer. This will free the cap **(see illustrations)**.

5 Remove the valves from the combustion chambers. It is essential that the valves and associated components are kept in their correct order, unless they are so badly worn that they are to be renewed. If they are going to be kept and used again, place them in labelled polythene bags, or in a compartmented box **(see illustrations)**.

6 On all petrol engines, the valve stem seals are integral with the valve spring lower seats, and may be difficult to remove.

7 On the K9K diesel engine, before removing the valve stem oil seals, measure their fitted height above the cylinder head and record it. Renault technicians use a special tool which is adjusted according to the fitted height of the

6.5a Withdrawing a valve from the combustion chamber

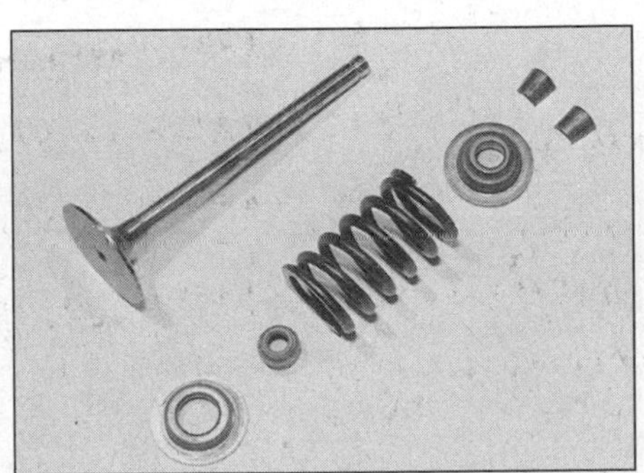

6.5b Valve components

6.5c Store the valve components in a labelled polythene bag

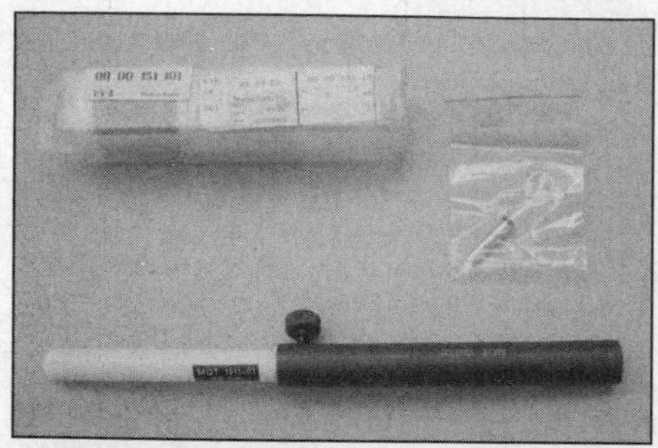

6.7a Renault tool for measuring the fitted height of the old valve stem oil seals, in order to fit the new seals at the same height

old seals; the tool is then used to tap the new seals to an identical height. Use a pair of pliers to pull the oil seals from the valve guides **(see illustrations)**.

7 Cylinder head and valves – cleaning and inspection

1 Thorough cleaning of the cylinder head and valve components, followed by a detailed inspection, will enable you to decide how much valve service work must be carried out during the engine overhaul. **Note:** *If the engine has been severely overheated, it is best to assume that the cylinder head is warped, and to check carefully for signs of this.*

Cleaning

2 Scrape away all traces of old gasket material and sealing compound from the cylinder head. Take care not to damage the cylinder head surfaces.

3 Scrape away the carbon from the combustion chambers and ports, then wash the cylinder head thoroughly with paraffin or a suitable solvent.

4 Scrape off any heavy carbon deposits that may have formed on the valves, then use a power-operated wire brush to remove deposits from the valve heads and stems.

Inspection and renovation

Note: *Be sure to perform all the following inspection procedures before concluding that the services of a machine shop or engine overhaul specialist are required. Make a list of all items that require attention.*

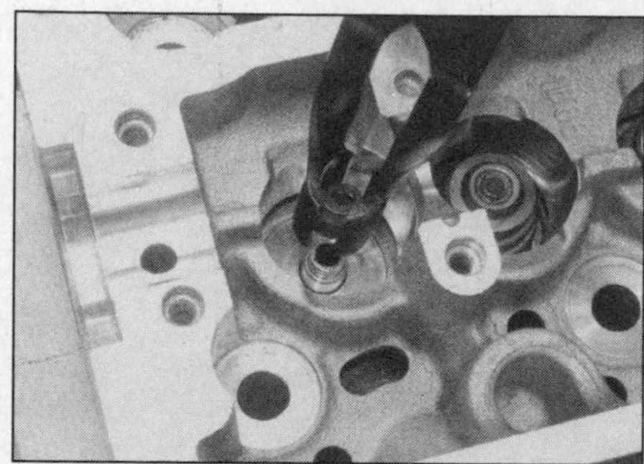

6.7b Removing the oil seal from the top of the valve guide

Cylinder head

5 Inspect the head very carefully for cracks, evidence of coolant leakage and other damage. If cracks are found, consult an automotive engineering specialist or manufacturer dealership, before purchasing a new head.

6 If warpage of the cylinder head gasket surface is suspected, use a straight-edge to check it for distortion **(see illustration)**. If feeler blades are used, the degree of distortion can be assessed more accurately, and compared with the value specified. Check for distortion along the length and across the width of the head, and along both diagonals. If the head is warped, it may be possible to have it machined flat ('skimmed') at an engineering works – check with an engine specialist.

7 Examine the valve seats in each of the combustion chambers. If they are severely pitted, cracked or burned, then they will need to be renewed or recut by an engine overhaul specialist. If they are only slightly pitted, this can be removed by grinding-in the valve heads and seats with fine valve-grinding compound, as described below. Note that on diesel engines the valve seats can only be recut to a limited depth, to avoid decreasing the compression ratio. Using a dial test indicator, check that valve depth below the cylinder head gasket surface is within the limits given in the Specifications.

8 If the valve guides are worn, indicated by a side-to-side motion of the valve, new guides must be fitted.

9 The renewal of valve guides is best carried out by an engine overhaul specialist, since if it is not done skilfully, there is a risk of damaging the cylinder head.

10 If the valve seats are to be recut, consult an automotive engineering specialist or manufacturer dealership.

11 Check the tappet bores in the cylinder head for wear. If excessive wear is evident, the cylinder head must be renewed.

Valves

12 Examine the head of each valve for pitting, burning, cracks and general wear, and check the valve stem for scoring and wear ridges. Rotate the valve, and check for any obvious indication that it is bent. Look for pits and excessive wear on the tip of each valve stem. Renew any valve that shows any such signs of wear or damage.

13 If the valve appears satisfactory at this stage, measure the valve stem diameter at several points, using a micrometer **(see illustration)**. Any significant difference in the readings obtained indicates wear of the valve stem. Should any of these conditions be apparent, the valve(s) must be renewed.

14 If the valves are in satisfactory condition, they should be ground (lapped) into their respective seats, to ensure a smooth gas-tight seal. If the seat is only lightly pitted, or if it has been recut, fine grinding compound only should be used to produce the required finish. Coarse valve-grinding compound should not be used unless a seat is badly burned or deeply pitted; if this is the case, the cylinder head and valves should be inspected by an expert, to decide whether seat recutting, or even the renewal of the valve or seat insert, is required.

15 Valve grinding is carried out as follows. Place the cylinder head upside-down on a bench, with a block of wood at each end to give clearance for the valve stems.

16 Smear a trace of valve-grinding compound on the seat face, and press a suction grinding tool onto the valve head. With a semi-rotary action, grind the valve head to its seat, lifting the valve occasionally to redistribute the grinding compound **(see illustration)**. A light spring placed under the

7.6 Checking the cylinder head surface for distortion with feeler blades

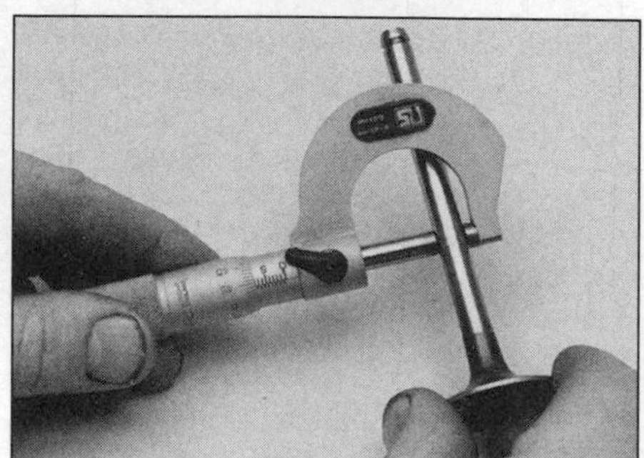

7.13 Measuring a valve stem using a micrometer

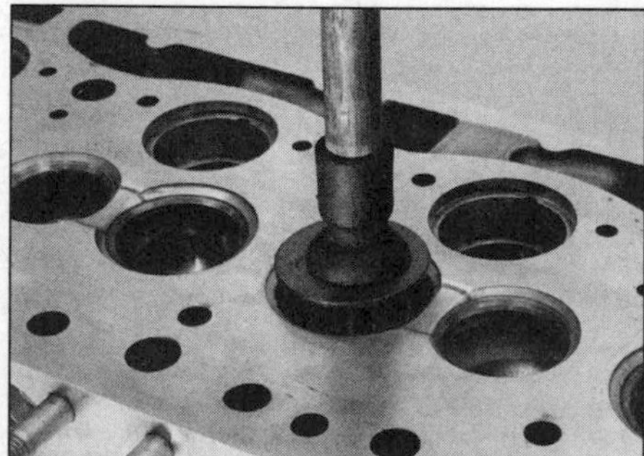

7.16 Grinding a valve to its seat – lift the valve to redistribute the paste

valve head will greatly ease this operation. If coarse grinding compound is being used, work only until a dull, matt even surface is produced on both the valve seat and the valve, then wipe off the used compound, and repeat the process with fine compound.

17 When a smooth unbroken ring of light grey matt finish is produced on both the valve and seat, the grinding operation is complete. Do not grind in the valves any further than absolutely necessary, or the seat will be prematurely sunk into the cylinder head.

18 When all the valves have been ground-in, carefully wash off all traces of grinding compound, using paraffin or a suitable solvent, before reassembly of the cylinder head.

Valve components

19 Examine the valve springs for signs of damage and discoloration and also measure their free length using vernier calipers or a steel rule **(see illustration)** or by comparing the existing spring with a new component.

20 Stand each spring on a flat surface and check it for squareness. If any of the springs are damaged, distorted or have lost their tension, obtain a complete new set of springs.

Rocker arms – D7F and D4F engines

21 Check the rocker arm contact surfaces for pits, wear, score marks or any indication that the surface-hardening has worn through. Dismantle the rocker shaft and check the rocker arm and rocker shaft pivot and contact areas in the same way. Measure the internal diameter of each rocker and check their fit on the shaft. Clean out the oil spill holes in each rocker using a length of wire. Renew the rocker arm or the rocker shaft itself if any are suspect.

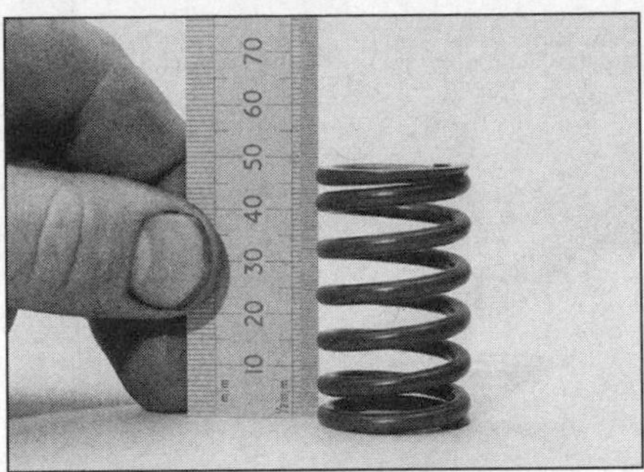

7.19 Checking a valve spring free length

Valve stem oil seals

22 The valve stem oil seals should be renewed as a matter of course.

8 Cylinder head – reassembly

1 Regardless of whether or not the head was sent away for repair work, make sure that it is clean before beginning reassembly. Be sure to remove any metal particles and abrasive grit that may still be present from operations such as valve grinding or head resurfacing. Use compressed air, if available, to blow out all the oil holes and passages.

2 Lubricate the valve stems, then insert the valves into their original locations. If new valves are being fitted, insert them into the locations to which they have been ground **(see illustration)**.

3 On petrol engines, ease the valve stem oil seals/seats over the valve stems, then press them onto the valve guides, using a large socket on the seat area. On the K9K diesel engine, press the new valve stem oil seals onto the guides to their previously-noted position, using the special guide to locate the seals over the valve stems **(see illustrations)**. **Do not** lubricate the oil seals before fitting them. Remove the guide after fitting the seal.

4 Working on each valve separately, locate the spring and cap over the valve stem. On the K9K diesel engine, the springs are tapered and the smaller diameter taper must be positioned at the top.

5 Compress the valve spring and locate the split collets in the recess in the valve stem. Release the compressor, then repeat the procedure on the remaining valves. Use a little grease to hold the collets in place **(see illustration)**.

6 With all the valves installed, place the cylinder head on the bench supported by blocks of wood and, using a hammer and interposed block of wood, tap the end of each valve stem to settle the components.

7 Refit as necessary the manifolds, lifting eyes and coolant outlet elbow.

8 On diesel engines, refit the brake vacuum pump (see Chapter 9), thermostat housing with a new seal **(see illustration)**, the fuel

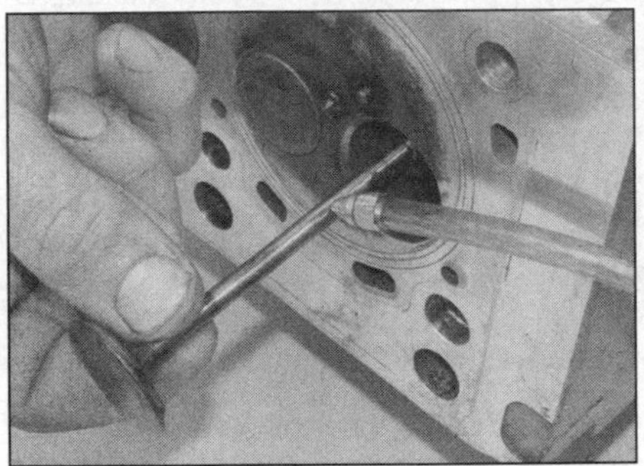

8.2 Lubricate the valve stems before inserting the valves

8.3a Fit the special guide onto the valve stem . . .

8.3b . . . then fit the oil seal . . .

8.3c . . . and press it on to its previously-noted position on the guide

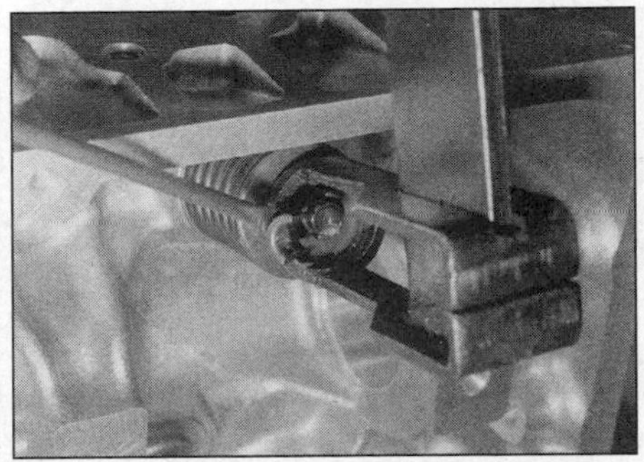

8.5 Use a little grease to hold the collets in place

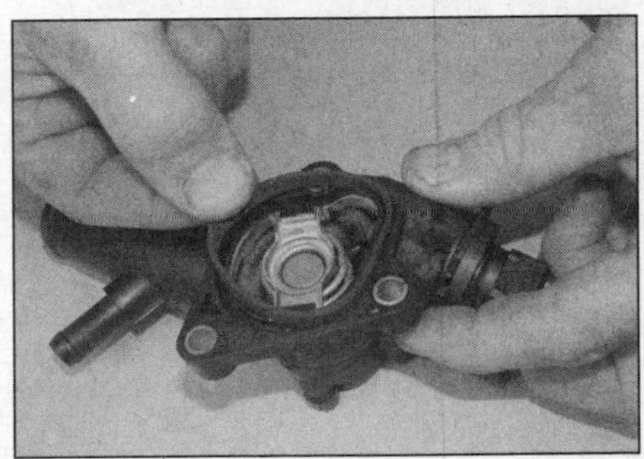

8.8 Locating a new seal on the thermostat housing – diesel engine

9.2 Big-end caps marked with a centre-punch

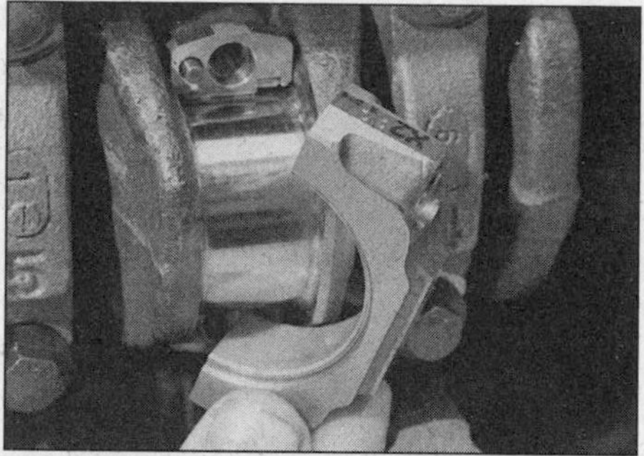

9.3 Removing a big-end bearing cap

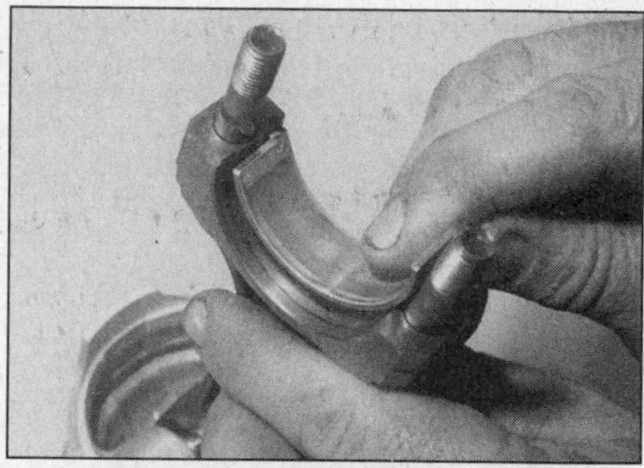

9.4 Removing a big-end bearing upper shell

injectors, injection pump and glow plugs (Chapter 4B or 5C).

9 Referring to Chapter 2A, 2B or 2C, refit the tappets and camshaft(s).

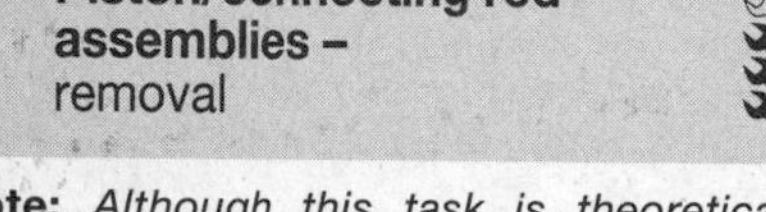

9 Piston/connecting rod assemblies – removal

Note: *Although this task is theoretically possible with the engine in the car, in practice, owners are advised to remove the engine first. The following paragraphs assume the engine is removed from the car.*

1 With the cylinder head, sump and oil pump removed (see Chapter 2A, 2B or 2C), proceed as follows.

2 Rotate the crankshaft so that No 1 big-end cap (nearest the flywheel/driveplate position) is at the lowest point of its travel. If the big-end cap and rod are not already numbered, mark them with a centre-punch **(see illustration)**. Mark both cap and rod to identify the cylinder they operate in.

3 Unscrew the big-end bearing cap nuts (K4J and K4M engines) or bolts (all other engines). Withdraw the cap, complete with shell bearing, from the connecting rod **(see illustration)**.

4 If only the bearing shells are being attended to, push the connecting rod up and off the crankpin and remove the upper bearing shell **(see illustration)**. Keep the bearing shells and cap together in their correct sequence if they are to be refitted.

5 Each piston has an arrow stamped on its crown, pointing towards the flywheel end of the engine.

6 Push the connecting rod up and remove the piston and rod from the top of the bore. Note that if there is a pronounced wear ridge at the top of the bore, there is a risk of damaging the piston rings as they foul the ridge. However, it is reasonable to assume that a rebore and new pistons will be required in any case if the ridge is so pronounced.

7 Repeat the procedure for the remaining piston/connecting rod assemblies. Ensure that the caps and rods are marked before removal, as described previously, and keep all components in order.

8 On diesel engines only, the gudgeon pins are a floating fit in the pistons, and can be removed after releasing the circlips. On petrol engines, do not attempt to separate the pistons from the connecting rods; have an engine overhaul specialist carry out the work.

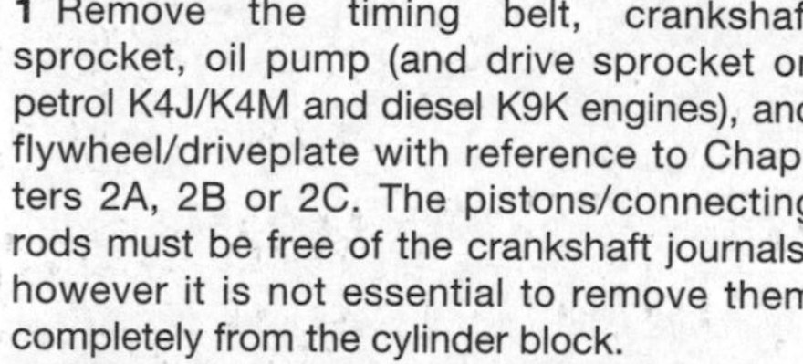

10 Crankshaft – removal

1 Remove the timing belt, crankshaft sprocket, oil pump (and drive sprocket on petrol K4J/K4M and diesel K9K engines), and flywheel/driveplate with reference to Chapters 2A, 2B or 2C. The pistons/connecting rods must be free of the crankshaft journals, however it is not essential to remove them completely from the cylinder block.

2 Unbolt the crankshaft left-hand oil seal housing from the cylinder block.

3 Before the crankshaft is removed, check the endfloat using a dial gauge in contact with the end of the crankshaft **(see illustration)**. Push the crankshaft fully one way and then zero the gauge. Push the crankshaft fully the other way and check the endfloat. The result can be compared with the specified amount and will give an indication as to whether new thrustwashers are required.

4 If a dial gauge is not available, feeler gauges can be used. First push the crankshaft fully towards the flywheel/driveplate end of the engine, then slip the feeler gauge between the web of No 2 crankpin and the thrustwasher of the centre main bearing.

5 Identification numbers should already be cast onto the base of each main bearing cap, together with arrows pointing towards the flywheel/driveplate end of the engine. If not, number them 1 to 5 from the flywheel/driveplate end of the engine using a centre-punch, as was done for the connecting rods and caps **(see illustration)**. Also mark the crankcase, so that the caps will be refitted the correct way round.

6 Unscrew the main bearing cap retaining bolts and withdraw the caps, complete with bearing shells **(see illustration)**. Tap the caps with a wooden or copper mallet if they are stuck.

7 Carefully lift the crankshaft from the crankcase **(see illustration)**.

8 Remove the thrustwashers at each side of the centre main bearing where they are separate (K9K engine), then remove the bearing shell upper halves from the crankcase **(see illustration)**. Place each shell with its

10.3 Checking the crankshaft endfloat with a dial gauge

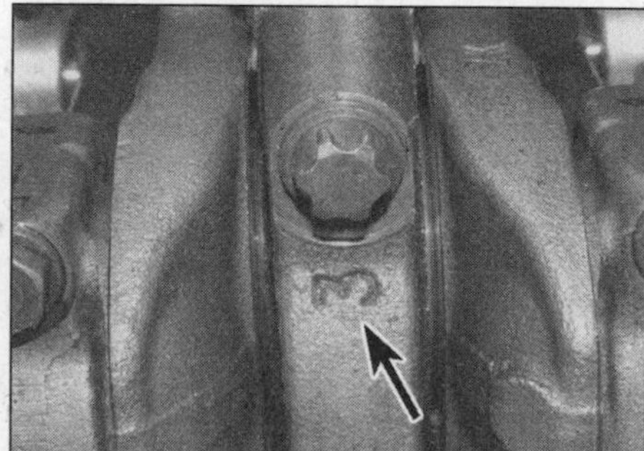

10.5 The main bearing caps are numbered for position

10.6 Removing a main bearing cap bolt

respective bearing cap, noting that the grooved shells are fitted on the crankcase and the plain shells in the caps.

11 Cylinder block/crankcase – cleaning and inspection

Cleaning

1 For complete cleaning, remove all external components and brackets, and all electrical switches/sensors. On the K4J and K4M petrol engine and K9K diesel engine, the piston-cooling oil jets are pressed into the cylinder block, and must be drilled in order to fit a removal tool; this work is best left to a specialist. If necessary, the core plugs can be removed. Drill a small hole in them, then insert a self-tapping screw and pull out the plugs using a pair of grips or a slide-hammer.

2 Scrape all traces of gasket or sealant from the cylinder block, taking care not to damage the head and sump mating faces.

3 If the block is extremely dirty, it should be steam-cleaned.

4 After the block has been steam-cleaned, clean all oil holes and oil galleries one more time. Flush all internal passages with warm water until the water runs clear, dry the block thoroughly and wipe all machined surfaces with a light rust-preventative oil. If you have access to compressed air, use it to speed up the drying process and to blow out all the oil holes and galleries.

5 If the block is not very dirty, you can do an adequate cleaning job with hot soapy water and a stiff brush. Take plenty of time and do a thorough job. Regardless of the cleaning method used, be sure to clean all oil holes and galleries very thoroughly, dry the block completely and coat all machined surfaces with light oil.

6 The threaded holes in the block must be clean to ensure accurate torque wrench readings during reassembly. Run the proper-size tap into each of the holes to remove rust, corrosion, thread sealant or sludge and to restore damaged threads. If possible, use compressed air to clear the holes of debris produced by this operation. Now is a good time to clean the threads on the head bolts and the main bearing cap bolts as well.

7 Refit the main bearing caps and tighten the bolts finger-tight.

8 After coating the mating surfaces of the new core plugs with suitable sealant, refit them in the cylinder block. Make sure that they are driven in straight and seated properly, or leakage could result. Special tools are available for this purpose, but a large socket, with an outside diameter that will just slip into the core plug, will work just as well.

9 If the engine is not going to be reassembled right away, cover it with a large plastic bag to keep it clean and prevent it rusting.

10.7 Lifting the crankshaft from the crankcase

Inspection

10 Visually check the castings for cracks and corrosion. Look for stripped threads in the threaded holes. If there has been any history of internal coolant leakage, it may be worthwhile having an engine overhaul specialist check the cylinder block/crankcase for cracks with special equipment. If defects are found, have them repaired, if possible, or renew the assembly.

11 Check each cylinder bore for scuffing and scoring.

12 If in any doubt as the condition of the cylinder block have the block/bores inspected and measured by an engine reconditioning specialist. They will be able to advise on whether the block is serviceable, whether a rebore is necessary, and supply the appropriate replacement pistons and rings.

13 If the bores are in reasonably good condition and not excessively worn, then it may only be necessary to renew the piston rings.

14 If this is the case, the bores should be honed, to allow the new rings to bed-in correctly and provide the best possible seal. Consult an engine reconditioning specialist

15 The cylinder block/crankcase should now be completely clean and dry, with all components checked for wear or damage, and repaired or overhauled as necessary. Refit as many ancillary components as possible, for safe-keeping. If reassembly is not to start immediately, cover the block with a large plastic bag to keep it clean, and protect the machined surfaces as described above to prevent rusting.

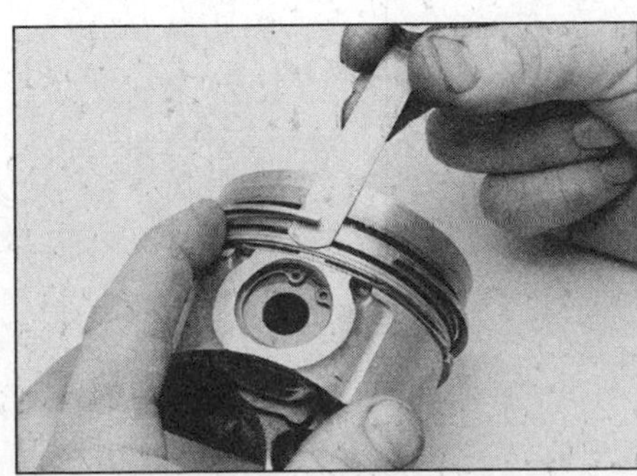

12.2 Removing a piston ring with the aid of a feeler blade

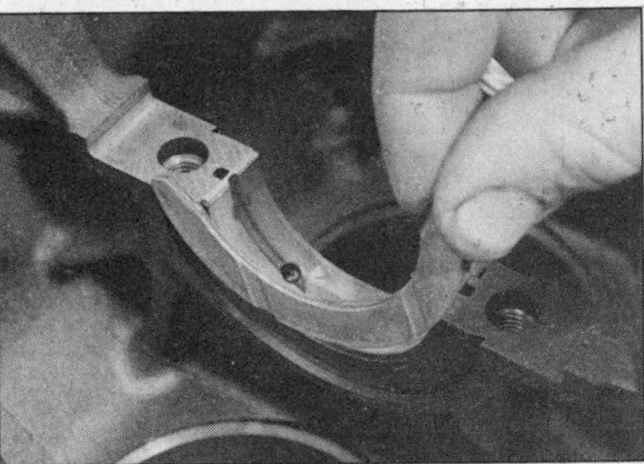

10.8 Removing the crankshaft thrustwashers – diesel engine

12 Piston/connecting rod assemblies – inspection

1 Before the inspection process can begin, the piston/connecting rod assemblies must be cleaned and the original piston rings removed from the pistons.

2 Carefully expand the old rings over the top of the pistons. The use of two or three old feeler blades will be helpful in preventing the rings dropping into empty grooves **(see illustration)**. Note that the oil control ring is in two sections.

3 Scrape away all traces of carbon from the top of the piston. A wire brush or a piece of fine emery cloth can be used once the majority of the deposits have been scraped away.

4 Remove the carbon from the ring grooves using a special groove-cleaning tool. If a tool is not available, use an old ring. Break the ring in half to do this. Be very careful to remove only the carbon deposits; do not remove any metal, or scratch the sides of the ring grooves. Protect your fingers – piston rings are sharp.

5 Once the deposits have been removed, clean the piston/connecting rod assembly with paraffin or a suitable solvent and dry thoroughly. Make sure the oil return holes in the ring grooves are clear.

6 If the pistons and cylinder bores are not damaged or worn excessively and if the cylinder block does not need to be rebored, the original pistons can be re-used. Normal piston wear appears as even vertical wear on the piston thrust surfaces and slight looseness of the top ring in its groove. New piston rings should always be used when the engine is reassembled.

7 Carefully inspect each piston for cracks around the skirt, at the gudgeon pin bosses and at the piston ring lands (between the piston ring grooves).

8 Look for scoring and scuffing on the sides of the skirt, holes in the piston crown and burned areas at the edge of the crown. If the skirt is scored or scuffed, the engine may have been suffering from overheating and/or abnormal combustion, which caused excessively-high

12.11a Use the piston to push the rings into the cylinder bores . . .

12.11b . . . then measure the ring end gaps

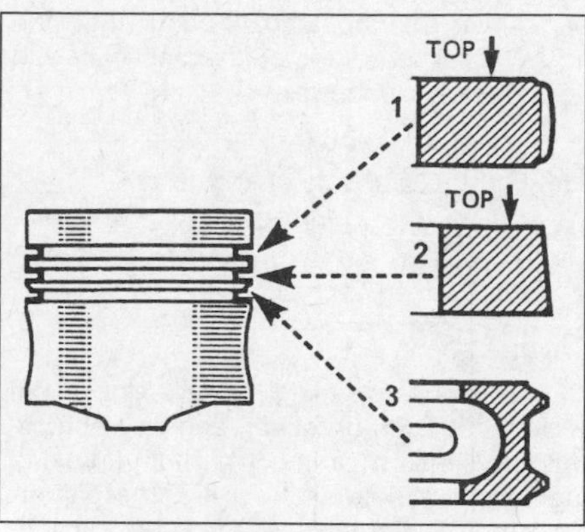

12.12 Piston ring profiles

1 Top compression ring
2 Lower compression ring
3 Oil control ring
Position the TOP markings as shown

operating temperatures. The cooling and lubricating systems should be checked thoroughly. Scorch marks on the sides of the pistons show that blow-by has occurred and the rings are not sealing correctly. A hole in the piston crown is an indication that abnormal combustion (pre-ignition, knocking or detonation) has been occurring. If any of the above problems exist, the causes must be corrected, or the damage will occur again.

9 Corrosion of the piston, in the form of small pits, indicates that coolant is leaking into the combustion chamber and/or the crankcase. Again, the cause must be corrected, or the problem may persist in the rebuilt engine.

10 Check the fit of the gudgeon pin by twisting the piston and connecting rod in opposite directions. Any noticeable play indicates excessive wear, which must be corrected. The piston/connecting rod assemblies should be taken to a dealer or engine reconditioning specialist to have the pistons, gudgeon pins and rods checked, and new components fitted as required.

11 Before refitting the rings to the pistons, check their end gaps by inserting each of them in their cylinder bores. Use the piston to make sure that they are square **(see illustrations)**. Renault rings are supplied pregapped; no attempt should be made to adjust the gaps by filing.

12 Refit the piston rings as follows. Where the original rings are being refitted, use the marks or notes made on removal, to ensure that each ring is refitted to its original groove and the same way up. New rings generally have their top surfaces identified by markings (often an indication of size, such as STD, or the word TOP) – the rings must be fitted with such markings uppermost **(see illustration)**. **Note:** *Always follow the instructions printed on the ring package or box.*

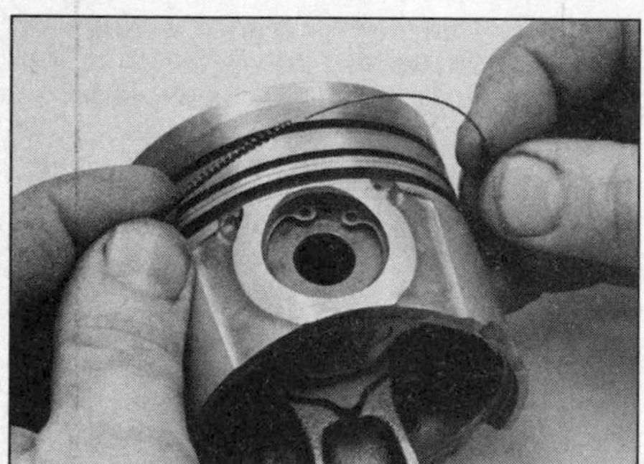

12.13a Fit the oil control ring expander . . .

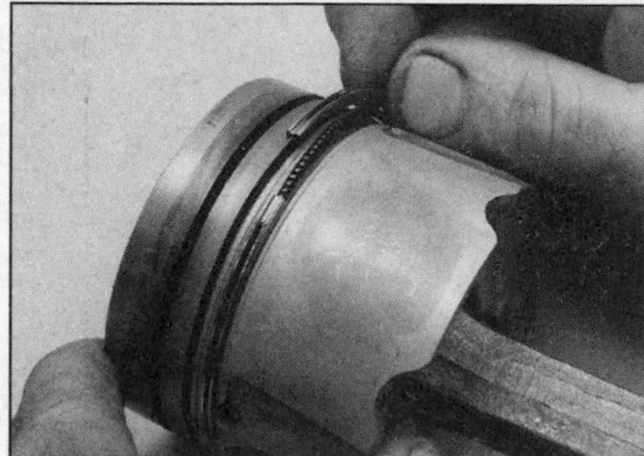

12.13b . . . followed by the ring

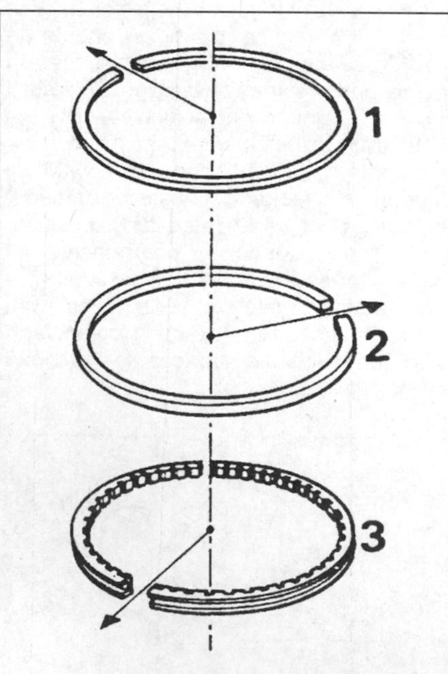

12.15 Position the piston ring end gaps 120° apart

1 Top compression ring
2 Lower compression ring
3 Oil control ring

13 The oil control ring (lowest one on the piston) is usually installed first. It is composed of three separate elements. Slip the spacer/expander into the groove. Next, install the lower side rail. Place one end of the side rail into the groove between the spacer/expander and the ring land, hold it firmly in place, and slide a finger around the piston while pushing the rail into the groove. Next, install the upper side rail in the same manner **(see illustrations)**. After the three oil ring components have been installed, check that both the upper and lower side rails can be turned smoothly in the ring groove.

14 The second compression (middle) ring is installed next, followed by the top compression ring – ensure their marks are uppermost. Do not expand either ring any more than necessary to slide it over the top of the piston.

15 With all the rings in position, space the ring gaps (including the elements of the oil control ring) uniformly around the piston at 120° intervals **(see illustration)**. Repeat the procedure for the remaining pistons and rings.

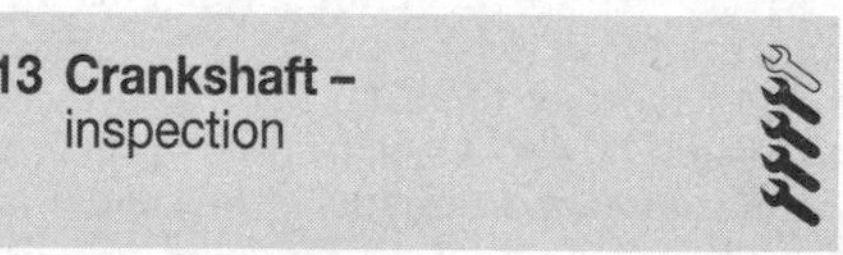

13 Crankshaft – inspection

1 Clean the crankshaft and dry it with compressed air if available. Be sure to clean the oil holes with a pipe cleaner or similar probe.

Warning: Wear eye protection when using compressed air.

2 Check the main and big-end bearing journals for uneven wear, scoring, pitting and cracking.

3 If the crankshaft has been reground, check for burrs around the crankshaft oil holes (the holes are usually chamfered, so burrs should not be a problem unless regrinding has been carried out carelessly). Remove any burrs with a fine file or scraper and thoroughly clean the oil holes as described previously.

4 Using a micrometer, measure the diameter of the main bearing and connecting rod journals and compare the results with the Specifications at the beginning of this Chapter **(see illustration)**. If in any doubt, take the crankshaft to an engine reconditioning specialist and have it measured.

5 By measuring the diameter at a number of points around each journal's circumference, you will be able to determine whether or not the journal is out-of-round. Take the measurement at each end of the journal, near the webs, to determine if the journal is tapered.

6 If the crankshaft journals are damaged, tapered, out-of-round, or worn beyond the limits specified in this Chapter, the crankshaft must be taken to an engine overhaul specialist, who will regrind it, and who can supply the necessary undersize bearing shells, where available. **Note:** *Renault state that regrinding the crankshaft on the K9K diesel engine is not allowed.*

7 Check the oil seal journals at each end of the crankshaft for wear and damage. If either seal has worn an excessive groove in its journal, consult an engine overhaul specialist, who will be able to advise whether a repair is possible, or whether a new crankshaft is necessary.

14 Main and big-end bearings – inspection

1 Even though the main and big-end bearing shells should be renewed during the engine overhaul (where possible), the old shells should be retained for close examination, as they may reveal valuable information about the condition of the engine.

2 Bearing failure occurs because of lack of lubrication, the presence of dirt or other foreign particles, overloading the engine, and corrosion **(see illustration)**. Regardless of the cause of bearing failure, it must be corrected before the engine is reassembled, to prevent it from happening again.

3 When examining the bearing shells, remove them from the cylinder block/crankcase and main bearing caps and from the connecting rods and the big-end bearing caps, then lay them out on a clean surface in the same general position as their location in the engine. This will enable you to match any bearing problems with the corresponding crankshaft journal. Do not touch any shell's bearing surface with your fingers while checking it, or the delicate surface may be scratched.

4 Dirt or other foreign matter gets into the engine in a variety of ways. It may be left in the engine during assembly, or it may pass through filters or the crankcase ventilation system. It may get into the oil, and from there into the bearings. Metal chips from machining operations and normal engine wear are often present. Abrasives are sometimes left in engine components after reconditioning, especially when parts are not thoroughly

13.4 Measuring a main bearing journal diameter using a micrometer

cleaned using the proper cleaning methods. Whatever the source, these foreign objects often end up embedded in the soft bearing material, and are easily recognised. Large particles will not embed in the material, and will score or gouge the shell and journal. The best prevention for this cause of bearing failure is to clean all parts thoroughly, and to keep everything spotlessly-clean during engine assembly. Frequent and regular engine oil and filter changes are also recommended.

5 Lack of lubrication (or lubrication breakdown) has a number of inter-related causes. Excessive heat (which thins the oil), overloading (which squeezes the oil from the bearing face) and oil leakage (from excessive bearing clearances, worn oil pump or high engine speeds) all contribute to lubrication breakdown. Blocked oil passages, which usually are the result of misaligned oil holes in a bearing shell, will also starve a bearing of oil, and destroy it. When lack of lubrication is the cause of bearing failure, the bearing material is wiped or extruded from the shell's steel backing. Temperatures may increase to the point where the steel backing turns blue from overheating.

6 Driving habits can have a definite effect on

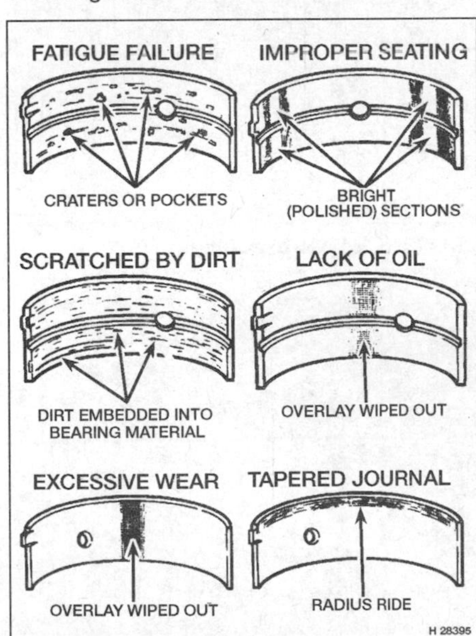

14.2 Typical bearing shell failures

bearing life. Full-throttle, low-speed operation (labouring the engine) puts very high loads on bearings, which tends to squeeze out the oil film. These loads cause the shells to flex, which produces fine cracks in the bearing face (fatigue failure). Eventually, the bearing material will loosen in pieces, and tear away from the steel backing. Short-distance driving leads to corrosion of bearings, because insufficient engine heat is produced to drive off condensed water and corrosive gases. These products collect in the engine oil, forming acid and sludge. As the oil is carried to the engine bearings, the acid attacks and corrodes the bearing material.

7 Incorrect shell refitting during engine assembly will lead to bearing failure as well. Tight-fitting shells leave insufficient bearing running clearance, and will result in oil starvation. Dirt or foreign particles trapped behind a bearing shell result in high spots on the bearing, which lead to failure. Do not touch any shell's bearing surface with your fingers during reassembly; there is a risk of scratching the delicate surface, or of depositing particles of dirt on it.

15 Engine overhaul – reassembly sequence

1 Before starting, ensure all new parts have been obtained and all necessary tools are available. Read through the entire procedure to familiarise yourself with the work involved and to ensure all items necessary for engine reassembly are at hand.

2 In addition to all normal tools and materials, obtain any necessary sealant and thread-locking fluid.

3 To save time and avoid problems, assembly can be carried out in the following order:

a) Crankshaft.
b) Pistons/connecting rod assemblies.
c) Oil pump.
d) Sump.
e) Flywheel/driveplate.
f) Cylinder head.
g) Timing belt and sprockets.
h) Engine external components.

4 At this stage, all engine components should be absolutely clean and dry, with all faults repaired. All components should be neatly arranged on a completely clean work surface or in individual containers.

16 Crankshaft – refitting

1 Crankshaft refitting is the first major step in engine reassembly. It is assumed at this point that the cylinder block/crankcase and crankshaft have been cleaned, inspected and repaired or reconditioned as necessary. Position the engine upside-down.

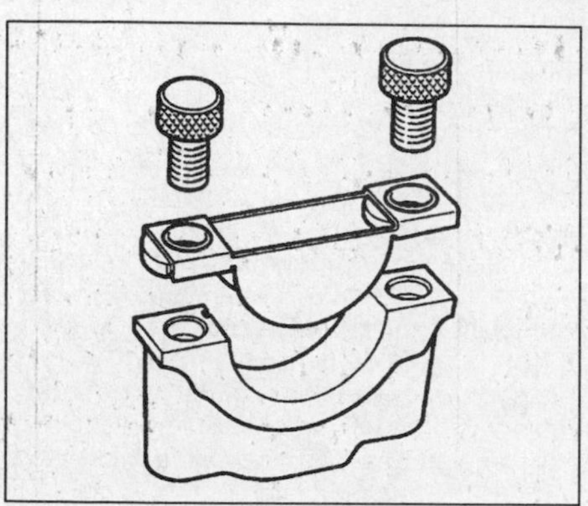

16.4a Tool for fitting main bearing shells – K4J and K4M petrol engines

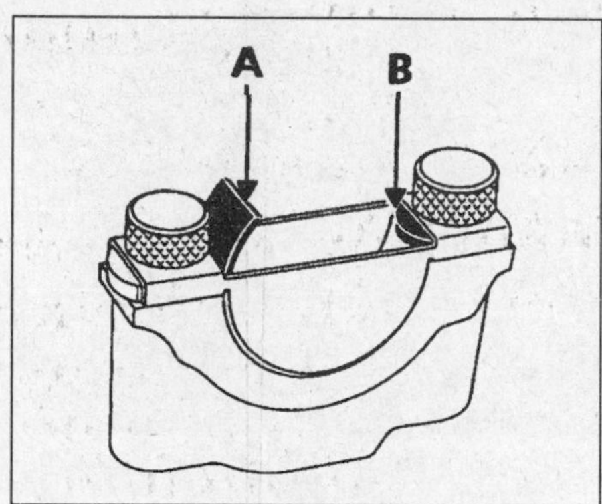

16.4b Press the bearing shell at (A) until it contacts (B)

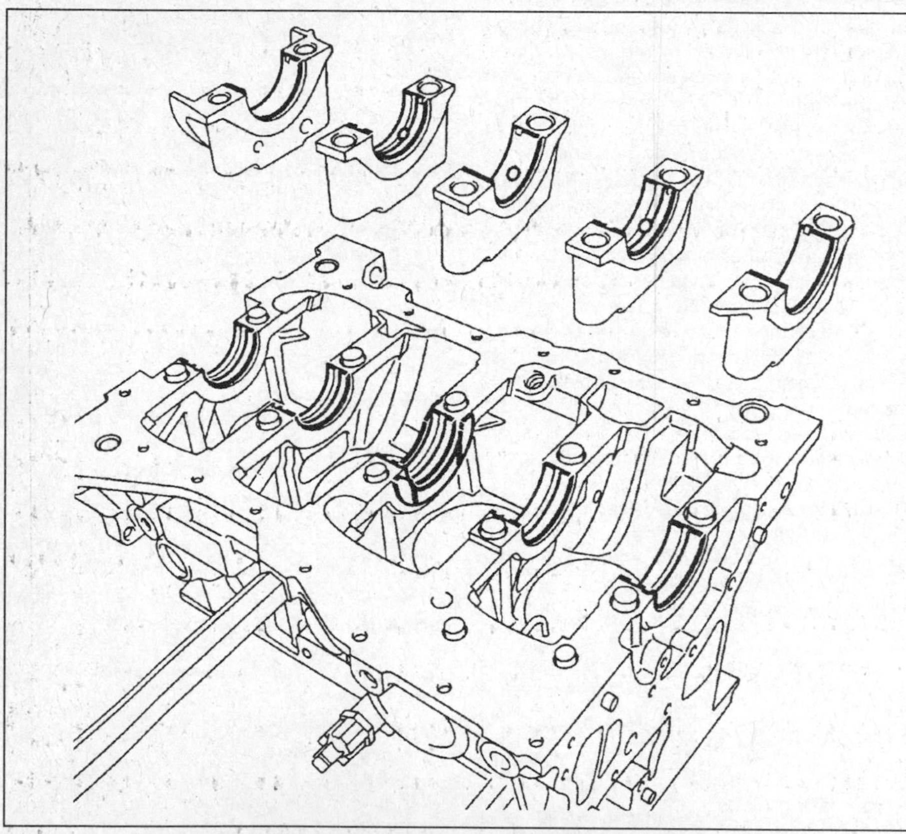

16.4c Bearing shell positions – K4J and K4M petrol engines

2 If temporarily refitted, remove the main bearing cap bolts, and lift out the caps. Lay the caps out in the proper order, to ensure correct installation.

3 If they are still in place, remove the old bearing shells from the block and the main bearing caps. Wipe the bearing recesses with a clean, lint-free cloth. They must be kept spotlessly clean.

4 Clean the backs of the new main bearing shells. Fit the shells with an oil groove in each main bearing location in the block. Note on petrol engines the thrustwashers are integral with the No 3 (centre) upper main bearing shell, ans on diesel engines the thrustwasher halves are fitted either side of No 3 upper main bearing location. Fit the other shell from each bearing set in the corresponding main bearing cap. Make sure the tag where fitted on each bearing shell fits into the notch in the block or cap/lower crankcase. On engines where tags are not incorporated in the shells, it is recommended that the Renault tool Mot. 1493-01 is obtained. Note that the oil holes in the block must line up with the oil holes in the bearing shell. Where separate, fit the thrustwasher halves to No 3 main bearing position and retain with grease **(see illustrations)**. Do not hammer the shells into place, and do not nick or gouge the bearing faces.

5 Clean the bearing surfaces of the shells in the block, then apply a thin, uniform layer of clean molybdenum disulphide-based grease, engine assembly lubricant, or clean engine oil to each surface **(see illustration)**. Coat the thrustwasher surfaces as well.

6 Lubricate the crankshaft oil seal journals with molybdenum disulphide-based grease, engine assembly lubricant, or clean engine oil.

7 Make sure the crankshaft journals are clean, then lay the crankshaft back in place in the block **(see illustration)**.

8 Refit and tighten the main bearing caps as follows **(see illustrations)**:

a) Clean the bearing surfaces of the shells in the caps, then lubricate them. Refit the caps in their respective positions, with the arrows pointing towards the flywheel/driveplate end of the engine.

b) Working on one cap at a time, from the centre main bearing outwards (and

16.4d Smear a little grease on the crankshaft thrustwashers . . .

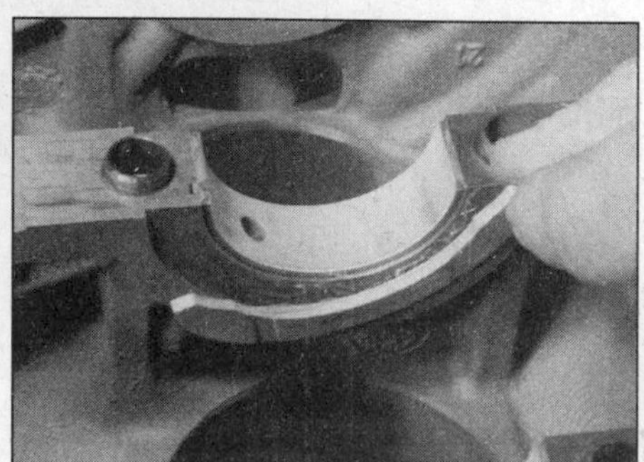

16.4e . . . and stick them to the centre main bearing

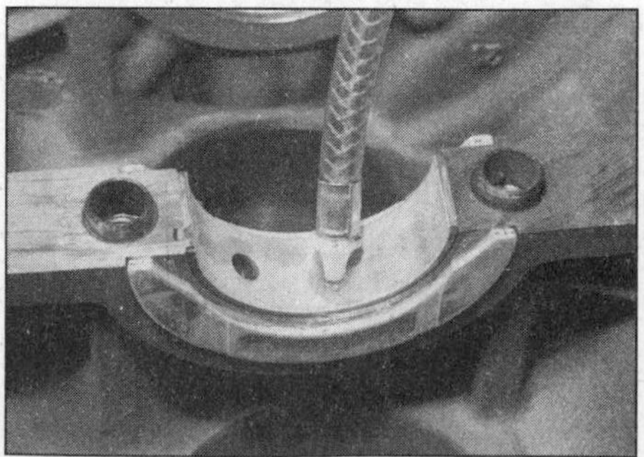

16.5 Lubricate the main bearing shells before fitting the crankshaft

ensuring that each cap is tightened down squarely and evenly onto the block), tighten the main bearing cap bolts to the specified torque wrench setting.

9 Rotate the crankshaft a number of times by hand, to check for any obvious binding.

10 Check the crankshaft endfloat (see Section 10). It should be correct if the crankshaft thrustwashers are not worn or damaged, or have been renewed.

11 Refit the crankshaft left-hand oil seal housing and install a new seal (Chapters 2A, 2B or 2C).

12 Refit the flywheel/driveplate, oil pump (and drive sprocket on petrol K4J/K4M and diesel K9K engines), crankshaft sprocket and timing belt (Chapters 2A, 2B or 2C).

17 Piston/connecting rod assemblies - refitting

1 Clean the backs of the big-end bearing shells and the recesses in the connecting rods and big-end caps. If new shells are being fitted, ensure that all traces of the protective grease are cleaned off using paraffin. Wipe the shells and connecting rods dry with a lint-free cloth.

2 Press the big-end bearing shells into the connecting rods and caps in their correct positions. On the D7F petrol engine, make sure that the location tabs are engaged with the cut-outs in the connecting rods. Note that on all other engines, tags are not incorporated in the shells and, to ensure correct fitting, it is recommended that the Renault tool Mot. 1492 is obtained **(see illustration)**.

3 Lubricate No 1 piston and piston rings and check that the ring gaps are still spaced at 120° intervals to each other. Also, lubricate the big-end bearing shell in the connecting rod **(see illustrations)**.

4 Fit a ring compressor to No 1 piston, then insert the piston and connecting rod into No 1 cylinder. The V arrow must point to the flywheel end of the engine. With No 1 crankpin at its lowest point, drive the piston carefully into the cylinder with the wooden handle of a hammer, at the same time guiding the connecting rod onto the crankpin **(see illustration)**.

16.7 Lay the crankshaft in position in the crankcase

16.8a Fitting No 5 main bearing cap - petrol engine

16.8b Tighten the main bearing cap bolts to the specified torque . . .

16.8c . . . and angle

5 Liberally lubricate the crankpin journal and big-end cap bearing shells, then refit the correct cap and insert the nuts/bolts. Tighten them to the specified torque and angle **(see illustrations)**. Turn the crankshaft to make sure that it is free before moving on to the next assembly.

6 Repeat the above procedures on the remaining piston/connecting rod assemblies.

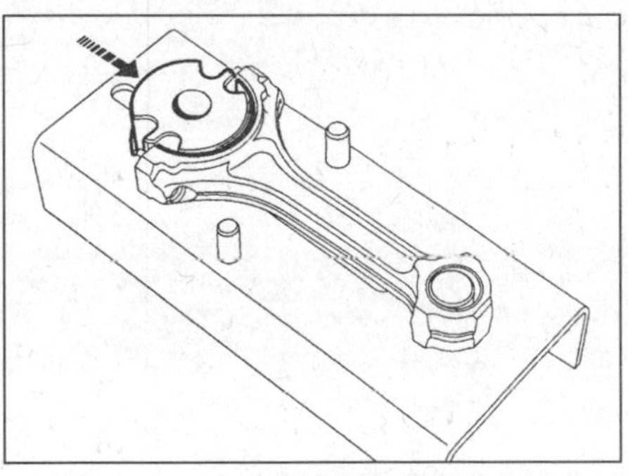

17.2 Using tool Mot. 1492 to fit the big-end shells

17.3a Lubricating the piston rings . . .

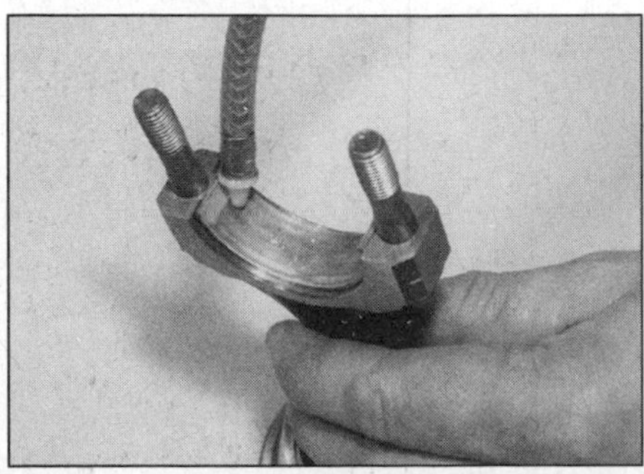

17.3b . . . and big-end bearing shell in the connecting rod

17.4 Using the wooden handle of a hammer to drive the piston into the bore

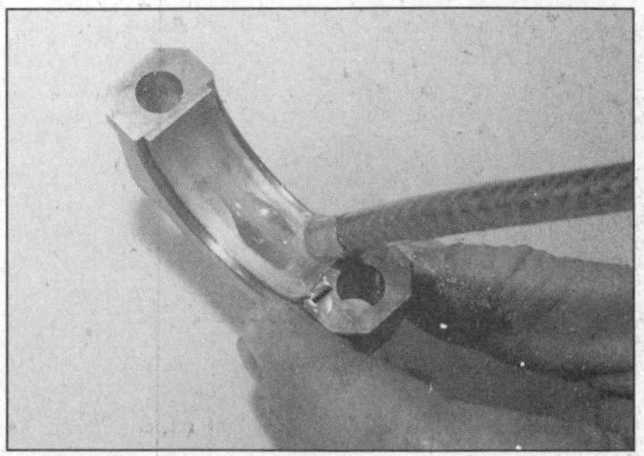

17.5a Lubricate the big-end cap bearing shell . . .

17.5b . . . then refit the cap . . .

17.5c . . . screw on the nuts . . .

17.5d . . . and tighten them to the specified torque and angle

7 On completion, refit the oil pump, sump and cylinder head as described in Chapter 2A, 2B or 2C.

18 Engine – initial start-up after overhaul

1 With the engine refitted in the vehicle, double-check the engine oil and coolant levels. Make a final check that everything has been reconnected, and that there are no tools or rags left in the engine compartment.

2 On petrol-engined models, carry out the following:

a) With the spark plugs removed and the engine management system disabled by removing the engine protection fuse from the engine compartment fusebox, crank the engine on the starter motor until the oil pressure light goes out.

b) Refit the spark plugs and the fuse.

c) Start the engine, noting that this may take a little longer than usual, due to the fuel system being empty.

3 On diesel-engined models, carry out the following:

a) Prime the fuel system as described in Chapter 4B.

b) Fully depress the accelerator pedal, turn the ignition key to position M and wait for the preheating warning light to go out.

c) Start the engine. Additional cranking may be necessary to bleed the fuel system before the engine starts.

4 Once started, keep the engine running at fast tickover. Check that the oil pressure light goes out, then check that there are no leaks of oil, fuel and coolant. Where applicable, check the power steering pipe/hose unions for leakage. Do not be alarmed if there are some odd smells and smoke from parts getting hot and burning off oil deposits.

5 While the engine is idling, check for fuel, water and oil leaks. Where applicable, check the power steering pipe/hose unions for leakage.

6 Keep the engine idling until hot water is felt circulating through the top hose, indicating that the engine is at normal operating temperature, then switch it off.

7 After a few minutes, recheck the oil and water levels and top-up as necessary (see *Weekly checks*).

8 There is no requirement to retighten the cylinder head bolts.

9 If new pistons, rings or crankshaft bearings have been fitted, the engine must be run-in for the first 500 miles (800 km). Do not operate the engine at full-throttle, nor allow it to labour in any gear during this period. It is recommended that the oil and filter be changed at the end of this period.

Chapter 3
Cooling, heating and air conditioning systems

Contents

Degrees of difficulty

Easy, suitable for novice with little experience 	**Fairly easy,** suitable for beginner with some experience 	**Fairly difficult,** suitable for competent DIY mechanic 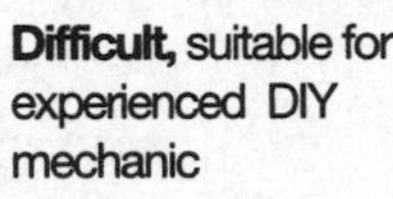	**Difficult,** suitable for experienced DIY mechanic	**Very difficult,** suitable for expert DIY or professional 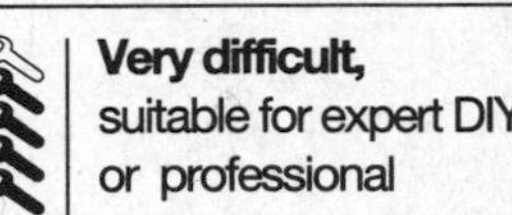

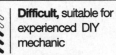

Specifications

General

Cooling system type	Pressurised sealed system, with belt-driven pump, front-mounted radiator and electric cooling fan	
Engine codes:		
1.2 litre:		
8V petrol engine	D7F	
16V petrol engine	D4F	
1.4 litre 16V petrol engine	K4J	
1.6 litre 16V petrol engine	K4M	
1.5 litre Diesel engine	K9K	
Cooling system pressure:		
Cap with yellow mark	1.4 bars	
Cap with brown valve	1.2 bars	
Air conditioning refrigerant type	R134a	
Thermostat	**Starts to open**	**Fully open**
Opening temperatures	89°C	99°C
Travel (closed to fully open)	7.5 mm	
Type	Wax	
Coolant temperature sensor		
Resistance:		
76 000 ± 7000 ohms	at – 40°C	
12 500 ± 1130 ohms	at – 10°C	
2252 ± 112 ohms	at + 25°C	
810 ± 40 ohms	at + 50°C	
280 ± 8 ohms	at + 80°C	
115 ± 3 ohms	at + 110°C	
88 ± 2 ohms	at + 120°C	
Thermo-plungers		
Make	Beru	
Resistance:		
0 to 1.2 ohms	at + 20°C	

Torque wrench settings

	Nm	lbf ft
Air conditioning:		
Compressor mounting bolts	21	16
Pressure relief valve	8	6
Condenser mounting bolts	8	6
Coolant pump bolts:		
D7F and D4F engine	9	7
K4J and K4M engines:		
M6 bolts	11	8
M8 bolts	22	16
K9K engine	11	8

1 General information

1 The cooling system is of the pressurised type. The main components are a belt-driven pump, an aluminium cross-flow radiator, an expansion bottle, an electric cooling fan, a thermostat, and the associated hoses **(see illustrations)**.

2 The system functions as follows. When the engine is cold, coolant is pumped around the cylinder block and head passages. After cooling the cylinder bores, combustion surfaces and valve seats, the coolant passes through the heater and inlet manifold, and is returned to the water pump.

3 When the coolant reaches a predetermined temperature, the thermostat opens, and the hot coolant passes through the top hose to the radiator. As the coolant circulates through the radiator, it is cooled by the inrush of air when the car is in motion. The airflow is supplemented by the action of the electric cooling fan when necessary. Upon reaching the bottom of the radiator, the coolant returns to the pump via the radiator bottom hose, and the cycle is repeated.

4 As the coolant warms up, it expands; the increased volume is accommodated in an expansion bottle. The bottle is 'hot': the coolant circulates through the bottle all the time that the engine is running.

5 The electric cooling fan is mounted behind the radiator and is controlled by the injection ECU, see Section 7 for details.

6 For details of the air conditioning system (when fitted) refer to Section 14.

Precautions

Warning: Do not attempt to remove the expansion bottle filler cap, or to disturb any part of the cooling system, while the engine is hot, as there is a high risk of scalding. If the expansion bottle filler cap must be removed before the engine and radiator have fully cooled (even though this is not recommended), the pressure in the cooling system must first be relieved. Cover the cap with a thick layer of cloth to avoid scalding, and slowly unscrew the filler cap until a hissing sound is heard. When the hissing has stopped, indicating that the pressure has reduced, slowly unscrew the

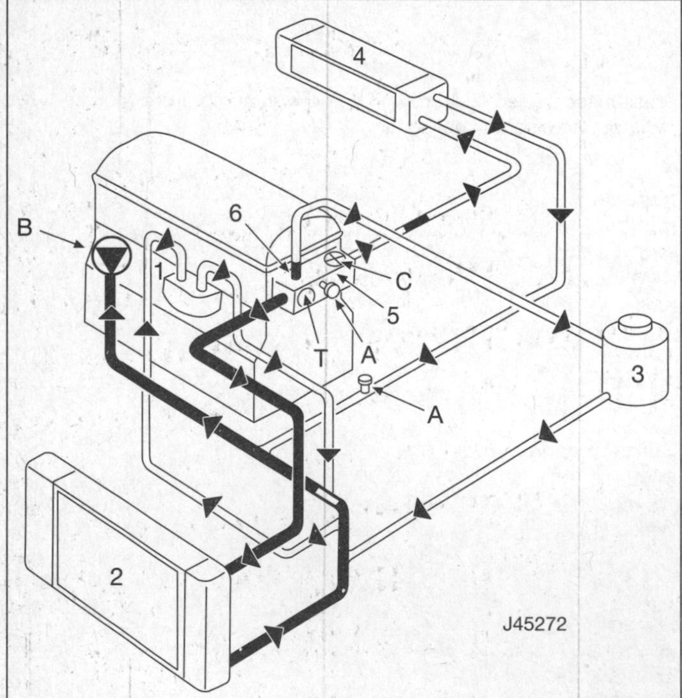

1.1a Cooling system schematic – K9K engine

1 Cylinder block
2 Radiator
3 Hot Expansion bottle with permanent degassing
4 Heater matrix/radiator
5 Thermostat mounting
6 3 mm diameter restriction
A Bleed screw
B Water pump
C Temperature switch
T Thermostat

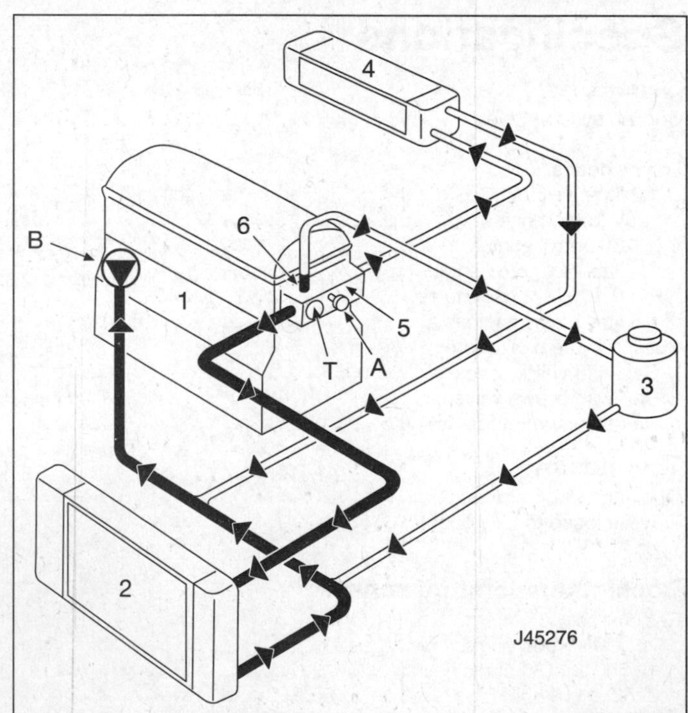

1.1b Cooling system schematic – D4F, K4J and K4M engines

See illustration 1.1a for key

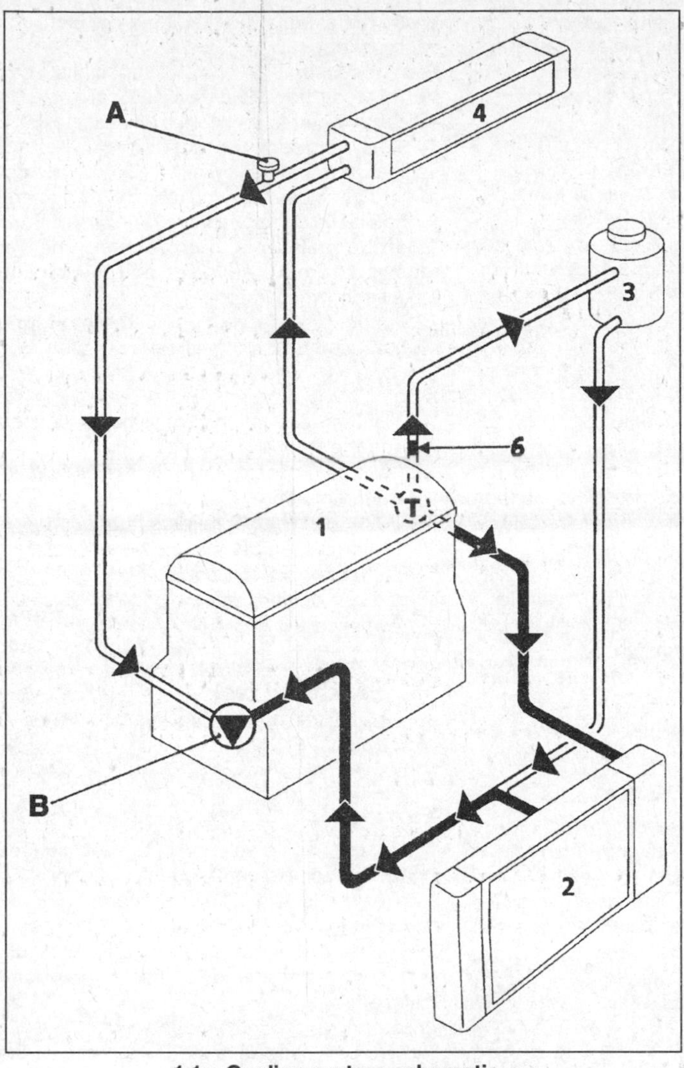

1.1c Cooling system schematic – D7F engine with air conditioning

See illustration 1.1a for key

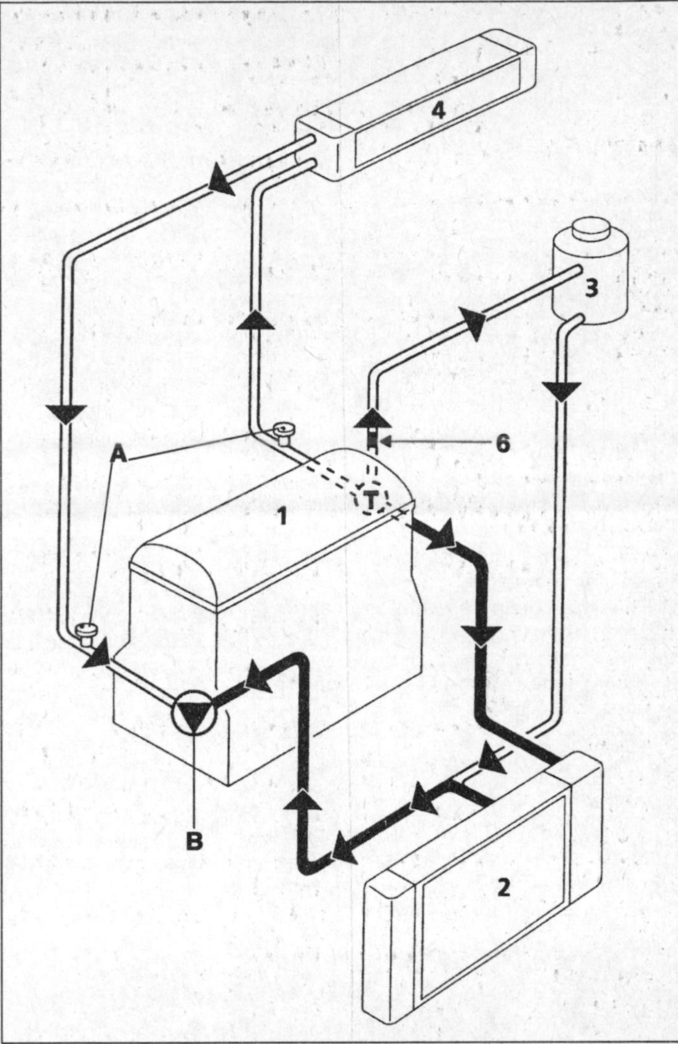

1.1d Cooling system schematic – D7F engine without air conditioning

See illustration 1.1a for key

filler cap until it can be removed; if more hissing sounds are heard, wait until they have stopped before unscrewing the cap completely. At all times, keep well away from the filler cap opening, and protect your hands.

Warning: Do not allow antifreeze to come into contact with your skin, or with the painted surfaces of the vehicle. Rinse off spills immediately, with plenty of water. Never leave antifreeze lying around in an open container, or in a puddle in the driveway or on the garage floor. Children and pets are attracted by its sweet smell, but antifreeze can be fatal if ingested.

Warning: If the engine is hot, the electric cooling fan may start rotating even if the engine is not running. Be careful to keep your hands, hair, and any loose clothing well clear when working in the engine compartment.

Warning: Refer to Section 14 for precautions to be observed when working on models equipped with air conditioning.

2 Cooling system hoses – renewal

Note: *Refer to the warnings given in Section 1 of this Chapter before proceeding. Hoses should only be disconnected once the engine has cooled sufficiently to avoid scalding.*

1 The number, routing and pattern of hoses will vary according to model, but the same basic procedure applies. Before commencing work, make sure that the new hoses are to hand, along with new hose clips if needed. It is good practice to renew the hose clips at the same time as the hoses.

2 Drain the cooling system, as described in Chapter 1A or 1B, saving the coolant if it is fit for re-use. Squirt a little penetrating oil onto the hose clips if they are rusty.

3 Release the hose clips from the hose concerned. Three clip types are used: worm-drive, spring and quick-release. The worm-drive clip is released by turning its screw anti-clockwise. The spring clip is released by squeezing its tags together with pliers **(see illustration)**, at the same time working the clip away from the hose stub. The quick-release clips twist or press to release **(see illustrations 11.23a and 11.23b)**.

4 Unclip any wires, cables or other hoses which may be attached to the hose being removed. Make notes for reference when reassembling if necessary.

5 Release the hose from its stubs with a twisting motion. Be careful not to damage the stubs on delicate components such as the radiator. If the hose is stuck fast, the best course is often to cut it off using a sharp knife, but again be careful not to damage the stubs.

2.3 Releasing a spring hose clip using self-locking grips

6 Before fitting the new hose, smear the stubs with washing-up liquid or a suitable rubber lubricant to aid fitting. **Do not** use oil or grease, which may attack the rubber.

7 Fit the hose clips over the ends of the hose, then fit the hose over its stubs. Work the hose into position. When satisfied, locate and tighten the hose clips.

8 Refill the cooling system as described in Chapter 1A or 1B. Run the engine, and check that there are no leaks.

9 Recheck the tightness of the hose clips on any new hoses after a few hundred miles.

3 Radiator - removal, inspection, cleaning and refitting

Note: *If the radiator is to be removed for a period of more than 48 hours, precautions must be taken against internal corrosion. Either rinse the radiator with clean water and dry it thoroughly by blowing air through it, or fill it with coolant and plug the hose stubs.*

Removal

1 Drain the cooling system by disconnecting the radiator bottom hose. Save the coolant in a clean container, if it is fit for re-use.

2 On models with a front-mounted expansion tank, remove the tank as described in Section 4.

3 Remove the radiator cooling fan as described in Section 6.

4 Release the hose clips and disconnect the remaining hoses from the radiator.

5 On models with air conditioning, separate the condenser from the radiator by removing the mounting bolts **(see illustration)**. **Do not** disconnect the refrigerant pipes. ***Note:*** *Support the condenser in position when the radiator is removed,* ***do not*** *let it hang by its pipes.*

6 Where applicable, unscrew the bolts securing the radiator plastic ducting/shield to the radiator, and leave the ducting/shield in place as the radiator is removed.

7 Carefully lift the radiator off its bottom mountings and remove it from the vehicle. Recover the rubber mountings; renew them if they are in poor condition **(see illustrations)**.

Inspection and cleaning

8 If the radiator has been removed due to suspected blockage, reverse-flush it as described in Chapter 1A or 1B. Clean dirt and debris from the radiator fins, using an airline (in which case, wear eye protection) or a soft brush. Be careful, as the fins are sharp, and easily damaged.

9 If necessary, a radiator specialist can perform a 'flow test' on the radiator, to establish whether an internal blockage exists.

10 A leaking radiator must be referred to a specialist for permanent repair. Do not attempt to weld or solder a leaking radiator, as damage to the plastic components may result.

11 If the radiator is to be sent for repair or renewed, remove all hoses and the cooling fan switch (where fitted).

12 Inspect the condition of the mounting rubbers, and renew them if necessary.

Refitting

13 Refitting is a reversal of removal, bearing in mind the following points.

a) Take care not to damage the radiator fins during refitting.
b) Where applicable, refit the front bumper, top crossmember and the bonnet catch with reference to Chapter 11.
c) On completion, refill the cooling system as described in Chapter 1A or 1B.

4 Expansion tank - removal and refitting

Removal

1 With the engine cold, drain the coolant (see Chapter 1A or 1B) until the tank is empty.

2 On models with the rear-mounted tank, undo the two nuts securing it to the bulkhead, then slide the bottle forwards off the studs, and upwards off the lower locating peg **(see illustration)**.

3 To remove the front-mounted tank, release the two turn-clips securing the top part of the bumper ('grille') to the front crossmember, and pull the plastic back to access the two tank securing bolts. Unscrew the bolts, then release the tank from its two side locating pegs, and withdraw it **(see illustration)**.

4 Disconnect the hose (or hoses) and remove the tank.

Inspection

5 Clean the tank and inspect it for cracks and other damage. Renew it if necessary. Also

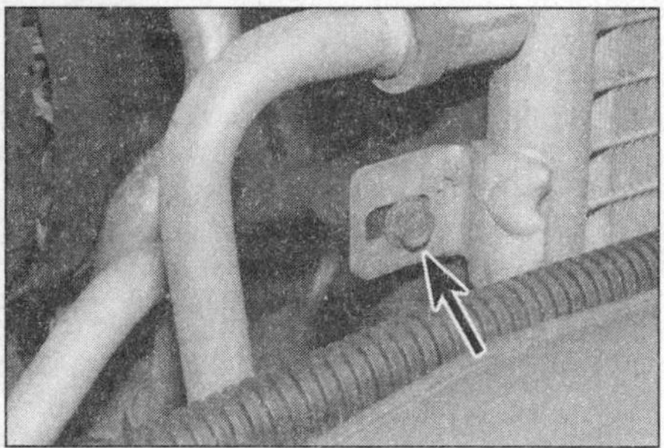

3.5 Undo the condenser retaining bolts from each end of the radiator (right-hand bolt arrowed)

3.7a Lower radiator rubber mounting (arrowed) . . .

3.7b . . . and upper radiator rubber mounting (arrowed)

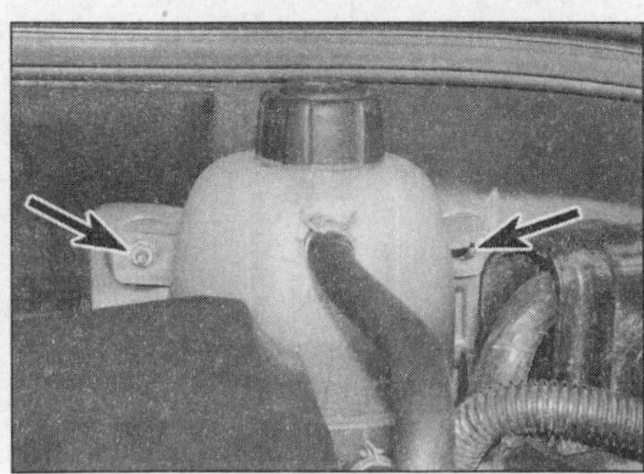

4.2a Undo the two retaining nuts on the rear-mounted tank . . .

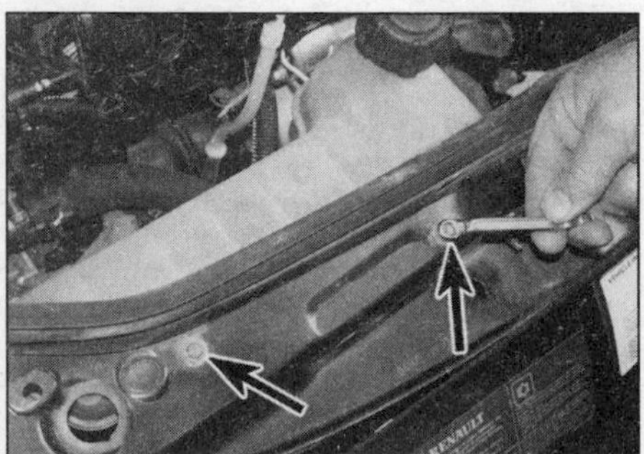

4.3 . . . or pull back the plastic to access the two bolts (front-mounted tank)

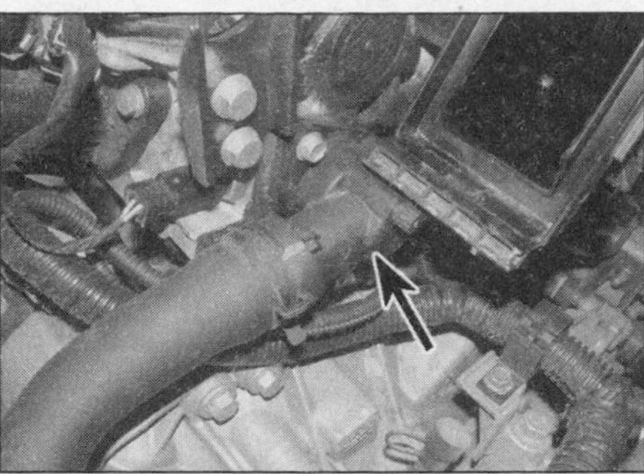

5.1 Thermostat housing (arrowed) on D4F engine (air filter removed for clarity)

inspect the cap; if there is evidence that coolant has been vented through the cap, renew it.

Refitting

6 Refit by reversing the removal operations. Refill and bleed the cooling system as described in Chapter 1A or 1B.

5 Thermostat – removal, testing and refitting

1 The thermostat is located in the cylinder head outlet elbow housing on the left-hand side of the engine **(see illustration)**, above the transmission bellhousing (see illustrations in Section 1 for location). On some models, it may be necessary to remove air intake hoses or air filter housing to make easier access to

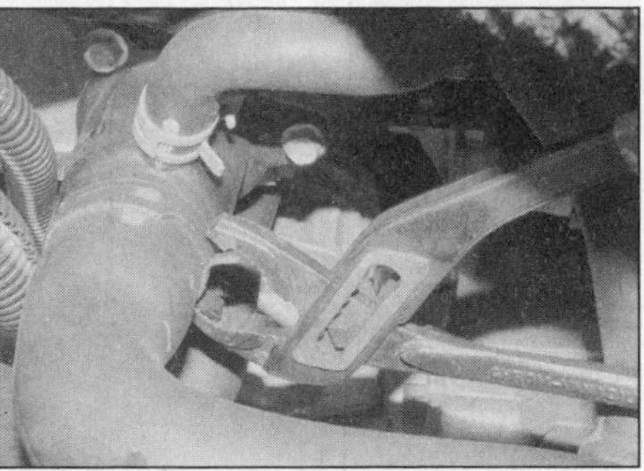

5.3 Releasing the clip securing the hose to the thermostat cover

the thermostat housing. See relevant Chapters for information on the removal and refitting procedures.

Removal

Note: *A new thermostat sealing ring may be required on refitting. Check with your local Renault dealer for the availability of parts, as the thermostat may be part of the coolant housing.*

2 Partially drain the cooling system, as described in Chapter 1A or 1B, so that the coolant level is below the thermostat location.

3 Where necessary, loosen the clip and disconnect the hose from the thermostat cover **(see illustration)**.

4 Unbolt the cover/thermostat assembly, noting that the thermostat may be integral with the cover. Recover the sealing ring from the housing **(see illustrations)**.

5 On some engine types, unbolt the cover and remove the thermostat, then remove the sealing ring from around the thermostat **(see illustrations)**.

Testing

6 To test whether the unit is serviceable, suspend it on a string in a saucepan of cold water, together with a thermometer. Heat the water, and note the temperature at which the thermostat begins to open. Continue heating the water until the thermostat is fully open, and then remove it from the water.

7 The temperature at which the thermostat should start to open is stamped on the unit. If the thermostat does not start to open at the specified temperature, does not fully open in boiling water, or does not fully close when removed from the water, then it must be discarded and a new one fitted.

Refitting

8 Refitting is a reversal of removal, bearing in mind the following points.

a) Where applicable renew the sealing ring.

b) On completion, refill the cooling system as described in Chapter 1A or 1B.

6 Electric cooling fan assembly – removal and refitting

Removal

1 Disconnect the battery negative lead.

2 On models with the D4F and D7F engines, unscrew the bolts securing the fan assembly to the radiator **(see illustration)**, then release

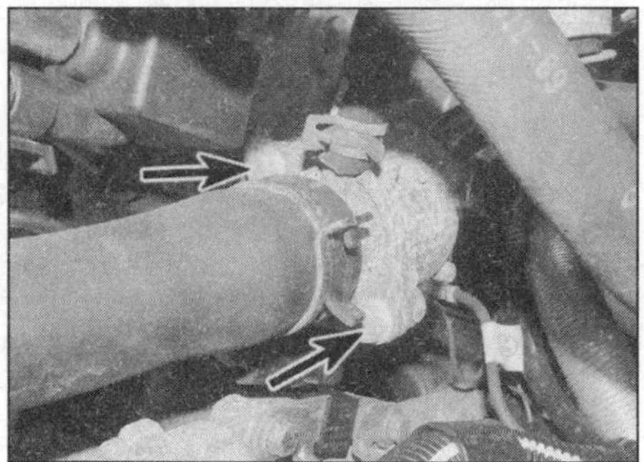

5.4a Undo the two retaining bolts (arrowed) . . .

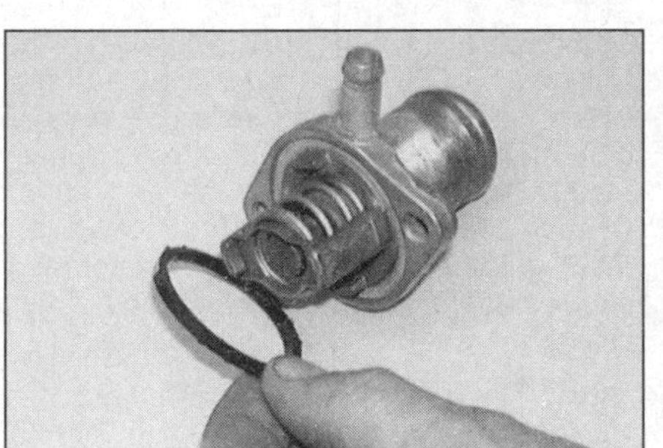

5.4b . . . and fit a new sealing ring to the thermostat/cover assembly on the D7F engine

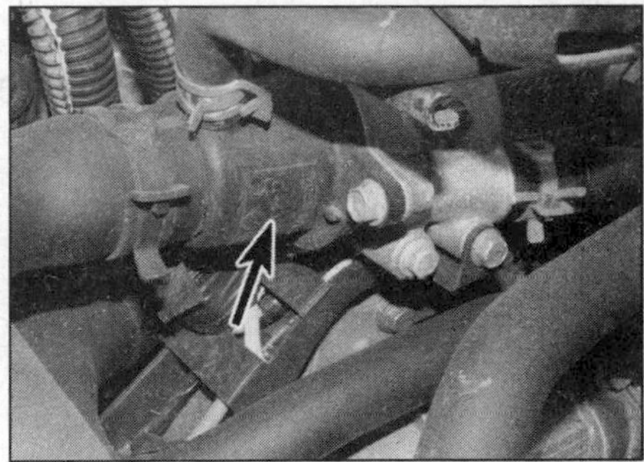

5.4c Thermostat housing (arrowed) on the K4J and K4M engines

5.5a On diesel models, slacken and remove the retaining bolts (arrowed) . . .

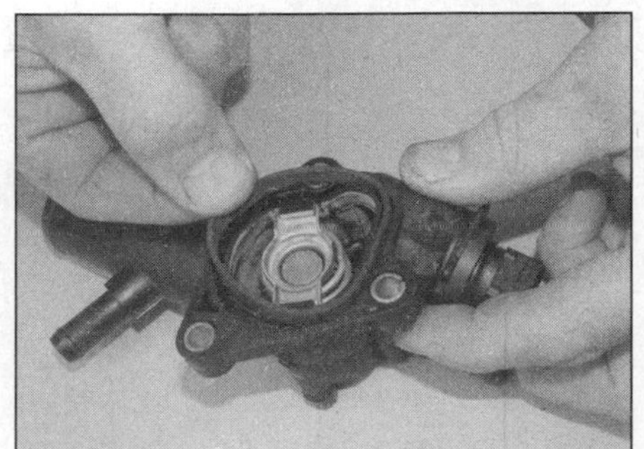

5.5b . . . then remove the thermostat housing cover and renew the sealing ring

6.2 Undo the retaining bolts (arrowed) and lift out the fan assembly

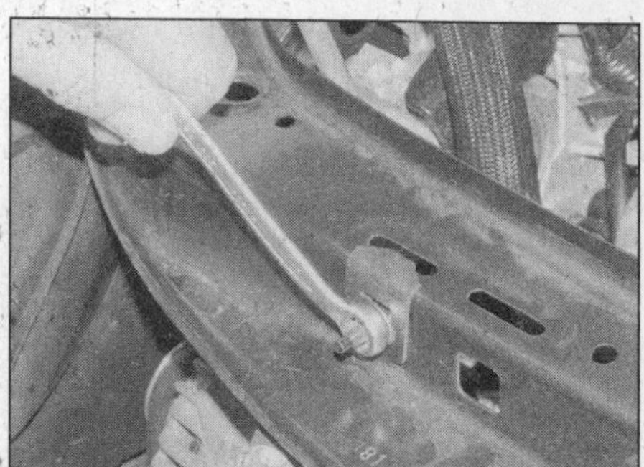
6.4a Slacken the two radiator mounting nuts (right-hand shown) . . .

6.4b . . . and withdraw the brackets to release the radiator from the crossmember

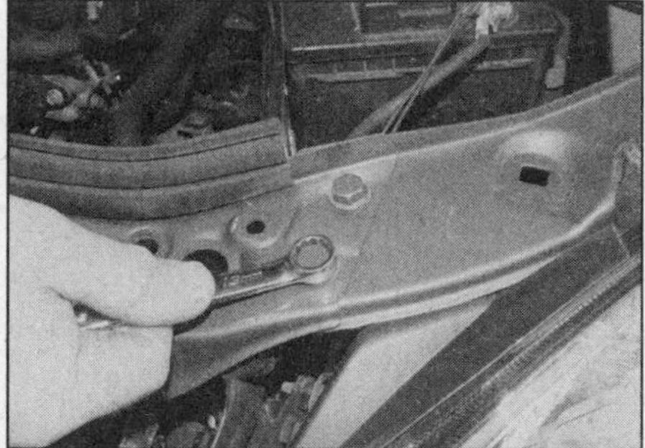
6.5 Remove the crossmember retaining bolts (left-hand side shown)

6.6a Lift fan assembly upwards to release it from the radiator retaining clips (arrowed) . . .

the wiring connector from fan frame, and disconnect it.

3 On other models, remove the front bumper/ grille assembly as described in Chapter 11, Section 6.

4 Remove the two radiator mounting nuts from the top crossmember. Note the position of each mounting brackets and remove them **(see illustrations)**.

5 Undo the four securing bolts and remove the crossmember from above the radiator **(see illustration)**. Move it to the rear of the engine bay leaving the bonnet release cable still connected.

6 Unclip the fan assembly from the radiator **(see illustration)**. Withdraw the fan assembly, disconnecting the wiring on removal.

Refitting

7 Refit by reversing the removal operations.

6.6b . . . unclip any wiring from the fan shroud

7 Electric cooling fan switch – general information

The operation of the fan is controlled by the fuel injection ECU and has a slow and high speed function, this is controlled when the air conditioning is selected on the instrument panel. See Section 16 at the end of this Chapter, for information on the removal and refitting procedures for the fan resistor/relay. ***Note:** If there is a fault on the slow speed circuit, the fan will run at high speed setting.*

a) At slow speeds – if the coolant temperature is greater than 99°C the fan will operate. When the coolant temperature is lower than 96°C the fan stops operating.

b) At high speeds – if the coolant temperature is greater than 102°C the fan will operate. When the coolant temperature is lower than 99°C the fan stops operating.

c) The coolant temperature warning light will illuminate if the temperature is greater than 114°C. When the coolant temperature is lower than 111°C the light will go out.

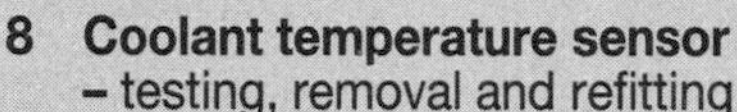

8 Coolant temperature sensor – testing, removal and refitting

1 The location of the temperature sensor varies according to model. It is located in the thermostat housing or the left-hand of the cylinder head, above the transmission bellhousing **(see illustrations)**.

Testing

2 The temperature gauge is fed with a stabilised voltage from the instrument panel feed (via the ignition switch and a fuse). The gauge earth is controlled by the sender. The sender contains a thermistor – an electronic component whose electrical resistance decreases as its temperature rises. When the coolant is cold, the sender resistance is high, current flow through the gauge is reduced, and the gauge needle points towards the cold end of the scale. As the coolant temperature rises and the sender resistance falls, current

8.1a Temperature sensor (arrowed) – K9K diesel engine

8.1b Temperature sensor (arrowed) – K4J and K4M engines

8.1c Temperature sensor (arrowed) – D4F engine

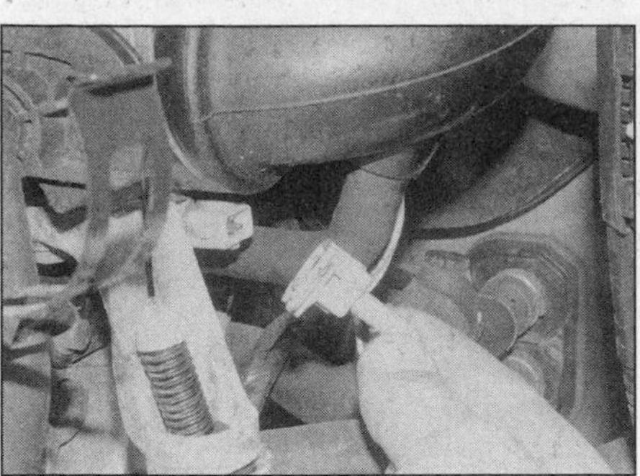

8.9 Disconnecting the multi-plug from the temperature sensor – D7F engine

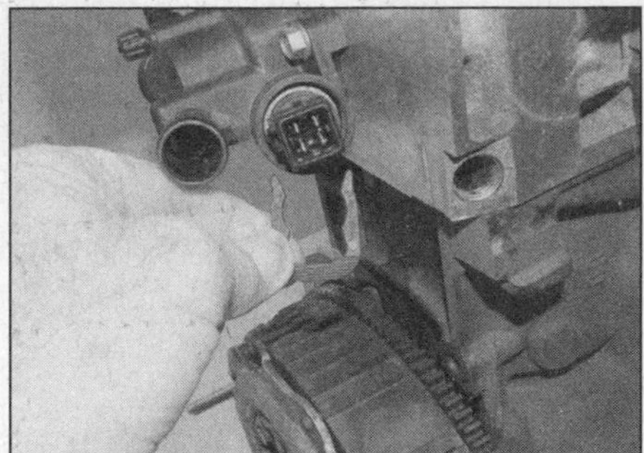

8.13a Release the retaining clip . . .

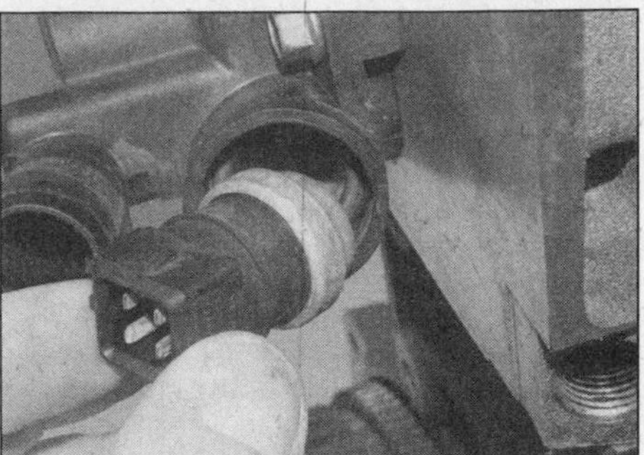

8.13b . . . and withdraw the sensor from the housing – K9K engine

flow increases, and the gauge needle moves towards the upper end of the scale. If the sender is faulty, it must be renewed.

3 The temperature warning light is fed with a voltage from the instrument panel. The light's earth is controlled by the sender. The sender is effectively a switch, which operates at a predetermined temperature to earth the light and complete the circuit.

4 If the gauge develops a fault, first check the other instruments; if they do not work at all, check the instrument panel electrical feed. If the readings are erratic, there may be a fault in the voltage stabiliser, which will necessitate renewal of the stabiliser (the stabiliser is integral with the instrument panel printed circuit board – see Chapter 12). If the fault lies in the temperature gauge alone, check it as follows.

5 If the gauge needle remains at the 'cold' end of the scale when the engine is hot, disconnect the sender wiring plug, and earth the relevant wire to the cylinder head. If the needle then deflects when the ignition is switched on, the sender unit is proved faulty, and should be renewed. If the needle still does not move, remove the instrument panel (Chapter 12) and check the continuity of the wire between the sender unit and the gauge, and the feed to the gauge unit. If continuity is shown, and the fault still exists, then the gauge is faulty, and the gauge unit should be renewed.

6 If the gauge needle remains at the 'hot' end of the scale when the engine is cold, disconnect the sender wire. If the needle then returns to the 'cold' end of the scale when the ignition is switched on, the sender unit is proved faulty, and should be renewed. If the needle still does not move, check the remainder of the circuit as described previously.

7 The same basic principles apply to testing the warning light. The light should illuminate when the relevant sender wire is earthed.

Removal and refitting

Petrol engines

Note: *Suitable sealant will be required to coat the sender threads on refitting.*

8 Drain the cooling system as described in Chapter 1A. Alternatively, remove the expansion bottle cap to depressurise the system, and have the new sensor or a suitable bung to hand.

9 Disconnect the multi-plug and unscrew the temperature sensor from the transmission end of the cylinder head **(see illustration)**.

10 Apply a little sealant to the temperature sensor threads, and screw it into the coolant housing. Reconnect the multi-plug.

11 Top-up or refill the cooling system, with reference to *Weekly checks* or Chapter 1A.

Diesel engines

12 Drain the cooling system as described in Chapter 1B. Alternatively, remove the expansion bottle cap to depressurise the system, and have the new temperature sensor or a suitable bung to hand.

13 Disconnect the multi-plug, release the securing clip and withdraw the temperature sensor from the coolant housing **(see illustrations)**.

14 Refit the temperature sensor into the coolant housing and secure it in place with the retaining clip. Reconnect the multi-plug.

15 Top-up or refill the cooling system, with reference to *Weekly checks* or Chapter 1B.

9 Coolant pump – removal and refitting

1 If the coolant pump is leaking, or is noisy in operation, it must be renewed.

K4J and K4M petrol engines

Note: *A tube of Loctite 518 sealant will be required on refitting.*

Removal

2 Disconnect the battery negative lead, then drain the cooling system as described in Chapter 1A.

3 Remove the timing belt and timing belt tensioner as described in Chapter 2B.

4 Slacken and remove the coolant pump retaining bolts, noting the locations of the different size bolts.

5 Withdraw the pump from the block, tapping it with a soft-faced mallet if it is stuck.

Refitting

6 Commence refitting by thoroughly cleaning the mating surfaces of the pump and cylinder block, ensuring that all traces of sealant are removed.

7 Apply a 0.6 to 1.0mm wide band of Loctite 518 sealant to the pump mating face **(see illustration)**.

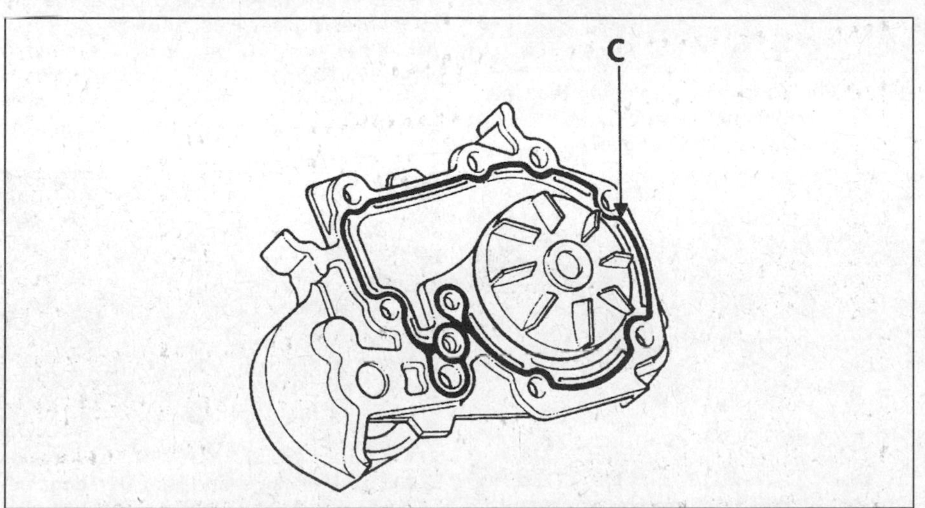

9.7 Apply a bead of sealant (C) to the coolant mating surface – K4J and K4M engines

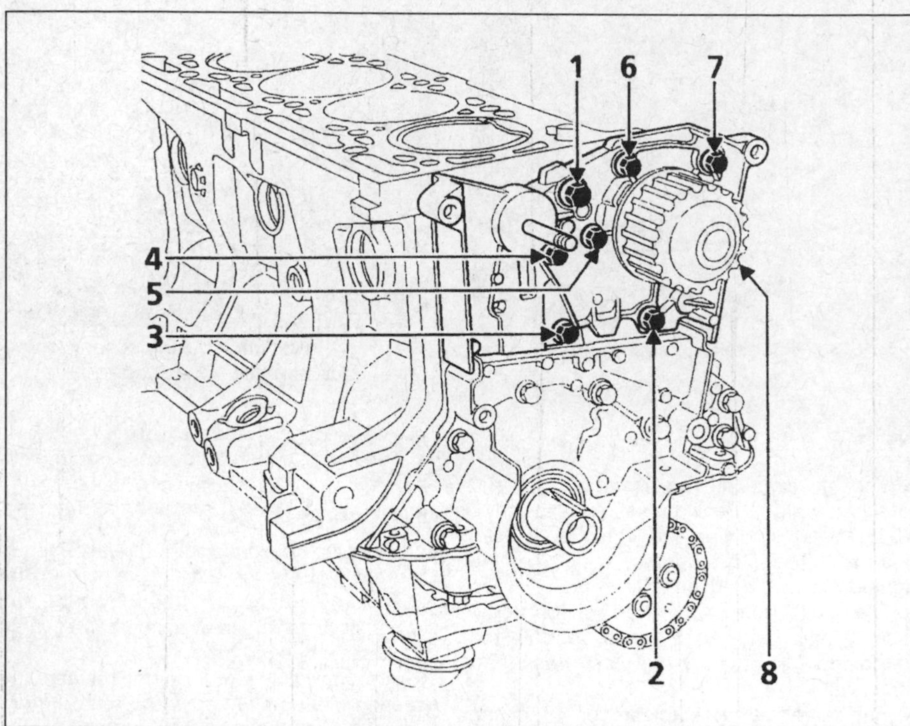

9.9 Coolant pump retaining bolt tightening sequence – K4J and K4M engines

8 Locate the pump in position and refit the retaining bolts to their correct locations, tightening them to their specified torque.

9 Work in sequence **(see illustration)**, to tighten all the bolts to the specified torque setting. **Note:** *The tightening torque of the M6 bolts and M8 bolts are different (see Specifications at the start of this Chapter).*

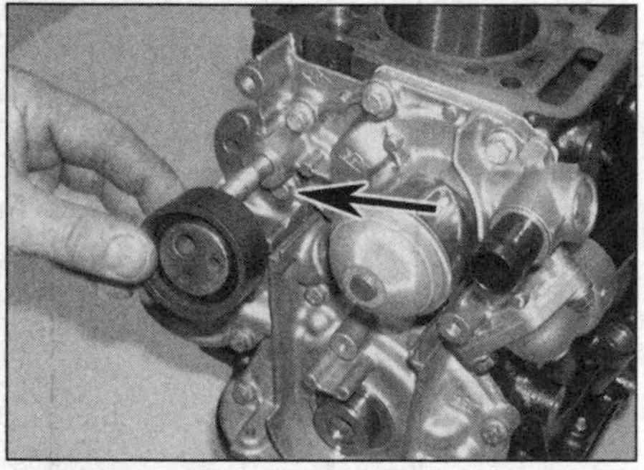

9.17 Remove the timing belt tensioner pulley for access to one of the pump securing bolts (arrowed) – D7F and D4F engines

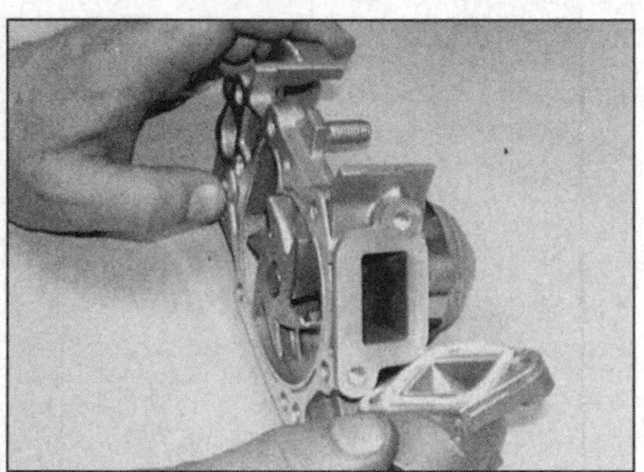

9.20a Apply a bead of sealant to the water elbow before refitting – D7F and D4F engines

10 Refit the timing belt tensioner and timing belt as described in Chapter 2B.

11 On completion, refill the cooling system as described in Chapter 1A.

D7F and D4F petrol engines

Note: *Check with Renault for the availability of a new gasket for your model. On later models there is a gasket available and on earlier models sealant will be required on refitting*

Removal

12 Disconnect the battery negative lead.

13 Drain the cooling system as described in Chapter 1A.

14 Apply the handbrake, then jack up the front of the car and support securely on axle stands (see *Jacking and vehicle support*).

15 Remove the timing belt as described in Chapter 2A. On some models, it may be necessary to unscrew and remove the upper alternator mounting bolt, and slacken the lower bolt.

16 Disconnect the coolant hoses from the coolant pump and, where applicable, unscrew the bolt securing the pump coolant pipe to the alternator mounting bracket.

17 Unscrew the nut and washer and remove the timing belt tensioner pulley (this is necessary for access to one of the coolant pump securing bolts) **(see illustration)**.

18 Unbolt and remove the coolant pump from the cylinder block (remove and discard the gasket – where fitted). Tapping it with a soft-faced mallet if it is stuck.

Refitting

19 Thoroughly clean all sealant from the mating faces of the coolant pump and the cylinder block.

20 If the water elbow has been removed from the pump, apply a thin bead of Loctite 518 or a suitable equivalent, to the sealing surface between the water elbow and the pump. On early D7F engines, if the plastic pipe has been removed from the pump elbow, renew the O-ring – note that the plastic pipe is a push-fit in the elbow, and relies on the O-ring as the only form of sealing **(see illustrations)**.

21 Fit new gasket (where applicable) or apply a bead of Rhodorseal 5661 (available from a Renault dealer), or similar sealant, to the mating face of the coolant pump. Offer the pump into

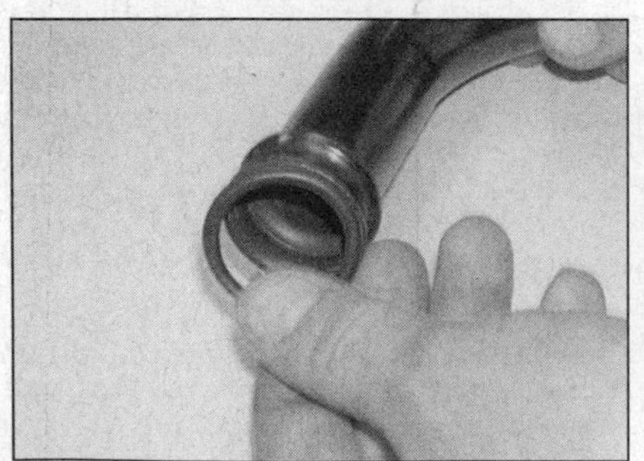

9.20b On D7F engines, renew the O-ring . . .

9.20c . . . then push the plastic pipe into the elbow

9.20d D4F engines (and later D7F engines) have plastic elbows (arrowed) with a standard hose fitting

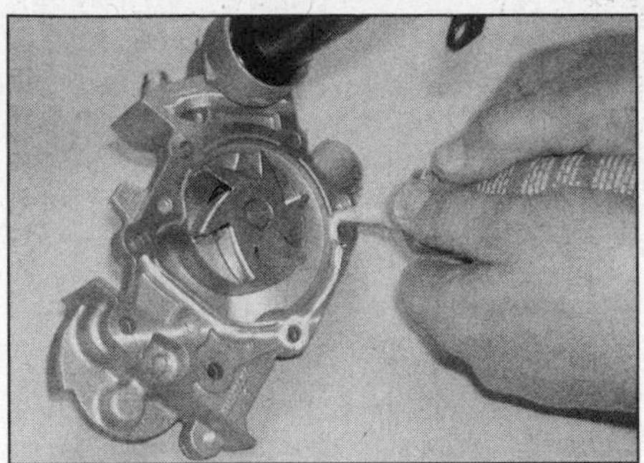

9.21a Apply a bead of sealant to the water pump mating surface . . .

position in the cylinder block, ensuring that it engages with the locating dowels, then refit the bolts and tighten securely in the recommended order **(see illustrations)**.

22 Further refitting is a reversal of removal, bearing in mind the following points.

a) Refit and tension the timing belt as described in Chapter 2A.

b) On completion, refill the cooling system as described in Chapter 1A.

K9K diesel engines

Note: *A new gasket will be required on refitting.*

Removal

23 Disconnect the battery negative lead, then drain the cooling system as described in Chapter 1B.

24 Remove the timing belt as described in Chapter 2C.

25 Undo the retaining bolts and remove the rear timing belt cover from the cylinder block **(see illustration)**.

26 Unscrew the retaining bolts, then manoeuvre the coolant pump out of position **(see illustration)**. Recover the pump gasket and discard it; a new one must be used on refitting.

Refitting

27 Ensure that pump and cylinder block/housing mating faces are clean and dry, and that the locating dowels are correctly positioned.

28 Offer up the new gasket (dry) and fit the pump assembly, tightening its retaining bolts securely **(see illustration)**.

29 Refit the rear timing belt cover to the cylinder block and securely tighten the retaining bolts.

30 Refit the timing belt as described in Chapter 2C.

31 On completion, refill the cooling system as described in Chapter 1B.

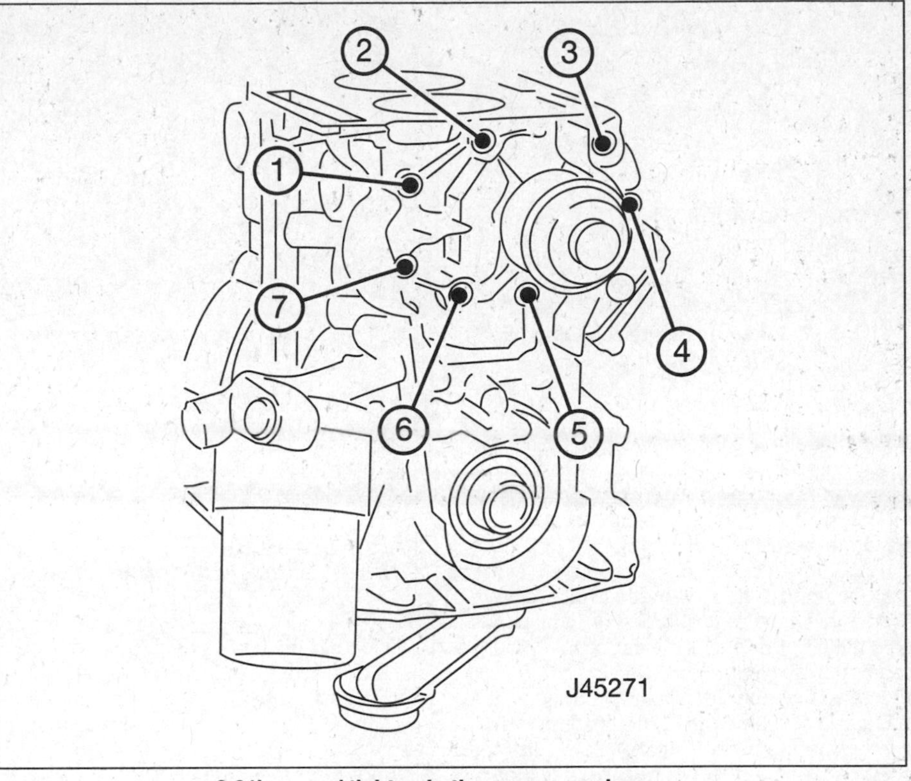

9.21b . . and tighten in the sequence shown – D7F and D4F engines

10 Heating system – general information and checks

General information

1 The heater and fresh air ventilation unit works on the principle of mixing hot and cold air in the proportions selected by means of the left-hand (temperature) control knob. Coolant flows through the heater radiator all the time that the engine is running, regardless of the temperature selected.

2 Air distribution is selected by the central control knob. Additional control is possible by opening, closing or redirecting individual vents in the facia panel. This also has a recirculation position which enables the outside air supply to be closed off, while the air inside the vehicle is recirculated. This can be useful to prevent unpleasant odours entering from outside the vehicle – for Instance, when driving in heavy traffic – but should only be used briefly, as the recirculated air inside the vehicle will soon become stale and may cause light misting.

3 A four-speed blower is controlled by the right-hand knob.

4 For details of the air conditioning system fitted to some models, refer to Section 14.

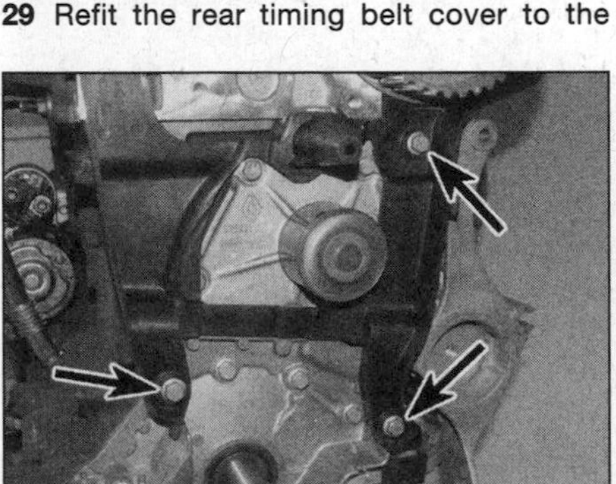

9.25 Unscrew the securing bolts (arrowed)

9.26 Undo the pump retaining bolts (arrowed)

9.28 Fitting a new gasket to the water pump

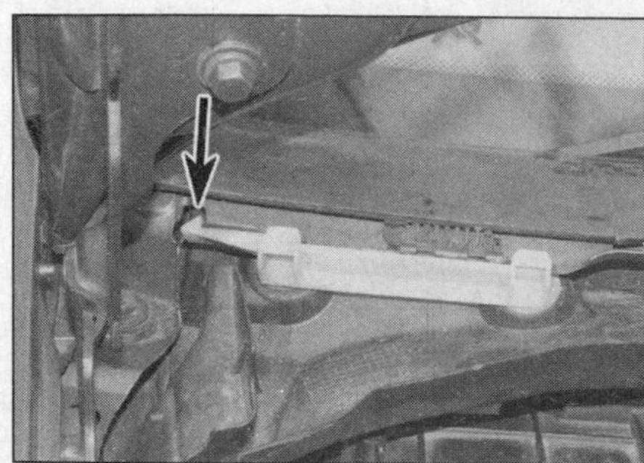

11.11a Release the white retaining clip (arrowed) . . .

Checks

5 Periodically check that all the controls operate as intended. Problems related to the temperature and air distribution controls may be due to cables being broken or disconnected (see Section 13).

6 If the blower does not operate at all, check the fuse and the blower multi-plug before condemning the motor. If one or two speeds do not work, the fault is almost certainly in the heater blower resistor (see Section 11).

7 Check the condition and security of the coolant hoses which feed the heater radiator. The radiator-to-hose joints are at the bulkhead under the bonnet. If water leaks inside the car seem to be coming from the heater, establish whether the leak is of coolant (indicating a leaking heater radiator) or of rainwater (indicating a defective scuttle seal). Cooling system antifreeze has a distinctive sweet smell.

11.11b . . . and remove the rain channel

11 Heater components – removal and refitting

Blower assembly (without air conditioning)

Removal

1 Disconnect the battery negative lead.

2 Remove the windscreen wiper arms as described in Chapter 12, and the windscreen cowl panel as described in Chapter 11.

3 Where required, remove the windscreen wiper motor and linkage as described in Chapter 12.

4 Disconnect the multi-plug from the side of the blower assembly.

5 Remove the three bolts which secure the blower assembly in place. Manoeuvre the blower and remove it through the right-hand side of the scuttle panel.

6 If the motor is to be renewed, release the clips and separate the half-housings. Use new clips or screws (supplied with a new motor) on reassembly.

7 Check the condition of the seal at the base of the blower. Renew it if its condition is in doubt. **Note:** *If the seal is defective, rainwater entering the scuttle will leak into the passenger compartment.*

Refitting

8 Refit by reversing the removal operations.

Blower assembly (with air conditioning)

Removal

9 Disconnect the battery negative lead.

10 Remove the windscreen wiper arms as described in Chapter 12, and the windscreen cowl panel as described in Chapter 11.

11 Release the retaining clip and withdraw the rain channel from the lower corner of the windscreen, on the right-hand side **(see illustrations)**.

12 Disconnect the multi-plug wiring connector and two pin wiring connector from the blower assembly **(see illustrations)**.

13 Remove the retaining screws which secure the blower motor in place. Manoeuvre the blower motor and remove it from the scuttle panel **(see illustration)**.

14 To remove the motor from the plastic housing, disconnect the wiring connector, undo the retaining screws and withdraw the fan from the housing **(see illustrations).**

11.12a Disconnecting the multi-plug . . .

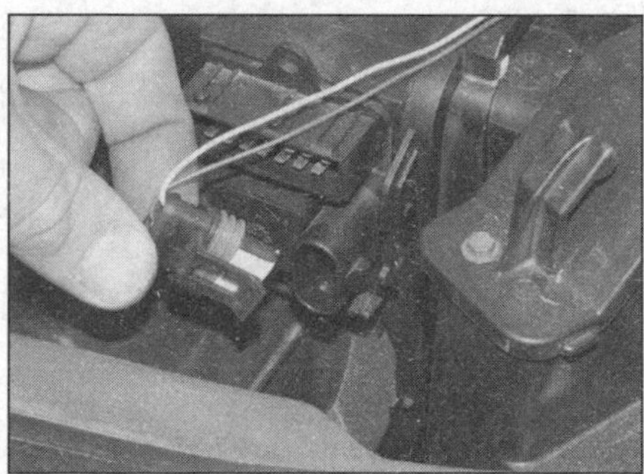

11.12b . . . and the small wiring connector from the heater blower

11.13 Withdraw the motor from the heater blower housing

11.14a Disconnect the wiring connector . . .

11.14b . . . undo the retaining screws . . .

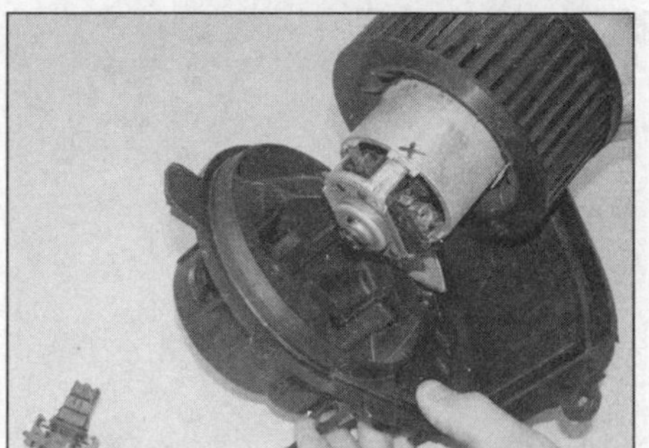

11.14c . . . and withdraw the motor

11.17a Undo the retaining bolt (arrowed) . . .

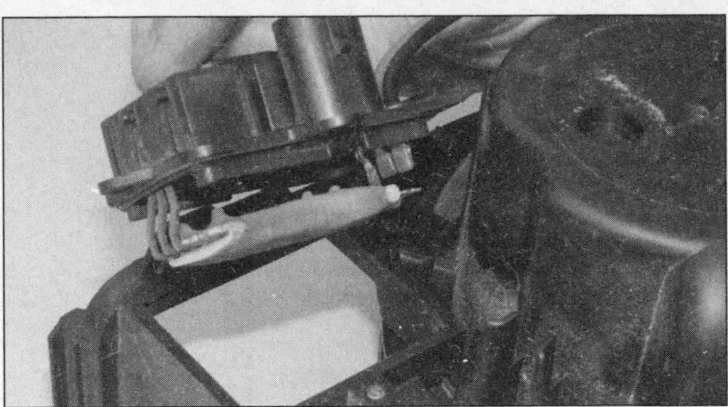
11.17b . . . and unclip the resistor from the heater housing

Refitting

15 Refit by reversing the removal operations.

Heater blower resistor

Note: *The resistor is located in the blower motor casing. It is switched into the circuit at low and intermediate speeds. If it fails, one or more speeds will not be operative.*

Removal

16 Disconnect the multi-plug wiring connector and two pin wiring connector from the blower assembly **(see illustrations 11.12a and 11.12b)**.

17 Remove the retaining bolt, release the clip and withdraw the resistor from the heater housing **(see illustrations)**.

Refitting

18 Refit by reversing the removal operations.

Air distribution unit

Removal

19 Remove the complete facia assembly as described in Chapter 11.

20 Undo the securing bolts from the facia mounting beam, and move it to one side.

21 If required, remove the blower assembly as described previously in this Section, to gain easier access.

22 Remove the retaining bolts now accessible from inside the scuttle panel.

23 Clamp the coolant hoses where they pass through the bulkhead. Alternatively, drain the cooling system as described in Chapter 1A or 1B. Disconnect the hoses from the heater radiator stubs. **Note:** *There are two types of clips fitted for the heater hoses. One type twists and releases, for the other press at each side and then pull hose to release* ***(see illustrations)****.*

24 Remove the air distribution unit, complete with control panel and cables (if still fitted), from inside the car. Be prepared for coolant spillage from the heater radiator.

Refitting

25 Refit by reversing the removal operations. Top up, or refill and bleed the cooling system as described in *Weekly checks*, Chapter 1A or 1B.

Heater radiator

Removal

26 Remove the air distribution unit as described previously in this Section.

27 Remove the foam seal and the closing plate from the heater radiator stubs **(see illustration)**.

28 Remove the two screws (if fitted), release the clips and withdraw the heater radiator **(see illustrations)**. Be careful not to damage the fins.

Refitting

29 Refit by reversing the removal operations. If the clips were damaged during removal,

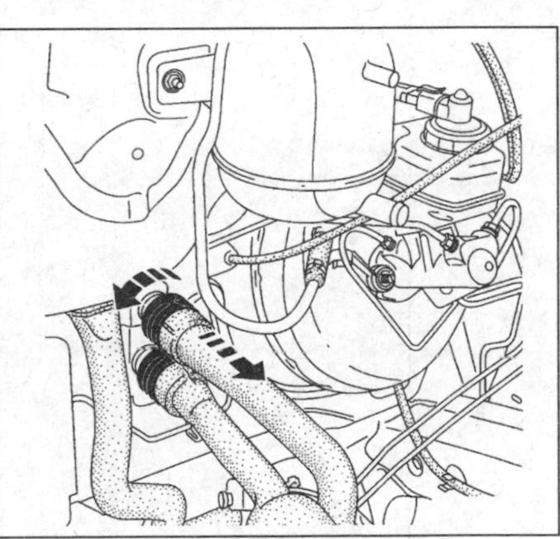
11.23a Quick-release type of heater hose fittings, twist and release . . .

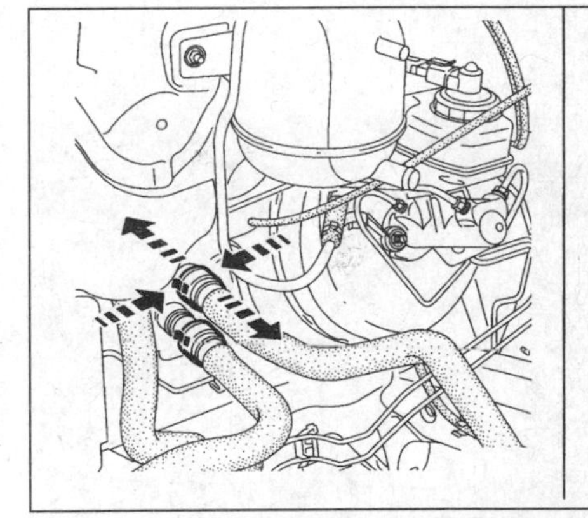
11.23b . . . or press at each side to release

11.27 Removing the foam seal and the closing plate from the heater radiator stubs

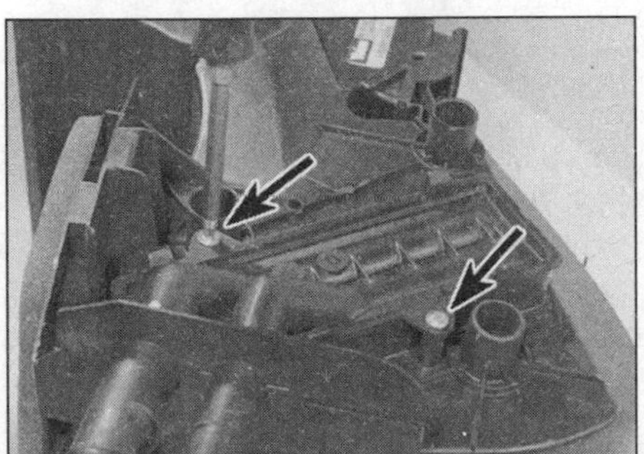
11.28a Remove the heater radiator securing screws (arrowed) – where fitted . . .

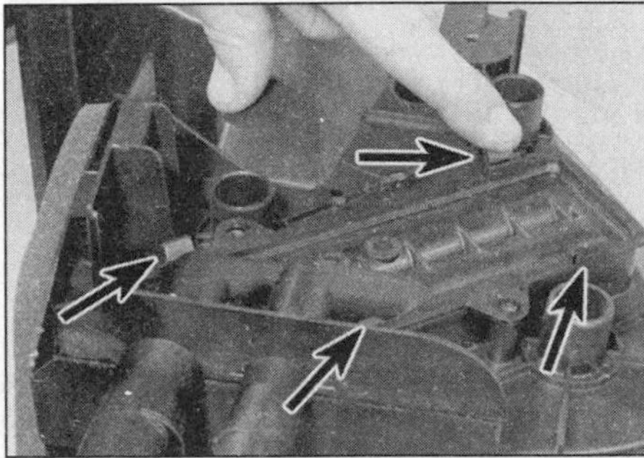
11.28b . . . release the retaining clips (arrowed) . . .

11.28c . . . and slide the heater radiator from the housing

secure the radiator using two screws in the holes provided.

Heater plugs (thermo-plungers)

30 The heater plugs (thermo-plungers) are located in a water housing attached to the transmission by a mounting bracket, between the engine and the heater radiator **(see illustration)**. They only operate when the temperature of the coolant and airflow is not up to temperature.

Removal

Note: *Suitable sealant will be required to coat the sender threads on refitting.*

31 Drain the cooling system as described in Chapter 1A or 1B. Alternatively, remove the expansion bottle cap to depressurise the system, and have the new heater plug or a suitable bung to hand.

32 Disconnect the multi-plug and unscrew the heater plug from the water housing.

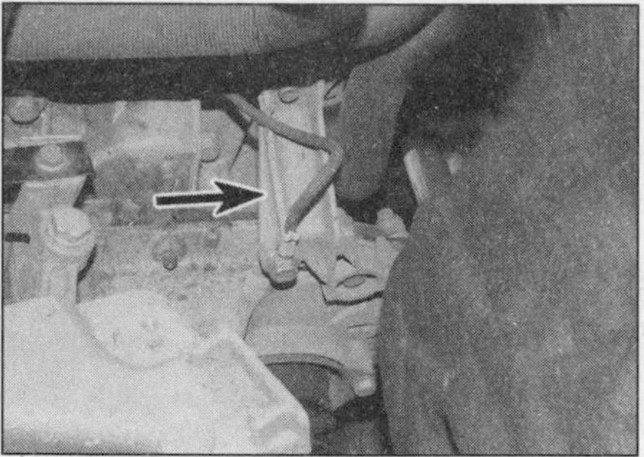

11.30 Mounting bracket (arrowed) for thermo-plunger housing

Refitting

33 Apply a little sealant to the threads, and screw the heater plug into position. Reconnect the multi-plug.

34 Top-up or refill the cooling system, with reference to *Weekly checks,* Chapter 1A or 1B.

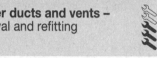

12 Heater ducts and vents – removal and refitting

Removal

1 Remove the upper facia panel as described in Chapter 11.

2 Undo the retaining screws from the side air vents, and withdraw them from the upper facia panel **(see illustration)**.

3 The facia central vents are each clipped

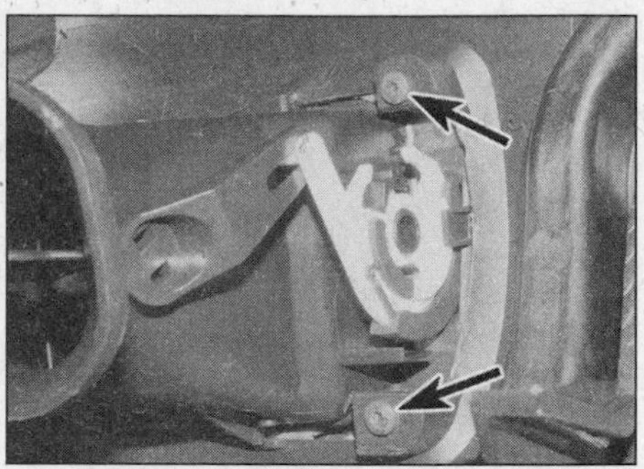

12.2 Undo the retaining screws (arrowed) and free the vent from the facia

into the upper part of the facia, unclip the retaining clips and withdraw the vent.

Refitting

4 Refitting is a reversal of removal.

13 Heater controls – removal and refitting

Note: *On models with automatic air conditioning, there are no heater control cables as it is all controlled electronically. The procedure for the removal and refitting of the control panel is the same, ignoring the references to the heater cables.*

Control panel and bulb

Removal

1 Disconnect the battery negative lead.

2 Remove the radio/cassette as described in Chapter 12, Section 23.

3 Unclip the trim cover and remove the two screws which secure the heater control panel and withdraw the control panel **(see illustrations)**. It may be necessary to disconnect the cables (where fitted) first, to give more room for removal of the control panel.

4 If the reason for removing the panel is to renew the bulb, this can be done without further dismantling **(see illustration)**

5 To remove the panel completely, disconnect the multi-plugs and the cables – where fitted **(see illustrations)**.

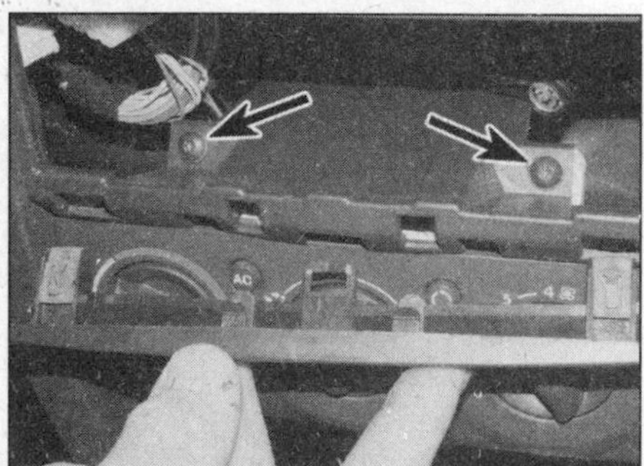

13.3a Unclip the trim and remove the retaining screws (arrowed) . . .

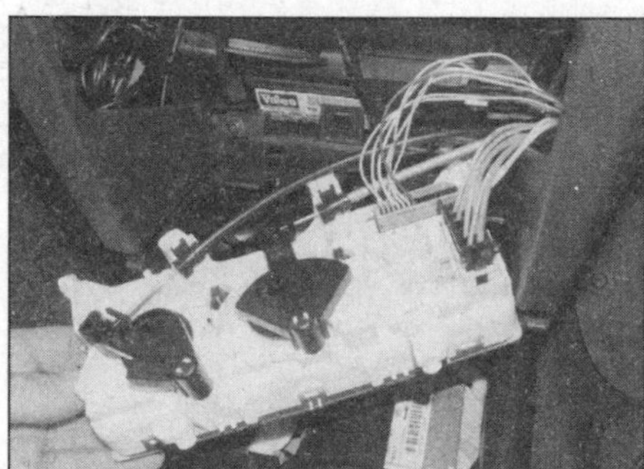

13.3b . . . and withdraw the heater control panel

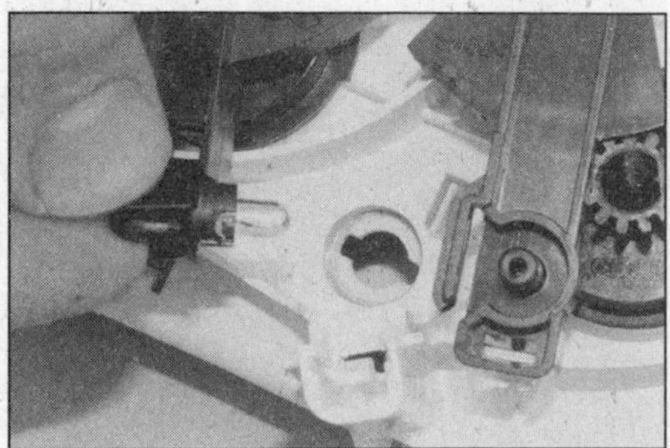

13.4 Free the bulb holder by twisting it a quarter of a turn, then separate the bulb and holder

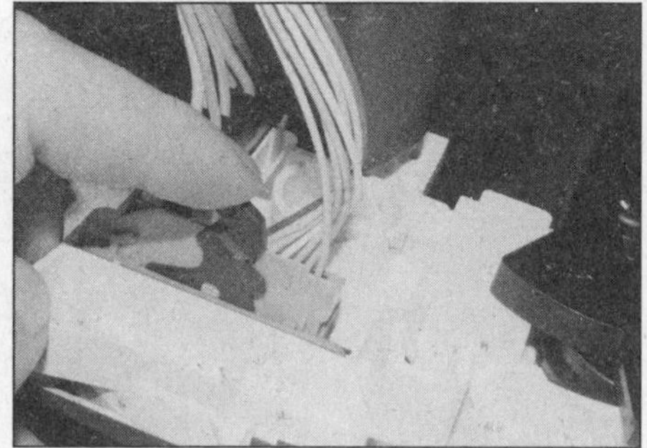

13.5a Release the locking clips to disconnect the wiring connectors . . .

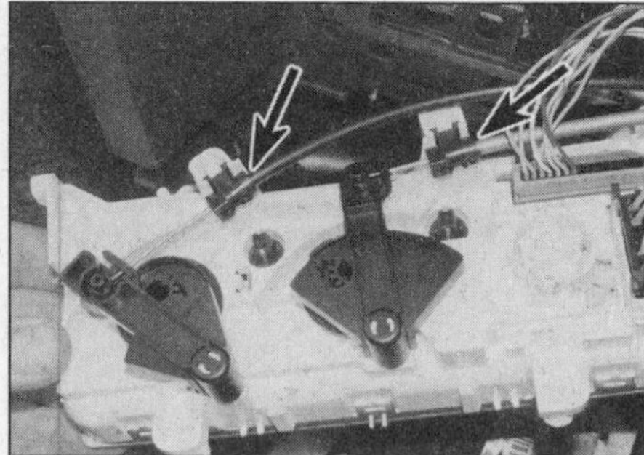

13.5b . . . and release the heater control cable securing clips (arrowed)

Refitting

6 Refit by reversing the removal operations. Check that the controls operate over their full range before securing the panel.

Control cables

Removal

7 Remove the control panel as described previously.

8 Unclip the outer cable securing clip from the back of the control panel. Disconnect each inner cable from its lever by turning the cable through 90° **(see illustrations)**.

9 To disconnect the cables from the right-hand side of the heater unit assembly **(see illustration)**, release the retaining clips and turn the cable(s) through 90° in the same way as described in paragraph 8.

10 Remove the cables, noting that the upper cable is grey in colour and the lower cable is black.

Refitting

11 Refitting is a reversal of removal. Connect the cables (where fitted) to the control levers making sure the clips are secure. Refit the control panel and check the operation of the controls.

14 Air conditioning system – general information and precautions

General information

1 An air conditioning system is available on some models. It enables the temperature of incoming air to be lowered; it also dehumidifies the air, which makes for rapid demisting and increased comfort **(see illustration overleaf)**.

2 The cooling side of the system works in the same way as a domestic refrigerator. Refrigerant gas is drawn into a belt-driven

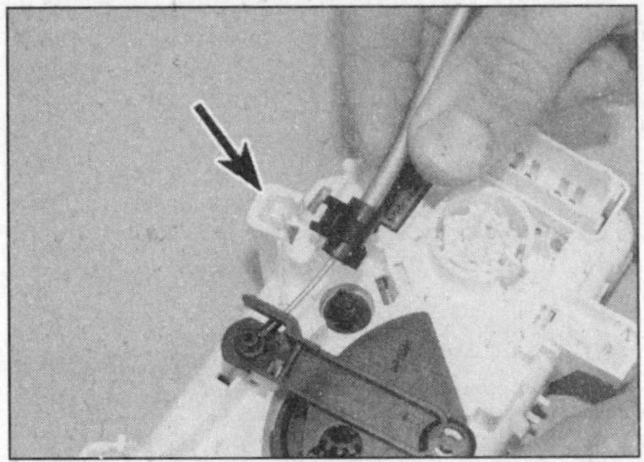

13.8a Release the securing clip to release the outer cable . . .

compressor, and passes into a condenser in front of the radiator, where it loses heat and becomes liquid. The liquid passes through an expansion valve to an evaporator, where it changes from liquid under high pressure to gas under low pressure. This change is accompanied by a drop in temperature, which cools the evaporator. The refrigerant returns to the compressor and the cycle begins again.

3 Air blown through the evaporator passes to the air distribution unit, where it is mixed with hot air blown through the heater radiator, to achieve the desired temperature in the passenger compartment.

4 The heating side of the system works in the same way as on models without air conditioning.

Precautions

Warning: The refrigerant is potentially dangerous, and should only be handled by qualified persons. If it is splashed onto the skin, it can cause frostbite. It is not itself poisonous, but in the presence of a naked flame (including a cigarette) it forms a poisonous gas.

- Uncontrolled discharging of the refrigerant is dangerous, and damaging to the environment. It follows that any work on the air conditioning system which involves opening the refrigerant circuit **must** only be carried out by a Renault dealer or an air conditioning specialist.
- Do not operate the air conditioning system if it is known to be short of refrigerant; the compressor may be damaged.

15 Air conditioning system – checking and maintenance

1 Routine maintenance is limited to checking the tension and condition of the compressor drivebelt, as described in Chapter 1A or 1B.

2 Periodic recharging of the system will be required, since there is inevitably a slow loss of refrigerant. It is suggested that the system be inspected by a specialist every year, or at once if a loss of performance is noticed.

TOOL TiP

Many car accessory shops sell one-shot air conditioning recharge aerosols. These generally contain refrigerant, compressor oil, leak sealer and system conditioner. Some also have a dye to help pinpoint leaks.

Warning: These products must only be used as directed by the manufacturer, and do not remove the need for regular maintenance.

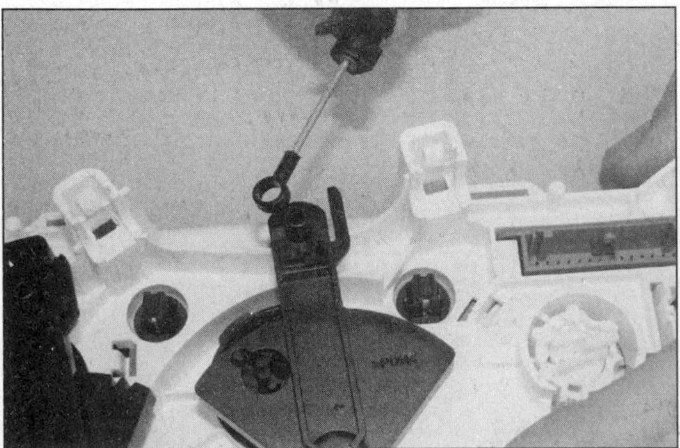

13.8b . . . and disconnect the inner cable from the lever

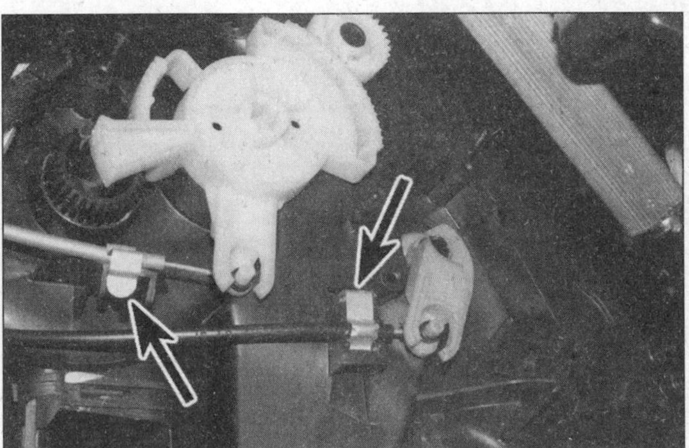

13.9 Cable securing clips (arrowed). The upper cable colour is grey, and the lower cable is black

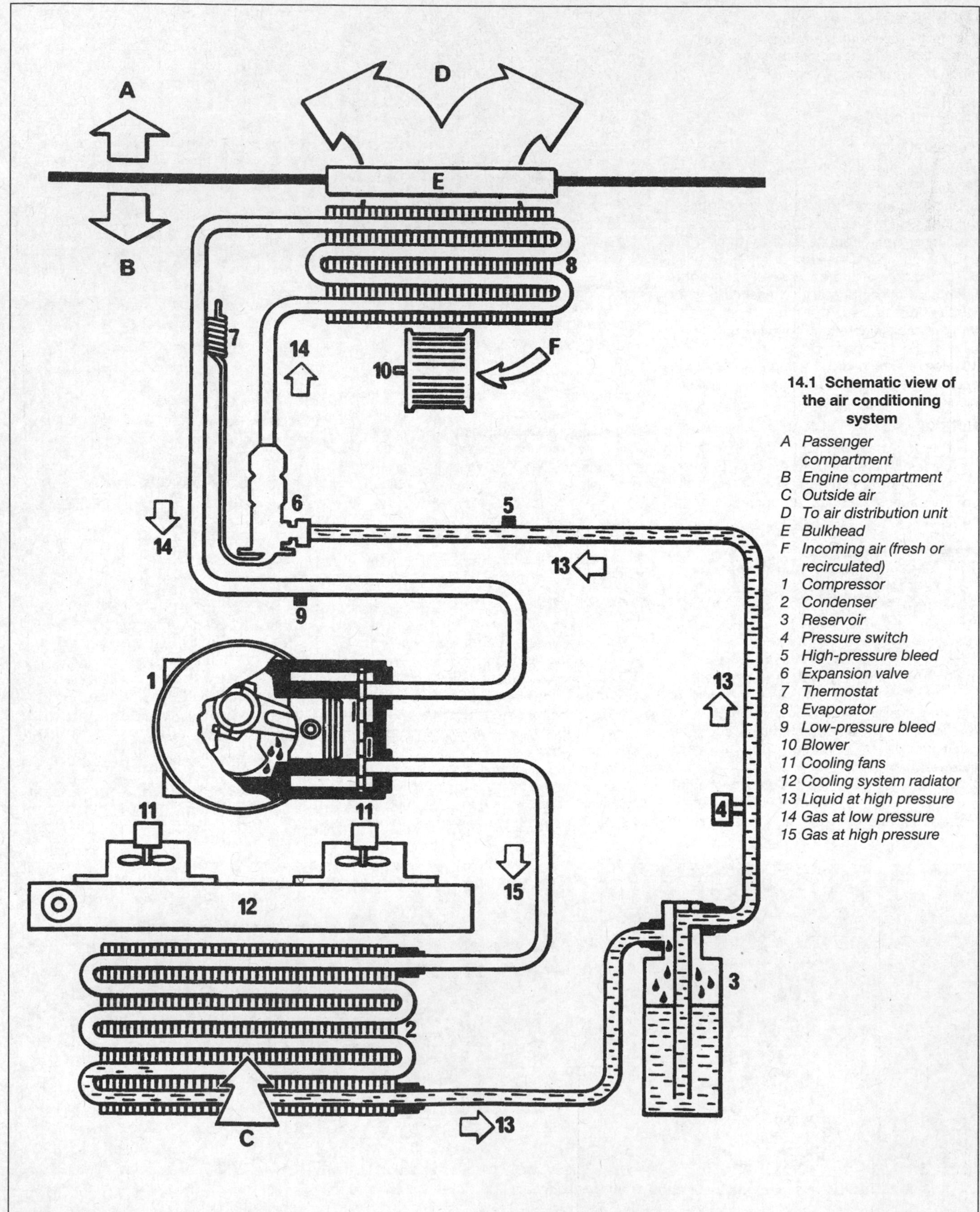

14.1 Schematic view of the air conditioning system

A Passenger compartment
B Engine compartment
C Outside air
D To air distribution unit
E Bulkhead
F Incoming air (fresh or recirculated)
1 Compressor
2 Condenser
3 Reservoir
4 Pressure switch
5 High-pressure bleed
6 Expansion valve
7 Thermostat
8 Evaporator
9 Low-pressure bleed
10 Blower
11 Cooling fans
12 Cooling system radiator
13 Liquid at high pressure
14 Gas at low pressure
15 Gas at high pressure

16.2 Compressor mounting bolts (arrowed)

16.4a Location of dehydration canister (arrowed)

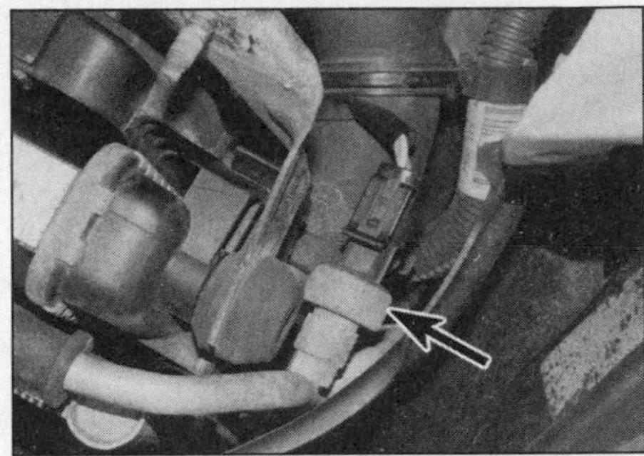

16.4b Location of pressure sensor (arrowed)

16 Air conditioning system – component removal and refitting

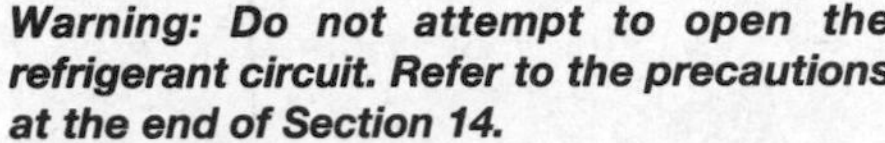

Warning: Do not attempt to open the refrigerant circuit. Refer to the precautions at the end of Section 14.

1 The only operations described here are those which can be carried out without discharging the refrigerant. All other operations must be referred to a specialist.

2 If necessary, the compressor can be unbolted and moved aside **(see illustration overleaf)**, without disconnecting its flexible hoses, after removing the drivebelt (see Chapter 1A or 1B).

Compressor drivebelt

3 Refer to *Auxiliary drivebelt check and renewal* in Chapter 1A or 1B.

Evaporator pressure sensor

Note: *The pressure sensor is located beside the condenser on the high-pressure pipe between the pressure relief valve and the dehydration canister. This can be removed without draining the system, as it is mounted on a 'schrader' valve.*

Removal

4 Disconnect the wiring connector from the sensor **(see illustrations)**.

5 Slacken and remove the pressure sensor from the high-pressure pipe.

Refitting

6 Refitting is a reversal of removal noting: The sensor is fitted with a seal, ensure it is in good condition and lubricate with P.A.G. SP10 oil.

Cooling fan relay/resistor

7 A two-speed cooling fan is fitted to models with air conditioning. The fan operates at low speed all the time that the air conditioning system is in use. If pressure rises in the refrigerant circuit or if the engine overheats, the fan operates at high speed.

8 The two fan speeds are obtained using a relay/resistor of 0.23 ohms. For low-speed operation, the resistor is switched in series with the fan motor. For high-speed operation, the resistor is bypassed.

9 Disconnect the wiring plug, release the retaining clips and slide the resistor up to disengage it from the cowling **(see illustrations)**. Refit by reversing the removal operations.

10 On most models, the resistor is located in the fan cowling to the left of the radiator. Its resistance can be checked without removing it, after disconnecting the multi-plug.

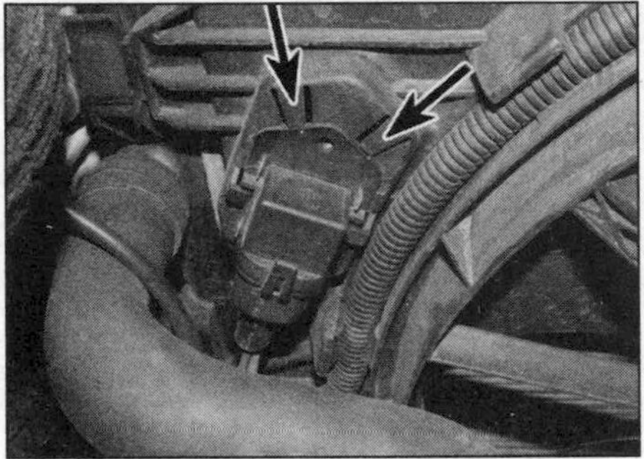

16.9a Release the retaining clips (arrowed) . . .

16.9b . . . slide upwards and unclip the resistor from the cowling

Chapter 4 Part A:
Petrol engine fuel and exhaust systems

Contents

Degrees of difficulty

Easy, suitable for novice with little experience 	**Fairly easy,** suitable for beginner with some experience 	**Fairly difficult,** suitable for competent DIY mechanic	**Difficult,** suitable for experienced DIY mechanic	**Very difficult,** suitable for expert DIY or professional

Specifications

System type

1.2 litre models:	
Engine code D7F 720	Sagem or Magneti Marelli semi-sequential multi-point injection
Engine code D4F 702/704/712	Magneti Marelli 5NR sequential multi-point injection
1.4 litre models	Siemens-Sirius 34 sequential multi-point injection
1.6 litre models	Siemens-Sirius 34 sequential multi-point injection

Fuel system data

Fuel pressure regulator control pressure	3.5 ± 0.06 bars
Fuel pump flow output (minimum):	
D7F engine	80 litres/hour at 3.0 bars fuel pressure
D4F engine	80 to 100 litres/hour (1.3 litres in 1 minute) at 3.5 bars fuel pressure
K4J engine	130 litres/hour at 3.5 bars fuel pressure
K4M engine	80 litres/hour at 3.0 bars fuel pressure
Air temperature sensor resistance:	
D7F engine:	
At 0°C	5000 to 7000 ohms
At 20°C	1700 to 3300 ohms
At 40°C	800 to 1550 ohms
D4F engine:	
At -10°C	10 450 to 8625 ohms
At 25°C	2065 to 2040 ohms
At 50°C	815 to 805 ohms
K4J and K4M engines:	
At 0°C	5290 to 6490 ohms
At 20°C	2400 to 2600 ohms
At 40°C	1070 to 1270 ohms

Fuel system data (continued)

Coolant temperature sensor resistance:	
D7F engine:	
At 20°C	2600 to 3000 ohms
At 40°C	1100 to 1300 ohms
At 80°C	270 to 300 ohms
At 90°C	200 to 215 ohms
D4F engine:	
At 25°C	2360 to 2140 ohms
At 50°C	850 to 770 ohms
At 80°C	290 to 275 ohms
At 110°C	117 to 112 ohms
K4J and K4M engines:	
At 20°C	3060 to 4045 ohms
At 40°C	1315 to 1600 ohms
At 80°C	300 to 370 ohms
At 90°C	210 to 270 ohms
Throttle potentiometer:	
D7F engine:	
Voltage	5.0 volts
Resistance:	
Track A-B	1300 ohms (no load), 1300 ohms (full load)
Track A-C	1360 ohms (no load), 2350 ohms (full load)
Track B-C	2300 ohms (no load), 1260 ohms (full load)
D4F engine	N/A
K4J and K4M engines:	
Voltage	5.0 volts
Resistance:	
Tracks A and B	1250 ohms (no load), 1250 ohms (full load)
Tracks A and C	1245 ohms (no load), 2230 ohms (full load)
Tracks B and C	2230 ohms (no load), 1245 ohms (full load)
Accelerator pedal sensor (D4F engine):	
Voltage	5 volts
Resistance:	
CTS (before June 2001):	
Track 1	1700 ± 900 ohms
Track 2	3000 ± 2200 ohms
Hella (from June 2001):	
Track 1	1200 ± 480 ohms
Track 2	1700 ± 680 ohms
Stepper motor:	
D7F engine:	
Voltage	12 volts
Resistance:	
Track A-D	100 ± 10 ohms
Track B-C	100 ± 10 ohms
K4J and K4M engines:	
Resistance	53.0 ± 5 ohms
Injector resistance	14.5 ± 0.7 ohms at 20°C
TDC sensor resistance:	
Except D4F engine	220 ohms
D4F engine	200 to 270 ohms at 25°C
Fuel tank level sender unit resistance at height of float pin (approx):	
At 164 mm	3.5 ± 3.5 ohms
At 143 mm	61 ± 7 ohms
At 110 mm	110 ± 10 ohms
At 81 mm	190 ± 16 ohms
At 52 mm	280 ± 20 ohms
At 47 mm	310 ± 10 ohms
Specified idle speed (non-adjustable):	
D7F engine	740 ± 50 rpm
D4F engine	750 ± 50 rpm
K4J and K4M engines	750 ± 50 rpm
Idle mixture CO content (non-adjustable)	0.5% maximum at 2500 rpm

Recommended fuel

Minimum octane rating	95 or 98 RON unleaded (if unavailable, 91 RON may be used). Leaded fuel or LRP must **not** be used

Torque wrench settings

	Nm	lbf ft
Exhaust manifold:		
D7F engine:		
Nut	25	18
Stud	10	7
Downpipe bolt	22	16
D4F engine:		
Nut	25	18
Stud	12	9
Heat shield	15	11
Downpipe nut	25	18
K4J and K4M engines:		
Nut	18	13
Downpipe nuts	20	15
Heat shield	10	7
Oxygen sensor	45	33
Fuel rail:		
Except D4F engine	10	7
D4F engine	7	5
Fuel tank	21	15
Inlet manifold:		
D7F engine:		
Nut	17	13
Stud	10	7
D4F engine	10	7
K4J and K4M engines	10	7
Knock sensor	20	15
Motorised throttle valve (D4F engine)	7	5
Throttle body (except D4F engine)	10	7

1 General information and precautions

The fuel system consists of a fuel tank which is mounted under the rear of the vehicle with an electric fuel pump immersed in it, and a fuel feed line leading to the fuel rail on the engine. A further line from the fuel tank leads to the charcoal canister located beneath the right-hand front wing. In comparison to the fuel system on earlier models, there is no return line to the fuel tank and no fuel filter is fitted, although the filter fitting clip is still located on the front of the fuel tank **(see illustration)**. The fuel pump supplies fuel to the fuel rail, which acts as a reservoir for the four fuel injectors which inject fuel into the inlet tracts. The fuel pressure regulator is located in the base of the fuel pump and not in the fuel rail as on earlier models. The Electronic Control Unit (ECU) is located on the left-hand side of the engine compartment, and the system includes various sensors, electrical components and related wiring.

Refer to Section 6 for further information on the operation of each fuel injection system, and to Section 15 for information on the exhaust system.

Warning: Many of the procedures in this Chapter require the removal of fuel lines and connections, which may result in some fuel spillage. Before carrying out any operation on the fuel system, refer to the precautions given in 'Safety first!' at the beginning of this manual, and follow them implicitly. Petrol is a highly-dangerous and volatile liquid, and the precautions necessary when handling it cannot be overstressed

Note: *Residual pressure will remain in the fuel lines long after the vehicle was last used. When disconnecting any fuel line, first depressurise the fuel system as described in Section 7.*

2 Air cleaner assembly and inlet ducts – removal and refitting

Removal

D7F engine

1 Disconnect the wiring plug from the absolute pressure (MAP) sensor on top of the air cleaner housing **(see illustration)**.

2 Disconnect the MAP sensor vacuum hose from the inlet manifold **(see illustration)**.

3 Release the wiring harness from the clip on the air cleaner housing.

4 Release the clips, and disconnect the inlet air trunking from the air cleaner and the air

1.1 The fuel filter clip is still located on the front of the fuel tank, although no filter is fitted

2.1 Disconnect the wiring plug from the MAP sensor . . .

2.2 . . . then disconnect the MAP sensor vacuum hose from the inlet manifold – D7F engine

2.4a Removing the inlet air trunking . . .

2.4b . . . and the air cleaner-to-inlet manifold trunking – D7F engine

2.5a Release the rubber straps . . .

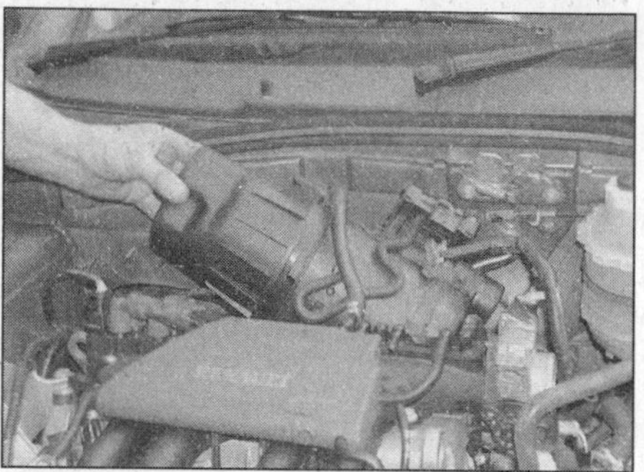
2.5b . . . then lift the air cleaner from the engine – D7F engine

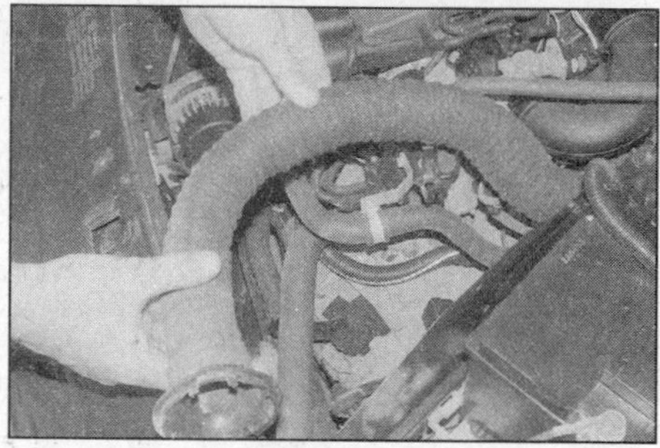
2.5c Removing the inlet duct from the front of the engine compartment – D7F engine

2.6 Disconnect the coolant hose from the air inlet elbow . . .

intake pipe, then remove the inlet air trunking securing screw, disconnect the breather hoses from the trunking, and remove the trunking. Similarly, remove the air cleaner-to-inlet manifold trunking **(see illustrations)**.

5 Release the two rubber securing straps, then lift the air cleaner assembly from the engine. If necessary, remove the inlet duct from the front of the engine compartment **(see illustrations)**.

D4F engine

6 Disconnect the coolant hose from the air inlet elbow on the front of the air cleaner **(see illustration)**.

7 If required, disconnect the inlet air duct, then unscrew the bolts and unhook the cover. Remove the element **(see illustrations)**.

8 Unbolt and remove the base.

K4J and K4M engines

9 Disconnect the rubber strap and release the hose from the side clip, then remove the resonator box and duct from the air cleaner housing on the rear of the cylinder head **(see illustrations)**.

10 Undo the retaining screws then unhook the air cleaner housing and remove it from the inlet manifold **(see illustration)**.

11 Note how the air cleaner element is fitted, then remove it from the housing **(see illustration)**.

2.7a . . . then unscrew the bolts . . .

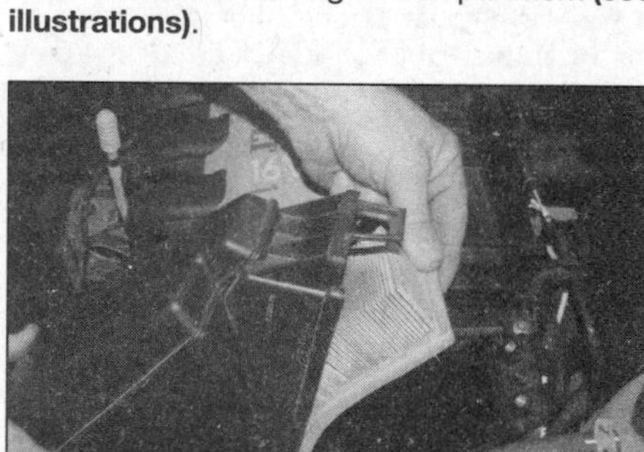
2.7b . . . unhook the cover and remove the element – D4F engine

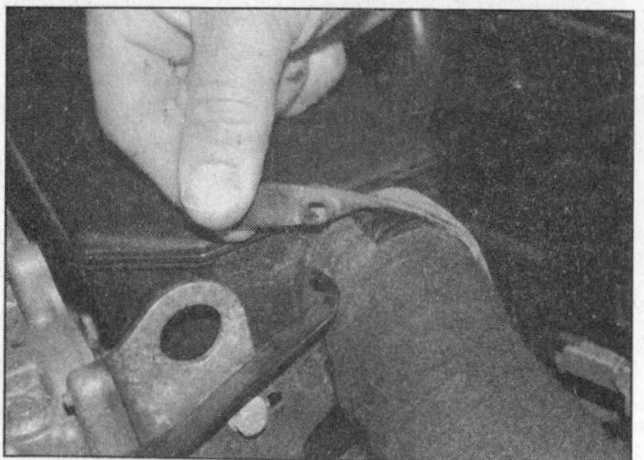
2.9a Disconnect the rubber strap . . .

2.9b . . . release the hose . . .

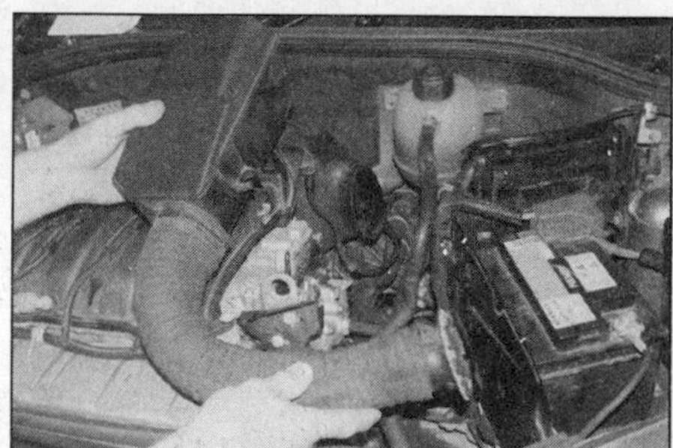
2.9c . . . and remove the resonator box and duct from the air cleaner housing – K4J and K4M engines

12 Unbolt the inlet duct plenum from the throttle body.

Refitting

13 Refitting is a reversal of removal.

3 Accelerator cable – removal, refitting and adjustment

Note: *Certain early models may be fitted with an accelerator cable, however, all later models do not have one. On 1.2 litre D4F engines manufactured before June 2001, an accelerator cable links the accelerator pedal to a potentiometer located on the bulkhead; on later models, no cable is fitted as the accelerator pedal potentiometer gives the information direct to the engine management ECU.*

Removal

1 Remove the air cleaner and inlet ducts as described in Section 2.

2 On the throttle body/housing, turn the throttle quadrant by hand to release the cable tension. Disconnect the inner cable from the quadrant **(see illustration).**

3 Remove the outer cable and ferrule from the support bracket **(see illustration)**. If necessary, remove the spring clip from the end of the cable noting its position in the groove.

4 Working inside the car, remove the lower trim panel from under the steering column. Disconnect the cable from the accelerator pedal by squeezing the lugs of the cable end fitting.

5 Return to the engine compartment, release the outer cable from the bulkhead and withdraw the cable.

Refitting

6 Refitting is a reversal of removal, but adjust the cable if necessary as follows.

Adjustment

7 With the spring clip removed from the accelerator outer cable, ensure that the throttle quadrant is fully against its stop. Gently pull the cable out of its grommet until all free play is removed from the inner cable.

8 With the cable held in this position, refit the spring clip to the last exposed outer cable groove in front of the rubber grommet and washer **(see illustration)**. When the clip is refitted and the outer cable is released, there should be only a small amount of free play in the inner cable. **Note:** *The idle speed control motor opens the throttle slightly when the ignition is switched off. There must be enough slack in the cable to allow the throttle to close past this position, otherwise a stable idle speed will not be obtained.*

9 Have an assistant depress the accelerator pedal, and check that the throttle quadrant opens fully and returns smoothly to its stop.

2.10 Removing the air cleaner housing from the inlet manifold – K4J and K4M

2.11 Removing the air cleaner element – K4J and K4M

4 Accelerator pedal – removal and refitting

Removal

1 Remove the lower trim panel from under the steering column.

2 Disconnect the cable or potentiometer link (as applicable) from the accelerator pedal.

3 Remove the nut which secures the accelerator pedal pivot and bush to the bulkhead.

4 Withdraw the accelerator pedal.

5 Examine the pedal and pivot for signs of wear and renew as necessary.

Refitting

6 Refitting is a reversal of removal. Check the adjustment of the accelerator cable as described in Section 3.

5 Unleaded petrol – general information and usage

All petrol models are designed to run on fuel with an octane rating of 95 or 98 RON, however, if unavailable, 91 octane fuel may be used. All models have a catalytic converter, and so must be run on unleaded fuel **only**. Under no circumstances should leaded fuel or LRP be used, as this will damage the converter.

6 Fuel injection systems – general information

1.2 litre (D7F)

1 1.2 litre models with the D7F engine are equipped with a Sagem or Magneti Marelli semi-sequential multi-point injection system with a Magneti Marelli throttle body. The system incorporates a closed-loop catalytic converter and an evaporative emission control system, and is of semi-sequential design with the injectors operating in pairs (1 and 4, then 2 and 3). There is one injection per revolution of the engine for each cylinder, ie, during the complete four-stroke cycle these take place on the induction **and** combustion strokes. The fuel injection side of the system operates as follows; refer to Chapter 5B for information on the ignition system.

2 The fuel pump is immersed in the fuel tank,

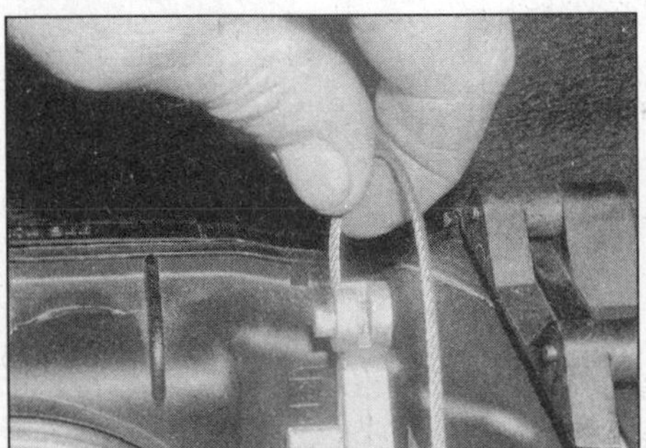

3.2 Disconnecting the accelerator cable from the quadrant

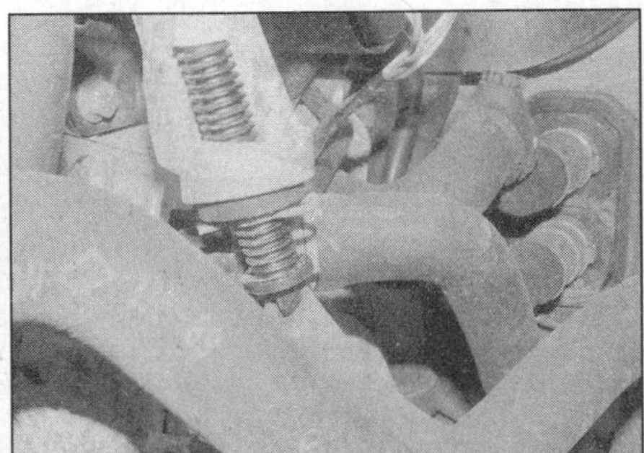

3.3 Accelerator cable adjustment ferrule and bracket – D7F engine

3.8 Fitting the spring clip to the ferrule on the outer cable

and pumps fuel from the fuel tank to the fuel rail on the engine. Fuel supply pressure is controlled by a pressure regulator in the fuel pump. The regulator operates by allowing excess fuel to return to the tank. There are four injectors (one per cylinder) located in the inlet manifold downstream of the throttle valve. All the injectors are fed from the fuel rail.

1.2 (D4F), 1.4 and 1.6 litre

3 1.2 litre models with the D4F engine are equipped with the Magneti Marelli 5NR sequential multi-point fuel injection/ignition system. 1.4 and 1.6 litre models are equipped with a Siemens-Sirius sequential multi-point fuel injection/ignition system. Both systems operate in a similar way.

4 The system is of closed-loop type incorporating two lambda (oxygen) sensors, one located upstream and the other downstream of the catalytic converter. An evaporative emission control system is fitted.

5 The multi-point injection system uses one injector and one ignition coil for each cylinder, and the injectors are operated individually and sequentially at the beginning of the inlet stroke. The electronic control unit (ECU) is able to determine which cylinder is on its inlet stroke without the use of a camshaft position sensor, however if the unit is renewed, the car must be taken for a road test lasting at least 25 minutes to enable the ECU to reprogram itself; on 1.4 and 1.6 litre models, the stepper motor must also be reset.

6 The system incorporates a closed-loop catalytic converter and an evaporative emission control system. The fuel injection side of the system operates as follows; refer to Chapter 5B for information on the ignition system.

7 The fuel pump is immersed in the fuel tank, and pumps fuel from the fuel tank to the fuel rail on the engine. Fuel supply pressure is controlled by a pressure regulator in the fuel pump. The regulator operates by allowing excess fuel to return to the tank. There are four injectors (one per cylinder) located in the inlet manifold downstream of the throttle valve. All the injectors are fed from the fuel rail.

8 Later models are not fitted with an accelerator cable, as the throttle valve is motorised and has an integral potentiometer; the accelerator pedal also incorporates a potentiometer.

All systems

9 The electrical control system consists of the ECU, along with the following sensors:

a) *Throttle potentiometer – informs the ECU of the throttle position, and the rate of throttle opening or closing.*
b) *Coolant temperature sensor – informs the ECU of engine temperature.*
c) *Inlet air temperature sensor – informs the ECU of the temperature of the air passing through the throttle body.*
d) *Lambda (oxygen) sensor – informs the ECU of the oxygen content of the exhaust gases (explained in greater detail in Part C of this Chapter).*
e) *Idle speed regulation stepper motor (where fitted) – controls the idle speed.*
f) *Crankshaft speed/position (TDC) sensor – informs the ECU of engine speed and crankshaft position.*
g) *Power steering pressure switch (early models) – informs the ECU when the power steering pump is working so the engine idle speed can be increased to prevent stalling.*
h) *Knock sensor (where fitted) – informs the ECU when pre-ignition ('pinking') is occurring (explained in greater detail in Part B of Chapter 5).*
i) *Manifold absolute pressure (MAP) sensor – informs the ECU of the engine load by monitoring the pressure in the inlet manifold.*
j) *Fuel vapour recirculation valve – operates the fuel evaporative control system (explained in greater detail in Part C of this Chapter).*
k) *Vehicle speed sensor (on D4F engine, only fitted before June 2001) – informs the ECU of the vehicle speed.*

10 All the above information is analysed by the ECU and, based on this, the ECU determines the appropriate ignition and fuelling requirements for the engine. The ECU controls the fuel injector by varying its pulse width – the length of time the injector is held open – to provide a richer or weaker mixture, as appropriate. The mixture is constantly varied by the ECU, to provide the best setting for cranking, starting (with either a hot or cold engine), warm-up, idle, cruising and acceleration. On automatic transmission models, information from sensors on the transmission is sent to the ECU for processing to determine the most efficient settings for the engine.

11 The ECU also has full control over the engine idle speed, via a stepper motor which is fitted to the throttle body. The motor pushrod rests against a cam on the throttle spindle. When the throttle is closed (accelerator pedal released), the ECU uses the motor to vary the opening of the throttle valve and so control the idle speed.

12 The ECU also controls the exhaust and evaporative emission control systems, which are described in detail in Part C of this Chapter.

13 If there is an abnormality in any of the readings obtained from either the coolant temperature sensor, the inlet air temperature sensor or the lambda sensor, the ECU enters its back-up mode. In this event, the ECU ignores the abnormal sensor signal, and assumes a preprogrammed value which will allow the engine to continue running (albeit at reduced efficiency). If the ECU enters this back-up mode, the warning light on the instrument panel will come on, and the relevant fault code will be stored in the ECU memory.

14 If the warning light comes on, the vehicle should be taken to a Renault dealer at the earliest opportunity. A complete test of the engine management system can then be carried out, using a special electronic diagnostic test unit (XR25) which is simply plugged into the system's diagnostic connector (located beneath the ashtray on the centre console).

7 Fuel injection system – depressurisation

Warning: Refer to the warning note in Section 1 before proceeding. The following procedure will merely relieve the pressure in the fuel system – remember that fuel will still be present in the system components, and take precautions accordingly before disconnecting any of them.

Note: *The fuel system referred to in this Section includes the tank-mounted fuel pump, the fuel injectors, the pressure regulator, the fuel rail and the metal pipes and flexible hoses of the fuel lines between these components. All these contain fuel which will be under pressure while the engine is running, and/or while the ignition is switched on. The pressure will remain for some time after the ignition has been switched off, and it must be relieved when any of these components are disturbed for servicing work.*

Method 1

1 Disconnect the battery negative lead (refer to *Disconnecting the battery* in the Reference Section).

2 Place a suitable container beneath the connection or union to be disconnected, and have a large rag ready to soak up any escaping fuel not being caught by the container.

3 Slowly loosen the connection or union nut to avoid a sudden release of pressure, and position the rag around the connection, to catch any fuel spray which may be expelled. Once the pressure is released, disconnect the fuel line. Plug the pipe ends, to minimise fuel loss and prevent the entry of dirt into the fuel system.

Method 2

4 Remove the fuel pump relay located behind the left-hand headlight in the engine compartment fuse/relay box (see Chapter 12).

5 Start the engine and allow it to idle until it stops due to lack of fuel. Operate the starter motor a couple more times, to ensure that all fuel pressure has been relieved.

6 Switch off the ignition and refit the fuel pump relay.

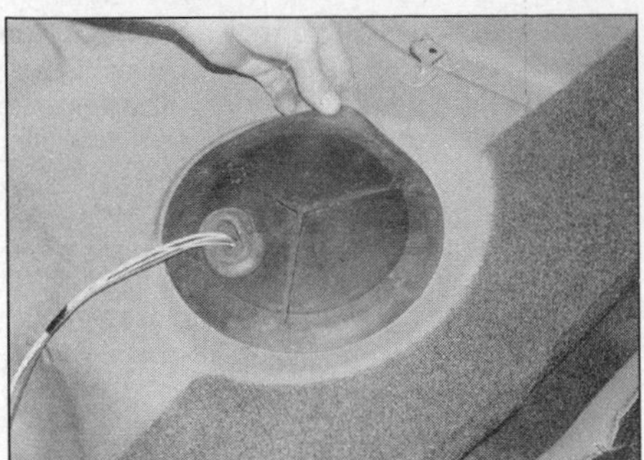
8.3 Prising the access cover from the rear floor

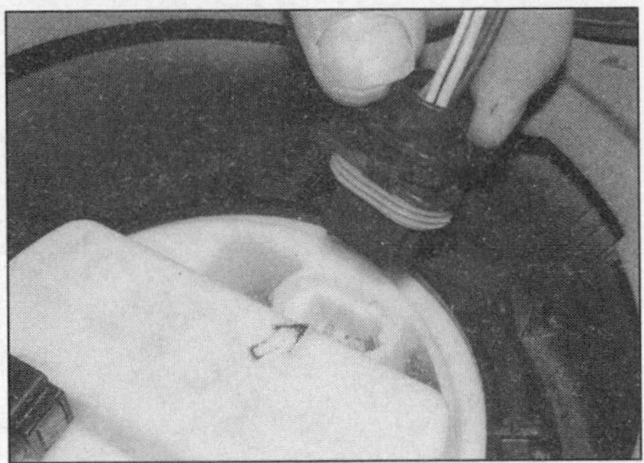
8.4 Disconnecting the wiring from the fuel pump

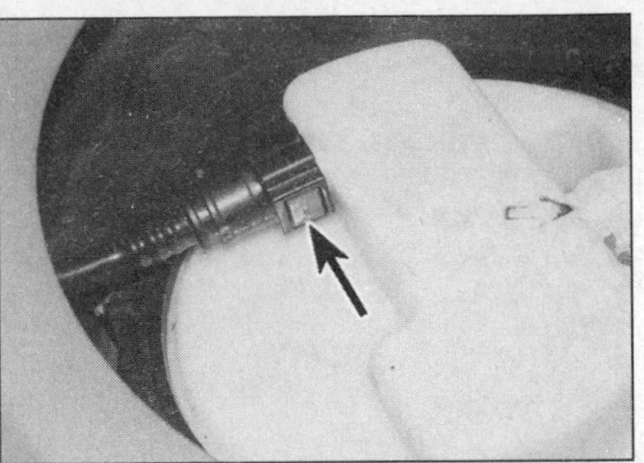
8.5 Fuel supply hose quick-release fitting on the fuel pump

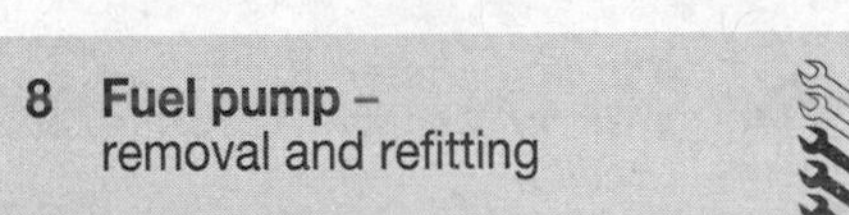

8 Fuel pump – removal and refitting

Warning: Refer to the warning note in Section 1 before proceeding.

Removal

1 Disconnect the battery negative lead (refer to *Disconnecting the battery* in the Reference Section).

2 Remove the rear seat, or rear seat cushion as described in Chapter 11, for access to the fuel pump cover.

3 Carefully prise the access cover from the floor to expose the fuel pump **(see illustration)**.

4 Disconnect the wiring connector from the fuel pump, and tape the connector to the vehicle body, to prevent it disappearing behind the tank **(see illustration)**.

5 Note that the fuel supply hose is equipped with a quick-release fitting to ease removal. To disconnect the hose, squeeze together the locking button, then pull off the hose **(see illustration)**.

6 Noting the alignment arrows on the pump cover, locking ring and fuel tank, unscrew the locking ring and remove it from the tank. This can be accomplished by using a screwdriver on the raised ribs of the locking ring – carefully tap the screwdriver to turn the ring anti-clockwise until it can be unscrewed by hand. Alternatively a removal tool can be fabricated out of metal bar and two bolts **(see illustrations)**.

7 Carefully lift the fuel pump assembly out of the fuel tank, taking great care not to damage the fuel level gauge sender arm, or to spill fuel in the interior of the vehicle. Remove the rubber sealing ring and check it for deterioration; if it is in good condition, it may be re-used, however if the pump is to remain out of the fuel tank for several hours, the locking ring should be refitted temporarily to prevent the sealing ring from distorting. If the sealing ring is unserviceable, obtain a new one **(see illustrations)**.

8 Note that the fuel pump/fuel gauge sender unit is only available as a complete assembly – no components are available separately.

Refitting

9 Ensure that the fuel pump pick-up filter is clean and free of debris. Fit the sealing ring to the top of the fuel tank.

10 Carefully manoeuvre the pump assembly into the fuel tank.

11 Align the arrow on the fuel pump cover with the arrow on the fuel tank (the arrow must point to the rear of the vehicle), then refit the

8.6a Alignment arrows on the pump cover, fuel tank and locking ring

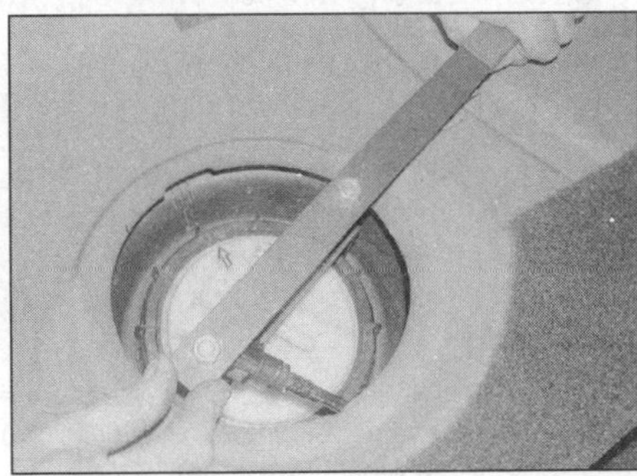
8.6b Using a home-made removal tool to unscrew the locking ring from the fuel tank

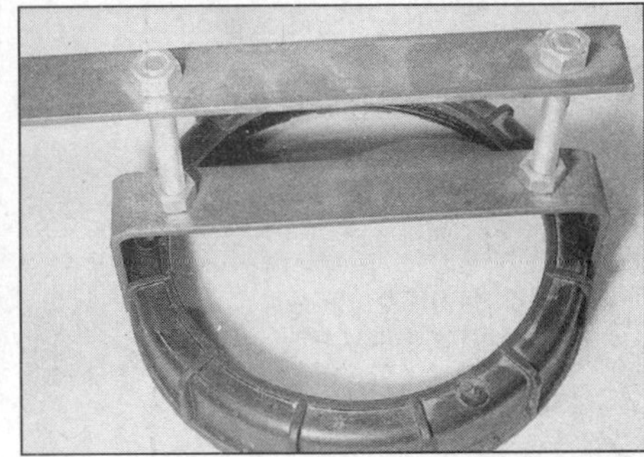
8.6c Home-made fuel pump locking ring removal tool

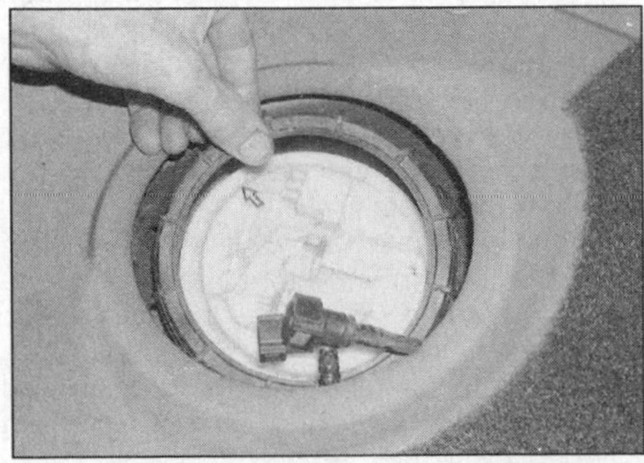
8.6d Removing the locking ring

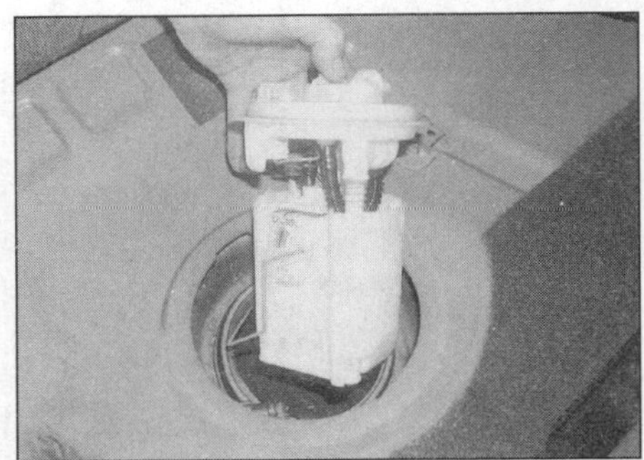
8.7a Removing the fuel pump from the tank

8.7b Removing the rubber sealing ring

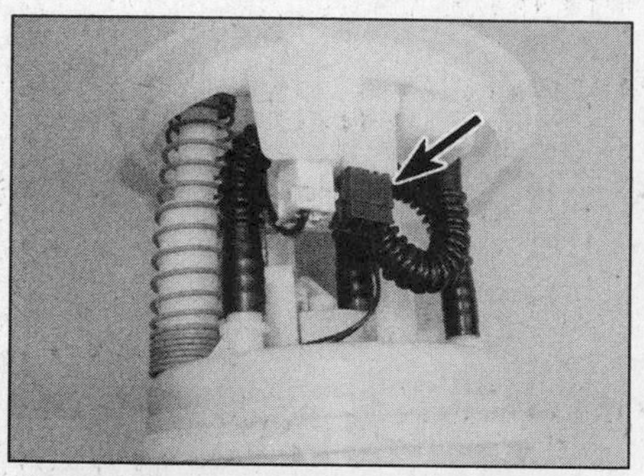

9.3 Disconnect the wiring from the cover

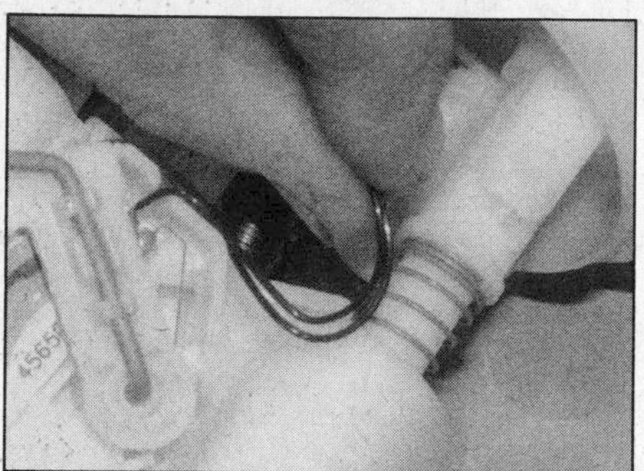

9.5a Remove the wiring from the clips . . .

locking ring. Securely tighten the locking ring until the arrow is pointing rearwards, then recheck that the pump cover and tank marks are all correctly aligned.

12 Reconnect the hose to the top of the fuel pump.

13 Reconnect the wiring connector.

14 Reconnect the battery and start the engine. Check the fuel pump and hose(s) for signs of leakage.

15 Refit the plastic access cover and the rear seat cushion.

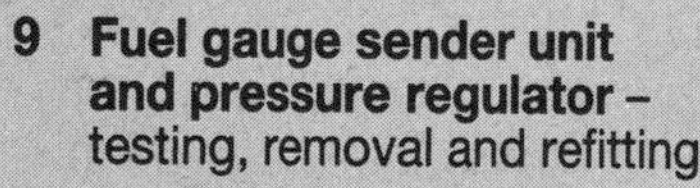

9 Fuel gauge sender unit and pressure regulator – testing, removal and refitting

Testing

1 The fuel gauge sender unit is supplied as part of the fuel pump assembly, however it is possible to test its operation and remove it.

2 To test the sender unit, first remove the pump as described in Section 8.

3 Disconnect the wiring plug from the cover and connect an ohmmeter to the two terminals **(see illustration)**.

4 With the pump assembly upright on the bench, measure the resistance of the sender unit at the different heights given in the Specifications **(see illustration)**. The resistances are approximate but is should be clear if the sender unit is not operating correctly.

Removal

5 To remove the sender unit, first release the wiring from the clips, then unclip the unit from the main body **(see illustrations)**.

6 To remove the fuel pressure regulator, unclip the base cover, then pull out the retaining spring clip and remove the regulator **(see illustrations)**.

7 Use a screwdriver to prise off the gauze filter, then clean any sediment from the filter and cover.

9.6a Release the clips and remove the base cover . . .

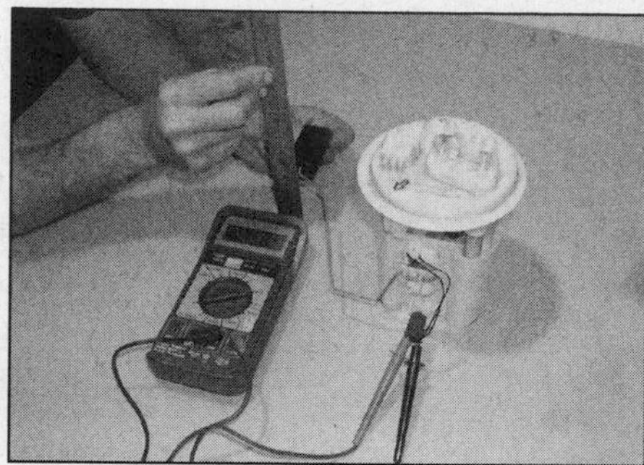

9.4 Testing the sender unit with an ohmmeter

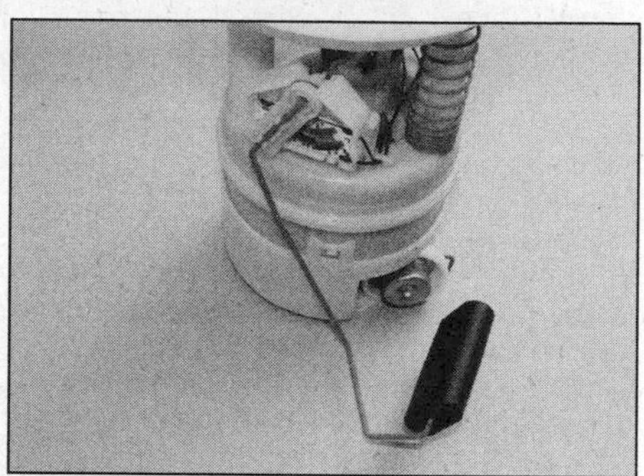

9.5b . . . then unclip the unit from the main body

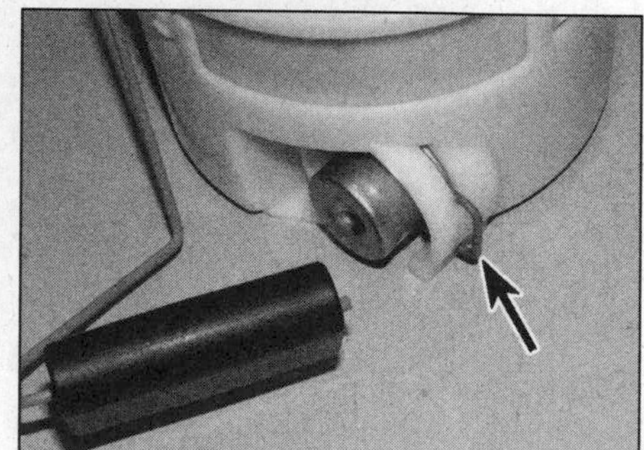

9.6b . . . then pull out the spring clip to remove the pressure regulator

Refitting

8 Refitting is a reversal of removal, but test the unit before refitting the pump assembly to the tank.

10 Fuel tank – removal and refitting

Warning: Refer to the warning note in Section 1 before proceeding

Removal

1 Before removing the fuel tank, all fuel must be drained from it. Since a drain plug is not provided, it is preferable to carry out the removal operation when the tank is nearly empty.

2 Remove the rear seat, or rear seat cushion (Chapter 11), for access to the fuel pump cover.

3 Using a screwdriver, carefully prise the plastic access cover from the floor to expose the fuel pump.

4 If there is any fuel remaining in the fuel tank, it can be removed by disconnecting the fuel delivery hose and connecting a suitable hose leading to a container outside the vehicle (refer to Section 8 for disconnecting the quick-release hose). Remove the fuel pump relay located behind the left-hand headlight in the engine compartment fuse/relay box (see Chapter 12), and connect a bridging wire between terminals 3 and 5 (the terminals with the thick wires). Allow the fuel pump to operate until the fuel flow is intermittent, then disconnect the bridging wire and refit the relay.

5 Disconnect the wiring connector from the fuel pump, and tape the connector to the vehicle body, to prevent it disappearing behind the tank.

6 Disconnect the battery negative lead (refer to *Disconnecting the battery* in the Reference Section).

7 Where applicable, disconnect the return hose from the fuel pump with reference to Section 8.

8 Chock the front wheels then jack up the rear of the vehicle and support on axle stands (see *Jacking and vehicle support*). Remove the right-hand rear wheel.

9 Remove the exhaust system and relevant heat shield(s) with reference to Section 15. Also unbolt and remove the central exhaust mounting.

10 On early models only, disconnect the hose from the fuel filter and also disconnect the union with the fuel gallery.

11 Remove the heat shield from below the fuel tank and below the handbrake cables.

12 Note the position of the adjustment nut on the rear of the handbrake lever equaliser rod, then unscrew and remove it and detach the handbrake cables from the supports on the underbody. Position the cables to one side away from the fuel tank.

13 Disconnect the hoses from the fuel tank to the fuel gallery.

14 Disconnect the overflow pipe.

15 Separate the filler neck from the fuel tank, then unclip the handbrake cables from under the tank **(see illustrations)**.

16 Place a trolley jack with an interposed block of wood beneath the tank, then raise the jack until it is supporting the weight of the tank.

17 Unscrew and remove the mounting bolts **(see illustrations)**, then slowly lower the fuel tank out of position, disconnecting any other relevant pipes as they become accessible (where necessary), and remove the tank from underneath the vehicle. Note that the tank must be slightly tilted to the right, and it may be necessary to bend the brake pipes to provide sufficient clearance. **Do not** bend the pipes excessively.

18 If the tank is contaminated with sediment or water, remove the fuel pump/sender unit (Section 8), and swill the tank out with clean fuel. The tank is injection-moulded from a synthetic material – if seriously damaged, it should be renewed. However, in certain cases, it may be possible to have small leaks or minor damage repaired. Seek the advice of a specialist before attempting to repair the fuel tank.

Refitting

19 Refitting is the reverse of the removal procedure, noting the following points:

a) When lifting the tank back into position, take care to ensure that the hoses are not trapped between the tank and vehicle body.

b) As the tank is located on the underbody, make sure that the positioning holes are correctly aligned with each other. There are two rear holes and one front hole.

c) Ensure that all pipes and hoses are correctly routed. Make sure the sealing rings are in position in the quick-release fittings prior to fitting and make sure they are securely clipped in position.

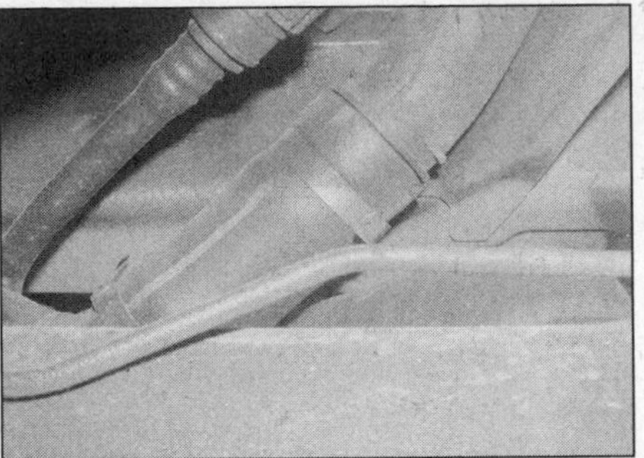

10.15a Filler neck connection to the tank

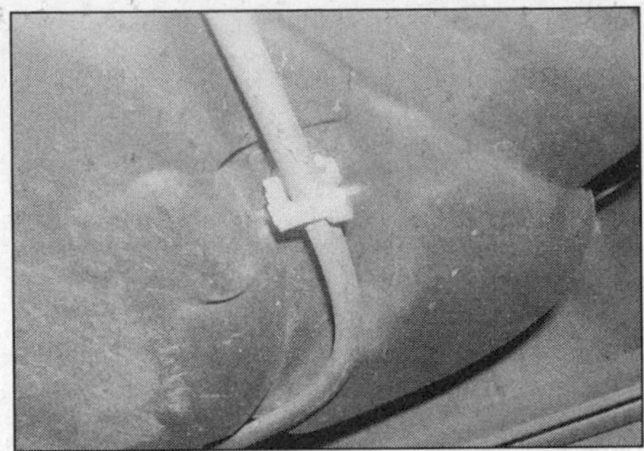

10.15b Handbrake cable clip on the bottom of the fuel tank

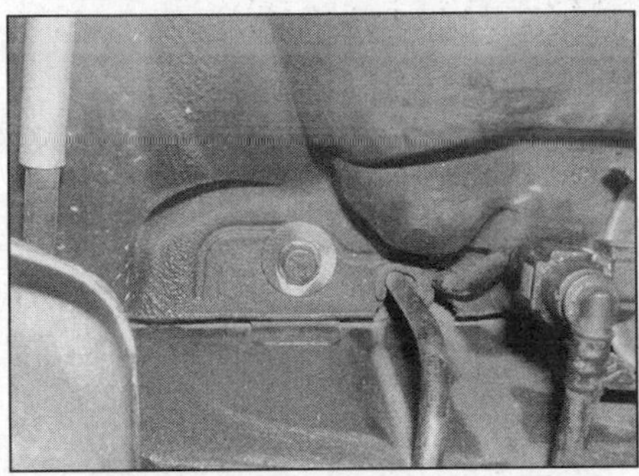

10.17a Fuel tank right-hand mounting bolt . . .

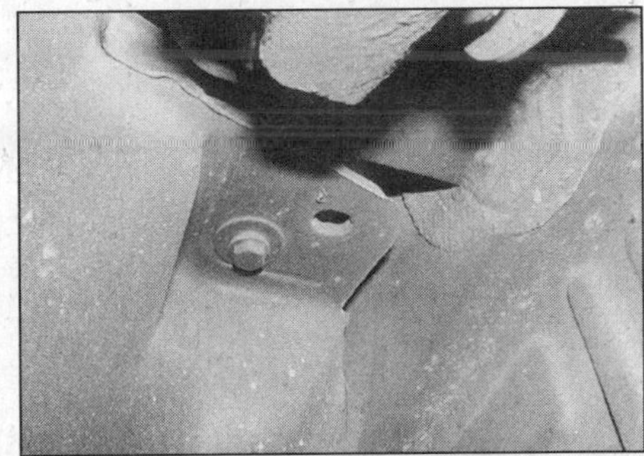

10.17b . . . and left-hand mounting bolt

d) On completion, refill the tank with a small amount of fuel, and check for signs of leakage prior to taking the vehicle out on the road.

11 Throttle body/housing – removal and refitting

Warning: Refer to the warning note in Section 1 before proceeding

Note: *It is not possible to repair the throttle body/housing – if faulty, it must be renewed complete.*

1 Depressurise the fuel system with reference to Section 7.

2 Disconnect the battery negative lead (refer to *Disconnecting the battery* in the Reference Section) and proceed as described under the relevant heading.

D7F engine

Note: *The inlet air temperature sensor, idle speed control valve and throttle potentiometer are integral with the throttle housing, and cannot be renewed independently. A new seal will be required on refitting.*

3 Slacken the hose clips, and remove the air ducting connecting the air cleaner assembly to the throttle body.

4 Disconnect the wiring from the idle speed control valve, the air temperature sensor, and the throttle position sensor **(see illustrations)**.

5 Where applicable, disconnect the accelerator cable from the throttle quadrant on the throttle housing, with reference to Section 3 **(see illustration)**.

11.4a Disconnect the wiring from the idle speed control valve . . .

11.4b . . . the air temperature sensor . . .

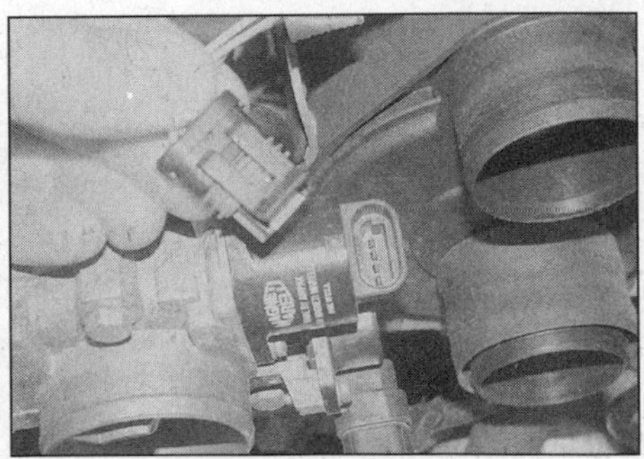

11.4c . . . and the throttle position sensor – D7F engine

11.5 Disconnecting the accelerator cable from the throttle quadrant – D7F engine

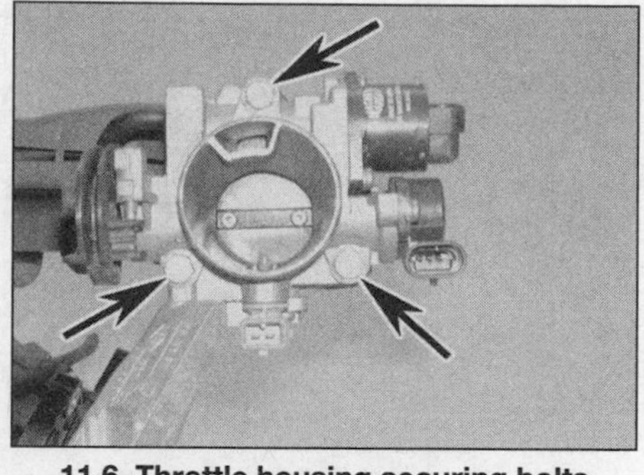

11.6 Throttle housing securing bolts (arrowed) – D7F engine

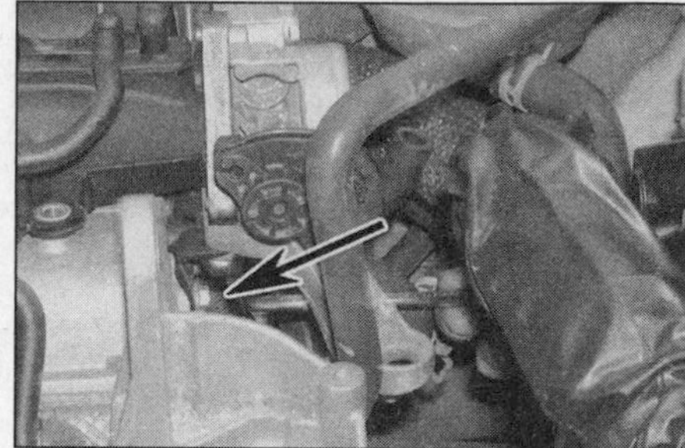

11.7a Throttle housing bracing bracket-to-cylinder head securing bolt (arrowed) – D7F engine

11.7b Withdraw the throttle housing . . .

11.7c . . . and recover the seal – D7F engine

6 Unscrew the three throttle housing securing bolts **(see illustration)**.

7 Unscrew the two bolts securing the bracing bracket to the cylinder head, or unscrew the bolts securing the bracing bracket to the throttle body bracket, then withdraw the throttle housing complete with the bracket(s). Recover the seal **(see illustrations)**.

8 Refitting is a reversal of removal, but use a new seal, and reconnect and if necessary adjust the accelerator cable.

D4F engine

Note: *On the D4F engine, the throttle valve is electrically-motorised and is not operated directly by an accelerator cable. If the throttle valve is renewed, the new unit must be reprogrammed. Although it is possible to carry out the reprogramming without dedicated equipment, any fault codes stored in the engine management ECU must be erased with a special diagnostic tool.*

Caution: Do not alter the settings of the stop screws on the motorised throttle valve.

9 Remove the inlet manifold as described in Section 14.

10 With the inlet manifold inverted on the bench, progressively unscrew the four mounting bolts and remove the motorised throttle valve. Recover the O-ring seal.

11 Clean the contact faces of the valve and inlet manifold, and the threads of the mounting bolts.

12 Refit the valve together with a new O-ring seal, and tighten the mounting bolts progressively to the specified torque.

13 Refit the inlet manifold as described in Section 14.

14 If a new throttle valve has been fitted, the minimum throttle stop must be reprogrammed as follows.

a) Switch on the ignition for approximately 3 seconds, then start the engine.

b) Switch off the ignition, and wait for approximately 5 seconds.

c) Restart the engine and allow the coolant temperature to reach 60°C (approximately 3 minutes from ambient temperature of 20°C).

d) Road test the car to allow the ECU to learn the throttle valve adaptives.

K4J and K4M engines

Note: *On later models, the throttle valve is electrically-motorised and is not operated directly by an accelerator cable. If the throttle valve is renewed, the new unit must be reprogrammed. Although it is possible to carry out the reprogramming without dedicated equipment, any fault codes stored in the engine management ECU must be erased with a special diagnostic tool.*

Caution: Do not alter the settings of the stop screws on the motorised throttle valve.

15 Remove the air cleaner assembly as described in Section 2. Also remove the airbox from the throttle housing.

16 Where applicable on early models, disconnect the accelerator cable from the throttle quadrant.

17 Disconnect the wiring from the throttle potentiometer or motorised throttle valve. Note that a locking plate must first be removed on the motorised throttle valve **(see illustrations)**.

11.17a Disconnecting the wiring from the throttle potentiometer (early models)

11.17b On later models, pull out the locking plate . . .

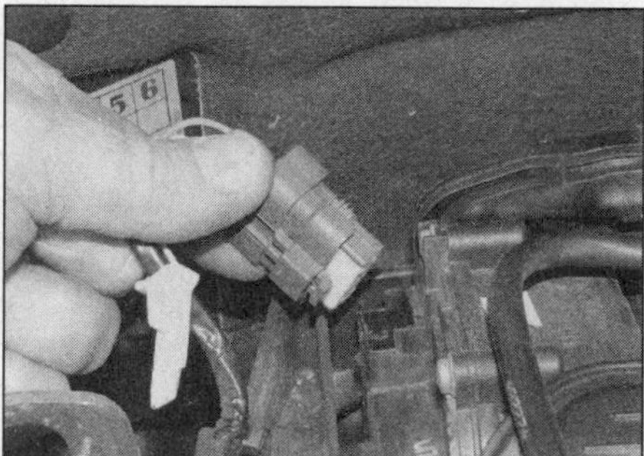

11.17c . . . and disconnect the wiring – K4J and K4M

18 Unscrew the bolts securing the throttle body assembly to the inlet manifold, then remove the assembly and gasket/seal. Discard the gasket/seal; a new one should be used on refitting.

19 Clean the mating faces of the throttle body/housing and inlet manifold.

20 Refitting is a reversal of removal, but, where applicable, fit a new gasket/seal and check the adjustment of the accelerator cable with reference to Section 3.

12 Fuel injection system – testing and adjustment

Testing

1 If a fault appears in the fuel injection system, first ensure that all the system wiring connectors are securely connected and free of corrosion. Ensure that the fault is not due to poor maintenance; ie, check that the air cleaner filter element is clean, the spark plugs are in good condition and correctly gapped, the cylinder compression pressures are correct, the ignition timing is correct, and that the engine breather hoses are clear and undamaged, referring to the relevant part of Chapters 1, 2 and 5 for further information.

2 If these checks fail to reveal the cause of the problem, the vehicle should be taken to a Renault dealer for testing. A diagnostic connector (located beneath the ashtray on the centre console) is incorporated in the engine management circuit, into which a special electronic diagnostic tester can be plugged. The tester will locate the fault quickly and simply, alleviating the need to test all the system components individually, which is a time-consuming operation that carries a risk of damaging the ECU. The Renault XR25 diagnostic tester is specific for Renault dealerships; at the time of writing there was no equivalent tester available. The tester uses a bar chart configuration on a LCD screen; a fiche for the particular model is placed on the screen and each circuit can be checked instantly. There is no code output as such, so it is not possible for the home mechanic to determine a faulty area of the fuel injection system.

3 If the 'electronic incident' warning light illuminates on the instrument panel whilst driving, or remains illuminated longer than 3 seconds after switching on the ignition, a fault is indicated in one or more of the following components:

a) Manifold absolute pressure sensor.
b) Throttle potentiometer.
c) Injectors.
d) Idle speed stepper motor (where fitted).
e) Vehicle speed sensor (only fitted before June 2001).
f) EGR solenoid valve (where fitted).
g) Automatic transmission.

4 Some individual components may be tested for resistance after removal using the

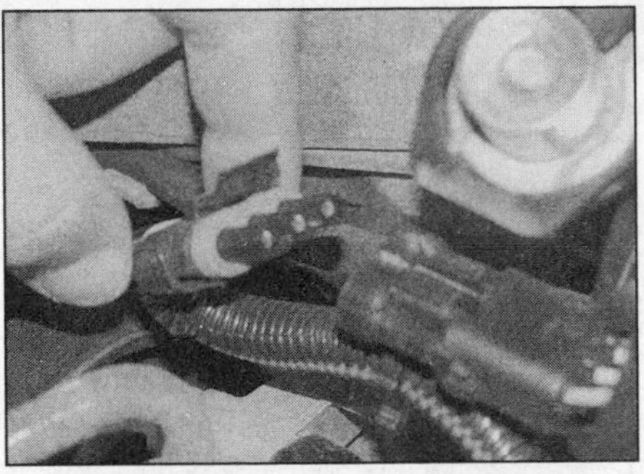

13.2 Separate the two halves of the fuel injection wiring connector – D7F engine

information given in the Specifications, however other items (such as the idle speed stepper motor) cannot be checked and are not adjustable.

Adjustment

5 Experienced home mechanics with a considerable amount of skill and equipment (including a tachometer and an accurately calibrated exhaust gas analyser) may be able to check the exhaust CO level and the idle speed. However, if these are found to be in need of adjustment, the car *must* be taken to a suitably-equipped Renault dealer for further testing. Neither the mixture adjustment (exhaust gas CO level) nor the idle speed are adjustable, and should either be incorrect, a fault must be present in the fuel injection system.

13 Multi-point injection system components – removal and refitting

Warning: Refer to the warning note in Section 1 before proceeding

Fuel rail and injectors

Note: *If a faulty injector is suspected, before condemning the injector, it is worth trying the effect of one of the proprietary injector-cleaning treatments.*

D7F engine

Note: *New O-rings will be required on refitting.*

13.4 Release the securing clip, then disconnect the fuel return pipe from the fuel rail – D7F engine

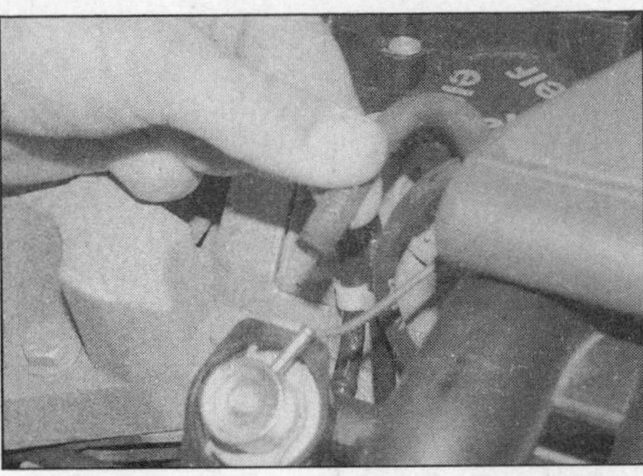

13.3 Disconnecting the vacuum pipe from the fuel pressure regulator – D7F engine

1 Depressurise the fuel system as described in Section 7, then disconnect the battery negative lead.

2 Separate the two halves of the fuel injector harness wiring connector. The connector is located in front of the fuel pressure regulator **(see illustration).**

3 Disconnect the vacuum pipe from the fuel pressure regulator **(see illustration).**

4 Disconnect the fuel return pipe from the end of the fuel rail **(see illustration).** Be prepared for fuel spillage. Plug or clamp the hose to prevent dirt entry and further fuel loss.

5 It is now necessary to disconnect the fuel feed hose from the fuel rail. To do this, a special tool will be required to release the connector. The appropriate Renault special tool (Mot. 1311-06) slides through the connector collar to release the securing lugs, but the same effect can be achieved using a small flat-bladed screwdriver to release the lugs. Note that some models have the Renault special tool built into the hose connection. Once the connector securing lugs have been released, the hose can be pulled from the end of the fuel rail **(see illustrations).** Plug or clamp the hose to prevent dirt entry and further fuel loss.

6 Working underneath the manifold, unscrew the two bolts securing the fuel rail to the manifold **(see illustration).**

7 Carefully slide the fuel rail and injector assembly towards the right-hand side of the vehicle, between the manifold and cylinder head.

8 To remove a fuel injector from the fuel rail, release the wiring clips from the injectors, and

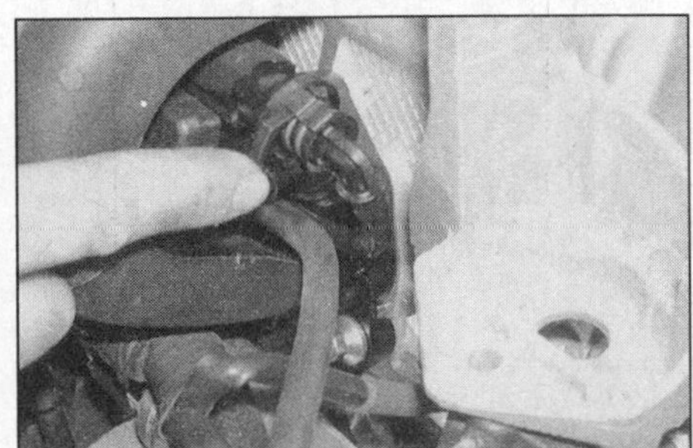

13.5a Push the built-in tool in to release the fuel feed hose connector securing lugs . . .

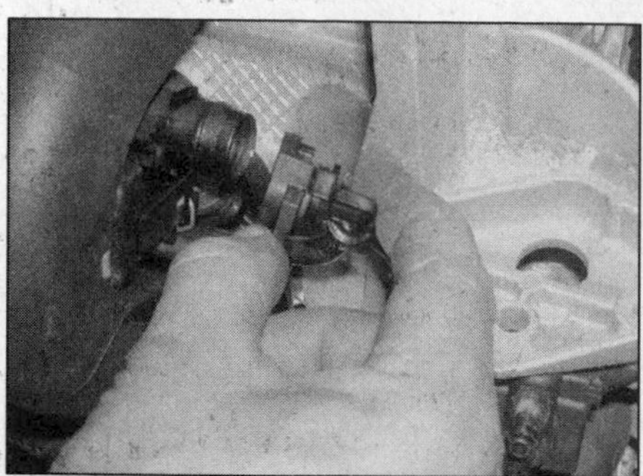
13.5b . . . then disconnect the hose from the fuel rail – D7F engine

13.6 Unscrew the fuel rail securing bolts (arrowed) (viewed with inlet manifold removed) – D7F engine

pull the wiring tube assembly from the top of the injectors. Release the relevant injector securing clip, and remove the fuel injector **(see illustrations)**.

9 Refitting is a reversal of removal, but renew the O-rings at the top and bottom of each injector (check on availability before removing the old O-rings), and ensure that the fuel feed hose is securely reconnected (the connector should click securely into position).

D4F engine

10 Depressurise the fuel system as described in Section 7, then disconnect the battery negative lead.

11 Remove the inlet manifold as described in Section 14.

12 Unscrew the two bolts and remove the fuel rail from the inlet manifold.

13 To remove the fuel injectors from the fuel rail, release the wiring clips from the injectors, and pull the wiring tube assembly from the top of the injectors. Release the injector securing clips, and remove the fuel injectors.

14 Refitting is a reversal of removal, but renew the O-rings at the top and bottom of each injector (check on availability before removing the old O-rings), and ensure that the fuel feed hose is securely reconnected (the connector should click securely into position).

K4J and K4M engines

15 Depressurise the fuel system as described in Section 7, then disconnect the battery negative lead.

16 Remove the cover for access to the fuel rail.

17 Disconnect the fuel feed and return hoses from the fuel rail.

18 Disconnect the vacuum hose connecting the pressure regulator (on the fuel rail) to the inlet manifold.

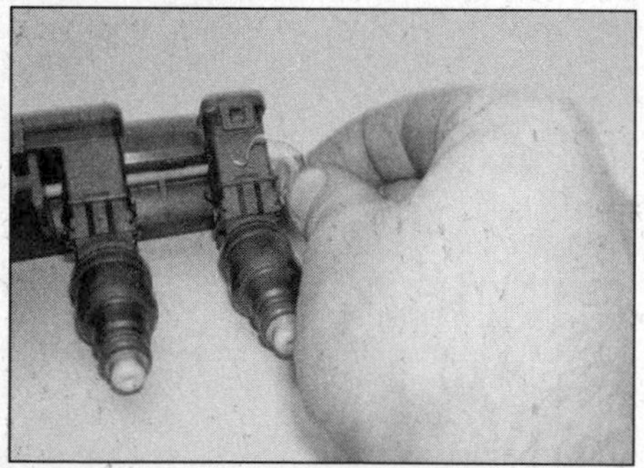
13.8a Release the injector wiring clips . . .

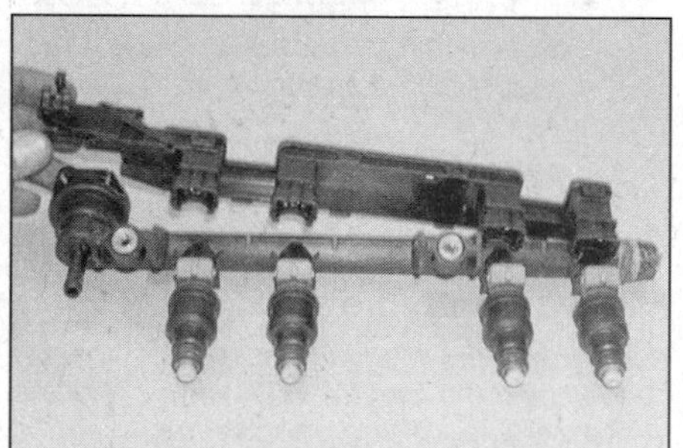
13.8b . . . and pull the wiring tube assembly from the top of the injectors – D7F engine

13.8c Release the injector securing clip . . .

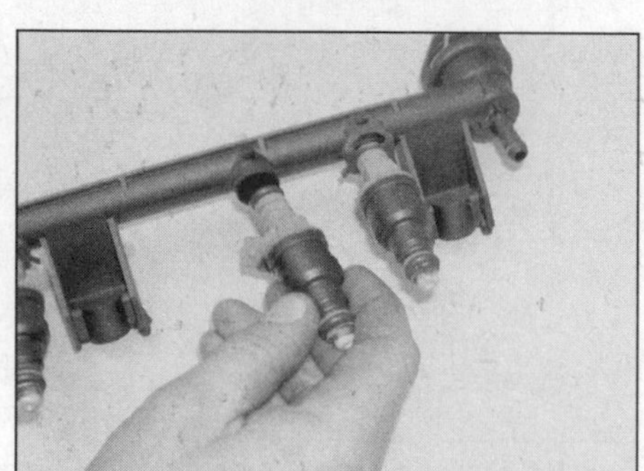
13.8d . . . and remove the fuel injector – D7F engine

19 Disconnect the wiring from the injectors and move the loom to one side.

20 Unscrew and remove the mounting bolts and carefully ease the fuel rail together with the injectors from the inlet manifold.

21 Note the fitted positions of the injectors, then remove the clips and ease the injectors from the fuel rail.

22 Remove the sealing rings from the grooves at each end of the injectors and obtain new ones.

23 Refitting is a reversal of the removal procedure, noting the following points:

a) Renew all sealing rings, using a smear of engine oil to aid installation.
b) Refit the fuel rail assembly to the manifold, making sure the sealing rings remain correctly positioned, and tighten the retaining bolts to the specified torque.
c) On completion start the engine and check for fuel leaks.

Fuel rail pressure regulator

Note: *On some early models with a fuel return line, the fuel pressure regulator is located on the fuel rail in the engine compartment, however, on later models with no return line, it is located on the fuel pump inside the fuel tank, and may be removed after removing the pump.*

Removal

24 Disconnect the vacuum pipe from the regulator.

25 Place a wad of rag over the regulator to catch any spilled fuel, then extract the retaining spring and ease the regulator from the fuel rail.

26 Remove the sealing rings from the grooves in the pressure regulator and obtain new ones.

Refitting

27 On refitting, fit new sealing rings to the regulator grooves and apply a smear of engine oil to them to ease installation. Ease the regulator back into the end of the fuel rail and refit the retaining spring and vacuum pipe.

Throttle potentiometer (early D7F engines)

Note: *It is not possible to remove the potentiometer on the D4F throttle housing.*

Removal

28 Remove the throttle housing as described in Section 11.

29 Undo the retaining screws and remove the potentiometer from the throttle housing. On some models, the potentiometer is not retained with screws, however, it can be removed by pulling it from the housing but this may destroy the old unit.

Refitting

30 Refitting is a reverse of the removal procedure ensuring that the potentiometer is correctly engaged with the throttle spindle. **Note:** *Renault recommend that the*

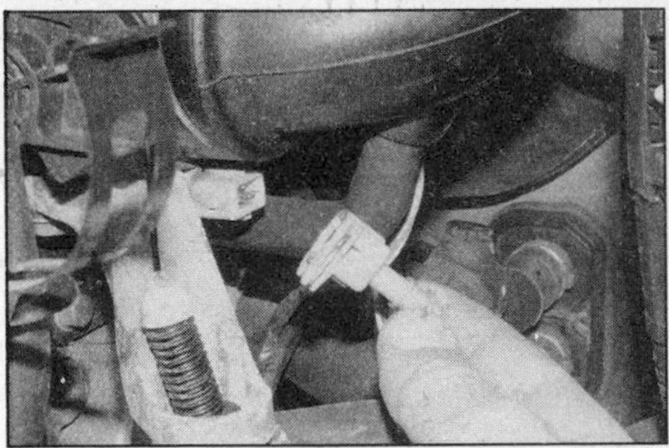

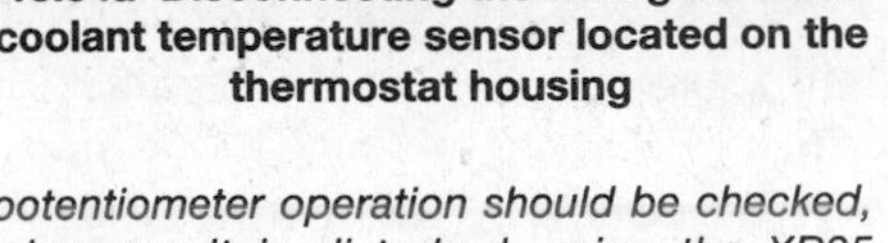

13.34a Disconnecting the wiring from the coolant temperature sensor located on the thermostat housing

potentiometer operation should be checked, whenever it is disturbed, using the XR25 diagnostic tester.

Inlet air temperature sensor

Removal

31 The air temperature sensor is located on the air inlet duct to the throttle housing on SOHC engines, and on the upper section of the inlet manifold on DOHC engines. To remove it, first disconnect the wiring from the sensor, then loosen the clips and remove the air inlet duct.

32 Unscrew and remove the inlet air temperature sensor from the air inlet duct.

Refitting

33 Refitting is a reversal of removal.

13.42a Disconnecting the wiring from the manifold absolute pressure sensor on the D7F engine . . .

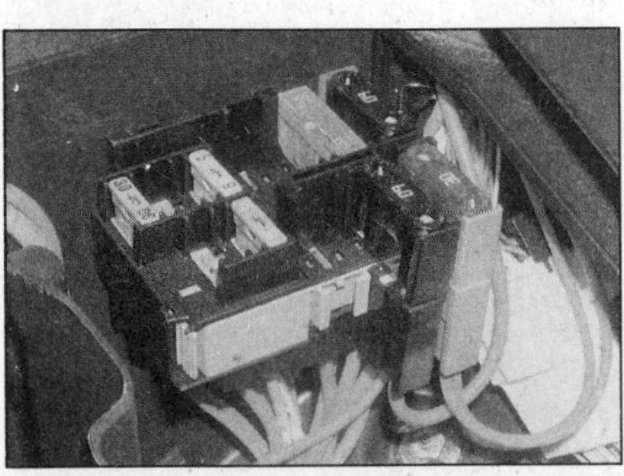

13.47 Fuse and relay box located on the left-hand side of the engine compartment

13.34b Coolant temperature sensor located on the front of the cylinder head

Coolant temperature sensor

34 The sensor is located on the thermostat housing or at the left-hand end of the cylinder head above the gearbox bellhousing **(see illustration)**. Refer to Chapter 3 for removal and refitting details.

Knock sensor

35 The knock sensor is located on the front of the cylinder block **(see illustration)**.

36 Refer to Chapter 5B for the removal and refitting procedures.

Idle speed control stepper motor

Note: *No separate idle speed motor is fitted to later models equipped with a motorised throttle valve (see Section 11).*

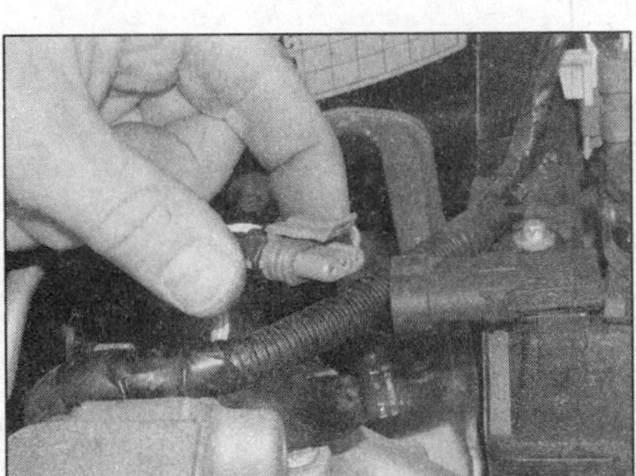

13.42b . . . and K4J engine

13.49 The crankshaft speed/position sensor is mounted on top of the transmission

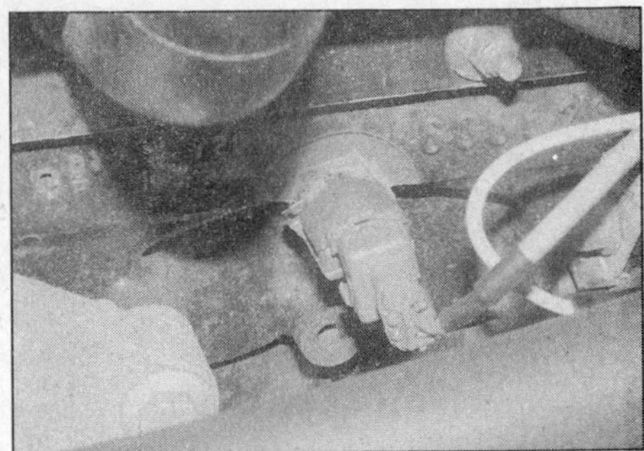

13.35 The knock sensor on the D7F engine

Removal

37 On D7F and D4F engines, the idle speed control stepper motor is mounted on the top of the throttle housing on the left-hand side of the engine. On K4J and K4M engines the stepper motor is located on the top of the inlet manifold plenum chamber on the right-hand rear side of the engine.

38 To remove the stepper motor, first remove the throttle housing as described in Section 11.

39 Undo the retaining screws and remove the stepper motor from the throttle housing. Recover the gasket and discard it; a new one should be used on refitting.

Refitting

40 Refitting is a reversal of the removal procedure using a new gasket.

Manifold absolute pressure (MAP) sensor

Removal

41 The manifold absolute sensor is mounted on the rear of the air cleaner.

42 Disconnect the wiring and (where applicable) the vacuum hose from the sensor **(see illustrations)**.

43 Unscrew the mounting nuts and remove the sensor.

Refitting

44 Refitting is a reversal of removal.

Fuel system and fuel pump relays

Removal

45 These relays are located behind the left-hand headlight in the engine compartment.

46 Remove the cover from the box.

47 Remove the relevant relay from the fuse/relay box **(see illustration)**.

Refitting

48 Refitting is the reverse of removal.

Crankshaft TDC sensor

Removal

49 The sensor is mounted on the top of the transmission bellhousing at the left-hand end of the cylinder block **(see illustration)**.

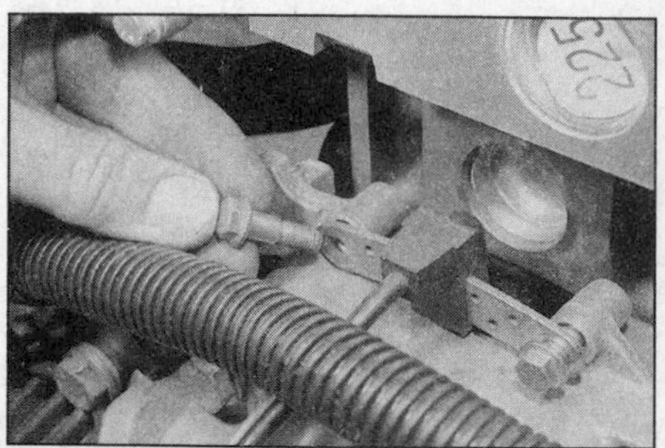
13.52 Note the special bolts used to locate and secure the crankshaft speed/position sensor

13.54 Fuel cut-off inertia switch

13.58 Position the power steering hydraulic fluid reservoir to one side . . .

50 To remove the sensor, remove the air cleaner housing as described in Section 2.
51 Trace the wiring back from the sensor to the wiring connector, and disconnect it from the main harness.
52 Unscrew the retaining bolts and remove the sensor **(see illustration)**.

Refitting

53 Refitting is a reversal of removal. Ensure that the sensor retaining bolts are securely tightened – note that only the special shouldered bolts originally fitted must be used to secure the sensor; these bolts locate the sensor precisely to give the correct air gap between the sensor tip and the flywheel/driveplate.

Fuel cut-off inertia switch

Removal

54 The switch is only fitted to some early models, and is located in the left-hand side of the engine compartment **(see illustration)**.
55 Unscrew and remove the switch retaining screws then disconnect its wiring connector and remove the switch from the engine compartment.

Refitting

56 Refitting is the reverse of removal. On completion, reset the switch by depressing its button.

Electronic control unit (ECU)

***Note:** The ECU is electronically-coded to match the engine immobiliser and certain other engine components. If the ECU is being removed in order to fit a new unit, it is highly recommended that the work be carried out by a Renault dealer.*
57 On all engines except the D4F, the ECU is located in the left-hand side of the engine compartment, behind the battery. On the D4F engine, it is located on the rear of the engine or inlet manifold. First disconnect the battery negative lead (refer to *Disconnecting the battery* in the Reference Section).

Removal – except D4F engine

58 On early models, unclip the power steering hydraulic fluid reservoir from the bulkhead and position it to one side **(see illustration)**.
59 Where applicable, unbolt the bracket from the top of the ECU and release the strap **(see illustration)**. Alternatively the bracket can remain on the ECU until the assembly is removed.
60 Undo the mounting screws and remove the ECU and mounting bracket **(see illustration)**.
61 Disconnect the wiring connector and remove the ECU from the engine compartment.

Removal – D4F engine

62 Remove the engine top cover **(see illustration)**. Lift the rear of the cover then push the front rearwards.
63 Reach over the rear of the engine and disconnect the wiring plug(s) from the computer **(see illustration)**.
64 Unscrew the ECU mounting screws. If necessary, use a mirror to locate the screws.
65 Withdraw the ECU and recover the seal.

Refitting

66 Refitting is a reverse of the removal procedure ensuring that the wiring is securely reconnected. On the D4F engine, renew the seal.

13.59 . . . then remove the upper bracket . . .

13.60 . . . followed by the ECU

13.62 Removing the engine top cover

13.63 ECU on the D4F engine

14 Manifolds – removal and refitting

Inlet manifold

D7F engine

1 Disconnect the battery negative (earth) lead and position it away from the terminal.
2 Remove the air cleaner assembly as described in Section 2.
3 Remove the fuel rail and injectors as described in Section 13.
4 Apply the handbrake, then jack up the front of the vehicle and support it on axle stands (see *Jacking and vehicle support*). Remove the right-hand roadwheel and wheel arch liner.
5 On the right-hand side of the engine, unbolt the support strut located to the rear of the right-hand driveshaft.
6 Loosen the clips and remove the air inlet duct from between the air cleaner and throttle body **(see illustration).**
7 Disconnect the accelerator cable from the throttle body with reference to Section 3 **(see illustration).**
8 Disconnect the wiring from the throttle body.
9 Disconnect the brake servo vacuum hose.
10 Progressively unscrew and remove the bolts and nuts securing the inlet manifold to the cylinder head **(see illustrations)**. Also unscrew the bolts securing the support bracket.

14.6 Remove the air ducting connecting the air cleaner assembly to the throttle body – D7F engine

11 Withdraw the inlet manifold from the cylinder head and recover the gasket or O-rings as applicable **(see illustration)**.
12 Refitting is a reversal of removal but use new O-rings or gasket (as applicable) and tighten the mounting nuts and bolts to the specified torque. Ensure that the cylinder head and manifold mating surfaces are clean.

D4F engine

13 Disconnect the battery negative (earth) lead and position it away from the terminal.
14 Unbolt the air cleaner unit and remove the engine top cover.
15 At the rear of the engine, disconnect the wiring from the engine management ECU. Also, disconnect the wiring from the engine wiring loom and inlet manifold absolute pressure sensor **(see illustration)**.
16 Remove the interference suppressor located on the inlet manifold.

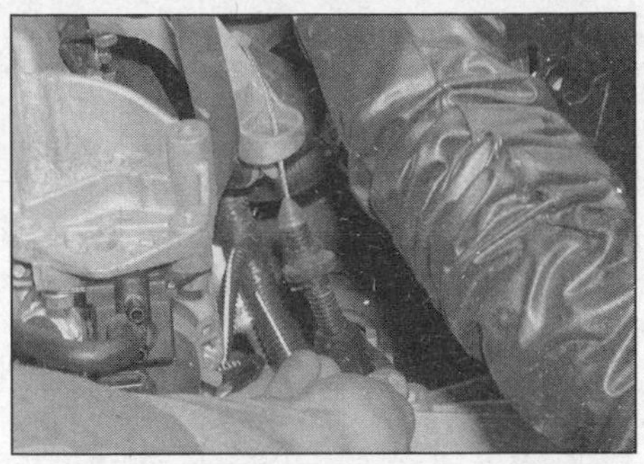

14.7 Disconnecting the accelerator cable – D7F engine

17 Disconnect the wiring from the engine oil pressure sensor.
18 Disconnect the wiring from the ignition coil.
19 Disconnect the ignition HT leads.
20 Disconnect the wiring from the coolant temperature sensor on the left-hand side of the engine.
21 Disconnect the wiring from the knock sensor on the front of the cylinder block.
22 Disconnect the starter motor wiring.
23 Release the brake vacuum pipe from the left-hand end of the inlet manifold.
24 From the right-hand end of the inlet manifold, disconnect the carbon canister purge pipe **(see illustration)**.
25 Disconnect the fuel pipe from the right-hand end of the fuel rail located beneath the inlet manifold **(see illustration)**.
26 Unscrew the four bolts securing the inlet manifold to the valve cover.

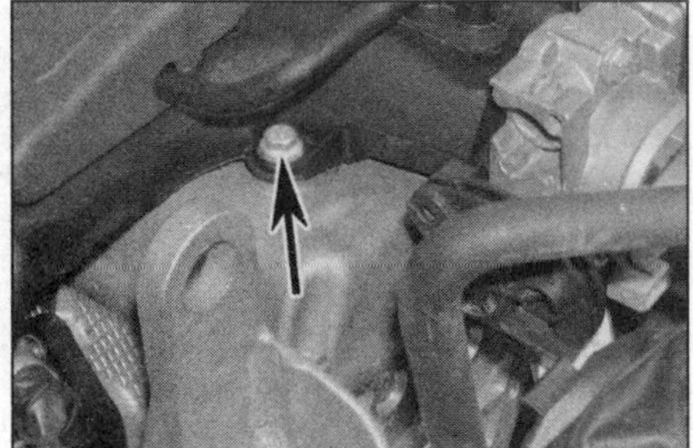

14.10a Unscrew the two bolts securing the inlet manifold to the top of the cylinder head . . .

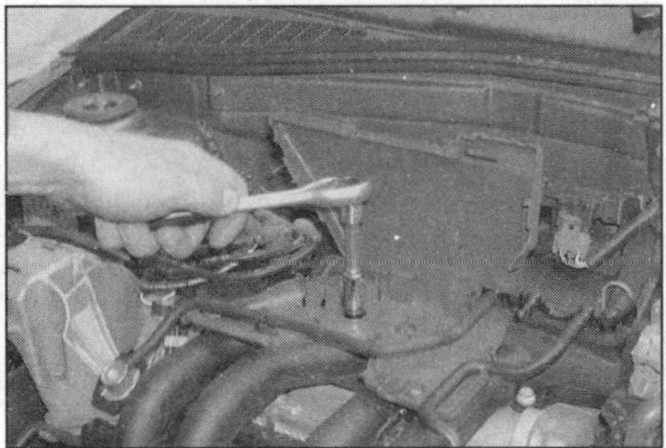

14.10b . . . noting that one of the bolts is accessed through the spark plug lead housing – D7F engine

14.11 Removing the inlet manifold – D7F engine

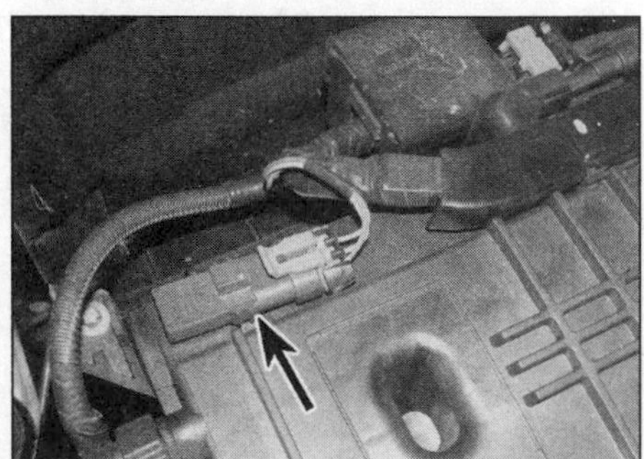

14.15 Inlet manifold absolute pressure sensor

14.24 Carbon canister purge pipe connection to the inlet manifold

14.25 Fuel pipe on the right-hand end of the fuel rail

27 Progressively unscrew the bolts securing the inlet manifold to the front of the cylinder head.
28 Release the inlet manifold from the head, then move it sideways while disconnecting the wiring from the motorised throttle valve, air temperature sensor and fuel injectors. Pull the wiring to one side and withdraw the inlet manifold. If required, unbolt the motorised throttle valve from the underside of the inlet manifold.
29 Refitting is a reversal of removal but use new seals for the inlet manifold, valve cover and purge pipe. It is important to apply Loctite Frenetanch (or similar) to the threads of the inlet manifold mounting bolts before refitting them, and they must be tightened using the following procedure.

1) *Refit and hand-tighten the bolts securing the manifold to the side of the cylinder head.*
2) *Working on the side bolts only, pretighten bolts 2 and 4 on top row to 6 Nm, then loosen and hand-tighten again.*
3) *Starting on the top middle bolt and working in a clockwise direction, tighten the side bolts to 10 Nm.*
4) *Progressively tighten the bolts securing the manifold to the valve cover to 10 Nm.*

K4J and K4M engines

30 Disconnect the battery negative (earth) lead and position it away from the terminal.
31 Remove the air cleaner assembly as described in Section 2.
32 Disconnect the wiring from the throttle potentiometer, absolute pressure sensor, ignition coils and air temperature sensor.
33 Disconnect the accelerator cable from the throttle body with reference to Section 3.
34 Unscrew and remove the throttle body mounting bolts and position the throttle body to one side.
35 Progressively unscrew and remove the bolts securing the inlet manifold to the cylinder head.
36 Withdraw the inlet manifold and recover the gasket.
37 Refitting is a reversal of removal but use a new gasket and tighten the mounting bolts to the specified torque. Ensure that the cylinder head and manifold mating surfaces are clean.

Exhaust manifold

D7F engine

38 Disconnect the battery negative (earth) lead and position it away from the terminal.
39 Apply the handbrake, then jack up the front of the vehicle and support it on axle stands (see *Jacking and vehicle support*). Remove the engine undertray.
40 On the right-hand side of the engine, remove the multi-function support.
41 Disconnect the exhaust front downpipe from the exhaust manifold on the front of the engine with reference to Section 15.
42 Unscrew the nuts and remove the heat shield from the exhaust manifold.

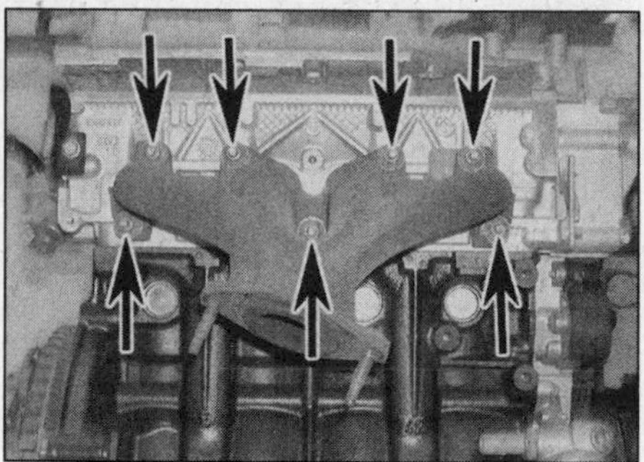

14.43 Exhaust manifold securing bolt locations – D7F engine

43 Progressively unscrew the bolts and remove the exhaust manifold from the cylinder head **(see illustration)**. Recover the gasket.
44 Refitting is a reversal of removal but use a new gasket and tighten the mounting bolts to the specified torque. Ensure that the cylinder head and manifold mating surfaces are clean.

D4F engine

45 Disconnect the battery negative (earth) lead and position it away from the terminal.
46 Apply the handbrake, then jack up the front of the vehicle and support it on axle stands (see *Jacking and vehicle support*). Remove the engine undertray.
47 Disconnect the wiring from the upstream and downstream oxygen sensors, and position the downstream wiring loom to one side.
48 Unscrew the nuts and disconnect the exhaust downpipe and catalytic converter from the exhaust manifold. Recover the gasket.
49 Unbolt and remove the heat shield.
50 Unscrew the mounting nuts and withdraw the exhaust manifold from the rear of the cylinder head. Access to the nuts is best gained using a flexible socket drive through the subframe. Recover the gasket.
51 Refitting is a reversal of removal but use new gaskets and tighten the mounting nuts to the specified torque. Ensure that the cylinder head and manifold mating surfaces are clean.

K4J and K4M engines

52 Disconnect the battery negative (earth) lead and position it away from the terminal.

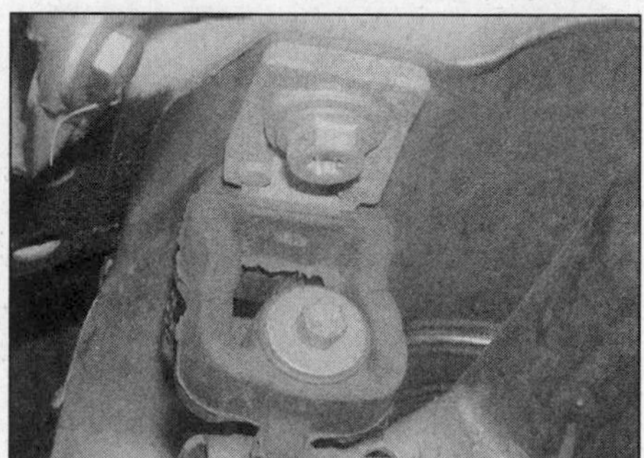

15.2 Exhaust rubber mounting

53 Apply the handbrake, then jack up the front of the vehicle and support it on axle stands (see *Jacking and vehicle support*). Remove the engine undertray.
54 Remove the air cleaner assembly as described in Section 2.
55 Remove the lambda/oxygen sensor as described in Chapter 4C.
56 Unbolt the heat shield from the top of the exhaust manifold on the rear of the engine. Also remove the subframe heat shield.
57 Disconnect the exhaust front downpipe from the exhaust manifold with reference to Section 15.
58 Remove the catalytic converter from the exhaust manifold and exhaust intermediate section. Note that the subframe can be slightly lowered to make it easier to remove the catalytic converter without damaging the underbody heat shield.
59 Unbolt the support strut from between the exhaust manifold and cylinder block.
60 Unscrew the mounting nuts, then tilt the exhaust manifold as required and withdraw it from the studs on the cylinder head. Recover the gasket.
61 Refitting is a reversal of removal but use a new gasket and tighten the mounting nuts to the specified torque. Ensure that the cylinder head and manifold mating surfaces are clean.

15 Exhaust system – general information, removal and refitting

General information

1 On new vehicles the exhaust system consists of just two sections; the front downpipe with catalytic converter and the remaining system consisting of a resonator (not all models), tailpipe and silencer. The downpipe is attached to the rear section by a cone-and-socket clamp joint.
2 The rear section of the exhaust is located above the rear suspension; the intermediate and tailpipe/silencer may be renewed separately by cutting the intermediate pipe with a hacksaw. The system is suspended throughout its entire length by rubber mountings **(see illustration)**.

Removal

3 To remove a part of the system, first jack up the front or rear of the car, and support it on axle stands (see *Jacking and vehicle support*). Alternatively, position the car over an inspection pit, or on car ramps. Where fitted, remove the engine compartment undertray.

Front downpipe and catalytic converter

4 Trace the wiring back from the lambda/oxygen sensors and disconnect it at the wiring connectors. Free the wiring from any relevant retaining clips so the sensors are free to be removed with the front pipe.

5 Where applicable, unbolt the front pipe from the mounting bracket on the transmission.

6 Unscrew and remove the nuts/bolts securing the front pipe flange joint to the manifold, and recover the gasket.

7 Unscrew and remove the clamp and disconnect the front pipe and catalytic converter from the rear section **(see illustration)**. Withdraw the pipe from under the vehicle.

Intermediate pipe and resonator

8 Unscrew and remove the clamp bolts attaching the front pipe and catalytic converter to the rear section.

9 If the original rear section is fitted, it must be cut in half using either a hacksaw or pipe cutter. Locate the cutting area which is situated approximately midway between the rear silencer and intermediate mounting. The cutting point is marked with two circular punch marks on the side of the pipe. The punch marks are 90 mm apart and the exhaust section should be cut at the mid-point between the two punch marks. **Note:** *Ensure that the exhaust pipe is cut squarely, or else it will be difficult to obtain a gas-tight seal when the exhaust is refitted.*

10 With the intermediate pipe cut, withdraw the intermediate exhaust section from under the vehicle.

11 If the rear section is in two halves, unscrew the bolt and slide the clamp sleeve on to the rear section then release the rubber mountings and withdraw the intermediate section from under the vehicle.

Rear tailpipe and silencer

12 If the original rear section is fitted, follow the instructions given in paragraph 9.

13 If the rear section is in two halves, unscrew the bolt and slide the clamp sleeve on to the intermediate section then release the rubber mountings and withdraw the tailpipe and silencer from under the vehicle.

Heat shields

14 The heat shields are secured to the underbody by various nuts and bolts. Each shield can be removed separately but note that they overlap making it necessary to loosen another section first. If a shield is being removed to gain access to a component located behind it, it may prove sufficient in some cases to remove the retaining nuts and/or bolts, and simply lower the shield, without disturbing the exhaust system. Otherwise remove the exhaust section as described earlier.

Refitting

15 Each section is refitted by reversing the removal sequence, noting the following points:

a) *Ensure that all traces of corrosion have been removed from the joints.*
b) *Inspect the rubber mountings for signs of damage or deterioration, and renew as necessary.*
c) *When reconnecting the intermediate pipe to the tailpipe, apply a smear of exhaust system jointing paste (Renault recommend the use of Sodicam) to the sleeve inner surface, to ensure a gas-tight seal. Make sure both inner ends of the cut pipe are positioned squarely against the stop of the clamp sleeve. Position the sleeve bolt vertically on the left-hand side of the pipe and securely tighten the nut until it is heard to click; the clamp bolt has a groove in it to ensure that the nut is correctly tightened (equivalent to a tightening torque of approximately 25 Nm).*
d) *Prior to tightening the exhaust system fasteners, ensure that all rubber mountings are correctly located, and that there is adequate clearance between the exhaust system and vehicle underbody.*

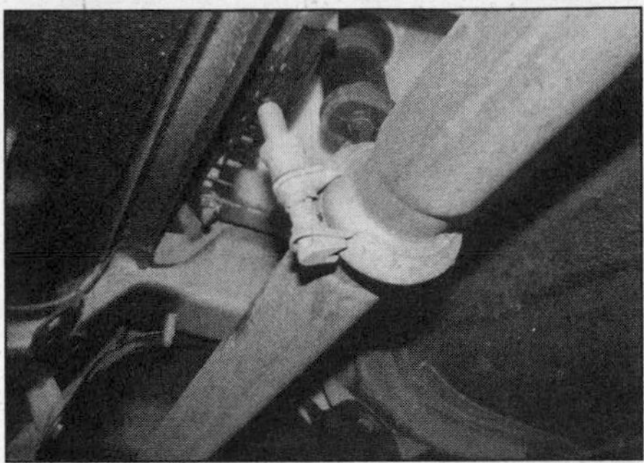

15.7 Exhaust clamp connecting the front to rear sections

Chapter 4 Part B:
Diesel engine fuel and exhaust systems

Contents

Degrees of difficulty

Easy, suitable for novice with little experience 	**Fairly easy,** suitable for beginner with some experience 	**Fairly difficult,** suitable for competent DIY mechanic	**Difficult,** suitable for experienced DIY mechanic 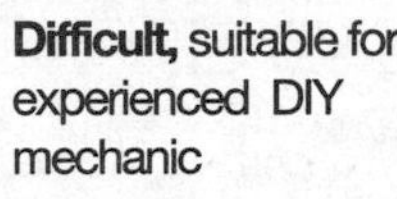	**Very difficult,** suitable for expert DIY or professional

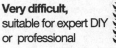

Specifications

General

Type	Lucas-Delphi
System type	Rear-mounted fuel tank, high-pressure pump with common-rail, direct injection
Firing order	1-3-4-2 (number 1 at flywheel end)
Fuel type	Diesel
Idle speed	800 ± 50 rpm
Maximum no-load speed	4500 ± 150 rpm
Maximum under-load speed	5000 ± 150 rpm

High-pressure pump

Type	Delphi
Direction of rotation	Clockwise viewed from sprocket end

Injectors

Type	Delphi solenoid injector
Maximum pressure	1400 bars
Resistance	Non-measurable

Sensor resistances

Air temperature sensor:	
At -40° C	50000 ± 6800 ohms
At -10° C	9500 ± 900 ohms
At 25° C	2051 ± 120 ohms
At 50° C	810 ± 47 ohms
At 80° C	310 ± 17 ohms
Engine speed sensor	760 ohms
Fuel flow actuator (on pump)	5.3 ± 0.5 ohms
Accelerator pedal potentiometer:	
Track 1 – 4 (earth) and 6 (+5V)	1.2 ± 0.5 kohms
Track 2 – 5 (earth) and 3 (+5V)	1.7 ± 0.7 kohms
Fuel temperature sensor (on pump)	2.2 kohms
Turbocharger pressure sensor:	
Tracks A and B	9.0 kohms
Tracks A and C	4.0 kohms
Tracks B and C	5.0 kohms

Turbocharger

Type	Garrett
Boost pressure	1300 ± 2 mbars

Fuel tank

Fuel tank level sender unit resistance at height of float pin (approx):	
At 164 mm	3.5 ± 3.5 ohms
At 143 mm	61 ± 7 ohms
At 110 mm	110 ± 10 ohms
At 81 mm	190 ± 16 ohms
At 52 mm	280 ± 20 ohms
At 47 mm	310 ± 10 ohms

Torque wrench settings

	Nm	lbf ft
Catalytic converter:		
Rear mounting	21	15
To side mounting strut	25	18
Converter to turbocharger	26	19
Strut to engine	44	32
EGR valve	21	15
EGR valve heat shield	12	9
Engine lifting eye	21	15
Exhaust manifold	26	19
Exhaust pipe clamp	21	15
Flow actuator	6	4
Fuel gauge sender unit	65	48
Fuel injectors to cylinder head	28	21
Fuel tank	21	15
Fuel temperature sensor (on high-pressure pump)	15	11
High-pressure pump	21	16
High-pressure pump sprocket nut:		
Stage 1	15	11
Stage 2	Angle-tighten a further 60° ± 10°	
High-pressure fuel rail	28	21
High-pressure pipe union nuts	38	28
High-pressure pump venturi	6	4
Turbocharger oil supply pipe:		
On cylinder head	23	17
On turbocharger	12	9
Turbocharger to exhaust manifold	26	19

1 General information and precautions

General information

1 The fuel system consists of a rear-mounted fuel tank, a fuel filter with integral water separator, a high-pressure pump with common-rail injection system, electronic injectors and associated components.

2 The main components of the system are as follows:

a) Priming bulb on the low pressure circuit.
b) Fuel filter.
c) High-pressure pump incorporating a low-pressure transfer pump.
d) Flow actuator attached to the pump.
e) Injector rail.
f) Pressure sensor located on the injector rail.
g) Four electronic solenoid injectors.
h) Fuel temperature sensor.
i) Coolant temperature sensor.
j) Upstream air temperature sensor.
k) Downstream air temperature sensor.
l) Cylinder reference sensor.
m) Engine speed sensor.
n) Turbocharging pressure sensor.
o) Accelerometer.
p) EGR solenoid valve.
q) Accelerator pedal potentiometer.
r) Atmospheric pressure sensor.
s) ECU
t) Knock sensor

3 The common-rail injection system operates as follows. Fuel is drawn from the fuel tank to the high-pressure pump by a low pressure transfer pump integrated in the high-pressure pump. Before reaching the high-pressure pump, the fuel passes through a fuel filter, where foreign matter and water are removed. As the fuel passes through the filter, it is heated by an electric heater. On reaching the high-pressure pump, the fuel is pressurised to a maximum of 1400 bars according to demand, and accumulates in the injection common-rail. The pressure is accurately maintained in the fuel rail by a flow actuator located on the rear of the pump, the actuator being controlled by the engine management ECU. This arrangement keeps heat generation to a minimum, and improves engine output. The rail pressure is also maintained by the injectors themselves; short electrical pulses which are not long enough to open the injector, allow fuel into the return (leak-off) circuit, and also the normal pulses which open the injectors cause a reduction in pressure. The ECU determines the exact timing and duration of the injection period according to engine operating conditions.

4 The four fuel injectors inject a homogeneous spray of fuel into the combustion chambers located in the cylinder head. The injectors operate sequentially according to the firing order of the cylinders, and each injector needle is lubricated by fuel, which accumulates in the spring chamber. Each injector has its own unique flow characteristics which are used by the system ECU to calculate the exact quantity of fuel to inject.

5 The knock sensor is mounted on the cylinder block to inform the ECU when the fuel injection timing needs to be retarded, in order to regain optimum engine efficiency **(see illustration)**.

6 Provided that the specified maintenance is carried out, the fuel injection equipment will

1.5 Knock sensor

give long and trouble-free service. The main potential cause of damage to the high-pressure pump and injectors is dirt or water in the fuel **(see Tool tip)**.

7 Servicing of the high-pressure pump, injectors, and electronic equipment and sensors is very limited for the home mechanic, and any dismantling or adjustment other than that described in this Chapter must be entrusted to a Renault dealer or fuel injection specialist.

8 If a fault appears in the injection system, first ensure that all the system wiring connectors are securely connected and free of corrosion. Should the fault persist, the vehicle should be taken to a Renault dealer or specialist who can test the system on a diagnostic tester. The tester will locate the fault quickly and simply, alleviating the need to test all the system components individually, which is a time-consuming operation that carries a risk of damaging the ECU. It is advisable to have any faulty components renewed by the dealer as in many instances the tester is required to reprogramme the ECU in the event of component or sensor renewal.

TOOL TiP

The fuel system is very sensitive to contamination; even a small amount could be sufficient to cause extensive damage to fuel system components such as the high-pressure pump and electronic injectors. It is highly recommended that a set of fuel line plugs is obtained from a Renault dealership.

Precautions

Warning: It is necessary to take certain precautions when working on the fuel system components, particularly the fuel injectors and high-pressure pump. Before carrying out any operations on the fuel system, refer to the precautions given in 'Safety first!' at the beginning of this manual, and to any additional warning notes at the start of the relevant Sections. Allow the engine to cool for 5 to 10 minutes to ensure the fuel pressure and temperature are at a minimum.

2 Air cleaner assembly – removal and refitting

Removal

1 Remove the engine top cover.

2 Disconnect the inlet stub from the front of the air cleaner **(see illustrations)**.

3 Release the wiring loom from the air cleaner.

4 Undo the four upper screws, then open the lid and withdraw the filter element **(see illustrations)**.

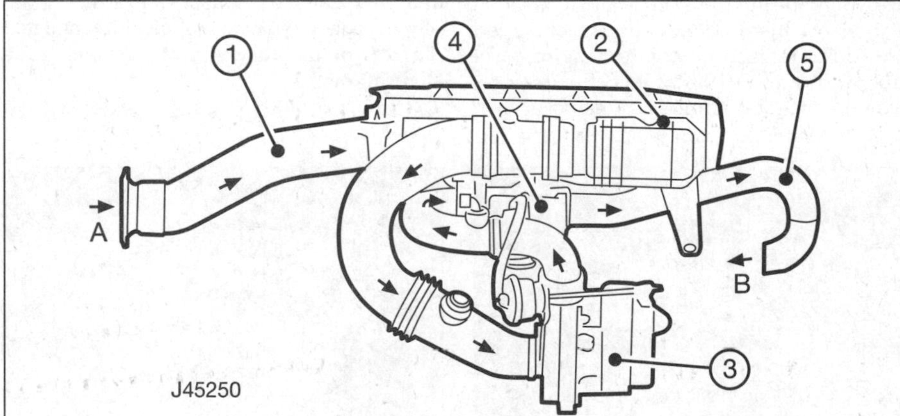

2.2a Air inlet system

1 Air inlet duct
2 Air cleaner assembly
3 Turbocharger
4 EGR unit
5 Metal air inlet tube
A Inlet to air cleaner
B Outlet to inlet manifold

2.2b Disconnecting the inlet stub

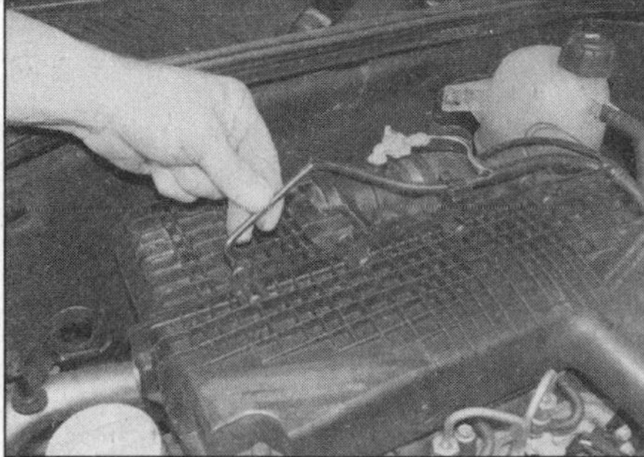

2.4a Undo the four upper screws . . .

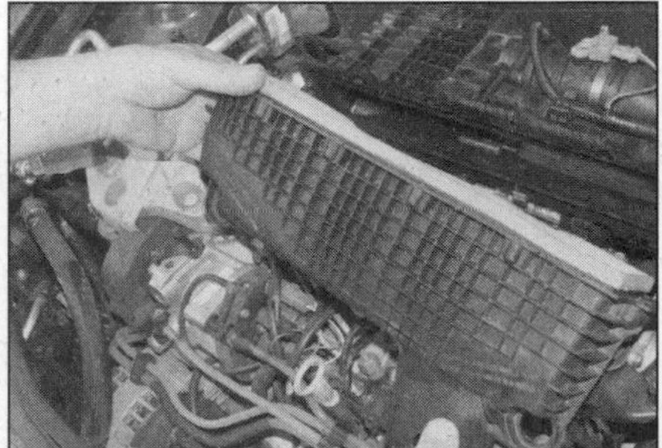

2.4b . . . open the lid . . .

2.4c . . . and withdraw the filter element

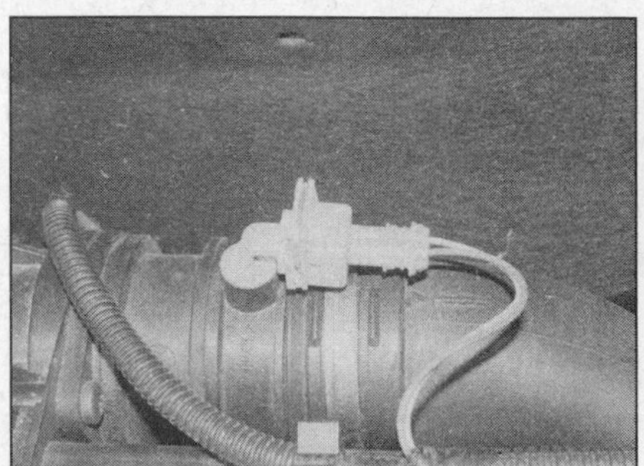

2.5 Upstream air temperature sensor

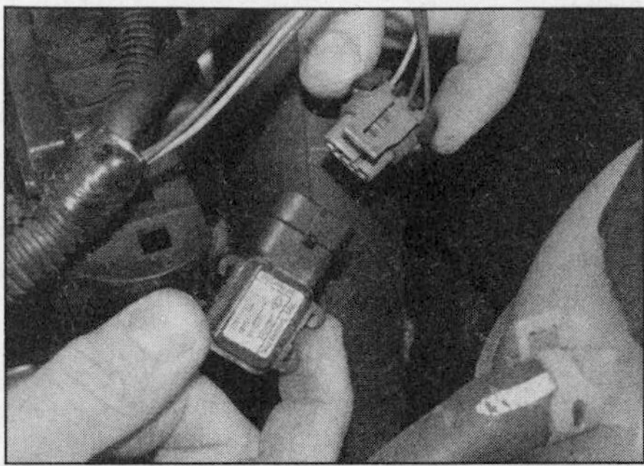

2.6 Disconnecting the wiring from the turbocharger pressure sensor

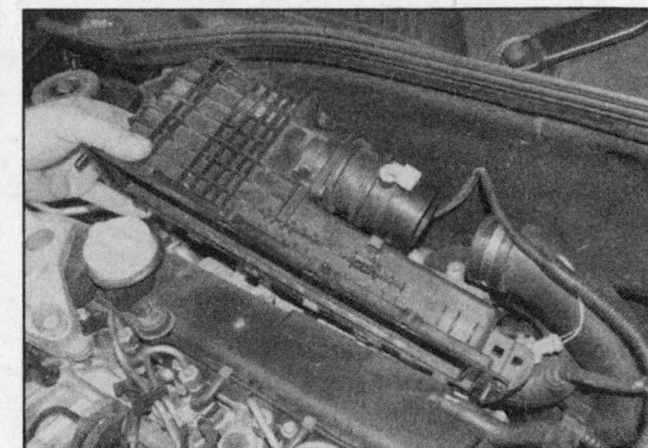

2.7 Removing the air cleaner housing from the engine

5 Disconnect the wiring from the upstream air temperature sensor **(see illustration)**.

6 Release then disconnect the wiring from the turbocharger pressure sensor **(see illustration)**.

7 Loosen the clip for the air inlet duct, then withdraw the air cleaner housing from the engine **(see illustration)**.

Refitting

8 Refitting is a reversal of removal.

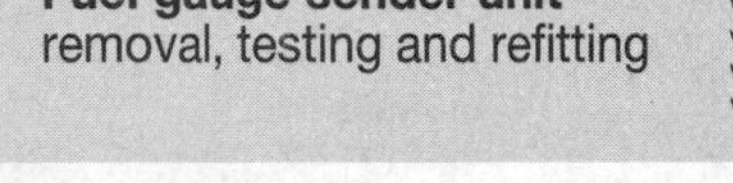

3 Fuel gauge sender unit – removal, testing and refitting

Warning: Refer to the warning note in Section 1 before proceeding.

Removal

1 Disconnect the battery negative lead (refer to *Disconnecting the battery* in the Reference Section).

2 Remove the rear seat, or rear seat cushion as described in Chapter 11, for access to the fuel gauge sender unit cover.

3 Carefully prise the access cover from the floor to expose the fuel gauge sender unit **(see illustration)**.

4 Disconnect the wiring connector, and tape it to the vehicle body, to prevent it disappearing behind the tank **(see illustration)**.

5 Identify the fuel hoses for position, then disconnect them. The hoses are equipped with quick-release fittings to ease removal **(see illustration)**. To disconnect each hose, slide out the locking tab from the collar then compress the collar and detach the hose from the pump. Renault technicians use a special tool to compress the collar – without this tool, it is possible to use a small screwdriver **carefully** to press back the locking collar inside the end of the special end fitting. Disconnect both hoses, then plug the hose ends to minimise fuel loss.

6 Noting the alignment arrows on the cover, locking ring and fuel tank, unscrew the locking ring and remove it from the tank. This can be accomplished by using a screwdriver on the raised ribs of the locking ring – carefully tap the screwdriver to turn the ring anti-clockwise until it can be unscrewed by hand. Alternatively a removal tool can be fabricated out of metal bar and two bolts **(see illustrations)**.

7 Carefully lift the fuel gauge sender unit out

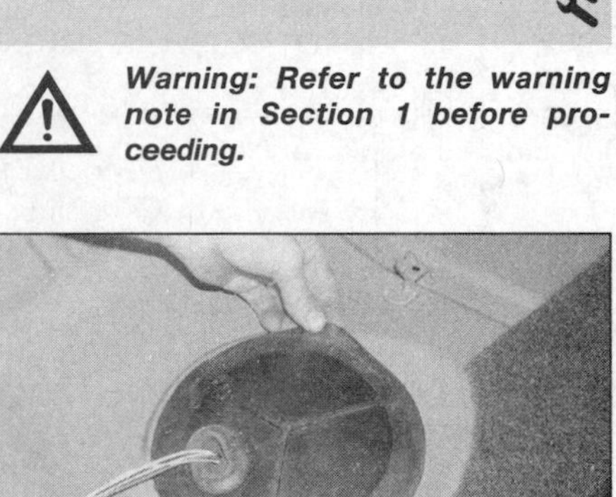

3.3 Prising the access cover from the rear floor

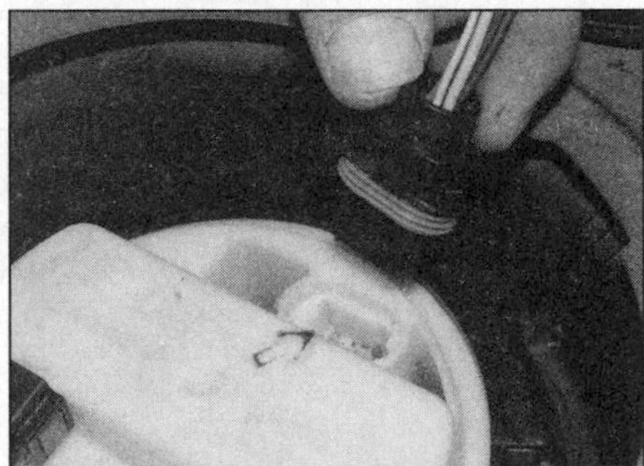

3.4 Disconnecting the wiring from the fuel gauge sender unit

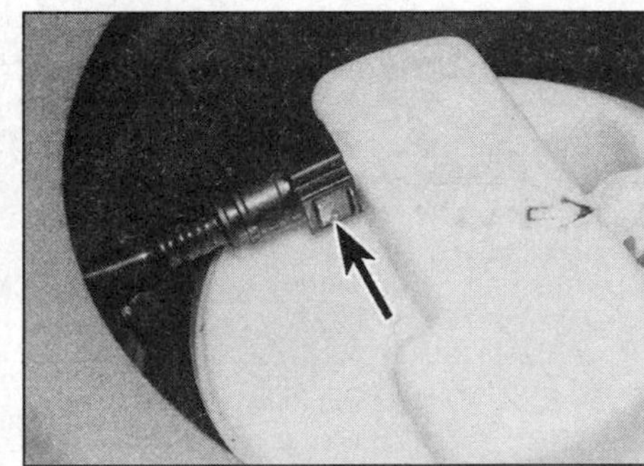

3.5 Fuel supply hose quick-release fitting on the fuel gauge sender unit

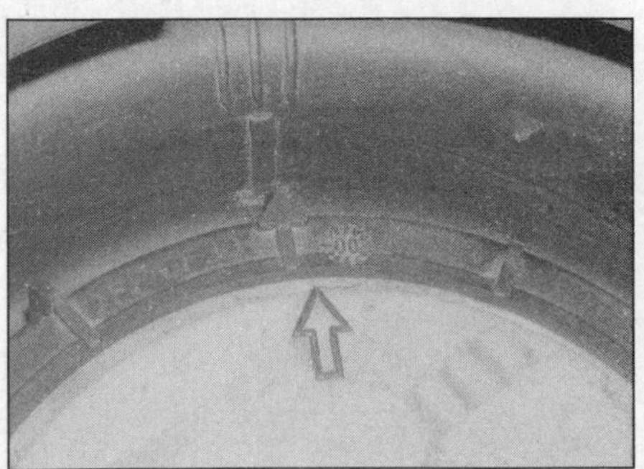

3.6a Alignment arrows on the pump cover, fuel tank and locking ring

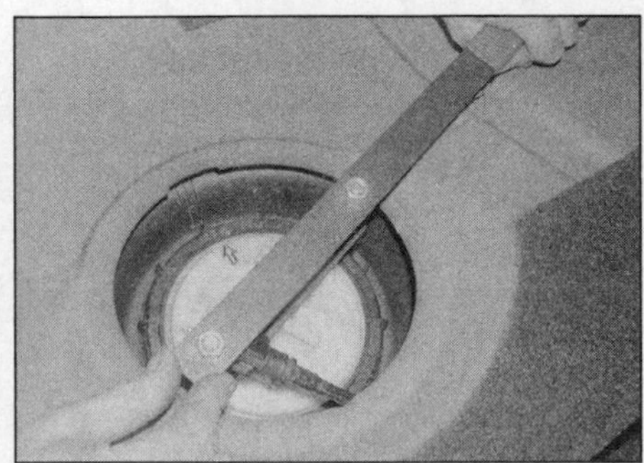

3.6b Using a home-made removal tool to unscrew the locking ring from the fuel tank

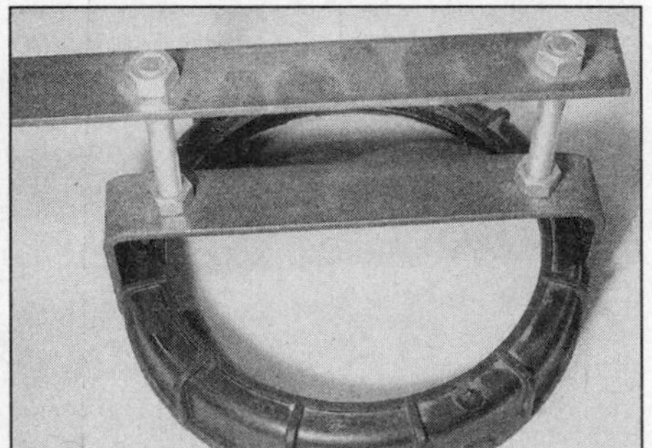

3.6c Home-made locking ring removal tool

of the fuel tank, taking great care not to damage the gauge sender arm, or to spill fuel in the interior of the vehicle. Remove the rubber sealing ring and check it for deterioration **(see illustration)**; if it is in good condition, it may be re-used, however if the pump is to remain out of the fuel tank for several hours, the locking ring should be refitted temporarily to prevent the sealing ring from distorting. If the sealing ring is unserviceable, obtain a new one.

Testing

8 Note that the fuel gauge sender unit is only available as a complete assembly, however it is possible to test its operation and to remove it. To test the unit, disconnect the wiring plug from the cover and connect an ohmmeter to the two terminals.

9 With the pump assembly upright on the bench, measure the resistance of the sender unit at the different heights given in the Specifications. The resistances are approximate but is should be clear if the sender unit is not operating correctly.

10 To remove the sender unit, first release the wiring from the clips, then unclip and remove the cover from the main body.

11 Using a screwdriver, prise off the gauze filter from the bottom of the unit. Also recover the O-ring seal from the spring location column.

12 Carefully unclip the bottom section, then disconnect the wiring and slide out the sender unit and float.

Refitting

13 Ensure that the fuel gauge sender unit pick-up filter is clean and free of debris. Fit the sealing ring to the top of the fuel tank.

14 Carefully manoeuvre the fuel gauge sender unit assembly into the fuel tank.

15 Align the arrow on the fuel gauge sender unit cover with the arrow on the fuel tank (the arrow must point to the rear of the vehicle), then refit the locking ring. Tighten the locking ring until the alignment marks on the unit and securing ring are aligned, then recheck that the fuel gauge sender unit cover and tank marks are all correctly aligned. **Note:** *If a suitable adapter is available tighten the locking ring to the specified torque.*

3.6d Removing the locking ring

3.7 Removing the rubber sealing ring

16 Reconnect the feed and return hoses to the top of the fuel gauge sender unit; it is not necessary to depress the collars when refitting the hoses. Check the hoses are securely in position.

17 Reconnect the wiring connector.

18 Reconnect the battery negative lead, and start the engine. Check the fuel gauge sender unit feed and return hoses for signs of leakage.

19 Refit the plastic access cover and the rear seat cushion.

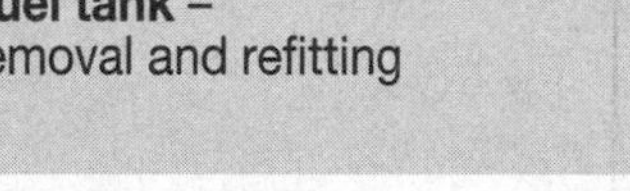

4 Fuel tank – removal and refitting

Warning: Refer to the warning note in Section 1 before proceeding.

Removal

1 Before removing the fuel tank, all fuel must be drained from it. Since a drain plug is not provided, it is preferable to carry out the removal operation when the tank is nearly empty.

2 Disconnect the battery negative lead (refer to *Disconnecting the battery* in the Reference Chapter).

3 Remove the rear seat, or rear seat cushion (Chapter 11), for access to the fuel gauge sender unit cover.

4 Using a screwdriver, carefully prise the plastic access cover from the floor to expose the sender unit.

5 If there is any fuel remaining in the fuel tank, it can be removed by disconnecting the fuel delivery hose and connecting an external syphoning pump to the tank outlet union.

6 Disconnect the wiring connector from the sender unit, and tape the connector to the vehicle body, to prevent it disappearing behind the tank.

7 Disconnect the feed and, where applicable, the return hoses.

8 Chock the front wheels then jack up the rear of the vehicle and support on axle stands (see *Jacking and vehicle support*). Remove the right-hand rear wheel.

9 Remove the exhaust system and relevant heat shield(s) with reference to Section 18. Also, where applicable, unbolt and remove the central exhaust mounting.

10 Where applicable, remove the heat shield from below the fuel tank and below the handbrake cables.

11 Note the position of the adjustment nut on the rear of the handbrake lever equaliser rod, then unscrew and remove it and detach the handbrake cables from the supports on the underbody. Unclip the cables and position them to one side away from the fuel tank.

12 Disconnect the overflow pipe.

13 Separate the filler neck from the fuel tank, then unclip the handbrake cables from under the tank **(see illustrations)**.

14 Place a trolley jack with an interposed block of wood beneath the tank, then raise the jack until it is supporting the weight of the tank.

15 Unscrew and remove the mounting bolts **(see illustrations)**, then slowly lower the fuel

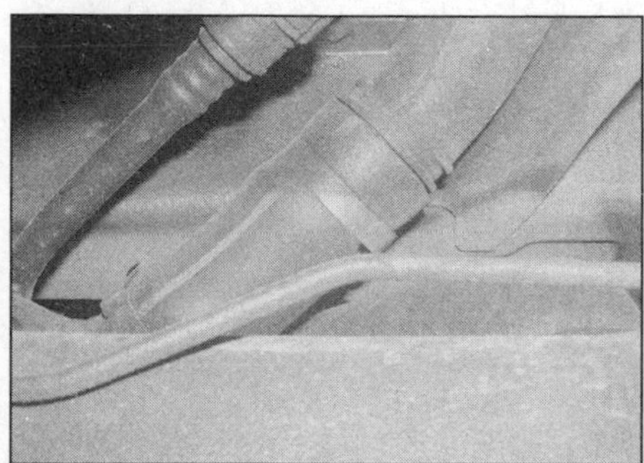

4.13a Filler neck connection to the tank

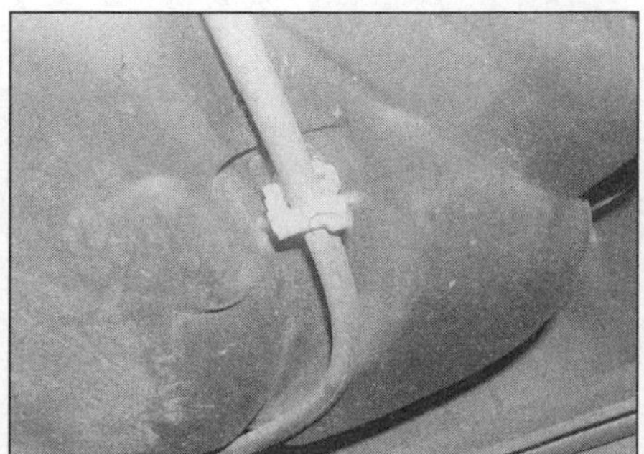

4.13b Handbrake cable clip on the bottom of the fuel tank

4.15a Fuel tank right-hand mounting bolt . . .

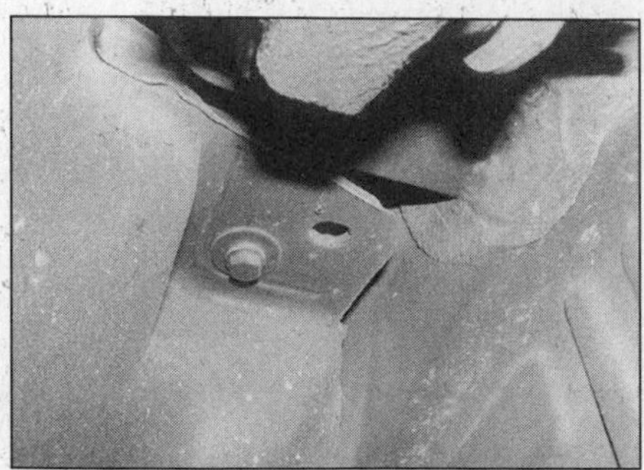

4.15b . . . and left-hand mounting bolt

tank, disconnecting any other relevant vent pipes as they become accessible, and remove the tank from underneath the vehicle. Note that the tank must be slightly tilted to the right, and it may be necessary to bend the brake pipes to provide sufficient clearance. **Do not** bend the pipes excessively.

16 If the tank is contaminated with sediment or water, remove the sender unit (Section 3), and swill the tank out with clean fuel. The tank is injection-moulded from a synthetic material – if seriously damaged, it should be renewed. However, in certain cases, it may be possible to have small leaks or minor damage repaired. Seek the advice of a specialist before attempting to repair the fuel tank.

Refitting

17 Refitting is the reverse of the removal procedure, noting the following points:

a) *When lifting the tank back into position, take care to ensure that the hoses are not trapped between the tank and vehicle body.*

b) *As the tank is located on the underbody, make sure that the positioning holes are correctly aligned with each other. There are two rear holes and one front hole.*

c) *Ensure that all pipes and hoses are correctly routed. Make sure the sealing rings are in position in the quick-release fittings prior to fitting and make sure they are securely clipped in position.*

d) *On completion, refill the tank with a small amount of fuel, and check for signs of leakage prior to taking the vehicle out on the road.*

5.3 Squeeze the priming bulb several times to purge the low-pressure fuel circuit

5 Fuel system – priming and bleeding

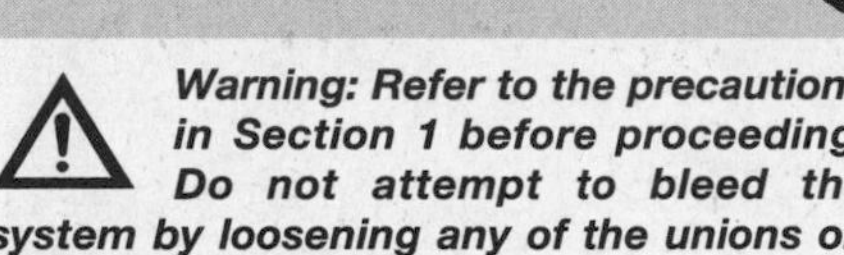

Warning: Refer to the precautions in Section 1 before proceeding. Do not attempt to bleed the system by loosening any of the unions on the high-pressure circuit.

Note: *Priming of the fuel system after filter renewal will be improved if the filter is filled with clean diesel fuel before securing it to the filter head. To avoid spillages of fuel, keep the filter upright during refitting.*

1 After disconnecting part of the fuel supply system or running out of fuel, it is necessary to prime the system low-pressure circuit before restarting the engine.

2 All models are fitted with a hand-operated priming bulb located next to the fuel filter, next to the battery, in the left-hand front corner of the engine compartment.

3 Squeeze the priming bulb several times to purge the low-pressure circuit of air **(see illustration)**.

4 Attempt to start the engine normally, however, do not operate the starter motor for more than 5 seconds. If necessary, operate the starter motor in 4 to 5 second bursts followed by pauses of 8 to 10 seconds. As soon as the engine starts, let it run at fast idle speed until a regular idle speed is reached. If difficulty in purging the air from the system is experienced (engine may hunt), disconnect the blue high-pressure return pipe from the fuel filter and plug this hole, then place the end of the pipe in a container and continue to squeeze the priming bulb until the air is removed. Reconnect the return pipe and start the engine.

6 Idle speed – general

1 The engine management ECU uses the following inputs to calculate the recommended idle speed according to the varying load on the engine by peripheral electrical or mechanical components.

a) *Engine coolant temperature.*

b) *Battery voltage.*

c) *The gear selected.*

d) *Electrical consumers (heater fan, climate control system, thermo-plungers, etc).*

2 At normal engine temperature with no electrical consumers switched on and neutral selected, the engine idle speed will be 850 rpm.

3 If the accelerator pedal potentiometer internal tracks are faulty, the ECU will override the idle speed to 1100 rpm, and the injection warning light will be illuminated on the instrument panel. If there is no output from the potentiometer, the idle speed will be 1300 rpm. In each case, if the brake pedal is depressed, the idle speed will revert to its normal level.

4 If there is an injector fault, the idle speed will be set to 1300 rpm and the warning light will be illuminated.

5 With Neutral, 1st or 2nd gear selected, the idle speed will be 850 rpm at an ambient temperature of more than 20°C; below this temperature the idle speed will increase accordingly. In 3rd, 4th or 5th gear, the idle speed will be 900 rpm.

6 Should the idle speed be incorrect, the car should be taken to a Renault dealer who will have the necessary diagnostic equipment to pin-point the faulty component responsible.

7 Accelerator pedal – removal and refitting

Removal

1 Remove the nut which secures the accelerator pedal pivot bush **(see illustration)**.

2 Disconnect the potentiometer link rod.

3 Remove the pedal and bush.

Refitting

4 Refit by reversing the removal operations.

8 Accelerator potentiometer and cable – removal and refitting

Removal

1 Disconnect the battery negative lead (refer to *Disconnecting the battery* in the Reference Chapter).

2 Disconnect the wiring from the potentiometer. Note on some LHD models, the potentiometer is located on the bulkhead, and it may be necessary to release it from the power steering fluid reservoir, and also move the engine management ECU to one side.

3 Disconnect the potentiometer-to-pedal link rod (or cable on some LHD models).

4 Unscrew the three mounting bolts and withdraw the potentiometer from inside the car.

Refitting

5 Refitting is a reversal of removal.

7.1 Remove the nut (arrowed) which secures the accelerator pedal pivot bush

10.13 Disconnect the wiring from the rear of the high-pressure pump

10.14a Disconnecting the wiring from the injectors . . .

9 Engine management ECU – removal and refitting

Note: *The engine management ECU is electronically-coded for the vehicle to which it is fitted, therefore new units are supplied without a code. If the ECU is being removed to enable a new unit to be fitted, the new unit must be programmed with the information from the old ECU by a Renault dealer. The information includes configuration for items such as the injectors, immobiliser, power-assisted steering pump and climate control system.*

Removal

1 The ECU is located in the left-hand rear corner of the engine compartment, behind the battery. First disconnect the battery negative lead (refer to *Disconnecting the battery* in the Reference Section).

2 Unclip the metal cover from the top of the ECU.

3 Unscrew the ECU mounting nuts on the battery tray.

4 Disconnect the wiring connector by hinging it upwards, then tilt the ECU slightly rearwards to release the studs, and lift it to release the location tab.

Refitting

5 Refitting is a reverse of the removal procedure ensuring that the wiring connector is securely reconnected. If a new ECU has been fitted, it must be programmed by a Renault dealer.

10 High-pressure pump – removal and refitting

Warning: Refer to the warning note in Section 1 before proceeding.

Caution: Before starting work, allow the engine to cool for 5 to 10 minutes, to ensure the fuel pressure and temperature are at a minimum.

Note: *The high pressure pump is removed after first removing the timing belt as described in Chapter 2C. However, if the special Renault locking tools Mot. 1525/1525-02/1606 are available, it is possible to remove the pump leaving the sprocket and timing belt supported independently. Using the latter method will prove quicker, as it will not be necessary to renew the timing belt. Note that all high-pressure pipes removed must be renewed as a matter of course.*

Removal

1 Disconnect the battery negative lead (refer to *Disconnecting the battery* in the Reference Chapter).

2 Jack up the right-hand front of the car and support on axle stands. Remove the front right wheel, engine undertray and wheel arch liner.

3 Remove the auxiliary drivebelt with reference to Chapter 1B.

4 Support the right-hand end of the engine with a support bar across the engine compartment, with a hoist, or alternatively with a jack and block of wood beneath the sump. If a hoist is being used, remove the bonnet with reference to Chapter 11.

5 Unbolt the right-hand engine mounting from the engine and body, then unclip the upper timing cover.

6 Unbolt the high-pressure pump position sensor from the lower timing cover.

7 Release the fuel pipes from the support clips, then remove the lower timing cover by releasing the clips and pulling out the plastic bolt. If necessary, slightly raise the engine to facilitate removal of the timing cover.

8 Unbolt and remove the engine mounting support bracket.

9 Unscrew the bolt securing the rear engine torque link to the bottom of the transmission. Raise the engine slightly to provide improved access to the high-pressure pump sprocket, however, take care not to pull out the right-hand driveshaft.

10 If the special Renault locking tools are not available, remove the timing belt as described in Chapter 2C. Also remove the high-pressure pump sprocket but note it is **strictly forbidden** to remove the high-pressure pump sprocket where it is marked with the number 070 575 (see Chapter 2C). In this case, the timing belt must be removed, and the sprocket removed together with the pump. New pumps with this type of sprocket are supplied together with a new sprocket already fitted.

11 Remove the engine top cover, then disconnect the air inlet duct from the air cleaner.

12 Remove the dipstick guide from the cylinder block, and tape over the opening.

13 Disconnect the wiring from the flow actuator and fuel temperature sensor on the rear of the high-pressure pump **(see illustration).**

14 Disconnect the wiring from the injectors and glow plugs **(see illustrations).**

15 Clean the area around the fuel supply and return pipes, then disconnect them from the high-pressure pump. The pipes are fitted with quick-release clips which must be depressed.

10.14b . . . and glow plugs

10.15a Clean the area around the fuel supply and return pipes before disconnecting them

Fit the protector plugs to the open apertures and lines **(see illustrations)**.

16 Disconnect the fuel injector leak-off pipe.

17 Disconnect the wiring from the oil level sensor on the cylinder block.

18 Unclip the wiring loom from the fuel rail.

19 Loosen the fuel rail mounting nuts a few turns

20 Disconnect the high-pressure pipe connecting the pump to the fuel rail. To do this, unscrew the nut on the pump followed by the nut on the fuel rail, then move the nut along the tube while keeping the oval-shaped handle in contact with the taper. **Note:** *The manufacturers stipulate that the return pipe is renewed whenever it is removed.* Tape over or plug the pump apertures.

21 Set the engine to TDC as described in Chapter 2C. **Note:** *If a sprocket holder tool is being used, this is unnecessary.*

22 Where the Renault locking tool is available, fit the tool to secure the pump sprocket, then unscrew and remove the centre nut while holding the sprocket with a suitable tool. Fit the outer part of the tool which acts as a puller, and hand-tighten the centre bolt onto the pump shaft.

23 Unscrew the pump mounting bolts. Where not using the locking tool, simply withdraw the high-pressure pump from the engine. Where using the tool, tighten the centre bolt until the pump shaft is forced out of the (stationary) sprocket, then withdraw the pump.

Refitting

24 Refitting is a reversal of removal, but take care not to place the new high-pressure pipe

10.15b The fuel supply and return pipes on the high-pressure pump

under any stress. Before fitting the new pipe, lubricate the threads of the union nuts with oil from the sachet provided, and finger-tighten the nuts before tightening them to the specified torque. Tighten all nuts and bolts to the specified torque and angle as applicable. When tightening the pipe union nuts onto the injectors, counter-hold the injectors with a further spanner. When angle-tightening the high-pressure pump sprocket nut, use an angle protractor. Prime and bleed the fuel system as described in Section 5.

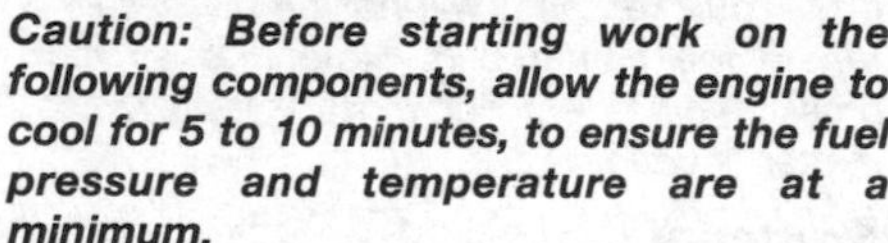

11 High-pressure pump components – removal and refitting

Caution: Before starting work on the following components, allow the engine to cool for 5 to 10 minutes, to ensure the fuel pressure and temperature are at a minimum.

1 Disconnect the battery negative lead (refer to *Disconnecting the battery* in the Reference Chapter).

Flow actuator

2 Remove the engine top cover.

3 Disconnect the wiring from the flow actuator (inner) and fuel temperature sensor (outer) located on the rear of the high-pressure pump.

4 Wrap some cloth rag over the fuel return pipe, then disconnect it by depressing the quick-release fitting.

5 Wrap some cloth rag over the union nuts, then unscrew them and remove the high-pressure pipe for No 4 injector. **Note:** *The manufacturers stipulate that the pipe is renewed whenever removed.* Plug or tape over the fuel apertures.

6 Disconnect the wiring from the glow plugs and injectors for cylinders 3 and 4.

7 Unscrew the retaining bracket bolts and withdraw the flow actuator from the high-pressure pump. **Do not** pull on the wiring connector, but ease it out by hand only.

8 Only remove the new unit from its packaging just before fitting it, and do not lubricate it with used fuel or grease.

9 Carefully locate the actuator on the pump, making sure that the seal is not damaged. Insert the mounting bolts and tighten to the specified torque.

10 Reconnect all wiring, then fit the new high-pressure pipe and tighten the union nuts to the specified torque.

11 Refit the fuel return pipe and engine top cover.

Fuel temperature sensor

12 Remove the engine top cover.

13 Disconnect the wiring from the fuel temperature sensor located on the rear of the high-pressure pump. The sensor is nearest the outer edge of the pump.

14 Wrap some cloth rag over the sensor, then unscrew and remove it and recover the O-ring seal.

15 Lubricate the new O-ring seal with the lubricant supplied with the new sensor, then locate it on the sensor.

16 Fit the sensor and seal to the pump and tighten to the specified torque.

17 Reconnect the wiring and refit the engine top cover.

Venturi

18 Remove the engine top cover.

19 Wrap some cloth rag over the fuel return pipe, then disconnect it by depressing the quick-release fitting.

20 Disconnect the injector leak-off pipe from the high-pressure pump.

21 Unscrew the bolts and remove the venturi from the pump. Recover the O-ring seal.

22 Lubricate the new O-ring seal with the lubricant supplied with the new venturi, then fit the unit to the pump and tighten to the specified torque.

23 Reconnect the leak-off pipe and return pipe.

24 Refit the engine top cover.

12 Fuel injectors – testing, removal and refitting

Warning: Exercise extreme caution when working on the high-pressure fuel system. Do not attempt to test the fuel injectors or disconnect the high-pressure lines with

10.15c Fuel supply pipe on the high-pressure pump

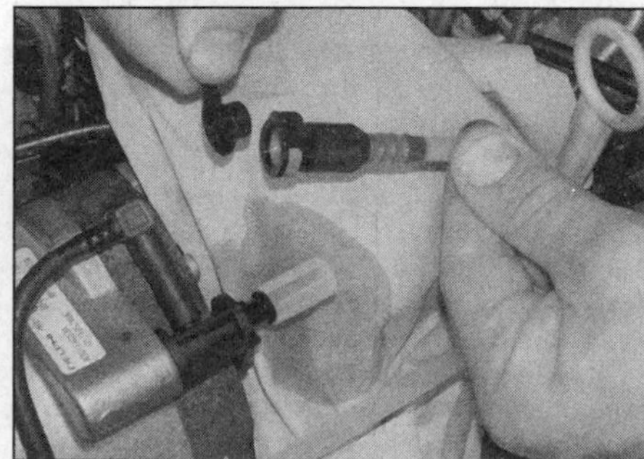

10.15d Fit the plugs to the open apertures and fuel lines

12.3 Thoroughly clean the area around the injectors

12.4 Releasing the wiring loom conduit from the fuel rail

12.5 Removing the oil level dipstick guide

the engine running. Never expose the hands or any part of the body to injector spray, as the high working pressure can cause the fuel to penetrate the skin, with possibly fatal results. You are strongly advised to have any work which involves testing the injectors under pressure carried out by a dealer or fuel injection specialist. Refer to the precautions given in Section 1 of this Chapter before proceeding. After switching off the engine, allow the engine to cool for 5 to 10 minutes to allow the fuel pressure to drop before disconnecting any of the high-pressure fuel pipes.

Note: *Each new injector is supplied with a unique 16-digit code which specifies its flow characteristics. This code must be programmed into the engine management ECU with a special diagnostic tool, therefore this work should be entrusted to a Renault dealer.*

Testing

1 It is not possible to test the fuel injectors without specialist equipment, therefore, if they are thought to be faulty, consult a Renault dealer or diesel specialist.

Removal

Note: *Take care not to allow dirt into the injectors or fuel pipes during this procedure; clean around the area before commencing work. Note that all high-pressure pipes removed must be renewed as a matter of course. The injector flame shield washers must also be renewed.*

2 Disconnect the battery negative lead (refer to *Disconnecting the battery* in the Reference Chapter).

3 Remove the engine top cover, then thoroughly clean the area around the injectors **(see illustration)**.

4 Unclip the wiring loom conduit from the high-pressure fuel rail **(see illustration)**.

5 Remove the engine oil level dipstick guide and tape over the hole **(see illustration)**.

6 Loosen the fuel rail mounting nuts a few turns, then unscrew the union nut securing the fuel return pipe to the high-pressure pump.

7 Disconnect the fuel injector wiring **(see illustration)**.

8 Using a screwdriver, release the clips from the two pairs of injector pipes **(see illustrations)**.

9 While holding the injector central unions with one spanner, unscrew the high-pressure pipe union nuts with a further spanner. Take care not to damage the leak-off stubs on the injectors, and wrap them in cloth rag before loosening them. Similarly, unscrew the union nuts from the fuel rail, then remove the pipes. Move the nuts and olives along the pipes when releasing the pipes from the rail and injectors **(see illustration)**.

10 Disconnect the fuel leak-off pipes from the injectors. Tape over or plug all fuel apertures to prevent entry of dust and dirt **(see illustrations)**.

11 Using a Torx key, unscrew the bolt securing each injector clamp plate to the cylinder head. Lift off the clamp plates and remove the injectors then recover the flame shield washers between the injectors and the cylinder head **(see illustrations)**. Take care not to drop the injectors or allow the needles at their tips to become damaged. The injectors are precision-made to fine limits and must not be handled roughly. In particular, do not mount them in a bench vice.

12.7 Disconnecting the fuel injector wiring

12.8a Use a screwdriver . . .

12.8b . . . to prise off the injector pipe clips

12.9a Unscrew the high-pressure pipe union nuts . . .

12.9b . . . and move them away before releasing the pipe from the injector

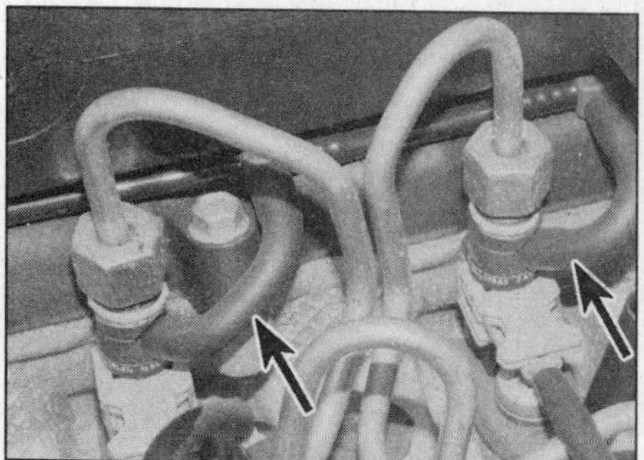

12.10a Fuel leak-off pipes on the injectors

12.10b Fit protective caps to prevent entry of dust

12.11a Unscrew the securing bolt . . .

Refitting

12 Clean the cylinder head and injectors, taking care to prevent foreign matter entering the fuel apertures.

13 Fit new sealing shims between the injectors and the cylinder head. Insert the injectors then fit the clamp plates. Tighten the clamp plate bolts to the specified torque.

14 Refit the leak-off pipes, then fit the new high-pressure fuel pipes together with the retaining clips. Before fitting the new pipes, lubricate the threads of the union nuts with oil from the sachet provided, and finger-tighten the nuts before tightening them to the specified torque. Use pliers to fit the retaining clips onto the fuel pipes **(see illustrations)**.

15 Reconnect the fuel injector wiring.

16 Fit the new fuel return pipe to the high-pressure pump and fuel rail.

17 Refit the engine oil level dipstick guide, the clip on the fuel rail, and the engine top cover.

18 Reconnect the battery negative lead (refer to *Disconnecting the battery* in the Reference Chapter).

19 Start the engine. If difficulty is experienced, bleed the fuel system as described in Section 7.

13 Injector rail (common rail) – removal and refitting

Warning: Refer to the warning note in Section 1 before proceeding. After switching off the engine, allow several minutes for the fuel pressure so subside before disconnecting any of the high-pressure fuel pipes.

Note: *Take care not to allow dirt into the fuel pipes during this procedure; clean around the area before commencing work. Note that all high-pressure pipes removed must be renewed as a matter of course.*

Removal

1 Disconnect the battery negative lead (refer to *Disconnecting the battery* in the Reference Chapter).

2 Remove the engine top cover.

3 Disconnect the following wiring:

a) Flow actuator on the rear of the high-pressure pump.

b) Fuel temperature sensor on the rear of the high-pressure pump.

c) Fuel injectors.

d) Heater (glow) plugs.

4 Disconnect the fuel supply and return pipes from the high-pressure pump.

5 Disconnect the fuel leak-off return pipe from the high-pressure pump.

12.11b . . . and remove the clamp plate . . .

12.11c . . . then remove the injector from the cylinder head . . .

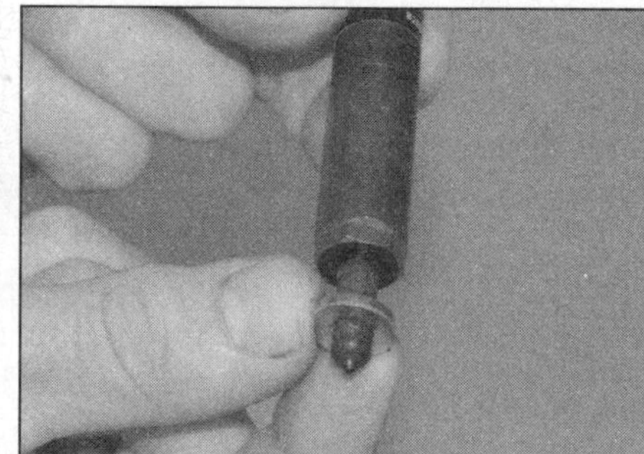

12.11d . . . and recover the flame shield washer

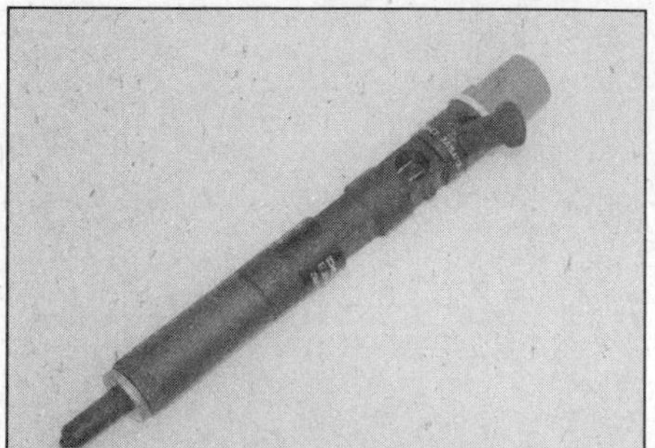

12.11e Fuel injector removed from the cylinder head

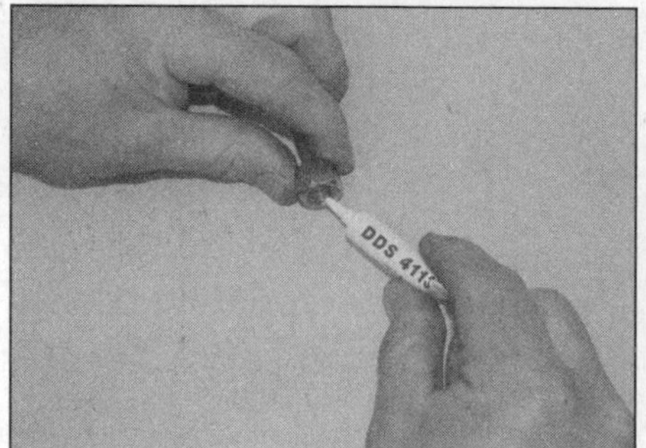

12.14a Lubricate the threads of the union nuts before tightening them

12.14b Fitting the plastic clips to the high-pressure fuel pipes

6 Unclip the wiring loom conduit from the high-pressure fuel rail.
7 Remove the engine oil level dipstick guide and tape over the hole.
8 Disconnect the wiring from the fuel pressure sensor on the fuel rail **(see illustration)**.
9 Release the clips from the two pairs of high-pressure injector pipes.
10 While holding the injector central unions with one spanner, unscrew the high-pressure pipe union nuts with a further spanner. As a precaution against remaining pressure in the pipes, first wrap them loosely in cloth rag. Take care not to damage the leak-off stubs on the injectors. Similarly, unscrew the union nuts from the fuel rail, then remove the pipes. Move the nuts and olives along the pipes when releasing the pipes from the rail and injectors.
11 Tape over or plug all fuel apertures to prevent entry of dust and dirt into the fuel system.
12 Unbolt and remove the fuel rail. Note that the pressure sensor cannot be separated from the fuel rail; if the sensor fails, the complete rail must be renewed.

Refitting

13 Refitting is a reversal of removal, but take care not to place the new high-pressure pipe under any stress. Before fitting the new pipe, lubricate the threads of the union nuts with oil from the sachet provided, and finger-tighten the nuts before tightening them to the specified torque. When tightening the pipe union nuts onto the injectors, counter-hold the injectors with a further spanner.

14 Manifolds – removal and refitting

Removal

1 The inlet manifold is incorporated into the cylinder head and therefore cannot be removed separately. To remove the exhaust manifold, first apply the handbrake, then jack up the front of the vehicle and support it on axle stands (see *Jacking and Vehicle Support*).

13.8 Disconnecting the wiring from the fuel pressure sensor on the fuel rail

2 Disconnect the exhaust downpipe from the exhaust manifold and support it to one side with reference to Section 18.
3 Remove the turbocharger as described in Section 16. If the reason of removing the manifold is simply to renew the gasket, the turbocharger can remain attached to the manifold.
4 Loosen the two clamps, then remove the EGR metal tube between the inlet and exhaust manifolds. The manufacturers recommend that the metal tube and clamps are renewed as a matter of course.
5 Unscrew the mounting bolts and remove the EGR unit from the inlet manifold.
6 Progressively unscrew the mounting nuts and remove the exhaust manifold from the studs on the cylinder head. Recover the metal gasket **(see illustrations)**.

Refitting

7 Clean the surfaces of the cylinder head and exhaust manifold.
8 Locate a new gasket on the cylinder head studs.
9 Refit the exhaust manifold and finger-tighten the retaining nuts. Tighten the nuts to the specified torque, working in a clockwise direction from the centre of the manifold.
10 Refit the EGR unit to the inlet manifold and tighten the mounting nuts to the specified torque.
11 Fit the new metal tube between the inlet and exhaust manifolds and secure with new clamps. Renault technicians use a special tool to tighten the clamps, however, it should be possible to tighten them using pliers and a screwdriver if care it taken.
12 Refit the turbocharger with reference to Section 16.
13 Refit the exhaust downpipe to the manifold with reference to Section 18.
14 Lower the vehicle to the ground.

15 Turbocharger – description

1 A turbocharger increases engine efficiency by raising the pressure in the inlet manifold above atmospheric pressure. Instead of the air simply being sucked into the cylinders, it is forced in. Additional fuel is supplied in proportion to the increased air intake.
2 Energy for the operation of the turbocharger comes from the exhaust gas. The gas flows through a specially-shaped housing (the turbine housing) and in so doing, spins the turbine wheel. The turbine wheel is attached to a shaft, at the end of which is another vaned wheel known as the compressor wheel. The compressor wheel spins in its own housing and compresses the inducted air on the way to the inlet manifold.
3 Between the turbocharger and the inlet manifold on certain engine types, the compressed air passes through an intercooler. This is an air-to-air heat exchanger, mounted behind the front bumper, between the air conditioning condenser and the coolant radiator. The purpose of the intercooler is to remove, from the inducted air, some of the heat gained in being compressed. Because cooler air is denser, removal of this heat further increases engine efficiency.
4 Boost pressure (the pressure in the inlet manifold) is limited by a wastegate, which diverts the exhaust gas away from the turbine wheel in response to a pressure-sensitive actuator. Turbocharging pressure is controlled by a pressure sensor located on the air cleaner outlet **(see illustration)**.
5 The turbo shaft is pressure-lubricated by an oil feed pipe from the main oil gallery. The shaft 'floats' on a cushion of oil. A drain pipe returns the oil to the sump.

14.6a Removing the exhaust manifold together with the turbocharger

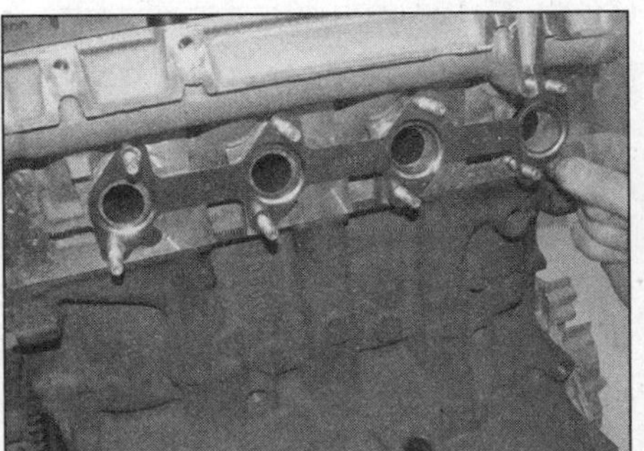

14.6b Removing the exhaust manifold gasket

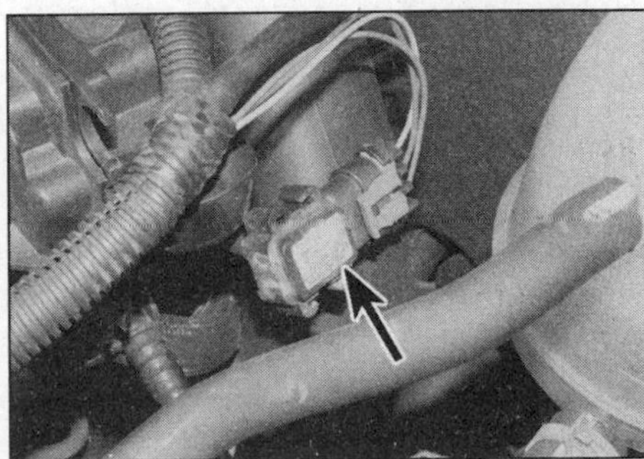

15.4 Turbocharger pressure sensor

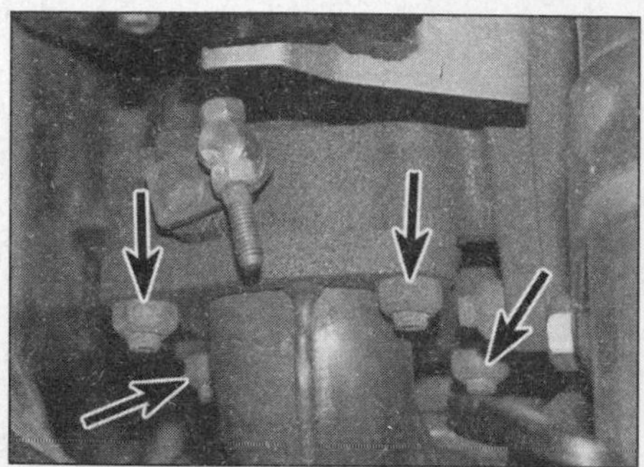

16.9 Nuts securing the catalytic converter to the turbocharger

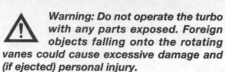

16.10 Unbolt the strut from the side of the catalytic converter

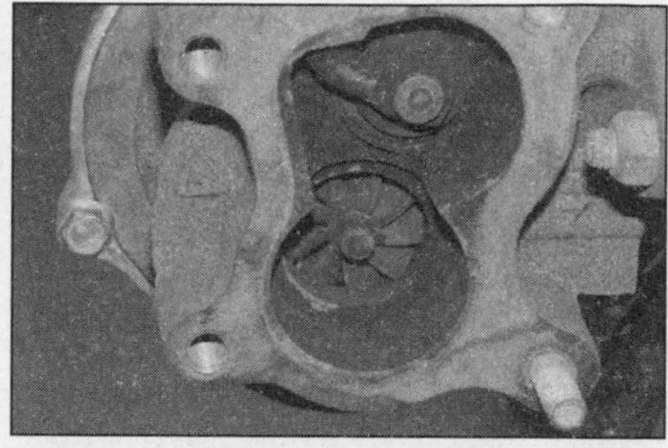

16.11 View of the turbocharger wastegate (upper) and vanes (lower) with the catalytic converter removed

Precautions

6 The turbocharger operates at extremely high speeds and temperatures. Certain precautions must be observed to avoid premature failure of the turbo or injury to the operator.

7 Do not race the engine immediately after start-up, especially if it is cold. Give the oil a few seconds to circulate.

8 Always allow the engine to return to idle speed before switching it off – do not blip the throttle and switch off, as this will leave the turbo spinning without lubrication.

9 Allow the engine to idle for several minutes before switching off after a high-speed run.

10 Observe the recommended intervals for oil and filter changing, and use a reputable oil of the specified quality. Neglect of oil changing, or use of inferior oil, can cause carbon formation on the turbo shaft and subsequent failure.

Warning: Do not operate the turbo with any parts exposed. Foreign objects falling onto the rotating vanes could cause excessive damage and (if ejected) personal injury.

16 Turbocharger – removal and refitting

Note: *New oil supply pipe O-rings and copper washers must be used on refitting.*

Removal

1 Apply the handbrake, then jack up the front of the vehicle, and support securely on axle stands (see *Jacking and vehicle support*). Remove the right-hand front roadwheel.

2 Disconnect the battery negative lead (refer to *Disconnecting the battery* in the Reference Chapter).

3 Remove the engine top cover, then remove the air cleaner unit as described in Section 2.

4 At the rear of the engine, disconnect the wiring from the downstream air temperature sensor and EGR solenoid valve.

5 Disconnect the tube from the turbocharging pressure adjustment valve on the air duct.

6 Loosen the clips and disconnect the air ducts from between the EGR unit and turbocharger.

7 Unbolt and remove the engine lifting eye from the right-hand rear of the cylinder head.

8 Unscrew the bolt and remove the air inlet metal tube.

9 Unscrew the four nuts securing the catalytic converter to the turbocharger **(see illustration)**.

10 Working under the front of the car, unscrew the nuts and disconnect the intermediate pipe flexible flange from the catalytic converter. Also, unbolt the strut from the side of the catalytic converter and block **(see illustration)**.

11 Unbolt the catalytic converter and lower it as far as possible **(see illustration)**.

12 In the engine compartment, unbolt the head shield from the EGR solenoid valve.

13 Unscrew the union and disconnect the oil supply pipe from the turbocharger, collect the copper sealing rings, then unscrew the union nut and disconnect the pipe from the cylinder head **(see illustrations)**.

14 Unscrew the bolts and detach the oil return pipe from the bottom of the turbocharger – if necessary, remove the pipe from the cylinder block **(see illustrations)**.

15 Unscrew the turbocharger upper and lower mounting nuts **(see illustrations)**, then remove the turbocharger together with the oil return pipe from the exhaust manifold. With the assembly on the bench, remove the oil return pipe. Do not attempt to separate the inlet and exhaust sections of the turbocharger.

Refitting

16 Refitting is a reversal of removal, but renew any damaged hose clamps, and use new turbocharger-to-exhaust manifold nuts which should be tightened to the specified torque. Fit new oil supply pipe O-rings and

16.13a Removing the oil supply pipe and copper sealing rings from the turbocharger

16.13b Removing the oil supply pipe from the cylinder head

16.14a Oil return pipe flange bolts on the bottom of the turbocharger

16.14b Removing the oil return pipe

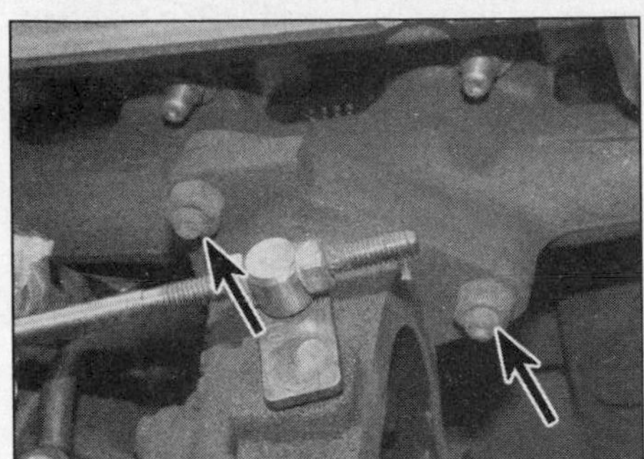

16.15a Turbocharger upper mounting nuts . . .

copper seals, then apply Loctite Frenetanch (or similar sealant) to the union threads before refitting the pipe and tightening the union nuts to the specified torque. Fit a new gasket to the top of the oil return pipe, and new O-ring seals to the grooves in the bottom of the pipe **(see illustrations)**. On completion, the following procedure must be observed before starting the engine in order to establish initial oil pressure in the turbocharger.

a) Disconnect the wiring from the fuel injectors.
b) Crank the engine on the starter motor until the instrument panel oil pressure warning light goes out (this may take several seconds).
c) Reconnect the wiring to the injectors, then start the engine using the normal procedure.
d) Run the engine at idle speed, and check the turbocharger oil unions for leakage.
e) After the engine has been run, check the engine oil level, and top-up if necessary.

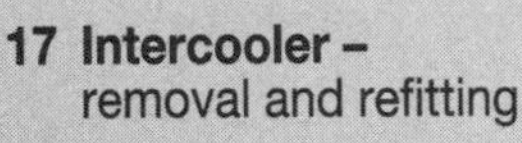

17 Intercooler – removal and refitting

Removal

1 The intercooler is located behind the air conditioning condenser, and in front of the radiator.
2 Remove the front bumper as described in Chapter 11.
3 Remove the plastic trim strip from the air conditioning condenser.
4 Loosen the clips and disconnect the air inlet and outlet ducts from the intercooler. Release the ducts from the diesel fuel filter.
5 Unscrew the bolts securing the right-hand side of the condenser to the intercooler.
6 Unscrew the bolts securing the intercooler to the radiator.
7 Lift the left-hand side of the condenser from the mounting brackets, without disconnecting the coolant pipes, and position the condenser as far forward as possible.
8 Carefully lift and tilt the intercooler from the radiator and withdraw it from between the condenser and radiator.

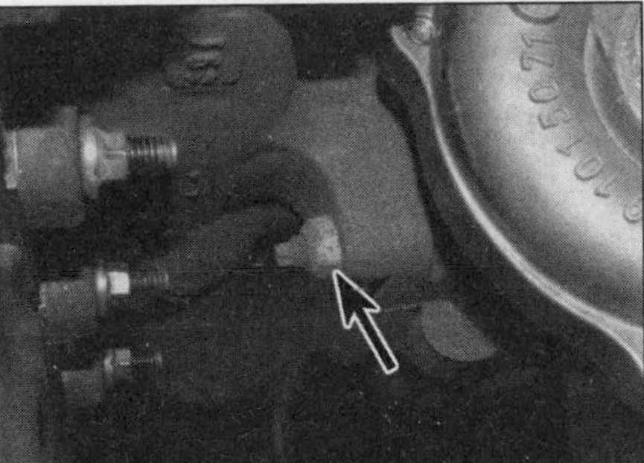

16.15b . . . and lower mounting nut

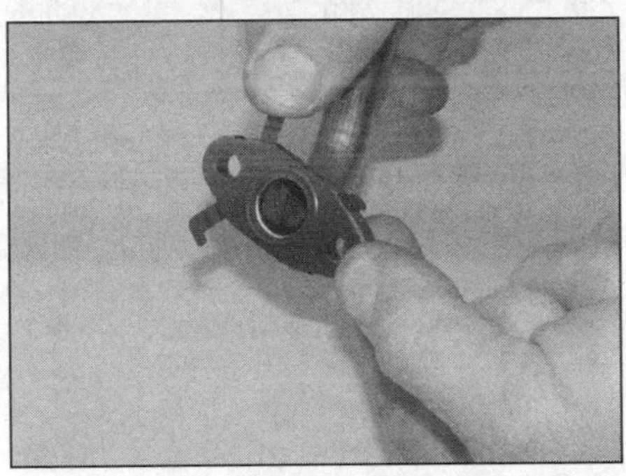

16.16b Fitting a new gasket to the top of the oil return pipe . . .

Refitting

9 Refitting is a reversal of removal, but tighten all nuts and bolts to the specified torque where given.

18 Exhaust system – general information and component renewal

General information

1 On new vehicles the exhaust system consists of just two sections; the catalytic converter (attached to the exhaust manifold), and the remaining system consisting of the intermediate pipe, tailpipe and silencer **(see illustration)**. The catalytic converter is attached to the intermediate pipe by a flexible flange joint.
2 The rear section of the exhaust is located above the rear suspension; the intermediate pipe and tailpipe may be renewed separately by cutting the intermediate pipe with a

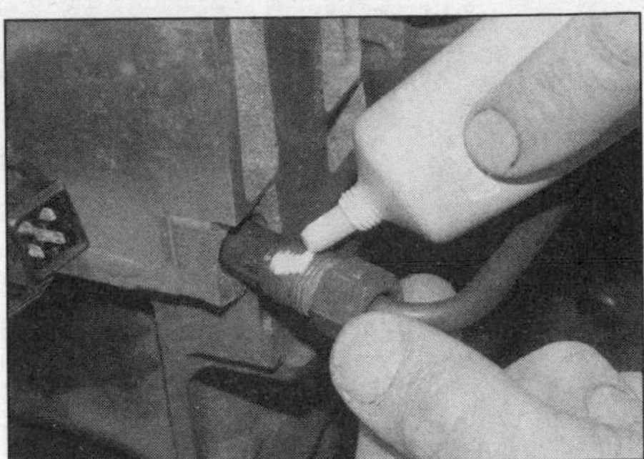

16.16a Applying sealant to the threads of the oil supply pipe union

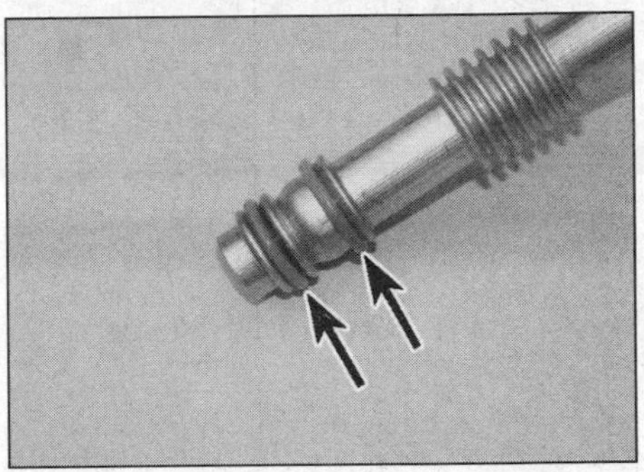

16.16c . . . and fit new O-ring seals to the grooves in the bottom of the pipe

hacksaw. The system is suspended throughout its entire length by rubber mountings.

Removal

3 To remove a part of the system, first jack up the front or rear of the car, and support it on axle stands (see *Jacking and vehicle support*). Alternatively, position the car over an inspection pit, or on car ramps. Where fitted, remove the engine compartment undertray.

Catalytic converter

4 Chock the rear wheels and firmly apply the handbrake, then jack up the front of the vehicle and support it on axle stands (*see Jacking and vehicle support*). Remove the right-hand front roadwheel.
5 Remove the engine undertray and top cover, then remove the air cleaner assembly as described in Section 2.
6 Working from above, unscrew the four nuts securing the catalytic converter to the exhaust manifold.
7 Remove the right-hand front driveshaft as described in Chapter 8.

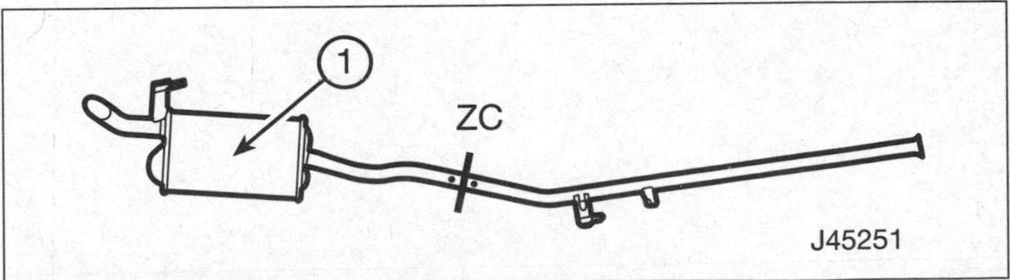

18.1 Factory-supplied exhaust system showing rear silencer (1) and cutting zone (ZC)

18.9 Removing the catalytic converter

8 Working beneath the car, loosen the clamp, then unscrew the two mounting nuts and disconnect the exhaust intermediate pipe flexible flange from the catalytic converter. Lower it as far as possible.

9 Unbolt the side strut from the catalytic converter, then unscrew and remove the rear mounting bolt from the rear strut. Withdraw the catalytic converter downwards from the engine compartment **(see illustration)**.

Intermediate pipe

10 Working beneath the car, loosen the clamp, then unscrew the two mounting nuts and disconnect the exhaust intermediate pipe flexible flange from the catalytic converter.

11 If the original rear section is fitted, it must be cut in half using either a hacksaw or pipe cutter. Locate the cutting area which is situated approximately midway between the rear silencer and intermediate mounting. The cutting point is marked with two circular punch marks on the side of the pipe. The punch marks are 9.0 mm apart and the exhaust section should be cut at the mid-point between the two punch marks. **Note:** *Ensure that the exhaust pipe is cut squarely, or else it will be difficult to obtain a gas-tight seal when the exhaust is refitted.*

12 With the intermediate pipe cut, withdraw the intermediate exhaust section from under the vehicle.

13 If the rear section is in two halves, unscrew the bolt and slide the clamp sleeve on to the rear section then release the rubber mountings and withdraw the intermediate section from under the vehicle.

Rear tailpipe and silencer

14 If the original rear section is fitted, follow the instructions given in paragraph 11.

15 If the rear section is in two halves, unscrew the bolt and slide the clamp sleeve on to the intermediate section then release the rubber mountings and withdraw the tailpipe and silencer from under the vehicle.

Heat shield(s)

16 The heat shields are secured to the underbody by various nuts and bolts. Each shield can be removed separately but note that they overlap making it necessary to loosen another section first. If a shield is being removed to gain access to a component located behind it, it may prove sufficient in some cases to remove the retaining nuts and/or bolts, and simply lower the shield, without disturbing the exhaust system. Otherwise remove the exhaust section as described earlier.

Refitting

17 Each section is refitted by reversing the removal sequence, noting the following points:

a) Ensure that all traces of corrosion have been removed from the joints.

b) Inspect the rubber mountings for signs of damage or deterioration, and renew as necessary.

c) When reconnecting the intermediate pipe to the tailpipe, apply a smear of exhaust system jointing paste (Renault recommend the use of Sodicam) to the sleeve inner surface, to ensure a gas-tight seal. Make sure both inner ends of the cut pipe are positioned squarely against the stop of the clamp sleeve. Position the sleeve bolt vertically on the left-hand side of the pipe and securely tighten the nut until it is heard to click; the clamp bolt has a groove in it to ensure that the nut is correctly tightened (equivalent to a tightening torque of approximately 25 Nm).

d) Prior to tightening the exhaust system fasteners, ensure that all rubber mountings are correctly located, and that there is adequate clearance between the exhaust system and vehicle underbody.

Chapter 4 Part C: Emissions control systems

Contents

Degrees of difficulty

Easy, suitable for novice with little experience 	**Fairly easy,** suitable for beginner with some experience 	**Fairly difficult,** suitable for competent DIY mechanic 	**Difficult,** suitable for experienced DIY mechanic 	**Very difficult,** suitable for expert DIY or professional

Specifications

General

Oxygen (lambda) sensor voltage at 850°C (petrol engines):

D7F and D4F engines:	
Rich mixture	> 625 mV
Lean mixture	0 to 80 mV
K4J and K4M engines:	
Rich mixture	840 ± 70 mV
Lean mixture	20 ± 50 mV
Lambda (oxygen) sensor resistance at ambient temperature (petrol engines):	
D7F and D4F engines	3 to 15 ohms
K4J and K4M engines:	
Upstream sensor	9.0 ohms
Downstream sensor	3.4 ohms

Torque wrench setting	Nm	lbf ft
Oxygen (lambda) sensor	44	32

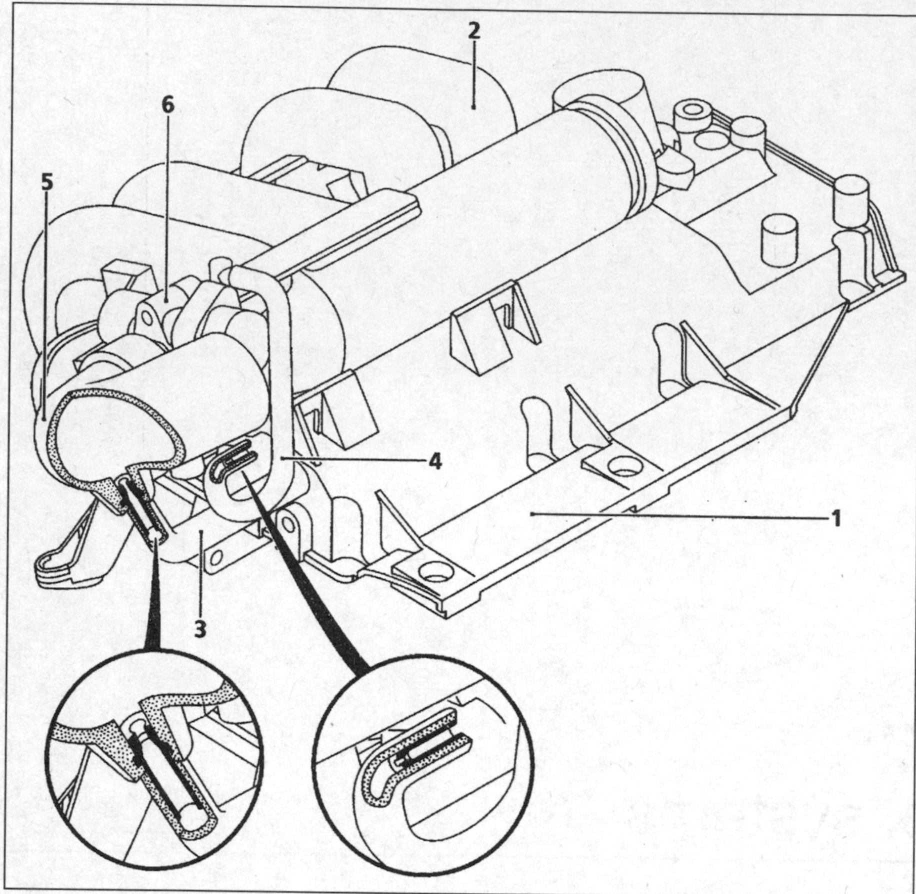

1.4a Crankcase emission control system – D7F petrol engine

1 *Cylinder head cover*
2 *Inlet manifold*
3 *Oil vapour rebreathing pipe connected upstream of the throttle body*
4 *Oil vapour rebreathing pipe connected downstream of the throttle body*
5 *Air pipe*
6 *Throttle body*

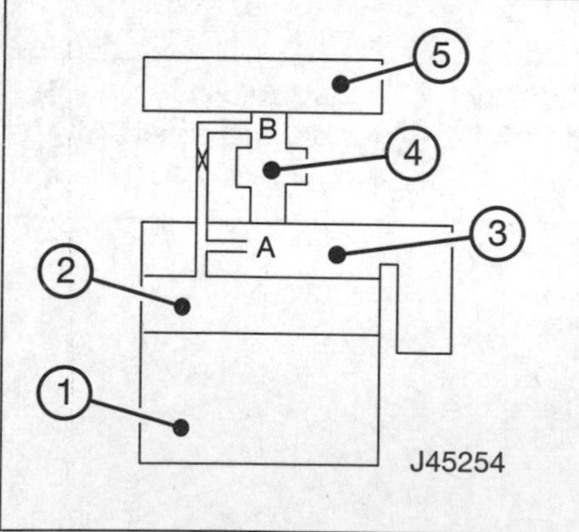

1.4b Crankcase emission control system – D4F petrol engine

1 *Engine*
2 *Cylinder head cover*
3 *Inlet manifold*
4 *Throttle housing*
5 *Air cleaner*
A *Area upstream of the throttle valve used for medium and high load conditions*
B *Area downstream of the throttle valve used for low load conditions via a calibrated orifice*

1 General information and precautions

Petrol models

1 All petrol engines are designed to use unleaded petrol and also have various other features built into the fuel system to help minimise harmful emissions.

2 All models are equipped with a crankcase emissions control system, a catalytic converter and an evaporative emissions control system.

3 The emissions control systems function as follows.

Crankcase emissions control

4 To reduce the emission of unburned hydrocarbons from the crankcase into the atmosphere, the engine is sealed and the blow-by gases and oil vapour are drawn from inside the crankcase, and into the inlet manifold or throttle body to be burned by the engine during normal combustion **(see illustrations)**.

5 Under all conditions the gases are forced out of the crankcase by the (relatively) higher crankcase pressure.

6 The crankcase ventilation hoses and restrictors should be periodically cleaned to ensure correct operation of the system.

Exhaust emissions control

7 To minimise the amount of pollutants which escape into the atmosphere, all models are fitted with a catalytic converter in the exhaust system. The system is of the closed loop type, in which a lambda (oxygen) sensor in the exhaust system provides the fuel injection/ ignition system ECU with constant feedback, enabling the ECU to adjust the mixture to provide the best possible conditions for the converter to operate. On D7F and D4F engines the oxygen sensor is located in the exhaust downpipe, however on K4J and K4M engines there are two sensors, one located on the top of the exhaust manifold and the other located downstream of the catalytic converter **(see illustration)**.

8 The lambda sensor has a heating element built-in that is controlled by the ECU through the sensor relay to bring the sensor's tip to an efficient operating temperature quickly. The sensor's tip is sensitive to oxygen and sends the ECU a varying voltage depending on the amount of oxygen in the exhaust gases; if the inlet air/fuel mixture is too rich, the exhaust gases are low in oxygen so the sensor sends a low voltage signal, the voltage rising as the mixture weakens and the amount of oxygen rises in the exhaust gases. Peak conversion efficiency of all major pollutants occurs if the inlet air/fuel mixture is maintained at the chemically correct ratio for the complete combustion of petrol of 14.7 parts (by weight) of air to 1 part of fuel (the 'stoichiometric' ratio). The sensor output voltage alters in a large step at this point, the ECU using the signal change as a reference point and correcting the inlet air/fuel mixture accordingly by altering the fuel injector pulse width.

Evaporative emissions control

9 To minimise the escape into the atmosphere of unburned hydrocarbons, an evaporative emissions control system is also fitted to all models **(see illustrations)**. The fuel tank filler cap is sealed and a charcoal canister is mounted behind the front right-hand wheel arch liner, behind the front bumper. The canister collects the petrol vapours generated in the tank when the car is parked and stores them until they can be cleared from the canister (under the control of the fuel injection/ignition system ECU) via the purge valve into the inlet manifold to be burned by the engine during normal combustion.

10 To ensure that the engine runs correctly when it is cold and/or idling and to protect the catalytic converter from the effects of an over-rich mixture, the purge control valve is not opened by the ECU until the engine has warmed-up, and the engine is under load; the valve solenoid is then modulated on and off to allow the stored vapour to pass into the inlet manifold.

Diesel models

11 All diesel engine models are designed to meet strict emission requirements and are also equipped with a crankcase emissions control system. In addition to this, all models are fitted with an unregulated catalytic converter to reduce harmful exhaust emissions. To further reduce emissions, an exhaust gas recirculation (EGR) system is also fitted.

12 The emissions control systems function as follows.

Crankcase emissions control

13 To reduce the emission of unburned hydrocarbons from the crankcase into the atmosphere, the engine is sealed and the blow-by gases and oil vapour are drawn from inside the crankcase, through the cylinder head cover, then through a pressure-sensitive recirculation valve into the turbocharger. From the turbocharger, the gases enter the inlet manifold to be burned by the engine during normal combustion **(see illustration overleaf)**.

14 There are no restrictors in the system hoses, since the minimal depression in the inlet manifold remains constant during all engine operating conditions.

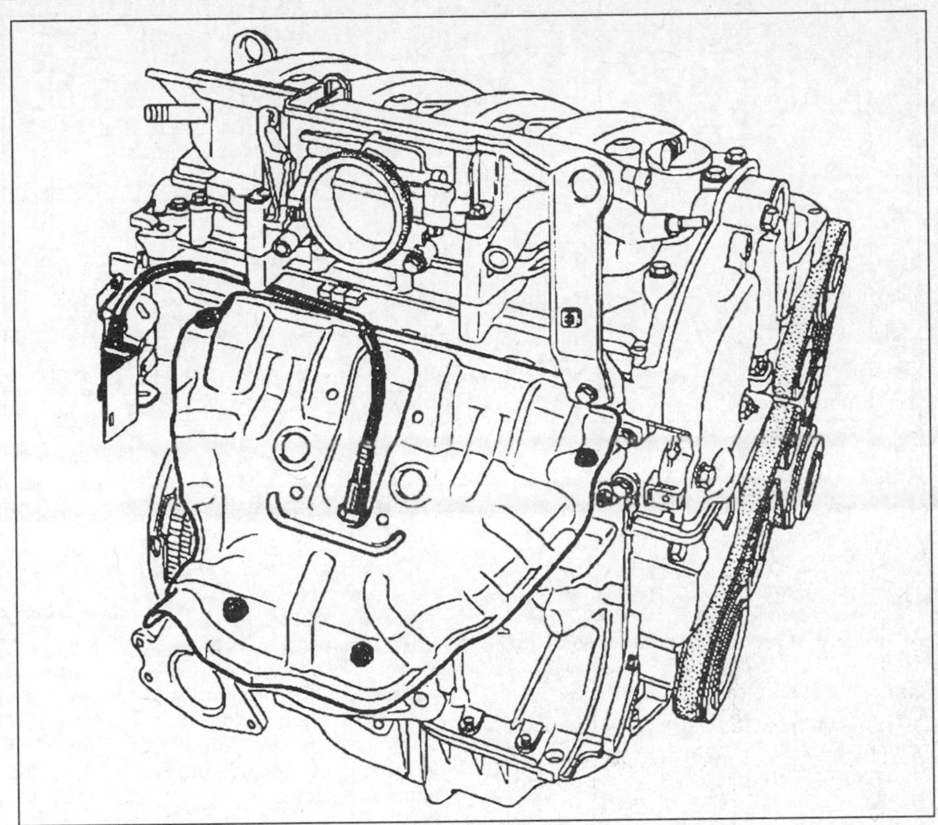

1.7 On the K4J and K4M engines, the upstream oxygen sensor is located on the exhaust manifold

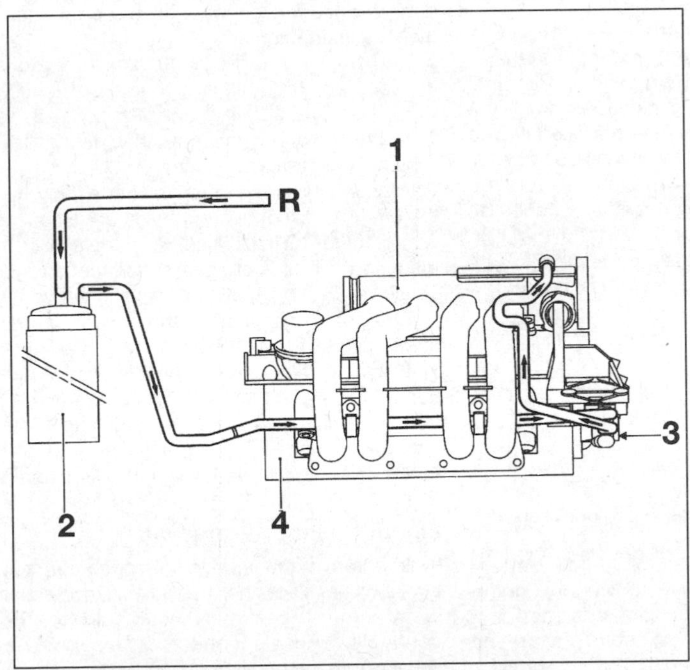

1.9a Evaporative emission control system – D7F petrol engine

1 Inlet manifold
2 Charcoal vapour canister
3 Solenoid valve (purge valve)
4 Cylinder head
R Pipe from fuel tank

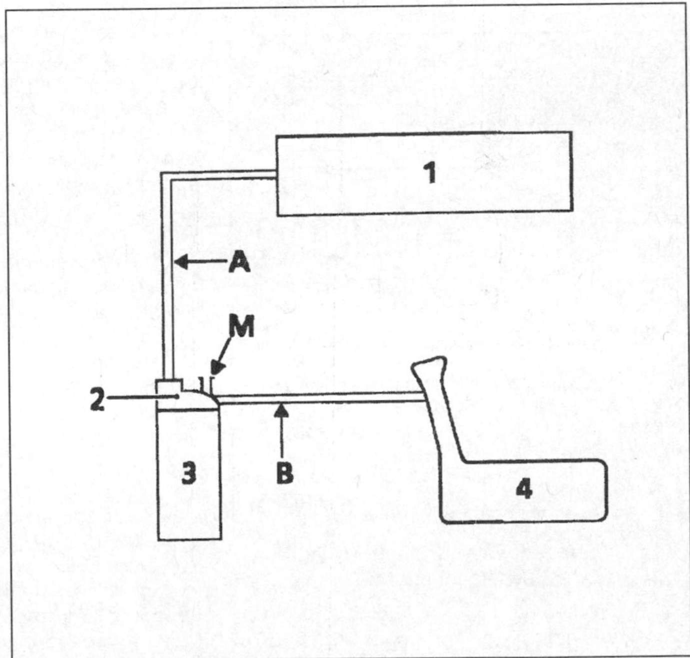

1.9b Evaporative emission control system – D4F and K4M petrol engines

1 Inlet manifold
2 Solenoid valve
3 Charcoal canister
4 Fuel tank
A Canister-to-inlet manifold pipe
B Fuel tank-to-canister pipe
M Breather

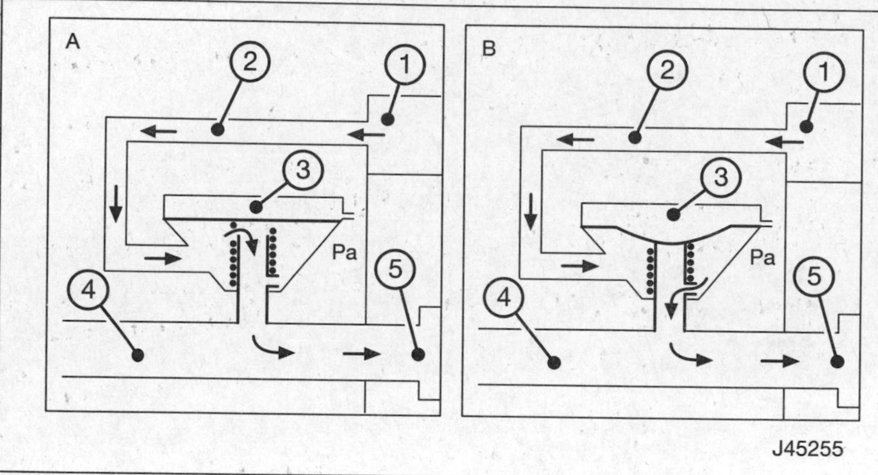

1.13 Crankcase emissions control system – K9K diesel engine

A Low load conditions
B Medium to high load conditions
1 Cylinder head cover
2 Oil vapour rebreathing hose
3 Pressure-sensitive recirculation valve
4 Air inlet duct
5 Turbocharger
Pa Atmospheric pressure

Exhaust emissions control

15 To minimise the amount of pollutants which escape into the atmosphere, an unregulated catalytic converter is fitted in the exhaust system. The catalytic converter consists of a canister containing a fine mesh impregnated with a catalyst material, over which the exhaust gases pass. The catalyst speeds up the oxidation of harmful carbon monoxide, unburnt hydrocarbons and soot, effectively reducing the quantity of harmful products reaching the atmosphere. The catalytic converter operates remotely in the exhaust system, and there is no lambda sensor as fitted to the petrol engines.

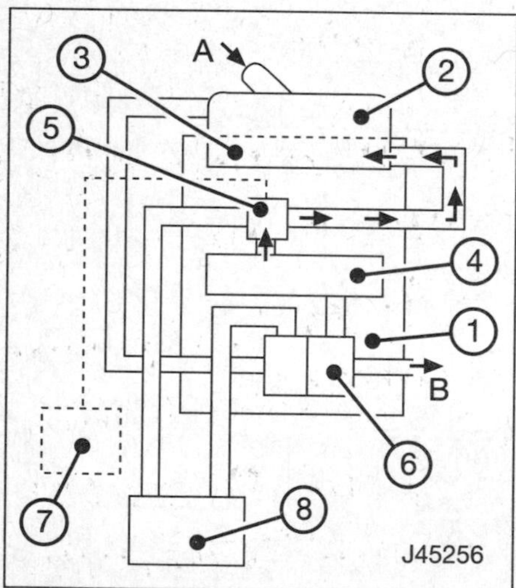

1.16 Exhaust gas recirculation system – K9K diesel engine

1 Engine
2 Air cleaner
3 Inlet manifold
4 Exhaust manifold
5 EGR unit with solenoid valve
6 Turbocharger
7 Engine management ECU
8 Intercooler (80 bhp engine only) – direct link on other engines
A Air inlet
B Outlet to exhaust system

Exhaust gas recirculation system

16 The system is designed to recirculate small quantities of exhaust gas into the inlet tract, and therefore into the combustion process **(see illustration)**, reducing the level of oxides of nitrogen present in the final exhaust gas which is released into the atmosphere. The system is controlled by the engine management ECU which uses several sensors to determine when to switch the system on and off. The system is switched on if:

a) The air temperature is greater than 15°C and the coolant temperature is greater than 70°C.
b) The air temperature is greater than 50°C and the coolant temperature is greater than 40°C.
c) The engine speed is between 850 and 1000 rpm.
d) The injected diesel fuel flow is between 2.0 and 5.0 mg/stroke.
e) The atmospheric pressure is between 980 and 1000 mbars.

The system is switched off if the battery voltage is less than 9 volts, if the engine speed is less than 500 rpm, the mapping (engine speed/load) exceeds a given threshold, or the air conditioning compressor is activated.

17 The volume of exhaust gas recirculated is controlled by an electrically-operated exhaust gas recirculation (EGR) valve on the exhaust manifold, activated by the engine management ECU.

Catalytic converter precautions

18 For long life and satisfactory operation of the catalytic converter, certain precautions must be observed. These are listed in Section 4 of this Chapter.

2 Petrol engine emissions control systems – testing and component renewal

Crankcase emissions control

Testing

1 There is no specific test procedure for the crankcase emissions control system. If problems are suspected, check that the hoses are clean internally, and that the restrictors are not blocked or missing.

Component renewal

2 This is self-evident. Mark the various hoses before disconnecting them if there is any possibility of confusion on reassembly.

Exhaust emissions control

Testing

3 An exhaust gas analyser (CO meter) will be needed. The ignition system must be in good condition, the air cleaner element must be clean, and the engine must be in good mechanical condition.

4 Bring the engine to normal operating temperature, then connect the exhaust gas analyser in accordance with the equipment maker's instructions.

5 Run the engine at 2500 rpm for about 30 seconds, then allow it to idle and check the CO level (Chapter 4A Specifications). If the CO level is within the specified limits, the system is operating correctly.

6 If the CO level is higher than specified, try the effect of disconnecting the lambda sensor wiring. If the CO level rises when the sensor is disconnected, this suggests that the lambda sensor is OK and that the catalytic converter is faulty. If disconnecting the sensor has no effect, this suggests a fault in the sensor.

7 If a digital voltmeter is available, the lambda sensor output voltage can be measured. Voltage should alternate betweenthe specified rich mixture and lean mixture values.

8 Renew the lambda sensor if it is proved faulty.

Lambda sensor – renewal

9 To remove the upstream sensor on the K4M engine, trace the wiring from the sensor located on the exhaust manifold to the connector and disconnect it. Unscrew the sensor from the manifold using a deep socket.

10 On all other engines (and to remove the downstream sensor on the K4M engine), raise the front of the vehicle and support it on axle stands (see *Jacking and vehicle support*). Remove the engine compartment undershield, where fitted, then disconnect the sensor wiring. Unscrew the sensor from the exhaust downpipe or catalytic converter (as applicable), and remove it **(see illustrations)**.

11 Clean the threads of the sensor (if it is to be refitted) and the threads in the exhaust pipe or manifold (as applicable).

12 Note that if the sensor wires are broken, the sensor must be renewed. No attempt should be made to repair them.

13 Apply high temperature anti-seize compound to the sensor threads. Screw the sensor in by hand, then tighten it to the specified torque.

14 Reconnect the sensor wiring, and where applicable refit the undershield and lower the vehicle to the ground.

Catalytic converter – renewal

15 The catalytic converter is renewed as part of the exhaust system. Refer to Part A of this Chapter.

Evaporative emissions control

Testing

16 The operating principle of the system is that the solenoid valve is open only when the engine is warm with the throttle at least at the part-throttle position.

17 Bring the engine to normal operating temperature, then switch it off. Connect a vacuum gauge (range 0 to 1000 mbars) into the hose between the canister and the solenoid valve. Connect a voltmeter to the solenoid valve terminals.

18 Start the engine and allow it to idle. There should be no vacuum shown on the gauge, and no voltage present at the solenoid.

19 If manifold vacuum is indicated although no voltage is present, the solenoid valve may be stuck open. Temporarily disconnect the hoses from the solenoid valve and blow through the outlets to dislodge any particles of carbon.

20 If voltage is present at idle, there is a fault in the wiring or the computer.

21 Depress the accelerator slightly. Voltage should appear momentarily at the solenoid terminals, and manifold vacuum be indicated on the gauge.

22 If vacuum is not indicated even though voltage is present, either there is a leak in the hoses, or the valve is not opening.

23 If no voltage appears, there is a fault in the wiring or the computer.

Canister renewal

24 Apply the handbrake, then jack up the front of the vehicle and support it on axle stands (see *Jacking and vehicle support*). Remove the right-hand front roadwheel.

25 Disconnect the battery negative lead (refer to *Disconnecting the battery* in the Reference Chapter).

26 Working under the right-hand front wing, remove the front section of the wheel arch liner.

27 Undo the three mounting bolts securing the canister to the underbody, then carefully lower it for access to the hoses and wiring.

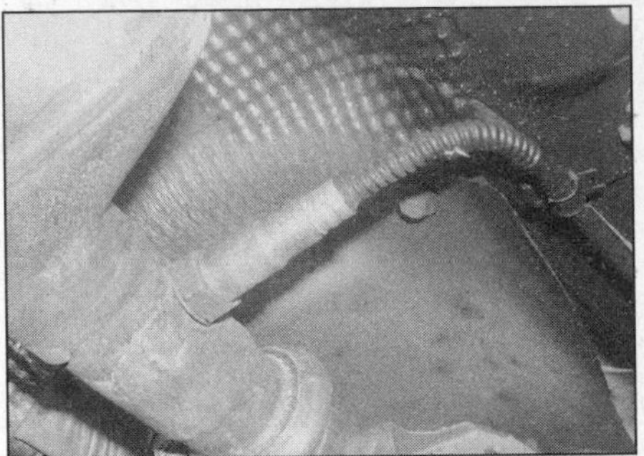

2.10a Downstream lambda sensor located on the catalytic converter – K4J petrol engine

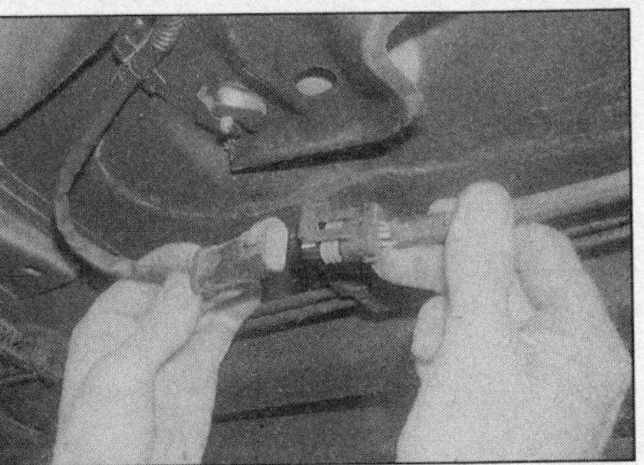

2.10b Disconnecting the lambda sensor wiring – K4J petrol engine

28 Disconnect the wiring plug.

29 Note the location of the hoses, then disconnect the vapour inlet hose leading from the fuel tank, and the rebreathing hose leading to the inlet manifold. Withdraw the canister from the vehicle.

30 If the canister is to be renewed, remove the solenoid valve and transfer it to the new unit.

31 Dispose of the old canister safely, bearing in mind that it may contain liquid fuel and/or fuel vapour.

32 Fit the new canister using a reversal of the removal procedure. Make sure that the hoses are connected correctly.

Solenoid valve

33 The solenoid valve is located on top of the canister, and the rebreathing hose is attached to it **(see illustration)**.

34 Remove the canister as described above.

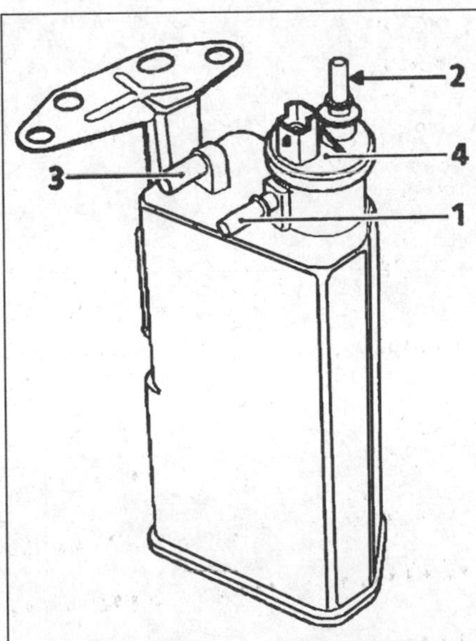

2.33 Connections to the top of the fuel evaporative canister – K4J and K4M petrol engines

1 From fuel tank (quick-release connection)
2 To engine
3 Canister breather
4 Solenoid valve

35 Disconnect the wiring plug and the vacuum hoses from the valve, noting the fitted locations of the hoses.

36 Unscrew the retaining nuts, and withdraw the valve complete with its bracket.

37 Refitting is a reversal of removal, ensuring that the vacuum hoses are securely reconnected.

3 Diesel engine emissions control systems – testing and component renewal

Crankcase emissions control

Testing

1 If the system is thought to be faulty, firstly, check that the hoses are unobstructed. On high mileage vehicles, particularly when regularly used for short journeys, a jellylike deposit may be evident inside the system hoses and oil separators. If excessive deposits are present, the relevant component(s) should be removed and cleaned.

2 Periodically inspect the system components for security and damage, and renew them as necessary.

Component renewal

3 This is self-evident. Mark the various hoses before disconnecting them if there is any possibility of confusion on reassembly.

Exhaust emissions control

Testing

4 The system can only be tested accurately using a suitable exhaust gas analyser (suitable for use with diesel engines).

Catalytic converter – renewal

5 The catalytic converter is renewed as part of the exhaust system. Refer to Part B of this Chapter.

Exhaust gas recirculation

Testing

6 Testing of the EGR system is best left to a Renault dealer who will have the dedicated equipment necessary to carry out the test.

3.10a EGR solenoid valve

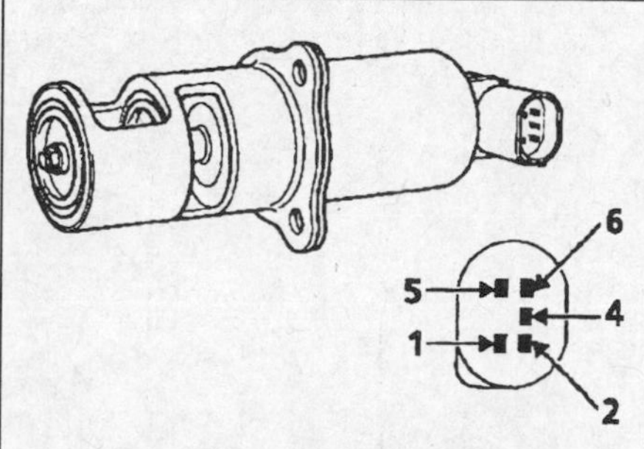

3.10b EGR valve wiring – K9K diesel engine

1 *Solenoid supply*
2 *Throttle position potentiometer supply*
4 *Not used*
5 *Throttle position potentiometer earth*
6 *Throttle position potentiometer output*

3.11 Disconnecting the turbocharging pressure adjustment valve hose from the air duct

EGR valve unit

7 The EGR valve is mounted on the inlet manifold at the rear of the cylinder head, and is connected to the exhaust manifold by a convoluted metal tube, and to the inlet manifold by an air duct.

8 Disconnect the battery negative lead (refer to *Disconnecting the battery* in the Reference Chapter).

9 Remove the engine top cover, then remove the air cleaner unit as described in Chapter 4B.

10 Disconnect the wiring from the EGR solenoid valve and downstream air temperature sensor **(see illustration).**

11 Disconnect the hose from the turbocharging pressure adjustment valve on the air duct **(see illustration).**

12 Loosen the clips and remove the air duct from between the EGR unit and turbocharger **(see illustration).**

13 Unbolt and remove the right-hand rear engine lifting eye.

14 Unscrew the bolt and remove the air inlet metallic tube **(see illustration).**

15 Where fitted, remove the heat shield from over the EGR solenoid valve.

16 Loosen both clamps and remove the EGR convoluted metal tube from the EGR valve and exhaust manifold **(see illustrations).**

17 Unscrew the mounting bolts and remove the EGR valve unit from its location on the inlet manifold. Note that the solenoid valve is not available separately.

18 Refitting is a reversal of removal, but renew the air inlet duct O-rings. Check the condition of the convoluted metal tube retaining clamps and if necessary, renew them – if the special tool is not available, use a pair of pincers to tighten the clamps until the clip is engaged **(see illustration).**

4 Catalytic converter – general information and precautions

The catalytic converter is a reliable and simple device which needs no maintenance in itself, but there are some facts of which an owner should be aware if the converter is to function properly for its full service life.

Petrol models

a) DO NOT use leaded petrol or LRP in a car equipped with a catalytic converter – the lead will coat the precious metals, reducing their converting efficiency and will eventually destroy the converter.

b) Always keep the ignition and fuel systems well maintained in accordance with the manufacturer's schedule.

c) If the engine develops a misfire, do not drive the car at all (or at least as little as possible) until the fault is cured.

d) DO NOT push or tow start the car – this will soak the catalytic converter in unburned fuel, causing it to overheat when the engine does start.

e) DO NOT switch off the ignition at high engine speeds.

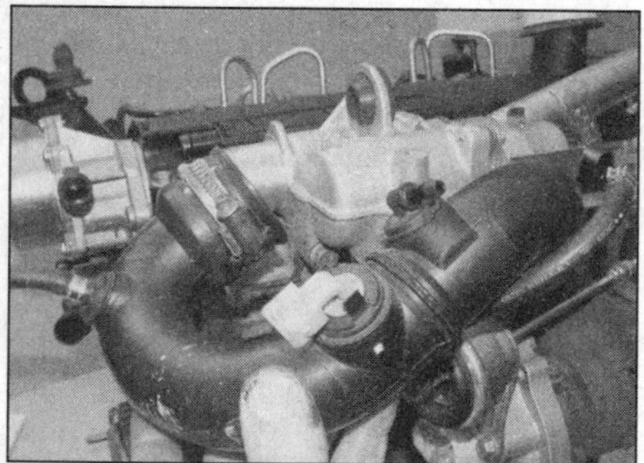

3.12 Removing the air duct from between the EGR unit and turbocharger

3.14 Removing the air inlet metallic tube

3.16a Release the clamps . . .

3.16b . . . and remove the EGR convoluted metal tube

3.18 Using pincers to tighten the metal tube retaining clamps

f) DO NOT use fuel or engine oil additives – these may contain substances harmful to the catalytic converter.
g) DO NOT continue to use the car if the engine burns oil to the extent of leaving a visible trail of blue smoke.
h) Remember that the catalytic converter operates at very high temperatures. DO NOT, therefore, park the car on dry undergrowth, over long grass or piles of dead leaves after a long run.
i) Remember that the catalytic converter is FRAGILE – do not strike it with tools during servicing work or drop it.
j) In some cases a sulphurous smell (like that of rotten eggs) may be noticed from the exhaust. This is common to many catalytic converter equipped cars and once the car has covered a few thousand miles the problem should disappear.
k) The catalytic converter, used on a well-maintained and well-driven car, should last for between 50 000 and 100 000 miles – if the converter is no longer effective it must be renewed.

Diesel models

a) DO NOT use fuel or engine oil additives – these may contain substances harmful to the catalytic converter.
b) DO NOT continue to use the car if the engine burns oil to the extent of leaving a visible trail of blue smoke.
c) Remember that the catalytic converter operates at very high temperatures. DO NOT, therefore, park the car on dry undergrowth, over long grass or piles of dead leaves after a long run.
d) Remember that the catalytic converter is FRAGILE – do not strike it with tools during servicing work or drop it.

Chapter 5 Part A: Starting and charging systems

Contents

Degrees of difficulty

Easy, suitable for novice with little experience 	**Fairly easy,** suitable for beginner with some experience 	**Fairly difficult,** suitable for competent DIY mechanic	**Difficult,** suitable for experienced DIY mechanic 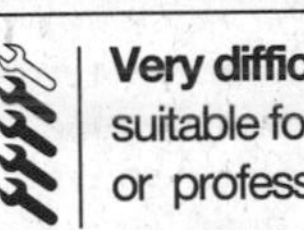	**Very difficult,** suitable for expert DIY or professional

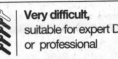

Specifications

Battery

Type	Lead-acid, low-maintenance or 'maintenance-free'
Charge condition:	
Poor	12.5 volts
Normal	12.6 volts
Good	12.7 volts

Alternator

Type	AC Delco, Valeo, Mitsubishi or Bosch
Output	75, 80, 110 or 125 amps
Regulated voltage	13.5 to 14.8 volts

Starter motor

Type	Valeo, Bosch or Mitsubishi

Torque wrench setting

	Nm	lbf ft
Alternator	25	18

1 General information and precautions

General information

The engine electrical system consists mainly of the charging and starting systems. Because of their engine-related functions, these components are covered separately from the body electrical devices such as the lights, instruments, etc (which are covered in Chapter 12). On petrol engine models, refer to Part B for information on the ignition system, and on diesel models, refer to Part C for information on the preheating system.

The electrical system is of the 12 volt negative earth type.

The battery is of the low maintenance or 'maintenance-free' (sealed for life) type, and is charged by the alternator, which is belt-driven from the crankshaft pulley.

The starter motor is of the pre-engaged type, incorporating an integral solenoid. On starting, the solenoid moves the drive pinion into engagement with the flywheel ring gear before the starter motor is energised. Once the engine has started, a one-way clutch prevents the motor armature being driven by the engine until the pinion disengages from the flywheel.

Precautions

Warning: It is necessary to take extra care when working on the electrical system, to avoid damage to semi-conductor devices (diodes and transistors), and to avoid the risk of personal injury. In addition to the precautions given in 'Safety first!' at the beginning of this manual, observe the following when working on the system:

- ***Always remove rings, watches, etc, before working on the electrical system.*** Even with the battery disconnected, capacitive discharge could occur if a component's live terminal is earthed through a metal object. This could cause a shock or nasty burn.
- ***Do not reverse the battery connections.*** Components such as the alternator, electronic control units, or any other components having semi-conductor circuitry could be irreparably damaged.
- ***Never disconnect the battery terminals, the alternator, any electrical wiring or any test instruments with the engine running.***
- ***Do not allow the engine to turn the alternator when the alternator is not connected.***
- ***Never 'test' for alternator output by 'flashing' the output lead to earth.***
- ***Never use an ohmmeter of the type incorporating a hand-cranked generator for circuit or continuity testing.***
- ***Always ensure that the battery negative lead is disconnected when working on the electrical system.***
- ***If the engine is being started using jump leads and a slave battery, connect the batteries positive-to-positive and negative-to-negative (see 'Jump starting' at the beginning of the manual). This also applies when connecting a battery charger.***

4.2 Disconnecting the battery negative terminal

• Before using electric-arc welding equipment on the car, disconnect the battery, alternator and components such as the electronic control units to protect them from the risk of damage.

• The radio/cassette unit fitted may be equipped with a built-in security code, to deter thieves. If the power source to the unit is cut, the anti-theft system will be activated.

Caution: If the radio/cassette in your vehicle is equipped with an anti-theft system, make sure you have the correct activation code before disconnecting the battery.

2 Electrical fault finding – general information

Refer to Chapter 12.

3 Battery – testing and charging

Testing

Standard and low maintenance battery

1 If the vehicle covers a small annual mileage, it is worthwhile checking the specific gravity of the electrolyte every three months to determine the state of charge of the battery.

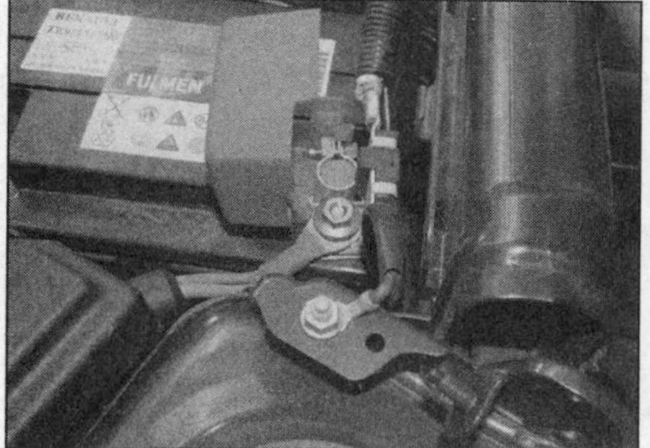

4.3 Open the cover for access to the positive battery terminal

Use a hydrometer to make the check and compare the results with the following table (the temperatures quoted are ambient temperatures). Note that the specific gravity readings assume an electrolyte temperature of 15°C (60°F); for every 10°C (18°F) below 15°C (60°F) subtract 0.007. For every 10°C (18°F) above 15°C (60°F) add 0.007.

	Above 25°C	Below 25°C
Fully-charged	*1.210 to 1.230*	*1.270 to 1.290*
70% charged	*1.170 to 1.190*	*1.230 to 1.250*
Discharged	*1.050 to 1.070*	*1.110 to 1.130*

2 If the battery condition is suspect, first check the specific gravity of electrolyte in each cell. A variation of 0.040 or more between any cells indicates loss of electrolyte or deterioration of the internal plates.

3 If the specific gravity variation is 0.040 or more, the battery should be renewed. If the cell variation is satisfactory but the battery is discharged, it should be charged as described later in this Section.

Maintenance-free battery

4 In cases where a 'sealed for life' maintenance-free battery is fitted, topping-up and testing of the electrolyte in each cell is not possible. The condition of the battery can therefore only be tested using a battery condition indicator or a voltmeter.

5 Certain models may be fitted with a Delco type maintenance-free battery, with a built-in charge condition indicator. The indicator is located in the top of the battery casing, and indicates the condition of the battery from its colour. If the indicator shows green, then the battery is in a good state of charge. If the indicator turns darker, eventually to black, then the battery requires charging, as described later in this Section. If the indicator shows clear/yellow, then the electrolyte level in the battery is too low to allow further use, and the battery should be renewed. **Do not** attempt to charge, load or jump start a battery when the indicator shows clear/yellow.

All batteries

6 If testing the battery using a voltmeter, connect it to the terminals and compare the result with that given in the Specifications. The test is only accurate if the battery has not been subjected to any kind of charge for the previous six hours. If this is not the case, switch on the headlights for 30 seconds, then wait four to five minutes before testing the battery after switching off the headlights. All other electrical circuits must be switched off, so check that the doors and tailgate are fully shut when making the test.

7 If the voltage reading is less than 12.2 volts, then the battery is discharged, whilst a reading of 12.2 to 12.4 volts indicates a partially-discharged condition.

8 If the battery is to be charged, remove it from the vehicle (Section 4) and charge it as described later in this Section.

Charging

Note: *The following is intended as a guide only. Always follow the maker's recommendations (often printed on a label attached to the battery) before charging a battery.*

Standard and low maintenance battery

9 Charge the battery at a rate equivalent to 10% of the battery capacity (eg, for a 45 Ah battery charge at 4.5A), and continue to charge the battery at this rate until no further rise in specific gravity is noted over a four-hour period.

10 Alternatively, a trickle charger charging at the rate of 1.5 amps can safely be used overnight.

11 Specially rapid 'boost' charges which are claimed to restore the power of the battery in 1 to 2 hours are not recommended, as they can cause serious damage to the battery plates through overheating.

12 While charging the battery, note that the temperature of the electrolyte should never exceed 37.8°C (100°F).

Maintenance-free battery

13 This battery type takes considerably longer to fully recharge than the standard type, the time taken being dependent on the extent of discharge, but it can take anything up to three days.

14 A constant voltage type charger is required, to be set, when connected, to 13.9 to 14.9 volts with a charger current below 25 amps. Using this method, the battery should be usable within three hours, giving a voltage reading of 12.5 volts, but this is for a partially-discharged battery and, as mentioned, full charging can take considerably longer.

15 If the battery is to be charged from a fully-discharged state (condition reading less than 12.2 volts), have it recharged by your Renault dealer or local automotive electrician, as the charge rate is higher and constant supervision during charging is necessary.

4 Battery – removal and refitting

Note: *Refer to the precautions given in 'Safety first!' and in Section 1 of this Chapter.*

Removal

1 The battery is located at the front left-hand corner of the engine compartment.

2 Disconnect the lead(s) at the negative (earth) terminal by unscrewing the retaining nut and removing the terminal clamp **(see illustration)**.

3 Disconnect the positive terminal lead(s) in the same way. Where necessary, flip open the cover for access to the terminal **(see illustration)**.

4 Unscrew the clamp bolt, remove the clamp assembly, then lift the battery from its location **(see illustration)**. Keep the battery in an upright position, to avoid spilling electrolyte on the bodywork.

4.4 The battery retaining clamp bolt

Refitting

5 Refitting is a reversal of removal. Smear petroleum jelly on the terminals after reconnecting the leads to reduce corrosion. Always reconnect the positive lead first, and the negative lead last.

5 Charging system – testing

Note: *Refer to the warnings given in 'Safety first!' and in Section 1 of this Chapter before starting work.*

1 If the ignition warning light fails to illuminate when the ignition is switched on, first check the alternator wiring connections for security. If satisfactory, check that the warning light bulb has not blown, and that the bulbholder is secure in its location in the instrument panel (see Chapter 12). If the light still fails to illuminate, check the continuity of the warning light feed wire from the alternator to the bulbholder. If all is satisfactory, the alternator is at fault, and should be renewed or taken to an auto-electrician for testing and repair.

2 If the ignition warning light illuminates when the engine is running, stop the engine and check that the drivebelt is correctly tensioned (see Chapter 1A or 1B) and that the alternator connections are secure. If all is so far satisfactory, have the alternator checked by an auto-electrician for testing and repair.

3 If the alternator output is suspect even though the warning light functions correctly, the regulated voltage may be checked as follows.

4 Connect a voltmeter across the battery terminals and start the engine.

5 Increase the engine speed until the voltmeter reading remains steady; the reading should be between 13.2 and 14.8 volts.

6 Switch on as many electrical accessories (eg, the headlights, heated rear window and heater blower) as possible, and check that the alternator maintains the regulated voltage between 13.2 and 14.8 volts.

7 If the regulated voltage is not as stated, the fault may be due to worn brushes, weak brush springs, a faulty voltage regulator, a faulty diode, a severed phase winding, or worn or damaged slip rings. The alternator should be renewed or taken to an auto-electrician for testing and repair.

6 Alternator – testing

If the alternator is thought to be suspect, it should be removed from the vehicle and taken to an auto-electrician for testing. Most auto-electricians will be able to supply and fit brushes at a reasonable cost. However, check on the cost of repairs before proceeding as it may prove more economical to obtain a new or exchange alternator.

7 Alternator – removal and refitting

Removal

1 Disconnect the battery negative lead (refer to *Disconnecting the battery* in the Reference Chapter).

D7F and D4F engines

2 Apply the handbrake, then jack up the front of the vehicle and support it on axle stands (see *Jacking and vehicle support*).

3 Remove the auxiliary drivebelt with reference to Chapter 1A.

4 On models with air conditioning, remove the radiator grille (Chapter 11), then unbolt and remove the radiator upper mountings.

5 On the D7F engine, remove the electric cooling fan assembly as described in Chapter 3, then lift the radiator from its lower mountings and position to provide access to the alternator.

6 Remove the cover (where fitted) from the alternator main terminal, then unscrew the retaining nut and disconnect the main cable. Also disconnect the wiring plug from the rear of the alternator **(see illustration)**.

7 Unscrew and remove the alternator upper mounting bolt, then support the alternator and unscrew the lower bolt. Withdraw the alternator from the engine **(see illustrations)**.

K4J and K4M engines

8 Apply the handbrake, then jack up the front of the vehicle and support it on axle stands (see *Jacking and vehicle support*). Remove the front right-hand roadwheel

9 Remove the engine undertray, the right-hand front roadwheel, and the wheel arch liner from under the right-hand front wing.

10 Remove the radiator grille with reference to Chapter 11.

11 Loosen only the engine compartment front crossmember centre lower mounting bolts, then unbolt the crossmember from the inner body on both sides **(see illustrations)**. Position the crossmember on the engine, or alternatively unhook the bonnet lock cable and remove the crossmember completely.

12 Remove the protective cover from the fuel rail.

13 Remove the front right-hand headlight unit as described in Chapter 12, Section 9.

14 Remove the auxiliary drivebelt as described in Chapter 1A.

7.6 Disconnecting the main cable from the alternator – D7F engine

7.7a Unscrew the upper alternator mounting/adjustment bolt . . .

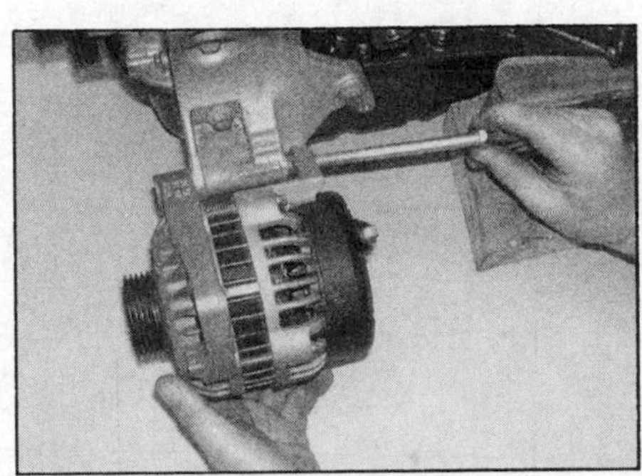

7.7b . . . and the lower through-bolt, then remove the alternator

7.11a Unscrew the bolts from the front crossmember . . .

7.11b ... then loosen the centre bolts and lift out the crossmember

7.15a Disconnecting the main cable ...

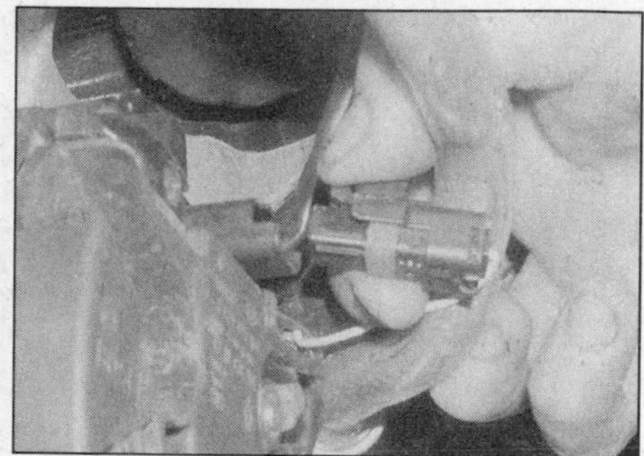
7.15b ... and wiring plug from the rear of the alternator

7.17a The alternator is located on the front right-hand side of the engine – K4M engine

7.17b Removing the alternator from the engine – K4M engine

15 Remove the cover (where fitted) from the alternator main terminal, then unscrew the retaining nut and disconnect the main cable. Also disconnect the wiring plug from the rear of the alternator **(see illustrations)**.

16 Disconnect the fuel supply pipe from the fuel rail, then disconnect the wiring from the fuel injector at the right-hand end of the engine.

17 Withdraw the alternator from the engine. If necessary to provide additional working room, the radiator and (where fitted) the air conditioning condenser may be unbolted and moved to one side with reference to the relevant Chapters of this Manual **(see illustrations)**. There is no need to drain the radiator or evacuate the refrigerant.

K9K engine

18 Apply the handbrake, then jack up the front of the vehicle and support it on axle stands (see *Jacking and vehicle support*). Remove the front right-hand roadwheel.

19 Remove the right-hand front wheel arch liner.

20 Remove the auxiliary drivebelt as described in Chapter 1B. Note that the inner groove of the air conditioning and crankshaft pulleys is not used.

21 Unscrew the alternator mounting bolts, and remove the upper one completely. Note that, due to the close proximity of the inner body panel, the lower bolt cannot be completely removed at this stage, but must be withdrawn so that it is visible in the slotted lower bracket **(see illustration)**.

22 Swivel the top of the alternator towards the front of the car, then ease the bottom of the alternator forwards so that the lower mounting bolt slides out of the slot.

Refitting

23 Refitting is a reversal of removal. Refer to the relevant part of Chapter 1A or 1B for details of fitting (and tensioning, where necessary) the auxiliary drivebelt. Note that the alternator mounting holes are fitted with adjustable spacers which are clamped to the mounting bracket when the bolts are tightened. This makes the task of refitting the alternator difficult, and it is suggested that the spacers are tapped out slightly to provide additional clearance **(see illustration)**.

7.21 The lower mounting bolt must be positioned as shown so that it engages the slot in the lower bracket

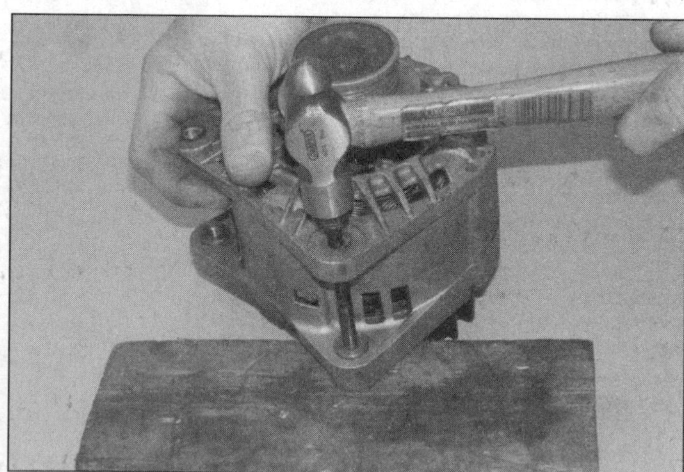
7.23 Using the mounting bolt to reposition the spacers before refitting the alternator – K9K engine

9.2 Starter motor on the D4F engine

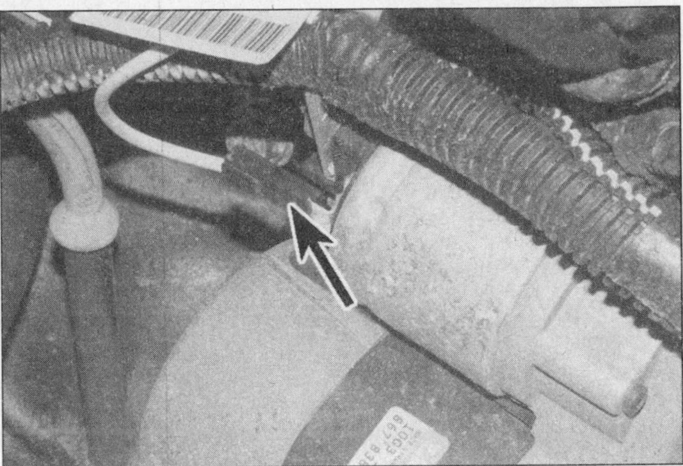
9.3 Trigger wire on the starter motor – D4F engine

8 Starting system – testing

Note: *Refer to the precautions given in 'Safety first!' and in Section 1 of this Chapter before starting work.*

1 If the starter motor fails to operate when the ignition key is turned to the appropriate position, the following may be the possible causes:

- *a) The battery is faulty.*
- *b) The electrical connections between the switch, solenoid, battery and starter motor are somewhere failing to pass the necessary current from the battery through the starter to earth.*
- *c) The solenoid is faulty.*
- *d) The starter motor is mechanically or electrically defective.*

2 To check the battery, switch on the headlights. If they dim after a few seconds, this indicates that the battery is discharged – recharge (see Section 3) or renew the battery. If the headlights glow brightly, operate the ignition switch and observe the lights. If they dim, then this indicates that current is reaching the starter motor, therefore the fault must lie in the starter motor. If the lights continue to glow brightly (and no clicking sound can be heard from the starter motor solenoid), this indicates that there is a fault in the circuit or solenoid – see the following paragraphs. If the starter motor turns slowly when operated, but the battery is in good condition, then this indicates that either the starter motor is faulty, or there is considerable resistance somewhere in the circuit.

3 If a fault in the circuit is suspected, disconnect the battery leads (including the earth connection to the body), the starter/solenoid wiring and the engine/transmission earth strap. Thoroughly clean the connections, and reconnect the leads and wiring, then use a voltmeter or test lamp to check that full battery voltage is available at the battery positive lead connection to the solenoid, and that the earth is sound. Smear petroleum jelly around the battery terminals to prevent corrosion – corroded connections are amongst the most frequent causes of electrical system faults.

4 If the battery and all connections are in good condition, check the circuit by disconnecting the wire from the solenoid blade terminal. Connect a voltmeter or test lamp between the wire end and a good earth (such as the battery negative terminal), and check that the wire is live when the ignition switch is turned to the 'start' position. If it is, then the circuit is sound – if not the circuit wiring can be checked as described in Chapter 12.

5 The solenoid contacts can be checked by connecting a voltmeter or test lamp between the battery positive feed connection on the starter side of the solenoid and earth. When the ignition switch is turned to the 'start' position, there should be a reading or lighted bulb, as applicable. If there is no reading or lighted bulb, the solenoid is faulty and should be renewed.

6 If the circuit and solenoid are proved sound, the fault must lie in the starter motor. In this event, it may be possible to have the starter motor overhauled by a specialist, but check on the cost of spares before proceeding, as it may prove more economical to obtain a new or exchange motor.

9 Starter motor – removal and refitting

Removal

1 Disconnect the battery negative lead (refer to *Disconnecting the battery* in the Reference Chapter).

D7F and D4F engines

2 The starter motor is located on the front of the cylinder block **(see illustration)**. Unscrew the nut and disconnect the main positive battery lead from the large terminal on the starter solenoid.

3 Disconnect the smaller trigger wire from the starter solenoid **(see illustration)**.

4 Support the starter motor, then unscrew and remove the two mounting bolts. The front bolt is on the motor side of the transmission flange, whereas the rear bolt is on the transmission side.

5 Withdraw the starter motor from the transmission.

K4J and K4M engines

6 Apply the handbrake, then jack up the front of the vehicle and support it on axle stands (see *Jacking and vehicle support*). Remove the right-hand front roadwheel. Also remove the engine undertray.

7 Remove the air inlet duct resonator with reference to Chapter 4A.

8 Refer to Chapter 8 and drive out the roll pin securing the right-hand driveshaft to the transmission sun gear (where fitted).

9 Disconnect the steering right-hand track rod end with reference to Chapter 10, then unscrew and remove the upper bolt securing the swivel hub to the bottom of the suspension strut, noting which way round it is fitted. Loosen *only* the lower bolt.

10 Tilt outwards the swivel hub and detach the driveshaft from the sun gear.

11 Remove the battery as described in Section 4.

12 Disconnect the wiring loom from the engine management ECU and disconnect the wiring from the impact sensor located on the left-hand side of the engine compartment. Remove the ECU.

13 Remove the heat shield from over the catalytic converter below the exhaust manifold.

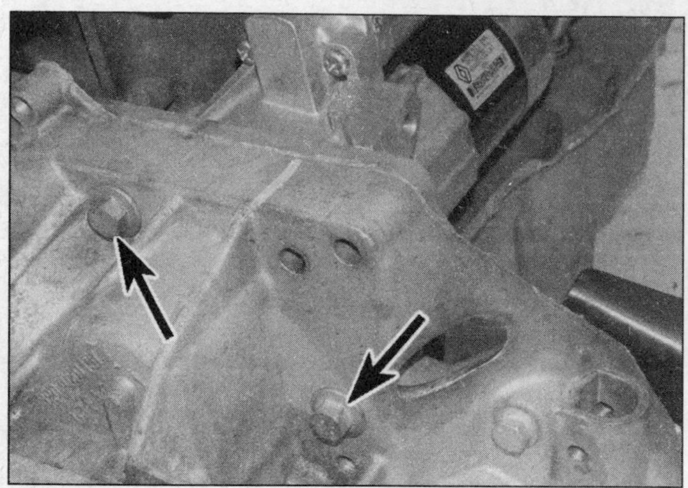

9.25a Unscrew the mounting bolts . . .

9.25b . . . and remove the starter motor from the gearbox

14 Disconnect the wiring from the oil level sensor and move the wiring loom to one side.

15 Unscrew the nut and disconnect the main positive battery lead from the large terminal on the starter solenoid.

16 Disconnect the smaller trigger wire from the starter solenoid.

17 Support the starter motor, then unscrew the mounting bolts and lower it from under the vehicle.

K9K engine

18 Apply the handbrake, then jack up the front of the vehicle and support it on axle stands (see *Jacking and vehicle support*). Remove the right-hand front roadwheel. Also remove the engine undertray.

19 Remove the right-hand driveshaft with reference to Chapter 8.

20 Remove the air cleaner assembly with reference to Chapter 4B.

21 Remove the exhaust catalytic converter with reference to Chapter 4B.

22 Unscrew the two mounting bolts securing the cooling system thermo-plunger unit (electric auxiliary heating) to the transmission, and move the unit to one side.

23 Unscrew the nut and disconnect the main positive battery lead from the large terminal on the starter solenoid.

24 Disconnect the smaller trigger wire from the starter solenoid.

25 Support the starter motor, then unscrew the mounting bolts and lower it from under the vehicle **(see illustrations)**.

Refitting

26 Refitting is a reversal of removal, but where necessary position the starter motor on the location dowel. Finally, tighten the mounting bolts securely.

Chapter 5 Part B:
Ignition system – petrol engines

Contents

Degrees of difficulty

Easy, suitable for novice with little experience 	**Fairly easy,** suitable for beginner with some experience 	**Fairly difficult,** suitable for competent DIY mechanic 	**Difficult,** suitable for experienced DIY mechanic	**Very difficult,** suitable for expert DIY or professional 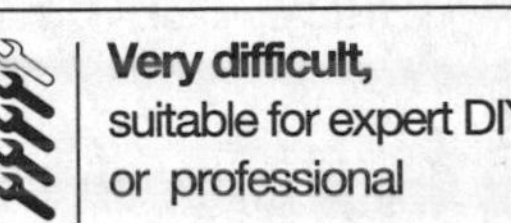

Specifications

General

Ignition system type:	
D7F and D4F engines	Fully-electronic, computer-controlled, with two dual output ignition coils serving cylinders 1 and 4, and 2 and 3
K4J and K4M engines	Fully-electronic, computer-controlled, with four individual ignition coils, one on each spark plug
Firing order	1-3-4-2
Location of No 1 cylinder	Flywheel end

Ignition timing

Ignition timing	Controlled by the ECU

Ignition HT coil resistances measured at ignition connector

D7F engine

Terminals 1 to 2	1.5 ohms
Terminals 1 to 3	1.0 ohms
Terminals 1 to 4	1.0 ohms
Terminals 2 to 3	1.0 ohms
Terminals 2 to 4	1.0 ohms
Terminals 3 to 4	0.6 ohms
HT terminal to HT terminal	8.0 ohms

D4F engine

Note: *The HT leads cannot be removed from the coils, therefore the secondary resistance includes the HT leads.*

Primary resistance:	
A to B	0.40 ± 0.02 ohms
C to D	0.40 ± 0.02 ohms
B to C	0.0 ± 0.02 ohms
Secondary resistance (incl HT leads):	
Leads 1 and 4	9.8 ± 0.5 kohms
Leads 2 and 3	9.6 ± 0.5 kohms

K4J and K4M engines

Nippondenso:	
Primary resistance	0.5 ± 0.02 ohms
Secondary resistance	5.8 to 8.5 kohms
Sagem:	
Primary resistance	0.54 ± 0.02 ohms
Secondary resistance	9.0 to 12.5 kohms

Torque wrench settings

Torque wrench settings	Nm	lbf ft
Ignition coil	15	11
Knock sensor:		
D7F and D4F engines	25	18
K4J, K4M engines	20	15
Spark plugs	See Chapter 1A	

1 Ignition system – general information and precautions

General information

The ignition system is integrated with the fuel injection system to form a combined engine management system under the control of one ECU (see Chapter 4A for further information). All engines are fitted with a distributorless ignition system.

On 1.2 litre engines the ignition system consists simply of two ignition HT coils, the crankshaft speed/position/TDC sensor and a knock sensor. Each coil supplies two cylinders (one coil supplies cylinders 1 and 4 and the other coil supplies cylinders 2 and 3). The ignition coils operate on the 'wasted spark' principle, ie, each spark plug sparks twice for every cycle of the engine, once on the compression stroke and once on the exhaust stroke.

On 1.4 and 1.6 litre engines the ignition system uses one coil for each cylinder, with each coil mounted on the relevant spark plug. The coils are fed in series, two at a time, and the system operates on the 'wasted spark' principle as for SOHC engines.

The TDC sensor (see Chapter 4A, Section 13) is used to determine piston position as well as engine speed.

The power module for the ignition is integrated in the engine management ECU. The ECU uses the inputs from the sensors to calculate the required ignition advance setting and coil charging time – an integral amplifier circuit within the ECU switches the ignition coil primary (LT) circuit.

The knock sensor is mounted on the cylinder block to inform the ECU when the engine is 'pinking'. Its sensitivity to a particular frequency of vibration allows it to detect the impulses which are caused by the shock waves set up when the engine starts to 'pink' (pre-ignite). The knock sensor sends an electrical signal to the ECU which retards the ignition advance setting until the 'pinking' ceases – the ignition timing is then gradually returned to the 'normal' setting. This maintains the ignition timing as close to the knock threshold as possible – the most efficient setting for the engine under normal running conditions.

Precautions

The following precautions must be observed, to prevent damage to the ignition system components and to reduce risk of personal injury.

a) *Ensure the ignition is switched off before disconnecting any of the ignition wiring.*
b) *Ensure that the ignition is switched off before connecting or disconnecting any ignition test equipment, such as a timing light.*
c) *Do not earth the coil primary or secondary circuits.*

Warning: Voltages produced by an electronic ignition system are considerably higher than those produced by conventional ignition systems. Extreme care must be taken when working on the system with the ignition switched on. Persons with surgically-implanted cardiac pacemaker devices should keep well clear of the ignition circuits, components and test equipment

2 Ignition system – testing

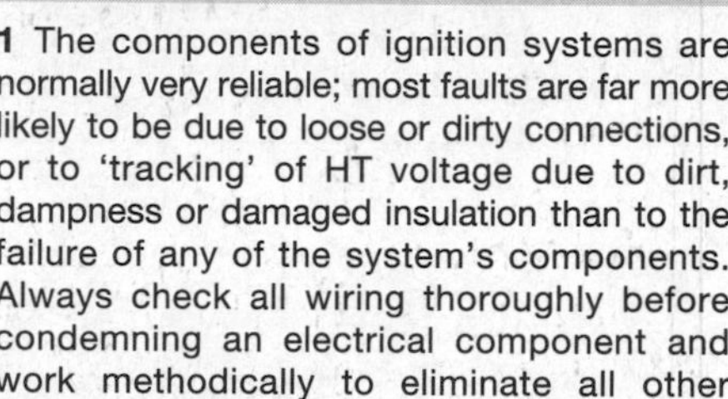

1 The components of ignition systems are normally very reliable; most faults are far more likely to be due to loose or dirty connections, or to 'tracking' of HT voltage due to dirt, dampness or damaged insulation than to the failure of any of the system's components. Always check all wiring thoroughly before condemning an electrical component and work methodically to eliminate all other possibilities before deciding that a particular component is faulty.

2 The old practice of checking for a spark by holding the live end of a spark plug HT lead a short distance away from the engine is not recommended; not only is there a high risk of a powerful electric shock, but the HT coil or ECU may be damaged. However, if necessary each plug can be checked individually by removing it, then reconnecting the HT lead or coil (as applicable) and connecting the body of the spark plug to a suitable earthing point on the engine using a battery jumper lead. It is important to make a good earth connection if using this method. Never try to 'diagnose' misfires by pulling off one HT lead at a time.

Engine will not start

3 If the engine either will not turn over at all, or only turns very slowly, first check the battery and starter motor as described in Chapter 5A.

4 If the engine turns over at normal speed but will not start, the HT circuit of 1.2 litre engines can be checked by connecting a timing light to an HT lead (following the manufacturer's instructions) and turning the engine over on the starter motor. If the light flashes, voltage is reaching the spark plugs, so these should be removed and checked. If the light does not flash, check the spark plug HT leads themselves with reference to Chapter 1A. **Note:** *On 1.4 and 1.6 litre engines, the coils are mounted on each individual spark plug, so it is not possible to use a conventional timing light to check the system.*

5 If there is still no spark, use an ohmmeter to check the resistances of the coils and compare with the information given in the Specifications. The tracks for 1.2 litre engines are as follows:

D7F engine

Track number	Allocation
1	Coil control for cylinders 1 and 4
2	Coil control for cylinders 3 and 2
3	+ after ignition
4	+ anti-interference condenser

D4F engine

Track number	Allocation
1	Coil control for cylinders 3 and 2
2	+ after ignition
3	+ anti-interference condenser
4	Coil control for cylinders 1 and 4

6 If these checks fail to reveal the cause of the problem, the vehicle should be taken to a Renault dealer for testing. A wiring block connector is incorporated in the engine management circuit, into which a special electronic diagnostic tester can be plugged. The tester will locate the fault quickly and simply, alleviating the need to test all the system components individually, which is a time-consuming operation that carries a high risk of damaging the ECU. If necessary, the system wiring and wiring connectors can be checked as described in Chapter 12, ensuring that the ECU wiring connector is first disconnected with the ignition switched off.

Engine misfires

7 An irregular misfire suggests either a loose connection or intermittent fault in the primary circuit, or an HT fault on the circuit between the coil and spark plugs.

8 With the ignition switched off, check carefully through the system ensuring that all connections are clean and securely fastened.

9 Check that the HT coil and the spark plug HT leads (where applicable) are clean and dry.

10 Regular misfiring of one spark plug may be due to a faulty spark plug, faulty injector, a faulty HT lead or loss of compression in the relevant cylinder. Regular misfiring of cylinders 1 and 4 only, or 2 and 3 only suggests a fault on the relevant coil. Regular misfiring of all the cylinders suggests a fuel supply fault, such as a clogged fuel filter or faulty fuel pump.

3 Ignition HT coils – removal, testing and refitting

Removal

1 Disconnect the battery negative lead (refer to *Disconnecting the battery* in Reference).

D7F and D4F engines

2 The ignition HT coils are located on the right-hand end of the valve cover **(see illustrations)**.

3 Note their location, then disconnect the spark

3.2a Ignition HT coils on the D7F engine . . .

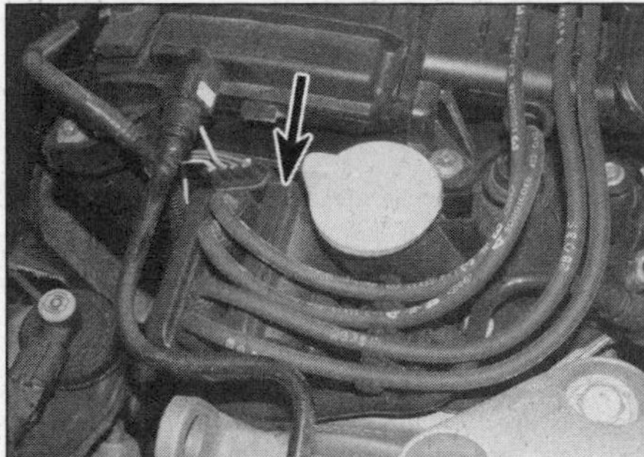
3.2b . . . and D4F engine

3.3a Disconnecting the HT leads from the coils . . .

3.3b . . . and from the spark plugs

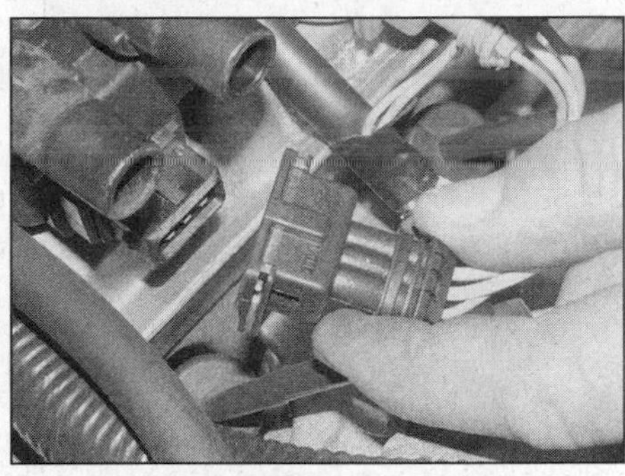
3.4 Disconnecting the wiring multi-plugs from the ignition coils

3.5 Note the location of the suppressor on one of the mounting screws

plug HT leads from the spark plugs and, on the D7F engine, from the coils **(see illustrations)**. If necessary, identify each lead to ensure correct refitting. On the D7F engine, the leads are located in a special retainer, and a tool for disconnecting the leads from the spark plugs is incorporated in the retainer. On the D4F engine, pull on the reinforced extension cables.

4 Disconnect the wiring multi-plug from each coil **(see illustration)**.

5 Undo the mounting screws and remove the coils from the mounting plate – note the location of the suppressor **(see illustration)**. **Note:** *The base of each coil is different to ensure that they only locate in one position.*

K4J and K4M engines

6 The ignition coils are accessible through the holes in the inlet manifold. First, remove the engine top cover, then carefully disconnect the wiring from each coil. Take care not to damage the connectors **(see illustrations)**.

7 Unscrew the mounting screws and withdraw each coil off of its spark plug **(see illustrations)**.

8 Check the condition of the O-rings where the coils enter the valve cover, and if necessary renew them.

Testing

9 On 1.2 litre engines, each coil can be tested as described in the previous Section, using an ohmmeter to check for the resistances given in the Specifications **(see illustrations)**.

10 On 1.4 and 1.6 litre engines, testing of the ignition system should be carried out by a Renault dealer using specialised equipment connected to the engine management diagnostic socket.

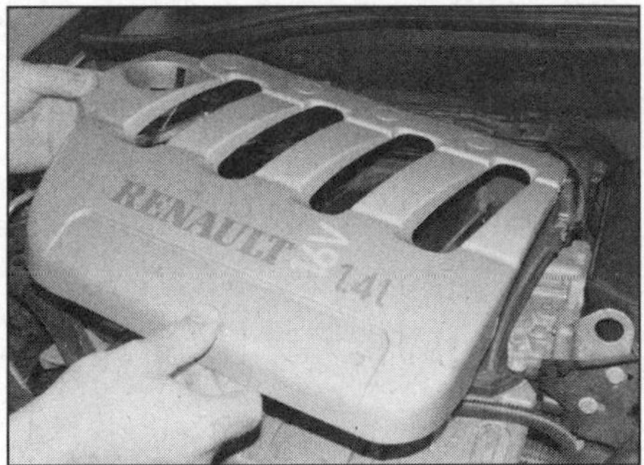

3.6a Remove the engine top cover . . .

3.6b . . . then disconnect the wiring from each ignition coil

3.7a Undo the mounting screw . . .

3.7b . . . and withdraw the coil off of its spark plug

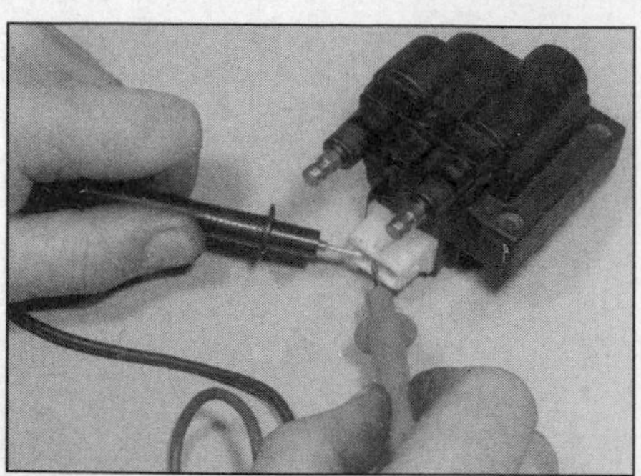

3.9a Testing an ignition coil's low tension circuits

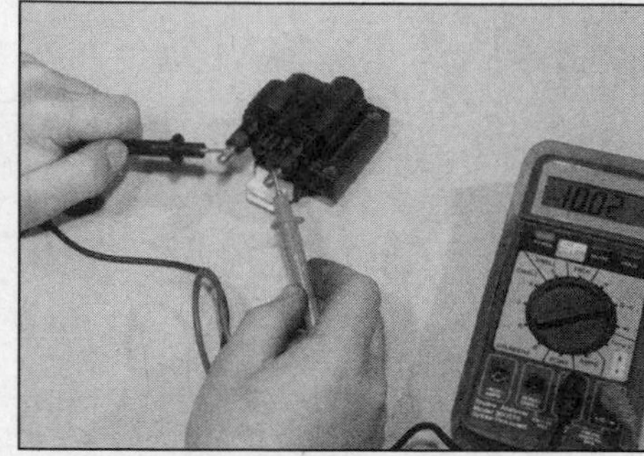

3.9b Testing an ignition coil's HT circuit

4.1 Knock sensor location – K4J engine

Refitting

11 Refitting is a reversal of removal, but tighten the mounting bolts to the specified torque, and ensure that the wiring connectors and spark plug HT leads are correctly and securely refitted.

4 Knock sensor – removal and refitting

Removal

1 On the D7F and D4F engines the knock sensor is located on the front of the cylinder block, below the inlet manifold, next to the engine oil level dipstick tube. On K4J and K4M engines, it is located on the front, right-hand side of the cylinder block **(see illustration)**.

2 To remove the sensor, first disconnect the wiring, then unscrew it from the cylinder block.

Refitting

3 Refitting is a reversal of removal. Ensure that the sensor and its seating on the cylinder block or head are completely clean and tighten the sensor to the specified torque wrench setting. It is essential that these measures are scrupulously observed, as if the sensor is not correctly secured to a clean mating surface it may not be able to detect the impulses caused by pre-ignition. If this were to happen the correction of ignition timing would not take place, with the consequent risk of severe engine damage.

5 Ignition timing – checking and adjustment

With the type of ignition fitted, the ignition timing is constantly being monitored and adjusted by the engine management ECU and nominal checking values cannot be given. Therefore, it is not possible for the home mechanic to check the ignition timing. The only way in which the ignition timing can be checked is using special electronic test equipment, connected to the engine management system diagnostic connector (refer to Chapter 4A). No adjustment of the ignition timing is possible. Should the ignition timing be incorrect, then a fault must be present in the engine management system.

Chapter 5 Part C:
Pre/post-heating system – diesel engines

Contents

Degrees of difficulty

Easy, suitable for novice with little experience 	**Fairly easy,** suitable for beginner with some experience 	**Fairly difficult,** suitable for competent DIY mechanic	**Difficult,** suitable for experienced DIY mechanic 	**Very difficult,** suitable for expert DIY or professional

Specifications

Glow plugs

Type	Bosch 0 250 202 022
Resistance	0.6 ohms

Coolant temperature sensor

Resistance at:	
-10° C	12 500 ± 7000 ohms
25° C	2252 ± 112 ohms
50° C	810 ± 40 ohms
80° C	280 ± 8 ohms
110° C	115 ± 3 ohms
120° C	88 ± 2 ohms

Fuel temperature sensor

Resistance at 25°C	2.2 kohms

Torque wrench setting

	Nm	lbf ft
Glow plugs	15	11

1 Pre/post-heating system – description and testing

Description

1 The preheating/post-heating system consists of glow plugs screwed into the combustion chambers, a control unit mounted next to the battery on the left-hand side of the engine compartment, and a coolant temperature sensor located on the thermostat housing. The control unit is itself activated by the engine management ECU.

2 The glow plugs are supplied with current from the control unit in several phases, namely variable preheating, fixed preheating, starting heating, and variable post-heating.

3 The variable preheating phase occurs when the ignition is switched on, and during this phase the preheating warning light is illuminated on the instrument panel. The period of preheating depends on the temperature of the coolant and battery voltage. The maximum period of 15 seconds occurs if the coolant temperature is low and the battery voltage is less than 9.3 volts. The period varies from 15 seconds to zero seconds according to the temperature of the coolant, and when the temperature reaches 80°C, no preheating occurs. With normal battery voltage the maximum period is 10 seconds.

4 The fixed preheating phase occurs immediately after the variable phase finishes, after the warning light has extinguished, and lasts for up to 5 seconds. Normally, the driver will start the engine at some point during this phase.

5 During the period when the starter motor is in operation, the glow plugs are continuously supplied with current.

6 The variable post-heating phase occurs immediately after the engine has been started, and the period of post-heating depends on the temperature of the coolant. The maximum period of variable post-heating is 60 seconds, at which point the system is switched off. Variable post-heating will cease if the coolant temperature exceeds 80°C.

Testing

7 If the system malfunctions, testing is best carried out by a Renault dealer using dedicated test equipment, however, some preliminary checks may be made as follows.

8 Connect a voltmeter or 12 volt test lamp between the glow plug supply cable and earth (engine or vehicle metal). Make sure that the live connection is kept clear of the engine and bodywork. Have an assistant switch on the ignition and check that voltage is applied to the glow plugs. Note the time for which the warning light is lit and the total time for which voltage is applied before the system cuts out, and compare to the times given in the description above.

9 If there is no supply at all, the relay, control unit or associated wiring is at fault.

10 To locate a defective glow plug, disconnect the main supply cable and the interconnecting wire from the top of the glow plugs. Using an ohmmeter, check for continuity between each glow plug terminal and earth. The resistance of a glow plug in good condition is very low (less than 1 ohm), so if the test lamp does not light or the continuity tester shows a high resistance, the glow plug is defective.

11 If an ammeter is available, the current

2.2 Disconnecting the wiring from the glow plugs

2.3a Clean the surrounding area . . .

2.3b . . . then unscrew and remove the glow plugs (note the rubber hose for removing and refitting No 4 glow plug)

draw of each glow plug can be checked. After an initial surge of around 15 to 20 amps, each plug should draw around 10 amps. Any plug which draws much more or less than 10 amps is probably defective.

12 As a final check, the glow plugs can be removed and inspected as described in Section 2.

13 If the pre/post-heating system is faulty, first check the wiring to each individual component. If this does not locate the fault, ideally each component should be substituted with known good units until the fault is located. If this is not possible, take the vehicle to a Renault dealer or diesel specialist who will have the diagnostic equipment necessary to pin-point the fault quickly.

2 Glow plugs – removal, inspection and refitting

Caution: If the preheating system has just been energised, or if the engine has been running, the glow plugs may be very hot.

Removal

1 Disconnect the battery negative (earth) lead and position it away from the terminal (refer to *Disconnecting the battery* in the Reference Section).

2 Disconnect the wiring plugs from the glow plugs **(see illustration)**.

3 Clean the surrounding area, then unscrew and remove the glow plugs from the cylinder head. Note that access to No 4 glow plug is difficult, and once loosened, a suitable tight-fitting hose may be used to unscrew it **(see illustrations)**.

Inspection

4 Inspect the glow plugs for physical damage. Burnt or eroded glow plug tips can be caused by a bad injector spray pattern. Have the injectors checked if this sort of damage is found.

5 If the glow plugs are in good physical condition, check them electrically using a 12 volt test lamp or continuity tester with reference to the previous Section.

6 The glow plugs can be energised by applying 12 volts to them to verify that they heat up evenly and in the required time. Observe the following precautions:

a) Support the glow plug by clamping it carefully in a vice or self-locking pliers. Remember it will become red-hot.

b) Make sure that the power supply or test lead incorporates a fuse or overload trip to protect against damage from a short-circuit.

c) After testing, allow the glow plug to cool for several minutes before attempting to handle it.

7 A glow plug in good condition will start to glow red at the tip after drawing current for 5 seconds or so. Any plug which takes much longer to start glowing, or which starts glowing in the middle instead of at the tip, is defective.

Refitting

8 Refit by reversing the removal operations. Apply a smear of copper-based anti-seize compound to the plug threads and tighten the glow plugs to the specified torque **(see illustration)**. Do not overtighten, as this can damage the glow plug element.

2.8 Tightening the glow plugs

3.2 Disconnecting the wiring from the pre/post-heating unit on the battery bracket

3 Pre/post-heating system control unit – removal and refitting

Removal

1 The pre/post-heating control unit is located on a bracket next to the battery, on the left-hand side of the engine compartment. Before proceeding, make sure that the ignition is switched off.

2 Disconnect the wiring from the control unit **(see illustration)**.

3 Unscrew the mounting nuts/bolts and remove the control unit from the mounting bracket.

Refitting

4 Refitting is a reversal of removal.

4 Coolant temperature sensor – removal, testing, and refitting

Note: *Also refer to Chapter 3, Section 8.*

Removal

1 The coolant temperature sensor is located on the thermostat housing on the left-hand end of the cylinder head.

2 Drain the cooling system as described in Chapter 1B. Alternatively, have the new sensor or a suitable bung to hand to quickly plug the hole and prevent liquid from being spilt while the sensor is being removed.

3 Pull out the retaining clip, then ease the sensor from the thermostat housing **(see illustrations)**.

Testing

Note: *A continuity tester or an ohmmeter will be required for testing.*

4 The sensor has two functions – the NTC (negative temperature coefficient) resistor informs the pre/post-heating control unit of the engine coolant temperature, and its switch interrupts the electrical supply to the EGR solenoid.

5 Connect a continuity tester or an ohmmeter to pins 1 and 4 of the sensor connector. There should be infinite resistance at room temperature, showing that the contacts of the thermoswitch are open.

6 Next suspend the sensor in a container of water (using string) so that it is immersed but not touching the sides or the base of the container. Dip a thermometer into the water, apply heat and then check that the contacts of the thermoswitch remain open up to 20°C but close at temperatures above 30°C. With the contacts closed, the ohmmeter must show zero resistance.

7 On all engines, connect an ohmmeter across the switch terminals 2 and 3. Heat the water and check that the resistance of the thermistor (coolant temperature sensor) is in accordance with the figures given in the Specifications.

8 If the results obtained are not as specified, the switch is proved faulty and should be renewed.

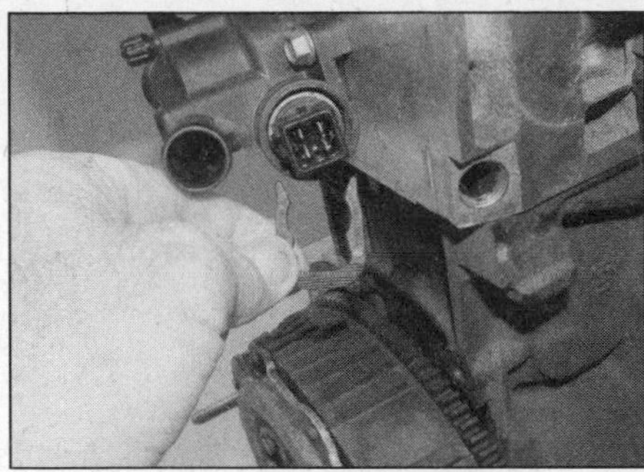

4.3a Pull out the retaining clip . . .

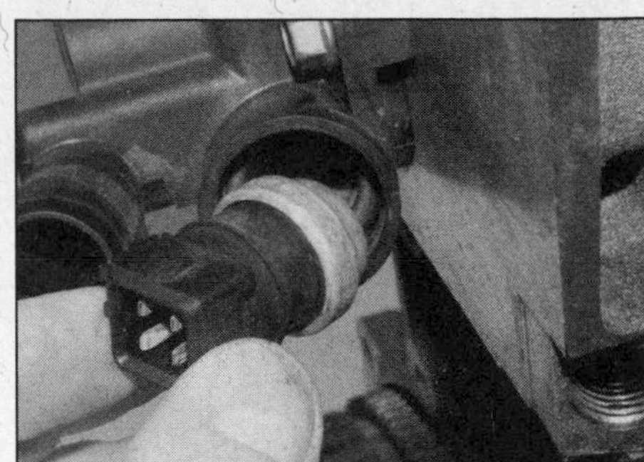

4.3b . . . and ease the sensor from the thermostat housing

Refitting

9 Refitting is the reverse of removal, but fit a new sealing ring.

10 On completion, top up or refill and bleed the cooling system, as necessary, as described in Chapter 1B.

Chapter 6
Clutch

Contents

Degrees of difficulty

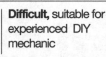

Easy, suitable for novice with little experience 	**Fairly easy,** suitable for beginner with some experience 	**Fairly difficult,** suitable for competent DIY mechanic 	**Difficult,** suitable for experienced DIY mechanic 	**Very difficult,** suitable for expert DIY or professional

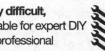

Specifications

General

Clutch type	Single dry plate, diaphragm spring, cable-operated
Adjustment	Automatic

Clutch disc

Diameter:	
D7F and D4F engines	181.5 mm
All other engines	200.0 mm
Lining thickness (new, and in compressed position):	
D7F and D4F engines	6.7 mm
All other engines	6.8 mm
Number of springs	6

Torque wrench setting	Nm	lbf ft
Clutch cover bolts	20	15

1 General information

Note: *This Chapter describes procedures for models fitted with the conventional manual gearbox. Information on the clutch fitted to the sequential gearbox is given in Chapter 7C.*

Manual gearbox models are equipped with a cable-operated clutch. The unit consists of a steel cover which is dowelled and bolted to the rear face of the flywheel, and contains the pressure plate and diaphragm spring.

The clutch friction disc is free to slide along the gearbox splined input shaft. The disc is held in position between the flywheel and the pressure plate by the pressure of the diaphragm spring. Friction lining material is riveted to the disc, which has a spring-cushioned hub to absorb transmission shocks and help ensure a smooth take-up of the drive.

The clutch is actuated by a cable, controlled by the clutch pedal. The clutch release mechanism consists of a release arm and bearing which are in permanent contact with the fingers of the diaphragm spring.

Depressing the clutch pedal actuates the release arm by means of the cable. The arm pushes the release bearing against the diaphragm fingers, so moving the centre of the diaphragm spring inwards. As the centre of the spring is pushed in, the outside of the spring pivots out, so moving the pressure plate backwards and disengaging its grip on the friction disc.

When the pedal is released, the diaphragm spring forces the pressure plate into contact with the friction linings on the disc. The disc is now firmly sandwiched between the pressure plate and the flywheel, thus transmitting engine power to the gearbox.

Wear of the friction material on the disc is automatically compensated for by a separate self-adjusting mechanism attached to the clutch pedal by a short link. The mechanism functions as follows. One end of the clutch cable is attached to the quadrant, which is free to pivot, but is kept in tension by a spring. When the pedal is depressed, the notched cam contacts the quadrant, thus locking it and allowing the pedal to pull the cable and operate the clutch. When the pedal is released, the tension spring causes the notched cam to move free of the quadrant, and at the same time tension is maintained on the cable, keeping the release bearing in contact with the diaphragm spring. As the friction material on the disc wears, the self-adjusting quadrant will rotate when the pedal is released, and the pedal free play will be maintained between the notched cam and the quadrant.

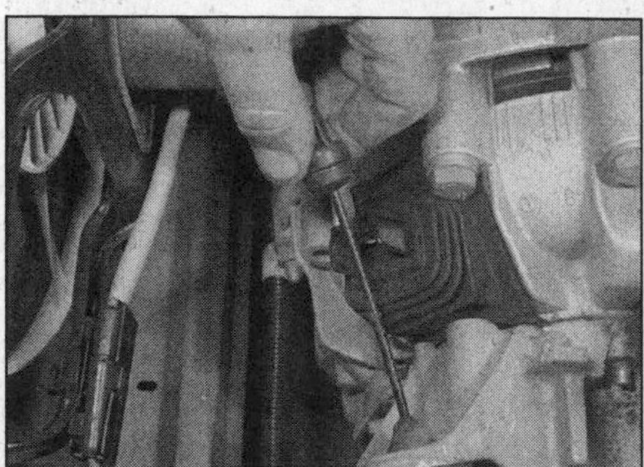

2.2a Disconnecting the clutch inner cable from the release fork

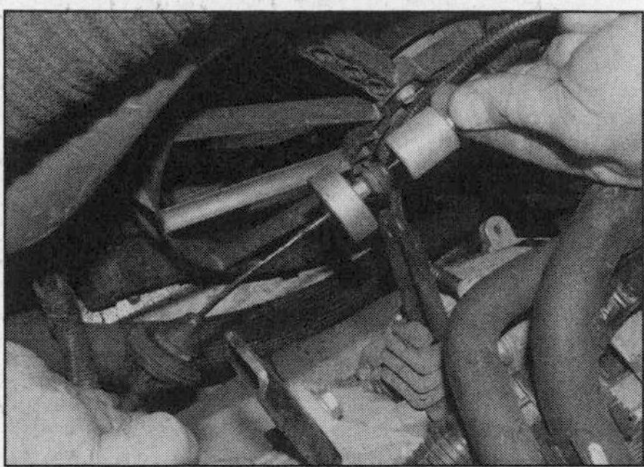

2.2b Withdrawing the clutch outer cable from the bracket on the bellhousing

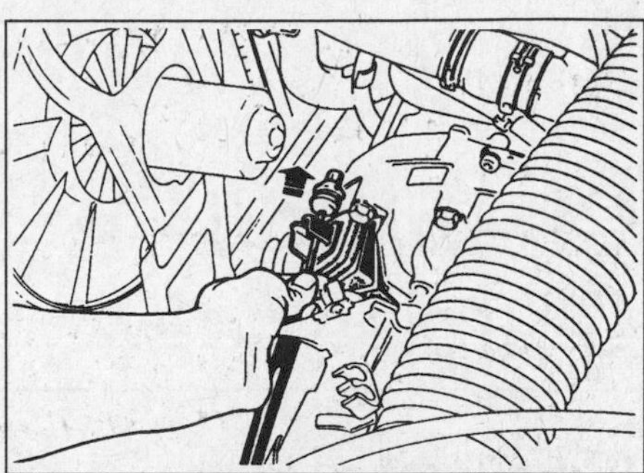

2.10 Checking the clutch inner cable slack at the release fork end

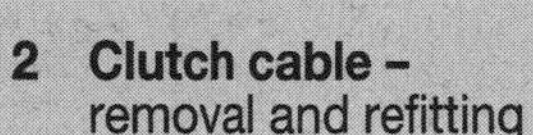

2 Clutch cable - removal and refitting

Removal

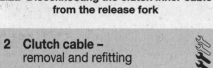

1 In order to gain access to the clutch cable on the gearbox bellhousing, remove the air cleaner or air inlet ducting, according to model as described in Chapter 4A or 4B.

2 Disengage the inner cable from the release fork, then withdraw the outer cable from the bracket on the bellhousing **(see illustrations)**.

Caution: Do not lift the release fork as it may become detached from the release bearing inside the bellhousing.

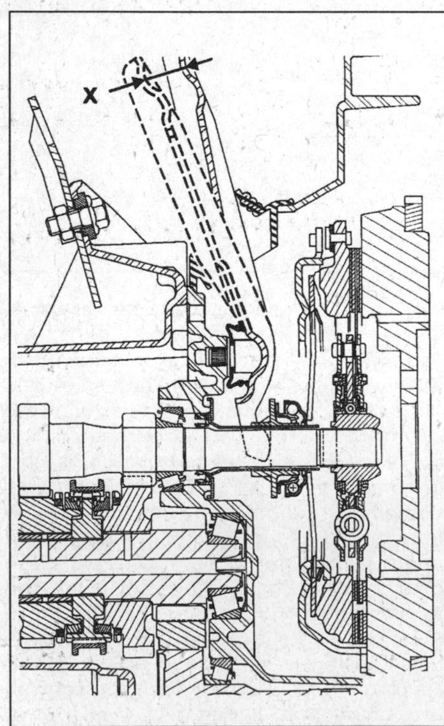

2.11 Checking the clutch release fork movement (X)

K4J and K4M engines: X = 27.0 to 31.6 mm
All other engines: X = 27.4 to 30.7 mm

3 Working inside the car, remove the lower facia panel. Press the clutch pedal to the floor, then pull it up and free the inner cable end from the serrated quadrant on the self-adjusting mechanism.

4 With the inner cable released, push the outer cable out of its location in the bulkhead.

5 Pull the cable through into the engine compartment, detach it from the support clips and remove it from the car.

Refitting

6 To refit the cable, thread it through from the engine compartment, place it over the self-adjusting cam, and connect the inner cable end to the quadrant.

7 Working in the engine compartment, slip the other end of the cable through the bellhousing bracket, and connect the inner cable to the release fork. Refit the cable to the support clips.

8 Depress the clutch pedal to draw the outer cable into its locating hole in the bulkhead, ensuring that it locates properly. At the same time, the inner cable guide (where fitted) will be automatically pulled onto the top of the pedal to hold the inner cable in position.

9 Depress the clutch pedal several times in order to allow the self-adjusting mechanism to set the correct free play.

10 When the self-adjusting mechanism on the clutch pedal is functioning correctly, there should be a minimum of 20 mm slack in the cable. To check this dimension, pull out the inner cable near the release fork on the gearbox **(see illustration)**. If there is less than the minimum slack in the cable, the self-adjusting quadrant should be checked for seizure or possible restricted movement.

11 Depress the clutch pedal fully, and check the total movement at the end of the release fork **(see illustration)**. This movement ensures that the clutch pedal stroke is correct. If not, make sure that the quadrant is free to turn, and that the spring has not lost its tension. If necessary, check the free length of the spring against a new one. Also check that the inner cable is not seizing in the outer cable.

12 Refit the lower facia panel, air cleaner and inlet ducting as applicable.

3 Clutch pedal - removal and refitting

Removal

1 Working in the engine compartment, remove the air cleaner or air inlet ducting (as applicable) as described in Chapter 4A or 4B, then disengage the inner cable from the release fork on the transmission.

Caution: Do not lift the release fork as it may become detached from the release bearing inside the bellhousing.

2 Inside the car, carefully prise the adjustment link bar from the top of the pedal using a screwdriver **(see illustration)**.

3 Unscrew and remove the pedal pivot bolt and withdraw the pedal.

Refitting

4 Apply some multi-purpose grease to the pedal pivot bush and upper link ball.

5 Locate the pedal on its bracket and insert the pivot bolt. Tighten the bolt securely.

6 Press the adjustment link bar onto the pedal upper ball.

7 If necessary, adjust the link bar so that the clutch pedal is the same height as the brake pedal. Tighten the lock nuts on completion.

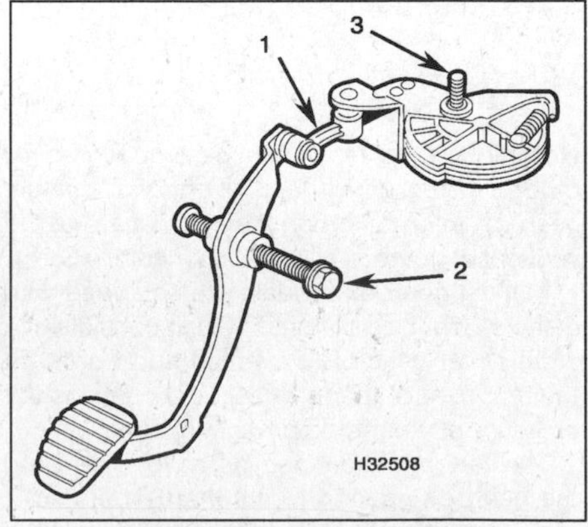

3.2 Clutch pedal components

1 Link bar
2 Pedal pivot bolt
3 Self-adjusting mechanism retaining bolt

4 Clutch cable adjusting mechanism – removal and refitting

Removal

1 Working in the engine compartment, remove the air cleaner or air inlet ducting (as applicable) as described in Chapter 4A or 4B, then disengage the inner cable from the release fork on the transmission.

Caution: Do not lift the release fork as it may become detached from the release bearing inside the bellhousing.

2 Inside the car, carefully prise the adjustment link bar from the top of the pedal using a screwdriver.

3 Free the inner cable end from the serrated quadrant on the self-adjusting mechanism **(see illustrations)**.

4 Unbolt and remove the adjusting mechanism.

Refitting

5 Refitting is a reversal of removal, but, on completion, adjust the link bar so that the clutch pedal is the same height as the brake pedal. Tighten the lock nuts on completion.
Note: *Adjustment of the link bar may not be possible on later models.*

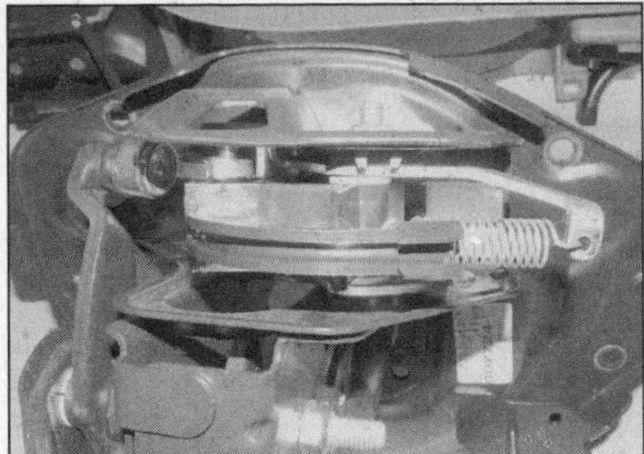

4.3a Self-adjusting mechanism showing return spring

4.3b Self-adjusting mechanism showing link

5.1 View of the clutch assembly with the gearbox removed

5.2 Mark the relationship of the clutch cover and flywheel

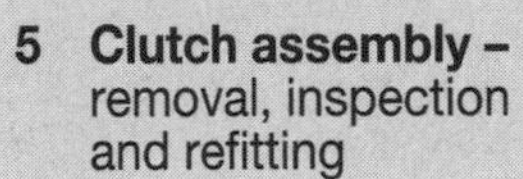

5 Clutch assembly – removal, inspection and refitting

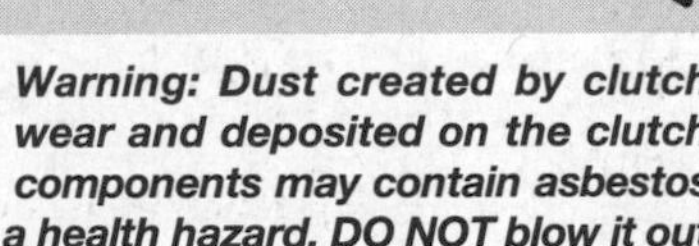

Warning: Dust created by clutch wear and deposited on the clutch components may contain asbestos which is a health hazard. DO NOT blow it out with compressed air or inhale any of it. DO NOT use petrol or petroleum-based solvents to clean off the dust. Brake system cleaner or methylated spirit should be used to flush the dust into a suitable receptacle. After the clutch components are wiped clean with rags, dispose of the contaminated rags and cleaner in a sealed, marked container.

Removal

1 Access to the clutch may be gained in one of two ways. Either the gearbox may be removed independently, as described in Chapter 7A, or the engine/gearbox unit may be removed as described in Chapter 2D, and the gearbox separated from the engine on the bench **(see illustration)**.

2 Having separated the gearbox from the engine, first use paint or a marker pen to mark the relationship of the clutch cover to the flywheel **(see illustration)**.

3 Unscrew and remove the clutch cover retaining bolts. Work in a diagonal sequence and slacken the bolts only a few turns at a time. Hold the flywheel stationary by positioning a screwdriver over the dowel on the cylinder block and engaging it with the starter ring gear **(see illustration)**.

4 Ease the cover assembly off its locating dowels. Be prepared to catch the friction disc, which will drop out as the assembly is removed. Note which way round the disc is fitted.

Inspection

5 With the clutch assembly removed, clean off all traces of asbestos dust using a dry cloth. This is best done outside or in a well-ventilated area (refer to the warning at the beginning of this Section).

6 Examine the linings of the friction disc for wear or loose rivets, and the disc rim for distortion, cracks, broken torsion springs and worn splines **(see illustration)**. The surface of

5.3 Unscrewing the clutch cover retaining bolts, showing a screwdriver engaged with the starter ring gear

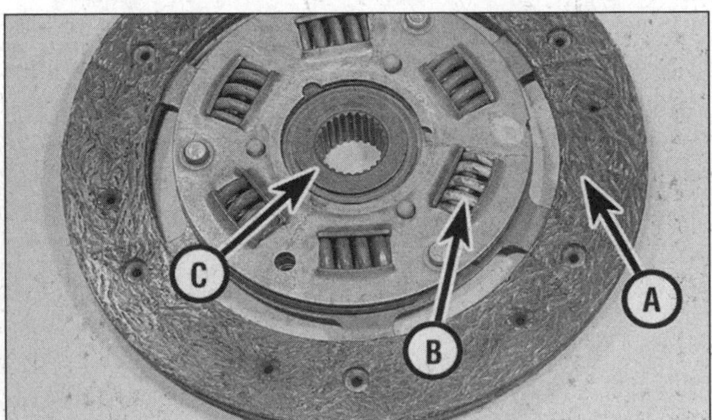

5.6 Inspect the friction disc linings (A), springs (B) and splines (C)

5.7a Check the machined face of the pressure plate (arrowed) . . .

5.7b . . . and the diaphragm spring, paying particular attention to the tips (arrowed)

the friction linings may be highly glazed, but as long as the friction material pattern can be clearly seen, this is satisfactory. If there is any sign of oil contamination, indicated by shiny black discoloration, the disc must be renewed and the source of the contamination traced and rectified. This will be a leaking crankshaft oil seal, gearbox input shaft oil seal, or both. The renewal procedure for the crankshaft oil seal is given in the relevant part of Chapter 2. Renewal of the gearbox input shaft oil seal should be entrusted to a Renault garage, as it involves dismantling the gearbox and the renewal of the clutch release bearing guide tube using a press. The disc must also be renewed if the linings have worn down to, or just above, the level of the rivet heads.

7 Check the machined faces of the flywheel and pressure plate. If either is grooved, or heavily scored, renewal is necessary. The pressure plate must also be renewed if any cracks are apparent, or if the diaphragm spring is damaged or its pressure suspect **(see illustrations)**.

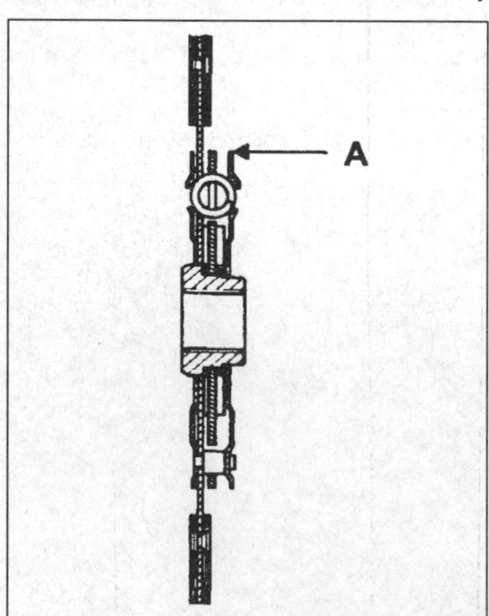

5.13 Clutch friction disc offset (A) faces away from flywheel

8 Take the opportunity to check the condition of the release bearing, as described in Section 6.

9 It is good practice to renew the friction disc, pressure plate and release bearing at the same time.

Refitting

10 Before commencing the refitting procedure, apply a little high-melting-point grease to the splines of the gearbox input shaft. Distribute the grease by sliding the friction disc on and off the splines a few times. Remove the disc and wipe away any excess grease. Also smear a little grease to the guide tube on the gearbox.

11 It is important that no oil or grease is allowed to come into contact with the friction material of the friction disc or the pressure plate and flywheel faces. It is advisable to refit the clutch assembly with clean hands, and to wipe the pressure plate and flywheel faces with a clean dry rag before assembly begins.

12 There are several different types of clutch alignment tool available to the home mechanic; the conventional type uses a spigot which centralises the disc with the hole in the end of the crankshaft, however, an alternative clamp-type tool centralises the disc onto the pressure plate before refitting them both to the flywheel.

Using a conventional alignment tool

13 Place the friction disc against the flywheel, with the side having the larger offset facing away from the flywheel, and hold the disc in position using the alignment tool **(see illustration)**.

14 Place the clutch cover assembly over the dowels, and where applicable, align it with the previously-made mark. Refit the retaining bolts and tighten them finger-tight so that the friction disc is gripped, but can still be moved.

15 The disc must now be centralised so that, when the engine and gearbox are reconnected, the splines of the gearbox input shaft will pass through the splines in the centre of the friction disc hub. If this is not done accurately, it will be impossible to refit the gearbox.

16 Centralisation can be carried out quite easily by inserting a round bar through the hole in the centre of the friction disc, so that the end of the bar rests in the hole in the end of the crankshaft. Note that a plastic centralising tube is supplied with Renault clutch kits, making the use of a bar unnecessary. If a non-Renault clutch is being fitted, an alternative and more accurate method of centralisation is to use a commercially-available clutch alignment tool obtainable from most accessory shops **(see illustration)**.

17 If a bar is being used, move it sideways or up-and-down until the friction disc is centralised. Centralisation can be judged by removing the bar and viewing the disc hub in relation to the bore in the end of the crankshaft. When the bore appears exactly in the centre of the disc hub, all is correct.

18 Once the disc is centralised, progressively tighten the cover bolts in a diagonal sequence to the correct torque setting **(see illustration)**. Remove the centralising tool.

19 The gearbox can now be refitted to the

5.16 Using a clutch alignment tool to centralise the friction disc

5.18 Tightening the clutch cover bolts

5.20a Centralise the pressure plate on the disc . . .

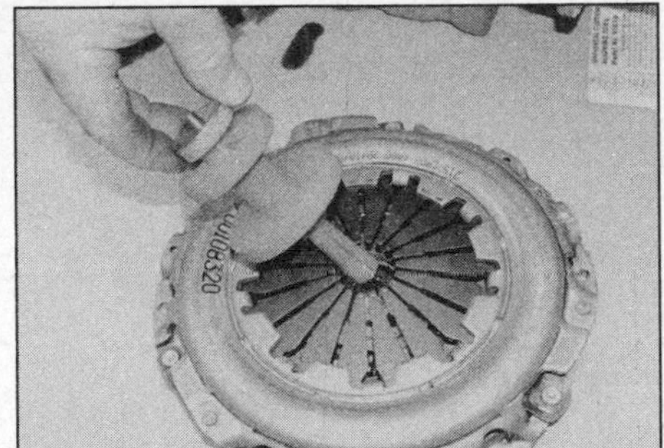
5.20b . . . fit the tool and tighten to clamp the disc to the pressure plate

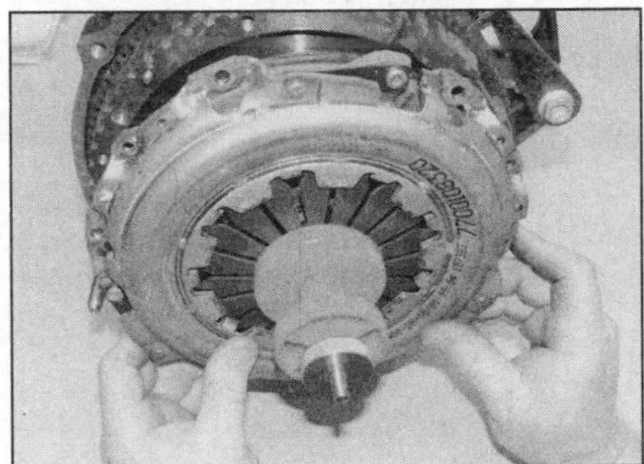
5.21 Locate the assembly on the flywheel . . .

5.22 . . . then progressively tighten the bolts to the specified torque

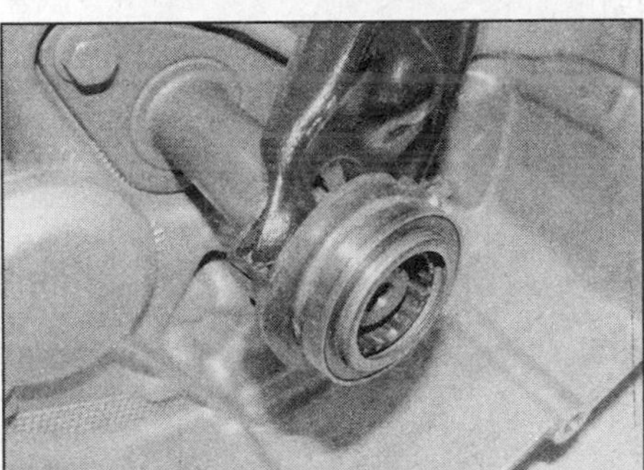
6.2 Removing the release bearing from the guide tube and fork

engine with reference to Chapter 7A or 2D as applicable.

Using a clamp-type alignment tool

20 Position the pressure plate centrally on the friction disc, then insert the alignment tool and clamp the two items together with the tool **(see illustrations)**. Check that the disc is correctly aligned with the pressure plate by viewing it from the flywheel side.

21 Position the plate and disc on the flywheel and insert the retaining bolts finger-tight **(see illustration)**. Where applicable, align the previously-made marks on the plate and flywheel.

22 Progressively tighten the pressure plate bolts to the specified torque, then remove the tool **(see illustration)**.

23 The gearbox can now be refitted to the engine with reference to Chapter 7A or 2D as applicable.

6 Clutch release bearing – removal, inspection and refitting

Removal

1 Access to the clutch release bearing may be gained in one of two ways. Either the gearbox may be removed independently, as described in Chapter 7A, or the engine/gearbox unit may be removed, as described in Chapter 2D, and the gearbox separated from the engine on the bench.

2 Having separated the gearbox from the engine, tilt the release fork and slide the bearing assembly off the gearbox input shaft guide tube **(see illustration)**. Note how the fork locates in the release bearing.

3 To remove the release fork, disengage the rubber cover and then pull the fork off its pivot ball stud **(see illustrations)**.

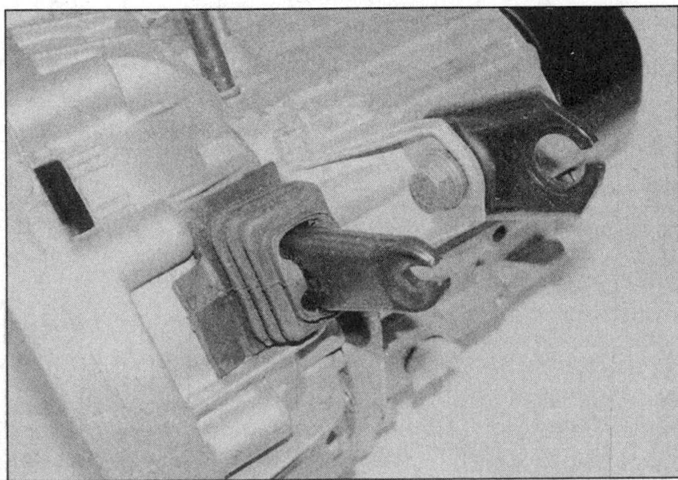
6.3a Showing the rubber cover on the release lever

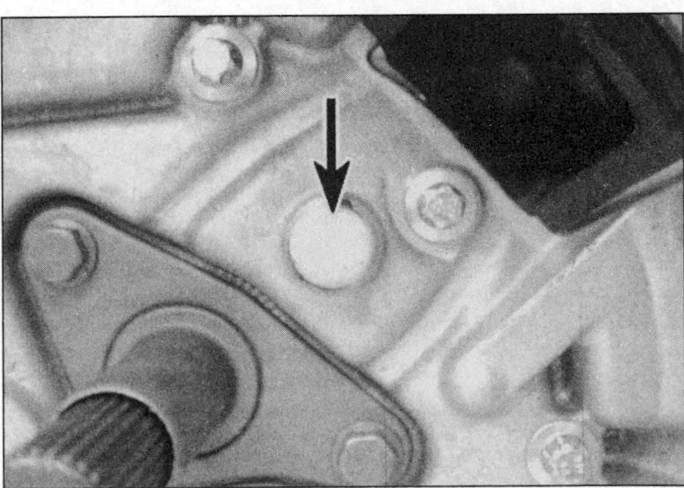
6.3b Release lever pivot ball stud

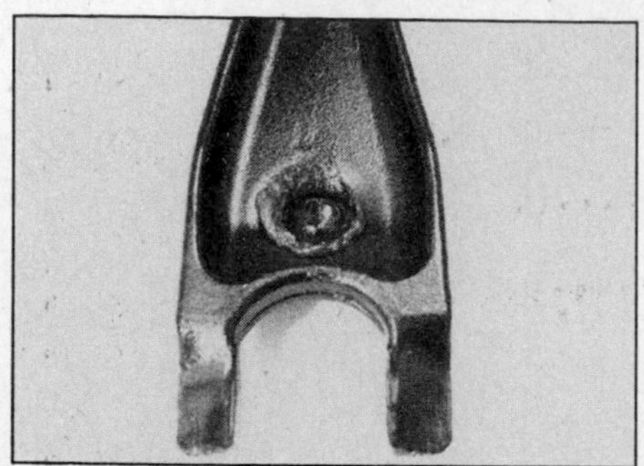

6.3c The release lever has an indentation to locate on the pivot ball stud

6.5a Smear molybdenum disulphide grease on the pivot stud before refitting the release fork

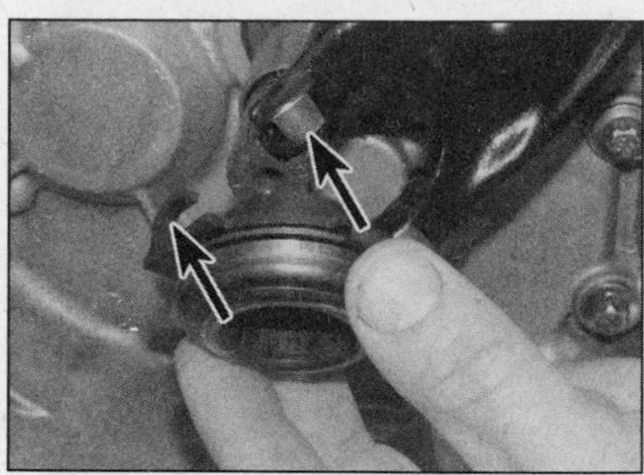

6.5b Clutch release components. The clip on the bearing carrier must engage with the release fork

Inspection

4 Check the bearing for smoothness of operation. Renew it if there is any roughness or harshness as the bearing is spun. It is good practice to renew the bearing as a matter of course during clutch overhaul, regardless of its apparent condition.

Refitting

5 Refitting the release fork and release bearing is a reversal of the removal procedure, but note the following points.

a) *Lubricate the release fork pivot ball stud, the release bearing-to-diaphragm spring contact areas and the guide tube sparingly with molybdenum disulphide grease **(see illustration)**.*

b) *Ensure that the release fork engages correctly with the lugs on the bearing **(see illustrations)**.*

6.5c Locating the release arm and bearing over the input shaft

Chapter 7 Part A:
Manual gearbox

Contents

Degrees of difficulty

Easy, suitable for novice with little experience 

Fairly easy, suitable for beginner with some experience 

Fairly difficult, suitable for competent DIY mechanic 

Difficult, suitable for experienced DIY mechanic 

Very difficult, suitable for expert DIY or professional 

Specifications

General

Type	Five forward speeds (all synchromesh) and reverse. Final drive differential integral with main gearbox

Designation

Except K4M and K9K engines	JB1 or JH1
K4M and K9K engines	JB3 or JH3

Gear ratios

1st	3.4 : 1
2nd	1.9 : 1
3rd	1.3 : 1
4th	1.0 : 1
5th	0.8 : 1
Reverse	3.6 : 1
Final drive	3.7:1, 3.9:1, 4.1:1 or 4.2:1

Lubrication

Type	See *Lubricants and fluids*
Capacity	3.4 litres

Torque wrench settings	Nm	lbf ft
Engine to gearbox tie bar	65	48
Gearbox bellhousing to engine	45	33
Rear engine mounting to gearbox	See Chapter 2A, 2B or 2C	
Starter motor mounting bolt	45	33

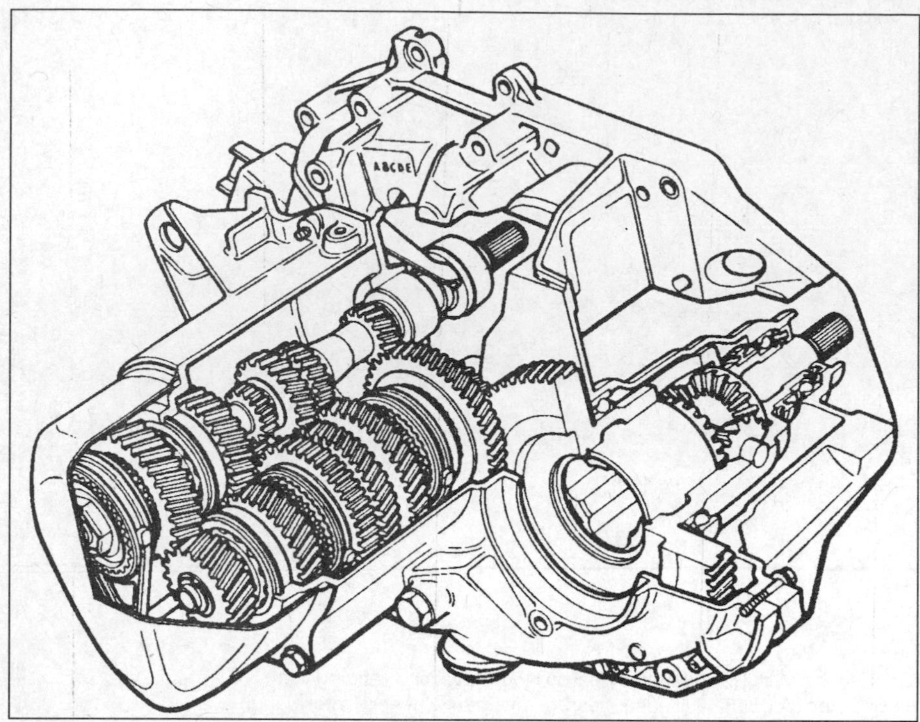
1.1a Cutaway view of the gearbox

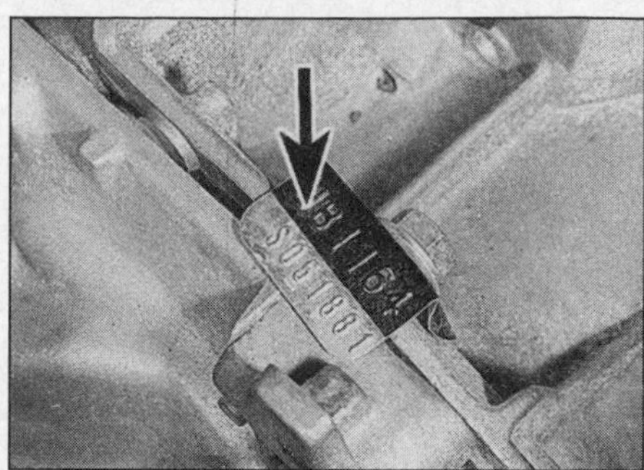
1.1b The identification number starts with the gearbox type code

1 General information

The gearbox is equipped with five forward gears, one reverse gear and a final drive differential, incorporated in one casing bolted to the left-hand end of the engine. The gearbox type code is stamped on an identification plate attached to the top of the gearbox **(see illustrations)**.

Drive is transmitted from the crankshaft via the clutch to the input shaft which rotates in sealed ball-bearings, and has a splined extension to accept the clutch friction disc. From the input shaft, drive is transmitted to the output shaft, which rotates in a roller bearing at its right-hand end, and a sealed ball-bearing at its left-hand end. From the output shaft, drive is transmitted to the differential crown wheel, which rotates with the differential case and planetary gears, thus driving the side gears and driveshafts. The rotation of the planetary gears on their shaft allows the inner roadwheel to rotate at a slower speed than the outer roadwheel when the car is cornering.

The input and output shafts are arranged side-by-side, parallel to the crankshaft and driveshafts, so that their gear pinion teeth are in constant mesh. In the neutral position, the output shaft gear pinions rotate freely, so that drive cannot be transmitted to the crown wheel. Synchromesh is provided on all forward speeds. Gear selection is via a floor-mounted lever and rod mechanism.

The gearbox selector rod causes the appropriate selector fork to move its respective synchro-sleeve along the shaft, in order to lock the gear pinion to the synchro-hub. Since the synchro-hubs are splined to the output shaft, this locks the pinion to the shaft, so that drive can be transmitted. To ensure that gearchanging can be made quickly and quietly, a synchromesh system is fitted to all forward gears, consisting of baulk rings and spring-loaded fingers, as well as the gear pinions and synchro-hubs. The synchromesh cones are formed on the mating faces of the baulk rings and gear pinions.

2 Gearbox oil – draining and refilling

Note: *The filler plug is also used as the level plug.*

1 This operation is much quicker and more efficient if the car is first taken on a journey of sufficient length to warm the engine/gearbox up to operating temperature.

2 Park the car on level ground, switch off the ignition and apply the handbrake firmly. For improved access, jack up the car and support it securely on axle stands (see *Jacking and vehicle support*), or alternatively position the vehicle over an inspection pit or on car ramps. Note that, to ensure accuracy, the car must be level when checking the oil level. Remove the engine compartment undertray or the small cover from the bottom of the gearbox (as applicable) **(see illustration)**.

3 Remove all traces of dirt from around the drain and filler plugs, then unscrew the filler/level plug from the front face of the gearbox **(see illustration)**.

4 Position a suitable container under the gearbox, then unscrew the drain plug and allow the oil to drain completely into the container **(see illustrations)**. If the oil is hot,

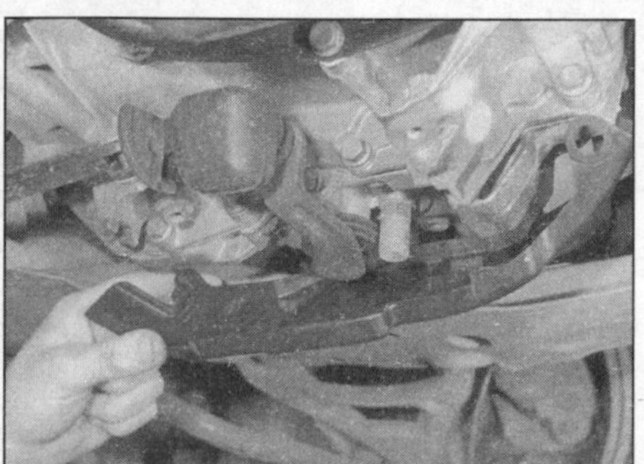
2.2 Removing the plastic cover from the bottom of the gearbox

2.3 Oil filler plug on the front of the gearbox

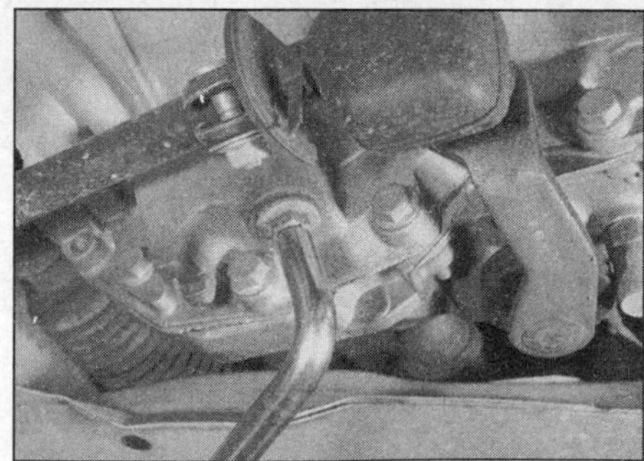
2.4a Unscrew the drain plug . . .

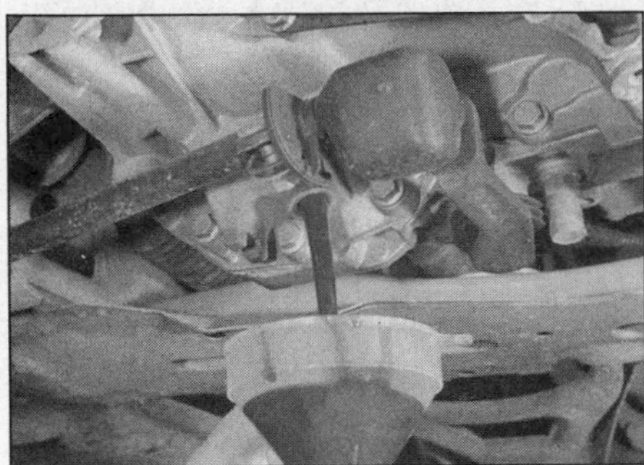

2.4b . . . and drain the oil

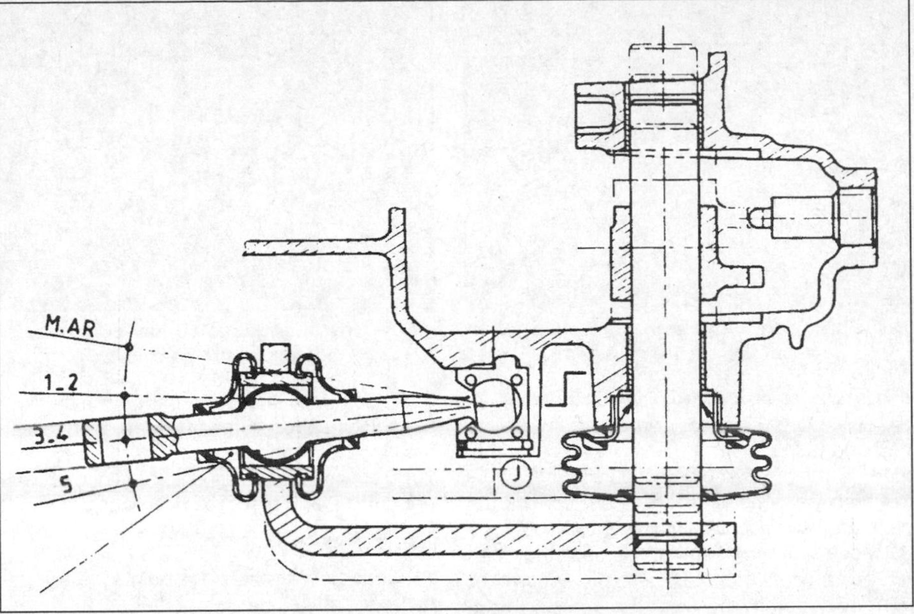

3.3a Gear positions for the gearbox lever

take precautions against scalding. Clean both the filler/level and the drain plugs, being especially careful to wipe any metallic particles off the magnetic inserts. The sealing washers should be renewed whenever they are disturbed.

5 When the oil has finished draining, clean the drain plug threads and those of the gearbox casing, and refit the drain plug, tightening it securely.

6 Refilling the gearbox is an extremely awkward operation. Above all, allow plenty of time for the oil level to settle properly before checking it. Note that the car must be level when checking the oil level.

7 Refill the gearbox with the exact amount of the specified type of oil, then check the oil level as described in Chapter 1A or 1B. When the level is correct, refit the filler level plug with a new sealing washer and tighten securely.

8 Refit the plastic cover to the gearbox or the engine undertray (as applicable), then lower the vehicle to the ground.

3 Gearchange mechanism – adjustment

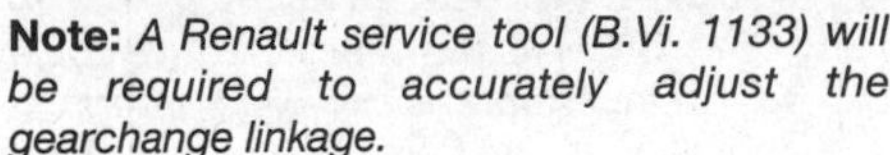

Note: *A Renault service tool (B.Vi. 1133) will be required to accurately adjust the gearchange linkage.*

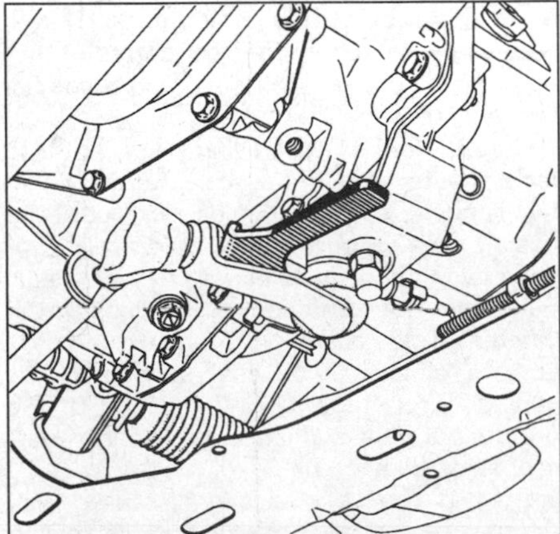

3.3b Using the Renault tool B.Vi. 1133 to hold the gearchange lever in position

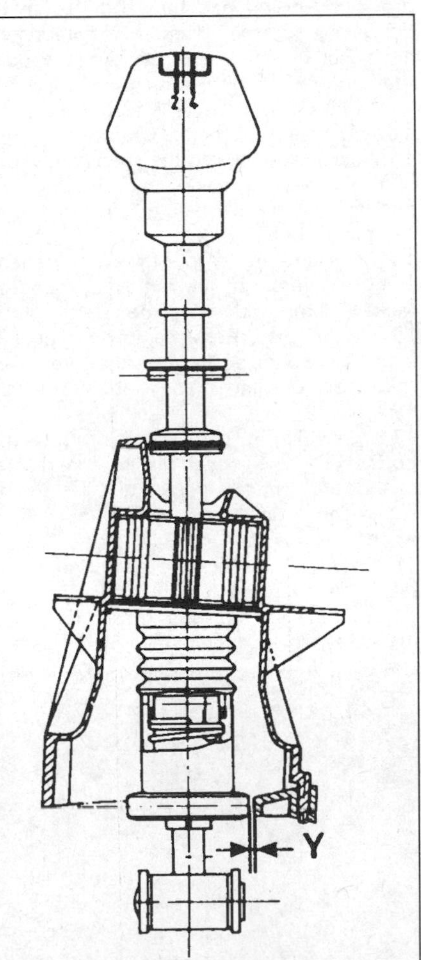

3.4 The clearance (Y) between the gear lever and housing should be between 7.0 and 10.0 mm

1 Firmly apply the handbrake, then jack up the front of the vehicle and support it securely on axle stands (see *Jacking and vehicle support*). As applicable, remove the engine compartment undertray or unclip the small cover from the bottom of the gearbox.

2 Unbolt the heat shields from the underbody to gain access to the bottom of the gear lever.

3 Select 1st gear at the gearbox by moving the lever to the appropriate position. To hold the lever securely in position, fit the Renault tool B.Vi. 1133 **(see illustrations)**. In the absence of the special tool, a suitable alternative can be made from a flat metal bar or a piece of wood.

4 Using a feeler gauge, check that the clearance between the reverse stop-ring on the gear lever and the inclined plane on the right-hand side of the gear lever housing is between 7.0 and 10.0 mm **(see illustration)**.

5 If adjustment is necessary, loosen the clamp bolt at the gearbox end of the gearchange rod so that the rod can be moved **(see illustration)**.

6 Move the gear lever so that the reverse stop-

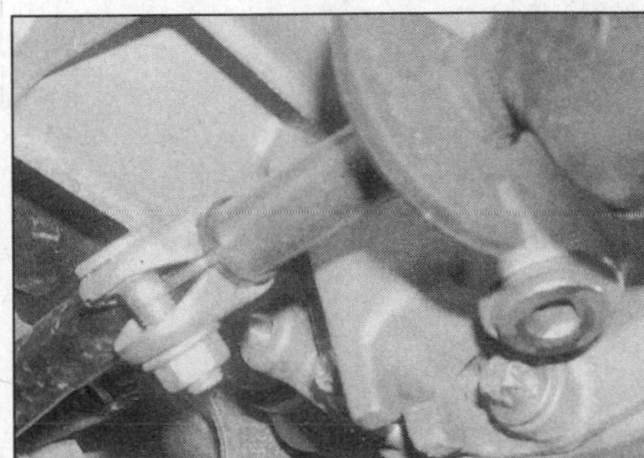

3.5 Adjustment clamp at the gearbox end of the gearchange rod

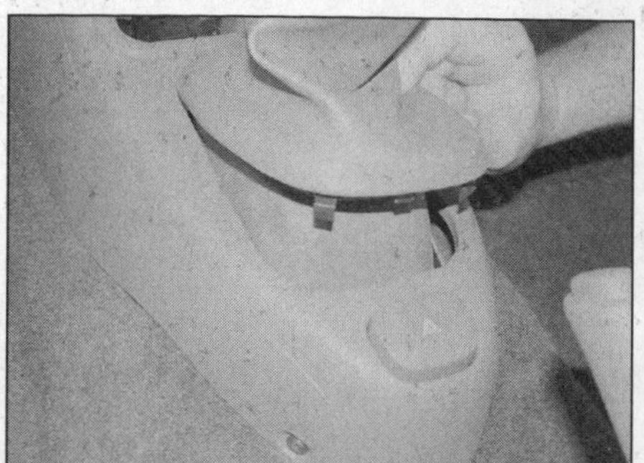

4.1 Removing the gearchange lever gaiter from the centre console

ring is against the inclined plane on the housing, then insert a 9.0 mm feeler gauge between the ring and plane. Hold the lever in this position, then tighten the clamp bolt securely.

7 Remove the holding tool, then recheck the clearance as described in paragraph 4.

8 Check that all gears can be selected, then refit the heat shields, plastic cover or undertray before lowering the vehicle to the ground.

4 Gearchange mechanism - removal and refitting

Removal

1 Working inside the vehicle, carefully prise the gearchange lever gaiter out of the centre console **(see illustration)**. Pull the knob off the top of the gearchange lever and remove it with the gaiter.

2 Firmly apply the handbrake, then jack up the front of the vehicle and support it on axle stands (see *Jacking and vehicle support*). As applicable, remove the engine compartment undertray or unclip the small cover from the bottom of the gearbox.

3 Unbolt and remove the exhaust heat shields for access to the bottom of the gear lever. If necessary, unscrew the clamp bolt and separate the exhaust system, then support the exhaust on an axle stand.

4 Unscrew the nut, then remove the washer and disconnect the gearchange rod from the bottom of the gear lever **(see illustration)**.

5 Unscrew the mounting nuts securing the gear lever base assembly to the floor, then lower the assembly and remove it from under the car. If the exhaust is still in position, it will be necessary to push it to one side while removing the gear lever assembly.

6 Remove the frame from the base.

7 Mount the gear lever in a soft-jawed vice, then extract the circlip and separate the base and gaiter.

8 To remove the gearchange rod, release the rubber gaiter and unscrew the clamp bolt at the front of the rod. Note the location of the bush and spacer **(see illustration)**. Remove the rod from the gearbox.

4.4 Gearchange rod connection to the bottom of the gear lever

9 To separate the gearchange clevis, first mark it in relation to the main rod, then loosen the clamp bolt and separate the two sections.

10 Examine all components for signs of wear or damage, and renew as necessary.

Refitting

11 Lubricate all the pivot points with multi-purpose grease.

12 Where the gearchange rod has been dismantled, locate the clevis on the rod in its previously-noted position, and tighten the clamp bolt securely. Where new components are being fitted, locate the clevis on the rod so that approximately 7.0 to 8.0 mm of the knurled section is visible. Make sure that the clevis is offset towards the gearbox.

13 Attach the clevis to the gearchange lever and refit the bolt, making sure that the bush and spacer are in their correct positions. Tighten the bolt securely.

14 Reassemble the gear lever components using a reversal of the removal procedure. Make sure the circlip is secure.

15 Lift the gear lever assembly into position in the floor aperture, then locate the frame and refit the mounting nuts. Tighten the nuts securely.

16 Connect the gearchange rod to the bottom of the gear lever, making sure that the bushes are correctly located and that the nut is positioned on the left-hand side. Refit the washer, then tighten the nut securely.

17 Check and adjust the gearchange with reference to Section 3.

18 Refit the heat shields, plastic cover and undertray, and exhaust system components

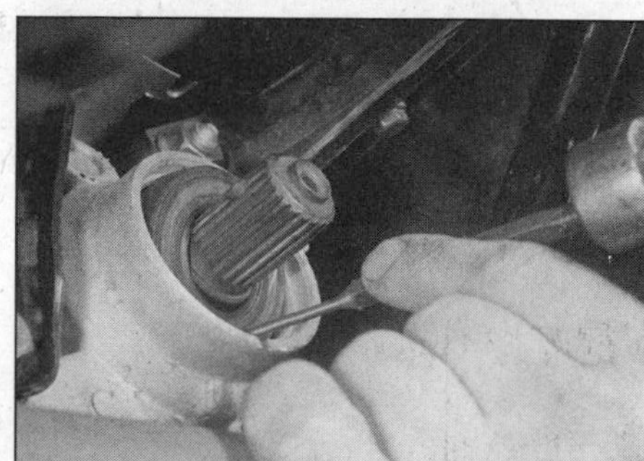

5.6 Tap the bottom of the driveshaft oil seal with a small drift to remove it

4.8 Clamp bolt at the front of the gearchange rod

as applicable, then lower the car to the ground.

19 Refit the gaiter and gear lever knob to the centre console. The knob should be bonded to the lever using suitable adhesive.

5 Oil seals - renewal

Right-hand driveshaft oil seal

Note: *New driveshaft-to-differential side gear roll pins may be required on refitting (see Chapter 8).*

1 Apply the handbrake, then jack up the front of the car and support it on axle stands (see *Jacking and vehicle support*). Remove the right-hand wheel.

2 Drain the gearbox oil as described in Section 2.

3 Referring to Chapter 8, disconnect the driveshaft from the gearbox. Note that it is not necessary to remove the driveshaft completely, the shaft can be left attached to the hub assembly and slid off from the differential gear splines as the hub assembly is pulled outwards. **Note:** *Do not allow it to hang down under its own weight, as this could damage the constant velocity joints/gaiters.*

4 Remove the O-ring from the side gear shaft.

5 Wipe clean the old oil seal, and measure its fitted depth below the casing edge. This is necessary to determine the correct fitted position of the new oil seal, if the special Renault fitting tool is not being used.

6 Free the old oil seal, using a small drift to tap the outer edge of the seal inwards so that the opposite edge of the seal tilts out of the casing **(see illustration)**. A pair of pliers or grips can then be used to pull out the oil seal. Take care not to damage the splines of the differential side gear.

7 Wipe clean the oil seal seating in the casing. Wrap tape around the end of the differential gear splines to prevent the new seal being damaged.

8 Apply a smear of grease to the sealing lip of the new oil seal and, making sure its sealing lip is facing inwards, carefully slide it onto the differential gear shaft. Press the seal squarely into the gearbox until it is positioned at the same depth as the original was prior to removal. If necessary, the seal can be tapped into position using a piece of metal tube or a socket which bears only on the hard outer edge of the seal **(see illustrations)**.

9 Remove the tape from the end of the differential shaft, and slide a new O-ring into position.

10 Reconnect the driveshaft to the gearbox as described in Chapter 8.

11 Refill the gearbox with oil as described in Section 2.

12 Refit the roadwheel and lower the car to the ground. Tighten the wheel bolts to the specified torque (Chapter 1A or 1B).

Left-hand driveshaft oil seal

13 On the left-hand side of the gearbox, there is no oil seal as the seal is formed by the driveshaft gaiter. If oil is leaking from the left-hand driveshaft-to-gearbox joint, renew the gaiter as described in Chapter 8.

Input shaft oil seal

14 It is not possible to renew the input shaft oil seal without first dismantling the gearbox. The guide tube assembly is a press-fit in the housing, and is removed inwards. Oil seal renewal should therefore be entrusted to a Renault dealer or gearbox overhaul specialist.

6 Reversing light switch – testing, removal and refitting

Testing

1 The reversing light circuit is controlled by a plunger-type switch that is screwed into the left-hand side of the gearbox casing, next to the driveshaft inner joint. If a fault develops in the circuit, first ensure that the circuit fuse has not blown.

2 To test the switch, disconnect the wiring connector, and use a multimeter (set to the resistance function) or a battery-and-bulb test circuit to check that there is continuity between the switch terminals only when reverse gear is selected. If this is not the case, and there are no obvious breaks or other damage to the wires, the switch is faulty, and must be renewed.

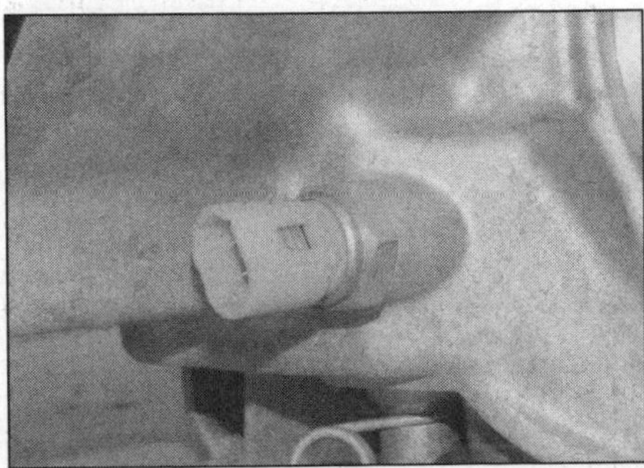

6.5 Reversing light switch on the bottom of the gearbox

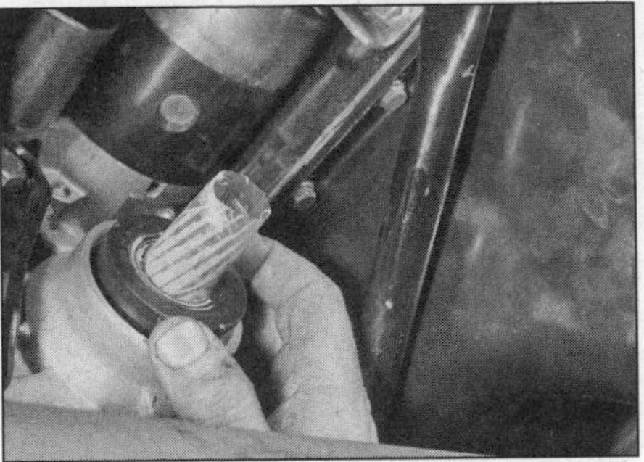

5.8a Locate the new oil seal carefully over the output shaft splines . . .

5.8b . . . and press into position with a socket or metal tube

Removal

3 Firmly apply the handbrake, then jack up the front of the vehicle and support it on axle stands (see *Jacking and vehicle support*).

4 Where fitted, remove the engine compartment undertray.

5 Disconnect the wiring, then unscrew the switch from the gearbox **(see illustration)**. Recover the sealing washer.

Refitting

6 Fit a new sealing washer to the switch, then screw it back into the gearbox casing and tighten it securely. Reconnect the wiring, and test the operation of the circuit. Where fitted, refit the engine compartment undertray, then lower the vehicle to the ground. If any oil was lost when the switch was removed, check the oil level as described in Chapter 1A or 1B.

7 Manual gearbox – removal and refitting

Note: *This Section describes the removal of the gearbox leaving the engine in position in the car. Alternatively, the engine and gearbox can be removed together, as described in Chapter 2D, then separated on the bench.*

Removal

1 Apply the handbrake, then jack up the front of the vehicle and support it on axle stands (see *Jacking and vehicle support*). Remove the engine compartment undertray and both front roadwheels.

2 Remove the battery as described in Chapter 5A.

3 On petrol engine models, disconnect the wiring from the engine management ECU with reference to Chapter 4A.

4 On diesel engine models, disconnect the wiring from the pre/post-heating control unit on the battery shield plate.

5 Remove the inlet air duct leading to the air cleaner.

6 Unbolt and remove the battery shield plate. The engine management ECU may be left attached, and the plate move to one side.

7 Disconnect the clutch cable and position it to one side with reference to Chapter 6.

8 Unscrew the mounting bolts and remove the TDC sensor from the top of the gearbox bellhousing **(see illustrations)**. Position the sensor to one side.

9 Unbolt the earth cables from the gearbox casing, then release the coolant hoses and wiring loom from the clips on the gearbox **(see illustrations)**.

10 Unscrew the gearbox-to-engine bolts but leave one upper bolt finger-tight until just before the gearbox is removed. Also unscrew and remove the front lower nut securing the gearbox to the engine, noting the location of the wiring harness support and bracket **(see illustrations)**.

11 Remove the right-hand driveshaft as described in Chapter 8 **(see illustration)**.

12 Remove the left-hand driveshaft together with the swivel hub with reference to Chapters 8

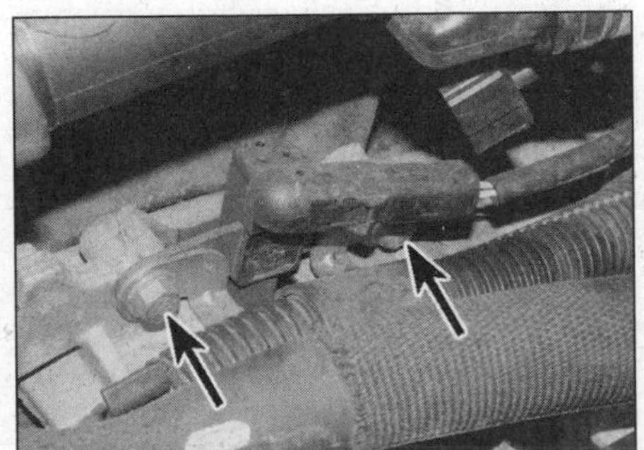

7.8a Unscrew the bolts . . .

7.8b . . . and remove the TDC sensor from the top of the gearbox bellhousing

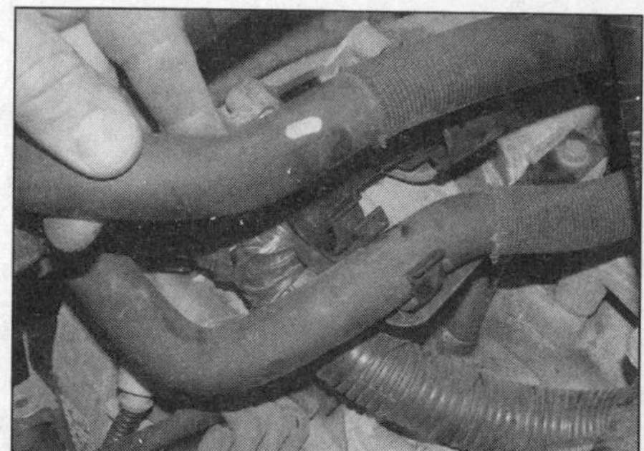

7.9a Release the hoses . . .

7.9b . . . and wiring loom from the retaining clips

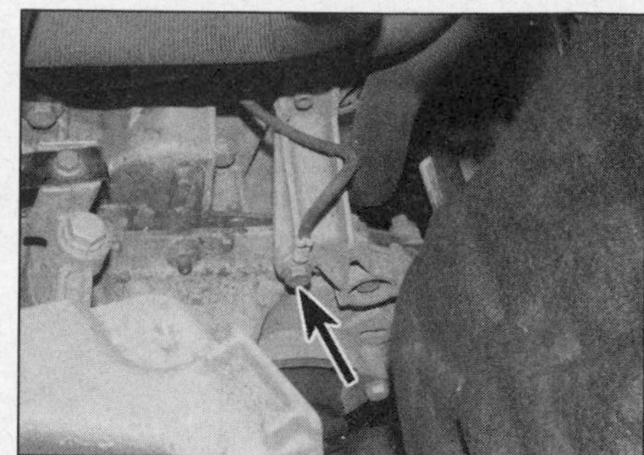

7.9c Earth cable on the rear . . .

7.9d . . . and front of the gearbox

7.10a Unscrew the lower front nut . . .

7.10b . . . and upper bolts securing the gearbox to the engine, noting the location of the wiring harness bracket

and 10. There is no need to separate the driveshaft from the swivel hub.

13 Unbolt and remove the subframe-to-inner wing panel brace from the left-hand side **(see illustration)**.

14 Remove the starter motor as described in Chapter 5A.

15 Disconnect the wiring from the reversing light switch and, where applicable, from the speedometer sensor. Note that later models with ABS are not fitted with a speedometer sensor – on these models, either unbolt and remove the left-hand ABS sensor or disconnect the wiring at the connector on the inner wing panel **(see illustrations)**.

7.10c Gearbox-to-engine upper mounting bolts

7.10d Bracket on the lower gearbox-to-engine bolts

7.11 Removing the right-hand driveshaft from the gearbox splined shaft

7.13 Subframe-to-inner wing panel brace

7.15a Removing the left-hand ABS sensor

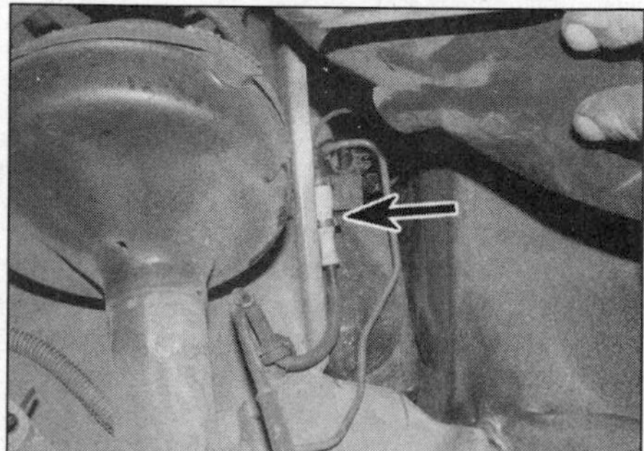

7.15b The ABS sensor wiring connector on the inner wing panel

7.15c Reversing light switch

7.18 Gearbox-to-engine lower rear mounting nut

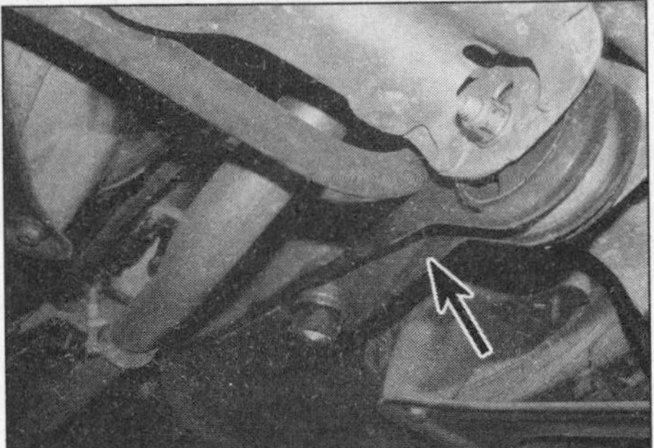

7.19 Engine rear mounting link

16 Remove the exhaust front downpipe as described in Chapter 4A or 4B.

17 Remove the gearchange mechanism control rod from the gear lever and gearbox with reference to Section 4.

18 Unscrew the nut securing the gearbox to the rear of the cylinder block. The nut is located above the right-hand gearbox output shaft **(see illustration)**.

19 Unscrew the engine rear mounting bolt securing the mounting link to the rear of the gearbox. Swivel the mounting link away from the gearbox **(see illustration)**.

20 Unbolt the coolant thermo-heater bracket from the gearbox **(see illustration)** – if necessary the heater housing can remain attached to the bracket which can then be tied to one side. Where applicable, unbolt the engine-to-gearbox tie rod bracket from the gearbox flange.

21 Unbolt the steering gear from the subframe with reference to Chapter 10. To improve access, temporarily wedge a block of wood between the rear of the engine and the bulkhead to tilt the engine forward.

22 Unbolt and remove the subframe rear support brackets, then support the front suspension subframe with a trolley jack and length of wood, unscrew the mounting bolts and lower the subframe to the ground. Use temporary threaded rods in the front mounting bolt holes to act as guides **(see illustrations)**.

23 Attach a suitable hoist or support bar to the left-hand end of the engine and take its weight **(see illustration)**.

24 Remove the left-hand engine mounting complete with brackets with reference to Chapter 2A, 2B or 2C. Also, unbolt the mounting bracket and centre pin from the top of the gearbox; this will prevent lowering the engine excessively **(see illustrations)**.

25 Lower the engine and gearbox as far as possible without straining the coolant hoses.

26 Support the gearbox with a trolley jack, then remove the final engine-to-gearbox bolt and, with the help of an assistant, withdraw the gearbox from the engine. Do not allow the gearbox to hang on the input shaft and keep the gearbox in line with the engine until the input shaft has cleared the clutch.

Refitting

27 Refitting is a reversal of removal, noting the following additional points.

a) *Before assembling the gearbox to the engine, make sure that the clutch release fork is correctly engaged with the release bearing. To ensure the fork remains engaged, tie it to the gearbox bellhousing.*

b) *Make sure that the location dowels are correctly positioned in the gearbox.*

c) *Apply a little high-melting-point grease to*

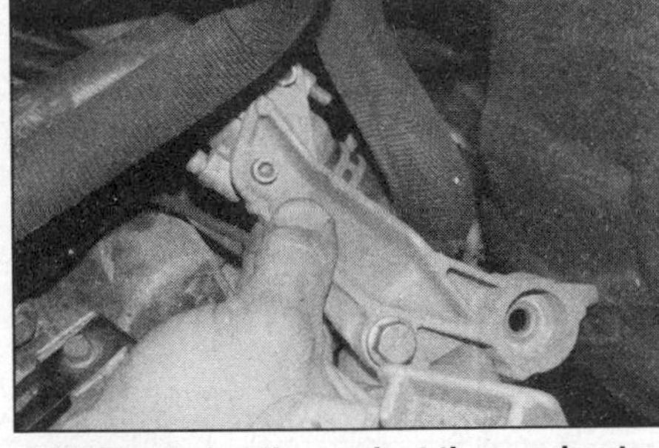

7.20 Removing the coolant thermo-heater bracket

7.22a Subframe rear support bracket

7.22b Fit threaded rods to the front mounting holes to act as guides

7.23 Support bar attached to the left-hand end of the engine

7.24a Left-hand engine mounting

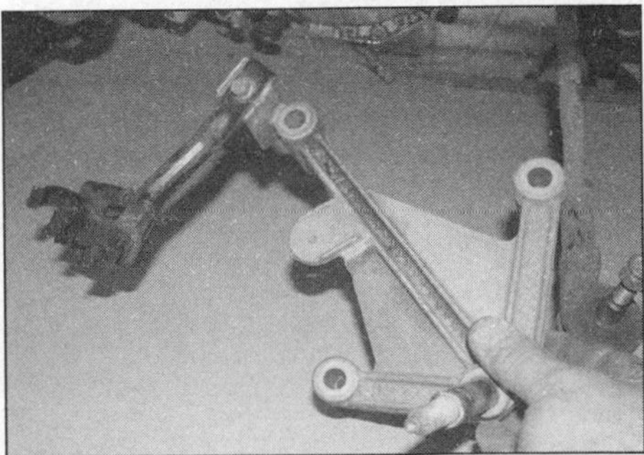

7.24b Removing the mounting bracket and centre pin from the top of the gearbox

the splines of the gearbox input shaft. Do not apply too much, otherwise there is the possibility of the grease contaminating the clutch friction disc.

d) Make sure that the locating dowel for the starter motor is correctly fitted.

e) Check the gearbox oil level with reference to Chapter 1A or 1B.

f) Tighten all nuts and bolts to the specified torque.

8 Manual gearbox overhaul – general information

Overhauling a manual gearbox is a difficult and involved job for the DIY home mechanic. In addition to dismantling and reassembling many small parts, clearances must be precisely measured and, if necessary, changed by selecting shims and spacers. Gearbox internal components are also often difficult to obtain, and in many instances, extremely expensive. Because of this, if the gearbox develops a fault or becomes noisy, the best course of action is to have the unit overhauled by a specialist repairer, or to obtain an exchange reconditioned unit.

Nevertheless, it is not impossible for the more experienced mechanic to overhaul a gearbox, provided the special tools are available and the job is done in a deliberate step-by-step manner so that nothing is overlooked.

The tools necessary for an overhaul include internal and external circlip pliers, bearing pullers, a slide-hammer, a set of pin punches, a dial test indicator, and possibly a hydraulic press. In addition, a large, sturdy workbench and a vice will be required.

During dismantling of the gearbox, make careful notes of how each component is fitted, to make reassembly easier and more accurate.

Before dismantling the gearbox, it will help if you have some idea what area is malfunctioning. Certain problems can be closely related to specific areas in the gearbox, which can make component examination and renewal easier. Refer to the *Fault finding* Section at the end of this manual for more information.

Chapter 7 Part B:
Automatic transmission

Contents

Degrees of difficulty

Easy, suitable for novice with little experience

Fairly easy, suitable for beginner with some experience

Fairly difficult, suitable for competent DIY mechanic

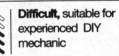

Difficult, suitable for experienced DIY mechanic

Very difficult, suitable for expert DIY or professional

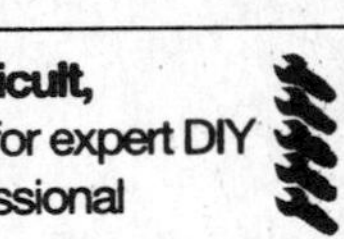

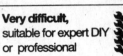

Specifications

General

Type	Electrically-controlled with four forward speeds and reverse. Final drive differential integral with transmission

Designation

All models	DP0

Ratios

1st	2.73 : 1
2nd	1.50 : 1
3rd	1.00 : 1
4th	0.71 : 1
Reverse	2.46 : 1
Final drive	3.04 : 1

Lubrication

Type	See *Lubricants and fluids*
Capacity (from dry)	6.0 litres

Torque wrench settings	**Nm**	**lbf ft**
Drain plug	25	18
Engine-to-transmission bolts/nuts	45	33
Fluid cooler bolt	50	37
Modular connector mounting plate bolts	20	15
Multi-function switch mounting bolts	10	7
Topping-up overflow	35	26
Torque converter-to-driveplate nuts	30	22

** Use new nuts*

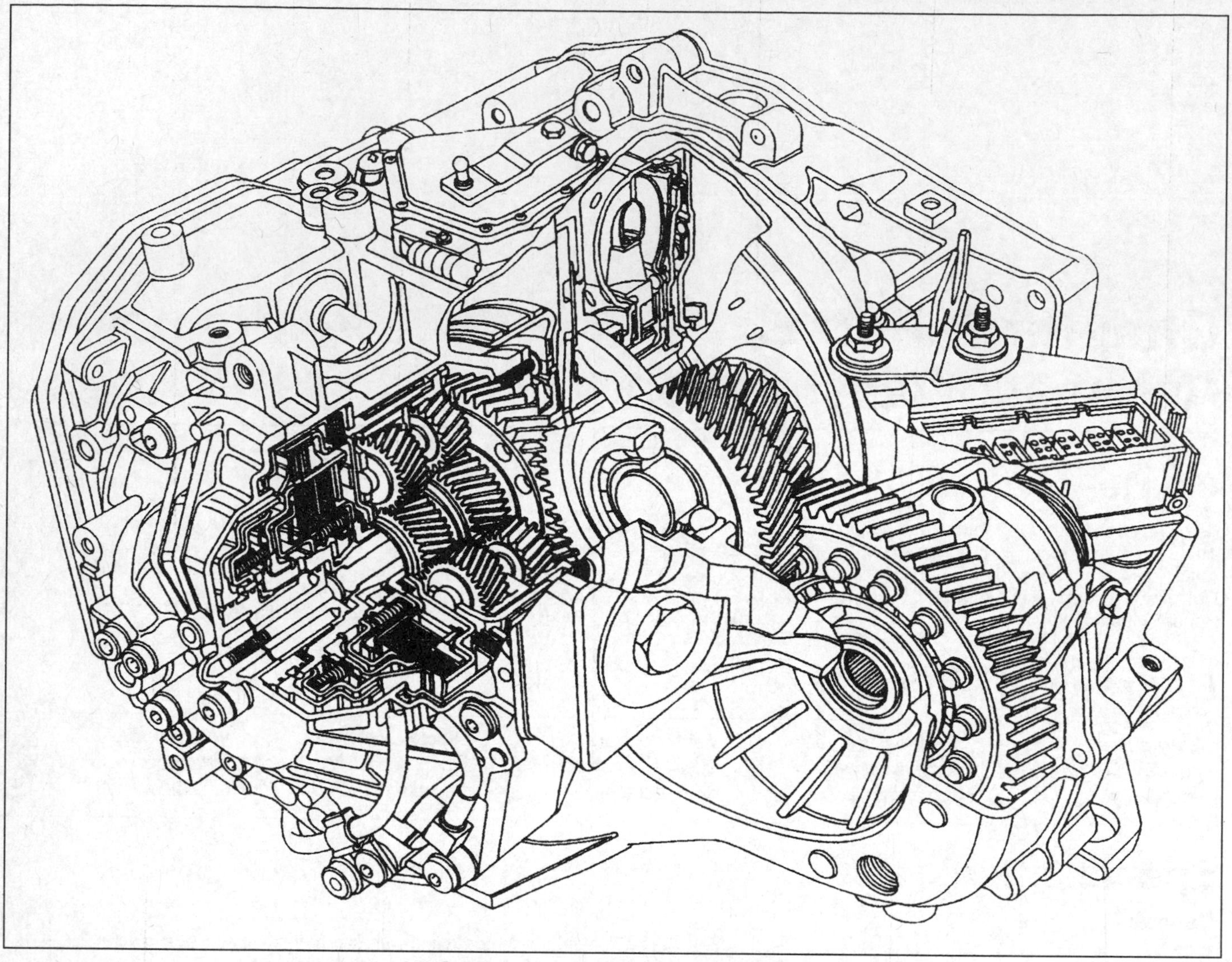

1.1 Cutaway view of the DP0 transmission unit

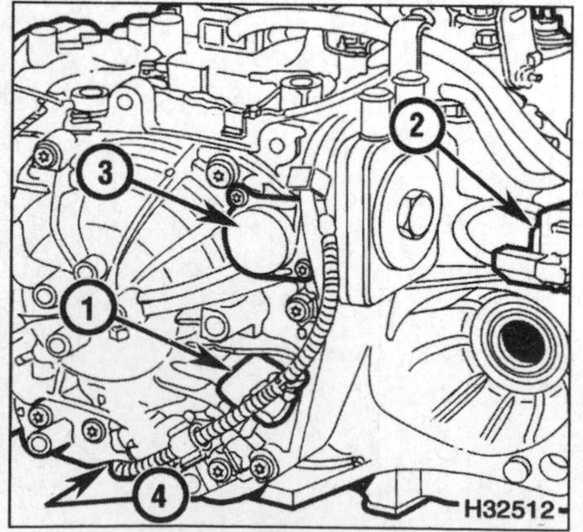

1.2 Sensor locations on the automatic transmission

1 *Input speed sensor*
2 *Output speed sensor*
3 *Fluid cooler flow control solenoid*
4 *Line pressure sensor*

1 General information

Automatic transmission models are fitted with the fully automatic four-speed, electronically controlled DP0-type transmission **(see illustration)**.

The transmission consists of a torque converter, an epicyclic geartrain, hydraulically-operated clutches and brakes, and an electronic control unit incorporated into the engine management ECU. Sensors fitted to the transmission include an input speed sensor, output speed sensor, fluid cooler flow control solenoid valve and a line pressure sensor **(see illustration)**.

The torque converter provides a fluid coupling between the engine and transmission, and acts as an automatic clutch, also providing a degree of torque multiplication when accelerating. The torque converter incorporates a lock-up function whereby the engine and transmission can be directly coupled by means of a small clutch unit inside the torque converter. The lock-up function is controlled by the ECU according to vehicle operating conditions.

The epicyclic geartrain provides the forward gears or reverse gear, depending on which of its component parts are held stationary or allowed to turn. The components of the geartrain are held or released by brakes and clutches which are activated by a hydraulic control unit. A fluid pump within the transmission provides the necessary hydraulic pressure to operate the brakes and clutches.

Impulses from switches and sensors connected to the transmission throttle and selector linkages are directed to the ECU computer module, which determines the ratio to be selected from the information received. The computer activates solenoid valves, which in turn open or close ducts within the hydraulic control unit. This causes the clutches and brakes to hold or release the various components of the geartrain, and provide the correct ratio for the particular engine speed or load. The information from the computer module can be overridden by use of the selector lever, and a particular gear can be held if required, regardless of engine speed. The selector lever also incorporates a shift-lock feature, which prevents the selector lever being moved from the P position unless the brake pedal is depressed.

The automatic transmission fluid is cooled by passing it through a cooler located on the top of the transmission. Coolant from the cooling system passes through the cooler.

Due to the complexity of the automatic transmission, any repair or overhaul work must be left to a Renault dealer with the necessary special equipment for fault diagnosis and repair. The contents of the following Sections are therefore confined to supplying general information, and any service information and instructions that can be used by the owner.

2 Automatic transmission fluid - draining and refilling

Note: *The transmission is a 'sealed-for-life' unit and fluid renewal is not required. The following procedure should only be necessary if there is any reason to believe that the fluid may be contaminated, or if repair work requiring the fluid to be drained is to be carried out. The transmission fluid filling and level checking procedure is particularly complicated, and the home mechanic would be well-advised to take the vehicle to a Renault dealer for the draining and refilling work carried out. To ensure accuracy, special test equipment is necessary to measure the fluid temperature when carrying out the level check. However, the following procedure is given for those who have access to this equipment.*

Draining

1 Take the vehicle on a short run, to warm the transmission up to normal operating temperature.
2 Park the car on level ground, then switch off the ignition and apply the handbrake firmly. Jack up the front of the car and support it securely on axle stands (see *Jacking and vehicle support*). Note that, when refilling and checking the fluid level, the car must be level to ensure accuracy.
3 Remove the engine compartment undertray.
4 Position a suitable container under the transmission. Unscrew the transmission drain plug and allow the fluid to drain completely into the container. Note that the drain plug and level checking plug are incorporated into one unit – the drain plug is the larger of the two hexagonal headed plugs forming the draining/level checking unit **(see illustrations)**.

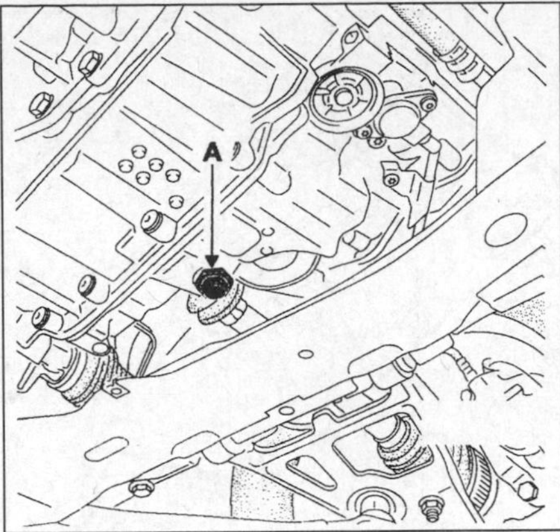

2.4a Combined drain plug and level checking plug unit (A)

Warning: If the fluid is hot, take precautions against scalding.

5 When the fluid has finished draining, clean the drain plug threads and those of the transmission casing. Fit a new sealing washer to the drain plug, and refit the plug to the transmission, tightening it securely.

Refilling

6 Refer to Chapter 4A and remove the air inlet duct from the engine compartment for access to the transmission filler plug. Unscrew the filler plug from the top of the transmission **(see illustration)**. Add 3.5 litres of the specified fluid to the transmission via the filler plug opening, using a clean funnel with a fine-mesh filter, then refit the plug.
7 Connect the Renault XR25 test meter to the diagnostic socket, and enter D14 then #04. With the selector lever in Park, run the engine at idle speed until the fluid temperature, as shown on the test meter, reaches 60° ± 1.0°C.
8 With the engine still running, unscrew the level plug from the centre of the draining/level checking unit. Allow the excess fluid to run out into a calibrated container drop-by-drop, then refit the plug. The amount of fluid should be more than 0.1 litre; if it is not, the fluid level in the transmission is incorrect.
9 If the level is incorrect, add an extra 0.5 litre of the specified fluid to the transmission, as described in paragraph 6. Allow the transmission to cool down to 50°C, then repeat the checking procedure again as described in the previous paragraphs. Repeat the procedure as required until more than the specified amount of fluid is drained as described in the previous paragraphs, indicating that the transmission fluid level is correct, then securely tighten the level plug. Refit the engine undertray and the air cleaner duct.
10 With the XR25 test meter still connected, enter the command G74* then the date to reset the oil ageing counter in the electronic control unit. Disconnect the test meter on completion.

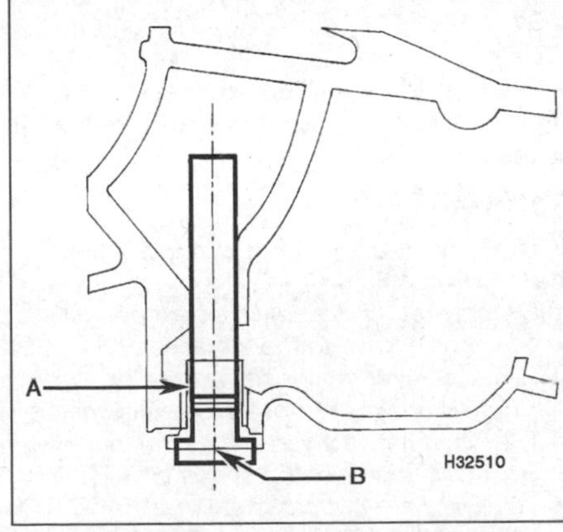

2.4b Cross-section of the combined drain/level plug unit

A Drain plug
B Level (overflow) plug

3 Selector cable - adjustment

1 Move the selector lever inside the car to the N position.
2 Disconnect the selector cable end fitting from the multi-function switch on top of the transmission. To improve access to the cable, remove the air cleaner inlet duct as described in Chapter 4A.
3 Check that the multi-function switch is in the N position, and if necessary set it accordingly.
4 Depress the tab on the side of the cable end fitting and suitably retain it in the released position.
5 Reconnect the selector cable to the multi-function switch then release the tab on the end fitting to lock the cable. Refit the air cleaner inlet duct as described in Chapter 4A.
6 Check that the selector lever moves freely, and that the starter motor will only operate with P or N selected. Also check that the Park function operates correctly.

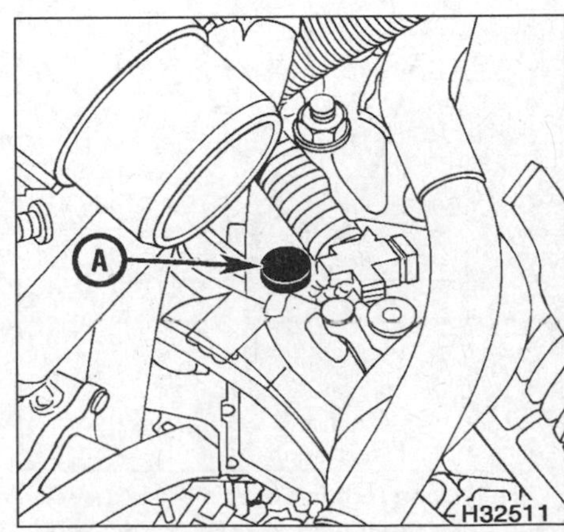

2.6 Transmission fluid filler plug (A)

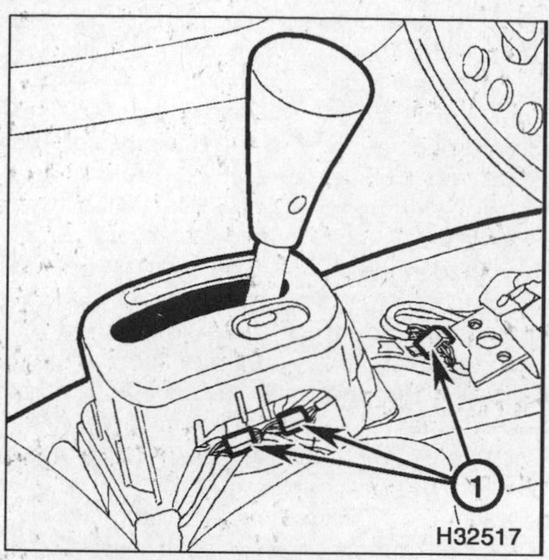

4.4 Wiring connectors (1) on the selector lever assembly

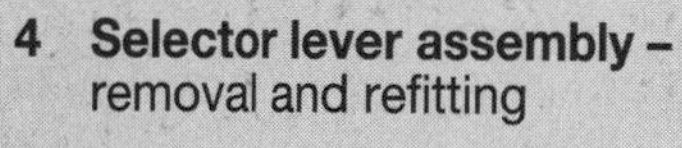

4 Selector lever assembly – removal and refitting

Removal

1 Apply the handbrake, then jack up the front of the vehicle and support it on axle stands (see *Jacking and vehicle support*).

2 Disconnect the battery negative (earth) lead and position it away from the terminal (refer to *Disconnecting the battery* in the Reference Section).

3 Remove the centre console as described in Chapter 11.

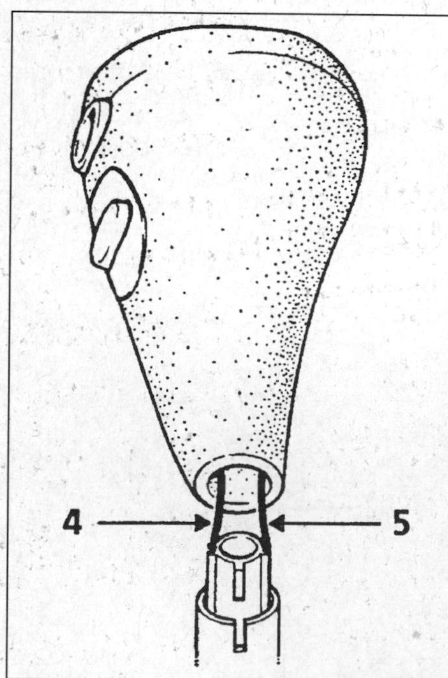

4.10 When refitting the selector lever knob, take great care to ensure the switch wires (4 and 5) are not crossed and are correctly routed down the lever guides

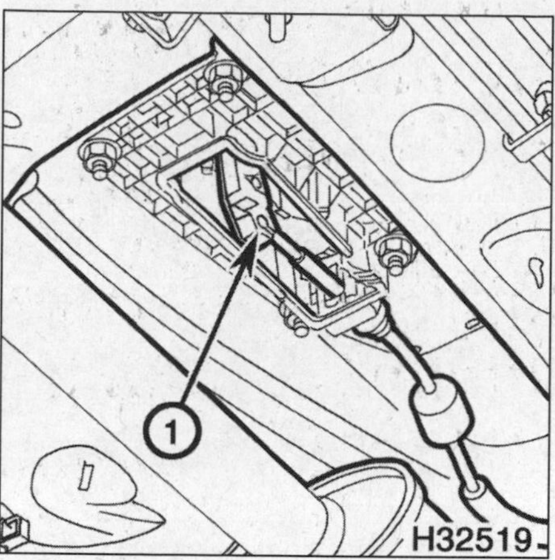

4.7a Selector cable end fitting (1) on the bottom of the selector lever

4 Disconnect the wiring from the selector lever assembly. There are two connectors under the right-hand side of the assembly, and one connector located just in front of the assembly **(see illustration)**.

5 Working under the vehicle, unclip the exhaust downpipe from its mounting, then unbolt the heat shields from the underbody for access beneath the selector assembly.

6 Remove the protector plate, then unscrew and remove the four mounting nuts securing the assembly to the floor. Recover the spacers.

7 Release the cable end fitting from its balljoint on the bottom of the lever, then prise out the clip and remove the outer cable from the assembly. Withdraw the assembly from under the vehicle **(see illustrations)**.

8 If necessary, the knob may be removed from the lever. To do this, undo the screw securing the knob to the lever and lift the knob to access the two wires. Identify the location of each wire, then disconnect them from the connector so that the knob may be removed separate. The wire locations are as follows.

Track	Colour
A1	Black
A2	Black
B1	White
B2	Light brown

9 Examine the selector lever assembly for signs of wear or damage and renew if necessary.

Refitting

10 Refitting is the reverse of removal, noting the following points.

a) Prior to refitting, apply a smear of multi-purpose grease to the surfaces of the selector lever mechanism.

*b) If the knob was removed, carefully feed the sport mode switch wires down the guides in the selector lever making sure the wires are not crossed **(see illustration)**. Seat the control knob in position and tighten its retaining screw. Crimp new wiring connectors onto the ends of the switch wires and locate the connectors in the connector.*

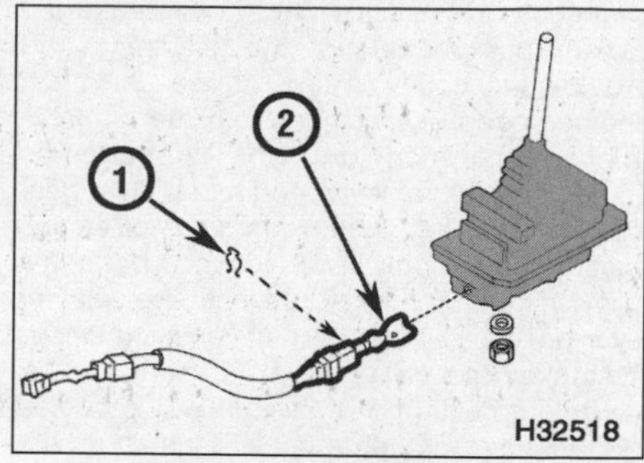

4.7b Selector cable retaining clip (1) and inner cable end fitting (2)

c) On completion check the operation of the selector lever and, if necessary, adjust the cable as described in Section 3.

5 Selector cable – removal and refitting

Removal

1 Remove the selector lever assembly as described in Section 4.

2 Working in the engine compartment, remove the air cleaner inlet duct with reference to Chapter 4A.

3 Disconnect the selector cable end fitting from the multi-function switch on top of the transmission. Release the outer cable from the support bracket by turning the two locking rings in opposite directions. **Do not** move the orange ring as the locking rings are released. Note that if the orange ring breaks during removal, this will not adversely affect the operation of the cable and is not grounds for cable renewal.

4 Release the selector cable from all relevant retaining clips and withdraw it from under the vehicle.

5 Examine the cable for worn end fittings or a damaged outer casing, and for signs of fraying of the inner wire. The cable inner wire should move smoothly and easily through the outer casing. If the adjuster mechanism is thought to be faulty the cable must be renewed.

Refitting

6 Refitting is a reversal of removal, and adjust the cable as described in Section 3.

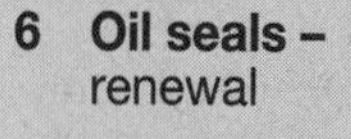

6 Oil seals – renewal

Differential oil seals

1 Disconnect the battery negative lead (refer to *Disconnecting the battery* in the Reference Chapter).

2 Apply the handbrake, then jack up the front

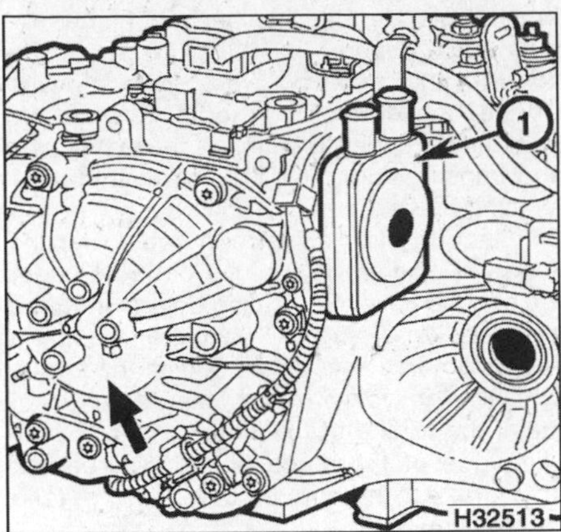

7.1 The fluid cooler (1) is located on the rear left-hand side of the transmission

Arrow indicates identification mark

of the car and support it on axle stands (see *Jacking and vehicle support*). Remove the relevant roadwheel.

3 Drain the transmission fluid as described in Section 2.

4 Referring to Chapter 8, disconnect the complete driveshaft assembly from the transmission on the side being worked on. Note that it is not necessary to remove the driveshaft completely, as the shaft can be left attached to the hub assembly and freed from the transmission as the hub assembly is pulled outwards. **Note:** *Do not allow it to hang down under its own weight as this could damage the constant velocity joints/gaiters.*

5 Note the fitted depth of the old seal, then carefully lever the seal out of position using a flat-bladed screwdriver. Be careful not to drop the seal or its inner spring into the automatic transmission.

6 Wipe clean the oil seal seating in the casing and apply a smear of oil to the seal lip. Making sure the seal lip is facing inwards, carefully ease the new seal into position. Press the seal squarely into the transmission until it is positioned at the same depth as the original was prior to removal. If necessary the seal can be tapped into position using a piece of metal tube or a socket which bears only on the hard outer edge of the seal.

7 Refit the driveshaft assembly with reference to Chapter 8.

8 Refill the transmission with new fluid as described in Section 2.

9 Refit the roadwheel, lower the car to the ground and tighten the wheel bolts to the specified torque (Chapter 1A).

10 Reconnect the battery negative cable.

Torque converter seal

11 Remove the transmission from the engine as described in Section 9.

12 Remove the retaining strap and carefully slide the torque converter from the transmission shaft. Be prepared for fluid loss as the converter is removed.

13 Using a flat-bladed screwdriver carefully lever the seal out from the centre of the torque converter, taking great care not to mark the metal bush.

14 Press the new seal squarely into position making sure its sealing lip is facing inwards.

15 Lubricate the lip of the seal with clean transmission fluid and carefully slide the converter onto the transmission shaft.

16 Make sure the torque converter is correctly engaged with the transmission shaft splines then refit the transmission as described in Section 9.

7 Fluid cooler – removal and refitting

Removal

1 The fluid cooler is located on the rear left-hand side of the transmission **(see illustration)**. To gain access to the cooler, remove the air cleaner and inlet duct as described in Chapter 4A.

2 To minimise coolant loss, clamp the coolant hoses on either side of the fluid cooler. Alternately, drain the cooling system as described in Chapter 1A.

3 Loosen the clips and disconnect the hoses from the fluid cooler – be prepared for some coolant spillage. Wash off any spilt coolant immediately with cold water, and dry the surrounding area before proceeding further.

4 Slacken and remove the mounting bolt(s), and remove the fluid cooler from the transmission. There will be some loss of fluid, so some clean rags should be placed around the cooler to absorb spillage. Make sure that dirt is prevented from entering the hydraulic system.

5 Remove the sealing ring from each mounting bolt and the sealing rings fitted between the cooler and transmission. Discard all sealing rings; new ones must be used on refitting.

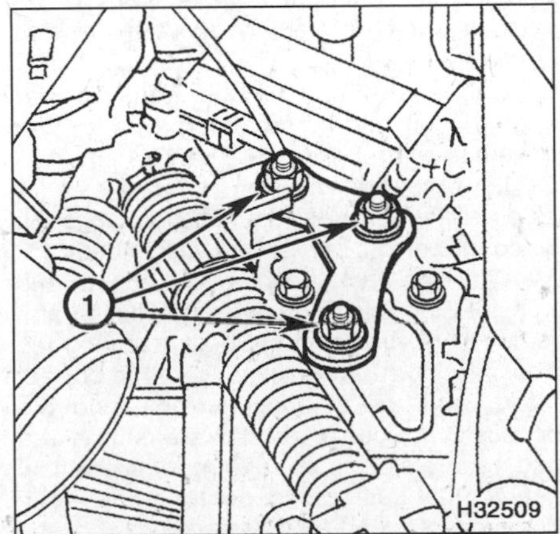

8.8 Modular connector mounting plate bolts (1)

Refitting

6 Lubricate the new seals with clean automatic transmission fluid, then fit the two new seals to the base of the fluid cooler, and a new seal to each mounting bolt.

7 Locate the fluid cooler on the top of the transmission housing, ensuring its lower seals remain in position. Refit the mounting bolt(s) and tighten them to the specified torque.

8 Reconnect the coolant hoses to the fluid cooler, and securely tighten their retaining clips. Remove the hose clamps.

9 Refit the air cleaner and inlet duct with reference to Chapter 4A.

10 On completion, top-up the cooling system and check the automatic transmission fluid level as described in Section 2.

8 Multi-function switch – removal, refitting and adjustment

Removal

1 Disconnect the battery negative lead (refer to *Disconnecting the battery* in the Reference Chapter).

2 The multi-function switch informs the electronic control unit of the selector lever position, prevents the starter motor operating when the transmission is in gear and also controls the reversing lights. The switch is located on the top of the transmission, below the air cleaner inlet duct.

3 Move the selector lever to position D.

4 To gain access to the switch, remove the air cleaner inlet duct with reference to Chapter 4A.

5 Pull out the locking tab and disconnect the transmission wiring harness modular connector.

6 Disconnect the selector cable end fitting from the multi-function switch lever.

7 Remove the lever then undo the two multi-function switch mounting bolts.

8 Undo the three mounting bolts and release the modular connector mounting plate from the top of the transmission **(see illustration)**.

9 Trace the switch wiring back to the modular connector plate and disconnect the 12-pin socket from the connector plate. Remove the multi-function switch from the transmission.

Refitting

10 Reconnect the multi-function switch wiring to the modular connector plate, then refit the plate and attach the connector. Tighten the mounting bolts.

11 Position the multi-function switch on the transmission and refit the two mounting bolts, finger tight only at this stage.

12 Reconnect the selector cable end fitting to the multi-function switch lever.

13 With the gear selector lever and multi-function switch in position N, connect an ohmmeter across the two test terminals on the side of the multi-function switch.

14 Turn the switch body until the internal switch contacts close and 0 ohms is indicated on the ohmmeter. Hold the switch body in this position and tighten the two retaining bolts.
15 Refit the air cleaner inlet duct with reference to Chapter 4A, then reconnect the battery negative lead.
16 Check that the starter motor will only operate with P or N selected.

9 Automatic transmission – removal and refitting

Note: *If a new transmission and/or torque converter is being fitted, note that the ECU auto-adaptive values must be reset by a Renault dealer using the XR25 test equipment.*

Removal

1 Remove the battery and battery tray as described in Chapter 5A.
2 Apply the handbrake, then jack up the front of the vehicle and support it on axle stands (see *Jacking and vehicle support*). Remove the engine undertray and both front roadwheels.
3 Remove the air cleaner assembly and the inlet duct as described in Chapter 4A.
4 Disconnect the selector cable end fitting from the multi-function switch on top of the transmission. Release the outer cable from the support bracket by turning the two locking rings in opposite directions. **Do not** move the orange ring as the locking rings are released. Note that if the orange ring breaks during removal, this will not adversely affect the operation of the cable and is not grounds for cable renewal.
5 Pull out the locking tab and disconnect the transmission wiring harness modular connector. To prevent entry of dust and dirt, wrap a polythene bag over the connector.
6 Unscrew the engine wiring harness support bolts, and remove the support.
7 Unbolt the TDC sensor from the top of the transmission and place to one side.
8 Clamp the coolant hoses on either side of the fluid cooler. Alternately, drain the cooling system as described in Chapter 1A. Loosen the clips and disconnect the hoses from the cooler.
9 Disconnect the oxygen sensor wiring at the connector.
10 Remove both the left-hand and right-hand driveshafts as described in Chapter 8.
11 Unscrew the bolts securing the steering gear to the subframe and tie it to the bulkhead making sure that, where applicable, the power steering fluid pipes are not strained.
12 Disconnect the wiring from the input and output speed sensors on the transmission. Note that later models with ABS are not fitted with an output sensor – on these models, either unbolt and remove the left-hand ABS sensor or disconnect the wiring at the connector on the inner wing panel.

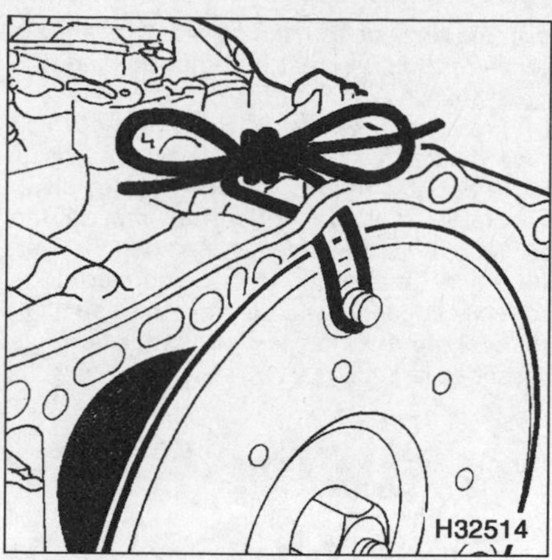

9.26 Torque converter secured in the transmission with string tied through the TDC sensor aperture

13 Remove the starter motor as described in Chapter 5A.
14 Unbolt the earthing cable from the transmission.
15 Remove the rear engine mounting as described in the relevant part of Chapter 2.
16 Remove the exhaust front downpipe as described in Chapter 4A.
17 Support the weight of the subframe on trolley jacks.
18 Support the weight of the engine with a suitable hoist attached to the lifting eyes.
19 Support the radiator by tying it to the engine compartment front crossmember, then unbolt and remove the subframe, lowering it to the ground.
20 The torque converter is attached to the driveplate by three nuts which are accessed through the starter motor aperture. Turn the engine as required to position the nuts in the aperture, then unscrew and remove them. **Note:** *The nuts must be renewed every time they are removed.* Where applicable, unbolt the access plate from the bottom of the transmission.
21 Support the weight of the transmission on a trolley jack, or (preferably) on a transmission cradle.
22 Unbolt and remove the transmission/engine left-hand mounting from the transmission and inner body panel.
23 Lower the transmission and engine as far as possible, but take care not to damage the air conditioning compressor (where fitted).
24 With the jack positioned beneath the transmission taking the weight, slacken and remove the remaining nut/bolts securing the transmission to the engine. Note the correct fitted positions of each nut/bolt, and the necessary brackets, as they are removed to use as a reference on refitting. Make a final check that all components have been disconnected, and are positioned clear of the transmission so that they will not hinder the removal procedure.
25 With the bolts removed, make sure the torque converter is pushed fully onto the transmission shaft then move the trolley jack and transmission to the left, to free it from its locating dowels.
26 Once the transmission is free, lower the jack and manoeuvre the unit out from under the car. Remove the locating dowels from the transmission or engine if they are loose, and keep them in a safe place. Secure the torque converter in position by bolting a length of metal bar to one of the housing holes, or by tying one of the studs to the TDC sensor aperture on the top of the housing **(see illustration)**.

Refitting

27 The transmission is refitted using a reversal of the removal procedure, bearing in mind the following points.

a) *Remove the retaining bar and ensure that the torque converter is pushed fully onto the transmission. Apply a smear of high-melting point grease (Renault recommend the use of Molykote BR2) to the converter centring ring.*
b) *Ensure the locating dowels are correctly positioned prior to installation and clean the torque converter-to-driveplate stud threads.*
c) *Align the torque converter studs with the driveplate holes as the transmission is refitted. Apply thread locking compound (Renault recommend the use of Loctite Frenbloc) to the new retaining nuts and tighten them to the specified torque.*
d) *Tighten all nuts and bolts to the specified torque (where given).*
e) *Refit the driveshafts as described in Chapter 8.*
f) *Connect the selector cable and adjust as described in Sections 5 and 3.*
g) *On completion, top-up/refill the transmission with the specified type and quantity of lubricant, as described in Section 2.*

10 Automatic transmission overhaul – general information

In the event of a fault occurring with the transmission, it is first necessary to determine whether it is of an electrical, mechanical or hydraulic nature, and to do this special test equipment is required. It is therefore essential to have the work carried out by a Renault dealer if a transmission fault is suspected.

Do not remove the transmission from the car for possible repair before professional fault diagnosis has been carried out, since most tests require the transmission to be in the vehicle.

Chapter 7 Part C: Sequential gearbox

Contents

Degrees of difficulty

Easy, suitable for novice with little experience 	**Fairly easy,** suitable for beginner with some experience 	**Fairly difficult,** suitable for competent DIY mechanic	**Difficult,** suitable for experienced DIY mechanic	**Very difficult,** suitable for expert DIY or professional

Specifications

General

Type	Five forward speeds (all synchromesh) and reverse, selected automatically or manually. Final drive differential integral with main gearbox

Designation

Code	JH1

Gear ratios

1st	3.4 : 1
2nd	1.9 : 1
3rd	1.3 : 1
4th	1.0 : 1
5th	0.8 : 1
Reverse	3.6 : 1
Final drive	4.1 : 1

Gearbox lubrication

Type	See *Lubricants and fluids* on page 0•18
Capacity	3.4 litres

Hydraulic control fluid

Type	See *Lubricants and fluids* on page 0•18

Torque wrench settings

	Nm	lbf ft
Engine to gearbox tie bar	65	48
Gearbox bellhousing to engine	45	33
Rear engine mounting to gearbox	See Chapter 2A, 2B or 2C	
Starter motor mounting bolt	45	33

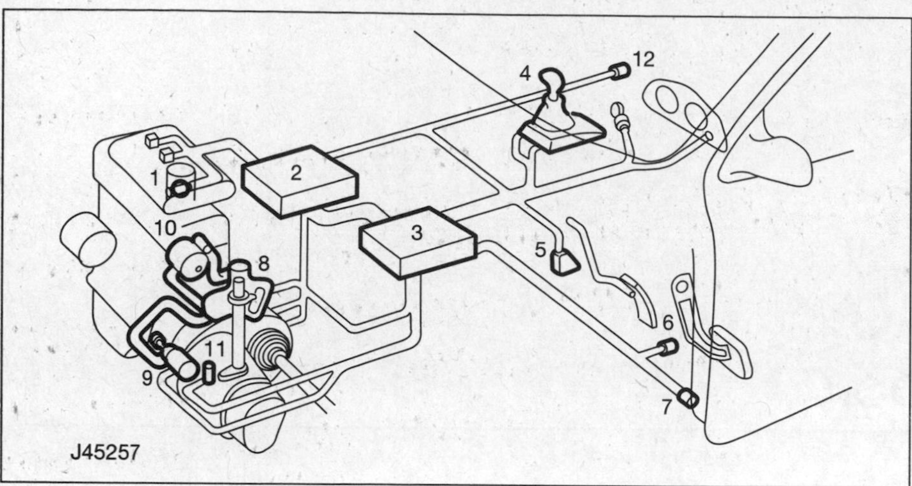

1.1a Diagram of the sequential gearbox control system

1 *Motorised throttle unit*
2 *Engine management ECU*
3 *Sequential gearbox computer*
4 *Selector lever*
5 *Accelerator pedal position sensor/load sensor*
6 *Footbrake pedal contact*
7 *Front door contacts*
8 *Select and change actuator*
9 *Clutch actuator*
10 *Power unit*
11 *Primary speed sensor*
12 *Handbrake lever contact*

1 General information and precautions

The Quickshift-5 sequential gearbox is fitted as an option to models with the D4F petrol engine, and is essentially an electro-hydraulically-controlled conventional manual gearbox. Clutch engagement and gear-changing is controlled by a specific computer which also acts as a link between the accelerator pedal and the engine; the computer also controls engine torque in order to give smooth gearchanges. The hydraulic control unit consists of two actuators; one for gearchanging and selection, and the other for clutch engagement. No clutch pedal is fitted, however, and in manual mode, gearchanges are made by a switch located in the base of the gear lever. The driver can select either automatic or manual mode by a switch located on the side of the gear lever knob. There is a comprehensive interlock safety system which includes brake pedal, hand-brake and door contacts **(see illustrations)**.

In automatic mode, the system takes into consideration the weight of the car, the road surface and driving style when deciding the correct moment to change gear. The accelerator pedal is fitted with a 'kickdown' switch which enables maximum performance to be obtained from the engine.

An acoustic warning will sound if the car is held on a hill without depressing the footbrake or applying the handbrake, as in this situation the clutch disc friction surfaces could be overheated and worn excessively. The warning will also sound if an attempt is made to open the driver's door with a gear selected and the ignition switched on.

The system has two relays located in the left-hand front corner of the engine compartment; one is for the hydraulic pump and the other for the reversing lights. There are three fuses, located in the engine compartment fusebox; a 5 amp fuse supplies the control area of the sequential gearbox computer, a 20 amp fuse supplies the power area of the computer, and a 30 amp fuse supplies the hydraulic pump.

Due to the complexity of the sequential gearbox control system, any repair or overhaul work must be left to a Renault dealer with the necessary special equipment for fault diagnosis and repair. The contents of the following Sections are therefore confined to supplying general information and minor work that can be carried out by the owner.

Caution: Do not attempt to remove any of the peripheral components from the gearbox, as most of them require that the accumulator is first discharged using the special Renault diagnostic tool.

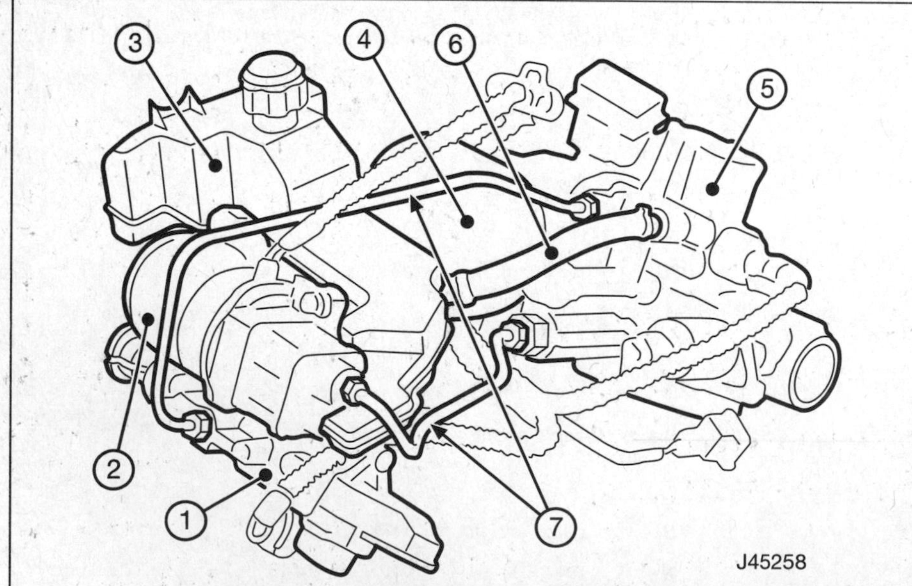

1.1b Hydraulic unit

1 *Clutch actuator*
2 *Pump*
3 *Fluid reservoir*
4 *Accumulator*
5 *Actuator module*
6 *Low pressure pipe*
7 *High pressure pipe*

2 Gearbox oil – draining and refilling

Refer to the information given in Chapter 7A for the conventional manual gearbox.

3 Hydraulic fluid – topping-up

1 Topping-up the hydraulic fluid is not a routine maintenance procedure, and will not normally be required unless fluid has been lost as a result of a fractured high- or low-pressure pipe, or faulty hydraulic component.
2 If all the fluid has been drained or lost, add fresh fluid to the reservoir until it is 32.0 to 38.0 mm above the MIN level mark.
3 Switch on the ignition. After 15 seconds, the accumulator will be fully pressurised and the fluid level will drop to the MIN mark.

4 Clutch position sensor – removal and refitting

Removal

1 Disconnect the battery negative lead (refer to *Disconnecting the battery* in the Reference Chapter).

2 Apply the handbrake, then jack up the front of the vehicle and support it on axle stands (see *Jacking and vehicle support*).

3 Disconnect the wiring from the clutch position sensor located on the front of the gearbox **(see illustration)**.

4 Unbolt and remove the sensor.

Refitting

5 Refitting is a reversal of removal, but make sure that it is free to rotate on its shaft. After fitting the sensor, the sequential gearbox control system should be reprogrammed and checked for faults by a Renault dealer.

5 Engagement position sensor – removal and refitting

Removal

1 Disconnect the battery negative lead (refer to *Disconnecting the battery* in the Reference Chapter).

2 Apply the handbrake, then jack up the front of the vehicle and support it on axle stands (see *Jacking and vehicle support*).

3 Disconnect the wiring from the engagement position sensor located on the left-hand side of the gearbox **(see illustration)**.

4 Unbolt and remove the sensor.

Refitting

5 Refitting is a reversal of removal, but make sure that it is free to rotate on its shaft. After fitting the sensor, the sequential gearbox control system should be reprogrammed and checked for faults by a Renault dealer.

6 Accelerator pedal potentiometer – removal and refitting

Removal

1 Disconnect the battery negative lead (refer to *Disconnecting the battery* in the Reference Chapter).

2 Working inside the car, disconnect the wiring from the accelerator pedal potentiometer located on top of the pedal assembly **(see illustration)**.

3 Disconnect the control lever.

4 Unscrew the mounting bolts and withdraw the potentiometer from the bulkhead.

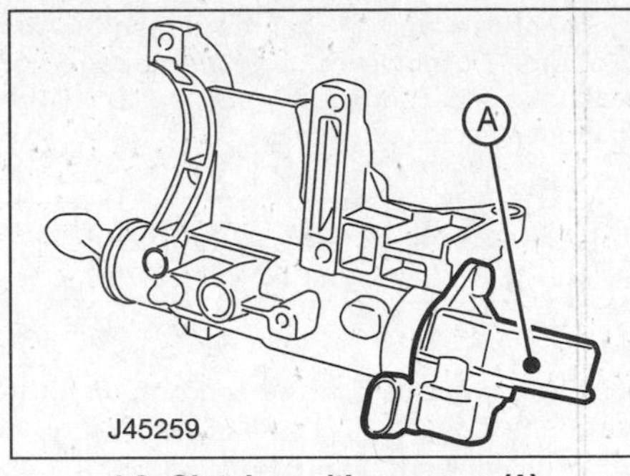

4.3 Clutch position sensor (A)

Refitting

5 Refitting is a reversal of removal.

7 Sequential gearbox computer – removal and refitting

Note: *The sequential gearbox computer is electronically-coded for the vehicle to which it is fitted. If it is being removed to enable a new unit to be fitted, the new unit must be reprogrammed by a Renault dealer using dedicated equipment.*

Removal

1 The sequential gearbox computer is located together with the engine management ECU in the left-hand rear corner of the engine compartment, behind the battery. First disconnect the battery negative lead (refer to *Disconnecting the battery* in the Reference Section).

2 Where applicable, unclip the power steering hydraulic fluid reservoir from the bulkhead and position it to one side.

3 Unscrew the mounting nuts on the battery tray.

4 Disconnect the wiring connector, then tilt the unit slightly rearwards to release the studs, and lift it to release the location tab.

Refitting

5 Refitting is a reverse of the removal procedure ensuring that the wiring connector is securely reconnected. If a new unit has been fitted, it must be reprogrammed by a Renault dealer.

8 Gear lever – removal and refitting

Removal

1 Disconnect the battery negative lead (refer to *Disconnecting the battery* in the Reference Chapter).

2 Unclip the gear lever console cover, followed by the console front plate.

3 Disconnect the wiring from the gear lever.

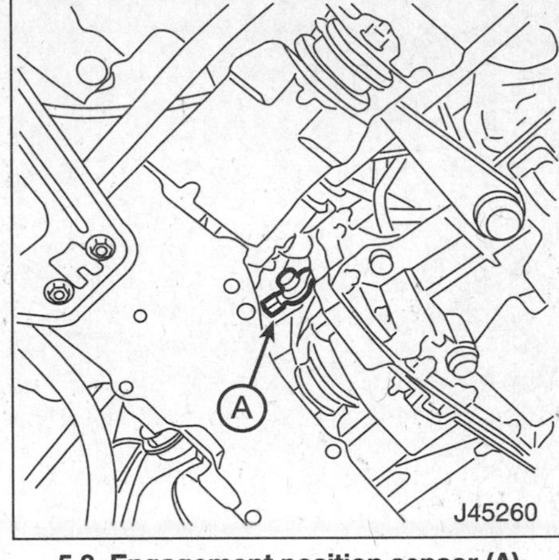

5.3 Engagement position sensor (A)

4 Unscrew the four baseplate bolts, and withdraw the gear lever assembly from inside the car.

Refitting

5 Refitting is a reversal of removal.

9 Oil seals – renewal

Refer to the information given in Chapter 7A for the conventional manual gearbox.

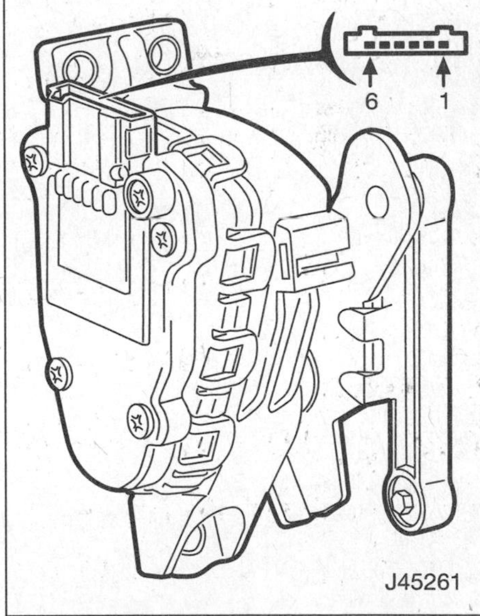

6.2 Accelerator pedal potentiometer

Socket numbers indicate tracks
1 Track 2 earth
2 Track 1 earth
3 Track 1 signal
4 Track 1 supply
5 Track 2 supply
6 Track 2 signal

10 Reversing light switch – testing, removal and refitting

Refer to the information given in Chapter 7A for the conventional manual gearbox.

11 Sequential gearbox – removal and refitting

The procedure is similar to that for the conventional manual gearbox described in Chapter 7A, however, note the location of each electrical wire disconnected to ensure correct refitting.

12 Sequential gearbox overhaul – general information

In the event of a fault occurring with the sequential gearbox, it is first necessary to determine whether it is of an electrical, mechanical or hydraulic nature, and to do this, special test equipment is required. It is therefore essential to have the work carried out by a Renault dealer if a transmission fault is suspected. The system incorporates its own self-diagnosis program which can only be accessed by a Renault dealer using dedicated equipment.

Do not remove the gearbox from the car for possible repair before professional fault diagnosis has been carried out, since most tests require the gearbox to be in the vehicle.

Chapter 8
Driveshafts

Contents

Degrees of difficulty

Easy, suitable for novice with little experience 

Fairly easy, suitable for beginner with some experience 

Fairly difficult, suitable for competent DIY mechanic

Difficult, suitable for experienced DIY mechanic 

Very difficult, suitable for expert DIY or professional

Specifications

General

Driveshaft type	Solid steel shafts, splined to inner and outer constant velocity joints, vibration damper fitted on some right-hand driveshafts
Lubricant type/specification	Special grease supplied in sachets with gaiter kits – joints are otherwise pre-packed with grease and sealed

Torque wrench settings	Nm	lbf ft
Driveshaft retaining nut (ENKO self-locking nut with integral washer)*	280	207
Left-hand driveshaft gaiter retaining plate bolts (manual and sequential gearbox)	25	18
Roadwheel bolts	90	66
Strut lower mounting bolts	105	77
Track rod end balljoint retaining nut	37	27

** Use new nuts*

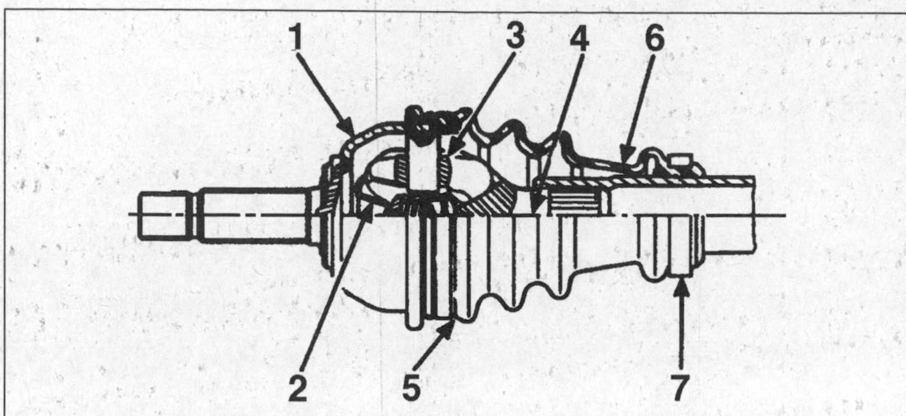

1.2 Sectional view of the spider-and-yoke type outer constant velocity joint

1 Outer member
2 Thrust plunger
3 Driveshaft spider
4 Driveshaft
5 Outer retaining clip
6 Gaiter
7 Inner retaining clip

1 General information

1 Drive is transmitted from the differential to the front wheels by means of two driveshafts.

2 Both driveshafts are fitted with a constant velocity (CV) joint at their outer ends, which are of the spider-and-yoke or ball-and-cage type **(see illustration)**. Each joint has an outer member, which is splined at its outer end to accept the wheel hub and is threaded so that it can be fastened to the hub by a large nut. The joint contains a spring-loaded plunger, which engages with the inner member. The complete assembly is protected by a thermoplastic flexible gaiter secured to the driveshaft and joint outer member.

3 On vehicles equipped with a manual or sequential gearbox, a different inner constant velocity joint arrangement is fitted to each driveshaft. On the right-hand side, the driveshaft is splined to engage with a tripod joint, containing needle roller bearings and cups. The tripod joint is free to slide within the yoke of the joint outer member, which is splined and retained by a roll-pin to the differential side gear stub shaft (on most later models, the roll-pin is deleted, and the splined end of the driveshaft joint is sprung to retain it in the differential side gear stub shaft). A rubber flexible gaiter secured to the driveshaft and outer member protects the complete assembly. On the left-hand side, the driveshaft also engages with a tripod joint, but the yoke in which the tripod joint is free to slide is an integral part of the differential side gear. On this side, the gaiter is secured to the transmission casing with a retaining plate, and to a ball-bearing on the driveshaft with a retaining clip. The bearing allows the driveshaft to turn within the gaiter, which does not revolve.

TOOL TiP

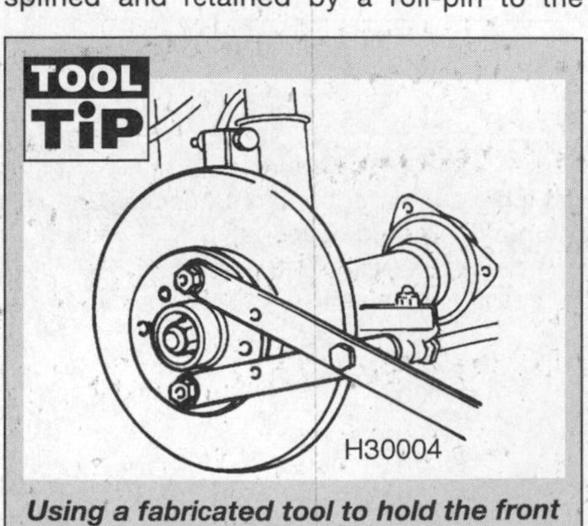

Using a fabricated tool to hold the front hub stationary whilst the driveshaft nut is slackened.

2 Driveshaft – removal and refitting

Note: *On some earlier models, there may be a roll-pin fitted to the inner joint of the driveshaft where it fits onto the differential splined shaft. Where applicable, new roll-pins will be required on refitting.*

Removal

1 Remove the wheel trim/hub cap (as applicable), then slacken the driveshaft nut with the vehicle resting on its wheels. Also slacken the wheel bolts.

2 Chock the rear wheels of the car, firmly apply the handbrake, then jack up the front of the car and support it on axle stands (see *Jacking and vehicle support*). Remove the appropriate front roadwheel.

3 On models equipped with ABS, remove the wheel sensor as described in Chapter 9, Section 23.

4 Slacken and remove the driveshaft retaining nut. If the nut was not slackened with the wheels on the ground (see paragraph 1), refit at least two roadwheel bolts to the front hub, tightening them securely, then have an assistant firmly depress the brake pedal to prevent the front hub from rotating, whilst you slacken and remove the driveshaft retaining nut. Alternatively, a tool can be fabricated from two lengths of steel strip (one long, one short) and a nut and bolt; the nut and bolt forming the pivot of a forked tool **(see Tool Tip)**.

5 Unscrew the two bolts securing the brake caliper assembly to the swivel hub, and slide the caliper assembly off the disc. Using a piece of wire or string, tie the caliper to the front suspension coil spring, to avoid placing any strain on the hydraulic brake hose.

6 Slacken and remove the nut securing the steering gear track rod end balljoint to the swivel hub. Release the balljoint tapered shank using a universal balljoint separator **(see illustration)**.

7 Slacken and remove the two nuts from the bolts securing the swivel hub to the suspension strut, noting that the nuts are positioned on the rear side of the strut. Withdraw the upper bolt, but leave the lower bolt in position at this stage **(see illustration)**. Now proceed as described under the relevant sub-heading.

Left-hand driveshaft – manual or sequential gearbox

8 Drain the gearbox oil as described in Chapter 7A.

9 Slacken and remove the three bolts securing the flexible gaiter retaining plate to the side of the gearbox **(see illustration)**.

10 Pull the top of the swivel hub outwards until the driveshaft tripod joint is released from its yoke; be prepared for some oil spillage as the joint is withdrawn **(see illustration)**. Be

2.6 Use a balljoint separator to release the track rod end balljoint from the swivel hub

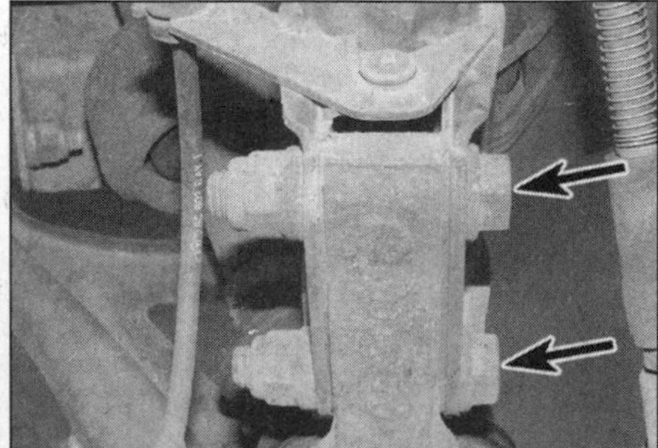

2.7 Note the fitted direction of the bolts (arrowed)

2.9 On the left-hand driveshaft, remove the flexible gaiter retaining plate bolts . . .

2.10 . . . and release the tripod joint from the manual and sequential gearbox

2.11 Using an extractor to press the driveshaft out of the front hub

careful that the rollers on the end of the tripod do not fall off.

11 Remove the lower bolt securing the swivel hub to the suspension strut. Taking care not to damage the driveshaft gaiters, release the outer constant velocity joint from the hub and remove the driveshaft. Note that it is likely the joint will be a tight fit in the hub splines (see Note at the start of this Section). Try tapping the joint out of position using a hammer and a soft metal drift, while an assistant supports the hub assembly. If this fails to move the joint, a suitable puller/extractor will be required to draw the hub assembly off the driveshaft end **(see illustration)**. While the driveshaft is removed, support the hub assembly by refitting the bolts to the base of the strut.

Right-hand driveshaft – all models

12 Where applicable, rotate the driveshaft until the double roll-pin, securing the inner constant velocity joint to the side gear shaft, is visible. Using a hammer and a 5 mm diameter pin punch, drive out the double roll-pin **(see illustration)**. New roll-pins must be used on refitting.

13 Pull the top of the swivel hub outwards until the inner constant velocity joint splines are released from the side gear shaft. Remove the sealing ring (where fitted) from the side gear shaft splines.

14 Remove the driveshaft as described in paragraph 11.

Left-hand driveshaft – automatic transmission

15 Pull the top of the swivel hub outwards, and disengage the inner constant velocity joint from the differential. Carefully use a lever to disengage the shaft as required.

16 Remove the driveshaft as described in paragraph 11.

Refitting

17 All new driveshafts supplied by Renault are equipped with cardboard or plastic protectors, to prevent damage to the gaiters. Even the slightest knock to the gaiter can puncture it, allowing the entry of water or dirt at a later date, which may lead to the premature failure of the joint. If the original driveshaft is being refitted, it is worthwhile making up some cardboard protectors as a precaution. They can be held in position with elastic bands. The protectors should be left on the driveshafts until the end of the refitting procedure.

Left-hand driveshaft – manual or sequential gearbox

18 Wipe clean the side of the gearbox and the outer constant velocity joint splines.

19 Insert the tripod joint into the side gear yoke, keeping the driveshaft horizontal as far as possible. Align the gaiter retaining plate with its bolt holes. Refit the retaining bolts, and tighten them to the specified torque. Ensure that the gaiter is not twisted.

20 Ensure both the hub and driveshaft outer constant velocity joint splines are clean and dry.

21 Move the top of the swivel hub inwards, at the same time engaging the driveshaft with the hub.

22 Slide the hub fully onto the driveshaft splines, then insert the two suspension strut mounting bolts from the front side of the strut. Refit the washers and nuts to the rear of the bolts, and tighten them to the specified torque (see Chapter 10 Specifications).

23 Fit the new driveshaft 'Enko type' **(see illustration)** retaining nut, tightening it by hand only at this stage.

24 Reconnect the steering track rod balljoint to the swivel hub, and tighten its retaining nut to the specified torque (see Chapter 10 Specifications).

25 Clean the threads of the caliper bracket mounting bolts, and coat them with thread locking compound (Renault recommend Loctite Frenbloc – available from your Renault dealer). Slide the caliper into position, making sure the pads pass either side of the disc, and tighten the caliper bracket bolts to the specified torque setting (see Chapter 9 Specifications).

2.12 Where applicable on the right-hand driveshaft, tap out the roll-pin with a suitable pin punch

26 Using the method employed during removal to prevent the hub from rotating, tighten a new driveshaft retaining nut to the specified torque. Alternatively, lightly tighten the nut at this stage, and tighten it to the specified torque once the vehicle is resting on its wheels again.

27 Check that the hub rotates freely, then remove the protectors (where fitted) from the driveshaft, taking great care not to damage the flexible gaiters.

28 Refit the roadwheel. Lower the car to the ground and tighten the roadwheel bolts to the specified torque. If not already done, also tighten the driveshaft retaining nut to the specified torque.

29 Refill the gearbox with the specified type and amount of oil, and check the level using the information given in Chapter 1A or 1B.

Right-hand driveshaft – all models

30 Ensure that the inner constant velocity joint and side gear shaft splines are clean and dry. Apply a smear of molybdenum disulphide grease to the splines (Renault recommend the use of Molykote BR2 – available from your Renault dealer). Where necessary, fit a new

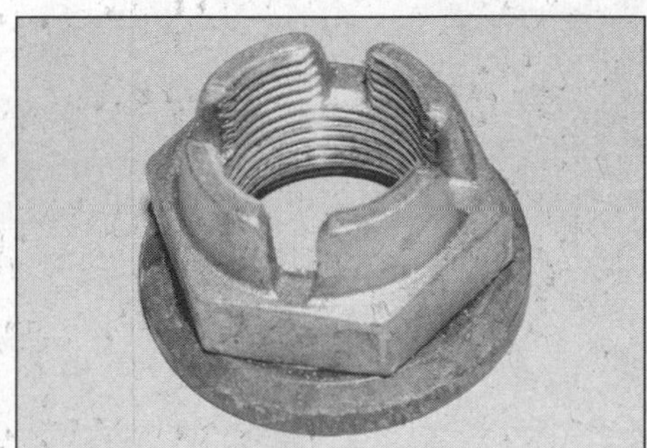
2.23 A new 'Enko type' driveshaft securing nut will be needed

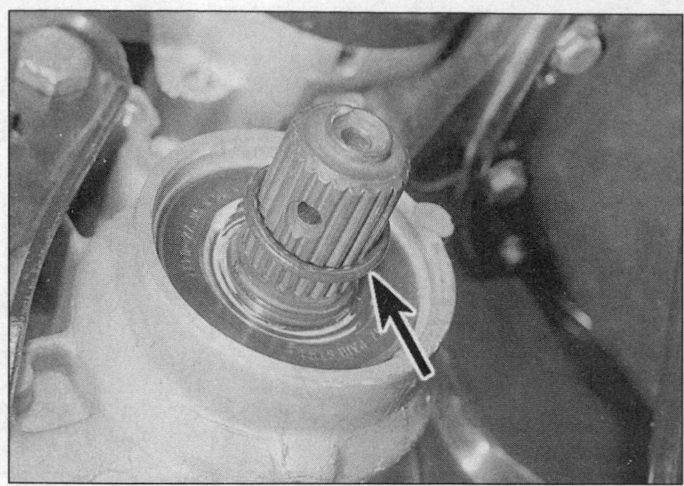
2.30 Where applicable, fit the new O-ring (arrowed) onto the side gear shaft . . .

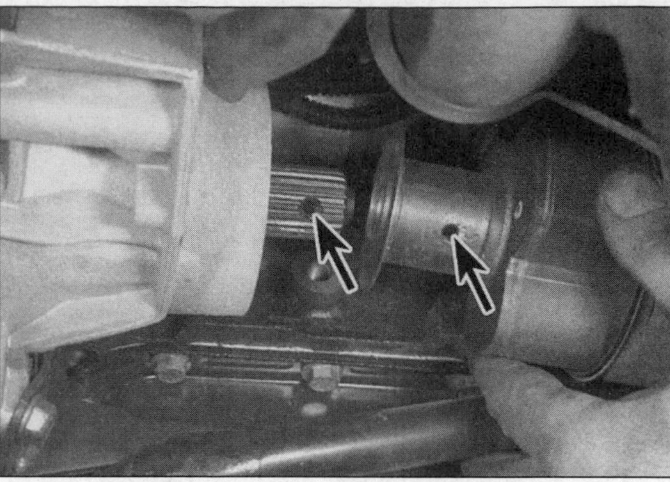
2.31 . . . and engage the driveshaft, ensuring that the roll-pin holes (arrowed) are correctly aligned

sealing ring over the end of the side gear shaft, and slide the O-ring along the shaft until it abuts the transmission oil seal **(see illustration)**.

31 Engage the driveshaft splines with those of the side gear shaft, where required, make sure that the roll-pin holes are in alignment **(see illustration)**. Slide the driveshaft onto the side gear shaft until the roll-pin holes are aligned.

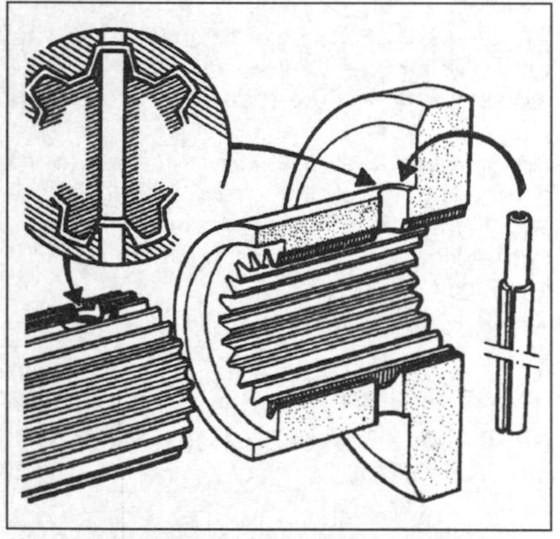
2.32a Right-hand driveshaft inner constant velocity joint roll-pin arrangement

2.32b On the right-hand driveshaft, tap the roll-pins securely into position and seal their ends with sealing compound

32 Where applicable, drive in new roll-pins with their slots 180° apart, then seal the ends of the pins with sealing compound (Renault recommend the use of CAF 4/60 THIXO or Rhodoseal 5661 – available from your Renault dealer) **(see illustrations)**.

33 Carry out the procedures described in paragraphs 20 to 28.

Left-hand driveshaft – automatic transmission

34 Ensure that the inner constant velocity joint and side gear shaft splines are clean and dry. Apply a smear of molybdenum disulphide grease to the splines (Renault recommend the use of Molykote BR2 – available from your Renault dealer).

35 Engage the driveshaft inner constant velocity joint with the side gear shaft splines.

36 Carry out the procedures described in paragraphs 20 to 28.

3 Outer constant velocity joint gaiter (manual and sequential gearbox) – renewal

Note: *The spider-and-yoke type joint is the most common type used. Check on the availability of a joint repair kit before removal.*

3.5 Removing the vibration damper from the driveshaft (where applicable)

The type of retaining clip for the gaiter may vary, check the fitment of the clip is correct according to the type supplied with the kit.

1 Remove the driveshaft as described in Section 2.

2 Cut through the gaiter retaining clip(s) or release the retaining spring and inner collar (as applicable), then slide the gaiter down the shaft to expose the outer constant velocity joint.

3 Scoop out as much grease as possible from the joint, and determine which type of constant velocity joint is fitted. Proceed as described under the relevant sub-heading.

Spider-and-yoke type joint

Note: *On some right-hand driveshafts, the vibration damper is an integral part of the driveshaft. If the gaiter is damaged on this type, then the complete driveshaft will need renewing.*

4 Remove the inner constant velocity joint, bearing and gaiter (as applicable), as described in Section 4 or 5 of this Chapter.

5 Where a vibration damper is fitted, check to see if it can be removed from the driveshaft. If it can, then clearly mark the position of the damper on the driveshaft, and use a puller or press to remove it from the inner end of the driveshaft, noting which way around it is fitted **(see illustration)**. Ensure that the legs of the puller or support plate rest only on the damper inner rubber bush, otherwise the damper will distort and break away from the outer metal housing as it is removed.

6 Slide the outer constant velocity joint gaiter off the inner end of the driveshaft.

7 Clean the outer constant velocity joint using paraffin or a suitable solvent, and dry it thoroughly. Carry out a visual inspection of the joint.

8 Check the driveshaft spider and outer member yoke for signs of wear, pitting or scuffing on their bearing surfaces. Also check that the outer member pivots smoothly and easily, with no traces of roughness.

9 If inspection reveals signs of wear or

3.9 Renault driveshaft repair kit

Note: Retaining clips may vary with supplier

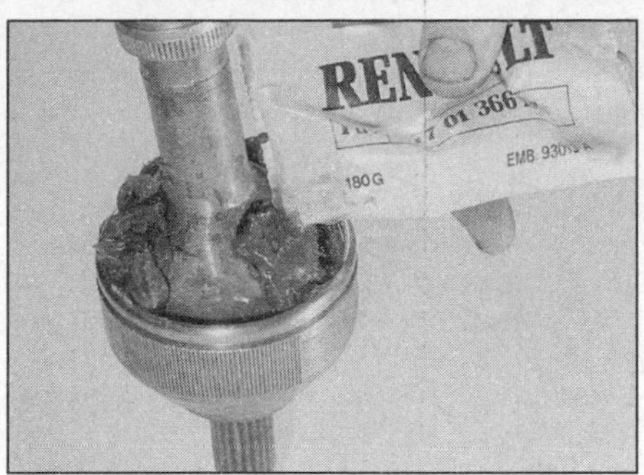
3.11 Pack the joint with the grease supplied in the repair kit . . .

3.12 . . . then slide the gaiter into position over the joint

damage, it will be necessary to renew the driveshaft complete, since no components are available separately. If the joint components are in satisfactory condition, obtain a repair kit consisting of a new gaiter, retaining clips, and the correct type and quantity of grease **(see illustration)**.

10 Tape over the splines on the inner end of the driveshaft, then carefully slide the outer gaiter onto the shaft.

11 Pack the joint with the grease supplied in the repair kit. Work the grease well into the joint, and fill the gaiter with any excess **(see illustration)**.

12 Ease the gaiter over the joint, and ensure that the gaiter lips are correctly located in the grooves on the driveshaft and on the joint **(see illustration)**. With the coupling aligned with the driveshaft, lift the lip of the gaiter to equalise the air pressure.

13 Fit the large metal retaining clip to the gaiter. Remove any slack in the gaiter retaining clip by carefully compressing the raised section of the clip. In the absence of the special tool, a pair of pincers may be used. Secure the small retaining clip using the same procedure **(see illustrations)**. Check that the constant velocity joint moves freely in all directions before proceeding further.

14 To refit the vibration damper (where applicable), lubricate the driveshaft with a solution of soapy water. Press or drive the vibration damper along the shaft, using a tubular spacer which bears only on the damper inner bush, until it is aligned with the mark made prior to removal.

15 Refit the inner constant velocity joint components as described in Section 4 or 5 (as applicable), then refit the driveshaft to the vehicle as described in Section 2.

Ball-and-cage type joint

16 Using circlip pliers, expand the joint internal circlip. At the same time, tap the exposed face of the ball hub with a mallet to separate the joint from the driveshaft. Slide off the gaiter and rubber collar.

17 With the constant velocity joint removed from the driveshaft, clean the joint using paraffin, or a suitable solvent, and dry it thoroughly. Carry out a visual inspection of the joint.

18 Move the inner splined driving member from side-to-side, to expose each ball in turn at the top of its track. Examine the balls for cracks, flat spots or signs of surface pitting.

19 Inspect the ball tracks on the inner and outer members. If the tracks have widened, the balls will no longer be a tight fit. At the same time, check the ball cage windows for wear or cracking between the windows.

20 If on inspection any of the constant velocity joint components are found to be worn or damaged, it will be necessary to renew the complete driveshaft assembly, since no components are available separately. If the joint is in satisfactory condition, obtain a repair kit from your Renault dealer consisting of a new gaiter, rubber collar, retaining spring, and the correct type and quantity of grease.

21 Tape over the splines on the end of the driveshaft, then slide the rubber collar and gaiter onto the shaft. Locate the inner end of the gaiter on the driveshaft, and secure it in position with the rubber collar.

22 Remove the tape, then slide the constant velocity joint coupling onto the driveshaft until the internal circlip locates in the driveshaft groove.

23 Check that the circlip holds the joint securely on the driveshaft, then pack the joint with the grease supplied. Work the grease well into the ball tracks, and fill the gaiter with any excess.

24 Locate the outer lip of the gaiter in the groove on the joint outer member. With the coupling aligned with the driveshaft, lift the lip of the gaiter to equalise the air pressure. Secure the gaiter in position with the large retaining clip as described in paragraph 13.

25 Check that the constant velocity joint moves freely in all directions, then refit the driveshaft to the vehicle as described in Section 2.

4 Right-hand driveshaft inner gaiter (manual and sequential gearbox) – renewal

Note: *On these models, two different types of inner constant velocity joint are used on the right-hand driveshaft: type RC 462 and type RC462 E. The RC 462 type has a roll-pin to hold the driveshaft onto the splines of the differential. The RC462 E joint has no roll-pin, this is held in position by a spring, fitted internally in the joint. Check on the availability of a joint repair kit before removal.*

1 Remove the driveshaft as described in Section 2.

2 Release the large outer retaining clip and the inner retaining clip, then slide the gaiter down the shaft to expose the joint.

3 Slide the outer member off the tripod joint. Be prepared to hold the rollers in place (where applicable), otherwise they may fall off the tripod ends as the outer member is withdrawn. If necessary, secure the rollers in place using tape after removal of the outer member. The rollers are matched to the tripod joint stems, and it is important that they are not interchanged.

4 On the RC 462 E Type joint (no roll-pin

3.13a Fit the large gaiter retaining clip . . .

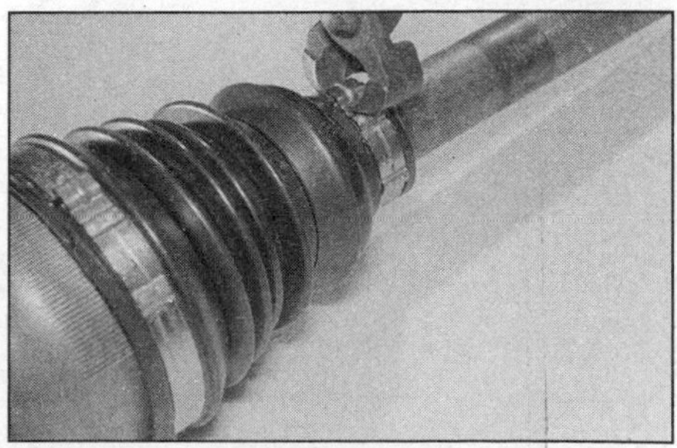
3.13b . . . and secure it in position by carefully compressing the raised section of the clip

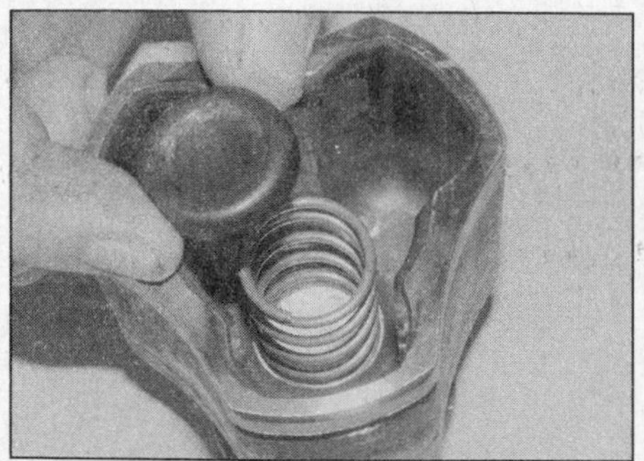
4.4 Spring and cup is fitted to the joint without a roll-pin

4.5 Remove the circlip . . .

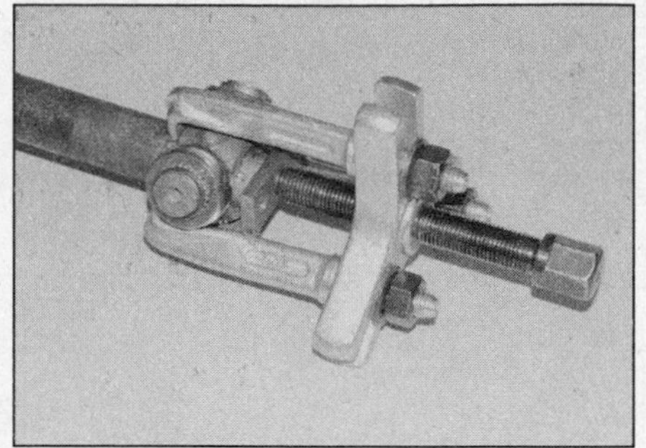
4.6 . . . and withdraw the tripod joint, using a puller if required

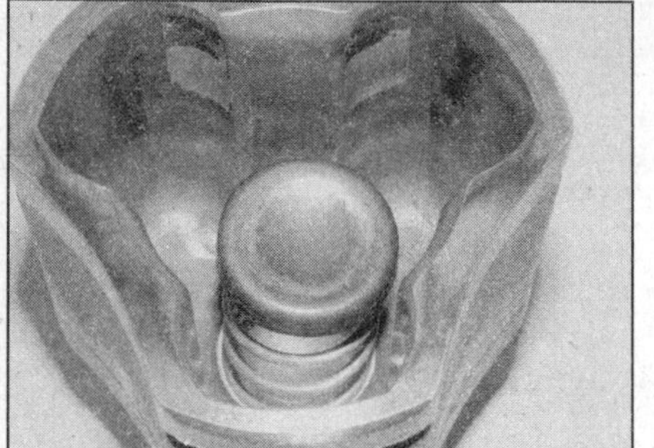
4.13a Refit the spring and cup into the outer part of the joint . . .

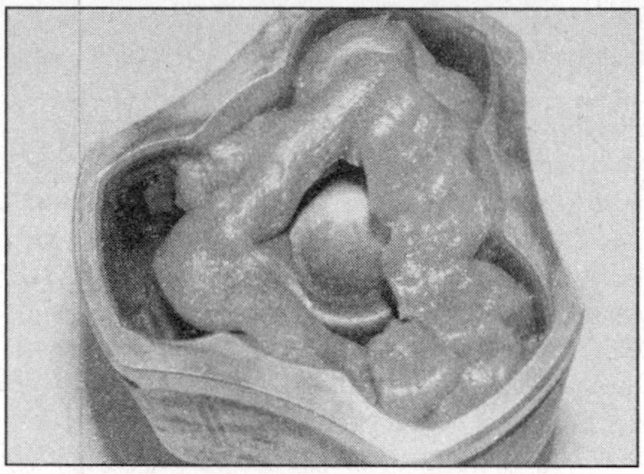

4.13b . . . and pack with the grease supplied in the repair kit

type), remove the spring and cup from inside the outer member of the joint **(see illustration)**.

5 Using circlip pliers, extract the circlip securing the tripod joint to the driveshaft **(see illustration)**. Note that on some models, the joint may be staked in position; if so, relieve the staking using a file. Mark the position of the tripod in relation to the driveshaft, using a dab of paint or a punch.

6 The tripod joint can now be removed **(see illustration)**. If it is tight, draw the joint off the driveshaft end using a puller. Ensure that the legs of the puller are located behind the joint inner member and do not contact the joint rollers. Alternatively, support the inner member of the tripod joint, and press the shaft out using a hydraulic press, again ensuring that no load is applied to the joint rollers.

7 With the tripod joint removed, slide the gaiter and inner retaining collar off the end of the driveshaft.

8 Wipe clean the joint components, taking care not to remove the alignment marks made on dismantling. **Do not** use paraffin or other solvents to clean this type of joint.

9 Examine the tripod joint, rollers and outer member for any signs of scoring or wear. Check that the rollers move smoothly on the tripod stems. If wear is evident, the tripod joint and roller assembly can be renewed, but it is not possible to obtain a new outer member. Obtain a new gaiter, retaining clips and a quantity of the special lubricating grease. These parts are available in the form of a repair kit from your Renault dealer.

10 Tape over the splines on the end of the driveshaft, then carefully slide the inner retaining clip and gaiter onto the shaft.

11 Remove the tape, then, aligning the marks made on dismantling, engage the tripod joint with the driveshaft splines. Use a hammer and soft metal drift to tap the joint onto the shaft, taking great care not to damage the driveshaft splines or joint rollers. Alternatively, support the driveshaft, and press the joint into position using a hydraulic press and suitable tubular spacer which bears only on the joint inner member.

12 Secure the tripod joint in position with the circlip, ensuring that it is correctly located in the driveshaft groove. Where no circlip is fitted, secure the joint in position by staking the end of the driveshaft in three places, at intervals of 120°, using a hammer and punch.

13 Refit the spring and cup in the outer member, then evenly distribute the grease contained in the repair kit around the tripod joint and inside the outer member **(see illustrations)**.

14 Pack the gaiter with the remainder of the grease and slide the two halves of the joint together **(see illustrations)**.

4.14a Pack the gaiter and tripod joint with the remainder of the grease . . .

4.14b . . . and slide the two halves of the joint together

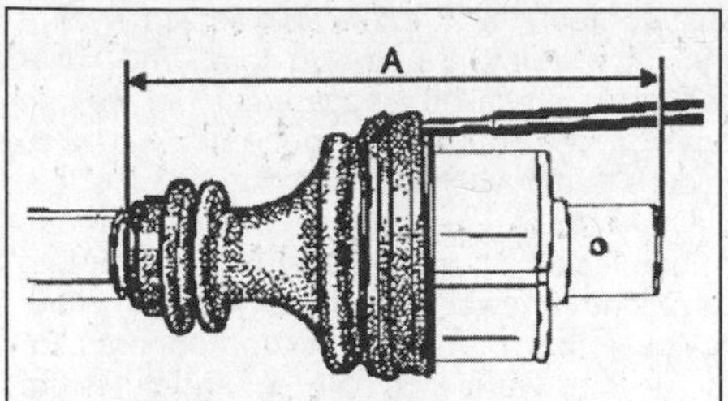

4.17a Fitting dimension for the right-hand driveshaft inner joint gaiter with roll-pin – RC 462-type joint

A = 190 ± 1 mm

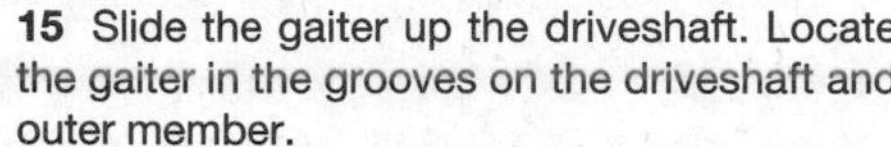

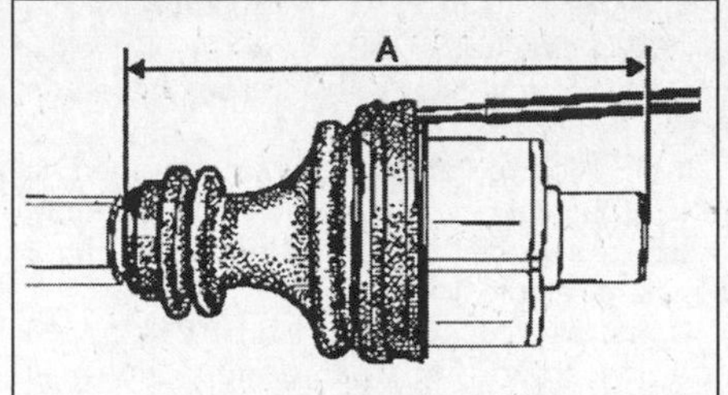

4.17b Fitting dimension for the right-hand driveshaft inner joint gaiter without roll-pin – RC 462 E-type joint

A = 203 ± 1 mm

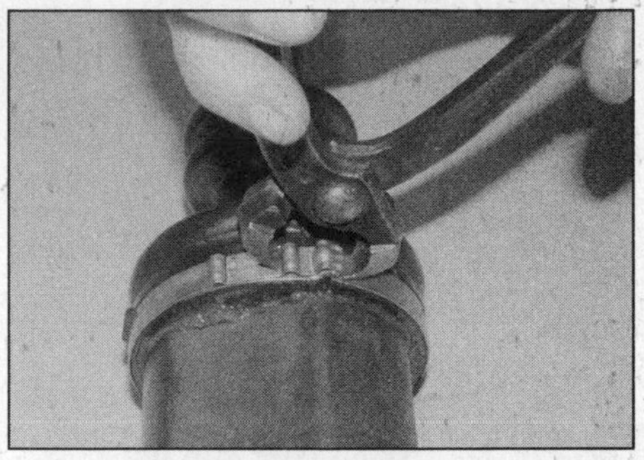

4.18 Using pincers to secure the gaiter retaining clip

15 Slide the gaiter up the driveshaft. Locate the gaiter in the grooves on the driveshaft and outer member.

16 Fit the inner retaining clip into place over the inner end of the gaiter.

17 Using a blunt rod, carefully lift the outer lip of the gaiter to equalise the air pressure. With the rod in position, compress the joint until the dimension from the inner end of the gaiter to the flat end face of the outer member is as shown **(see illustrations)**. Hold the outer member in this position and withdraw the rod.

18 Slip the new retaining clip into place to secure the outer lip of the gaiter to the outer member. Remove any slack in the gaiter retaining clip by carefully compressing the raised section of the clip (depending on type of clip supplied). In the absence of the special tool, a pair of pincers may be used **(see illustration)**. Secure the small retaining clip using the same procedure.

19 Check that the constant velocity joint moves freely in all directions, then refit the driveshaft as described in Section 2.

5 Left-hand driveshaft inner gaiter (manual and sequential gearbox) – renewal

Note: *Check on the availability of a joint repair kit before removal.*

1 Remove the driveshaft as described in Section 2.

2 Using circlip pliers, extract the circlip securing the tripod joint to the driveshaft. Note that on some models, the joint may be staked in position; if so, relieve the stakings using a file. Using a dab of paint or a hammer and punch, mark the position of the tripod joint in relation to the driveshaft, to use as a guide to refitting.

3 The tripod joint can now be removed. If it is tight, draw the joint off the driveshaft end using a puller. Ensure that the legs of the puller are located behind the joint inner member and do not contact the joint rollers. Alternatively, support the inner member of the tripod joint and press the shaft out of the joint, again ensuring that no load is applied to the joint rollers.

4 The gaiter and bearing assembly is removed in the same way, either by drawing the bearing off the driveshaft, or by pressing the driveshaft out of the bearing. Remove the retaining plate, noting which way round it is fitted.

5 Obtain a new gaiter, which is supplied complete with the small bearing.

6 Owing to the lip-type seal used in the bearing, the bearing and gaiter must be pressed into position. If a hammer and tubular drift are used to drive the assembly onto the driveshaft, there is a risk of distorting the seal.

7 Refit the retaining plate to the driveshaft, ensuring that it is fitted the correct way around.

8 Support the driveshaft, and press the gaiter bearing onto the shaft, using a tubular spacer which bears only on the bearing inner race. Position the bearing so that the distance from the end of the driveshaft to the inner face of the bearing is as shown **(see illustrations)**.

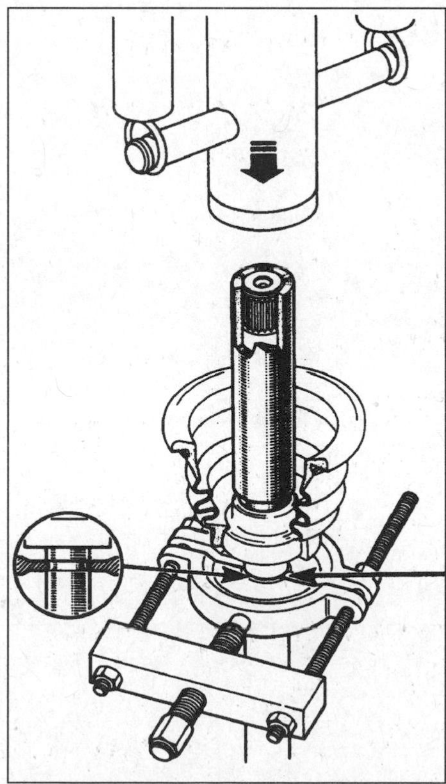

5.8a Pressing the inner bearing/gaiter onto the end of the left-hand driveshaft – manual and sequential gearbox models

9 Align the marks made on dismantling, and engage the tripod joint with the driveshaft splines. Use a hammer and soft metal drift to tap the joint onto the shaft, taking care not to damage the driveshaft splines or joint rollers. Alternatively, support the driveshaft, and press the joint into position using a tubular spacer which bears only on the joint inner member.

10 Secure the tripod joint in position with the circlip, ensuring that it is correctly located in the driveshaft groove. Where no circlip is fitted, secure the joint in position by staking the end of the driveshaft in three places, at intervals of 120°, using a hammer and punch.

11 Refit the driveshaft to the vehicle as described in Section 2.

6 CV joint gaiter renewal (automatic transmission) – general information

At the time of writing, no information on driveshaft dismantling was available for these models, although the driveshafts are very similar in design to the manual and sequential gearbox models. If gaiter renewal is necessary, and further information required, then the driveshaft should be removed from the vehicle, as described in Section 2, and taken to a Renault dealer.

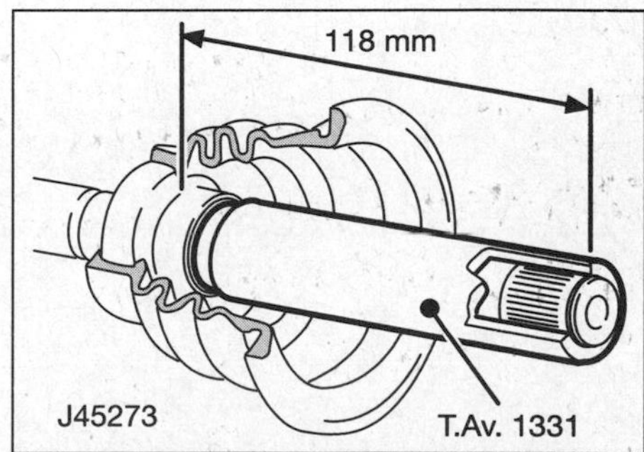

5.8b Fitting dimension for the left-hand driveshaft inner bearing/gaiter – manual and sequential gearbox models

7 Driveshaft overhaul – general information

If any of the checks described in Chapter 1A or 1B reveal wear in a driveshaft joint, first remove the roadwheel trim or centre cap (as appropriate) and check that the driveshaft retaining nut is still correctly tightened; if in doubt, use a torque wrench to check it. Refit the centre cap or trim, and repeat the check on the other driveshaft.

Road test the vehicle, and listen for a metallic clicking from the front as the vehicle is driven slowly in a circle on full-lock. If a clicking noise is heard, this indicates wear in the outer constant velocity joint.

If vibration, consistent with road speed, is felt through the vehicle when accelerating, there is a possibility of wear in the inner constant velocity joints.

Constant velocity joints can be dismantled and inspected for wear as described in Sections 3, 4 and 5.

On models with a manual or sequential gearbox, wear in the outer constant velocity joint can only be rectified by renewing the driveshaft. This is necessary since no outer joint components are available separately. For the inner joint, the tripod joint and roller assembly is available separately, but wear in any of the other components will also necessitate driveshaft renewal.

On models equipped with automatic transmission, it will necessitate a complete driveshaft renewal if there is any wear in either of the joints; no separate components for either joint were available separately at the time of writing.

On models with ABS, you will need to check with your Renault dealer to see if the reluctor ring can be purchased separately from the driveshaft. See Chapter 9, Section 23.

Chapter 9
Braking system

Contents

Degrees of difficulty

Easy, suitable for novice with little experience 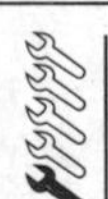	**Fairly easy,** suitable for beginner with some experience 	**Fairly difficult,** suitable for competent DIY mechanic 	**Difficult,** suitable for experienced DIY mechanic 	**Very difficult,** suitable for expert DIY or professional

Specifications

General

System type	Servo assisted hydraulic circuit, split diagonally with ABS anti-locking braking system
Front brakes	Disc, with single-piston sliding caliper
Rear brakes	Self-adjusting drum or disc, according to model
Handbrake	Cable-operated, to rear wheels

Front brakes

Disc diameter:		
1.2 8-valve models	238 mm	
All other models	259 mm	
Disc run-out (all models)	0.07 mm maximum	
Disc thickness:	**New**	**Minimum**
Solid discs brakes	12.0 mm	10.5 mm
Vented disc brakes	20.0 mm	17.7 mm
Brake pad thickness (friction material and backing plate)	18.2	6.0 mm

Rear drum brakes

Drum diameter:		
New	203.20 mm	
Maximum diameter after machining	204.20 mm	
Brake shoe thickness (friction material only):	**New**	**Minimum**
Leading shoe	4.60 mm	2.00 mm
Trailing shoe	3.30 mm	2.00 mm

Rear disc brakes

Brake pad thickness (friction material and backing plate):	
New	15.0 mm
Minimum	6.0 mm
Disc diameter	238 mm
Disc thickness:	
New	8.0 mm
Minimum	7.0 mm
Disc run-out (all models)	0.07 mm maximum

Anti-lock braking system (ABS)

Wheel sensor-to-reluctor ring clearance	0.10 to 1.90 mm
Sensor electrical resistance	1130 ohms (approx)

Torque wrench settings

Torque wrench settings	Nm	lbf ft
ABS system components:		
Hydraulic unit brake pipe union nuts	17	13
Wheel sensor retaining bolts	8 to 10	6 to 7
Brake caliper mounting bolts	100	74
Brake disc retaining screw	20	15
Brake hose and pipe unions	15	11
Front brake caliper guide pin bolts*	40	30
Master cylinder brake pipe union nuts	15	11
Master cylinder-to-servo unit nuts	18	13
Rear brake caliper frame retaining bolts	65	48
Rear brake compensator adjustment bolt	10	7
Rear brake compensator mounting bolts	18	13
Rear hub nut*	175	129
Roadwheel bolts	90	66
Vacuum servo unit mounting nuts	23	17

* *Use new bolts or nuts*

1 General information

ABS anti-lock braking system is fitted to all models as standard. The braking system is of the servo-assisted, dual circuit hydraulic type. All models are fitted with front disc brakes, but the rear brakes may be of drum or disc type, depending on model. Refer to Sections 22 and 23 for further information on ABS operation and components.

The front disc brakes are actuated by single-piston sliding type calipers, which ensure that equal pressure is applied to each disc pad.

The rear drum brakes incorporate leading and trailing shoes, which are actuated by twin-piston wheel cylinders (one cylinder per drum). The wheel cylinders incorporate integral pressure-regulating valves, which control the hydraulic pressure applied to the rear brakes. The regulating valves help to prevent rear wheel lock-up during emergency braking. As the brake shoe linings wear, footbrake operation automatically operates a self-adjuster mechanism, which effectively lengthens the strut between the shoes and reduces the lining-to-drum clearance.

On models with rear disc brakes, the brakes are actuated by single-piston sliding calipers which incorporate mechanical handbrake mechanisms. A load-sensitive pressure-regulating valve is connected into the brake lines to the rear calipers. The regulating valve is similar to that fitted to the rear wheel cylinders (on rear drum brake models), and helps to prevent rear wheel lock-up during emergency braking. It does this by varying the hydraulic pressure applied to the rear calipers in proportion to the load being carried by the vehicle.

On all models, the handbrake provides an independent mechanical means of rear brake application.

Note: *When servicing any part of the braking system, work carefully and methodically; also observe scrupulous cleanliness when overhauling any part of the hydraulic system. Always renew components (in axle sets, where applicable) if in doubt about their condition, and use only genuine Renault parts, or at least those of known good quality. Note the warnings given in 'Safety first!' and at relevant points in this Chapter, concerning the dangers of asbestos dust and hydraulic fluid.*

2.2 Release the retaining clip (arrowed)

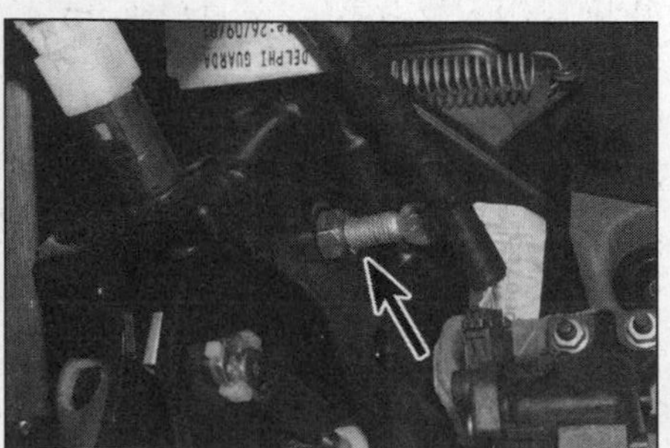

2.3 Withdraw the cross-shaft/bolt (arrowed) and manoeuvre the brake pedal out of the mounting bracket

2 Brake pedal – removal and refitting

Removal

1 Remove the clutch pedal as described in Chapter 6.

2 Extract the spring clip, then withdraw the clevis pin securing the servo unit pushrod to the brake pedal **(see illustration)**. Note the position of any spacers/bushes which may be located on the inside of the pedal.

3 Fully withdraw the pedal cross-shaft/bolt and manoeuvre the brake pedal out of the pedal mounting bracket, noting the fitted positions of the pivot bushes **(see illustration)**.

4 Inspect the bushes for signs of wear or damage, and renew as necessary.

Refitting

5 Apply a smear of multi-purpose grease to the contact surfaces of the pivot bushes (where fitted). Fit the bushes to the brake pedal, in the position noted on removal, and correctly locate the pedal.

6 Slide the pedal and bush assembly into position in the mounting bracket. Ensure that the pedal is correctly engaged with the servo pushrod, then insert the cross-shaft/bolt through the mounting bracket.

7 Position the spacer on the inside of the pedal **(see illustration)**. Refit the clevis pin, and secure it in position with the spring clip.

8 Refit the clutch pedal (see Chapter 6).

2.7 Ensure that the lugs on the spacer are correctly engaged with the pushrod

3 Vacuum servo unit – general information, testing, removal and refitting

General information

1 The vacuum servo unit can be removed from within the engine compartment. To do this the brake master cylinder will have to be removed first as described in Section 8. This procedure will mean that, depending on model, it will be necessary to remove the inlet manifold, heat shields, coolant expansion bottle, injection ECU and, on diesel models, the driveshaft. The removal and refitting of these components can be found in their relevant Chapters. The removal procedure that is described in this Section is from inside the vehicle in the driver's footwell.

Testing

2 To test the operation of the servo unit, depress the footbrake several times to exhaust the vacuum, then start the engine whilst keeping the pedal firmly depressed. As the engine starts, there should be a noticeable 'give' in the brake pedal as the vacuum builds-up. Allow the engine to run for at least two minutes, then switch it off. If the brake pedal is now depressed it should feel normal, but further applications should result in the pedal feeling firmer, with the pedal stroke decreasing with each application.

3 If the servo does not operate as described, inspect the servo unit check valve as described in Section 4. If the check valve is in good working order, try renewing the servo air filter (Section 5).

4 If the servo unit still fails to operate satisfactorily, the fault lies within the unit itself. Apart from external components, no spares are available, so a defective servo must be renewed.

Removal

Note: *A new master cylinder/servo O-ring seal will be required on refitting.*

5 Disconnect the battery negative lead (refer to *Disconnecting the battery* in the Reference Section).

6 Apply the handbrake, then jack up the front of the vehicle and support it on axle stands (see *Jacking and vehicle support*). Remove the right-hand front roadwheel and wheel arch liner **(see illustration)**.

7 Undo the two retaining nuts and remove the bracket off the servo studs, then undo the master cylinder securing nuts to disengage it from the servo unit **(see illustration)**, discard the O-ring seal.

8 Disconnect the vacuum hose from the check valve on the servo unit **(see illustration)**.

9 Working inside the vehicle, disconnect the accelerator wiring connector from the pedal. Undo the accelerator pedal securing nuts and remove the pedal **(see illustration)**.

10 Disconnect the brake light switch wiring connector from above the brake pedal.

11 Remove the clutch pedal travel stop, and disconnect the clutch cable from its linkage on the top of the pedal assembly **(see illustrations)**.

12 Undo the five retaining nuts from around

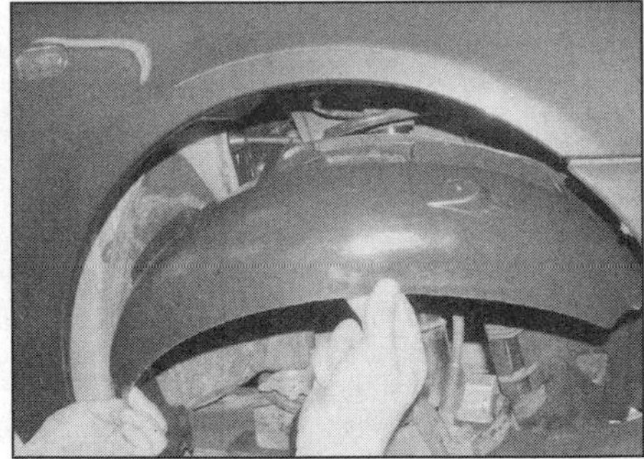

3.6 Removing the right-hand front wheel arch liner

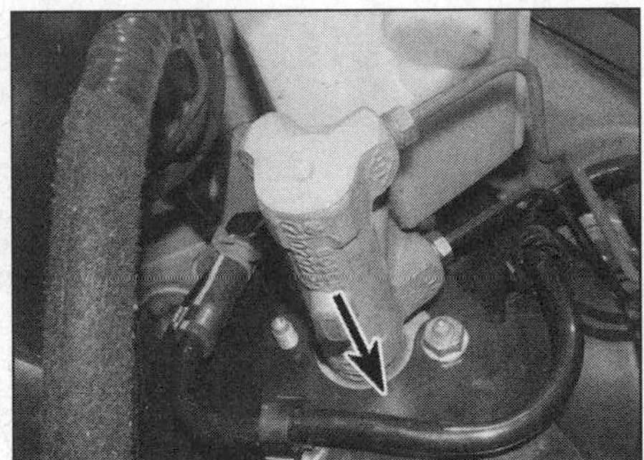

3.7a Remove the vacuum pipe mounting bracket (arrowed) from the studs . . .

3.7b . . . then remove the master cylinder securing nuts (one side arrowed)

3.8 Release the securing clip (arrowed) for the vacuum hose

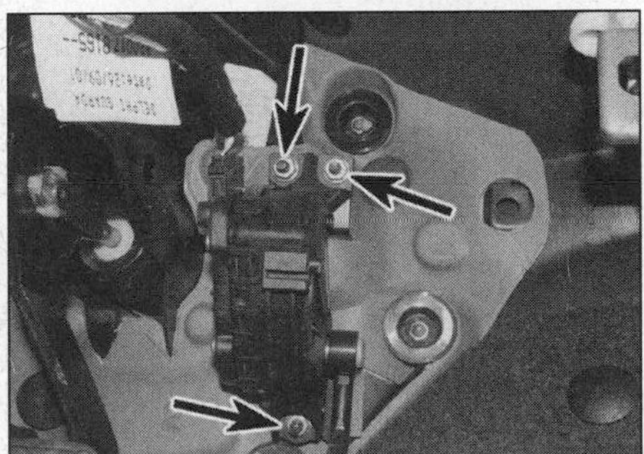

3.9 Remove the accelerator pedal mounting nuts (arrowed)

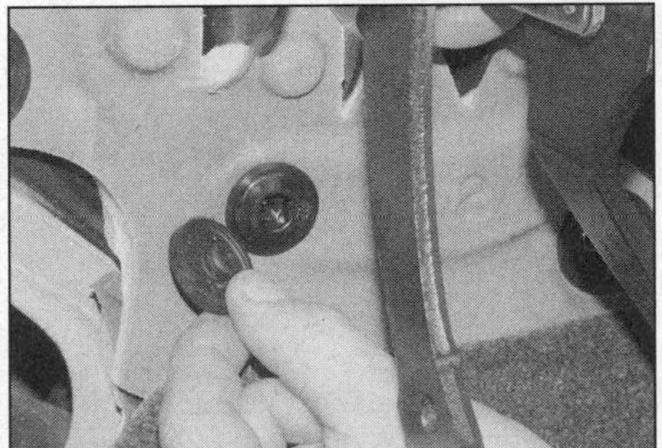

3.11a Unclip the clutch pedal stop . . .

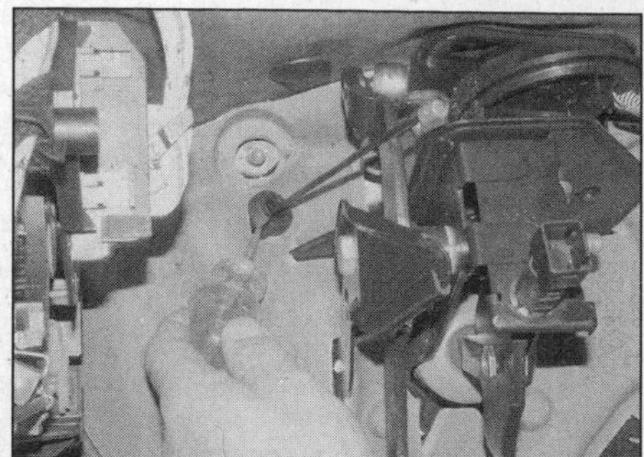
3.11b . . . and release the clutch cable

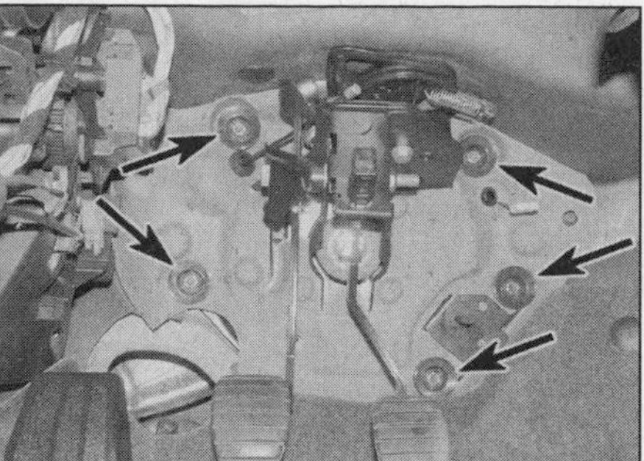
3.12a Remove the five retaining nuts (arrowed) . . .

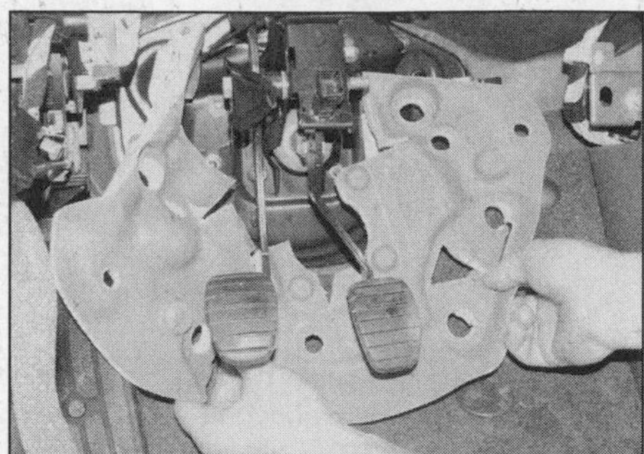
3.12b . . . and remove the soundproofing

3.13 Withdraw the assembly from the bulkhead – check the master cylinder does not foul the servo

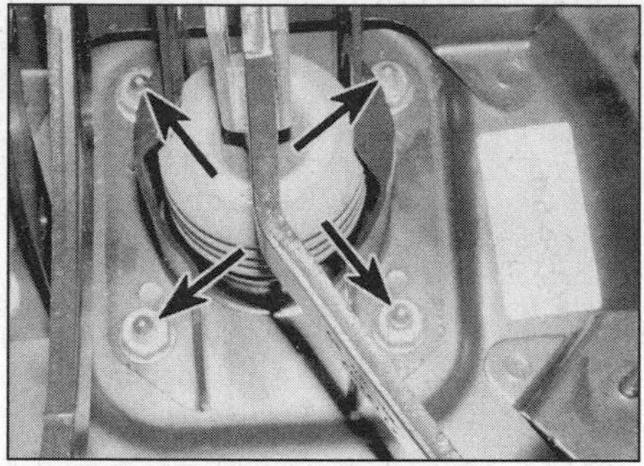
3.14 Remove the four securing nuts (arrowed) to release the servo from the pedal assembly

the pedal assembly, and remove the soundproofing **(see illustrations)**.

13 The pedal assembly, complete with mounting plate and servo, can be withdrawn from inside the footwell **(see illustration)**.

14 To remove the servo from the pedal assembly, remove the four nuts securing the servo unit to the pedal assembly mounting plate **(see illustration)**.

15 Extract the spring clip and withdraw the clevis pin securing the servo unit pushrod to the brake pedal. Note the spacer which is located on the inside of the pedal as described in Section 2.

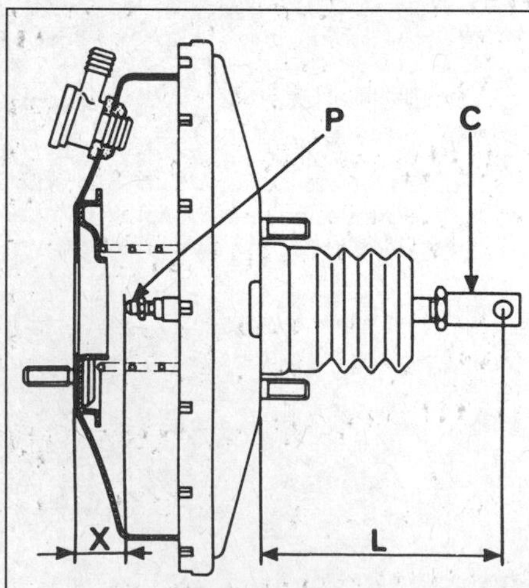

3.16 Vacuum servo unit adjustment dimensions

C Pushrod clevis
L = 104.8 mm
P Pushrod nut
X = 22.3 mm

Refitting

16 Prior to refitting, check that the servo unit pushrod is correctly adjusted as follows. With the gasket removed, check the dimensions **(see illustration)**. If adjustment is necessary, dimension L can be altered by slackening the locknut and repositioning the pushrod clevis, and dimension X can be altered by repositioning the nut (P). After adjustment ensure that the clevis locknut is securely tightened.

17 Inspect the check valve sealing grommet for signs of damage or deterioration, and renew if necessary.

18 Fit a new O-ring seal to the rear of the master cylinder, and reposition the unit in the engine compartment.

19 Working inside the vehicle, refit the servo unit to the pedal assembly mounting plate. Ensure that the servo unit pushrod is correctly engaged with the brake pedal and tighten the four mounting nuts to their specified torque.

20 Position the spacer on the inside of the brake pedal. Refit the clevis pin, and secure it in position with the spring clip.

21 Offer the assembly into position, aligning the servo with the master cylinder.

22 Refit the soundproofing around the pedal assembly, and tighten the five mounting plate retaining nuts securely.

23 Reconnect the clutch cable to the pedal linkage, making sure the outer cable is located in the mounting plate correctly. Refit the clutch pedal travel stop.

24 Refit the accelerator pedal and reconnect the wiring connectors, including the wiring to the brake light switch.

25 Working inside the engine bay, reconnect the vacuum hose to the servo unit check valve, and refit the master cylinder retaining nuts, tighten them to their specified torque.

26 Reconnect the battery.

27 Refit the wheel arch liner and roadwheel, tighten the wheel bolts to their specified torque.

28 On completion, start the engine and check that there are no air leaks at the servo vacuum hose connection. Check the operation of the servo as described at the beginning of this Section.

4 Vacuum servo unit check valve – removal, testing and refitting

Removal

1 Apply the handbrake, then jack up the front of the vehicle and support it on axle stands (see *Jacking and vehicle support*). Remove the right-hand front roadwheel and wheel arch liner **(see illustration 3.6)**.

2 Slacken the retaining clip, and disconnect the vacuum hose from the check valve on the servo unit **(see illustration)**.

3 Withdraw the valve from its rubber sealing grommet, using a pulling and twisting motion. Remove the grommet from the servo.

4.2 Vacuum servo unit check valve (arrowed)

Testing

4 Examine the check valve for signs of damage, and renew if necessary. The valve may be tested by blowing through it in both directions. Air should flow through the valve in one direction only – when blown through from the servo unit end of the valve. Renew the valve if this is not the case.

5 Examine the rubber sealing grommet and flexible vacuum hose for signs of damage or deterioration, and renew as necessary.

Refitting

6 Fit the sealing grommet into position in the servo unit.

7 Ease the check valve into position, taking care not to displace or damage the grommet. Reconnect the vacuum hose to the valve, and securely tighten its retaining clip.

8 On completion, start the engine and check that there are no air leaks.

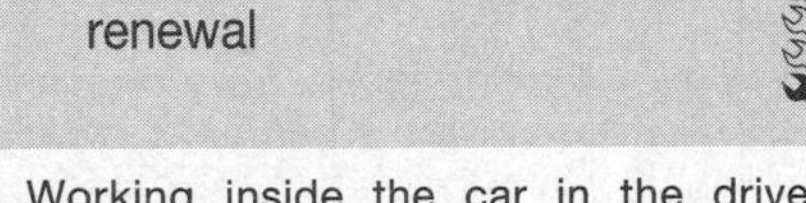

5 Vacuum servo unit air filter – renewal

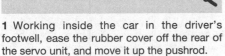

1 Working inside the car in the driver's footwell, ease the rubber cover off the rear of the servo unit, and move it up the pushrod.

2 Using a screwdriver or scriber, hook out the old air filter and remove it from the servo.

3 Make a cut in the new filter **(see illustration)**. Place the filter over the pushrod and into position in the servo end (check that it fills the complete opening to prevent any non-filtered air from passing through).

4 Refit the rubber cover, and check the operation of the brake pedal.

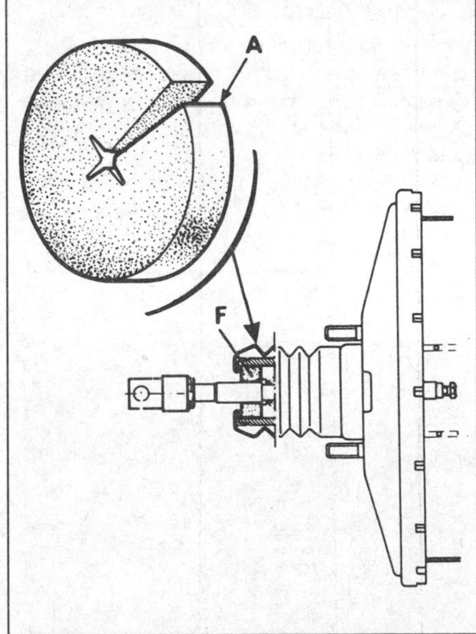

5.3 Vacuum servo unit air filter renewal

A Cut the new filter as shown
F Correct fitted position of filter in servo unit

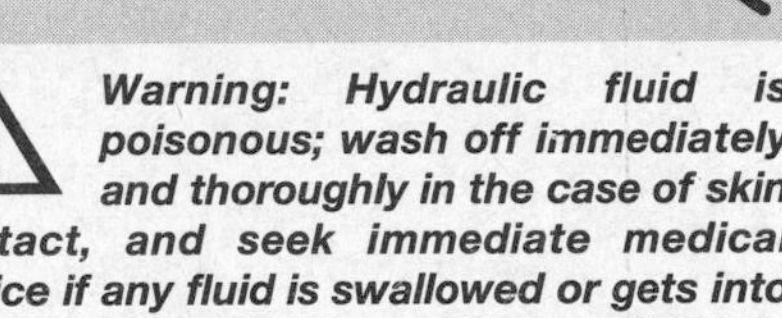

6 Hydraulic system – bleeding

Warning: Hydraulic fluid is poisonous; wash off immediately and thoroughly in the case of skin contact, and seek immediate medical advice if any fluid is swallowed or gets into the eyes. Certain types of hydraulic fluid are inflammable, and may ignite when allowed into contact with hot components; when servicing any hydraulic system, it is safest to assume that the fluid is inflammable, and to take precautions against the risk of fire as though it is petrol that is being handled. Finally, hydraulic fluid is hygroscopic (it absorbs moisture from the air) – old fluid may be contaminated and unfit for further use. When topping-up or renewing the fluid, always use the recommended type (see 'Lubricants and fluids'), and ensure that it comes from a freshly-opened, previously-sealed container.

Hydraulic fluid is an effective paint stripper, and will attack plastics; if any is spilt, it should be washed off immediately using copious quantities of fresh water.

Caution: Make sure the ignition switch is in the OFF position before disconnecting any braking system hydraulic union and do not switch it on until after the hydraulic system has been bled. Failure to do this could lead to air entering the ABS hydraulic unit. If air enters the hydraulic unit pump, it will prove very difficult (in some cases impossible) to bleed the unit.

General

1 The correct operation of any hydraulic system is only possible after removing all air from the components and circuit; this is achieved by bleeding the system.

2 During the bleeding procedure, add only clean, unused hydraulic fluid of the recommended type; never re-use fluid that has already been bled from the system. Ensure that sufficient fluid is available before starting work.

3 If there is any possibility of incorrect fluid being already in the system, the system must be flushed completely with uncontaminated, correct fluid, and new seals should be fitted to the various components.

4 If air has entered the hydraulic system because of a leak, ensure that the fault is cured before proceeding further.

5 Park the vehicle on level ground, switch off the engine and select first or reverse gear (or P on automatic transmission models). Chock the wheels and release the handbrake.

6 Check that all pipes and hoses are secure, unions tight and bleed screws closed. Clean any dirt from around the bleed screws.

7 Unscrew the master cylinder reservoir cap and top the master cylinder reservoir up to the MAX level line; refit the cap loosely. Remember to maintain the fluid level at least above the MIN level line throughout the procedure, or there is a risk of further air entering the system.

8 There is a number of one-man, do-it-yourself brake bleeding kits currently available from motor accessory shops. It is recommended that one of these kits is used whenever possible, as they greatly simplify the bleeding operation, and also reduce the risk of expelled air and fluid being drawn back into the system. If such a kit is not available, the basic (two-man) method must be used, which is described in detail below.

9 If a kit is to be used, prepare the vehicle as described previously, and follow the kit manufacturer's instructions. The procedure may vary slightly according to the type of kit being used; general procedures are as outlined below in the relevant sub-section.

10 Whichever method is used, the same sequence must be followed (paragraphs 11 and 12) to ensure the removal of all air from the system.

Bleeding sequence

Note: *The engine must not be running when bleeding the brakes.*

11 If the system has been only partially disconnected, and the correct precautions were taken to minimise fluid loss, it should be necessary only to bleed that part of the system (ie, the primary or secondary circuit).

12 If the complete system is to be bled, then it should be done working in the following sequence:

a) Left-hand front brake.
b) Right-hand front brake.
c) Left-hand rear brake.
d) Right-hand rear brake.

Bleeding

Basic (two-man) method

13 Collect a clean glass jar, a length of plastic or rubber tubing which is a tight fit over the bleed screw, and a ring spanner to fit the screw. The help of an assistant will also be required.

14 Remove the dust cap from the first screw in the sequence. Fit the spanner and tube to the screw, place the other end of the tube in the jar, and pour in sufficient fluid to cover the end of the tube.

15 Ensure that the master cylinder reservoir fluid level is maintained at least above the MIN level line throughout the procedure.

16 Have the assistant fully depress the brake pedal several times to build-up pressure, then maintain it on the final stroke.

17 While pedal pressure is maintained, unscrew the bleed screw (approximately one turn) and allow the compressed fluid and air to

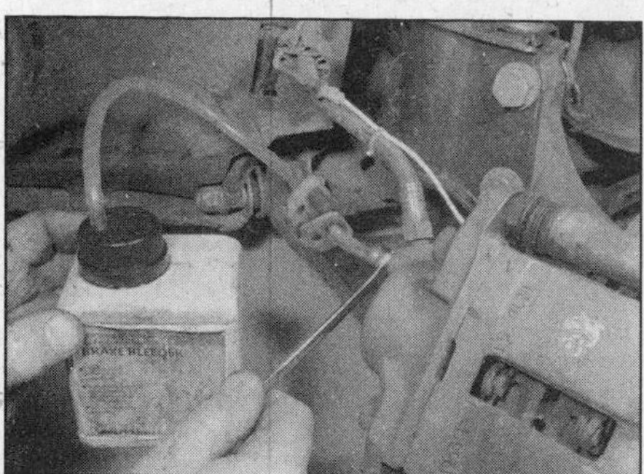

6.21 Bleeding a front brake caliper

flow into the jar. The assistant should maintain pedal pressure, following it down to the floor if necessary, and should not release it until instructed to do so. When the flow stops, tighten the bleed screw again. Have the assistant release the pedal slowly.

18 Repeat the steps given in paragraphs 16 and 17 until the fluid emerging from the bleed screw is free from air bubbles. Remember to recheck the fluid level in the master cylinder reservoir every five strokes or so. If the master cylinder has been drained and refilled, and air is being bled from the first screw in the sequence, allow approximately five seconds between strokes for the master cylinder passages to refill.

19 When no more air bubbles appear, tighten the bleed screw securely, remove the tube and spanner, and refit the dust cap. Do not overtighten the bleed screw.

20 Repeat the procedure on the remaining screws in the sequence until all air is removed from the system and the brake pedal feels firm.

Using a one-way valve kit

21 As their name implies, these kits consist of a length of tubing with a one-way valve fitted to prevent expelled air and fluid being drawn back into the system; some kits include a translucent container, which can be positioned so that the air bubbles can be more easily seen flowing from the end of the tube **(see illustration)**.

22 The kit is connected to the bleed screw, which is then opened. The user returns to the driver's seat and depresses the brake pedal with a smooth, steady stroke and slowly releases it; this is repeated until the expelled fluid is clear of air bubbles.

23 Note that these kits simplify work so much that it is easy to forget the master cylinder reservoir fluid level; ensure that this is maintained at least above the MIN level line at all times.

Using a pressure-bleeding kit

24 These kits are usually operated by the reservoir of pressurised air contained in the spare tyre, although it may be necessary to reduce the pressure in the tyre to lower than normal; refer to the instructions supplied with the kit.

25 By connecting a pressurised, fluid-filled container to the master cylinder reservoir, bleeding can be carried out simply by opening each screw in turn (in the specified sequence) and allowing the fluid to flow out until no more air bubbles can be seen in the expelled fluid.

26 This method has the advantage that the large reservoir of fluid provides an additional safeguard against air being drawn into the system during bleeding.

27 Pressure-bleeding is particularly effective when bleeding 'difficult' systems, or when bleeding the complete system at the time of routine fluid renewal.

All methods

28 When bleeding is complete and firm pedal feel is restored, wash off any spilt fluid, tighten the bleed screws securely and refit their dust caps.

29 Check the hydraulic fluid level, and top-up if necessary (see *Weekly checks*).

30 Discard any hydraulic fluid that has been bled from the system; it will not be fit for re-use.

31 Check the feel of the brake pedal. If it feels at all spongy, air must still be present in the system, and further bleeding is required. Failure to bleed satisfactorily after several repetitions of the bleeding procedure may be due to worn master cylinder seals.

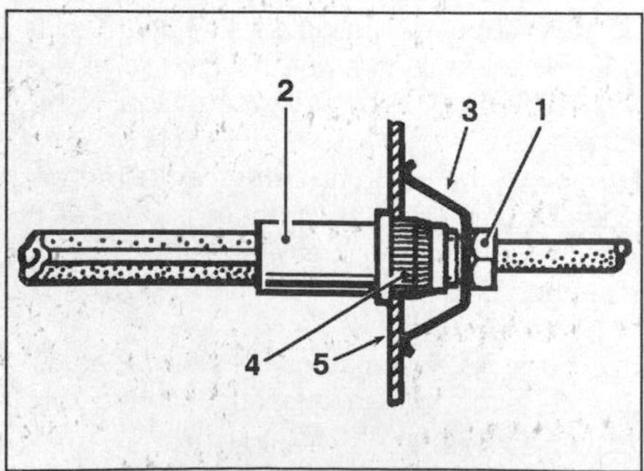

7.2a Hydraulic pipe connection to a flexible hose

1 *Union nut*
2 *Flexible hose*
3 *Spring clip support*
4 *Splined end fitting*
5 *Bodywork*

7 Hydraulic pipes and hoses – renewal

Note: *Before starting work, refer to the warning at the beginning of Section 6 concerning the dangers of hydraulic fluid.*

1 If any pipe or hose is to be renewed, minimise fluid loss by removing the master cylinder reservoir cap and then tightening it down onto a piece of polythene (taking care not to damage the sender unit) to obtain an airtight seal. Alternatively, flexible hoses can be sealed, if required, using a proprietary brake hose clamp; metal brake pipe unions can be plugged (if care is taken not to allow dirt into the system) or capped immediately they are disconnected. Place a wad of rag under any union that is to be disconnected, to catch any spilt fluid.

2 If a flexible hose is to be disconnected, unscrew the brake pipe union nut before removing the spring clip which secures the hose to its mounting bracket **(see illustrations)**.

3 To unscrew the union nuts, it is preferable to obtain a brake pipe spanner of the correct size (split ring); these are available from motor accessory shops. Failing this, a close-fitting open-ended spanner will be required, though if the nuts are tight or corroded, their flats may be rounded off if the spanner slips. In such a case, a self-locking wrench is often the only way to unscrew a stubborn union, but it follows that the pipe and the damaged nuts must be renewed on reassembly. Always clean a union and surrounding area before disconnecting it. If disconnecting a component with more than one union, make a careful note of the connections before disturbing any of them.

4 If a brake pipe is to be renewed, it can be obtained, cut to length and with the union nuts and end flares in place, from Renault dealers. All that is then necessary is to bend it to shape, following the line of the original, before fitting it to the car. Alternatively, most motor accessory shops can make up brake pipes from kits, but this requires very careful measurement of the original to ensure that the new pipe is of the correct length. The safest answer is usually to take the original to the shop as a pattern.

5 On refitting, do not over tighten the union nuts. The specified torque wrench settings (where given) are not high, and it is not necessary to exercise brute force to obtain a sound joint.

6 Ensure that the pipes and hoses are correctly routed with no kinks, and that they are secured in the clips or brackets provided. In the case of flexible hoses, make sure that they cannot contact other components during movement of the steering and/or suspension assemblies.

7 After fitting, remove the polythene from the reservoir (or remove the plugs or clamps, as applicable), and bleed the hydraulic system as described in Section 6. Wash off any spilt fluid, and check carefully for fluid leaks.

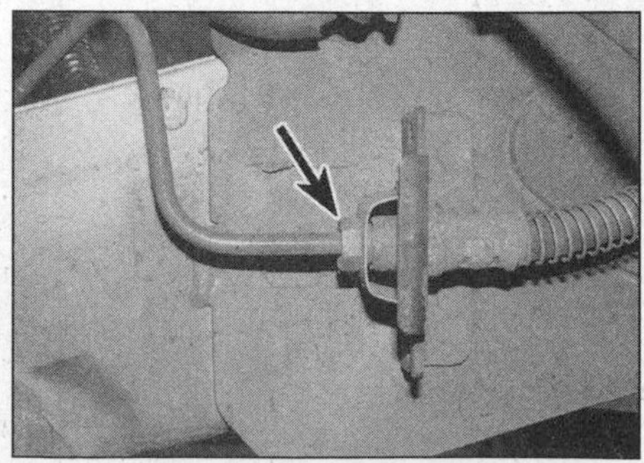

7.2b Use a brake pipe spanner to unscrew a hydraulic union nut (arrowed)

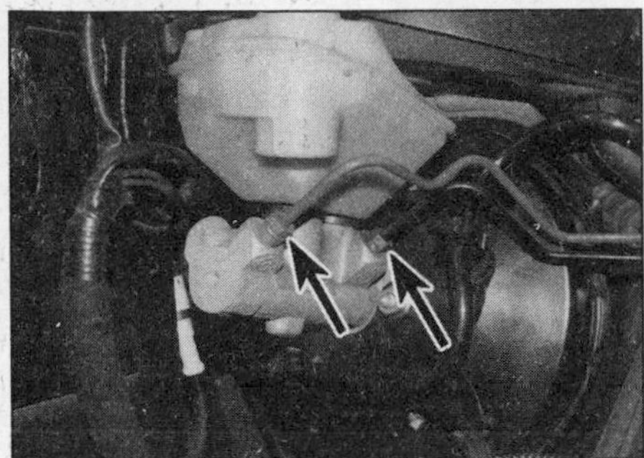
8.8 Slacken the brake fluid pipe unions (arrowed)

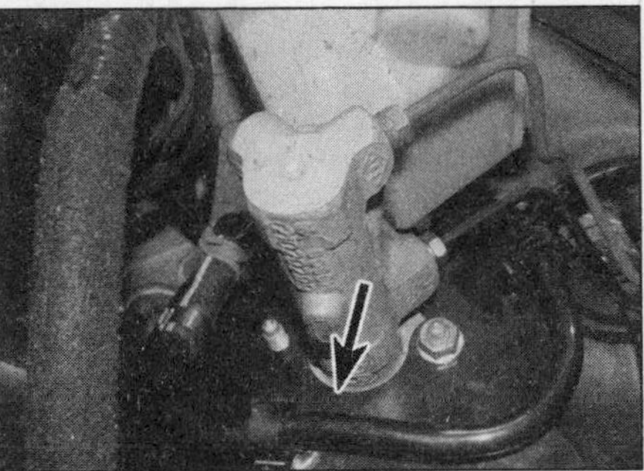
8.9 Remove the vacuum pipe mounting bracket (arrowed)

8.10 Remove the master cylinder securing nuts (one side arrowed)

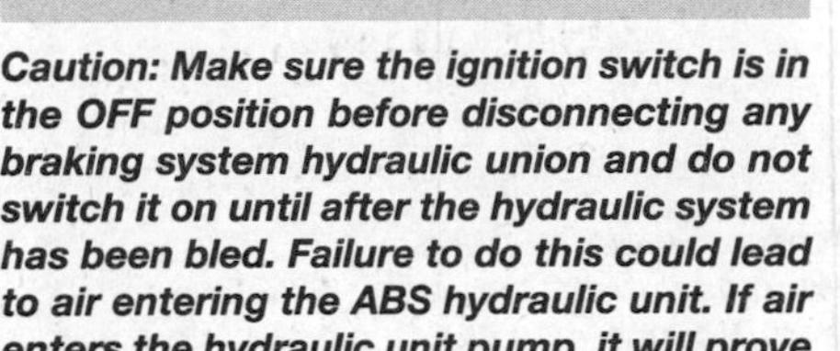

8 Master cylinder – removal and refitting

Caution: Make sure the ignition switch is in the OFF position before disconnecting any braking system hydraulic union and do not switch it on until after the hydraulic system has been bled. Failure to do this could lead to air entering the ABS hydraulic unit. If air enters the hydraulic unit pump, it will prove very difficult (in some cases impossible) to bleed the unit (see Section 6).

Note: *Before starting work, refer to the warning at the beginning of Section 6 concerning the dangers of hydraulic fluid.*

Removal

1 Disconnect the battery negative lead (refer to *Disconnecting the battery* in the Reference Section)

2 Apply the handbrake, then jack up the front of the vehicle and support it on axle stands (see *Jacking and vehicle support*).

3 On right-hand drive models, remove the right-hand front roadwheel and wheel arch liner.

4 On left-hand drive models, remove the left-hand front roadwheel and wheel arch liner.

5 On left-hand drive models, also remove the injection ECU (depending on model) from the inner wing. Also release the power steering reservoir and move it to one side.

6 On all models, remove the master cylinder reservoir cap, having disconnected the sender unit wiring connector, and syphon the hydraulic fluid from the reservoir. **Note:** *Do not syphon the fluid by mouth, as it is poisonous; use a syringe or an old antifreeze hydrometer.* Alternatively, open any convenient pair of bleed screws in the system (one in each hydraulic circuit) and gently pump the brake pedal to expel the fluid through plastic tubes connected to the screws (see Section 6).

7 Once drained, remove the reservoir from the master cylinder by pulling it upwards.

8 Wipe clean the area around the brake pipe unions on the side of the master cylinder, and place absorbent rags beneath the pipe unions to catch any surplus fluid. Make a note of the correct fitted positions of the unions, then unscrew the union nuts and carefully withdraw the pipes **(see illustration)**. Plug or tape over the pipe ends and master cylinder orifices, to minimise the loss of brake fluid and to prevent the entry of dirt into the system. Wash off any spilt fluid immediately with cold water.

9 Undo the two vacuum pipe retaining bracket nuts **(see illustration)**.

10 Slacken and remove the two nuts securing the master cylinder to the vacuum servo unit **(see illustration)**, then withdraw the master cylinder from the engine compartment. Remove the O-ring seal from the rear of the master cylinder, and discard it.

11 At the time of writing it was not possible to obtain internal components for the master cylinder, although it is worth checking. If parts are not available, it must be renewed as a complete unit. The reservoir mounting bush seals may be renewed if necessary. The O-ring seal fitted between the master cylinder and the vacuum servo must be renewed as a matter of course whenever the unit is removed, as a leak at this point will allow atmospheric pressure into the servo unit.

Refitting

12 Before refitting the master cylinder, check that the distance between the tip of the master cylinder end of the pushrod and the front of the servo unit, dimension X **(see illustration 3.16)**. If necessary, adjust by repositioning the pushrod nut P.

13 Remove all traces of dirt from the master cylinder and servo unit mating surfaces. Fit a new O-ring seal to the groove on the master cylinder body.

14 Fit the master cylinder to the servo, ensuring that the servo pushrod enters the master cylinder bore centrally. Refit the master cylinder mounting nuts, and tighten them to the specified torque.

15 Wipe clean the brake pipe unions, then refit them to the master cylinder ports. Tighten the union nuts to the specified torque.

16 Carefully align the reservoir with the mounting bush seals. Push the reservoir firmly into position.

17 On left-hand drive models, where applicable; refit the injection ECU and power steering reservoir back into their correct position.

18 On all models, refill the master cylinder reservoir with new fluid, and bleed the hydraulic system as described in Section 6.

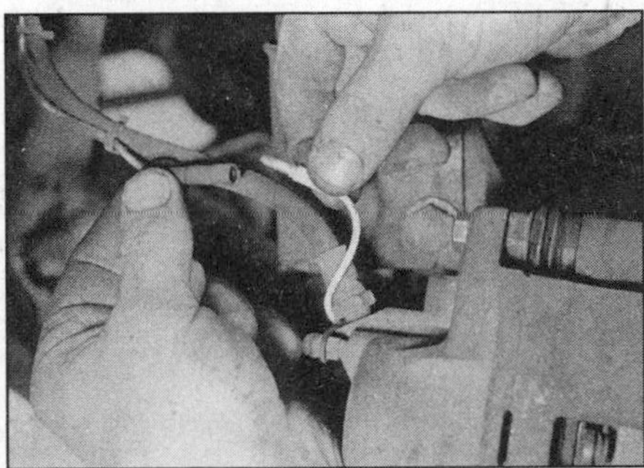
9.2 Disconnecting the pad wear sensor wiring connector

9 Front brake pads – renewal

Warning: Renew both sets of front brake pads at the same time – never renew the pads on only one wheel, as uneven braking may result. Note that the dust created by wear of the pads may contain asbestos, which is a health hazard. Never blow it out with compressed air, and don't inhale any of it. An approved filtering mask should be worn when working on the brakes. DO NOT use petroleum-based solvents to clean brake parts – use brake cleaner or methylated spirit only.

Note: *Thread-locking compound will be required to coat the threads of the caliper guide pin bolts on refitting.*

1 Apply the handbrake, then jack up the front of the vehicle and support it on axle stands (see *Jacking and vehicle support*). Remove the front roadwheels.

2 Where fitted, trace the brake pad wear sensor wiring back from the inner pad, and disconnect it at the wiring connector **(see illustration)**.

3 Push the piston a short way into its bore by pulling the caliper outwards (do not overdo it, or the master cylinder reservoir may overflow).

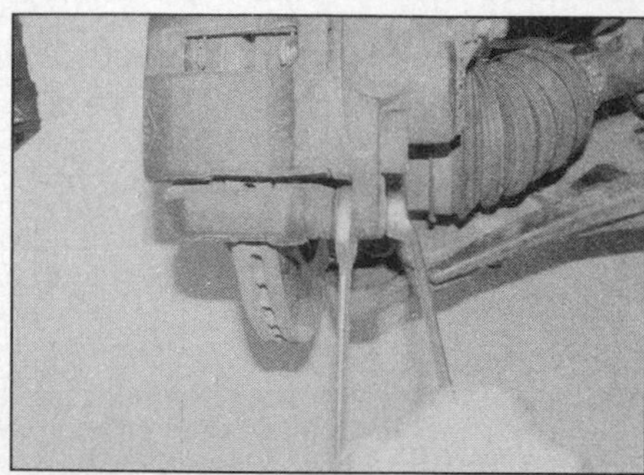

9.4 Slacken the guide pin bolts whilst holding the guide pins with an open-ended spanner

9.11 Ensure that the brake pads are fitted the correct way round, with friction material facing the disc

4 Slacken and remove the caliper upper and lower guide pin bolts, using a slim open-ended spanner to prevent the guide pin itself from rotating **(see illustration)**. Discard the guide pin bolts; new bolts must be used on refitting. If genuine Renault brake pads are purchased, the bolts will be supplied with the pad set.

5 With the guide pins removed, lift the caliper away from the brake pads and mounting bracket, and tie it to the suspension strut using a length of wire/string. Do not allow the caliper to hang unsupported on the flexible hose.

6 Withdraw the two brake pads from the caliper mounting bracket, and examine them.

7 First measure the thickness of each brake pad (friction material and backing plate). If any pad is worn at any point to the specified minimum thickness or less, all four pads must be renewed. Also, the pads should be renewed if any are fouled with oil or grease; there is no satisfactory way of degreasing friction material once contaminated. If any of the brake pads are worn unevenly or fouled with oil or grease, trace and rectify the cause before reassembly. New brake pads and spring kits are available from Renault dealers.

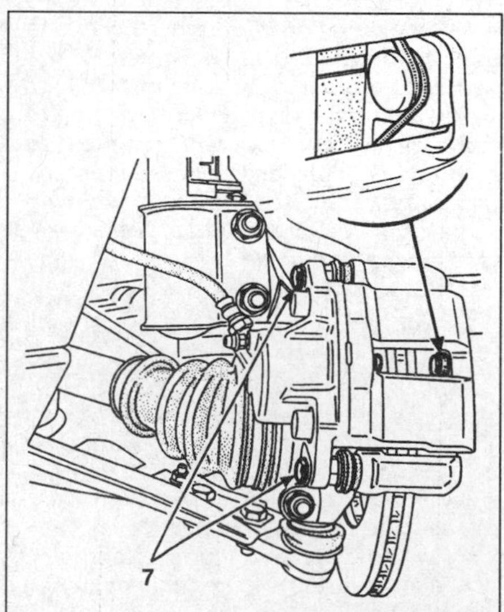

9.12 Girling caliper showing guide pin bolts (7) and correct fitted position of anti-rattle spring

8 If the brake pads are still serviceable, carefully clean them using a clean, fine wire brush or similar, paying particular attention to the sides and back of the metal backing. Clean out the grooves in the friction material, and pick out any large embedded particles of dirt or debris. Carefully clean the pad locations in the caliper body/mounting bracket.

9 Prior to fitting the pads, check that the guide sleeves are free to slide easily in the caliper body, and check that the rubber guide sleeve gaiters are undamaged. Brush the dust and dirt from the caliper and piston, but *do not inhale it as it is injurious to health*. Inspect the dust seal around the piston for damage, and the piston for evidence of fluid leaks, corrosion or damage. If attention to any of these components is necessary, refer to Section 10. Also inspect the brake disc as described in Section 11.

10 If new brake pads are to be fitted, the caliper piston must be pushed back into the cylinder to make room for them. Either use a G-clamp or similar tool to do this. Provided that the master cylinder reservoir has not been overfilled with hydraulic fluid, there should be no spillage, but keep a careful watch on the fluid level while retracting the piston. If the fluid level rises above the MAX level line at any time, the surplus should be syphoned off (not by mouth – use an old syringe or antifreeze hydrometer) or ejected via a plastic tube connected to the bleed screw (see Section 6).

11 Install the pads in the caliper mounting bracket, ensuring that the friction material of each pad is against the brake disc. Where applicable, the pad with the wear sensor is fitted on the inside **(see illustration)**.

12 Position the caliper over the pads. Coat the threads of the new lower guide pin bolt with locking fluid, and fit the bolt. Apply locking fluid to the new upper guide pin bolt, press the caliper into position, and fit the bolt. Check that the anti-rattle springs are correctly located **(see illustration)**, then tighten the guide pin bolts to the specified torque, starting with the lower bolt.

13 Reconnect the brake pad wear sensor wiring connector, ensuring that the wire is correctly routed.

14 Depress the brake pedal several times to bring the pads into firm contact with the brake disc.

15 Repeat the above procedure on the other front brake caliper.

16 Refit the roadwheels, then lower the vehicle to the ground and tighten the bolts to the specified torque.

17 Check the hydraulic fluid level as described in *Weekly checks*.

18 If new pads have been fitted, full braking efficiency will not be obtained until the linings have bedded-in. Be prepared for longer stopping distances, and avoid harsh braking as far as possible for the first hundred miles or so after fitting new pads.

10 Front brake caliper – removal, overhaul and refitting

Note: *Before starting work, refer to the warnings at the beginning of Sections 6, 8 and 9 concerning the dangers of hydraulic fluid and asbestos dust.*

Removal

1 Apply the handbrake, then jack up the front of the vehicle and support it on axle stands (see *Jacking and vehicle support*). Remove the appropriate roadwheel.

2 Minimise fluid loss, either by removing the master cylinder reservoir cap and then tightening it down onto a piece of polythene to obtain an airtight seal (taking care not to damage the sender unit), or by using a brake hose clamp, a G-clamp or a similar tool with protected jaws to clamp the flexible hose.

3 Clean the area around the hose union, then loosen the brake hose union nut **(see illustration)**.

4 Slacken and remove the upper and lower caliper guide pin bolts, using a slim open-ended spanner to prevent the guide pin itself from rotating **(see illustration 9.4)**. Discard the guide pin bolts; new bolts must be used on refitting. With the guide pin bolts removed, lift the caliper away from the brake disc, then

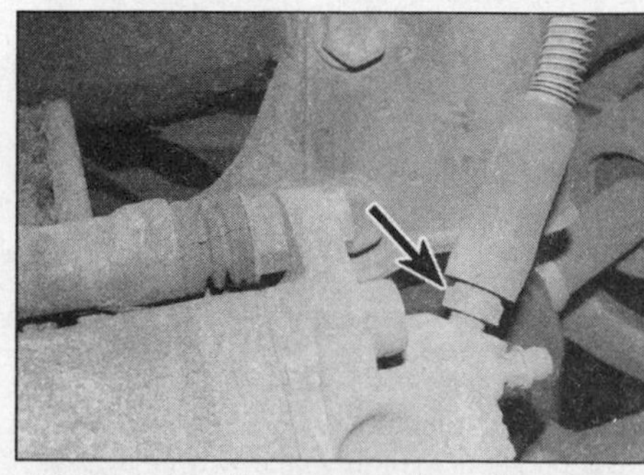

10.3 Slacken the front brake caliper hose union nut (arrowed)

unscrew the caliper from the end of the brake hose. Note that the brake pads need not be disturbed, and can be left in position in the caliper mounting bracket.

Overhaul

Note: *Ensure that an appropriate caliper overhaul kit is obtained before starting work.*

5 With the caliper on the bench, wipe away all traces of dust and dirt, but avoid inhaling the dust, as it is injurious to health.

6 Using a small flat-bladed screwdriver, carefully prise the dust seal retaining clip out of the caliper bore.

7 Withdraw the partially-ejected piston from the caliper body and remove the dust seal. The piston can be withdrawn by hand, or if necessary forced out by applying compressed air to the union bolt hole.

Caution: The piston may be ejected with some force. Only low pressure should be required, such as is generated by a foot pump.

8 Extract the piston hydraulic seal using a blunt instrument such as a knitting needle or a crochet hook, taking care not to damage the caliper bore.

9 Withdraw the guide sleeves or pins from the caliper body or mounting bracket (as applicable) and remove the rubber gaiters.

10 Thoroughly clean all components using only methylated spirit, isopropyl alcohol or clean hydraulic fluid as a cleaning medium. Never use mineral-based solvents, such as petrol or paraffin, which will attack the hydraulic system rubber components. Dry the components immediately, using compressed air or a clean, lint-free cloth. Use compressed air to blow clear the fluid passages.

11 Check all components and renew any that are worn or damaged. Check particularly the cylinder bore and piston; if they are scratched, worn or corroded in any way, they must be renewed (note that this means the renewal of the complete body assembly). Similarly check the condition of the guide sleeves or pins and their bores; they should be undamaged and (when cleaned) a reasonably tight sliding fit in the body or mounting bracket bores. If there is any doubt about the condition of a component, renew it.

12 If the assembly is fit for further use, obtain the appropriate repair kit.

13 Renew all rubber seals, dust covers and caps disturbed on dismantling as a matter of course; these should never be re-used.

14 Before commencing reassembly, ensure that all components are absolutely clean and dry.

15 Dip the piston and the new piston (fluid) seal in clean hydraulic fluid. Smear clean fluid on the cylinder bore surface.

16 Fit the new piston (fluid) seal, using only the fingers to manipulate it into the cylinder bore groove. Fit the new dust seal to the piston. Refit the piston to the cylinder bore using a twisting motion, ensuring that the piston enters squarely into the bore. Press the piston fully into the bore, then press the dust seal into the caliper body.

17 Install the dust seal retaining clip, ensuring that it is correctly seated in the caliper groove.

18 Apply the grease supplied in the repair kit, or a good quality high-temperature brake grease or anti-seize compound to the guide sleeves or pins. Fit the sleeves or pins to the caliper body or mounting bracket. Fit the new rubber gaiters, ensuring that they are correctly located in the grooves on both the sleeve or pin, and body or mounting bracket (as applicable).

Refitting

19 Screw the caliper body fully onto the flexible hose union nut. Check that the brake pads are still correctly fitted in the caliper mounting bracket.

20 Position the caliper over the pads. Coat the threads of the new lower guide pin bolt with locking fluid, and fit the bolt. Apply locking fluid to the new upper guide pin bolt, press the caliper into position, and fit the bolt. Check that the anti-rattle springs are correctly located **(see illustration 9.12)**, then tighten the guide pin bolts to the specified torque, starting with the lower bolt.

21 Tighten the brake hose union nut to the specified torque.

22 Remove the brake hose clamp or polythene, where fitted, and bleed the hydraulic system as described in Section 6. Providing the precautions described were taken to minimise brake fluid loss, it should only be necessary to bleed the relevant front brake.

23 Refit the roadwheel, then lower the vehicle to the ground and tighten the roadwheel bolts to the specified torque.

11 Front brake disc – inspection, removal and refitting

Note: *Before starting work, refer to the warning at the beginning of Section 9 concerning the dangers of asbestos dust. If either disc requires renewal, both should be renewed at the same time, to ensure even and consistent braking. In principle, new pads should be fitted also.*

Inspection

1 Chock the rear wheels, firmly apply the handbrake, jack up the front of the vehicle and support on axle stands (see *Jacking and vehicle support*). Remove the appropriate front roadwheel.

2 Slowly rotate the brake disc so that the full area of both sides can be checked; remove the brake pads, as described in Section 9, if better access is required to the inboard surface. Light scoring is normal in the area swept by the brake pads, but if heavy scoring is found, the disc must be renewed.

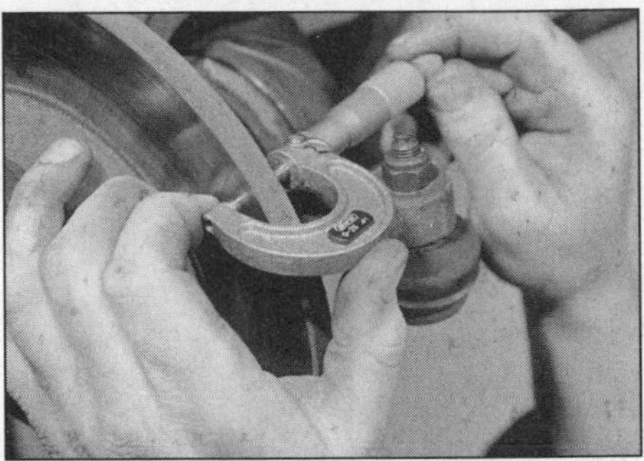

11.3 Measuring brake disc thickness with a micrometer

3 It is normal to find a lip of rust and brake dust around the disc's perimeter; this can be scraped off if required. If, however, a lip has formed due to wear of the brake pad swept area, the disc thickness must be measured using a micrometer **(see illustration)**. Take measurements at several places around the disc at the inside and outside of the pad swept area; if the disc has worn at any point to the specified minimum thickness or less, it must be renewed.

4 If the disc is thought to be warped, it can be checked for run-out, ideally by using a dial gauge mounted on any convenient fixed point, while the disc is slowly rotated **(see illustration)**. In the absence of a dial gauge, use feeler blades to measure (at several points all around the disc) the clearance between the disc and a fixed point such as the caliper mounting bracket. If the measurements obtained are at the specified maximum or beyond, the disc is excessively warped, and must be renewed; however, it is worth checking first that the hub bearing is in good condition (Chapters 1A or 1B and 10). Also try the effect of removing the disc and turning it through 180° to reposition it on the hub; if run-out is still excessive, the disc must be renewed.

5 Check the disc for cracks (especially around the wheel bolt holes), and for any other wear or damage. Renew the disc if necessary.

Removal

Note: *Thread-locking fluid will be required to coat the threads of the brake caliper mounting bolts on refitting.*

11.4 Measuring brake disc run-out with a dial gauge

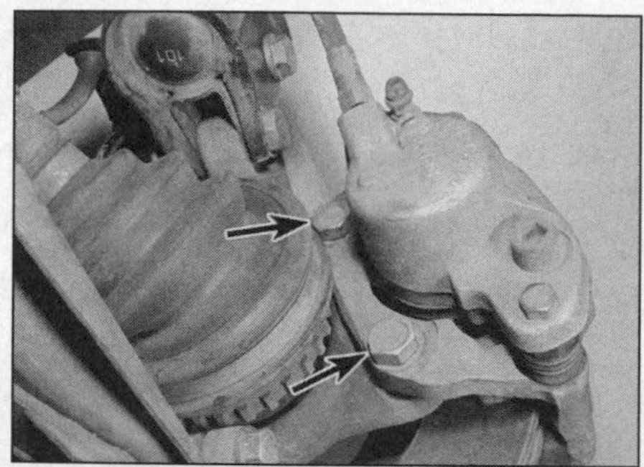

11.6a Undo the two bolts (arrowed) securing the caliper to the swivel hub . . .

11.6b . . . then slide the caliper off the disc, and tie it to the suspension strut spring – Girling caliper

11.7 Remove the two brake disc retaining screws (arrowed)

6 Unscrew the two bolts securing the brake caliper and bracket to the swivel hub, and slide the caliper assembly off the disc. Using a piece of wire or string, tie the caliper to the front suspension coil spring, to avoid placing any strain on the hydraulic brake hose **(see illustrations)**.

7 If the same disc is to be refitted, use chalk or paint to mark the relationship of the disc to the hub. Remove the two screws securing the brake disc to the hub **(see illustration)**, and remove the disc. If it is tight, lightly tap its rear face with a hide or plastic mallet.

Refitting

8 Refitting is the reverse of the removal procedure, noting the following points:

a) *Ensure that the mating surfaces of the disc and hub are clean and flat.*
b) *If applicable, align the marks made on removal.*
c) *Securely tighten the disc retaining screws.*
d) *If a new disc has been fitted, use a suitable solvent to wipe any preservative coating from the disc before refitting the caliper.*
e) *Apply locking fluid to the threads of the brake caliper mounting bolts, and tighten them to the specified torque.*
f) *Refit the roadwheel, then lower the vehicle to the ground and tighten the roadwheel bolts to the specified torque. On completion, depress the brake pedal several times to bring the brake pads into contact with the disc.*

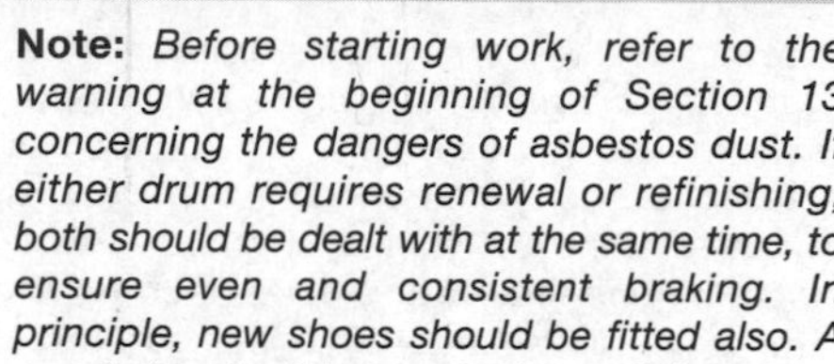

12 Rear brake drum – removal, inspection and refitting

Note: *Before starting work, refer to the warning at the beginning of Section 13 concerning the dangers of asbestos dust. If either drum requires renewal or refinishing, both should be dealt with at the same time, to ensure even and consistent braking. In principle, new shoes should be fitted also. A new hub nut will be required on refitting.*

Removal

1 Chock the front wheels, engage reverse gear (or P) and release the handbrake. Jack up the rear of the vehicle and support it on axle stands (see *Jacking and vehicle support*). Remove the appropriate rear wheel.

2 Using a hammer and large flat-bladed screwdriver, carefully tap and prise the cap out of the centre of the brake drum **(see illustration)**.

3 Using a socket and long bar, slacken and remove the rear hub nut, and withdraw the thrustwasher (where fitted) **(see illustration)**. Discard the hub nut; a new nut must used on refitting.

4 It should now be possible to withdraw the brake drum and hub bearing assembly from the stub axle by hand. It may be difficult to remove the drum due to the tightness of the hub bearing on the stub axle, or due to the brake shoes binding on the inner circumference of the drum. If the bearing is tight, tap the periphery of the drum using a hide or plastic mallet, or use a universal puller, secured to the drum with the wheel bolts, to pull it off. If the brake shoes are binding, proceed as follows.

5 First ensure that the handbrake is fully off. From underneath the vehicle, slacken the handbrake cable adjuster locknut, then back off the adjuster nut on the handbrake lever rod. Note that on most models, it will first be necessary to remove the mounting nut(s) and lower the exhaust heat shield to gain access to the adjuster nut.

6 Insert a screwdriver through one of the wheel bolt holes in the brake drum, so that it contacts the handbrake operating lever on the trailing brake shoe **(see illustration)**. Push the

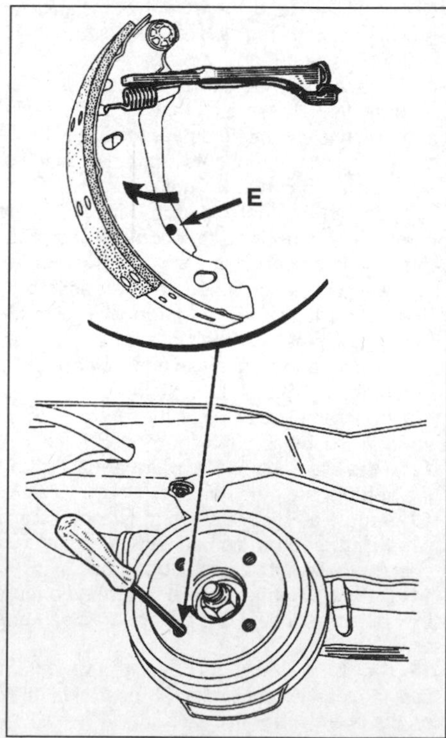

12.6 Using a screwdriver inserted through the brake drum to release the handbrake operating lever

E Handbrake operating lever stop-peg location

12.2 Lever out the cap from the centre of the brake drum . . .

12.3 . . . then remove the rear hub nut

lever until the stop-peg slips behind the brake shoe web, allowing the brake shoes to retract fully. Withdraw the brake drum off the stub axle.

Inspection

7 Working carefully, remove all traces of brake dust from the drum, but *avoid inhaling the dust, as it is injurious to health.*

8 Scrub clean the outside of the drum, and check it for obvious signs of wear or damage such as cracks around the roadwheel bolt holes; renew the drum if necessary.

9 Examine carefully the inside of the drum. Light scoring of the friction surface is normal, but if heavy scoring is found, the drum must be renewed. It is usual to find a lip on the drum's inboard edge which consists of a mixture of rust and brake dust; this should be scraped away to leave a smooth surface which can be polished with fine (120 to 150 grade) emery paper. If the lip is due to the friction surface being recessed by wear, then the drum must be refinished (within the specified limits) or renewed.

10 If the drum is thought to be excessively worn or oval, its internal diameter must be measured at several points using an internal micrometer. Take measurements in pairs, the second at right-angles to the first, and compare the two to check for signs of ovality. Minor ovality can be corrected by machining; otherwise, renew the drum.

Refitting

11 If a new brake drum is to be installed, use a suitable solvent to remove any preservative coating that may have been applied to its interior.

12 Ensure that the handbrake lever stop-peg is correctly repositioned against the edge of the brake shoe web **(see illustration)**. Apply a smear of gear oil to the stub axle, and slide on the brake drum, being careful not to get oil onto the brake shoes or the friction surface of the drum. Fit the thrustwasher (where fitted) and a new hub nut; tighten the nut to the specified torque. Tap the hub cap into place in the centre of the brake drum.

13 Depress the footbrake several times to operate the self-adjusting mechanism.

14 Repeat the above procedure on the

12.12 Check that the handbrake lever stop-peg is correctly positioned against the trailing shoe edge

remaining rear brake assembly (where necessary), then adjust the handbrake as described in Chapter 1A or 1B.

15 On completion, refit the roadwheel(s), lower the vehicle to the ground and tighten the wheel bolts to the specified torque.

13 Rear brake shoes - inspection and renewal

Warning: Brake shoes must be renewed on both rear wheels at the same time - never renew the shoes on only one wheel, as uneven braking may result. Also, the dust created by wear of the shoes may contain asbestos, which is a health hazard. Never blow it out with compressed air, and don't inhale any of it. An approved filtering mask should be worn when working on the brakes. DO NOT use petroleum-based solvents to clean brake parts - use brake cleaner or methylated spirit only.

Inspection

1 Remove the brake drum as described in Section 12.

2 Working carefully, remove all traces of brake dust from the brake drum, backplate and shoes.

3 Measure the thickness of each brake shoe (friction material and shoe) at several points; if either shoe is worn at any point to the specified minimum thickness or less, all four

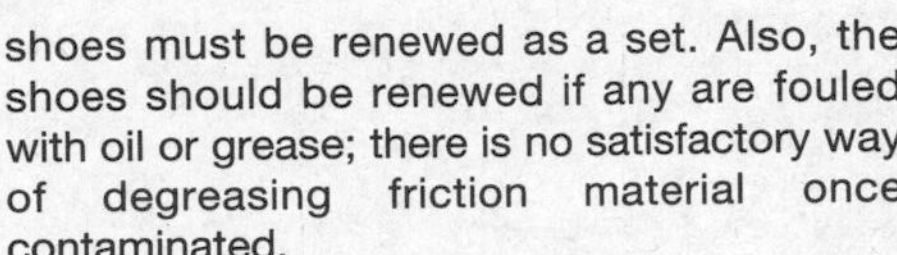

shoes must be renewed as a set. Also, the shoes should be renewed if any are fouled with oil or grease; there is no satisfactory way of degreasing friction material once contaminated.

4 If any of the brake shoes are worn unevenly, or fouled with oil or grease, trace and rectify the cause before reassembly.

Renewal

Note: *High-temperature brake grease or anti-seize compound will be required to apply to the shoe contact surfaces on the brake backplate on refitting.*

5 Make a note of the correct fitted positions of the springs and adjuster strut, to use as a guide on reassembly.

6 Carefully unhook the lower return spring, and remove it from the brake shoes.

7 Using a pair of pliers, remove the leading shoe retainer spring cup by depressing it and turning through 90°. With the cup removed, lift off the spring, then withdraw the retainer pin and remove the shoe from the backplate. Unhook the adjusting lever spring, and remove it from the leading shoe **(see illustrations)**.

8 Detach the adjuster strut and upper return spring, then remove them from the trailing shoe.

9 Remove the trailing shoe retainer spring cup **(see illustration)**, spring and pin as described above, then detach the handbrake cable and remove the shoe from the vehicle. Do not depress the brake pedal until the brakes are reassembled; wrap a strong elastic band around the wheel cylinder pistons to retain them.

10 If genuine Renault brake shoes are being installed, it will be necessary to remove the adjusting lever from the original leading shoe and install it on the new shoe. All return springs should be renewed, regardless of their apparent condition; spring kits are also available from Renault dealers.

11 Withdraw the forked end from the adjuster strut. Carefully examine the assembly for signs of wear or damage, paying particular attention to the threads and the knurled adjuster wheel, and renew if necessary. Note that left-hand and right-hand struts are not interchangeable; the left-hand fork has a

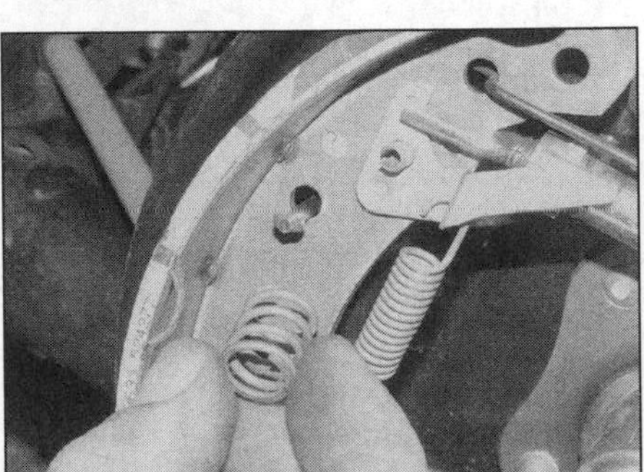

13.7a Remove the brake shoe retaining spring . . .

13.7b . . . and the adjusting lever return spring

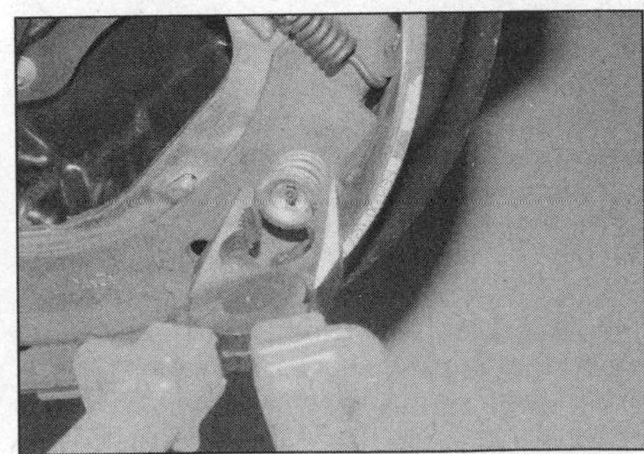

13.9 Removing the locking cup from the brake shoe retaining spring

13.13 Apply a little high-melting point grease to shoe contact points on the backplate

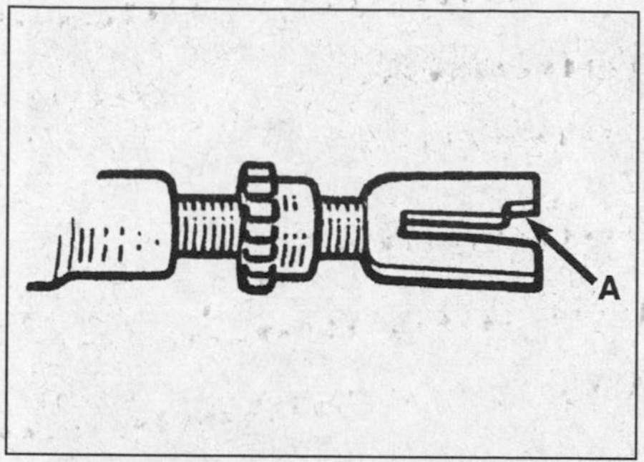

13.16a On Girling rear brakes, adjuster strut fork cut-out (A) must engage with leading shoe adjusting lever on refitting

13.16b Locating the adjusting lever in the cut-out in the adjuster strut fork

13.18 Fitted position (arrowed) of the lever

right-hand thread, and **the right-hand fork has a left-hand thread.** The forks can also be identified by their colour: the left-hand fork is silver, and the right-hand fork is gold.

12 Remove the elastic band fitted to the wheel cylinder. Peel back the rubber protective caps, and check the wheel cylinder for fluid leaks or other damage. Check that both cylinder pistons are free to move easily. Refer to Section 14, if necessary, for information on wheel cylinder renewal.

13 Prior to installation, clean the backplate and apply a thin smear of high-temperature brake grease or anti-seize compound to all those surfaces of the backplate which bear on the shoes **(see illustration)**, particularly the wheel cylinder pistons and lower pivot point. Do not allow the lubricant to foul the friction material.

14 Ensure that the handbrake lever stop-peg is correctly located against the edge of the trailing shoe.

15 Locate the upper end of the trailing shoe in the wheel cylinder piston, then refit the retainer pin and spring, and secure it in position with the spring cup. Connect the handbrake cable to the lever.

16 Screw in the adjuster wheel until the minimum strut length is obtained, then hook the strut into position on the trailing shoe. Rotate the adjuster strut forked end so that the cut-out of the fork will engage with the leading shoe adjusting lever **(see illustrations)**.

17 Fit the spring to the leading shoe adjusting lever, so that the shorter hook of the spring engages with the lever.

18 Slide the leading shoe assembly into position, ensuring that it is correctly engaged with the adjuster strut fork, and that the fork cut-out is engaged with the adjusting lever **(see illustration)**. Engage the upper end of the shoe in the wheel cylinder piston, then secure the shoe in position with the retainer pin, spring and spring cup.

19 Install the upper and lower return springs, then tap the shoes to centralise them on the backplate.

20 Using a screwdriver, turn the strut adjuster wheel until the brake drum will just pass over the brake shoes.

21 Slide the drum into position over the linings, but do not refit the hub nut yet.

22 Repeat the above procedure on the remaining rear brake.

23 Once both sets of rear shoes have been renewed, adjust the lining-to-drum clearance by repeatedly depressing the brake pedal. Whilst depressing the pedal, have an assistant listen to the rear drums, to check that the adjuster strut is functioning correctly; if this is so, a clicking sound will be emitted by the strut as the pedal is depressed.

24 Remove both the rear drums, and check that the handbrake lever stop-pegs are still correctly located against the edges of the trailing shoes, and that each lever operates smoothly. If all is well, with the aid of an assistant, adjust the handbrake cable so that the handbrake lever on each rear brake assembly starts to move as the handbrake is moved between the first and second notch (click) of its ratchet mechanism, ie, so that the stop-pegs are still in contact with the shoes when the handbrake is on the first notch of the ratchet, but no longer contact the shoes when the handbrake is on the second notch. Once the handbrake adjustment is correct, hold the adjuster nut and securely tighten the locknut. Where necessary, refit the exhaust system heat shield to the vehicle underbody.

25 Refit the brake drums as described in Section 12.

26 On completion, check the hydraulic fluid level as described in *Weekly checks*.

27 If new shoes have been fitted, full braking efficiency will not be obtained until the linings have bedded-in. Be prepared for longer stopping distances, and avoid harsh braking as far as possible for the first hundred miles or so after fitting new shoes.

14.3 Brake hose clamp fitted to rear brake flexible hose

14 Rear wheel cylinder – removal and refitting

Note: *Before starting work, refer to the warnings at the beginning of Section 6 concerning the dangers of hydraulic fluid, and at the beginning of Section 13 concerning the dangers of asbestos dust.*

Removal

1 Remove the brake drum as described in Section 12.

2 Using pliers, carefully unhook the brake shoe upper return spring and remove it from the brake shoes. Pull the upper ends of the shoes away from the wheel cylinder to disengage them from the pistons.

3 Minimise fluid loss, either by removing the master cylinder reservoir cap and then tightening it down onto a piece of polythene to obtain an airtight seal (taking care not to damage the sender unit), or by using a brake hose clamp, a G-clamp or a similar tool with protected jaws to clamp the flexible hose at the nearest convenient point to the wheel cylinder **(see illustration)**.

4 Wipe away all traces of dirt around the brake pipe union at the rear of the wheel cylinder, and unscrew the union nut **(see**

illustration). Carefully ease the pipe out of the wheel cylinder, and plug or tape over its end to prevent dirt entry. Wipe off any spilt fluid immediately.

5 Unscrew the two wheel cylinder retaining bolts from the rear of the backplate **(see illustration)**. Remove the cylinder, taking care not to allow hydraulic fluid to contaminate the brake shoe linings.

6 It is not possible to overhaul the cylinder, since no components are available separately. If faulty, the complete wheel cylinder assembly must be renewed.

Refitting

7 Ensure the backplate and wheel cylinder mating surfaces are clean, then spread the brake shoes and manoeuvre the wheel cylinder into position.

8 Engage the brake pipe, and screw in the union nut two or three turns to ensure that the thread has started.

9 Insert the two wheel cylinder retaining bolts, and tighten them securely. Now fully tighten the brake pipe union nut.

10 Remove the clamp from the brake hose, or the polythene from the master cylinder reservoir (as applicable).

11 Ensure that the brake shoes are correctly located in the cylinder pistons. Carefully refit the brake shoe upper return spring, using a screwdriver to stretch the spring into position.

12 Refit the brake drum as described in Section 12.

13 Bleed the brake hydraulic system as described in Section 6. Providing the correct precautions were taken to minimise loss of fluid, it should only be necessary to bleed the relevant rear brake.

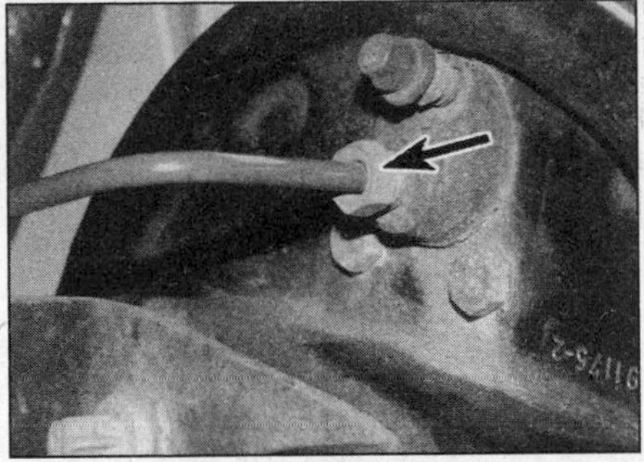

14.4 Unscrew the brake union nut (arrowed) from the rear of the wheel cylinder

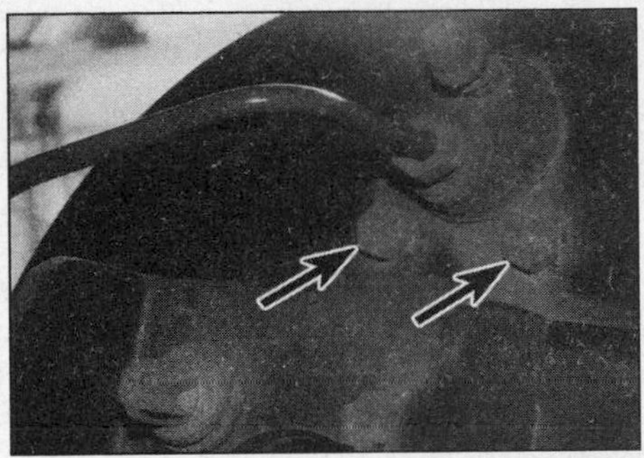

14.5 Undo the two wheel cylinder retaining bolts (arrowed)

15 Handbrake lever – removal and refitting

Removal

1 Chock the front wheels, engage reverse gear (or P) and release the handbrake. Jack up the rear of the vehicle and support it on axle stands (see *Jacking and vehicle support*).

2 Working from inside the vehicle, move the front seats as far forwards as possible. Undo the two retaining screws in the rear of the console and lift it off from around the handbrake lever **(see illustration)**.

3 Working from underneath the vehicle, undo the nuts securing the exhaust system heat shield to the vehicle underbody. Manoeuvre the heat shield out from under the vehicle **(see illustration)**.

4 Unscrew the handbrake cable adjuster locknut from the end of the handbrake linkage rod under the vehicle **(see illustration)**.

5 Disengage the cable equaliser plate from the end of the cable/linkage rod.

6 Working inside the vehicle, unscrew the two nuts securing the lever to the floor, and remove the assembly from the vehicle **(see illustration)**. Disconnect the handbrake warning light switch wire from the rear of the lever.

Refitting

7 Refitting is a reversal of removal. Adjust the handbrake as described in Chapter 1A or 1B.

16 Handbrake cables – removal and refitting

Removal

1 The handbrake cable consists of two sections, a right- and left-hand section, which are linked to the lever assembly by an equaliser plate. Each section can be removed individually as follows.

2 Chock the front wheels, engage reverse gear (or P) and release the handbrake. Jack up the rear of the vehicle and support it on axle stands (see *Jacking and vehicle support*).

3 Working from underneath the vehicle, undo the nut(s) securing the exhaust system heat shield to the vehicle underbody. Manoeuvre the heat shield out from under the vehicle, to gain access to the handbrake cable adjuster nuts (see Section 15, paragraphs 3 and 4).

4 Slacken the adjuster locknut until there is sufficient slack in the cables to allow it to be disconnected from the equaliser plate **(see illustration)**.

5 On models with rear drum brakes, remove the rear brake shoes from the appropriate side as described in Section 13. Using a

15.2 Remove the retaining screws and lift off the handbrake lever trim

15.3 Withdrawing the heat shield from above the exhaust system

15.4 The handbrake adjuster nut is under the vehicle

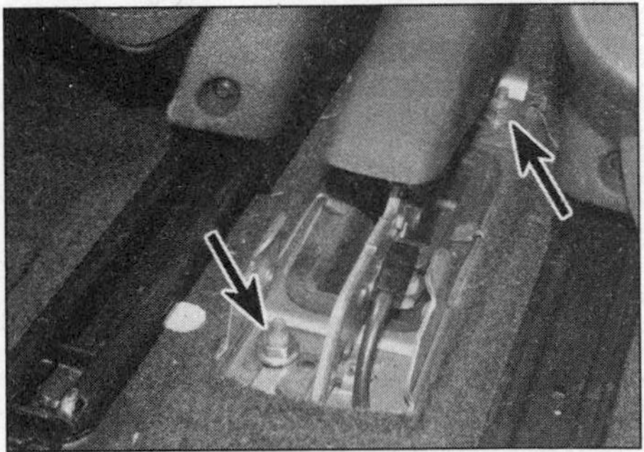

15.6 Unscrew the two handbrake lever mounting nuts (arrowed)

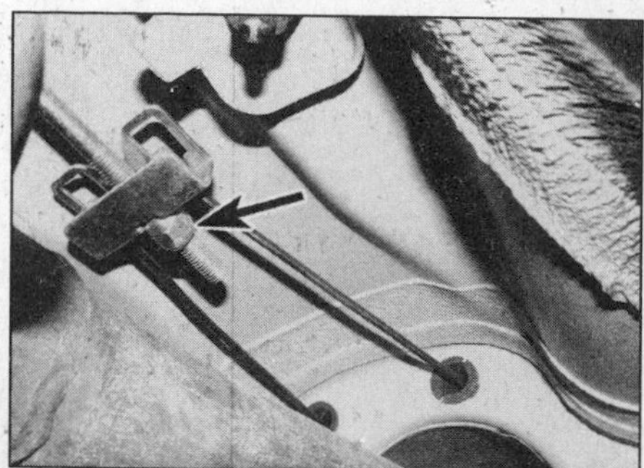

16.4 Slacken the adjuster nut (arrowed) under the vehicle to release the equaliser plate

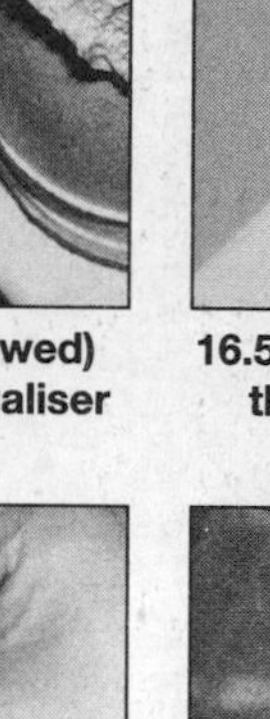

16.5 Drive the handbrake outer cable from the brake backplate (rear drum brake models)

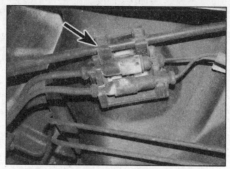

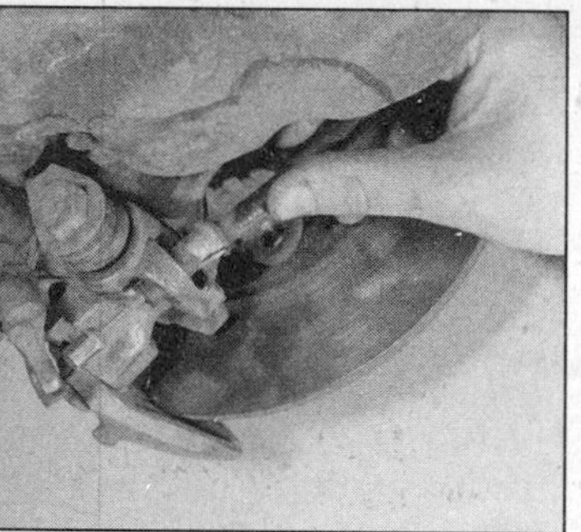

16.6 On rear disc brake models, disconnect the handbrake cable from the brake caliper

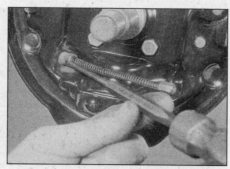

16.7 Release the handbrake cable (arrowed) from the retaining clips

hammer and pin punch, carefully tap the outer cable from the brake backplate **(see illustration)**.

6 On models with rear disc brakes, disengage the inner cable from the caliper handbrake lever. Using a hammer and pin punch, tap the outer cable out of its mounting bracket on the caliper **(see illustration)**.

7 Working along the length of the cable, remove any retaining bolts and screws, and free the cable from the retaining clips and ties **(see illustration)**. Remove the cable from under the vehicle.

Refitting

8 Refitting is a reversal of removal. Adjust the handbrake as described in Chapter 1A or 1B.

17 Rear brake pads - inspection and renewal

Warning: Renew both sets of rear brake pads at the same time - never renew the pads on only one wheel, as uneven braking may result. Note that the dust created by wear of the pads may contain asbestos, which is a health hazard. Never blow it out with compressed air, and don't inhale any of it. An approved filtering mask should be worn when working on the brakes. DO NOT use petroleum-based solvents to clean brake parts - use brake cleaner or methylated spirit only.

Inspection

1 Chock the front wheels, engage reverse gear (or P) and release the handbrake. Jack up the rear of the vehicle and support it on axle stands (see *Jacking and vehicle support*). Remove the rear wheels.

2 Extract the small spring clip from the pad retaining plate. Slide the plate out of the caliper **(see illustrations)**.

3 Withdraw the inner pad from the caliper, using pliers if necessary. Slacken and remove the two outer pad retaining screws, then withdraw the outer pad from the caliper **(see illustrations)**. Make a note of the correct fitted position of the anti-rattle springs, and remove the springs from each pad.

4 First measure the thickness of each brake pad (friction material and backing plate). If either pad is worn at any point to the specified minimum thickness or less, all four pads must be renewed. Also, the pads should be renewed if any are fouled with oil or grease; there is no satisfactory way of degreasing

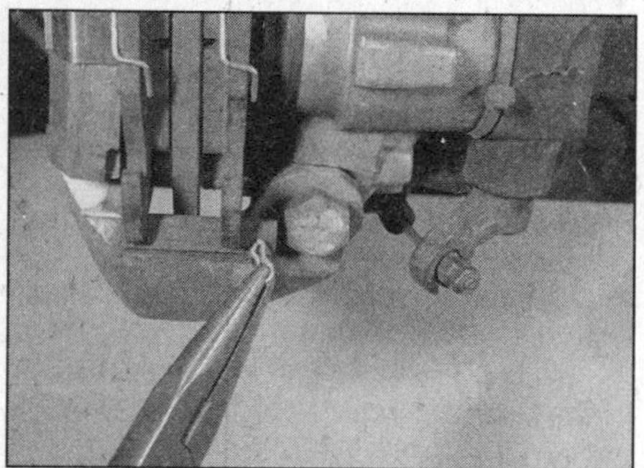

17.2a To remove rear brake pads, remove the spring clip . . .

17.2b . . . then withdraw the retaining plate from the caliper

17.3a Slide out the inner brake pad . . .

17.3b . . . undo the two retaining screws . . .

17.3c . . . and withdraw the outer brake pad

friction material once contaminated. If any of the brake pads are worn unevenly, or fouled with oil or grease, trace and rectify the cause before reassembly. New brake pads and spring kits are available from Renault dealers.

5 If the brake pads are still serviceable, carefully clean them using a clean, fine wire brush or similar, paying particular attention to the sides and back of the metal backing. Clean out the grooves in the friction material, and pick out any large embedded particles of dirt or debris. Clean the pad locations in the caliper body/mounting bracket.

6 Prior to fitting the pads, check that the guide sleeves are free to slide easily in the caliper body, and that the guide sleeve rubber gaiters are undamaged. Brush the dust and dirt from the caliper and piston, but *do not inhale it, as it is injurious to health.* Inspect the dust seal around the piston for damage, and the piston for evidence of fluid leaks, corrosion or damage. If attention to any of these components is necessary, refer to Section 18.

Renewal

7 If new brake pads are to be fitted, it will be necessary to retract the piston fully into the caliper bore by rotating it in a clockwise direction. This can be achieved using a length of square-section bar, such as the shaft of a screwdriver, which locates snugly in the caliper piston slots **(see illustration)**. Provided that the master cylinder reservoir has not been overfilled with hydraulic fluid, there should be no spillage, but keep a careful watch on the fluid level while retracting the piston. If the fluid level rises above the MAX level, the surplus should be syphoned off (not by mouth – use an old syringe or antifreeze tester), or ejected via a plastic tube connected to the bleed screw (see Section 6).

8 Position the caliper piston so that the small groove scribed across the piston points in the direction of the caliper bleed screw. This is necessary to ensure that the lug on the inner pad will locate with the caliper piston slot on installation **(see illustration)**.

9 Refit the anti-rattle springs to the pads, so that when the pads are installed in the caliper, the spring end will be located at the opposite end of the pad in relation to the pad retaining plate. The brake pad with the lug on its backing plate is the inner pad **(see illustration)**.

10 Locate the outer brake pad in the caliper body, ensuring that its friction material is against the brake disc. Insert the retaining screws and tighten them securely.

11 Slide the inner pad into position in the caliper, ensuring that the lug on the pad backing plate is aligned with the slot in the caliper piston. Recheck that the anti-rattle spring ends on both pads are at the opposite end of the pad to which the retaining plate is to be inserted.

12 Slide the retaining plate into place, and install the small spring clip at its inner end. It may be necessary to file an entry chamfer on the edge of the retaining key, to enable it to be fitted without difficulty.

17.7 Retract the piston using a square-section bar

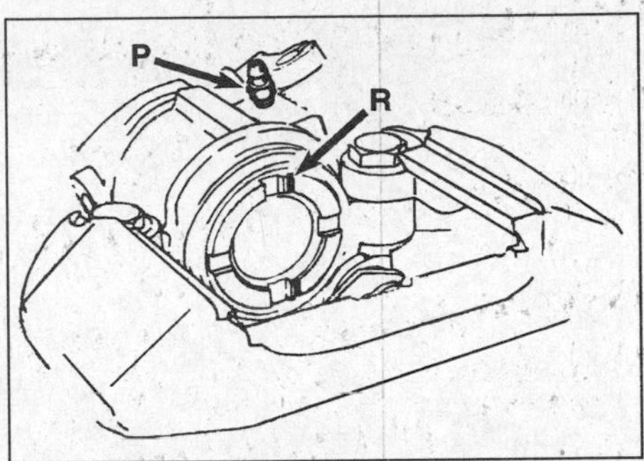

17.8 Prior to installing rear brake pads, align groove on caliper piston (R) with bleed screw (P)

13 Depress the brake pedal repeatedly until the pads are pressed into firm contact with the brake disc. Check that the inner pad lug is correctly engaged with one of the caliper piston slots **(see illustration)**.

14 Repeat the procedure on the remaining rear brake caliper.

15 Check the handbrake cable adjustment as described in Chapter 1A or 1B, then refit the roadwheels and lower the vehicle to the ground. Tighten the roadwheel bolts to the specified torque.

16 Check the hydraulic fluid level as described in *Weekly checks*.

17 If new pads have been fitted, full braking efficiency will not be obtained until the linings have bedded-in. Be prepared for longer stopping distances, and avoid harsh braking as far as possible for the first hundred miles or so after fitting new pads.

18 Rear brake caliper – removal, overhaul and refitting

Note: *Before starting work, refer to the warnings at the beginning of Section 6 concerning the dangers of hydraulic fluid, and at the beginning of Section 17 concerning the dangers of asbestos dust.*

Removal

1 Chock the front wheels, engage reverse gear (or P) and release the handbrake. Jack up the rear of the vehicle and support it on axle stands (see *Jacking and vehicle support*). Remove the relevant rear wheel.

2 Remove the brake pads as described in Section 17.

3 Free the handbrake inner cable from the caliper handbrake operating lever, then tap the outer cable out of its bracket on the caliper body.

4 Minimise fluid loss, either by removing the master cylinder reservoir cap and then tightening it down onto a piece of polythene to obtain an airtight seal (taking care not to damage the sender unit), or by using a brake hose clamp, a G-clamp or a similar tool with protected jaws to clamp the flexible hose at the nearest convenient point to the brake caliper.

5 Wipe away all traces of dirt around the brake pipe union on the caliper, and unscrew the union nut. Carefully ease the pipe out of position, and plug or tape over its end to prevent dirt entry. Wipe off any spilt fluid immediately.

6 Slacken the two bolts securing the caliper assembly to the trailing arm, and remove them along with the mounting plate, noting which way around the plate is fitted **(see illustration)**. Lift the caliper assembly away from the brake disc.

Overhaul

Note: *Ensure the correct caliper overhaul kit is obtained before starting work.*

7 With the caliper on the bench, wipe away all

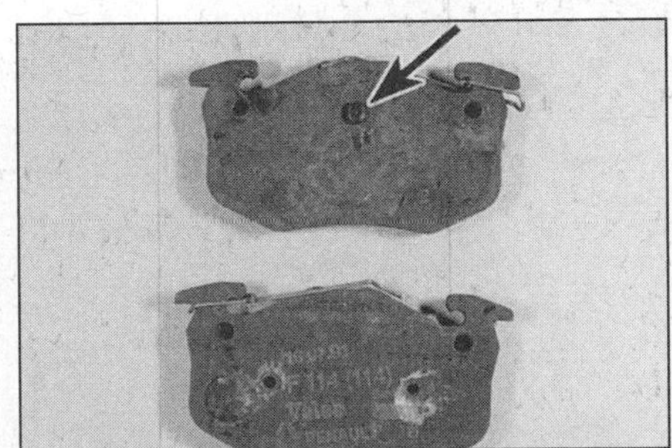

17.9 Inner brake pad can be identified by its locating lug (arrowed). Note correct fitted positions of anti-rattle springs

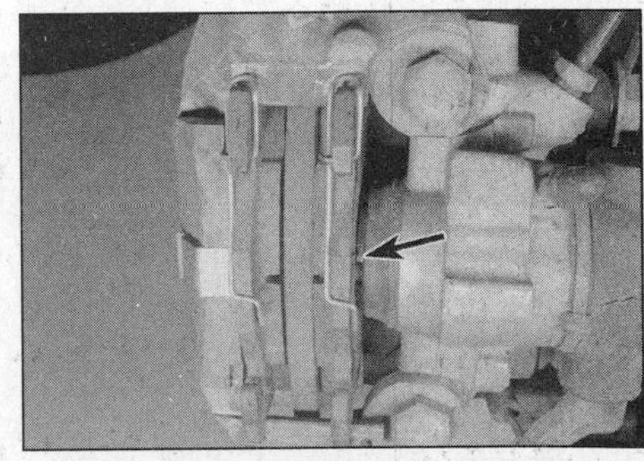

17.13 Ensure inner pad locating lug is correctly located in piston slot (arrowed)

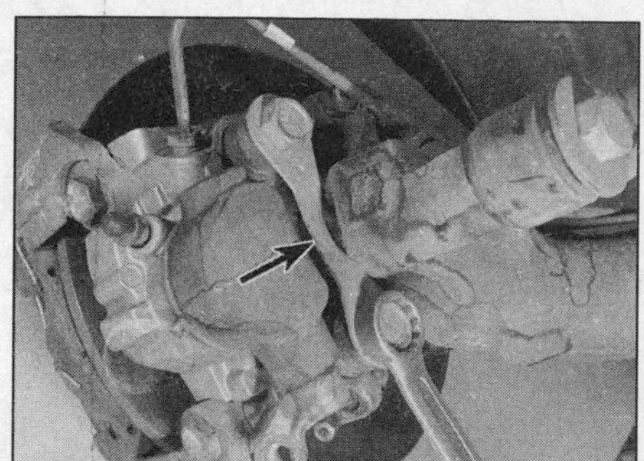

18.6 Remove the caliper mounting bolts, noting which way around the mounting plate is fitted (arrowed)

traces of dust and dirt, but avoid inhaling the dust, as it is injurious to health.

8 Using a small screwdriver, carefully prise out the dust seal from the caliper bore, taking care not to damage the piston **(see illustration)**.

9 Remove the piston from the caliper bore by rotating it in an anti-clockwise direction. This can be achieved by using a square-section bar, such as the shaft of a screwdriver, which locates snugly in the caliper piston slots. Once the piston turns freely but does not come out any further, the piston can be withdrawn by hand, or if necessary pushed out by applying compressed air to the union bolt hole.

Caution: The piston may be ejected with some force - only low pressure should be required, such as is generated by a foot pump.

10 Using a blunt instrument such as a knitting needle or a crochet hook, extract the piston hydraulic seal, taking care not to damage the caliper bore.

11 Withdraw the guide sleeves from the caliper body, and remove the guide sleeve gaiters.

12 Inspect the caliper components as described in Section 10 for the front calipers. Renew as necessary, noting that the inside of the caliper piston must **not** be dismantled. If necessary, the handbrake mechanism can be overhauled as described in the following paragraphs. If it is not wished to overhaul the handbrake mechanism, proceed to paragraph 16.

13 Release the handbrake dust cover retaining clip, and peel the cover away from the rear of the caliper. Make a note of the correct fitted positions of the relative components to use as a guide on reassembly. Remove the circlip from the base of the operating lever shaft, then compress the adjusting screw spring washers, and withdraw the operating lever and dust cover from the caliper body. With the lever withdrawn, remove the return spring, plunger cam, adjusting screw, spring washers and thrustwasher from the rear of the caliper body. Using a pin punch, carefully tap the adjusting screw bush out of the caliper body and remove the O-ring.

14 Clean all the handbrake components in methylated spirit, and examine them for wear. If there is any sign of wear or damage, the complete handbrake mechanism assembly should be renewed.

15 Ensure that all components are clean and dry. Install the O-ring, then press the adjusting screw bush into position until its outer edge is flush with the rear of the caliper body; if necessary, tap the bush into position using a tubular drift. Fit the thrustwasher, then install the adjusting screw and spring washers, ensuring that the washers are correctly positioned **(see illustration)**. Locate the plunger cam in the end of the adjusting screw, and position the return spring in the caliper housing. Fit the new dust cover to the operating lever, then compress the adjusting screw spring washers and insert the lever shaft through the caliper body, ensuring that it is correctly engaged with the return spring and plunger cam. Secure the operating lever in position with the circlip, then release the spring washers and check the operation of the handbrake mechanism. Apply a smear of high-melting point grease to the operating lever shaft and adjusting screw. Slide the dust cover over the caliper body, and secure it in position with a cable tie.

16 Soak the piston and the new piston (fluid) seal in clean hydraulic fluid. Smear clean fluid on the cylinder bore surface.

17 Fit the new piston (fluid) seal, using only the fingers to manipulate it into the cylinder bore groove, and refit the piston assembly. Turn the piston in a clockwise direction, using the method employed on dismantling, until it is fully retracted into the caliper bore.

18 Fit the dust seal to the caliper, ensuring that it is correctly located in the caliper and also the groove on the piston.

19 Apply the grease supplied in the repair kit, or a good-quality high-temperature brake grease or anti-seize compound to the guide sleeves. Fit the guide sleeves to the caliper body, and fit the new gaiters, ensuring that the gaiters are correctly located in the grooves on both the guide sleeve and caliper body.

Refitting

20 Position the caliper over the brake disc. Refit the two caliper mounting bolts and the mounting plate, noting that the mounting plate must be fitted so that its bend curves towards the caliper body. With the plate correctly positioned, tighten the caliper bolts to the specified torque.

21 Wipe clean the brake pipe union. Refit the pipe to the caliper, and tighten its union nut securely.

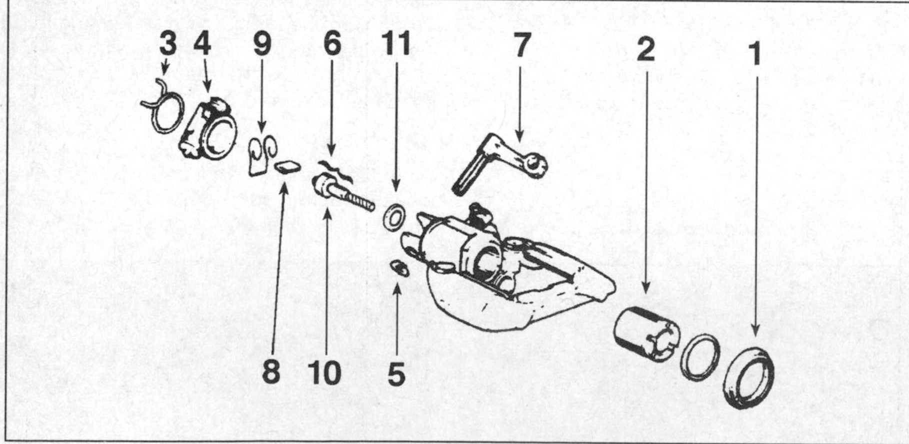

18.8 Exploded view of the rear brake caliper

1 Dust seal
2 Piston
3 Retaining clip
4 Handbrake mechanism dust cover
5 Circlip
6 Spring washers
7 Handbrake operating lever
8 Plunger cam
9 Return spring
10 Adjusting screw
11 Thrustwasher

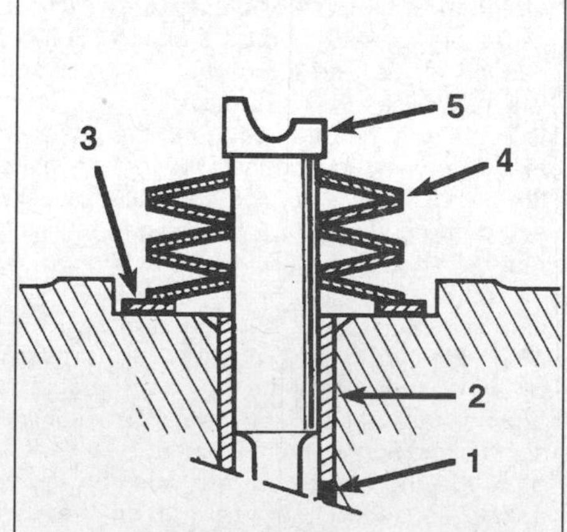

18.15 Correct fitted positions of rear brake caliper handbrake mechanism adjuster screw and associated components

1 O-ring
2 Adjusting screw bush
3 Thrustwasher
4 Correct arrangement of spring washers
5 Adjusting screw

22 Remove the clamp from the brake hose, or the polythene from the master cylinder reservoir (as applicable).
23 Insert the handbrake cable through its bracket on the caliper, and tap the outer cable into position using a hammer and a pin punch **(see illustration)**. Reconnect the inner cable to the caliper operating lever.
24 Refit the brake pads as described in Section 17.
25 Bleed the hydraulic system as described in Section 6. Note that, providing the precautions described were taken to minimise brake fluid loss, it should only be necessary to bleed the relevant rear brake.
26 Repeatedly apply the brake pedal to bring the pads into contact with the disc. Check and if necessary adjust the handbrake cable as described in Chapter 1A or 1B.
27 Refit the roadwheel, lower the vehicle to the ground and tighten the wheel bolts to the specified torque. On completion, check the hydraulic fluid level as described in *Weekly checks*.

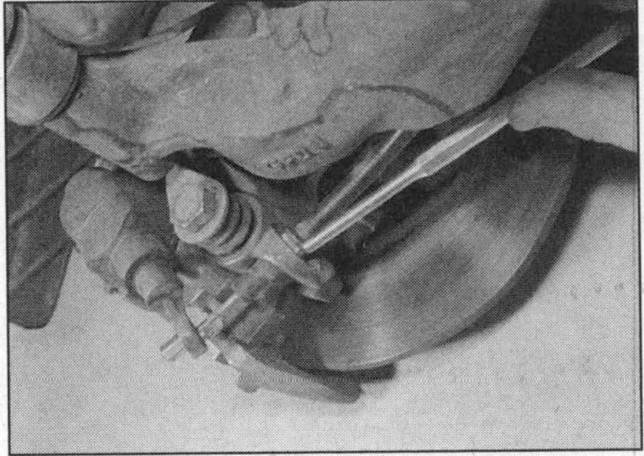

18.23 Tap the handbrake outer cable into position using a hammer and punch

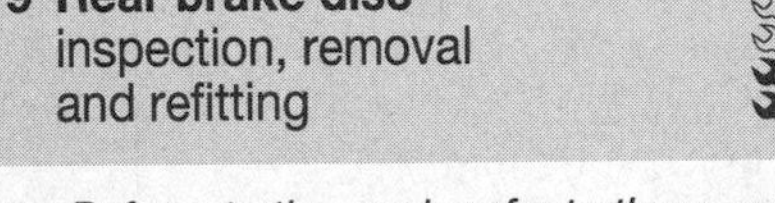

19 Rear brake disc – inspection, removal and refitting

Note: *Before starting work, refer to the warning at the beginning of Section 17 concerning the dangers of asbestos dust. If either disc requires renewal, both should be renewed at the same time, to ensure even and consistent braking. A new rear hub nut will be required on refitting.*

Inspection

1 Chock the front wheels, engage reverse gear (or P) and release the handbrake. Jack up the rear of the vehicle and support it on axle stands (see *Jacking and vehicle support*). Remove the appropriate rear roadwheel.
2 Inspect the disc as described in Section 11.

Removal

3 Remove the brake pads as described in Section 17.
4 Remove the two caliper frame retaining bolts. Remove the frame from the caliper body.
5 Using a hammer and a large flat-bladed screwdriver, carefully tap and prise the cap out of the centre of the brake disc **(see illustration)**.
6 Using a socket and long bar, slacken and remove the rear hub nut and withdraw the thrustwasher. Discard the hub nut; a new nut must be used on refitting.
7 It should now be possible to withdraw the brake disc and hub bearing assembly from the stub axle by hand. It may be difficult to remove the disc, due to the tightness of the hub bearing on the stub axle. If the bearing is tight, tap the periphery of the disc using a hide or plastic mallet, or use a universal puller, secured to the disc with the wheel bolts, to pull it off. Remove the spacer from the rear of the disc, noting which way round it is fitted.

Refitting

8 Prior to refitting the disc, smear the stub axle shaft with gear oil. Be careful not to contaminate the friction surfaces with oil. If a new disc is to be fitted, use a suitable solvent to wipe any preservative coating from its surface.
9 Refit the spacer to the rear of the disc, noting that its slightly bigger protrusion should face the hub bearing. Slide the disc onto the stub axle, and tap it into position using a soft-faced mallet **(see illustrations)**.
10 Slide on the thrustwasher, then fit the new rear hub nut and tighten it to the specified torque **(see illustration)**. Tap the cap back into position in the centre of the disc.
11 Apply a few drops of locking fluid to the threads of the caliper frame retaining bolts. Offer up the frame and refit the bolts. Tighten both bolts to the specified torque **(see illustrations)**.
12 Refit the brake pads as described in Section 17.
13 Check the handbrake cable adjustment as described in Chapter 1A or 1B.

19.5 Prising out the rear disc hub cap

19.9a Refit the spacer to the rear of the brake disc . . .

19.9b . . . and slide the disc onto the stub axle

19.10 Tighten the new rear hub nut to the specified torque

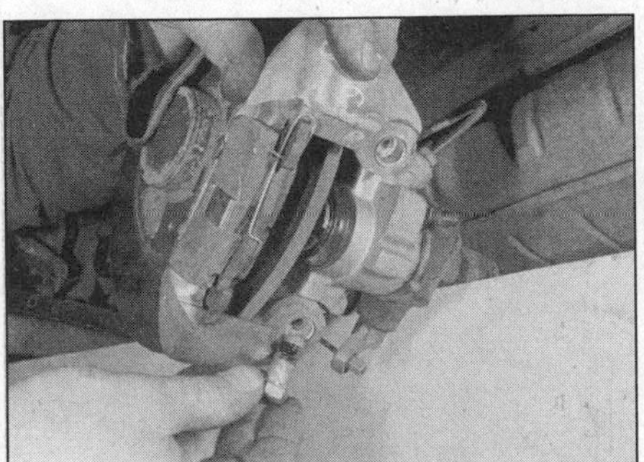

19.11a Apply locking fluid to the retaining bolts, then refit the caliper frame . . .

19.11b . . . and tighten the bolts

20.6 Disconnect the brake pipe unions (arrowed) from the load-sensitive pressure-regulating valve

14 Refit the roadwheels and lower the vehicle to the ground. Tighten the roadwheel bolts to the specified torque.

20 Load-sensitive pressure-regulating valve – testing, removal and refitting

Testing

1 Depending on model, a load-sensitive pressure regulating valve may be fitted into the hydraulic circuit to the rear brakes. The valve is mounted onto the underside of the rear of the vehicle and is attached to the rear axle. The valve measures the load on the rear axle, via the movement of the axle, and regulates the hydraulic pressure being applied to the rear brakes to help prevent rear wheels locking up under hard braking.

2 Specialist equipment is required to check the performance of the valve(s), therefore if the valve is thought to be faulty the car should be taken to a suitably-equipped Renault dealer for testing. Repairs are not possible and, if faulty, the valve must be renewed.

Removal

Caution: On models equipped with ABS, disconnect the battery before disconnecting any braking system hydraulic union and do not reconnect the battery until after the hydraulic system has been bled. Failure to do this could lead to air entering the hydraulic unit. If air enters the hydraulic unit pump, it will prove very difficult (in some cases impossible) to bleed the unit (see Section 6).

Note: *Before starting work, refer to the warning at the beginning of Section 6 concerning the dangers of hydraulic fluid.*

3 Minimise fluid loss by first removing the master cylinder reservoir cap, and then tightening it down onto a piece of polythene, to obtain an airtight seal.

4 Check the front wheels then jack up the rear of the vehicle and support it on axle stands (see *Jacking and vehicle support*).

5 Wipe clean the area around the brake pipe unions on the valve, and place absorbent rags beneath the pipe unions to catch any surplus fluid. To avoid confusion on refitting, make alignment marks between the pipes and valve assembly.

6 Slacken the union nuts and disconnect the brake pipes from the valve **(see illustration)**. Plug or tape over the pipe ends and valve orifices, to minimise the loss of brake fluid, and to prevent the entry of dirt into the system. Wash off any spilt fluid immediately with cold water.

7 Slacken and remove the retaining bolts then unclip the valve link rod **(see illustration)** and remove the valve assembly from underneath the vehicle. **Note:** *Do not slacken the link rod clamp bolt. If the bolt is slackened and the link rod length altered the valve will need to be adjusted on refitting.*

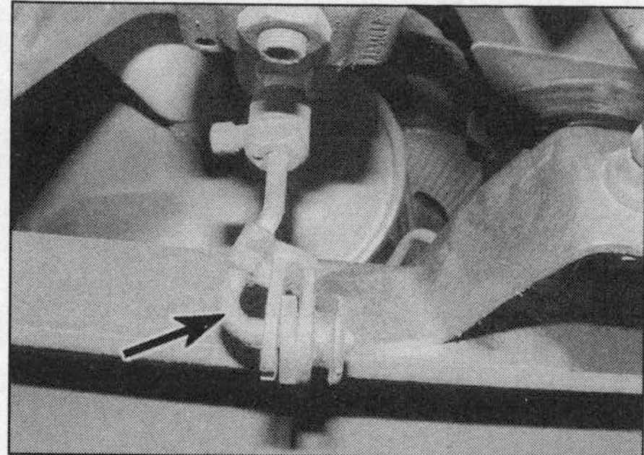

20.7 Unclip the link rod from the bracket on the axle

Refitting

8 Manoeuvre the valve assembly into position and tighten its retaining bolts securely.

9 Refit the brake pipes to their specific unions on the valve and tighten the union nuts to the specified torque setting.

10 Clip the valve link rod back into position in its retaining clip and lower the vehicle to the ground.

11 If a new valve assembly is being fitted, it will be noted that a spacer is fitted to the link rod; this is to adjust the link rod length. With the vehicle resting on its wheels, with a full tank of fuel and one person in the driver's seat, slacken the link rod clamp bolt and allow the valve spring to set the link rod length. Securely tighten the clamp bolt and remove the spacer from the link rod. Although not strictly necessary, it is recommended that the valve operation is tested by a Renault dealer.

12 Remove the polythene from the master cylinder reservoir and bleed the complete hydraulic system as described in Section 6.

21 Stop-light switch – removal, refitting and adjustment

Removal

1 The stop-light switch is located on the pedal bracket beneath the facia.

2 To remove the switch, reach up behind the facia, disconnect the wiring connector and unscrew the switch from the bracket **(see illustrations)**.

Refitting and adjustment

3 Refitting is a reversal of removal. Before fitting the switch, the plunger should be reset as follows. Pull the plunger out firmly – it should extend on its ratchet mechanism by several clicks. When the switch is refitted and the pedal pressed for the first few times, the plunger will be pushed back in automatically to the correct setting.

4 On completion, check the operation of the stop-lights.

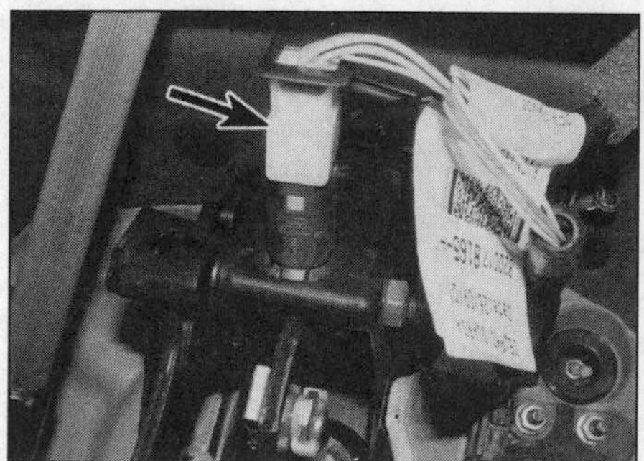

21.2a Disconnect the wiring connector (arrowed) . . .

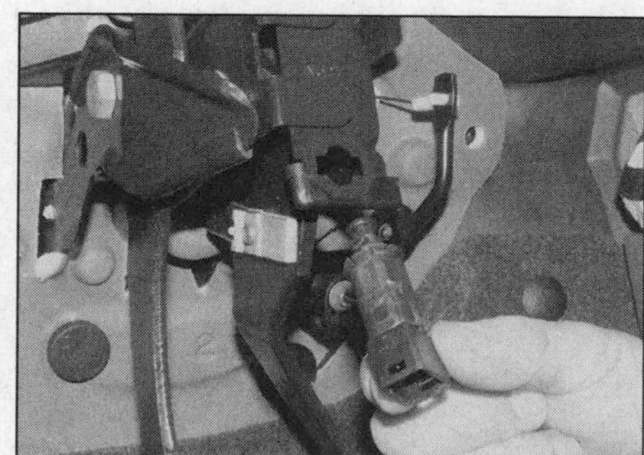

21.2b . . . and unscrew the stop-light switch (facia panel removed for clarity)

22 Anti-lock braking system (ABS) – general information

1 The purpose of the system is to prevent the wheel(s) locking during heavy braking. This is achieved by automatic release of the brake on the relevant wheel, followed by reapplication of the brake **(see illustration)**.

2 The main components of the system are four wheel sensors (one per wheel), and a modulator

block which contains the ABS computer, the hydraulic solenoid valves and accumulators, and an electrically-driven return pump.

3 The solenoids are controlled by the computer, which receives signals from the wheel sensors. The sensors detect the speed of rotation of a toothed ring, known as a reluctor ring, attached to the wheel hub. By comparing the speed signals from the four wheels, the computer can determine when a wheel is decelerating at an abnormal rate, and can therefore predict when a wheel is about to lock. During normal operation, the system functions in the same way as a non-ABS braking system does.

4 If the computer senses that a wheel is about to lock, the ABS system enters the 'pressure-maintain' phase. The computer operates the relevant solenoid valve in the modulator block; this isolates the brake on the wheel in question from the master cylinder, effectively sealing-in the hydraulic pressure.

5 If the speed of rotation of the wheel continues to decrease at an abnormal rate, the ABS system then enters the 'pressure-decrease' phase. The return pump operates and pumps the hydraulic fluid back into the master cylinder, releasing pressure on the brake. When the speed of rotation of the wheel returns to an acceptable rate, the pump stops and the solenoid valve opens, allowing hydraulic pressure to return and reapply the brake. This cycle can be carried out at up to 10 times a second.

6 The action of the solenoid valves and return pump creates pulses in the hydraulic circuit. When the ABS system is functioning, these pulses can be felt through the brake pedal.

7 The solenoid valves connected to the front calipers operate independently, but the valve connected to the rear brakes operates both simultaneously. Since the braking circuit is split diagonally, a separate mechanical plunger valve in the modulator block divides the rear solenoid valve hydraulic outlet into two separate circuits.

8 The operation of the ABS system is entirely dependent on electrical signals. To prevent the system responding to any inaccurate signals, a built-in safety circuit monitors all signals received by the computer. If an inaccurate signal or low battery voltage is detected, the ABS system is automatically shut down, and the warning lamp on the instrument panel is illuminated to inform the driver that the ABS system is not operational. Normal braking is unaffected.

9 If a fault does develop in the ABS system, the vehicle must be taken to a Renault dealer for fault diagnosis and repair. Check first, however, that the problem is not due to loose or damaged wiring connections, or badly-routed wiring picking up spurious signals from the ignition system.

Warning: If the ABS fuse is removed, be careful during road tests not to brake hard as the Electronic Braking Distributor Function is no longer activated.

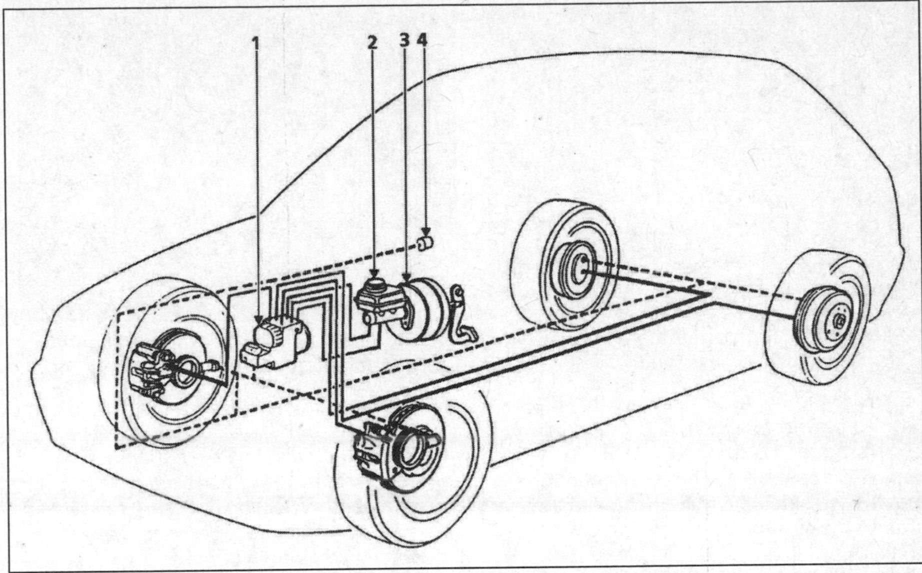

22.1 Location of the Bosch anti-lock braking system (ABS) components

1 Hydraulic assembly
2 Master cylinder
3 Brake servo
4 Brake fluid level warning light

23 Anti-lock braking system (ABS) components – removal and refitting

Caution: Disconnect the battery before removing any braking system hydraulic unions and do not reconnect the battery until after the hydraulic system has been bled. Failure to do this could lead to air entering the hydraulic unit. If air enters the hydraulic unit pump, it will prove very difficult (in some cases impossible) to bleed the unit (see Section 6).

Hydraulic Unit

Note: *Before starting work, refer to the warning at the beginning of Section 6 concerning the dangers of hydraulic fluid.*

Removal

1 Disconnect the battery negative lead (refer to *Disconnecting the battery* in the Reference Section).

2 Detach the coolant expansion bottle and move it to one side.

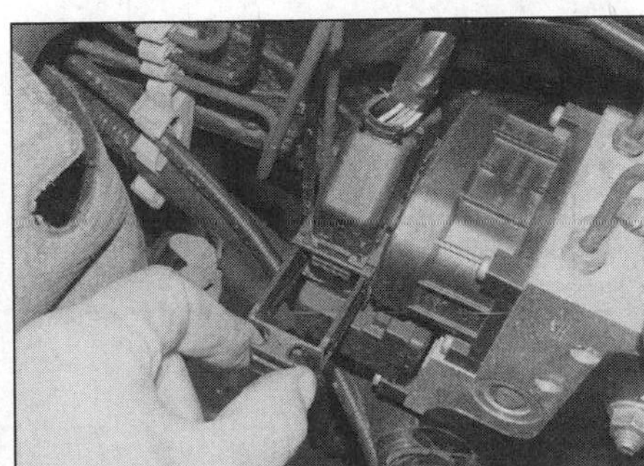

23.3a Slide the locking clip out . . .

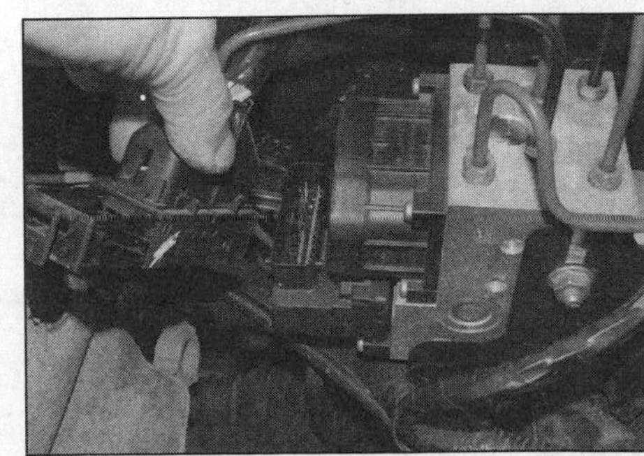

23.3b . . . and disconnect the wiring block connector

3 Disconnect the large block connector from the hydraulic unit **(see illustrations)**.

4 Release any earth leads and wiring loom retaining clips from the mounting bracket.

5 Remove the master cylinder reservoir filler cap. Place a piece of polythene over the filler neck, and securely refit the cap (taking care not to damage the sender unit). This will minimise brake fluid loss during subsequent operations. On all models, be prepared for some fluid spillage. As a precaution, place absorbent rags beneath the modulator brake pipe unions.

6 Wipe clean the area around the hydraulic unit brake pipe unions. Make a note of how the pipes are arranged, to use as a reference on refitting; the pipes may be colour-coded, and the hydraulic unit unions marked to aid refitting **(see illustration)**. Unscrew the union nuts and carefully withdraw the pipes. Plug or tape over the pipe ends and valve orifices, to minimise the loss of brake fluid and to prevent the entry of dirt into the system. Wash off any spilt fluid immediately with cold water.

7 Slacken and remove the upper mounting bolt **(see illustration)**, and the lower mounting

23.6 Note the position of the hydraulic unit brake pipe union

23.7 Unscrew the upper mounting bolt (arrowed), then the lower mounting bolts

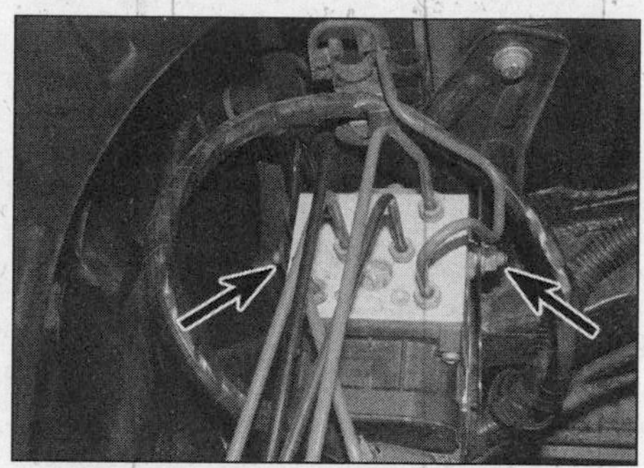
23.8 Slacken the two securing nuts (arrowed)

bolts from the hydraulic unit support bracket and withdraw from the engine compartment.

8 To remove the hydraulic unit from the support bracket, undo the two securing nuts (one at each side). If required, remove the two studs to make removal of the unit easier **(see illustration)**.

Caution: Do not attempt to dismantle the hydraulic unit assembly. Overhaul of the unit is a complex job, and should be entrusted to a Renault dealer.

Refitting

9 Refitting is the reverse of the removal procedure, noting the following points:

a) *Tighten the hydraulic unit mounting nuts securely.*

b) *Refit the brake pipes to the correct unions, and tighten the union nuts to the specified torque.*

c) *Ensure the wiring is correctly routed, and the connectors firmly pressed into position.*

d) *Before reconnecting the battery, bleed the complete braking system as described in Section 6. Ensure the system is bled in the correct order, to prevent air entering the return pump.*

ABS computer

10 The computer is an integral part of the hydraulic unit assembly **(see illustration)**, and cannot be renewed separately. If renewal is necessary, the hydraulic unit must be renewed as a complete assembly, as described in this Section.

Front wheel sensor

Removal

11 Chock the rear wheels and apply the handbrake. Jack up the front of the vehicle and support it on axle stands (see *Jacking and vehicle support*). Remove the appropriate front roadwheel.

12 Release the sensor wiring connector from its clip on the side of the suspension turret and disconnect the connector **(see illustration)**.

13 Pull the sensor wiring lead through from under the wheel arch, and free the sensor wiring from its bracket on the suspension strut **(see illustration)**.

14 Remove the bolt securing the sensor to the swivel hub, and remove the sensor and lead assembly from the vehicle **(see illustrations)**.

Refitting

15 Prior to refitting, apply a thin coat of multi-purpose grease to the sensor tip.

16 Ensure that the sensor and swivel hub sealing faces are clean. Fit the sensor, using

23.10 The computer (arrowed) is part of the ABS hydraulic brake unit

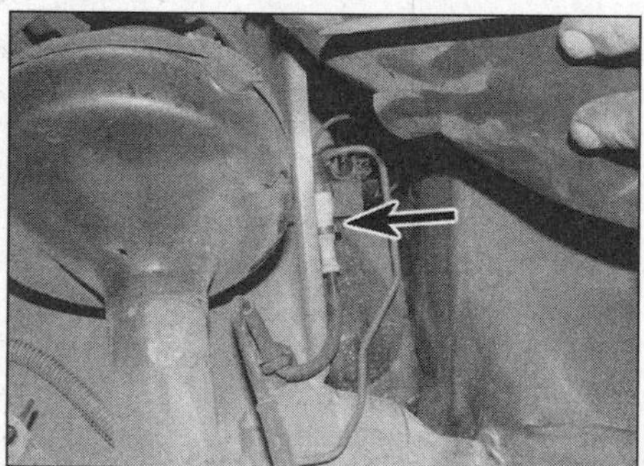
23.12 Release the sensor wiring (arrowed) from the suspension strut bracket

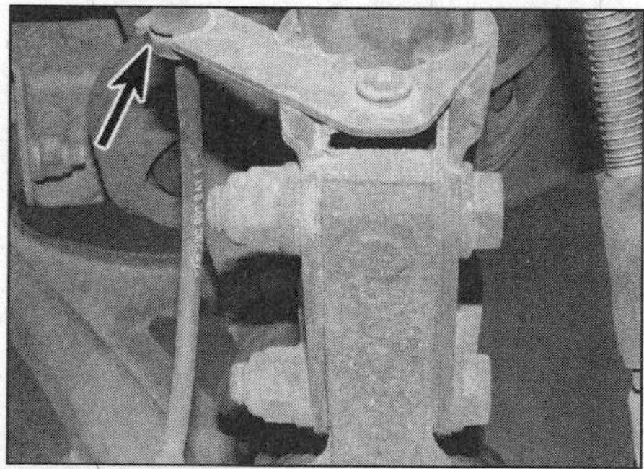
23.13 Unclip the sensor wire (arrowed) from the strut bracket

23.14a Undo the retaining screw (arrowed) . . .

23.14b . . . and withdraw the sensor from the swivel hub

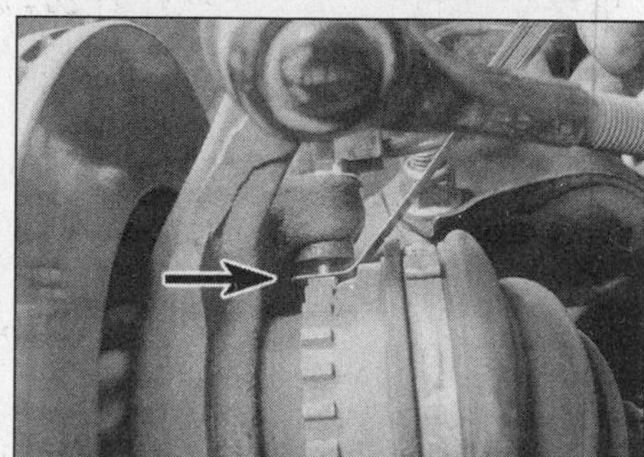
23.17 Checking front wheel sensor-to-reluctor ring clearance

hand pressure only; in particular, do not hit it with a hammer. Fit the sensor retaining bolt, and tighten it to the specified torque.

17 Rotate the hub until one of the reluctor ring teeth is aligned with the sensor tip. Using feeler gauges, measure the air gap between the tooth and the sensor tip **(see illustration)**. Rotate the hub and repeat the check on several other teeth. If the air gap is not within the range given in the Specifications, then the advice of a Renault dealer must be sought to supply shims.

18 Ensure the sensor wiring is correctly routed, then clip it back into position in the strut bracket.

19 Feed the wiring through into the engine compartment, and reconnect the wiring connector. Refit the connector to its retaining clip, then refit the sealing grommet to the wing valance.

20 Refit the roadwheel. Lower the vehicle to the ground and tighten the roadwheel bolts to the specified torque.

Rear wheel sensor

Removal

21 Chock the front wheels, engage reverse gear (or P) and release the handbrake. Jack up the rear of the vehicle and support it on axle stands (see *Jacking and vehicle support*). Remove the appropriate roadwheel.

22 Trace the wiring back from the sensor, and disconnect the wiring from the main wiring loom **(see illustration)**.

23 Work back along the sensor wiring, and free it from any retaining clips.

24 Remove the bolt securing the sensor unit to the rear hub **(see illustration)**. Remove the sensor and lead assembly from the vehicle.

Refitting

25 Prior to refitting, apply a thin coat of multi-purpose grease to the sensor tip.

26 Ensure that the sensor and trailing arm sealing faces are clean. Fit the sensor, using hand pressure only; in particular, do not hit it with a hammer. Tighten the retaining bolt to the specified torque.

27 The rear sensors are not adjustable. If the air gap is not within the range given in the Specifications, then the advice of a Renault dealer must be sought.

28 Ensure that the sensor wiring is correctly routed and retained by all the necessary retaining clips. Reconnect the wiring connector, and clip it into its retaining bracket.

29 Refit the roadwheel. Lower the vehicle to the ground and tighten the roadwheel bolts to the specified torque.

Front reluctor ring

Note: *Reluctor rings may be part of the driveshaft or hub assemblies, check on the availability of a new reluctor ring at your local dealer before removal.*

Removal

30 The front reluctor rings are a press-fit on

23.22 Rear wheel sensor wiring connectors (arrowed) under the left-hand side of the vehicle

23.30 Front reluctor ring (arrowed) is part of the driveshaft

the driveshaft outer constant velocity (CV) joints **(see illustration)**. They should not normally need any attention, but if damage is found such as chipped or missing teeth, they may be renewed as follows.

31 Remove the appropriate driveshaft as described in Chapter 8.

32 Using a heavy-duty puller, carefully draw the reluctor ring off the end of the CV joint.

Refitting

33 Ensure the mating surfaces of the reluctor ring and CV joint are clean and dry. Apply a thin coat of locking fluid to the inside of the ring.

34 Locate the reluctor ring on the CV joint, and tap the ring squarely onto the locating shoulder. Note that, to ensure the correct operation of the ABS system, it is important that the ring is correctly and squarely seated against the CV joint shoulder.

24.1 Unclip the cover from the top of the engine

23.24 Remove the rear wheel sensor retaining bolt (arrowed) – rear drum brakes

23.36 Rear reluctor ring (arrowed) on inside of rear drum brake

35 Refit the driveshaft to the vehicle as described in Chapter 8, then check the sensor tip air gap as described in paragraph 17 of this Section.

Rear reluctor ring

36 At the time of writing, the rear reluctor rings where an integral part of the rear hub **(see illustration)**, and could not be renewed separately. Examine the rings for signs of damage such as chipped or missing teeth, and renew as necessary. If renewal is necessary, the hub may need to be renewed (as described in Chapter 10).

24 Vacuum pump (diesel engines) – removal and refitting

Note: *The vacuum pump is bolted to the transmission end of the cylinder head, a new gasket will be required before refitting.*

Removal

1 Unclip the engine cover from the top of the engine **(see illustration)**.

2 If required, to give better access to the vacuum pump, remove the air filter housing as described in Chapter 4B.

3 Release the retaining clip and disconnect the vacuum hose from the pump.

4 Slacken and remove the two mounting bolts securing the pump to the end of the cylinder head **(see illustration)**, then remove the

24.4 Undo the two retaining bolts (arrowed) – one out of view

24.5 Fitting new gasket to vacuum pump

pump. Recover the pump gasket and discard it; a new one should be used on refitting.

Refitting

5 Ensure that the pump and cylinder head mating surfaces are clean and dry and fit the new gasket to the head **(see illustration)**.

6 Manoeuvre the pump into position, then refit the pump mounting bolts and tighten them securely.

25 Vacuum pump (diesel engines) – testing and overhaul

1 The operation of the braking system vacuum pump can be checked using a vacuum gauge.

2 Disconnect the vacuum pipe from the pump, and connect the gauge to the pump union using a length of hose.

3 Start the engine and allow it to idle, then measure the vacuum created by the pump. As a guide, after one minute, a minimum of approximately 500 mm Hg should be recorded. If the vacuum registered is significantly less than this, it is likely that the pump is faulty. However, seek the advice of a Renault dealer before condemning the pump.

4 Overhaul of the vacuum pump may not be possible; check for availability of spares.

Chapter 10
Suspension and steering

Contents

Degrees of difficulty

Easy, suitable for novice with little experience 	**Fairly easy,** suitable for beginner with some experience 	**Fairly difficult,** suitable for competent DIY mechanic 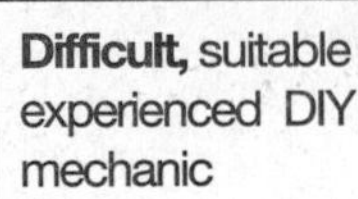	**Difficult,** suitable for experienced DIY mechanic 	**Very difficult,** suitable for expert DIY or professional

Specifications

Front suspension

Type	Independent, MacPherson struts, with coil springs and integral shock absorbers. Anti-roll bar fitted to all models
Hub bearing endfloat	0 to 0.05 mm
Front ride height – difference between sides must not exceed	5.0 mm

Rear suspension

Type	Independent, incorporating trailing arms with telescopic dampers and separate coil springs.
Hub bearing endfloat	0 to 0.05 mm
Ride height – difference between sides must not exceed	5.0 mm

Steering

Type	Power-assisted steering, rack-and-pinion

Wheel alignment and steering angles

Front wheel camber angle at ride height (H1 minus H2) stated:	
14 inch wheels:	
87 mm	- 0° 22' ± 1°
96 mm	- 0° 25' ± 1°
105 mm	- 0° 28' ± 1°
113 mm	- 0° 30' ± 1°
122 mm	- 0° 33' ± 1°
15 inch wheels:	
92 mm	- 0° 25' ± 1°
101 mm	- 0° 27' ± 1°
110 mm	- 0° 28' ± 1°
119 mm	- 0° 30' ± 1°
128 mm	- 0° 31' ± 1°
Maximum difference between left- and right-hand sides	1°
Castor angle at ride height (H5 minus H2) stated:	
14 inch wheels:	
125 mm	1° 41' ± 30'
115 mm	1° 56' ± 30'
105 mm	2° 11' ± 30'
95 mm	2° 26' ± 30'
85 mm	2° 41' ± 30'
15 inch wheels:	
124 mm	1° 42' ± 30'
114 mm	1° 59' ± 30'
103 mm	2° 15' ± 30'
93 mm	2° 32' ± 30'
83 mm	2° 48' ± 30'
Maximum difference between left- and right-hand sides	1°
Steering axis inclination/kingpin inclination at ride height (H1 minus H2) stated:	
14 inch wheels:	
87mm	10° 42' ± 30'
96 mm	10° 53' ± 30'
105 mm	11° 05' ± 30'
113 mm	11° 18' ± 30'
122 mm	11° 30' ± 30'
15 inch wheels:	
92mm	10° 54' ± 30'
101 mm	10° 04' ± 30'
110 mm	11° 15' ± 30'
119 mm	11° 25' ± 30'
128 mm	11° 36' ± 30'
Maximum difference between left- and right-hand sides	1°
Front wheel toe setting (vehicle unladen)	+0° 10' ± 10' (+1.0 mm ± 1.0 mm) toe-out
Rear wheel camber setting (vehicle unladen)	- 0° 46' ± 20'
Rear wheel toe setting (vehicle unladen)	- 0° 40' ± 30' (-7.0 mm ± 5.0 mm) toe-in

Tyres

Tyre size	175/65 R 14T or 185/55 R 15H (depending on model)
Pressures	See end of *Weekly checks* on page 0•18

Roadwheels

Type	Pressed-steel or aluminium alloy (depending on model)
Size	5.5J x 14 or 6J x 15 (depending on model)
Maximum run-out at rim	1.2 mm

Torque wrench settings

	Nm	lbf ft
Front suspension		
Anti-roll bar mounting clamp bolts	30	22
Anti-roll bar-to-lower arm bolt/nut	15	11
Engine tie-bar bolt	65	48
Lower arm balljoint clamp bolt	55	41
Lower arm balljoint retaining nuts	75	55
Lower arm pivot bolts	90	66
Strut upper mounting nut	60	44
Strut-to-swivel hub bolts	105	77

Torque wrench settings (continued)

	Nm	lbf ft
Rear suspension		
Hub nut*	175	129
Rear trailing arm mounting bracket-to-chassis securing bolts	60	44
Rear trailing arm-to-mounting bracket securing bolt	70	52
Shock absorber lower mounting bolt	105	77
Shock absorber upper mounting nut	20	15
Stub axle/back plate mounting bolts	55	41
Steering		
Intermediate shaft universal joint eccentric bolt	25	18
Power steering pump mounting bolts	20	15
Steering column mounting bolts	20	15
Steering gear mounting bolts	50	37
Steering wheel bolt*	45	33
Track rod end balljoint adjustment clamp bolt	18	13
Track rod end balljoint-to-swivel hub retaining nut	37	27
Track rod-to-steering rack axial balljoint:		
SMI steering gear assembly	50	37
TRW steering gear assembly	80	59
Roadwheels		
Wheel bolts	90	66

** Renew every time*

1 General information

The independent front suspension is of the MacPherson strut type, incorporating coil springs and integral telescopic shock absorbers. The MacPherson struts are located by transverse lower suspension arms, which utilise rubber inner mounting bushes and incorporate a balljoint at the outer ends. The front swivel hubs, which carry the wheel bearings, brake calipers and the hub/disc assemblies, are bolted to the MacPherson struts and connected to the lower arms via the balljoints. A front anti-roll bar is fitted to all models. The anti-roll bar is rubber-mounted onto the subframe, and connects both the lower suspension arms.

The rear suspension incorporates a beam axle, trailing arms, coil springs and separate telescopic dampers. The front ends of the trailing arms are attached to the vehicle underbody by rubber bushes, and the rear ends are located by the shock absorbers, which are bolted to the underbody at their upper ends. The coil springs are mounted separately from the shock absorbers, and act directly between the axle and the underbody.

The steering column is connected by a universal joint to an intermediate shaft, which has a second universal joint at its lower end. The lower universal joint is attached to the steering gear pinion by means of an eccentric clamp bolt.

The steering gear is mounted onto the front subframe. It is connected by two track rods and balljoints to steering arms projecting rearwards from the swivel hubs. The track rod ends are threaded to enable wheel alignment adjustment.

An electrically-powered motor is used to power the steering. The motor is attached to the steering column and at the time of writing could only be purchased as a complete unit with the steering column shaft, check with your local dealer for availability of parts.

2 Front swivel hub assembly – removal and refitting

Removal

1 Chock the rear wheels, firmly apply the handbrake, then jack up the front of the vehicle and support it on axle stands *(see Jacking and vehicle support)*. Remove the appropriate front roadwheel.

2 Refit at least two roadwheel bolts to the front hub, and tighten them securely. Remove and discard the driveshaft nut; a new one should be used on refitting.

2.3 Undo the mounting bracket bolts and slide the brake caliper off the disc

3 If the hub bearings are to be disturbed, remove the brake disc as described in Chapter 9. If not, unscrew the two bolts securing the brake caliper assembly to the swivel hub, and slide the caliper assembly off the disc **(see illustration)**. Using a piece of wire or string, tie the caliper to the front suspension coil spring, to avoid straining the brake hose.

4 Undo the retaining bolt and withdraw the front wheel sensor from the swivel hub **(see illustration)**. Tie the sensor to the suspension strut, so that it does not get damaged during the remainder of the removal procedure.

5 Remove the nut securing the track rod end balljoint to the swivel hub. Release the balljoint tapered shank using a universal balljoint separator.

6 Remove the nut and clamp bolt securing the lower suspension arm to the swivel hub **(see illustration)**. Carefully lever the balljoint out of the swivel hub, taking care not to damage the balljoint or driveshaft gaiters. Note the plastic protector plate which is fitted to the balljoint shank.

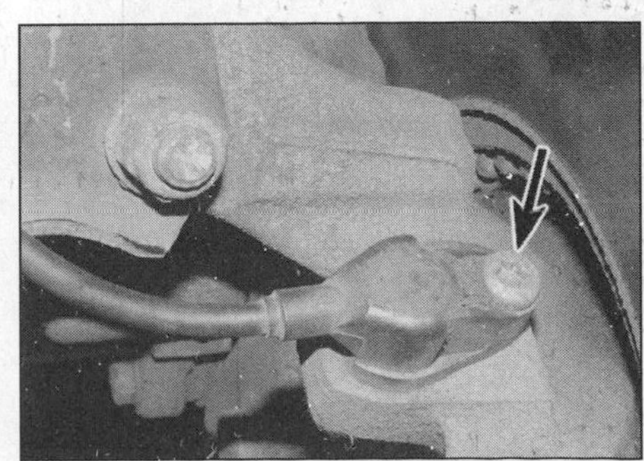

2.4 Front wheel sensor for ABS (arrowed)

2.6 Slacken the lower suspension arm balljoint clamp bolt and nut (arrowed)

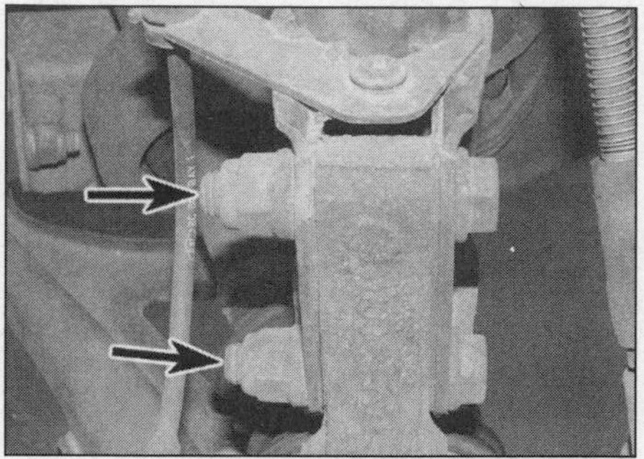

2.7 Note the fitted direction of the lower strut bolts (arrowed)

2.12 Make sure the plastic protector (arrowed) is fitted the correct way around

7 Remove the two nuts from the bolts securing the swivel hub to the suspension strut, noting that the nuts are positioned on the rear side of the strut **(see illustration)**. Withdraw the bolts and support the swivel hub assembly.

8 Release the driveshaft joint from the hub, and remove the swivel hub assembly from the vehicle.

Refitting

9 Ensure that the driveshaft joint and hub splines are clean and dry.

10 Engage the joint splines with the hub, and slide the hub fully onto the driveshaft. Insert the two swivel hub-to-suspension strut mounting bolts from the front side of the strut, then refit the nuts to the bolts and tighten them to the specified torque.

11 Fit the new driveshaft nut, tightening it by hand only at this stage.

12 Ensure that the plastic protector is still fitted to the lower arm balljoint **(see illustration)**, then locate the balljoint shank in the swivel hub. Refit the balljoint clamp bolt, and tighten its retaining nut to the specified torque.

13 Reconnect the track rod end balljoint to the swivel hub, and tighten its retaining nut to the specified torque.

14 Refit the sensor to the hub, and tighten its retaining bolt to the specified torque (see Chapter 9).

15 Refit the brake disc (if removed), aligning the marks made on removal, and securely tighten its retaining screws. Slide the brake caliper assembly into position over the brake disc. Apply a few drops of locking fluid to the caliper bolt threads. Refit the bolts and tighten them to the specified torque (Chapter 9).

16 Insert and tighten two wheel bolts. Tighten the driveshaft nut to the specified torque (Chapter 8), using the method employed during removal to prevent the hub from rotating.

17 Check that the hub rotates freely, then refit the roadwheel and lower the vehicle to the ground. Tighten the roadwheel bolts to the specified torque.

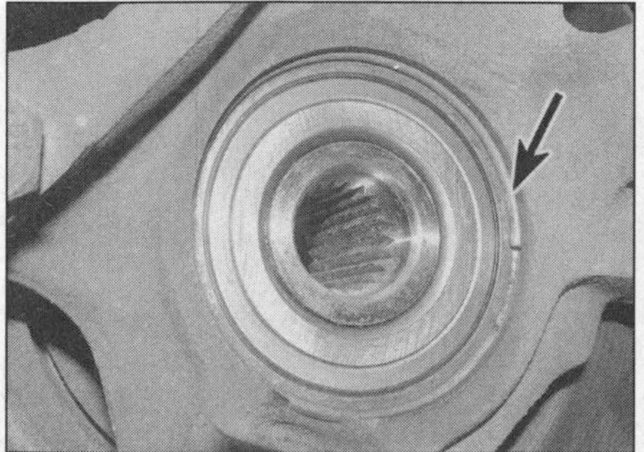

3.4 Circlip fitted to retain the bearing in the hub assembly (arrowed)

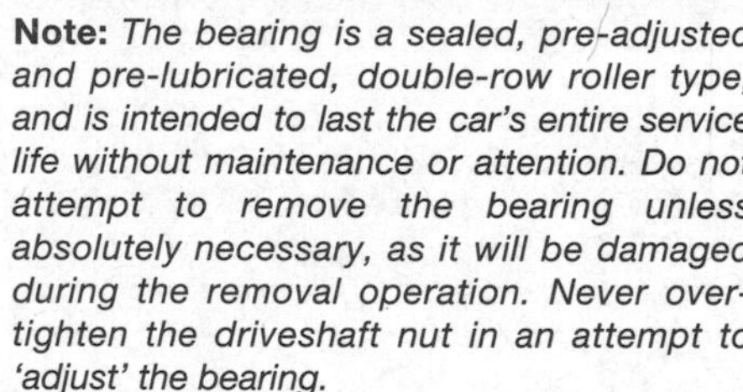

3 Front hub bearings – checking, removal and refitting

Note: *The bearing is a sealed, pre-adjusted and pre-lubricated, double-row roller type, and is intended to last the car's entire service life without maintenance or attention. Do not attempt to remove the bearing unless absolutely necessary, as it will be damaged during the removal operation. Never over-tighten the driveshaft nut in an attempt to 'adjust' the bearing.*

Note: *A press will be required to dismantle and rebuild the assembly; if such a tool is not available, a large bench vice and spacers (such as large sockets) will serve as an adequate substitute. The bearing's inner races are an interference fit on the hub; if the inner race remains on the hub when it is pressed out of the hub carrier, a knife-edged bearing puller will be required to remove it.*

Checking

1 Wear in the front hub bearings can be checked by measuring the amount of side play (endfloat) present. To do this, a dial gauge should be fixed so that its probe is in contact with the disc face of the hub. The play should be as Specified. If it is greater than this, the bearings are worn excessively, and should be renewed.

Removal

Note: *A new bearing circlip will be required on refitting.*

2 Remove the swivel hub assembly as described in Section 2.

3 Support the swivel hub securely on blocks or in a vice. Using a tubular spacer which bears only on the inner end of the hub flange, press the hub flange out of the bearing. If the bearing outboard inner race remains on the hub, remove it using a bearing puller (see note above).

4 Extract the bearing retaining circlip from the inner end of the swivel hub assembly **(see illustration)**.

5 Where necessary, refit the inner race in position over the ball cage, and securely support the inner face of the swivel hub. Using a tubular spacer which bears only on the inner race, press the complete bearing assembly out of the swivel hub.

6 Thoroughly clean the hub and swivel hub, removing all traces of dirt and grease. Polish away any burrs or raised edges which might hinder reassembly. Check for cracks or any other signs of wear or damage, and renew the components if necessary. As noted above, the bearing and its circlip must be renewed whenever they are disturbed. A bearing kit, which consists of the bearing, circlip and thrust-washer, is available from Renault dealers.

Refitting

7 On reassembly, check (if possible) that the new bearing is packed with grease. Apply a light film of oil to the bearing outer race and to the hub flange shaft.

8 Before fitting the new bearing, remove the plastic covers protecting the seals at each end, but leave the inner plastic sleeve in position to hold the inner races together.

9 Securely support the swivel hub, and locate the bearing in the hub. Press the bearing into position, ensuring that it enters the hub squarely, using a tubular spacer which bears only on the outer race.

10 Once the bearing is correctly seated, secure it with the new circlip and remove the plastic sleeve. Apply a smear of grease to the seal lips.

11 Locate the bearing inner race over the end of the hub flange. Press the bearing onto the hub, using a tubular spacer which bears only on the inner race, until it seats against the thrustwasher/hub flange **(see illustration)**. Check that the hub flange rotates freely. Wipe off any excess oil or grease.

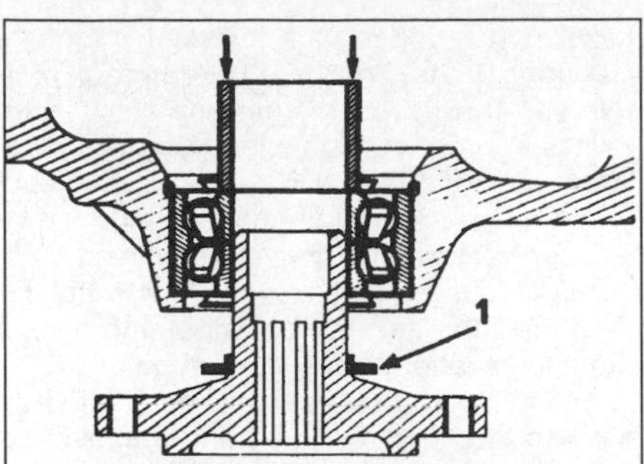

3.11 Refitting the hub flange

1 Thrustwasher (where applicable)

12 Refit the swivel hub assembly as described in Section 2.

4 Front strut – removal and refitting

Removal

1 Chock the rear wheels, firmly apply the handbrake, then jack up the front of the vehicle and support it on axle stands *(see Jacking and vehicle support)*. Remove the appropriate roadwheel.

2 Remove the two nuts from the bolts securing the swivel hub to the suspension strut, noting that the nuts are positioned on the rear side of the strut. Withdraw the bolts, and support the swivel hub assembly.

3 Unclip the brake pipe hose and ABS wiring from the strut assembly.

4 From within the engine compartment, slacken the suspension strut upper mounting nut, holding the strut piston rod with an Allen key **(see illustration)**. Remove the nut.

5 Lower the assembly from under the wing, releasing the strut from the swivel hub. Withdraw the strut from under the wheel arch, taking care not to damage the driveshaft gaiter **(see illustration)**.

Refitting

6 Manoeuvre the strut assembly into position, taking care not to damage the driveshaft gaiter.

7 Insert the two swivel hub-to-suspension strut mounting bolts from the front side of the strut. Refit the nuts to the rear of the bolts, and tighten them to the specified torque **(see illustration)**.

8 Refit the upper mounting nut and tighten it to the specified torque.

9 Refit the roadwheel, lower the vehicle to the ground and tighten the roadwheel bolts to the specified torque.

5 Front strut – dismantling, inspection and reassembly

Warning: Before attempting to dismantle the front suspension strut, a special tool to hold the coil spring in compression must be obtained. Adjustable coil spring compressors are readily available, and are recommended for this operation. Any attempt to dismantle the strut without such a tool is likely to result in damage or personal injury.

Dismantling

1 With the strut removed from the vehicle as described in Section 4, clean away all external dirt. Mount the strut upright in a vice.

2 Remove the upper mounting rubber. Fit the spring compressor, and compress the coil spring until all tension is relieved from the upper mounting plate. Ensure that the compressor tool is securely located on the spring according to the tool manufacturer's instructions **(see illustration)**.

3 Slacken and remove the retaining nut from the top of the strut.

4 Remove the upper mounting plate, the bearing and the upper spring seat **(see illustration)**.

5 Carefully remove the coil spring, complete with the spring compressor, and store in a safe place for refitting. (It may be safer to release the spring compressor from the spring.)

6 Slide the rubber bump stop/dust cover off the strut piston.

Inspection

7 With the strut assembly now completely dismantled, examine all the components for wear, damage or deformation, and check the upper bearing for smoothness of operation. Renew any of the components as necessary.

8 Examine the strut for signs of fluid leakage. Check the strut piston for signs of pitting along its entire length, and check the strut body for signs of damage. Test the operation of the strut, while holding it in an upright position, by moving the piston through a full stroke and then through short strokes of 50 to 100 mm. In both cases, the resistance felt should be smooth and continuous. If the resistance is jerky or uneven, or if there is any visible sign of wear or damage, renewal is necessary.

9 If any doubt exists about the condition of the coil spring, gradually release the spring compressor (if not already done), and check the spring for distortion and signs of cracking. Since no minimum free length is specified by Renault, the only way to check the tension of

4.4 Slacken the suspension strut upper mounting nut, holding the strut piston rod with an Allen key

4.5 Removing the front suspension strut

4.7 Tightening the swivel hub-to-strut nut and bolts. Note that the bolt heads face forwards

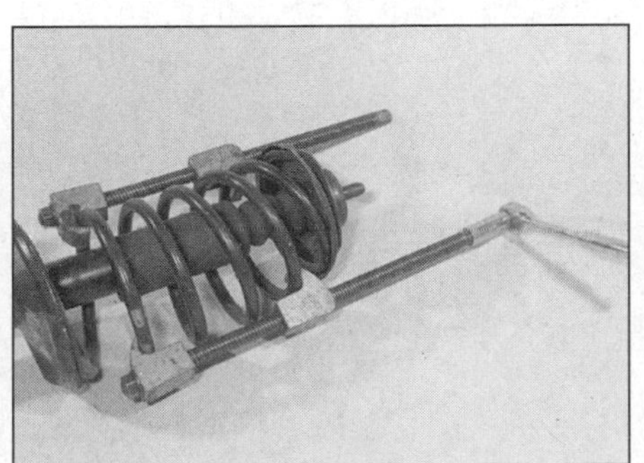

5.2 Using spring compressors, compress the suspension strut coil spring

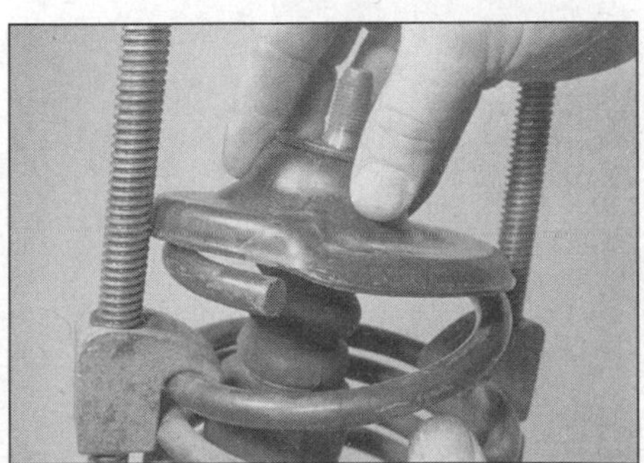

5.4 Remove the upper spring seat and coil spring

5.11 Refit the rubber dust cover to the strut piston

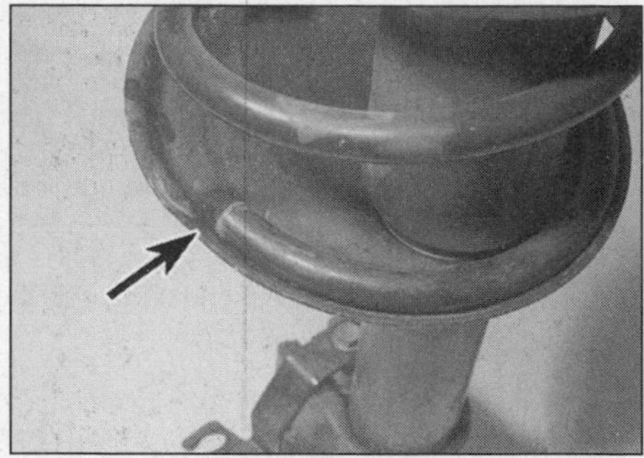
5.12 Coil spring lower end correctly located in spring seat

the spring is to compare it to a new component. Renew the spring if it is damaged or distorted, or if there is any doubt as to its condition.

10 Inspect all other components for signs of damage or deterioration, and renew any that are suspect.

Reassembly

Note: *Apply grease between the ends of the spring and its stops.*

11 Ensure that all components are clean and dry. Slide the bump stop/dust cover into position over the strut piston **(see illustration)**.

12 Refit the compressed coil spring, followed by the upper spring seat. Ensure that both ends of the spring are correctly located in the spring seats **(see illustration)**.

13 Refit the strut bearing and upper mounting plate.

14 Slide the retaining collar (where fitted) onto the strut piston, and secure it in position with the retaining nut. Slowly and carefully release the spring compressor, watching to make sure that both ends of the spring remain correctly located in the spring seats.

15 Refit the strut to the vehicle as described in Section 4.

6 Front anti-roll bar – removal and refitting

Removal

1 Chock the rear wheels, apply the hand-brake, then jack up the front of the vehicle and support it on axle stands *(see Jacking and vehicle support)*. Remove both front roadwheels.

2 Remove the exhaust downpipe as described in the relevant part of Chapter 4.

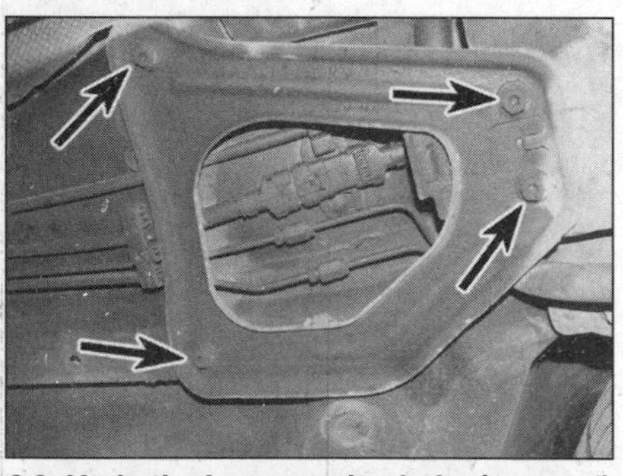
6.3 Undo the four securing bolts (arrowed) – left-hand reinforcement plate shown

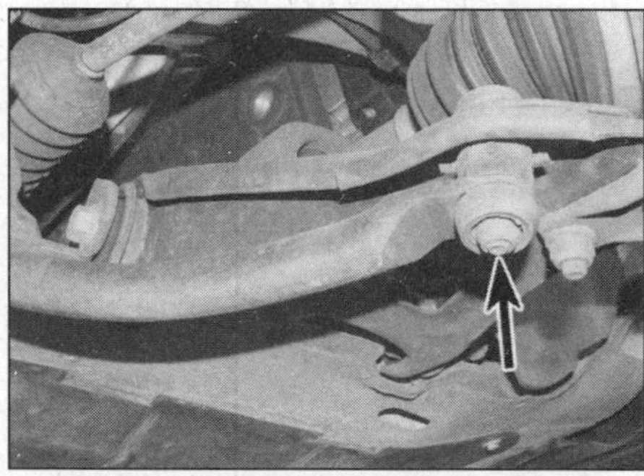
6.4 Remove the front anti-roll bar mounting bolt (arrowed)

6.5 Front anti-roll bar mounting clamp (arrowed) – one side shown

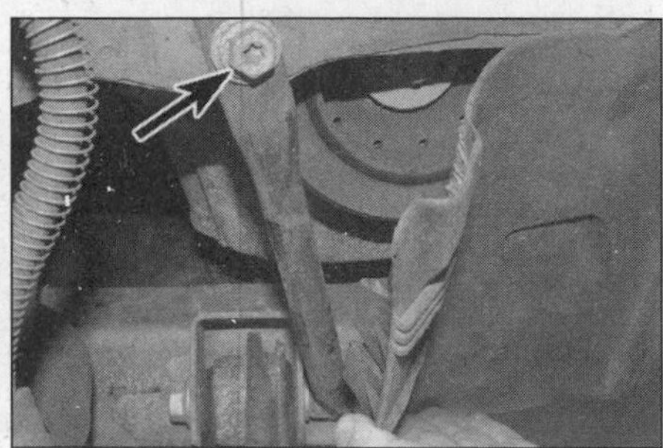
7.3a Unclip the splash shield, undo the support bar upper mounting bolt (arrowed) . . .

3 Working under the vehicle, undo the securing bolts from the two reinforcement plates (4 bolts each side) and remove the plates from the subframe **(see illustration)**.

4 Remove the nuts and bolts securing each end of the anti-roll bar to the lower suspension arms, noting the positions of the rubber mounting spacers **(see illustration)**.

5 Unbolt the anti-roll bar mounting clamps from the subframe **(see illustration)**.

6 Manoeuvre the anti-roll bar out from underneath the vehicle, and remove the rubber mounting bushes.

7 Carefully examine the anti-roll bar components for signs of wear, damage or deterioration, paying particular attention to the mounting bushes. Renew worn components as necessary.

Refitting

8 Fit the bushes onto the anti-roll bar, then manoeuvre the anti-roll bar into position underneath the vehicle. Do not tighten the mounting clamp bolts fully yet.

9 Secure the ends of the anti-roll bar to the lower suspension arms, ensuring that the rubber mounting spacers are correctly positioned. Fit the nuts and bolts, but do not tighten them fully yet.

10 Refit the exhaust downpipe.

11 Refit the reinforcement plates to the subframe.

12 Refit the roadwheels, lower the vehicle to the ground and tighten the wheel bolts to the specified torque.

13 Tighten the anti-roll bar fastenings to the specified torque, starting with the mounting clamps.

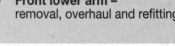

7 Front lower arm – removal, overhaul and refitting

Removal

1 Chock the rear wheels, apply the hand-brake, jack up the front of the vehicle and support it on axle stands. *(see Jacking and vehicle support)*. Remove the appropriate front roadwheel.

2 Disconnect the end of the anti-roll bar from the lower suspension arm, as described in the previous Section.

3 Unclip the inner plastic splash guard. Remove the bolt securing the upper part of the support bar to the front wing valance and the nut securing it to the front pivot bolt. Remove the support bar from the vehicle **(see illustrations)**.

4 Remove the nut and clamp bolt securing the lower suspension arm balljoint to the swivel hub. Carefully lever the balljoint out of the swivel hub, taking care not to damage the balljoint or driveshaft gaiters. Remove the plastic protector plate which is fitted to the balljoint shank **(see illustrations)**.

5 Remove the two pivot nuts and bolts, and

remove the lower suspension arm from the vehicle **(see illustration)**.

Overhaul

6 Clean the lower arm and the area around the arm mountings, then check for cracks, distortion or any other signs of damage. On some models, a brake disc cooling shield is clipped to the arm; this should also be removed. Check that the lower arm balljoint moves freely, without any sign of roughness, and that the balljoint gaiter is free from cracks and splits. Examine the shank of the pivot bolts for signs of wear or scoring. Renew worn components as necessary.

7 Inspect the lower arm pivot bushes. If they are worn, cracked, split or perished, they must be renewed. To renew the bushes, support the lower arm, and press the first bush out using a tubular spacer, such as a socket, which bears only on the hard, outer edge of the bush (make a note of the distance between the two bushes before removal). **Note:** *Remove only one bush at a time from the arm, to ensure that each new bush is correctly positioned on installation.* Thoroughly clean the lower arm bore, removing all traces of dirt and grease, and polish away any burrs or raised edges which might hinder reassembly. Apply a smear of grease to the outer edge of the new bush. Press the bush into position until the distance between the inner edges of the lower arm bushes is as shown **(see illustration)**. Wipe away surplus grease and repeat the procedure on the remaining bush.

Refitting

8 Offer up the lower suspension arm, and insert the two pivot bolts from the rear of the suspension arm. Refit the nuts, but tighten them by hand only at this stage.

9 Refit the plastic protector to the lower arm balljoint, then locate the balljoint shank in the swivel hub. Refit the balljoint clamp bolt, and tighten its retaining nut to the specified torque **(see illustration)**.

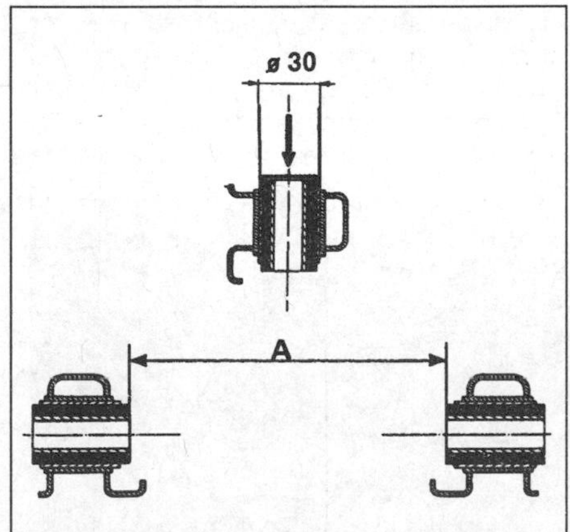

7.7 Front suspension lower arm pivot bush fitting dimension

A = 146.5

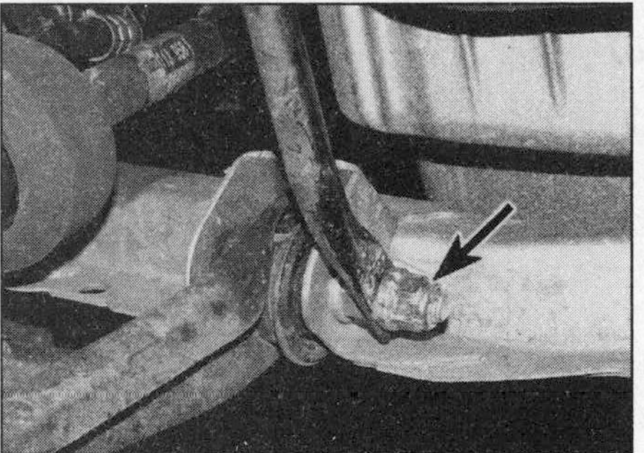

7.3b . . . and remove nut from the suspension arm pivot bolt (arrowed)

7.4b . . . then free the balljoint from the swivel hub, and remove the plastic protector plate

10 When applicable, refit the support bar on the front pivot bolt shank. Fit the retaining bolt and nut, tightening both by hand only at this stage.

11 Reconnect the end of the anti-roll bar to the lower suspension arm, ensuring that the rubber mounting spacers are correctly positioned. Do not fully tighten the fastenings yet.

12 Refit the roadwheel, lower the vehicle and tighten the roadwheel bolts to the specified torque.

13 With the vehicle standing on its wheels, rock the vehicle to settle the lower arm bushes in position. Tighten the lower arm pivot bolts and the anti-roll bar fixing to the specified torque. When the pivot bolts have been tightened, secure the support bar in position (if applicable) by securely tightening its retaining nut and bolt.

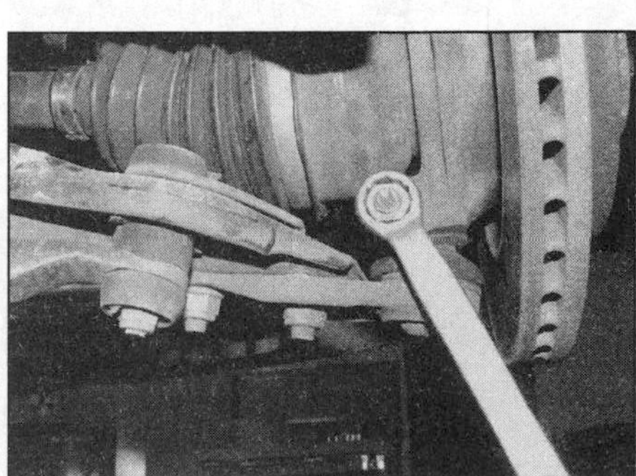

7.9 Tightening the balljoint clamp bolt

7.4a Remove the balljoint clamp bolt . . .

7.5 Remove the lower suspension arm pivot bolts (arrowed)

8 Front lower arm balljoint – removal and refitting

Removal

1 Chock the rear wheels, apply the handbrake, jack up the front of the vehicle and support it on axle stands *(see Jacking and vehicle support)*. Remove the appropriate front roadwheel.

2 Disconnect the end of the anti-roll bar from the lower suspension arm, as described in Section 6.

3 Slacken the nut securing the support bar to the lower arm front pivot bolt **(see illustration)**, then slacken both the lower suspension arm pivot bolts, so as to allow the arm to move down freely.

8.3 Remove nut (arrowed) from the suspension arm pivot bolt

8.5 Front lower suspension arm balljoint retaining nuts (arrowed)

4 Remove the nut and clamp bolt securing the lower suspension arm to the swivel hub. Carefully lever the balljoint out of the swivel hub, taking care not to damage the balljoint or driveshaft gaiters. Remove the plastic protector plate which is fitted to the balljoint shank **(see illustrations 7.4a and 7.4b)**.

5 Remove the two nuts and bolts securing the balljoint to the lower suspension arm **(see illustration)**. Remove the balljoint.

6 Check that the balljoint moves freely, without any sign of roughness or free play. Examine the balljoint gaiter for signs of damage and deterioration such as cracks or splits. Renew the complete balljoint assembly if damaged; it is not possible to renew the balljoint gaiter separately. The balljoint renewal kit obtainable from Renault dealers contains the balljoint, the plastic protector plate and all fixings.

Refitting

7 Fit the balljoint to the suspension arm. Insert the bolts and washers, and tighten the retaining nuts to the specified torque.

8 Fit the plastic protector to the balljoint shank, then locate the shank in the swivel hub. Refit the balljoint clamp bolt, and tighten its retaining nut to the specified torque.

9 Reconnect the end of the anti-roll bar to the lower suspension arm, ensuring that the rubber mounting spacers are correctly positioned. Do not fully tighten the fastenings yet.

10 Refit the roadwheel, lower the vehicle and tighten the roadwheel bolts to the specified torque.

11 With the vehicle standing on its wheels, rock the vehicle to settle the lower arm bushes in position. Tighten the lower arm pivot bolts and the anti-roll bar fixing to the specified torque. When the pivot bolts have been tightened, secure the support bar in position by securely tightening its retaining nut.

9 Rear hub bearings – checking, removal and refitting

Note: *The bearing is a sealed, pre-adjusted and pre-lubricated, double-row tapered-roller type, and is intended to last the car's entire service life without maintenance or attention. Never overtighten the hub nut in an attempt to 'adjust' the bearings.*

Checking

1 Chock the front wheels and engage reverse gear (or P on automatic models). Jack up the rear of the vehicle and support it on axle stands *(see Jacking and vehicle support)*. Remove the appropriate rear roadwheel, and fully release the handbrake.

2 Wear in the rear hub bearings can be checked by measuring the amount of side play (endfloat) present. To do this, a dial test indicator should be fixed so that its probe is in contact with the hub outer face. The play should be as Specified. If it is greater than this, the bearings are worn excessively and should be renewed.

Removal

3 Remove the rear brake disc or drum, as described in Chapter 9.

4 Using circlip pliers, extract the bearing retaining circlip from the centre of the brake disc or drum **(see illustration)**.

5 Securely support the disc or drum hub. Press or drive the bearing out of the hub, using a tubular tube as a drift **(see illustration)**.

6 Thoroughly clean the hub, removing all traces of dirt and grease. Polish away any burrs or raised edges which might hinder reassembly. Check the hub for cracks or any other signs of damage, and renew if necessary. The bearing and its circlip must be renewed whenever they are disturbed. A bearing kit is available from Renault dealers, consisting of the bearing, circlip, spacer, thrustwasher, hub nut and grease cap.

Refitting

7 On reassembly, check (if possible) that the new bearing is packed with grease. Apply a light film of gear oil to the bearing outer race and stub axle.

8 Securely support the hub. Press the bearing into position, ensuring that it enters the hub squarely, using a tube which presses only on the bearing outer race.

9 Ensure that the bearing is correctly seated against the hub shoulder, and secure it in position with the new circlip. Ensure that the circlip is correctly seated in its groove.

10 Refit the brake disc or drum as described in Chapter 9.

10 Rear shock absorber – removal, testing and refitting

Removal

1 Chock the front wheels and engage reverse gear (or P). Jack up the rear of the vehicle and support it on axle stands *(see Jacking and vehicle support)*. Remove the appropriate rear roadwheel.

2 Using a jack, raise the trailing arm slightly until the shock absorber is slightly compressed. Remove the lower mounting bolt **(see illustration)**.

3 Working inside the luggage compartment, unclip the cover from the shock absorber upper mounting. Slacken and remove the upper mounting nut **(see illustrations)**, and remove the shock absorber from the vehicle.

Testing

4 Mount the shock absorber in a vice, and test as described in Section 5 for the front suspension strut. Also check the rubber mounting bushes for damage and deterioration. Renew the shock absorber complete if any damage or wear is evident; the mounting bushes are not available

9.4 Extract the circlip . . .

9.5 . . . then drive the bearing out of the hub using a suitable tubular drift

10.2 Removing the rear shock absorber lower mounting bolt

separately. Inspect the mounting bolts for signs of wear or damage, and renew as necessary.

Refitting

5 Prior to refitting the shock absorber, mount it upright in the vice, and operate it fully through several strokes in order to prime it. (This is necessary even if a new unit is being fitted, as it may have been stored horizontally, and so need priming.) Apply a smear of multi-purpose grease to the shock absorber mounting bolts.
6 Offer up the shock absorber, then refit its upper mounting securing nut, tightening it by hand only at this stage.
7 Refit the lower shock absorber mounting bolt, again tightening it by hand only. Lower and remove the jack from under the trailing arm.
8 Refit the roadwheel, lower the vehicle to the ground and tighten the roadwheel bolts to the specified torque.
9 Rock the vehicle to settle the shock absorber mounting bushes in position, then tighten both the upper and lower mountings to the specified torque.

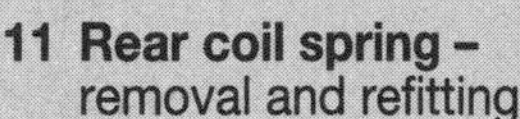

11 Rear coil spring – removal and refitting

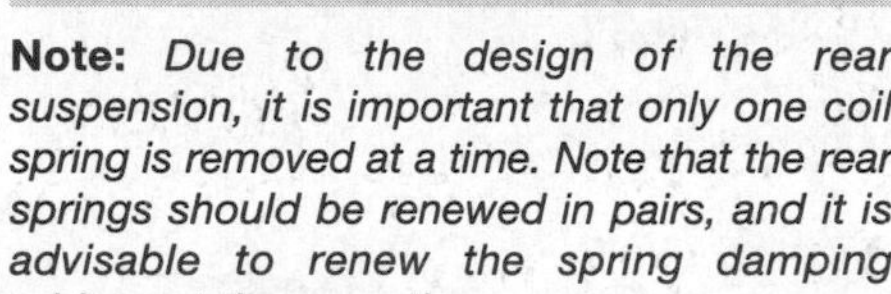

Note: *Due to the design of the rear suspension, it is important that only one coil spring is removed at a time. Note that the rear springs should be renewed in pairs, and it is advisable to renew the spring damping rubbers at the same time.*

Removal

1 Chock the front wheels and engage reverse gear (or P on automatic models). Jack up the rear of the vehicle and support it on axle stands. Remove the appropriate roadwheel.
2 Raise the relevant trailing arm slightly using a jack.
3 Unscrew and remove the bolt securing the lower end of the shock absorber to the trailing arm **(see illustration)**.
4 Carefully lower the jack supporting the trailing arm, and remove the coil spring and its damping rubbers from between the axle and underbody. Lever the trailing arm down slightly if necessary to remove the spring **(see illustration)**.

Refitting

5 Refitting is a reversal of removal, remembering the following points.
6 Ensure that the spring locates correctly on the damping rubbers, between the trailing arm and the underbody. The spring has a coloured paint mark **(see illustration)**, which must be at the top and facing towards the rear of the vehicle.
7 Tighten the lower shock absorber bolt as described in Section 10.

10.3a Unclip the upper shock absorber mounting cover .....

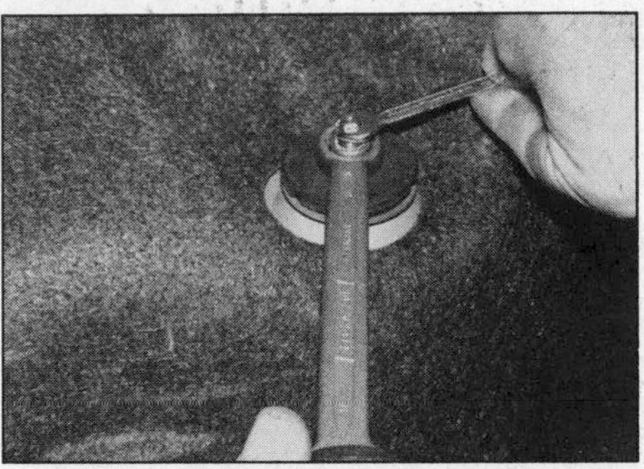

10.3b .... and slacken the retaining nut, holding the strut piston rod secure

8 If the coil spring is being renewed, repeat the procedure on the other side of the vehicle.

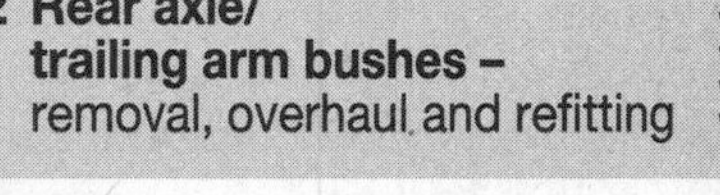

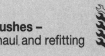

12 Rear axle/trailing arm bushes – removal, overhaul and refitting

Removal

1 Chock the front wheels and engage reverse gear (or P on automatic models). Jack up the rear of the vehicle and support it on axle stands. Remove both rear roadwheels.
2 If a new rear axle is to be installed, remove the brake disc or drums as described in Chapter 9.
3 Remove the rear wheel sensors as described in Chapter 9, Section 23.
4 Where fitted, unhook the level sensor link rod (for the Xenon headlamps) from the axle crossmember and the link-rod for the pressure regulating valve **(see illustration)**.
5 Use a brake hose clamp, a G-clamp or a similar tool with protected jaws to clamp the brake flexible hose at the nearest convenient point.
6 Disconnect the rear brake pipes at the flexible hose unions which are clipped to the axle crossmember **(see illustration)**. Remove the retaining clips, free the flexible hoses from the crossmember, and plug or tape over the union ends to prevent dirt entry. Wash off any spilt fluid immediately.
7 Disconnect the handbrake cables from the rear brakes as described in Chapter 9.
8 Slacken, but do not remove the nuts securing the front ends of the trailing arms to the vehicle underbody **(see illustration)**.

11.3 Removing the lower shock absorber mounting bolt

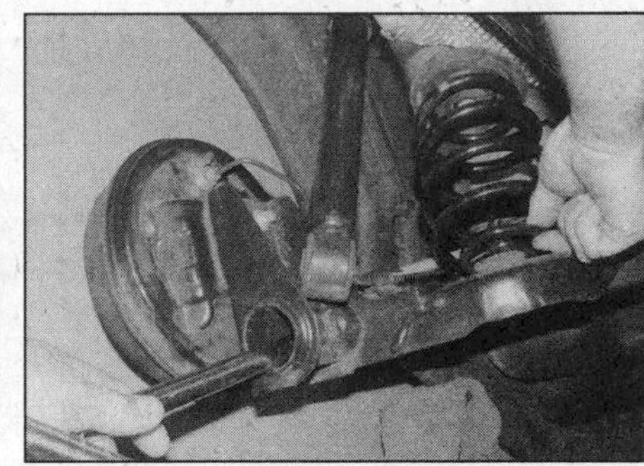

11.4 Lever the trailing arm downwards and remove the coil spring

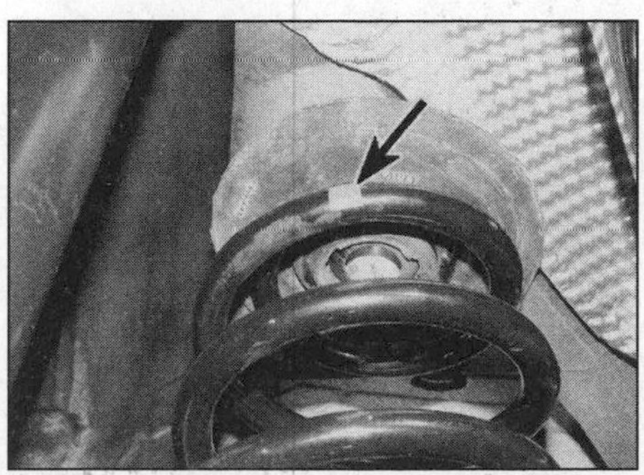

11.6 Coloured paint mark (arrowed) at the top, facing towards the rear of the vehicle

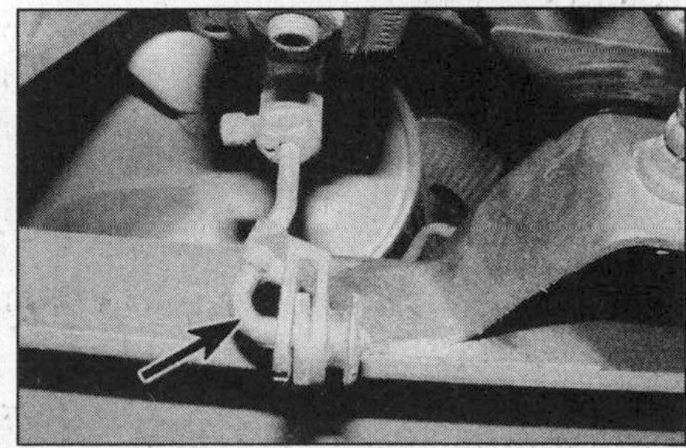

12.4 Unclip the pressure regulating valve linkage rod (arrowed) from the axle crossmember

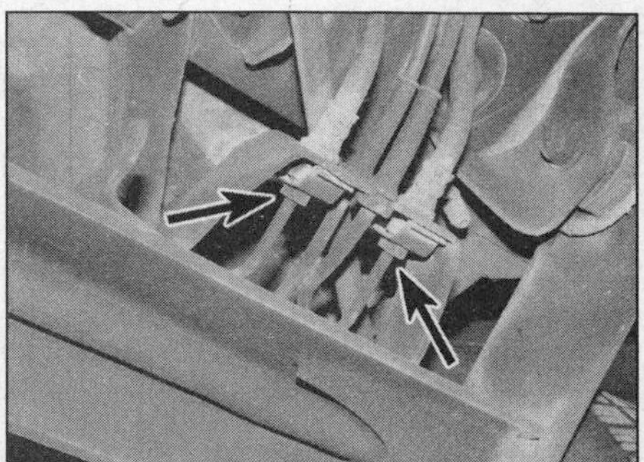

12.6 Disconnect the brake pipe connections (arrowed) from the axle crossmember

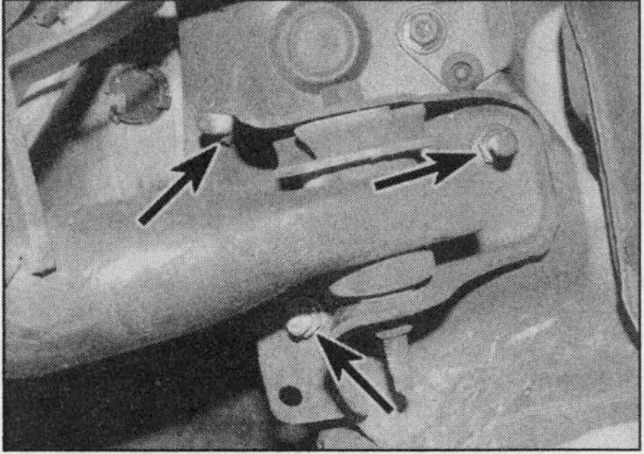

12.8 Slacken the three mounting nuts arrowed (left-hand side shown)

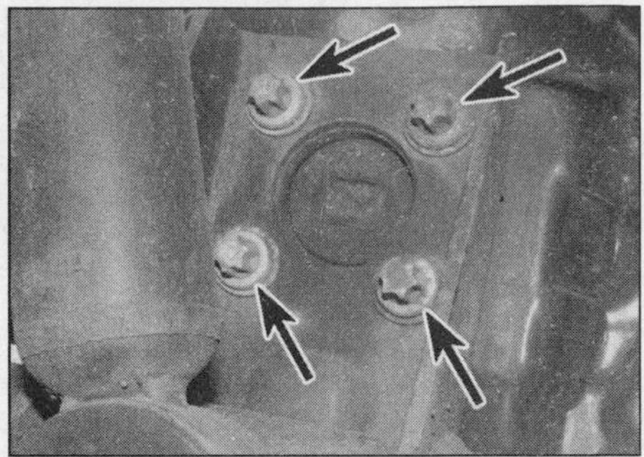

12.13 When refitting, use locking fluid on the threads of the bolts (arrowed)

9 Remove the rear coil springs as described in Section 11.

10 Support the weight of the rear axle on a trolley jack.

11 The help of an assistant at this point will ease this task to ensure that the axle beam does not slip off the jack. Remove the six securing nuts (three each side – illustration 12.8) from the axle mountings to the vehicle body. Withdraw the axle from underneath the vehicle.

12 If necessary, the trailing arm bushes can be renewed, referring to the later paragraphs.

13 If a new axle is being fitted, remove the brake pipes from the original and fit them to the new axle. Also transfer the brake assemblies as described in Chapter 9. Transfer the brake mounting brackets, using locking fluid on the threads of the retaining bolts **(see illustration)**.

Refitting

14 Place the rear axle on a trolley jack, and lift it into position underneath the vehicle. Insert the trailing arm mounting bolts from under the vehicle, ensuring that the mounting plate is correctly fitted. Refit the nuts and tighten them to the specified torque.

15 Refit the coil springs as described in Section 11.

16 Refit the brake hoses to the brackets on the crossmember, and secure them in position with the retaining clips. Reconnect the brake pipes to the hoses, and securely tighten the union nuts.

17 Where applicable, refit the headlight level sensor link-rod and the pressure regulating valve link-rod onto their locating brackets on the axle crossmember.

18 Feed the handbrake cables along the trailing arms. Refit the handbrake cables as described in Chapter 9.

19 Refit the ABS wheel sensors and bleed the brake hydraulic system on completion. Refer to the relevant Sections of Chapter 9.

20 Refit the roadwheels, lower the vehicle to the ground and tighten the wheel bolts to the specified torque.

21 Check the rear underbody height as described in Section 13.

Trailing arm bush renewal

22 Examine all the axle components for wear and damage. If the trailing arm bushes require renewal, proceed as described below.

23 Make a note of the position of the bush in the trailing arm before removal, as the new bush will need to be fitted in the same position.

24 A special Renault tool is required for removal and refitting of the bushes, the tool is made up of three parts: T.Ar. 1454, T.Av. 1420 and T.Av. 1420-01 **(see illustration)**. An alternative can be improvised using a long bolt, nut, washers, and a length of metal tubing or a socket.

25 Removal of the bush may be made easier if the bush housing in the trailing arm is heated using a heat gun, or similar. Do not use a naked flame, due to the close proximity of the fuel tank (if renewing the bushes while the axle is still on the vehicle).

26 Draw the bush from the trailing arm using the tool described in paragraph 24.

27 Refit the new bush using the special tool used on removal. Draw the new bush back into the trailing arm, ensuring that it is fitted in the correct position in the trailing arm.

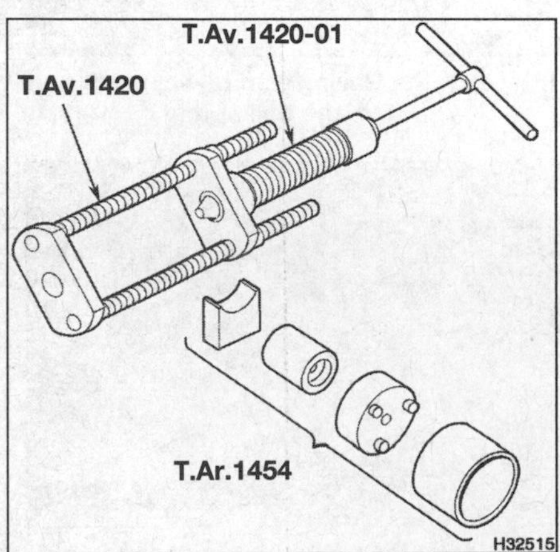

12.24 Renault tooling for removing and refitting the trailing arm bushes

13 Vehicle ride height – general information and checking

Note: *As from January 2003, Renault have given new designations for the underbody height measuring points on all vehicles in the range.*

New designation shown in brackets

H1 (R1) *Dimension between the front wheel axle and the ground*

H2 (W1) *Dimension between the front underbody measuring point and the ground*

H4 (R2) *Dimension between the rear wheel axle and the ground*

H5 (W2) *Dimension between the rear underbody measuring point and the ground*

General information

1 The vehicle ride height measurements are

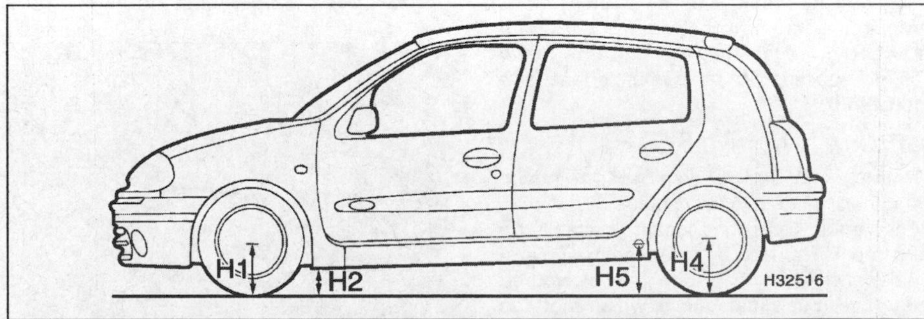

13.1 Underbody height measuring points. Note that H5 (W2 from January 2003 MY) is measured from the centre of the trailing arm rubber bush

For values, refer to Specifications

used to ensure accuracy when checking the front suspension and steering angles (see Section 20). This is because the angles will vary slightly according to the ride height of the vehicle (see Specifications). The ride height measuring points are as shown **(see illustration).** The front and rear ride heights can also be calculated as follows.

Checking

2 To accurately check the ride height, position the unladen vehicle on a level surface, with the tyres correctly inflated and the fuel tank full.

Ride height

Note: *As from January 2003, see new designations (eg, H1 = R1) in this section, for the underbody height measuring points.*

3 To check the front ride height, measure and record the dimensions H1 (centre of the wheel axis to the ground) and H2 (subframe to the ground) on both sides of the vehicle. Subtract H2 from H1 to find the ride height dimension.

4 To check the rear ride height, measure and record the dimensions H4 (centre of the wheel axis to the ground) and H5 (centre of the rear trailing arm bush to the ground) on both sides of the vehicle. Subtract H4 from H5 to find the ride height.

5 Note that the difference between the heights on each side must not exceed 5 mm, with the driver's side slightly higher than the passenger side.

6 Note that no adjustment of the ride height is possible. If the ride heights differ greatly, examine the suspension components for signs of wear or damage.

7 If further checks are required, take your vehicle to your local dealer who will have the specialised equipment to do this.

14 Steering wheel – removal and refitting

Note: *A new steering wheel retaining bolt will be required on refitting.*

Removal

1 Set the front wheels in the straight-ahead position. Release the steering lock by inserting the ignition key.

2 Remove the airbag (referring to the warnings) as described in Chapter 12.

3 Disconnect the wiring connector for the horn **(see illustration)**.

4 Slacken but do not remove the steering wheel retaining bolt (see illustration). **Note:** *The steering wheel splines are designed so that they can only be fitted in one position* ***(see illustration).***

5 Lift the steering wheel off the column splines, carefully feeding the wiring through the steering wheel as it is removed **(see illustration)**. If it is tight tap the steering wheel, using the palm of the hand, or rock it from side-to-side whilst pulling upwards to release it from the shaft splines. Remove the bolt and lift off the steering wheel. ***Note:*** *Do not turn the airbag contact ring assembly or the steering column shaft whilst the steering wheel is removed.*

Refitting

6 Refitting is a reversal of removal, bearing in mind the following points.

a) Make sure the steering wheel splines are aligned correctly with the steering column shaft.

b) Tighten the new retaining bolt to the specified torque ***(see illustration).***

c) Check that all the wiring plugs are connected securely.

d) Refit the airbag as described in Chapter 12 (referring to the warnings).

15 Steering column/motor – removal, checking and refitting

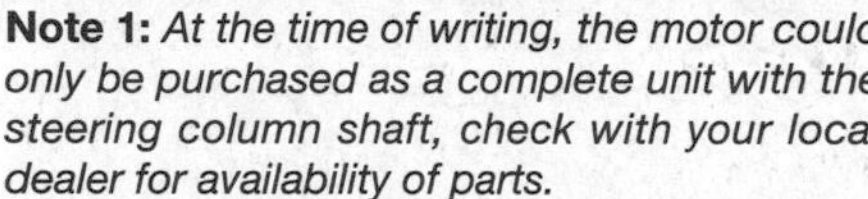

Note 1: *At the time of writing, the motor could only be purchased as a complete unit with the steering column shaft, check with your local dealer for availability of parts.*

Note 2: *A new steering wheel bolt will be required on refitting. For more information on removal of individual components, check in the relevant Chapters.*

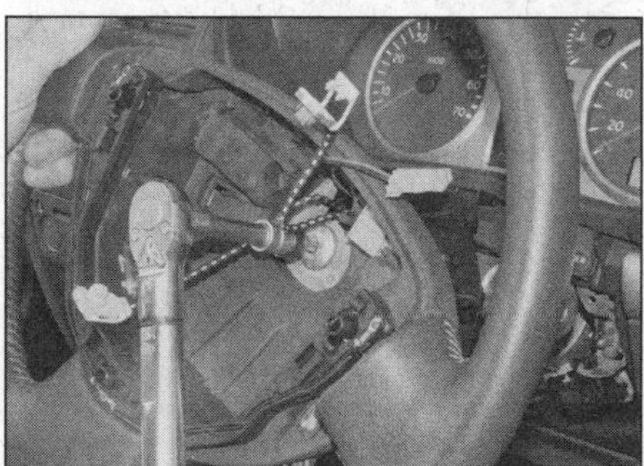

14.4a Slackening the steering wheel retaining bolt

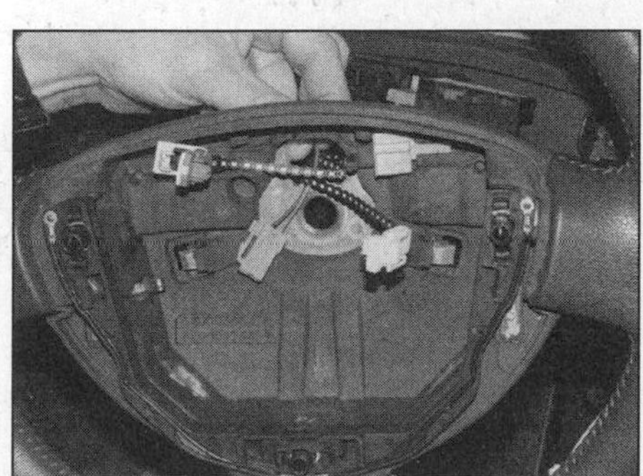

14.5 Withdrawing the wiring through the steering wheel as it is removed

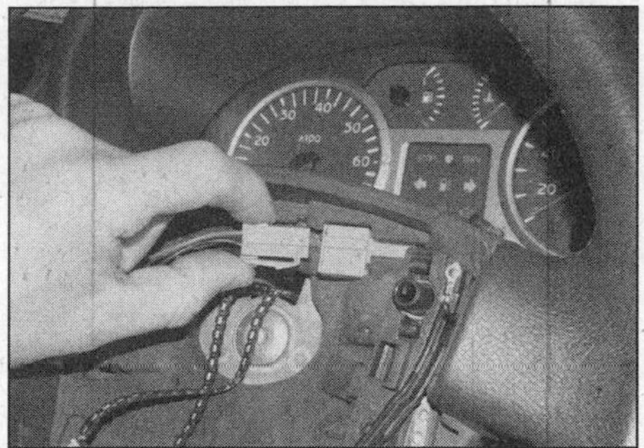

14.3 Disconnecting the wiring connector for the horn

Removal

1 Disconnect the battery negative lead.

2 Remove the steering wheel as described in Section 14.

3 Remove the upper and lower facia trim panels as described in Chapter 11, Section 29.

4 Chock the rear wheels, apply the handbrake, jack up the front of the vehicle and support it on axle stands *(see Jacking and vehicle support)*.

5 Working from underneath the vehicle, cut the retaining clip (where applicable), then fold the protective cover back from the steering gear to gain access to the lower universal joint clamp eccentric bolt **(see illustration)**.

6 Mark the relationship between the lower universal joint and the steering gear drive pinion, using a hammer and punch, white paint or similar. Remove the nut and clamp

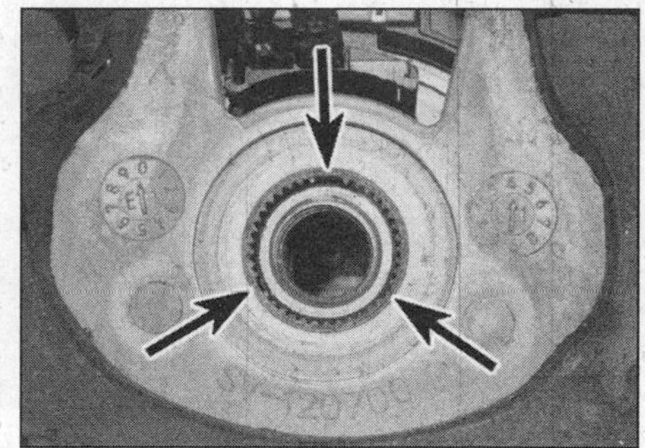

14.4b Note locating splines (arrowed) so that the steering wheel can only be fitted in one position

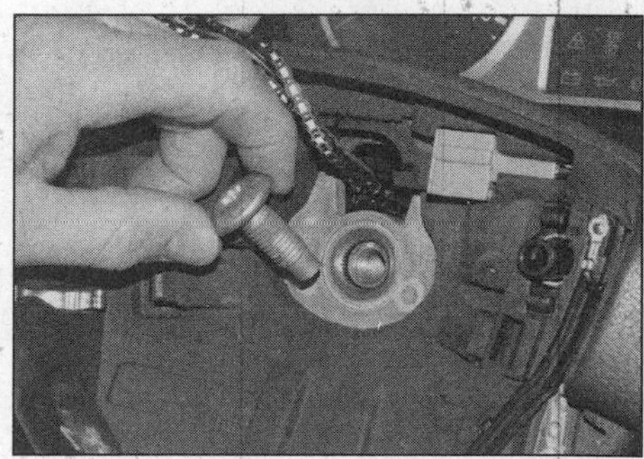

14.6 Use a new retaining bolt on refitting

15.5 Remove the lower universal clamp bolt (arrowed)

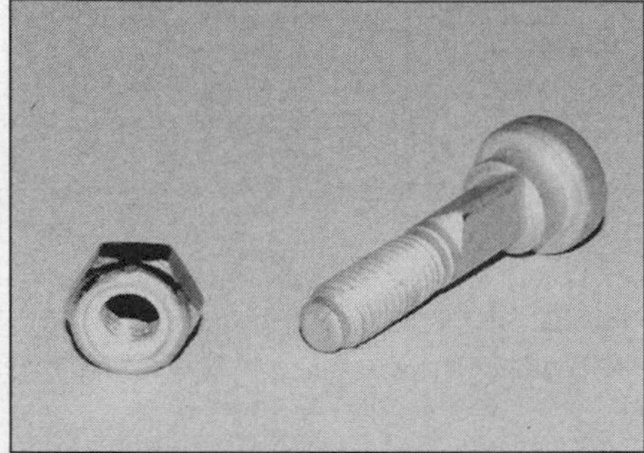
15.6 Lower universal joint clamp eccentric bolt

15.7a Undo the two upper mounting bolts (arrowed) . . .

15.7b . . . lower mounting bolts (arrowed) . . .

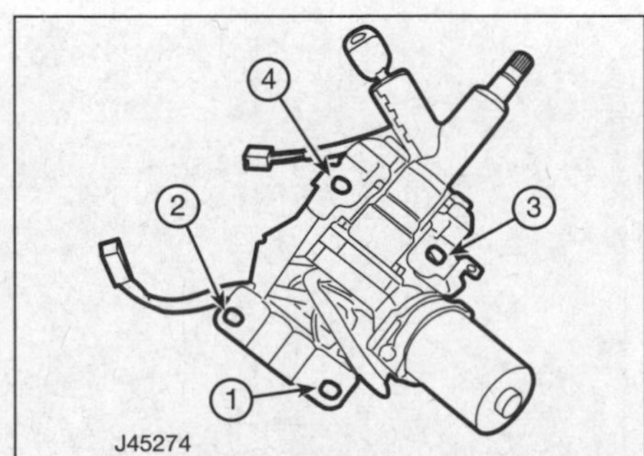
15.7c . . . and release the gaiter from the bulkhead

eccentric bolt securing the joint to the pinion **(see illustration)**.

7 Make sure the steering column height adjuster is in the locked position, then remove the steering column mounting bolts. Release the steering column from its mountings and the facia panel, also release the steering column lower gaiter from the bulkhead **(see illustrations)**.

8 Disengage the universal joint from the steering gear pinion, and remove the steering column assembly from the vehicle. Unclip any wiring from the steering column on removal.

Checking

9 The intermediate shaft attached to the bottom of the steering column incorporates a telescopic safety feature. In the event of a front-end crash, the shaft collapses and prevents the steering wheel injuring the driver. Before refitting the steering column, the length of the intermediate shaft must be checked **(see illustration)**. If the length is shorter than specified, the complete steering column must be renewed. Damage to the intermediate shaft is also implied if it is found that the clamp bolt at its base cannot be inserted freely when refitting the column.

10 Check the steering shaft for signs of free play in the column bushes, and check the universal joints for signs of damage or roughness in the joint bearings. If damage or wear is found on the steering shaft universal joints or shaft bushes, the column must be renewed as an assembly.

11 Refer to Chapter 12, Section 6, for information on ignition switch renewal.

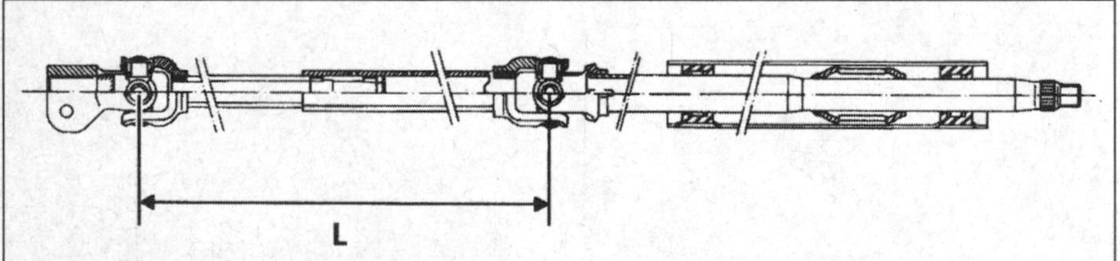

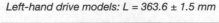

15.9 Steering column intermediate shaft checking dimension (L)

Right-hand drive models: L = 386.6 ± 1.5 mm

Left-hand drive models: L = 363.6 ± 1.5 mm

Refitting

12 Making sure the steering column height adjuster is still in the locked position, manoeuvre the steering column assembly into position. Engage the universal joint with the steering gear pinion splines, aligning the marks made prior to removal.

13 Refit the column gaiter to the bulkhead by tying a piece of string or using a cable tie through the holes in the gaiter and pulling it through the bulkhead into position from under the vehicle **(see illustration)**, cut the string off when the gaiter is in position.

14 From underneath the vehicle, refit the universal joint clamp eccentric bolt and nut, aligning it with the marks made on removal. Tighten the bolt to its specified torque. Relocate the protective cover on the steering gear, and secure it in position. Lower the vehicle to the ground.

15 Refit the steering column mounting bolts.

16 Refit the upper and lower facia trim panels as in Chapter 11, Section 29.

17 Tighten the steering column mounting bolts to their specified torque. **Note:** *If the steering column height adjuster is not in the locked position, then the mounting bolts must be tightened in the sequence shown* ***(see illustration)****.*

18 Refit the steering wheel as described in Section 14, and reconnect the battery negative terminal.

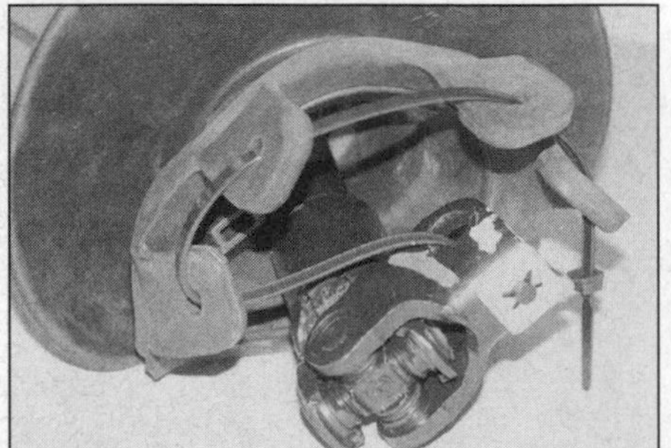
15.13 Using a cable tie through the gaiter flaps to pull gaiter into position

(Figure 15.17)

15.17 Tightening sequence for mounting bolts

16 Steering gear rubber gaiter – renewal

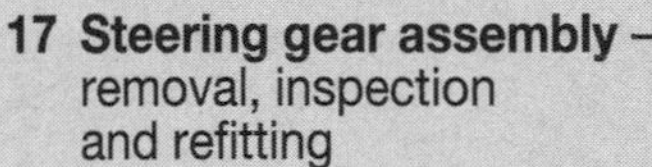

1 Remove the track rod end balljoint as described in Section 18.
2 Mark the correct fitted position of the gaiter on the track rod. Release the retaining clips **(see illustration)**, and slide the gaiter off the steering gear housing and track rod end.
3 Thoroughly clean the track rod and the steering gear housing, using fine abrasive paper to polish off any corrosion, burrs or sharp edges which might damage the sealing lips of the new gaiter on installation.
4 Recover the grease from inside the old gaiter. If it is uncontaminated with dirt or grit, apply it to the track rod inner balljoint. If the old grease is contaminated, or it is suspected that some has been lost, apply some new molybdenum disulphide grease.
5 Grease the inside of the new gaiter. Carefully slide the gaiter onto the track rod, and locate it on the steering gear housing. Align the outer edge of the gaiter with the mark made on the track rod prior to removal, then secure it in position with new retaining clips.
6 Refit the track rod balljoint as described in Section 18.

17 Steering gear assembly – removal, inspection and refitting

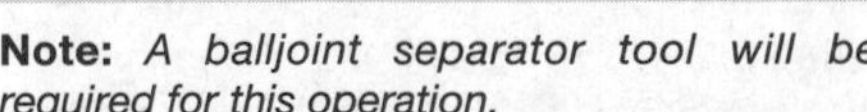

Note: *A balljoint separator tool will be required for this operation.*

Removal

1 Chock the rear wheels, apply the handbrake, jack up the front of the vehicle and support it on axle stands *(see Jacking and vehicle support)*. Remove both front roadwheels.

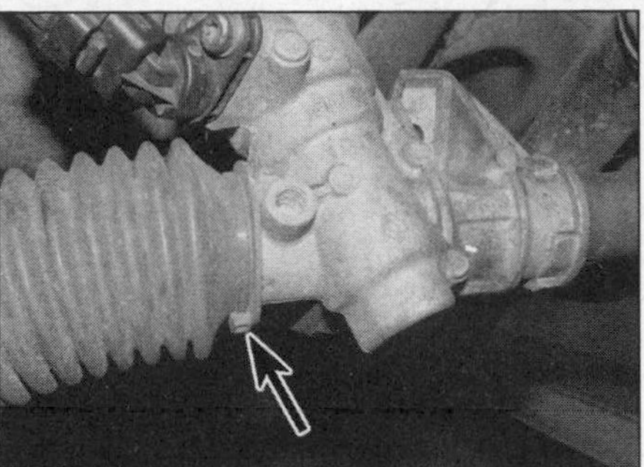

16.2 Steering rack gaiter inner retaining clip (arrowed)

17.3 Disconnecting the wiring connector from the steering angle sensor

2 Remove the nuts securing the track rod balljoints to the swivel hubs. Release the balljoint tapered shanks using a universal balljoint separator.
3 Working from underneath the vehicle, disconnect the wiring connector from the steering angle sensor **(see illustration).**
4 Cut the retaining clip (where fitted), then fold the protective cover back from the steering gear to gain access to the lower universal joint clamp eccentric bolt.
5 Mark the relationship between the intermediate shaft universal joint and the steering gear drive pinion, using a hammer and punch, white paint or similar. Remove the nut and clamp eccentric bolt securing the joint to the pinion **(see illustration)**.
6 Remove the nuts and bolts securing the steering gear assembly to the rear of the front subframe **(see illustration)**. Release the steering gear pinion from the universal joint, and manoeuvre the assembly sideways out of position.

Refitting

7 Manoeuvre the steering gear assembly into position. Engage the universal joint with the steering gear pinion splines, aligning the marks made prior to removal.
8 Insert the steering gear mounting bolts from the rear of the subframe. Refit the nuts and tighten them to the specified torque.
9 Refit the universal joint clamp eccentric bolt and nut, and tighten it to the specified torque. Relocate the protective cover on the steering gear, and secure it in position with a new cable tie (where applicable).
10 Reconnect the wiring connector to the angle sensor.
11 Reconnect the track rod balljoints to the swivel hubs, and tighten their retaining nuts to the specified torque.
12 Refit the roadwheels, lower the vehicle to the ground and tighten the wheel bolts to the specified torque.
13 Check the front wheel toe setting as described in Section 20.

Inspection

14 Renewal procedures for the gaiters, the track rod end balljoints and the track rods (complete with inner balljoints) are given in Sections 16, 18 and 19 respectively.
15 Examine the steering gear assembly for signs of wear or damage. Check that the rack moves freely over the full length of its travel, with no signs of roughness or excessive free play between the steering gear pinion and rack. Internal wear or damage can only be cured by renewing the steering gear assembly.

17.5 Remove the lower universal clamp bolt (arrowed)

17.6 Remove the steering rack mounting bolts – left-hand side mounting bolt (arrowed)

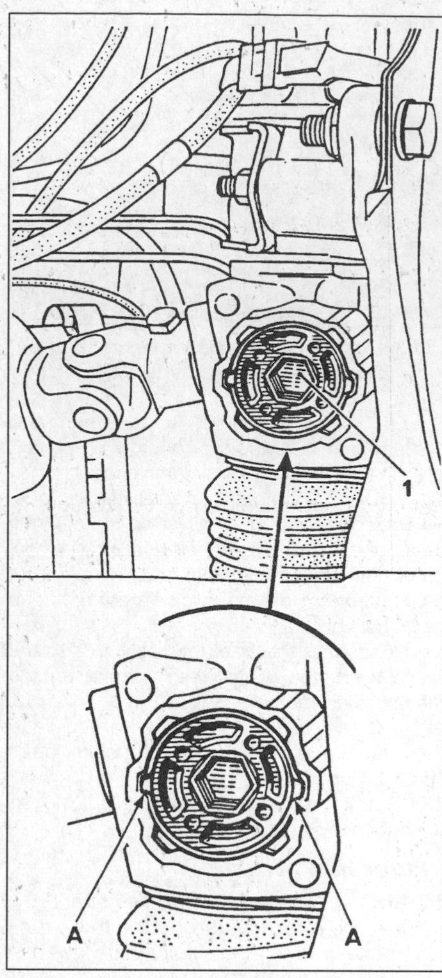

17.17 Steering rack thrust plunger adjustment
1 Adjusting nut *A Staking points*

16 Overhaul of the steering rack and pinion assembly is not possible. The only components which can be renewed are the steering gear gaiters, the track rod balljoints and the track rods.

Rack pinion adjustment

Note: *At the time of writing, no adjustment information was available for the TRW steering rack.*

17 If there is excessive free play of the rack in the steering gear housing, accompanied by a knocking noise, it may be possible to correct this by adjusting the rack pinion adjuster. On SMI steering racks, relieve the staking on the rack pinion adjusting nut. Using a 10 mm Allen key, tighten the adjusting nut until the free play disappears (but by no more than 1 notch). Check that the rack still moves freely over its full travel, then secure the adjusting nut by staking it **(see illustration)**.

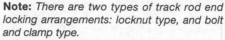

18 Track rod end balljoint – removal and refitting

Note: *There are two types of track rod end locking arrangements: locknut type, and bolt and clamp type.*
Note: *A balljoint separator tool will be required for this operation.*

Removal

1 Apply the handbrake, then jack up the front of the vehicle and support it on axle stands (see *Jacking and vehicle support*). Remove the appropriate front roadwheel.
2 If the balljoint is to be re-used, use a straight-edge and a scriber, or similar, to mark its relationship to the track rod.
3 Holding the balljoint, unscrew its locknut or clamp **(see illustrations)**. If a locknut type is used, slacken it by half a turn only, do not move the locknut from this position as it will serve as a reference mark on refitting.
4 Remove the nut securing the track rod balljoint to the swivel hub. Release the balljoint tapered shank using a universal balljoint separator. If the balljoint is to be re-used, protect the threaded end of the shank by screwing the nut back on a few turns before using the separator **(see illustration)**.
5 Counting the **exact** number of turns necessary to do so, unscrew the balljoint from the track rod end.
6 Count the number of exposed threads between the end of the balljoint and the locknut, and record this figure. If a new balljoint is to be fitted, unscrew the locknut from the old balljoint.
7 Carefully clean the balljoint and the threads. Renew the balljoint if its movement is sloppy or if it is too stiff, if it is excessively worn, or if it is damaged in any way. Carefully check the shank taper and threads. If the balljoint gaiter is damaged, the complete balljoint must be renewed; it is not possible to obtain the gaiter separately.

Refitting

8 If applicable, screw the locknut onto the new balljoint, and position it so that the same number of exposed threads are visible as was noted prior to removal.
9 Screw the balljoint into the track rod by the number of turns noted on removal. This should bring the balljoint locknut to within a quarter of a turn of the end of the track rod, with the alignment marks that were made (if applicable) on removal lined up.
10 Refit the balljoint shank to the swivel hub, and tighten the retaining nut to the specified torque. If difficulty is experienced due to the balljoint shank rotating, jam it by exerting pressure on the underside of the balljoint, using a tyre lever or a jack.
11 Refit the roadwheel, lower the vehicle to the ground and tighten the roadwheel bolts to the specified torque.
12 Check the front wheel toe setting as described in Section 20, then tighten the balljoint locknut/clamp bolt securely.

19 Track rod and inner balljoint – removal and refitting

Note: *In order to safely remove the track rod, without the risk of damaging the steering rack, a special track rod wrench (Renault number Dir.1305) and rack retaining clamp (Renault number Dir.1306 for SMI steering rack or 1306-01 for TRW steering rack) will be required. The special wrench engages with the track rod inner balljoint housing allowing the track rod to be easily slackened/tightened, and the retaining clamp secures the rack to the steering gear housing to prevent any stress being exerted on the steering gear pinion assembly* ***(see illustrations)****. Note that without access to the special tools, track rod*

18.3a Locknut (arrowed) used for locking one type of track rod end . . .

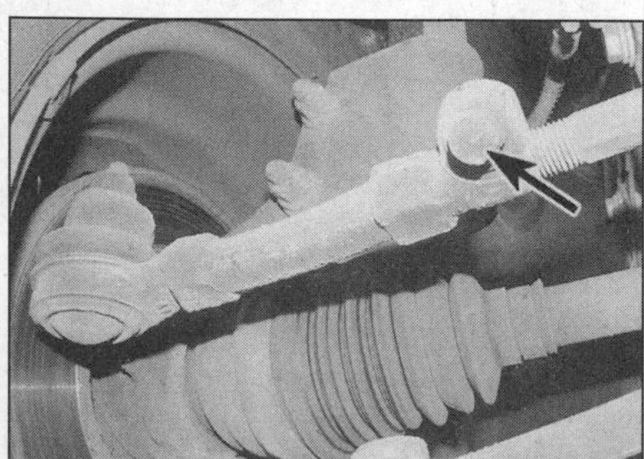

18.3b . . . and clamp type (arrowed) used for locking other types of track rod end

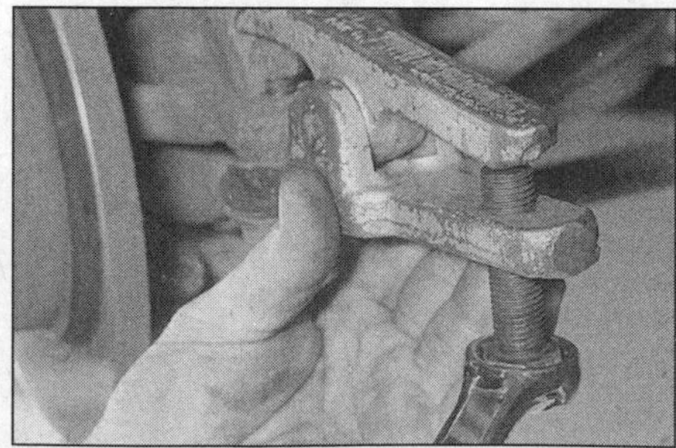

18.4 Using a universal balljoint separator to release the track rod balljoint from the swivel hub

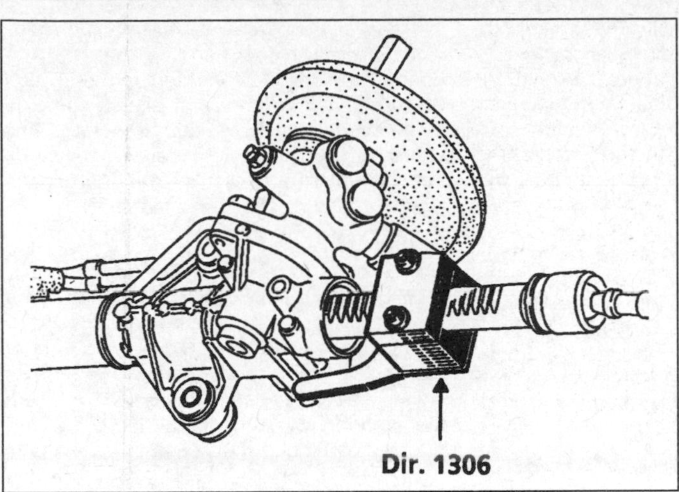

19.0a Steering rack secured with a retaining clamp

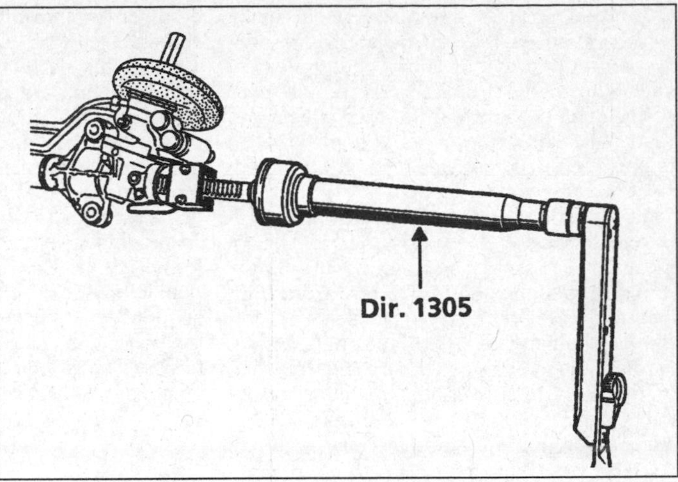

19.0b Track rod balljoints slackened with a special wrench

removal will be difficult, especially without causing damage.

Note: *There are two different types of steering gear assemblies fitted to these vehicles; the steering racks are manufactured by either SMI or TRW; the type of rack fitted can be identified from the manufacturing markings cast onto the steering gear housing. If work is being carried out on a SMI steering rack note that a new track rod locking washer assembly must be used on refitting.*

Removal

1 Remove the track rod end balljoint as described in Section 18.

2 Cut the retaining clips, and slide the steering gear gaiter off the track rod. It is recommended that the gaiter is renewed, regardless of its apparent condition.

3 In the absence of the special tools, using a pair of grips, unscrew the track rod inner balljoint from the steering rack end. Prevent the steering rack from turning by holding the balljoint lockwasher/steering rack with a second pair of grips.

Caution: Take care not to mark the surfaces of the rack and balljoint.

4 Remove the track rod assembly from the steering rack. On SMI steering gear assemblies, discard the lockwasher assembly; a new one must be used on refitting.

5 Examine the inner balljoint for signs of slackness or tight spots. Check that the track rod itself is straight and free from damage. If necessary, renew the track rod.

Refitting

6 Prior to refitting the track rod remove all traces of locking compound from the rack and track rod threads.

7 On models fitted with a SMI steering gear assembly, ensure the new lockwasher and locking ring are correctly assembled and fit them to the end of the track rod **(see illustration)**.

8 Apply a coat of locking compound (Renault recommend the use of Loctite Frenbloc – available from your Renault dealer) to the threads of the track rod then fit the track rod to the end of the steering rack. Using the method employed on removal, tighten the track rod inner balljoint to the specified torque, taking great care not to marks either the rack or the balljoint. On the SMI steering gear, whilst tightening the track rod ensure the tabs on the lock washer engage with the flats on the steering end.

9 Slide the new gaiter onto the track rod end, and locate it on the steering gear housing. Turn the steering from lock-to-lock to check that the gaiter is correctly positioned, then secure it with new retaining clips.

10 Refit the track rod end balljoint as described in Section 18.

20 Wheel alignment and steering angles – general information

General information

1 A car's steering and suspension geometry is defined in four basic settings **(see illustration)**. For this purpose, all angles are expressed in degrees (toe settings are also expressed as a measurement of length). The steering axis is defined as an imaginary line drawn through the axis of the suspension strut, extended where necessary to contact the ground.

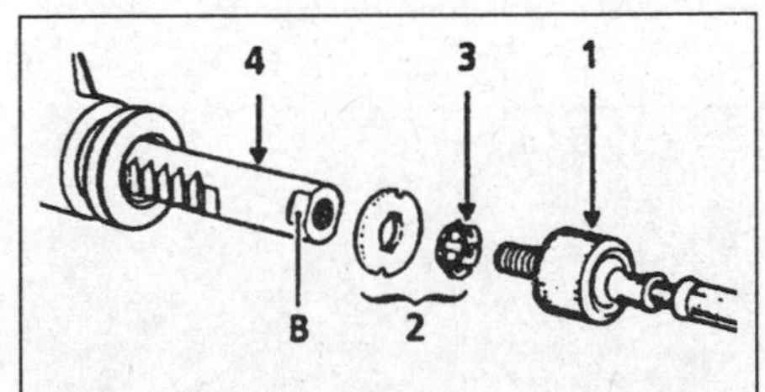

19.7 On models fitted with a SMI steering gear assembly, ensure the new lockwasher and locking ring are correctly assembled and fit them to the end of the track rod

1 Track rod
2 Locking ring
3 Lock washer
4 Steering gear
B Flats on steering end

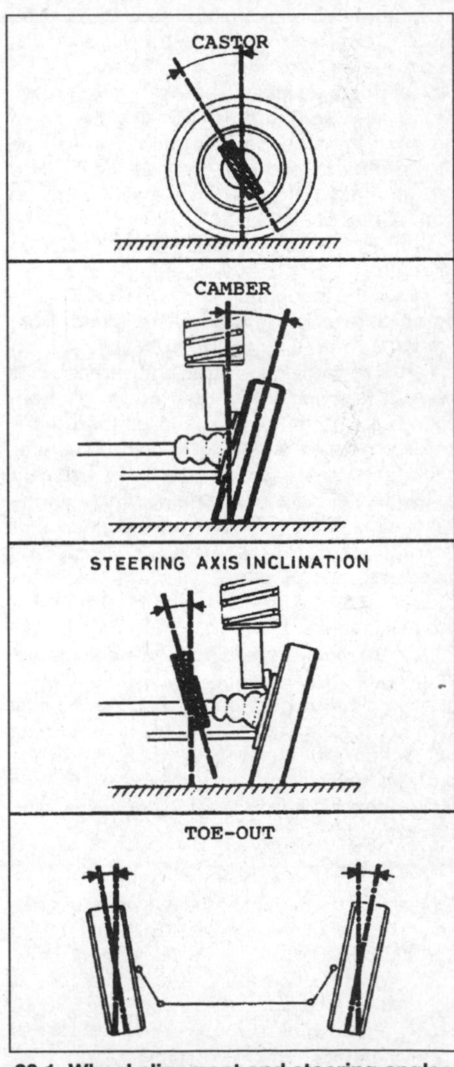

20.1 Wheel alignment and steering angles

2 Camber is the angle between each roadwheel and a vertical line drawn through its centre and tyre contact patch, when viewed from the front or rear of the car. Positive camber is when the roadwheels are tilted outwards from the vertical at the top; negative camber is when they are tilted inwards.

3 Camber is not adjustable. Values are given for reference only. Checking is possible using a camber checking gauge, but if the figure obtained is significantly different from that specified, the vehicle must be taken for careful checking by a professional. Wrong camber settings can only be caused by wear or damage to the body or suspension components.

4 Castor is the angle between the steering axis and a vertical line drawn through each roadwheel's centre and tyre contact patch, when viewed from the side of the car. Positive castor is when the steering axis is tilted so that it contacts the ground ahead of the vertical; negative castor is when it contacts the ground behind the vertical.

5 Castor is not adjustable. As with camber, values are given for reference only; deviation can only be due to wear or damage.

6 Steering axis inclination/SAI – also known as **kingpin inclination/KPI** – is the angle between the steering axis and a vertical line drawn through each roadwheel's centre and tyre contact patch, when viewed from the front or rear of the car.

7 SAI/KPI is not adjustable, and is given for reference only.

8 Toe is the amount by which the roadwheels point outwards or inwards, viewed from above. Toe-in is when the roadwheels point inwards, towards each other at the front, while toe-out is when they splay outwards from each other at the front. The value for toe can be expressed as an angle (taking the centre-line of the car as zero), or as a measurement of length (taking measurements between the inside rims of the wheels at hub height).

9 The front wheel toe setting is adjusted by screwing the balljoints in or out of their track rods to alter the effective length of the track rod assemblies.

10 Rear wheel toe setting is not adjustable, and is given for reference only. While it can be checked, if the figure obtained is significantly different from that specified, the vehicle must be taken for careful checking by a professional, as the fault can only be caused by wear or damage to the body or suspension components.

Checking - general

11 Due to the special measuring equipment necessary to check the wheel alignment, and the skill required to use it properly, the checking and adjustment of these settings is best left to a Renault dealer or similar expert. Most tyre-fitting shops now possess sophisticated checking equipment.

12 For accurate checking, the vehicle must be at the kerb weight specified in *Dimensions and weights* in the Reference Section.

13 Before starting work, check first that the tyre sizes and types are as specified, then check tyre pressures and tread wear. Also check roadwheel run-out, the condition of the hub bearings, the steering wheel free play and the condition of the front suspension components (Chapter 1A or 1B). Correct any faults.

14 Park the vehicle on level ground, with the front roadwheels in the straight-ahead position. Rock both ends to settle the suspension. Release the handbrake and roll the vehicle backwards 1 metre (3 feet), then forwards again, to relieve any stresses in the steering and suspension components.

Front wheels toe setting

Checking

15 Two methods are available to the home mechanic for checking the front wheel toe setting. One method is to use a gauge to measure the distance between the front and rear inside edges of the roadwheels. The other method is to use a scuff plate, in which each front wheel is rolled across a movable plate which records any deviation, or scuff, of the tyre from the straight-ahead position as it moves across the plate. Such gauges are available in relatively-inexpensive form from accessory outlets. It is up to the owner to decide whether the expense is justified, in view of the small amount of use such equipment would normally receive.

16 Prepare the vehicle as described previously in paragraphs 12 to 14.

17 If the measurement procedure is being used, carefully measure the distance between the front edges of the roadwheel rims and the rear edges of the rims. Subtract the rear measurement from the front measurement, and check that the result is within the specified range. If not, adjust the toe setting as described in paragraph 19.

18 If scuff plates are to be used, roll the vehicle backwards, check that the roadwheels are in the straight-ahead position, then roll it across the scuff plates so that each front roadwheel passes squarely over the centre of its respective plate. Note the angle recorded by the scuff plates. To ensure accuracy, repeat the check three times, and take the average of the three readings. If the roadwheels are running parallel, there will of course be no angle recorded; if a deviation value is shown on the scuff plates, compare the reading obtained for each wheel with that specified. If the value recorded is outside the specified tolerance, the toe setting is incorrect, and must be adjusted as follows.

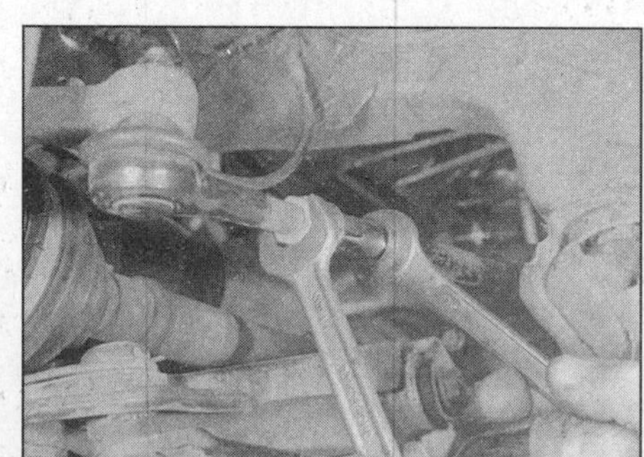

20.22 Adjusting the front wheel toe setting

Adjustment

Note: *There are two types of track rod end locking arrangements: locknut type, and bolt and clamp type.*

19 Apply the handbrake, jack up the front of the vehicle and support it securely on axle stands (see *Jacking and vehicle support*). Turn the steering wheel onto full-left lock, and record the number of exposed threads on the right-hand track rod end. Now turn the steering onto full-right lock, and record the number of threads on the left-hand side. If there are the same number of threads visible on both sides, then subsequent adjustment should be made equally on both sides. If there are more threads visible on one side than the other, it will be necessary to compensate for this during adjustment. **Note:** *It is important that, after adjustment, the same number of threads be visible on each track rod end.*

20 First clean the track rod threads; if they are corroded, apply penetrating fluid before starting adjustment. Release the rubber gaiter outboard clips, then peel back the gaiters and apply a smear of grease, so that both gaiters are free and will not be twisted or strained as their respective track rods are rotated.

21 Use a straight-edge and a scriber or similar to mark the relationship of each track rod to its balljoint. Holding each track rod in turn, unscrew its locknut or clamp fully.

22 Alter the length of the track rods, bearing in mind the note in paragraph 19, by screwing them into or out of the balljoints. Rotate the track rod using an open-ended spanner fitted to the flats provided. Shortening the track rods (screwing them onto their balljoints) will reduce toe-in and increase toe-out. Each complete turn of the track rod effectively adjusts the toe setting by 30' or 3 mm (depending on the method being used) **(see illustration)**.

23 When the setting is correct, hold the track rods and securely tighten the balljoint locknuts or clamps. Check that the balljoints are seated correctly in their sockets, and count the exposed threads. If the number of threads exposed is not the same on both sides, then the adjustment has not been made equally, and problems will be encountered with tyre scrubbing in turns; also, the steering wheel spokes will no longer be horizontal when the wheels are in the straight-ahead position.

24 When the track rod lengths are the same, lower the vehicle to the ground and recheck the toe setting; readjust if necessary. Ensure that the rubber gaiters are seated correctly and are not twisted or strained; secure them in position with new retaining clips.

21.0a Steering computer (arrowed) location

21.0b Steering angle sensor (arrowed) location

21.2 Unclipping the headlight adjuster panel from the facia

Rear wheels toe setting

25 The procedure for checking the rear toe setting is same as described for the front in paragraph 17. However, no adjustment is possible.

21 Steering computer (ECU) and angle sensor – removal and refitting

Note: *The steering computer (ECU) is located behind the facia panel on the right-hand side and the angle sensor is located on the steering rack* **(see illustrations)**.

Steering computer

Removal

1 Disconnect the battery negative lead.
2 Using a screwdriver, carefully prise the headlight adjuster control switch panel from the facia, taking care not to damage the facia trim **(see illustration)**.
3 Working under the facia from the driver's side footwell, disconnect the wiring connectors from the steering computer **(see illustrations). Note:** *To give better access to the ECU, unclip the heater ducting pipe from under the facia panel.*
4 Remove the retaining screw from the upper part of the mounting bracket and withdraw the steering computer (ECU) from under the facia panel **(see illustrations)**.

Refitting

5 Refitting is a reversal of removal, making sure that the wiring plugs are connected securely.

Steering angle sensor

Removal

6 Disconnect the battery negative lead.
7 Chock the rear wheels, apply the handbrake, jack up the front of the vehicle and support it on axle stands *(see Jacking and vehicle support)*. Remove engine undertray (where fitted).
8 Working under the vehicle, disconnect the

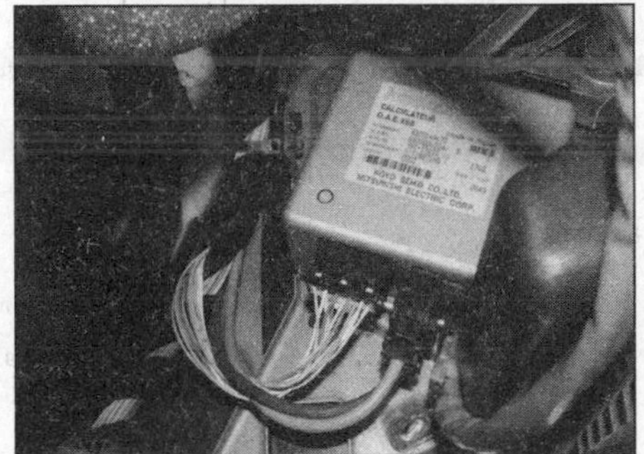
21.3a Steering computer viewed from under facia . . .

21.3b . . . disconnecting the three wiring connectors from the computer

wiring connector from the steering angle sensor **(see illustration).**
9 Remove the retaining screw and withdraw the steering angle sensor from the steering rack **(see illustration)**.

Refitting

10 Refitting is a reversal of removal, making sure that the wiring plug is connected securely.

21.4a Remove the retaining screw (arrowed) . . .

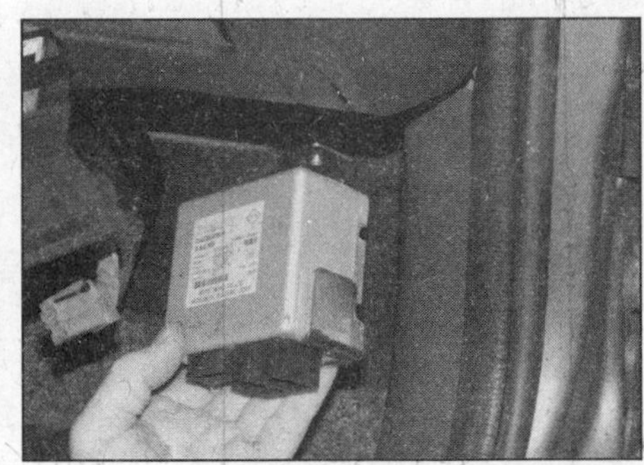
21.4b . . . and withdraw the computer from under the facia

21.8 Disconnecting the wiring connector from the sensor

21.9 Undo the retaining bolt (arrowed) to remove the sensor

Notes

Chapter 11
Bodywork and fittings

Contents

Degrees of difficulty

Easy, suitable for novice with little experience 

Fairly easy, suitable for beginner with some experience 

Fairly difficult, suitable for competent DIY mechanic 

Difficult, suitable for experienced DIY mechanic 

Very difficult, suitable for expert DIY or professional 

Specifications

Torque wrench setting	Nm	lbf ft
Seat belt and seat belt height adjuster mountings	25	18

1 General information

The bodyshell and floorpan are manufactured from pressed-steel, and form an integral part of the vehicle's structure (monocoque), without the need for a separate chassis. The Clio is available in 3- and 5-door Hatchback body styles, with a Van version also available in some markets.

Various areas of the structure are strengthened to provide for suspension, steering and engine mounting points, and load distribution.

All models are fitted with front wings manufactured from a polymer compound, which can withstand an impact of up to 10 mph (16 km/h) without sustaining permanent damage.

Corrosion protection is applied to all new vehicles. Various anti-corrosion preparations are used, including galvanising, zinc phosphatisation, and PVC underseal. An 'anti-gravel' undercoat is applied to the front section of the bonnet, to prevent corrosion and paint chipping caused by stones and other road debris hitting the front of the vehicle. Protective wax is injected into the box sections and other hollow cavities.

Extensive use is made of plastic for peripheral components, such as the radiator grille, bumpers and wheel trims, and for much of the interior trim. Plastic wheel arch liners are fitted, to protect the metal body panels against corrosion due to a build-up of road dirt.

Interior fittings are to a high standard on all models, and a wide range of optional equipment is available throughout the range.

2 Maintenance – bodywork and underframe

The general condition of a vehicle's bodywork is the one thing that significantly affects its value. Maintenance is easy, but needs to be regular. Neglect, particularly after minor damage, can lead quickly to further deterioration and costly repair bills. It is important also to keep watch on those parts of the vehicle not immediately visible, for instance the underside, inside all the wheel arches, and the lower part of the engine compartment.

The basic maintenance routine for the bodywork is washing – preferably with a lot of water, from a hose. This will remove all the loose solids which may have stuck to the vehicle. It is important to flush these off in such a way as to prevent grit from scratching the finish. The wheel arches and underframe need washing in the same way, to remove any accumulated mud which will retain moisture and tend to encourage rust. Paradoxically enough, the best time to clean the underframe and wheel arches is in wet weather, when the mud is thoroughly wet and soft. In very wet weather, the underframe is usually cleaned of large accumulations automatically, and this is a good time for inspection.

Periodically, except on vehicles with a wax-based underbody protective coating, it is a good idea to have the whole of the underframe of the vehicle steam-cleaned, engine compartment included, so that a thorough inspection can be carried out to see what minor repairs and renovations are necessary. Steam-cleaning is available at many garages, and is necessary for the removal of the accumulation of oily grime, which sometimes is allowed to become thick in certain areas. If steam-cleaning facilities are not available, there are one or two excellent grease solvents available, which can be brush-applied; the dirt can then be simply hosed off. Note that these methods should not be used on vehicles with wax-based underbody protective coating, or the coating will be removed. Such vehicles should be inspected annually, preferably just prior to Winter, when the underbody should be washed down, and any damage to the wax coating repaired. Ideally, a completely fresh coat should be applied. It would also be worth considering the use of such wax-based protection for injection into door panels, sills, box sections, etc, as an additional safeguard against rust damage, where such protection is not provided by the vehicle manufacturer.

After washing paintwork, wipe off with a chamois leather to give an unspotted clear finish. A coat of clear protective wax polish will give added protection against chemical pollutants in the air. If the paintwork sheen has dulled or oxidised, use a cleaner/polisher combination to restore the brilliance of the shine. This requires a little effort, but such dulling is usually caused because regular washing has been neglected. Care needs to be taken with metallic paintwork, as special non-abrasive cleaner/polisher is required to avoid damage to the finish. Always check that the door and ventilator opening drain holes and pipes are completely clear, so that water can be drained out. Brightwork should be treated in the same way as paintwork. Windscreens and windows can be kept clear of the smeary film which often appears, by the use of proprietary glass cleaner. Never use any form of wax or other body or chromium polish on glass.

3 Maintenance – upholstery and carpets

Mats and carpets should be brushed or vacuum-cleaned regularly, to keep them free of grit. If they are badly stained, remove them from the vehicle for scrubbing or sponging, and make quite sure they are dry before refitting. Seats and interior trim panels can be kept clean by wiping with a damp cloth. If they do become stained (which can be more apparent on light-coloured upholstery), use a little liquid detergent and a soft nail brush to scour the grime out of the grain of the material. Do not forget to keep the headlining clean in the same way as the upholstery. When using liquid cleaners inside the vehicle, do not over-wet the surfaces being cleaned. Excessive damp could get into the seams and padded interior, causing stains, offensive odours or even rot. If the inside of the vehicle gets wet accidentally, it is worthwhile taking some trouble to dry it out properly, particularly where carpets are involved. *Do not leave oil or electric heaters inside the vehicle for this purpose.*

4 Minor body damage – repair

Minor scratches

If the scratch is very superficial, and does not penetrate to the metal of the bodywork, repair is very simple. Lightly rub the area of the scratch with a paintwork renovator, or a very fine cutting paste, to remove loose paint from the scratch, and to clear the surrounding bodywork of wax polish. Rinse the area with clean water.

Apply touch-up paint to the scratch using a fine paint brush; continue to apply fine layers of paint until the surface of the paint in the scratch is level with the surrounding paintwork. Allow the new paint at least two weeks to harden, then blend it into the surrounding paintwork by rubbing the scratch area with a paintwork renovator or a very fine cutting paste. Finally, apply wax polish.

Where the scratch has penetrated right through to the metal of the bodywork, causing the metal to rust, a different repair technique is required. Remove any loose rust from the bottom of the scratch with a penknife, then apply rust-inhibiting paint, to prevent the formation of rust in the future. Using a rubber or nylon applicator, fill the scratch with bodystopper paste. If required, this paste can be mixed with cellulose thinners, to provide a very thin paste which is ideal for filling narrow scratches. Before the stopper-paste in the scratch hardens, wrap a piece of smooth cotton rag around the top of a finger. Dip the finger in cellulose thinners, and quickly sweep it across the surface of the stopper-paste in the scratch; this will ensure that the surface of the stopper-paste is slightly hollowed. The scratch can now be painted over as described earlier in this Section.

Dents

When deep denting of the vehicle's bodywork has taken place, the first task is to pull the dent out, until the affected bodywork almost attains its original shape. There is little point in trying to restore the original shape completely, as the metal in the damaged area will have stretched on impact, and cannot be reshaped fully to its original contour. It is better to bring the level of the dent up to a point which is about 3 mm below the level of the surrounding bodywork. In cases where the dent is very shallow anyway, it is not worth trying to pull it out at all. If the underside of the dent is accessible, it can be hammered out gently from behind, using a mallet with a wooden or plastic head. Whilst doing this, hold a block of wood firmly against the outside of the panel, to absorb the impact from the hammer blows and thus prevent a large area of the bodywork from being 'belled-out'.

Should the dent be in a section of the bodywork which has a double skin, or some other factor making it inaccessible from behind, a different technique is called for. Drill several small holes through the metal inside the area – particularly in the deeper section. Then screw long self-tapping screws into the holes, just sufficiently for them to gain a good purchase in the metal. Now the dent can be pulled out by pulling on the protruding heads of the screws with a pair of pliers.

The next stage of the repair is the removal of the paint from the damaged area, and from an inch or so of the surrounding 'sound' bodywork. This is accomplished most easily by using a wire brush or abrasive pad on a power drill, although it can be done just as effectively by hand, using sheets of abrasive paper. To complete the preparation for filling, score the surface of the bare metal with a screwdriver or the tang of a file, or alternatively, drill small holes in the affected area. This will provide a really good 'key' for the filler paste.

To complete the repair, see the Section on filling and respraying.

Rust holes or gashes

Remove all paint from the affected area, and from an inch or so of the surrounding 'sound' bodywork, using an abrasive pad or a wire brush on a power drill. If these are not available, a few sheets of abrasive paper will do the job most effectively. With the paint removed, you will be able to judge the severity of the corrosion, and therefore decide whether to renew the whole panel (if this is possible) or to repair the affected area. New body panels are not as expensive as most people think, and it is often quicker and more satisfactory to fit a new panel than to attempt to repair large areas of corrosion.

Remove all fittings from the affected area, except those which will act as a guide to the original shape of the damaged bodywork (e.g. headlamp shells etc). Then, using tin snips or a hacksaw blade, remove all loose metal and any other metal badly affected by corrosion. Hammer the edges of the hole inwards, in order to create a slight depression for the filler paste.

Wire-brush the affected area to remove the powdery rust from the surface of the remaining metal. Paint the affected area with rust-inhibiting paint; if the back of the rusted area is accessible, treat this also.

Before filling can take place, it will be necessary to block the hole in some way. This can be achieved by the use of aluminium or plastic mesh, or aluminium tape.

Aluminium or plastic mesh, or glass-fibre matting is probably the best material to use for a large hole. Cut a piece to the approximate size and shape of the hole to be filled, then position it in the hole so that its edges are below the level of the surrounding bodywork. It can be retained in position by several blobs of filler paste around its periphery.

Aluminium tape should be used for small or very narrow holes. Pull a piece off the roll, trim it to the approximate size and shape required, then pull off the backing paper (if used) and stick the tape over the hole; it can be overlapped if the thickness of one piece is insufficient. Burnish down the edges of the tape with the handle of a screwdriver or similar, to ensure that the tape is securely attached to the metal underneath.

Filling and respraying

Before using this Section, see the Sections on dent, deep scratch, rust holes and gash repairs.

Many types of bodyfiller are available, but generally speaking, those proprietary kits which contain a tin of filler paste and a tube of resin hardener are best for this type of repair. A wide, flexible plastic or nylon applicator will be found invaluable for imparting a smooth and well-contoured finish to the surface of the filler.

Mix up a little filler on a clean piece of card or board – measure the hardener carefully (follow the maker's instructions on the pack), otherwise the filler will set too rapidly or too slowly. Using the applicator, apply the filler paste to the prepared area; draw the applicator across the surface of the filler to achieve the correct contour and to level the surface. As soon as a contour that approximates to the correct one is achieved, stop working the paste – if you carry on too long, the paste will become sticky and begin to 'pick-up' on the applicator. Continue to add thin layers of filler paste at 20-minute intervals, until the level of the filler is just proud of the surrounding bodywork.

Once the filler has hardened, the excess can be removed using a metal plane or file. From then on, progressively-finer grades of abrasive paper should be used, starting with a 40-grade production paper, and finishing with a 400-grade wet-and-dry paper. Always wrap the abrasive paper around a flat rubber, cork, or wooden block – otherwise the surface of the filler will not be completely flat. During the smoothing of the filler surface, the wet-and-dry paper should be periodically rinsed in water. This will ensure that a very smooth finish is imparted to the filler at the final stage.

At this stage, the 'dent' should be surrounded by a ring of bare metal, which in turn should be encircled by the finely 'feathered' edge of the good paintwork. Rinse the repair area with clean water, until all of the dust produced by the rubbing-down operation has gone.

Spray the whole area with a light coat of – this will show up any imperfections in the surface of the filler. Repair these imperfections with fresh filler paste or bodystopper, and once more smooth the surface with abrasive paper. If bodystopper is used, it can be mixed with cellulose thinners, to form a really thin paste which is ideal for filling small holes. Repeat this spray-and-repair procedure until you are satisfied that the surface of the filler, and the feathered edge of the paintwork, are perfect. Clean the repair area with clean water, and allow to dry fully.

The repair area is now ready for final spraying. Paint spraying must be carried out in a warm, dry, windless and dust-free atmosphere. This condition can be created artificially if you have access to a large indoor working area, but if you are forced to work in the open, you will have to pick your day very carefully. If you are working indoors, dousing the floor in the work area with water will help to settle the dust which would otherwise be in the atmosphere. If the repair area is confined to one body panel, mask off the surrounding panels; this will help to minimise the effects of a slight mis-match in paint colours. Bodywork fittings (e.g. chrome strips, door handles etc) will also need to be masked off. Use genuine masking tape, and several thicknesses of newspaper, for the masking operations.

Before commencing to spray, agitate the aerosol can thoroughly, then spray a test area (an old tin, or similar) until the technique is mastered. Cover the repair area with a thick coat of primer; the thickness should be built up using several thin layers of paint, rather than one thick one. Using 400 grade wet-and-dry paper, rub down the surface of the primer until it is really smooth. While doing this, the work area should be thoroughly doused with water, and the wet-and-dry paper periodically rinsed in water. Allow to dry before spraying on more paint.

Spray on the top coat, again building up the thickness by using several thin layers of paint. Start spraying at the top of the repair area, and then, using a side-to-side motion, work downwards until the whole repair area and about 2 inches of the surrounding original paintwork is covered. Remove all masking material 10 to 15 minutes after spraying on the final coat of paint.

Allow the new paint at least two weeks to harden, then, using a paintwork renovator or a very fine cutting paste, blend the edges of the paint into the existing paintwork. Finally, apply wax polish.

Plastic components

With the use of more and more plastic body components by the vehicle manufacturers (e.g. bumpers, spoilers, wings and in some cases major body panels), rectification of more serious damage to such items has become a matter of either entrusting repair work to a specialist in this field, or renewing complete components. Repair of such damage by the DIY owner is not really feasible, owing to the cost of the equipment and materials required for effecting such repairs. The basic technique involves making a groove along the line of the crack in the plastic, using a rotary burr in a power drill. The damaged part is then welded back together, using a hot air gun to heat up and fuse a plastic filler rod into the groove. Any excess plastic is then removed, and the area rubbed down to a smooth finish. It is important that a filler rod of the correct plastic is used, as body components can be made of a variety of different types (e.g. polycarbonate, ABS, polypropylene).

Damage of a less serious nature (abrasions, minor cracks etc) can be repaired by the DIY owner using a two-part epoxy filler repair. Once mixed in equal, this is used in similar fashion to the bodywork filler used on metal panels. The filler is usually cured in twenty to thirty minutes, ready for sanding and painting.

If the owner is renewing a complete component himself, or if he has repaired it with epoxy filler, he will be left with the problem of finding a suitable paint for finishing which is compatible with the type of plastic used. At one time, the use of a universal paint was not possible, owing to the complex range of plastics encountered in body component applications. Standard paints, generally speaking, will not bond to plastic or rubber satisfactorily, but suitable paints to match any plastic or rubber finish, can be obtained from dealers. However, it is now possible to obtain a plastic body parts finishing kit which consists of a pre-primer treatment, a primer and coloured top coat. Full instructions are normally supplied with a kit, but basically, the method of use is to first apply the pre-primer to the component concerned, and allow it to dry for up to 30 minutes. Then the primer is applied, and left to dry for about an hour before finally applying the special-coloured top coat. The result is a correctly-coloured component, where the paint will flex with the plastic or rubber, a property that standard paint does not normally posses.

5 Major body damage – repair

Where serious damage has occurred, or large areas need renewal due to neglect, it means that complete new panels will need welding-in, and this is best left to professionals. If the damage is due to impact, it will also be necessary to check completely the alignment of the bodyshell, and this can only be carried out accurately by a Renault dealer using special jigs. If the body is left misaligned, it is primarily dangerous, as the car will not handle properly, and secondly, uneven stresses will be imposed on the steering, suspension and possibly transmission, causing abnormal wear, or complete failure, particularly to such items as the tyres.

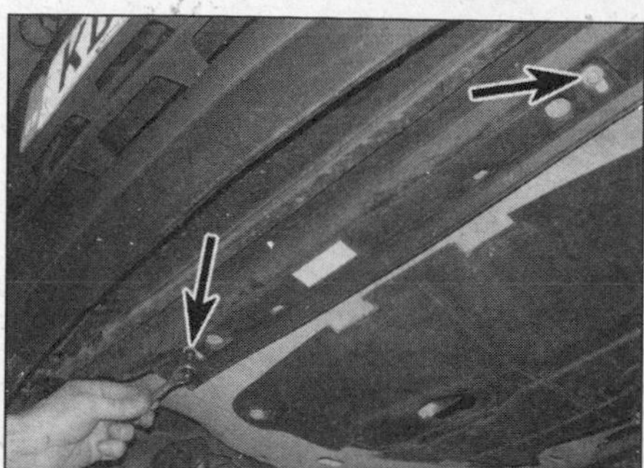

6.3 Undo the two retaining screws arrowed

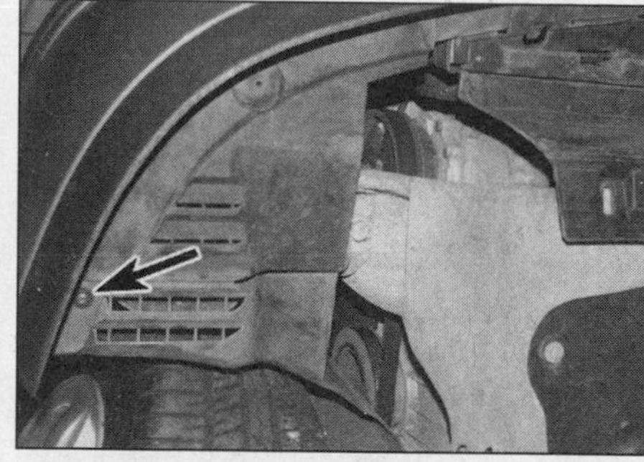

6.4a Unscrew the lower retaining screw (arrowed) . . .

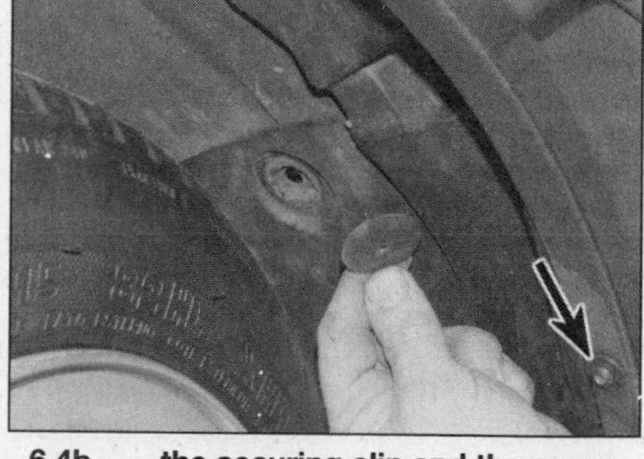

6.4b . . . the securing clip and the screw (arrowed)

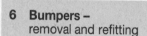

6 Bumpers – removal and refitting

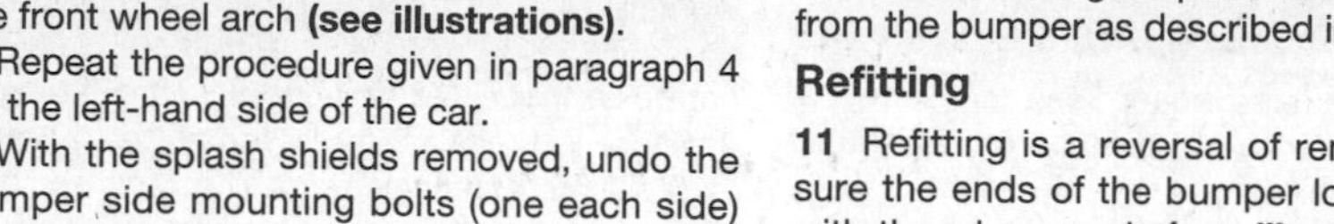

Front bumper

Removal

1 On models fitted with front foglights, make sure the ignition and light switches are in the off position.

2 To improve access, jack up the front of the car and support it securely on axle stands (see *Jacking and vehicle support*).

3 From under the front bumper, undo and remove the securing bolts from the splash shield below the radiator to the subframe **(see illustration)**.

4 Working under the right-hand side of the car, undo the two retaining screws and release the securing clips from the liner under the front wheel arch **(see illustrations)**.

5 Repeat the procedure given in paragraph 4 on the left-hand side of the car.

6 With the splash shields removed, undo the bumper side mounting bolts (one each side) **(see illustration)**.

7 From under the left-hand side of the bumper, locate the front foglight wiring main loom and disconnect it from the rear of the foglight. **Note:** *There is a wiring loom that runs across the rear of the bumper to the right-hand foglight – this can be left in place.*

8 Withdraw the two upper mounting clips/screws from the top of the grille **(see illustration)**.

9 Have an assistant support one end of the bumper, then unclip the outer ends of the bumper from the front wings **(see illustration)** then withdraw the bumper, complete with grille from the vehicle.

10 The radiator grille panel can be separated from the bumper as described in Section 7.

Refitting

11 Refitting is a reversal of removal, making sure the ends of the bumper locate correctly with the wing panels **(see illustrations)**. Refit the front grille with reference to Section 7.

Rear bumper

Removal

12 Make sure the ignition and light switches are in the off position.

13 To improve access, chock the front wheels, then jack up the rear of the car and support it securely on axle stands (see *Jacking and vehicle support*).

14 Working under the rear wheel arches, remove the securing nut and retaining screws **(see illustrations)**, and remove the splash shields from both sides of the car.

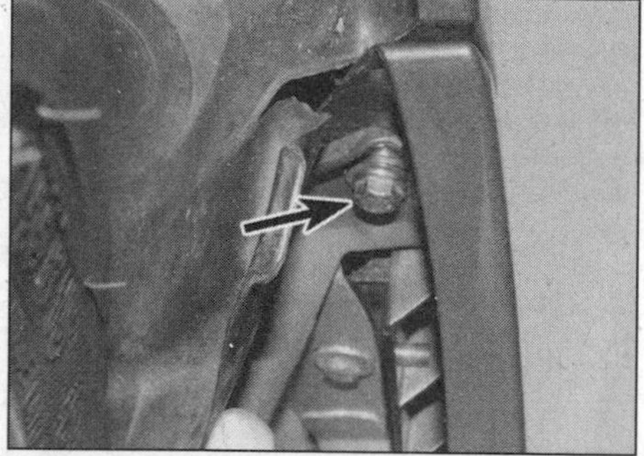

6.6 Front bumper side securing bolt (arrowed), behind wheel arch splash shield

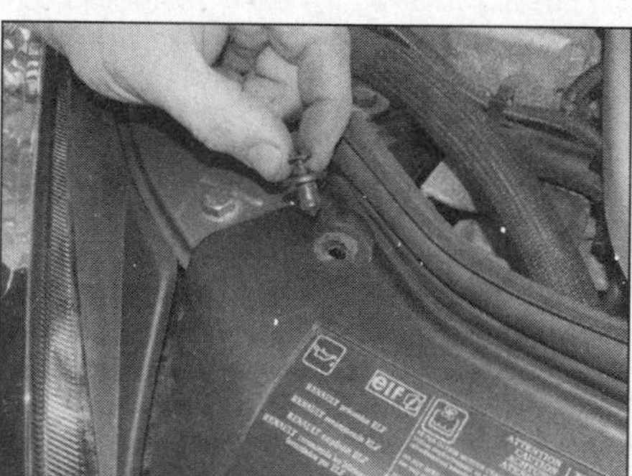

6.8 Front bumper/grille upper securing screws/clips

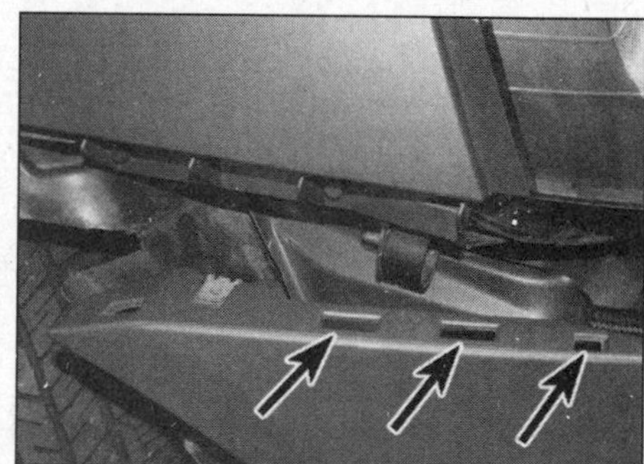

6.9 Slots (arrowed) to locate front bumper to wing panel

6.11a Make sure the lugs on the front wing panel . . .

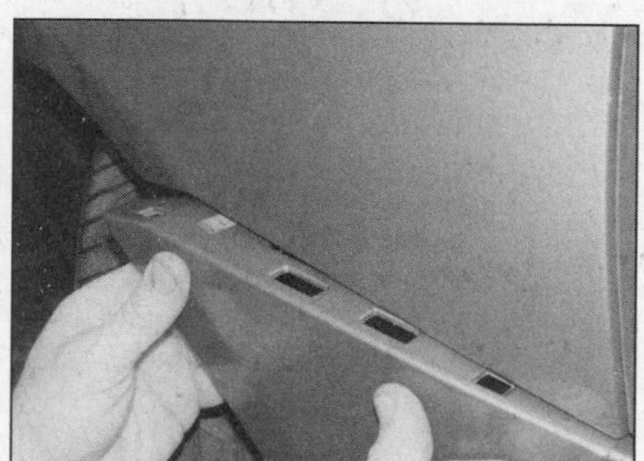

6.11b . . . line up with the slots in the bumper

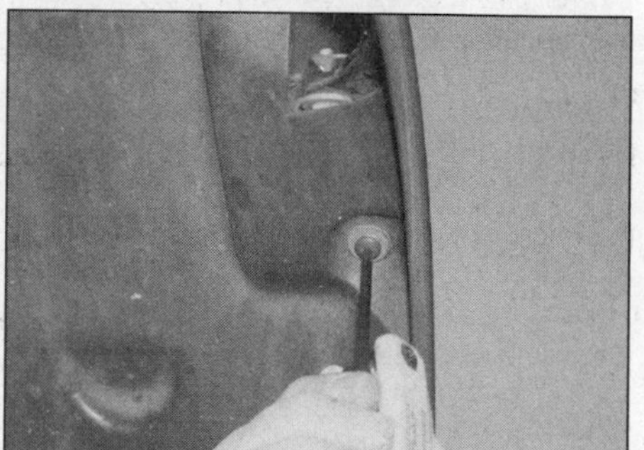

6.14a Removing the splash shield upper retaining screw . . .

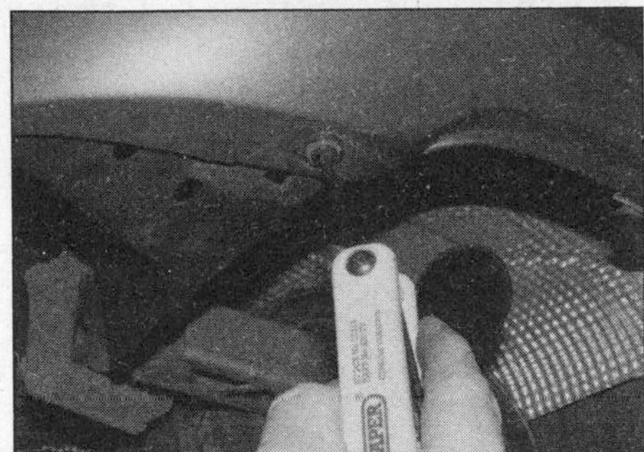
6.14b . . . and the lower retaining screw

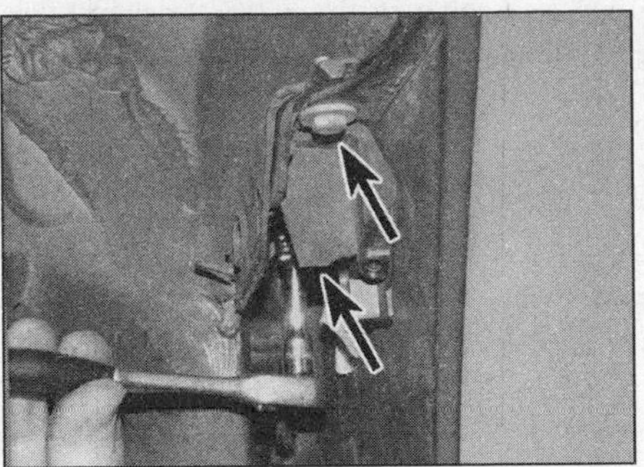
6.15 Remove the rear bumper side-mounting bolts (arrowed)

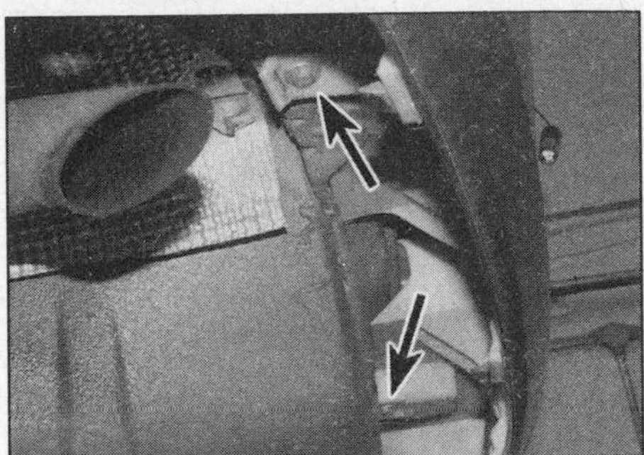
6.16 Remove the two rear lower mounting bolts (arrowed)

15 Remove the now-exposed bumper side-mounting bolts **(see illustration)** (two at each end of the bumper).
16 Working under the rear of the car, slacken the two lower securing bolts from the bumper **(see illustration)**.
17 Using a flat-bladed screwdriver, unclip the number plate light and disconnect the wiring **(see illustration)**.
18 Undo and remove the two upper securing bolts from the bumper **(see illustration)**.
19 Have an assistant support one side of the bumper, then unclip the bumper at each side and withdraw it from the rear of the vehicle **(see illustration)**.

Refitting

20 Refitting is a reversal of removal. Make sure the plastic locating brackets are correctly located on each end of the bumper **(see illustration)**

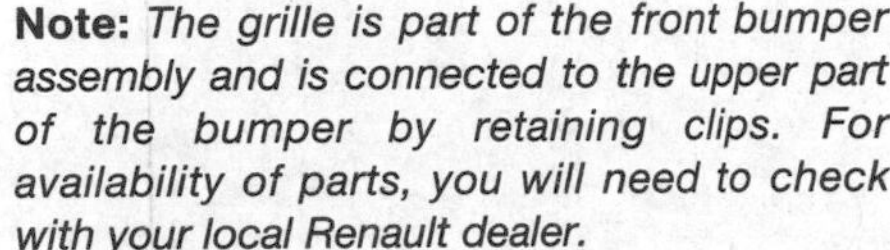

7 Radiator grille panel – removal and refitting

Note: *The grille is part of the front bumper assembly and is connected to the upper part of the bumper by retaining clips. For availability of parts, you will need to check with your local Renault dealer.*

Removal

1 Open the bonnet and remove the front bumper as described in Section 6.
2 Unclip the air duct from the rear of the grille **(see illustration)**.
3 Working your way along the lower part of the grille, release the retaining clips **(see illustration)** and withdraw the grille panel from the front bumper.

Refitting

4 Refitting is a reversal of removal.

8 Windscreen cowl panels – removal and refitting

Note: *The right-hand panel (as seen from the driver's seat) must be removed first, before removing the left-hand panel.*

Removal

1 Open the bonnet and remove the weather-seal from along the windscreen cowl panels **(see illustration)**.
2 Remove the windscreen wiper arms, as described in Chapter 12.
3 Carefully release the cowl panel securing clips by pushing the centre pin down about

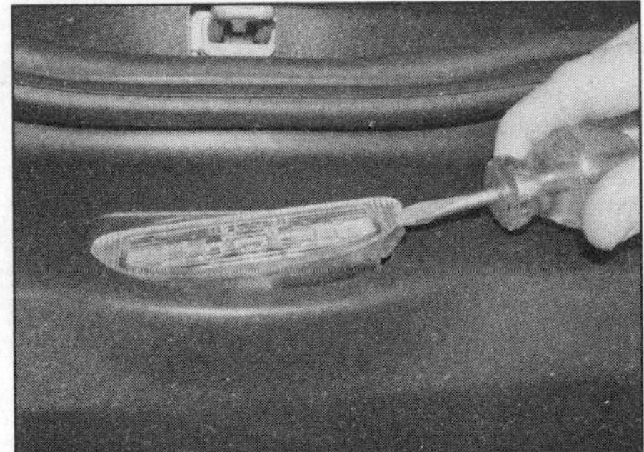
6.17 Unclipping the rear number plate light unit

6.18 Unscrew the two upper mounting bolts (arrowed)

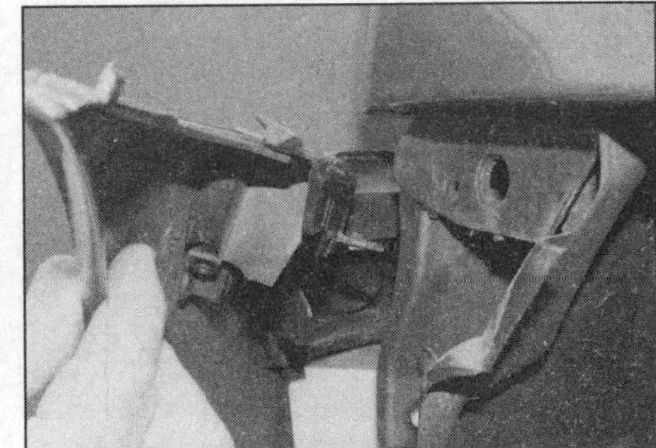
6.19 Release the bumper from the side mounting brackets

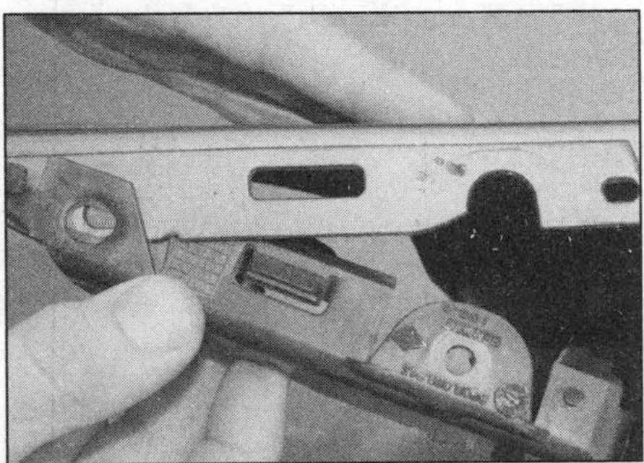
6.20 Locate the brackets onto each end of the bumper

7.2 Unclipping the cover from the grille panel

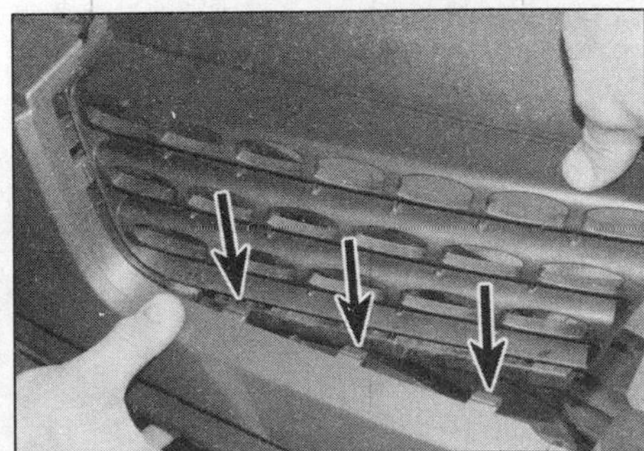
7.3 Unclip the grille from the retaining clips (arrowed) on edge of the front bumper

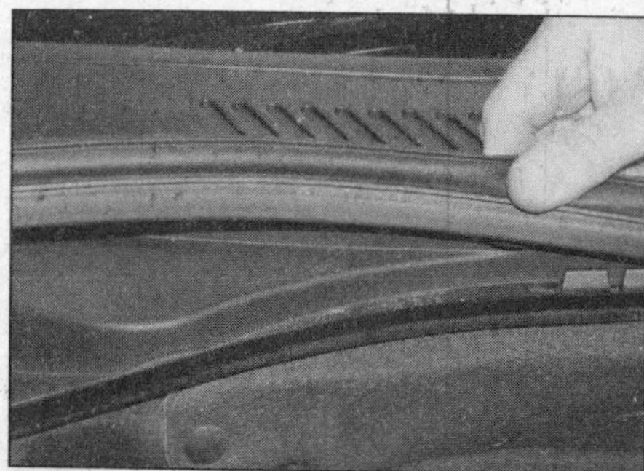
8.1 Removing the weather seal from along the scuttle panel

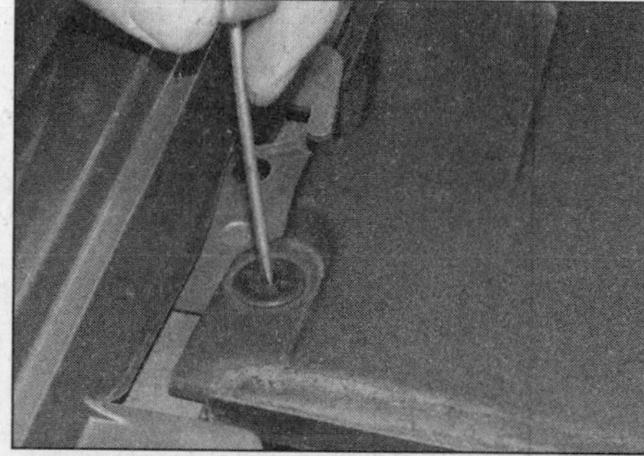
8.3 Releasing the securing clip from the windscreen cowl panel

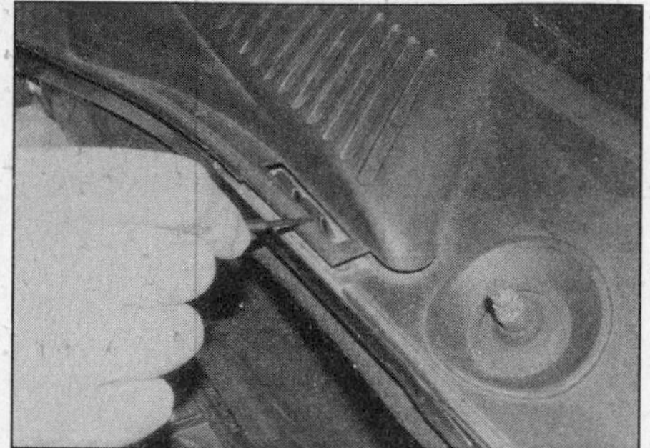
8.4a Unclip the right-hand windscreen cowl panel from the left-hand panel . . .

8.4b . . . release the right-hand cowl panel . . .

8.4c . . . then the left-hand cowl panel from the windscreen

5 mm **(see illustration)**. One securing clip at each side, in the top of the inner wing panel.

4 Unclip the panels at the centre, then release them from the lower part of the windscreen. Unclip the panels from the locating pin at the top edge of the inner wing, taking care not to damage the wing panel **(see illustrations)**.

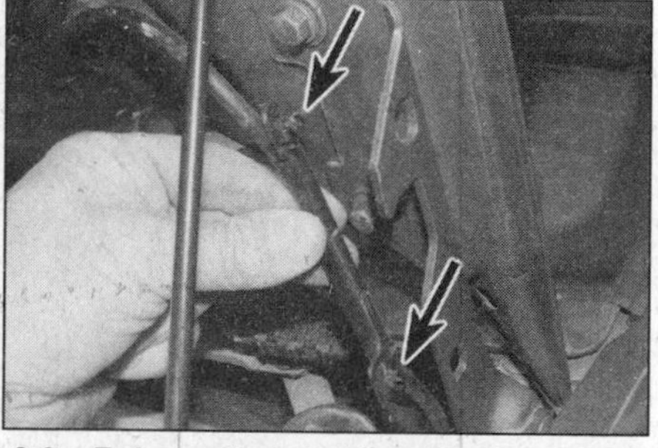
9.2a Release the retaining clips (arrowed) to disengage the washer hose from the bonnet hinge . . .

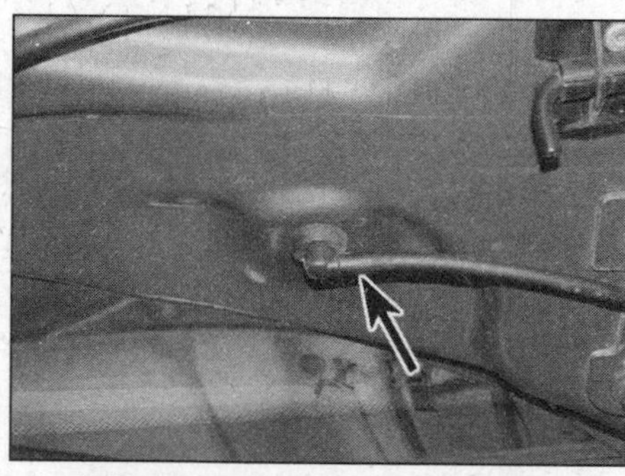
9.2b . . . and disconnect the hose (arrowed) from the washer jet

9.4a Undo the two bolts (arrowed) from the right-hand hinge . . .

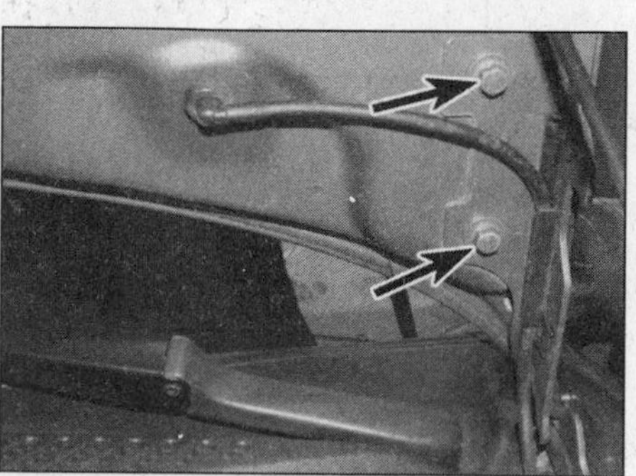
9.4b . . . and the bolts (arrowed) from the left-hand hinge

Refitting

5 Refitting is a reversal of removal, bearing in mind the following points.

6 Check the two halves of the cowling are securely clipped together.

7 Ensure that the weatherseal is correctly located over the front of the panels, and that the panel securing clips are correctly engaged.

8 Refit the windscreen wiper arms with reference to Chapter 12.

9 Push the centre pin so that it protrudes about 5 mm through the top of the securing clip, before refitting. Then, when in place, push the centre pin down flush with the clip to secure.

9 Bonnet and hinges – removal and refitting

Bonnet

Removal

1 Have an assistant support the bonnet in the open position.

2 Disconnect the windscreen washer hose from the left-hand bonnet hinge and the washer jet **(see illustrations)**.

3 If the original bonnet is to be refitted, mark the position of the hinges on the bonnet to aid alignment on refitting (a line can be drawn around the hinge using a suitable pen).

4 Remove the bolts securing the bonnet to the hinges (two bolts at each side) **(see illustrations)**, then carefully withdraw the bonnet from the car.

Refitting

5 Refitting is a reversal of removal, bearing in mind the following points.

6 Where applicable, align the hinges with the marks made on the bonnet before removal.

7 Close the bonnet (carefully, in case it fouls the surrounding bodywork), and check the alignment with the surrounding body panels.

8 If necessary, the alignment of the bonnet can be adjusted by altering the position of the bonnet on the hinges, using the elongated holes provided. The alignment of the front of the bonnet can also be adjusted by altering the position of the bonnet lock assembly, using the elongated bolt holes provided.

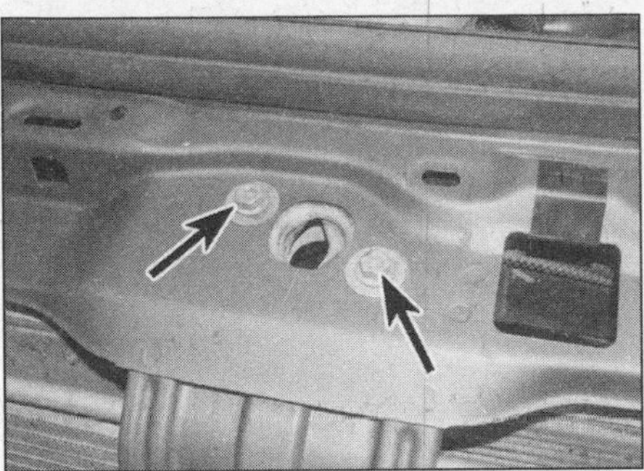

10.3a Undo the bonnet lock assembly securing bolts (arrowed) . . .

Hinges

9 The bonnet hinges are bolted to the inner wing panel, and can only be removed after the outer wing has been removed. This cannot easily be removed and may require special equipment, this can only be carried out accurately by a Renault dealer or bodyshop specialists.

10 Bonnet lock components – removal and refitting

Lock assembly

Removal

1 Open the bonnet.
2 Note and mark the position of the lock on the panel, to aid correct alignment when refitting.
3 Unscrew the two securing bolts, then lift the lock assembly from the panel **(see illustrations)**.
4 Release the outer cable from the lock assembly.
5 Disconnect the end of the inner release cable from the lock operating lever, and withdraw the lock assembly.

Refitting

6 Refitting is a reversal of removal, but align the assembly with the marks made on the panel before removal.

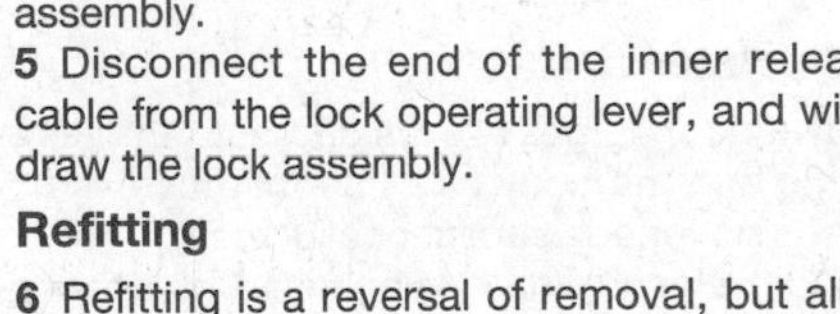

7 Make sure that the outer and inner cables are located correctly before closing the bonnet **(see illustration)**.
8 On completion, if necessary adjust the alignment of the bonnet with the surrounding body panels by altering the position of the lock/striker assembly, using the elongated bolt holes provided.

Lock striker

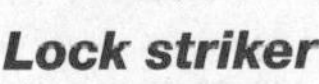

9 Open the bonnet. (The lock striker is bolted to the bonnet.)
10 Note and mark the position of the lock striker on the bonnet, to aid correct alignment when refitting.
11 Unscrew the two securing nuts from the lock striker mounting bracket **(see illustration)**.

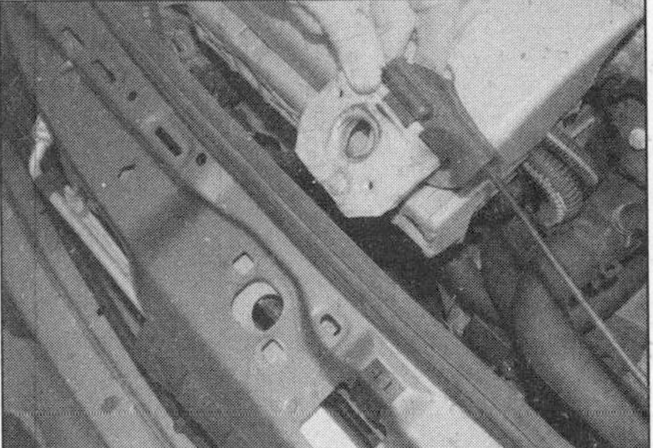

10.3b . . . then withdraw the lock assembly from the cross-panel

12 Unclip the bonnet safety catch pull and remove the lock striker from the bonnet **(see illustration)**.

Refitting

13 Refitting is a reversal of removal, but align the assembly with the marks made on the panel before removal.
14 On completion, if necessary adjust the alignment of the bonnet with the surrounding body panels by altering the position of the lock/striker assembly, using the elongated bolt holes provided.

Lock release cable/lever

Removal

15 Working inside the vehicle, use a screwdriver to carefully prise the bonnet release lever off **(see illustration)**.

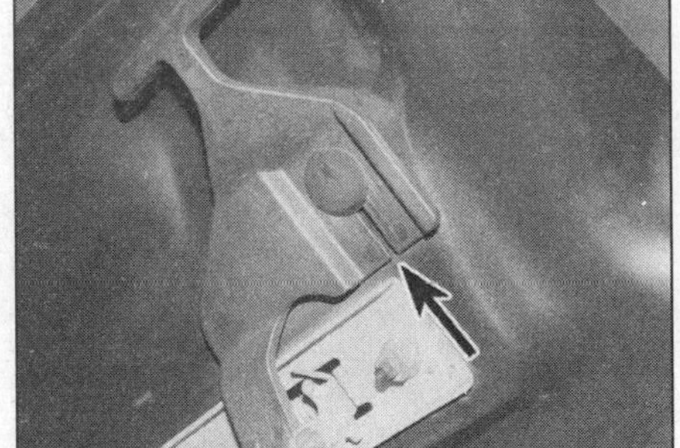

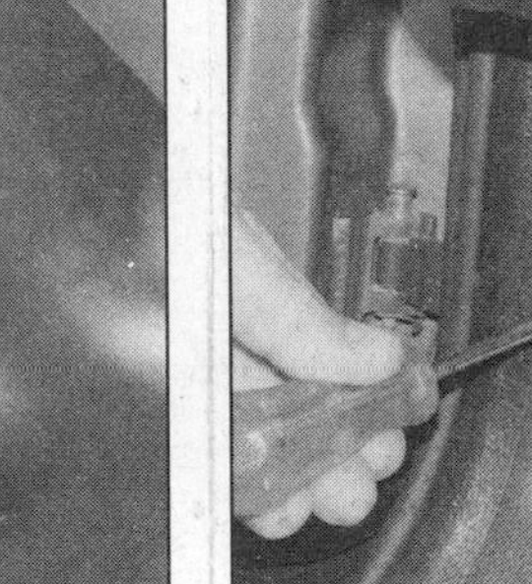

10.12 Slide the safety catch pull out, in the direction of the arrow

10.17a Undo the retaining screw (arrowed) . . .

10.7 Check the cable is fitted correctly

10.11 Undo the two retaining nuts (arrowed)

16 Remove the left-hand side front sill panel, as described in Section 27.
17 Undo the retaining screw and unclip the assembly from the body **(see illustrations)**.

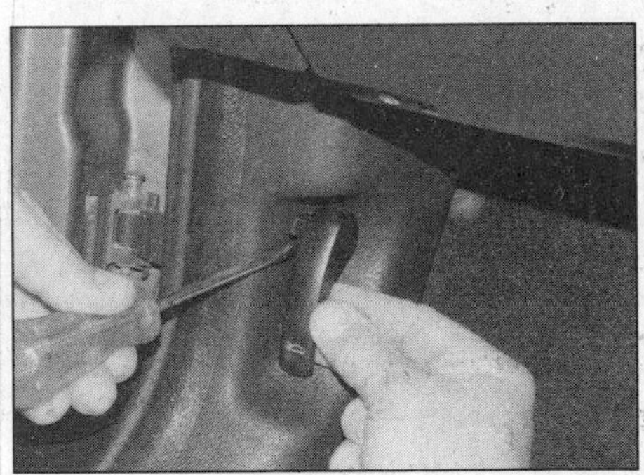

10.15 Carefully prise the bonnet release lever off

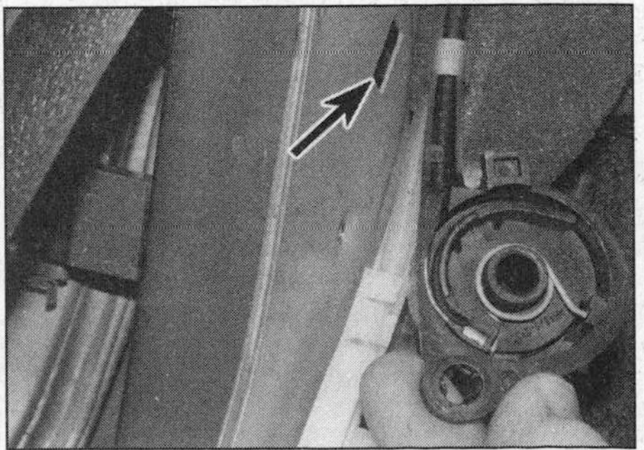

10.17b . . . and unclip the assembly from the sill panel (arrowed)

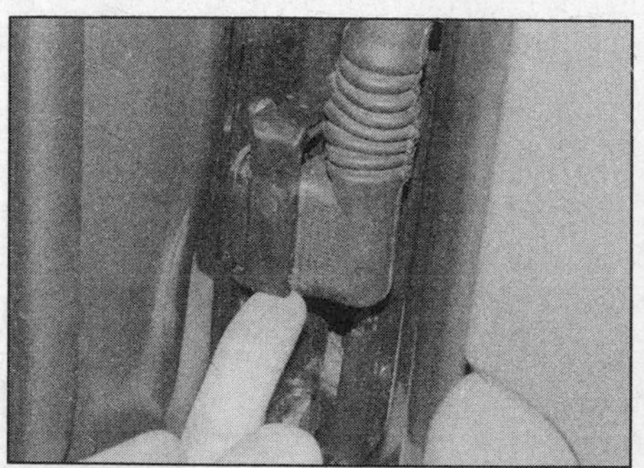

11.3a Slide the securing clip upwards . . .

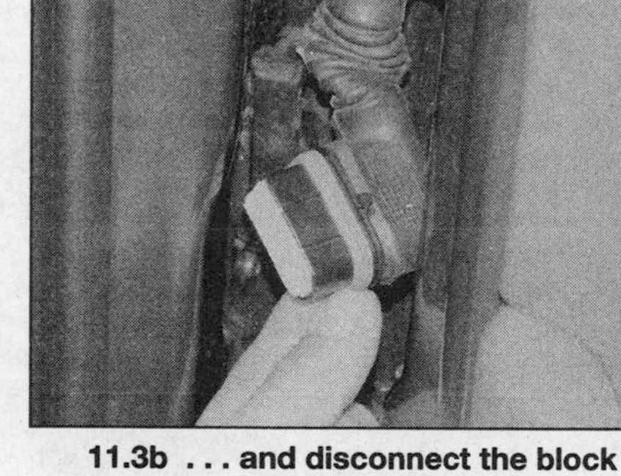

11.3b . . . and disconnect the block connector

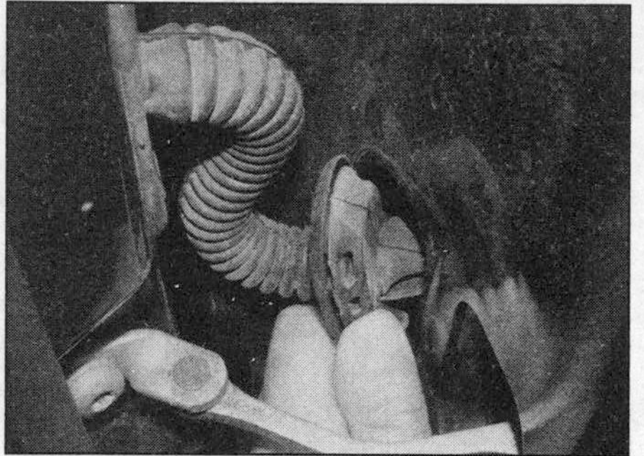

11.4a Unclip the rubber grommet from the door pillar . . .

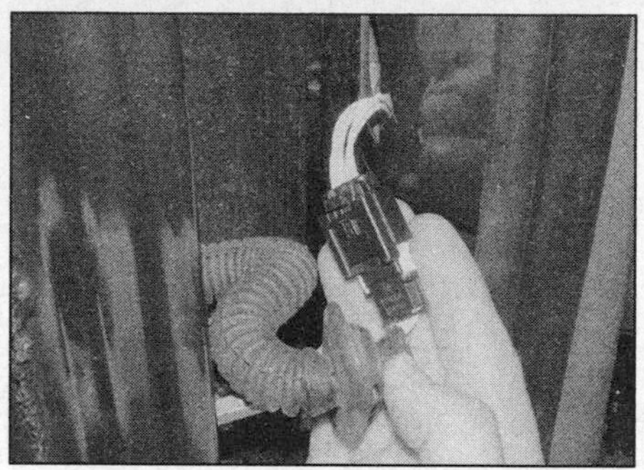

11.4b . . . and disconnect the wiring connector

18 Working in the engine compartment, release the outer cable from the lock assembly and disconnect the inner cable from the lock operating lever **(see illustration 10.7)**.

19 Tie string to the end of the bonnet release cable then, from inside the car, carefully pull the cable through the bulkhead grommet into the car, noting the cable routing. Leave the string in position through to the engine bay, to aid refitting.

11.5 Door check strap securing screw (arrowed)

11.6a Remove the clip (arrowed) from the hinge pin . . .

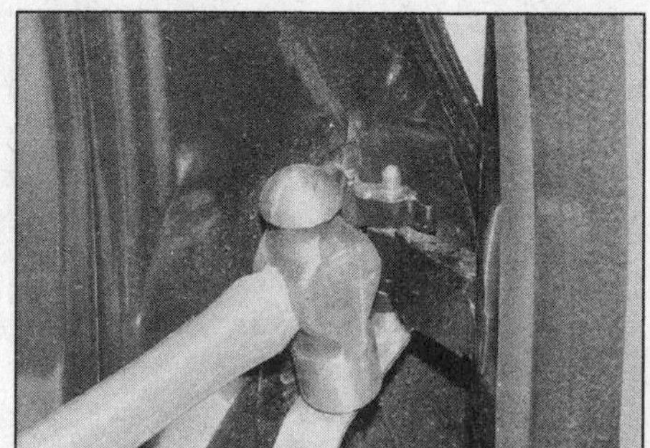

11.6b . . . then tap the hinge pin out using a forked tool

11.13 Undo the two check strap securing nuts (arrowed)

Refitting

20 Refitting is a reversal of removal, but ensure that the bulkhead grommet is securely located in the bulkhead. Route the cable as noted during removal, using the string to pull the cable back through the bulkhead grommet.

11 Doors and check straps - removal, refitting and adjustment

Doors

Removal

1 To remove a door, open it fully, and support it under its lower edge on blocks covered with pads of rag.

2 Disconnect the battery negative lead.

3 On the front doors, disconnect the door wiring connector by sliding the securing clip upwards, then pull the connector from its socket **(see illustrations)**.

4 On the rear doors (where applicable), disconnect the door wiring by unclipping the rubber grommet and disconnecting the wiring block connector **(see illustrations)**.

5 Unbolt the door check strap from the body **(see illustration)**.

6 Have an assistant support the door, then remove the securing clips from the hinge pins. Using a suitable tool and hammer, remove the two hinge pins from the hinges and withdraw the door from the car **(see illustrations)**.

Refitting

7 Refitting is a reversal of removal.

Adjustment

8 The door hinges are welded onto the door frame and the body pillar, so that there is no provision for adjustment or alignment.

9 Door closure may be adjusted by altering the position of the lock striker on the body pillar, using a Torx bit (see Section 12).

Door check straps

Removal

10 Open the door fully.

11 Unbolt the door check strap from the body **(see illustration 11.5)**.

12 Remove the door inner trim panel, as described in Section 27.

13 Working at the outer front edge of the door, unscrew the two nuts securing the check strap to the door **(see illustration)**.

14 Withdraw the check strap through the inside of the door.

Refitting

15 Refitting is a reversal of removal.

12 Door handle and lock components – removal and refitting

Door interior handle

Removal

1 Remove the single screw securing the door interior handle to the door **(see illustration)**.

2 On front doors, withdraw the handle and disconnect the operating cable from the rear of the handle by releasing the outer cable and unclipping the inner cable **(see illustration)**.

3 On rear doors, unclip the linkage rod from the rear of the door handle **(see illustration)**.

4 Withdraw the handle from the door.

Refitting

5 Refitting is a reversal of removal.

Front door exterior handle

Removal

6 Remove the door inner trim panel as described in Section 27.

7 Working inside the door, release the securing clip and disconnect the exterior handle operating rod from the lock or handle (if disconnecting from the handle, note the position of the rod for adjustment) **(see illustration)**.

8 Unscrew the two exterior handle securing nuts from inside the door **(see illustration)**, then tilt the handle and remove it from outside the door.

Refitting

9 Refitting is a reversal of removal, refit the door inner trim panel as described in Section 27.

Rear door exterior handle

Removal

10 Remove the door inner trim panel as described in Section 27.

11 Unclip the anti-theft cover from the door **(see illustration)**.

12 Working inside the door, release the securing clip and disconnect the exterior handle operating rod from the lock or handle (if disconnecting from the handle, note the position of the rod for adjustment) **(see illustration 12.7)**.

13 Unscrew the two exterior handle securing nuts from inside the door **(see illustration)**, then tilt the handle and remove it from outside the door.

Refitting

14 Refitting is a reversal of removal, refit the door inner trim panel as described in Section 27.

Front door lock

Removal

15 Remove the door inner trim panel as described in Section 27.

12.1 Remove the interior handle securing screw

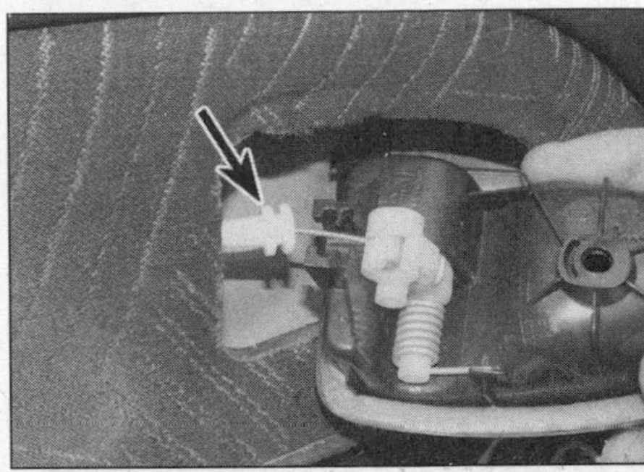

12.2 Disconnect the operating cable (arrowed) from the front interior handle

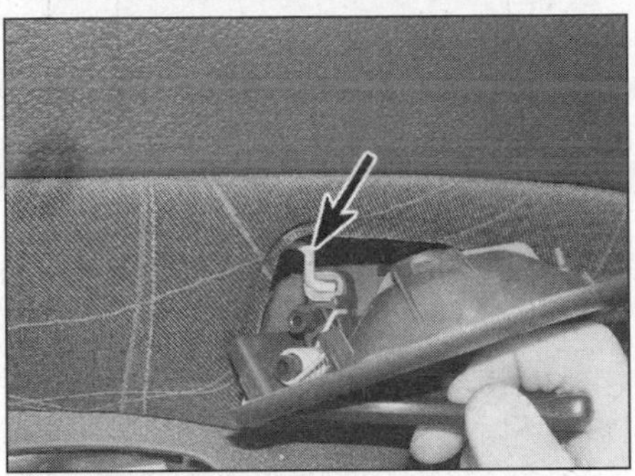

12.3 Disconnect the operating rod (arrowed) from the rear interior handle

12.7 Note the position of the retaining clip (arrowed) on the linkage rod before removal

16 Unscrew the three lock securing screws from the rear edge of the door **(see illustration). Note:** *It may be necessary to remove the anti-theft bracket from around the lock cylinder* ***(see illustrations 12.30a and 12.30b)****.*

17 Working inside the door, release the securing clip and disconnect the exterior

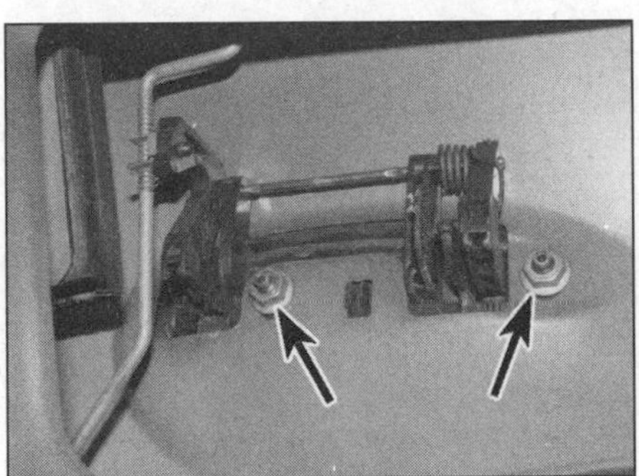

12.8 Removing the front door exterior handle securing nuts (arrowed)

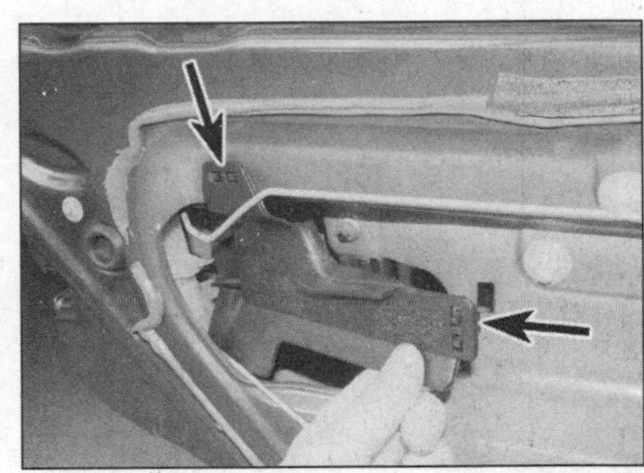

12.11 Release the clips (arrowed) and withdraw the anti-theft cover

12.13 Remove the rear door exterior handle securing nuts (arrowed)

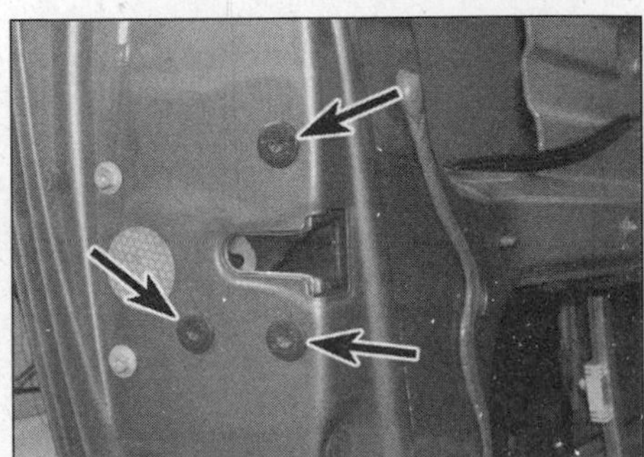

12.16 Remove the three door lock securing screws (arrowed)

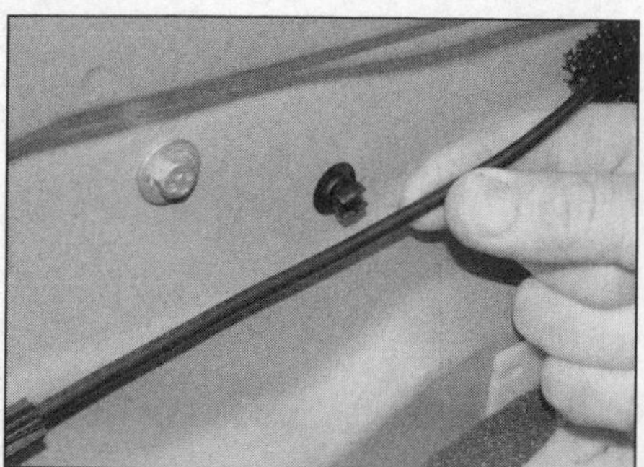

12.17 Releasing the door lock cable from the door panel

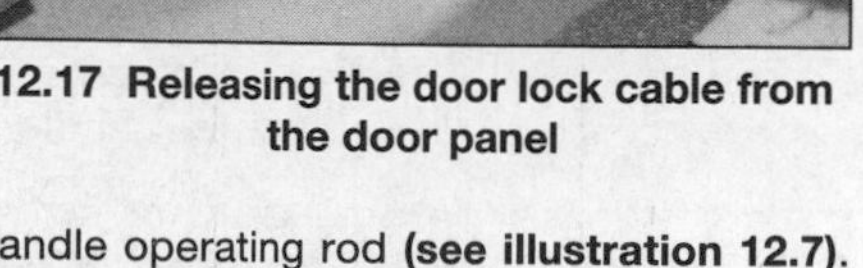

12.19 Disconnecting the wiring plug from the door lock operating motor

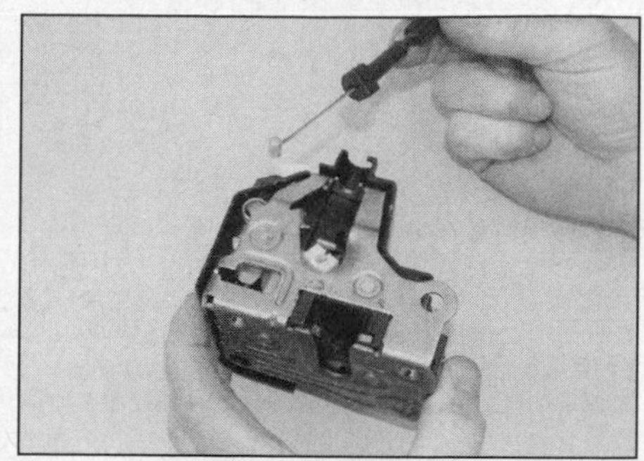

12.20 Unclip the outer cable, then disengage the inner cable

handle operating rod **(see illustration 12.7)**. Unclip the interior door handle cable from the door panel **(see illustration)**.

18 Twist the lock assembly, to release it from the control lever on the lock cylinder, then move the lock assembly downwards and out through the door aperture.

19 Disconnect the wiring plug(s) from the lock operating motor as it is removed **(see illustration)**.

20 The door handle release cable can be disconnected from the lock assembly when the lock assembly is removed **(see illustration)**.

Refitting

21 Refitting is a reversal of removal, refitting the door inner trim panel as described in Section 27.

Rear door lock

Removal

22 Remove the door inner trim panel, as described in Section 27.

23 Unclip the anti-theft cover from the door **(see illustration 12.11)**.

24 Working inside the door, release the securing clip, and disconnect the operating rod from the exterior door handle.

25 Unscrew the three lock securing screws from the rear edge of the door **(see illustration)**.

26 Disconnect the interior handle and lock button linkage rods from the door panel and locking button **(see illustrations)**.

27 Withdraw the lock assembly through the door aperture. Disconnect the wiring plug from the lock operating motor as it is being withdrawn **(see illustrations)**.

Refitting

28 Refitting is a reversal of removal, refitting the door inner trim panel as described in Section 27.

Front door lock cylinder

Removal

29 Remove the door inner trim panel, as described in Section 27.

30 Unscrew the two securing screws from the rear edge of the door and from inside the door, remove the anti-theft bracket from around the lock cylinder **(see illustrations)**.

31 From inside the door, turn the retaining clip anti-clockwise to release the lock

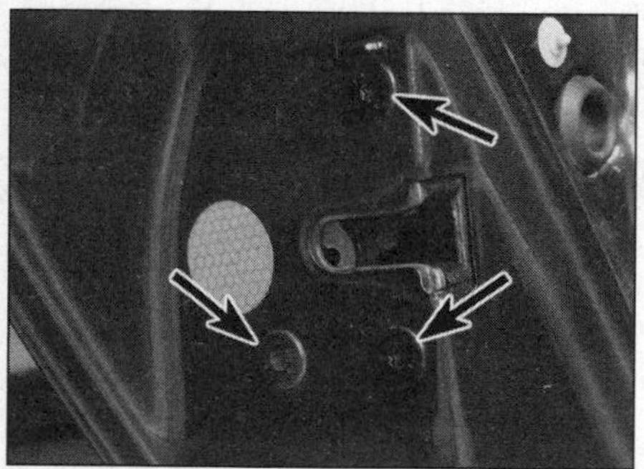

12.25 Remove the three door lock securing screws (arrowed)

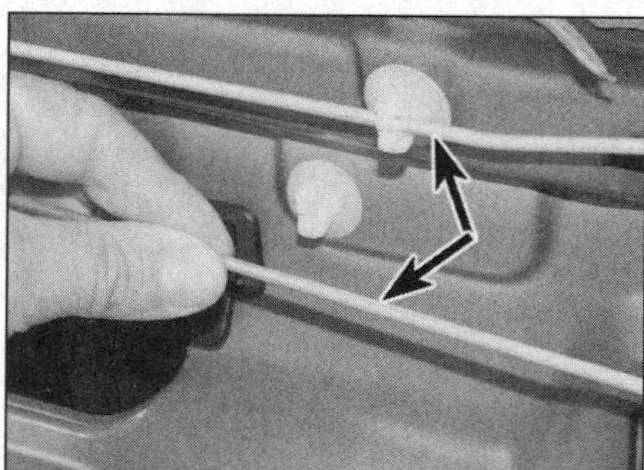

12.26a Unclip the linkage rods (arrowed) from the door panel . . .

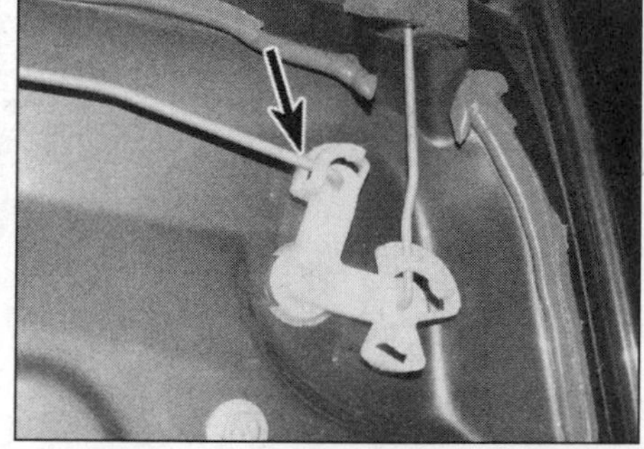

12.26b . . . then disengage the rod (arrowed) from the door lock button

12.27a Withdraw the rear door lock from the door

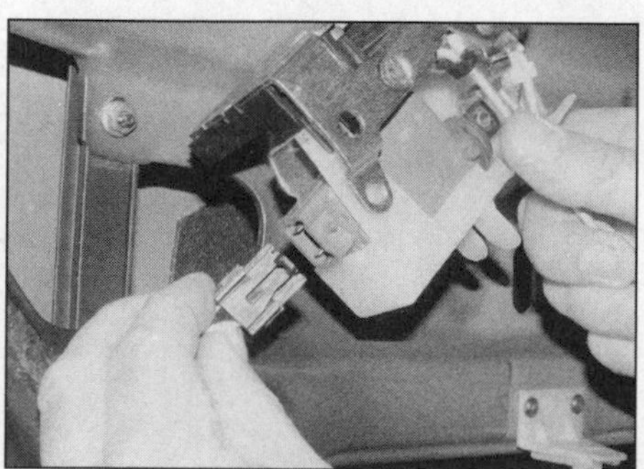

12.27b . . . then disconnect the wiring plug

12.30a Undo the two securing screws (arrowed) . . .

cylinder, then withdraw the lock cylinder from outside the door **(see illustrations)**.

Refitting

32 Refitting is a reversal of removal, bearing in mind the following points.

33 When refitting the lock cylinder, ensure that the lugs on the assembly engage with the corresp

Lock striker

Removal

35 The lock striker is screwed onto the door pillar on the body **(see illustration)**.

36 Before removing the striker, mark its position, so that it can be refitted in exactly the same place.

37 To remove the striker, simply unscrew the securing screws using a Torx bit.

Refitting

38 Refitting is a reversal of removal, but if necessary, adjust the position of the striker to achieve satisfactory closing of the door.

Central locking components

39 Refer to Section 16.

13 Door window glass and regulators – removal and refitting

Front door window

Removal

1 Remove the door inner trim panel, as described in Section 27.

2 Lower the window glass, temporarily reconnect the battery negative lead (if disconnected), and reconnect the wiring plug to the electric window operating switch to enable the window to be lowered.

3 Carefully prise the weatherseal from the inner lower edge of the window aperture **(see illustration)**.

4 Remove the retaining clip from the rear of the window guide **(see illustration)**, then disengage the lug from the hole in the glass. Support the glass.

5 Working at the rear edge of the window glass, release the window pad guide (riveted to the rear upper edge of the glass). Carefully disengage the window pad guide from the lower end of the weatherseal/guide channel inside the door **(see illustration)**.

6 Carefully push the glass upwards tilting the rear edge forwards, and manipulate the glass out from the door panel **(see illustration)**.

Refitting

7 Refitting is a reversal of removal, bearing in mind the following points.

8 Ensure that the guide plate at the rear upper edge of the glass is correctly engaged with the weatherseal/guide channel inside the door.

9 Before refitting the door inner trim panel, reconnect the battery and the electric window's operating switch and check the operation of the window mechanism.

10 Refit the door inner trim panel as described in Section 27.

Rear door fixed window

Removal

11 Remove the door inner trim panel, as described in Section 27.

12.30b . . . and withdraw the anti-theft bracket

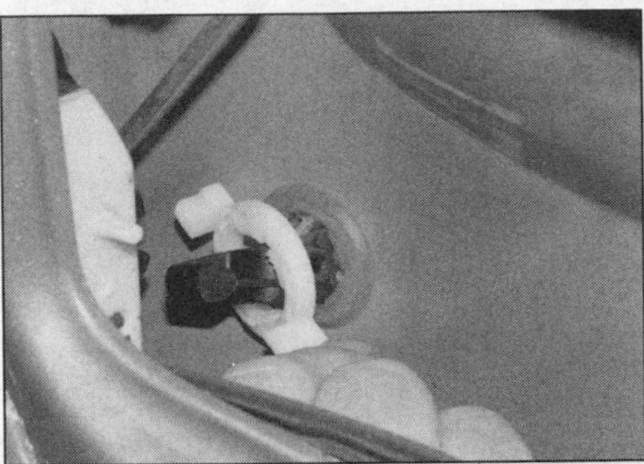

12.31a Remove the plastic retaining clip – turn anti-clockwise . . .

12.31b . . . and withdraw the lock cylinder

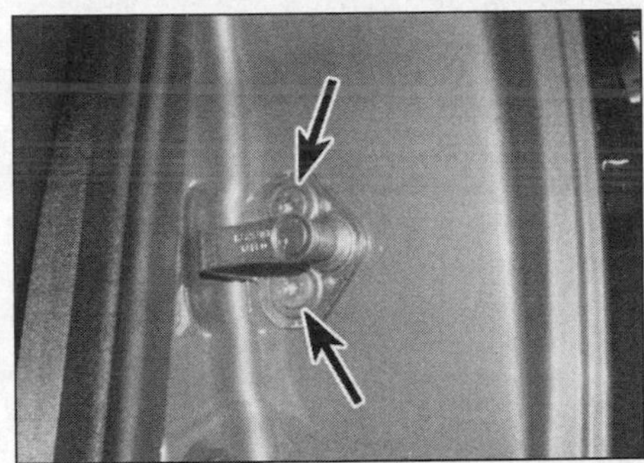

12.35 Lock striker securing screws (arrowed)

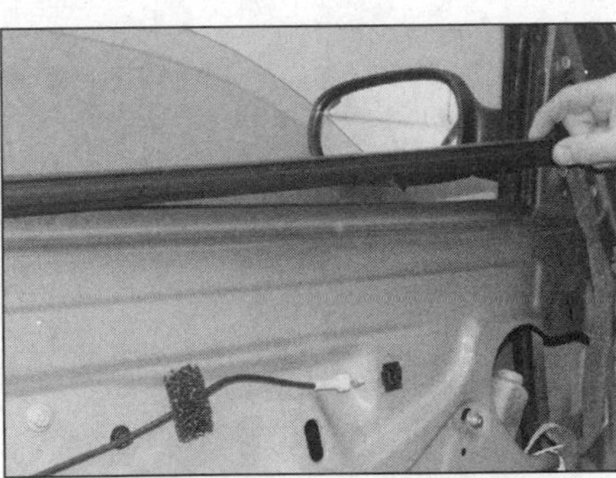

13.3 Unclip the inner sealing strip and remove it from the top of the door

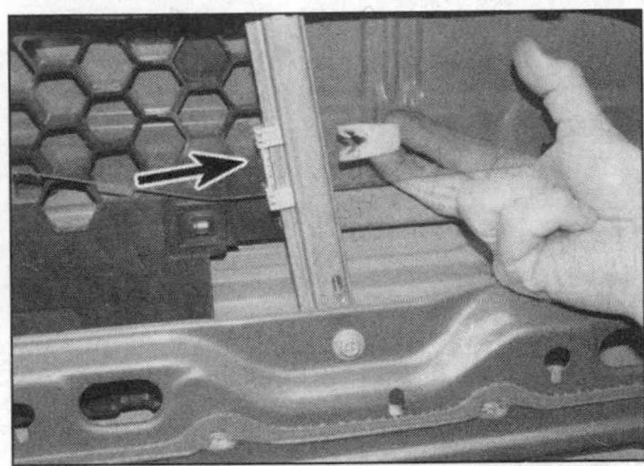

13.4 Remove the plastic clip in the direction of the arrow

13.5 Press down the ends of the guide to release the window

13.6 Removing the front door window glass

13.15 Remove door window glass-to-regulator bracket securing screws (arrowed)

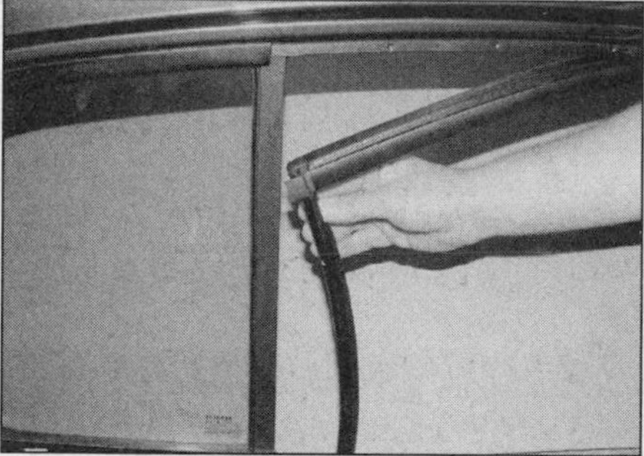
13.16 Removing the rubber seal from the window aperture

13.17a Remove the upper Torx screw inside the window channel (arrowed) . . .

12 Lower the sliding window.

13 Carefully prise the inner and outer weatherseals from the lower edge of the window aperture.

14 Temporarily refit the window winder handle. Raise the window until the bolts securing the window glass to the regulator bracket are accessible.

15 If the original sliding glass is to be refitted, mark the positions of the two screws securing the window glass to the regulator bracket, then remove the screws and carefully lower the window glass into the door **(see illustration).**

16 Carefully prise out the rubber guide seal from the window aperture in the door frame **(see illustration).**

17 Remove the upper mounting bolt and lower mounting nut securing the window rear guide rail to the door. Support the fixed window glass, and carefully twist the guide rail and withdraw it through the window aperture **(see illustrations).**

18 Carefully slide the fixed window glass from its location, complete with surrounding seal **(see illustration).**

Refitting

19 Refitting is a reversal of removal, bearing in mind the following points.

20 When refitting the fixed window glass, ensure that the glass engages correctly with the seals around the edges of the window aperture.

21 Where applicable, refit the screws securing the sliding window glass to the regulator bracket in the positions marked before removal.

22 Make sure that the weatherseals are correctly located on the lower edge of the window aperture.

23 Before refitting the door inner trim panel, temporarily refit the window winder handle, and check the operation of the regulator mechanism. If necessary, the alignment of the glass can be adjusted by altering the position of the bolts securing the window glass to the regulator bracket, using the elongated holes provided.

24 Refit the door inner trim panel, as described in Section 27.

Rear door sliding window

Removal

25 Carry out the procedures in paragraphs 11 to 17, as described earlier in this Section.

26 With the fixed window glass left in position, carefully lift the sliding window glass out through the inside of the window aperture.

Refitting

27 Lower the window glass into the door, then refit as described earlier in this Section.

Front door regulator

Removal

28 Remove the door inner trim panel, as described in Section 27.

29 Remove the front door window glass as described earlier in this Section (or slide the glass up to the top of the window frame and tape in position).

30 Remove the three nuts securing the regulator assembly (**Note:** *Two of the retaining nuts do not need to be completely removed*), and the two bolts securing the window guide rail to the door **(see illustrations).**

31 Disconnect the wiring plug connector from the window motor, as it becomes accessible **(see illustration).**

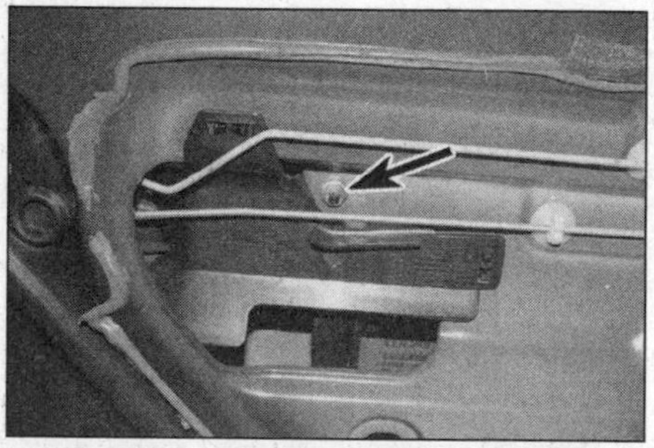
13.17b . . . and the lower securing nut (arrowed), then withdraw the window guide rail

13.18 Removing the fixed rear window glass, complete with seal

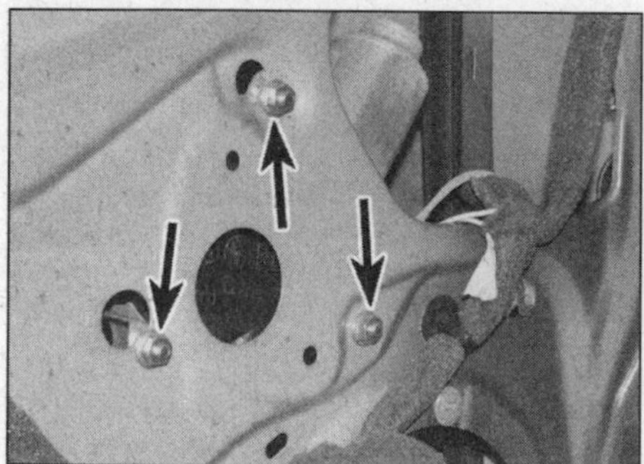
13.30a Remove the three motor securing nuts (arrowed) . . .

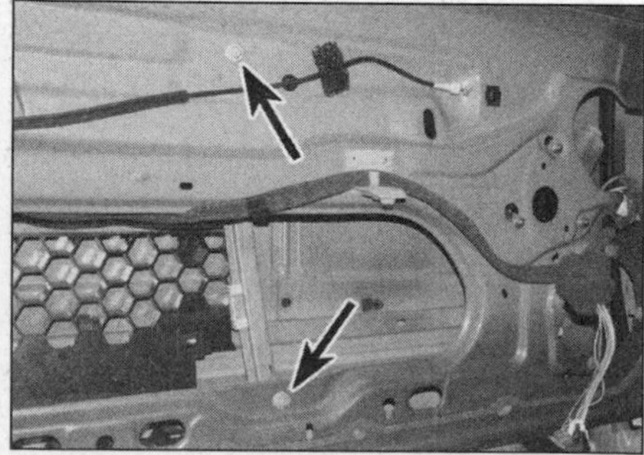
13.30b . . . and the two guide rail securing bolts (arrowed)

13.31 Disconnecting the wiring block connector from the electric window motor

32 Carefully manipulate the window regulator assembly out through the lower aperture in the door **(see illustration)**.

Refitting

33 Refitting is a reversal of removal, bearing in mind the following points.
34 Before refitting the door inner trim panel, make sure the window motor is located correctly in the door **(see illustration)**. Reconnect the battery and the electric window's operating switch and check the operation of the window mechanism.
35 Refit the door inner trim panel as described in Section 27.

Rear door regulator

Removal

36 Remove the door inner trim panel, as described in Section 27.
37 Temporarily refit the window winder handle. Lower the window glass until the screws securing the window glass to the regulator bracket are accessible.
38 Mark the positions of the screws securing the window glass to the regulator bracket, then remove the screws and lower the window glass. To give more room for removal, slide the glass up to the top of the window frame and tape in position.
39 On models fitted with electric windows, disconnect the wiring plug from the electric window motor.
40 Remove the four securing bolts (two bolts securing the regulator, and two bolts securing the window guide rail), then carefully manipulate the regulator assembly out through the door aperture **(see illustrations)**.

Refitting

41 Refitting is a reversal of removal, bearing in mind the following points.
42 Ensure that the bolts securing the sliding window glass to the regulator bracket are refitted in their original positions marked before removal.
43 Before refitting the door inner trim panel, check the operation of the window mechanism, reconnecting the battery and the electric windows operating switch, or refitting the window winder handle, as applicable.
44 If necessary, the alignment of the glass can be adjusted by altering the position of the bolts securing the window glass to the regulator bracket, using the elongated holes provided.
45 Refit the door inner trim panel as described in Section 27.

Electric window components

46 The motors are an integral part of the window regulator assemblies, and cannot be renewed independently.
47 Removal and refitting of the regulator assemblies are described in this Section. Refer to Section 17 for the switches.

13.32 Removing the window regulator assembly

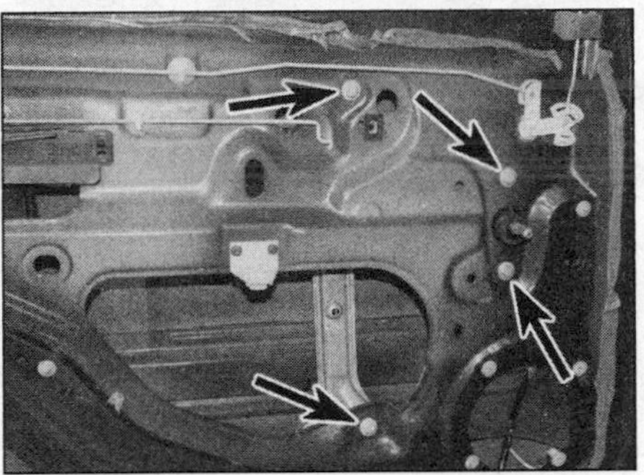

13.40a Rear door window regulator assembly securing bolts (arrowed)

14 Tailgate, hinges and support struts – removal and refitting

Tailgate

Removal

1 Disconnect the battery negative (earth) lead, and position it away from the terminal.
2 Open the tailgate, then undo the retaining screw from the right-hand side of the tailgate inner trim panel and carefully pull the trim panel from the tailgate **(see illustration)**. If necessary, release the trim clips using a forked tool.
3 Disconnect the wiring from the heated rear window, tailgate wiper motor, and central locking motor, as applicable. Release the wiring loom from any securing clips **(see illustrations)**.

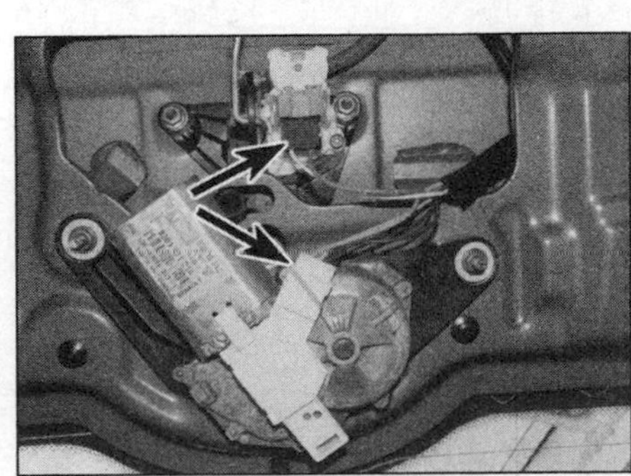

14.3a Disconnect the wiring connectors (arrowed) . . .

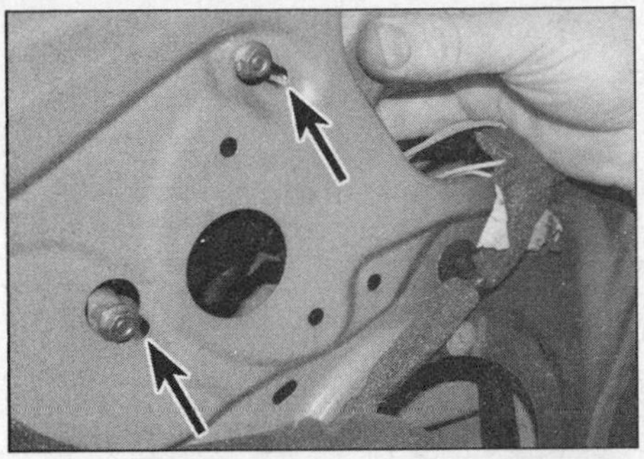

13.34 Slide the window motor into place using the elongated holes (arrowed)

13.40b Removing the rear door window regulator mechanism

4 Undo the rear spoiler securing screws and remove spoiler as described in Section 22. Disconnect the high-level stop-light and washer fluid hose, where applicable; be prepared for fluid spillage.

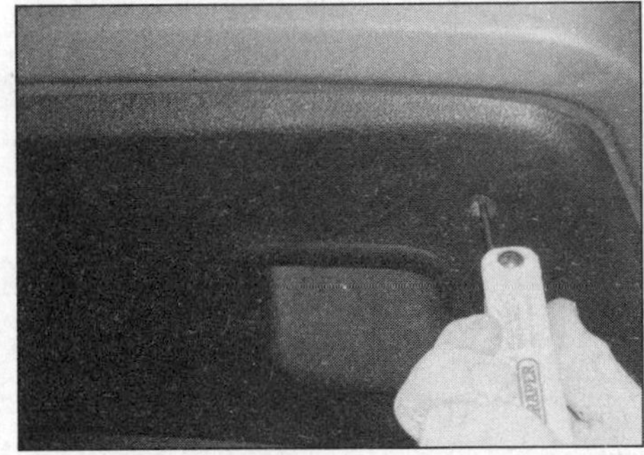

14.2 Undo the tailgate trim retaining screw

14.3b . . and disengage the wiring connector from the tailgate panel

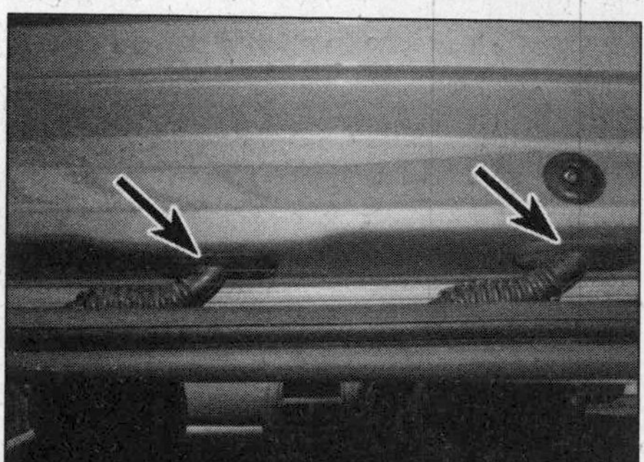
14.5 Remove the wiring loom grommets (arrowed)

14.6 Prising out a tailgate support strut securing clip (arrowed)

14.8 Undo the two tailgate securing nuts

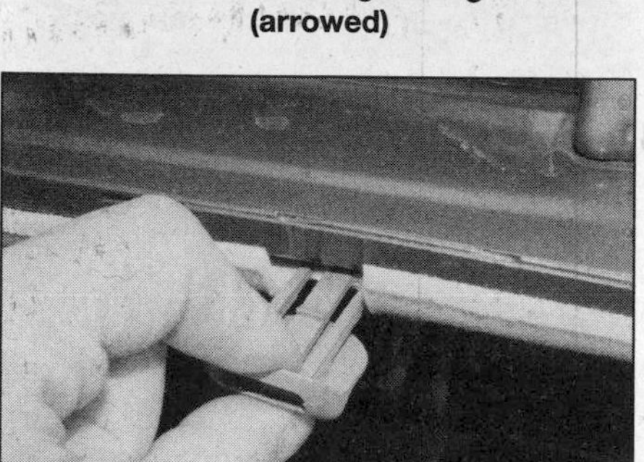
14.9a Prise out the plastic clip . . .

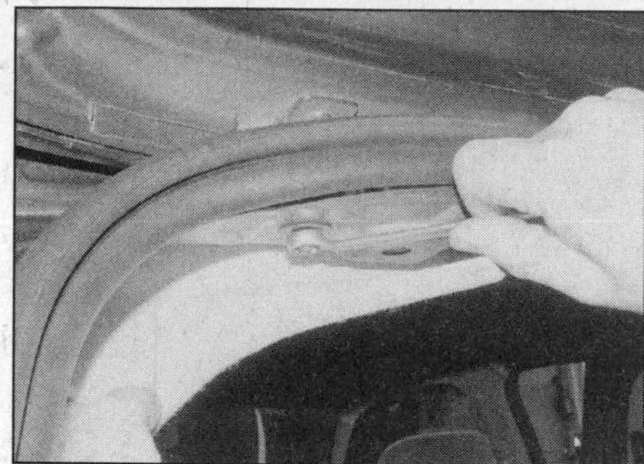
14.9b . . . and pull down the headlining to undo the hinge securing nuts

5 Release the wiring loom and hose grommets from the edge of the tailgate **(see illustration)**. Tie string to the wiring loom and hose, and pull them through the edge of the tailgate. Leave the string in position in the tailgate, to aid refitting.
6 Have an assistant support the tailgate. Disconnect the support struts from the tailgate by prising out the retaining clips using a screwdriver **(see illustration)**.
7 If the original tailgate is to be refitted, mark the positions of the securing nuts on the tailgate.
8 Unscrew the two nuts from under the spoiler **(see illustration)**, and carefully withdraw the tailgate from the vehicle.
9 To remove the hinges, prise the plastic clips from the headlining for access to the tailgate hinge securing nuts **(see illustrations)**.

Refitting

10 Refitting is a reversal of removal, but where applicable, fit the tailgate securing nuts in their original positions, as noted before removal.
11 Do not fully tighten the tailgate securing nuts until the top of the tailgate is aligned correctly with the roof panel and the rear body pillars.
12 On completion, if adjustment of the tailgate lower edge alignment is required, adjust the tailgate lock striker on the lower body panel.
13 Alter the position of the lock striker on the body (by means of the elongated screw holes) to give correct alignment of the lower edge of the tailgate with the surrounding body panels.
14 Using the string left in the tailgate on removal, pull the wiring loom and hose back up through the tailgate.

Hinges

15 The tailgate hinges can be removed as described in paragraph 9.

Support struts

Removal

16 Open the tailgate, and have an assistant support it in the fully-open position.
17 Disconnect the support strut from the tailgate by prising out the securing clip using a small screwdriver **(see illustration 14.6)**.
18 Repeat the procedure for the clip securing the strut to the body, and withdraw the strut from the vehicle.

Refitting

19 Refitting is a reversal of removal.

15 Tailgate lock components - removal and refitting

Lock assembly

Removal

1 Disconnect the battery negative (earth) lead, and position it away from the terminal.
2 Open the tailgate, then undo the retaining screw from the right-hand side of the tailgate inner trim panel and carefully pull the trim panel from the tailgate **(see illustration 14.2)**. If necessary, release the trim clips using a forked tool.
3 Disconnect the wiring connector from the lock mechanism **(see illustration)**.
4 Slacken and remove the three retaining nuts from the lock assembly, and withdraw the outer trim cover from the tailgate **(see illustrations)**.

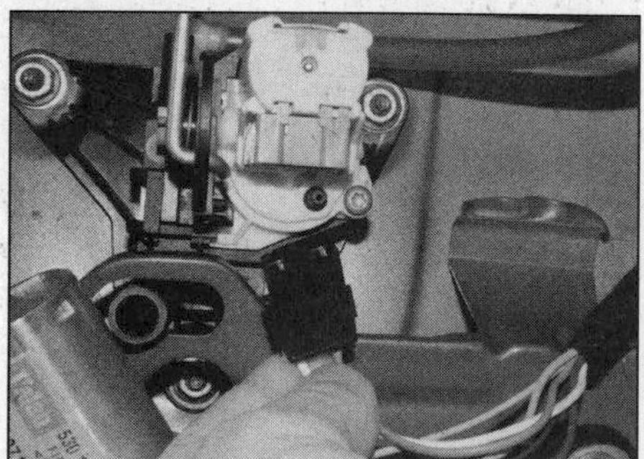
15.3 Disconnecting the wiring connector

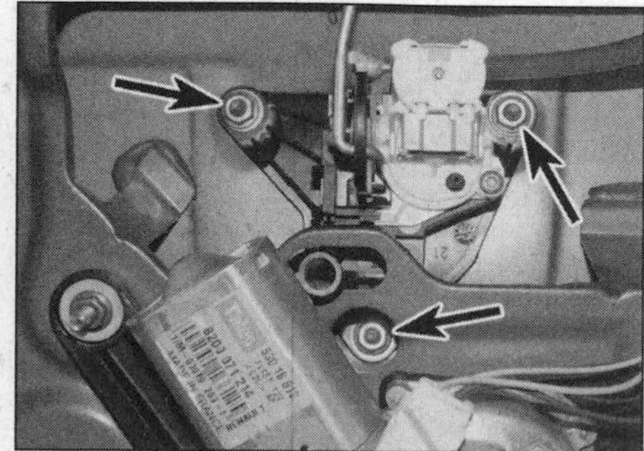
15.4a Remove the lock assembly securing nuts (arrowed) . . .

15.4b . . . and withdraw the outer trim panel

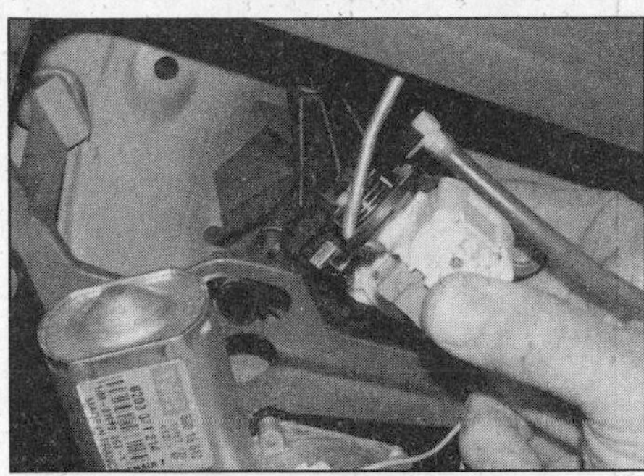

15.5a Unclip the linkage rod from the lock cylinder . . .

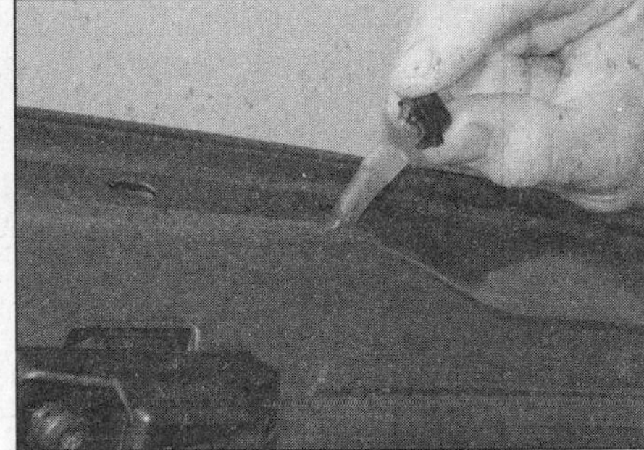

15.5b . . . and disconnect the drain tube from the lower edge of the tailgate

15.6a Remove the lock catch securing screws (arrowed) . . .

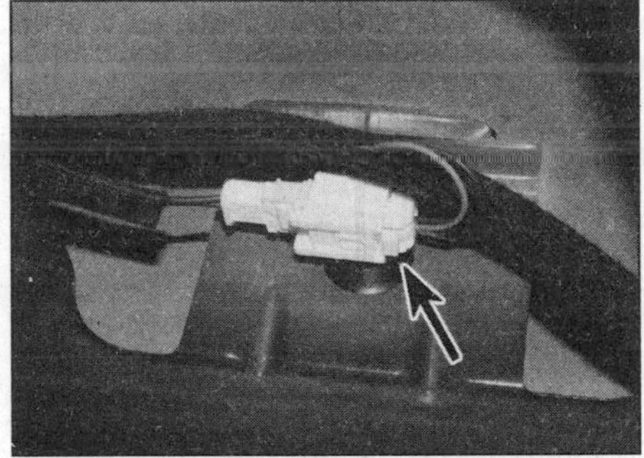

15.6b . . . disconnect the wiring connector (arrowed) . . .

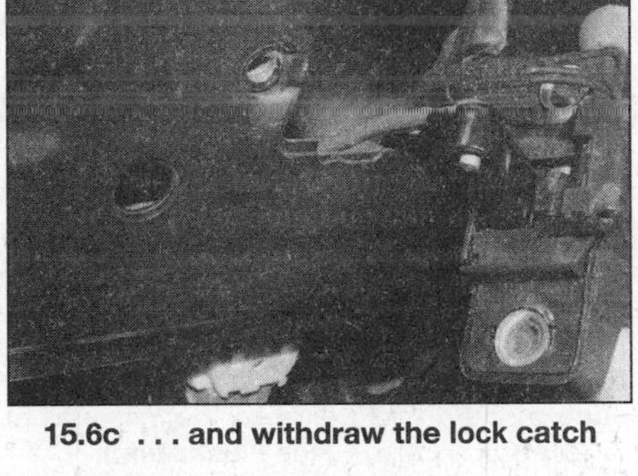

15.6c . . . and withdraw the lock catch

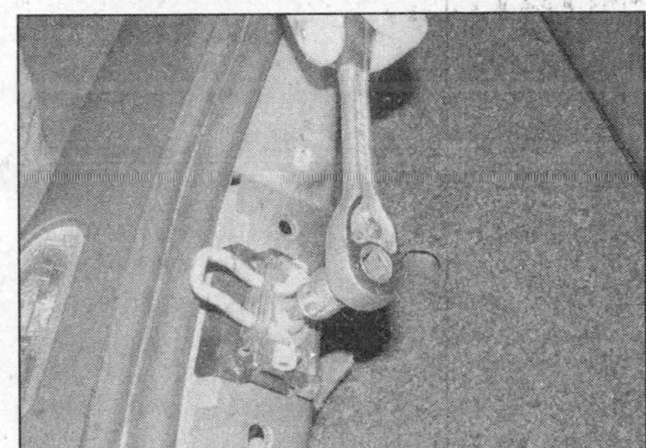

15.10 Removing the mounting bolt from the tailgate lock striker

5 Twist the lock as it is removed and unhook the linkage rod from the lock assembly. Disconnect the drain tube from the lower part of the tailgate **(see illustrations)**.

6 To remove the lock catch and linkage rod, undo the two retaining screws, disconnect the wiring connector and withdraw from the lower part of the tailgate **(see illustrations)**.

Refitting

7 Refitting is a reversal of removal.

Lock striker

Removal

8 The lock striker is attached to the lower body panel.

9 Remove the securing screws, and withdraw the rear trim from the rear body panel.

10 Remove the mounting bolt now exposed and withdraw the lock striker assembly **(see illustration)**.

Refitting

11 Refitting is a reversal of removal, but if necessary adjust the position of the striker **(see illustration)** (by means of the elongated bolt hole) to achieve satisfactory alignment of the bottom of the tailgate with the surrounding body panels.

16 Central locking components - general information

The central locking is operated by radio frequency and is controlled by the Multi-timer unit (see Chapter 12, Section 5, for further information), which also holds a number of relays. It is located under the left-hand side of the facia (as seen from the driver's seat) above the bonnet release lever. If there is a fault with this unit, it will require checking with a fault code reader.

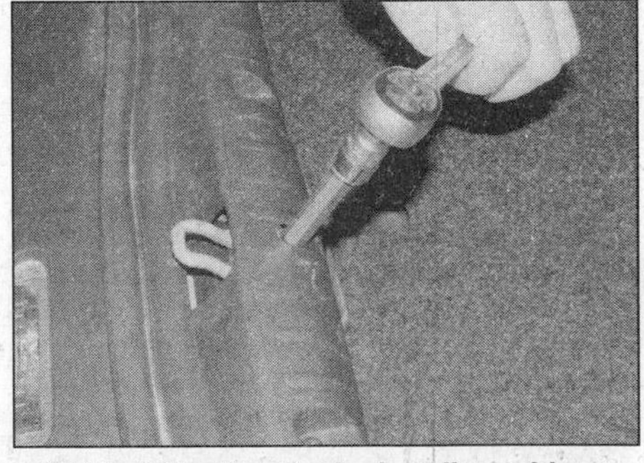

15.11 Adjusting the lock striker without removing the trim panel

The door lock motors and switches are an integral part of the door lock assembly, see Section 12 of this Chapter for removal and refitting of the door locking components. Also see Section 15, for the removal and refitting of the tailgate locking components.

17 Electric window components - removal and refitting

Switches

Removal

1 Disconnect the battery negative (earth) lead, and position it away from the terminal.

2 Remove the blanking plug and undo the securing screw in the door grab handle, then carefully lift and pull back the handle to release it from the door **(see illustrations)**.

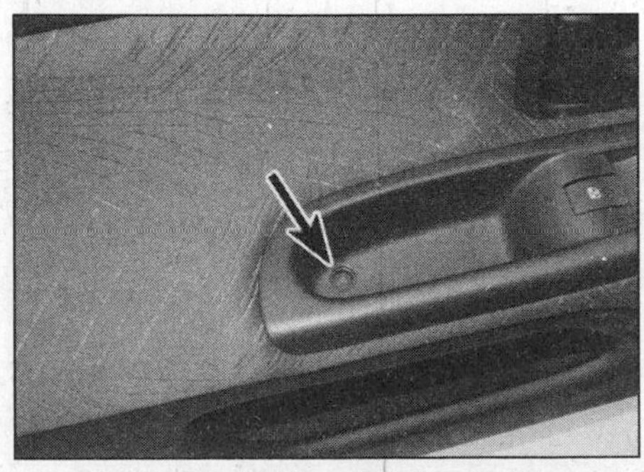

17.2a Undo the retaining screw (arrowed) . . .

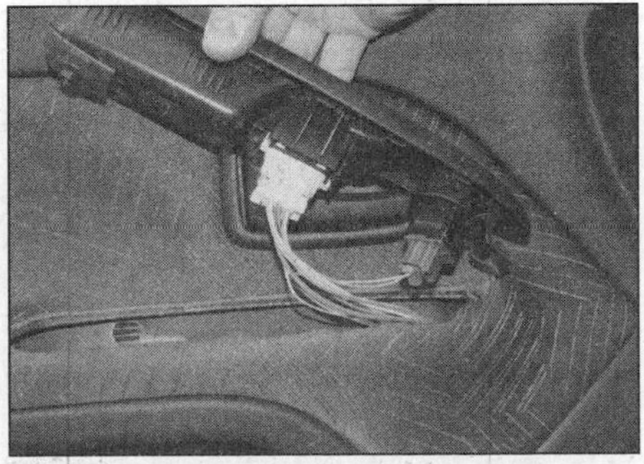

17.2b . . . and withdraw the switches panel from the door trim

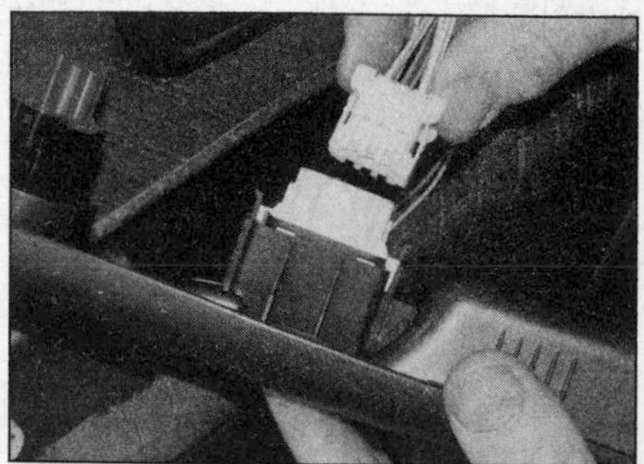

17.3a Disconnect the wiring plugs . . .

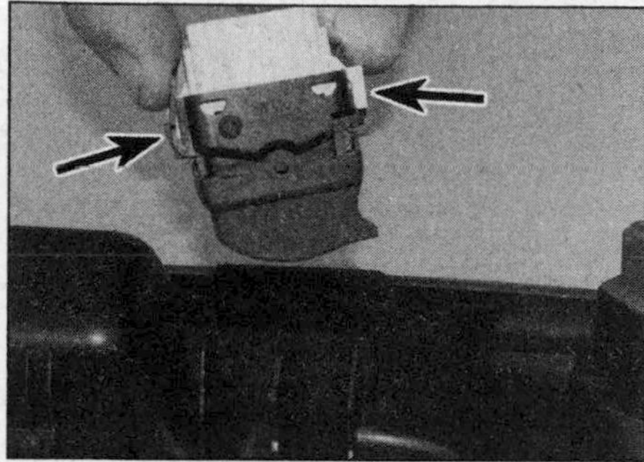

17.3b . . . press the retaining clips (arrowed) and withdraw the switch

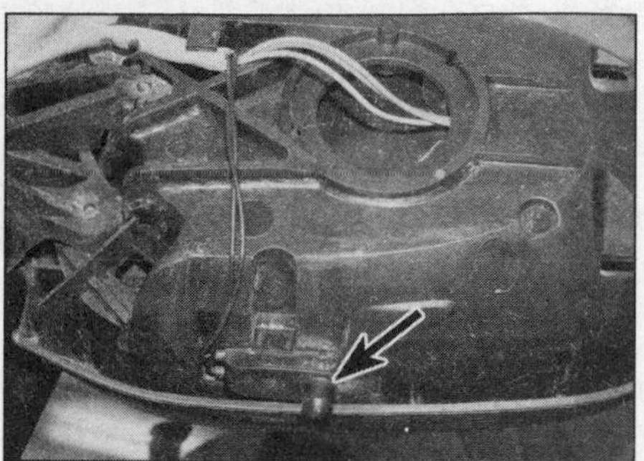

18.1 Outside temperature sensor located in the passenger mirror (arrowed) – cover removed

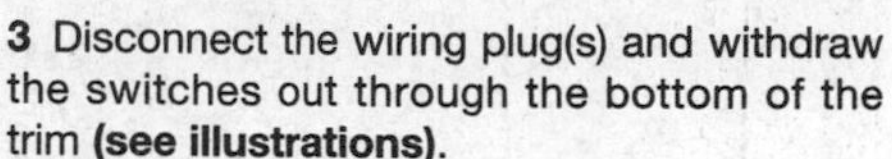

3 Disconnect the wiring plug(s) and withdraw the switches out through the bottom of the trim **(see illustrations)**.

Refitting

4 Refitting is a reversal of removal.

Operating motors

5 The motors are an integral part of the window regulator assemblies, and cannot be renewed independently. Removal and refitting of the regulator assemblies are described in Section 13.

18 Mirrors – removal, refitting and glass renewal

Note: *The outside temperature sensor (where fitted) is located in the passenger side mirror behind the mirror shell* ***(see illustration).***

Door mirror

Removal

1 On models fitted with electric mirrors, disconnect the battery negative (earth) lead, and position it away from the terminal.

2 Carefully prise the mirror trim panel from the front edge of the door **(see illustration)**.

3 Prise the plastic grommet from the front edge of the door to expose the mirror front lower securing screw **(see illustration)**.

4 On models fitted with electrically-operated mirrors, unplug the wiring connector from the mirror **(see illustration)**.

5 Undo the two retaining screws now exposed and the one from behind the grommet **(see illustration)**.

6 Withdraw the mirror from the door, by lifting it upwards and releasing it from the door frame **(see illustration)**.

Refitting

7 Refitting is a reversal of removal.

Glass renewal

8 Using a flat-bladed tool, carefully prise behind the top edge of the mirror glass **(see illustration)**.

9 Support the glass, lever the tool forwards and the mirror glass will unclip from the mirror assembly. Take care not to drop the mirror glass as the clip is released.

10 Where applicable, disconnect the wiring connectors from the rear of the mirror glass **(see illustration)**.

11 To refit the glass, press the glass into position until it engages securely **(see**

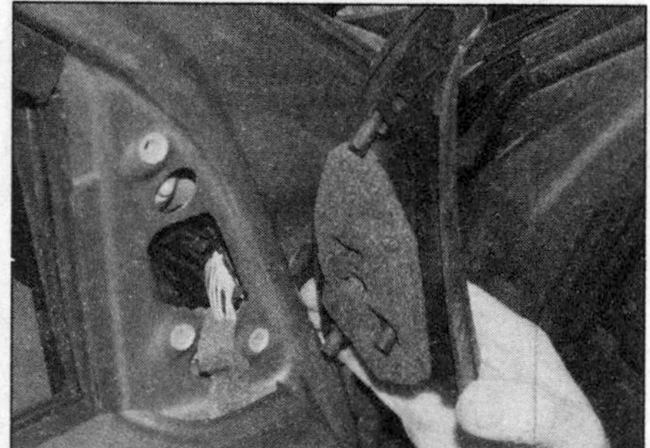

18.2 Removing the mirror inner trim panel

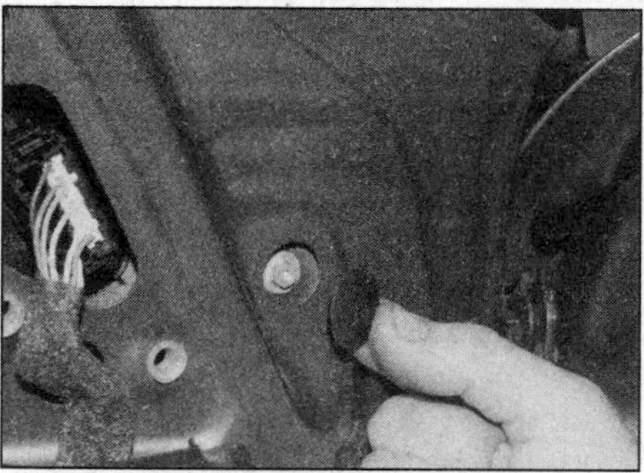

18.3 Unclipping the grommet to locate the mirror front securing screw

18.4 Disconnecting the wiring connector

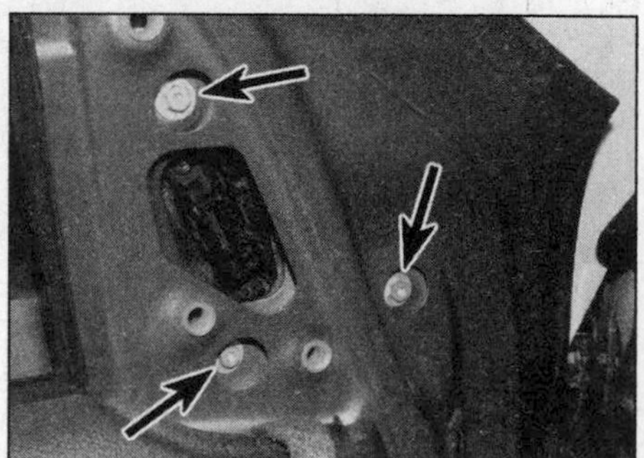

18.5 Undo the securing screws (arrowed) . . .

18.6 . . . and withdraw the mirror

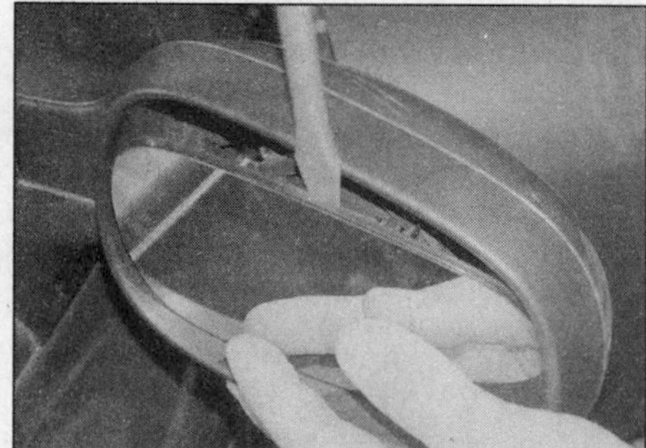

18.8 Carefully lever the mirror glass from its retaining clips

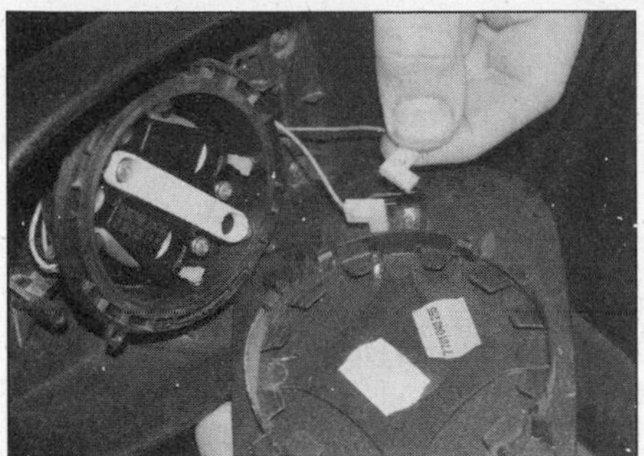
18.10 Where applicable, disconnect the wiring connectors for heated mirror glass

18.11 Carefully press the glass into position to secure the retaining clips

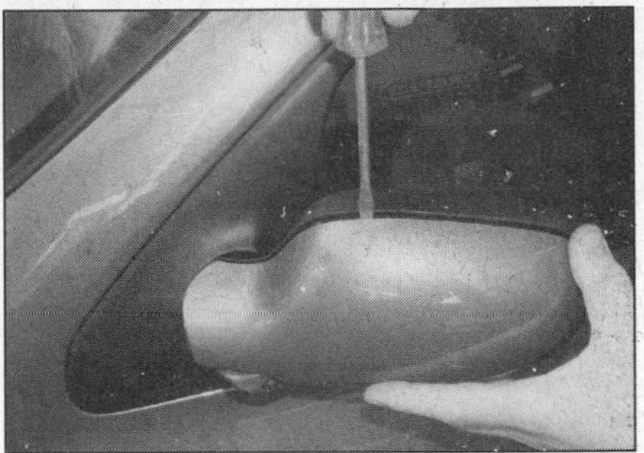
18.12a Using a screwdriver . . .

illustration), taking care not to damage the glass.

Shell renewal

12 Fold the mirror assembly inwards, then carefully prise the shell from the mirror **(see illustrations)**.

13 If the shell is difficult to remove, it may be necessary to remove the mirror glass as described in this Section. The retaining clips can then be released from the inside of the mirror assembly **(see illustration)**.

Electric mirror switch

14 Remove the blanking plug and undo the securing screw in the driver's door grab handle, then carefully lift and pull back the handle to release it from the door **(see illustration)**.

15 Disconnect the wiring plug(s) and withdraw the switch out through the top of the trim **(see illustrations)**. Refitting is a reversal of removal.

Electric mirror motor

16 The motor is not available separately from the mirror. If it is faulty, the complete mirror assembly must be renewed.

Interior mirror

Removal

17 The mirror can be removed by carefully lifting it upwards from the mounting bracket attached to the windscreen **(see illustration)**.

18 The mounting bracket is fixed to the windscreen using a special adhesive, and should not be disturbed unless absolutely necessary. Note that there is a risk of cracking the windscreen glass if an attempt is made to remove a securely-bonded mounting bracket.

Refitting

19 Refitting is a reversal of removal. If necessary, the special adhesive required to fix the mounting bracket to the windscreen can be obtained from a Renault dealer.

19 Windscreen and tailgate window glass – general information

1 The windscreen and the tailgate window glass are bonded in position using a special adhesive. Special tools, adhesives and expertise are required for successful removal and refitting of glass fixed by this method. Such work must therefore be entrusted to a Renault dealer, a windscreen specialist, or other competent professional.

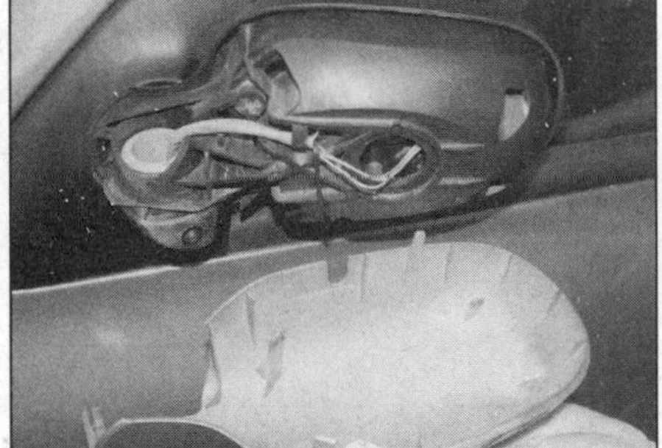
18.12b . . . carefully prise off the outer shell

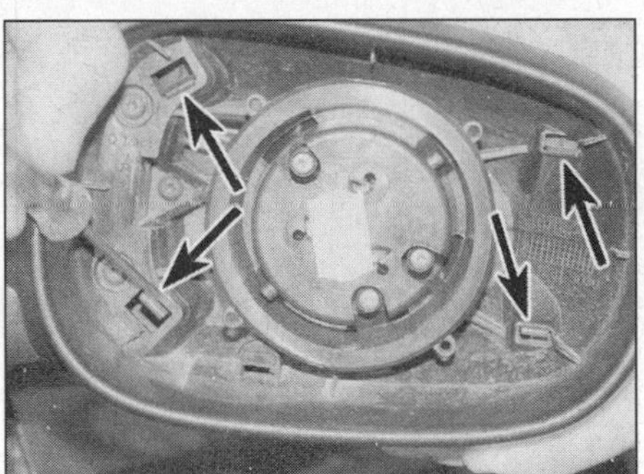
18.13 Release the retaining clips (arrowed) using a small screwdriver

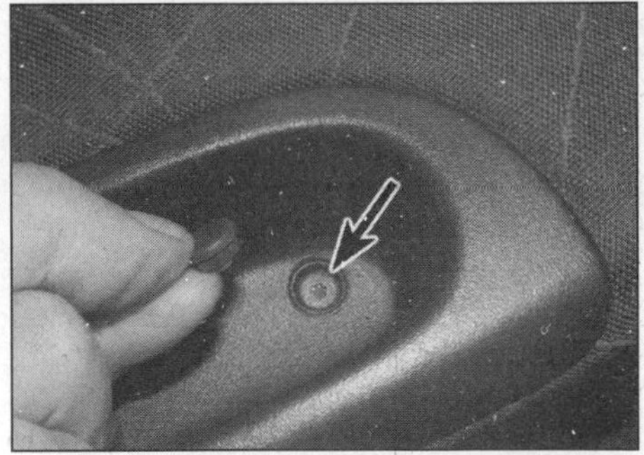
18.14 Remove the blanking plug, then undo the retaining screw (arrowed)

18.15a Withdraw the switch panel, disconnect the wiring plug . . .

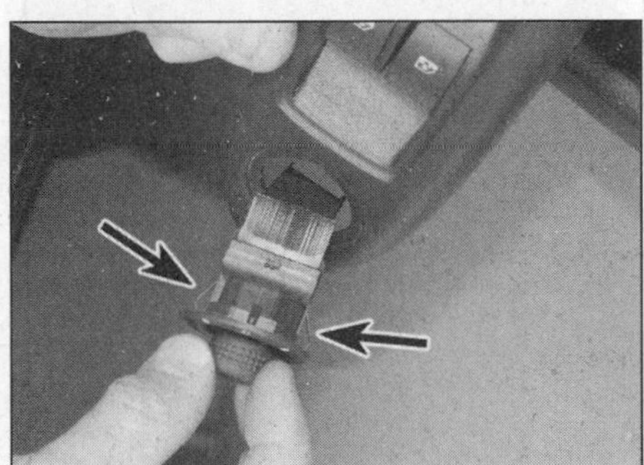
18.15b . . . and withdraw the switch, releasing the clips (arrowed)

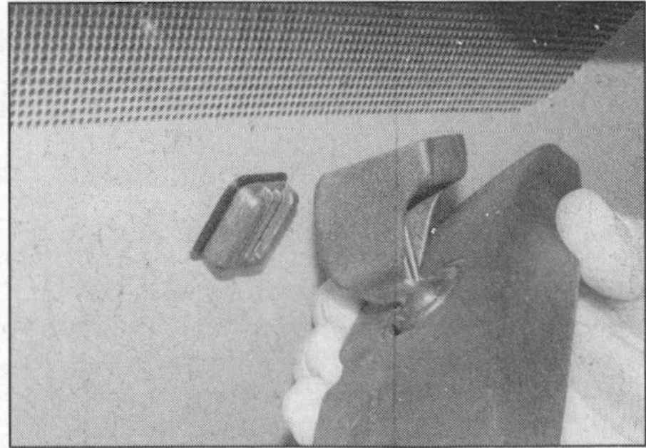
18.17 Lift the interior mirror from its mounting bracket

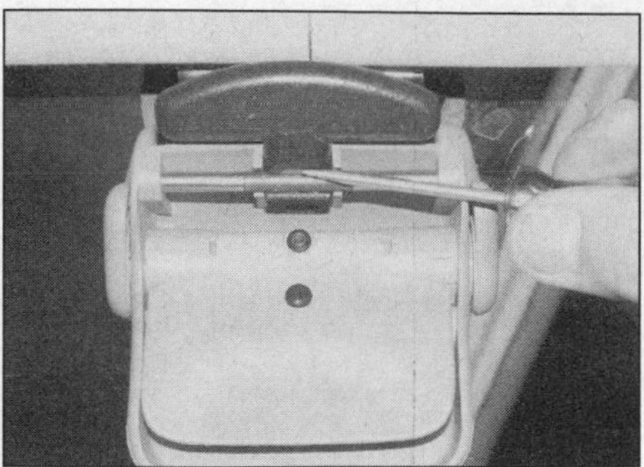

21.1 Press the red button in to release the handle assembly

21.2 Unhook the hinges from the front of the sunroof frame

20 Rear quarter window components – removal and refitting

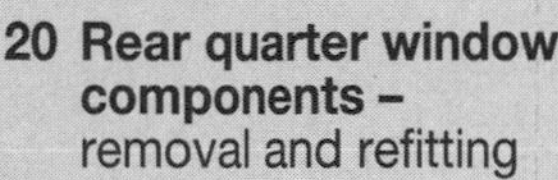

1 The fixed rear quarter window glass is bonded in position using a special adhesive. Special tools, adhesives and expertise are required for successful removal and refitting of glass fixed by this method. Such work must therefore be entrusted to a Renault dealer, a windscreen specialist, or other competent professional.

21 Sunroof components – removal and refitting

Manual sunroof

Glass panel

1 Open the sunroof to its first stage, then press the button on the handle to release it from the locating pin **(see illustration)**.

2 Lift the glass almost vertically, and unhook the hinges from the front of the sunroof frame **(see illustration)**. Lift the glass panel from the roof taking care not to damage it.

3 Refitting is a reversal of removal.

Handle and hinges

4 Remove the glass panel as described in paragraphs 1 and 2 of this Section.

5 Undo the two securing screws and remove the handle assembly from the glass panel.

6 Unclip the plastic covers, then undo the securing screws, and withdraw the hinges from the glass panel.

7 Refitting is a reversal of removal.

Electric sunroof

8 This type of sunroof is a complex piece of equipment, consisting of a large number of components. It is strongly recommended that the sunroof mechanism is not disturbed unless absolutely necessary. If the sunroof mechanism is faulty, or requires overhaul, consult a Renault dealer for advice.

22 Body exterior fittings – removal and refitting

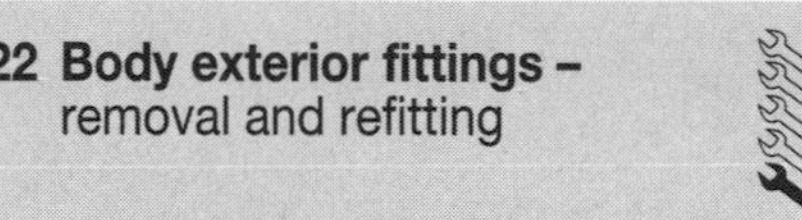

Splash shields and wheel arch liners

1 Various plastic shields may be fitted to the wheel arches and various engine components to protect against road dirt and moisture.

2 The shields are secured by a combination of plastic clips, screws, nuts or pop-rivets. Removal and refitting should be self-evident. Take particular care not to break plastic clips when removing them. Renew any pop-rivets on refitting where necessary.

Rubbing strips

Note: *Take care not to damage the paintwork when removing the rubbing strips.*

Front door

3 Open the door, and remove the plastic cover from the rear edge of the door to expose the rubbing strip securing clip **(see illustration)**. Where applicable, it may be necessary to remove a retaining screw.

4 Working outside the door, unclip the end of the rubbing strip and slide it towards the rear of the door **(see illustrations)**.

5 To refit a rubbing strip, align the clips in the strip with the corresponding holes in the door. Push the strip towards the front of the door to engage the holes.

6 On completion, refit the retaining screw (where fitted) and its plastic cover in the end of the door.

Rear door

7 Open the door, and remove the plastic cover from the front edge of the door to expose the rubbing strip securing clip. Where applicable, it may be necessary to remove a retaining screw.

8 Working outside the door, unclip the end of the rubbing strip and push it towards the front of the door **(see illustration)**.

9 To refit a rubbing strip, align the clips in the strip with the corresponding holes in the door. Push the strip towards the rear of the door to engage the holes.

10 On completion, refit the securing screw (where fitted) and its plastic cover.

Rear quarter panel (3-door)

11 Using a small screwdriver unclip the front retaining clip for the rubbing strip, then gently tap the rubbing strip towards the front of the

22.3 Remove the blanking plug from inside the door edge

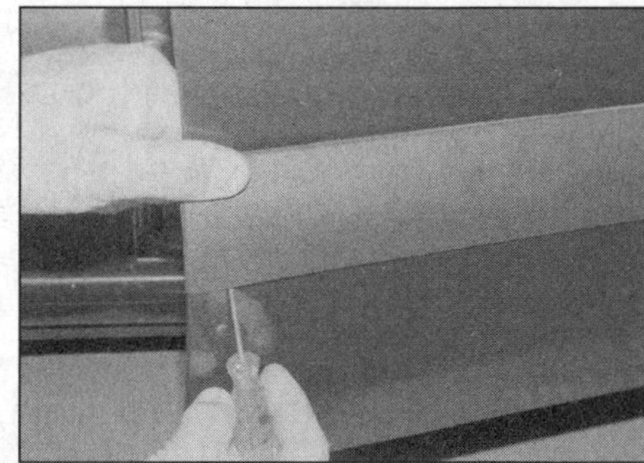

22.4a Use a small screwdriver to unclip the door rubbing strip . . .

22.4b . . . then slide rubbing strip towards the rear of the door to remove

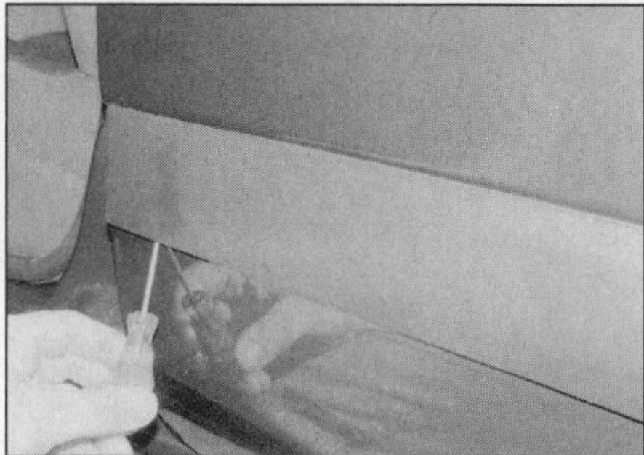

22.8 Using a small screwdriver to unclip the front of the door rubbing strip

22.11a Use a small screwdriver to unclip the rear panel rubbing strip . . .

22.11b . . . then slide rubbing strip towards the front of the vehicle to remove

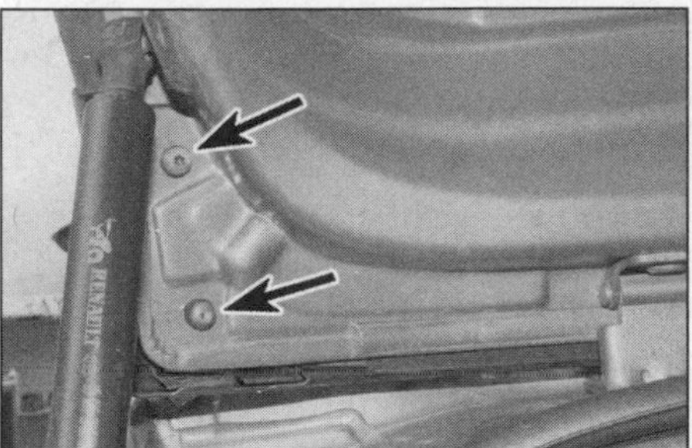

22.15a Unscrew the retaining screws (arrowed) from the end of the spoiler – one side shown

22.15b Undo the two inner retaining screws (arrowed)

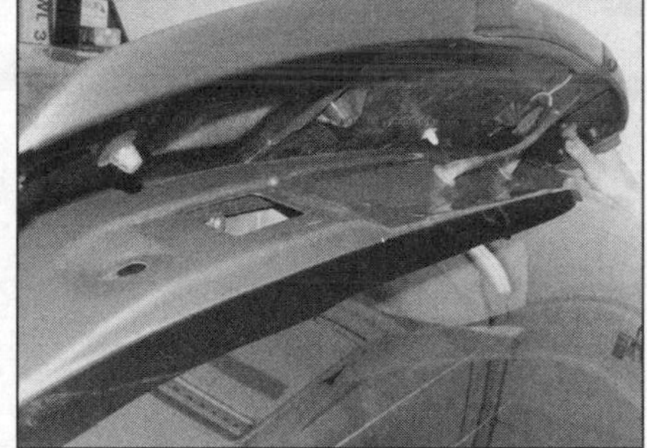

22.16 Unclipping the spoiler from the tailgate

22.17 Disconnecting the washer hose from the spoiler

vehicle to release it from its remaining clips **(see illustrations)**.

Badges

Removal

12 The various badges may be secured with adhesives. To remove them, either soften the adhesive using a hot air gun or hairdryer (taking care to avoid damage to the paint-work), or separate the badge from the body by 'sawing' through the adhesive using a length of nylon cord. **Note:** *Some badges are located by pegs in plastic grommets, these will need to be carefully prised from the bodywork.*

Refitting

13 Clean off all traces of adhesive using white spirit, then wash the area with warm soapy water to remove all traces of spirit, and allow to dry. Ensure that the surface to which the new badge is to be fastened is completely clean, and free from grease and dirt.

14 Use the hot air gun to soften the adhesive on the new badge, then press it firmly into position.

Tailgate spoiler

Removal

15 Open the tailgate, and remove the six spoiler securing screws (two at each end of the spoiler and two in the middle) **(see illustrations)**.

16 With the tailgate closed, carefully release the spoiler from its retaining clips by lifting it upwards from the tailgate, starting at the ends **(see illustration)**.

17 Disconnect the high-level stop-light wiring and washer hose **(see illustration)**, before withdrawing the spoiler.

Refitting

18 Refitting is a reversal of removal.

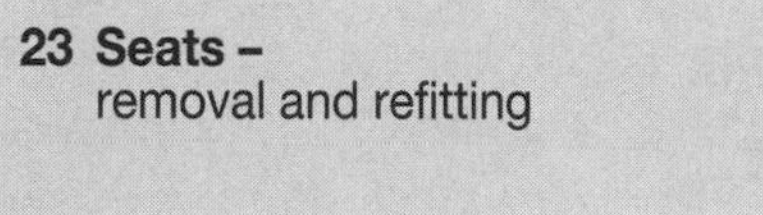

23 Seats – removal and refitting

Front seat

Warning: Disconnect the battery negative lead (see* Disconnecting the battery*), then wait for five minutes before proceeding. If this waiting period is not observed, there is danger of activating the side airbags and seat belt tensioners.

Removal

Note: *On some models, there is a storage tray fitted under the front passenger seat. This is held in place by one retaining screw* ***(see illustration)****.*

1 If desired, remove the seat side trim panels for improved access.

2 Working underneath the car, remove the rubber grommets (where fitted) and unscrew the four nuts securing the seat rails to the floor **(see illustrations)**. When removing the inner seat securing nuts, take care not to burn yourself if the exhaust is still hot.

3 Carefully lift the seat from the vehicle, disconnect any wiring on removal **(see illustration)**.

Refitting

4 Refitting is a reversal of removal, making sure the spacers are in place in the carpet before refitting.

23.0 Undo the retaining screw to remove the storage tray

23.2a Prise out the rubber grommet . . .

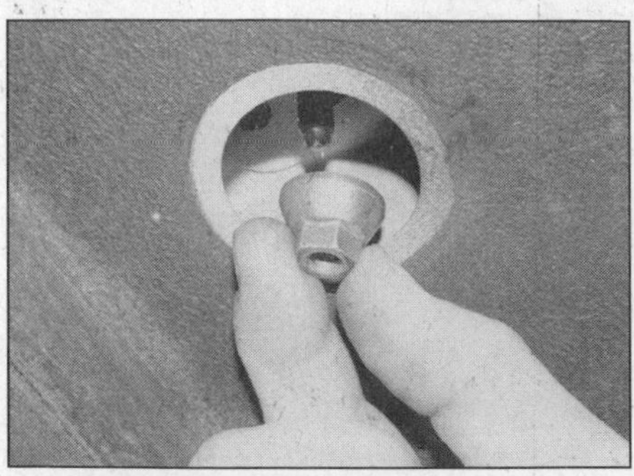

23.2b . . . and remove an outer seat securing nut

23.6 Undo the retaining screw to release the seat runner trim

Front seat runners

Removal

5 Remove the seat as described in this Section.

6 Undo the retaining screws (one on each

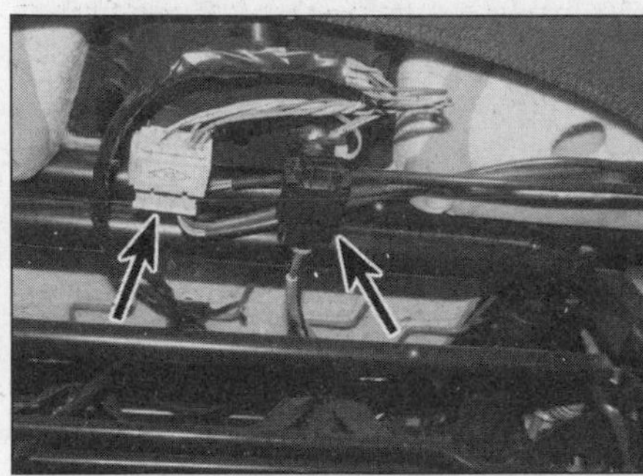

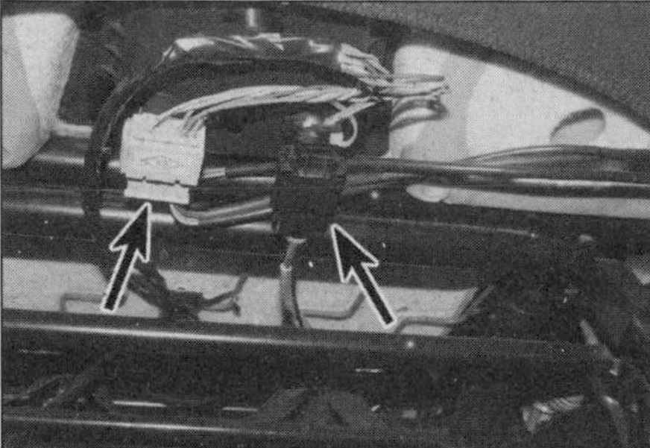

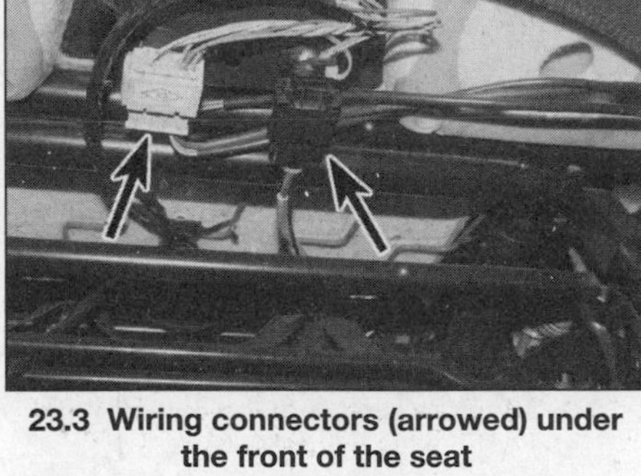

23.3 Wiring connectors (arrowed) under the front of the seat

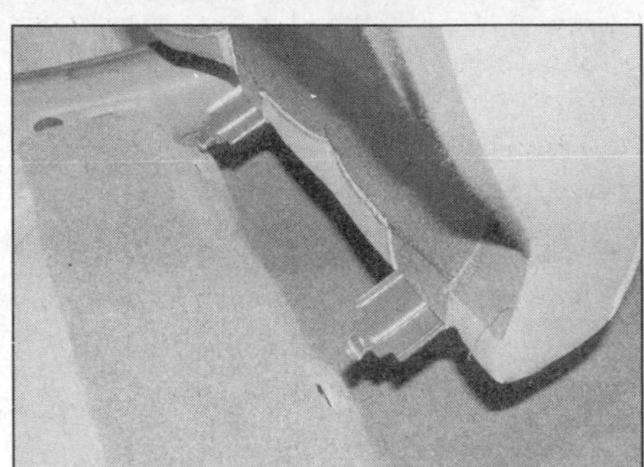

23.10 Disengaging the rear seat cushion from the floor panel

side) and remove the seat side trim panels **(see illustration)**.

7 Slacken and remove the securing bolts and withdraw the seat runners from the seat frame.

8 On three-door models, disconnect the control cable from the seat runner assembly.

Refitting

9 Refitting is a reversal of removal.

Rear seat cushion

Removal

10 Tilt the seat cushion forwards, then lift it to disengage the securing lugs from the holes in the floor **(see illustration)**.

Refitting

11 Refitting is a reversal of removal.

Rear seat back

Removal

12 Remove the luggage compartment carpet. Undo the two securing bolts from the rear luggage compartment reinforcement bar, and remove from the car **(see illustrations)**.

13 Slacken, but do not remove, the seat centre bracket front retaining bolt from the floor panel.

14 Release the securing catches at the top of the seat backs. Fold the seat backs forwards.

15 Remove the seat centre bracket rear retaining bolt from the floor panel and disengage the bracket from the front bolt **(see illustrations)**.

16 Working at the lower ends of the seat backs, lift out the locating pegs from the brackets in front of the wheel arches **(see illustration)**, then withdraw the assembly from the car.

17 To split the two seat backs, undo the two

23.12a Undo the securing bolts – left-hand bolt arrowed . . .

23.12b . . . and remove the reinforcement bar

23.15a Remove the rear retaining bolt from the centre seat bracket . . .

23.15b . . . then release the bracket from the front locating bolt

23.16 Lift the seat locating peg from the bracket on the wheel arch

23.17a Undo the two securing nuts, to split the rear seat backs

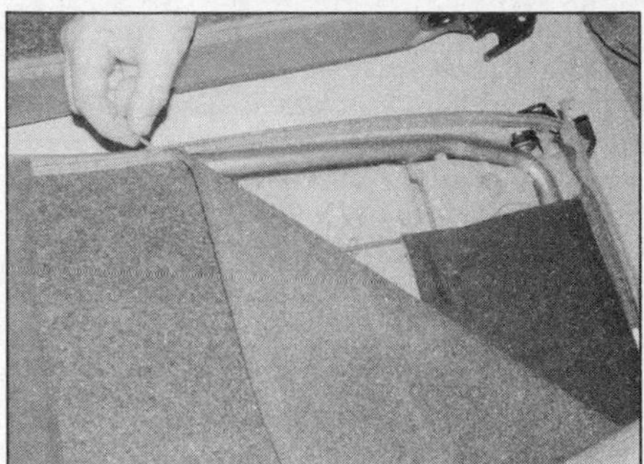

23.17b The seat covers can be unzipped from the seat backs

securing nuts from the centre bracket. The seat covers can be unzipped for removal **(see illustrations)**.

Refitting

18 Refitting is a reversal of removal.

24 Seat belt components – removal and refitting

Warning: If the vehicle has been in an accident, all the seat belt components must be renewed.

Front belt

Removal

1 Remove the footwell side/sill trim panels and B-pillar panel, as described in Section 27.
2 Undo the seat belt lower mounting bolt, if not already removed with the sill trims.
3 Unscrew the mounting bolt, and withdraw the inertia reel assembly from the door pillar **(see illustration)**. Remove the seat belt assembly from the car.

Refitting

4 Refitting is a reversal of removal. Tighten the seat belt mounting bolts to the specified torque.

Front belt height adjuster

Removal

5 Remove the B-pillar trim panel, as described in Section 27.

24.11 The rear seat belt buckles can be unbolted (arrow) from the floor panel

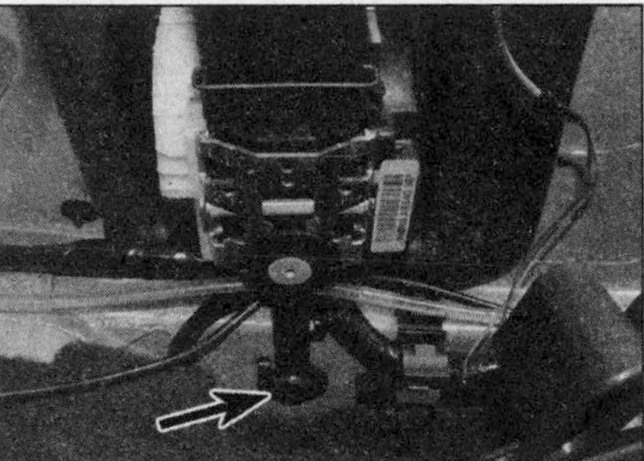

24.3 Undo the inertia reel mounting bolt (arrowed)

6 Unscrew the two securing bolts, and withdraw the adjuster from the pillar **(see illustration)**.

Refitting

7 Refitting is a reversal of removal. Ensure that the B-pillar trim panel locates correctly over the door aperture weatherseals. Tighten the seat belt mountings to the specified torque.

Rear inertia reel side belt

Removal

8 Remove the rear seat cushion, with reference to Section 23, for access to the seat belt lower mounting bolt. Unscrew the bolt **(see illustration)**.
9 Fold the seat back forwards and remove the rear side shelf trim panels as described in Section 27

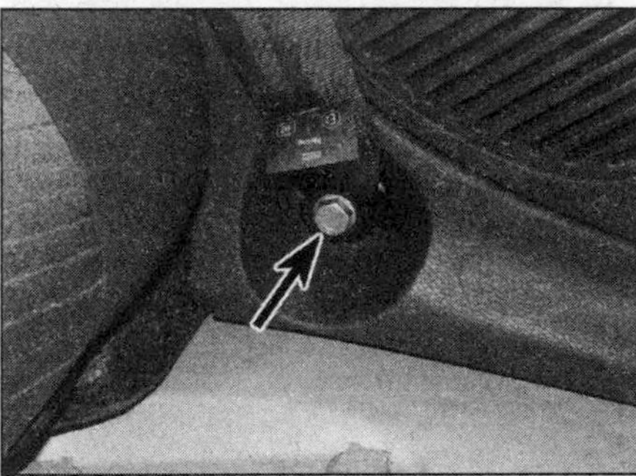

24.8 Remove the lower seat belt mounting bolt (arrowed)

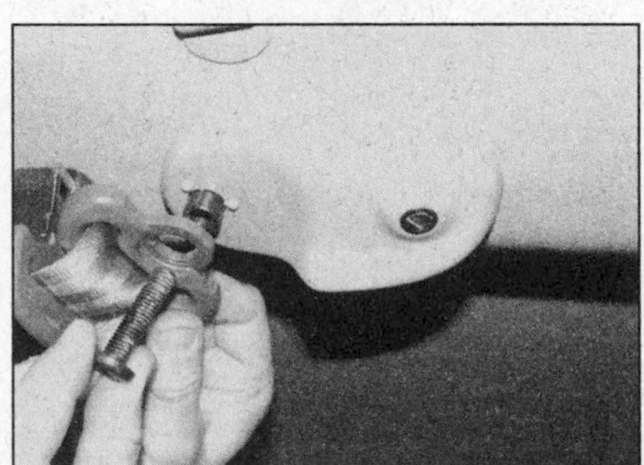

24.14a Unbolt the seat belt mounting from the roof panel . . .

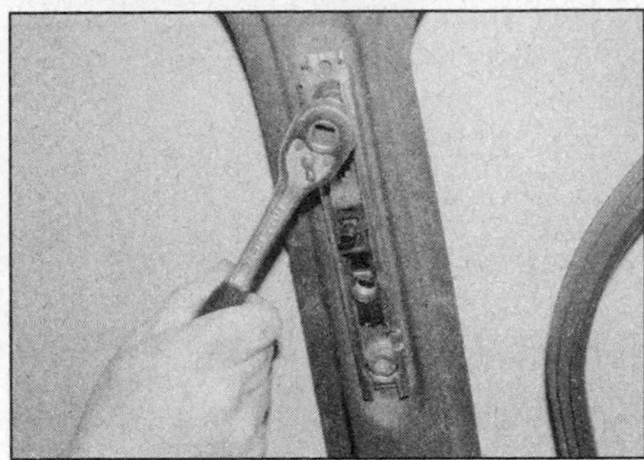

24.6 Remove the height adjuster mounting bolts

10 Unscrew the securing bolt and withdraw the inertia reel from its location **(see illustration)**.
11 The seat belt buckle can be unbolted from the floor, after removing the rear seat cushion for access **(see illustration)**.

Refitting

12 Refitting is a reversal of removal. Tighten the seat belt mountings to the specified torque.

Rear inertia reel centre belt

Removal

13 Carry out the procedures as described in paragraph 9 in this Section (on the left-hand side of the car).
14 Unscrew the seat belt securing bolt from the rear of the headlining, then feed the seat belt through the hole in the rear quarter trim panel **(see illustrations)**.

24.10 Undo the rear inertia reel mounting bolt (arrowed)

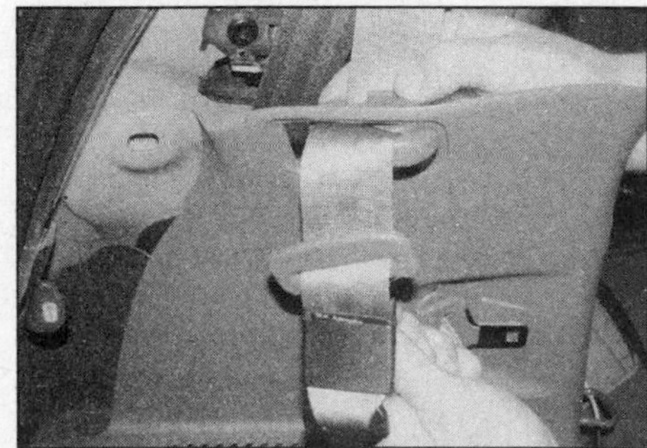

24.14b . . . then feed the belt through the rear quarter trim panel

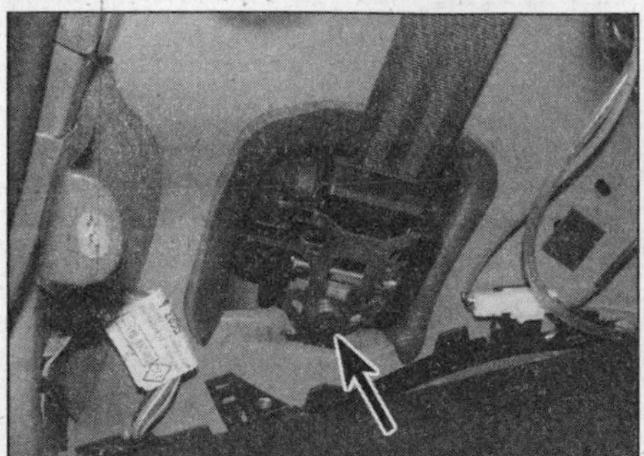

24.16 Undo the inertia reel mounting bolt (arrowed) for the centre seat belt

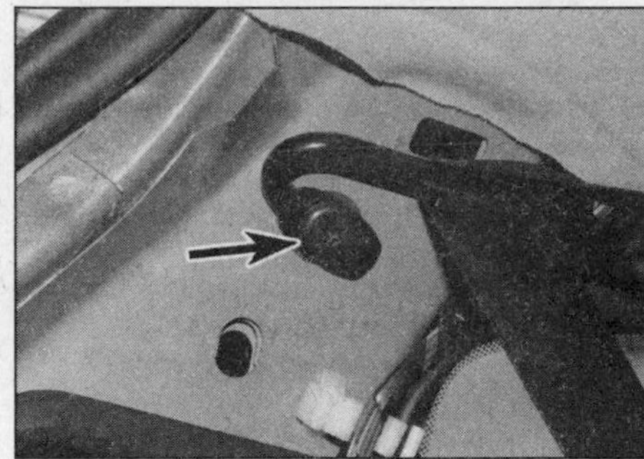

24.17 Undo the bolt (arrowed) to remove the guide rail

15 Working in the luggage compartment, pull back the side trim to expose the inertia reel mounting bolt.

16 Undo the securing bolt and withdraw the inertia reel from its location **(see illustration)**.

17 Unbolt the metal guide bracket from the rear quarter body panel to release the seat belt **(see illustration)**.

18 The seat belt buckle can be unbolted from the floor, after removing the rear seat cushion for access.

Refitting

19 Refitting is a reversal of removal. Tighten the securing bolts to the specified torque.

25 Seat belt pretensioner system – general information and component renewal

General information

1 Seat belt pretensioners are fitted to remove any slack from the front seat belts in the event of a frontal impact. The system is designed to reduce the chances of injury to the driver and front seat passenger in the event of an accident, due to the seat belts being slack.

2 The system consists of two special seat belt tensioner/stalk assemblies mounted directly on the front seats, and an electronic control unit.

3 Each tensioner/stalk assembly consist of a special buckle attached to a cable. The end of the cable is attached to a piston inside the tensioner cylinder.

4 The electronic control unit is mounted under the centre console, and incorporates a deceleration sensor and a trigger unit. If the sensor senses a deceleration greater than a predetermined limit, the trigger unit sends signals to the ignition modules in both seat belt tensioner units. Note that, on most models, the seat belt tensioner electronic control unit is integrated with the airbag electronic control unit.

5 When a tensioner ignition module is triggered, a small capsule is energised, which rapidly releases gas into the tensioner cylinder. As the gas is released, the piston is forced along the cylinder, pulling the cable (approximately 70 mm) and hence the seat belt stalk, which in turn removes any slack from the seat belt, pulling the belt tight against the wearer.

6 Once a seat belt tensioner has been triggered, it must be renewed.

Warning: Do not expose the pretensioner system to excessive heat.

Warning: If any work is to be carried out under the vehicle (eg, exhaust renewal) in the vicinity of the pretensioner system components which involves impacts or hammering, remove the pretensioner system fuse then wait for at least five minutes before proceeding.

Warning: When installing any electrical accessories (such as loudspeakers or alarm systems) which emit a magnetic field, the components must not be fitted near the pretensioner control unit.

Warning: If an attempt has been made to steal the vehicle, if the vehicle has been stolen, or if the vehicle has been involved in an impact which did not trigger the pretensioners, the pretensioner system should be tested using Renault special test tool XRBAG.

Pretensioner system

Note: *Renault recommend that special test tool XRBAG is used to test the operation of the system before reactivation.*

De-activation

7 To de-activate the pretensioner system, in order to make the system safe, proceed as follows.

a) *Switch off the ignition.*
b) *Disconnect the battery negative lead.*
c) *Wait for a minimum of 5 minutes before carrying out any further work.*
d) *Working under each front seat in turn, separate the two halves of the seat belt pretensioner wiring connector.*

Re-activation

8 To re-activate the pretensioner system after carrying out work, proceed as follows.

a) *Reconnect the pretensioner wiring connectors under the seats.*
b) *Reconnect the battery negative lead.*
c) *Switch the ignition on. Check that all the warning lights on the instrument panel are working correctly.*
d) *Renault recommend that the operation of the system is checked using Renault special test tool XRBAG.*

Pretensioner assembly

Removal

9 De-activate the pretensioner system as described previously in this Section.

10 Remove the seat (see Section 23).

11 Undo the securing screw and remove the trim panel from the seat **(see illustration)**.

12 Disconnect the wiring plug from the top of the pretensioner assembly **(see illustration)**, and feed the wiring through the trim panel (leave the wiring clipped in place under the seat).

13 Undo the securing bolt from the pretensioner assembly **(see illustration)**, then

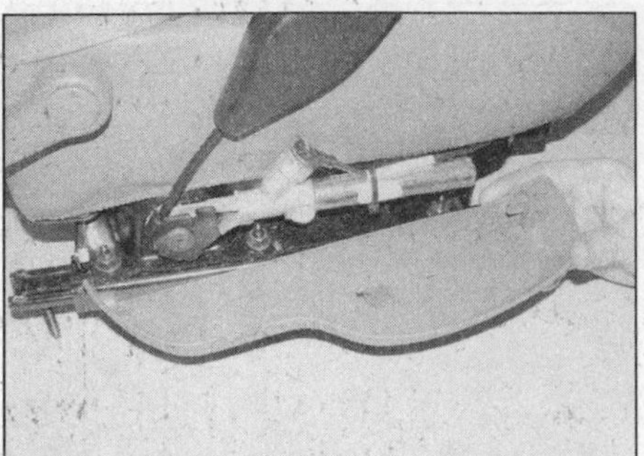

25.11 Remove the screw and unclip the trim panel from the seat runner

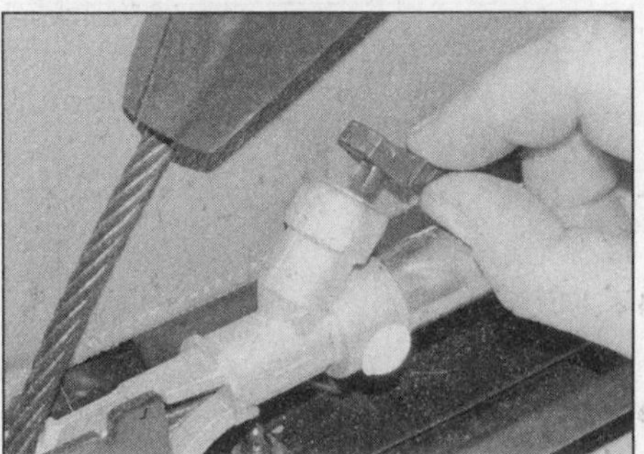

25.12 Disconnecting the wiring plug from the pretensioner assembly

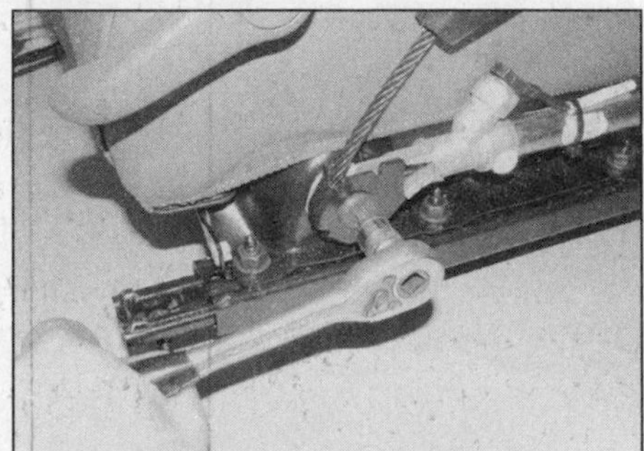

25.13 Unbolting the pretensioner assembly from the seat frame

withdraw the tensioner assembly from the seat frame.

Warning: Do not expose the pretensioner assembly to shocks or excessive heat.

Warning: Before discarding a pretensioner assembly which has not been triggered, the assembly must be rendered safe using the appropriate Renault special equipment.

Refitting

14 Feed the pretensioner wiring through the slot in the seat trim panel, and reconnect the wring connector to the top of the pretensioner unit.

15 Refit the tensioner to the seat, ensuring that the pretensioner is correctly located, then refit and tighten the securing bolt.

16 Refit the trim panel to the seat frame.

17 Refit the seat as described in Section 23.

18 Re-activate the system as described previously in this Section.

Electronic control unit

19 The pretensioner system shares the same control unit as the airbag system. If the control unit is to be removed, follow the procedure for the removal and refitting of the airbag control unit as described in Chapter 12, Section 28.

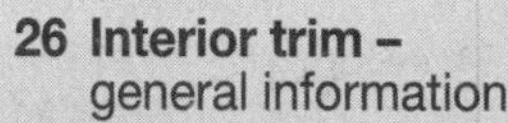

26 Interior trim – general information

Interior trim panels

Removal

1 The interior trim panels are all secured using either screws or various types of plastic fasteners.

2 Before removing a panel, study it carefully, noting how it is secured. Often, other panels or ancillary components (such as seat belt mountings, grab handles, etc) must be removed before a particular panel can be withdrawn.

3 Once any such components have been removed, check that there are no other panels overlapping the one to be removed. Usually, the sequence to be followed will become obvious on close inspection.

26.4 Suitable forked tool for releasing plastic trim panel securing clips

4 Remove all obvious fasteners, such as screws, which may have plastic covers fitted. If the panel cannot be freed, it is probably secured by hidden clips or fasteners on the rear of the panel. Such fasteners are usually situated around the edge of the panel, and can be prised up to release them. Note that plastic clips can break quite easily, so it is advisable to have a few new clips of the correct type available for refitting. Generally, the best way of releasing such clips is to use a forked tool **(see illustration)**. If this is not available, an old, broad-bladed screwdriver with the edges rounded-off and wrapped in insulating tape will serve as a good substitute.

5 The following Section and the accompanying illustrations describe removal and refitting of all the major trim panels. Note that the type and number of fasteners used often varies during the production run of a particular model, so differences may be found to the procedures provided.

6 When removing a panel, **never** use excessive force, or the panel may be damaged. Always check carefully that all fasteners have been removed or released before attempting to withdraw a panel.

Refitting

7 When refitting, secure the fasteners by pressing them firmly into place. Ensure that all disturbed components are correctly secured, to prevent rattles. If adhesives were found at any point during removal, use white spirit to remove the old adhesive, then wash off the white spirit using soapy water. Use a trim adhesive (a Renault dealer should be able to recommend a proprietary product) on reassembly.

Carpets

8 The carpet is not bonded and rests on the floor, it is held in position by the sill trim panels and other surrounding panels and components.

9 Carpet removal and refitting is reasonably straightforward, but very time-consuming, due to the fact that many of the adjoining trim panels must be removed first. It will also be necessary to remove components such as the seats and their mountings, the centre console, etc.

Headlining

10 The headlining is bonded to the rear section of the roof, and is also held in place by the grab handles, sun visors, sunroof trim, door pillar trim panels, rear quarter trim panels, weatherseals, etc. When all the fittings have been removed or prised clear, it can then be withdrawn out through the tailgate aperture.

11 Note that headlining removal requires considerable skill and patience if it is to be carried out without damage, and is therefore best entrusted to an expert.

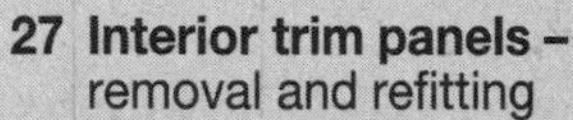

27 Interior trim panels – removal and refitting

Front door inner trim panel

Removal

1 Make sure the ignition is in the off position, before disconnecting any electrical connectors. If preferred, disconnect the battery negative lead.

2 Unclip the mirror inner trim panel and the speaker cover grille **(see illustrations)**.

3 Remove the securing screw and cover, then carefully lift and pull back the grab handle/switch panel to release it from the door **(see illustration)**.

4 Remove the screw securing the inner door

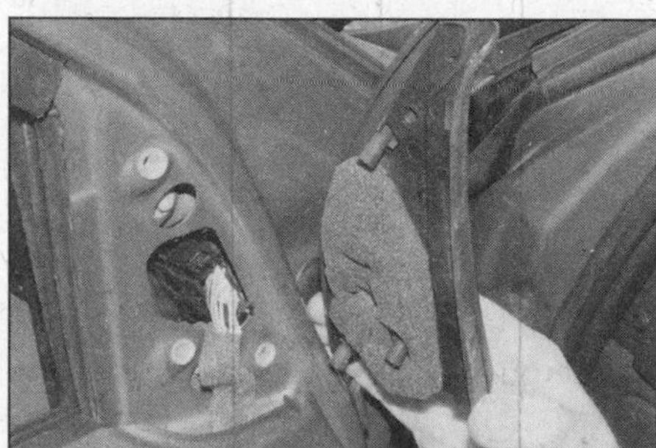

27.2a Unclip the mirror inner trim panel . . .

27.2b . . . and unclip the speaker grille surround

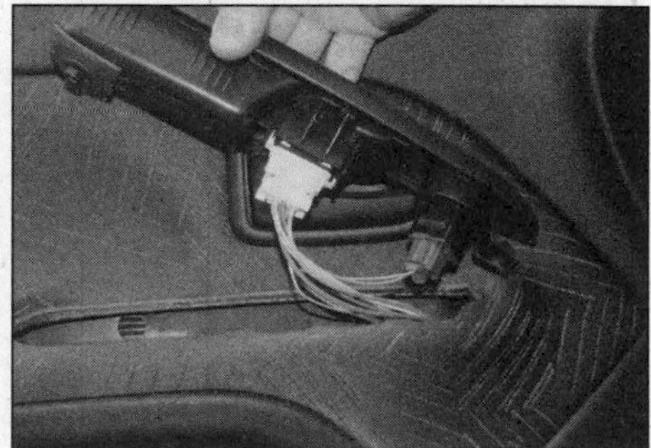

27.3 Undo the retaining screw and remove the switch panel

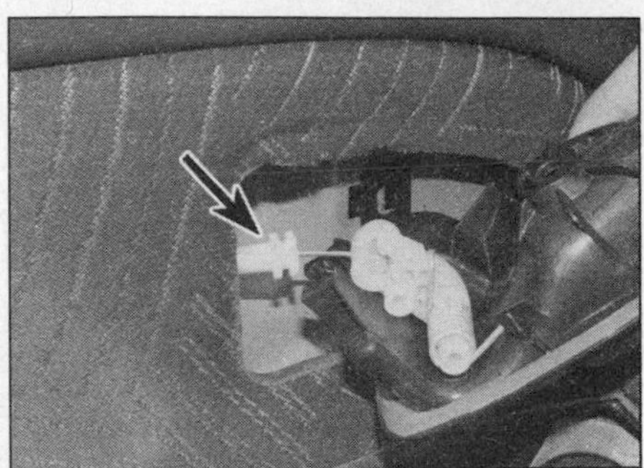
27.4 Release the operating cable (arrowed) from the handle

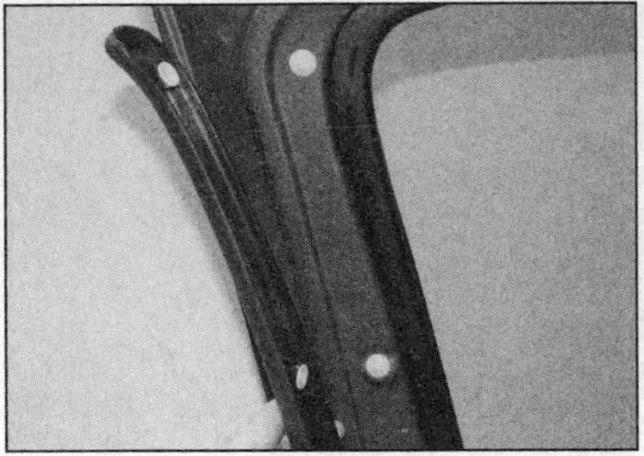
27.6a On 3-door models, unclip the trim from the door frame . . .

27.6b . . . then release it from the inner door trim panel

handle to the door. Withdraw the handle and disconnect the outer part of the operating cable from the rear of the handle, then unclip the inner cable **(see illustration)**.

5 Disconnect the wiring plugs from the electric window switches. Also disconnect the wiring plug from the electric mirror switch or airbag switch, where applicable.

6 On 3-door models, unclip the upper trim panel from the rear of the window frame, then carefully release it from the top of the door inner trim panel **(see illustrations)**.

7 Remove the securing screws and withdraw the speaker from the door, disconnecting the wiring connector **(see illustration)**.

8 Slacken and remove the retaining screws from the lower edge of the door trim panel **(see illustration)**.

9 Carefully release the securing clips around the edge of the trim panel, preferably using a forked tool. Pull the trim panel from the door, and lift upwards off the inner weather strip to remove (noting that it is secured with sealing compound around its edge).

Refitting

10 Refitting is a reversal of removal, bearing in mind the following points.

11 When refitting the panel to the door, ensure that the sealing compound provides a good seal between the door and the panel. If necessary, apply new sealing compound of a suitable type (available from a Renault dealer).

12 Make sure all the wiring connectors are fitted correctly, before switching the ignition on or reconnecting battery.

Front door impact absorbers

13 With the door inner trim panel removed as described in this Section, using a flat-bladed screwdriver, unclip the side impact absorber **(see illustration)**. The impact absorber can then be withdrawn through the aperture in the door frame.

Refitting

14 Refitting is a reversal of removal.

Rear door inner trim panel

Removal

15 Remove the blanking plug and undo the securing screw, then carefully lift and pull forward the grab handle to release it from the door panel **(see illustrations)**.

16 On models fitted with manual window winders, note the position of the window winder handle with the window fully open, then pull the handle firmly to release it from the window regulator **(see illustration)**.

17 Remove the screw securing the inner door handle to the door. Withdraw the handle and disconnect the operating rod from the rear of the handle **(see illustrations)**.

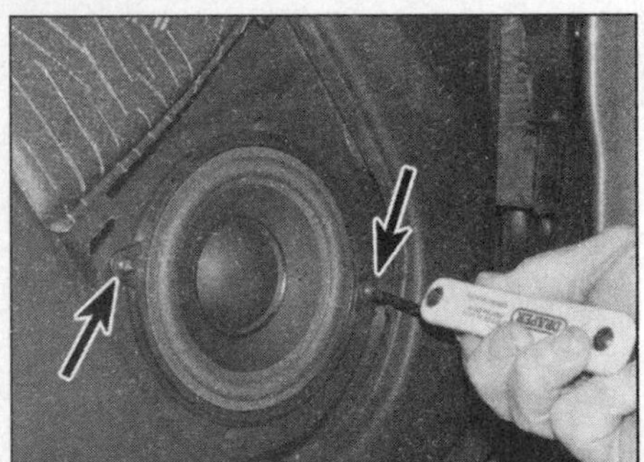
27.7 Removing the speaker securing screws (arrowed)

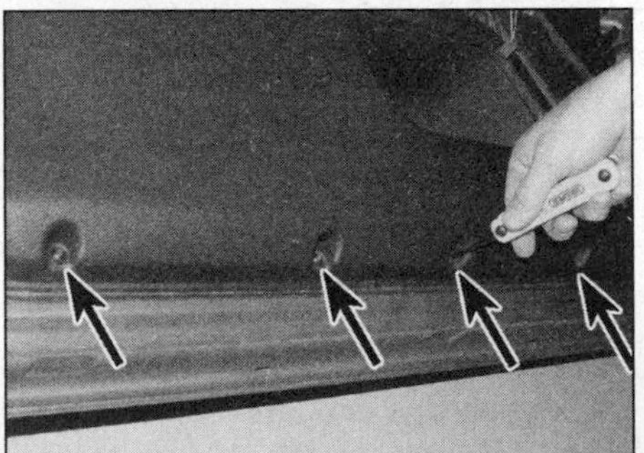
27.8 Remove the retaining screws (arrowed) from the lower edge of the door panel

27.13 Securing clips (arrowed) for the door impact absorber

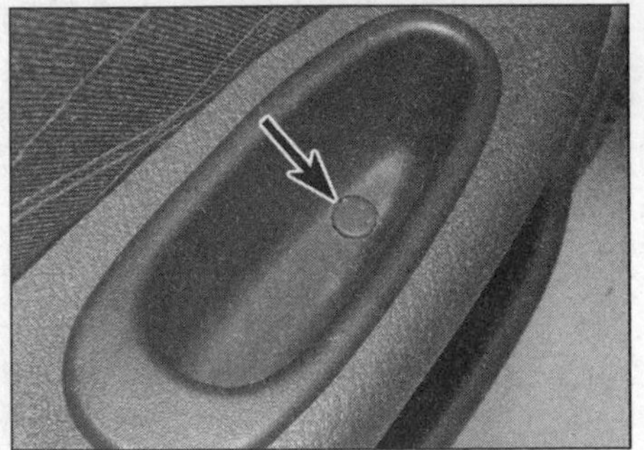
27.15a Remove the blanking plug (arrowed) and remove the retaining screw . . .

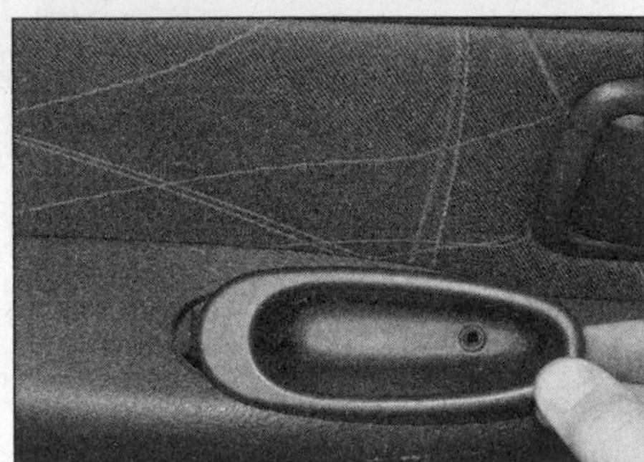
27.15b . . . and lift the door grab handle out of the door trim panel

27.16 Removing the rear door window winder handle

18 On models fitted with electric windows, disconnect the wiring plugs from the electric window switches.

19 Turn the speaker cover anti-clockwise to remove, then undo the four securing screws and withdraw the speaker from the door panel, disconnecting the wiring connector **(see illustration).**

20 Carefully release the securing clips around the edge of the trim panel, preferably using a forked tool. Pull the trim panel from the door, and lift upwards of the inner weather strip and door locking button **(see illustration)** to remove (noting that it is secured with sealing compound around its edge). **Note:** *There is a spacer on the window regulator spindle, under the door trim panel* **(*see illustration*).**

Refitting

21 Proceed as described in paragraphs 10 to 12 in this Section.

Footwell side/sill trim panels

Removal

22 Remove the front seat as described in Section 23.

23 Carefully pull off the lower part of the door seals, taking care not to damage the seal.

24 For the front left-hand sill trim to be removed, the bonnet release lever will have to be unclipped first.

25 On 3-door models, unscrew the bolt securing the seat belt mounting rail. Note the position of any washers and/or spacers. Carefully manipulate the rail to release the rear end from the trim panel **(see illustrations).**

26 On 5-door models, unbolt the front and rear seat belt lower mountings **(see illustrations).**

27 Carefully pull the panel from the body to release the securing clips, and withdraw the panel from the sill **(see illustration).**

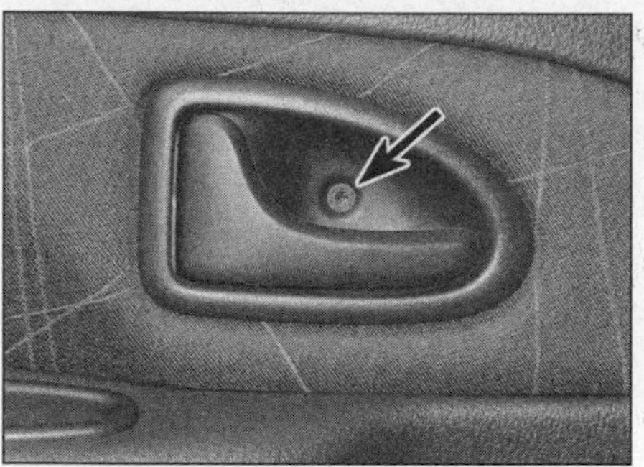

27.17a Remove the interior door handle securing screw (arrowed) . . .

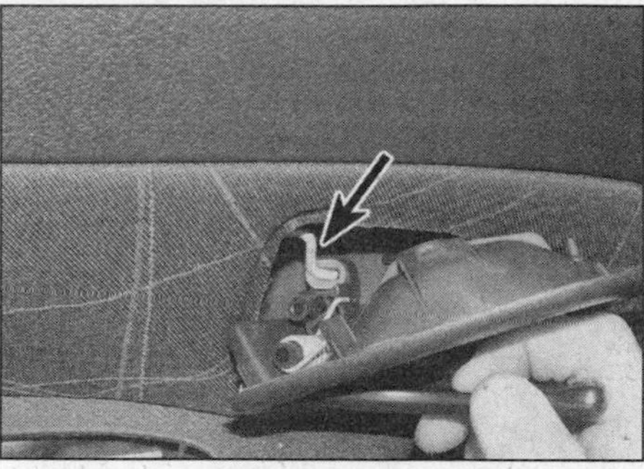

27.17b . . . then disconnect the operating rod (arrowed)

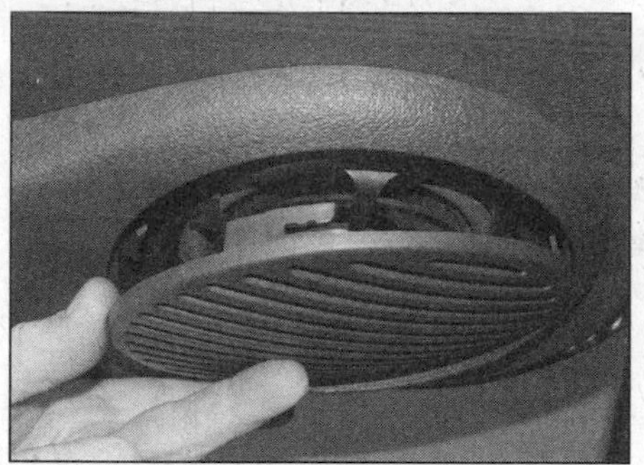

27.19 Turn the speaker cover anti-clockwise to remove

27.20a Lift the door trim panel up over the door lock button

27.20b Make sure the spacer is fitted to the window regulator spindle, before refitting the door trim panel

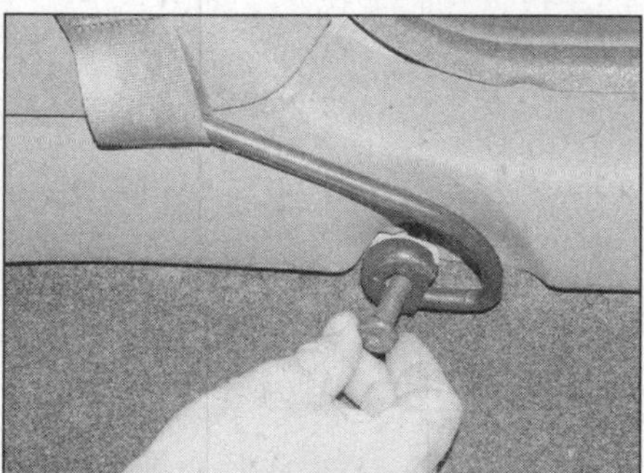

27.25a Remove the seat belt rail mounting bolt . . .

27.25b . . . then release the rail from the pillar – 3-door model

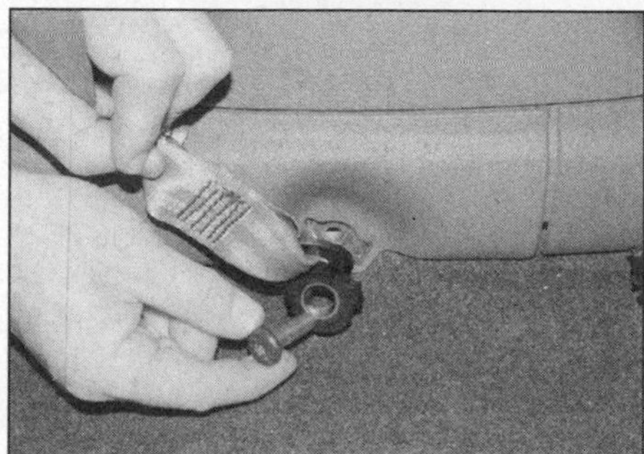

27.26a Removing the front seat belt lower mounting bolt – 5-door model

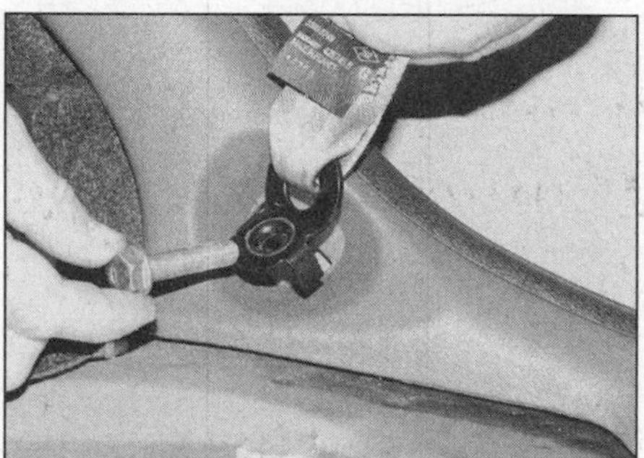

27.26b Removing the rear seat belt lower mounting bolt – 5-door model

27.27 Removing a front footwell/side trim panel

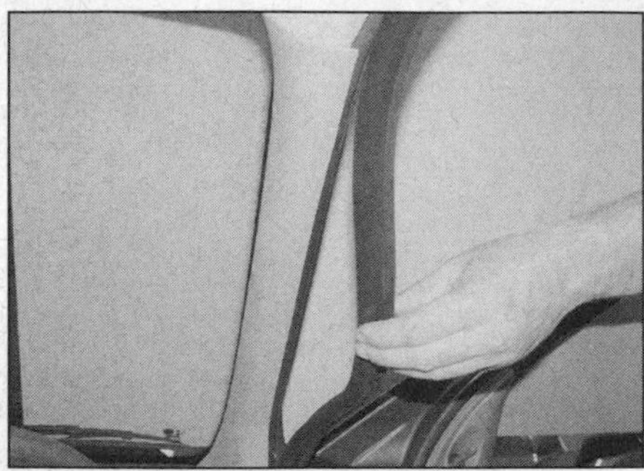

27.29 Take care not to damage the seal on removal

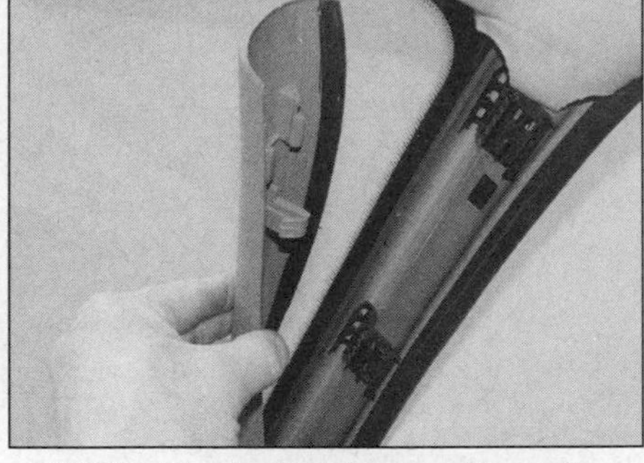

27.30a Unclip the trim panel from the A-pillar . . .

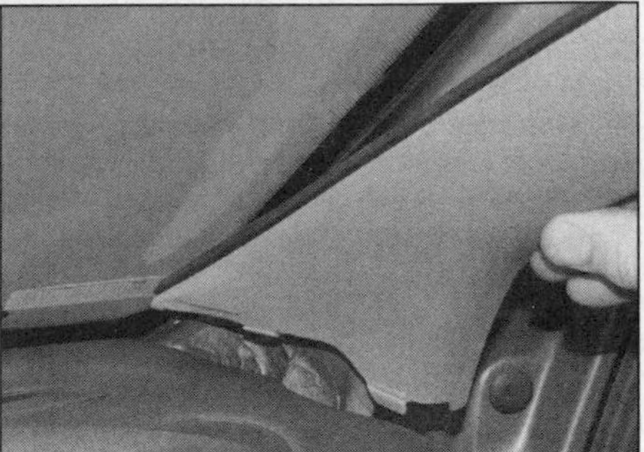

27.30b . . . then release it from the top of the facia panel

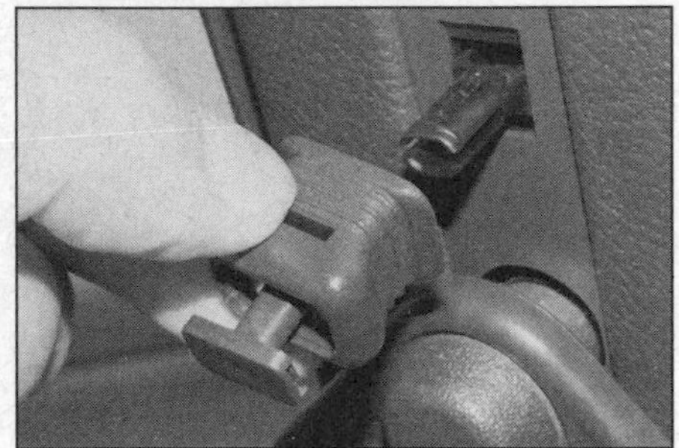

27.33 Prise the clip from the seat belt height adjustment knob, then pull the knob from the adjuster

Refitting

28 Refitting is a reversal of removal. Ensure that the securing clips are correctly engaged, and tighten the seat belt mounting bolts to the specified torque.

27.34 Prise off the cover and remove the upper seat belt mounting bolt

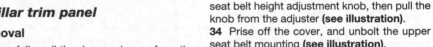

A-pillar trim panel

Removal

29 Carefully pull the door seal away from the front windscreen pillar where it touches the trim panel, taking care not to damage the seal **(see illustration)**.

30 Carefully pull back the top of the panel from the pillar to release the securing clips. Withdraw the panel, lifting it upwards from the facia panel **(see illustrations)**.

Refitting

31 Refitting is a reversal of removal.

B-pillar trim panel (5-door)

Removal

32 Remove the footwell side/sill trim panels as described previously in this Section.

33 If applicable, prise the centre clip from the seat belt height adjustment knob, then pull the knob from the adjuster **(see illustration)**.

34 Prise off the cover, and unbolt the upper seat belt mounting **(see illustration)**.

35 Unclip the seat belt trim and remove the retaining clip from above the upper mounting bolt **(see illustrations)**.

36 Carefully pull the panel from the pillar to release the securing clips, and withdraw the panel.

Refitting

37 Refitting is a reversal of removal. Ensure that the panel locates correctly with the door aperture weatherseals, and tighten the seat belt mountings to the specified torque.

Rear side/B-pillar trim panel (3-door)

Removal

38 Proceed as described in paragraphs 32 to 34.

39 Tilt the seat cushion forwards, then lift it to disengage the securing lugs from the holes in the floor.

40 Unscrew the bolt securing the seat belt mounting rail. Note the position of any washers and/or spacers. Carefully manipulate the rail to release the rear end from the trim panel **(see illustrations 27.25a and 27.25b)**.

41 Carefully release the securing clips around the edge of the trim panel, preferably using a forked tool, then lift the panel upwards to withdraw from the vehicle.

42 Carefully pull the roof side trim panel from the body to release the securing clips, and withdraw the panel **(see illustration)**.

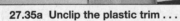

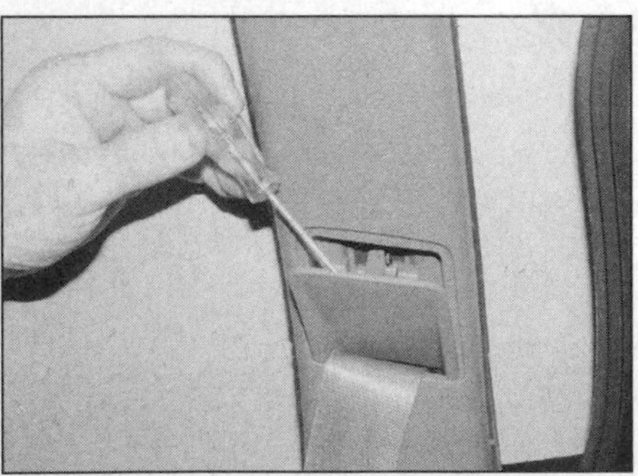

27.35a Unclip the plastic trim . . .

27.35b . . . and remove the retaining clip

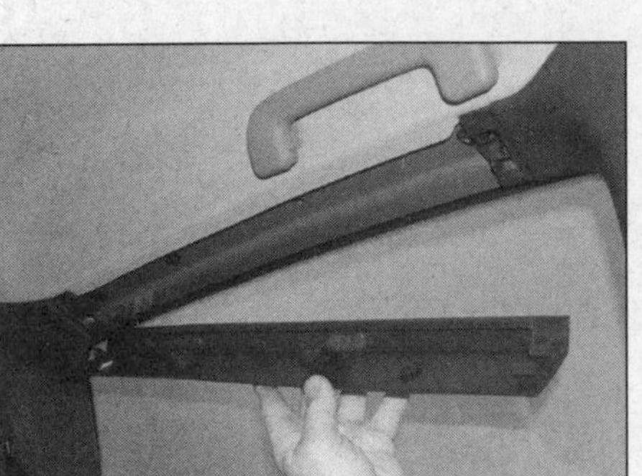

27.42 Removing the roof side trim panel

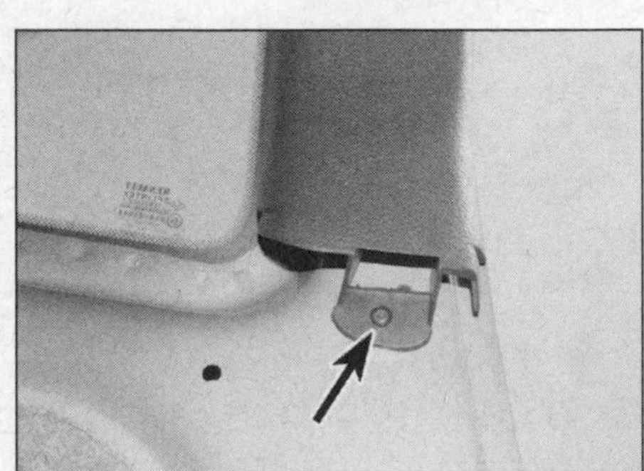

27.43a B-pillar trim lower retaining screw (arrowed) . . .

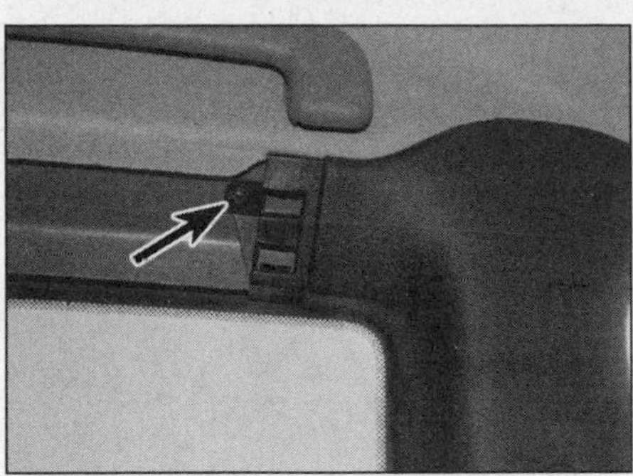

27.43b . . . and upper retaining screw (arrowed)

43 Remove the two securing screws from the B-pillar upper trim panel (one at the bottom and one at the top) **(see illustrations)**. Carefully pull the panel from the pillar to release the securing clips, and withdraw the panel.

Refitting

44 Refitting is a reversal of removal. Tighten the seat belt mountings to the specified torque.

Roof side trim panel (3-door)

Removal

45 Carefully pull the roof side trim panel from the body to release the securing clips, and withdraw the panel **(see illustration 27.42)**.

Refitting

46 Refitting is a reversal of removal.

Rear side shelf trim panels

Note: *See illustrations in Section 24.*

47 Carefully pull the rear door seal and the tailgate seal away from where it touches the trim panel, taking care not to damage the seals.

48 Unbolt the rear seat belt lower mounting.

49 Unclip the rear of the inner sill trim on 5-door models to gain access to the screw at the front of the shelf trim panel. On 3-door models, remove the inner side trim and roof side trim panel as described in this Section, and remove the securing screws and retaining clip from the shelf trim panel **(see illustrations)**.

50 Unclip and disconnect the luggage compartment light and tailgate switch where fitted.

51 Unclip the trim from the centre rear seat belt, undo the retaining bolt in the roof panel and pass the seat belt through the panel as it is removed **(see illustrations)**.

52 Carefully release the securing clips around the edge of the trim panel, preferably using a forked tool. Move the panel forwards to unhook it from the seat catch, then pass seat belt through the panel and withdraw from the vehicle.

Refitting

53 Refitting is a reversal of removal.

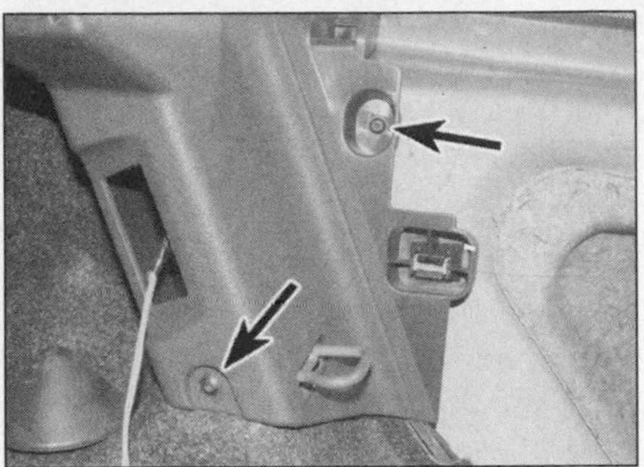

27.49a Rear shelf trim panel lower securing screws (arrowed) . . .

Rear wheel arch trim panel

Removal

54 Remove the rear seat backs as described in Section 23.

55 Remove the side shelf trim panels as described in this Section.

56 Remove the rear shock absorber upper mounting cover.

57 Unclip the seat back side anchor plate bracket.

58 Remove the luggage compartment rear trim panel as described in this Section.

59 Carefully pull the panel from the inner wheel arch and withdraw towards the front of the vehicle.

Refitting

60 Refitting is a reversal of removal. Tighten the seat belt mounting bolt to the specified torque.

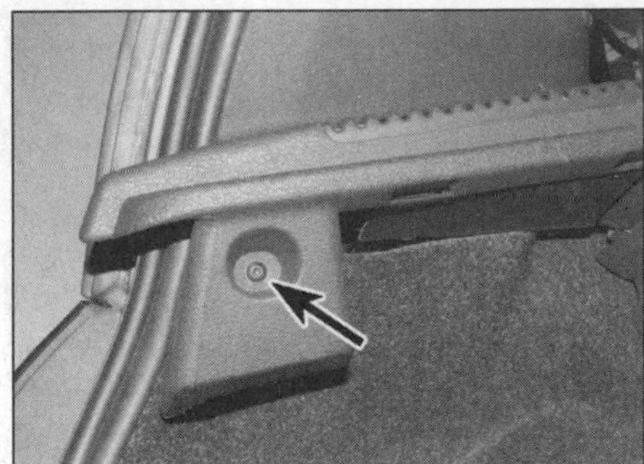

27.49c . . . and rear retaining screw (arrowed)

27.51b . . . then undo the retaining bolt (arrowed)

27.49b . . . upper retaining clip (arrowed) . . .

Roof console panel

Removal

61 Remove the interior courtesy light assembly as described in Chapter 12, Section 10.

62 Unclip the console from the headlining, then slide it away from the windscreen to remove **(see illustration)**.

63 Where applicable, disconnect any wiring connectors as the panel is removed.

Refitting

64 Refitting is a reversal of removal.

Luggage area rear trim panel

65 The luggage compartment rear trim panel has four securing screws, it can then be lifted upwards to release the retaining clips on the upper edge. Withdraw the trim panel from the rear of the luggage compartment.

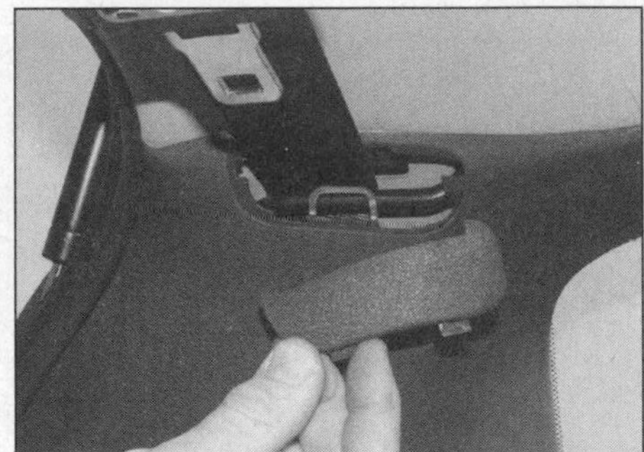

27.51a Unclip the seat belt plastic trim . . .

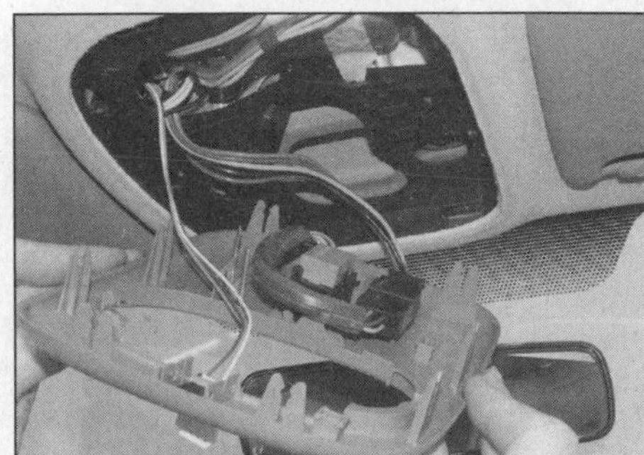

27.62 Withdrawing the roof console panel

27.66 Removing the tailgate trim panel

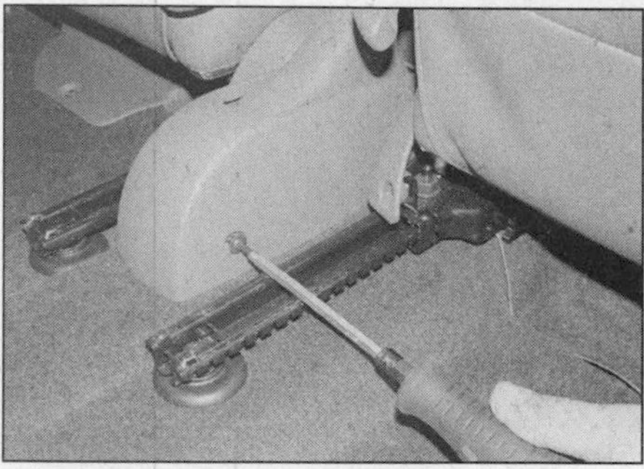
27.68a Undo the securing screws . . .

27.68b . . . and lift the trim from the handbrake

Tailgate trim panel

66 The panel is secured by one retaining screw and a number of plastic clips around the panel. Carefully pull the panel from the tailgate to release the clips **(see illustration)**, or release the clips using a forked tool.

Front seat trim panels

67 The seat side trim panels are secured by a single screw, then clipped in place. Removal and refitting are self-evident.

Handbrake lever trim

68 Move the two front seats as far forwards as possible. Undo the two securing screws from the rear of the handbrake trim, then push the trim forwards to remove **(see illustrations)**.

28 Centre console – removal and refitting

Warning: On models fitted with seat belt pretensioners, de-activate the pretensioner system as described in Section 25.

Removal

1 Disconnect the battery negative lead, then unclip the trim panel from below the heater control panel **(see illustration)** .

2 Remove the ashtray from the centre console, then unclip the cigarette lighter surround from the console **(see illustrations)**. Disconnect the wiring connector on removal.

3 On models fitted with a manual gearbox, unclip the gear lever gaiter from the centre console **(see illustration)**.

4 On models fitted with automatic transmission, unclip the selector lever surround from the centre console. Where applicable, undo the retaining screws.

5 Release the securing clips (one each side) at the front of the console **(see illustration)**.

6 Pull the centre console back towards the rear of the vehicle, releasing it from the Velcro pad which holds it in place **(see illustration)**. Where applicable, take care not to strain any wiring.

7 Lift the centre console over the gear lever and gaiter (or selector lever surround and selector lever), and withdraw it from the car.

Refitting

8 Refitting is a reversal of removal.

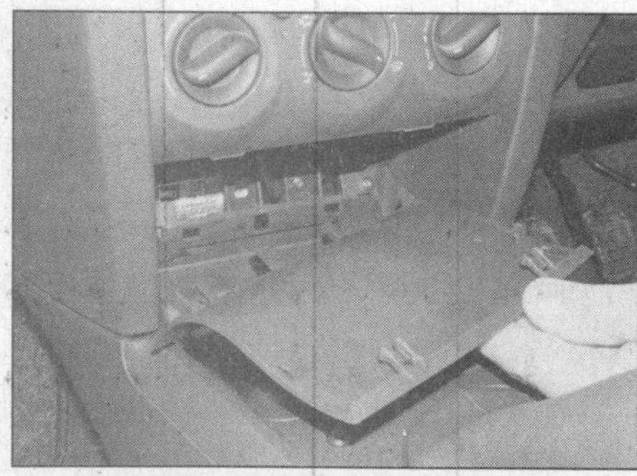
28.1 Unclipping the trim panel from below the heater control panel

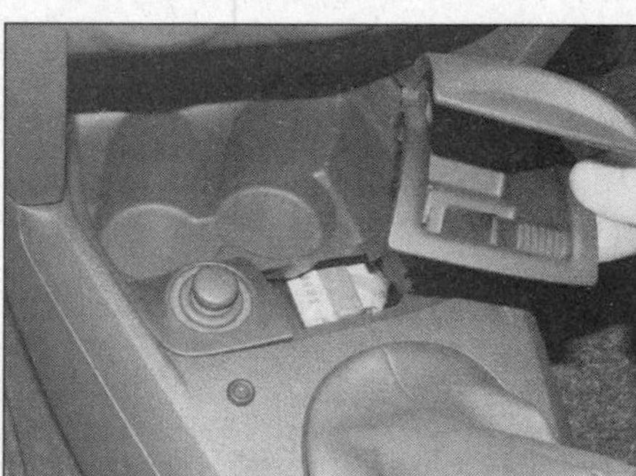
28.2a Lift out the ashtray . . .

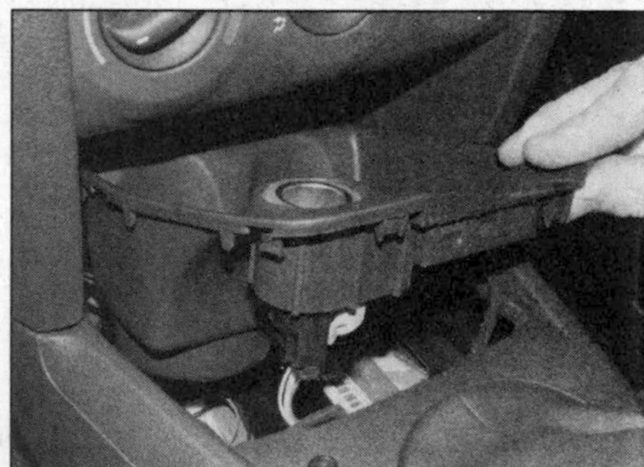
28.2b . . . then unclip the cigarette lighter surround from the console

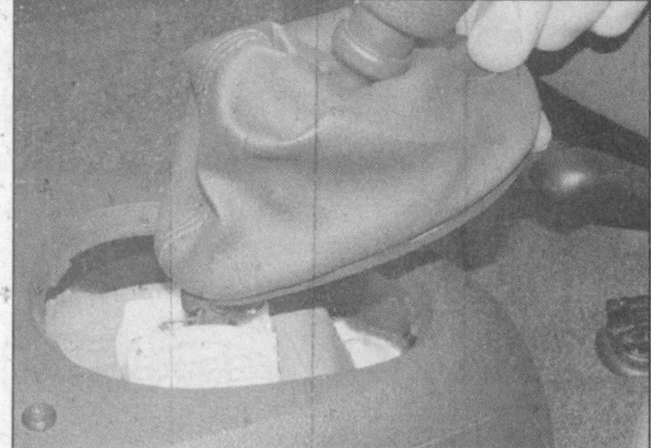
28.3 Unclipping the gear lever gaiter from the centre console

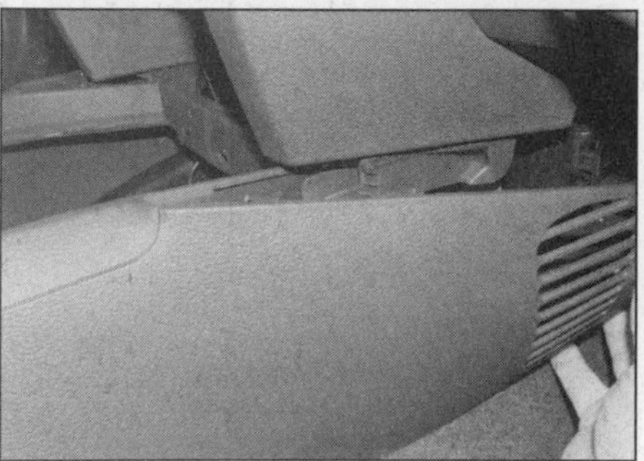
28.5 Unclip the front edges of the centre console

28.6 Withdraw the centre console and release the Velcro pad (arrowed)

29.2 Unclip and withdraw the upper shroud

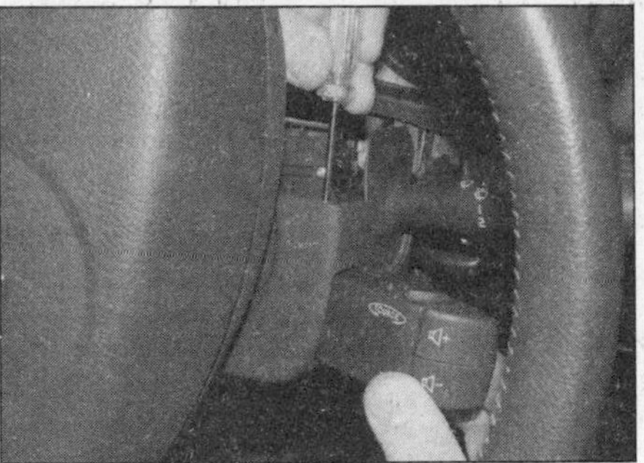

29.3a Release the radio control stalk . . .

29.3b . . . by pressing down on the securing clip (arrowed)

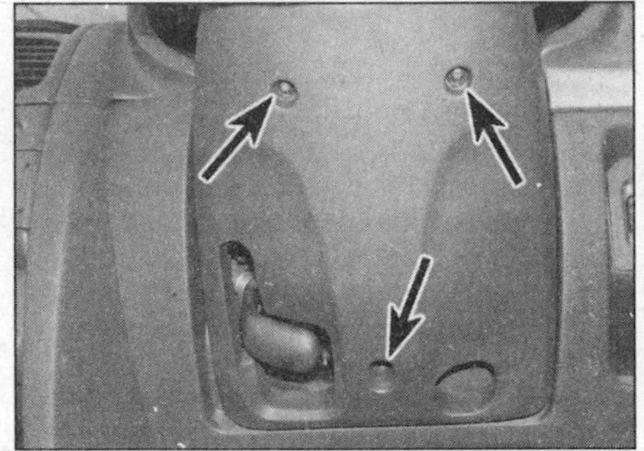

29.4 Unscrew the lower retaining screws (arrowed)

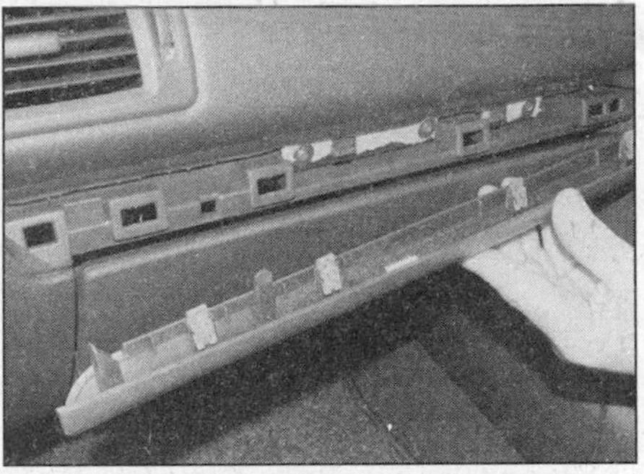

29.7a Unclip the trim from the left-hand side of the facia . . .

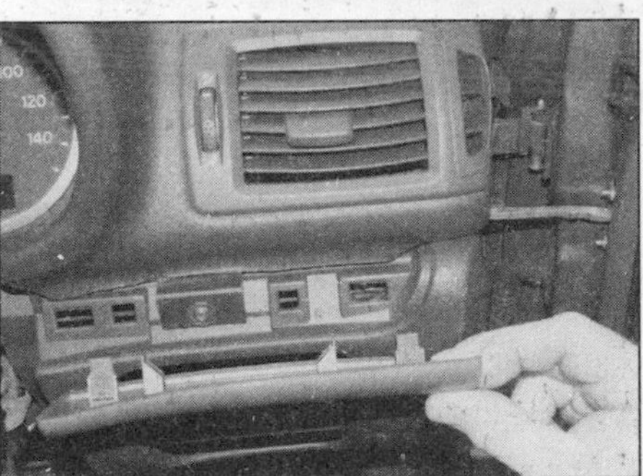

29.7b . . . and the trim from the right-hand side

29 Facia panels and components – removal and refitting

Warning: Before carrying out any work on the facia panel, read and follow the precautions given in Chapter 12, Section 27, on airbags.

Steering column shrouds

Removal

1 Release the steering column height lever and lower the steering column as far as it will go. Remove the ignition switch.

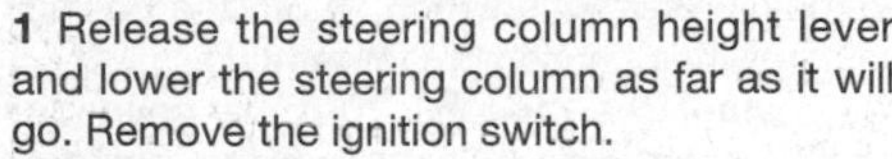

2 Unclip the upper shroud from the steering column **(see illustration)**.

3 Using a small screwdriver, release the retaining clip and withdraw the radio control stalk from the steering column **(see illustrations).** Disconnect the wiring connector on removal.

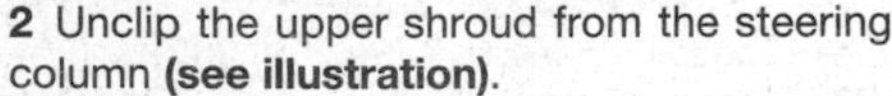

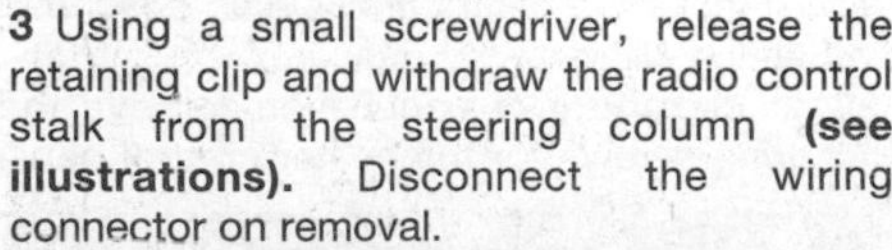

4 Working under the steering column, unscrew the three securing screws and withdraw the lower shroud from the steering column **(see illustration)**.

Refitting

5 Refitting is a reversal of removal.

Upper facia trim panel

Removal

6 Remove the A-pillar trim panels as described in Section 27 and the steering column shrouds as described in this Section.

7 Carefully unclip the trim from above the glovebox and the trim from above the headlight beam adjusting switch to locate the upper facia retaining screws **(see illustrations)**.

8 Undo the four securing screws from behind the trim panels and two from below the instrument panel **(see illustrations)**.

9 Undo the three screws along the top edge of the facia near to the windscreen and one

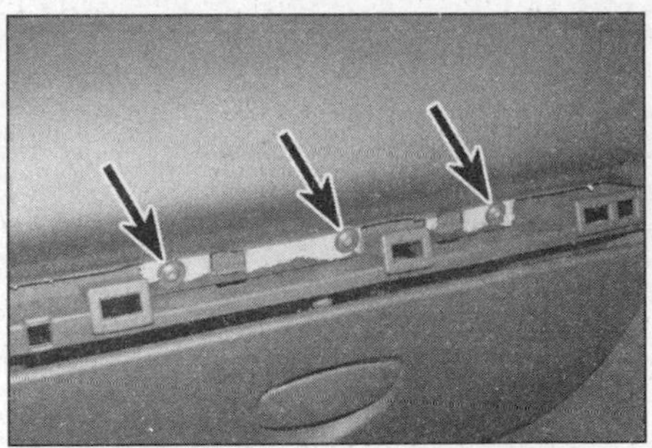

29.8a Remove the securing screws (arrowed) from the left-hand side of the facia . . .

29..8b . . . the right-hand side . . .

29.8c . . . and the two screws (arrowed) from below the instrument panel

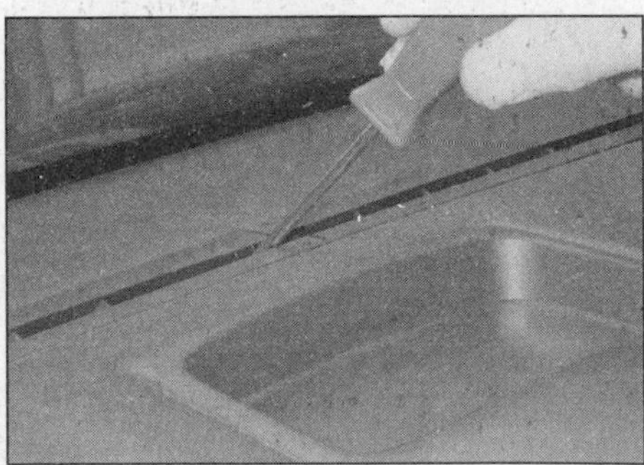

29.9a Unscrewing an upper facia trim panel top securing screw . . .

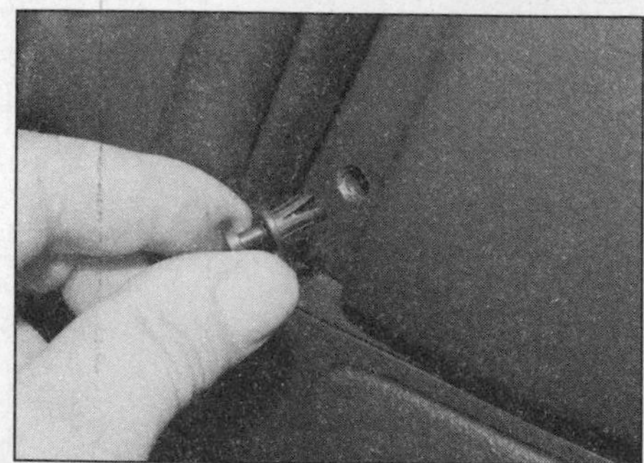
29.9b . . . and side securing screw

29.10 Removing the upper facia trim panel

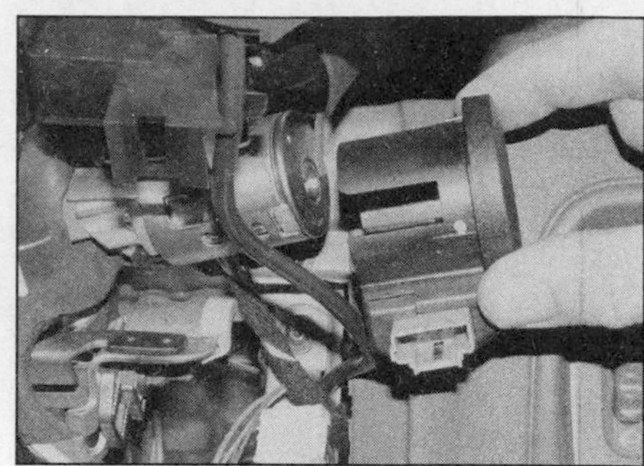
29.19 Unclipping the immobiliser antenna ring from the ignition switch

plastic screw/clip at each end of the facia **(see illustrations)**.

10 With the aid of an assistant, slide the upper facia panel towards you, away from the windscreen, to remove from the lower part of the facia **(see illustration)**.

Refitting

11 Refitting is a reversal of removal.

Heater ducts and vents

12 Refer to Chapter 3.

Glovebox lid

Note: *Check with your Renault dealer for availability of parts. The glovebox lid is held in position in the facia by four rivets.*

Removal

13 Drill out the four rivets from along the lower edge of the glovebox lid.

14 Open the glovebox and slide the two hinge/stays out from the facia panel and remove the glovebox lid from the vehicle.

Refitting

15 Refitting is a reversal of removal.

Complete facia assembly

Note: *This is an involved procedure, which is likely to take some time. It is advisable to make careful notes as the procedure progresses, to ensure correct refitting of all components, and correct routing of all wiring, etc. Specific details of fixings and components may vary from model to model, but the following will serve as a guide. Provided plenty of time is allowed, removal of the facia assembly should not present any problems.*

Removal

16 Disconnect the battery negative lead.

17 Remove the steering wheel as described in Chapter 10.

18 Remove the upper facia trim panel and steering column shrouds as described previously in this Section.

19 Unclip the immobiliser antenna ring from around the ignition switch and disconnect the wiring connector **(see illustration)**.

20 Lift the instrument panel up and unclip it from the facia, disconnect the wiring block connectors on removal **(see illustration)**. See Chapter 12, Section 12, for further information on the instrument panel.

21 Release the retaining clips and withdraw the auxiliary display, and disconnect the wiring connectors **(see illustration)**. See Chapter 12, Section 14, for further information on the auxiliary display.

22 Disconnect the wiring connector from the passenger airbag assembly, then undo the mounting screws to remove, with reference to Chapter 12, Section 28.

23 Remove the screws along the top of the reinforcement beam behind the facia, each screw secures an earth wire **(see illustration)**.

24 Disconnect the wiring connectors from the tweeters at each end of the facia **(see illustration)**.

25 Unclip the switch trim panel and disconnect the wiring block connector as it is removed **(see illustration)**. Note the position of the wiring connectors for refitting.

26 Using the special tool, remove the radio/cassette and disconnect the wiring as described in Chapter 12, Section 23.

27 Remove the centre console as described in Section 28.

28 Unclip the trim panel then remove the securing screws for the heater control panel

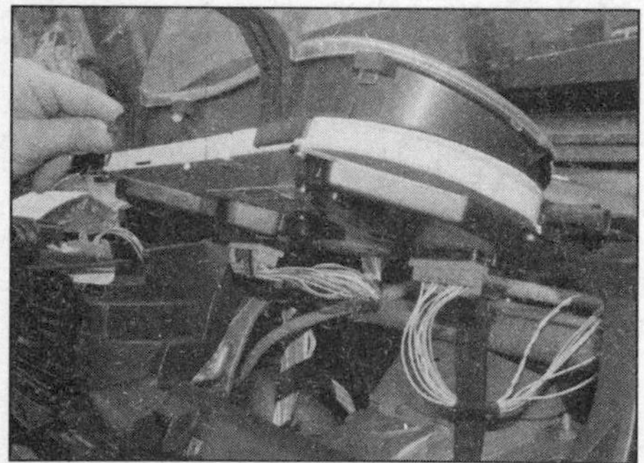
29.20 Hinge the instrument panel up to unclip from the facia

29.21 Release the retaining clips (arrowed) for the auxiliary display unit

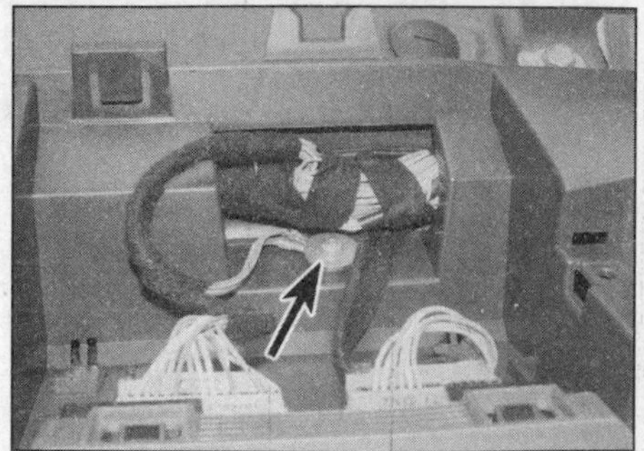
29.23 Release the earth wire retaining screws (one shown)

29.24 Disconnecting one of the tweeters

29.25 Unclipping the switch panel from the facia

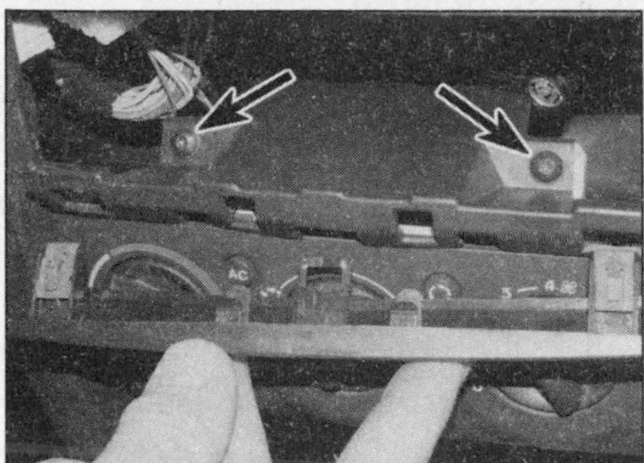
29.28 Unclip trim panel and remove retaining screws (arrowed)

29.30 Unclipping the headlight adjustment switch panel from the facia

29.31 Disconnect the ignition switch wiring block connector (arrowed)

29.33 Unclipping the fusebox cover

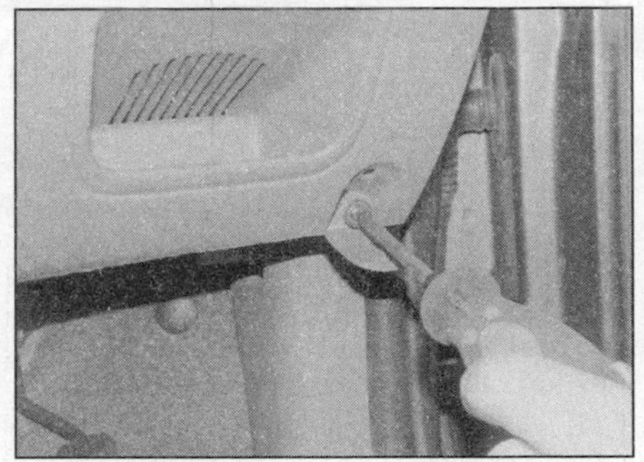
29.34 Removing one of the lower facia panel securing screws

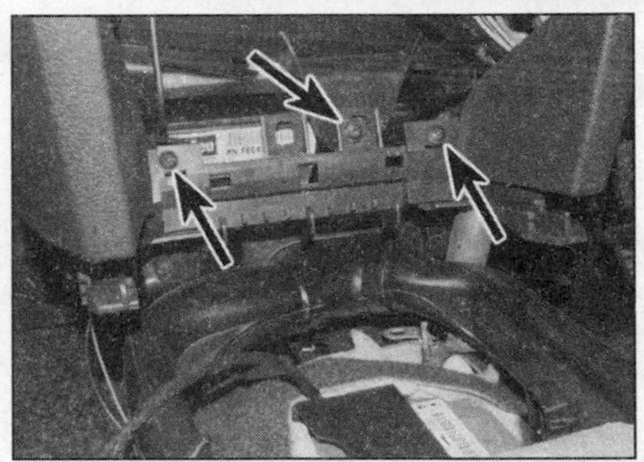
29.35 Undo the lower centre securing screws (arrowed)

(see illustration), and unclip it from the facia with reference to Chapter 3.

29 Remove the steering column switches as described in Chapter 12, Section 6.

30 Unclip the headlight height adjustment switch trim from the facia panel and disconnect the wiring connector **(see illustration)**.

31 Slide the retaining clip up and disconnect the wiring block connector for the ignition switch **(see illustration)**.

32 Slacken and remove the steering column as described in Chapter 10.

33 Remove the cover from the fusebox at the end of the facia **(see illustration)**.

34 Unclip the covers from the lower edge of the facia panel and undo the securing screws (one at each end of the facia) **(see illustration)**.

35 Undo the facia lower securing screws from the heater unit at the centre **(see illustration)**.

36 Make a final check to ensure that all wires, cables and hoses are disconnected and moved clear of the facia.

37 With the aid of an assistant, carefully lift and withdraw the right-hand side of the facia assembly from the bulkhead first. Remove the facia from the car through one of the front doors.

38 If the facia is difficult to remove, do not use excessive force – check that all necessary wiring has been disconnected, and that the harnesses are not fouling surrounding components.

Refitting

39 Refitting is a reversal of removal, bearing in mind the following points.

40 As the facia assembly is offered to the bulkhead, ensure that none of the wiring harnesses, plugs, cables or hoses are trapped.

41 Ensure that all wiring connectors are securely reconnected, and that all connector securing clips are in place.

42 On completion, check that all switches, lights and instruments function correctly.

Chapter 12
Body electrical system

Contents

Degrees of difficulty

Easy, suitable for novice with little experience 	**Fairly easy,** suitable for beginner with some experience 	**Fairly difficult,** suitable for competent DIY mechanic 	**Difficult,** suitable for experienced DIY mechanic 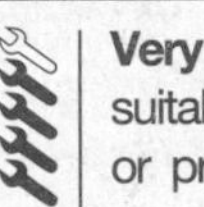	**Very difficult,** suitable for expert DIY or professional

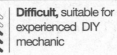

Specifications

General

System type	12 volt, negative earth

Bulbs

	Wattage
Exterior lights	
Dual headlight with halogen bulbs:	
Main beam	55 (H1 type*)
Dip Beam	55 (H7 type*)
Dual headlight with Xenon bulbs:	
Main beam	55 (H7 type*)
Dip Beam	37 (D2S type*)
Front foglight	55 (H1 type)
Front sidelight	5
Direction indicator (orange-coloured)	21
Direction indicator side repeater	5
Stop/tail	21/5
Reversing light	21
Rear foglight	21
Rear sidelight	5
Number plate light	5
Interior light	
Courtesy lights	
Bayonet	5
Festoon	7
Luggage compartment light (festoon)	7
Glovebox illumination light	5

*** Note***: As the headlights have plastic lenses,* ***anti-UV type bulbs*** *are used (the headlight may be damaged if any other type of H1, H4, or H7 bulb is used). Do not touch the glass of the bulbs, hold it by the base only.*

Torque wrench setting

	Nm	lbf ft
Passenger airbag securing bolts	6	4

1 General information and precautions

Warning: Before carrying out any work on the electrical system, read through the precautions given in 'Safety first!' at the beginning of this manual, and in Chapter 5A.

The electrical system is of 12 volt negative earth type. Power for the lights and all electrical accessories is supplied by a lead-acid type battery, which is charged by the alternator.

This Chapter covers repair and service procedures for the various electrical components not associated with engine. Information on the battery, alternator and starter motor can be found in Chapter 5A.

It should be noted that, prior to working on any component in the electrical system, the battery negative terminal should first be disconnected, to prevent the possibility of electrical short-circuits and/or fires.

Caution: Before disconnecting the battery, refer to the information given in 'Disconnecting the battery' in the Reference Section of this manual.

2 Electrical fault finding – general information

Note: *Refer to the precautions given in 'Safety first!' and at the beginning of Chapter 5A before starting work. The following tests relate to testing of the main electrical circuits, and should not be used to test delicate electronic circuits (such as anti-lock braking systems), particularly where an electronic control module is used.*

General

1 A typical electrical circuit consists of an electrical component, any switches, relays, motors, fuses, fusible links or circuit breakers related to that component, and the wiring and connectors which link the component to both the battery and the chassis. To help to pinpoint a problem in an electrical circuit, wiring diagrams are included at the end of this Chapter.

2 Before attempting to diagnose an electrical fault, first study the appropriate wiring diagram, to obtain a more complete understanding of the components included in the particular circuit concerned. The possible sources of a fault can be narrowed down by noting whether other components related to the circuit are operating properly. If several components or circuits fail at one time, the problem is likely to be related to a shared fuse or earth connection.

3 Electrical problems usually stem from simple causes, such as loose or corroded connections, a faulty earth connection, a blown fuse, a melted fusible link, or a faulty relay (refer to Section 4 for details of testing relays). Visually inspect the condition of all fuses, wires and connections in a problem circuit before testing the components. Use the wiring diagrams to determine which terminal connections will need to be checked, in order to pinpoint the trouble-spot.

4 The basic tools required for electrical fault finding include a circuit tester or voltmeter (a 12 volt bulb with a set of test leads can also be used for certain tests); a self-powered test light (sometimes known as a continuity tester); an ohmmeter (to measure resistance); a battery and set of test leads; and a jumper wire, preferably with a circuit breaker or fuse incorporated, which can be used to bypass suspect wires or electrical components. Before attempting to locate a problem with test instruments, use the wiring diagram to determine where to make the connections.

5 To find the source of an intermittent wiring fault (usually due to a poor or dirty connection, or damaged wiring insulation), a 'wiggle' test can be performed on the wiring. This involves wiggling the wiring by hand, to see if the fault occurs as the wiring is moved. It should be possible to narrow down the source of the fault to a particular section of wiring. This method of testing can be used in conjunction with any of the tests described in the following sub-Sections.

6 Apart from problems due to poor connections, two basic types of fault can occur in an electrical circuit – open-circuit, or short-circuit.

7 Open-circuit faults are caused by a break somewhere in the circuit, which prevents current from flowing. An open-circuit fault will prevent a component from working, but will not cause the relevant circuit fuse to blow.

8 Short-circuit faults are caused by a 'short' somewhere in the circuit, which allows the current flowing in the circuit to 'escape' along an alternative route, usually to earth. Short-circuit faults are normally caused by a breakdown in wiring insulation, which allows a feed wire to touch either another wire, or an earthed component such as the bodyshell. A short-circuit fault will normally cause the relevant circuit fuse to blow.

Finding an open-circuit

9 To check for an open-circuit, connect one lead of a circuit tester or voltmeter to either the negative battery terminal or a known good earth.

10 Connect the other lead to a connector in the circuit being tested, preferably nearest to the battery or fuse.

11 Switch on the circuit, bearing in mind that some circuits are live only when the ignition switch is moved to a particular position.

12 If voltage is present (indicated either by the tester bulb lighting or a voltmeter reading, as applicable), this means that the section of the circuit between the relevant connector and the battery is problem-free.

13 Continue to check the remainder of the circuit in the same fashion.

14 When a point is reached at which no voltage is present, the problem must lie between that point and the previous test point with voltage. Most problems can be traced to a broken, corroded or loose connection.

Finding a short-circuit

15 To check for a short-circuit, first disconnect the load(s) from the circuit (loads are the components which draw current from a circuit, such as bulbs, motors, heating elements, etc).

16 Remove the relevant fuse from the circuit, and connect a circuit tester or voltmeter to the fuse connections.

17 Switch on the circuit, bearing in mind that some circuits are live only when the ignition switch is moved to a particular position.

18 If voltage is present (indicated either by the tester bulb lighting or a voltmeter reading, as applicable), this means that there is a short-circuit.

19 If no voltage is present, but the fuse still blows with the load(s) connected, this indicates an internal fault in the load(s).

Finding an earth fault

20 The battery negative terminal is connected to 'earth' – the metal of the engine/transmission unit and the car body – and most systems are wired so that they only receive a positive feed, the current returning via the metal of the car body. This means that the component mounting and the body form part of that circuit. Loose or corroded mountings can therefore cause a range of electrical faults, ranging from total failure of a circuit, to a puzzling partial fault. In particular, lights may shine dimly (especially when another circuit sharing the same earth point is in operation), motors (eg, wiper motors or the radiator cooling fan motor) may run slowly, and the operation of one circuit may have an apparently-unrelated effect on another. Note that on many vehicles, earth straps are used between certain components, such as the engine/transmission and the body, usually where there is no metal-to-metal contact between components, due to flexible rubber mountings, etc.

21 To check whether a component is properly earthed, disconnect the battery, and connect one lead of an ohmmeter to a known good earth point. Connect the other lead to the wire or earth connection being tested. The resistance reading should be zero; if not, check the connection as follows.

22 If an earth connection is thought to be faulty, dismantle the connection, and clean back to bare metal both the bodyshell and the wire terminal or the component earth connection mating surface. Be careful to remove all traces of dirt and corrosion, then use a knife to trim away any paint, so that a clean metal-to-metal joint is made. On reassembly, tighten the joint fasteners securely; if a wire terminal is being refitted, use serrated washers between the terminal and the bodyshell, to ensure a clean and secure connection. When the connection is remade, prevent the onset of corrosion in the future by applying a coat of petroleum jelly or silicone-based grease, or by spraying on (at regular intervals) a proprietary ignition sealer.

3 Fusebox – removal and refitting

Note: *Additional fuses are located in an auxiliary fusebox under the bonnet* ***(see illustrations 4.4a and 4.4b)****.*

Removal

1 Disconnect the battery negative lead.
2 Unclip the fusebox cover from the left-hand side of the facia panel **(see illustration)**.
3 Unscrew the two securing screws from the fusebox **(see illustration)**.
4 Carefully lower the fusebox from under the facia.

Refitting

5 Refitting is a reversal of removal.

3.2 Unclip the lower part of the fusebox cover to remove

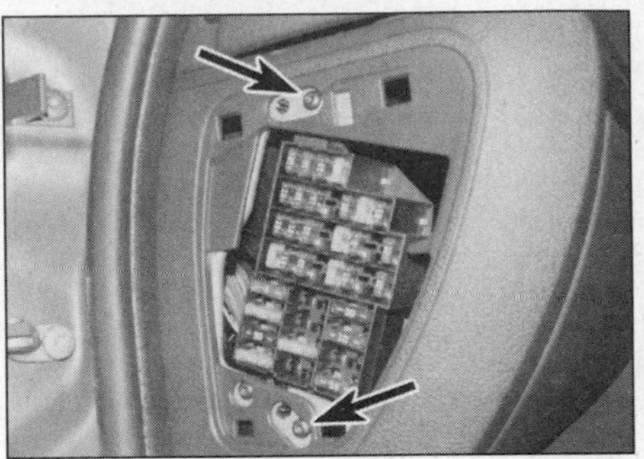

3.3 Undo the two securing screws (arrowed)

4 Fuses and relays – testing and renewal

Fuses

1 Fuses are designed to break a circuit when a predetermined current is reached, in order to protect components and wiring which could be damaged by excessive current flow. Any excessive current flow will be due to a fault in the circuit, usually a short-circuit (see Section 2).
2 The main fuses are located in the fusebox, in the left-hand side of the facia panel **(see illustration)**.
3 For access to the fuses, unclip the cover and withdraw from the facia. The circuits protected by the fuses are marked on a the inside of the fusebox cover.
4 Additional fuses are located in an auxiliary fusebox under the bonnet **(see illustrations)**, beneath a plastic cover alongside the battery on the left-hand side of the engine compartment. For access to these fuses, unclip the plastic cover from the fusebox. The circuits protected by the fuses are marked on the inside of the panel cover. The fuse for the radio/cassette player is mounted on the rear of the unit.
5 A blown fuse can be recognised from its melted or broken wire.
6 To remove a fuse, first ensure that the relevant circuit is switched off.
7 Using the plastic tool provided on the fusebox cover, pull the fuse from its location.
8 Spare fuses are provided on the inside of the cover.
9 Before renewing a blown fuse, trace and rectify the cause, and always use a fuse of the correct rating. Never substitute a fuse of a higher rating, or make temporary repairs using wire or metal foil; more serious damage, or even fire, could result.
10 Note that the fuses are colour-coded as follows. Refer to the wiring diagrams for details of the fuse ratings and the circuits protected.

Colour	Rating
Orange	*5A*
Red	*10A*
Blue	*15A*
Yellow	*20A*
Clear or white	*25A*
Green	*30A*

Relays

11 A relay is an electrically-operated switch, which is used for the following reasons.

a) A relay can switch a heavy current remotely from the circuit in which the current is flowing, therefore allowing the use of lighter gauge wiring and switch contacts.
b) A relay can receive more than one control input, unlike a mechanical switch.
c) A relay can have a 'timer' function – for example, the intermittent wiper relay.

12 Some of the relays are located inside the vehicle, under the facia on the left-hand side **(see illustrations)**, along with the multi-timer unit – see Section 5.
13 Other relays are located in the engine compartment fusebox, on the left-hand side front, of the engine compartment **(see illustrations 4.4a and 4.4b)**. Depending on model, the box contains relays for the fuel injection system, ignition, cooling fan, air conditioning and the power steering pump.
14 If a circuit controlled by a relay develops a

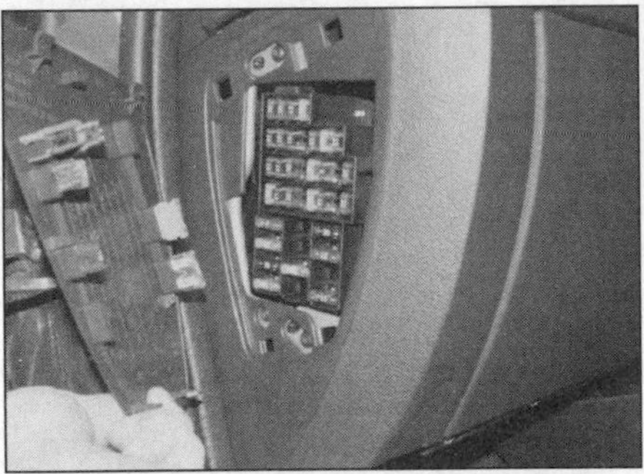

4.2 Most fuses are located behind the cover on the left-hand side of the facia

4.4a Unclip the cover in the engine compartment . . .

4.4b . . . to access other fuses and relays

4.12a Disconnecting relay from the multi-timer control unit

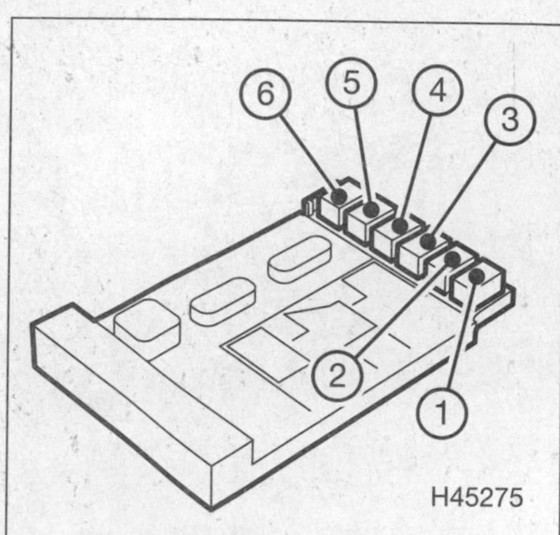

4.12b Identification of relays attached to the multi-timer unit

1 *Main daytime running lights relay*
2 *Daytime running sidelights relay*
3 *Front foglights relay*
4 *Daytime running lights code relay*
5 *Headlight washer pump relay*
6 *Headlight washer pump relay*

fault, and the relay is suspect, operate the circuit. If the relay is functioning, it should be possible to hear the relay click as it is energised. If this is the case, the fault lies with the components or wiring in the system. If the relay is not being energised, then either the relay is not receiving a switching voltage, or the relay itself is faulty (do not overlook the relay socket terminals when tracing faults). Testing is by the substitution of a known good unit, but be careful; while some relays are identical in appearance and in operation, others look similar, but perform different functions.

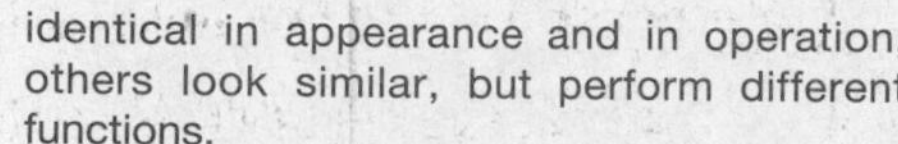

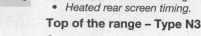

5 Multi-timer unit – removal, refitting and general information

General information

1 The multi-timer unit is located under the left-hand side of the facia panel, along with the relays **(see illustration).** Note that once removed, the immobiliser, remote control, engine configuration, etc, will all need reprogramming, if this is not done correctly it will prevent the vehicle from starting. Because of the specialised equipment required, this may have to be entrusted to your local Renault dealer.

2 For models covered in this manual, there are two types of multi-timer units available, depending on the equipment level in the vehicle.

Bottom of the range – Type N2

Controlling:

- *Indicators and hazard warning lights.*
- *Front and rear wipers.*
- *Door and window controls.*
- *Door locking when driving (unlocking on impact).*
- *Door opening indicator light.*
- *Central door locking indicator light.*
- *Timed courtesy lighting.*
- *Radio frequency remote control.*
- *One-touch windows.*
- *Engine immobiliser.*
- *Positive after ignition supply/starter control.*
- *Passenger compartment horn (alarm).*
- *Alarm connections.*
- *Multiplex network interface.*
- *Interface with fault finding.*
- *Heated rear screen timing.*

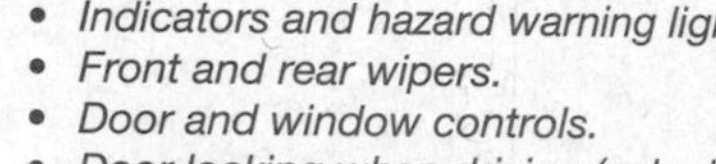

Top of the range – Type N3

Controlling (in addition to the bottom of the range – type N2):

- *Daytime running lights.*
- *Light controls.*
- *Light sensors.*
- *Headlight washer controls.*
- *Rain sensors.*

Removal

3 Disconnect the battery negative lead.

4 Open the passenger side front door and carefully prise off the bonnet release lever **(see illustration).**

5 Peel back the door seal and unclip the inner sill trim panel **(see illustration).**

6 Unclip the cover from the fusebox, at the left-hand end of the facia panel and undo the multi-timer unit retaining screw **(see illustration).**

7 Working under the left-hand end of the facia panel, undo the lower retaining bolt and withdraw the retaining bracket **(see illustration).**

8 Release the securing clip at the top of the multi-timer unit and lower it out from under the facia.

5.1 Multi-timer unit under left-hand side of facia

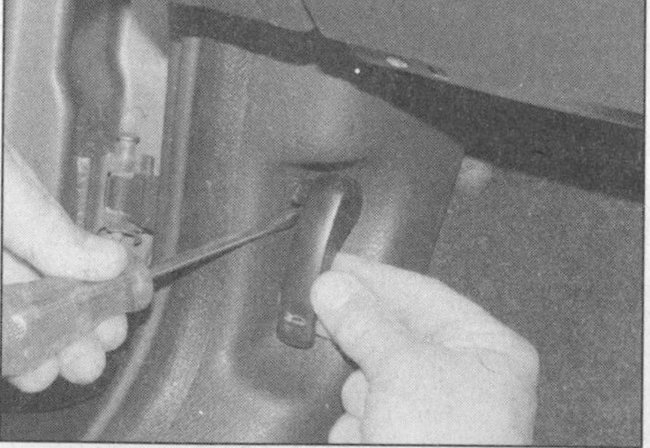

5.4 Prise off the bonnet release lever

5.5 Unclipping the inner sill trim panel

5.6 Remove the multi-timer unit retaining screw (arrowed)

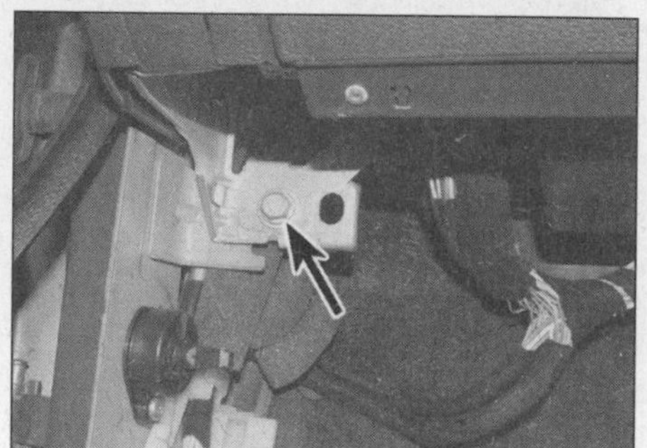

5.7a Remove the retaining bolt (arrowed) . . .

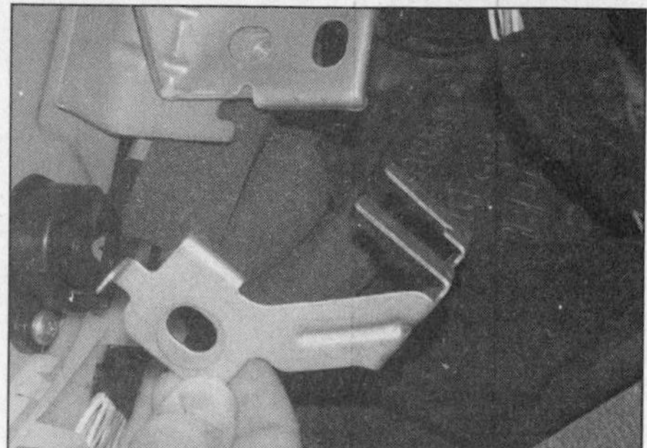

5.7b . . . and withdraw the mounting bracket

5.9 Disconnecting the wiring connectors from the multi-timer unit

9 The relay(s) can now be unclipped from the end of the multi-timer unit and the wiring block connectors disconnected **(see illustration)**.

Refitting

10 Refitting is a reversal of removal, bearing in mind the following points.
11 Make sure that the multi-timer unit is located correctly behind the facia panel.
12 Ensure that the wiring is routed correctly.

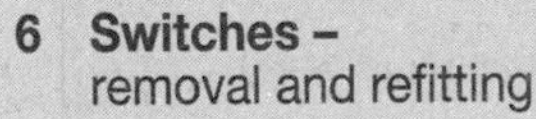

6 Switches – removal and refitting

Ignition switch and immobiliser

Removal

1 Disconnect the battery negative lead.

6.3 Unclip the immobiliser from around the ignition switch

2 Remove the steering column shrouds as described in Chapter 11, Section 29.
3 Unclip the immobiliser from around the ignition switch, then disconnect the wiring connector **(see illustration)**.
4 Follow the switch wiring behind the facia, and disconnect the wiring connectors **(see illustration)**. Take note of the routing of the wiring.
5 Insert the ignition key into the switch, and turn it midway between A and M (arrow).
6 Using a Torx key, remove the grub screw securing the switch assembly to the steering column **(see illustration)**.
7 Using a screwdriver, depress the securing clip located at the bottom of the switch assembly, then pull the assembly from the steering column using the key **(see illustration)**.
8 Feed the wiring through the steering column as the switch is withdrawn **(see illustration)**.

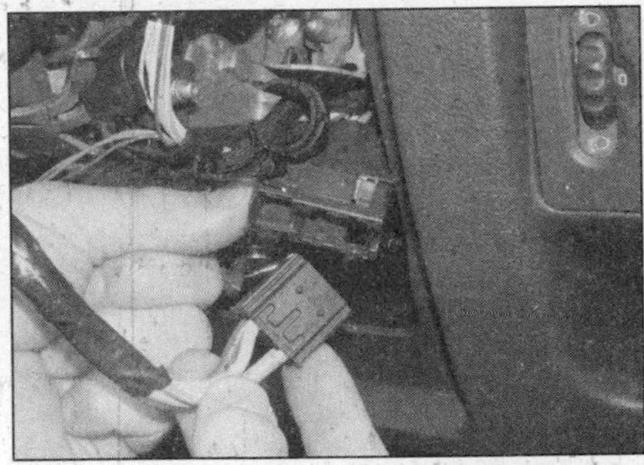

6.4 Disconnecting the wiring connector from ignition switch

Refitting

9 Refitting is a reversal of removal, bearing in mind the following points.
10 Note that the switch will only fit in one position.
11 Ensure that the switch wiring is routed as noted before removal.

Wash/wipe stalk switch

Removal

12 Disconnect the battery negative lead.
13 Remove the steering column shrouds as described in Chapter 11, Section 29. Unclip the immobiliser from around the ignition switch **(see illustration)**.
14 Disconnect the wiring plug from the switch assembly **(see illustration)**.
15 Unscrew the two securing screws and withdraw the switch from the steering column **(see illustrations)**.

6.6 Unscrew the ignition switch grub screw

6.7 Depressing the ignition switch securing clip

6.8 Feeding the wiring out through the housing

6.13 Unclipping the immobiliser from around the ignition switch

6.14 Disconnect the wiring plug from the switch

6.15a Unscrew the securing screws (arrowed) . . .

6.15b . . . and withdraw the stalk switch

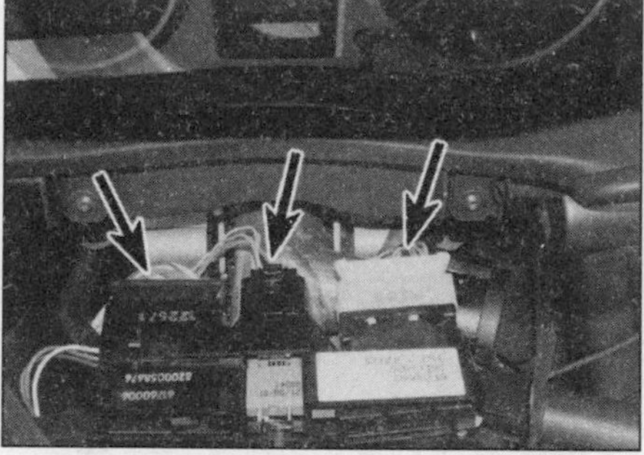
6.20 Disconnect the wiring plugs (arrowed) from the switch assembly

6.21a Align the 0 with the mark (arrowed) on the rotary switch

Refitting

16 Refitting is a reversal of removal.

Lights/indicators/horn stalk

17 Proceed as just described for the wash/wipe stalk switch, except ignore the procedure for unclipping the immobiliser from around the ignition switch.

Stalk switch assembly

Removal

18 Remove the steering wheel as described in Chapter 10, Section 14.

19 Remove the steering column shrouds as described in Chapter 11, Section 29.

20 Disconnect the wiring plugs from the switches **(see illustration)**.

21 Note: *Before removing the assembly, the position of the rotary switch MUST be noted. Either by ensuring the wheels are in the straight-ahead position or by checking that the 0 mark on the rotary switch is in line with the fixed reference mark* ***(see illustration).*** Slacken the retaining screw from the lower part of the switch assembly **(see illustration)**.

22 Release the clip at the upper part of the of the switch assembly, then withdraw the assembly from the steering column **(see illustrations)**.

Refitting

23 Refitting is a reversal of removal. **Note:** *Prior to refitting it is necessary to ensure that the contact unit is correctly centralised as noted before removal* ***(see illustration)****, with the front wheels pointing in the straight-ahead position.* Refit the steering wheel and steering column shrouds as described in their relevant Chapters.

Radio/cassette player control

24 Unclip the upper shroud from the steering column then, using a small screwdriver, release the retaining clip and withdraw the radio control stalk from the steering column. Disconnect the wiring connector on removal. See illustrations in Chapter 11, Section 29.

Heater-related switches

25 These switches are built into the heater control panel **(see illustration)**, remove the panel as described in Chapter 3, Section 13.

Headlight aim adjustment control

Removal

26 Using a screwdriver, carefully prise the control panel from the facia, taking care not to damage the facia trim **(see illustration)**.

27 Unclip the switche(s) from the rear of the

6.21b Slacken the retaining screw (arrowed)

6.22a Release the retaining clip (arrowed) . . .

6.22b . . . to withdraw the switch assembly from the column

6.23 Masking tape used to hold rotary switch in position

6.25 Switches are located in the heater control panel

6.26 Carefully prise the control panel from the facia

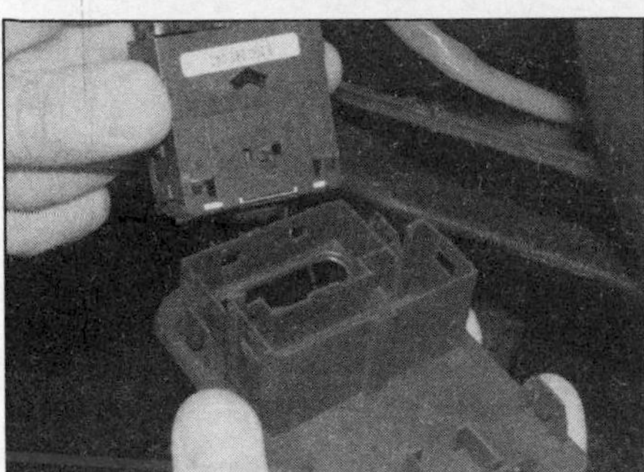
6.27 Unclip the switch from the rear of the panel

6.29 Unclip the switch from rear of the panel

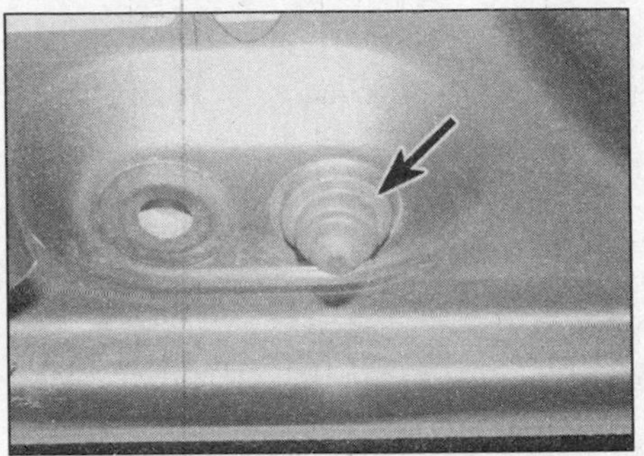
6.34 Unclip the rubber cover (arrowed) from the courtesy light switch

control panel **(see illustration)**. Disconnect the wiring connector from the switches as required.

Refitting

28 Refitting is a reversal of removal.

Instrument panel illumination

29 The switch (where fitted) is located in the same control panel as the headlight aim adjustment control **(see illustration)**.

30 To remove the switch, proceed as described in paragraphs 26 to 28.

Electric window switches

31 Refer to Chapter 11, Section 17.

Courtesy light switches

Removal

32 The switches are located in the door pillars.

33 Disconnect the battery negative lead.

34 Pull the rubber cover from the switch **(see illustration)**.

35 Carefully prise the switch from the door pillar and disconnect the wiring plug **(see illustration)**. Take care not to allow the wiring to drop down into the door pillar while the switch is removed – tape it to the door pillar if necessary.

Refitting

36 Refitting is a reversal of removal. **Note:** *Fit the rubber cover to the switch before refitting it into the pillar **(see illustration)**.*

Hazard warning light switch

Removal

37 Using a screwdriver, carefully prise the switch panel from the facia, taking care not to damage the facia trim **(see illustration)**.

38 Unclip the switch from the panel **(see illustration)**. Disconnect the wiring connector from the switches as required.

Refitting

39 Refitting is a reversal of removal.

Heated rear window switch

Removal

40 Using a screwdriver, carefully prise the switch panel from the facia, taking care not to damage the facia trim **(see illustration 6.38)**.

41 Unclip the switch from the panel **(see illustration)**. Disconnect the wiring connector from the switches as required.

Refitting

42 Refitting is a reversal of removal.

Door locking switch

Removal

43 Using a screwdriver, carefully prise the switch panel from the facia, taking care not to damage the facia trim **(see illustration 6.38)**.

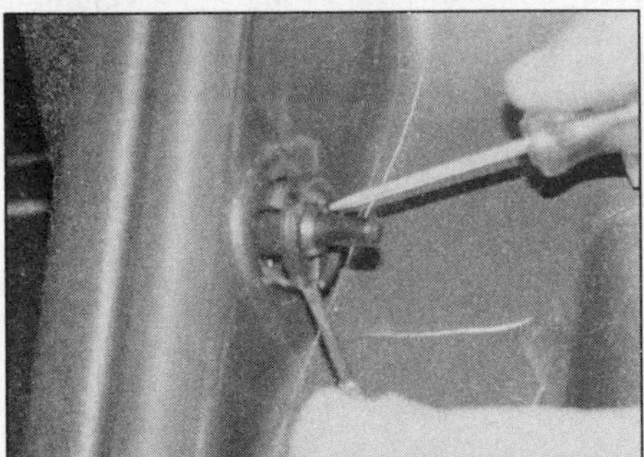
6.35 Using screwdrivers to release the switch from the door pillar

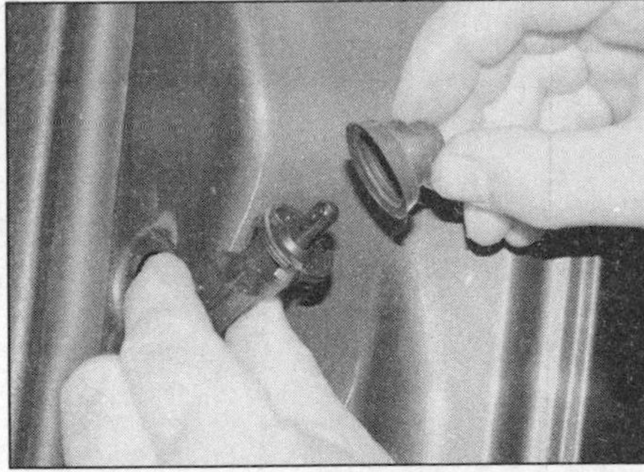
6.36 Fit the rubber cover to the switch before refitting the switch

6.37 Unclip the switch panel from the facia

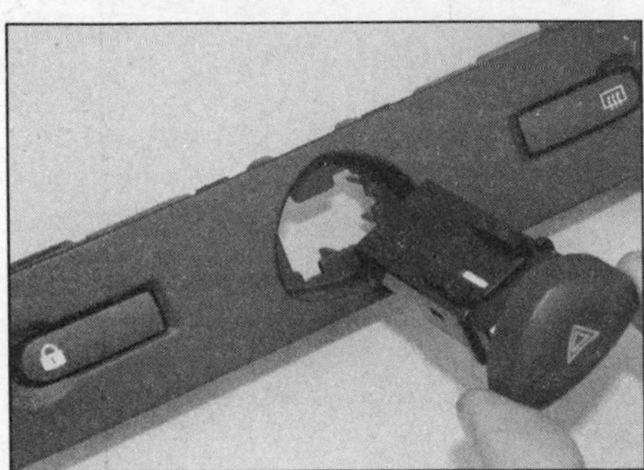
6.38 Unclip the hazard switch from the front of the switch panel

6.41 Unclip the heated rear window switch from the rear of the panel

6.44 Unclip the door locking switch from the rear of the panel

44 Unclip the switch from the panel **(see illustration)**. Disconnect the wiring connector from the switches as required.

Refitting

45 Refitting is a reversal of removal.

Luggage area light switch

Removal

46 The switch is part of the tailgate lock catch **(see illustration)**.

47 To remove the switch/lock catch assembly, carry out the procedure as described in Chapter 11, Section 15.

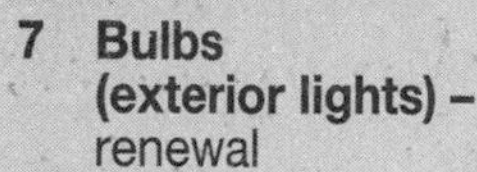

7 Bulbs (exterior lights) – renewal

General

1 Whenever a bulb is renewed, note the following points.

a) Disconnect the battery negative lead, or at least make sure that the lighting circuit is switched off, before starting work.

b) Remember that if the light has recently been in use, the bulb may be extremely hot.

c) Always check the bulb contacts and/or holder (as applicable). Ensure that there is clean metal-to-metal contact between the bulb contacts and the contacts in the holder, and/or the holder and the wiring plug. Clean off any corrosion or dirt before fitting a new bulb.

7.2 Unclip the rubber cover from the rear of the headlight unit

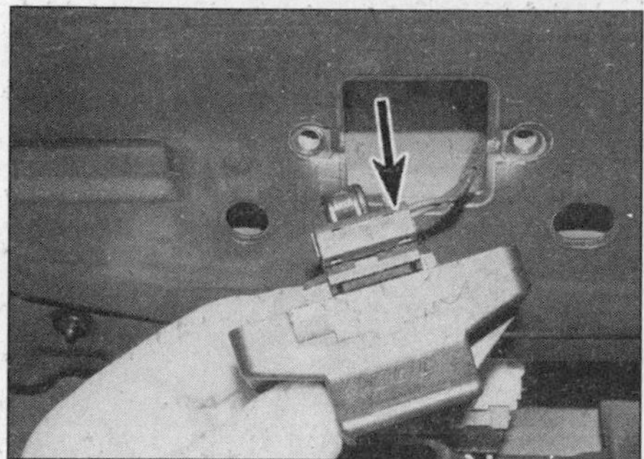

6.46 Luggage compartment light switch (arrowed)

d) Ensure that the new bulb is of the correct rating and that it is completely clean before fitting; this applies particularly to headlight bulbs.

Headlight (halogen)

Note: *Some headlights may vary slightly, depending on model. Check the specifications at the beginning of the Chapter for recommended bulb type. The headlight lenses are plastic and may melt if the correct bulbs are not fitted.*

Removal

2 Working in the engine compartment, remove the relevant rubber cover from the rear of the headlight **(see illustration)**.

3 For main beam bulb, disconnect the wiring connector from the rear of the headlight bulb. Release the bulb retaining spring clip and remove the bulb, without touching the glass **(see illustrations)**.

7.3a Disconnect the wiring plug from the rear of the headlight

4 For dipped beam bulb, withdraw the bulbholder and bulb from the headlight unit. Grasp the bulb, without touching the glass and carefully disconnect it from the wiring connector **(see illustrations)**.

Refitting

5 When handling the new bulb, use a tissue or clean cloth to avoid touching the glass with the fingers; moisture and grease from the skin can cause blackening and rapid failure of this type of bulb.

6 Refitting is a reversal of removal.

Headlight (Xenon)

Warning: Before carrying out any operations on Xenon headlight units, it is recommended that protective gloves and safety glasses are worn. It is essential that the wiring connectors are disconnected from the rear of the headlight unit, then wait until the computer module and bulbs have cooled down before removal. DO NOT switch the headlamps on with the bulb removed as it is harmful to the eyes.

7 Remove the headlight unit as described in Section 9.

8 Unclip the rubber cover from the rear of the headlight unit.

9 Turn the high voltage unit on the rear of the bulb anti-clockwise about an eighth of a turn and withdraw it from the bulb.

10 Turn the bulb locking ring anti-clockwise about an eighth of a turn and withdraw the bulb from the light unit. The external conductor of the bulb is fragile, take care not to damage or knock it.

Refitting

11 When handling the new bulb, use a tissue or clean cloth to avoid touching the glass with the fingers; moisture and grease from the skin can cause blackening and rapid failure of this type of bulb.

12 Refitting is a reversal of removal.

Front sidelight

Removal

13 Working in the engine compartment,

7.3b . . . then release the spring clip

7.4a Withdraw the bulbholder and bulb . . .

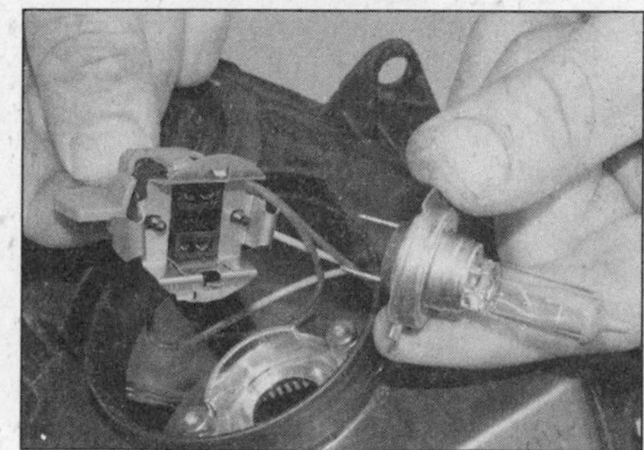

7.4b . . . then remove the bulb

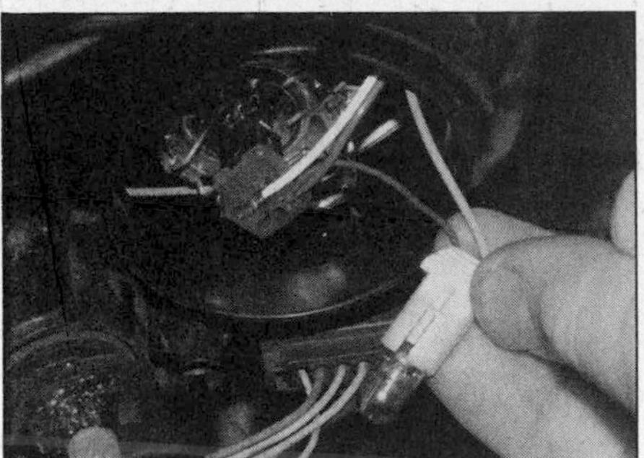
7.14 Removing the sidelight bulb and holder

unclip the cover from the rear of the light unit **(see illustration 7.2)**.

14 Withdraw the bulbholder from the rear of the headlight assembly **(see illustration)**.

15 The bulb is a push-fit (capless) in the bulbholder.

Refitting

16 Refitting is a reversal of removal, bearing in mind the following points.

17 Ensure that the cover is in good condition and is correctly fitted.

Front indicator

Removal

18 Working in the engine compartment, twist the bulbholder anti-clockwise, and remove it from the rear of the indicator assembly **(see illustration)**.

19 The bulb is a bayonet fit in the bulbholder **(see illustration)**.

7.18 Twist the bulbholder to remove

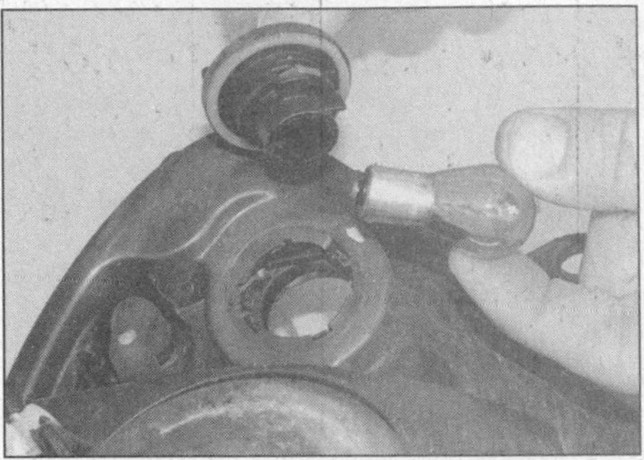
7.19 Press and twist the bulb to remove

Refitting

20 Refitting is a reversal of removal.

Front indicator side repeater

Removal

21 Carefully prise the light unit from the front wing **(see illustrations in Section 9)**.

22 Twist the bulbholder anti-clockwise, and withdraw it from the rear of the light unit **(see illustration)**.

23 The bulb is a push-fit in the bulbholder **(see illustration)**.

Refitting

24 Refitting is a reversal of removal.

Front foglight

Removal

25 Remove the securing clip(s) and hinge the splash shield downwards **(see illustration)**.

26 Release the retaining clips and disconnect the wiring connector **(see illustration)**.

27 Twist the plastic cover anti-clockwise, and withdraw the bulb from the rear of the light **(see illustration)**.

Refitting

28 When handling the new bulb, use a tissue or clean cloth to avoid touching the glass with the fingers; moisture and grease from the skin can cause blackening and rapid failure of this type of bulb. If the glass is accidentally touched, wipe it clean using methylated spirit.

29 Refitting is a reversal of removal.

Rear light cluster

Removal

30 Open the tailgate, and unscrew the rear light cluster securing nut **(see illustrations in Section 9)**.

31 Withdraw the light cluster from outside the car, taking care not to damage the locating lugs, then disconnect the wiring plug.

32 Release the securing clips outwards, and pull the bulbholder from the rear of the light cluster **(see illustrations)**.

33 The bulbs are a bayonet fit in their holders **(see illustration)**.

Refitting

34 Refitting is a reversal of removal, making sure the locating pegs are aligned correctly.

High-level stop-light

35 If the light unit is faulty, it will have to be renewed as a complete unit as it has an LED

7.22 Twist the bulbholder to remove it from the light unit

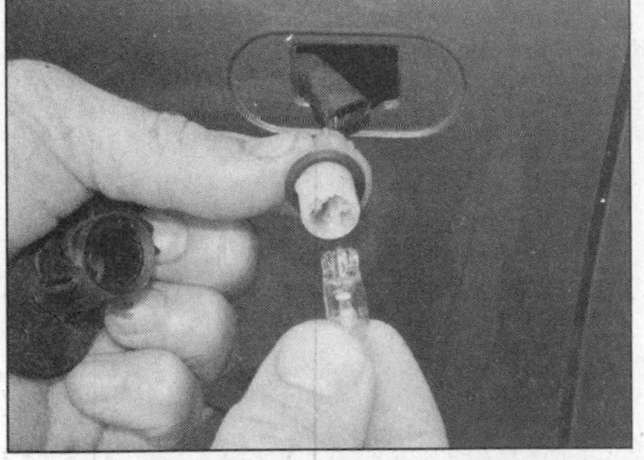
7.23 Withdraw bulb from the bulbholder

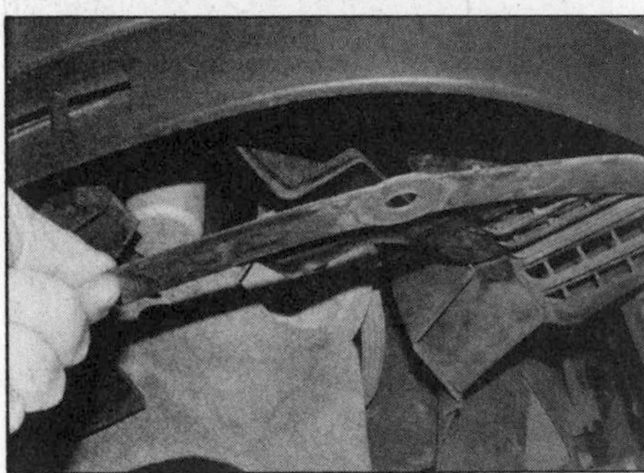
7.25 Unclipping shield to access rear of light unit

7.26 Disconnecting a front foglight wiring plug

7.27 Twist and withdraw the foglight bulb

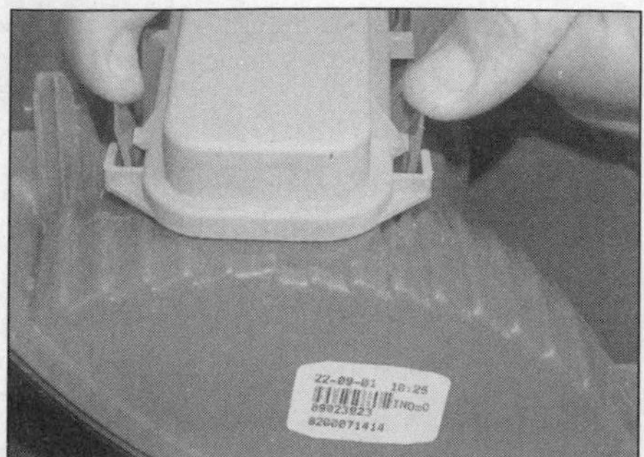

7.32a Release the securing clips . . .

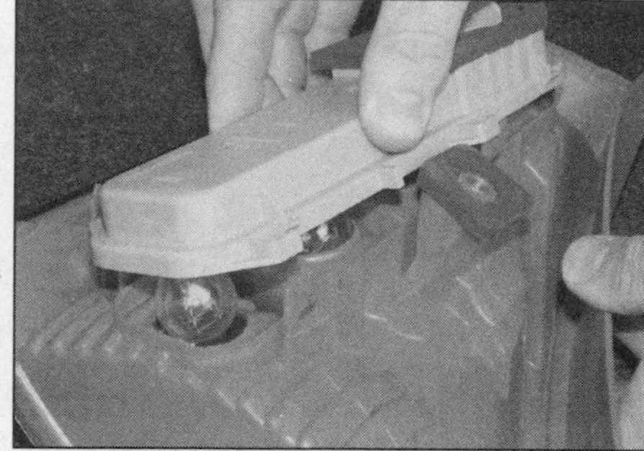

7.32b . . . and remove the bulbholder

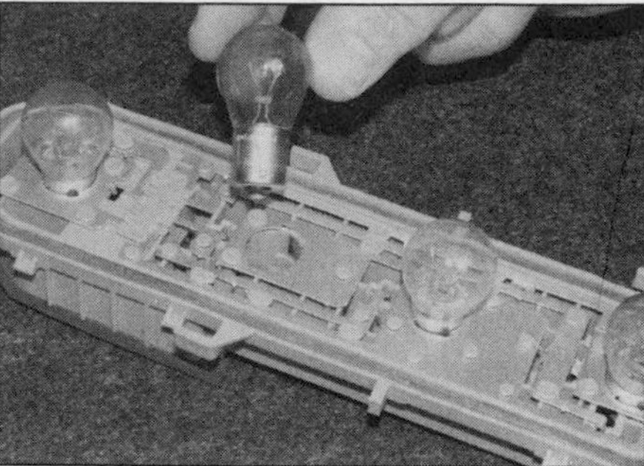

7.33 Press and twist the bulb to remove

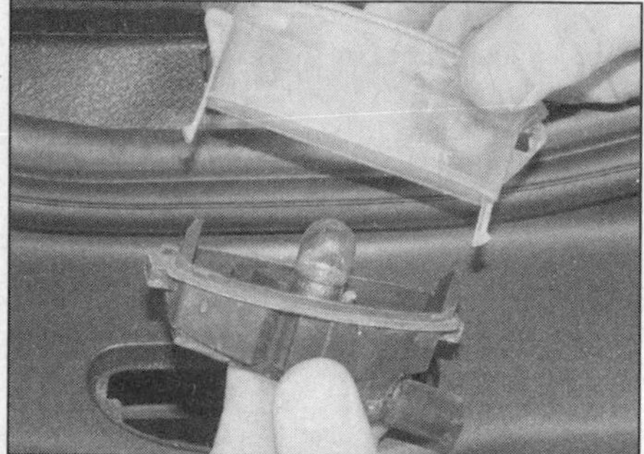

7.37 Unclip the lens to expose the bulb

7.38 Removing the number plate light bulb

sealed unit. Remove the light unit as described in Section 9.

Rear number plate light

Removal

36 Using a screwdriver, carefully prise the number plate light assembly from its location in the bumper. See illustrations in Section 9.

37 Release the securing tabs and unclip the lens from the light assembly **(see illustration)**.

38 The bulb is a bayonet fit in the holder **(see illustration)**.

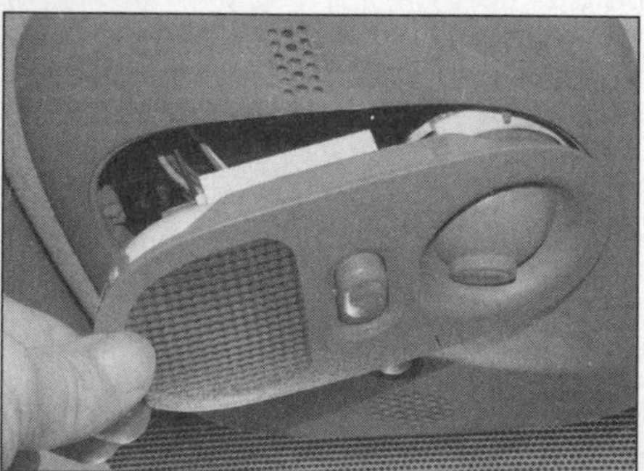

8.2 Unclipping the interior light from the roof console

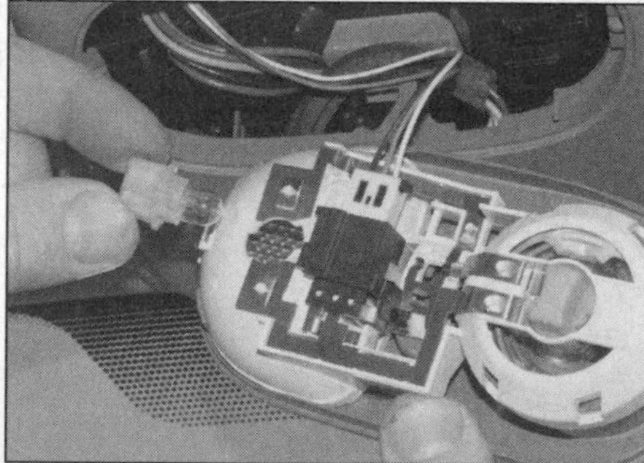

8.3 Twist and release the relevant bulbholder from the light unit

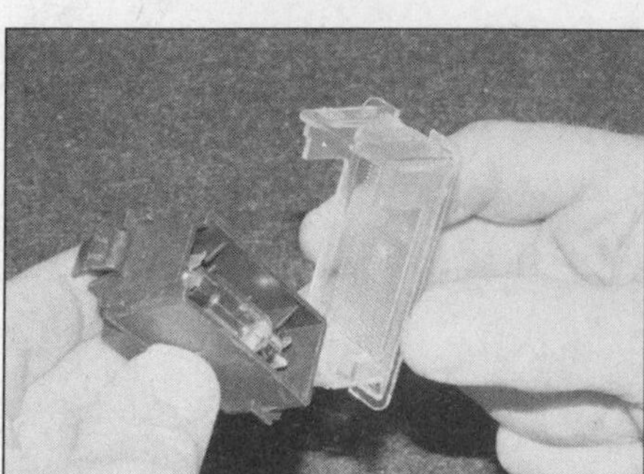

8.6a Unclip the lens from the boot light . . .

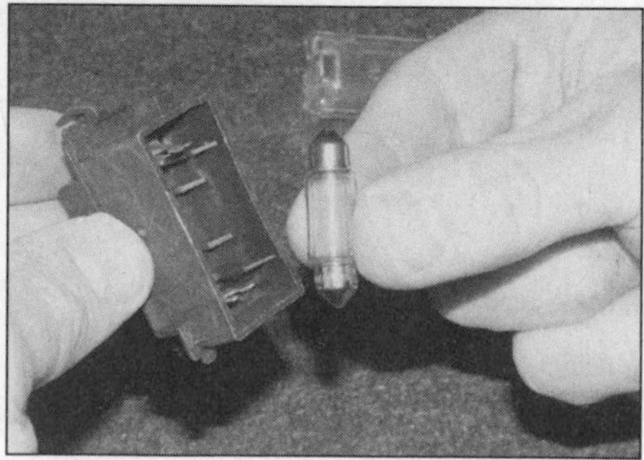

8.6b . . . and remove the festoon bulb

Refitting

39 Refitting is a reversal of removal.

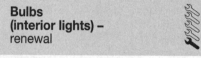

8 Bulbs (interior lights) – renewal

General

1 Refer to Section 7, paragraph 1.

Courtesy light

2 Unclip the interior light from the roof console for access to the bulb **(see illustration)**.

3 Twist the bulbholder and remove the capless bulb from the rear of the light assembly **(see illustration)**.

4 Refitting is a reversal of removal.

Luggage compartment light

5 Release the tabs and withdraw the light assembly from its location in the luggage compartment.

6 Unclip the lens, and remove the festoon bulb **(see illustrations)**.

7 Refitting is a reversal of removal.

Instrument panel and warning lights

8 The bulbs cannot be renewed on these instrument panels, as they are soldered LEDs.

Auxiliary display illumination

9 Refer to Section 14.

Cigarette lighter illumination

10 Remove the cigarette lighter as described in Section 17.

11 The bulb may have to be renewed as part of the holder, check with your Renault dealer for availability. Reassemble and refit the cigarette lighter using a reversal of the removal procedure.

Ashtray illumination

12 The ashtray shares the same illumination bulb as the cigarette lighter. Refer to paragraphs 10 and 11 for details.

Clock illumination

13 The clock is part of the instrument panel or

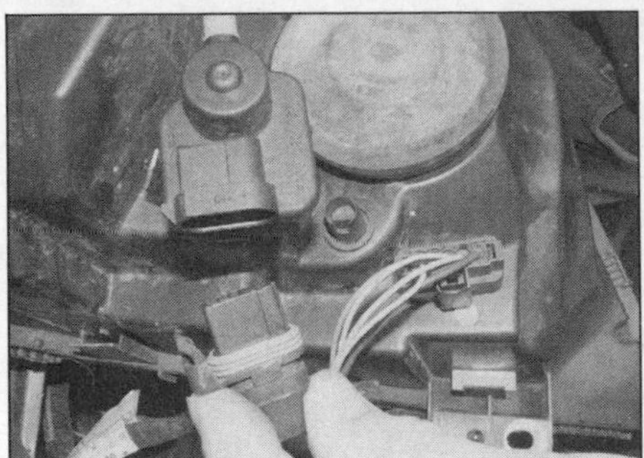

9.2a Disconnect the height adjustment wiring connector . . .

9.2b . . . and the headlight wiring plug

9.3 Remove the lower headlight securing bolts (arrowed)

the auxiliary display unit. Refer to Section 12 or 14 depending on specification of the vehicle.

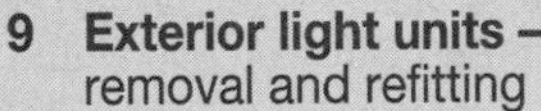

9 Exterior light units – removal and refitting

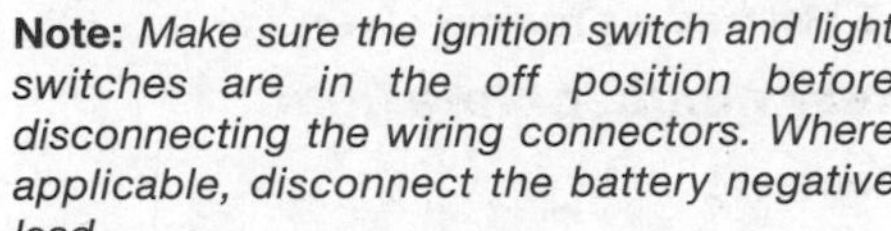

Note: *Make sure the ignition switch and light switches are in the off position before disconnecting the wiring connectors. Where applicable, disconnect the battery negative lead.*

Headlight/front indicator unit

Warning: Before carrying out any operations on Xenon headlight units, it is recommended that protective gloves and safety glasses are worn. It is essential that the wiring connectors are disconnected from the rear of the headlight unit, then wait until the computer module and bulbs have cooled down before removal. DO NOT switch the headlamps on with the bulb removed as it is harmful to the eyes.

Removal

1 Remove the front bumper/grille panel, as described in Chapter 11, Section 6.

2 Disconnect the wiring plugs from the rear of the headlight unit **(see illustrations)**.

3 Unscrew and remove the two lower headlight unit securing bolts **(see illustration)**.

4 Unscrew the headlight unit upper securing screw **(see illustration)**.

5 Withdraw the headlight unit from the vehicle taking care not to damage the light unit or wing panel **(see illustration)**.

Refitting

6 Refitting is a reversal of removal.

Beam alignment

7 On completion, the headlight beam alignment should be checked, ideally using optical setting equipment. This check should be carried out by a Renault dealer or a suitably-equipped garage (see Section 11). The beam alignment is adjusted using the two screws provided on the light unit **(see illustrations)**.

Front indicator side repeater

Removal

8 Carefully prise the light unit from the front wing and disconnect the bulbholder **(see illustrations)**.

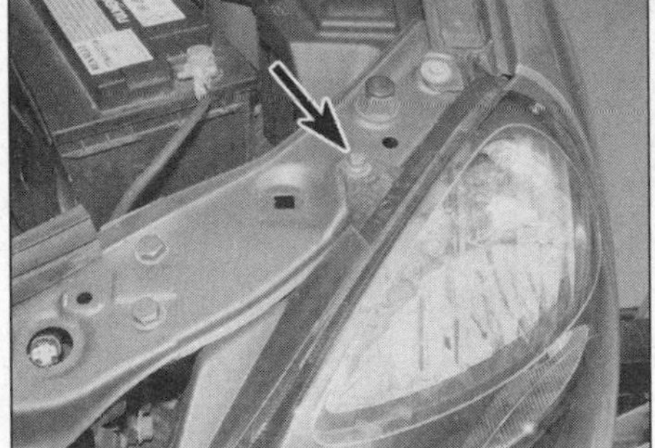

9.4 Unscrew the upper headlight securing bolt (arrowed)

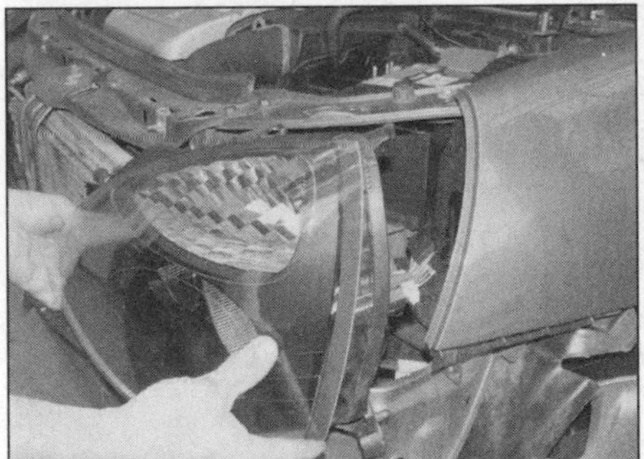

9.5 Carefully withdraw the headlight from the vehicle

9.7a Adjusting the direction of the headlamp . . .

9.7b . . . and adjusting the height of the headlamp

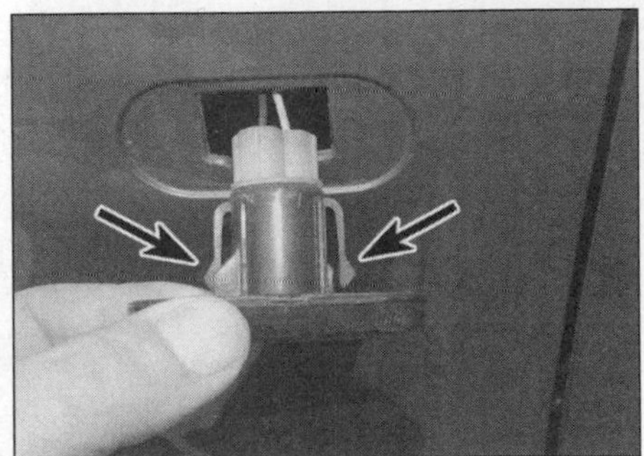

9.8a Retaining clips (arrowed) for the indicator side repeaters

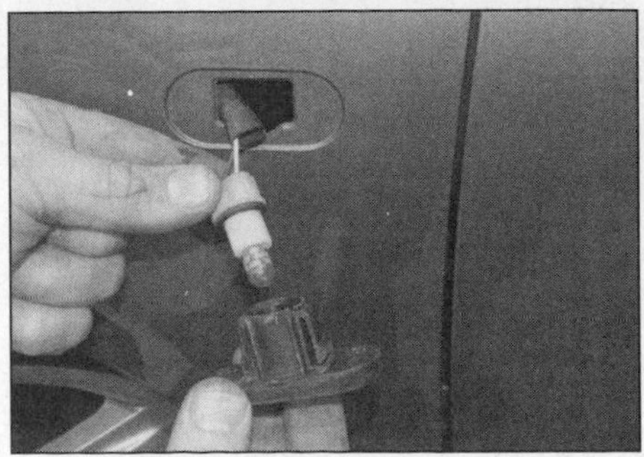

9.8b Withdraw the bulbholder from the light unit

9.10a Disconnect the wiring plug from the rear light unit . . .

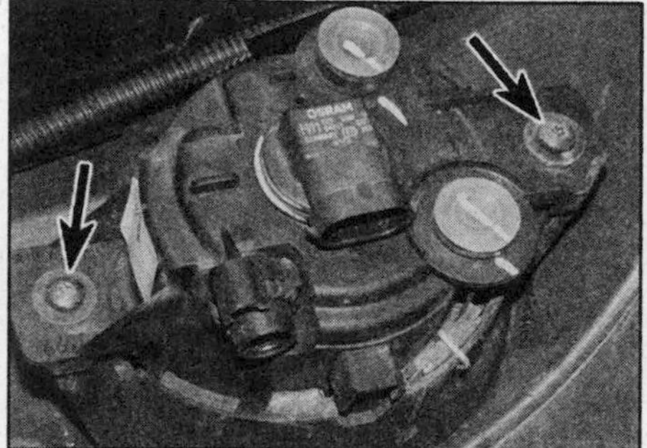
9.10b . . . undo the retaining bolts (arrowed) and remove the foglight

9.11 Front foglight beam adjustment screw (arrowed)

Refitting

9 Refitting is a reversal of removal.

Front foglight

Removal

10 Disconnect the wiring connector from the rear of the foglight, then undo the two mounting screws and remove the light from the bumper **(see illustrations).** If required, the foglight surround can be unclipped from the bumper.

Refitting

11 Refitting is a reversal of removal. If necessary, the vertical alignment of the beam can be adjusted by turning the adjustment screw from under the bumper **(see illustration).**

Rear light cluster

Removal

12 Open the tailgate, and unscrew the rear light cluster securing nut **(see illustration).**

13 Withdraw the light cluster from outside the car, taking care not to damage the locating lugs, then disconnect the wiring plugs **(see illustration).**

Refitting

14 Refitting is a reversal of removal, bearing in mind the following points.

15 Ensure that the locating lugs are correctly engaged with the corresponding holes in the body **(see illustration).**

High-level stop-light

Removal

16 Open the tailgate, and remove the rear spoiler as described in Chapter 11, Section 22.

17 Disconnect the wiring, and undo the two retaining nuts to release the light unit from the rear spoiler **(see illustrations).**

18 If the light unit is faulty, it will have to be renewed as a complete unit as it has an LED sealed unit.

Refitting

19 Refitting is a reversal of removal.

Rear number plate light

Removal

20 Using a screwdriver, carefully prise the number plate light assembly from its location in the bumper. Disconnect the wiring connector **(see illustrations).**

Refitting

21 Refitting is a reversal of removal.

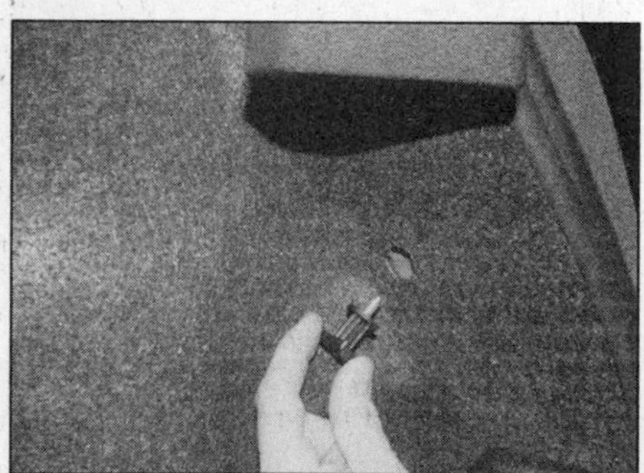
9.12 Unscrew the rear light cluster securing nut

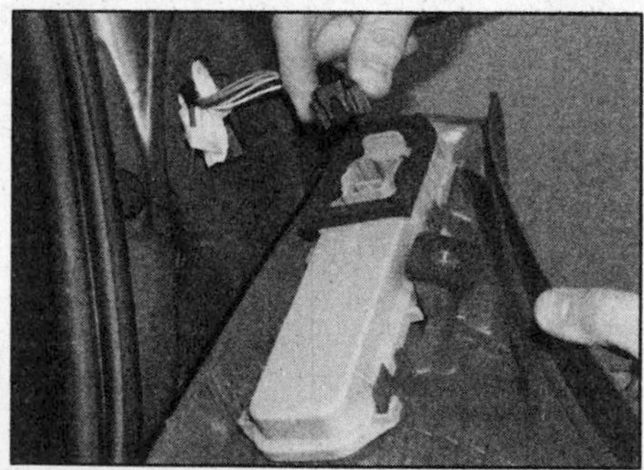
9.13 Disconnecting the wiring plug from the rear light unit

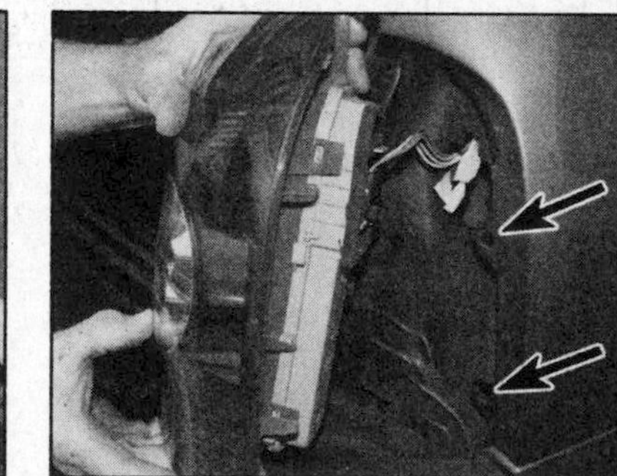
9.15 The lugs on the light unit align with the holes (arrowed) in the panel

9.17a Disconnecting the wiring plug, undo the retaining nuts . . .

9.17b . . . and remove the high-level brake light from the spoiler

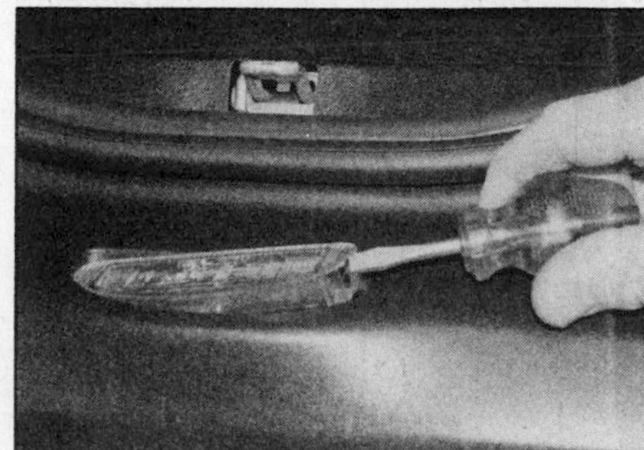
9.20a Careful unclip the light unit from the bumper . . .

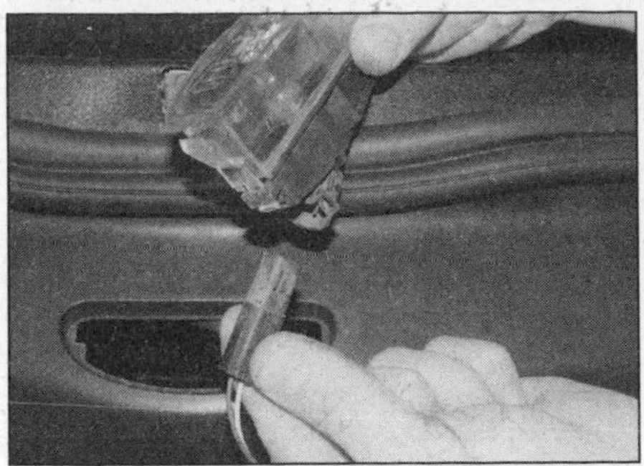

9.20b . . . and disconnect the wiring plug

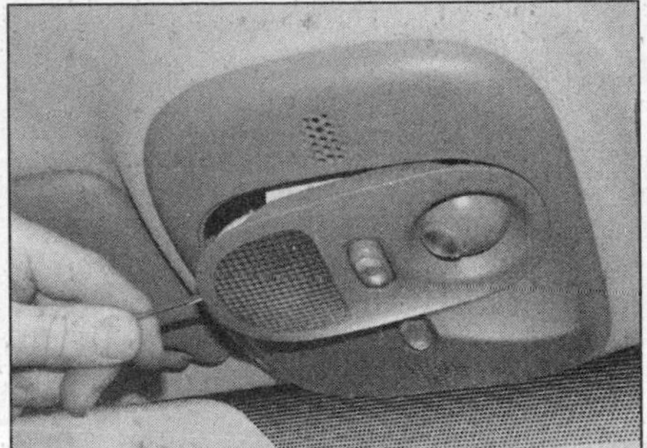

10.2 Release the courtesy light from the roof console

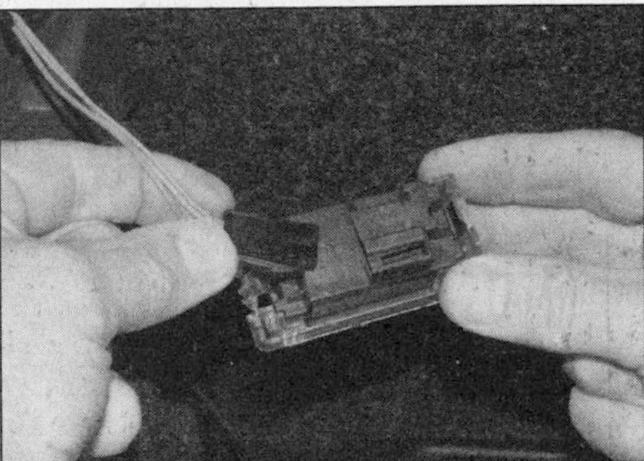

10.5 Disconnecting the wiring connector from the luggage compartment light unit

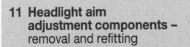

10 Interior light units – removal and refitting

Courtesy light

1 Disconnect the battery negative lead.

2 Carefully prise the light assembly from its location in the roof panel, and disconnect the wiring plugs **(see illustration)**.

3 Refitting is a reversal of removal.

Luggage compartment light

4 Prise the light assembly from its location in the luggage compartment.

5 Disconnect the wiring plug as the light is withdrawn **(see illustration)**.

6 Refitting is a reversal of removal.

11 Headlight aim adjustment components – removal and refitting

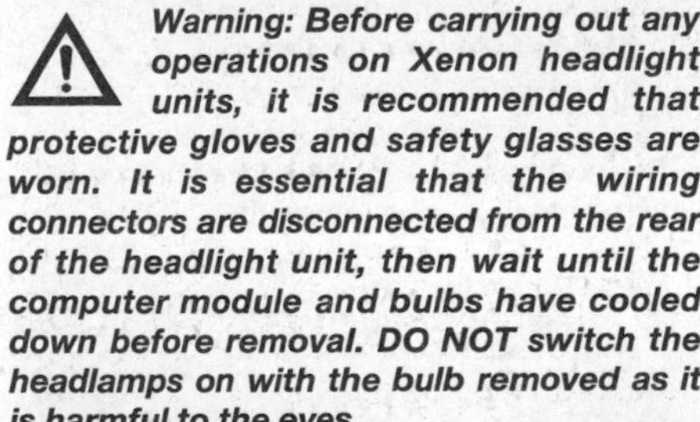

Warning: Before carrying out any operations on Xenon headlight units, it is recommended that protective gloves and safety glasses are worn. It is essential that the wiring connectors are disconnected from the rear of the headlight unit, then wait until the computer module and bulbs have cooled down before removal. DO NOT switch the headlamps on with the bulb removed as it is harmful to the eyes.

1 Accurate adjustment of the headlight beam is only possible using optical beam-setting equipment, and this work should therefore be carried out by a Renault dealer or suitably-equipped workshop.

2 To make a temporary adjustment of the headlights, position the vehicle on a level surface 10 metres from a wall. The tyres must all be at the correct pressure, the fuel tank half full, and a person be sitting in the driver's seat. Turn on the ignition, and where applicable check that the manual adjustment inside the vehicle is set at 0. Measure the distance from the ground to the cross in the centre of the headlight, then deduct 5.0cm for models with halogen lights and 7.5cm for models with Xenon lights. Draw a mark on the wall at this height, then adjust the headlight beam centre point onto this mark by turning the adjustment screws on the rear of the headlight unit, refer to Section 9, paragraph 7.

3 Certain models have a headlight beam manual adjustment control, which allows the aim of the headlights to be adjusted to compensate for variation in the vehicle's payload. The aim is altered by means of facia-mounted switch, which controls electric adjuster motors located in the rear of the headlight assemblies.

4 Models with Xenon headlights have an automatic levelling system. If a fault occurs in the system, a warning light will show up on the instrument panel, and the headlights will be angled down to avoid dazzling oncoming traffic. If this happens, the driving speed must be adjusted accordingly to allow for decreased visibility.

Headlight adjuster

Removal

5 Working in the engine compartment, disconnect the wiring connector from the rear of the headlight adjuster unit **(see illustration)**.

6 Release the actuator retaining clip, then twist the actuator anti-clockwise. Unclip the balljoint from the headlight unit **(see illustrations)**.

7 To remove the headlight aim adjustment control switch, refer to Section 6.

Refitting

8 Refitting is a reversal of removal, bearing in mind the following points.

9 Take care not to damage the actuator balljoints when reconnecting them to the headlights.

10 To initially set the beam alignment, refer to paragraph 2.

Xenon headlight control

Note: *If the module is to be renewed, it must be programmed by a Renault dealer using specialist equipment.*

Removal

11 Remove the headlight unit as described in Section 9.

12 Undo the control module retaining screws from the rear of the headlight unit.

13 Carefully withdraw the module from the headlight unit, disconnecting it from the wiring block connector.

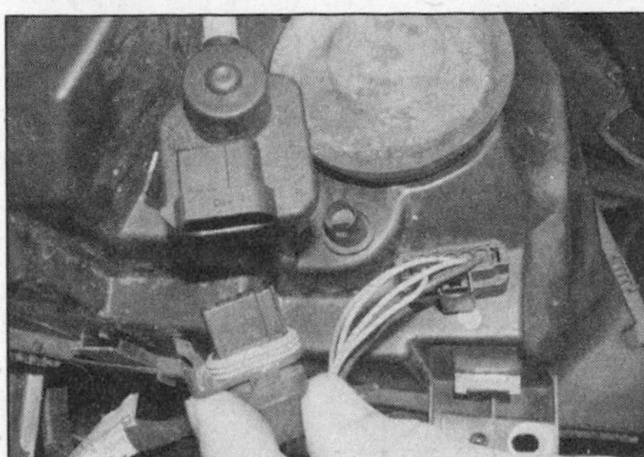

11.5 Disconnecting the headlight adjuster wiring plug

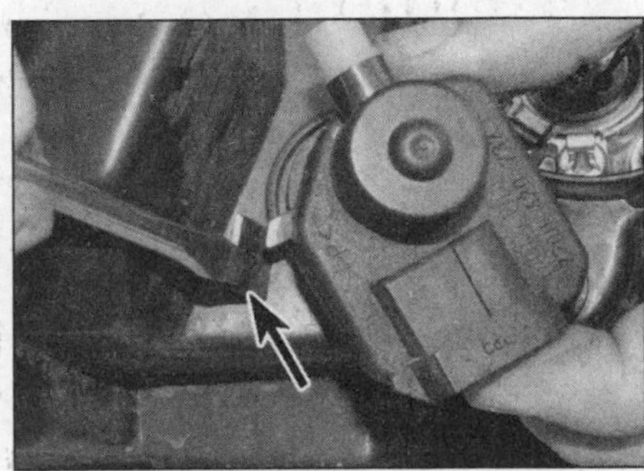

11.6a Release the retaining clip (arrowed) . . .

11.6b . . . remove the headlight aim adjustment actuator from headlight assembly

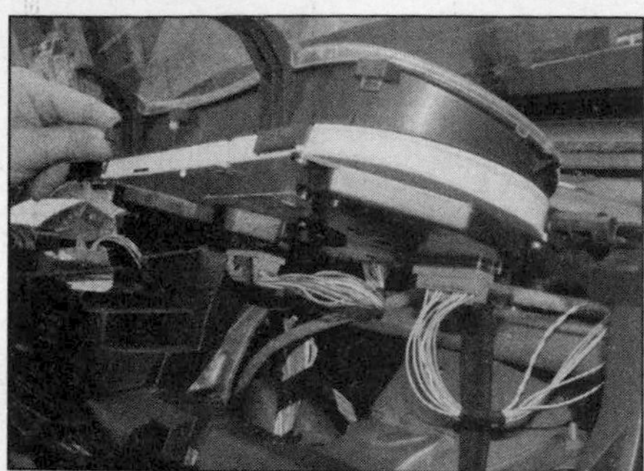

12.3a Hinge the instrument panel up . . .

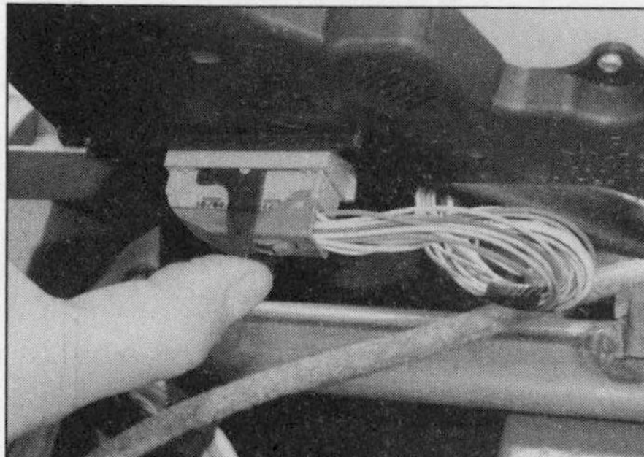

12.3b . . . and release the securing clips . . .

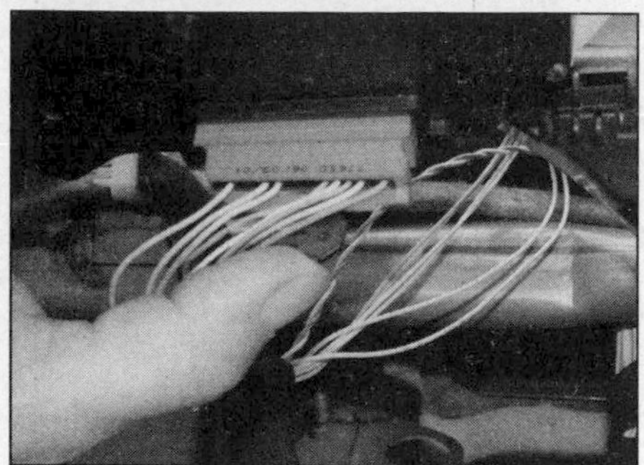

12.3c . . . to disconnect the wiring plugs

12.4 Release the instrument panel from the retaining clips (arrowed)

Refitting

14 Refitting is a reversal of removal. Refer to Section 9 for refitting the headlight unit.

Xenon headlight sensor/ computer

Note: *If the sensor/computer is to be renewed, it must be programmed by a Renault dealer using specialist equipment.*

15 Working under the rear of the vehicle, disconnect the wiring connector from the sensor.

16 Unclip the sensor linkage from the rear suspension arm.

17 Undo the retaining bolt and withdraw the sensor from the vehicle.

Refitting

18 Refitting is a reversal of removal.

12 Instrument panel – removal and refitting

Removal

1 Disconnect the battery negative lead.

2 Remove the steering column shrouds and the facia upper trim panel, as described in Chapter 11, Section 29.

3 Lift the instrument panel upwards and disconnect the wiring connectors from the rear of the instrument panel **(see illustrations)**.

4 Pull the instrument panel and unclip the upper part from the facia **(see illustration)**.

Refitting

5 Refitting is a reversal of removal, ensuring that all wiring plugs are securely reconnected.

13 Instrument panel components – general information

1 Depending on model specification, the instrument panel has the following functions:

- *Electronic speedometer.*
- *Rev counter (tachometer).*
- *Fuel gauge.*
- *Engine coolant temperature gauge.*
- *Various warning light illuminations.*
- *Automatic transmission display.*
- *Display for total mileage, trip mileage, oil level and on-board computer (ADAC).*
- *Clock.*
- *Trip reset button.*

2 The instrument panel is a sealed unit and the only part that can be renewed is the instrument glass. If any other components are faulty, the entire instrument panel has to be renewed.

3 The illumination bulbs cannot be renewed on these instrument panels, as they are soldered LEDs.

Self Test

4 Press and hold down the ADAC button on the end of the wiper stalk and switch the ignition on without starting the engine, release the ADAC button after approx 5 seconds.

5 The system then checks the following functions simultaneously:

- *The speedometer, by the needle moving in increments of 40 km/h.*
- *The rev counter, by the needle moving in increments of 1000 rpm.*
- *The fuel gauge, by the needle moving in increments of approximately 1/4 of the scale.*
- *The coolant temperature gauge, by the needle moving in increments of approximately 1/4 of the scale.*
- *The digital display, by making all the segments illuminate at once.*

6 This will carry on checking the instruments until the ignition is switched off.

14 Auxiliary display – removal and refitting

Note: *There is an auxiliary display fitted in the top of the facia panel at the centre. This display is for the radio, temperature and clock.*

Removal

1 Disconnect the battery negative lead.

2 Remove the steering column shrouds and the facia upper trim panel, as described in Chapter 11, Section 29.

3 Release the two securing clips, then pull the panel from the facia **(see illustrations)**.

4 Release the securing clips and disconnect the wiring plugs from the rear of the panel **(see illustration)**, then withdraw the panel from the facia.

14.3a Release the retaining clips (arrowed) . . .

14.3b . . . and withdraw the auxiliary display panel

5 The auxiliary display panel can be unclipped from the surround trim panel as required **(see illustrations)**.

6 To renew a bulb, twist the appropriate bulbholder anti-clockwise, and withdraw it from the panel **(see illustration)**.

Refitting

7 Refitting is a reversal of removal.

15 Clock – general information

1 The clock, depending on model specification, is either located in the instrument panel or the auxiliary display unit. Both the instrument panel and auxiliary unit are sealed units and if faulty must be renewed as a complete unit.

2 If the clock is in the instrument panel, refer to Sections 12 and 13.

3 If the clock is in the auxiliary display unit, refer to Section 14.

16 Outside air temperature display components – removal and refitting

Instrument panel-mounted display

1 Proceed as described in Sections 12 and 13.

Auxiliary display

2 Proceed as described in Section 14.

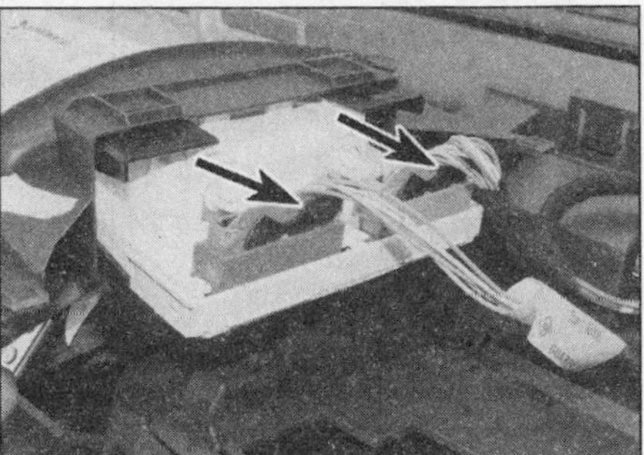

14.4 Disconnect the wiring block connectors (arrowed)

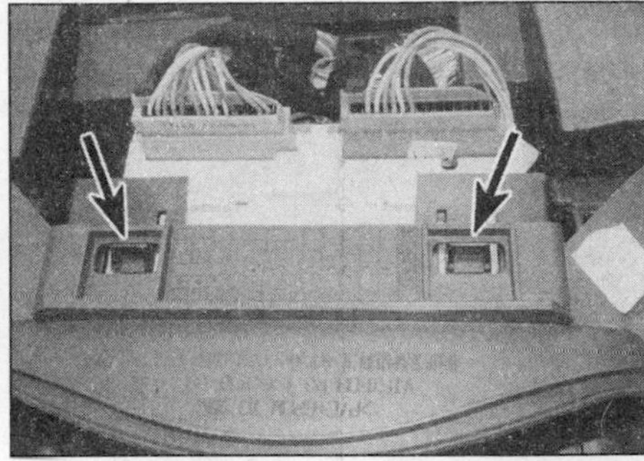

14.5a Release the retaining clips (arrowed) . . .

14.5b . . . and withdraw the surround trim panel

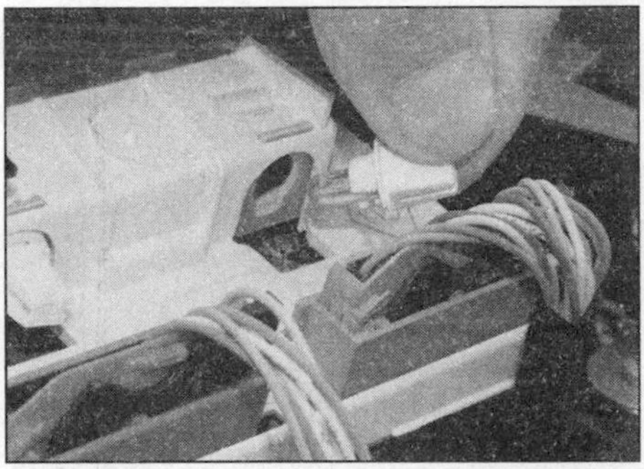

14.6 Withdrawing a bulb from the display unit

Sensor (air temperature)

Note: *Check with your local Renault dealer for availability of parts, the sensor may only be available as part of the mirror as a complete assembly.*

Removal

3 The sensor is mounted in the bottom of the exterior mirror on the passenger side.

4 Disconnect the battery negative lead.

5 Open the door, and carefully prise the mirror trim panel from the front edge of the door.

6 Unscrew the two screws securing the mirror cover panel to the door, then disconnect the sensor wiring plug.

7 Remove the mirror cover **(see illustration)**, as described in Chapter 11, Section 18.

8 Unclip the sensor from the mirror, feeding the wiring through the mirror body **(see illustration)**.

Refitting

9 Refitting is a reversal of removal.

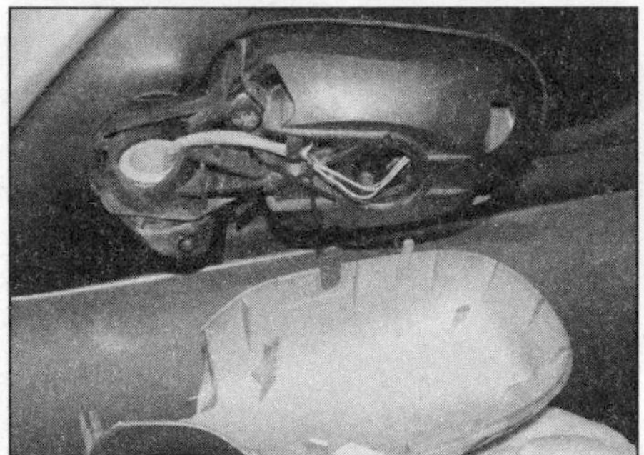

16.7 Carefully unclip the outer shell/cover from the passenger mirror

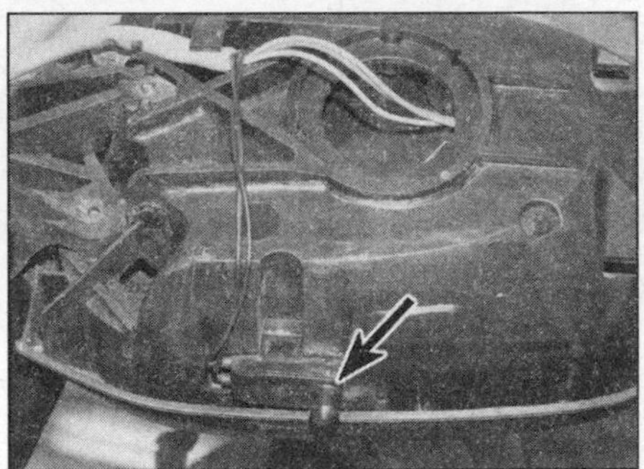

16.8 Air temperature sensor (arrowed) – with cover removed

17 Cigarette lighter – removal and refitting

Removal

1 Disconnect the battery negative lead.

2 Unclip the trim panel from below the heater control panel **(see illustration)**.

3 Remove the ashtray from the centre console, then unclip the cigarette lighter surround from the console. Disconnect the wiring connector on removal **(see illustrations)**.

4 Working at the rear of the cigarette lighter,

17.2 Unclipping the trim panel

17.3a Unclip the cigarette lighter surround . . .

17.3b ... and disconnect the wiring connector

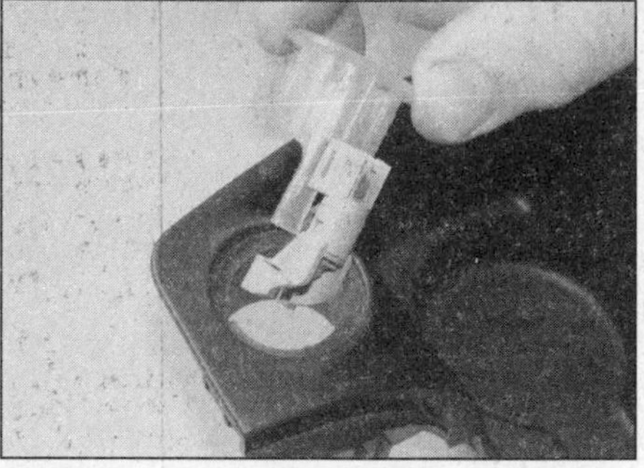

17.5a Withdraw the plastic outer ring surround ...

push the centre part of the lighter out and remove it from the plastic outer ring **(see illustrations)**.

5 Withdraw the plastic outer ring and bulbholder from the cigarette lighter surround,

18.1 Horn location, left-hand front – viewed with the front bumper removed

19.3a Lift the hinged cover ...

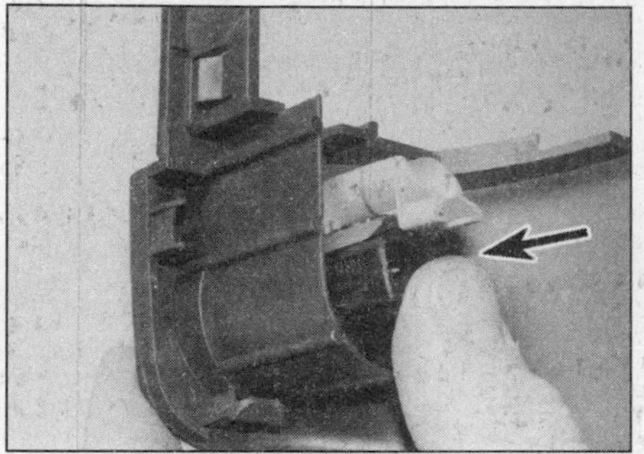

17.4a Press the centre of the lighter, in the direction of the arrow ...

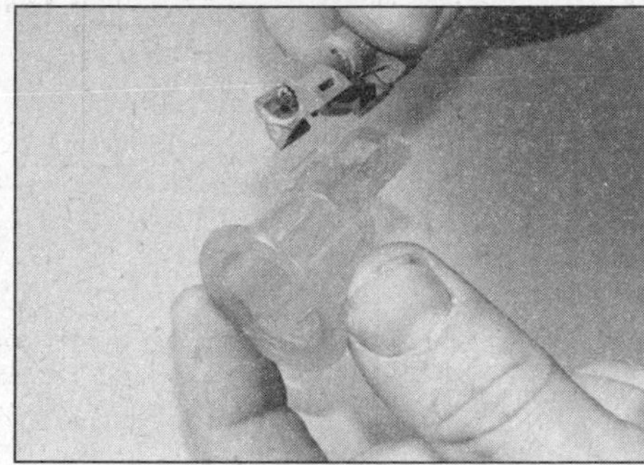

17.5b ... and unclip the bulb and holder

then unclip the bulbholder from the outer ring **(see illustrations)**.

Refitting

6 Refitting is a reversal of removal.

18.4 Disconnect the wiring connector(s)

19.3b ... or unclip the plastic cap ...

17.4b ... and withdraw it out of its plastic outer ring

18 Horn – removal and refitting

Removal

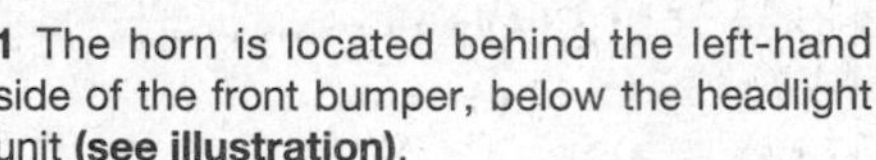

1 The horn is located behind the left-hand side of the front bumper, below the headlight unit **(see illustration)**.

2 Disconnect the battery negative lead.

3 To gain access to the horn, remove the front wheel arch liner. Refer to Chapter 11, Section 22, if necessary.

4 Disconnect the wiring from the horn **(see illustration)**.

5 Unscrew the securing nut, and withdraw the horn from its mounting bracket.

Refitting

6 Refitting is a reversal of removal.

19 Wiper arms – removal and refitting

Removal

1 The wiper motor should be in the parked position before removing the wiper arm. Mark the position of the blade on the glass with adhesive tape, as a guide to refitting.

2 If both windscreen wiper arms are to be removed, identify them so that they can be refitted in their original positions (the arms are of different lengths).

3 Lift the hinged cover or unclip the plastic cap, and remove the nut securing the arm to the spindle **(see illustrations)**.

4 Pull or prise the arm from the spindle, using a puller or screwdriver if necessary **(see illustration)**. Take care not to damage the trim or paintwork.

Refitting

5 Refitting is a reversal of removal. Position the arms so that the blades align with the tape applied to the glass before removal.

19.3c . . . and undo the wiper arm securing nut

19.4 Using a puller to remove the wiper arm

20.5 Disconnecting the windscreen wiper motor wiring plug

20 Windscreen wiper motor and linkage – removal and refitting

Removal

1 Make sure that the wipers are parked.

2 Disconnect the battery negative lead.

3 Remove the windscreen wiper arms, as described in Section 19.

4 Remove the windscreen cowl panels, as described in Chapter 11, Section 8.

5 Release the securing clip (where applicable), and disconnect the wiring plug from the motor **(see illustration)**.

6 Unscrew the motor/linkage assembly securing bolts, and recover the washers **(see illustrations)**.

7 Note that the assembly has to be disengaged from the locating peg at the rear of the scuttle panel **(see illustration)**.

8 Manipulate the assembly out through the scuttle, taking care not to damage surrounding components **(see illustration)**.

9 To remove the motor from the linkage, mark the relative positions of the motor shaft and crank then unscrew the retaining nut and washer and free the wiper linkage from the motor spindle. Unscrew the motor retaining bolts and manoeuvre the motor out of position and remove it from the vehicle **(see illustrations)**.

Refitting

10 Refitting is a reversal of removal, bearing in mind the following points.

11 Ensure that the assembly is mounted on the locating peg before refitting the mounting bolts.

12 Refit the windscreen wiper arms with reference to Section 19.

21 Tailgate wiper motor and linkage – removal and refitting

Removal

1 Disconnect the battery negative lead.

20.6a Unscrew the centre mounting bolts (arrowed) . . .

20.6b . . . and the left-hand mounting bolt (arrowed)

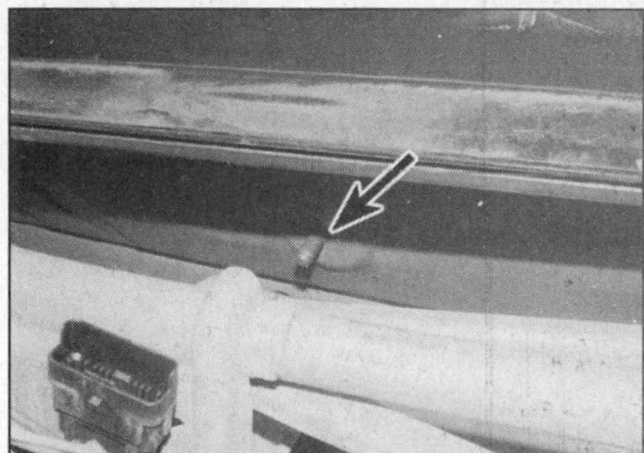
20.7 Locating peg (arrowed) at the rear of the scuttle panel

20.8 Withdraw the wiper motor/linkage from the scuttle panel

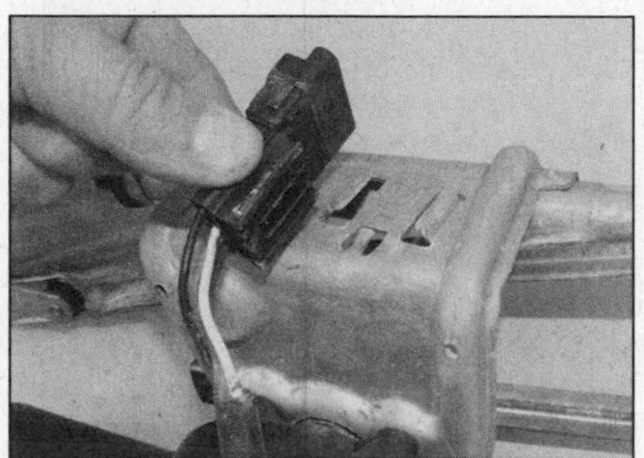
20.9a Unclip the wiring block connector from the mounting bracket . . .

20.9b . . . undo the linkage retaining nut (arrowed) and remove wiper motor securing screws

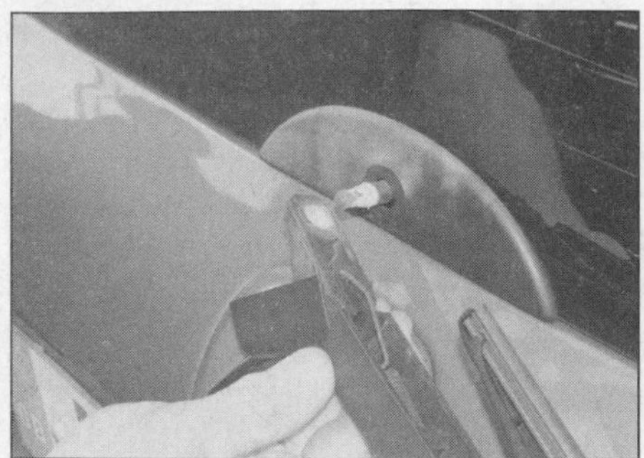

21.2 Remove the rear wiper arm

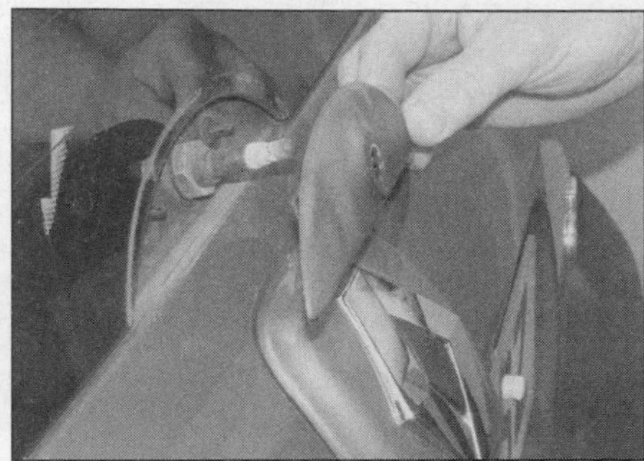

21.3a Unclip the plastic surround from the wiper spindle . . .

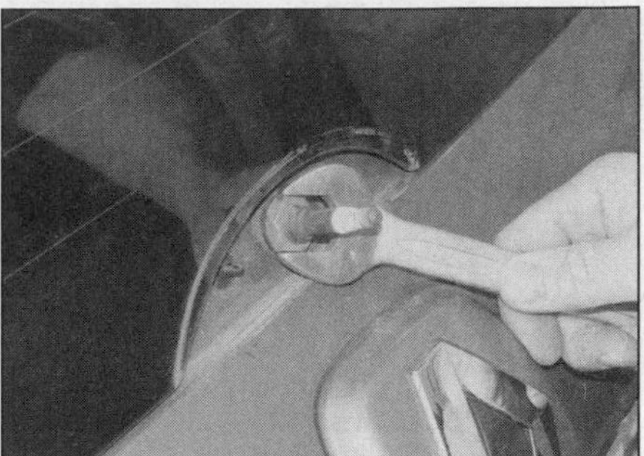

21.3b . . . remove the securing nut . . .

21.3c . . . and sealing washer

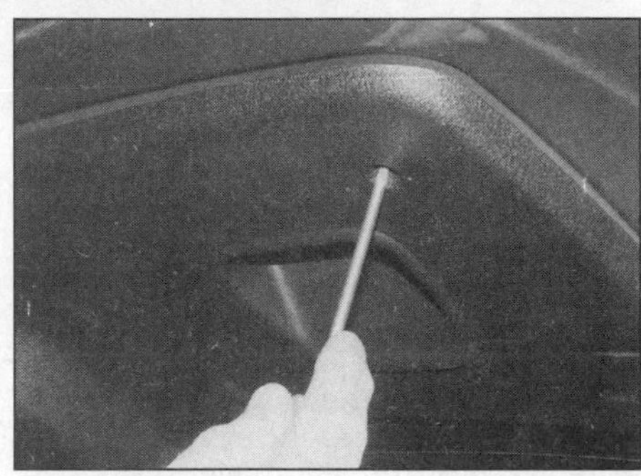

21.4 Remove the tailgate trim retaining screw

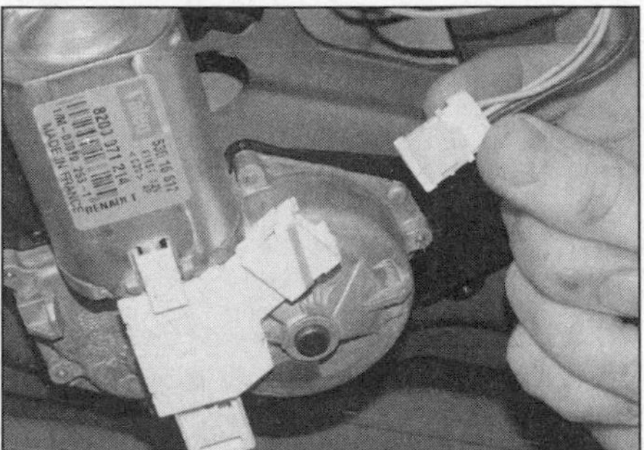

21.5 Disconnecting the wiring plug from the wiper motor

2 Remove the tailgate wiper arm **(see illustration)**, with reference to Section 19.

3 Unclip the plastic cover from around the wiper motor spindle, and remove the securing nut and washer **(see illustrations)**.

4 Open the tailgate, undo the retaining screw and unclip the tailgate interior trim panel **(see illustration)**.

5 Disconnect the wiper motor wiring plug **(see illustration)**.

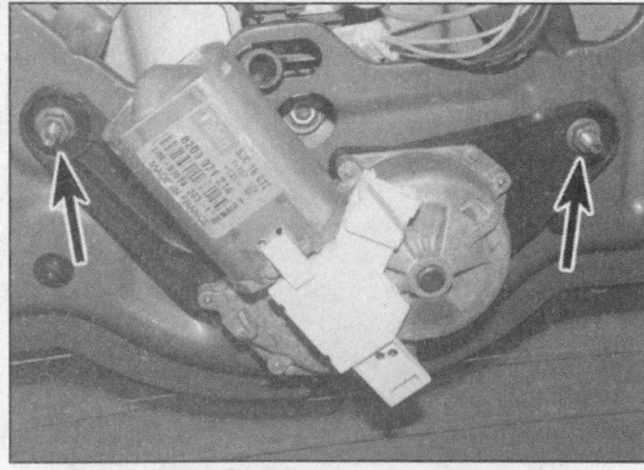

21.6a Remove the wiper motor retaining nuts (arrowed)

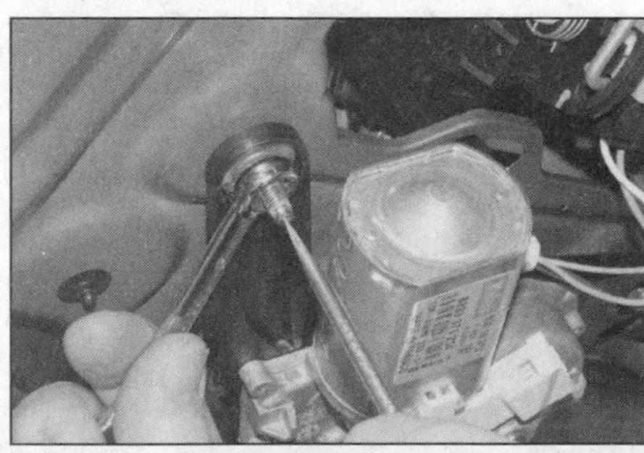

21.6b Using a screwdriver to hold the mounting studs, while unscrewing the securing nuts . . .

21.6c . . . and retrieving the sealing washer as the motor is removed

22.4 Disconnect the wiring plug (arrowed) from the washer pump

6 Unscrew the nuts securing the motor mounting bracket to the tailgate (use a screwdriver to hold the studs). Withdraw the motor assembly and (where applicable) retrieve the washers from the mounting studs **(see illustrations)**.

Refitting

7 Refitting is a reversal of removal.

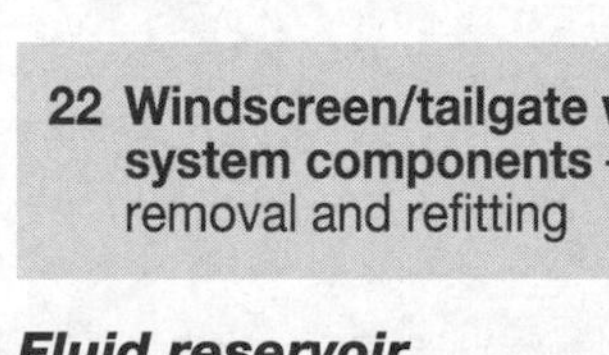

22 Windscreen/tailgate washer system components – removal and refitting

Fluid reservoir

Removal

1 Disconnect the battery negative lead.

2 Remove the windscreen wiper arms as described in Section 19.

3 Remove the windscreen cowl panels as described in Chapter 11, Section 8.

4 Disconnect the wiring plug from the top of the washer pump **(see illustration)**.

5 Unscrew the fluid reservoir securing bolt, then lift the reservoir sufficiently to disconnect the hoses from the pump **(see illustrations)**. Be prepared for fluid spillage.

6 Manipulate the reservoir out from the scuttle.

Refitting

7 Refitting is a reversal of removal. Refit the windscreen wiper arms and windscreen cowl panels with reference to Section 19 and Chapter 11, Section 8.

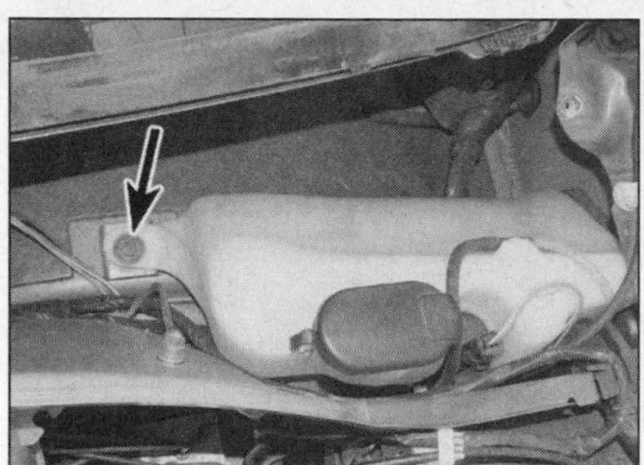
22.5a Unscrew the washer fluid reservoir securing bolt (arrowed) . . .

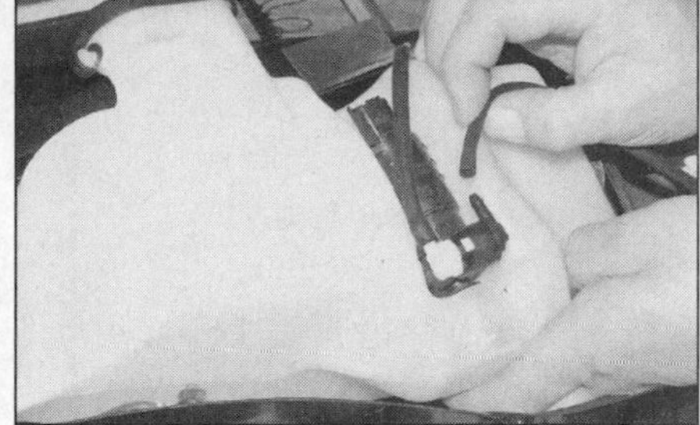
22.5b . . . and disconnect the two washer hoses (one for the front, and one for the rear)

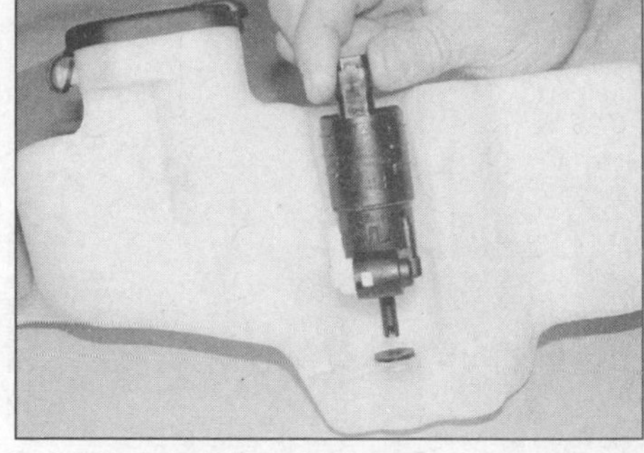
22.9 Carefully pull the pump from the sealing grommet in the reservoir

Fluid pump

Removal

8 Remove the fluid reservoir as described in this Section.

9 Carefully disconnect the hoses from the pump, then pull the pump from the reservoir **(see illustration)**. Be prepared for fluid spillage. Note that one pump supplies the front and rear washer jets.

Refitting

10 Refitting is a reversal of removal. Check the sealing grommet in the fluid reservoir, before inserting the pump.

Windscreen washer jet

Removal

11 With the bonnet open, disconnect the fluid hose, then carefully prise the jet from the bonnet **(see illustrations)**. Take care not to damage the trim or paintwork.

Refitting

12 Refitting is a reversal of removal. The jet can be adjusted by inserting a pin into the jet, and swivelling it to the required position.

Tailgate washer jet

Removal

13 Remove the rear spoiler as described in Chapter 11, Section 22.

14 Disconnect the fluid hose, then carefully prise the jet from the spoiler **(see illustrations)**. Take care not to damage the trim or paintwork.

Refitting

15 Refitting is a reversal of removal. The jet can be adjusted by inserting a pin into the jet, and swivelling it to the required position.

23 Radio/cassette player – removal and refitting

Removal

1 All the radio/cassette players fitted to the Clio range have DIN standard fixings. A pair of removal clips, obtainable from in-car entertainment specialists, will be required for removal.

2 Disconnect the battery negative lead. **Note:** *If the vehicle has a security-coded radio, check that you have a copy of the code number before disconnecting the battery. Refer to your Renault dealer if in doubt.*

3 Where applicable, prise the plastic covers from the sides of the radio/cassette player.

4 Insert the clips into the holes at the sides of the unit until they snap into place. Pull the clips rearwards (away from the facia) to release the unit **(see illustration)**.

5 Withdraw the radio/cassette unit from the facia. Disconnect the wiring plugs and the aerial cable from the rear of the unit **(see illustration)**.

Refitting

6 Reconnect the wiring plugs and the aerial cable to the rear of the unit.

7 Push the unit into its housing in the facia until the retaining lugs snap into place.

8 Where applicable, refit the covers to the sides of the unit, then reconnect the battery negative lead.

22.11a Disconnecting the hose from the washer jet . . .

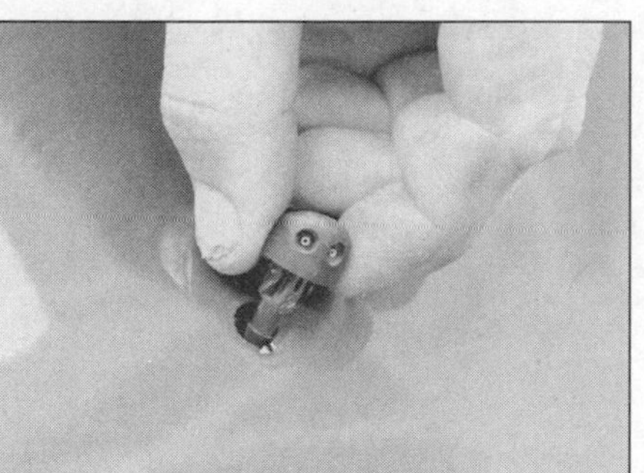
22.11b . . . and removing the washer jet from the bonnet

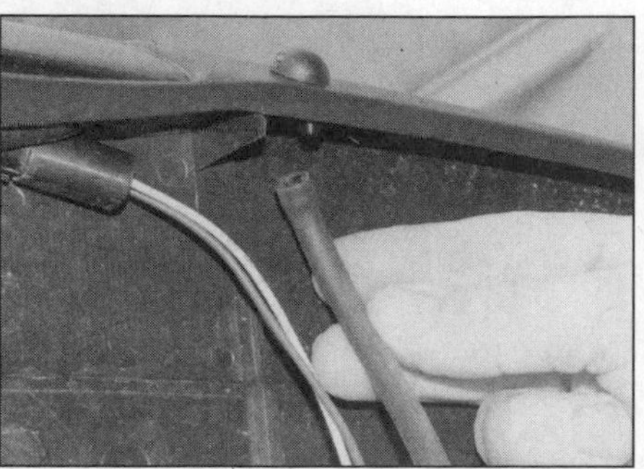
22.14a Disconnect the rear washer hose

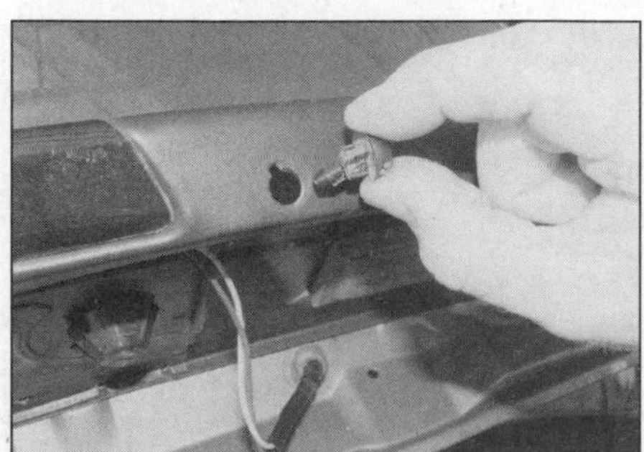
22.14b . . . and remove the washer jet from the spoiler

23.4 Using DIN standard removal clips to remove the radio/cassette player

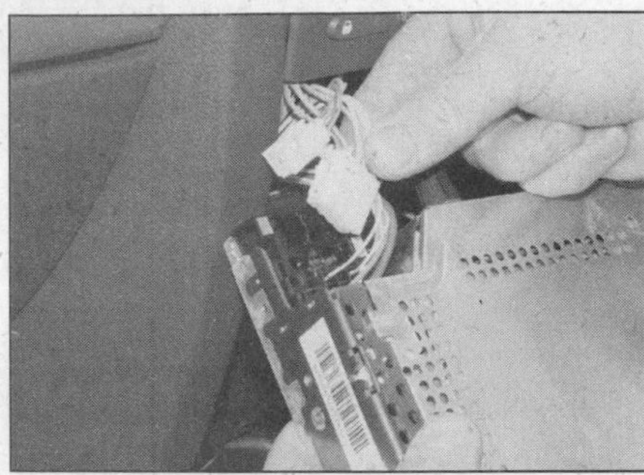

23.5 Disconnecting the radio/cassette player wiring plugs

24 Loudspeakers – removal and refitting

Front door-mounted

Removal

1 Make sure the ignition and radio/cassette/CD player is switched off.

2 Unclip the speaker grille from the door inner trim panel.

3 Remove the securing screws, then withdraw the loudspeaker from the housing in the door **(see illustration)**.

4 Disconnect the wiring and remove the loudspeaker **(see illustration)**.

Refitting

5 Refitting is a reversal of removal.

Front facia-mounted

Removal

6 Disconnect the battery negative lead.

7 Remove the upper facia trim panel as described in Chapter 11, Section 29.

8 Disconnect the wiring plug and unclip the speaker from the lower facia trim panel **(see illustrations)**.

Refitting

9 Refitting is a reversal of removal.

Rear door-mounted (5-door)

Removal

10 Make sure the ignition and radio/cassette/CD player is switched off.

11 Twist the speaker grille from the speaker housing **(see illustration)**.

12 Remove the four securing screws, then withdraw the loudspeaker from the housing in the door **(see illustration)**.

13 Disconnect the wiring and remove the loudspeaker **(see illustration)**.

Refitting

14 Refitting is a reversal of removal.

Rear inner panel-mounted (3-door)

Removal

15 Make sure the ignition and radio/cassette/CD player is switched off.

16 Fold the seat cushion base forward and unclip the speaker grille from the inner trim panel **(see illustration)**.

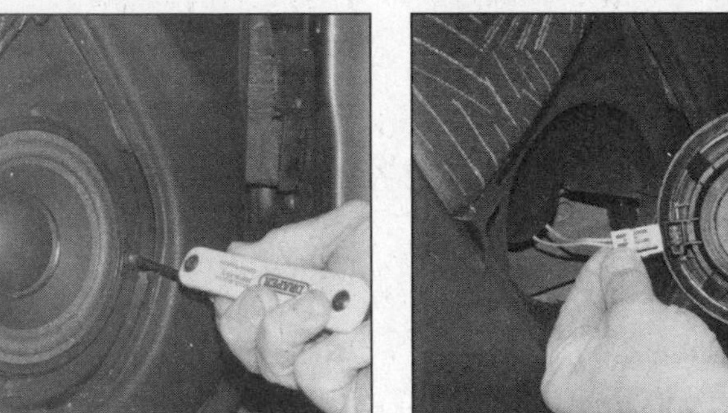

24.3 Undo the speaker securing screws

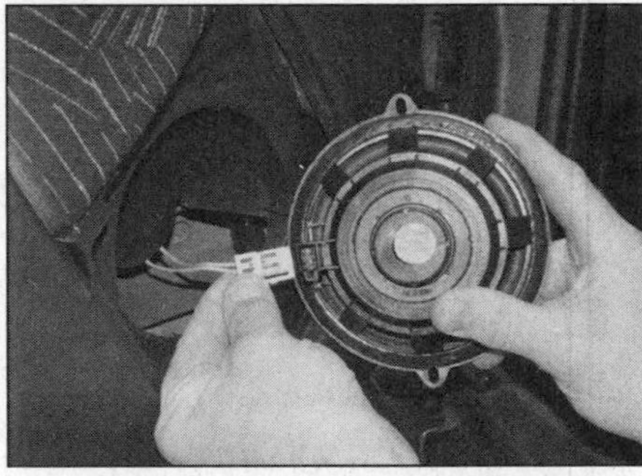

24.4 Disconnect the wiring from the speaker on removal

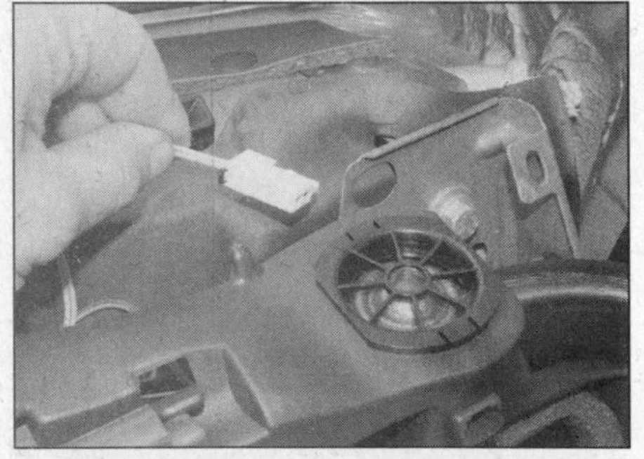

24.8a Disconnect the wiring plug . . .

24.8b . . . and unclip the speaker

24.11 Twist the speaker grille (in the direction of the arrow) to remove

24.12 Undo the speaker securing screws (arrowed)

24.13 Disconnect the wiring plug from the speaker

24.16 Unclip the speaker grille from the rear panel

17 Remove the securing screws, then withdraw the loudspeaker from the housing in the door **(see illustration)**.

18 Disconnect the wiring and remove the loudspeaker.

Refitting

19 Refitting is a reversal of removal.

25 Radio aerial – removal and refitting

Aerial assembly

Removal

1 Open the tailgate, peel back the aperture seal and remove the plastic clips from the headlining **(see illustrations)**.

2 Unclip the plastic bung from the centre of the rear headlining **(see illustration).**

3 Undo the securing bolt and withdraw the seat belt anchorage from the rear of the headlining **(see illustration)**.

4 For further movement of the headlining, to expose the base of the aerial, it may be necessary to remove the right- and left-hand rear inner trim panels as described in Chapter 11, Section 27.

5 Unscrew the securing nut, and disconnect the aerial lead from the base of the aerial. Lift the aerial from the roof panel.

6 The aerial mast can be unscrewed from the base of the aerial if required **(see illustration)**.

24.17 Undo the speaker securing screws (arrowed)

Refitting

7 Refitting is a reversal of removal.

Aerial lead

Removal

8 With the lead disconnected from the aerial as described previously in this Section, observe the routing of the lead.

9 Remove the relevant inner trim panels as described in Chapter 11, Section 27.

10 Remove the radio/cassette player as described in Section 23, then disconnect the aerial lead from the rear of the unit **(see illustration)**,

11 Pull the lower end of the lead and feed the lead from behind the facia.

Refitting

12 Refitting is a reversal of removal. Take care not to damage the lead or surrounding components when feeding it through behind the facia and behind the trim panels.

13 Refit the radio/cassette player with reference to Section 23.

26 Anti-theft alarm system – general information

1 Certain models are fitted with an anti-theft alarm system, which uses various sensing systems and warning sirens, depending on model. No information was available for the alarm systems at the time of writing. Any faults should be referred to a Renault dealer for diagnosis.

2 All models are fitted with an engine immobiliser device which is activated by the coded ignition key. When the immobiliser is armed, the indicator light on the instrument panel will flash continuously. When the ignition is switched on, an antenna ring around the ignition switch interrogates and captures the code from the head of the key and transmits it to the multi-timer unit (see Section 5). If the multi-timer unit recognises the code, the engine can be started.

27 Airbag system – general information and precautions

All models are equipped with an airbag system. In addition to front airbags for the

25.1a Carefully peel back the tailgate seal . . .

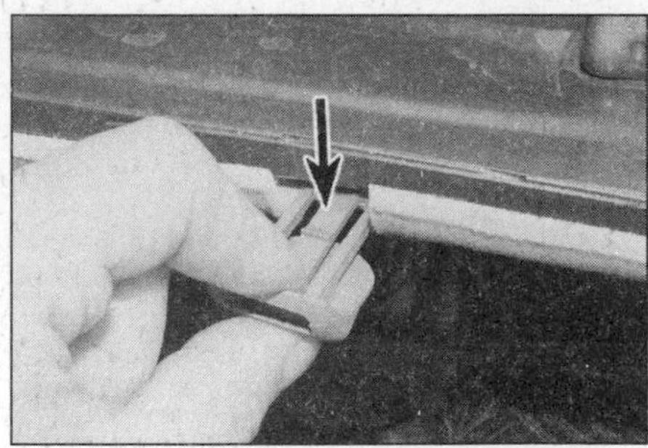

25.1b . . . and press down the clip (arrowed) to remove the retaining clips from the headlining

25.2 Unclip the bung from the centre of the headlining at the rear

25.3 Undo the securing bolt (arrowed) from the rear of the headlining

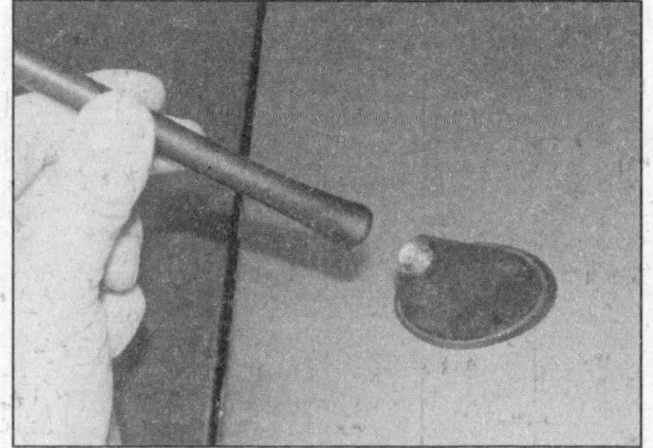

25.6 Aerial mast will unscrew from the base

25.10 Disconnect the aerial lead from the radio/cassette

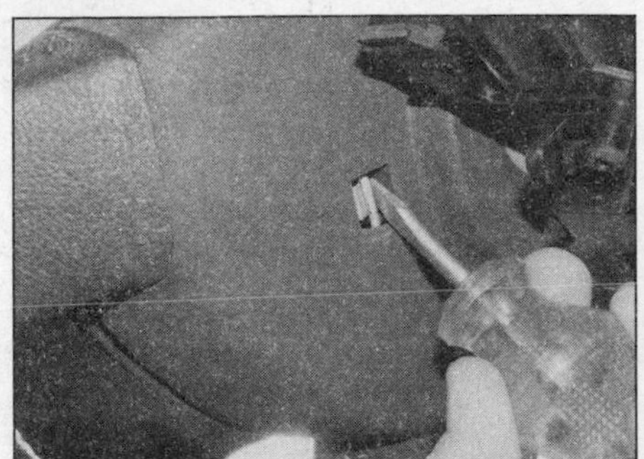
28.2 Using a screwdriver to release the airbag retaining clip (one side shown)

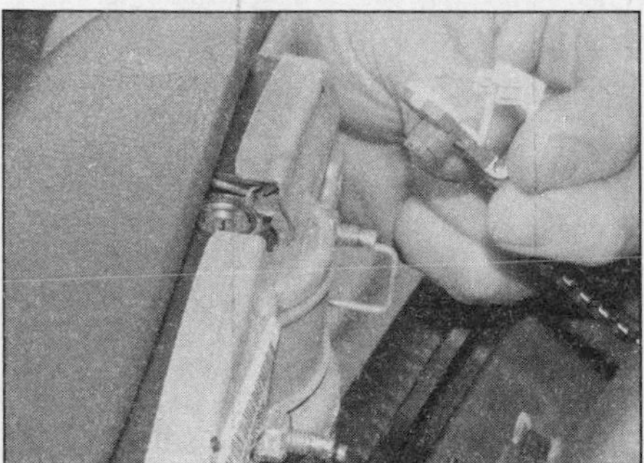
28.3a Disconnect the airbag upper wiring connector . . .

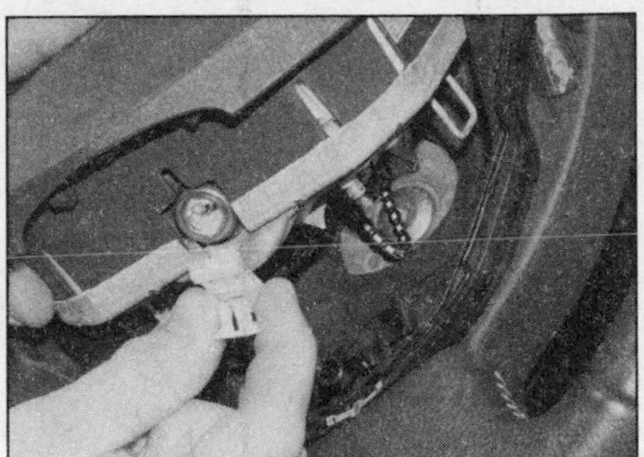
28.3b . . . and disconnect the airbag lower wiring connector

driver and front passenger, there are side airbags fitted to the front seats.

The airbag system is triggered in the event of a heavy frontal or side impact; depending on the point of impact, not all the airbags will be fired. The airbags inflate rapidly to form a safety cushion which prevents contact with the inside of the car, greatly reducing the risk of injury, after which they deflate.

The system is armed only when the ignition is on. However, a reserve power source maintains power to the system for a short period – for this reason, it is essential to disconnect the battery and wait before disconnecting any of the system wiring.

The system is activated by a 'g' sensor in the electronic control unit, fitted under the centre console. The airbag control unit also controls the seat belt tensioners. Impact sensors in the B-pillars or door sills detect side impacts, which if severe enough, will cause the side airbag to be fired on the side concerned.

Linked to the airbag system are the seat belt tensioners fitted to the front belts (see Chapter 11). The seat belt tensioners are fired with the airbags in the event of an accident, to take up the slack in the belts, and hold the occupants in their seats.

When the ignition is switched on, the system performs a self-test (the airbag warning light should come on, then go out). If the light stays on, or comes on while driving, consult a Renault dealer without delay.

Precautions

Warning: Before carrying out any operations on the airbag system, to prevent the risk of injury if the system is triggered inadvertently when working on the vehicle, disconnect the battery and disable the system (wait for at least five minutes). This will allow the reserve power capacitors in the control unit to discharge. When operations are complete, make sure no one is inside the vehicle when the battery is reconnected then, with the driver's door open, switch the ignition on from outside the vehicle.

Warning: Before carrying out any operations in the vicinity of the airbag or steering wheel, to prevent the risk of injury if the system is triggered inadvertently when working on the vehicle, remove the airbag unit as described in Section 28.

Warning: Note that the airbag(s) must not be subjected to excess temperatures. When the airbag is removed, ensure that it is stored the correct way up to prevent possible inflation.

Warning: Do not allow any solvents or cleaning agents to contact the airbag assemblies. They must be cleaned using only a damp cloth.

Warning: The airbags and control unit are both sensitive to impact. If either is dropped or damaged they should be renewed.

Warning: Do not refit the airbag unit to the steering wheel once the steering wheel has been removed from the vehicle.

Warning: Do not attempt to test the airbag electrical circuit using anything except the Renault special test tool. Using a conventional multimeter or ohmmeter is likely to trigger the airbag.

Warning: If the airbag has been triggered, the control unit must be renewed.

Warning: If the airbag is to be renewed, the control unit must also be renewed.

Warning: Disconnect the airbag control unit wiring plug prior to using arc-welding equipment on the vehicle.

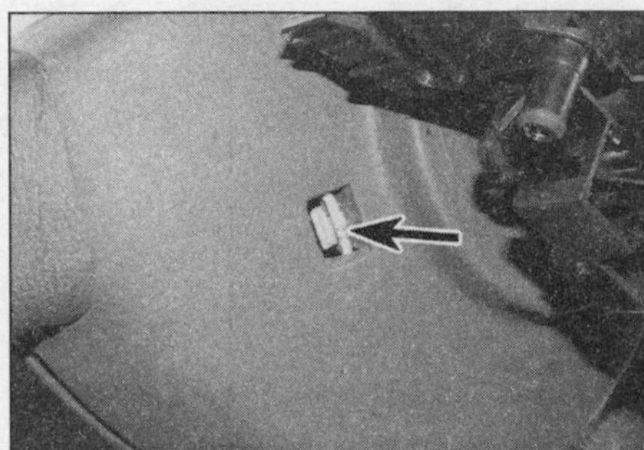
28.4 Make sure the retaining clips (one side shown) is located correctly

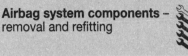

28 Airbag system components – removal and refitting

Note: *Refer to the warnings in Section 27 before carrying out the following operations.*

1 Disconnect the battery negative lead and wait for at least five minutes. This will allow the reserve power capacitors in the control unit to discharge and disable the airbag system (see Section 27).

Driver's airbag

Removal

2 Using a screwdriver unclip the airbag from the steering wheel **(see illustration)**, rotating the wheel as necessary to gain access to the retaining clips.

3 Return the steering wheel to the straight-ahead position then carefully lift the airbag assembly away from the steering wheel. Release the centre locking tabs and disconnect the wiring connectors (upper and lower) from the rear of the unit **(see illustrations)**. Note that the airbag must not be knocked or dropped and should be stored with its padded surface uppermost.

Refitting

4 Ensure that the wiring connectors are securely reconnected and seat the airbag unit centrally in the steering wheel, making sure the wires do not become trapped. Press the airbag squarely in to place until the retaining clips locate in the steering wheel **(see illustration)**.

5 Ensuring no one is inside the vehicle, reconnect the battery. With the driver's door open, turn on the ignition switch and check the operation of the airbag warning light.

Passenger airbag

Removal

6 Remove the upper facia panel, referring to Chapter 11, Section 29.

7 Unclip the centre locking tab from the wiring connector, then disconnect the wiring connector from the airbag unit **(see illustration)**.

8 Slacken and remove the retaining screws,

28.7 Unclip the locking tab and disconnect the wiring plug (arrowed) from the airbag

28.8 Undo the securing screws (arrowed) and carefully remove the airbag

then release the airbag unit from its mountings and remove it from the facia **(see illustration)**. Note that the airbag must not be knocked or dropped and should be stored with its padded surface uppermost.

Refitting

9 Manoeuvre the airbag into position, then refit the mounting screws securely. Reconnect the wiring connector, ensuring that the wiring is correctly routed and retained by its locking tab.

10 Refit the upper facia panel as described in Chapter 11, Section 29.

11 Ensuring no one is inside the vehicle, reconnect the battery. With the driver's door open, turn on the ignition switch and check the operation of the airbag warning light.

Airbag control unit

Removal

12 Remove the centre console as described in Chapter 11 to gain access to the control unit which is mounted in front of the gearchange/selector lever.

13 Undo the retaining screws and remove the heater ducting going to the rear footwell **(see illustration)**. If required, lift up the carpet to gain access to the control unit.

14 Unscrew the retaining nuts and remove the control unit from the vehicle **(see illustration)**. Release the retaining clip and disconnect the wiring connector as the unit is removed.

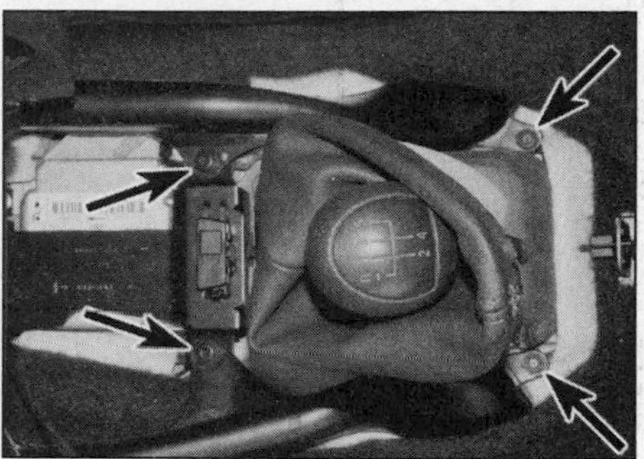
28.13 Remove the retaining screws (arrowed) from the air ducting

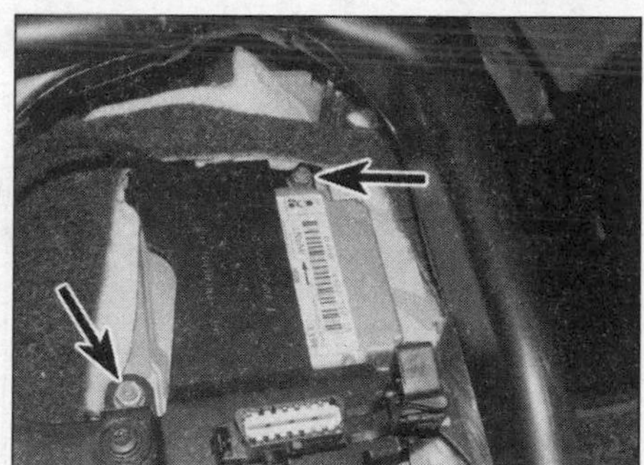
28.14 Undo the control unit mounting nuts (arrowed)

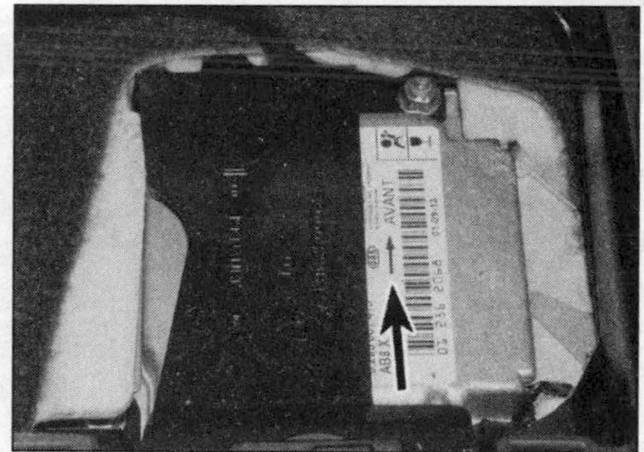

28.15 Arrow on the control unit (arrowed) must be pointing forwards

Refitting

15 Refit the control unit, making sure the arrow on the top of the unit is pointing towards the front of the vehicle **(see illustration)**. Refit the mounting nuts and tighten them securely.

16 Reconnect the wiring connector and refit the centre console as described in the relevant Section of Chapter 11.

17 Ensuring no one is inside the vehicle, reconnect the battery. With the driver's door open, turn on the ignition switch and check the operation of the airbag warning light.

Airbag contact unit/switch assembly

18 Follow the procedures as described in Section 6 for the removal and refitting of the complete stalk switch assembly.

Side airbags

19 The side airbags are located internally within the front seat backrests, and no attempt should be made to remove them. Any suspected problems with the side airbag system should be referred to a Renault dealer.

Clio 2001 on

Diagram 1

Key to symbols

Bulb

Switch

Fuse/fusible link and current rating — F5 10A

Multiple contact switch (ganged)

Resistor

Variable resistor

Connecting wires

Item no. — 2

Pump/motor — M

Earth point and location — E12

Wire joint

Solenoid actuator

Diode

Light emitting diode (LED)

Wire colour (brown with black tracer) — Br/Bk

Screened cable

Dashed outline denotes part of a larger item, containing in this case an electronic or solid state device.
Pin types:
2 - Unspecified colour connector, pin 2.
Bk 1 - Black Connector, pin 1.

Earth points

E1	Battery earth	**E8**	Heater casing electrical earth
E2	RH instrument panel	**E9**	Engine electrical earth
E3	Instrument panel radio earth	**E10**	Bodywork earth
E4	RH instrument panel electrical earth	**E11**	Passenger air bag earth
E5	LH instrument panel electrical earth	**E12**	RH front electrical earth
E6	ABS earth	**E13**	LH front pillar electrical earth
E7	LH front electrical earth		

Key to circuits

Diagram 1	Information for wiring diagrams
Diagram 2	Starting and charging, airbag and radio with CD player
Diagram 3	Electric windows, central locking, ABS, sunroof and cigarette lighter
Diagram 4	Air conditioning and horn
Diagram 5	Engine cooling, electric mirrors and wash/wipe
Diagram 6	Power steering, carphone, instrument panel, heated rear window and mirrors
Diagram 7	Multitimer
Diagram 8	Interior lights, headlight adjustment, xenon headlight adjustment and diagnostic connector power
Diagram 9	Headlights, side lights, brake lights, fog lights and direction indicators

Fuse table

Engine fuse box

Fuses	*Rating*	*Fuses*	*Rating*	*Fuses*	*Rating*
F1	30A	**F5**	7.5A	**F9**	60A
F2	25A	**F6**	70A	**F10**	60A
F3	30A	**F7**	50A	**F11**	30A
F4	5A	**F8**	60A	**F1a**	60A

Main fuse box

Fuses	*Rating*	*Circuit protected*
F1	15A	Air bag
F2	15A	Brake lights, carphone, instrument panel, diagnostic connector
F3	15A	Wash/wipe, multitimer, reversing lights, starter, headlight adjuster, air conditioning
F4	20A	Wash/wipe
F5	10A	ABS
F6	10A	Air conditioning, multitimer
F7	10A	Radio, cigarette lighter, mirror lights
F8	15A	Horn
F9	15A	LH dipped beam
F10	15A	RH dipped beam
F11	10A	RH main beam
F12	10A	LH main beam
F13	20A	Rear wiper via multitimer
F14	-	Not used
F15	-	Not used
F16	-	Not used
F17	10A	Heated mirrors
F18	20A	Front fog light
F19	20A	Driver's electric window via multitimer
F20	30A	Passenger's electric window via multitimer
F21	5A	Central locking, diagnostic connector, multitimer, instrument panel
F22	15A	Hazard lights via multitimer
F23	15A	ABS, power steering
F24	-	Not used
F25	-	Not used
F26	10A	LH side lights
F27	10A	RH side lights
F28	2A	Alarm
F29	20A	Radio, multitimer, electric mirrors interior lights via multitimer, automatic air conditioning
F30	30A	Heated rear window via multitimer
F31	20A	Central locking via multitimer
F32	-	Not used
F33	20A	Headlight washer
F34	20A	Air conditioning
F35	-	Not used
F36	30A	Electric windows via multitimer
F37	10A	Multitimer
F38	30A	Caravan connection
F39	15A	Power steering

H32958

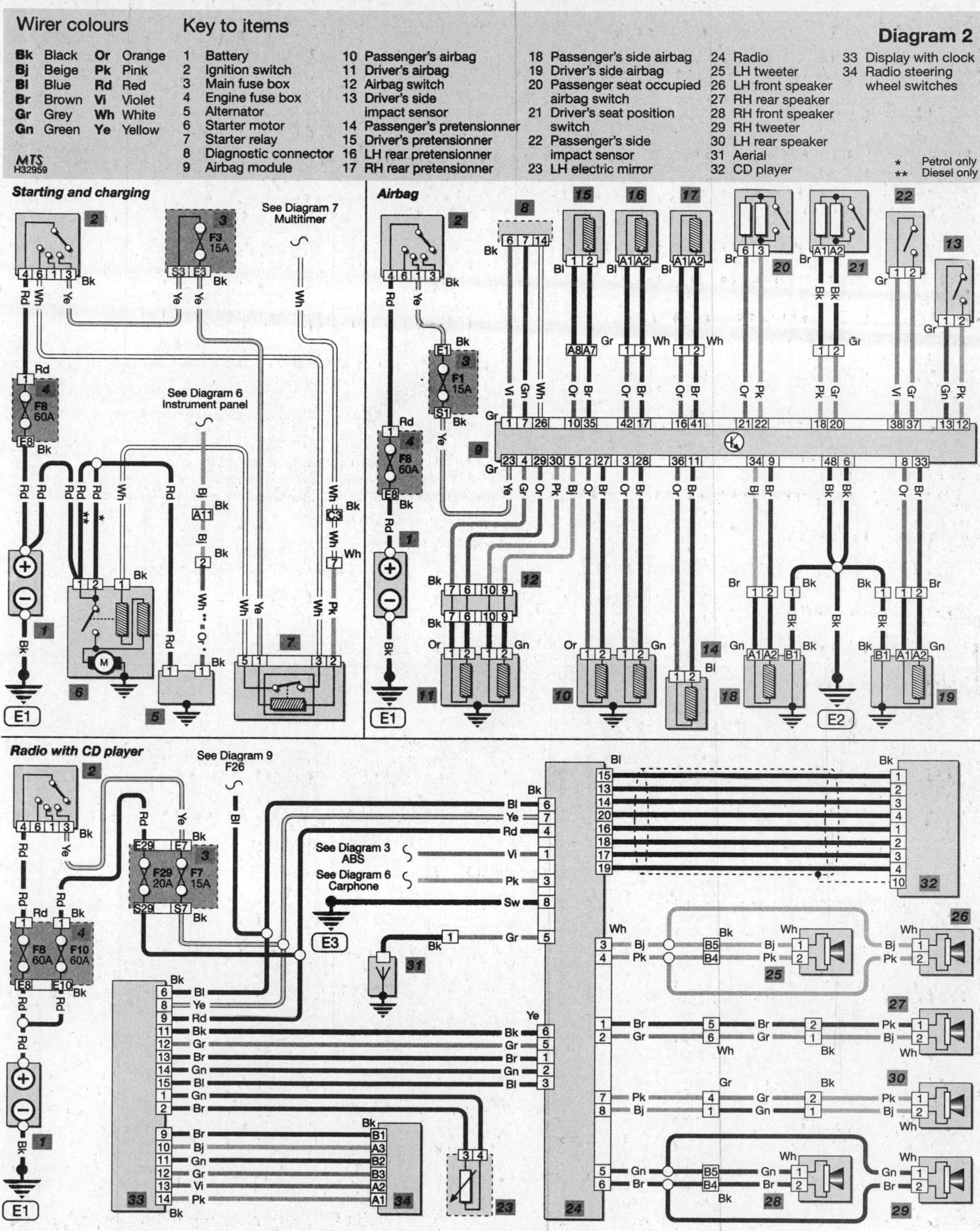
Diagram 2
Wirer colours
Bk Black
Bj Beige
Bl Blue
Br Brown
Gr Grey
Gn Green
Or Orange
Pk Pink
Rd Red
Vi Violet
Wh White
Ye Yellow
Key to items
1 Battery
2 Ignition switch
3 Main fuse box
4 Engine fuse box
5 Alternator
6 Starter motor
7 Starter relay
8 Diagnostic connector
9 Airbag module
10 Passenger's airbag
11 Driver's airbag
12 Airbag switch
13 Driver's side impact sensor
14 Passenger's pretensionner
15 Driver's pretensionner
16 LH rear pretensionner
17 RH rear pretensionner
18 Passenger's side airbag
19 Driver's side airbag
20 Passenger seat occupied airbag switch
21 Driver's seat position switch
22 Passenger's side impact sensor
23 LH electric mirror
24 Radio
25 LH tweeter
26 LH front speaker
27 RH rear speaker
28 RH front speaker
29 RH tweeter
30 LH rear speaker
31 Aerial
32 CD player
33 Display with clock
34 Radio steering wheel switches
* Petrol only
** Diesel only
MTS
H32959
Starting and charging
See Diagram 7 Multitimer
See Diagram 6 Instrument panel
Airbag
Radio with CD player
See Diagram 9 F26
See Diagram 3 ABS
See Diagram 6 Carphone

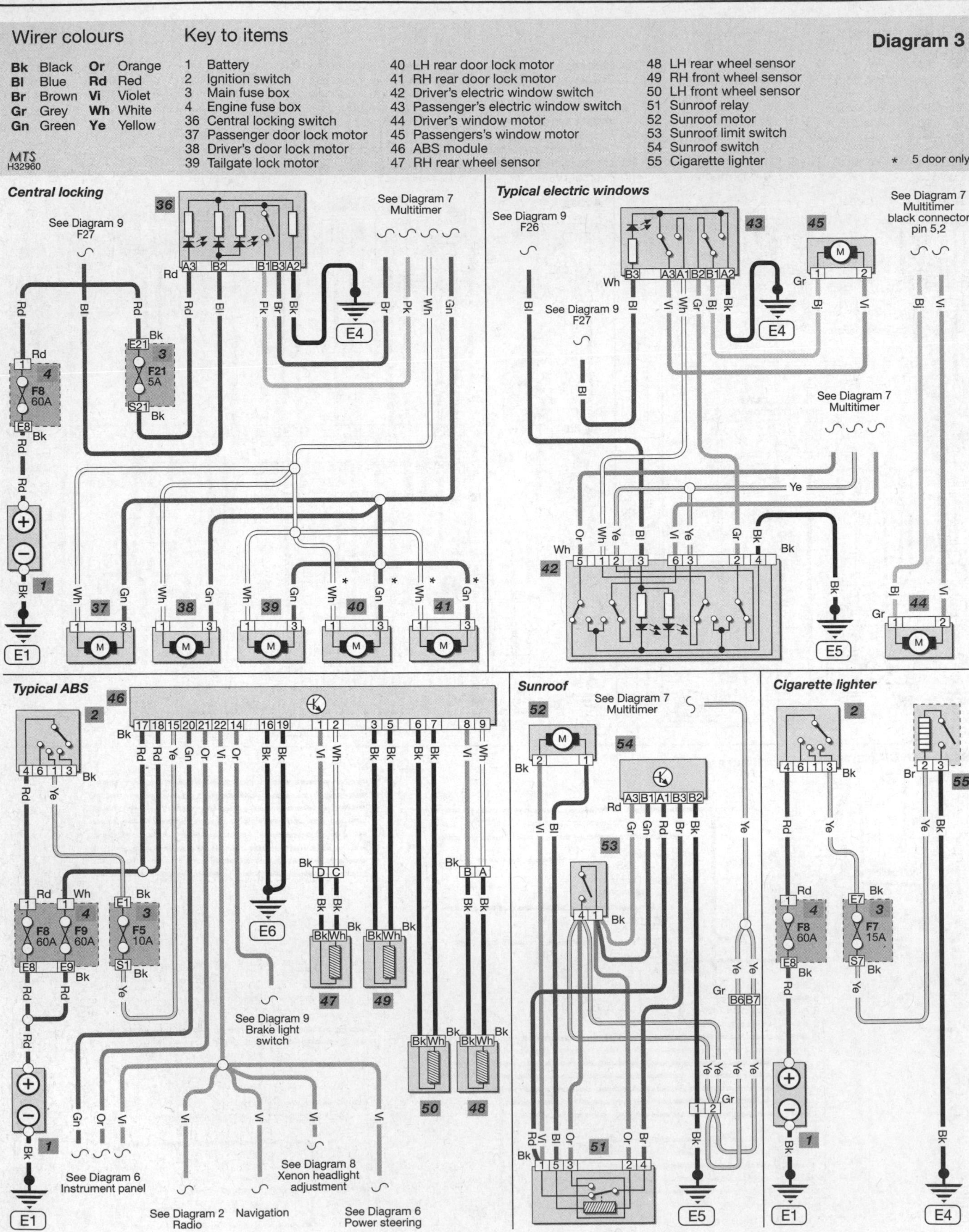
Wirer colours
Bk Black
Bl Blue
Br Brown
Gr Grey
Gn Green
Or Orange
Rd Red
Vi Violet
Wh White
Ye Yellow
MTS
H32960
Key to items
1 Battery
2 Ignition switch
3 Main fuse box
4 Engine fuse box
36 Central locking switch
37 Passenger door lock motor
38 Driver's door lock motor
39 Tailgate lock motor
40 LH rear door lock motor
41 RH rear door lock motor
42 Driver's electric window switch
43 Passenger's electric window switch
44 Driver's window motor
45 Passengers's window motor
46 ABS module
47 RH rear wheel sensor
48 LH rear wheel sensor
49 RH front wheel sensor
50 LH front wheel sensor
51 Sunroof relay
52 Sunroof motor
53 Sunroof limit switch
54 Sunroof switch
55 Cigarette lighter
Diagram 3
* 5 door only
Central locking
See Diagram 9 F27
See Diagram 7 Multitimer
F8 60A
F21 5A
Typical electric windows
See Diagram 9 F26
See Diagram 9 F27
See Diagram 7 Multitimer black connector pin 5,2
See Diagram 7 Multitimer
Typical ABS
F8 60A
F9 60A
F5 10A
See Diagram 9 Brake light switch
See Diagram 6 Instrument panel
See Diagram 2 Radio
Navigation
See Diagram 8 Xenon headlight adjustment
See Diagram 6 Power steering
Sunroof
See Diagram 7 Multitimer
Cigarette lighter
F8 60A
F7 15A

Diagram 4

Wirer colours

Bk	Black	**Or**	Orange
Bl	Blue	**Rd**	Red
Br	Brown	**Vi**	Violet
Gr	Grey	**Wh**	White
Gn	Green	**Ye**	Yellow

MTS
H32961

Key to items

1 Battery
2 Ignition switch
3 Main fuse box
4 Engine fuse box
8 Diagnostic connector
56 Air conditioning unit
57 Interior light rheostat
58 Passenger compartment temperature sensor and fan
59 Central communication unit
60 Air recirculation flap motor
61 Air conditioning fan power unit
62 Air conditioning fan
63 Cold air blower relay
64 Footwell fan
65 Air mixing flap motor
66 Blown air temperature sensor
67 Air conditioning control panel
68 Cold air blower unit
69 Air conditioning control relay
70 Power steering/AC diode
71 Air conditioning compressor
72 Light switch with horn button
73 Horn

* Manual air conditioning only

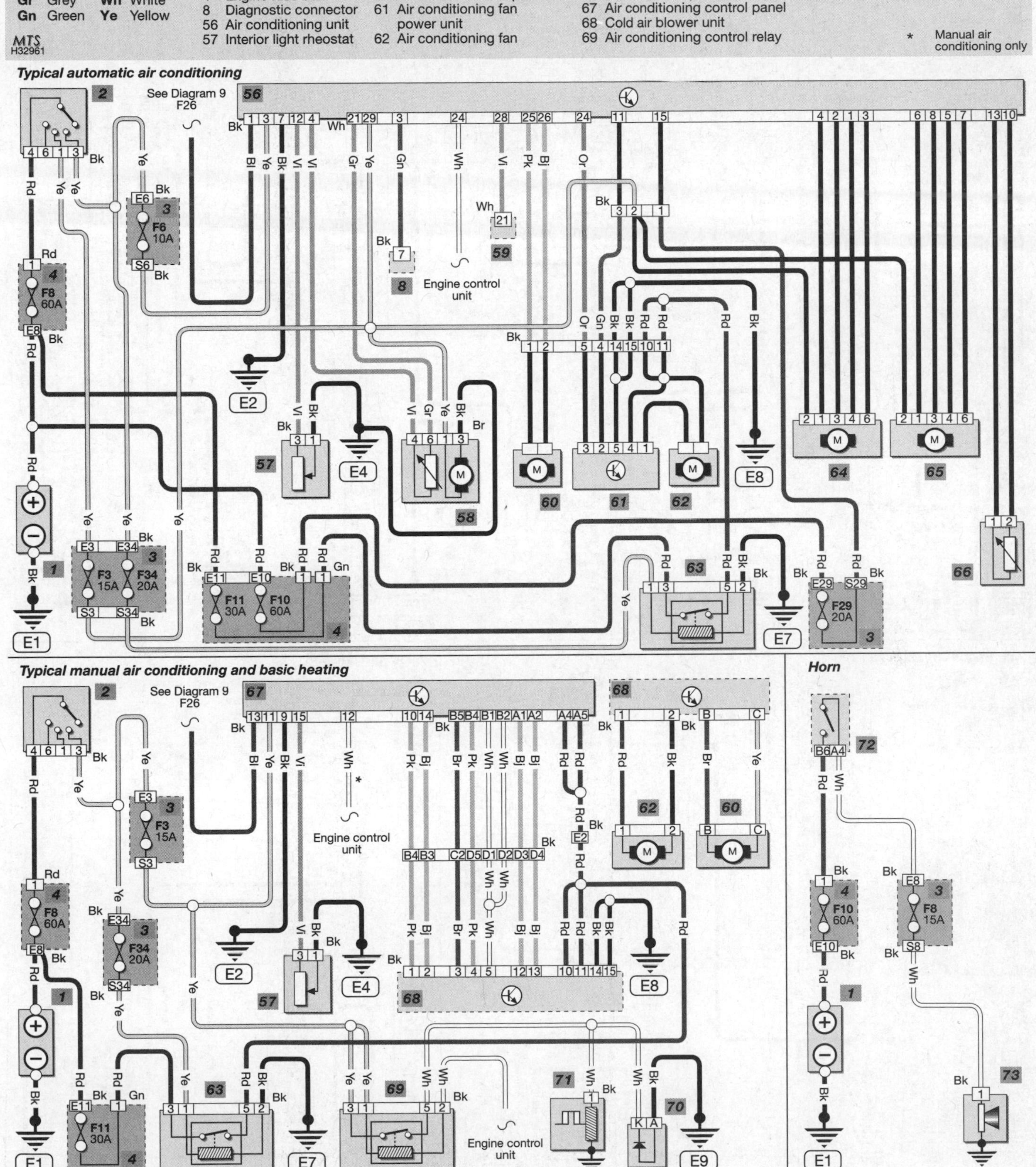

Diagram 5

Wirer colours

Bk	Black	**Or**	Orange
Bl	Blue	**Rd**	Red
Br	Brown	**Vi**	Violet
Gr	Grey	**Wh**	White
Gn	Green	**Ye**	Yellow

Key to items

1 Battery
2 Ignition switch
3 Main fuse box
4 Engine fuse box
23 LH electric mirror
74 Injection relay
75 Engine cooling fan low speed relay
76 Engine cooling fan
77 Engine cooling fan relay
78 Engine cooling fan resistor
79 Electric mirror switch
80 RH electric mirror
81 Wash/wipe switch
82 Rain sensor
83 Washer pump
84 Windscreen wiper
85 Rear wiper
86 Headlight washer relay 1
87 Headlight washer relay 2
88 Headlight washer pump

MTS H32962

Petrol engine cooling

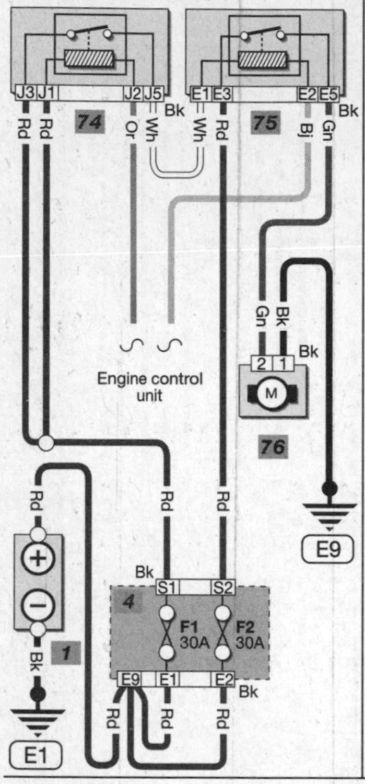
74
75
76
Engine control unit
F1 30A
F2 30A
E1
E9

Diesel engine cooling

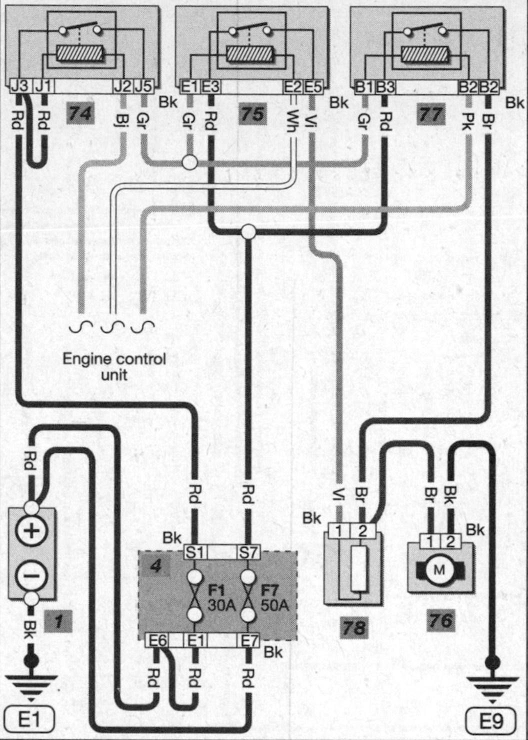
74
75
77
76
78
Engine control unit
F1 30A
F7 50A
E1
E9

Electric mirrors

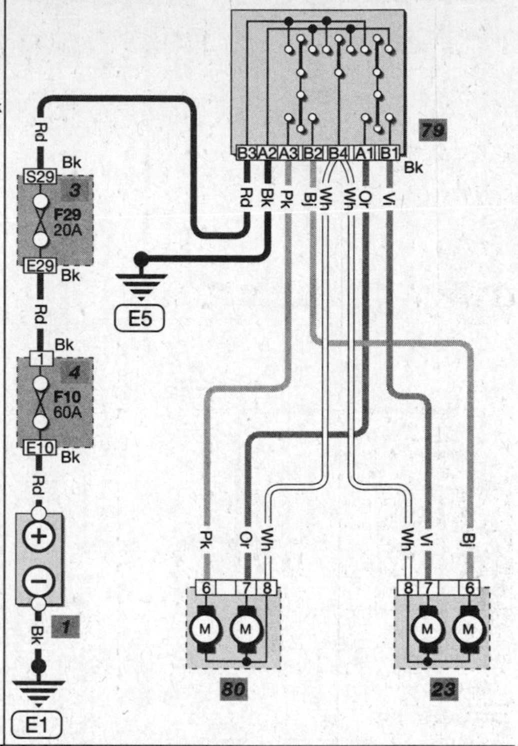
79
F29 20A
F10 60A
E5
E1
80
23

Wash/wipe with rain sensor

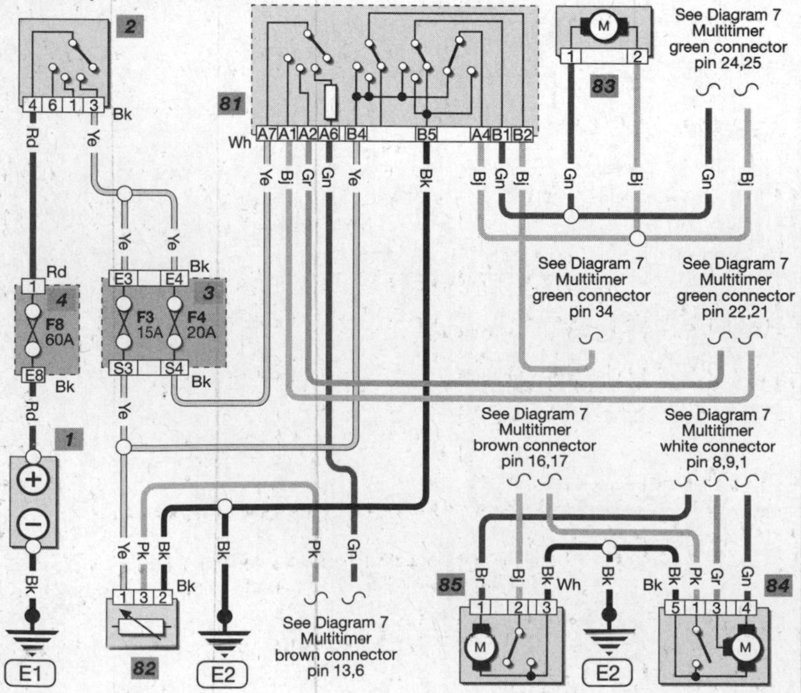
2
81
83
F8 60A
F3 15A
F4 20A
See Diagram 7 Multitimer green connector pin 24,25
See Diagram 7 Multitimer green connector pin 34
See Diagram 7 Multitimer green connector pin 22,21
See Diagram 7 Multitimer brown connector pin 16,17
See Diagram 7 Multitimer white connector pin 8,9,1
See Diagram 7 Multitimer brown connector pin 13,6
82
85
84
E1
E2

Headlight washer

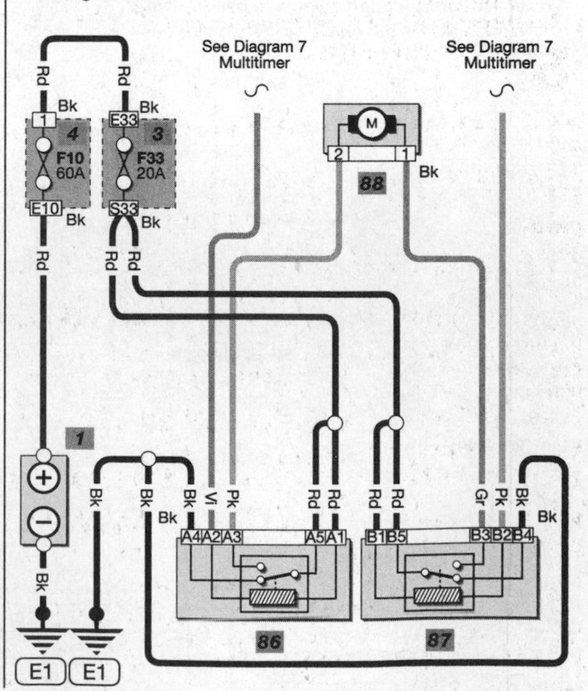
See Diagram 7 Multitimer
See Diagram 7 Multitimer
F10 60A
F33 20A
88
86
87
E1

Diagram 6

Wirer colours

Bk	Black	**Or**	Orange
Bl	Blue	**Rd**	Red
Br	Brown	**Vi**	Violet
Gr	Grey	**Wh**	White
Gn	Green	**Ye**	Yellow

Key to items

1 Battery
2 Ignition switch
3 Main fuse box
4 Engine fuse box
8 Diagnostic connector
23 LH electric mirror
57 Interior lighting rheostat
80 RH electric mirror
81 Wash wipe switch
a) trip computer switch
89 Heated rear window switch
90 Heated rear window
91 Power steering control unit
92 Steering wheel angle sensor
93 Steering wheel torque sensor
94 Power steering motor
95 Mobile phone connector
96 Microphone
97 Speaker
98 Instrument panel
99 Oil level sensor
100 Brake fluid level sensor
101 Oil pressure switch
102 Handbrake switch
103 Fuel level sensor
104 Seatbelt switch

MTS H32963

Heated rear window and mirrors

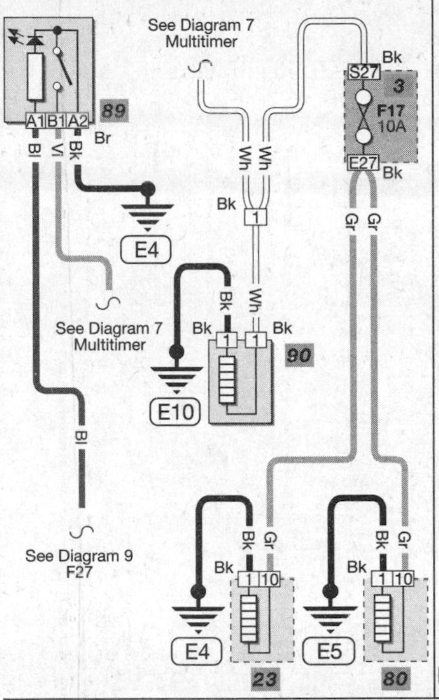

See Diagram 7 Multitimer
See Diagram 7 Multitimer
See Diagram 9 F27

Power steering

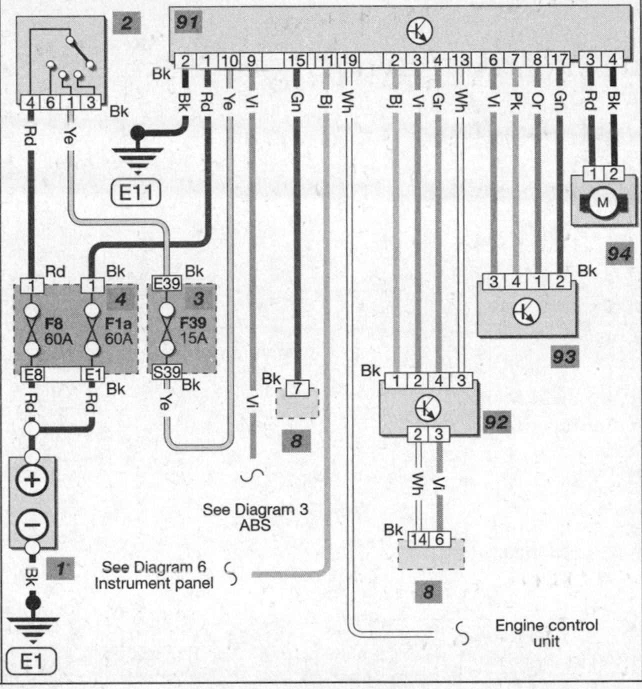

See Diagram 3 ABS
See Diagram 6 Instrument panel
Engine control unit

Carphone

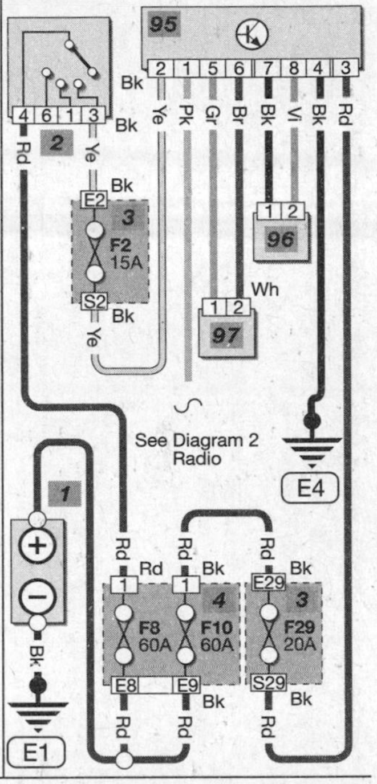

See Diagram 2 Radio

Instrument panel

See Diagram 6 Power steering
See Diagram 7 Multitimer white connector pin 3,2
See Diagram 7 Multitimer brown connector pin 5
See Diagram 3 ABS
See Diagram 2 Alternator
See Diagram 9 Fog lights
See Diagram 9 F26
See Diagram 9 F23
See Diagram 9 F10
See Diagram 9 F12

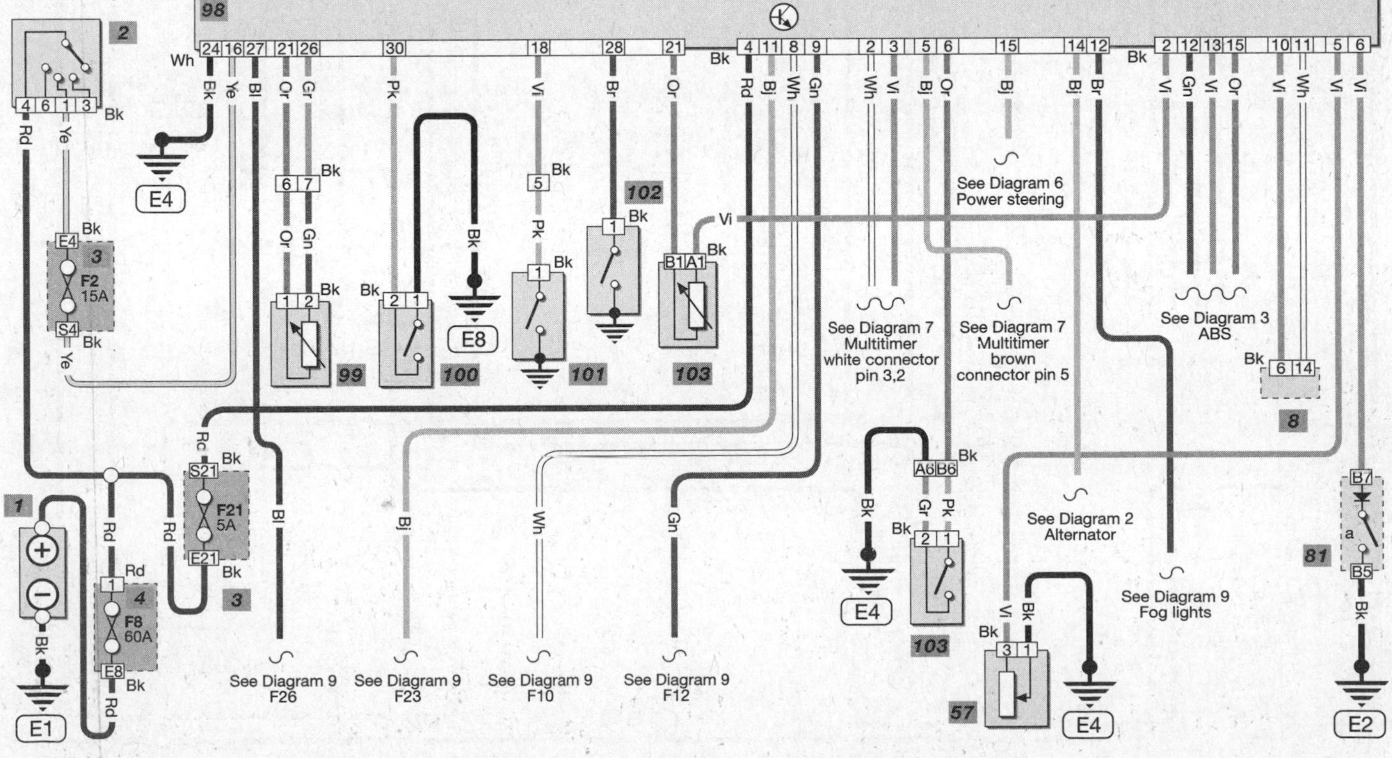

Wire colours

Bk	Black	**Or**	Orange
Bl	Blue	**Rd**	Red
Br	Brown	**Vi**	Violet
Gr	Grey	**Wh**	White
Gn	Green	**Ye**	Yellow

Key to items

1 Battery
2 Ignition switch
3 Main fuse box
4 Engine fuse box
8 Diagnostic connector
105 Multitimer

Diagram 7

MTS
H32964/a

Multitimer

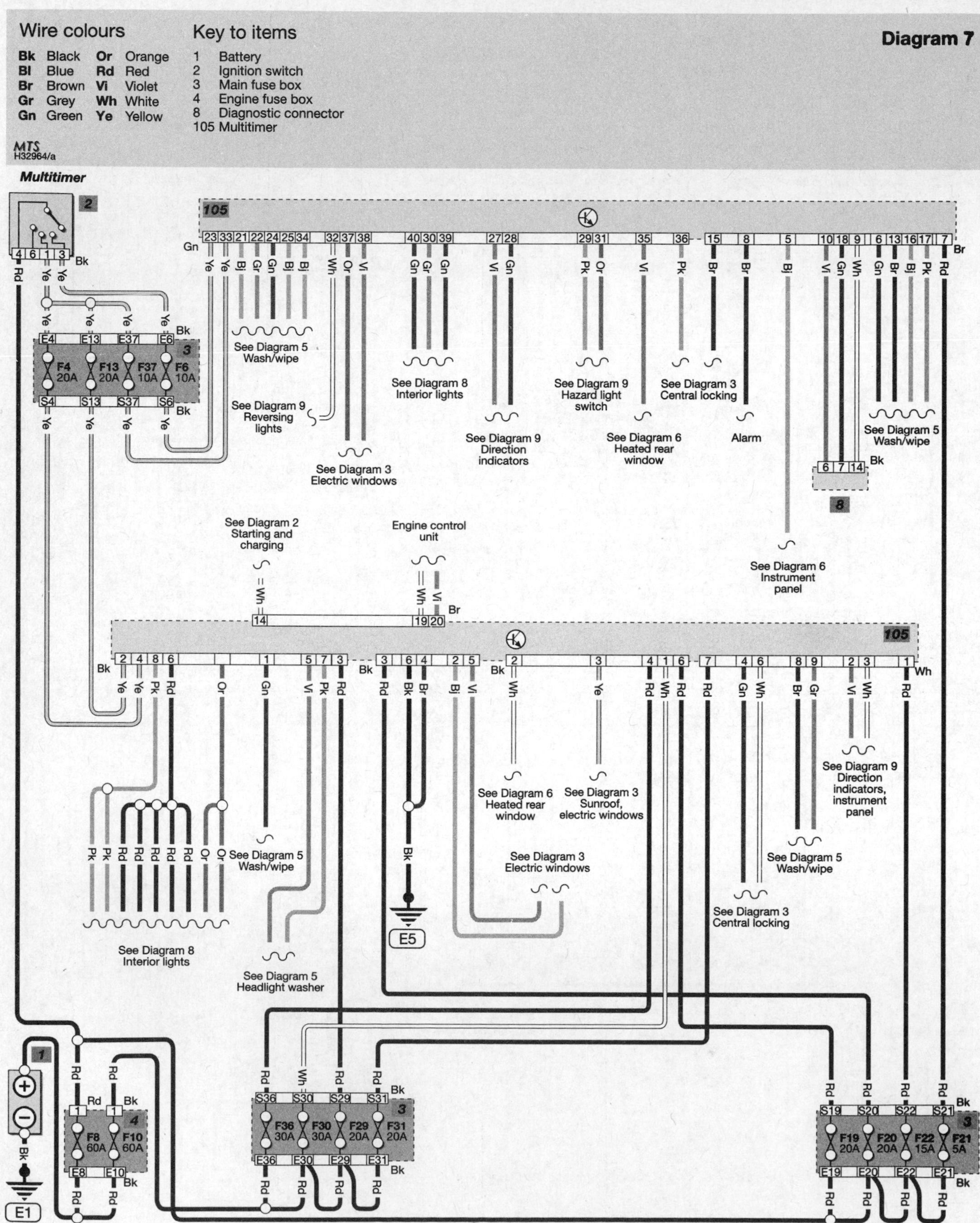

Diagram 8

Wirer colours

Bk	Black	**Or**	Orange
Bl	Blue	**Rd**	Red
Br	Brown	**Vi**	Violet
Gr	Grey	**Wh**	White
Gn	Green	**Ye**	Yellow

Key to items

1 Battery
2 Ignition switch
3 Main fuse box
4 Engine fuse box
8 Diagnostic connector
55 Cigarette lighter
106 RH mirror light
107 LH mirror light
108 Glovebox light
109 Glovebox light switch
110 Boot light switch
111 Boot light
112 RH rear door switch
113 LH rear door switch
114 Driver's door switch
115 Passenger's door switch
116 RH rear courtesy light
117 LH rear courtesy light
118 Central courtesy light
119 Driver's door sill light
120 Passenger's door sill light
121 Headlight adjustment switch
122 Xenon headlight control unit
123 RH headlight adjustment motor
124 LH headlight adjustment motor
125 RH headlight
a) dipped beam
126 LH headlight (as 125)

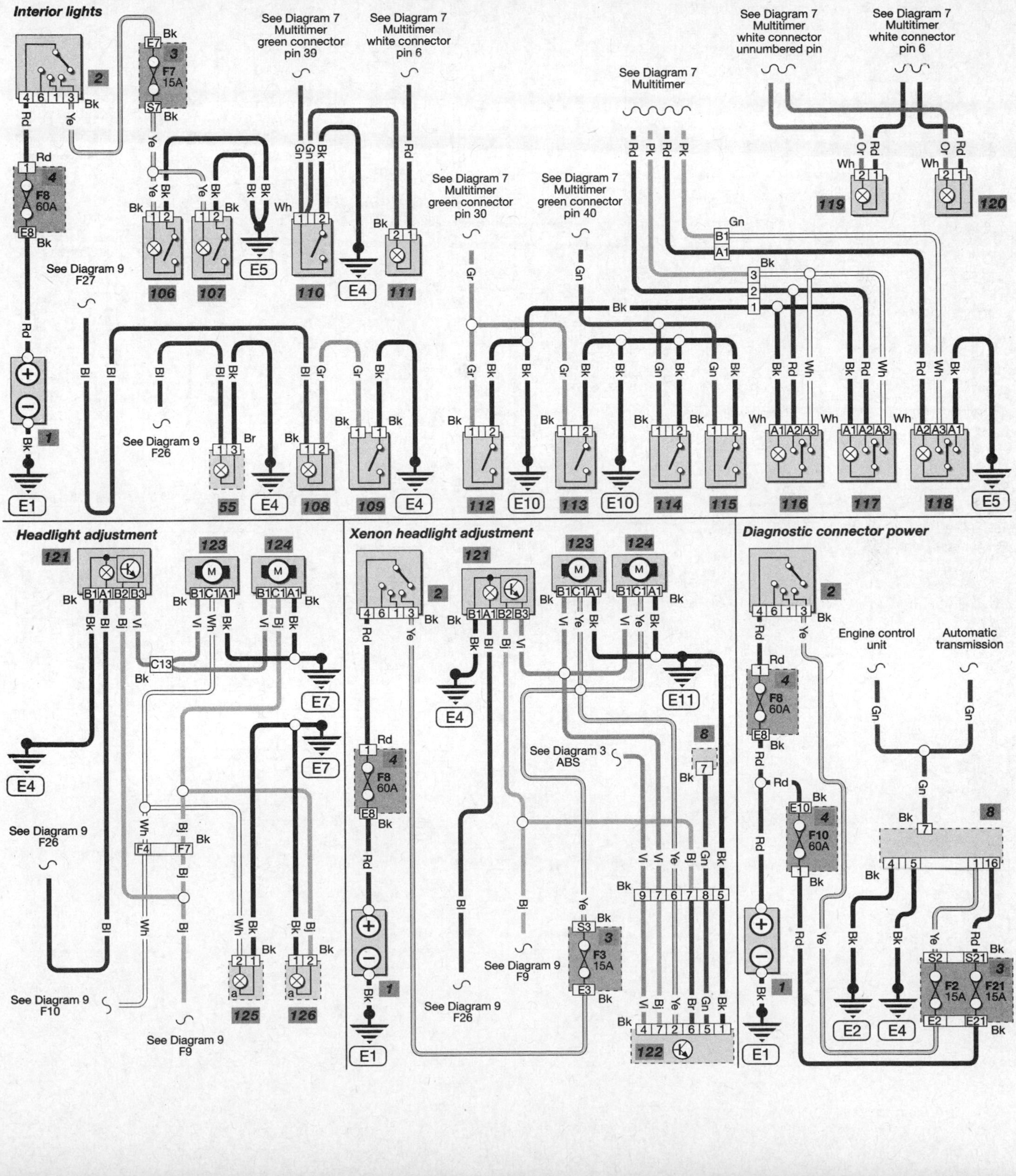

MTS H32965

Interior lights

Headlight adjustment

Xenon headlight adjustment

Diagnostic connector power

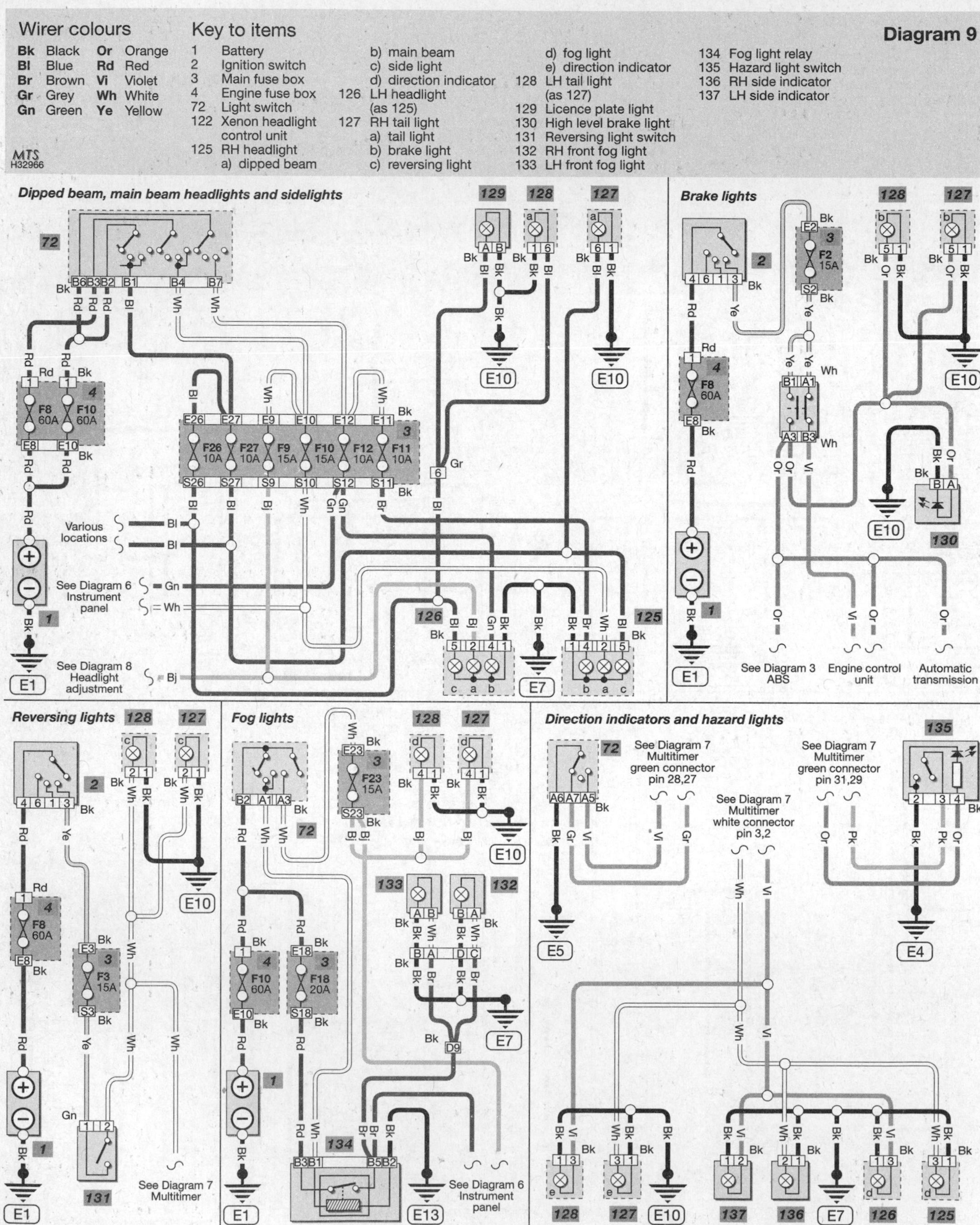

Wirer colours
Bk Black
Bl Blue
Br Brown
Gr Grey
Gn Green
Or Orange
Rd Red
Vi Violet
Wh White
Ye Yellow
Key to items
1 Battery
2 Ignition switch
3 Main fuse box
4 Engine fuse box
72 Light switch
122 Xenon headlight control unit
125 RH headlight
a) dipped beam
b) main beam
c) side light
d) direction indicator
126 LH headlight (as 125)
127 RH tail light
a) tail light
b) brake light
c) reversing light
d) fog light
e) direction indicator
128 LH tail light (as 127)
129 Licence plate light
130 High level brake light
131 Reversing light switch
132 RH front fog light
133 LH front fog light
134 Fog light relay
135 Hazard light switch
136 RH side indicator
137 LH side indicator
Diagram 9
MTS
H32966
Dipped beam, main beam headlights and sidelights
Various locations
See Diagram 6 Instrument panel
See Diagram 8 Headlight adjustment
Brake lights
See Diagram 3 ABS
Engine control unit
Automatic transmission
Reversing lights
See Diagram 7 Multitimer
Fog lights
See Diagram 6 Instrument panel
Direction indicators and hazard lights
See Diagram 7 Multitimer green connector pin 28,27
See Diagram 7 Multitimer white connector pin 3,2
See Diagram 7 Multitimer green connector pin 31,29

Dimensions and weights

Note: *All figures are approximate and may vary according to model. Refer to manufacturer's data for exact figures.*

Dimensions

Overall length	3773 mm
Overall width (including door mirrors)	1940 mm
Overall height (unladen)	1417 mm
Wheelbase	2472 mm
Front track	1406 mm
Rear track	1385 mm
Turning circle (between walls)	10.7 or 11.2 metres (according to equipment level)

Weights

	3-door models	5-door models
Kerb weight:		
1.2 litre 8V	880 kg	900 kg
1.2 litre 16V manual	910 kg	930 kg
1.2 litre 16V sequential	920 kg	940 kg
1.4 litre manual	980 kg	1000 kg
1.4 litre automatic	1010 kg	1030 kg
1.6 litre manual	1020 kg	1040 kg
1.6 litre automatic	1045 kg	1065 kg
1.5 litre (diesel)	960 kg	980 kg
Maximum gross vehicle weight:		
1.2 litre 8V	1420 kg	1440 kg
1.2 litre 16V manual	1450 kg	1470 kg
1.2 litre 16V sequential	1460 kg	1480 kg
1.4 litre manual	1525 kg	1545 kg
1.4 litre automatic	1550 kg	1570 kg
1.6 litre manual	1515 kg	1535 kg
1.6 litre automatic	1540 kg	1560 kg
1.5 litre (diesel) models	1520 kg	1540 kg
Maximum roof rack load (all models)	60 kg	70 kg
Maximum towing weight:		
1.2 litre (all models)	800 kg	
1.4 litre (all models)	900 kg	
1.6 litre (all models)	900 kg	
1.5 litre diesel	950 kg	900 kg

Conversion factors

Length (distance)

Inches (in)	x 25.4	= Millimetres (mm)	x 0.0394	= Inches (in)
Feet (ft)	x 0.305	= Metres (m)	x 3.281	= Feet (ft)
Miles	x 1.609	= Kilometres (km)	x 0.621	= Miles

Volume (capacity)

Cubic inches (cu in; in^3)	x 16.387	= Cubic centimetres (cc; cm^3)	x 0.061	= Cubic inches (cu in; in^3)
Imperial pints (Imp pt)	x 0.568	= Litres (l)	x 1.76	= Imperial pints (Imp pt)
Imperial quarts (Imp qt)	x 1.137	= Litres (l)	x 0.88	= Imperial quarts (Imp qt)
Imperial quarts (Imp qt)	x 1.201	= US quarts (US qt)	x 0.833	= Imperial quarts (Imp qt)
US quarts (US qt)	x 0.946	= Litres (l)	x 1.057	= US quarts (US qt)
Imperial gallons (Imp gal)	x 4.546	= Litres (l)	x 0.22	= Imperial gallons (Imp gal)
Imperial gallons (Imp gal)	x 1.201	= US gallons (US gal)	x 0.833	= Imperial gallons (Imp gal)
US gallons (US gal)	x 3.785	= Litres (l)	x 0.264	= US gallons (US gal)

Mass (weight)

Ounces (oz)	x 28.35	= Grams (g)	x 0.035	= Ounces (oz)
Pounds (lb)	x 0.454	= Kilograms (kg)	x 2.205	= Pounds (lb)

Force

Ounces-force (ozf; oz)	x 0.278	= Newtons (N)	x 3.6	= Ounces-force (ozf; oz)
Pounds-force (lbf; lb)	x 4.448	= Newtons (N)	x 0.225	= Pounds-force (lbf; lb)
Newtons (N)	x 0.1	= Kilograms-force (kgf; kg)	x 9.81	= Newtons (N)

Pressure

Pounds-force per square inch (psi; lbf/in^2; lb/in^2)	x 0.070	= Kilograms-force per square centimetre (kgf/cm^2; kg/cm^2)	x 14.223	= Pounds-force per square inch (psi; lbf/in^2; lb/in^2)
Pounds-force per square inch (psi; lbf/in^2; lb/in^2)	x 0.068	= Atmospheres (atm)	x 14.696	= Pounds-force per square inch (psi; lbf/in^2; lb/in^2)
Pounds-force per square inch (psi; lbf/in^2; lb/in^2)	x 0.069	= Bars	x 14.5	= Pounds-force per square inch (psi; lbf/in^2; lb/in^2)
Pounds-force per square inch (psi; lbf/in^2; lb/in^2)	x 6.895	= Kilopascals (kPa)	x 0.145	= Pounds-force per square inch (psi; lbf/in^2; lb/in^2)
Kilopascals (kPa)	x 0.01	= Kilograms-force per square centimetre (kgf/cm^2; kg/cm^2)	x 98.1	= Kilopascals (kPa)
Millibar (mbar)	x 100	= Pascals (Pa)	x 0.01	= Millibar (mbar)
Millibar (mbar)	x 0.0145	= Pounds-force per square inch (psi; lbf/in^2; lb/in^2)	x 68.947	= Millibar (mbar)
Millibar (mbar)	x 0.75	= Millimetres of mercury (mmHg)	x 1.333	= Millibar (mbar)
Millibar (mbar)	x 0.401	= Inches of water (inH_2O)	x 2.491	= Millibar (mbar)
Millimetres of mercury (mmHg)	x 0.535	= Inches of water (inH_2O)	x 1.868	= Millimetres of mercury (mmHg)
Inches of water (inH_2O)	x 0.036	= Pounds-force per square inch (psi; lbf/in^2; lb/in^2)	x 27.68	= Inches of water (inH_2O)

Torque (moment of force)

Pounds-force inches (lbf in; lb in)	x 1.152	= Kilograms-force centimetre (kgf cm; kg cm)	x 0.868	= Pounds-force inches (lbf in; lb in)
Pounds-force inches (lbf in; lb in)	x 0.113	= Newton metres (Nm)	x 8.85	= Pounds-force inches (lbf in; lb in)
Pounds-force inches (lbf in; lb in)	x 0.083	= Pounds-force feet (lbf ft; lb ft)	x 12	= Pounds-force inches (lbf in; lb in)
Pounds-force feet (lbf ft; lb ft)	x 0.138	= Kilograms-force metres (kgf m; kg m)	x 7.233	= Pounds-force feet (lbf ft; lb ft)
Pounds-force feet (lbf ft; lb ft)	x 1.356	= Newton metres (Nm)	x 0.738	= Pounds-force feet (lbf ft; lb ft)
Newton metres (Nm)	x 0.102	= Kilograms-force metres (kgf m; kg m)	x 9.804	= Newton metres (Nm)

Power

Horsepower (hp)	x 745.7	= Watts (W)	x 0.0013	= Horsepower (hp)

Velocity (speed)

Miles per hour (miles/hr; mph)	x 1.609	= Kilometres per hour (km/hr; kph)	x 0.621	= Miles per hour (miles/hr; mph)

Fuel consumption*

Miles per gallon, Imperial (mpg)	x 0.354	= Kilometres per litre (km/l)	x 2.825	= Miles per gallon, Imperial (mpg)
Miles per gallon, US (mpg)	x 0.425	= Kilometres per litre (km/l)	x 2.352	= Miles per gallon, US (mpg)

Temperature

Degrees Fahrenheit = (°C x 1.8) + 32

Degrees Celsius (Degrees Centigrade; °C) = (°F - 32) x 0.56

** It is common practice to convert from miles per gallon (mpg) to litres/100 kilometres (l/100km), where mpg x l/100 km = 282*

Spare parts are available from many sources, including maker's appointed garages, accessory shops, and motor factors. To be sure of obtaining the correct parts, it will sometimes be necessary to quote the vehicle identification number. If possible, it can also be useful to take the old parts along for positive identification. Items such as starter motors and alternators may be available under a service exchange scheme – any parts returned should be clean.

Our advice regarding spare parts is as follows.

Officially-appointed garages

This is the best source of parts which are peculiar to your car, and which are not otherwise generally available (eg, badges, interior trim, certain body panels, etc). It is also the only place at which you should buy parts if the vehicle is still under warranty.

Accessory shops

These are very good places to buy materials and components needed for the maintenance of your car (oil, air and fuel filters, light bulbs, drivebelts, greases, brake pads, touch-up paint, etc). Components of this nature sold by a reputable shop are usually of the same standard as those used by the car manufacturer.

Besides components, these shops also sell tools and general accessories, usually have convenient opening hours, charge lower prices, and can often be found close to home. Some accessory shops have parts counters where components needed for almost any repair job can be purchased or ordered.

Motor factors

Good factors will stock all the more important components which wear out comparatively quickly, and can sometimes supply individual components needed for the overhaul of a larger assembly (eg, brake seals and hydraulic parts, bearing shells, pistons, valves). They may also handle work such as cylinder block reboring, crankshaft regrinding, etc.

Tyre and exhaust specialists

These outlets may be independent, or members of a local or national chain. They frequently offer competitive prices when compared with a main dealer or local garage, but it will pay to obtain several quotes before making a decision. When researching prices, also ask what 'extras' may be added – for instance fitting a new valve and balancing the wheel are both commonly charged on top of the price of a new tyre.

Other sources

Beware of parts or materials obtained from market stalls, car boot sales or similar outlets. Such items are not invariably sub-standard, but there is little chance of compensation if they do prove unsatisfactory. in the case of safety-critical components such as brake pads, there is the risk not only of financial loss, but also of an accident causing injury or death.

Second-hand components or assemblies obtained from a car breaker can be a good buy in some circumstances, but this sort of purchase is best made by the experienced DIY mechanic.

Vehicle identification numbers

Modifications are a continuing and unpublicised process in vehicle manufacture, quite apart from major model changes. Spare parts manuals and lists are compiled upon a numerical basis, the individual vehicle identification numbers being essential to correct identification of the component concerned.

When ordering spare parts, always give as much information as possible. Quote the car model, year of manufacture, body and engine numbers as appropriate.

The *Vehicle Identification Number (VIN)* plate is located on the door pillar behind the driver's door. The plate carries the VIN number, chassis number, vehicle weight information and various other information, depending on territory **(see illustrations)**.

The *engine number* is located on a metal plate attached to the front of the engine **(see illustration)**.

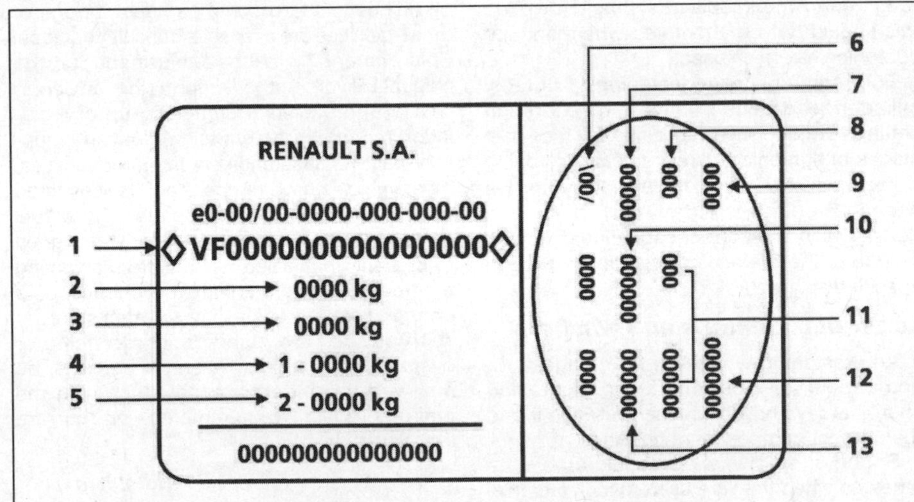

VIN plate information

1 *Type and chassis number*
2 *Maximum permissible all-up weight*
3 *Maximum permissible total train weight*
4 *Maximum permissible front axle loading*
5 *Maximum permissible rear axle loading*
6 *Technical specifications*
7 *Paint code*
8 *Equipment level*
9 *Vehicle type*
10 *Trim code*
11 *Additional equipment code*
12 *Fabrication number*
13 *Interior matching trim code*

VIN plate location on the door pillar

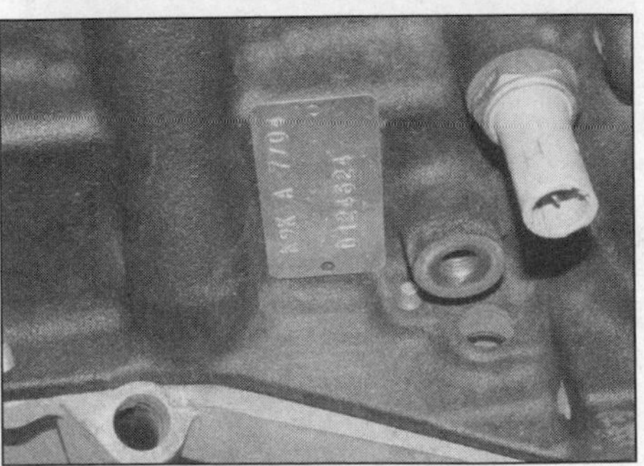

Engine number plate – diesel engine

Whenever servicing, repair or overhaul work is carried out on the car or its components, observe the following procedures and instructions. This will assist in carrying out the operation efficiently and to a professional standard of workmanship.

Joint mating faces and gaskets

When separating components at their mating faces, never insert screwdrivers or similar implements into the joint between the faces in order to prise them apart. This can cause severe damage which results in oil leaks, coolant leaks, etc upon reassembly. Separation is usually achieved by tapping along the joint with a soft-faced hammer in order to break the seal. However, note that this method may not be suitable where dowels are used for component location.

Where a gasket is used between the mating faces of two components, a new one must be fitted on reassembly; fit it dry unless otherwise stated in the repair procedure. Make sure that the mating faces are clean and dry, with all traces of old gasket removed. When cleaning a joint face, use a tool which is unlikely to score or damage the face, and remove any burrs or nicks with an oilstone or fine file.

Make sure that tapped holes are cleaned with a pipe cleaner, and keep them free of jointing compound, if this is being used, unless specifically instructed otherwise.

Ensure that all orifices, channels or pipes are clear, and blow through them, preferably using compressed air.

Oil seals

Oil seals can be removed by levering them out with a wide flat-bladed screwdriver or similar implement. Alternatively, a number of self-tapping screws may be screwed into the seal, and these used as a purchase for pliers or some similar device in order to pull the seal free.

Whenever an oil seal is removed from its working location, either individually or as part of an assembly, it should be renewed.

The very fine sealing lip of the seal is easily damaged, and will not seal if the surface it contacts is not completely clean and free from scratches, nicks or grooves. If the original sealing surface of the component cannot be restored, and the manufacturer has not made provision for slight relocation of the seal relative to the sealing surface, the component should be renewed.

Protect the lips of the seal from any surface which may damage them in the course of fitting. Use tape or a conical sleeve where possible. Lubricate the seal lips with oil before fitting and, on dual-lipped seals, fill the space between the lips with grease.

Unless otherwise stated, oil seals must be fitted with their sealing lips toward the lubricant to be sealed.

Use a tubular drift or block of wood of the appropriate size to install the seal and, if the seal housing is shouldered, drive the seal down to the shoulder. If the seal housing is unshouldered, the seal should be fitted with its face flush with the housing top face (unless otherwise instructed).

Screw threads and fastenings

Seized nuts, bolts and screws are quite a common occurrence where corrosion has set in, and the use of penetrating oil or releasing fluid will often overcome this problem if the offending item is soaked for a while before attempting to release it. The use of an impact driver may also provide a means of releasing such stubborn fastening devices, when used in conjunction with the appropriate screwdriver bit or socket. If none of these methods works, it may be necessary to resort to the careful application of heat, or the use of a hacksaw or nut splitter device.

Studs are usually removed by locking two nuts together on the threaded part, and then using a spanner on the lower nut to unscrew the stud. Studs or bolts which have broken off below the surface of the component in which they are mounted can sometimes be removed using a stud extractor. Always ensure that a blind tapped hole is completely free from oil, grease, water or other fluid before installing the bolt or stud. Failure to do this could cause the housing to crack due to the hydraulic action of the bolt or stud as it is screwed in.

When tightening a castellated nut to accept a split pin, tighten the nut to the specified torque, where applicable, and then tighten further to the next split pin hole. Never slacken the nut to align the split pin hole, unless stated in the repair procedure.

When checking or retightening a nut or bolt to a specified torque setting, slacken the nut or bolt by a quarter of a turn, and then retighten to the specified setting. However, this should not be attempted where angular tightening has been used.

For some screw fastenings, notably cylinder head bolts or nuts, torque wrench settings are no longer specified for the latter stages of tightening, "angle-tightening" being called up instead. Typically, a fairly low torque wrench setting will be applied to the bolts/nuts in the correct sequence, followed by one or more stages of tightening through specified angles.

Locknuts, locktabs and washers

Any fastening which will rotate against a component or housing during tightening should always have a washer between it and the relevant component or housing.

Spring or split washers should always be renewed when they are used to lock a critical component such as a big-end bearing retaining bolt or nut. Locktabs which are folded over to retain a nut or bolt should always be renewed.

Self-locking nuts can be re-used in non-critical areas, providing resistance can be felt when the locking portion passes over the bolt or stud thread. However, it should be noted that self-locking stiffnuts tend to lose their effectiveness after long periods of use, and should then be renewed as a matter of course.

Split pins must always be replaced with new ones of the correct size for the hole.

When thread-locking compound is found on the threads of a fastener which is to be re-used, it should be cleaned off with a wire brush and solvent, and fresh compound applied on reassembly.

Special tools

Some repair procedures in this manual entail the use of special tools such as a press, two or three-legged pullers, spring compressors, etc. Wherever possible, suitable readily-available alternatives to the manufacturer's special tools are described, and are shown in use. In some instances, where no alternative is possible, it has been necessary to resort to the use of a manufacturer's tool, and this has been done for reasons of safety as well as the efficient completion of the repair operation. Unless you are highly-skilled and have a thorough understanding of the procedures described, never attempt to bypass the use of any special tool when the procedure described specifies its use. Not only is there a very great risk of personal injury, but expensive damage could be caused to the components involved.

Environmental considerations

When disposing of used engine oil, brake fluid, antifreeze, etc, give due consideration to any detrimental environmental effects. Do not, for instance, pour any of the above liquids down drains into the general sewage system, or onto the ground to soak away. Many local council refuse tips provide a facility for waste oil disposal, as do some garages. If none of these facilities are available, consult your local Environmental Health Department, or the National Rivers Authority, for further advice.

With the universal tightening-up of legislation regarding the emission of environmentally-harmful substances from motor vehicles, most vehicles have tamperproof devices fitted to the main adjustment points of the fuel system. These devices are primarily designed to prevent unqualified persons from adjusting the fuel/air mixture, with the chance of a consequent increase in toxic emissions. If such devices are found during servicing or overhaul, they should, wherever possible, be renewed or refitted in accordance with the manufacturer's requirements or current legislation.

OIL CARE
FOLLOW THE CODE
OIL BANK LINE
0800 66 33 66
www.oilbankline.org.uk

Note: It is antisocial and illegal to dump oil down the drain. To find the location of your local oil recycling bank, call this number free.

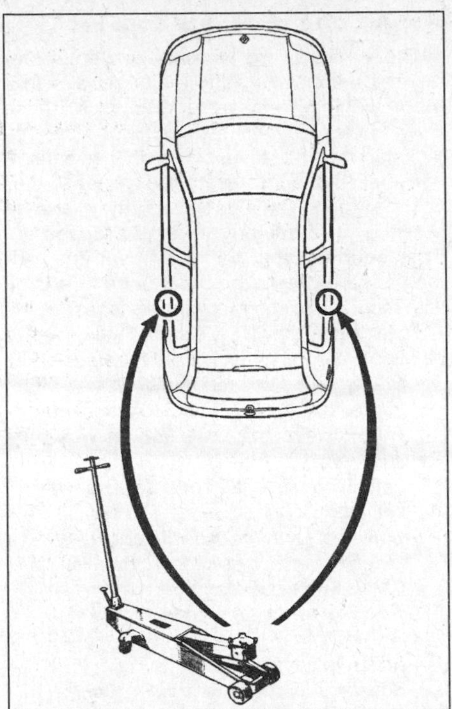
Rear jacking point for use with trolley jack

The jack supplied with the car should only be used for changing the roadwheels – see *Wheel changing* at the front of this manual. When carrying out any other kind of work, raise the vehicle using a hydraulic trolley jack, and always supplement the jack with axle stands positioned under the vehicle jacking points.

When using a hydraulic jack or axle stands, always position the jack head or axle stand head under one of the relevant jacking points **(see illustrations)**.

Do not jack the vehicle under any other part of the sill, sump, floor pan, or any of the steering or suspension components. With the vehicle raised, the axle stands should be positioned beneath the vehicle jack location points on the sill.

Warning: Never work under, around, or near a raised car, unless it is adequately supported.

The jacking points are indicated by an arrow on the sill

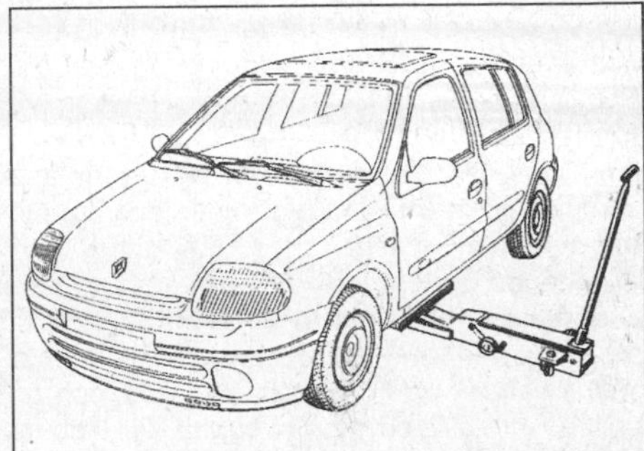
Use a piece of wood between the jack head and sill when jacking the side of the vehicle

Disconnecting the battery

Several systems fitted to the vehicle require battery power to be available at all times, either to ensure their continued operation (such as the clock), or to maintain electronic memory settings which would otherwise be erased. Whenever the battery is to be disconnected, first note the following points, to ensure there are no unforeseen consequences:

a) First, on any vehicle with central door locking, it is a wise precaution to remove the key from the ignition, and to keep it with you, so that it does not get locked in if the central locking engages when the battery is reconnected.

b) If a security-coded audio unit is fitted, and the unit and/or the battery is disconnected, the unit will not function again on reconnection until the correct security code is entered. Details of this procedure, which varies according to the unit fitted and vehicle model, are given in the vehicle owner's handbook. Where necessary, ensure you have the correct code before you disconnect the battery. If you do not have the code or details of the correct procedure, but can supply proof of ownership and a legitimate reason for wanting this information, a Renault dealer may be able to help.

c) On vehicles equipped with an original equipment anti-theft alarm system, before disconnecting the battery, de-activate the alarm siren, using the dedicated key. When reconnecting the battery, as soon as the battery is reconnected, the alarm is automatically activated. Use the remote control transmitter to turn off the alarm, then activate the alarm siren using the dedicated key.

Devices known as 'memory-savers' or 'code-savers' can be used to avoid some of the above problems. Precise details of use vary according to the device used. Typically, it is plugged into the cigar lighter socket, and is connected by its own wiring to a spare battery; the vehicle battery is then disconnected from the electrical system, leaving the memory-saver to pass sufficient current to maintain audio unlt security codes and other memory values, and also to run permanently-live circuits such as the clock.

Warning: Some of these devices allow a considerable amount of current to pass, which can mean that many of the vehicle's systems are still operational when the main battery is disconnected. If a 'memory-saver' is used, ensure that the circuit concerned is actually 'dead' before carrying out any work on it!

Introduction

A selection of good tools is a fundamental requirement for anyone contemplating the maintenance and repair of a motor vehicle. For the owner who does not possess any, their purchase will prove a considerable expense, offsetting some of the savings made by doing-it-yourself. However, provided that the tools purchased meet the relevant national safety standards and are of good quality, they will last for many years and prove an extremely worthwhile investment.

To help the average owner to decide which tools are needed to carry out the various tasks detailed in this manual, we have compiled three lists of tools under the following headings: *Maintenance and minor repair, Repair and overhaul*, and *Special*. Newcomers to practical mechanics should start off with the *Maintenance and minor repair* tool kit, and confine themselves to the simpler jobs around the vehicle. Then, as confidence and experience grow, more difficult tasks can be undertaken, with extra tools being purchased as, and when, they are needed. In this way, a *Maintenance and minor repair* tool kit can be built up into a *Repair and overhaul* tool kit over a considerable period of time, without any major cash outlays. The experienced do-it-yourselfer will have a tool kit good enough for most repair and overhaul procedures, and will add tools from the *Special* category when it is felt that the expense is justified by the amount of use to which these tools will be put.

Maintenance and minor repair tool kit

The tools given in this list should be considered as a minimum requirement if routine maintenance, servicing and minor repair operations are to be undertaken. We recommend the purchase of combination spanners (ring one end, open-ended the other); although more expensive than open-ended ones, they do give the advantages of both types of spanner.

- ☐ *Combination spanners:*
  Metric - 8 to 19 mm inclusive
- ☐ *Adjustable spanner - 35 mm jaw (approx.)*
- ☐ *Spark plug spanner (with rubber insert) - petrol models*
- ☐ *Spark plug gap adjustment tool - petrol models*
- ☐ *Set of feeler gauges*
- ☐ *Brake bleed nipple spanner*
- ☐ *Screwdrivers:*
  Flat blade - 100 mm long x 6 mm dia
  Cross blade - 100 mm long x 6 mm dia
  Torx - various sizes (not all vehicles)
- ☐ *Combination pliers*
- ☐ *Hacksaw (junior)*
- ☐ *Tyre pump*
- ☐ *Tyre pressure gauge*
- ☐ *Oil can*
- ☐ *Oil filter removal tool*
- ☐ *Fine emery cloth*
- ☐ *Wire brush (small)*
- ☐ *Funnel (medium size)*
- ☐ *Sump drain plug key (not all vehicles)*

Repair and overhaul tool kit

These tools are virtually essential for anyone undertaking any major repairs to a motor vehicle, and are additional to those given in the *Maintenance and minor repair* list. Included in this list is a comprehensive set of sockets. Although these are expensive, they will be found invaluable as they are so versatile - particularly if various drives are included in the set. We recommend the half-inch square-drive type, as this can be used with most proprietary torque wrenches.

The tools in this list will sometimes need to be supplemented by tools from the *Special* list:

- ☐ *Sockets (or box spanners) to cover range in previous list (including Torx sockets)*
- ☐ *Reversible ratchet drive (for use with sockets)*
- ☐ *Extension piece, 250 mm (for use with sockets)*
- ☐ *Universal joint (for use with sockets)*
- ☐ *Flexible handle or sliding T "breaker bar" (for use with sockets)*
- ☐ *Torque wrench (for use with sockets)*
- ☐ *Self-locking grips*
- ☐ *Ball pein hammer*
- ☐ *Soft-faced mallet (plastic or rubber)*
- ☐ *Screwdrivers:*
  Flat blade - long & sturdy, short (chubby), and narrow (electrician's) types
  Cross blade – long & sturdy, and short (chubby) types
- ☐ *Pliers:*
  Long-nosed
  Side cutters (electrician's)
  Circlip (internal and external)
- ☐ *Cold chisel - 25 mm*
- ☐ *Scriber*
- ☐ *Scraper*
- ☐ *Centre-punch*
- ☐ *Pin punch*
- ☐ *Hacksaw*
- ☐ *Brake hose clamp*
- ☐ *Brake/clutch bleeding kit*
- ☐ *Selection of twist drills*
- ☐ *Steel rule/straight-edge*
- ☐ *Allen keys (inc. splined/Torx type)*
- ☐ *Selection of files*
- ☐ *Wire brush*
- ☐ *Axle stands*
- ☐ *Jack (strong trolley or hydraulic type)*
- ☐ *Light with extension lead*
- ☐ *Universal electrical multi-meter*

Sockets and reversible ratchet drive

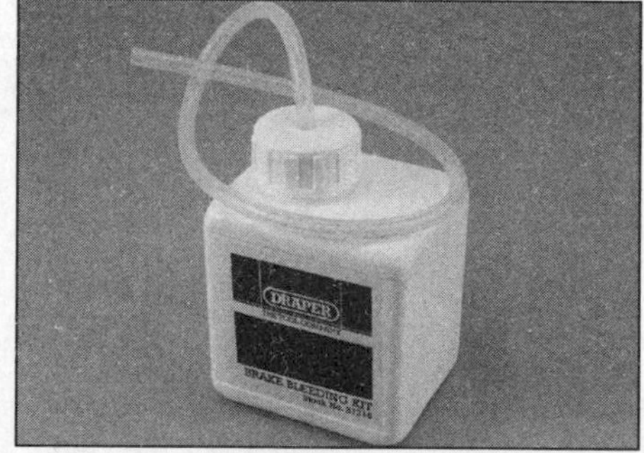

Brake bleeding kit

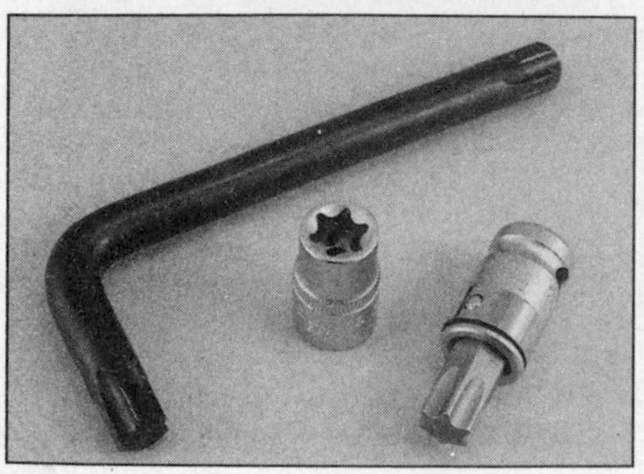

Torx key, socket and bit

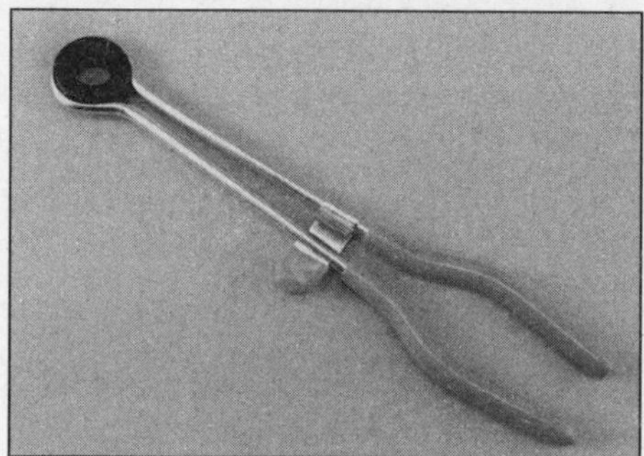

Hose clamp

Angular-tightening gauge

Special tools

The tools in this list are those which are not used regularly, are expensive to buy, or which need to be used in accordance with their manufacturers' instructions. Unless relatively difficult mechanical jobs are undertaken frequently, it will not be economic to buy many of these tools. Where this is the case, you could consider clubbing together with friends (or joining a motorists' club) to make a joint purchase, or borrowing the tools against a deposit from a local garage or tool hire specialist. It is worth noting that many of the larger DIY superstores now carry a large range of special tools for hire at modest rates.

The following list contains only those tools and instruments freely available to the public, and not those special tools produced by the vehicle manufacturer specifically for its dealer network. You will find occasional references to these manufacturers' special tools in the text of this manual. Generally, an alternative method of doing the job without the vehicle manufacturers' special tool is given. However, sometimes there is no alternative to using them. Where this is the case and the relevant tool cannot be bought or borrowed, you will have to entrust the work to a dealer.

- ☐ *Angular-tightening gauge*
- ☐ *Valve spring compressor*
- ☐ *Valve grinding tool*
- ☐ *Piston ring compressor*
- ☐ *Piston ring removal/installation tool*
- ☐ *Cylinder bore hone*
- ☐ *Balljoint separator*
- ☐ *Coil spring compressors (where applicable)*
- ☐ *Two/three-legged hub and bearing puller*
- ☐ *Impact screwdriver*
- ☐ *Micrometer and/or vernier calipers*
- ☐ *Dial gauge*
- ☐ *Stroboscopic timing light*
- ☐ *Dwell angle meter/tachometer*
- ☐ *Fault code reader*
- ☐ *Cylinder compression gauge*
- ☐ *Hand-operated vacuum pump and gauge*
- ☐ *Clutch plate alignment set*
- ☐ *Brake shoe steady spring cup removal tool*
- ☐ *Bush and bearing removal/installation set*
- ☐ *Stud extractors*
- ☐ *Tap and die set*
- ☐ *Lifting tackle*
- ☐ *Trolley jack*

Buying tools

Reputable motor accessory shops and superstores often offer excellent quality tools at discount prices, so it pays to shop around.

Remember, you don't have to buy the most expensive items on the shelf, but it is always advisable to steer clear of the very cheap tools. Beware of 'bargains' offered on market stalls or at car boot sales. There are plenty of good tools around at reasonable prices, but always aim to purchase items which meet the relevant national safety standards. If in doubt, ask the proprietor or manager of the shop for advice before making a purchase.

Care and maintenance of tools

Having purchased a reasonable tool kit, it is necessary to keep the tools in a clean and serviceable condition. After use, always wipe off any dirt, grease and metal particles using a clean, dry cloth, before putting the tools away. Never leave them lying around after they have been used. A simple tool rack on the garage or workshop wall for items such as screwdrivers and pliers is a good idea. Store all normal spanners and sockets in a metal box. Any measuring instruments, gauges, meters, etc, must be carefully stored where they cannot be damaged or become rusty.

Take a little care when tools are used. Hammer heads inevitably become marked, and screwdrivers lose the keen edge on their blades from time to time. A little timely attention with emery cloth or a file will soon restore items like this to a good finish.

Working facilities

Not to be forgotten when discussing tools is the workshop itself. If anything more than routine maintenance is to be carried out, a suitable working area becomes essential.

It is appreciated that many an owner-mechanic is forced by circumstances to remove an engine or similar item without the benefit of a garage or workshop. Having done this, any repairs should always be done under the cover of a roof.

Wherever possible, any dismantling should be done on a clean, flat workbench or table at a suitable working height.

Any workbench needs a vice; one with a jaw opening of 100 mm is suitable for most jobs. As mentioned previously, some clean dry storage space is also required for tools, as well as for any lubricants, cleaning fluids, touch-up paints etc, which become necessary.

Another item which may be required, and which has a much more general usage, is an electric drill with a chuck capacity of at least 8 mm. This, together with a good range of twist drills, is virtually essential for fitting accessories.

Last, but not least, always keep a supply of old newspapers and clean, lint-free rags available, and try to keep any working area as clean as possible.

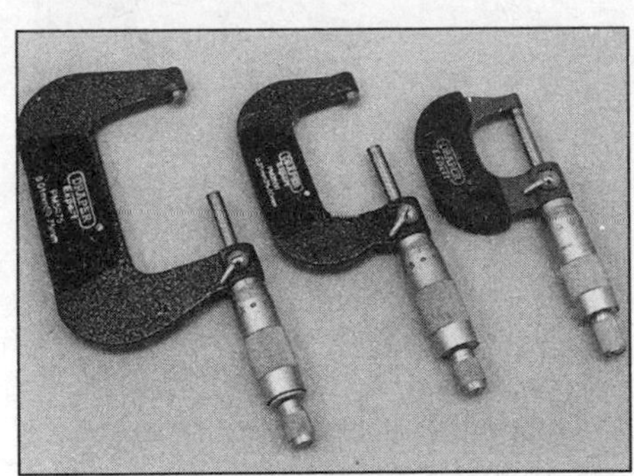

Micrometers

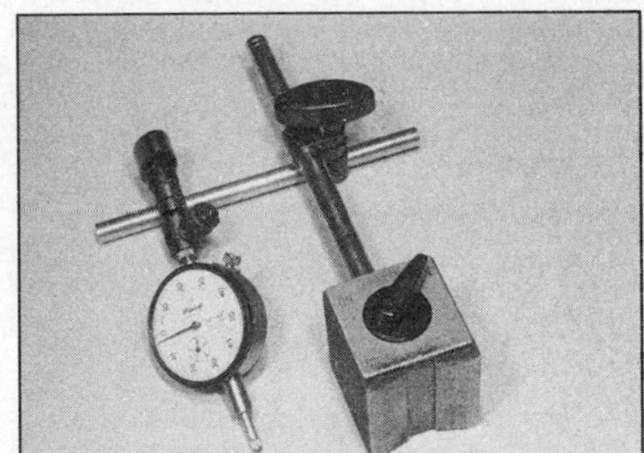

Dial test indicator ("dial gauge")

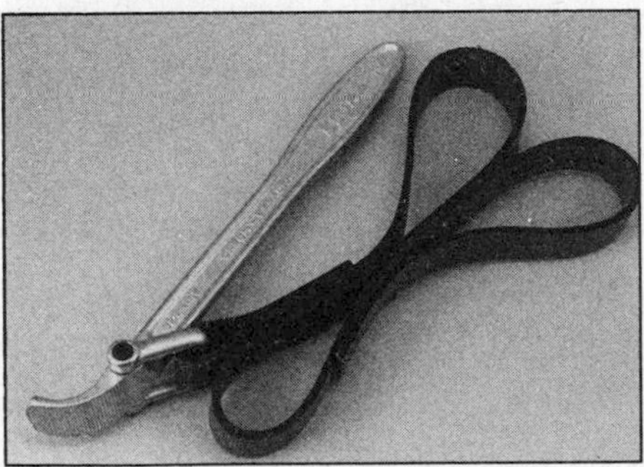

Strap wrench

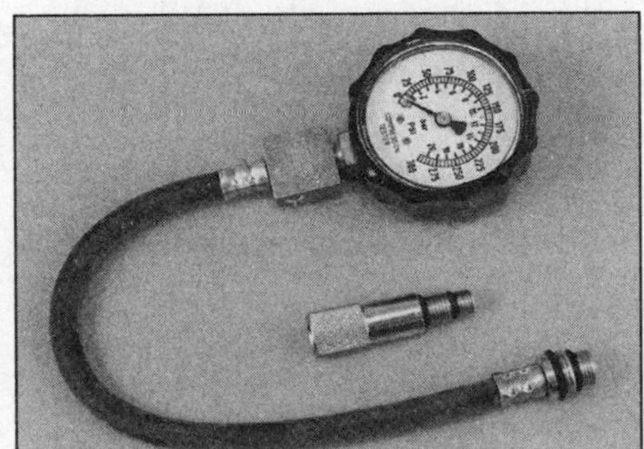

Compression tester

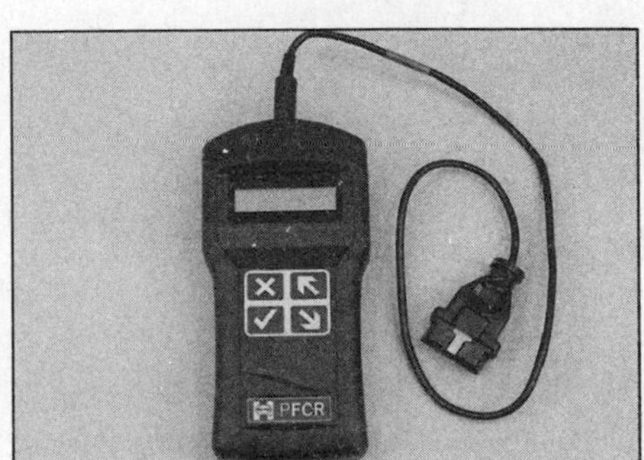

Fault code reader

This is a guide to getting your vehicle through the MOT test. Obviously it will not be possible to examine the vehicle to the same standard as the professional MOT tester. However, working through the following checks will enable you to identify any problem areas before submitting the vehicle for the test.

Where a testable component is in borderline condition, the tester has discretion in deciding whether to pass or fail it. The basis of such discretion is whether the tester would be happy for a close relative or friend to use the vehicle with the component in that condition. If the vehicle presented is clean and evidently well cared for, the tester may be more inclined to pass a borderline component than if the vehicle is scruffy and apparently neglected.

It has only been possible to summarise the test requirements here, based on the regulations in force at the time of printing. Test standards are becoming increasingly stringent, although there are some exemptions for older vehicles.

An assistant will be needed to help carry out some of these checks.

The checks have been sub-divided into four categories, as follows:

1 Checks carried out **FROM THE DRIVER'S SEAT**

2 Checks carried out **WITH THE VEHICLE ON THE GROUND**

3 Checks carried out **WITH THE VEHICLE RAISED AND THE WHEELS FREE TO TURN**

4 Checks carried out on **YOUR VEHICLE'S EXHAUST EMISSION SYSTEM**

1 Checks carried out FROM THE DRIVER'S SEAT

Handbrake

☐ Test the operation of the handbrake. Excessive travel (too many clicks) indicates incorrect brake or cable adjustment.

☐ Check that the handbrake cannot be released by tapping the lever sideways. Check the security of the lever mountings.

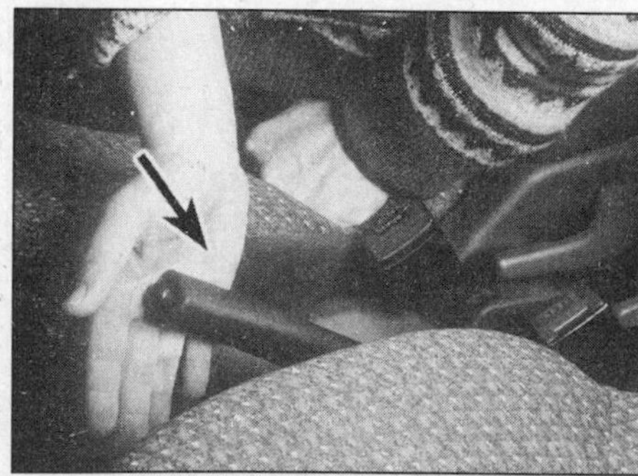

Footbrake

☐ Depress the brake pedal and check that it does not creep down to the floor, indicating a master cylinder fault. Release the pedal, wait a few seconds, then depress it again. If the pedal travels nearly to the floor before firm resistance is felt, brake adjustment or repair is necessary. If the pedal feels spongy, there is air in the hydraulic system which must be removed by bleeding.

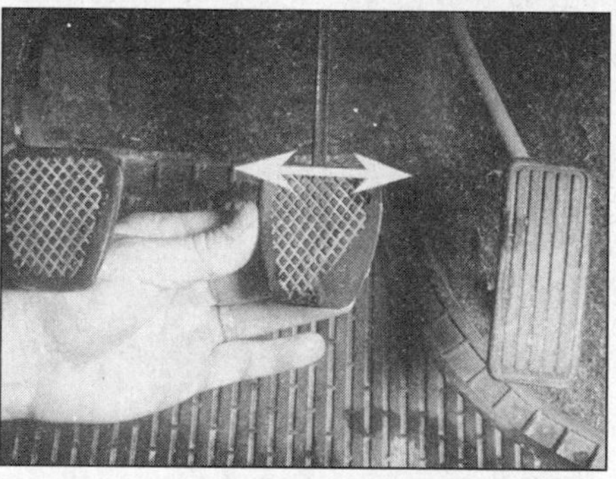

☐ Check that the brake pedal is secure and in good condition. Check also for signs of fluid leaks on the pedal, floor or carpets, which would indicate failed seals in the brake master cylinder.

☐ Check the servo unit (when applicable) by operating the brake pedal several times, then keeping the pedal depressed and starting the engine. As the engine starts, the pedal will move down slightly. If not, the vacuum hose or the servo itself may be faulty.

Steering wheel and column

☐ Examine the steering wheel for fractures or looseness of the hub, spokes or rim.

☐ Move the steering wheel from side to side and then up and down. Check that the steering wheel is not loose on the column, indicating wear or a loose retaining nut. Continue moving the steering wheel as before, but also turn it slightly from left to right.

☐ Check that the steering wheel is not loose on the column, and that there is no abnormal

movement of the steering wheel, indicating wear in the column support bearings or couplings.

Windscreen, mirrors and sunvisor

☐ The windscreen must be free of cracks or other significant damage within the driver's field of view. (Small stone chips are acceptable.) Rear view mirrors must be secure, intact, and capable of being adjusted.

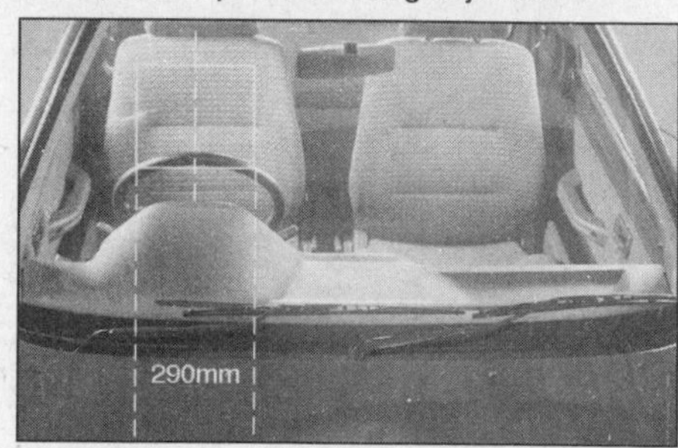

☐ The driver's sunvisor must be capable of being stored in the "up" position.

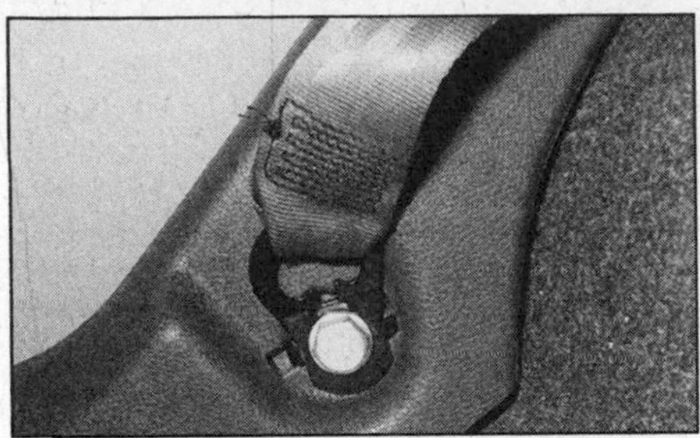

Seat belts and seats

Note: *The following checks are applicable to all seat belts, front and rear.*

☐ Examine the webbing of all the belts (including rear belts if fitted) for cuts, serious fraying or deterioration. Fasten and unfasten each belt to check the buckles. If applicable, check the retracting mechanism. Check the security of all seat belt mountings accessible from inside the vehicle.

☐ Seat belts with pre-tensioners, once activated, have a "flag" or similar showing on the seat belt stalk. This, in itself, is not a reason for test failure.

☐ The front seats themselves must be securely attached and the backrests must lock in the upright position.

Doors

☐ Both front doors must be able to be opened and closed from outside and inside, and must latch securely when closed.

2 Checks carried out **WITH THE VEHICLE ON THE GROUND**

Vehicle identification

☐ Number plates must be in good condition, secure and legible, with letters and numbers correctly spaced – spacing at (A) should be at least twice that at (B).

☐ The VIN plate and/or homologation plate must be legible.

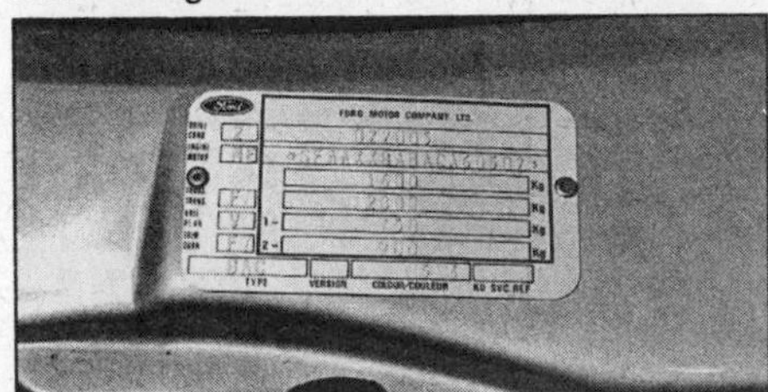

Electrical equipment

☐ Switch on the ignition and check the operation of the horn.

☐ Check the windscreen washers and wipers, examining the wiper blades; renew damaged or perished blades. Also check the operation of the stop-lights.

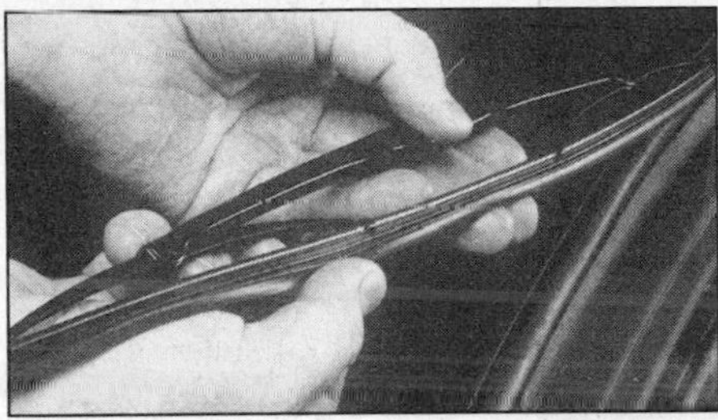

☐ Check the operation of the sidelights and number plate lights. The lenses and reflectors must be secure, clean and undamaged.

☐ Check the operation and alignment of the headlights. The headlight reflectors must not be tarnished and the lenses must be undamaged.

☐ Switch on the ignition and check the operation of the direction indicators (including the instrument panel tell-tale) and the hazard warning lights. Operation of the sidelights and stop-lights must not affect the indicators - if it does, the cause is usually a bad earth at the rear light cluster.

☐ Check the operation of the rear foglight(s), including the warning light on the instrument panel or in the switch.

☐ The ABS warning light must illuminate in accordance with the manufacturers' design. For most vehicles, the ABS warning light should illuminate when the ignition is switched on, and (if the system is operating properly) extinguish after a few seconds. Refer to the owner's handbook.

Footbrake

☐ Examine the master cylinder, brake pipes and servo unit for leaks, loose mountings, corrosion or other damage.

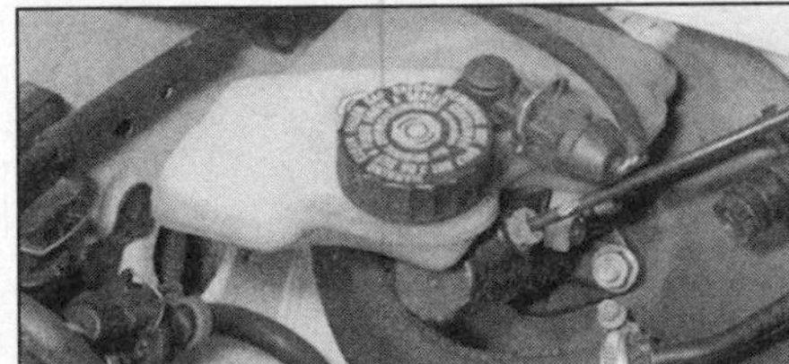

☐ The fluid reservoir must be secure and the fluid level must be between the upper (**A**) and lower (**B**) markings.

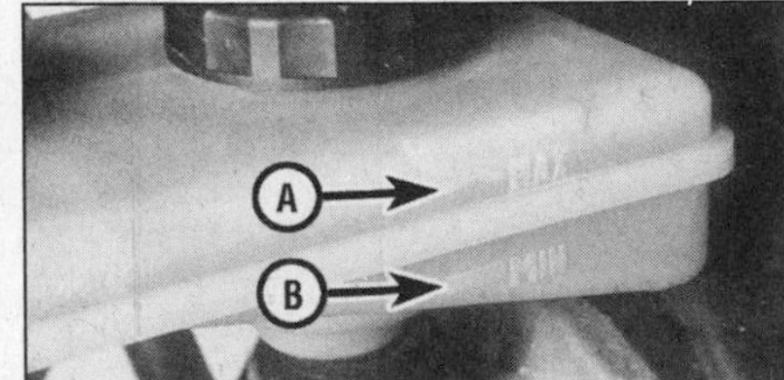

☐ Inspect both front brake flexible hoses for cracks or deterioration of the rubber. Turn the steering from lock to lock, and ensure that the hoses do not contact the wheel, tyre, or any part of the steering or suspension mechanism. With the brake pedal firmly depressed, check the hoses for bulges or leaks under pressure.

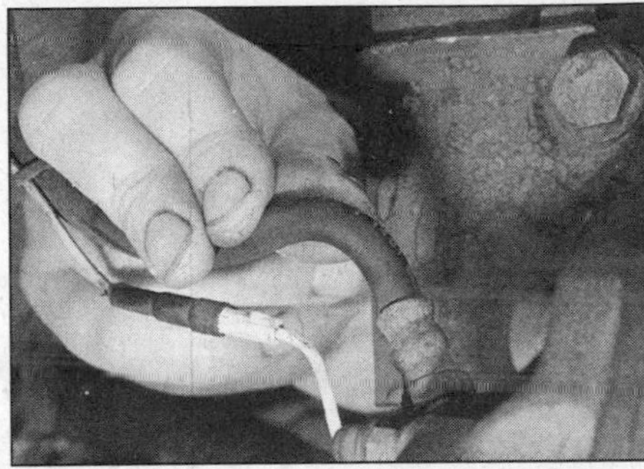

Steering and suspension

☐ Have your assistant turn the steering wheel from side to side slightly, up to the point where the steering gear just begins to transmit this movement to the roadwheels. Check for excessive free play between the steering wheel and the steering gear, indicating wear or insecurity of the steering column joints, the column-to-steering gear coupling, or the steering gear itself.

☐ Have your assistant turn the steering wheel more vigorously in each direction, so that the roadwheels just begin to turn. As this is done, examine all the steering joints, linkages, fittings and attachments. Renew any component that shows signs of wear or damage. On vehicles with power steering, check the security and condition of the steering pump, drivebelt and hoses.

☐ Check that the vehicle is standing level, and at approximately the correct ride height.

Shock absorbers

☐ Depress each corner of the vehicle in turn, then release it. The vehicle should rise and then settle in its normal position. If the vehicle continues to rise and fall, the shock absorber is defective. A shock absorber which has seized will also cause the vehicle to fail.

Exhaust system

☐ Start the engine. With your assistant holding a rag over the tailpipe, check the entire system for leaks. Repair or renew leaking sections.

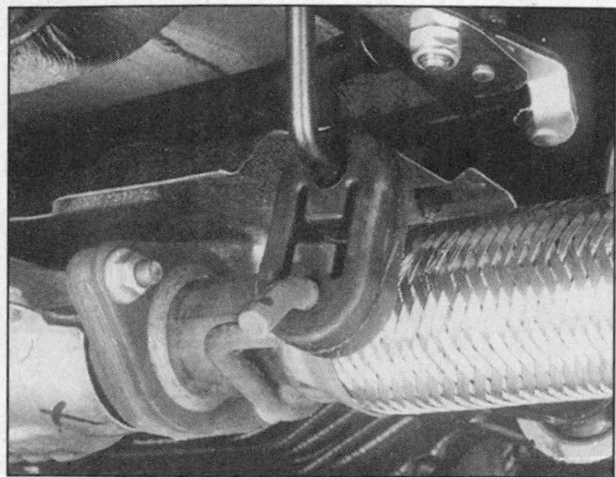

3 Checks carried out WITH THE VEHICLE RAISED AND THE WHEELS FREE TO TURN

Jack up the front and rear of the vehicle, and securely support it on axle stands. Position the stands clear of the suspension assemblies. Ensure that the wheels are clear of the ground and that the steering can be turned from lock to lock.

Steering mechanism

☐ Have your assistant turn the steering from lock to lock. Check that the steering turns smoothly, and that no part of the steering mechanism, including a wheel or tyre, fouls any brake hose or pipe or any part of the body structure.

☐ Examine the steering rack rubber gaiters for damage or insecurity of the retaining clips. If power steering is fitted, check for signs of damage or leakage of the fluid hoses, pipes or connections. Also check for excessive stiffness or binding of the steering, a missing split pin or locking device, or severe corrosion of the body structure within 30 cm of any steering component attachment point.

Front and rear suspension and wheel bearings

☐ Starting at the front right-hand side, grasp the roadwheel at the 3 o'clock and 9 o'clock positions and rock gently but firmly. Check for free play or insecurity at the wheel bearings, suspension balljoints, or suspension mountings, pivots and attachments.

☐ Now grasp the wheel at the 12 o'clock and 6 o'clock positions and repeat the previous inspection. Spin the wheel, and check for roughness or tightness of the front wheel bearing.

☐ If excess free play is suspected at a component pivot point, this can be confirmed by using a large screwdriver or similar tool and levering between the mounting and the component attachment. This will confirm whether the wear is in the pivot bush, its retaining bolt, or in the mounting itself (the bolt holes can often become elongated).

☐ Carry out all the above checks at the other front wheel, and then at both rear wheels.

Springs and shock absorbers

☐ Examine the suspension struts (when applicable) for serious fluid leakage, corrosion, or damage to the casing. Also check the security of the mounting points.

☐ If coil springs are fitted, check that the spring ends locate in their seats, and that the spring is not corroded, cracked or broken.

☐ If leaf springs are fitted, check that all leaves are intact, that the axle is securely attached to each spring, and that there is no deterioration of the spring eye mountings, bushes, and shackles.

☐ The same general checks apply to vehicles fitted with other suspension types, such as torsion bars, hydraulic displacer units, etc. Ensure that all mountings and attachments are secure, that there are no signs of excessive wear, corrosion or damage, and (on hydraulic types) that there are no fluid leaks or damaged pipes.

☐ Inspect the shock absorbers for signs of serious fluid leakage. Check for wear of the mounting bushes or attachments, or damage to the body of the unit.

Driveshafts (fwd vehicles only)

☐ Rotate each front wheel in turn and inspect the constant velocity joint gaiters for splits or damage. Also check that each driveshaft is straight and undamaged.

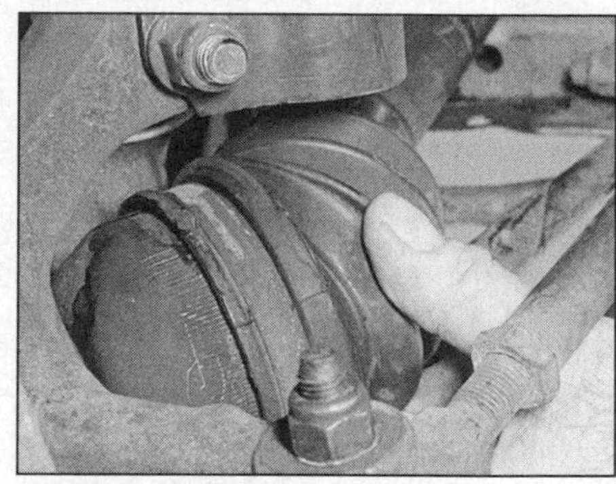

Braking system

☐ If possible without dismantling, check brake pad wear and disc condition. Ensure that the friction lining material has not worn excessively, (A) and that the discs are not fractured, pitted, scored or badly worn (B).

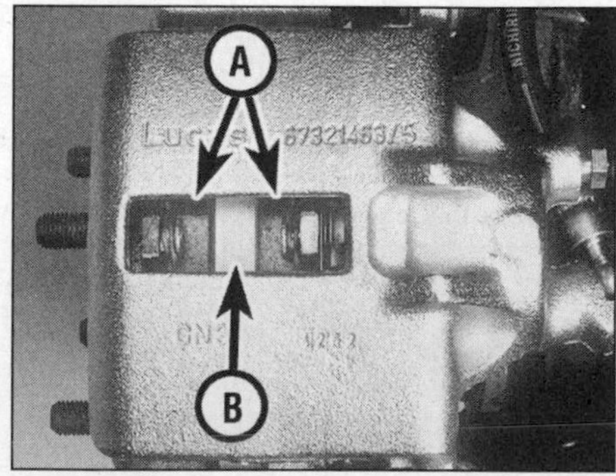

☐ Examine all the rigid brake pipes underneath the vehicle, and the flexible hose(s) at the rear. Look for corrosion, chafing or insecurity of the pipes, and for signs of bulging under pressure, chafing, splits or deterioration of the flexible hoses.

☐ Look for signs of fluid leaks at the brake calipers or on the brake backplates. Repair or renew leaking components.

☐ Slowly spin each wheel, while your assistant depresses and releases the footbrake. Ensure that each brake is operating and does not bind when the pedal is released.

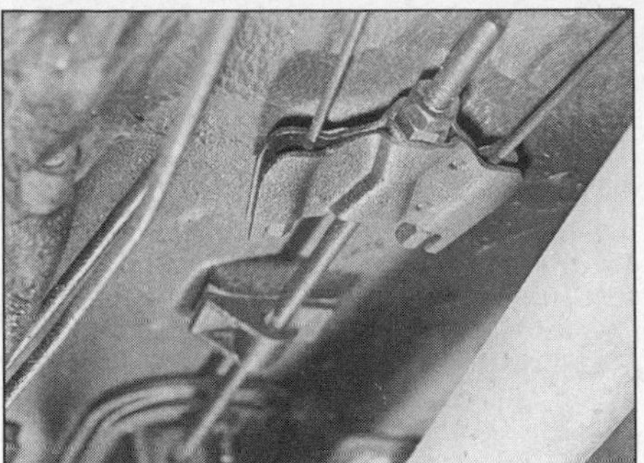

☐ Examine the handbrake mechanism, checking for frayed or broken cables, excessive corrosion, or wear or insecurity of the linkage. Check that the mechanism works on each relevant wheel, and releases fully, without binding.

☐ It is not possible to test brake efficiency without special equipment, but a road test can be carried out later to check that the vehicle pulls up in a straight line.

Fuel and exhaust systems

☐ Inspect the fuel tank (including the filler cap), fuel pipes, hoses and unions. All components must be secure and free from leaks.

☐ Examine the exhaust system over its entire length, checking for any damaged, broken or missing mountings, security of the retaining clamps and rust or corrosion.

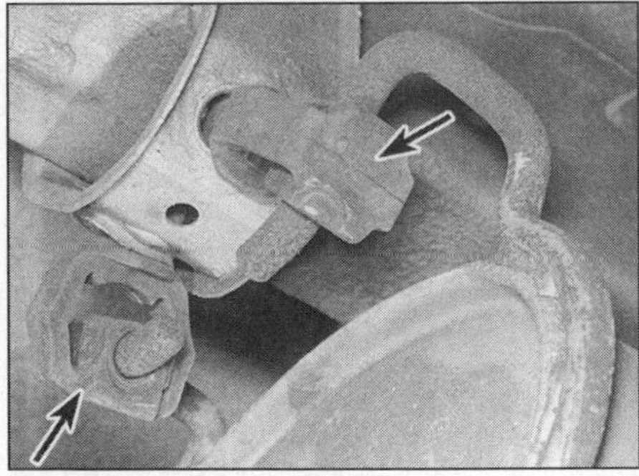

Wheels and tyres

☐ Examine the sidewalls and tread area of each tyre in turn. Check for cuts, tears, lumps, bulges, separation of the tread, and exposure of the ply or cord due to wear or damage. Check that the tyre bead is correctly seated on the wheel rim, that the valve is sound and properly seated, and that the wheel is not distorted or damaged.

☐ Check that the tyres are of the correct size for the vehicle, that they are of the same size and type on each axle, and that the pressures are correct.

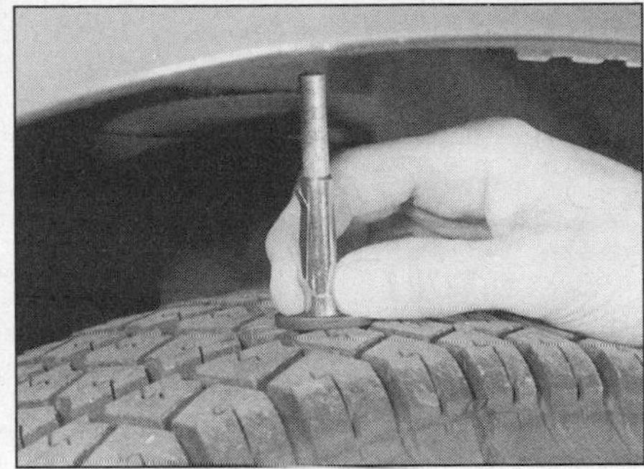

☐ Check the tyre tread depth. The legal minimum at the time of writing is 1.6 mm over at least three-quarters of the tread width. Abnormal tread wear may indicate incorrect front wheel alignment.

Body corrosion

☐ Check the condition of the entire vehicle structure for signs of corrosion in load-bearing areas. (These include chassis box sections, side sills, cross-members, pillars, and all suspension, steering, braking system and seat belt mountings and anchorages.) Any corrosion which has seriously reduced the thickness of a load-bearing area is likely to cause the vehicle to fail. In this case professional repairs are likely to be needed.

☐ Damage or corrosion which causes sharp or otherwise dangerous edges to be exposed will also cause the vehicle to fail.

4 Checks carried out on YOUR VEHICLE'S EXHAUST EMISSION SYSTEM

Petrol models

☐ The engine should be warmed up, and running well (ignition system in good order, air filter element clean, etc).

☐ Before testing, run the engine at around 2500 rpm for 20 seconds. Let the engine drop to idle, and watch for smoke from the exhaust. If the idle speed is too high, or if dense blue or black smoke emerges for more than 5 seconds, the vehicle will fail. Typically, blue smoke signifies oil burning (engine wear); black smoke means unburnt fuel (dirty air cleaner element, or other fuel system fault).

☐ An exhaust gas analyser for measuring carbon monoxide (CO) and hydrocarbons (HC) is now needed. If one cannot be hired or borrowed, have a local garage perform the check.

CO emissions (mixture)

☐ The MOT tester has access to the CO limits for all vehicles. The CO level is measured at idle speed, and at 'fast idle' (2500 to 3000 rpm). The following limits are given as a general guide:

At idle speed – Less than 0.5% CO
At 'fast idle' – Less than 0.3% CO
Lambda reading – 0.97 to 1.03

☐ If the CO level is too high, this may point to poor maintenance, a fuel injection system problem, faulty lambda (oxygen) sensor or catalytic converter. Try an injector cleaning treatment, and check the vehicle's ECU for fault codes.

HC emissions

☐ The MOT tester has access to HC limits for all vehicles. The HC level is measured at 'fast idle' (2500 to 3000 rpm). The following limits are given as a general guide:

At 'fast idle' – Less then 200 ppm

☐ Excessive HC emissions are typically caused by oil being burnt (worn engine), or by a blocked crankcase ventilation system ('breather'). If the engine oil is old and thin, an oil change may help. If the engine is running badly, check the vehicle's ECU for fault codes.

Diesel models

☐ The only emission test for diesel engines is measuring exhaust smoke density, using a calibrated smoke meter. The test involves accelerating the engine at least 3 times to its maximum unloaded speed.

Note: *On engines with a timing belt, it is VITAL that the belt is in good condition before the test is carried out.*

☐ With the engine warmed up, it is first purged by running at around 2500 rpm for 20 seconds. A governor check is then carried out, by slowly accelerating the engine to its maximum speed. After this, the smoke meter is connected, and the engine is accelerated quickly to maximum speed three times. If the smoke density is less than the limits given below, the vehicle will pass:

Non-turbo vehicles: 2.5m-1
Turbocharged vehicles: 3.0m-1

☐ If excess smoke is produced, try fitting a new air cleaner element, or using an injector cleaning treatment. If the engine is running badly, where applicable, check the vehicle's ECU for fault codes. Also check the vehicle's EGR system, where applicable. At high mileages, the injectors may require professional attention.

Engine

- ☐ Engine fails to rotate when attempting to start
- ☐ Engine rotates, but will not start
- ☐ Engine difficult to start when cold
- ☐ Engine difficult to start when hot
- ☐ Starter motor noisy or rough in engagement
- ☐ Engine starts, but stops immediately
- ☐ Engine idles erratically
- ☐ Engine misfires at idle speed
- ☐ Engine misfires throughout the driving speed range
- ☐ Engine hesitates on acceleration
- ☐ Engine stalls
- ☐ Engine lacks power
- ☐ Engine backfires
- ☐ Oil pressure warning light illuminated with engine running
- ☐ Engine runs-on after switching off
- ☐ Engine noises

Cooling system

- ☐ Overheating
- ☐ Overcooling
- ☐ External coolant leakage
- ☐ Internal coolant leakage
- ☐ Corrosion

Fuel and exhaust systems

- ☐ Excessive fuel consumption
- ☐ Fuel leakage and/or fuel odour
- ☐ Excessive noise or fumes from exhaust system

Clutch

- ☐ Pedal travels to floor – no pressure or very little resistance
- ☐ Clutch fails to disengage (unable to select gears)
- ☐ Clutch slips (engine speed increases, with no increase in vehicle speed)
- ☐ Judder as clutch is engaged
- ☐ Noise when depressing or releasing clutch pedal

Manual and sequential transmission

- ☐ Noisy in neutral with engine running
- ☐ Noisy in one particular gear
- ☐ Difficulty engaging gears
- ☐ Jumps out of gear
- ☐ Vibration
- ☐ Lubricant leaks

Automatic transmission

- ☐ Fluid leakage
- ☐ Transmission fluid brown, or has burned smell
- ☐ General gear selection problems
- ☐ Transmission will not downshift (kickdown) with accelerator fully depressed
- ☐ Engine will not start in any gear, or starts in gears other than Park or Neutral
- ☐ Transmission slips, shifts roughly, is noisy, or has no drive in forward or reverse gears

Driveshafts

- ☐ Clicking or knocking noise on turns (at slow speed on full-lock)
- ☐ Vibration when accelerating or decelerating

Braking system

- ☐ Vehicle pulls to one side under braking
- ☐ Noise (grinding or high-pitched squeal) when brakes applied
- ☐ Excessive brake pedal travel
- ☐ Brake pedal feels spongy when depressed
- ☐ Excessive brake pedal effort required to stop vehicle
- ☐ Judder felt through brake pedal or steering wheel when braking
- ☐ Pedal pulsates when braking hard
- ☐ Brakes binding
- ☐ Rear wheels locking under normal braking

Suspension and steering systems

- ☐ Vehicle pulls to one side
- ☐ Wheel wobble and vibration
- ☐ Excessive pitching and/or rolling around corners, or during braking
- ☐ Wandering or general instability
- ☐ Excessively-stiff steering
- ☐ Excessive play in steering
- ☐ Lack of power assistance
- ☐ Tyre wear excessive

Electrical system

- ☐ Battery will only hold a charge for a few days
- ☐ Ignition/no-charge warning light remains illuminated with engine running
- ☐ Ignition/no-charge warning light fails to come on
- ☐ Lights inoperative
- ☐ Instrument readings inaccurate or erratic
- ☐ Horn inoperative, or unsatisfactory in operation
- ☐ Wipers inoperative, or unsatisfactory in operation
- ☐ Washers inoperative, or unsatisfactory in operation
- ☐ Electric windows inoperative, or unsatisfactory in operation
- ☐ Central locking system inoperative, or unsatisfactory in operation

Introduction

The vehicle owner who does his or her own maintenance according to the recommended service schedules should not have to use this section of the manual very often. Modern component reliability is such that, provided those items subject to wear or deterioration are inspected or renewed at the specified intervals, sudden failure is comparatively rare. Faults do not usually just happen as a result of sudden failure, but develop over a period of time. Major mechanical failures in particular are usually preceded by characteristic symptoms over hundreds or even thousands of miles. Those components which do occasionally fail without warning are often small and easily carried in the vehicle.

With any fault-finding, the first step is to decide where to begin investigations. Sometimes this is obvious, but on other occasions, a little detective work will be necessary. The owner who makes half a dozen haphazard adjustments or replacements may be successful in curing a fault (or its symptoms), but will be none the wiser if the fault recurs, and ultimately may have spent more time and money than was necessary. A calm and logical approach will be found to be more satisfactory in the long run. Always take into account any warning signs or abnormalities that may have been noticed in the period preceding the fault – power loss, high or low gauge readings, unusual smells, etc – and remember that failure of components such as fuses or spark plugs may only be pointers to some underlying fault.

The pages which follow provide an easy-reference guide to the more common problems which may occur during the operation of the vehicle. These problems and their possible causes are grouped under headings denoting various components or systems, such as Engine, Cooling system, etc. The general Chapter which deals with the problem is also shown in brackets; refer to the relevant part of that Chapter for system-specific information. Whatever the fault, certain basic principles apply. These are as follows:

Verify the fault. This is simply a matter of being sure that you know what the symptoms are before starting work. This is particularly important if you are investigating a fault for someone else, who may not have described it very accurately.

Don't overlook the obvious. For example, if the vehicle won't start, is there fuel in the tank? (Don't take anyone else's word on this particular point, and don't trust the fuel gauge either!) If an electrical fault is indicated, look for loose or broken wires before digging out the test gear.

Cure the disease, not the symptom. Substituting a flat battery with a fully-charged one will get you off the hard shoulder, but if the underlying cause is not attended to, the new battery will go the same way. Similarly, changing oil-fouled spark plugs for a new set will get you moving again, but remember that the reason for the fouling (if it wasn't simply an incorrect grade of plug) will have to be established and corrected.

Don't take anything for granted. Particularly, don't forget that a 'new' component may itself be defective (especially if it's been rattling around in the boot for months), and don't leave components out of a fault diagnosis sequence just because they are new or recently-fitted. When you do finally diagnose a difficult fault, you'll probably realise that all the evidence was there from the start.

Engine

Engine fails to rotate when attempting to start

- ☐ Battery terminal connections loose or corroded (*Weekly checks*).
- ☐ Battery discharged or faulty (Chapter 5A).
- ☐ Broken, loose or disconnected wiring in the starting circuit (Chapter 5A).
- ☐ Defective starter solenoid or switch (Chapter 5A).
- ☐ Defective starter motor (Chapter 5A).
- ☐ Starter pinion or flywheel ring gear teeth loose or broken (Chapters 2A, 2B, 2C and 5A).
- ☐ Engine earth strap broken or disconnected (Chapter 5A).

Engine rotates, but will not start

- ☐ Fuel tank empty.
- ☐ Battery discharged (engine rotates slowly) (Chapter 5A).
- ☐ Battery terminal connections loose or corroded (Chapters 1A or 1B).
- ☐ Ignition components damp or damaged – petrol models (Chapters 1A, 1B and 5B).
- ☐ Broken, loose or disconnected wiring in the ignition circuit – petrol models (Chapters 1A, 1B and 5B).
- ☐ Worn, faulty or incorrectly-gapped spark plugs – petrol models (Chapter 1A).
- ☐ Preheating system faulty – diesel models (Chapter 5C).
- ☐ Fuel injection system fault – petrol models (Chapter 4A).
- ☐ Air in fuel system – diesel models (Chapter 4B).
- ☐ Major mechanical failure (eg camshaft drive) (Chapter 2A, 2B or 2C).

Engine difficult to start when cold

- ☐ Battery discharged (Chapter 5A).
- ☐ Battery terminal connections loose or corroded (Chapter 1A or 1B).
- ☐ Worn, faulty or incorrectly-gapped spark plugs – petrol models (Chapter 1A).
- ☐ Preheating system faulty – diesel models (Chapter 5C).
- ☐ Fuel injection system fault – petrol models (Chapter 4A).
- ☐ Other ignition system fault – petrol models (Chapters 1A and 5B).
- ☐ Fast idle valve incorrectly adjusted – diesel models (Chapter 4B).
- ☐ Low cylinder compressions (Chapter 2A, 2B or 2C).

Engine difficult to start when hot

- ☐ Air filter element dirty or clogged (Chapter 1A or 1B).
- ☐ Fuel injection system fault – petrol models (Chapter 4A).
- ☐ Low cylinder compressions (Chapter 2A, 2B or 2C).

Starter motor noisy or rough in engagement

- ☐ Starter pinion or flywheel ring gear teeth loose or broken (Chapters 2A, 2B, 2C and 5A).
- ☐ Starter motor mounting bolts loose or missing (Chapter 5A).
- ☐ Starter motor internal components worn or damaged (Chapter 5A).

Engine starts, but stops immediately

- ☐ Loose or faulty electrical connections in the ignition circuit – petrol models (Chapters 1A and 5B).
- ☐ Vacuum leak at the throttle body or inlet manifold – petrol models (Chapter 4A).
- ☐ Blocked injector/fuel injection system fault – petrol models (Chapter 4A).

Engine idles erratically

- ☐ Air filter element clogged (Chapter 1A or 1B).
- ☐ Vacuum leak at the throttle body, inlet manifold or associated hoses – petrol models (Chapter 4A).
- ☐ Worn, faulty or incorrectly-gapped spark plugs – petrol models (Chapter 1A).
- ☐ Uneven or low cylinder compressions (Chapter 2A or 2B).
- ☐ Camshaft lobes worn (Chapter 2A, 2B or 2C).
- ☐ Timing belt incorrectly tensioned (Chapter 2A, 2B or 2C).
- ☐ Blocked injector/fuel injection system fault – petrol models (Chapter 4A).
- ☐ Faulty injector(s) – diesel models (Chapter 4B).

Engine misfires at idle speed

- ☐ Worn, faulty or incorrectly-gapped spark plugs – petrol models (Chapter 1A).
- ☐ Faulty spark plug HT leads – 1.2 petrol models (Chapter 1A).
- ☐ Vacuum leak at the throttle body, inlet manifold or associated hoses – petrol models (Chapter 4A).
- ☐ Blocked injector/fuel injection system fault – petrol models (Chapter 4A).
- ☐ Faulty injector(s) – diesel models (Chapter 4B).
- ☐ Ignition fault – petrol models (Chapter 5B).
- ☐ Uneven or low cylinder compressions (Chapter 2A, 2B or 2C).
- ☐ Disconnected, leaking, or perished crankcase ventilation hoses (Chapter 4C).

Engine misfires throughout the driving speed range

- ☐ Fuel filter choked (Chapter 1A or 1B).
- ☐ Fuel pump faulty, or delivery pressure low – petrol models (Chapter 4A).
- ☐ Fuel tank vent blocked, or fuel pipes restricted (Chapter 4A or 4B).
- ☐ Vacuum leak at the throttle body, inlet manifold or associated hoses – petrol models (Chapter 4A).
- ☐ Worn, faulty or incorrectly-gapped spark plugs – petrol models (Chapter 1A).
- ☐ Faulty spark plug HT leads – 1.2 petrol models (Chapter 1A).
- ☐ Faulty injector(s) – diesel models (Chapter 4B).
- ☐ Faulty ignition coil – petrol models (Chapter 5B).
- ☐ Uneven or low cylinder compressions (Chapter 2A, 2B or 2C).
- ☐ Blocked injector/fuel injection system fault – petrol models (Chapter 4A).

Engine (continued)

Engine hesitates on acceleration

- ☐ Worn, faulty or incorrectly-gapped spark plugs – petrol models (Chapter 1A).
- ☐ Vacuum leak at the throttle body, inlet manifold or associated hoses – petrol models (Chapter 4A).
- ☐ Blocked injector/fuel injection system fault – petrol models (Chapter 4A).
- ☐ Faulty injector(s) – diesel models (Chapter 4B).

Engine stalls

- ☐ Vacuum leak at the throttle body, inlet manifold or associated hoses – petrol models (Chapter 4A).
- ☐ Fuel filter choked (Chapter 1A or 1B).
- ☐ Fuel pump faulty, or delivery pressure low – petrol models (Chapter 4A).
- ☐ Fuel tank vent blocked, or fuel pipes restricted (Chapter 4A or 4B).
- ☐ Blocked injector/fuel injection system fault – petrol models (Chapter 4A).
- ☐ Faulty injector(s) – diesel models (Chapter 4B).

Engine lacks power

- ☐ Timing belt incorrectly fitted or tensioned (Chapter 2A, 2B or 2C).
- ☐ Fuel filter choked (Chapter 1A or 1B).
- ☐ Fuel pump faulty, or delivery pressure low – petrol models (Chapter 4A).
- ☐ Uneven or low cylinder compressions (Chapter 2A, 2B or 2C).
- ☐ Worn, faulty or incorrectly-gapped spark plugs – petrol models (Chapter 1A).
- ☐ Vacuum leak at the throttle body, inlet manifold or associated hoses – petrol models (Chapter 4A).
- ☐ Blocked injector/fuel injection system fault – petrol models (Chapter 4A).
- ☐ Faulty injector(s) – diesel models (Chapter 4B).
- ☐ Injection pump timing incorrect – diesel models (Chapter 4B).
- ☐ Brakes binding (Chapter 9).
- ☐ Clutch slipping (Chapter 6).

Engine backfires

- ☐ Timing belt incorrectly fitted or tensioned (Chapter 2A, 2B or 2C).
- ☐ Vacuum leak at the throttle body, inlet manifold or associated hoses – petrol models (Chapter 4A).
- ☐ Blocked injector/fuel injection system fault – petrol models (Chapter 4A).

Oil pressure warning light illuminated with engine running

- ☐ Low oil level, or incorrect oil grade (*Weekly checks*).
- ☐ Faulty oil pressure sensor (Chapter 5A).
- ☐ Worn engine bearings and/or oil pump (Chapter 2A, 2B or 2C).
- ☐ High engine operating temperature (Chapter 3).
- ☐ Oil pressure relief valve defective (Chapter 2A, 2B or 2C).
- ☐ Oil pick-up strainer clogged (Chapter 2A, 2B or 2C).

Engine runs-on after switching off

- ☐ Excessive carbon build-up in engine (Chapter 2A, 2B or 2C).
- ☐ High engine operating temperature (Chapter 3).
- ☐ Fuel injection system fault – petrol models (Chapter 4A).

Engine noises

Pre-ignition (pinking) or knocking during acceleration or under load

- ☐ Ignition system fault – petrol models (Chapters 1A and 5B).
- ☐ Incorrect grade of spark plug – petrol models (Chapter 1A).
- ☐ Incorrect grade of fuel (Chapters 1A or 1B).
- ☐ Vacuum leak at the throttle body, inlet manifold or associated hoses – petrol models (Chapter 4A).
- ☐ Excessive carbon build-up in engine (Chapter 2A, 2B or 2C).
- ☐ Blocked injector/fuel injection system fault – petrol models (Chapter 4A).

Whistling or wheezing noises

- ☐ Leaking inlet manifold or throttle body gasket – petrol models (Chapter 4A).
- ☐ Leaking exhaust manifold gasket or pipe-to-manifold joint (Chapter 4A or 4B).
- ☐ Leaking vacuum hose (Chapters 4A, 4B or 4C, 5B and 9).
- ☐ Blowing cylinder head gasket (Chapter 2A, 2B or 2C).

Tapping or rattling noises

- ☐ Worn valve gear or camshaft (Chapter 2A, 2B or 2C).
- ☐ Ancillary component fault (water pump, alternator, etc) (Chapters 3, 5A, etc).

Knocking or thumping noises

- ☐ Worn big-end bearings (regular heavy knocking, perhaps less under load) (Chapter 2C).
- ☐ Worn main bearings (rumbling and knocking, perhaps worsening under load) (Chapter 2C).
- ☐ Piston slap (most noticeable when cold) (Chapter 2C).
- ☐ Ancillary component fault (water pump, alternator, etc) (Chapters 3, 5A, etc).

Cooling system

Overheating

- ☐ Insufficient coolant in system (*Weekly checks*).
- ☐ Thermostat faulty (Chapter 3).
- ☐ Radiator core blocked, or grille restricted (Chapter 3).
- ☐ Electric cooling fan or thermostatic switch faulty (Chapter 3).
- ☐ Inaccurate temperature gauge sender unit (Chapter 3).
- ☐ Airlock in cooling system (Chapter 3).
- ☐ Expansion tank pressure cap faulty (Chapter 3).

Overcooling

- ☐ Thermostat faulty (Chapter 3).
- ☐ Inaccurate temperature gauge sender unit (Chapter 3).

External coolant leakage

- ☐ Deteriorated or damaged hoses or hose clips (Chapters 1A or 1B).
- ☐ Radiator core or heater matrix leaking (Chapter 3).
- ☐ Pressure cap faulty (Chapter 3).
- ☐ Coolant pump internal seal leaking (Chapter 3).
- ☐ Coolant pump-to-block seal leaking (Chapter 3).
- ☐ Boiling due to overheating (Chapter 3).
- ☐ Core plug leaking (Chapter 2A, 2B or 2C).

Internal coolant leakage

- ☐ Leaking cylinder head gasket (Chapter 2A, 2B or 2C).
- ☐ Cracked cylinder head or cylinder block (Chapter 2A, 2B or 2C).

Corrosion

- ☐ Infrequent draining and flushing (Chapters 1A or 1B).
- ☐ Incorrect coolant mixture or inappropriate coolant type (Chapters 1A or 1B).

Fuel and exhaust systems

Excessive fuel consumption

- ☐ Air filter element dirty or clogged (Chapters 1A or 1B).
- ☐ Fuel injection system fault – petrol models (Chapter 4A).
- ☐ Faulty injector(s) – diesel models (Chapter 4B).
- ☐ Ignition system fault – petrol models (Chapters 1A and 5B).
- ☐ Tyres under-inflated (*Weekly checks*).

Fuel leakage and/or fuel odour

- ☐ Damaged or corroded fuel tank, pipes or connections (Chapter 4A or 4B).

Excessive noise or fumes from exhaust system

- ☐ Leaking exhaust system or manifold joints (Chapters 1A, 1B, 4A or 4B).
- ☐ Leaking, corroded or damaged silencers or pipe (Chapters 1A, 1B, 4A or 4B).
- ☐ Broken mountings causing body or suspension contact (Chapters 1A or 1B).

Clutch

Pedal travels to floor – no pressure or very little resistance

- ☐ Badly stretched or broken cable (Chapter 6).
- ☐ Leak or other fault in clutch hydraulic system – where applicable (Chapter 6).
- ☐ Incorrect clutch adjustment (Chapter 6).
- ☐ Broken clutch release bearing or arm (Chapter 6).
- ☐ Broken diaphragm spring in clutch pressure plate (Chapter 6).

Clutch fails to disengage (unable to select gears)

- ☐ Incorrect clutch adjustment (Chapter 6).
- ☐ Clutch friction plate sticking on gearbox input shaft splines (Chapter 6).
- ☐ Clutch friction plate sticking to flywheel or pressure plate (Chapter 6).
- ☐ Faulty pressure plate assembly (Chapter 6).
- ☐ Clutch release mechanism worn or badly assembled (Chapter 6).

Clutch slips (engine speed increases, with no increase in vehicle speed)

- ☐ Clutch friction plate linings excessively worn (Chapter 6).
- ☐ Clutch friction plate linings contaminated with oil or grease (Chapter 6).
- ☐ Faulty pressure plate or weak diaphragm spring (Chapter 6).

Judder as clutch is engaged

- ☐ Clutch friction plate linings contaminated with oil or grease (Chapter 6).
- ☐ Clutch friction plate linings excessively worn (Chapter 6).
- ☐ Faulty or distorted pressure plate or diaphragm spring (Chapter 6).
- ☐ Worn or loose engine or gearbox mountings (Chapter 2A, 2B or 2C).
- ☐ Clutch friction plate hub or gearbox input shaft splines worn (Chapter 6).

Noise when depressing or releasing clutch pedal

- ☐ Worn clutch release bearing (Chapter 6).
- ☐ Worn or dry clutch pedal pivot (Chapter 6).
- ☐ Faulty pressure plate assembly (Chapter 6).
- ☐ Pressure plate diaphragm spring broken (Chapter 6).
- ☐ Broken clutch friction plate cushioning springs (Chapter 6).

Manual and sequential transmission

Note: *On sequential transmission models, also refer to Chapter 7C for electrical or hydraulic problems.*

Noisy in neutral with engine running

- ☐ Input shaft bearings worn (noise apparent with clutch pedal released, but not when depressed) (Chapter 7).*
- ☐ Clutch release bearing worn (noise apparent with clutch pedal depressed, possibly less when released) (Chapter 6).

Noisy in one particular gear

- ☐ Worn, damaged or chipped gear teeth (Chapter 7).*

Difficulty engaging gears

- ☐ Clutch fault (Chapter 6).
- ☐ Worn or damaged gear linkage (Chapter 7).
- ☐ Worn synchroniser units (Chapter 7).*

Jumps out of gear

- ☐ Worn or damaged gear linkage (Chapter 7).
- ☐ Worn synchroniser units (Chapter 7).*
- ☐ Worn selector forks (Chapter 7).*

Vibration

- ☐ Lack of oil (Chapters 1A or 1B).
- ☐ Worn bearings (Chapter 7).*

Lubricant leaks

- ☐ Leaking oil seal (Chapter 7).
- ☐ Leaking housing joint (Chapter 7).*

** Although the corrective action necessary to remedy the symptoms described is beyond the scope of the home mechanic, the above information should be helpful in isolating the cause of the condition, so that the owner can communicate clearly with a professional mechanic.*

Automatic transmission

Note: *Due to the complexity of the automatic transmission, it is difficult for the home mechanic to properly diagnose and service this unit. For problems other than the following, the vehicle should be taken to a dealer service department or automatic transmission specialist. Do not be too hasty in removing the transmission if a fault is suspected, as most of the testing is carried out with the unit still fitted.*

Fluid leakage

- ☐ Automatic transmission fluid is usually dark in colour. Fluid leaks should not be confused with engine oil, which can easily be blown onto the transmission by airflow.
- ☐ To determine the source of a leak, first remove all built-up dirt and grime from the transmission housing and surrounding areas using a degreasing agent, or by steam-cleaning. Drive the vehicle at low speed, so airflow will not blow the leak far from its source. Raise and support the vehicle, and determine where the leak is coming from. The following are common areas of leakage:
  - *a) Oil pan (Chapter 1A and 7B).*
  - *b) Dipstick tube (Chapter 1A and 7B).*
  - *c) Transmission-to-fluid cooler pipes/unions (Chapter 7B).*

Transmission fluid brown, or has burned smell

- ☐ Transmission fluid level low, or fluid in need of renewal (Chapter 7B).

General gear selection problems

- ☐ Chapter 7B deals with checking and adjusting the selector cable on automatic transmissions. The following are common problems which may be caused by a poorly-adjusted cable:
  - *a) Engine starting in gears other than Park or Neutral.*
  - *b) Indicator panel indicating a gear other than the one actually being used.*
  - *c) Vehicle moves when in Park or Neutral.*
  - *d) Poor gear shift quality or erratic gear changes.*
- ☐ Refer to Chapter 7B for the selector cable adjustment procedure.

Transmission will not downshift (kickdown) with accelerator pedal fully depressed

- ☐ Low transmission fluid level (Chapter 1 and 7B).
- ☐ Incorrect selector cable adjustment (Chapter 7B).

Engine will not start in any gear, or starts in gears other than Park or Neutral

- ☐ Incorrect starter/inhibitor switch adjustment (Chapter 7B).
- ☐ Incorrect selector cable adjustment (Chapter 7B).

Transmission slips, shifts roughly, is noisy, or has no drive in forward or reverse gears

- ☐ There are many probable causes for the above problems, but the home mechanic should be concerned with only one possibility – fluid level. Before taking the vehicle to a dealer or transmission specialist, check the fluid level and condition of the fluid as described in Chapters 1A, 1B or 7B, as applicable. Correct the fluid level as necessary, or change the fluid and filter if needed. If the problem persists, professional help will be necessary.

Driveshafts

Clicking or knocking noise on turns (at slow speed on full-lock)

- ☐ Lack of constant velocity joint lubricant, possibly due to damaged gaiter (Chapter 8).
- ☐ Worn outer constant velocity joint (Chapter 8).

Vibration when accelerating or decelerating

- ☐ Worn inner constant velocity joint (Chapter 8).
- ☐ Damaged or distorted driveshaft (Chapter 8).
- ☐ Worn right-hand driveshaft intermediate bearing – where applicable (Chapter 8).

Braking system

Note: *Before assuming that a brake problem exists, make sure that the tyres are in good condition and correctly inflated, that the front wheel alignment is correct, and that the vehicle is not loaded with weight in an unequal manner. Apart from checking the condition of all pipe and hose connections, any faults occurring on the anti-lock braking system should be referred to a Renault dealer for diagnosis.*

Vehicle pulls to one side under braking

- ☐ Worn, defective, damaged or contaminated front or rear brake pads/shoes on one side (Chapters 1A, 1B and 9).
- ☐ Seized or partially-seized front or rear brake caliper/wheel cylinder piston (Chapter 9).
- ☐ A mixture of brake pad/shoe lining materials fitted between sides (Chapter 9).
- ☐ Brake caliper or rear brake backplate bolts loose (Chapter 9).
- ☐ Worn or damaged steering or suspension components (Chapters 1A, 1B and 10).

Noise (grinding or high-pitched squeal) when brakes applied

- ☐ Brake pad or shoe friction lining material worn down to metal backing (Chapters 1A, 1B and 9).
- ☐ Excessive corrosion of brake disc or drum – may be apparent after the vehicle has been standing for some time (Chapters 1A, 1B and 9).

Excessive brake pedal travel

- ☐ Faulty rear drum brake self-adjust mechanism (Chapter 9).
- ☐ Faulty master cylinder (Chapter 9).
- ☐ Air in hydraulic system (Chapter 9).
- ☐ Faulty vacuum servo unit (Chapter 9).
- ☐ Faulty vacuum pump – diesel models (Chapter 9).

Brake pedal feels spongy when depressed

- ☐ Air in hydraulic system (Chapter 9).
- ☐ Deteriorated flexible rubber brake hoses (Chapters 1A, 1B and 9).
- ☐ Master cylinder mountings loose (Chapter 9).
- ☐ Faulty master cylinder (Chapter 9).

Excessive brake pedal effort required to stop vehicle

- ☐ Faulty vacuum servo unit (Chapter 9).
- ☐ Disconnected, damaged or insecure brake servo vacuum hose (Chapters 1A, 1B and 9).
- ☐ Faulty vacuum pump – diesel models (Chapter 9).
- ☐ Primary or secondary hydraulic circuit failure (Chapter 9).
- ☐ Seized brake caliper or wheel cylinder piston(s) (Chapter 9).
- ☐ Brake pads or brake shoes incorrectly fitted (Chapter 9).
- ☐ Incorrect grade of brake pads or brake shoes fitted (Chapter 9).
- ☐ Brake pads or brake shoe linings contaminated (Chapter 9).

Braking system (continued)

Judder felt through brake pedal or steering wheel when braking

- ☐ Excessive run-out or distortion of brake disc(s) or drum(s) (Chapter 9).
- ☐ Brake pad or brake shoe linings worn (Chapters 1A, 1B and 9).
- ☐ Brake caliper or rear brake backplate mounting bolts loose (Chapter 9).
- ☐ Wear in suspension or steering components or mountings (Chapters 1A, 1B and 10).

Pedal pulsates when braking hard

- ☐ Normal feature of ABS – no fault

Brakes binding

- ☐ Seized brake caliper piston(s) or wheel cylinder piston(s) (Chapter 9).
- ☐ Incorrectly-adjusted handbrake mechanism or linkage (Chapter 9).
- ☐ Faulty master cylinder (Chapter 9).

Rear wheels locking under normal braking

- ☐ Seized brake caliper piston(s) or wheel cylinder piston(s) (Chapter 9).
- ☐ Faulty brake pressure regulator (Chapter 9).

Steering and suspension

Note: *Before diagnosing suspension or steering faults, be sure that the trouble is not due to incorrect tyre pressures, mixtures of tyre types, or binding brakes.*

Vehicle pulls to one side

- ☐ Defective tyre (Chapter 1A or 1B).
- ☐ Excessive wear in suspension or steering components (Chapters 1A, 1B and 10).
- ☐ Incorrect front wheel alignment (Chapter 10).
- ☐ Accident damage to steering or suspension components (Chapters 1A, 1B and 10).

Wheel wobble and vibration

- ☐ Front roadwheels out of balance (vibration felt mainly through the steering wheel) (Chapter 10).
- ☐ Rear roadwheels out of balance (vibration felt throughout the vehicle) (Chapter 10).
- ☐ Roadwheels damaged or distorted (Chapter 10).
- ☐ Faulty or damaged tyre (*Weekly checks*).
- ☐ Worn steering or suspension joints, bushes or components (Chapters 1A, 1B and 10).
- ☐ Wheel bolts loose (Chapter 10).

Excessive pitching and/or rolling around corners, or during braking

- ☐ Defective shock absorbers (Chapters 1A, 1B and 10).
- ☐ Broken or weak coil spring and/or suspension component (Chapters 1A, 1B and 10).
- ☐ Worn or damaged anti-roll bar or mountings (Chapter 10).

Wandering or general instability

- ☐ Incorrect front wheel alignment (Chapter 10).
- ☐ Worn steering or suspension joints, bushes or components (Chapters 1A, 1B and 10).
- ☐ Roadwheels out of balance (Chapter 10).
- ☐ Faulty or damaged tyre (*Weekly checks*).
- ☐ Wheel bolts loose (Chapter 10).
- ☐ Defective shock absorbers (Chapters 1A, 1B and 10).

Excessively-stiff steering

- ☐ Lack of steering gear lubricant (Chapter 10).
- ☐ Seized track rod end balljoint or suspension balljoint (Chapters 1A, 1B and 10).
- ☐ Broken or incorrectly adjusted auxiliary drivebelt (Chapters 1A or 1B).
- ☐ Incorrect front wheel alignment (Chapter 10).
- ☐ Steering rack or column bent or damaged (Chapter 10).

Excessive play in steering

- ☐ Worn steering column universal joint(s) (Chapter 10).
- ☐ Worn steering track rod end balljoints (Chapters 1A, 1B and 10).
- ☐ Worn rack-and-pinion steering gear (Chapter 10).
- ☐ Worn steering or suspension joints, bushes or components (Chapters 1A, 1B and 10).

Lack of power assistance

- ☐ Faulty power steering motor (Chapter 10).
- ☐ Faulty rack-and-pinion steering gear (Chapter 10).

Tyre wear excessive

Tyres worn on inside or outside edges

- ☐ Tyres under-inflated (wear on both edges) (*Weekly checks*).
- ☐ Incorrect camber or castor angles (wear on one edge only) (Chapter 10).
- ☐ Worn steering or suspension joints, bushes or components (Chapters 1A, 1B and 10).
- ☐ Excessively-hard cornering.
- ☐ Accident damage.

Tyre treads exhibit feathered edges

- ☐ Incorrect toe setting (Chapter 10).Tyres worn in centre of tread
- ☐ Tyres over-inflated (*Weekly checks*).

Tyres worn on inside and outside edges

- ☐ Tyres under-inflated (*Weekly checks*).
- ☐ Worn shock absorbers (Chapters 1A, 1B and 10).

Tyres worn unevenly

- ☐ Tyres out of balance (*Weekly checks*).
- ☐ Excessive wheel or tyre run-out (Chapters 1A or 1B).
- ☐ Worn shock absorbers (Chapters 1A, 1B and 10).
- ☐ Faulty tyre (*Weekly checks*).

Electrical system

Note: *For problems associated with the starting system, refer to the faults listed under Engine earlier in this Section.*

Battery will only hold a charge for a few days

- ☐ Battery defective internally (Chapter 5A).
- ☐ Battery electrolyte level low – where applicable (*Weekly checks*).
- ☐ Battery terminal connections loose or corroded (*Weekly checks*).
- ☐ Auxiliary drivebelt worn – or incorrectly adjusted, where applicable (Chapters 1A or 1B).
- ☐ Alternator not charging at correct output (Chapter 5A).

Electrical system (continued)

Battery will only hold a charge for a few days (continued)

- ☐ Alternator or voltage regulator faulty (Chapter 5A).
- ☐ Short-circuit causing continual battery drain (Chapters 5A and 12).

Ignition/no-charge warning light remains illuminated with engine running

- ☐ Auxiliary drivebelt broken, worn, or incorrectly adjusted (Chapters 1A or 1B).
- ☐ Alternator brushes worn, sticking, or dirty (Chapter 5A).
- ☐ Alternator brush springs weak or broken (Chapter 5A).
- ☐ Internal fault in alternator or voltage regulator (Chapter 5A).
- ☐ Broken, disconnected, or loose wiring in charging circuit (Chapter 5A).

Ignition/no-charge warning light fails to come on

- ☐ Warning light bulb blown (Chapter 12).
- ☐ Broken, disconnected, or loose wiring in warning light circuit (Chapter 12).
- ☐ Alternator faulty (Chapter 5A).

Lights inoperative

- ☐ Bulb blown (Chapter 12).
- ☐ Corrosion of bulb or bulbholder contacts (Chapter 12).
- ☐ Blown fuse (Chapter 12).
- ☐ Faulty relay (Chapter 12).
- ☐ Broken, loose, or disconnected wiring (Chapter 12).
- ☐ Faulty switch (Chapter 12).

Instrument readings inaccurate or erratic

Instrument readings increase with engine speed

- ☐ Faulty voltage regulator (Chapter 12).

Fuel or temperature gauges give no reading

- ☐ Faulty gauge sender unit (Chapters 3, 4A or 4B).
- ☐ Wiring open-circuit (Chapter 12).
- ☐ Faulty gauge (Chapter 12).

Fuel or temperature gauges give continuous maximum reading

- ☐ Faulty gauge sender unit (Chapters 3, 4A or 4B).
- ☐ Wiring short-circuit (Chapter 12).
- ☐ Faulty gauge (Chapter 12).

Horn inoperative, or unsatisfactory in operation

Horn operates all the time

- ☐ Horn contacts permanently bridged or horn push stuck down (Chapter 12).

Horn fails to operate

- ☐ Blown fuse (Chapter 12).
- ☐ Cable or cable connections loose, broken or disconnected (Chapter 12).
- ☐ Faulty horn (Chapter 12).

Horn emits intermittent or unsatisfactory sound

- ☐ Cable connections loose (Chapter 12).
- ☐ Horn mountings loose (Chapter 12).
- ☐ Faulty horn (Chapter 12).

Wipers inoperative, or unsatisfactory in operation

Wipers fail to operate, or operate very slowly

- ☐ Wiper blades stuck to screen, or linkage seized or binding (*Weekly checks* and Chapter 12).
- ☐ Blown fuse (Chapter 12).
- ☐ Cable or cable connections loose, broken or disconnected (Chapter 12).
- ☐ Faulty relay (Chapter 12).
- ☐ Faulty wiper motor (Chapter 12).

Wiper blades sweep over too large or too small an area of the glass

- ☐ Wiper arms incorrectly positioned on spindles (Chapter 12).
- ☐ Excessive wear of wiper linkage (Chapter 12).
- ☐ Wiper motor or linkage mountings loose or insecure (Chapter 12).

Wiper blades fail to clean the glass effectively

- ☐ Wiper blade rubbers worn or perished (*Weekly checks*).
- ☐ Wiper arm tension springs broken, or arm pivots seized (Chapter 12).
- ☐ Insufficient windscreen washer additive to adequately remove road film (*Weekly checks*).

Washers inoperative, or unsatisfactory in operation

One or more washer jets inoperative

- ☐ Blocked washer jet (Chapter 12).
- ☐ Disconnected, kinked or restricted fluid hose (Chapter 12).
- ☐ Insufficient fluid in washer reservoir (*Weekly checks*).

Washer pump fails to operate

- ☐ Broken or disconnected wiring or connections (Chapter 12).
- ☐ Blown fuse (Chapter 12).
- ☐ Faulty washer switch (Chapter 12).
- ☐ Faulty washer pump (Chapter 12).

Washer pump runs for some time before fluid is emitted from jets

- ☐ Faulty one-way valve in fluid supply hose (Chapter 12).

Electric windows inoperative, or unsatisfactory in operation

Window glass will only move in one direction

- ☐ Faulty switch (Chapter 12).

Window glass slow to move

- ☐ Regulator seized or damaged, or in need of lubrication (Chapter 11).
- ☐ Door internal components or trim fouling regulator (Chapter 11).
- ☐ Faulty motor (Chapter 11).

Window glass fails to move

- ☐ Blown fuse (Chapter 12).
- ☐ Faulty relay (Chapter 12).
- ☐ Broken or disconnected wiring or connections (Chapter 12).
- ☐ Faulty motor (Chapter 12).

Central locking system inoperative, or unsatisfactory in operation

Complete system failure

- ☐ Blown fuse (Chapter 12).
- ☐ Faulty relay (Chapter 12).
- ☐ Broken or disconnected wiring or connections (Chapter 12).

Latch locks but will not unlock, or unlocks but will not lock

- ☐ Faulty switch (Chapter 12).
- ☐ Broken or disconnected latch operating rods or levers (Chapter 11).
- ☐ Faulty relay (Chapter 12).

One motor fails to operate

- ☐ Broken or disconnected wiring or connections (Chapter 12).
- ☐ Faulty motor (Chapter 11).
- ☐ Broken, binding or disconnected lock operating rods or levers (Chapter 11).
- ☐ Fault in door lock (Chapter 11).

Note: *References throughout this index are in the form* **"Chapter number" • "Page number"**

O

P

R

S

T

U

Haynes Manuals – The Complete **UK Car** List

Title	Book No.
ALFA ROMEO Alfasud/Sprint (74 - 88) up to F *	**0292**
Alfa Romeo Alfetta (73 - 87) up to E *	**0531**
AUDI 80, 90 & Coupe Petrol (79 - Nov 88) up to F	**0605**
Audi 80, 90 & Coupe Petrol (Oct 86 - 90) D to H	**1491**
Audi 100 & 200 Petrol (Oct 82 - 90) up to H	**0907**
Audi 100 & A6 Petrol & Diesel (May 91 - May 97) H to P	**3504**
Audi A3 Petrol & Diesel (96 - May 03) P to 03	**4253**
Audi A4 Petrol & Diesel (95 - 00) M to X	**3575**
Audi A4 Petrol & Diesel (01 - 04) X to 54	**4609**
AUSTIN A35 & A40 (56 - 67) up to F *	**0118**
Austin/MG/Rover Maestro 1.3 & 1.6 Petrol (83 - 95) up to M	**0922**
Austin/MG Metro (80 - May 90) up to G	**0718**
Austin/Rover Montego 1.3 & 1.6 Petrol (84 - 94) A to L	**1066**
Austin/MG/Rover Montego 2.0 Petrol (84 - 95) A to M	**1067**
Mini (59 - 69) up to H *	**0527**
Mini (69 - 01) up to X	**0646**
Austin/Rover 2.0 litre Diesel Engine (86 - 93) C to L	**1857**
Austin Healey 100/6 & 3000 (56 - 68) up to G *	**0049**
BEDFORD CF Petrol (69 - 87) up to E	**0163**
Bedford/Vauxhall Rascal & Suzuki Supercarry (86 - Oct 94) C to M	**3015**
BMW 316, 320 & 320i (4-cyl) (75 - Feb 83) up to Y *	**0276**
BMW 320, 320i, 323i & 325i (6-cyl) (Oct 77 - Sept 87) up to E	**0815**
BMW 3- & 5-Series Petrol (81 - 91) up to J	**1948**
BMW 3-Series Petrol (Apr 91 - 99) H to V	**3210**
BMW 3-Series Petrol (Sept 98 - 03) S to 53	**4067**
BMW 520i & 525e (Oct 81 - June 88) up to E	**1560**
BMW 525, 528 & 528i (73 - Sept 81) up to X *	**0632**
BMW 5-Series 6-cyl Petrol (April 96 - Aug 03) N to 03	**4151**
BMW 1500, 1502, 1600, 1602, 2000 & 2002 (59 - 77) up to S *	**0240**
CHRYSLER PT Cruiser Petrol (00 - 03) W to 53	**4058**
CITROËN 2CV, Ami & Dyane (67 - 90) up to H	**0196**
Citroën AX Petrol & Diesel (87 - 97) D to P	**3014**
Citroën Berlingo & Peugeot Partner Petrol & Diesel (96 - 05) P to 55	**4281**
Citroën BX Petrol (83 - 94) A to L	**0908**
Citroën C15 Van Petrol & Diesel (89 - Oct 98) F to S	**3509**
Citroën C3 Petrol & Diesel (02 - 05) 51 to 05	**4197**
Citroën CX Petrol (75 - 88) up to F	**0528**
Citroën Saxo Petrol & Diesel (96 - 04) N to 54	**3506**
Citroën Visa Petrol (79 - 88) up to F	**0620**
Citroën Xantia Petrol & Diesel (93 - 01) K to Y	**3082**
Citroën XM Petrol & Diesel (89 - 00) G to X	**3451**
Citroën Xsara Petrol & Diesel (97 - Sept 00) R to W	**3751**
Citroën Xsara Picasso Petrol & Diesel (00 - 02) W to 52	**3944**
Citroën ZX Diesel (91 - 98) J to S	**1922**
Citroën ZX Petrol (91 - 98) H to S	**1881**
Citroën 1.7 & 1.9 litre Diesel Engine (84 - 96) A to N	**1379**
FIAT 126 (73 - 87) up to E *	**0305**
Fiat 500 (57 - 73) up to M *	**0090**
Fiat Bravo & Brava Petrol (95 - 00) N to W	**3572**
Fiat Cinquecento (93 - 98) K to R	**3501**
Fiat Panda (81 - 95) up to M	**0793**
Fiat Punto Petrol & Diesel (94 - Oct 99) L to V	**3251**
Fiat Punto Petrol (Oct 99 - July 03) V to 03	**4066**
Fiat Regata Petrol (84 - 88) A to F	**1167**
Fiat Tipo Petrol (88 - 91) E to J	**1625**
Fiat Uno Petrol (83 - 95) up to M	**0923**
Fiat X1/9 (74 - 89) up to G *	**0273**
FORD Anglia (59 - 68) up to G *	**0001**
Ford Capri II (& III) 1.6 & 2.0 (74 - 87) up to E *	**0283**
Ford Capri II (& III) 2.8 & 3.0 V6 (74 - 87) up to E	**1309**
Ford Cortina Mk I & Corsair 1500 ('62 - '66) up to D*	**0214**
Ford Cortina Mk III 1300 & 1600 (70 - 76) up to P *	**0070**
Ford Escort Mk I 1100 & 1300 (68 - 74) up to N *	**0171**
Ford Escort Mk I Mexico, RS 1600 & RS 2000 (70 - 74) up to N *	**0139**
Ford Escort Mk II Mexico, RS 1800 & RS 2000 (75 - 80) up to W *	**0735**
Ford Escort (75 - Aug 80) up to V *	**0280**
Ford Escort Petrol (Sept 80 - Sept 90) up to H	**0686**
Ford Escort & Orion Petrol (Sept 90 - 00) H to X	**1737**
Ford Escort & Orion Diesel (Sept 90 - 00) H to X	**4081**
Ford Fiesta (76 - Aug 83) up to Y	**0334**
Ford Fiesta Petrol (Aug 83 - Feb 89) A to F	**1030**
Ford Fiesta Petrol (Feb 89 - Oct 95) F to N	**1595**
Ford Fiesta Petrol & Diesel (Oct 95 - Mar 02) N to 02	**3397**
Ford Fiesta Petrol & Diesel (Apr 02 - 05) 02 to 54	**4170**
Ford Focus Petrol & Diesel (98 - 01) S to Y	**3759**
Ford Focus Petrol & Diesel (Oct 01 - 05) 51 to 05	**4167**
Ford Galaxy Petrol & Diesel (95 - Aug 00) M to W	**3984**
Ford Granada Petrol (Sept 77 - Feb 85) up to B *	**0481**
Ford Granada & Scorpio Petrol (Mar 85 - 94) B to M	**1245**
Ford Ka (96 - 02) P to 52	**3570**
Ford Mondeo Petrol (93 - Sept 00) K to X	**1923**
Ford Mondeo Petrol & Diesel (Oct 00 - Jul 03) X to 03	**3990**
Ford Mondeo Petrol & Diesel (July 03 - 07) 03 to 56	**4619**
Ford Mondeo Diesel (93 - 96) L to N	**3465**
Ford Orion Petrol (83 - Sept 90) up to H	**1009**
Ford Sierra 4-cyl Petrol (82 - 93) up to K	**0903**
Ford Sierra V6 Petrol (82 - 91) up to J	**0904**
Ford Transit Petrol (Mk 2) (78 - Jan 86) up to C	**0719**
Ford Transit Petrol (Mk 3) (Feb 86 - 89) C to G	**1468**
Ford Transit Diesel (Feb 86 - 99) C to T	**3019**
Ford 1.6 & 1.8 litre Diesel Engine (84 - 96) A to N	**1172**
Ford 2.1, 2.3 & 2.5 litre Diesel Engine (77 - 90) up to H	**1606**
FREIGHT ROVER Sherpa Petrol (74 - 87) up to E	**0463**
HILLMAN Avenger (70 - 82) up to Y	**0037**
Hillman Imp (63 - 76) up to R *	**0022**
HONDA Civic (Feb 84 - Oct 87) A to E	**1226**
Honda Civic (Nov 91 - 96) J to N	**3199**
Honda Civic Petrol (Mar 95 - 00) M to X	**4050**
Honda Civic Petrol & Diesel (01 - 05) X to 55	**4611**
Honda Jazz (01 - Feb 08) 51 - 57	**4735**
HYUNDAI Pony (85 - 94) C to M	**3398**
JAGUAR E Type (61 - 72) up to L *	**0140**
Jaguar MkI & II, 240 & 340 (55 - 69) up to H *	**0098**
Jaguar XJ6, XJ & Sovereign; Daimler Sovereign (68 - Oct 86) up to D	**0242**
Jaguar XJ6 & Sovereign (Oct 86 - Sept 94) D to M	**3261**
Jaguar XJ12, XJS & Sovereign; Daimler Double Six (72 - 88) up to F	**0478**
JEEP Cherokee Petrol (93 - 96) K to N	**1943**
LADA 1200, 1300, 1500 & 1600 (74 - 91) up to J	**0413**
Lada Samara (87 - 91) D to J	**1610**
LAND ROVER 90, 110 & Defender Diesel (83 - 07) up to 56	**3017**
Land Rover Discovery Petrol & Diesel (89 - 98) G to S	**3016**
Land Rover Discovery Diesel (Nov 98 - Jul 04) S to 04	**4606**
Land Rover Freelander Petrol & Diesel (97 - Sept 03) R to 53	**3929**
Land Rover Freelander Petrol & Diesel (Oct 03 - Oct 06) 53 to 56	**4623**
Land Rover Series IIA & III Diesel (58 - 85) up to C	**0529**
Land Rover Series II, IIA & III 4-cyl Petrol (58 - 85) up to C	**0314**
MAZDA 323 (Mar 81 - Oct 89) up to G	**1608**
Mazda 323 (Oct 89 - 98) G to R	**3455**
Mazda 626 (May 83 - Sept 87) up to E	**0929**
Mazda B1600, B1800 & B2000 Pick-up Petrol (72 - 88) up to F	**0267**
Mazda RX-7 (79 - 85) up to C *	**0460**
MERCEDES-BENZ 190, 190E & 190D Petrol & Diesel (83 - 93) A to L	**3450**
Mercedes-Benz 200D, 240D, 240TD, 300D & 300TD 123 Series Diesel (Oct 76 - 85)	**1114**
Mercedes-Benz 250 & 280 (68 - 72) up to L *	**0346**
Mercedes-Benz 250 & 280 123 Series Petrol (Oct 76 - 84) up to B *	**0677**
Mercedes-Benz 124 Series Petrol & Diesel (85 - Aug 93) C to K	**3253**
Mercedes-Benz C-Class Petrol & Diesel (93 - Aug 00) L to W	**3511**
MGA (55 - 62) *	**0475**
MGB (62 - 80) up to W	**0111**
MG Midget & Austin-Healey Sprite (58 - 80) up to W *	**0265**
MINI Petrol (July 01 - 05) Y to 05	**4273**
MITSUBISHI Shogun & L200 Pick-Ups Petrol (83 - 94) up to M	**1944**
MORRIS Ital 1.3 (80 - 84) up to B	**0705**
Morris Minor 1000 (56 - 71) up to K	**0024**
NISSAN Almera Petrol (95 - Feb 00) N to V	**4053**
Nissan Almera & Tino Petrol (Feb 00 - 07) V to 56	**4612**
Nissan Bluebird (May 84 - Mar 86) A to C	**1223**
Nissan Bluebird Petrol (Mar 86 - 90) C to H	**1473**
Nissan Cherry (Sept 82 - 86) up to D	**1031**
Nissan Micra (83 - Jan 93) up to K	**0931**
Nissan Micra (93 - 02) K to 52	**3254**
Nissan Primera Petrol (90 - Aug 99) H to T	**1851**
Nissan Stanza (82 - 86) up to D	**0824**
Nissan Sunny Petrol (May 82 - Oct 86) up to D	**0895**
Nissan Sunny Petrol (Oct 86 - Mar 91) D to H	**1378**
Nissan Sunny Petrol (Apr 91 - 95) H to N	**3219**
OPEL Ascona & Manta (B Series) (Sept 75 - 88) up to F *	**0316**
Opel Ascona Petrol (81 - 88)	**3215**
Opel Astra Petrol (Oct 91 - Feb 98)	**3156**
Opel Corsa Petrol (83 - Mar 93)	**3160**
Opel Corsa Petrol (Mar 93 - 97)	**3159**
Opel Kadett Petrol (Nov 79 - Oct 84) up to B	**0634**
Opel Kadett Petrol (Oct 84 - Oct 91)	**3196**
Opel Omega & Senator Petrol (Nov 86 - 94)	**3157**
Opel Rekord Petrol (Feb 78 - Oct 86) up to D	**0543**
Opel Vectra Petrol (Oct 88 - Oct 95)	**3158**
PEUGEOT 106 Petrol & Diesel (91 - 04) J to 53	**1882**
Peugeot 205 Petrol (83 - 97) A to P	**0932**
Peugeot 206 Petrol & Diesel (98 - 01) S to X	**3757**
Peugeot 206 Petrol & Diesel (02 - 06) 51 to 06	**4613**
Peugeot 306 Petrol & Diesel (93 - 02) K to 02	**3073**
Peugeot 307 Petrol & Diesel (01 - 04) Y to 54	**4147**
Peugeot 309 Petrol (86 - 93) C to K	**1266**
Peugeot 405 Petrol (88 - 97) E to P	**1559**
Peugeot 405 Diesel (88 - 97) E to P	**3198**
Peugeot 406 Petrol & Diesel (96 - Mar 99) N to T	**3394**
Peugeot 406 Petrol & Diesel (Mar 99 - 02) T to 52	**3982**
Peugeot 505 Petrol (79 - 89) up to G	**0762**
Peugeot 1.7/1.8 & 1.9 litre Diesel Engine (82 - 96) up to N	**0950**
Peugeot 2.0, 2.1, 2.3 & 2.5 litre Diesel Engines (74 - 90) up to H	**1607**
PORSCHE 911 (65 - 85) up to C	**0264**

* Classic reprint

Title	Book No.
Porsche 924 & 924 Turbo (76 - 85) up to C	0397
PROTON (89 - 97) F to P	3255
RANGE ROVER V8 Petrol (70 - Oct 92) up to K	0606
RELIANT Robin & Kitten (73 - 83) up to A *	0436
RENAULT 4 (61 - 86) up to D *	0072
Renault 5 Petrol (Feb 85 - 96) B to N	1219
Renault 9 & 11 Petrol (82 - 89) up to F	0822
Renault 18 Petrol (79 - 86) up to D	0598
Renault 19 Petrol (89 - 96) F to N	1646
Renault 19 Diesel (89 - 96) F to N	1946
Renault 21 Petrol (86 - 94) C to M	1397
Renault 25 Petrol & Diesel (84 - 92) B to K	1228
Renault Clio Petrol (91 - May 98) H to R	1853
Renault Clio Diesel (91 - June 96) H to N	3031
Renault Clio Petrol & Diesel (May 98 - May 01) R to Y	3906
Renault Clio Petrol & Diesel (June '01 - '05) Y to 55	4168
Renault Espace Petrol & Diesel (85 - 96) C to N	3197
Renault Laguna Petrol & Diesel (94 - 00) L to W	3252
Renault Laguna Petrol & Diesel (Feb 01 - Feb 05) X to 54	4283
Renault Mégane & Scénic Petrol & Diesel (96 - 99) N to T	3395
Renault Mégane & Scénic Petrol & Diesel (Apr 99 - 02) T to 52	3916
Renault Megane Petrol & Diesel (Oct 02 - 05) 52 to 55	4284
Renault Scenic Petrol & Diesel (Sept 03 - 06) 53 to 06	4297
ROVER 213 & 216 (84 - 89) A to G	1116
Rover 214 & 414 Petrol (89 - 96) G to N	1689
Rover 216 & 416 Petrol (89 - 96) G to N	1830
Rover 211, 214, 216, 218 & 220 Petrol & Diesel (Dec 95 - 99) N to V	3399
Rover 25 & MG ZR Petrol & Diesel (Oct 99 - 04) V to 54	4145
Rover 414, 416 & 420 Petrol & Diesel (May 95 - 98) M to R	3453
Rover 45 / MG ZS Petrol & Diesel (99 - 05) V to 55	4384
Rover 618, 620 & 623 Petrol (93 - 97) K to P	3257
Rover 75 / MG ZT Petrol & Diesel (99 - 06) S to 06	4292
Rover 820, 825 & 827 Petrol (86 - 95) D to N	1380
Rover 3500 (76 - 87) up to E *	0365
Rover Metro, 111 & 114 Petrol (May 90 - 98) G to S	1711
SAAB 95 & 96 (66 - 76) up to R *	0198
Saab 90, 99 & 900 (79 - Oct 93) up to L	0765
Saab 900 (Oct 93 - 98) L to R	3512
Saab 9000 (4-cyl) (85 - 98) C to S	1686
Saab 9-3 Petrol & Diesel (98 - Aug 02) R to 02	4614
Saab 9-5 4-cyl Petrol (97 - 04) R to 54	4156
SEAT Ibiza & Cordoba Petrol & Diesel (Oct 93 - Oct 99) L to V	3571
Seat Ibiza & Malaga Petrol (85 - 92) B to K	1609
SKODA Estelle (77 - 89) up to G	0604
Skoda Fabia Petrol & Diesel (00 - 06) W to 06	4376
Skoda Favorit (89 - 96) F to N	1801
Skoda Felicia Petrol & Diesel (95 - 01) M to X	3505
Skoda Octavia Petrol & Diesel (98 - Apr 04) R to 04	4285
SUBARU 1600 & 1800 (Nov 79 - 90) up to H *	0995
SUNBEAM Alpine, Rapier & H120 (67 - 74) up to N *	0051
SUZUKI SJ Series, Samurai & Vitara (4-cyl) Petrol (82 - 97) up to P	1942
Suzuki Supercarry & Bedford/Vauxhall Rascal (86 - Oct 94) C to M	3015
TALBOT Alpine, Solara, Minx & Rapier (75 - 86) up to D	0337
Talbot Horizon Petrol (78 - 86) up to D	0473
Talbot Samba (82 - 86) up to D	0823
TOYOTA Avensis Petrol (98 - Jan 03) R to 52	4264
Toyota Carina E Petrol (May 92 - 97) J to P	3256
Toyota Corolla (80 - 85) up to C	0683
Toyota Corolla (Sept 83 - Sept 87) A to E	1024
Toyota Corolla (Sept 87 - Aug 92) E to K	1683
Toyota Corolla Petrol (Aug 92 - 97) K to P	3259
Toyota Corolla Petrol (July 97 - Feb 02) P to 51	4286
Toyota Hi-Ace & Hi-Lux Petrol (69 - Oct 83) up to A	0304
Toyota Yaris Petrol (99 - 05) T to 05	4265
TRIUMPH GT6 & Vitesse (62 - 74) up to N *	0112
Triumph Herald (59 - 71) up to K *	0010
Triumph Spitfire (62 - 81) up to X	0113
Triumph Stag (70 - 78) up to T *	0441
Triumph TR2, TR3, TR3A, TR4 & TR4A (52 - 67) up to F *	0028
Triumph TR5 & 6 (67 - 75) up to P *	0031
Triumph TR7 (75 - 82) up to Y *	0322
VAUXHALL Astra Petrol (80 - Oct 84) up to B	0635
Vauxhall Astra & Belmont Petrol (Oct 84 - Oct 91) B to J	1136
Vauxhall Astra Petrol (Oct 91 - Feb 98) J to R	1832
Vauxhall/Opel Astra & Zafira Petrol (Feb 98 - Apr 04) R to 04	3758
Vauxhall/Opel Astra & Zafira Diesel (Feb 98 - Apr 04) R to 04	3797
Vauxhall/Opel Astra Petrol (04 - 07) 04 - 07	4732
Vauxhall/Opel Astra Diesel (04 - 07) 04 - 07	4733
Vauxhall/Opel Calibra (90 - 98) G to S	3502
Vauxhall Carlton Petrol (Oct 78 - Oct 86) up to D	0480
Vauxhall Carlton & Senator Petrol (Nov 86 - 94) D to L	1469
Vauxhall Cavalier Petrol (81 - Oct 88) up to F	0812
Vauxhall Cavalier Petrol (Oct 88 - 95) F to N	1570
Vauxhall Chevette (75 - 84) up to B	0285
Vauxhall/Opel Corsa Diesel (Mar 93 - Oct 00) K to X	4087
Vauxhall Corsa Petrol (Mar 93 - 97) K to R	1985
Vauxhall/Opel Corsa Petrol (Apr 97 - Oct 00) P to X	3921
Vauxhall/Opel Corsa Petrol & Diesel (Oct 00 - Sept 03) X to 53	4079
Vauxhall/Opel Corsa Petrol & Diesel (Oct 03 - Aug 06) 53 to 06	4617
Vauxhall/Opel Frontera Petrol & Diesel (91 - Sept 98) J to S	3454
Vauxhall Nova Petrol (83 - 93) up to K	0909
Vauxhall/Opel Omega Petrol (94 - 99) L to T	3510
Vauxhall/Opel Vectra Petrol & Diesel (95 - Feb 99) N to S	3396
Vauxhall/Opel Vectra Petrol & Diesel (Mar 99 - May 02) T to 02	3930
Vauxhall/Opel Vectra Petrol & Diesel (June 02 - Sept 05) 02 to 55	4618
Vauxhall/Opel 1.5, 1.6 & 1.7 litre Diesel Engine (82 - 96) up to N	1222
VW 411 & 412 (68 - 75) up to P *	0091
VW Beetle 1200 (54 - 77) up to S	0036
VW Beetle 1300 & 1500 (65 - 75) up to P	0039
VW 1302 & 1302S (70 - 72) up to L *	0110
VW Beetle 1303, 1303S & GT (72 - 75) up to P	0159
VW Beetle Petrol & Diesel (Apr 99 - 01) T to 51	3798
VW Golf & Jetta Mk 1 Petrol 1.1 & 1.3 (74 - 84) up to A	0716
VW Golf, Jetta & Scirocco Mk 1 Petrol 1.5, 1.6 & 1.8 (74 - 84) up to A	0726
VW Golf & Jetta Mk 1 Diesel (78 - 84) up to A	0451
VW Golf & Jetta Mk 2 Petrol (Mar 84 - Feb 92) A to J	1081
VW Golf & Vento Petrol & Diesel (Feb 92 - Mar 98) J to R	3097
VW Golf & Bora Petrol & Diesel (April 98 - 00) R to X	3727
VW Golf & Bora 4-cyl Petrol & Diesel (01 - 03) X to 53	4169
VW Golf & Jetta Petrol & Diesel (04 - 07) 53 to 07	4610
VW LT Petrol Vans & Light Trucks (76 - 87) up to E	0637
VW Passat & Santana Petrol (Sept 81 - May 88) up to E	0814
VW Passat 4-cyl Petrol & Diesel (May 88 - 96) E to P	3498
VW Passat 4-cyl Petrol & Diesel (Dec 96 - Nov 00) P to X	3917
VW Passat Petrol & Diesel (Dec 00 - May 05) X to 05	4279
VW Polo & Derby (76 - Jan 82) up to X	0335
VW Polo (82 - Oct 90) up to H	0813
VW Polo Petrol (Nov 90 - Aug 94) H to L	3245
VW Polo Hatchback Petrol & Diesel (94 - 99) M to S	3500
VW Polo Hatchback Petrol (00 - Jan 02) V to 51	4150
VW Polo Petrol & Diesel (02 - May 05) 51 to 05	4608
VW Scirocco (82 - 90) up to H *	1224
VW Transporter 1600 (68 - 79) up to V	0082
VW Transporter 1700, 1800 & 2000 (72 - 79) up to V *	0226
VW Transporter (air-cooled) Petrol (79 - 82) up to Y *	0638
VW Transporter (water-cooled) Petrol (82 - 90) up to H	3452
VW Type 3 (63 - 73) up to M *	0084
VOLVO 120 & 130 Series (& P1800) (61 - 73) up to M *	0203
Volvo 142, 144 & 145 (66 - 74) up to N *	0129
Volvo 240 Series Petrol (74 - 93) up to K	0270
Volvo 262, 264 & 260/265 (75 - 85) up to C *	0400
Volvo 340, 343, 345 & 360 (76 - 91) up to J	0715
Volvo 440, 460 & 480 Petrol (87 - 97) D to P	1691
Volvo 740 & 760 Petrol (82 - 91) up to J	1258
Volvo 850 Petrol (92 - 96) J to P	3260
Volvo 940 petrol (90 - 98) H to R	3249
Volvo S40 & V40 Petrol (96 - Mar 04) N to 04	3569
Volvo S40 & V50 Petrol & Diesel (Mar 04 - Jun 07) 04 to 07	4731
Volvo S70, V70 & C70 Petrol (96 - 99) P to V	3573
Volvo V70 / S80 Petrol & Diesel (98 - 05) S to 55	4263
AUTOMOTIVE TECHBOOKS	
Automotive Electrical and Electronic Systems Manual	3049
Automotive Gearbox Overhaul Manual	3473
Automotive Service Summaries Manual	3475
Automotive Timing Belts Manual – Austin/Rover	3549
Automotive Timing Belts Manual – Ford	3474
Automotive Timing Belts Manual – Peugeot/Citroën	3568
Automotive Timing Belts Manual – Vauxhall/Opel	3577
DIY MANUAL SERIES	
The Haynes Air Conditioning Manual	4192
The Haynes Car Electrical Systems Manual	4251
The Haynes Manual on Bodywork	4198
The Haynes Manual on Brakes	4178
The Haynes Manual on Carburettors	4177
The Haynes Manual on Diesel Engines	4174
The Haynes Manual on Engine Management	4199
The Haynes Manual on Fault Codes	4175
The Haynes Manual on Practical Electrical Systems	4267
The Haynes Manual on Small Engines	4250
The Haynes Manual on Welding	4176

* Classic reprint

All the products featured on this page are available through most motor accessory shops, cycle shops and book stores. Our policy of continuous updating and development means that titles are being constantly added to the range. For up-to-date information on our complete list of titles, please telephone: (UK) +44 1963 442030 • (USA) +1 805 498 6703 • (Sweden) +46 18 124016 • (Australia) +61 3 9763 8100

CL23.12/07

Duesenberg
SFF 402

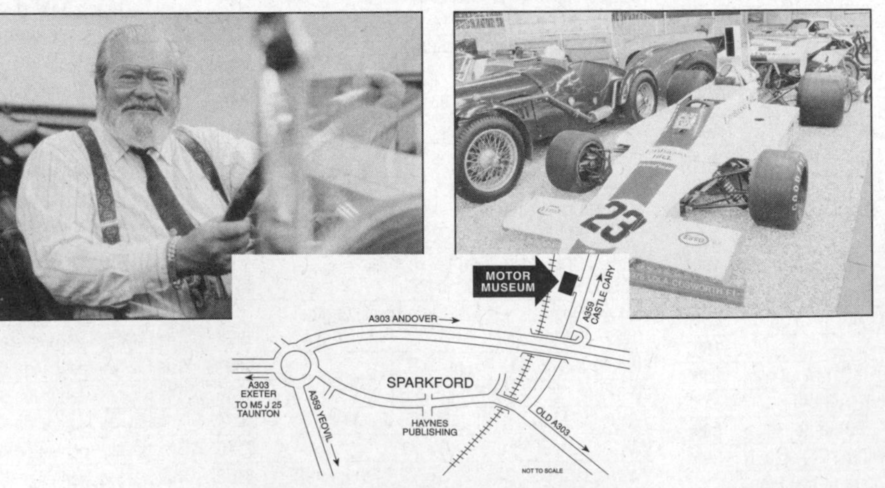

23
MOTOR MUSEUM
A303 ANDOVER
A359 CASTLE CARY
SPARKFORD
A303 EXETER TO M5 J 25 TAUNTON
A359 YEOVIL
HAYNES PUBLISHING
OLD A303
NOT TO SCALE